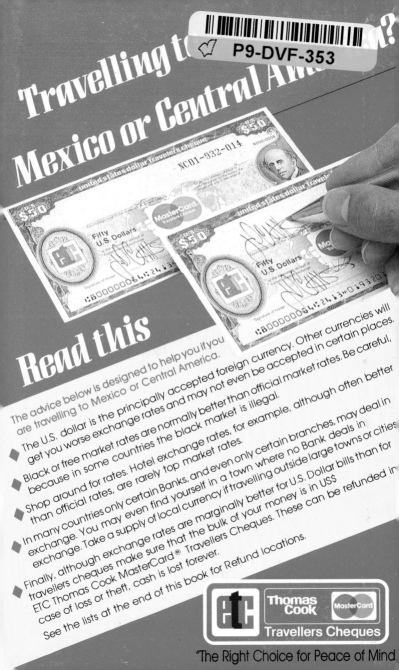

Travelling to Mexico or Central America?

P9-DVF-353

Read this

The advice below is designed to help you if you are travelling to Mexico or Central America.

- The U.S. dollar is the principally accepted foreign currency. Other currencies will get you worse exchange rates and may not even be accepted in certain places.

- Black or free market rates are normally better than official market rates. Be careful, because in some countries the black market is illegal.

- Shop around for rates. Hotel exchange rates, for example, although often better than official rates, are rarely top market rates.

- In many countries only certain Banks, and even only certain branches, may deal in exchange. You may even find yourself in a town where no Bank deals in exchange. Take a supply of local currency if travelling outside large towns or cities

- Finally, although exchange rates are marginally better for U.S. Dollar bills than for travellers cheques make sure that the bulk of your money is in US$ ETC Thomas Cook MasterCard® Travellers Cheques. These can be refunded in case of loss or theft, cash is lost forever.

See the lists at the end of this book for Refund locations.

Thomas Cook **MasterCard** **Travellers Cheques**

"The Right Choice for Peace of Mind

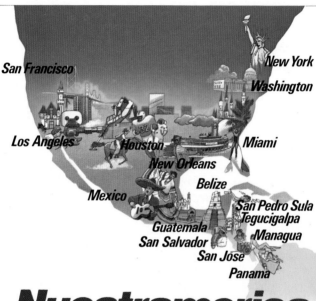

Nuestramerica

TACA's America means a whole new continent of advantages.
Discover it aboard Central America's largest and most efficient airline;
with recently acquired Boeing Aircraft, complimentary cocktails, two menus
to choose from, the most convenient itineraries and all that Central American warmth!

Consult your travel agent or TACA.
Reservations and information (800) 535-8780.

Love at first flight!

1991
MEXICO & CENTRAL AMERICAN HANDBOOK

Editor
Ben Box
Assistant Editor
Sarah Cameron

"There's no moon and no cloud; by eight o'clock the sky is obsidian speckled with the luminous dust of the Milky Way. I lie on my back and watch stars fall whenever a Maya god throws down his spent cigar."

Ronald Wright

TRADE & TRAVEL PUBLICATIONS

TRADE & TRAVEL PUBLICATIONS LTD
6 RIVERSIDE COURT
RIVERSIDE ROAD
BATH BA2 3DZ
ENGLAND
TEL 0225 469141
FAX 0225 462921

ISBN 0 900751 32 0

Published in the United States of America and Canada by
Prentice Hall Press
Division of Simon & Schuster Inc.
15 Columbus Circle
New York, NY 10023

In North America, ISBN 0-13-578964-8

Excerpt from *Time among the Maya* by Ronald Wright.
© Ronald Wright 1989.
First published by Weidenfeld and Nicholson in the USA in 1989.
Reprinted with kind permission of the Bodley Head Ltd.

COVER—THE QUETZAL

Quetzals inhabit the dense rain forests of Mexico and Central America, feeding on fruit, insects and small invertebrates. They nest in a hole in a tree where 2 or 3 eggs are laid after a period of 17 or 18 days.

Of the Trogon family, these birds grow to about 12 inches high. The male has brilliantly coloured plumage and elongated upper tail coverts, forming a magnificent train of approximately 36 inches. He helps to incubate the eggs and whilst sitting on the nest, the tail plumes are bent forward over his head and hang out of the hole in the tree. This damages the feathers and they are shed and regrown after each breeding season. The quetzal was once sacred to the Maya Aztec civilizations which made ceremonial use of these red and green contrasted feathers. The female is much plainer in appearance, with her upper tail coverts extending only to the end of the tail.

The Quetzal is the national bird of Guatemala. The currency is named after it, with the bird appearing on the coinage, stamps, and the national

ration by Jeremy Pyke
nd in Great Britain by Clays Ltd., Bungay, Suffolk.

CONTENTS

PREFACE

Over many years, the *South American Handbook*, including Mexico and Central America, expanded with the help of countless travellers who sent in details of their experiences, corrections to the text and additions of new routes and places to visit. The point was reached where it was no longer possible to accommodate all the information in a single volume. Having separated the Caribbean islands in 1990 into a companion volume to the *South American Handbook*, it was decided to do the same in 1991 for Mexico and Central America and this is the first edition. The *Mexico and Central American Handbook* appears simultaneously with the 67th edition of the *South American Handbook* and the second edition of the *Caribbean Islands Handbook*.

The procedure followed in preparing this *Handbook* is identical to that used for the *South American Handbook*, in that the text is updated annually on the strength of travellers' letters, details from correspondents resident in the region, the editor's visits and the many sources of information available in the UK. We hope that readers of this book will continue to send their constructive criticisms (and praise where due) as they have done for the *South American Handbook*. For this edition we acknowledge especially the invaluable assistance of Simon Ellis in Costa Rica, Mike Shawcross in Guatemala and Jorge Valle-Aguiluz in Honduras, and Nigel Gallop, who wrote the introduction to the music of the region. We are also grateful to the subeditors, Sylvia Brooks and Peter Pollard, for their work in incorporating into the text the details contained in the many hundreds of readers' letters, and to Debbie Wylde who transferred most of the new material to disk. The *Mexico and Central American Handbook* is designed very much as a companion volume to both the *South American Handbook* and the *Caribbean Islands Handbook*. For this reason there is overlapping material between all three where frequently used routes occur. One example of this is San Andrés and Providencia, which are in all three books: they are Colombian territory, they are located in the Caribbean Sea and they are a popular stopover for flights between Central America and South America. Many new maps have been prepared for this volume, mostly for cities and towns, in response to readers' requests. Thanks are due to Katherine Jarvis for drawing the majority of the new maps.

Mexico's good road connections with the USA have made it a natural holiday destination for North Americans. A number of mass tourism developments have received considerable attention from the package tourist industry: Acapulco, Cancún and latterly Huatulco. However, for the independent traveller there is still a wealth of precolumbian, colonial and natural attractions, as well as many undeniably beautiful beaches not yet touched by the mass market. This book sets out to encourage travellers to seek the less well-known areas as well as the major sites of interest, such as Teotihuacán, Palenque, Chichén Itzá, Cuernavaca or Guadalajara.

It is to be hoped that this new edition will coincide with progress under the various peace initiatives for Central America and that this will foster a desire to travel in the region. We recognize, nevertheless, that there are still many unresolved issues and that fighting continues in several areas. This should not deter travellers from exploring these countries' culture, history, flora and fauna. We shall follow with great interest the proposal by Mexico, Guatemala, Belize, El Salvador and Honduras to link the archaeological sites of the Maya, incorporating a new system of national parks, to be called the Ruta Maya. Already in Central America there have been moves to protect endangered species and unique environments. This plan will augment a growing system of National Parks extending beyond the Maya area northwards in Mexico and southwards to Panama and Costa Rica, which has the most extensive network of all. The quetzal on our cover, once highly prized by precolumbian societies, has become a symbol of the need for ecological protection.

The Editor

HOW TO USE THIS HANDBOOK

The Mexican and Central Amercian Handbook is the most complete and up-to-date package of information for independent travellers on Mexico and the Central American republics currently in print. Its text is updated every year for the new edition which is published on 1 September. The text is based on the Editors' travels, contributions from national tourist authorities, notes from correspondents living in the countries we cover, detailed material and maps which Handbook users send us, and the extensive sources of information on Latin America available in London and elsewhere.

Editorial Logic Users of the Handbook will find that we employ a logical system of arrangement, which we believe is the most useful for travellers. The capital city is (with two exceptions, Mexico—dictated by geography, and Panama) the first place covered in detail. The territory is then divided into subsections; in Mexico and Guatemala, these subsections are numbered on the country contents and map as well as in the text. In the subsections, towns appear in sequence along a route, which falls within the natural geography of the region. The routes cover the most interesting places to visit and do not necessarily constitute the shortest possible distance from A to B. Details are also given of any interesting excursions or other sights that are off the route. Travellers can therefore plan their own itineraries according to the time available, and their own special interests.

Cross Referencing and Indexing There is a complete index of place names at the end of the book.

To make it easier for Readers to find their way around the text, we have a comprehensive system of cross-references. For ease of use, the "see page" entry has been highlighted in heavier type. On the page referred to, you will find the entry again emphasised in some form of heavier type.

Maps Three types are used:
A. Country Maps These appear at the start of each country chapter and show main access routes (not necessarily major roads in all cases), main towns, and divisions of the country as described in the text. These divisions are numbered on the map, in the country's contents list and at the text divisions in the chapter. The numbers are not recommenda- tions as to which parts of the country are most interesting to visit, they are only for easy identification.
B. Regional Maps These give extra information on a more detailed

Map Symbols

Roads	————	Capital Cities	■SANTIAGO
Railways	+++++++++++	Cities/Towns	●córdoba
Trails/Paths/Tracks	_ _ _ _	Archaeological sites	▲
Rivers	RÍO ARUÑA	Mountains	⌂
Ferries	....	Streets	SAN MARTÍN
Waterfall	⫠	Parks	
Barrier Reef	∼ ∼ ∼	Train station	T
Borders		Bus Station	B
Country Subdivisions	//////	Airport	✈
Metropolitan areas	▨	Key Numbers	6
Major Highway	▭		

scale and show the main physical features, towns, means of communication and points of interest.

C. City and Town Maps Generally these are detailed maps of town centres, showing means of access to bus and railway stations and airports. The main points of interest are indicated by means of a numbered key.

Introduction and Hints This first section in the book gives information and hints that apply generally to all the countries we cover on

- travel to and in Latin America
- money
- law enforcement
- security
- travelling with children
- camping
- language

- photography
- surface transport
- hitch-hiking
- motoring and motorcycling
- hiking and trekking
- river boats
- cycling

Health Information This major section by Dr David Snashall of St Thomas's Hospital Medical School, London, gives details of the health risks common in Mexico and Central America, and the sensible precautions travellers should take to combat them.

Country Sections Information is set out country by country in a constant sequence as follows:

- List of contents

● Description of physical geography

> history
>
> people
>
> economic report
>
> present form of government

● Survey of Cities, Towns and places of interest

> things to do
>
> things worth seeing
>
> where to stay
>
> eating out
>
> services for visitors

● Information for visitors

> what documents are necessary
>
> how to get there
>
> food
>
> health precautions
>
> the best time for visiting
>
> clothing
>
> currency regulations
>
> other essential information

All those readers who have written with valuable updating material are listed with thanks at the end of each chapter.

Hotels and Restaurants In large cities, lists of hotels and restaurants include only those establishments for which positive recommendations have been received. In smaller towns, these lists contain both the favourable recommendations and others. In general, restaurants are grouped by neighbourhood and by type of cuisine.

Prices Our hotel price ranges, for double rooms with taxes and service charges but without meals unless stated, are as follows:

L+—Over US$125	**L**—US$71-US$125	**A**—US$46-70
B—US$31-45	**C**—US$21-30	**D**—US$12-20
E—US$7-11	**F**—US$4-6	**G**—Up to US$3

Other abbreviations used in the book (apart from p.p. = per person; a/c = air conditioned; rec. = recommended; T = telephone) should be self-explanatory.

We are also grateful to those travellers, listed below, who have sent us important information for the "Introduction and Hints" section which follows: Tam Agosti-Gisler (Anchorage, Alaska), Vladimir Antonowych (Toronto), Peter Caesar (Bogotá), Bryan Crawford (Beauly, Inverness-shire), Philipp Dyckerhoff (München), Dag K Ellingsen (Oslo 2), Pauline Fearon (Hornchurch), Margaret Fleming (Karlsfeld, W Ger), C Gammell (London SE 20), Jim Hardy (Waukesha, Wis), Dr Paul Heaton (London NW6), Bill Hite (Forest, VA), Marcel Kersten (Roosendaal, Neth), Ole W Lund (Oslo 3), Sasha Macmiadhachain (Swanage), Herbert P Minderhond (Amsterdam), S D Minks (Thos and Jas Harrison Ltd, Liverpool), Eitan Nir (Beit Ha'emek, Israel) and Orit Sela (Cabri), Barry Oldham (Plymouth, Devon), Sarah Parry (Southampton), Sandrine Pétremand and Gilles Maitre (Bevaix, Switz), John M Raspey, Louise Santamera (Liverpool 3), Piero Scaruffi (Redwood City, CA), Karen Schulpzand and Rudy Cruysbergs (Dilbeek, Belgium), von Schubert (Kehl, W Ger), R W Le Sueur (Jersey), Eileen Synnott and Paul Gurn (Waterbury, CT), Marian Temple (Mérida, Mexico), Ingrid Walter and Norbert Eisinger (Schnelldorf, W Ger), Jonathan Weiland (Philadelphia, PA) and Meg Worley (Maryville, TE).

WARNING: Whilst every endeavour is made to ensure that the facts printed in this book are correct at the time of going to press, travellers are cautioned to obtain authoritative advice from consulates, airlines, etc. concerning current travel and visa requirements and conditions before embarkation. The publishers cannot accept legal responsibility for errors, however caused, which are printed in this book.

INTRODUCTION AND HINTS

AIR TRAVEL TO AND WITHIN THE REGION

Travel to and in Mexico and Central America All the main airlines plying to each country are given in the "Information for Visitors" sections. Weight allowances if going direct from Europe are 20 kg. for economy and business class or 30 kg. for first class. Many people travel to Mexico and Central America via the USA, and this usually means a luggage allowance of *2 pieces*. This varies from airline to airline, but allows you more than 20 kg. However, weight limits for internal flights are often lower; best to enquire beforehand.

Chris Parrott and Paul Davies, of Journey Latin America, have told us:
1. Generally it is cheaper to fly from London rather than a point in Europe to South American destinations.

2. Most airlines offer discounted (cheaper than official) fares of one sort or another on scheduled flights. These are not offered by the airlines direct to the public, but through agencies who specialize in this type of fare*. The very busy seasons are as follows: 7 December–15 January and July to mid-September. If you intend travelling during those times, book as far ahead as possible.

3. In the last two years there have been a number of charter flights to Acapulco in Mexico. The fares offered have been very cheap in low season (May) but less so at busy periods. At the time of going to press, charters from Britain to Mexico have an uncertain future; their continuation depends on Acapulco receiving a

*In London, these include **Journey Latin America**, 16 Devonshire Road, Chiswick, London W4 2HD (T 081-747 3108); **Trailfinders**, 48 Earl's Court Road, London W8 6EJ (T 071-938 3366); **Melia Travel Ltd.**, 12 Dover Street, London W1X 4NS (T 071-491 3881); **Steamond Ltd.**, 23 Eccleston Street, London SW1W 9LX (T 071-730 8646) and **Transatlantic Wings**, 70 Pembroke Road, London W8 (T 071-602 4021). (Ed.)

better press than of late.

4. Other fares fall into three groups, and are all on scheduled services:

A. Excursion (return) fares with restricted validity 7-180 days (Mexico); 7-90 days (Central America). These are fixed date tickets where the dates of travel cannot be changed after issue of ticket.

B. Yearly fares: these may be bought on a one-way or return basis, and usually the returns can be issued with the return date left open. You must, however, fix the route.

C. Student (or Under 26) fares. Some airlines are flexible on the age limit, others strict. One way and returns available, or "Open Jaws" (see below). NB Some student tickets carry standby status only, and should be avoided in the busy seasons (see above).

5. For people intending to travel a linear route and return from a different point from that which they entered, there are "Open Jaws" fares, which are available on student or yearly fares, or occasionally on excursion fares.

6. Many of these fares require a change of plane at an intermediate point, and a stopover may be permitted, or even obligatory, depending on schedules. Simply because a flight stops at a given airport does not mean you can break your journey there—the airline must have traffic rights to pick up or set down passengers between points A and B before it will be permitted. This is where dealing with a specialized agency (like Journey Latin America!) will really pay dividends. On multi-stop itineraries, the specialized agencies can often save clients hundreds of pounds.

7. Although it's a little more complicated, it's possible to sell tickets in London for travel originating in Latin America at substantially cheaper fares than those available locally. But, in the case of Mexico, the opposite is true. It is cheaper to buy flights from Mexico to London than London to Mexico. This is useful for the traveller who doesn't know where he or she will end up, or who plans to travel for more than a year. But a oneway ticket from Latin America is more expensive than a oneway in the other direction, so it's always best to buy a return.

8. Certain Central American countries impose local tax on flights originating there. Among these are Guatemala and Mexico.

9. There are several cheap French charters to Mexico and Guatemala, but no-one in the UK sells them. Try: Uniclam-Voyages, 63 rue Monsieur-le Prince, 75006 Paris. A cheap Swiss charter firm is Sindbad, 3 Schoffelgasse, 8025 Zürich. Aeroflot flies from Shannon to Mexico, Managua and Havana; these can be booked and bought through Journey Latin America. In addition there are a number of "packages" that include flights from Mexico to Cuba which can be bought locally in Mexico, or in advance from London.

10. If you buy discounted air tickets *always* check the reservation with the airline concerned to make sure the flight still exists. Also remember the IATA airlines' schedules change in March and October each year, so if you're going to be away a long time it's best to leave return flight coupons open.

In addition, check whether you are entitled to any refund or re-issued ticket if you lose, or have stolen, a discounted air ticket.

N.B. At the time of going to press, American Airlines were on the point of taking over Eastern Airlines' routes to the region. American's precise schedules had not been released and we advise readers to check in advance before planning a route. Continental Airlines is also rapidly expanding its routes to Central America.

Beware buying tickets from the general sales agents in Europe of minor Latin American airlines. They are sometimes incorrectly made out and therefore impossible to transfer or cash in. If you buy internal airline tickets in Latin American countries you may find cash refunds difficult to get if you change your plans: better to change your ticket for a different one. On the other hand you can save money by buying tickets in a country with a black exchange market, for local currency, for flights on its national airline. Overbooking by Latin American airlines is very common (largely due to repeated block bookings by travel agents, which everyone knows will not be used), so always reconfirm the next stage of your flight within 72 hours of your intended departure. And it does no harm to reconfirm yet again in the last 24 hours, just to show them you mean it, and turn up for the flight in good time (at least 2 hours before departure).

We advise people who travel the cheap way in Latin America to pay for all transport as they go along, and not in advance. This advice does not apply to people on a tight schedule: paying as you go along may save money, but it is likely to waste your time somewhat. The one exception to this general principle is in transatlantic flights; here money is saved by booking as far as possible in one operation.

The Amerbuspass covers the whole of Latin America, from Mexico City to Ushuaia, and entitles the holder to 15-20% discounts on tickets with participating operators; bookable in all Latin American capitals, Europe, Asia, Africa, Oceania, it is valid for 9,999 miles, up to 180 days. Unlimited stopovers, travel with either a confirmed or open itinerary. Contact TISA Internacional, B. Irigoyen 1370, Oficina 25/26, 1138 Buenos Aires, Argentina, T 642-7028, or Av. Larrazabal 493, 1408 Buenos Aires, P.O. Box 40 Suc. 1 (B), 1401 Buenos Aires.

Travel to the USA Until July 1988 all foreigners (except Canadians) needed visas to enter the USA. Despite subsequent relaxations of visa requirements for British air travellers with round-trip tickets to the USA, it is advisable to have a visa to allow entry by land, or on airlines from South and Central America which are not "participating carriers" on the Visa Waiver scheme. If you are thinking of travelling via the USA, or of visiting the USA after Latin America, you are strongly advised to get your visa from a US Consulate in your own country, not while travelling.

If you wish to visit a little-known part of the USA (and W Canada), David Stanley's *Alaska-Yukon Handbook* (Chico, CA 96927, Moon Publications), 230 pages, will be of the very greatest use. It costs only US$8 (book postage anywhere).

Shipping   There are few shipping services which carry passengers to Central America from Europe, the USA or elsewhere. Those that do are the Harrison Line, MV *Author*, which on its round trip from Liverpool to Felixstowe, UK, via the Caribbean and Central America, calls at Santo Tomás de Castilla (Guatemala), Puerto Cortés (Honduras) and Puerto Limón (Costa Rica). The total fare for the trip is £2,750 p.p. in a double cabin, or approximately £63 per day full board; the full round trip takes 6 weeks.

The only other Central American destination is the Panama Canal through which the following passenger-carrying freight lines pass: Columbus Line on round trip voyages from the USA to Australia and New Zealand; Chilean Line between East Coast USA and West Coast South America; Associated Container Transportation between USA and Australia/New Zealand; Lykes Line from Miami/New Orleans to Colombia, Ecuador and Chile; and Egon Oldendorff from the USA.

Our thanks are due to John Alton of Weider Travel, Charing Cross Shopping Concourse, The Strand, London WC2N 4HZ, T 071-836 6363, Telex 918791, for the above information. Enquiries regarding passages should be made through agencies in your own country, or through Weider Travel.

Details on shipping cars are given in the relevant country sections.

Warning   Many countries in Latin America are reluctant to let travellers enter their territory if they do not already have onward or return tickets. (Look under "Information for Visitors" sections for the countries you intend to visit.) The purchase of a Miscellaneous Charges Order (open ticket) from an IATA airline for (say) US$100 will satisfy this requirement in many but not all countries; it is valid for 12 months, can be exchanged for a ticket, or cashed at the airline offices in the country of issue. (The onward ticket requirement does not apply to travellers with their own vehicles.) If you have no onward ticket, a consular letter verifying a statement from your bank at home, giving details of your account with them, might be helpful.

DOCUMENTATION AND SECURITY

Passports   Remember that Latin Americans, especially officials, are very document-minded. You should always carry your passport in a safe place about your person, or if not going far, leave it in the hotel safe. If staying in a country for several weeks, it is worth while registering at your Embassy or Consulate. Then, if your passport is stolen, the process of replacing it is simplified and speeded up. Keeping photocopies of essential documents, and some additional passport-sized photographs, is recommended

Remember that it is your responsibility to ensure that your passport is stamped in and out when you cross frontiers. The absence of entry and exit stamps can cause serious difficulties: seek out the proper migration offices if the stamping process is not carried out as you cross. Also, do not lose your entry card; replacing one causes a lot of trouble, and possibly expense.

If travelling from the West Coast of the USA to Latin America and you require visas, most can be obtained in one building in San Francisco, at 870 Market Street (in 1989, represented here were Mexico, Guatemala, Honduras, Costa Rica, Panama, Colombia, Venezuela, Argentina, Chile, Paraguay, Bolivia, Peru, Ecuador—and Brazil only 300 m. away). You are advised to check in advance that the office you want is still there.

Identity and Membership Cards Membership cards of British, European and US motoring organizations have been found useful for discounts off hotel charges, car rentals, maps, towing charges, etc. Student cards must carry a photograph if they are to be of any use in Latin America for discounts. (If you describe yourself as a student on your tourist card you may be able to get discounts, even if you haven't a student card.). Business people should carry a good supply of visiting cards, which are essential for good business relations in Latin America.

Money is best carried in US dollar travellers' cheques (denominations of US$50 and US$100 are preferable, though one does need a few of US$20) or cash. Sterling and other currencies are not recommended. Travellers' cheques are convenient but they attract thieves (though refunds can of course be arranged) and you will find that they are more difficult than dollar bills to change in small towns. Though the risk of loss is greater, many travellers take part of their funds in US dollar notes; better rates can usually be obtained for them. Low-value US dollar bills are very useful for shopping: shopkeepers and exchange shops (*casas de cambio*) tend to give better exchange rates than hotels or banks. The better hotels will normally change travellers' cheques for their guests (often at a rather poor rate), but if you're travelling on the cheap it is essential to keep in funds; watch weekends and public holidays carefully and never run out of local currency. Take plenty of local currency, in small denominations, when making trips into the interior. Spread your money around your person: less chance of thieves finding it all. Don't leave cash in your shoe for a long time, it may become too damaged to exchange or use.

American Express (Amex), Carte Blanche and Diners Club credit cards are useful, and so are those of the Visa and Master Charge groups. Conceal them very carefully (*not* under the insole of a shoe, however: that may render them unusable!), and make sure you know the correct procedure if they are lost or stolen. We advise using credit cards only for dollar transactions, or in countries where there is no black market exchange rate. Remember that credit card transactions are always at an officially recognized rate of exchange (sometimes, if there are several, the least favourable one); you may find it much cheaper to pay cash and get the parallel rate. Note that the Eurocard/Eurocheque system is virtually unknown in Latin America. For credit card security, insist that imprints are made in your presence and that any imprints incorrectly completed should be torn into tiny pieces. Also destroy the carbon papers after the form is completed (signatures can be copied from them).

We recommend in general the use of American Express or Thomas Cook US$ travellers' cheques, but should point out that less commission is often charged on Citibank or Bank of America cheques, if they are cashed at Latin American branches of those banks. These cheques are always accepted by banks, even though they may not be as well known outside banks as those of American Express or Thomas Cook. It is a good idea to take two kinds of cheque: if large numbers of one kind have recently been forged or stolen, making people suspicious, it is unlikely to have happened simultaneously with the other kind. Several banks charge a high fixed commission for changing travellers' cheques—sometimes as much as US$5-10 a cheque—because they don't really want to be bothered. Exchange houses (*casas de cambio*) are usually much better for this service. Some establishments may ask to see the customer's record of purchase before accepting travellers' cheques.

In those countries where there is a black market, find out how much of their currency you are allowed to take in, and *buy before you enter*, preferably in a big city where banks are unlikely to make a charge on the transaction. (In small places the bank may charge up to 50 cents on a 10-dollar travellers' cheque.) There is always an active (but illegal) black market in local currency in all those countries that have no free exchange; it is, however, not illegal to buy currency outside the country you are about to enter, up to any limit that may be imposed. The City of London currency dealers are worth checking with: some find themselves overloaded from time to time with exotic currencies they can't get rid of, and let them go at a large discount. Check in the publication *Banknotes of the World* (the dealers usually have it for consultation) that the notes you are being offered are still current, however.

N.B. Remember that a transfer of funds, even by telex, can take several days, and charges can be high; a recommended method is, before leaving, to find out which local bank is correspondent to your bank at home, then when you need funds, telex your own bank and ask them to telex the money to the local bank (confirming by air mail). It is possible to obtain money within hours by this method.

Whenever you leave a country, sell any local currency before leaving, because the further away you get, the less the value of a country's money.

Americans (we are told) should know that if they run out of funds they can expect no help from the US Embassy or Consul other than a referral to some welfare organization. In this regard, find out before you go precisely what services and assistance your embassy or consulate can provide if you find yourself in difficulties.

Law Enforcement   Whereas in Europe and North America we are accustomed to law enforcement on a systematic basis, in general, enforcement in Latin America is achieved by periodic campaigns. The most typical is a round-up of criminals in the cities just before Christmas. In December, therefore, you may well be asked for identification at any time, and if you cannot produce it, you will be jailed. At first sight, on arrival, it may seem that you can flout the law with impunity, because everybody else is obviously doing so. If a visitor is jailed his friends should take him food every day. This is especially important for people on a diet, such as diabetics. It must also be borne in mind that in the event of a vehicle accident in which anyone is injured, all drivers involved are automatically detained until blame has been established, and this does not usually take less than two weeks. Sometimes these problems can be avoided by offering a bribe, but this, naturally, is illegal and may be extremely dangerous. Imported cigarettes from airport duty-free shops are very much appreciated by customs officials.

Never offer a bribe unless you are fully conversant with the customs of the country. Wait until the official makes the suggestion, or offer money in some form which is apparently not bribery, e.g. "In our country we have a system of on-the-spot fines. Is there a similar system here?" Do not assume that an official who accepts a bribe is prepared to do anything else that is illegal. You bribe him to persuade him to do his job, or to persuade him not to do it, or to do it more quickly, or more slowly. You do not bribe him to do something which is against the law. The mere suggestion would make him very upset.

Security Try and look as little like a tourist as possible, especially in poor areas of cities. Most crime is opportunistic so if you are aware of the dangers, act confidently and use your common sense you will lessen many of the risks. The following tips, all endorsed by travellers, are meant to forewarn, but not alarm, you. Keep all documents secure; hide your main cash supply in different places or under your clothes (extra pockets sewn inside shirts and trousers, moneybelts, neck or leg pouches, and elasticated support bandages for keeping money and cheques above the elbow or below the knee have been repeatedly recommended—the last by John Hatt in *The Tropical Traveller*). Keep cameras in bags (preferably with a chain or wire in the strap to defeat the slasher) or briefcases; take spare spectacles (eyeglasses); don't wear wrist-watches (unless they're digital—too cheap and plentiful to attract thieves nowadays) or jewellery. If you wear a shoulder-bag in a market, carry it in front of you. Backpacks are vulnerable to slashers: a good idea is to cover with a sack with maybe a layer of wire netting between. Use a pack which is lockable at its base.

Ignore mustard smearers and paint or shampoo sprayers, and strangers' remarks like "what's that on your shoulder?" or "have you seen that dirt on your shoe?". Furthermore, don't bend over to pick up money or other items in the street. These are all ruses intended to distract your attention and make you easy for an accomplice to steal from. If someone follows you when you're in the street, let him catch up with you and "give him the eye".

Be wary of "plainclothes policemen"; insist on seeing identification and on going to the police station by main roads. Do not hand over your identification (or money—which he should not need to see anyway) until you are at the station. Be even more suspicious if he seeks confirmation of his status from a passer-by. If attacked, remember your assailants may well be armed, and try not to resist.

It is best, if you can trust your hotel, to leave any valuables you don't need in safe-deposit there, when sightseeing locally. If you don't trust the hotel, lock everything in your pack and secure that in your room (some people take eyelet-screws for padlocking cupboards or drawers). If you lose valuables, always report to police and note details of report—for insurance purposes.

When you have all your luggage with you at a bus or railway station, be especially careful: don't get into arguments—or even conversations—with any locals if you can help it, and lock all the items together with a chain or cable if you are waiting for some time. Take a taxi between airport/bus station/railway station and hotel, if you can possibly afford it. Avoid night buses; never arrive at night; and watch your belongings whether they are stowed inside or outside the cabin. Finally, never accept food, drink, sweets or cigarettes from unknown fellow-travellers on buses or trains. They may be drugged, and you would wake up hours later without your belongings. In this connection, never accept a bar drink from an opened bottle (unless you can see that that bottle is in general use): always have it uncapped in front of you.

A last point, from Canadian film-maker Russ Bentley: a courteous, friendly manner of speaking, including to beggars and market vendors, may avoid your being "set up" for robbery or assault. For specific local problems, see under the individual countries in the text.

It has been reported that women travelling alone or in pairs have suffered from sexual harassment, particularly in Mexico. On the other hand, several women have written to stress the enjoyment they have had travelling alone in Latin America. The most common advice is to "take care with your dress code" and exercise reasonable caution (i.e. don't explore night-life on your own, don't go for long walks on deserted beaches, speak the language, etc.) to ensure a successful trip.

ACCOMMODATION

Hotels A cheap but not bad hotel might be in the region of US$5-7 a night in Mexico. For the indigent, it is a good idea to ask for a boarding house—*casa de huéspedes, hospedaje, pensión, casa familial* or *residencial*, according to country; they are normally to be found in abundance near bus and railway stations and markets. Good value hotels can also be found near truckers' stops/service stations; they are usually secure. There are often great seasonal variations in hotel prices in resorts. Remember, cheaper hotels don't always supply soap, towels and toilet paper. A useful tip: ask the car rental agency employees at the airport for advice when you arrive—as long as they are not busy. And another, always ask for the best room.

Warning The electric showers used in innumerable cheap hotels are extremely dangerous. If you can't avoid using them, check the wiring for obvious flaws and try not to touch the rose while it is producing hot water.

Youth Hostels Organizations affiliated to the Youth Hostels movement exist in Mexico, Costa Rica and Guatemala. Further information in the country sections and from the IYHA.

Meals There is a paragraph on each nation's food under "Information for Visitors". For reliable cheap meals, look in and near the markets and eat what the locals are eating, making sure that you can see it being cooked.

Camping There is a growing network of organized campsites, to which reference is made in the text immediately below hotel lists, under each town. If there is no organized site in town, a football pitch or gravel pit might serve. Géraldine des Cressonnières, of Linkebeek, Belgium, gives the following rules for "wild" camping: (1) arrive in daylight; (2) ask permission to camp from the parish priest, or the fire chief, or the police, or a farmer regarding his own property; (3) never ask a group of people— especially young people; (4) never camp on a beach (because of sandflies and thieves). If you can't get information from anyone, camp in a spot where you can't be seen from the nearest inhabited place.

Gas cylinders and bottles are usually exchangeable, but if not can be recharged; specify whether you use butane or propane. (Liquid fuels are readily available.)

Hammocks A hammock can be an invaluable piece of equipment, especially if travelling on the cheap. It will be of more use than a tent because many places have hammock-hooks, or you can sling a hammock between trees, etc. Bryan Crawford, of Beauly, Inverness-shire, Scotland, recommends carrying a 10-metre rope and some plastic sheeting. "The rope gives a good choice of tree distances and the excess provides a hanging frame for the plastic sheeting to keep the rain off. Metal S-hooks can be very useful, especially under lorries". Don't forget a mosquito net if travelling in insect-infected areas. Tips on buying a hammock are given in the Mérida (Yucatán) **Shopping** section. Good hammocks are also sold in Guatemala. If in any doubt about quality or size, seek advice before buying. And as Remo Bulgheroni of Killroergen (Switzerland) says: "don't make a mess with your end strings because it makes your hammock useless and only the sellers can help you fast."

Toilets Many of the cheapest hotels in the poorer areas, also restaurants and bars, have inadequate water supplies. This may mean that used toilet paper should not be flushed down the pan, but placed in the receptacle provided. This is not very sanitary, of course, but a blocked pan or drain is infinitely more of a health risk.

Cockroaches These are ubiquitous and unpleasant, but not dangerous. Take some insecticide powder if staying in cheap hotels; Baygon (Bayer) has been recommended. Stuff toilet paper in any holes in walls that you may suspect of being parts of cockroach runs.

ETIQUETTE AND LANGUAGE

Travellers' Appearance There is a natural prejudice in all countries against travellers who ignore personal hygiene and have a generally dirty and unkempt appearance. Most Latin Americans, if they can afford it, devote great care to their clothes and appearance; it is appreciated if visitors do likewise. The general prejudice previously reported against backpacks has virtually disappeared, unless carried by those whom officials identify as "hippies". One tip we have received; young people of informal dress and life-style may find it advantageous to procure a letter from someone in an official position testifying to their good character, on official-looking notepaper. John Oliver, of Durban, tells us that a photograph of a pretty blonde young woman inside one's passport can have a similar salutary effect on Latin American officials!

Some countries have laws or prejudices against the wearing by civilians of army-surplus clothing. In many places there is also a prejudice against shorts, which are only appropriate on the beach, or for jogging, or for sports and games. A medium weight shawl with some wool content is recommended for women: it can double as pillow, light blanket, bathrobe or sunscreen as required.

Drugs Users of drugs, even of soft ones, without medical prescription should be particularly careful, as some countries impose heavy penalties— up to ten years' imprisonment—for even the simple possession of such substances. In this connection, the planting of drugs on travellers—by traffickers or the police—is not unknown. If offered drugs on the street, make no response at all and keep walking. Note that people who roll their own cigarettes are often suspected of carrying drugs and subjected to intensive searches. Advisable to stick to commercial brands of cigarettes—but better still not to smoke at all.

Courtesy Remember that politeness—even a little ceremoniousness— is much appreciated. In this connection professional or business cards are useful (and have even been known to secure for their owners discount prices in hotels). Michael Davison makes the following suggestions: men should always remove any headgear and say "con permiso" when entering offices, and be prepared to shake hands (this is much commoner in Latin America than in Europe or North America); always say "Buenos días" or "Buenas tardes" and wait for a reply before proceeding further; in a word, don't rush them! Always remember that the traveller from abroad has enjoyed greater advantages in life than most Latin American minor officials, and should be friendly and courteous in consequence. N. F. Hawkes adds: never be impatient or criticize situations in public: the officials may know more English than you think and they can certainly interpret gestures and facial expressions. Be judicious about discussing politics with strangers (especially in Guatemala, Honduras and El Salvador). Politeness can be a liability, however, in some situations; most Latin Americans are disorderly queuers. Russ Bentley stresses that politeness and friendliness, with small useful gifts for children such as pencils and scratchpads, not only increase the pleasure of one's trip, but may well improve one's personal security.

Moira Chubb, from New Zealand, suggests that if you are a guest and are offered food that arouses your suspicions, the only courteous way out is to feign an allergy or a stomach ailment.

Language Without some knowledge of Spanish you can become very frustrated and feel helpless in many situations. English is absolutely useless off the beaten track. Some initial study, to get you up to a basic Spanish vocabulary of 500 words or so, and a pocket dictionary and phrase-book, are most strongly recommended: your pleasure will be doubled if you can talk to the locals. Not all the locals speak Spanish, of course; you will find that some Indians in the more remote highland parts of Guatemala speak only their indigenous languages, though there will usually be at least one person in each village who can speak Spanish.

The basic Spanish of Hispanic America is that of south-western Spain, with soft "c's" and "z's" pronounced as "s", and not as "th" as in the other parts of Spain. Castilian Spanish is readily understood, but is not appreciated when spoken by non-Spaniards; try and learn the basic Latin American pronunciation. Differences in vocabulary also exist, both between peninsular Spanish and Latin American Spanish, and between the usages of the different countries.

INTERNAL SURFACE TRANSPORT

Surface Transport The continent has a growing road system for motor traffic, with frequent bus services. Some bus services in Mexico and Central America are excellent. In mountainous country, however, do not expect buses to get to their destination, after long journeys, anywhere near on time. When the journey takes more than 3 or 4 hours, meal stops at country inns or bars, good and bad, are the rule. See what the locals are eating—and buy likewise, or make sure you're stocked up well on food and drink at the start. For drinks, stick to bottled water or soft drinks or coffee (black). The food sold by vendors at bus stops may be all right: watch if locals are buying, though unpeeled fruit is of course reliable. (See above on **Security** in buses.)

In most countries trains are slower than buses. They do tend, however, to provide finer scenery, and you can normally see much more wildlife than from the road—it is less disturbed by one or two trains a day than by the more frequent road traffic. Moreover, so many buses now show video films that you can't see the countryside because the curtains are drawn. Complaining loudly to the conductor that you cannot see the beautiful landscape may persuade him to give you his seat at the front.

Hitch-hiking This custom is increasing in Latin America, and travellers have reported considerable success in virtually all countries. Neatness of appearance certainly helps. Costa Rica and Panama are reported as good. If trying to hitchhike away from main roads and in sparsely-populated areas, however, allow plenty of time.

Hitch-hiking in Latin America is reasonably safe and straightforward for males and couples, provided one speaks some Spanish. It is a most enjoyable mode of transport—a good way to meet the local people, to improve one's languages and to learn about the country. Truck drivers in particular are often well versed in things of interest one is passing, e.g. crops and industries.
    A few general hints: in remoter parts, make enquiries first about the volume of traffic on the road. On long journeys, set out at crack of dawn, which is when trucks usually leave. They tend to go longer distances than cars.

Motoring The car freely crosses international frontiers without payment of customs duties provided it is eventually returned to its country of origin. In Central America, this is controlled by an entry made in your passport.
    A separate insurance policy has to be issued in each country if a claim is to be legally payable in the country where an accident occurs. Very few companies have the necessary international connections, but one which does is American International Underwriters, 700 Pine Street, New York, T (212) 770-7000. Give them at least four months' notice of your requirements. Also Sanborn's Mexican Insurance Service, with branches in US-Mexican border towns, can extend insurance beyond Mexico. Remember that in many countries third-party insurance for drivers may not be compulsory, or if compulsory, not enforced; you may have no claim on the other driver after an accident, except through the courts—a time-consuming exercise. If you are injured in an accident, people may refuse to take you to hospital; if you are found dead on arrival they could be jailed until it is proved that they were not responsible for the accident. An additional reason for always driving carefully.
    The normal saloon car reaches most destinations of interest to the tourist. High ground clearance is useful for badly surfaced or unsurfaced roads and can

be of greater value than 4-wheel drive. The latter is recommended for mountainous terrain and unmade roads off the beaten track. In some places, service is not available for sophisticated items like automatic transmission, electronic ignition and fuel injection, so the simpler the car the better. Most mechanics in Latin America are great improvisers, preferring to repair rather than replace. Japanese makes are a good choice (e.g. Toyota or Nissan) since they are represented in every country. It's an advantage if you can sleep comfortably in your vehicle; hence the liking for minibuses such as the VW, which can be "Africanized" by the makers, with protective grills and additional cranked exhaust pipe added and a converter for high altitudes; there is also a good VW service network throughout the continent. VW drivers should note that, despite VW's wide network in South America, post-1985 models from Europe are difficult to service and repair, not so the earlier models. VW minibuses should have the normal diesel engine, not a turbo, or 4-wheel drive version, for the same reason.

Theft of all vehicles is common. Apply at least two anti-theft devices when parked, even in car parks, and remove easily detachable items such as hub-caps, mirrors and windscreen wipers. At least one locking wheel nut per wheel is useful. A policy of insurance may not satisfactorily solve the problem of a car stolen outside its country of origin. There will be a delay of at least a month in paying the claim, and the sum insured may be inadequate if the theft occurs in a country where cars are more expensive than in the country of origin. Import duty becomes payable on the stolen car, and again on any car bought for the return trip home. If, on the other hand, a cash settlement is made, there may be difficulties with exchange control. The same is largely true if a vehicle becomes a total loss in an accident.

Unleaded petrol (gasoline) is not available, except in parts of Mexico. Spare fuel should be in steel, not plastic, cans. You won't have travelled far before the plastic can will spring a leak, and there is danger of a spark from static electricity igniting the petrol when pouring. In remote areas, gas stations (few and far between, so keep well topped up) are unmarked. Look for a building with empty oil drums outside or ask. In this connection, it is wise to carry a funnel and/or hose to help fill the tank; often in rural areas there are no pumps and fuel must be taken from a drum. An in-line fuel filter is an advantage. In Mexico, there are not many gas stations on the main roads: you need to look in the villages off the road. You can reduce the risk of a broken windscreen on gravel roads by not following closely behind other vehicles, and reducing speed when other vehicles (especially trucks with double rear wheels) are passing.

In addition to the normal spares carried, fan belt, spark plugs etc., the more adventurous driver needs a spade, tow cable, planks for placing under the wheels when stuck in dust or sand, filters for fuel, air, water and oil, light bulbs, wiper blades, spare parts for the suspension and steering, jump leads in case of battery failure, extra battery as back-up, and either an extra spare wheel or repair patches, air pump and valve screw. Help to repair a tyre is sometimes only available if you can provide these items yourself. An emergency fan belt which can be fitted without the use of tools is available from Flexicom Ltd, North Wing Mills, Bradford BD1 4EP, England.

Make a check list to ensure you have everything before you start each journey. The list is also useful for establishing what it is essential to replace after the theft of a car's contents. If you carry a cooler for food and drink, any official on the highway who spots it is likely to ask for refreshments, so take plenty or you may end up with none for yourself.

If driving and camping, the purchase of a 12-volt low-consumption neon light will add greatly to convenience.

Motorcycling The following advice was received from Charles and Lucia Newall: *Machine*: The bike should be tough and simple and capable of handling dirt roads.

If riding solo a large 4-stroke trail bike, e.g. Honda or Yamaha 500, would be ideal; if carrying a passenger a larger machine might be needed. We used an 800cc BMW road bike which handled a variety of conditions with ease.

Preparations: Fit a handlebar windscreen rather than a large touring fairing, which will hamper low-speed handling and complicate shipping from Panama if continuing south. Standard air filters should be replaced by cleanable types e.g. K and N. You may need to carry a set of smaller carburettor jets to adapt the engine for high altitudes; chech with the manufacturer.

The standard rear suspension on motorcycles may give trouble if you are going to travel on unmade roads; again, check with the manufacturer. If so, fit high-quality replacement units (Konis) with springs matched for the weight carried.

The luggage panniers and rack should be very robust; distribute the weight of luggage around the bike rather than just piling it on the back. A fuel range of about 250 (400 km.) miles is useful and also the ability to run on 80-octane fuel.

Spares: A modern well-maintained machine shouldn't need any major repairs on a 25,000-mile trip. Take the usual consumables with you, such as plugs, points, filters, bulbs, chains, tubes and a set of cables; add to this any other parts which might be weak points on your machine. If possible, take spare tyres. Make arrangements to have parts sent out from home if you need anything unusual; a parts book and a good manual are invaluable. Find out how to service your machine and carry the correct tools. (Local mechanics are very good at making do without the proper parts.)

Clothes: Your clothing should keep you comfortable from 20° to 85°F and include a tough waterproof outer layer complete with overboots and overgloves.

Security: Security is not a problem; use a strong chain and lock. Hotel owners are very helpful and good about letting you bring your machine inside, but don't leave a loaded machine unattended. In general much safer than taking night buses or trains; cheaper too.

Documents: Passports, international driving licences, motoring association membership card (for discounts etc.), registration certificate, *Carnet de Passages*, or *Libreta de Paso* if intending to ride in those South American countries which require it (check at consulates). A letter from your Embassy, saying that you are a bona-fide tourist and have no intention of selling your bike, is very useful.

Warning: Do not attempt to take a bike through the Darién Gap.

Travelling with Children We are grateful to Tim and Arlene Frost, of New Zealand, for the following notes:

People contemplating overland travel in Latin America with children should remember that a lot of time can be spent waiting for buses, trains, and especially for aeroplanes. On bus journeys, if the children are good at amusing themselves, or can readily sleep while travelling, the problems can be considerably lessened. Travel on trains, while not as fast or at times as comfortable as buses, allows more scope for moving about. Some trains provide tables between seats, so that games can be played.

Food can be a problem if the children are not adaptable. It is easier to take biscuits, drinks, bread etc. with you on longer trips than to rely on meal stops where the food may not be to taste. A small immersion heater and jug for making hot drinks is invaluable, but remember that electric current varies. Try and get a dual-voltage one (110v and 220v).

Fares: On all long-distance buses you pay for each seat, and there are no half-fares if the children occupy a seat each. For shorter trips it is cheaper, if less comfortable, to seat small children on your knee. Often there are spare seats which children can occupy after tickets have been collected. In city and local excursion buses, small children generally do not pay a fare, but are not entitled to a seat when paying customers are standing. On sightseeing tours you should *always* bargain for a family rate—often children can go free. (In trains, reductions for children are general, but not universal.)

All civil airlines charge half for children under 12, but some military services don't have half-fares, or have younger age limits.

Hotels: In all hotels, bargain for rates. If charges are per person, always insist that two children will occupy one bed only, therefore counting as one tariff. If rates are per bed, the same applies. In either case you can almost always get a reduced rate at cheaper hotels. (In restaurants, you can normally buy children's helpings, or divide one full-size helping between two children.)

Generally, travel with children presents no special problems—in fact the path is often smoother for family groups. Officials tend to be more amenable where children are concerned. Moreover, even thieves and pickpockets seem to have some of the traditional respect for families, and may leave you alone because of it!

Cycling Hallam Murray writes: Over the past decade, bicycle technology has improved in leaps and bounds. With the advent of Kevlar tyres and puncture-resistant inner tubes it is now theoretically possible to cycle from Alaska to Tierra del Fuego without so much as a single puncture. For the traveller with a zest for adventure and a limited budget there is unlikely to be a finer way to explore. At first glance a bicycle may not appear to be the most obvious vehicle for a major journey, but given ample time and reasonable energy it most certainly is the best. It can be ridden, carried by almost every form of transport from an aeroplane to a canoe, and can even be lifted across one's shoulders over short distances. On my most recent journey from Lake Titicaca to Tierra del Fuego—largely on unpaved roads, many of which would have defeated even the most robust car or truck—I was often envied by travellers using more orthodox transport, for I was able to travel at my own pace, to explore more remote regions and to meet people who are not normally in contact with tourists.

Choosing a Bicycle: The choice of bicycle depends on the type and length of expedition being undertaken and on the terrain and road surfaces likely to be encountered. Unless you are planning a journey almost exclusively on paved roads—when a high quality touring bike such as a Dawes Super Galaxy would probably suffice—I would strongly recommend a mountain bike. The good quality ones (and the cast iron rule is **never** to skimp on quality) are incredibly tough and rugged, with low gear ratios for difficult terrain, wide tyres with plenty of tread for good road-holding, cantilever brakes, and a low centre of gravity for improved stability. Expect to pay upwards of US$800 for such a machine. Although touring bikes, and to a lesser extent mountain bikes, and spares are available in the larger Latin American cities, remember that in the developing world most indigenous manufactured goods are shoddy and rarely last. In some countries, such as Mexico, Chile and Uruguay, imported components can be found but they tend to be extremely expensive. Buy everything you possibly can before you leave home.

Bicycle Equipment : A small but comprehensive tool kit (to include chain rivet and crank removers, a spoke key and possibly a block remover), a spare tyre and inner tubes, a puncture repair kit with plenty of extra patches and glue, a set of brake blocks, brake and gear cables and all types of nuts and bolts, at least 12 spokes (best taped to the chain stay), a light oil for the chain, tube of waterproof grease, a pump secured by a pump lock, a Blackburn stopblock (my choice for the most invaluable accessory and they are cheap and virtually weightless), a cyclometer, a loud bell, and a secure lock and chain. *Richard's Bicycle Book* makes useful reading for even the most mechanically minded.

Luggage and equipment: Strong and waterproof front and back panniers are a must. A top bag cum rucksack (e.g. Carradice) makes a good addition for use on and off the bike. I used a Cannondale front bag for my maps, camera, compass, altimeter, notebook and small tape-recorder. My total luggage weighed 27 kg.—on the high side, but I never felt seriously overweight. "Gaffa" tape is excellent for protecting vulnerable parts of panniers and for carrying out all manner of repairs. My most vital equipment included a light and waterproof tent, a 3 season sleeping bag, an Optimus petrol stove (the best I have ever used for it is light and efficient and petrol can be found almost everywhere), a plastic survival bag for storing luggage at night when camping, 4 elastic straps, 4 one-litre water bottles, Swiss Army knife, torch, comprehensive medical kit, money belts, a hat to protect against hours of ferocious tropical sun and small presents such as postcards of home, balloons and plastic badges. A rubber mouse can do wonders for making contact with children in isolated villages.

All equipment and clothes should be packed in plastic bags to give extra protection against dust and rain. Always take the minimum clothing. It's better to buy extra items en route when you find you need them. Naturally the choice will depend on whether you are planning a journey through tropical lowlands, deserts, high mountains or a combination, and whether rain is to be expected. Generally it is best to carry several layers of thin light clothes than fewer bulky, heavy ones. Always keep one set of dry clothes, including long trousers, to put on at the end of the day. I would not have parted with my incredibly light, strong, waterproof and wind resistant goretex jacket and overtrousers. I could have sold them 100 times over and in Bolivia was even offered a young mule in exchange! I took two pairs of training shoes and found these to be ideal for both cycling and walking.

Useful Tips: Wind, not hills is the enemy of the cyclist. Try to make the best use of the times of day when there is little; mornings tend to be best but there is no steadfast rule. Take care to avoid dehydration, by drinking regularly. In hot, dry areas with limited supplies of water, be sure to carry an ample supply. For food I carried the staples (sugar, salt, dried milk, tea, coffee, porridge oats, raisins, dried soups, etc.) and supplemented these with whatever local foods I could find in the markets. Give your bicycle a thorough daily check for loose nuts or bolts or bearings. See that all parts run smoothly. A good chain should last 2,000 miles, 3,200 km. or more but be sure to keep it as clean as possible—an old toothbrush is good for this—and to oil it lightly from time to time. Always camp out of sight of aroad. Remember that thieves are attracted to towns and cities, so when sight-seeing, try to leave your bicycle with someone such as a café owner or a priest. Country people tend to be more honest and are usually friendly and very inquisitive. However, don't take unnecessary risks; always see that your bicycle is secure. In more remote regions dogs can be vicious; carry a stick or some small stones to frighten them off. Traffic on main roads can be a nightmare; it is usually far more rewarding to keep to the smaller roads or to paths if they exist. Most towns have a bicycle shop of some description, but it is best to do your own repairs and adjustments whenever possible. In an emergency it is amazing how one can improvise with wire, string, dental floss, nuts and bolts, odd pieces of tin or "Gaffa" tape!

The Expedition Advisory Centre, administered by the Royal Geographical Society, 1, Kensington Gore, London SW7 2AR has published a useful monograph entitled *Bicycle Expeditions*, by Paul Vickers. Published in March 1990, it is available direct from the Centre, price £6.50 (postage extra if outside the UK).

Matthias Müller of Berlin 31 adds: From Guatemala to Panama, border officials ask for a document of ownership and a frame number for your bicycle. Without these you will have a lot of trouble crossing frontiers.

Hiking and Trekking Hilary Bradt, the well-known trekker, author and publisher, writes: A network of paths and tracks covers much of Central America and is in constant use by the local people. In Guatemala, which has a large Indian population, you can walk just about anywhere, but in the more European countries, particularly Costa Rica you must usually limit yourself to the many excellent national parks with hiking trails. Most Central American countries have an Instituto Geográfico Militar which sells topographical maps, scale 1:100,000 or 1:50,000. The physical features shown on these are usually accurate; the trails and place names less so. National Parks offices also sell maps.

Hiking and backpacking should not be approached casually. Even if you only plan to be out a couple of hours you should have comfortable, safe footwear and a daypack to carry your sweater and waterproof. At high altitudes the difference in temperature between sun and shade is remarkable. The longer trips mentioned in this book require basic backpacking equipment. Essential items are: backpack with frame, sleeping bag, closed cell foam mat for insulation, stove, tent or tarpaulin, dried food (not tins), water bottle, compass. Some but not all of these things are available locally.

Hikers have little to fear from the animal kingdom apart from insects (although it's best to avoid actually stepping on a snake), and robbery and assault are very rare. You are much more of a threat to the environment than vice versa. Leave no evidence of your passing; don't litter and don't give gratuitous presents of sweets or money to rural villagers. Respect their system of reciprocity; if they give you hospitality or food, then is the time to reciprocate with presents.

Maps Those from the Instituto Geográficos Militares in the capitals (see above) are often the only good maps available in Latin Amercica. It is therfore wise to get as many as possible in your home country before leaving, especially if travelling by land. A recommended series of general maps is that published by International Travel Map Productions (ITM), PO Box 2290, Vancouver BC, V6B 2WF, Canada, compiled with historical notes, by Kevin Healey. Available are South America South, North East and North West (1:4,000,000), Amazon Basin (1:4,000,000),

Central America (1:1,800,000), Costa Rica (1:500,000), the Yucatán (1:1,000,000) and Baja California (1:1,000,000).

Other Travel Books We should mention the "Backpacking Guide Series" published by Bradt Publications, 41 Nortoft Road, Chalfont St. Peter, Bucks, SL9 0LA, UK. They give detailed descriptions of hiking trails and much fascinating information, with many illustrations; a new edition of *Backpacking in Mexico and Central America* is due in 1991. (Bradt Publications also publish and sell other trail guides, and import trekking and topographical maps from South America, including the ITM series.) *South America on a Shoestring*, by Geoff Crowther (Lonely Planet Publications) has been recommended repeatedly for the quality of its maps. Lonely Planet's growing number of individual country guides have also been praised.

Another very useful book, highly recommended, aimed specifically at the budget traveller is *The Tropical Traveller*, by John Hatt (Pan Books, 2nd edition, 1985).

GENERAL ADVICE

Souvenirs Remember that these can almost invariably be bought more cheaply away from the capital, though the choice may be less wide. Bargaining seems to be the general rule in most countries' street markets. Visitors should remember that souvenirs made from endangered species, for example, sea-turtle shells, may not be imported into their home countries, and are advised to ask the responsible government agency at home for a complete list of the endangered species concerned.

If British travellers have no space in their luggage, they might like to remember Tumi, the Latin American Craft Centre, at 23 Chalk Farm Road, London NW1 (T 071-485 4152) and 2 New Bond Street Place, Bath (T 0225 62367), who specialize in Mexican and Andean products. There are similar shops in the USA; one good one is on the ground floor of Citicorp Center, Lexington Avenue and 53rd Street, New York.

Photography Take as much film in from home as you can; it is expensive in most places. Some travellers have advised against mailing exposed films home; better to take them with you. The postal authorities may use less sensitive equipment for X-ray screening than the airports do.

Dan Buck and Anne Meadows write: A note on developing film in Latin America. Black and white is a problem. Often it is shoddily machine-processed and the negatives are ruined. Ask the store if you can see an example of their laboratory's work and if they hand-develop.

Jeremy Till and Sarah Wigglesworth suggest that exposed film can be protected in humid areas by putting it in a balloon and tying a knot.

Mail Postal services in most countries are not very efficient, and pilfering is frequent. All mail, especially packages, should be registered. Some travellers recommend that mail should be sent to one's Embassy (or, if a card- or cheque holder, American Express agent) rather than to the Poste Restante/General Delivery (*Lista de Correos*) department of a country's Post Office. Some Embassies and post offices, however, do not keep mail for more than a month. If there seems to be no mail at the

WILL YOU HELP US?

We do all we can to get our facts right in **The Mexico & Central American Handbook.** Each chapter is thoroughly revised each year, but the territory covered is vast, and our eyes cannot be everywhere. A new highway or airport is built; a hotel, a restaurant, a cabaret dies; another, a good one is born; a building we describe is pulled down, a street renamed. Names and addresses of good hotels and restaurants for "budget-minded" travellers are always very welcome. We would especially like to receive diagrams of walks, national parks and other interesting areas to use as source material for the Handbook and other forthcoming titles.

Your information may be far more up-to-date than ours. If your letter reaches us early enough in the year it will be used in the next edition, but write whenever you want to, for all your letters are used sooner or later.

Thank you very much indeed for you help.

Trade & Travel Publications Limited
6 Riverside Court
Riverside Road
Lower Bristol Road
Bath BA2 3DZ. England

Lista under the initial letter of your surname, ask them to look under the initial of your forename or your middle name. For the smallest risk of misunderstanding, use title, initial and surname only. (If you're a British male, and all else fails, ask them to look under "E" for "Esquire"!—Geoffrey van Dulken.)

Explorers   The South American Explorers Club has a wealth of information for travellers to any part of Latin America: 1510 York Street, Denver, CO 80206, T (303) 320-0388; 1254 Toledo, Apartado 21-431, Eloy Alfaro, Quito, Ecuador, T 566-076; Av. Portugal 146, Casilla 3714, Lima, Peru, T 31-44-80.

Final Hints   Everybody has his/her own list. Items most often mentioned include a small portable stove (liquid fuel is more readily available than gas— though the latter is becoming more common—and you need a combination canteen to go with it), air cushions for slatted seats, strong shoes (and remember that footwear over 9½ English size, or 42 European size, is difficult to obtain in Latin America except Argentina and Brazil), money-belt or neck pouch, obtainable from Journey Latin America (address on **page** 11); a small first-aid kit and handbook, rubber window wedges, fully waterproof top clothing, wax earplugs and airline-type eye mask to help you sleep in noisy and poorly curtained hotel rooms, rubber-thong Japanese-type sandals (flip-flops), a polyethylene sheet 2 x 1 metres to cover possibly infested beds and train floors and shelter your luggage, polyethylene bags of varying sizes, a toilet bag you can tie round your waist, a sheet sleeping-bag and pillow-case or a separate pillow-case—in some countries they are not changed often in cheap hotels, a mosquito net (or a hammock with a fitted net), a clothes line, a nailbrush (useful for scrubbing dirt off clothes as well as off oneself), a vacuum flask, a water bottle, a small dual-voltage immersion heater, a small dual-voltage (or battery-driven) electric fan, tea bags, a light nylon waterproof shopping bag, a universal bath- and basin-plug of the flanged type that will fit any waste-pipe (or improvise one from a sheet of thick rubber), string, electrical insulating tape, large penknife preferably with tin and bottle openers, scissors and corkscrew—the famous Swiss Army range has been repeatedly recommended, collapsible drinking beaker, electric motor-cycle alarm for luggage protection, a flour sack and roll of wire mesh for ditto, alarm clock or watch, candle, torch (flashlight)—especially one that will clip on to a pocket or belt, small transistor radio or battery cassette-player (Walkman type) with earphones, pocket calculator, an adaptor and flex to enable you to take power from an electric-light socket (the Edison screw type is the most commonly used), a padlock for the doors of the cheapest and most casual hotels, spare chain-lengths and padlock for securing luggage to bed or bus/train seat. Small coins, postage stamps, visiting cards and postcards of views from your own country to give away as souvenirs to friendly locals. Useful medicaments are given at the end of the "Health Information" section (**page** 41); to these might be added some lip salve ("Lypsil" has been recommended), and pre-moistened wipes (such as "Wet Ones"). Always carry toilet paper. Women travelling alone may find it useful to wear a wedding ring. Extra passport photos may be useful, also photocopies of essential documents (passport, credit cards, air tickets). **Never** carry firearms. Their possession could land you in serious trouble.

A note for **contact lens wearers**: most countries have a wide selection of products for the care of lenses, so you don't need to take kilos of lotions.

Be careful when asking directions. Women probably know more about the neighbourhood; men about more distant locations. Policemen are often helpful. However, many Latin Americans will give you the wrong answer rather than admit they do not know; this may be partly because they fear losing face, but is also because they like to please. You are more likely to get reliable information if you carefully refrain from asking leading questions.

Lastly, a good principle is to take half the clothes (trousers with plenty of pockets are very useful), and twice the money, that you think you will need.

HEALTH INFORMATION

The following information has been very kindly compiled for us by Dr. David Snashall, who is presently Senior Lecturer in Occupational Health at St. Thomas's Hospital Medical School in London and Chief Medical Advisor of the British Foreign and Commonwealth Office. He has travelled extensively in Central and South America, worked in Peru and in East Africa and keeps in close touch with developments in preventative and tropical medicine. We incorporate also some welcome observations on the text by Dr. C. J. Schofield, editor of Parasitology Today. The publishers have every confidence that the following information is correct, but cannot assume any direct responsibility in this connection.

THE TRAVELLER to Central America is inevitably exposed to health risks not encountered in Britain or the USA, especially if he spends time in the tropical regions. Epidemic diseases have been largely brought under control by vaccination programmes and public sanitation but, in rural areas, the latter is rudimentary and the chances of contracting infections of various sorts are much higher than at home.

There are English-speaking doctors in most major cities. If you fall ill the best plan may be to attend the out-patient department of a local hospital or contact your Embassy representative for the name of a reputable doctor. (We give the names of hospitals and some recommended doctors in the main city sections.—Ed.) Medical practices vary from those at home but remember they have particular experience in dealing with locally-occurring diseases.

Self-medication is undesirable except for minor complaints but may be forced on you by circumstances. Whatever the circumstances, be wary of medicines prescribed for you by pharmacists; many are poorly trained and unscrupulous enough to sell you potentially dangerous drugs or old stock they want to get rid of. The large number of pharmacies throughout Central America is a considerable surprise to most people, as is the range of medicines you can purchase over the counter. There is a tendency towards over-prescription of drug mixtures and in general this should be resisted. Many drugs are manufactured under licence from American or European companies so the trade names may be familiar to you. This means that you do not need to carry a whole chest of medicines, but remember that the shelf-life of some items, especially vaccines and antibiotics, is markedly reduced in tropical conditions. Buy your supplies at the better outlets where they have refrigerators, even though it is more expensive. Check the expiry date of all preparations you buy.

Immigration officials sometimes confiscate scheduled drugs (Lomotil is an example) if they are not accompanied by a doctor's prescription.

With the following precautions and advice, you should keep as healthy as usual. Make local enquiries about health risks if you are apprehensive and take the general advice of European or North American families who have lived or are living in the country.

Before you go take out medical insurance. You should have a dental check-up, obtain a spare glasses prescription and, if you suffer from a chronic illness (such as diabetes, high blood pressure, ear or sinus troubles, cardiopulmonary disease or a nervous disorder) arrange for a check-up with your doctor, who can at the same time provide you with a letter explaining the details of your disability, if possible in English and Spanish. Check current practice in malaria prophylaxis (prevention).

Inoculations Smallpox vaccination is no longer required anywhere in the world. Cholera vaccination is not required for Latin America. The following vaccinations are recommended:

Yellow fever: this is a live vaccine not to be given to children under nine months of age or persons allergic to eggs. Immunity lasts ten years. An international certificate of yellow fever vaccination will be given and should be kept because it is sometimes asked for.
Typhoid (monovalent): one dose followed by a booster in a month's time; Immunity from this course lasts two to three years.
Poliomyelitis: this is a live vaccine generally given orally and a full course consists of three doses with a booster in tropical regions every three to five years.
Tetanus: one dose should be given with a booster (vital) at six weeks and another at six months, and ten-yearly boosters thereafter are recommended.

Children should, in addition, be properly protected against diphtheria, and against pertussis (whooping cough) and measles, both of which tend to be more serious infections than at home. Measles, mumps and rubella vaccine is now widely available but those teenage girls who have not had rubella (German measles) should be tested and vaccinated. Consult your doctor for advice on tuberculosis inoculation: the disease is still widespread.

Infectious Hepatitis (jaundice) is endemic throughout Mexico and Central America and seems to be frequently caught by travellers. The main symptoms are pains in the stomach, lack of appetite, lassitude, and the typical yellow colour of the skin. Medically speaking there are two different types, the less serious but more common is hepatitis A, for which the best protection is the careful preparation of food, the avoidance of contaminated drinking water and scrupulous attention to toilet hygiene. Human normal immunoglobulin (gamma globulin) confers considerable protection against the disease and is particularly useful in epidemics; it should be obtained from a reputable source and is certainly useful for travellers who intend to live rough: they should have a shot before leaving and have it repeated every six months. The dose is 250 mg under 10 years of age and 750 mg above. The dose of gamma globulin depends on the concentration of the particular preparation used, so the manufacturer's advice should be taken. A smaller dose than usual can be given if exposure is for one or two months only.

The other, more serious, version is hepatitis B which is acquired usually by injections with unclean needles, blood transfusions, as a sexually transmitted disease and possibly by insect bites. This disease can be effectively prevented by a specific vaccination requiring three shots over six months before travelling but this is quite expensive. If you have had jaundice in the past it would be worthwhile having a blood test to see if you are immune to either of the two types because this might avoid the neccessity for vaccination or gamma globulin.

If at a particular occupational risk (e.g. zoologists or veterinarians), or in the case of epidemics, there are vaccines against other diseases such as rabies.

AIDS in Mexico and Central America is increasing in its prevalence, as in most countries, but is still largely confined to the well known high risk sections of the population, i.e. homosexual men, intravenous drug abusers, prostitutes and children of infected mothers. The main risk to travellers is from from casual sex in the main cities, and the same precautions should be taken as when encountering any sexually transmitted disease. The AIDS virus (HIV) can be passed via unsterilized needles which have been previously used to inject an HIV positive patient, but the risk of this is very small indeed. It would however be sensible to check that needles have been properly sterilised or disposable needles used. Be wary of carrying disposable needles yourself: customs officials find them suspicious. The risk of receiving a blood transfusion with blood infected with the HIV virus is greater than from dirty needles because of the amount of fluid exchanged. Supplies of blood for transfusion should now be screened for HIV in all reputable hospitals so again the risk must be very small indeed. Catching the AIDS virus does not usually produce an illness in itself; the only way to be sure if you feel you have been put at risk is to have a blood test for HIV antibodies on your return to a place where there are reliable laboratory facilities. The test does not become positive for many weeks.

Common Problems, some of which will almost certainly be encountered, are:

Heat and Cold Full acclimatization to high temperatures takes about two weeks and during this period it is normal to feel relatively apathetic, especially if the relative humidity is high. Drink plenty of water (up to 15 litres a day are required when working physically hard in the tropics), use salt on your food and avoid extreme exertion. Tepid showers are more cooling than hot or cold ones. Large hats do not cool you down, but do prevent sunburn. Remember that, especially in the highlands, there can be a large and sudden drop in temperature between sun and shade and between night and day, so dress accordingly. Warm jackets and woollens are essential after dark at high altitude.

Altitude The highest major city in Mexico/Central America is Mexico City at 2,240 metres which is unlikely to cause any symptons more serious than some breathlessness and heart pounding. The following remarks therefore apply mainly to hill walkers and mountain climbers. Acute mountain sickness or *soroche* can strike from about 3,000 metres upwards. It is more likely to affect those who ascend rapidly (e.g. by plane) and those who over-exert themselves. Teenagers are particularly prone. Past experience is not always a good guide: the author, having spent years in Peru travelling constantly between sea level and very high altitude, never suffered the slightest symptoms, then was severely affected climbing Kilimanjaro in Tanzania.

On reaching heights above 3,000 metres, heart pounding and shortness of breath, especially on exertion, are almost universal and a normal response to the lack of oxygen in the air. *Soroche* takes a few hours or days to come on and presents with headache, lassitude, dizziness, loss of appetite, nausea and vomiting. Insomnia is common and often associated with a suffocating feeling when lying in bed. Keen observers may note their breathing tends to wax and wane at night and their face tends to be puffy in the mornings—this is all part of the syndrome. The treatment is rest, pain killers (preferably not aspirin-based) for the headache and anti-sickness pills for vomiting. Oxygen may help at very high altitudes. Various local panaceas ("Coramina glucosada", "Effortil", "Micoren") have their advocates. (The drug acetazolamide (Diamox) is said to facilitate acclimatization to altitude; detailed information is available from the Mountain Medicine Centre, c/o Dr. Charles Clarke, Dept. of Neurological Sciences, St. Bartholomew's Hospital, 38 Little Britain, London EC1A 7BE.—Ed.)

On arrival at places over 3,000 metres, a few hours' rest in a chair and avoidance of alcohol, cigarettes and heavy food will go a long way towards preventing *soroche*. Should the symptoms be severe and prolonged it is best to descend to lower altitude and re-ascend slowly or in stages. If this is impossible because of shortage of time or if the likelihood of acute mountain sickness is high then the drug Acetazoleamide (Diamox) can be used as a preventative and continued during the ascent. There is good evidence of the value of this drug in the prevention of *soroche* but some people do experience funny side effects. The usual dose is 500 mg of the slow-release preparation each night, starting the night before ascending above 3,000 metres.

Other problems experienced at high altitude are sunburn, excessively dry air causing skin cracking, sore eyes (it may be wise to leave your contact lenses out) and stuffy noses. It is unwise to ascend to high altitude if you are pregnant, especially in the first 3 months, or if you have any history of heart, lung or blood disease, including sickle-cell.

There is a further, albeit rare, hazard due to rapid ascent to high altitude called acute pulmonary oedema. The condition comes on quite rapidly with breathlessness, noisy breathing, cough, blueness of the lips and frothing at the mouth. Anybody developing this must be brought down as soon as possible, given oxygen and taken to hospital.

Rapid descent from high places will aggravate sinus and middle ear infections, and make bad teeth ache painfully. The same problems are sometimes experienced during descent at the end of a flight.

Despite these various hazards (mostly preventable) of high-altitude travel, many people find the environment healthier and more invigorating than at sea-level.

Intestinal Upsets Practically nobody escapes this one, so be prepared for it. Most of the time it is due to the insanitary preparation of food. Don't eat uncooked fish or vegetables, fruit with the skin on (always peel your fruit yourself), food that is exposed to flies, or salads. Tap water is rarely safe outside the major cities, especially in the rainy season, and stream water is often contaminated by communities living surprisingly high in the mountains. Filtered or bottled (make sure it is opened in your presence—Ed.) water is usually available and safe. If your hotel has a central hot-water supply, this is safe to drink after cooling. (In Mexico, many hotels provide chilled drinking water.) Ice for drinks should be made from boiled water but rarely is, so stand your glass on the ice cubes rather than putting them in the drink. Dirty water should first be strained through a filter bag (available from camping shops) and then boiled or treated. Water in general can be rendered safe in the following ways: boil for 5 minutes at sea level, longer at higher altitudes; or add three drops of household bleach to 1 pint of water and leave for 15 minutes; or add 1 drop of tincture of iodine to 1 pint of water and leave for 3 minutes. Commercial water-sterilizing tablets are available, for instance Sterotabs from Boots, England.

Fresh, unpasteurized milk is a source of food poisoning germs, tuberculosis and brucellosis. This applies equally to ice-cream, yoghurt and cheese made from unpasteurized milk. Fresh milk can be rendered safe by heating it to 62°C for 30 minutes followed by rapid cooling, or by boiling it. Matured or processed cheeses are safer than fresh varieties. Heat-treated (UHT), pasteurized or sterilized milk is becoming more available.

The most effective treatment for simple diarrhoea is rest and plenty to drink. Seek medical advice, however, if there is no improvement after three days. Much of the exhaustion of travellers' diarrhoea derives from the dehydration: water and salts are lost from the body and are not replaced. This can be remedied by proprietary preparations of salts which are dissolved in water, e.g. Electrosol (Macarthys) Dioralyte (Armour) Rehidrat (Searle) or ask for "suero oral" at a pharmacy or health centre. Marsha Stuart, of Save the Children, Westport, Conn. states that adding ½ teaspoon of salt (3.5g) and 4 tablespoons of sugar (40 g) to a litre of pure water makes a perfectly good substitute for the proprietary preparations. If rest is not possible, or the lavatory is full of other people with the same trouble, or if the stomach cramps are particularly bad, then the following drugs may help:

Loperamide (Imodium, Janssen, or Arret) up to eight capsules a day. This is now available in the UK without prescription.
Diaphenoxylate with atropine (Lomotil, Searle) up to 16 tablets in any 24 hours, but do *not* use for simple diarrhoea, only to relieve cramps and never in children.
Codeine phosphate 30 mg. One tablet every 4 hours.

Kaolin and morphine or Paregoric, as directed by the pharmacist.

Severe vomiting may be calmed by metoclopramide (Maxolon, Beechams; Primperan, Berk) 10 mg. tablet or injection every 8 hours, but not more frequently.

The vast majority of cases of diarrhoea and/or vomiting are due to microbial infections of the bowel plus an effect from strange food and drink. They represent no more than a temporary inconvenience which you learn to live with and need no special treatment. Fortunately, as you get accustomed to Latin American germs, the attacks become less frequent and you can be more daring in your eating habits.

If, in addition to cramps and diarrhoea, you pass blood in the bowel motion, have severe abdominal pain, fever and feel really terrible, you may well have dysentery and a doctor should be consulted at once. If this is not possible, the recommended treatment for bacillary dysentery is Tetracycline or Ampicillin 500 mg. every 6 hours plus replacement of water and salts. If you catch amoebic dysentery, which has rather similar symptoms, do not try to cure yourself but put yourself in proper medical hands; the treatment can be complex and self-medication may just damp down the symptoms with the risk of serious liver involvement later on.

Another common bowel infection is with the parasite Giardia Lamblia, which causes prolonged diarrhoea, bloating, persistent indigestion and sometimes loss of weight. This needs treating with a drug such as Metronidazole, best taken under medical supervision.

There are many travellers' tales about special diets, herbal medicines and the consumption of vast quantities of yoghurt as an aid to rehabilitating one's bowels after such attacks. None of them has proved to be useful, in contrast to the widespread success of oral rehydration (water and salt replenishment by mouth) in thousands of children seriously ill with diarrhoea throughout the third world. There is some evidence that alcohol and milk products can prolong diarrhoea so these are best avoided after an attack.

Enterovioform (Ciba), "Mexaform" in Latin America, can have serious side effects (nerve damage, especially to the eyes) if taken for long periods. The active agent, diodochlor-hydroxy-quinoline, is used in many antidiarrhoeals sold in Central America. If it is impossible to control the source of your food and you are likely to be far from medical attention (such as on Amazonian river trips) it is justifiable to take diloxanide furoate (Furamide) 500 mg. daily *plus* a sulphonamide drug e.g. Phthalylsulphathiazole (Thalazole, May & Baker) 500 mg. twice daily. Many businessmen and, for example, athletes who are on short visits of great importance take Streptotriad (May & Baker) one tablet twice daily to prevent diarrhoea and this has been proved to be effective.

Paradoxically, constipation is also common, probably induced by dietary change, inadequate fluid intake in hot places and long bus journeys. Simple laxatives are useful in the short term (the Editor recommends Senokot) and bulky foods such as maize, beans and plenty of fruit are also useful.

Insects These can be a great nuisance, especially in the tropics, and some, of course, are carriers of serious diseases. The best way of keeping them away at night is to sleep off the ground with a mosquito net and to burn mosquito coils containing pyrethrum. The best way to use insecticide aerosol sprays is to spray the room thoroughly in all areas and then shut the door for a while, re-entering when the smell has dispersed. Tablets of insecticide are also available which, when placed on a heated mat plugged into a wall socket, fill the room with insecticide fumes in the same way. The best repellants contain di-ethyl-meta-toluamide (DET) or di-methyl phthalate—sold as "Deet", "Six-Twelve Plus", "Off", "Boots' Liquid Insect Repellant", "Autan", "Flypel". Liquid is best for arms and face (care around eyes) and aerosol spray for clothes and ankles to deter chiggers, mites and ticks. Liquid DEET suspended in water can be used to impregnate cotton clothes and mosquito nets.

If you are bitten, itching may be relieved by baking-soda baths, anti-histamine tablets (care with alcohol or driving), corticosteroid creams (great care—never use if any hint of sepsis) or by judicious scratching. Calamine lotion and cream have limited effectiveness and antihistamine creams (e.g. Antihisan, May & Baker) have a tendency to cause skin allergies and are, therefore, not generally recommended.

Bites which become infected (commonly in the tropics) should be treated with a local antiseptic or antibiotic cream, such as Cetrimide BP (Savlon, ICI) as should infected scratches.

Skin infestations with body lice (crabs) and scabies are, unfortunately, easy to pick up. Use gamma benzene hexachloride for lice and benzene benzoate solution for scabies. Crotamiton cream (Eurax, Geigy) alleviates itching and also kills a number of skin parasites. Malathion lotion 5% (Prioderm) kills lice effectively, but do not use the toxic agricultural insecticide Malathion.

In remote grassland or jungle areas, insect larvae such as that of the bot-fly, which burrow into the flesh, are best removed by covering the breathing hole in your skin with vaseline, then a circular piece of adhesive tape with more vaseline round the edges. If this is allowed to dry well, with no lymph leaking out round the edges, you will be able to squeeze the maggot out next day. The condition is identifiable by a clear hole in the middle of a growing boil or pimple.

Malaria in Central America is theoretically confined to coastal and jungle zones. The disease is not common. Mosquitoes do not thrive above 2,500 metres so you are safe at altitude. There are different varieties of malaria, some resistant to the normal drugs. Make local enquiries if you intend to visit possibly infected zones and use one of the following prophylactic regimes. Start taking the tablets a few days before exposure and continue to take them for six weeks after leaving the malarial zone. Remember to give the drugs to babies and children also. Opinion varies on the precise drugs and dosage to be used for protection; all the drugs may have some side effects, and it is important to balance the risk of catching the disease against the albeit rare side effects. The increasing complexity of the subject as the malarial parasite becomes immune to the new generation of drugs has made concentration on the physical prevention of being bitten by mosquitoes more important, i.e. the use of long-sleeved shirts/blouses and long trousers, repellants and nets.

Prophylactic regimes:
Proguanil (Paludrine ICI 100 mg, 2 tablets daily) *or* Chloroquin (Avloclor; ICI, Malarivon; Wallace MFG, Nivaquine, May & Baker; Resochin, Bayer; Aralen 300 mg base (2 tablets) weekly).

Where there is a high risk of Chloroquin-resistant falciparum malaria, take Chloroquin plus Proguanil in the above-mentioned doses and carry Fansidar (Roche, also spelt Falsidar) for treatment; *or* add Paludrine 2 tablets per day to your routine Chloroquin prophylaxis.

You can catch malaria even when sticking to the above rules, although it is unlikely. If you do develop symptoms (high fever, shivering, headache, sometimes diarrhoea) seek medical advice immediately. If this is not possible, and there is a great likelihood of malaria, the *treatment* is:

Normal types: Chloroquin, a single dose of 4 tablets (600mg) followed by two tablets (300 mg) in 6 hours and 300 mg each day following.
Falciparum type or type in doubt: Fansidar, single dose of 3 tablets. (We have been told that this drug does not combine well with alcohol, so best to avoid drinking during treatment period.)

If Falciparum type malaria is definitely diagnosed, it is wise to get to a good hospital as the treatment can be complex and the illness very serious.

Pregnant women are particularly prone to malaria and should stick to Proguanil as a prophylactic. Chloroquin may cause eye damage if taken over a long period. The safety of Fansidar has been questioned and, at the time of writing, it is not recommended for prophylaxis.

Sunburn The burning power of the tropical sun, especially at high altitude, is phenomenal. Always wear a wide-brimmed hat and use some form of suncream lotion on untanned skin. Normal temperate-zone suntan lotions (protection factor up to 7) are not much good; you need to use the types designed specifically for the tropics, or for mountaineers or skiers, with a protection factor between 7 and 15. These are often not available in Central America; a reasonable substitute is zinc oxide ointment. Glare from the sun can cause conjunctivitis, so wear sunglasses. especially on tropical beaches, where high protection-factor sunscreen cream should also be used.

Snakebite If you are unlucky enough to be bitten by a venomous snake, spider, scorpion or sea creature, try (within limits) to catch the animal for identification. The reactions to be expected are: fright, swelling, pain and bruising around the bite, soreness of the regional lymph glands, nausea, vomiting and fever. If any of the following symptoms supervene, get the victim to a doctor without delay: numbness and tingling of the face, muscular spasms, convulsion, shortness of breath and haemorrhage. The tiny coral snake, with red, black and white bands, is the most dangerous, but is very timid.

Commercial snakebite and scorpion kits are available, but only useful for the specific type of snake or scorpion for which they are designed. The serum has to be given intravenously so is not much good unless you have had some practice at making injections into veins. If the bite is on a limb, immobilize the limb and apply a tight bandage between the bite and the body, releasing it for 90 seconds every 15 minutes. Reassurance of the bitten person is very important because death from snakebite is very rare. Do not slash the bite area and try to suck out the poison because this sort of heroism does more harm than good. Hospitals usually hold stocks of snake bite serum. Best precaution: don't walk in snake territory with bare feet or sandals—wear proper shoes or boots.

Spiders and Scorpions These may be found in the more basic hotels. The sting of some species of Mexican scorpions can be quite dangerous. Anti-venom is available in the larger hospitals. If bitten by a spider, or stung by a scorpion, rest and take plenty of fluids, and call a doctor. Precaution: keep beds away from the walls, investigate the underside of the toilet seat and look inside shoes before putting them on in the morning.

Other Afflictions Remember that **rabies** is endemic throughout Latin America so avoid dogs that are behaving strangely, and cover your toes at night to foil the vampire bats, which also carry the disease. If you are bitten, try to have the animal captured for observation and see a doctor at once. Treatment with human diploid vaccine is now extremely effective and worth seeking out if the likelihood of having contracted rabies is high.

Dengue fever has made its appearance in southern Mexico and the lower-lying parts of Central America; also in Brazil. No treatment: you must just avoid mosquito bites.

Typhus can still occur, carried by ticks. There is usually a reaction at the site of the bite and a fever: seek medical advice.

Intestinal worms are common, and the more serious ones such as **hookworm** can be contracted from walking barefoot on infested earth or beaches. Various other tropical diseases can be caught in jungle areas, usually transmitted by biting insects; they are often related to African diseases and were probably introduced by the slave trade from Africa.

Onchocerciasis (river-blindness), carried by blackflies, is found in parts of Mexico. Cutaneous **leishmaniasis** (Espundia) is carried by sandflies and causes a sore that won't heal; wearing long trousers and long-sleeved shirt in infectious areas helps one to avoid the fly. Epidemics of meningitis occur from time to time.

Dangerous animals Apart from mosquitoes, the most dangerous animals are men, be they bandits or behind steering wheels. Think carefully about violent confrontations and wear a seatbelt, if you are lucky enough to have one available to you.

Prickly heat, a very common itchy rash, is avoided by frequent washing and by wearing loose clothing. Cured by allowing skin to dry off through use of powder, and spending 2 nights in an air-conditioned hotel! **Athlete's foot** and other fungal infections are best treated with Tinaderm.

When you return home, remember to take your anti-malarial tablets for 6 weeks. Thousands of people develop malaria after tropical holidays because they do not take this precaution and some of them die, because it is not realized at home that they are suffering from malaria. If you have had attacks of diarrhoea, it is worth having a stool specimen tested in case you may have picked up amoebic dysentery. If you have been living in the bush, a blood test may be worthwhile to detect worms and other parasites.

Basic supplies The following items you may find useful to take with you from home:

Sunglasses.

Suntan cream.

Insect repellant, flea powder, mosquito net and coils.

Tampons (they can be bought in the main cities), and contraceptives (not easy to obtain everywhere).

Water-sterilizing tablets, e.g. Sterotabs (Boots), Globaline, Puritabs (Kirby & Co. Ltd.).

Antimalarials.

Anti-infective ointment, e.g. Savlon (ICI).

Dusting powder for feet, e.g. Tinaderm (Glaxo), Desenex.

Travel-sickness pills, e.g. Dramamine (Searle), Gravol (Carter-Wallace).

Antacids, e.g. Maalox.

("Tiger balm", an apparently all-purpose remedy, recommended by two overland travellers from New Zealand).

Antidiarrheals, e.g. Lomotil (Searle), Imodium (Janssen) or Arret. (Charcoal tablets are useful for minor stomach ailments.)

First-aid kit.

The following organizations give information regarding well-trained, English-speaking physicians in Latin America:

International Association for Medical Assistance to Travellers, 745 Fifth Avenue, New York 10022.

Intermedic, 777 Third Avenue, New York 10017 (Tel.: 212-486-8974).

Information regarding country-by-country malaria risk can be obtained from the World Health Organization (WHO), or the Ross Institute, London School of Hygiene and Tropical Medicine, Keppel Street, London WC1E 7HT, which publishes a book strongly recommended, entitled *Preservation of Personal Health in Warm Climates*. Medical Advisory Services for Travellers Abroad (Masta), at the Keppel Street address above, prepares health briefs on every country for a fee.

The new edition of *Travellers' Health: How to Stay Healthy Abroad*, edited by Dr. Richard Dawood (Oxford University Press, 1989, paperback, £5.95), has been fully revised and updated, and will even help you survive travel closer to home. We strongly recommend this book, especially to the intrepid travellers who go to the more out-of-the-way places.

PRE-CONQUEST HISTORY

The Aztec empire which Hernán Cortés encountered in 1519 and subsequently destroyed was the third major power to have dominated what is now known as Mexico. Before it, the empires of Teotihuacan and Tula each unified what had essentially been an area of separate Indian groups. All three, together with their neighbours such as the Maya (dealt with below) and their predecessors, belong to a more-or-less common culture called Mesoamerica. Despite the wide variety of climates and terrains that fall within Mesoamerica's boundaries, from northern Mexico to El Salvador and Honduras, the civilizations that developed there were interdependent, sharing the same agriculture (based on maize, beans and squash) and many sociological features. These included an enormous pantheon, with the god of rain and the feathered serpent hero predominant; the offering of blood to the gods, from oneself and from sacrificial victims usually taken in war; pyramid-building; a game played with a rubber ball; trade in feathers, jade and other valuable objects, possibly from as far away as the Andean region of South America; hieroglyphic writing; astronomy; an elaborate calendar.

The Mesoamerican calendar was a combination of a 260-day almanac year and the 365-day solar year. A given day in one of the years would only coincide with that in the other every 52 years, a cycle called the Calendar Round. In order to give the Calendar Round a context within a larger timescale, a starting date for both years was devised; the date chosen was equivalent to 3113 B.C. in Christian time. Dates measured from this point are called Long Count dates.

Historians divide Mesoamerican civilizations into three periods, the Pre-classic, which lasted until about A.D. 300, the Classic, until A.D. 900, and the Post-classic, from 900 until the Spanish conquest. An alternative delineation is: Olmec, Teotihuacan and Aztec, named after the dominant civilizations within each of those periods.

Who precisely the Olmecs were, where they came from and why they disappeared, is a matter of debate. It is known that they flourished from about 1400 to 400 B.C., that they lived in the Mexican Gulf Coast region between Veracruz and Tabasco, and that all later civilizations have their roots ultimately in Olmec culture. They carved colossal heads, stelae (tall, flat monuments), jade figures and altars; they gave great importance to the jaguar and the serpent in their imagery; they built large ceremonial centres, such as San Lorenzo and La Venta. Possibly derived from the Olmecs and gaining importance in the first millenium B.C. was the centre in the Valley of Oaxaca at Monte Albán. This was a major city, with certain changes of influence, right through until the end of the

Classic period. Also derived from the Olmecs was the Izapa civilization, on the Pacific border of present day Mexico and Guatemala. Here seems to have taken place the progression from the Olmec to the Maya civilization, with obvious connections in artistic style, calendar-use, ceremonial architecture and the transformation of the Izapa Long-lipped God into the Maya Long-nosed God.

Almost as much mystery surrounds the origins of Teotihuacan as those of the Olmecs. Teotihuacan, "the place where men become gods", was a great urban state, holding in its power most of the central highlands of Mexico. Its influence can be detected in the Maya area, Oaxaca and the civilizations on the Gulf Coast which succeeded the Olmecs. The monuments in the city itself are enormous, the planning precise; it is estimated that by the seventh century A.D. some 125,000 people were living in its immediate vicinity. Yet there is little evidence to suggest that Teotihuacan's power was gained by force. Again for reasons unknown, Teotihuacan's influence over its neighbours ended around 600 A.D. Its glory coincided with that of the Classic Maya, but the latter's decline occurred some 300 years later, at which time a major change affected all Mesoamerica.

The start of the Post-classic period, between the Teotihuacan and Aztec horizons, was marked by an upsurge in militarism. In the semi-deserts to the north of the settled societies of central Mexico and Veracruz lived groups of nomadic hunters. These people, who were given the general name of Chichimecs, began to invade the central region and were quick to adopt the urban characteristics of the groups they overthrew. The Toltecs of Tula were one such invading force, rapidly building up an empire stretching from the Gulf of Mexico to the Pacific in central Mexico. Infighting by factions within the Toltecs split the rulers and probably hastened the empire's demise sometime after 1150. The exiled leader Topíltzin Quetzalcóatl (Featherd Serpent) is possibly the founder of the Maya-Toltec rule in the Yucatán (the Maya spoke of a Mexican invader named Kukulcán—Feathered Serpent). He is certainly the mythical figure the Aztec ruler, Moctezuma II, took Cortés to be, returning by sea from the east.

Another important culture which developed in the first millenium A.D. was the Mixtec, in western Oaxaca. They infiltrated all the territory held by the Zapotecs, who had ruled Monte Albán during the Classic period and had built many other sites in the Valley of Oaxaca, including Mitla. The Mixtecs, in alliance with the Zapotecs successfully withstood invasion by the Aztecs.

The process of transition from semi-nomadic hunter-gatherer to city and empire-builder continued with the Aztecs, who bludgeoned their way into the midst of rival city states in the vacuum left by the destruction of Tula. They rose from practically nothing to a power almost as great as Teotihuacan in about 200 years. From their base at Tenochtitlán in Lake Texcoco in the Valley of Mexico they extended through aggression their sphere of influence from the Tarascan Kingdom in the north to the Maya lands in the south. Not only did the conquered pay heavy tribute to their Aztec overlords, but they also supplied the constant flow of sacrificial victims needed to satisfy the deities, at whose head was Huitzilopochtli, the warrior god of the Sun. The speed with which the Aztecs adapted to a settled existence and fashioned a highly effective political state is remarkable. Their ability in sculpting stone, in pottery, in writing books, and in architecture (what we can gather from what the Spaniards did not destroy), was great. Surrounding all this activity was a strictly ritual existence, with ceremonies and feasts dictated by the two enmeshing calendars.

It is impossible to say whether the Aztec empire would have gone the way of its predecessors had not the Spaniards arrived to precipitate its collapse. Undoubtedly, the Europeans received much assistance from people who had been oppressed by the Aztecs and wished to be rid of them. Needless to say, Cortés, with his horses and an unknown array of military equipment in relatively few hands, brought to an end in two years an extraordinary culture.

The best known of the pre-Conquest Indian civilizations of the present Central American area was the Maya, which is thought to have evolved in a formative period in the Pacific highlands of Guatemala and El Salvador between 1500 B.C. and about A.D. 100. After 200 years of growth it entered what is known today as its Classic period when the civilization flourished in Guatemala, Belize and Honduras, and in Chiapas, Campeche and Yucatán (Mexico).

The Maya civilization was based on independent and antagonistic city states, including Tikal, Uaxactún, Kaminaljuyú, Iximché, Zaculeu and Quiriguá in Guatemala; Copán in Honduras; Altún Ha, Caracol, Lamanai in Belize; Tazumal and San Andrés in El Salvador; and Palenque, Bonampak (both in Chiapas), Uxmal, Mayapán, Túlum and the Puuc hill cities of Sayil, Labná and Kabah (all on the Yucatán peninsula) in Mexico. Recent research has revealed that these cities, far from being the peaceful ceremonial centres as once imagined, were warring adversaries, striving to capture victims for sacrifice. Furthermore, much of the cultural activity, controlled by a theocratic minority of priests and nobles, involved blood-letting, by even the highest members of society. Royal blood was the most precious offering that could be made to the gods. This change in perception of the Maya was the result of the discovery of defended cities and of a greater understanding of the Maya's hieroglyphic writing. Although John Lloyd Stephens' prophecy that "a key surer than that of the Rosetta stone will be discovered" has not been fulfilled, the painstaking decipherment of the glyphs has uncovered many of the secrets of Maya society.

Alongside the preoccupation with blood was an artistic tradition rich in ceremony, folklore and dance. They achieved paper codices and glyphic writing, which also appears on stone monuments and their fine ceramics; they were skilful weavers and traded over wide areas, though they did not use the wheel and had no beasts of burden. The cities were all meticulously dated. Mayan art is a mathematical art: each column, figure, face, animal, frieze, stairway and temple expresses a date or a time relationship. When, for example, an ornament on the ramp of the

Hieroglyphic Stairway at Copán was repeated some 15 times, it was to express that number of elapsed "leap" years. The 75 steps stand for the number of elapsed intercalary days. The Mayan calendar was a nearer approximation to sidereal time than either the Julian or the Gregorian calendars of Europe; it was only .000069 of a day out of true in a year. They used the zero centuries in advance of the Old World, plotted the movements of the sun, moon, Venus and other planets, and conceived a cycle of more than 1,800 million days.

Their tools and weapons were flint and hard stone, obsidian and fire-hardened wood, and yet with these they hewed out and transported great monoliths over miles of difficult country, and carved them over with intricate glyphs and figures which would be difficult enough with modern chisels. Also with those tools they grew lavish crops. To support urban populations now believed to number tens of thousands, and a population density of 150 per square kilometre (compared with less than one per square kilometre today), an agricultural system was developed of raised fields, fertilized by fish and vegetable matter from surrounding canals.

The height of the Classic period lasted until A.D. 900-1000, after which time the Maya concentrated into Yucatán after a successful invasion of their other lands by non-Maya people (this is only one theory: another is that they were forced to flee after a peasants' revolt against them), came under the influence of the Toltecs who invaded that area. Chichén Itzá in the Yucatán is considered to be an example of a Maya city which displays a great many Toltec features. From that time their culture declined. The Toltecs, who had firm control in Yucatán in the 10th century, gradually spread their empire as far as the southern borders of Guatemala. They in turn, however, were conquered by the Aztecs, who did not penetrate into Central America.

THE MUSIC OF THE REGION

Mexico

Mexican Music is particularly attractive and vibrant and a vigorous radio, film and recording industry has helped make it highly popular throughout Latin America. There can be no more representative an image of Mexico than the Mariachi musician and his Charro costume. The Spanish conquistadores and the churchmen that followed them imposed European musical culture on the defeated natives with a heavy hand and it is this influence that remains predominant. Nobody knows what precolumbian music sounded like and even the music played today in the Indian communities is basically Spanish in origin. African slaves introduced a third ingredient, but there is no Afro-Mexican music as such and indeed there are few black Mexicans. The music brought from Europe has over the centuries acquired a highly distinctive sound and style of which every Mexican is justly proud, even if many of the young now prefer to listen to Anglo-American rock and pop, like their counterparts the world over.

There is a basic distinction between Indian and Mestizo music. The former is largely limited to the Indians' own festive rituals and dances, religious in nature and solemn in expression. The commonest instruments are flute and drum, with harp and violin also widely used. Some of the most spectacular dances are those of the Concheros (mainly urban), the Quetzales (from the Sierra de Puebla), the Voladores (flying pole - also Sierra de Puebla), the Tarascan dances from around Lake Pátzcuaro and the Yaqui deer dance (Sonora).

Mestizo music clearly has more mass appeal in what is an overwhelmingly mixed population. The basic form is the *son* (also called *huapango* in eastern areas), featuring a driving rhythm overlaid with dazzling instrumentals. Each region has its own style of *son*, such as the *son huasteco* (Northeast), *son calentano* (Michoacán/Guerrero), *chilena* (Guervero coast), *son mariachi* (Jalisco), *jarana* (Yucatán) and *son jarocho* (Veracruz). One *son jarocho* that has achieved world status is "La Bamba". Instrumental backing is provided in almost all these areas by a combination of large and small guitars, with the violin as virtuoso lead in the *huasteca* and the harp in Veracruz. The *chilena* of Guerrero is said to have been introduced by Chilean seamen and miners on their way to the California gold rush, while Yucatán features a version of the Colombian *bambuco*. The *son* is a dance form for flirtation between couples, as befits a land of passionate men and women, and often involves spectacular heel-and-toe stamping by the man. Another widespread dance rhythm is the *jarabe*, including the patriotic "Jarabe Tapatío", better known to the English-speaking world as the "Mexican Hat Dance". Certain regions are known for more sedate rhythms and a quite different choice of instruments. In the north, the Conjunto Norteño leads with an accordion and favours the polka as a rhythm. In Yucatán they prefer wind and brass instruments, while the Isthmus of Tehuantepec is the home of the *marimba* (xylophone), which it shares with neighbouring Guatemala.

For singing, as opposed to dancing, there are three extremely popular genres. First is the *corrido*, a narrative form derived from old Spanish ballads, which swept across the country with the armies of the Revolution and has remained a potent vehicle for popular expression ever since. A second is the *canción* (literally "Song"), which gives full rein to the romantic, sentimental aspect of the Mexican character and is naturally slow and languid. "Las Mañanitas" is a celebrated song for serenading people on their birthdays. The third form is the *ranchera*, a sort of Mexican Country and Western, associated originally with the cattle-men of the Bajío region. Featured in a whole series of Mexican films of the 1930s and 1940s, *rancheras* became known all over the Spanish-speaking world as the typical Mexican music. The film and recording industry turned a number of Mexican artists into household names throughout Latin America. The "immortals" are Pedro Infante, Jorge Negrete, Pedro Vargas, Miguel Aceves Mejía and the Trio Los Panchos, with Agustín Lara as an equally celebrated and prolific songwriter and composer, particularly of romantic *boleros*. To all outsiders and most Mexicans however there is nothing more musically Mexican than *mariachi*, a word said to be derived from the French "mariage", introduced at the time of Maximilian and Carlota.

Originating in the state of Jalisco, *mariachi* bands arrived in Mexico City in the 1920s and have never looked back. Trumpets now take the lead, backed by violins and guitars and the players all wear *charro* (cowboy) costume, including the characteristic hat. They play all the major musical forms and can be found almost every evening in Mexico City's Plaza Garibaldi, where they congregate to be seen, heard and, they hope, hired. This is the very soul of Mexico.

Finally, there are a number of distinguished 20th century composers who have produced symphonies and other orchestral works based on indigenous and folk themes. Carlos Chávez is the giant and his "Sinfonía India" a particularly fine example. Other notable names are Silvestre Revueltas ("Sensemayá"), Pablo Moncayo ("Huapango"), Blas Galindo ("Sones de Mariachi") and Luis Sandi ("Yaqui Music").

Central America

Native music is at its most vigorous and flourishing at either end of the region, in Guatemala and Panama. In the intervening four republics its presence is more localized and indeed elusive. From Guatemala southwards a rich musical tradition based largely on the *marimba* (xylophone) as an instrument and the *son* as a song/dance genre fades fast but continues tenuously all the way down to Costa Rica, while

Panama has its own very distinctive vein of traditional music, with a combination of Spanish and African elements. While the influence of Mexican music is all pervasive in the northern five republics, Panama is more closely linked with the Caribbean coasts of Colombia and Venezuela in its musical idioms.

Guatemala is the heartland of the *marimba*, which it shares with parts of southern Mexico. How this came about has been much debated between adherents of a native precolombian origin and those who believe the *marimba* came from Africa with colonial slavery. Whatever its origins, it is now regarded as the national instrument in Guatemala, belonging equally to Indian and *ladino*. Among the Indians the more rustic *marimba de tecomate* with gourds as resonators is still to be found, whereas most instruments now have the box resonator. The manufacture and playing of *marimbas* has developed to the point where a number of them are now combined to form an orchestra, as with the Pans of Trinidad. Among the best known *marimba* orchestras are the Marimba Tecún Umán, Marimba Antigua and highly sophisticated Marimba Nacional de Concierto. Every village has its *marimba* players and no wedding or other secular celebration would be complete with them. The music played is generally either a fast or slow *son*, but the modern repertoire is likely to include many Mexican numbers.

Although the *marimba* is basic to the Indians as well as to the *ladinos*, the former have other instruments for their religious rituals and processions, such as the *tun* (a precolombian drum), *tzicolaj* (flute), *chirimía* (oboe) and violin. These are the instruments that accompany the colourful vernacular dances of the "Culebra" (snake), "Venado" (deer) and "Palo Volador" (flying pole), as also the "Baile de las Canastas" and "Rabinal Achí", two precolombian historical dramas that have amazingly survived the conquest and colonial period and are still performed at Chajul and Rabinal (Alta Verapaz) respectively.

El Salvador and **Honduras** are two countries that tend to "hide their light under a bushel" as regards native music. It is here above all that the Mexican music industry seems to exert an overwhelming cultural influence, while the virtual absence of an Indian population may also be partly responsible, since it is so often they who maintain traditions and hold to the past, as in Guatemala. Whatever the reason, the visitor who is seeking specifically Salvadorean or Honduran native music will find little to satisfy him or her. El Salvador is an extension of "marimba country", but in both republics popular songs and dances are often accompanied by the guitar and seem to lack a rhythm or style that can be pinpointed as specifically local. Honduras does share with Belize and Guatemala the presence of Garifuna or Black Caribs on the Caribbean coast. These descendants of Carib Indians and escaped black slaves were deported to the area from St. Vincent in the late 18th century and continue to maintain a very separate identity, including their own religious observances, music and dances, profoundly African in spirit and style.

In **Nicaragua** we again find ourselves in "marimba country" and here again the basic musical genre is the *son*, here called the "Son Nica". There are a number of popular dances for couples with the names of animals, like "La Vaca" (cow), "La Yeguita" (mare) and "El Toro" (bull). The folklore capital of Nicaragua is the city of Masaya and the musical heart of Masaya is the Indian quarter of Monimbó. Here the *marimba* is king, but on increasingly rare occasions may be supported by the *chirimía* (oboe), *quijada de asno* (asses jaw) and *quijongo*, a single-string bow with gourd resonator. Some of the most traditional Sones are "El Zañate", "Los Novios" and "La Perra Renca", while the more popular dances still to be found are "Las Inditas", "Las Negras", "Los Diablitos" and "El Torovenado", all involving masked characters. Diriamba is another centre of tradition, notable for the folk play known as "El Güeguense", accompanied by violin, fife and drum and the dance called "Toro Guaco". The Caribbean coast is a totally different cultural region, home to the Miskito Indians and English speaking black people of Jamaican origin concentrated around Bluefields. The latter have a maypole dance and their music is typically Afro-Caribbean, with banjos, accordeons, guitars and of course drums as the preferred instruments.

Costa Rica is the southernmost in our string of "marimba culture" countries. The guitar is also a popular instrument for accompanying folk dances, while the *chirimía* and *quijongo*, already encountered further north, have not yet totally died out in the Chorotega region of Guanacaste Province. This province is indeed the heartland of Costa Rican folklore and the "Punto Guanacasteco", a heel-and-toe dance for couples, has been officially decreed to be the "typical national dance", although it is not in fact traditional, but was composed at the turn of the century by Leandro Cabalceta Brau during a brief sojourn in gaol. There are other dances too, such as the "Botijuela Tamborito" and "Cambute", but it must honestly be said that they will not be found in the countryside as a tradition, but are performed on stage when outsiders need to be shown some native culture. Among the country's most popular ntive performers are the duet Los Talolingas, authors of "La Guaria Morada", regarded as the "second national anthem" and Lorenzo "Lencho" Salazar, whose humorous songs in the vernacular style are considered quintessentially "tico".

Some of the republic's rapidly deculturizing Indian groups have dances of their own, like the "Danza de los Diablitos" of the Borucas, the "Danza del Sol" and "Danza de la Luna" of the Chorotegas and the "Danza de los Huesos" of the Talamancas. A curious ocarina made of beeswax, the *dru mugata* is still played by the Guaymí Indians and is said to be the only truly precolombian instrument still to be found. The drum and flute are traditional among various groups, but the guitar and accordeon are moving in to replace them. As in the case of Nicaragua, the Caribbean coast of Costa Rica, centred on Puerto Limón, is inhabited by black people who came originally from the English speaking islands and whose music reflects this origin. The *sinkit* seems to be a strictly local rhythm, but the *calypso* is popular and the *cuadrille*, square dance and maypole dance are also found. There is too a kind of popular hymn called the *saki*. Brass, percussion and string instruments are played, as also the accordeon.

Panama is the crossroads of the Americas, where Central America meets South America and the Caribbean backs onto the Pacific. One of the smallest Latin American republics and the last to achieve independence, from Colombia, it nonetheless possesses an outstandingly rich and attractive musical culture. Albeit related to that of the Caribbean coast of Colombia and Venezuela, it is extremely distinctive. The classic Panamanian folk dances are the *tambor* or *tamborito*, *cumbia*, *punto* and *mejorana*, largely centred on the central provinces of Coclé and Veraguas and those of Herrera and Los Santos on the Azuero Peninsula. Towns that are particularly noted for their musical traditions are Los Santos, Ocú, Las Tablas, Tonosí and Chorrera. The dances are for couples and groupds of couples and the rhythms are lively and graceful, the man often fanning the girl with his hat. The woman's *pollera* costume is arguably the most beautiful in Latin America and her handling of the voluminous skirt is an important element of the dance. The *tamborito* is considered to be Panama's national dance and is accompanied by three tall drums. The *cumbia*, which has a common origin with the better known Colombian dance of the same name, has a fast variant called the *atravesado*, while the *punto* is slower and more stately. The name *mejorana* is shared by a small native guitar, a dance, a song form and a specific tune. The commonest instruments to be found today are the tall drums that provide the basic beat, the violin, the guitar and the accordeon, with the last named rapidly becoming predominant. The *tuna* is a highly rhythmic musical procession with womens' chorus and massed hand-clapping.

Turning to song, there are two traditional forms, both of Spanish origin, the *copla*, sung by women and accompanying the *tamborito*, and the *mejorana*, which is a male solo preserve, with the lyrics in the form of *décimas*, a verse form used by the great Spanish poets of the Golden Age. It is accompanied by the ukulele-like guitar of the same name. Quite unique to Panama are the *salomas* and *gritos*, the former between two or more men. The yodelling and falsetto of the *salomas* are in fact carried over into the singing style and it is this element, more than any other, that gives Panamanian folk song its unique and instantly recognizable sound. There are other traditional masked street dances of a carnavalesque nature, such as the very African "Congos", the "Diablicos Sucios" (dirty little devils) and the "Grandiablos" (big devils). In the area of the Canal there is a significant English speaking black population, similar to those in Nicaragua and Costa Rica, who also sing *calypso*, while the Guaymí Indians in the west and the Cuna and Chocó of the San Blas islands and Darién isthmus possess their own song, rituals and very attractive flute music.

MEXICO

INTRODUCTION

CORTES, asked what the country looked like, crushed a piece of parchment in his fist, released it and said: "That is the map of Mexico." This crumpled land is so splendid to the eye, and so exotic to the other senses, that millions, mainly from the USA, visit it each year.

Mexico is the third largest country in Latin America and the most populous Spanish-speaking country anywhere (86.7 million people). Its geography ranges from swamp to desert, from tropical lowland jungle to high alpine vegetation above the tree line, from thin arid soils to others so rich that they grow three crops a year. Over half the country is at an altitude of over 1,000 metres and much at over 2,000 metres;

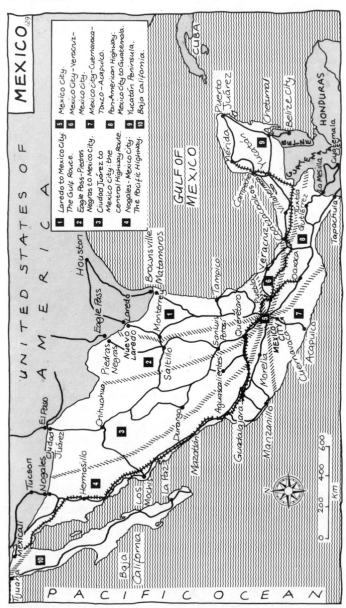

MEXICO

1 Laredo to Mexico City:
The Gulf Route.
2 Eagle Pass-Piedras
Negras to Mexico City.
3 Ciudad Juárez to
Mexico city: the
central Highway Route.
4 Nogales-Mexico City:
The Pacific Highway.
5 Mexico City.
6 Mexico City-Veracruz-
Mexico City.
7 Mexico City-Cuernavaca-
Toxco-Acapulco.
8 Pan-American Highway:
Mexico city to Guatemala.
9 Yucatán Peninsula.
10 Baja California.

over half is arid and another 30% semi-arid. Only about 30 million hectares (16% of the total land area) can be cultivated, and of these 33% are irrigable.

Mexico has an area equal to about a quarter of the United States, with which it has a frontier of 2,400 km. The southern frontier of 885 km. is with Guatemala and Belize. It has a coast line of 2,780 km. on the Gulf of Mexico and the Caribbean, and of 7,360 km. on the Pacific and the Gulf of California.

The structure of the land mass is extremely complicated, but may be simplified (with large reservations) as a plateau flanked by ranges of mountains roughly paralleling the coasts. The northern part of the plateau is low, arid and thinly populated; it takes up 40% of the total area of Mexico but holds only 19% of its people. From the Bolsón de Mayrán as far S as the Balsas valley, the level rises considerably; this southern section of the central plateau is crossed by a volcanic range of mountains in which the intermont basins are high and separated. The basin of Guadalajara is at 1,500 metres, the basin of México at 2,300 metres, and the basin of Toluca, W of Mexico City, is at 2,600 metres. Above the lakes and valley bottoms of this contorted middle-land rise the magnificent volcano cones of Orizaba (5,700 metres), Popocatépetl (5,452 metres), Ixtaccíhuatl (5,286 metres), Nevado de Toluca (4,583 metres), Matlalcueyetl or La Malinche (4,461 metres), and Cofre de Perote (4,282 metres). This mountainous southern end of the plateau, the heart of Mexico, has ample rainfall. Though only 14% of the area of Mexico, it holds nearly half of the country's people. Its centre, in a small high intermont basin measuring only 50 km. square, is Mexico City, with 20 or so million inhabitants.

The two high ranges of mountains which rise E and W of the plateau, between it and the sea, are great barriers against communications: there are far easier routes N along the floor of the plateau to the United States than there are to either the east coast or the west. In the W there are rail and road links across the Sierra Madre Occidental from Guadalajara to the Pacific at the port of Mazatlán; both continue northward through a coastal desert to Nogales. The Sierra Madre Oriental is more kindly; in its mountain ramparts a pass inland from Tampico gives road-rail access to Monterrey, a great industrial centre, and the highland basins; and another from Veracruz leads by a fair gradient to the Valley of México.

South of the seven intermont basins in the south-central region the mountainland is still rugged but a little lower (between 1,800 and 2,400 metres), with much less rainfall. After some 560 km. it falls away into the low-lying Isthmus of Tehuantepec. Population is sparse in these southern mountains and is settled on the few flat places where commercial crops can be grown—subsistence crops are sown on incredibly steep slopes. The Pacific coast here is forbidding and its few ports of little use, though there is massive development of tourism in such places as Acapulco, Zihuatanejo, Puerto Escondido and now Huatulco. Very different are the Gulf Coast and Yucatán; half this area is classed as flat, and much of it gets enough rain the year round, leading to its becoming one of the most important agricultural and cattle raising areas in the country. The Gulf Coast also provides most of Mexico's oil and sulphur. Geographically, North America may be said to come to an end in the Isthmus of Tehuantepec. South of the Isthmus the land rises again into the thinly populated highlands of Chiapas.

Climate and vegetation depend upon altitude. The *tierra caliente* takes in the coastlands and plateau lands below 750 metres. The *tierra templada*, or temperate zone is at 750 to 2,000 metres. The *tierra fría*, or cold zone, is from 2,000 metres upwards. Above the tree line at 4,000 metres are high moorlands (*páramos*).

The climate of the inland highlands is mostly mild, but with sharp changes of temperature between day and night, sunshine and shade. Generally, winter is the dry season and summer the wet season. There are only two areas where rain falls the year round: S of Tampico along the lower slopes of the Sierra Madre Oriental and across the Isthmus of Tehuantepec into Tabasco state; and along the Pacific coast of the state of Chiapas. Both areas together cover only 12% of Mexico. These wetter parts get most of their rain between June and September, when the skies are so full of clouds that the temperature is lowered: May is a hotter month than July. Apart from these favoured regions, the rest of the country suffers from a climate in which the rainy season hardly lives up to its name and the dry season almost always does.

History Of the many Indian nations in the vast territory of Mexico, the two most important before the Conquest were the Aztecs of Tenochtitlán (now Mexico City) and the Mayas of Yucatán. The Aztecs, a militarist, theocratic culture, had obtained absolute control over the whole Valley of México and a loose control of some other regions. The Mayas were already in decline by the time the Spaniards arrived. A brief history of these and other pre-Conquest, Mexican people is given in the introduction.

The 34-year-old Cortés disembarked near the present Veracruz with about 500 men, some horses and cannon, on 21 April, 1519. They marched into the interior; their passage was not contested; they arrived at Tenochtitlán in November and were admitted into the city as guests of the reigning monarch, Moctezuma. There they remained until June of the next year, when Pedro de Alvarado, in the absence of Cortés, murdered hundreds of Indians to quell his own fear of a rising. At this treacherous act the Indians did in fact rise, and it was only by good luck that the Spanish troops, with heavy losses, were able to fight their way out of the city on the Noche Triste (the Night of Sorrows) of 30 June. Next year Cortés came back with reinforcements and besieged the city. It fell on 30 August, 1521, and was utterly razed. Cortés then turned to the conquest of the rest of the country. One of the main factors in his success was his alliance with the Tlaxcalans, old rivals of the Aztecs. The fight was ruthless, and the Aztecs were soon mastered.

There followed 300 years of Spanish rule. In the early years all the main sources of gold and silver were discovered. Spanish grandees stepped into the shoes of dead Aztec lords and inherited their great estates and their wealth of savable souls with little disturbance, for Aztec and Spanish ways of holding land were not unlike: the *ejido* (or agrarian community holding lands in common), the *rancho*, or small private property worked by the owner; and that usually huge area which paid tribute to its master—the Spanish *encomienda*—soon to be converted into the *hacienda*, with its absolute title to the land and its almost feudal way of life. Within the first 50 years all the Indians in the populous southern valleys of the plateau had been christianized and harnessed to Spanish wealth-getting from mine and soil. The more scattered and less profitable Indians of the north and south had to await the coming of the missionizing Jesuits in 1571, a year behind the Inquisition. Too often, alas, the crowded Jesuit missions proved as fruitful a source of smallpox or measles as of salvation, with the unhappy result that large numbers of Indians died; their deserted communal lands were promptly filched by some neighbouring *encomendero*: a thieving of public lands by private interests which continued for 400 years.

By the end of the 16th century the Spaniards had founded most of the towns which are still important, tapped great wealth in mining, stock raising and sugar-growing, and firmly imposed their way of life and belief. Government was by a Spanish-born upper class, based on the subordination of the Indian and *mestizo* populations and a strict dependence on Spain for all things. As throughout all Hispanic America, Spain built up resistance to itself by excluding from government both Spaniards born in Mexico and the small body of educated *mestizos*.

The standard of revolt was raised in 1810 by the curate of Dolores, Miguel Hidalgo. The Grito de Dolores: "Perish the Spaniards", collected 80,000 armed supporters, and had it not been for Hidalgo's loss of nerve and failure to engage the Spaniards, the capital might have been captured in the first month and a government created not differing much from the royal Spanish government. But eleven years of fighting created bitter differences. A loyalist general, Agustín de Iturbide, joined the rebels and proclaimed an independent Mexico in 1821. His Plan of Iguala proposed an independent monarchy with a ruler from the Spanish royal family, but on second thoughts Iturbide proclaimed himself Emperor in 1822: a fantasy which lasted one year. A federal republic was created on 4 October, 1824, with General Guadalupe Victoria as President. Conservatives stood for a highly centralized government; Liberals favoured federated sovereign states. The tussle of interests expressed itself in endemic civil war. In 1836, Texas, whose cotton-growers and cattle-ranchers had been infuriated by the abolition of slavery in 1829, rebelled against the dictator, Santa Ana, and declared its independence. It was annexed by the United States in 1845. War broke out and US troops occupied Mexico City in 1847. Next year, under the terms of the treaty of Guadalupe Hidalgo, the US acquired half Mexico's territory: all the land from Texas to California and from the Río Grande to Oregon.

A period of reform dominated by independent Mexico's great hero, the pure-blooded Zapotec Indian, Benito Juárez, began in 1857. The church, in alliance with the conservatives, hotly contested by civil war his liberal programme of popular education, freedom of the press and of speech, civil marriage and the separation of church and state. Juárez won, but the constant civil strife wrecked the economy, and Juárez was forced to suspend payment on the national debt. Promptly, Spain, France and Britain landed a joint force at Veracruz to protect their financial rights. The British and the Spanish soon withdrew, but the French force pushed inland and occupied Mexico City in 1863. Juárez took to guerrilla warfare against the invaders. The Archduke Maximilian of Austria became Emperor of Mexico with Napoleon III's help, but United States insistence and the gathering strength of Prussia led to the withdrawal of the French troops in 1867. Maximilian, betrayed and deserted, was captured by the Juaristas at Querétaro, tried, and shot on 19 June. Juárez resumed control and died in July 1872. He was the first Mexican leader of any note who had died naturally since 1810.

Sebastián Lerdo de Tejada, the distinguished scholar who followed him, was soon tricked out of office by General Porfirio Díaz, who ruled Mexico from 1876 to 1910. But Díaz's paternal, though often ruthless, central authority did introduce a period of 35 years of peace. A superficial prosperity followed upon peace; a civil service was created, finances put on a sound basis, banditry put down, industries started, railways built, international relations improved, and foreign capital protected. But the main mass of peasants had never been so wretched; their lands were stolen from them, their personal liberties curtailed, and many were sold into forced labour on tobacco and henequen plantations from which death was the only release.

It was this open contradiction between dazzling prosperity and hideous distress which led to the upheaval of November 1910 and to Porfirio Díaz's self-exile in Paris. A new leader, Francisco Madero, who came from a landowning family in Coahuila, championed a programme of political and social reform, including the restoration of stolen lands. Madero was initially supported by revolutionary leaders such as Emiliano Zapata in Morelos, Pascual Orozco in Chihuahua and Pancho Villa in the north. During his presidency (1911-13), Madero neither satisfied his revolutionary supporters, nor pacified his reactionary enemies. After a coup in February 1913, led by General Victoriano Huerta, Madero was brutally murdered, but the great new cry, *Tierra y Libertad* (Land and Liberty) was not to be quieted until the revolution was made safe by the election of Alvaro Obregón to the Presidency in 1920. Before then, Mexico was in a state of civil war, leading first to the exile of Huerta in 1914, then the dominance of Venustiano Carranza's revolutionary faction over that of Zapata (assassinated in 1919) and Villa. Later, President Lázaro Cárdenas fulfilled some of the more important economic objectives of the revolution; it was his regime (1934-40) that brought about the division of the great estates into *ejidos* (or communal lands), irrigation, the raising of wages, the spread of education, the beginnings of industrialization, the nationalization of the oil wells and the railways. Later presidents nationalized electric power, most of the railways, the main airlines and parts of industry, but at the same time encouraged both Mexican and foreign (mainly US) entrepreneurs to develop the private sector. All presidents have pursued an independent and non-aligned foreign policy.

In 1946, the official party assumed the name Partido Revolucionario Institucional (PRI), since when it held a virtual monopoly over all political activity. Having comfortably won all elections against small opposition parties, in the 1980s electoral majorities were cut as opposition to dictatorship by the Party grew. Corruption and fraud were claimed to be keeping the PRI in power. The PRI candidate in 1988, Carlos Salinas de Gortari, saw his majority dramatically reduced when Cuauhtémoc Cárdenas (son of the former president), at the head of a breakaway PRI faction, stood in opposition to him. The disaffected PRI members and others subsequently formed the Partido de la Revolución Democrática (PRD), which rapidly gained support as liberalisation of many of the PRI's long-held political and economic traditions became inevitable. In 1989, for the first time, a state governorship was conceded by the PRI, to the right wing party, Partido de Acción Nacional (PAN). President Gortari will remain in office until 1994.

The People The population is growing at the rate of 2.4% a year. Birth rate per thousand, 34; death rate, 7. Urban growth is 3.3%; 50% of the population is under 20. About 5% consider themselves pure white and about 25% pure Indian; about 60% are *mestizos*, a mixture in varying proportions of Spanish and Indian bloods; a small percentage (mostly in the coastal zones of Veracruz, Guerrero and Chiapas) are a mixture of black and white or black and Indian or *mestizo*. Mexico also has infusions of other European, Arab and Chinese blood. About 12% are still illiterate; 70% live in towns or cities; 30% are rural. There is a national cultural prejudice in favour of the Indian rather than the Spanish element, though this does not prevent Indians from being looked down on by the more hispanicized elements. There is hardly a single statue of Cortés in the whole of Mexico, but he does figure, pejoratively, in the frescoes of Diego Rivera and his contemporaries. On the other hand the two last Aztec emperors, Moctezuma and Cuauhtémoc, are national heroes.

Among the estimated 20 million Indians there are 56 groups or sub-divisions, each with its own language. The Indians are far from evenly distributed; 36% live on the Central Plateau (mostly Puebla, Hidalgo, and México); 35% are along the southern Pacific coast (Oaxaca, Chiapas, Guerrero), and 23% along the Gulf coast (mostly Yucatán and Veracruz): 94% of them, that is, live in these three regions.

The issue of access to the land has always been the country's fundamental problem, and it was a despairing landless peasantry that rose in the Revolution of 1910 and swept away Porfirio Díaz and the old system of huge estates. The accomplishments of successive PRI governments have been mixed. Life for the peasant is still hard. His minimum wage barely allows him a simple diet of beans, rice, and *tortillas*. His home is still, possibly, a shack with no windows, no water, no sanitation, and he may still not be able to read or write, but something has been done to redistribute the land in the so-called *ejido* system, which does give the peasant either communal or personal control of the land he cultivates, though the purely economic benefit of the system is in doubt. At least the peasant is freed from the landowner, and his family receives some basic health and educational facilities from the state.

The Economy   Mexico has been an oil producer since the 1880s and was the world's leading producer in 1921, but by 1971 had become a net importer. This position was reversed in the mid-1970s with the discovery in 1972 of major new oil reserves. Mexico is now the world's fourth largest producer, 65% of crude output coming from offshore wells in the Gulf of Campeche, and 28% from onshore fields in the Chiapas-Tabasco area in the southeast. Proven reserves of 48.6bn barrels in the mid-1980s were sufficient to last 54 years. Mexico depends on oil and gas for about 85% of its primary energy supply and exports of crude oil, oil products and natural gas account for a third of exports and about two-fifths of government revenues.

Mexico's mineral resources are legendary. Precious metals make up about 36% of non-oil mineral output. The country is the world's leading producer of silver, fluorite and arsenic, and is among the world's major producers of strontium, graphite, copper, iron ore, sulphur, mercury, lead and zinc. Mexico also produces gold, molybdenum, antimony, bismuth, cadmium, selenium, tungsten, magnesium, common salt, celestite, fuller's earth and gypsum. It is estimated that although 60% of Mexico's land mass has mineral potential, only 25% is known, and only 5% explored in detail.

Agriculture employs 27% of the labour force but has been losing importance since the beginning of the 1970s and now contributes only 9% of gdp. About 12% of the land surface is under cultivation, of which only about one-quarter is irrigated. Over half of the developed cropland lies in the interior highlands. Mexico's agricultural success is almost always related to rainfall and available water for irrigation. On average, four out of every ten years are good, while four are drought years.

Manufacturing, including oil refining and petrochemicals, contributes a quarter of gdp. Mexico City is the focal point for manufacturing activity and the metropolitan area holds about 45% of the employment in manufacturing and 30% of the country's industrial establishments. The government offers tax incentives to companies relocating away from Mexico City and the other major industrial centres of Guadalajara and Monterrey; target cities are Tampico, Coatzacoalcos, Salina Cruz and Lázaro Cárdenas, while much of the manufacturing export activity takes place in the in-bond centres along the border with the USA.

Tourism is a large source of foreign exchange and the largest employer, with about a third of the workforce. About 4.5m tourists visit Mexico every year, of whom about 85% come from the USA. The government is actively encouraging new investment in tourism and foreign investment is being welcomed in hotel construction projects.

During 1978-81 the current account of the balance of payments registered increasing deficits because of domestic expansion and world recession. Mounting public sector deficits were covered by foreign borrowing of increasingly shorter terms until a bunching of short-term maturities and a loss of foreign exchange reserves caused Mexico to declare its inability to service its debts in August 1982, thus triggering what became known as the interna-tional debt crisis. Under the guidance of an IMF programme and helped by commercial bank debt rescheduling agreements, Mexico was able to improve its position largely because of a 40% drop in imports in both 1982 and 1983. In 1986, however, the country was hit by the sharp fall in oil prices, which reduced export revenues by 28%, despite a rapid growth of 37% in non-oil exports through vigorous promotion and exchange rate depreciation policies. Several debt rescheduling and new money agreements were negotiated during the 1980s with the IMF, the World Bank and the commercial banks. Mexico managed to secure progressively easier terms, helped by the US administration's concern for geopolitical reasons, and debt growth was contained. Prepayment of private debt and debt/equity conversions even reduced the overall level of foreign debt. In 1989, Mexico negotiated the first debt reduction package with commercial banks, which was designed to cut debt servicing and restructure debt over a 30-year period supported by collateral from multinational creditors and governments.

Government Under the 1917 Constitution Mexico is a federal republic of 31 states and a Federal District containing the capital, Mexico City. The President, who appoints the Ministers, is elected for 6 years and can never be re-elected. Congress consists of the 64-seat Senate, half elected every 3 years on a rotational basis, and the 500-seat Chamber of Deputies, elected every 3 years. There is universal suffrage, and one Deputy for 60,000 inhabitants.

Local Administration The States enjoy local autonomy and can levy their own taxes, and each State has its Governor, legislature and judicature. The President appoints the Chief of the Federal District.

Religion Roman Catholicism is the principal religion, but the State is determinedly secular. Because of its identification firstly with Spain, then with the Emperor Maximilian and finally with Porfirio Díaz, the Church has been severely persecuted in the past by reform-minded administrations, and priests are still not supposed to wear ecclesiastical dress (see *The Lawless Roads* and *The Power and the Glory*, by Graham Greene).

LAREDO TO MEXICO CITY: THE GULF ROUTE (1)

We are concerned here with the four great road routes from the US border to Mexico City: the Gulf Route from Laredo (by Pan-American Highway), the Eagle Pass/Piedras Negras route, the Central Route from El Paso, and the Pacific Route, from Nogales. The first of these to be opened was the Gulf Route: Nuevo Laredo-Mexico City: 1,226 km. (760 miles).

Traffic from the central and eastern parts of the United States can enter north-eastern Mexico through four gateways along the Río Bravo; at Matamoros, opposite Brownsville (which has 90% Mexican population, despite being in the USA; cheap hotel, *Hotel Bienvenidos*, about 200 metres from Río Grande bridge, D, if you don't want to cross the border at night); at Reynosa (*Hotel San Carlos*, on Zócalo, D, recommended) opposite McAllen; at Ciudad Miguel Alemán, opposite Roma; and at **Nuevo Laredo** (400,000), opposite Laredo—by far the most important of them. The roads from these places all converge upon Monterrey, though there are alternative roads from Reynosa and Matamoros which join the Nuevo Laredo-Mexico City highway at Montemorelos and Ciudad Victoria, respectively: the latter runs along the tropical Gulf coastal plain and then climbs sharply through the Sierra Madre Oriental to Ciudad Victoria, at 333 metres.

Hotels at Nuevo Laredo, *Dos Laredos*, D, Matamoros y 15 de Junio; *Alameda*, on plaza, D; many others.

Motels: *Hacienda*, Prol. Reforma 5530, A; *Reforma*, Av. Guerrero 822, B. Cheap hotel in Laredo, *The Bender*, D/E.

Crafts Shop Centro Artesanal Nuevo Laredo, Maclovio Herrera 3030. T 2-63-99.

Train Regiomontano (*servicio estrella*—**see page** 164) leaves for Mexico City at 1515, stopping at Monterrey (1900) and Saltillo (0935); it leaves Mexico City at 1800, 18 hrs., reserved seat US$21.80, single sleeper, US$41, double US$82. Aguila Azteca to Mexico City from Nuevo Laredo, US$13 *primera especial*, a/c, US$10 1st, US$7 2nd class, daily at 1855, 24 hrs., little difference between 1st and 2nd classes (leaves Mexico City for the border at 0800). Information: Av. López César de Lara y Mina, Apdo. Postal 248, Nuevo Laredo, Tamps. 88000 Mexico, T (871) 280-97; or P.O. Box 595, Laredo, TX 78042.

Buses Buses to Mexico City with Tres Estrellas de Oro, mid-afternoon, from the Nuevo Laredo bus station. Transportes del Norte is generally rec.; 5 buses a day to Mexico City. Buses for Monterrey (4 hrs, US$5.50, leaves at 0800), Mexico City (15 hrs., US$25, leaves at 1400) and intermediate points, Guadalajara (13 hrs., US$12.25, leaves at 1730). Bus Nuevo Laredo-Tampico leaves at 1600, US$13, arrives in the middle of next day. Bus Nuevo Laredo-Morelia 17 hrs., US$26, leaves at 1730.

The Nuevo Laredo bus station is not near the border; take a bus to the border, then walk across. It is not possible to get a bus from the Laredo Greyhound terminal to the Nuevo Larado terminal unless you have a ticket to the interior. Connecting tickets from Houston via Laredo to Monterrey are available, 14 hrs. Overland Greyhound bus New York-Laredo, US$129 with as many stops as you want, but only valid for 15 days. Some buses to Laredo connect with Greyhound buses in the U.S.

If pressed for time, avoid 20 November and other national holidays as there are delays at customs owing to Mexicans visiting the USA in large numbers. Border formalities can take 2 hrs. or more. We have been informed that at the border crossing at Matamoros guards have demanded bribes of from US$5 to US$20 or even US$50, especially from car drivers.

Matamoros (470,000 people), has a bright and unforbidding museum, designed to let a prospective tourist know what he can expect in Mexico. It is well worth a visit.

Hotels *Ritz*, Matamoros y Siete, D. There are 4 motels on the road to the beach, all C/B.

Craft shop: Centro Artesanal Matamoros, Calle 5a Hurtado and Alvaro Obregón (T 2-03-84).

Buses Several lines run first-class buses to Mexico City in 18 hrs. for US$28. Transportes del Norte to Ciudad Victoria for US$6 (4 hrs.).

Rail Tamaulipeco *servicio estrella* train leaves Matamoros at 1400 for Reynosa (opposite McAllen, Texas, arrives 1520) and Monterrey (arrives 1850, US$6).

Visas can be obtained in Brownsville from the Mexican Consulate at 940, E Washington. About 8 km. outside Matamoros there is an immigration check-point; to cross this point a visa must be shown which must be signed at the bus station by an immigration official. Without this signature you will be sent back. For drivers at least, this border crossing has been described as "chaotic".

After 130 km. of grey-green desert, the road from Nuevo Laredo climbs the Mamulique Pass, which it crosses at 700 metres, and then descends to

Monterrey, capital of Nuevo León state, third largest city in Mexico, 253 km. S of the border and 915 km. from Mexico City. The city is dominated by the Cerro de la Silla from the E. Its population now approaches 3 million and is still growing in spite of its unattractive climate—too hot in summer, too cold in winter, dusty at most times—and its shortage of water. It now turns out (using cheap gas from near the Texas border and increasingly from the new gas fields in the South), over 75% of Mexico's iron and steel, and many other products accompanied by an almost permanent industrial smog. Its people are highly skilled and educated, but its architecture is drab. In its main centre, Plaza Zaragoza, there is a pleasant 18th century Cathedral badly damaged in the war against the US in 1846-47, when it was used by Mexican troops as a powder magazine. Plaza Zaragoza, Plaza 5 de Mayo and many surrounding blocks now form the Gran Plaza, claimed to be the biggest civic square in the world; its centrepiece is the Laser Beam Tower. (There is a clean public convenience beneath the Gran Plaza, on Matamoros between Avs. Zua Zua and Zaragoza, near the Neptune Fountain.) Calle Morelos is a pedestrians-only shopping centre. Its famous Technological Institute has valuable collections of books on 16th century Mexican history, of rare books printed in Indian tongues, and 2,000 editions of Don Quixote in all languages. Altitude: 538 metres, and evenings are cool.

Students of architecture should see the remarkable church of San José Obrero built in a working-class district by Enrique de la Mora and his team. The Monterrey Museum is in the grounds of the Cuauhtémoc Brewery, Av. Universidad (beer—in small bottles—is handed out free in the gardens). The Mexican Baseball Hall of Fame is in part of the museum, as is a museum of Modern Art; open Tues.-Fri. 0930-1800, Sat.-Sun. 1030-1730. The Alfa Cultural Centre, in the Garza García suburb, has a fine planetarium and an astronomy and physics section with do-it-yourself illustrations of mechanical principles, etc. In a separate building is a Rufino Tamayo stained-glass window. Reached by special bus from W end of Alameda, hourly on the hour 1500-2000, the centre is open 1500-1920, closed Mon. The Alameda Gardens, between Avs. Aremberri and Washington, on Av. Pino Suárez, are a pleasant place to sit. The Obispado (Bishop's Palace Hill) affords good views, smog permitting. The Palace (1787) is a regional museum; it served as H.Q. for both Pancho Villa and Gen. Zachary Taylor. Take No. 1 bus which stops at the foot of the hill.

Hotels It is difficult to obtain accommodation because of the constant movement of people travelling north/south. *Holiday Inn Crowne Plaza*, Av. Constitución 300 Oriente, near Plaza Zaragoza, L, best, T (91-83) 44-60-00; *Holiday Inn*, Av. Universidad 101, L, T 766555; *Ancira*, Hidalgo y Escobedo, T 432060, A; *Ambassador*, Hidalgo y Galeana, T 422040, A; *Río*, Padre Mier 194 Poniente, T 449510, A; *Colonial*, Escobedo y Hidalgo, T 436791, B; *Yamallel*, Zaragoza 912, Nte Madero, T 753400, D, good; *Nuevo León*, Amado Nervo 1007 Norte con Av. Madero, T 741900, C with bath (hot water), very clean, pleasant, close to bus station.

Victoria, E, with shower, hot water only in day time, 2 blocks from railway station, clean, safe, but do not get room opposite station (less 10% if you show student card); *Reforma*, Av. Universidad, 1132, F, one of the better cheap ones; *Estación*, Guadalupe Victoria 1450, opp. train station, E, bath, reasonable; *Posada*, Juan Méndez 1515, Norte, with bath E, rec. Many hotels between Colón and Reforma, 2 blocks from the bus station.

Motels *El Paso Autel*, Zaragoza y Martínez, T 400690, B; *Motel/Trailerpark Nueva Castilla*, on Highway 85 before Saltillo bypass, E, hot showers, reasonable restaurant; several on Nuevo Laredo highway.

Restaurant *La Cabaña*, Calle Pino Suárez, meals and snacks. 23 eating places around the "Pink Zone" and Plaza Zaragoza in the heart of town.

British Consulate (Honorary) Mr Edward Lawrence, Privada de Tamazunchale 104, Colonia del Valle, Garza García. T (91-83) 782565/569114.

Tourist Office Infotur on Gran Plaza (W side). Large city maps available at bookshops.

Railways Regiomontano (*servicio estrella*) calls here en route to Mexico City at 1900, and to border at 0800; fares to Mexico City, reserved seat US$17, single sleeper US$31.80, double US$63.70. To Nuevo Laredo 0830. Tamaulipeco (*servicio estrella*) connects with Regiomontano at 0840 for Reynosa (arr. 1205, US$4.30) and Matamoros (arr. 1330, US$6). To Mexico City (US$6.30 2nd class, US$10.60 1st) and the port of Tampico. Day trains are slow.

Bus Terminal on Av. Colón, between Calzada B. Reyes and Av. Pino Suárez. Monterrey-Mexico City, US$13, 12 hrs. A more scenic trip is from Mexico City (northern bus terminal) to Ciudad Valles, 10 hrs., from where there are many connecting buses to Monterrey. To San Luis Potosí, US$7. To Chihuahua with Omnibus México, 1845, 12 hrs., US$14. Frequent buses to Saltillo, but long queues for tickets. To Santiago for Cola de Caballo falls, US$0.50.

Airport Aeropuerto del Norte, 24 km. from centre. Daily flights from Mexico City take 1¼ hrs.

In the hills around are the bathing resort of Topo Chico, 6½ km. to the NW; water from its hot springs is bottled and sold throughout Mexico; and 18 km. away Chipinque Mesa, at 1,280 metres in the Sierra Madre, with magnificent views of the Monterrey area.

W of Monterrey, off the Saltillo road are the García Caves (about 10 km. from Villa García, which is 40 km. from Monterrey). The entrance is 800 metres up, by cable car, and inside are beautiful stalagmites and stalactites. At the foot of the cable car are a pool and recreational centre.

A tour of the caves takes 1½ hrs., and it is compulsory to go in a group with a guide. You can take a bus to Villa García, but it is a dusty walk to the caves. On Sun. Transportes Saltillo-Monterrey run a bus to the caves at 0900, 1000 and 1100. Otherwise, take an agency tour, e.g. Osetur (details from Infotur); book at *Hotel Ancira* (on Tues., US$3.50).

Leaving Monterrey, the road threads the narrow and lovely Huajuco canyon; from Santiago village a road runs to within 2 km. of the Cola de Caballo, or Horsetail, Falls. (First-class hotel on the way, and you can get a colectivo, US$1.50, from the bus stop to the falls, and a horse, US$1.50, to take you to the top of the falls, entrance US$0.60; cost of guide US$5.) The road drops gradually into lower and warmer regions, passing through a succession of sub-tropical valleys with orange groves, banana plantations and vegetable gardens.

At **Montemorelos**, just off the highway, 79 km. S of Monterrey, a branch road from the Matamoros-Monterrey highway comes in. On 53 km. is **Linares** (100,000 people), a fast-expanding town.

Hotels *Hotel Guidi*, C, nr. bus station; *Escondido Court*, motel, D, clean, a/c, pool and restaurant, rec., 1½ km. N of Linares on Route 855.

Bus Linares to San Luis Potosí, US$7.

A most picturesque 96 km. highway runs west from Linares up the lovely Santa Rosa canyon, up and over the Sierra Madre after Iturbide, turn S on top of the Sierra Madre and continue on good road through the unspoilt Sierra via La Escondida and Dr. Arroyo. At San Roberto, N of Matehuala (**see page** 71) join the Highway 57 route from Eagle Pass to Mexico City.

(Km. 706) **Ciudad Victoria**, capital of Tamaulipas state, a quiet, unhurried city with a shaded plaza and a tiny church perched on the top of a hill. It is often used as a stop-over. Alt.: 336 metres; pop.: 300,000.

Hotels *Sierra Gorda*, Hidalgo 990 Oriente, T 32280, C, garage US$0.70 a night. *Trailer Park*, Libramiento 101-85, follow signs, good service, hot showers. Owner has travel information, US$5 for 2 plus vehicle.
    Motels *Panorámica*, Lomas de Santuario, T 25506, C; *Los Monteros*, Plaza Hidalgo, T 20300, downtown, C.

Buses Omnibuses Blancos to Ciudad Valles (see below) for US$4. Bus Ciudad Victoria-Mexico City 12 hrs., US$13.

After crossing the Tropic of Cancer the road enters the solid green jungle of the tropical lowlands.
    Monterrey trains run via Ciudad Victoria to the Caribbean port of **Tampico**, population: 560,000, definitely not a tourist attraction, reached by a fine road from (Km. 570) El Mante, in a rich sugar-growing area, a deviation of 156 km. Tampico is on the northern bank of the Río Pánuco, not far from a large oilfield: there are storage tanks and refineries for miles along the southern bank. The summer heat, rarely above 35°C, is tempered by sea breezes, but June and July are trying. Cold northerlies blow now and again during the winter. There are two

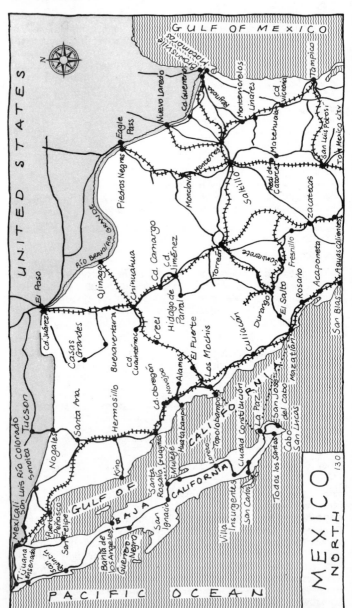

pleasant plazas, Plaza de Armas at Colón y Carranza, with squirrels in the trees, and Plaza de la Libertad, Madero y Juárez. Fishing (both sea and river) is excellent. Huge, interesting market, but watch your possessions carefully. The Playa de Miramar, a beach resort, is a tram or bus-ride from the city, but is reported dirty. If walking there, go along the breakwater (Escollera Norte) on N side of Río Pánuco, for views of the shipping and to see the monument to Mexican merchant seamen killed in World War II. The Museo de la Cultura Huasteca in Ciudad Madero, an adjacent town, is worth visiting (Instituto Tecnológico, Av. 1 de Mayo y Sor Juana Inés de la Cruz—in poor condition); take a colectivo, "Madero", from the centre of Tampico to the Zócalo in Ciudad Madero, then another to the Instituto; open 1000-1500, except Mon., small but select collection. Ciudad Madero claims to be Mexico's petroleum capital, with a huge oil refinery.

A second paved road from Tampico joins the Nuevo Laredo-México highway further S at Ciudad Valles. There are direct buses to Brownsville (Texas), leaving at 2400 and 0545, US$12. A splendid new bridge was opened at the end of 1988 to replace the ferry to Villa Cuauhtémoc. Further S, the coast road, Route 180, enters Veracruz state, leading to Tuxpan, Poza Rica and Veracruz (the northern towns of that state are described on **page** 195**).**

Hotels *Camino Real*, Av. Hidalgo 2000, T 38811, A; *Impala*, Mirón 220 Pte., T 20990, B; *Inglaterra*, Mirón y Olmos, A; *Imperial*, Aurora Sur 201, T 25678, D, clean, shower, fan, but noisy; *Tampico*, Carranza 513, T 24970, C; *Nuevo León*, D, Aduana N. 107, T 24370, a/c, shower, clean; *Ritz*, on Miramar beach, E, beautiful beach, deserted at night.

Several cheap hotels nr. Plaza de la Libertad: e.g. *Sevilla* (always full), *Rex*, F, dirty, no hot water; *América*, nr. market on Olmos, F, dirty but safe. All hotels downtown near market should be treated with discretion; many have a rapid turnover.

Restaurant *El Diligencias*, Héroes del Canonero Tampico 415 Oriente y Gral. López de Lara, excellent seafood; *Emir*, F.A. Olmos between Diaz Mirón y Madero, good; for breakfast, *El Selecto*, opp. market. To the N of Tampico on the Pan-American Highway, at Soto de Marina, *Colonial*—rec. Also, 4 good Chinese places in town.

West German Consul 2 de Enero, 102 Sur-A, Hon. Consul Dieter Schulze. Postal Address: Apdo. 775, T (91-72) 129784/129817. Also deals with British affairs.

Tourist Office Plaza de Armas, above *Chantal* ice cream parlour on Calle F.A. Olmos, helpful.

Trains To Monterrey at 0845 (2nd class), arrive 1930. To San Luis Potosí.

(Km. 548) Antiguo Morelos. A road turns off W to San Luis Potosí (**see page** 72) 314 Km., and Guadalajara (**see page** 113).

(Km. 476) **Ciudad Valles** (pop. 320,000), on a winding river and a popular stop-over with many hotels (*San Fernando*, T 20184; *Valles*, T 20050, both on Carretera México-Laredo, B). Museo Regional Huasteco, Calles Rotarios y Artes (or Peñaloza), open 1000-1200, 1400-1800, Mon.-Fri., centre of archaeological and ethnographic research for the Huastec region. Omnibus Oriente to San Luis Potosí for US$3 (4 hrs.); Mexico City 10 hrs. The road to Tampico (145 Km.) goes through the oil camp of El Ebano.

(Km. 370) **Tamazunchale** (alt. 206 metres, 150,000 people), with riotous tropical vegetation, is perhaps the most popular of all the overnight stops. (*San Antonio Hotel; Mirador*, D, good, but passing traffic by night is noisy; *Hotel OK*, F, cheapest but not rec.; *Pemex Tourist Camp*, US$2 p.p., nice position, poor plumbing.) The road S of here begins a spectacular climb to the highland, winding over the rugged terrain cut by the Río Moctezuma and its tributaries. The highest point on the road is 2,502 metres. From (Km. 279) Jacala there is a dizzying view into a chasm. **Zimapán** (*Posada del Rey*, fascinating but very run down, out on the highway), with a charming market place and a small old church in the plaza, is as good a place as any to stay the night. From (Km. 178) **Portezuelo** a paved road runs W to Querétaro (**see page 74**), 140 Km.

In an area of 23,300 sq. Km. N and S of (Km. 169) **Ixmiquilpan**, just off the highway, 65,000 Otomí Indians "live the bitterest and saddest life". The beautifully worked Otomí belts and bags may sometimes be bought at the Monday market, and also in the Artesanía shop in the main street almost opposite the government aid offices.

See early Indian frescoes in the main church, which is one of the 16th century battlemented Augustinian monastery-churches; the monastery is open to the public. John Streather writes: "At sunset each day white egrets come to roost in the trees outside the church; it's worth going up on to the battlements to see them swoop down. The church of El Carmen is worth a visit too, lovely west façade and gilded altars inside. There is also a 16th century bridge over the river; beautiful walk along the ahuehuete-lined banks".

Hotel Diana, E, rear buildings slightly dearer rooms but much cleaner, rec., safe parking.

Near Ixmiquilpan are several warm swimming pools, both natural and man-made—San Antonio, Dios Padre, Las Humedades, and near Tephé (the only warm-water bath, clean, entry US$0.40) and Tzindejé (this is about 20 mins. from town). The Otomí villages of La Lagunita, La Pechuga and La Bonanza, in a beautiful valley, have no modern conveniences, but the people are charming and friendly.

Actopán (km. 119) has another fine 16th century Augustinian church and convent (*Hotel Rira*, D). From Actopán a 56 km. branch road runs to one of Mexico's great archaeological sites: Tula, capital of the Toltecs (**see page 171**).

On the way to Tula there is an interesting cooperative village, **Cruz Azul**. Free concerts on Sun. mornings at 1000 in front of main market. At (Km. 85) Colonia, a road runs left for 8 km. to

Pachuca, one of the oldest silver-mining centres in Mexico and capital of Hidalgo state. Pop.: 320,000; alt.: 2,445 metres. The Aztecs mined here before the Spaniards came and the hills are honeycombed with old workings and terraced with tailings. Even today the silver output is one of the largest of any mine in the world. A large number of colonial buildings among its narrow, steep and crooked streets include the treasury for the royal tribute, La Caja, in Calle Cajas (1670), now used as offices; Las Casas Coloradas (1785), now the Escuela Vicente Guerrero; and a former Franciscan convent (1596) on Plaza Bartolomé de Medina, 5 blocks S of the Zócalo at Arista y Hidalgo, now a Regional History Museum displaying chronological exhibits of the state's history. It is known as the Centro Cultural Hidalgo (open Tues.-Sun., 1000-1400, 1600-1900—may close early on Sun. p.m.). An outstanding photographic museum is in the large cloister on the far side of the convent. In the complex there are a souvenir shop with reproductions of ceramic and metal anthropological items and recordings of indigenous music. Casa de las Artesanías for Hidalgo state is at the junction of Avenidas Revolución y Juárez. In the Plaza Independencia is a huge clock with four Carrara marble figures. The modern buildings include a notable theatre, the Palacio de Gobierno (which has a mural depicting ex-President Echeverría's dream of becoming Secretary-General of the UN), and the Banco de Hidalgo. An electric railway and a road run 10 km. to the large silver-mining camp of Real (or Mineral) del Monte, picturesque and with steep streets. Collective taxis also run frequently from beside La Caja (US$0.40 p.p.).

Hotels *De los Baños*, D, good but unreliable water supply; *América*, F with bath, one block from Zócalo, quiet, rec.; *Colonial*, Guerrero 505, central, E; *Juárez*, Barreda 107, E, with bath, some rooms without windows. just before Real del Monte, in superb wooded surroundings. CREA Youth Hostel at the turn off to El Chico.

Restaurant *Casino Español*, Matamoros 207, 2nd floor, old-time favourite. "Paste" is the local survivor from Cornish miners' days; a good approximation of the real pastie, but a bit peppery!

Transport Bus terminal is outside town; take any bus marked "Central". Train from the capital at 1013 (2nd class, 3 hrs.). Servicio Estrella to Mexico City.

Cornish miners settled at Real del Monte in the 19th century; their descendants can be recognized among the people. At each entry to the town is a mural commemorating the first strike in the Americas, by silver miners in 1776. The Panteón Inglés (English cemetery) is on a wooded hill opposite the town (ask the caretaker for the key). Mineral del Chico is a beautiful little town 30 km. from Pachuca in the **El Chico National Park**. The Park has many campsites and the town weekend homes for the wealthy of Mexico City. There are huge rock formations covered in pine forests; splendid walks. Bus from Pachuca bus station.

N of Pachuca via Atotonilco el Grande, where there are a chapel and convent half-way down a beautiful canyon, is the impressive Barranca de Metztitlán which has a wealth of different varieties of cacti, including the "hairy old man" cactus, and a huge 17th century monastery. Farther N (difficult road) is Molango, where there is a restored convent. 34 km. NE of Pachuca is *San Miguel Regla*, a mid-18th century *hacienda* built by the Conde de Regla, and now run as a resort, fine atmosphere, excellent service. A road continues to Tulancingo, on the Pachuca-Poza Rica road, Route 130. 17 km. from Pachuca, and a further 4 km. off Route 130 to the right is Epazoyucan, a village with an interesting convent. After Tulancingo, Route 119 branches off to the right to **Zacatlán**, famous for its apple orchards and now also producing plums, pears and cider. Its alpine surroundings include an impressive national park, **Valle de las Piedras Encimadas** (stacked rocks), camping possible. Nearby is *Posada Campestre al Final de la Senda*, a ranch with weekend accommodation, horse riding, walks, D, p.p. full board, T Puebla 413 821 for reservations. Some 16 km. S. of Zacatlán is Chignahuapan (about 1½ hrs. from Puebla), a leading producer of *sarapes*, surrounded by several curative spas.

30 km. from Tulancingo on Route 130 is *La Cabaña* restaurant, of log-cabin construction, cheap; thereafter, the road descends with many bends and slow lorries, and in winter there may be fog. At Huauchinango, an annual flower fair is held in March; 22 km. from here is Xicotepec de Juárez (*Mi Ranchito*, one of the nicest small hotels in Mexico; *Italia*, near main square, E). Along the route are the villages of Pahuatlan and San Pablito, where sequined headbands are made, and paintings are done on flattened *amate* bark. The entire route from desert to jungle is 190 km., taking 5 hours.

A 4-lane highway now runs from Pachuca to Mexico City via (Km. 27) Venta de Carpio, from which a road runs E to Acolman, 12 km., and Teotihuacán, another 10 km. Neither of these places should be missed (**see page** 170); buses are available from Pachuca; get them at the tollbooth on the highway to Mexico City.

At Santa Clara, 13 km. short of the Capital, the road forks. The right-hand fork (easy driving) goes direct to the City; the left fork goes through Villa Madero, where you can see the shrine of Guadalupe.

EAGLE PASS—PIEDRAS NEGRAS TO MEXICO CITY (2)

This route, 1,328 km. (825 miles), is 102 km. longer than the Laredo route, but is very wide, very fast and much easier to drive. It is by now the most popular route, but is far from being the most interesting. Take in enough gasoline at Monclova to cover the 205 km. to Saltillo. Hotel, restaurant and camping prices have risen rapidly.

Piedras Negras, pop. 150,000, altitude 220 metres, is across the Río Bravo from Eagle Pass, Texas. (Artesanía shop—Centro Artesanal Piedras Negras, Edificio la Estrella, Puerta México, T 2-10-87.) Beyond Hermanas (137 km.) the highway begins to climb gradually up to the plateau country.

Rail Coahuilense *servicio estrella* train leaves for Saltillo at 1300 (arr. 2030), US$8.70 for reclining seat.

Monclova (243 km. from border) has one of the largest steel mills in Mexico, and 250,000 people.

Then comes **Saltillo** (448 km.; alt.: 1,600 metres; population: 650,000), capital of Coahuila state, a cool, dry popular resort noted for the excellence of its *sarapes*. Its 18th century cathedral is the best in northern Mexico and it has a grand market. Good golf, tennis, swimming. College students from the US attend the popular Summer

School at the Universidad Interamericana. Good views from El Cerro del Pueblo overlooking city. An 87-km. road runs E to Monterrey. You turn right for Mexico City.

Festival Local *feria* in first half of August; cheap accommodation impossible to find at this time. Indian dances during 30 May and 30 August; picturesque ceremonies and bullfights during October *fiestas*. *Pastorelas*, the story of the Nativity, are performed in the neighbourhood in Christmas week.

Saltillo Hotels Several hotels a short distance from the plaza at the intersection of Allende and Aldama, the main streets, e.g. *San Jorge*, Manuel Acuña 240, T 30600, A; *Saade*, Aldama 397, T 33400, C; *Urdiñola*, Victoria 211, T 40940, reasonable, C; *Metropolí*, D, Allende 436, basic, with shower, a little dark but adequate, quiet. *De Avila*, Padre Flores 211, T 37272, D, basic, cold water, safe motorcycle parking. Cheaper are *Hidalgo*, on Padre Flores, E, without bath, not worth paying for bath in room, cold water only (hot baths open to public and guests for small fee). *Zamora*, Ramos Arzipe (Poniente) 552, F, cheap; also cheap *El Conde*, Pérez Treviño y Acuña.
    Several good **motels** in this area, e.g. *Huizache*, Blvd. Carranza 1746, T 28112, B; *La Fuente*, A, Blvd. Fundadores, T 22090; *Camino Real*, Carretera 57, Km. 865, T 41515, A.

Restaurants *Viena*, Acuña 519, rec.; *Victoria*, by *Hotel Hidalgo* has reasonable comida; *Dik-Dik*, Aldama 548. Drinks and night-time view can be had at the *Rodeway Inn* on the N side of town; *Kentucky Fried Chicken*, Victoria Pte. 358.

Tourist Office Near crossroads of Allende and Blvd. Francisco Coss in old railway station, long way from centre. Map with all useful addresses, incl. hotels.

Bus Terminal is a long way from centre; minibuses to Pérez Treviño y Allende (for centre) will take luggage. To Monterrey and Nuevo Laredo with Transportes del Norte. For Torreón, all buses originate in Monterrey and tickets only sold when bus arrives; be prepared to stand.

Train Regiomontano (*servicio estrella*) calls here en route to Mexico City at 2130, and to Monterrey and Nuevo Laredo at 0600. Coahuilense (*servicio estrella*) connects with Regiomontano for Piedras Negras 0700 (7½ hrs.). Fares to Mexico City: reserved seat US$15, single sleeper US$28.20, double US$56.40; to Piedras Negras, US$8.70.

San Roberto junction (581 km. from Saltillo), where a 96-km. road runs E over the Sierra Madre to Linares, on the Gulf Route (**see page** 65).
    After about 720 km. we reach *Matehuala*, an important road junction. Fiesta, 6-20 January.

Accommodation *Motel Trailerpark Las Palmas*, on the N edge of town, T 20001, clean, B, English spoken and paperbacks sold, bowling alley and miniature golf, tours to Real de Catorce (see below) arranged; *El Dorado* nearby, T 20174, cheaper, rec.; *Hotel Matehuala*, F, rooms shocking pink, full of furniture, adequate; *Motel Palapa*, on highway, C, excellent dining room. *Restaurant La Fontella* in the centre, good regional food.

Bus To San Luis Potosí, with Estrella Blanca, 2½ hrs., US$3.50; Mexico City, Monterrey and Queretaro.

Chris and Miyuki Kerfoot write: From Saltillo to Matehuala by 2nd class bus, Estrella Blanca, 1½ hrs., US$2 to San Roberto, which is no more than a road junction with a Pemex petrol station, hitch to the junction of Highways 58 and 68 and catch a bus (Transportes Tamaulipas) to Matehuala (US$3, 4 hrs.). From these junctions near Caleana to La Soledad the scenery is worthwhile, as the road winds its way up and down through wooded valleys. The final section to Matehuala passes through undulating scrub country.

56 km. W of Matehuala is one of Mexico's most interesting "ghost towns", **_Real De Catorce_**, founded in 1772.

Tim Connell writes: To get there, turn left along the Zacatecas road (not signposted) through Cedral. After 27 km. turn left off the paved road, on to a gravel one. The road passes through Potrero, a big centre for nopal cactus. Some people live in the old mine workings and old buildings. Huichol Indians are seen here occasionally. A silver mine is still being worked at Santana.

Real de Catorce is approached through Ogarrio, an old mine gallery widened (only just) to allow trucks through. It is 2½ km. long, and very eerie, with the odd tunnel leading off into the gloom on either side. There is an overtaking bay half way through. A small chapel to the Virgen de los Dolores is by the entrance. The tunnel opens out abruptly into the old city, once a major mining centre with its own mint and nearly 40,000 inhabitants. About 700 people still live here, mainly round the Zócalo, looking for silver. The cockpit and the 16 chapels are worth seeing; the Church of San Francisco is believed to be miraculous. There is a pilgrimage here, on foot from Matehuala, overnight on 4 October. The floor of the church is made of wooden panels, which can be lifted up to see the catacombs below. In a room to one side of the main altar are _retablos_, touchingly simple paintings on tin, as votive offerings to the Saint for his intercession. This remarkable city, clustering around the sides of a valley, is so quiet that you can hear the river in the canyon, 1,000 metres below. Next to the church is a small museum (entry US$0.10) showing mining equipment, etc., worth a visit.

Hotels one in the main street, very comfortable with restaurant and bar, expensive, another, _Hotel Real_, in a side street, clean, E.

Transport Four minibuses a day go there from the agency by the _Hotel Matehuala_ (US$3 return, journey 1½ hrs., with 2 hrs. to wander around). A taxi can be hired nearby for US$12.50—economic for 4 people; local buses from office 1 block N of the Zócalo. Tours can be arranged with Turismos del Altiplano, Bustamante 128, T 3-40. Real de Catorce is also easily reached from Saltillo or San Luis Potosí by train. Jeeps collect passengers from the station (US$8-10 per jeep) and follow a more spectacular route than the minibuses.

Huizache (785 km.) is the junction with the Guadalajara-Antiguo Morelos-Tampico highway. At 901 km. we come to San Luis Potosí.

San Luis Potosí, 423 km. from Mexico City, capital of its state, is the centre of a rich mining and agricultural area, which has expanded industrially in recent years. Alt.: 1,880 metres; pop.: 800,000. Glazed, many-coloured tiles are a feature of the city: one of its shopping streets, the main plaza, and the domes of many of its churches are covered with them. It became an important centre after the discovery of the famous San Pedro silver mine in the 16th century, and a city in 1658. The

Cathedral is on Plaza Hidalgo. See the churches of San Francisco, with its white and blue tiled dome and suspended glass boat in the transept (try and get into the magnificent sacristy); Carmen, in Plaza Morelos, with a grand tiled dome, an intricate façade, and a fine pulpit and altar inside (the Teatro de la Paz is next door); the baroque Capilla de Aránzazu, behind San Francisco inside the regional museum (see below); the Capilla de Loreto with a baroque façade; Iglesia de San Miquelito, in the oldest part of the city; San Agustín, with its ornate baroque tower; and the startling modern Templo de la Santa Cruz, in the Industria Aviación district, designed by Enrique de la Mora. The Palacio de Gobierno, begun 1770, contains oil-paintings of past governors, and the colonial treasury, Antigua Real Caja, built 1767. Other points of interest are the pedestrian precinct in Calle Hidalgo and the Caja del Agua fountain (1835) in Av. Juárez. Plaza de San Francisco is very pleasant. The modern railway station has frescoes by Fernando Leal. The Teatro Alarcón is by Tresguerras (see under Celaya, **page** 95). Locally made *rebozos* (the best are from Santa María del Río) are for sale in the markets. The University was founded in 1804. A scenic road leads to Aguascalientes airport.

Feria In the second fortnight of August.

Hotels Many between the railway station and the cathedral. *Panorama*, Av. Venustiano Carranza 315, T 21777, B; *María Cristina*, C, with swimming pool on roof (Juan Sarabia 110, Altos, T 29403); *Nápoles*, Juan Sarabia 120, T 42104, C, rec.; *Progreso*, Aldama 415, T 20366, D. *Universidad*, Universidad 1435, between train and bus station, E, clean, friendly, hot showers; *Jardín*, Los Bravos 530, T 23152, E, good, restaurant rec.; *Gran*, Bravo 235, F without bath, hot water, friendly; CREA Youth Hostel, Diagonal Sur, on the SW side of the Glorieta Juárez, 5 min. walk from central bus station, F, C.P. 78320, T 26603.
   Motels all along Highway 57: *Hostal del Quijote*, A, five-star, convention facilities, 6 km. S on the San Luis Potosí-Mexico City highway, one of the best in Mexico, T 81312; *Santa Fe*, T 25109, B; *Cactus*, T 21871, B; all with pools.

Restaurants *Panorama*, roof-garden restaurant, Plaza de la Universidad, good; *Los Molinos*, in *Hostal del Quijote*, excellent well-served food; *Posada del Virrey*, Plaza Hidalgo, clean, pleasant, reasonable; *Tokio*, Los Bravos 510, excellent comida. *La Lonja*, Aldama 300, and *La Virreina*, Carranza 830, both popular eating places; *Café Versalles*, Madero 145, excellent coffee and yoghurt; *El Girasol*, Guerrero 345, vegetarian; good cafeteria at bus station. *Café Florida*, Juan Sarabia 230, *Pacífico*, Juan Sarabia y Manuel José Othon, clean bathroom, good menu, open 24 hrs., highly rec.; and many other reasonably-priced eating places at western end of Alameda Juan Sarabia.

Museums Museo Regional de Arte Popular, open Tues.-Sat. 1000-1345, 1600-1745; Sun. 1000-1400, Mon. 1000-1500, next to San Francisco church. Nearby is **Museo Regional Potosino**, archaeological, and a collection of wrought iron work, Capilla Aránzazu on 2nd floor, open Tues.-Fri. 1000-1300, 1500-1800, Sat. 1000-1200, Sun. 1000-1300. **La Casa de la Cultura** on Av. Carranza, halfway between the centre and university, is a converted mansion with frequent art displays and musical recitals, open Tues.-Fri, 1000-1400, 1600-1800, Sat. 1000-1400, 1800-2100. **Museo Nacional de la Máscara**, in Palacio Federal, has most complete collection of masks in the country, open Tues.-Fri. 1000-1400, 1600-1800, Sat.-Sun. 1000-1400. In Parque Tangamanga (still under development S of city) is **Museo Tangamanga** in an old hacienda, also a

Planetarium, observatory and open air theatre (open 0600-1800). In Plaza España, next to the Plaza de Toros, is a **Museo Taurino** (E of Alameda on Universidad y Triana, Tues.-Sat. 1100-1330, 1730-1930). **Casa Othon**, Manuel José Othón 225, is the birthplace and home of the poet, open Tues.-Fri. 0800-1900, Sat. and Sun. 1000-1300; in the Palacio de Gobierno some rooms may be visited Mon.-Fri. 0930-1330.

Shopping Local sweets and craftwork at Plaza del Carmen 325, Los Bravos 546 and Escobedo 1030. The famous local painter, Vicente Guerrero, lives in a modest neighbourhood at Plata 407, Colonia Morales (T 3-80-57) where he also has his studio. Markets: head north on Hidalgo and you come to Mercado Hidalgo, then Mercado República, and Mercado 16 de Septiembre.

Post Office Morelos y González Ortega.

Tourist Office Dirrección Estatal de Turismo, Manuel José Othon 130, opp. Cathedral; Coordinación Regional de Turismo, Jardín Guerrero 14 (Plaza San Francisco), both helpful.

Buses Station on outskirts of town 1½ km. from centre. Bus to centre US$0.10. Flecha Amarilla to Querétaro, US$3.50, 2 hrs. (50-odd km. of 4-lane highway have been built N of Querétaro, about half the way, and 40 km. have also been completed to the S of San Luis Potosí); to Nuevo Laredo, US$20. To Mexico City, US$6.10, 6 hrs.

Train to Querétaro, US$2.25 1st class, US$1.20 2nd, supposed to leave at 1015 but arrives full and late from Nuevo Laredo; to Mexico City, 10-11 hrs.; to San Miguel de Allende, 3-4 hrs.

Excursions   Hot springs at Ojocaliente, Balneario de Lourdes and Gogorrón. Balneario de Lourdes (hotel, clean, nice atmosphere, small pool, D) is S of San Luis Potosí. Gogorrón is clean and relaxing, with pools, hot tubs, picnic grounds and campsites. There is a restaurant. A day trip or overnight camp-out is recommended in the lightly wooded hills and meadows near the microwave station (at 2,600 metres) 40 km. E of San Luis Potosí: go 35 km. along the Tampico highway and continue up 5 km. of cobblestone road to the station. Good views and flora.

(1,021 km. from border) *San Luis De La Paz*, the junction with Route 110 leading west to three of the most attractive towns in Mexico: Dolores Hidalgo, Guanajuato, and San Miguel de Allende. (**See pages 92-98.**) No one who yields to the temptation of this detour can hope to get back to the main route for three or four days.

Near San Luis is another of Mexico's mining ghost-towns, Pozos, where the population has fallen from 10,000 to 500 in the course of this century. One can explore everywhere in complete tranquillity.

(1,105 km.) *Querétaro*, pop.: 550,000; alt.: 1,865 metres (can be quite cold at night); 215 km. from the capital. The city was founded in 1531 and the name means "Place of Rocks" in Tarascan. It is now an important industrial centre and capital of Querétaro state, an old and beautiful city, dotted with attractive squares. (No buses in the centre.) Hidalgo's rising in 1810 was plotted here, and it was also here that Emperor Maximilian surrendered after defeat, was tried, and was shot, on 19 June, 1867, on the Cerro de las Campanas (the Hill of Bells), outside the city.

La Corregidora (Doña Josefa Ortiz de Domínguez, wife of the Corregidor, or Mayor), a member of the group of plotters for independence masquerading as a society for the study of the fine arts, was able, in 1810, to get word to Father Hidalgo that their plans for revolt had been discovered. Hidalgo immediately gave the cry (*grito*) for independence. Today, the Corregidor gives the Grito from the balcony of the Palacio Municipal (on Plaza Independencia) every 15 September at 1100 (it is echoed on every civic balcony thoughout Mexico on this date). La Corregidora's home may be visited.

Buildings to see: the Santa Rosa de Viterbo church and monastery, remodelled by Francisco Tresguerras; his reconstruction of Santa Clara, one of the loveliest churches in Mexico, and that is saying much; the church and monastery of Santa Cruz, which served as the HQ of Maximilian and his forces (view from the bell tower); the church of San Felipe, now being restored for use as the Cathedral; the splendid Federal Palace, once an Augustinian convent with exceptionally fine cloisters, now restored with an art gallery containing some beautiful works; the important and elegant Regional Museum on the main plaza, known as the Plaza de Armas or as Plaza Obregón (not all its galleries are always open) which contains much material on the revolution of 1810 and the 1864-67 period; the Teatro de la República, where Maximilian and his generals were tried, and where the Constitution of 1917 (still in force) was drafted; the aqueduct, built in 1726 and 9 km. long, very impressive. Several *andadores* (pedestrian walkways) have been developed, greatly adding to the amenities of the city; prices are high here. The *andadores* replace particular roads in places—e.g. Av. 16 de Septiembre becomes Andador de la Corregidora in the centre, and then reverts to its original name. There are local opals, amethysts and topazes for sale; remarkable mineral specimens are shaped into spheres, eggs, mushrooms, and then polished until they shine like jewels (US$10-30, cheaper than San Juan del Río, but more expensive than Taxco). Recommended is Lapidaría Querétaro, Pasteur Norte 72 (Hermanos Ramírez), for fine opals. City tour plus execution site and Juárez monument, excellent value, from J. Guadalupe Velásquez 5, Jardines de Oro, Santa Cruz, T 21298, daily at 1130, US$10. On Sun., family excursions leave the Plaza de Armas at 1000. Try local Hidalgo Pinot Noir wine.

There is a *feria agrícola* from 2nd week of December until Christmas; bull fights and cock fights. On New Year's Eve there is a special market and special performances are given in the main street.

Hotels *Holiday Inn*, Av. 5 de Febrero y Pino Suárez, on Highway 57, T 60202, restaurant, bars, A-L; *Mirabel*, A, Constituyentes 2, T 43585, good, garage, restaurant; *Real de Minas*, Constituyentes 124, T 604-44/602-57, 4 star; *Danés* at No. 32, T 602243; *Corregidora*, Corregidora 138, T 40406, D, reasonable but noisy; *Del Marqués*, Juárez Norte 104, T 20414, D, clean; *Plaza*, airy, lovely inner patio, modernized, safe, clean, comfortable, D; *El Cid*, E, Prolongación Corregidora, T 23518, more of a motel, clean, good value, close to bus station (left out of bus station and first left); *Impala* Zargoza y Corregidora, W of Alameida Park, T 22570, close to bus station, D, clean; *Hidalgo*, near Zócalo, Madero 11 Poniente, T 20081, E with bath, quite helpful; *San Agustín*, Pino Suárez 12, T 23919, E, clean, quiet, rec.; *Avenida*, Invierno 21, F. CREA Youth

Hostel, Av. del Ejército Republicano, ex-Convento de la Cruz, F, running water a.m. only, T 43050.

Motels *Holiday Inn*, near highway junction, T 60202, A; *Posada Campestre*, Madero y Circunvalación, T 6-27-28; *La Mansión*, B, 6½ km. S of town, excellent dining facilities, gorgeous grounds; *Flamingo*, on Constituyentes Poniente 138, T 62093, C, comfortable; *Azteca*, 15 km. N on road to San Luis Potosí, T 22060, C; *Jurica*, edge of town on road to San Luis Potosí, A, former *hacienda*, with gardens, squash, golf-course, opulent, T 21081.

Restaurants *Mesón Santa Rosa*, Pasteur 17, good but expensive, restored colonial building; *Fonda del Refugio*, Jardín Corregidora, pretty but food is poor; *La Corregidora*, on the other side of the street, is reportd as greatly superior. *Don Juan*, Jardín Corregidora, rec; *Flor de Querétaro*, on Plaza Obregón, Juárez Norte 5; *Salón del Valle*, Corregidora 91; *La Cocina Mexicana*, opp. *Hotel San Agustín*, cheap and good, à la carte better value than corrida corrida; *Le Bon Vivant*, Pino Suárez, cheap, good value, rec; *Ostionería Tampico*, Corregidora Nte 3, good cheap fish; *El Mirador*, roadhouse on highway 57, overlooking city, popular.

Entertainment *Corral de Comedias*, Carranza 39, T 207-65, an original theatre company, colonial surroundings and suppers; *JBJ Disco*, Blvd. Zona Dorada, Fracc. Los Arcos.

Post Office Arteaga Poniente 5 (inadequate). DHL, International courier service, Blvd. Zona Dorada 37, Fracc. Los Arcos, T 425-26 or 452-56, open Mon.-Fri. 0900-1800, Sat. 0900-1200.

Tourist Office State office, 5 de Mayo 61 y Pasteur; federal office Pte. de Alvarado 102-A (away from centre T 4-01-79).

Bus Mexico City (Terminal del Norte) 1st class with Transportes Chihuahuenses US$2.70, frequently 2nd class with Estrella Blanca or Flecha Amarilla, US$2, 3 hrs.; to San Miguel de Allende, 1 hr., hourly with Flecha Amarilla, US$1. To Guadalajara; US$4.45. To San Juan del Río, US$0.70, ½ hr., frequent. To Tula US$2.30. To Guanajuato, US$1.20, 3½ hrs. (Flecha Amarilla); to Pachuca, US$2.20, 4½ hrs. (Estrella Blanca, poor buses).

Rail Constitucionalista (*servicio estrella*) leaves Mexico City for Querétaro 0735, arriving 3 hrs. later (US$7); returns to Mexico City at 1800. arr. 2100. At Querétaro, the service divides to San Miguel Allende at 1055 (arr. 1210) and Guanajato at 1042 (arr. 1345). To Guadalajara US$3 1st class, US$1.80 2nd. Daily fast train from Mexico City at 0700, 1st class US$2.

Excursions There is a Huapango dance festival on 15 April at San Joaquín in the Sierra de Querétaro. Interesting wood carvings may be seen at Apaseo el Grande 28 km. away.

Tim Connell writes: **The Missions of Quérataro**. A little-known feature of Quérataro is the existence of eighteenth-century missions in the far north-east of the state. They were founded by Fray Junípero de la Serra, who later went on to establish missions in California with names like Nuestra Señora de los Angeles and San Francisco de Asís. (He is also said to have planted a miraculous tree in the convent of the Santa Cruz in Querétaro by thrusting his staff into the ground. The tree is apparently the only one of its kind in the world to have cruciform thorns.)

All five missions have been restored, and two of them have state-run hotels nearby. (Both hotels highly recommended and inexpensive. The restaurant at Concá is not very good however.) The journey itself requires something of a head for heights in that there are said to be seven hundred curves en route. (There is a slightly shorter way, but that has over a thousand...) The road (Route 120) goes through the small market town of Ezequiel Montes (pop. 5,000). 25 km. beyond the town of Colón it passes within 10 km. of the quite remarkable Peñón de Bernal, a massive rocky outcrop 350 metres high. The bends really start after Vizarrón, a local centre for marble. Much of the journey from here on is through rather arid and yet dramatic terrain with gorges and panoramic views. The high point (aptly enough) is called la Puerta del Cielo, as you can actually look down on the clouds. As the road begins to descend so the vegetation becomes more tropical and the weather gets much warmer. (Jalpan is at only 700 metres above sea level, Concá 500). There is a petrol station at Cadeyreta (Km. 75) and Ahuacatlán (Km. 166) as well as Vizarrón. There are ruins at San Joaquín (Km. 138) but the road is very steep and the ruins often swathed in mist. San Joaquín is famous for the annual Huapango dance festival (see above). Cadeyreta itself is colonial in style, and has two noteworthy churches in the main square, one dedicated to St Peter, the other St Paul. The latter houses an important collection of colonial religious art. Nearby is the Casa de los Alemanes, which houses an enormous collection of cacti.

Jalpan, the first of the missions, becomes visible way below in a broad lush valley. It is the largest of the missions, which are located in valleys that spread out from here. Jalpan was the first to be founded in 1774 and has cloisters as well as the main church. Opposite is the hotel, well appointed in colonial style with swimming pool. The town itself is picturesque without being spoilt. All the churches are distinguished by the profusion of baroque carving, their superb location and the care with which they have been conserved: Landa, 18 km. to the north, Tilaco 25 km. beyond Landa to the east, and Tancoyol 37 km. to the northwest. (The roads are good apart from the last 15 km. into Tilaco).

38 km. further on from Jalpan is **Concá**. There is a larger hotel in its own grounds a few kilometres from the village and mission, again in colonial style with a pool fed by warm spring water. *Acamaya*, freshwater crayfish, is a local speciality. At the bridge of Concá nearby a hot water river flows into one with cold water. The church itself is built on a ridge, creating a dramatic skyline when viewed from below. The village is very small. Two restaurants and a general stores.

It is reported to be possible to drive from Concá to San Luis Potosí, which is about three hours further on. The journey to Jalpan from Querétaro takes about six hours. At least three days should be allowed to see everything properly.

There is a 4-lane motorway (US$3 a car) from Irapuato past Querétaro to Mexico City. Along it (48 km. from Querétaro) is **San Juan Del Río** (*Hotel Mansión Galindo*, A, T 20050, restored hacienda—apparently given by Cortés to his mistress Malinche—beautiful building; several picturesque hotels, E-D), near where the best fighting bulls are raised; the town is a centre for handicrafts, and also for polishing gemstones—opals and amethysts. There is one friendly and reasonable shop: La Guadalupana, 16 de Septiembre 5; others are expensive and less friendly. Several *balnearios* in San Juan (try *Venecia*, cold water, very quiet mid-week, US$1.30). A branch road runs NE from San Juan to the picturesque town of **Tequesquiapán**, with thermal baths, fine climate, water sports, good and cheap hotels (*Los Virreyes; El Reloj*, etc, *Relax*, spa pool open to non-residents, US$4.50), *Artesanías Bugambilia*, on the main square, rec. The dam near the town is worth a visit. There is a geyser, at Tecozautla, 1¼ hrs. from Tequisquiapán. Between San Juan del Río and Tequesquiapán, a small track leads off the main road 4 km. to the village of La Trinidad, near which lie some of the opal mines which are still in operation. Bernal, a city some 60 km. from Querétaro, is a centre for clothing, blankets, wall hangings and carpets made by cottage industry, barter politely for good prices. Then at 1,167 km., Palmillas, 153 km. to Mexico City.

Bus   San Juan del Río-Tequesquiapán US$0.30, 20 mins.

The Mexico City motorway passes close to Tula and Tepozotlán (**see page** 171). There are various country clubs along the road: *San Gil Ciudad Turística* 7 km. along the road to Amealco; *El Ocotal; Bosques del Lago*.

CIUDAD JUAREZ TO MEXICO CITY (3)

Ciudad Juárez, opposite El Paso, Texas, to Mexico City: 1,866 km. Ciudad Juárez is at an altitude of 1,150 metres; Airport. Juárez, like Tijuana on the California border, attracts a nightly horde of tourists to be fascinated by a swarm of bead and spinach-jade peddlers, strip joints, doll shops blazing in magenta and green, dubious book stores, and "native dance" halls, mitigated by nightly bouts of that swift and beautiful ball game, *jai-alai*. It has a famous race course, too. There are pleasant markets. A monument in the form of a giant head of Father Hidalgo, who sparked off the 1810 revolution, surmounts a hill. See the cheerful Museum which acts as a Mexican "shop window"—well worth it for the uninitiated tourist.

Hotels   *Calinda Quality Inn*, A, Calz. Hermanos Escobar 3515, T 137250; *Continental*, Lerdo Sur 112 (downtown), T 150084, C, clean, TV, noisy, not friendly, restaurant good; *Gardner*, 3 blocks from bus station, E, pleasant, it doubles as a youth hostel; many others in all price ranges.

Restaurants   *Denny's*, Lincoln 1345, modern; *Le Pavos*, nr. bus station, good Mexican food; many reasonable Chinese places.

Exchange   There is a *cambio* in the bus station, open all night but will not change travellers' cheques.

British Consul (Honorary) Mr C.R. Maingot, Calle Fresno 185, Campestre Juárez, T (91-16) 75791.

Rail   Train from Ciudad Juárez to Mexico City (1,970 km.), leaves 1825, 36 hrs., US$20.80 1st class, no reserved seats, run when train arrives. Exciting or awful according to your view of travel, food and drink sellers at every stop. Reverse journey leaves at 1950 from Mexico City. The route is through Chihuahua, Torreón, Zacatecas, Aguascalientes, León, Silao (for Guanajuato), Celaya and Querétaro. Rápido de la Frontera (*servicio estrella*) leaves Ciudad Juárez at 1800 for Chihuahua (arr. 2210, US$8). Information: T (161) 225-57, or P.O. Box 2200,

El Paso, Tx 79951.

Road Pemex Travel Club, Chamber of Commerce Building, El Paso. A.A.A. office: 916 Mesa Avenue, El Paso.

Buses Terminal dirty, ticket counter sluggish. To El Paso US$2, hourly, to Greyhound Terminal; to Chihuahua (Transportes Chihuahuenses) every ½ hr. 375 km, 5 hrs., US$6; to Mexico City takes about 26 hrs., US$30. Taxi, El Paso airport to bus station US$20.

The road is wide, mostly flat, easy to drive, and not as interesting as the Gulf and Pacific routes. From Ciudad Juárez, for some 50 km. along the Río Bravo, there is an oasis which grows cotton of an exceptionally high grade. The next 160 km. of the road to Mexico City are through desert; towns en route are Salamayuca (restaurant), at Km. 58; Villa Ahumada (131 km.). *Dunas Motel*, D, scruffy. At 180 Km. is Moctezuma (restaurant). The road leads into grazing lands and the valley of Chihuahua. This is the country of the long-haired, fleet-footed Tarahumara Indians, able, it is said, to outstrip a galloping horse and to run down birds.

About 210 km. S of Juárez, near the village of El Sueco (restaurant), is the turnoff to the **Casas Grandes** ruins. Follow paved State Highway 10 for about 105 km. W, then turn NW for about 55. The place is spectacular: pyramids, a large ball court, an irrigation system and a great number of large adobe-brick houses. The ruins are signposted from the plaza in Casas Grandes, about 1 km. (entry US$0.30, guide booklet US$0.45).

No **accommodation** in the Casas Grandes village, but in the nearby Nueva Casas Grandes, *Motel Casa Grande* has air-conditioning, good dining room, fair accommodation; *Hotel California*, C, good looking; *Hotel Juárez*, next to bus stop, E, adequate; cheap hotels between the two bus stations.

Bus There are frequent buses from Nueva Casas Grandes to Casas Grandes village, leaving from near the railway station, one at 0800, US$0.15. Bus Ciudad Juárez-Nuevas Casas Grandes, 4 hrs., with Chihuahuenses. Three bus companies ply from Casas Grandes to Chihuahua, hourly, 5 hrs., US$4.80, passing through pleasant landscapes (especially between Casa Grandes and Madera).

Chihuahua, capital of Chihuahua state; alt.: 1,420 metres; pop.: 800,000; centre of a mining and cattle area (375 km. from the border, 1,479 km. from the capital). Worth looking at are the Cathedral on Plaza Constitución, begun 1717, finished 1789; the old tower of the Capilla Real (in the modern Federal Palace on Calle Libertad) in which Hidalgo awaited his execution; the Museo Regional, Bolívar 401, with interesting exhibits and extremely fine Art-Nouveau rooms: child's room features Little Red Riding Hood scenes; bathroom, frogs playing among reeds, etc.; Museo de Arte Popular, Av. Reforma e Independencia (Tarahumara art); Museo de Casa Juárez, Calle Juárez y Séptima, house and office of Benito Juárez; and the murals in the Palacio de Gobierno. Good Sunday market. The famous Santa Eulalia mining camp is 16 km. away; 8 km. from town is one of the largest smelting plants in the world. Pancho Villa operated in the country around, and once captured the city by disguising his men as peasants going to market. The Quinta Luz, Calle

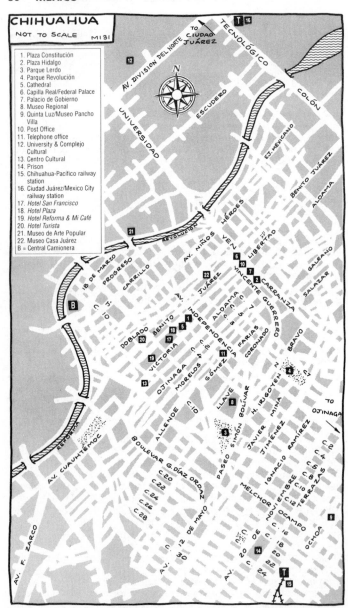

CHIHUAHUA
NOT TO SCALE   M131

1. Plaza Constitución
2. Plaza Hidalgo
3. Parque Lerdo
4. Parque Revolución
5. Cathedral
6. Capilla Real/Federal Palace
7. Palacio de Gobierno
8. Museo Regional
9. Quinta Luz/Museo Pancho Villa
10. Post Office
11. Telephone office
12. University & Complejo Cultural
13. Centro Cultural
14. Prison
15. Chihuahua-Pacifico railway station
16. Ciudad Juárez/Mexico City railway station
17. *Hotel San Francisco*
18. *Hotel Plaza*
19. *Hotel Reforma & Mi Café*
20. *Hotel Turista*
21. Museo de Arte Popular
22. Museo Casa Juárez
B = Central Camionera

10 No. 3014, where Pancho Villa lived, is now a museum, well worth a visit, open 0700-1300 and 1500-1800. In the SE of the town near Calle Zarco are ancient aqueducts. Summer temperatures often reach 40°C but be prepared for ice at night as late as November. Rain falls from July to September. The local hairless small dog has a constant body temperature of 40°C (104°F)—the world's only authentic "hot dog".

Hotels *Exalaris Hyatt*, Independencia y Niños Héroes, T 166000, A; *San Francisco*, Victoria 504, T 167770, B, restaurant good for steaks; *El Campanario*, Blvd. Díaz Ordaz 1405, 2 blocks SW of Cathedral, T 154545, C, good rooms, clean, TV, rec.; *El Cobre*, C, Calle 10A y Progreso, with bathroom, beside bus terminal, restaurant, bar and laundry; *Victoria*, Juárez y Colón, T 128893, courtyard, pleasant, D; *Balflo*, Niños Héroes 321, T 160300, modern, C; *Plaza*, behind cathedral, Calle 4, No. 206, T 155833, clean, D, rec.; *San Juan*, Victoria 823, T 128941, in old colonial house, D, nice atmosphere, reasonable food, water sometimes scarce; *Victoria*, opp. at No. 218, F.

Posada Aída, Calle 10, E, very clean, no hot water in p.m.; *Maceyra*, Ocampo Antigua 302, F, with shower, simple but clean, despite occasional beetles; *Reforma*, Calle Victoria 809, T 125808, E, basic, friendly, rec.; *Santa Fe*, near bus, friendly, clean, but hourly rentals too. *Turista*, Juárez 817, E, with bath, very clean, but reported to be very damp. *Casa de Huéspedes*, Libertad 1405, F with bath, basic but clean. The cheaper hotels are in Calle Juárez and its cross-streets; the cheapest are behind the cathedral.

Motels *Mirador*, Universidad 1309, T 132205, B; *Nieves*, Tecnológico y Ahuehuetes, T 132516, C.

Restaurants Best: *Los Parados de Tomy Vega*, followed by *La Calesa* and *La Olla*, excellent steaks. *La Parilla*, Victoria 450, rec.; *El Trastevere*, opp *Hotel San Francisco*, rec.; *Mi Café*, Victoria 807, good, friendly; *Ostionería de la Monja*, nr. main Plaza, good seafood. Corn (maize) is sold on the streets, excellent with cheese, lime, salt and chile.

Taxis work on a zone system. Agree price before boarding, to avoid unpleasant surprises.

Post Office Calle Libertad in the Federal Palace.

Travel Agents Wagon-Lits, Independencia 1412, very helpful, Guillermo Bechman, T 3-02-53, arranges stays at cabins above Bahuichivo, nr. Copper Canyon, 2 nights US$50.

Tourist Office Av. Carranza, very helpful.

Airport 20 km. from centre, airport buses collect passengers from hotels, fare US$1.50. Also minibuses.

Buses Bus station, Revolución y Progreso, in the centre. To El Paso, Texas, US$7.95 first class, 5 hrs. Change buses at Ciudad Juárez (get a seat number) at Customs. One meal stop. Zacatecas, US$6.45 1st, US$3.45 2nd class, Omnibus de México, several a day, 12 hrs. 2nd class bus, to Hidalgo del Parral, US$3.20, 2½ hrs. To Mazatlán, 1400, US$16 1st class, 19 hrs., heart-stopping view. To Mexico City, 1,488 km., US$21, 21 hrs., every 2 hours; Silao, US$13. León US$16, Durango, US$7. At busy times allow several hours to buy tickets for buses going North.

Chihuahua may also be reached from the border at *Ojinaga*, be sure to stop at the border, not the bus station 2 km. further on, otherwise an easy crossing, used infrequently by foreigners. *Hotel Parral*, cheap; cheap meals at *Lonchería Avenida*, across from bus station). On the way to Chihuahua from Ojinaga is Ciudad Delicias (*Hotel Delicias*, nr. market, several others of similar quality nearby). If leaving Mexico here, make sure they stamp your papers.

Bus to Ciudad Cuauhtémoc, 1½ hrs.; this is where the Mennonite order from Germany established its headquarters in 1920.

Railway There are two railway stations in Chihuahua: the station for Ciudad Juárez and Mexico City is 3 km. walk along Av. Niños Héroes, left at Av. Colón, which becomes Av. Tecnológico, past the river and right along Av. División Norte. Train to Mexico City, daily at midnight, US$5.95 2nd, US$9.90 1st class reserved, US$7.40 ordinary first, sleeper US$12.20, plus US$12.20 for bed or US$20 for private cabin, 30 hours, no food provided, soft drinks available, book in advance if you can. Train to Zacatecas about 16 hrs. Rápido de la Frontera (*servicio estrella*) for Ciudad Juárez leaves 0700 (4 hrs., US$8).

The station for the 631-km. Chihuahua-Pacífico railway is one block behind the prison (nr. Av. 20 de Noviembre and Blvd. Díaz Ordaz—take bus marked C. Rosario, or walk up Av. Independencia, then right along Paseo Bolívar or Av. 20 de Noviembre). Information: Apdo. Postal 46, Chihuahua, CHIH, Mexico, T (141) 2-2284/3867, or Av. Central 140, piso 6, Ala "C" 06358 Mexico D.F., T (905) 547-8545/6939.

The train journey to Los Mochis is very spectacular and exciting: book seats in advance. Sit on left hand side of carriage going to Los Mochis. As the train weaves through the mountains it crosses over 39 bridges and passes through 86 tunnels. It crosses the Sierra of the Tarahumara Indians, who call themselves the Raramuri ("those who run fast"), and were originally cave-dwellers and nomads. They now work as day-labourers in the logging stations and have settled around the mission churches built by the Spanish in the 17th century. The train stops about 15 mins. at Divisadero Barrancas in the Urique Canyon popularly known as the Copper Canyon and said, by some, to be finer than the Grand Canyon in the USA. Deep in the canyon are orange, banana and avocado trees, and jungles inhabited by pumas and parrots. High above, turning green in July, are the rocky mountain sides. The most beautiful part of the trip is between Creel (just east of the Barranca) and Los Mochis. Local women sell their handicrafts at bargain prices. Only *Hotel Cabañas Divisadero*, at Divisadero Barrancas by the station, is on the canyon's edge, A, bookable at Calle 7, No. 1216, Chihuahua, T 12-33-62, reported overpriced and not very clean, full board available; *Posada Barrancas Hotel* has its own stop on the railway between Divisadero Barrancas and San Rafael, good value accommodation and excursions; also *Florentio's Ranchito*, no sign, in an orchard, C, lovely place, no comfort but romantic. There are motels at the following places along the railway between Creel and Los Mochis: Temoris, Chinipas, Alamos, Bahuichivo, Cuiteco (*Posada Barranca*, A with full board, good cabins and food, friendly, bookable in Los Mochis by Flamingo Travel) and San Rafael.

The *servicio estrella* leaves daily at 0700, supposedly arriving at Creel at about 1130, Divisadero at 1215 and Los Mochis at 1900, local time (reserved seat US$20, breakfast, included; fare to Creel US$9.30); double check all details as they are subject to frequent change, the windows do not open. There is food at 2-3 stations along the way (e.g. Divisadero). An ordinary train to Los Mochis leaves at 0800, but often late (2nd class only, carriages are 1st Class, a/c and comfortable, windows do not open, mixed reports on cleanliness, US$6; fare to Creel US$2.60, arrives 1600-1700) reaching Divisadero at 1700 and Los Mochis at 2300, therefore best part is done in the dark. (Fares and schedule as of April 1990.) As the most interesting part of the journey is near Los Mochis it is better to travel from Los Mochis. Recommended places for taking photos, on the engine or between the carriages. There is a freight train (*carguero*), which stops overnight at San Rafael. **N.B.** If you leave the train at Creel you may not get a train back next day, but on most days there are 1 or 2 services to Los Mochis and Chihuahua. No heating on Creel train. The train Creel-Chihuahua may take up to 27 hrs. instead of the scheduled 13; be prepared. Watch your luggage and cameras, thefts occur. (For return journey, and for alternative route to Los Mochis, **see page** 104.) If taking this route with a view to connecting with a train to the North or South buy a ticket to Sufragio, leaves 1300, US$11 Pullman, clean, luxury, arrives after dark (**see page** 290) not Los Mochis (service in either direction at 2430).

On the Chihuahua-Los Mochis line is **Creel**, at 2,300 metres (very cold in winter), the centre of the Tarahumara region, an important timber centre and tourist resort, colourful and pleasant. Maps of the region (simple), description of the train ride and other good buys (such as excellent photographs of Indians) available at the mission, which acts as a quasi-tourist office (none in town, in spite of sign). *The National Parks of NW Mexico* is sold in the mission, also obtainable from R. Fisher. P.O. Box 40092, Tucson, Arizona 85717. There is an interesting mural just W of the station showing the tourist defiling the Indian with dollars.

Hotels *Motel Parador La Montaña*, T 7586, A (full board available), will exchange foreign currency at reasonable rates (horses can be hired here, US$5 and a tip for guides—2 hrs. are necessary to get anywhere; spectacular countryside); *Nuevo*, E, meals overpriced, but nice and clean; *Casa de Huéspedes Margarita*, López Mateos 11, T 6-00-45, no sign, between two churches, friendly, F-E inc. good meals, organizes tours to waterfalls and thermal springs, horses can be hired, highly rec. (if full, her sister will put you up for E with dinner and breakfast, enjoyable); *Korachi*, D, opp. railway, clean; *Creel*, F, basic, but friendly, 3 blankets, no running water (jug and basin), buses leave from outside hotel, filthy toilets; *Ejido*, very basic but nice people, F. Cheap meals at *Café El Manzano* next to railway station; other cheap restaurants nearby. A few km. out of town is *Cabaña de las Barrancas de Urique*, B, with 3 meals, with minibus service to and from station. 7 km. out, on lake, Jan Milburn runs *Tarahumara Indian Park*, shared or individual cabins. About 40 mins. drive from station is *Copper Canyon Lodge* (Apdo 3, Creel, Chihuahua, A, full board), which has a minibus to collect travellers, rustic woodstoves and oil-lamps, basic cuisine; set in high grassland near waterfall, considerable distance from canyon.

Services There is a bank in Creel, Serfín, next door to the mission at the railway station, very friendly, changes travellers' cheques between 1030 and 1200, but charges 2% commission, hotels cash travellers' cheques at poor rates. Post Office on W side of main square, large building, no sign.

Buses daily at 0700 and 1300, 5 hrs., US$2.50, from *Hotel Creel* to Chihuahua.

N.B. There is a time change (one hour back) between Creel and Los Mochis.

Guachochi, with a wild west appearance, 156 km. from Creel buses to Creel daily at 0700, Sun. at 1400, 8 hours (check at *Korachi Hotel* for schedule from Creel); also reached from Hidalgo del Parral, bus leaves for Parral at 0800 and 1200, a dusty trip, not spectacular. Hotels of questionable quality; try *Hotel Ejidal*, E, clean, friendly, belongs to the Creel-Guachochi bus driver; *Chaparre*, E, overpriced but good restaurant; *Orpimel*, F, in same building as bus station. There is a bank. From Guachochi one can walk 4 hrs. to the impressive Barranca de Sinforosa. Outside the town take road to the left of a wooden hut, after 6 km. take another left turn, keep walking, the Canyon is not visible until you reach the edge of it. Marlen Wolf and Markus Tobler of Switzerland write: "You will reach a point several hundred metres above the Río Verde where you can see an unforgettable extended system of immense canyons, grander than you can see from the Divisadero or on crossing the Barranca del Cobre. You can descend to the river on a path". This is not advisable for women alone. To the South, walk to San Ignacio, passing the Valle de Hongos (mushrooms), then continue to Laguna Arareco, a round trip of 20 km. There are hot springs at Tararecua Canyon. Margharita travel agency has tours to the railhead, US$8. **San Juanito**, 30 km. NE, a little larger than Creel, dusty, has an annual *fiesta* on 20-24 June, one hour away by train; bus from Creel at 0700, returns at 2000, paved roads. The Laguna is a little lake 7 km. S of Creel, but is polluted, hire a truck to get there, horses for hire once there, caves. S of Creel is **Cuzarare** ("Place of the Eagles") 20 km. from Creel with Jesuit church (1767) painted by Indians; **Norogachi** (80 km. away), with Tarahumara school and authentic costumes worn on Sun., typical *fiestas*; El Tejabán (Copper Canyon); **Basihuara** ("Sash") village, surrounded by pink and white rock formations (40 km. from Creel); Puente del Río Urique, spans the Urique canyon, ideal camping climate. **Samachique**, where the *rari-pame* race, consisting of kicking a wooden ball in a foot-race of 241 km. without rest, often takes 2-3 days and nights in September. **Kirare**, 65 km. from Creel and on the road to La Bufa mine, offers sights of Batopilas canyon, of great beauty. At the T junction Creel-Guachochi-Bufa is a small restaurant/hotel, *La Casita*, very primitive and romantic, F.

Batopilas (on a 120-km. dirt road from Creel after La Bufa) is a little town of 600 inhabitants, quiet, palm-fringed, subtropical and delightful, hemmed in by the swirling river and the cactus-studded canyon walls. There are good parties in the Plaza at Christmas and New Year. It is a good centre for walking—the Urique canyon can be reached. Horses, pigs, goats and chickens wander freely along the cobblestone streets; the town now has electricity and accommodation.

Hotels *Batopilas*, F, clean, friendly and pleasant, also *Parador Batopilas*. Basic rooms also at *Restaurant Clarita* (basic accommodation, F) and Sra. Monsé, E—ask prices first—at plaza (curio shop), rooms with gas lamps, who can give information in English (which she likes to practice on tourists) and can change travellers' cheques at a worse rate than in Creel *Don Mario*; close to the bridge, F, where the bus driver stays, is becoming popular; *Carmen's Youth Hostel*, basic accommodation, good food, friendly. In the village there are only basic supplies in shops, no bread or alcohol. Pleasant unnamed restaurant in the top right-hand corner of the little plaza beyond the main Zócalo, fixed, good menu. (Bring insect repellant against locally-nicknamed "assassin bug" or bloodsucking insect.)

Bus from Creel, Tues., Thurs., and Sat. at 0700, 8-10 hours, US$4.50, buy ticket the day before, very crowded, returns Mon., Wed., and Fri.

There is a 350-year-old, bat-infested church in Satevo, a 7-km. walk from Batopilas along the river, a poor place with 15 houses, 2 of them sell drinks. The area is inhabited by the Tarahumaras known as Gentiles (women don't look at, or talk to, men). It is possible to walk in a day to Cerro Colorado, also Cerro Yerbanis from which there are amazing views of Batopilas Canyon. A 2-3 day hike goes from Batopilas Canyon via Urique Canyon, then get a ride to Bahuichivo for a train to Creel or Las Mochis. **Chomachi**, famous for its caves, some 10 km. deep, inhabited in the past by Apaches. **Basaseachi**, with highest (311 metres) single-jump waterfall in North America. Tours arranged by the more expensive hotels to the places mentioned above require a minimum of 4 people and cost from US$8 p.p. to Cuzarare to US$28 p.p. to places further away such as La Bufa. The Creel-Batopilas bus journey passes through or close to Cuzarare, Basihuare, Urique Canyon, Samachique, Kirare, before awesome 14 km. descent into Batopilas Canyon at La Bufa. The road ends 30 km. later at Batopilas. If you want to take photographs better try to get a lift.

Recommended for guided tours deep into the Urique Canyon is Adventure Specialists, Inc. (president Gary Ziegler), Bear Basin Ranch, Westcliffe, CO. 81252 (303/783-2519, 800/621-8385, ext. 648), US$700-800 for 11-day tours from El Paso, vigorous, knowledgeable.

Ciudad Camargo (Km. 1,332), a small cattle town in a green valley, quiet save for its eight days of *fiesta* for Santa Rosalía beginning on Sept. 4, when there are cockfights, horse racing and dancing. Black bass fishing at the dam lake, and warm sulphur springs 5 km. away.

Hotel *Santa Rosalía Courts*. **Motel** *Baca*.

From Ciudad Jiménez (1,263 km. from Mexico City; *Motel Florido*, C, hot water) there are two routes to Fresnillo and Zacatecas: the Central Highway through Durango or a more direct route via Torreón (237 km. from Ciudad Jiménez), passing Escalón (restaurant), Ceballos (*Hotel San José*, F, basic), Yermo (restaurants) and Bermejillo (restaurant), on Route 49.

Torreón is the principal city of La Laguna cotton and wheat district. Population, 700,000. Here is the Bolsón de Mayrán (altitude 1,137 metres) an oasis of about 28,500 square km. which might be irrigated, but only about 2,000 square km. have been developed and much of that is stricken with drought. On the opposite side of the mostly dry Nazas river are the two towns of Gómez Palacio (*feria* first half of August; *Motel La Cabaña*, E, hot water) and Lerdo.

Hotels *Paraíso del Desierto*, Independencia y Jiménez, T 61122, B, resort; *Río Nazas*, highrise, very good, B, on Av. Morelos y Treviño; *Palacio Real*, Morelos 1280, T 60000, A; *Galicia*, Cepeda 273, E, good; *Laguna*, Carrillo 333, D; *Princesa*, Av. Morelos nr. Parque Central, F.

Restaurant *La República*, Musquiz 360, abundant comida corrida, cheap; *Kentucky Fried Chicken*, good, 2 locations.

Buses Bus companies all located within 2 blocks of Zócalo. To Chihuahua, 6 ½ hrs.; to Tepic, US$12; to Ciudad Juárez, US$11; about 6 a day to Durango, 4½ hrs. 2nd class. The new bus station is 5 km. S of the city; if coming from the N, drivers allow you to leave the bus in the centre. There is a shuttle service between the centre and the bus station. There is also an airport.

Between Gómez Palacio and Zacatecas are Cuencame (*Motel la Posta*, F, hot water), Río Grande (*Hotel Río*, F); Fresnillo (*Motel La Fortuna*, E, comfortable, hot water, *Hotel Cuauhtémoc*, F, basic).

From Ciudad Jiménez it is 77 km. to (Km. 1,138) **Hidalgo Del Parral**, an old picturesque mining town of 100,000 people with steep and narrow streets. It is rapidly becoming a modern commercial centre. See the parochial church and one dedicated to the Lightning Virgin (Virgen del Rayo). The Museum of Pancho Villa, which is also the public library, is worth seeing for the many old photos and newspaper clippings related to the 1910 revolution and Villa, who was assassinated in Parral on July 20, 1923 on the orders of Obregón and Calles.

Hotels *Savoy*, off Morelos, E, rec.; *Acosta*, Barbachano, T 20221, F, clean, hot water, friendly; *Pinos Altos*, E, clean, friendly; *Fuente*, Herrera 79, T 20016, E, basic but clean, can be cold, the desecrators of Pancho Villa's body stayed here.
     Motel *Camino Real*, Pan-American Highway, T 22050, C, good restaurant.

Restaurants *Mariscos Esquinapa*, on same block as **Hotel Fuente**, serves good seafood; *Nutrivida*, Herrera, good yoghurt and health food.

Buses There is a new bus station outside the town; 20 mins walk, taxi about US$1. To Durango, Transportes Chihuahuenses US$5.75, 6 hrs. To Zacatecas, Omnibuses de México, US$10, 9 hrs. To Chihuahua, TCH-Bus, frequent departures, 2½ hrs., US$3.20. Also to Guachochi (see page 84). Few bus lines start here so it is difficult to reserve seats.

On this road, between Rodeo and Durango, is the "Western landscape" beloved of Hollywood film-makers. Cinema enthusiasts can visit the Western sets of Villa del Oeste (9 km. from Durango) and Chupaderos (10.5 km.), both decaying but smelling authentically of horse (Cía San Juan del Río buses go there).

(Km. 926) (Victoria de) **Durango**, capital of Durango state: alt.: 1,924 metres; pop.: 600,000; founded in 1563. It is a pleasant city, with parks, a Cathedral (1695) and a famous iron-water spring. Parque Guadiana at W edge of town, with huge eucalyptus trees, is a nice place to relax. Good views of the city from Cerro de Los Remedios: many flights of steps up to a chapel. Presa Victoria can be reached by bus from Durango; one can swim in the lake enclosed by the dam.

Festival *Feria* first half of July.

Hotels *Casa Blanca*, 20 de Noviembre 811, T 13599, C, nice, big old hotel in the centre, unguarded parking lot; *Posada Durán* (D, T 12412), *Campo México Courts*, both on 20 de Noviembre, C, T 15560, good but restaurant service poor; *Reyes*, 20 de Noviembre 220, T 15050, clean, E; *Gallo*, 5 de Febrero, F, with bath, good. *Oasis*, Zarco between 20 de Noviembre y 5 de Febrero, F with bath, rooms on the top floor have a good view, rec.; *Motel Los Arcos*, nr. bus station, T 19880,

H.C. Militar 2204, good restaurant; *Villa*, P. Juárez 206, T 23491, across roundabout from bus station, D, clean, pleasant, TV; *Karla*, same street opp. bus station, T 16348, E, small, clean, friendly but noisy. Cheap hotels: *Roma*, Noviembre 20, E-F, clean, comfortable; *Patoni*, Patoni entre P.Suárez y 5 de Febrero, *Casa de Huéspedes Buenos Aires*, Constitución 126, Norte, also around the cathedral. CREA Youth Hostel, Av. Heróica Colegio Militar s/n, T 24516/11775, C.P. 34000.

Restaurants *La Bohemia* rec., reasonable food, good breakfasts; good breakfasts also at *Café Salum*, 5 de Febrero y Progreso; *Mariscos Ramírez*, in front of the market, good sea food. There is a good food store on the first block of Progreso where local foodstuffs are displayed in bulk. *El Zocabón*, off main plaza opp. Cathedral, rec.

Tourist Offices Hidalgo 408 Sur and 20 de Noviembre y Independencia; both good.

Rail Centauro del Norte *servicio estrella* to Zacatecas at 1100 (6 hrs. 35 mins., US$7 reserved seat).

Airport 5 km. from centre.

Buses Bus station out of town: minibus No. 2 to centre, US$0.15. Several buses a day cross the Sierra Madre Occidental to Mazatlán (Transportes Chihuahuenses, 1st class, 7 hrs., US$4.10), 0400 and 1000. This is rec. if you cannot do the Los Mochis-Chihuahua journey, sit on left side. Second class buses for camera buffs stop more frequently. Guadalajara, US$6; Chihuahua, US$7. Second class bus to Hidalgo del Parral, 7 hrs., US$5 with Transportes Chihuahuenses. Zacatecas, Omnibus de México, 4½ hrs., US$4.25. Chihuahua 10 hrs., US$7. Town buses stop running early in evening, so try to arrive before dark if you wish to avoid a long walk or taxi ride to centre.

Durango is on the Coast-to-Coast Highway from Mazatlán to Matamoros. The 320 km. stretch of road from Durango W to Mazatlán is through splendid mountain scenery. For a one day trip, go as far as El Salto (96 km.), 7 buses a day, but go early to get ticket. Durango is some 260 km. SW of Torreón.

Balneario La Florida on the outskirts is pleasant (take green "Potreros" bus on Calle Pasteur). Take a bus from Plaza Boca Ortiz to the big *hacienda* in Ferreria, a 7 km. walk along mostly deserted roads leads to the Mirador la Ventana with great views. Santiago Papasquiaro is 3 hrs. N (on the way, in Canatlán, are Mennonite colonies), *Hotel División del Norte*, Madero 35, E, in a former convent; the owner's husband was in Pancho Villa's División del Norte. *Restaurant Miradors*, across from the market, good food. There are a number of hot springs in the area, Hervideros is the most popular, take the bus to Herreras, then ½ hr. walk. Tepehuancas, one hour further on, is a small pleasant town with 2 hotels. Walk to Purisima and then to a small, spectacular canyon. A dirt road continues to Guanacevi, a mining town in the Sierra.

Between Durango and Zacatecas is Sombrerete, a small colonial mining town with good churches. (Hotels: *Real de Minas*, *Avenida Real*, *Hidalgo*).

Zacatecas, founded 1548, capital of Zacatecas state; alt.: 2,495 metres; pop. 150,000 (Km. 636 from capital). This picturesque up-and-down mining city is built in a ravine, pink stone houses towering above one another and sprinkled over the hills. The largest silver mine in the world, processing 10,000 tonnes of ore a day or 220 tonnes of silver, is at Real de Angeles. Places to see are the Cathedral (1730-52); the San Agustín church, with interior carvings now being restored; the Jesuit church of Santo Domingo and the little houses behind it; the Pedro Coronel museum on Plaza Santo Domingo, admission US$0.80; Plaza Hidalgo and its statues; the Casa Moneda (better known as the Tesorería); the Calderón theatre, and the chapel of Los Remedios (1728), on the Cerro de La Bufa (cablecar, US$1.20 return, starts at 1230, crowded Sun.) which dominates the city, through which an old aqueduct runs; the market; and the Museo Francisco Goitia, housed in what was once the Governor's mansion, near the aqueduct and park, with modern paintings by Zacatecans, admission US$0.80. La Mina Edén (admission US$1) is accessible from the upper end of the Alameda, behind the Seguro Social hospital.

Zacatecas is famous for its *sarapes* and has two delicacies: the local cheese, and *queso de tuna*, a candy made from the fruit of the nopal cactus (do not eat too much, it has laxative properties). Visit the small *tortilla* factories near the station, on the main road. Zacatecas is reckoned by many travellers to be the pleasantest town in this part of Mexico.

Fiesta spreads over most of September, a rainy month here. There are bullfights on Sundays.

Hotels *Aristos*, Lomas de Soledad, T 21788, A; *Gallery*, near old bus station, very comfortable, D; *Barranca*, D, opp. bus terminal, Blvd. López Mateos 401, T 21494, T 21093, pleasant, but noisy traffic; *Reina Cristina* on Zócalo, T 21130, D, run down, with bath, clean; *Posada de La Moneda*, nr. Cathedral, Av. Hidalgo 415, T 20881, nice and clean, D; *Posada del Conde*, Juárez 18, T 21093, good-looking, D. *Condesa*, opp. *Posada del Conde*, D, T 21160, OK. *Baños*, F, with bath, very hot water, at Hidalgo 203. *Insurgentes*, off Plaza del Vivar, E without bath, hot showers extra; *Zamora*, on Av. Independencia off Plazuela del Vivar, E, central, pleasant; *Río Grande*, Calzada de la Paz 313, F, rec; the cheap hotels (very few) are all within 5 minutes walk of the old bus station, towards Av. Hidalgo. CREA Youth Hostel, Parque del Encantado, T 20223/21891, C.P. 98000, on bus route to centre from bus station, F (no singles).

    Motels *Del Bosque*, C, Fortín de la Peña; *Parador Zacatecas*, excellent, C, Pan-American Highway.

Restaurants *La Cuija*, in old Centro Comercial on Av. Tacuba, good food, music, atmosphere; *El Jacalito*, Juárez 18, excellent comida corrida and breakfast. *El Fortín*, near Cathedral, good, nice coffee shop. *Pizzería Bambino*, Juárez, good and cheap, live music in the evening; *El Carnerito*, Av. Juárez 110, cheap. Several cheap restaurants (corrida for less than US$1.50) along Av. Independencia. *Café Nevería*, good cappuccino. Young people hang out at *La Bohemia*, Av. González Artegú.

Exchange Banamex rec.

Post Office, Calle Allende.

Travel Agent Cantera Tours, Centro Comercial El Mercado, Local A-21, T 29065, tour to Chicomostoc and Jérez at 0930, US$8.50.

Tourist Office opposite Cathedral friendly, helpful, English spoken, free maps, good hotel information, including cheaper hotels. Ask here about language classes at the University.

Trains San Marqueño-Zacarecano (*servicio estrella*) leaves Mexico City 2130, arrives Zacatecas 1000; returns 0720, via Aguascalientes; reserved seat US$14.80, single sleeper US$29.30, double US$58.65. To Mexico City at 0500 and at 1600, 1st class US$4.90, 2nd US$3.25; to Chihuahua 1030, US$6.45, 1st class, US$3.65, 2nd class to Aguascalientes, 4 hrs. US$1.60 2nd class. To Durango, 1st class US$3, 2nd class US$1.50, very crowded to Pescador (where you change trains), standing room only; after Pescador, train quite empty, 9½ hrs. in all. Also Centauro del Norte *servicio estrella* at 1010 (arr. 1645, reserved seat US$7).

Bus New terminal 4 km. N of town; yellow No. 8 buses from Plaza Independencia, or white *camionetas* from Av. González Artegú (old bus station on Blvd. A. López Mateos only serves local destinations). To Durango with Estrella Blanca, 5 hrs., US$3.40. To Chihuahua via Torreón, 12 hrs., US$12.50; Jiménez, US$9; to Hidalgo del Parral with Chihuahuenses at 0030 and 0130, Omnibus de México, 0220 and 0500, US$10, 10 hrs; San Luis Potosí with Estrella Blanca; Ciudad Juárez 1st class with Omnibus de México at 1930, 11 hrs; to Guadalajara, 6½ hrs., several companies, US$4, but shop around for different journey times. To Mexico City, 8 hrs., US$10.

Airport 25 km. N of city, daily flights to Mexico City and Tijuana.

Excursions Beyond Zacatecas to the east lies the Convento de Guadalupe, a national monument, with a fine church and convent, which now houses a museum of colonial religious art; admission US$0.35 (Tues.-Sun. 1000-1700). Next door is Museo Regional de Historia, under development. Frequent buses from old terminal, white-turquoise, Ruta 12 from Centro Comercial, US$0.15, 20 mins. Visit also the **Chicomostoc** ruins 56 km. S by taking the 0930 Línea Verde bus from main terminal to Adjuntas (about 45 mins., US$0.60), on the Villanueva road. Then walk ½ hr. through beautiful, silent, nopal-cactus scenery to the ruins, which offer an impressive view (may have to hitch back). Admission US$0.25; no information on site, so ask for explanations. Women are advised to keep at a distance from the caretaker! Jerez is an old colonial town about 65 km. from Zacatecas, where the wide brimmed *sombrero charro* is still worn, worth a visit; *Hotel Felix*, E, rec., frequent buses from new bus terminal.

(Km. 508) **Aguascalientes** was founded in 1575 and is capital of its state; alt.: 1,987 metres; pop.: 750,000; its name comes from its many hot mineral springs. An oddity is that the city is built over a network of tunnels dug out by a forgotten people. It has pretty parks, a pleasant climate, delicious fruits, and specializes in drawn linen threadwork, pottery, and leather goods. Places to see are the Government Palace (once the castle of the Marqués of Guadalupe, with colourful murals round inner courtyards), the churches of San Marcos and San Antonio on Zaragoza (somewhat odd) and the Municipal Palace. There is much industrial development on the outskirts.

On items of interest in Aguascalientes, Tim Connell writes:

Museo de Aguascalientes, Calle Zaragoza 505, is by the Church of San Antonio. The José Guadalupe Posada museum is in a gallery, by the Templo del Cristo Negro, close to a pleasant garden—Díaz de León (known locally as the Jardín del Encino); it has a remarkable collection of prints by the lithographer Posada, best known for his *cadaveras*, macabre skeletal figures illustrating and satirizing the Revolution and events leading up to it. Admission free, Tues.-Sun. 1000-1400, 1700-2100, shut Mon; cultural events in the courtyard on Sat. and Sun. The Casa de las Artesanías is near the main square. The Casa de la Cultura, on Venustiano Carranza and Galeana Norte, is a fine colonial building. It holds a display of *artesanía* during the *feria*.

Teatro Morelos next to the Cathedral; T 5-00-97. The University is ½ hr. from the city centre. Its administrative offices are in the ex-Convento de San Diego, by the attractive Jardín del Estudiante, and the Parián, a shopping centre. The market is not far away. There is carp fishing at El Jocoqui and Abelardo Rodríguez. The bull ring is on Avenida López Mateos.

Hacienda de San Blas, 34 km. away, contains the Museo de la Insurgencia, with murals by Alfredo Zermeño. The area is famous for viticulture; the local wine is called after San Marcos, and the *feria* in his honour lasts for 3 weeks, starting in the middle of April, with processions, cockfights (in Mexico's largest *palenque*, seating 4,000), bullfights, agricultural shows etc. The Plaza de Armas is lavishly decorated. The *feria*, covered by national TV networks, is said to be the biggest in Mexico. Accommodation can be very difficult and prices double during the *feria*.

Hotels *Francia*, Plaza Principal, T 56080, A, airy, colonial style; good restaurant (*El Fausto*) for breakfast and lunch; *Hotel Suites Alamo*, Alameda 129, T 5-68-85, D, pool; *Praga*, E, with TV, Zaragoza 214, T 5-23-57. *Continental*, Av. 5, No. 307, nr. Zócalo, F with bath, good, cafeteria; another *Continental* at Guatemala y Brasil, T 55548, E, near bus terminal. At Rep. de Brasil 403, *Casa de Huéspedes*, nr. main square, F, and at No. 602 *Gómez*, D, T 70409. On main square, *Señorial*, Colón 104, T 52179, E, helpful lady speaks English; *Don Jesús*, Juárez 427, T 55598, E, cold water, good value; *Maser*, 3 blocks from Cathedral on Montaro, T 53562, D, *comedor* for breakfast. Cheap hotels around Juárez market (Av. Guadalupe y Calle Guadalupe Victoria), e.g. *Brasil*, Guadalupe 110, F with bath, quiet, and *Bahía*, No. 144, E with bath, *Mexico*, F, no bath or hot water. CREA Youth Hostel, Av. de la Juventud y Rancho del Charro s/n, C.P. 20190, T 80863.

Motel *El Medrano*, Chávez 904, T 55500, A; *La Cascada*, Chávez 1501, T 61411, B.

Restaurants *Mitla*, Madero 220, cheap and clean, good Mexican menu; *Cascada*, main plaza; *Bugambilia*, Chávez 102, quite plush, reasonable menu, but service can be morose. *Café de los Artesanos*, Calle José María Chávez 122, good atmosphere and coffee, friendly owners welcome foreigners.

Market Main one at 5 de Mayo y Unión, large and clean, with toilet on upper floor.

Bookshop Librería Universal, Madero 427.

Post Office Hospitalidad, nr. El Porián shopping centre.

Tourist Office Next to Cathedral in main square (Plaza de la Patria).

Taxis There is a ticket system for taxis from the Central Camionera, with the city divided into different fare zones. There is no need to pay extra; a phone number for complaints is on the ticket.

Rail San Marqueño-Zacatecano (*servicio estrella*) between Mexico City and Zacatecas calls here at 0740; fare from the capital, US$12.25 for reclining seat, US$24.35 single sleeper, US$48.65 double. Twice a day to Mexico City, due from Ciudad Juárez at 1840 and from Torreón at 0815. Train to San Luis Potosí daily at 0740. Train station at E end of Av. Madero.

Buses Bus station about 1 km. S of centre on Av. Circunvalación Sur. Bus: to Guadalajara, 5 hrs. US$3.55 1st, US$3.40 2nd class, but 0900 and 1415 bus take 4 hrs. To Guanajuato US$2.60 with Flecha Amarilla. To Zacatecas: US$1.90. Some 170 km. to the E is San Luis Potosí (**see page 72**).

Thermal Baths Balneario Ojo Caliente, E end of town beyond train station, at end of Calzada Revolución (Alameda), claims to have been founded in 1808, some private hot baths and 2 excellent public pools (US$0.75), take bus marked "Alameda"; saunas, squash and tennis courts on the site. At end of Alameda fork right to Deportivo Ojocaliente, a large complex with several pools (not so warm water), US$0.65.

Encarnación de Díaz (hotel and restaurant) is halfway to **Lagos De Moreno** (Km. 425), a charming old town with fine baroque churches; the entry over the bridge, with domes and towers visible on the other side, is particularly impressive. See the ex-convent of the Capuchins and the Rosas Moreno Theatre. *Feria* last week of July and first of August. A road turns off right to Guadalajara, 197 km. away; the same road leads, left, to Antiguo Morelos via San Luis Potosí. Lagos de Moreno has several hotels (on main plaza: *París, Colonial*—both D, *Plaza,* F, and *Victoria,* nr. river, E) and restaurants. 46 km. south west is the colonial town of San Juan de los Lagos, a major pilgrimage centre, crowded during Mexican holidays, famous for glazed fruit; many hotels.

After about 1,600 km. of desert or semi-arid country, we now enter, surprisingly, the basin of Guanajuato, known as the Bajío, greener, more fertile, higher (on average over 1,800 metres), and wetter, though the rainfall is still not more than 635 to 740 mm. a year. The Bajío is the granary of central Mexico, growing maize, wheat, and fruit. The towns we pass through, León, Irapuato, and Celaya, have grown enormously in population and importance. Tim Connell writes that 50 km. before León there are some impressive buttes (isolated, steep hills).

(Km. 382) **León** (de los Aldamas), in the fertile plain of the Gómez river, is now said to be Mexico's fifth city, with a population of 1.2 million. The business centre is the Plaza de Constitución. There are a striking municipal palace, a cathedral, many shaded plazas and gardens. The Templo Expiatorio has been under construction for most of this century, catacombs open 1000-1300, well worth seeing; the Doblado theatre on Av. Hermanos Aldama; the modernized zoo, reached by the Ibarilla bus. León is the main shoe centre of the country (high quality shoes in the Plaza del Zapato, Hilario Medina, and cheaper ones in places round the bus station), and is noted for its leather work (buy in the shops round the jail, and along Belisario Domínguez), fine silver-trimmed saddles, and *rebozos.* Alt.: 1,885 metres. Frequent buses to Torreón (10 hrs.).

Hotels Rec.: *Real de Minas*, A. López, T 43677, 5 star; *Estancia*, Blvd. López Mateos 1313 Ote, T 63939, B; *León*, Madero 113, T 41050, 3 star; *Roma*, P. Vallarta 202, T 61500, 3 star; *Robert*, Blvd. L. Mateos Oriente 1503, T 69500, D; *Señorial*, D, near Plaza, Juárez 221, T 45896, and *Condesa*, on Plaza, Portal Bravo 14, T 31120, C; *Fénix*, Comonfort 338, T 32291; *Colón*, 20 de Enero 131, T 34353; *Tepeyac*, Av. Miguel Alemán, E; *Río*, P. Vallarta 203, T 43201, E; *Niza* at No. 10, T 31705, same price range. Also several cheaper ones near market.

Restaurants Two good and cheap Japanese: *Towaki*, near Plaza, English-speaking owner, and *Eiki*.

Airport San Carlos, 15 km. from centre. Daily flights to Mexico City, Mazatlán and Tijuana, and twice weekly to Houston, Monterrey and Puerto Vallarta. New international airport is being built between León and Silao, to be opened 1990.

(Km. 430) Silao (hotel). Between León and Silao, left off Highway 45 at Km. 387 (going S) are the famous swimming pools of Comanjilla fed by hot sulphurous springs (rustic, semi-tropical with hotel and restaurant at moderate rates). Eleven km. beyond Silao, at Los Infantes, a short side road through the picturesque Marfil canyon leads to Guanajuato.

Guanajuato, the beautiful capital of Guanajuato state and a university city, now declared a national monument, has been important for its silver since 1548. Population, 70,000 in 1880, now 150,000, altitude, 2,010 metres. The town is reported to be very dirty and poorly kept. It stands in a narrow gorge amid wild and striking scenery; the Guanajuato river cutting through it has been covered over and an underground street opened—an unusual and effective attraction. The streets, steep, twisted and narrow, follow the contours of the hills and are sometimes steps cut into the rock: one, the Street of the Kiss (Callejón del Beso), is so narrow that kisses can be—and are—exchanged from opposite balconies. Over the city looms the shoulder of La Bufa mountain.

A most interesting building is the massive Alhóndiga de Granadita, built as a granary, turned into a fortress, and now an attractive museum (US$0.35, theoretically closed Mon.). Guanajuato contains a series of fine museums, as well as the most elegant marble-lined public lavatories in Mexico. The best of many colonial churches are San Francisco (1671); La Compañía (Jesuit, 18th century); San Diego (1663) on the Plaza de la Unión; and the splendid church of La Valenciana, one of the most impressive in Mexico, 5 km. out of town and built for the workers of the Valenciana silver mine, once the richest in the world. The mine is surrounded by a wall with triangular projections on top, said to symbolize the crown of the King of Spain. (A local "Valenciana" bus starts in front of *Hotel Mineral de Rayas*, Alhóndiga 7, US$0.10, 10 minutes ride; 10 mins. walk between church and mine pit-head; don't believe anyone who tells you a taxi is necessary, but don't walk to it along the highway, it is narrow and dangerous). A gruesome sight shown to visitors is of mummified bodies in the small Museo de las Momias, arranged in glass cases along one wall (US$0.20—long queues); buses go there ("Momias", sign posted Panteón Municipal, US$0.06, 10 mins., along Av. Juárez), but you can walk; there is a free guide (Spanish-speaking). A new Don Quixote museum was opened in 1987 on Plaza Dr. Enrique Romero: paintings, drawings, sculptures of the Don (see **Festivals** below for Festival Cervantino). The Cathedral (Basilica) and the church of San Roque should also be visited. Local pottery can be bought at the Hidalgo market and along the potters' street. Good bargaining for *rebozos* in the plaza opposite the *Hotel San Diego*. The University was founded in 1732. The painter Diego Rivera was born in Calle de Pocitos; visit the museum there with permanent collection of his drawings, paintings and Popol Vuh collection. On the E side of the city is the Presa de la Olla, a favourite picnic spot; several parks and monuments in the vicinity, a *circuito panorámico* is sign posted, frequent buses (US$0.08). The area is being industrialized.

When Father Hidalgo took the city in 1810, the Alhóndiga was the last place to surrender, and there was a wanton slaughter of Spanish soldiers and royalist prisoners. When Hidalgo was himself caught and executed, along with three other leaders, at Chihuahua, their heads, in revenge, were fixed at the four corners of the Alhóndiga. There is a fine view from the monument to Pipila, the man who fired the door of the Alhóndiga so that the patriots could take it, which crowns the high hill of Hormiguera. Look for the "Al Pipila" sign. Steep climb. Local buses go from *Hotel Central*, on the hour, to the Pipila.

Festivals   Arts festival, the Festival Cervantino de Guanajuato (in honour of Cervantes), is an important cultural event in the Spanish-speaking world, encompassing theatre, song and dance (usually held in May). *Viernes de las Flores* is held on the Friday before Good Friday—starting with the Dance of the Flowers on Thurs. night at about 2200 right through the night, adjourning at Jardín de la Unión to exchange flowers. Very colourful and crowded.

Hotels   Bus station very helpful in finding hotels. Check hotel prices, as cheaper central hotels try to put up prices when foreigners appear, and they also try to insist on a room with two beds, which is more expensive than with a double bed. Hotel rooms can be hard to find after 1400. There are frequent water shortages, so that hotels with no reservoirs of their own have no water on certain days.
On Jardín de la Unión are **Castillo de Santa Cecilia**, Dolores road, tourist-bus haven, T 20485, A; **Parador San Javier**, Plaza Aldama 92, opp. side of Dolores road, T 20626, genuine hacienda style, B; **Posada Santa Fe**, No. 12, T 20084, B, and **San Diego**, No. 1, T 21300, C, good bar, better run; **Real de Minas**, Nejayote 17 at city entrance, T 21460, B; **La Abadía**, San Matías 50, T 22464, C. **Hostería del Frayle**, Sopeña 3, T 21179, C; **El Insurgente**, Juárez 226, C, pleasant and quiet, good breakfasts; several others on same street: **Granadita** (No. 109) clean and friendly, D; **Central**, Juárez 111, T 20080, near bus station, restaurant, good value, clean but noisy, E; **Posada San Francisco**, Av. Juárez y Gavira, T 22467, E, on Zócalo, good value but noisy on outside rooms, no hot water, lovely inner patio; **Reforma**, Av. Juárez 113, E, with bath, clean and quiet. Near the bus terminal is **Mineral de Rayas**, Alhóndiga 7, T 21967, D, with bath, small rooms, clean linen. **Alhóndiga**, Insurgencia 49, T 20525, good, E, clean, quiet, near to bus station; **Molino del Rey**, Campañero 15, T 22223, simple and quaint, E. **Casa Kloster**, E, very friendly, rooms for 4 (although few with private bath), very good value, rec., gardens. Very close to the main street is a street full of **casas de huéspedes**.
Motels   Many on Dolores Hidalgo road exit: **Guanajuato**, C, T 20689, good pool and food, quiet, rec.; **Valenciana**, T 20799, C; **Villa de Plata**, T 21173, C; **El Carruaje**, T 22140, C. **De Los Embajadores**, Paseo Embajadores, T 20081, Mexican décor, C, restaurant, famous Sun. lunch. Trailer Park 1 km. N of **Mineral de Rayas**, there is a sign on the Ruta Panorámica, hot showers.

Restaurants Good coffee and reasonable food at *El Retiro*, Sopeña 12, nr. Jardín de la Unión. *Pizza Piazza*, Plaza San Fernando; *Cuatro Ranas*, Jardín Unión 1, most popular; *Valdez* on the same street, excellent menu del día; *La Bohemia*, Calle Alonso, cheap, good sandwiches, at night it becomes a marvellous peña; *BBQ Chicken* on Av. Juárez about 200 metres up from Mercado Hidalgo; *Las Palomas*, near post office, reasonable comidas. *El Granero*, Juárez 25, good comida, US$1.50, until 1700. *El Figón*, open after 1830 (closed 2-3 days a week), family run, small, on same street as Teatro Principal, heading towards Teatro Cervantes. *Hamburguesa Feliz*, Sopeña 10, good value. Good small café on N side of Plaza de la Unión. *El Claustro*, can see food being cooked, cheap, reasonable food; *La Dolce Vita*, nr. Juárez theatre, excellent food and service.

Entertainment Sketches from classical authors out of doors in lovely old plazas from April to August. Teatro Juárez (a magnificent French-type Second Empire building, US$0.25 to view), shows art films and has symphony concerts, US$1.50, the programme may be seen in the Zócalo. The Teatro Principal is opposite this. A band plays in Jardín de la Unión (next to the theatre) thrice weekly.

Laundry E of Jardín de la Unión, US$2.10 for a load, including drying.

Tourist Office Excellent, 5 de Mayo y Juárez near bus terminal. They have all hotel rates (except the cheapest) and give away folders. Federal representative office, Insurgencia 6, T 20123/19. A tourist office outside the town on the road from Querétaro will book accommodation. Federal represenative office, Insurgencia 6, T 20123/19.

Bus A new bus terminal was due to open in 1990. San Miguel de Allende, 1st class, US$6, 0700 and 1715, 2 hrs; Flecha Amarilla or Servicios Coordinados, 2nd class, ½ hourly between 0630 and 2300, 2 hrs. via Dolores Hidalgo, a spectacular trip (most of them go on to Mexico City), US$2; to Guadalajara 1st class US$4.20; via Léon (US$1) and Lagos de Moreno with Flecha Amarilla, 2nd class, hourly (0550-2235) US$4 (7 hrs.). Also daily at 1500 with Omnibus de México, US$5. To Zacatecas, with Omnibus de México 1st class, US$3.90, 5½ hrs. Hourly service to Morelia (6 hrs.) US$2.20. To Mexico City, 1st class, Estrella Blanca, 5½ hrs. US$4.80, book well in advance. To San Luis Potosí, US$3. To Querétaro, US$1.20, 3½ hrs. by Flecha Amarilla.

Rail Constitucionalista (*servicio estrella*) from Mexico City via Querétaro leaves 0735, arrives 1345; returns from Guanajato 1430, arr. Querétaro 1350 and Mexico City 1900; fare to the capital, US$11.70 reservations can be made in Mexico City on 547-3190, 5819, 4114. One train a day to Irapuato, at 0820.

Excursions A very good round trip is through Dolores Hidalgo to San Miguel de Allende, taking in Atotonilco (**see page** 98). See also the three local silver mines of La Raya (you can walk up from town; it is still operating), La Valenciana and La Cata. It is possible to visit the separating plant at La Cata, but visitors are not admitted to mines. At old site of La Cata mine (local bus near market), a church with a magnificent baroque façade, also the shrine of El Señor de Villa Seca (the patron of adulterers) with *retablos* and crude drawings of miraculous escapes from harm, mostly due to poor shooting by husbands. 15 km. along the road to Dolores Hidalgo is Santa Rosa; in a story book setting in the forest is *Hotel El Crag*, D, new, clean, restaurant next door, frequent buses. 30 km. from Guanajuato is Cerro Cubilete, with a statue of Christ the King; local buses take 1½ hrs., spectacular view of the Bajío, US$1, hourly from Guanajuato (also from Silao for US$0.60). Dormitory at the site (US$1.50) food available; last bus up leaves at 1600 from Silao and

Guanajuato. Visit the *Rancho de Enmedio* midway between Guanajuato and Dolores Hidalgo. Good dried meat specialities and beautiful scenery. A profusion of wild pears is sold from the roadside by children. Go also to San Gabriel de Barrera with the bus to Marfil, beautiful garden and *hacienda*, 15 patios, quiet. Tours to local sights leave from the main square.

(Km. 315) **Irapuato**, 475,000 people (*Hotel Real de Minas*, T 62380, overpriced, with equally overpriced restaurant, on Portal Carrillo Puerto, quiet rooms on church side; *Restaurant El Gaucho*, Díaz Ordaz y Lago), noted for delicious strawberries, which should on no account be eaten unwashed.

A divided-lane highway goes to (Km. 265) **Celaya** (pop 420,000; altitude, 1,800 metres), famous for its confectionery, especially a caramel spread called *cajeta*, and its churches, built by Mexico's great baroque architect Tresguerras (1765-1833), a native of the town. His best church is El Carmen (1807), with a fine tower and dome; see also his fine bridge over the Laja river.

Accommodation and food *Hotel Isabel*, Hidalgo 207, T 22095, D; *Hotel Diplomático*, Carretera Panamericana, excellent restaurant, *El Gran Chaparral*, especially for steaks, good service, also **Los Guajolotes**, Insurgentes 929; there is a 24-hour pharmacy at the bus station.

From Celaya to Querétaro, where we join the route from Eagle Pass (**see page 72**), there is a 56-km. limited-access toll motorway (US$0.40 a car), or the old road through Apaseo el Alto. Between Celaya and San Miguel de Allende is Comonfort; from there go 3 km. N to Rancho Arias: on a hilltop to the W are precolumbian pyramids. Cross the river N of the church and climb to ruins via goat-tracks.

San Miguel De Allende, a charming old town at 1,850 metres, on a steep hillside facing the broad sweep of the Laja River and the distant blue of the Guanajuato mountains, is 50 km. N of Querétaro by paved road. Population, 150,000. The city was founded as San Miguel in 1542, and Allende added in honour of the independence patriot born there. Its twisting cobbled streets rise in terraces to the mineral spring of El Chorro, from which the blue and yellow tiled cupolas of some 20 churches can be seen. It has been declared a national monument and all changes in the town are strictly controlled. In recent years there has been a large influx of American residents (now numbering over a thousand) and tourists, with a consequent rise in prices.

Social life centres around the market and the Jardín, or central plaza, an open-air living room for the whole town. Around it are the colonial city hall, several hotels, and the parish church, adorned by an Indian mastermason in the late 19th century, Zeferino Gutiérrez, who provided the austere Franciscan front with a beautiful façade and a Gothic tower; see also mural in chapel. The church of San Felipe Neri, with its fine baroque façade, is at the SW end of the market. Notable among the baroque façades and doors rich in churrigueresque details is the Casa del Mayorazgo de Canal, and San Francisco church, designed by Tresguerras. The Convent of La Concepción, built in 1734, now houses an art school, the Centro Cultural Nigromonte, locally known as Bellas Artes; the summer residence of the Condes del Canal, on San Antonio, contains a language school, the Instituto Allende (which has an English-language library; Spanish courses, US$70 a week, US$230 a month, without accommodation, but some rooms can be rented). The Academia América-Española offers full time Spanish courses; Casa de la Luna teaches Spanish less formally. Handicrafts are the traditional pottery, cotton cloth and brasswork. Tours of old houses and gardens start from the public library, Sun. 1200, 1½-2 hrs (US$7). A magnificent view of the city can be gained from the mirador on the Querétaro road.

Fiestas   End-July to mid-August, classical chamber music festival, information from Bellas Artes. One every 10 days or so. Main ones are Independence Day (15-16 Sept.); Fiesta of San Miguel (28 Sept.-1 Oct., with Conchero dancers from many places); Day of the Dead (2 Nov.); the Christmas Posadas, celebrated in the traditional colonial manner (16-24 Dec.); the pre-Lenten carnival, Easter Week, and Corpus Christi (June).

Hotels   Many weekend visitors from Mexico City: book ahead if you can. *Mansión del Bosque*, Aldama 65, T 20277, B, half-board; *Posada La Aldea*, T 21022, Calle Ancha de San Antonio, B, colonial style, clean, quiet, swimming pool, gardens. *Posada de San Francisco*, main square, T 20072, C; *Parador San Miguel Aristos*, at Instituto Allende, Ancha de San Antonio 30, T 20149, students given priority, D; *Vista Hermosa Taboada*, Allende 11, D, very popular, nice old colonial building, some ground floor rooms dark and noisy; *Rancho-Hotel El Atascadero*, T 20206, Querétaro road entrance, in an old colonial hacienda, very satisfactory, C; *Posada de las Monjas*, Canal 37, T 20171, C, with shower, excellent set meals in restaurant, clean and attractive, very good value, a converted convent. *Misión de los Angeles*, de luxe, 2 km. out on Celaya road, T 21026, colonial style, swimming pool, convenient facilities, C. Near Jardín, on Calle Vinaron, *Posada La Fuente* has a few rooms, good food (by arrangement), D, Ancha de San Antonio 95, T 20629. *Monteverdi*, T 21814, 2 blocks from station, D, new, clean, hot water; *Posada Carmina*, Cuña de Allende 7, T 20485, D, colonial building, courtyard for meals, rec.; *Mesón San Antonio*, D, Mesones 80, T 20580, renovated mansion, clean, friendly, quiet; *Sautto*, Dr. Macías 59, T 20072, D, rustic, pleasant but little hot water.

   San Sebastián, Mesones 7, T 20707, nr. market, rec., E, but reports of overcharging, large rooms with fireplace, clean, car park, noisy, courtyard. *Quinta Loreto*, Loreto 13, T 22380, modern rooms, swimming pool, pleasant garden, E, splendid value, good food (but beware of mosquitoes); *Hidalgo*, Hidalgo 22, E, hot water, good value, but rooms vary in quality. *La Huerta*, E, nice and quiet at the bottom of a dead-end street 4 blocks from the market, "gringo place"; *Vianey*, del Fecolo, F; *Casa de Huéspedes*, Mesones 27, family atmosphere, clean, good value.

   Motels *Villa del Molino*, Mexico City road entrance A; *Siesta*, road to Guanajuato, with trailer park, C, gardens; KAO campgrounds further out on same road.

Restaurants   *Bugambilia*, excellent, rec.; *Mama Mía*, near main square, jazz evenings, good but expensive; *Señor Plato*, Jesús 7, pricey, but has amazing 1920s atmosphere piano bar, and colonial-style patio filled with plants and parrots, excellent steaks, free garlic bread. *Alejandra*, small, near market, all home-cooked food, closed evenings, highly rec.; *El Circo*, Insurgentes by the library, Italian, singing waiters, fancy; opposite library at Insurgentes 74 is *Parroquiazo*, French atmosphere, attractive and not expensive. On Aldama *Posada Carmen*, OK but expensive; *Café Colón*, San Francisco 21, "folksy",

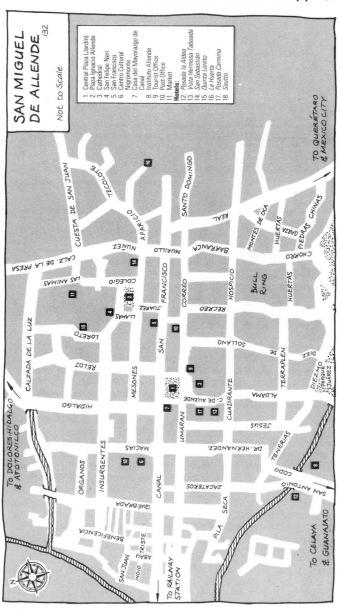

SAN MIGUEL
DE ALLENDE   132

Not to Scale

1. Central Plaza (Jardin)
2. Plaza Ignacio Allende
3. Cathedral
4. San Felipe Neri
5. San Francisco
6. Centro Cultural Nigromonte
7. Casa del Mayorazgo de Canal
8. Instituto Allende
9. Tourist Office
10. Post Office
11. Market

Hotels:
12. Posada la Aldea
13. Vista Hermosa Taboada
14. San Sebastián
15. Quinta Loreto
16. La Huerta
17. Posada Carmina
18. Sautto.

clean and inexpensive, rec. *Pepe Pizza*, Hidalgo 15, strudel too. *Matador*, Hernández Maciás, rec.; *El Jardín*, close to Plaza, friendly service, good food, also vegetarian; *Vegetarian* restaurant at Correo 4½ (on right-hand side as you walk away from centre), clean, cheap; *El Trigal*, opp. *Mama Mía*, vegetarian and meat, good value. *Café La Dolce Vita*, excellent coffee, cakes, fruit salads, Italian-owned. Try the licuados (fruit-shakes) in the market; ask for a campechana!

Bookshop El Colibrí, near Zócalo, French and English books.

Laundromat on Pasaje de Allende, US$1.50 wash and dry, same day service.

Immigration for tourist card extensions, etc., in Instituto Allende building, has an arrangement with Guadalajara and can issue a tourist card extension, or, if qualified, a *Rentista-Visitante* permit.

Tourist Office on Plaza next to the church, helpful with finding hotels, English spoken.

Trains The *servicio estrella* train, *El Constitucionalista*, leaves 1625 for Mexico City (via Querétaro); leaves the capital 0735, arrives San Miguel 1210 (US$10); T 20007 for reservations. The El Paso train stops at Celaya and Querétaro, 1309 (arr. 1920) and 1610 (arr. 2057); also one train to Nuevo Laredo daily.

Buses There is a new bus station on the outskirts, regular bus to the centre US$0.15, returns from the market. Frequent buses to Guanajuato (2 hrs.) with Flecha Amarilla and Estrella Blanca, via Dolores Hidalgo, US$2. To Dolores Hidalgo, US$0.50. Spectacular scenery between Dolores Hidalgo and Guanajuato as the road corkscrews up to a watershed from which you look down to arid lands on the east and tree-covered slopes on the west. Buses to Mexico City via Querétaro 4 a day before 1200, US$4, 2nd class, crowded but interesting. Buses to Morelia until 2040 daily, 4 hrs., US$2.30, 2nd class. Bus to Atotonilco US$0.30, plus short walk.

Excursions A good all-day hike can be made to the Palo Huérfano mountain on the S side of town. Take the road to just before the radio pylon then take the trails to the summit, where there are oaks and pines. Twenty mins. away is the small town of **Atotonilco**, where there is a church built around 1740 whose inside walls and ceiling are covered with frescoes done in black, red and grey earth: unrivalled anywhere for sheer native exuberance. There is a spa, the Balneario Taboada (admission US$1.70), between San Miguel and El Cortijo (about 20 mins. bus ride on the way to Dolores Hidalgo very near Atotonilco), a warm and hot pool, a fine swimming pool and good fishing in a nearby lake—very popular. Near the Spa is *Hacienda Taboada* hotel (5-star, large thermal pool, swimming pool, prior booking necessary). **Dolores Hidalgo**, (135,000) the home of Father Hidalgo, is 29 km. on, another most attractive small town; celebrations are held there on September 15 and 16. Visit Hidalgo's house, Casa Hidalgo, Morelos 1, entry US$0.30 and the Museo de la Independencia. Traditional Talavera tiles still made there.

Hotels *Hotel María Dolores*, between by-pass and centre coming from **San Miguel de Allende**; *Posada Las Campanas*, Guerrero 15, T 20427, D; *Posada*,Clocomacán, on the plaza, E, pleasant colonial house where Juárez stayed. *Posada Dolores*, F.

NOGALES—MEXICO CITY: THE PACIFIC HIGHWAY (4)

From Nogales (across the border from Nogales, Arizona) to Mexico City via Guadalajara is 2,043 km. (1,492 miles).

In summer, west coast drivers prefer the Central Route from El Paso, Texas, unless they love heat. It is dangerous to drive on retread tyres over the hot desert. Do not drive at night and never park or sleep along the road.

The Pacific Highway down the coast to Acapulco and Salina Cruz is completely paved but has military searches in the State of Guerrero (for narcotics and arms). The amount of accommodation along the Pacific Highway has increased greatly in recent years. There are many motels along the whole route, so that each town of any importance has one or more nearby. All available accommodation is listed in the American Automobile Association's *Mexico by Motor*.

From Nogales to Guaymas on the Gulf, the road runs along the western slopes of the Sierra Madre, whose summits rise to 3,000 metres. From Guaymas on to Mazatlán it threads along the lowland, with the Sierra Madre Occidental's bold and commanding escarpment to the E. Like the W coasts of all continents between latitudes 20° and 30°, the whole area is desert, but fruitful wherever irrigated by water flowing from the mountains. Summers are very hot, sometimes rainy, but winters are mild and very dry. Within the Sierra Madre nomadic people hunt the many wild animals; along the coasts available water determines the spots of concentrated settlement and of agriculture. Mexico gets most of its wheat from the southern part of Sonora state, and the irrigated valley bottoms (around Hermosillo) are also used for maize, cotton and beans. Farther S, in frost-free Sinaloa and Nayarit, sugar, rice, winter vegetables, tomatoes, and tobacco are grown. The three coastal states the route passed through make up 21% of Mexico's area, but include only 6% of its population.

(Km. 2,403) **Nogales** lies astride a mountain pass at 1,180 metres. It is a mining centre, with walnut groves and cattle ranches. It has the usual border night life. Population, 140,000.

Festival Cinco de Mayo festival, lasting four days, celebrates the defeat of the French army at Puebla on 5 May, 1862.

Hotel *Fray Marcos de Niza*, Campillo 91, B, not too good; many others.

Restaurant *Caverna* Greca, Elias 3, in a cave.

Train Pacific Railway as far as Guadalajara, and on by National Railways of Mexico. Guadalajara, 1,759 km. away, is reached in 29 hrs., at a speed of 60 k.p.h., and Mexico City (after changing in Guadalajara) in 52 hrs. (Mexicali-Mexico City costs US$20, 2nd, US$40, 1st class). Conditions vary in both 1st and 2nd class carriages, several unpleasant experiences reported, e.g. lack of air conditioning, dirt, overcrowding, etc. 1st class trains go only to Guadalajara and journey on to Mexico City has to be made in slower 2nd-class train. 2nd class train to Guadalajara 48 hours, crowded. *Servicio estrella* now reported to be operating. Train Nogales-Hermosillo, daily at 1000, US$3.50 2nd class, 5 hrs., continues to Mazatlán.

Bus to Mexico City, 42 hrs. with Transportes de Pacífico or Norte de Sonora, US$40, Tres Estrellas de Oro, 36 hrs. To Guadalajara 1st class, US$15, 26 hrs., very clean, fold-down seats, many food stops, leaves 1600, arrives 0700. Bus from Nogales to Tepic, 24 hrs., US$20. Nogales-Obregón via Hermosillo, US$8.50. There is a customs check after Nogales.

The highway passes through the Magdalena Valley. The Cocospera mines are near Imuris and there are famous gold and silver mines near Magdalena, which has a great Indian *fiesta* in the first week of October. Beyond, the cactus-strewn desert begins. At 120 km. from Nogales is Santa Ana, where the road from Tijuana and Mexicali comes in.

From Baja California There is a good road—**Route 2**—from Tijuana (**see page** 292), which runs close to the border, going through Mexicali (**see page** 288), Sonoita (*Desert Sun Motel; Motel Sono Inn*, E, American style, others nearby; customs inspection and immigration check), and Caborca to Santa Ana, where it joins the West Coast Highway (Route 15) to Mexico City. East of Mexicali the fast 4-lane highway crosses the fertile Mexicali valley to a toll bridge over the diminished Colorado River, and continues to **San Luis Río Colorado** (pop. 134,000), a cheerfully tourist-oriented border town in the "free zone" and serving cotton country: summer bullfights, small night-life district like those of the old west.

Motel *Naranjo* (first class); *El Rey* and others. Economy hotel: *Capra*.

Excursion North of San Luis (35 km.) is Baja's last international border crossing point, the farming town of **Algodones**. Border open 0600-2000. One hotel, cafés, a grassy park, souvenir crafts and a gas station. Just S of town is the Morelos Dam, which diverts from the Colorado all the water used to irrigate the Valle de Mexicali.

9 km. S of San Luis is Pozos, which 40 years ago had 60,000 inhabitants, now only 2,500. It has ruins of large buildings, churches, but no hotels. State highway 40 runs S to Riíto (petrol and a few stores) then follows the railway across the edge of the barren Gran Desierto to El Golfo de Santa Clara, a good-sized fishing town which has a fish-processing plant, supermarket, general store, church and a couple of eating places. The tidal range at the head of the Gulf is wide but there are good sandy beaches nearby at high tide. Public camping area (no facilities) at the end of a 3km. sandy track past the town. The highway is paved, a round-trip from San Luís of 230 km.

After leaving San Luís Rio Colorado, Highway 2 crosses the sandy wastes of the Desierto de Altar—Mexico's own mini-Sahara. For 150 km. there are no facilities (gas at Los Vidrios), only three houses and an enveloping landscape of sand dunes, cinder cones and a dark lava flow from the Cerro del Pinacate, so extensive that it stands out vividly on photographs from space. All the area around the central range is protected by the **Pinacate Natural Park**; a gravel road 10 km. E of Los Vidrios gives access to the northern sector of the park, which contains much wildlife: e.g., puma, deer, antelope, wild boar, Gila monster, wild sheep, quail, red-tailed eagle. Several unique volanic craters, the treacherous lava fields and an interesting cinder mine may also be visited.

After a hot and monotonous 200 km. from San Luís, Route 2 reaches the sun-bleached bordertown of **Sonoita**, a short distance from Lukeville, Arizona. (Note: If coming from Lukeville to San Luís Río Colorado, make sure you turn right (west) at Sonoita and not left (south) to San Luisito; they are both on Highway 2 but 320 km. apart in opposite directions!). Sonoita is a good base for exploring the Kino missions (see below) and there are a number of very interesting archaeological ruins in the desert nearby. Sonoita has a motel and a trailer park. Transportes Norte de Sonora and Tres Estrellas de Oro both run first-class bus services. Water and snacks should be carried anywhere in this very arid region, and, if driving your own vehicle, the tank should be kept full and replenished wherever possible. Arizona's picturesque Organ Pipe National Monument is just across the border from Sonoita.

Excursion Highway 8 goes SE from Sonoita through 100 km. of sand dunes to **Puerto Peñasco** (pop, 60,000), a popular fishing, surfing and beach resort on the Gulf of California. It lies on the Mexicali railway and also has a regular air service. Hotel accommodation is limited but there is the *Playa de Oro Trailer Resort*, 2 km. E, laundry, boat ramp, 200 sites, US$12 for 2. A few km. W is the town of La Choya and several fine beaches. Fishing tournaments are held in the Bahía La Choya; Playa de Oro has Puerto Peñasco, 29 May-1 June, with a colourful parade, dancing and a widely-attended sporting contest. Good souvenirs are the mirrors, necklaces and figurines locally made from coral, seashells and snail shells. Recently-paved state highway 37 continues on S and E, roughly following the rail line to Caborca (180 km.)—an alternative to the inland Highway 2 route.

Route 2 continues from Sonoita to Caborca (150 km.), passing through a number of small towns (San Emeterio, San Luisito) and a more mountainous but still arid land. Customs and Immigration station near Quitovac (28 km. S of Sonoita), where tourist cards and vehicle papers are validated as you enter the Mexican "mainland".

Caborca (pop. 37,000, alt. 286m) lies on the Mexicali-Benjamín Hill railway in the midst of a gently sloping plain. *Motel Posada San Cristóbal* and several hotels, service station and general facilities. A "Grape Fair" is held 21-26 June, with wine exhibitions and industrial and agricultural show. Caborca's restored Church of Nuestra Señora de la Concepción was one of the 25 missions founded by Padre Kino in Sonora and Arizona between 1687 and 1711. (It was also used in 1857 as a fortress during a raid by U.S. renegades under self-styled "General" Crabb; their defeat is still commemorated by a fair held each 6 April.)

Father Eusebio Francisco Kino was the foremost pioneer missionary of Northwest Mexico and Baja, California. He attempted the first major settlement of the Baja peninsula (San Bruno, 1683); after its failure he was assigned to the mainland, where he blazed a *ruta de misiones* as far as present-day Tucson. Kino was a versatile and hardy Jesuit of Italian origin—astronomer, cartographer, farmer, physician, navigator, explorer and a man of unlimited faith. Most of his adobe mission buildings were later replaced by substantial Franciscan churches, such as at nearby Pitiquito, Oquitoa and at Magdalena, where his grave was discovered as recently as 1966; the remains are enclosed in glass *in situ* and the site is a colonial monument.

Highway 2 continues east through Altar (café, gas station) to join Highway 15 at **Santa Ana** (pop. 12,500, alt. 690m), a small town of little note. *Motel San Francisco*, C, a/c, shower baths, restaurant. The Fiesta of Santa Ana is held 17-26 July: horse racing, fireworks, etc. 2 km. W is San Francisco, with another Kino mission.

42 km. S the Pacific Highway reaches Benjamín Hill, where the Mexicali railway joins the main Nogales-Guadalajara track; brightening up this forgettable junction is the Children's Park, with an amusement park, lake, zoo, and a delightful scaled-down children's railway.

There is little of note on the straight run S to Hermosillo through semi-arid farming and rangeland, apart from the little towns of El Oasis and nearby Carbo (on the rail line)—both have gasoline supplies. 158 km. from Santa Ana the land becomes greener and the irrigated fields and citrus groves begin to enclose.

Hermosillo (pop. 685,000 alt. 237m), capital of Sonora state, a modern city, resort town and centre of a rich orchard area. There is a modern jet airport on the road to Bahía Kino; the La Colorada copper mines are to the E. Near the city the Rodríguez Dam captures the fickle flow of the Río Sonora, producing a rich strip of cotton fields, vegetables, melons, oranges and grapes. Reminders of Hermosillo's illustrious colonial past can be found in the imposing Cathedral of La Asunción (neoclassical, baroque dome, three naves) facing the Plaza de la Constitutción and surrounded by a traditional quarter. The Palacio de Gobierno, with its intricately-carved pillars and pediment, has several grandiose statues amid landscaped gardens. See also the attractive Madero Park in the SE sector, a favourite promenade and sports centre, and the University City, with its modern buildings of Mexican architecture blended tastefully with Moorish and Mission influences. The main building contains a large library auditorium and interesting museum, open daily 0900-1300, closed holidays.

Hotels Generally poor standard of hotels, although there is a *Holiday Inn* on Blvd. Eusebio Kino 368, T 51112, L, with restaurant, bars, entertainment, etc. *Kino*, Pino Suárez 151, Sur, T 24599, B; *San Alberto*, Serdán y Rosales, T 21800, B; *San Andrés*, Oaxaca 14, T 20653, D with bath, *Washington*, Dr. Noriega, T 31183, E, with bath, but gloomy; *Monte Carlo*, Juárez y Sonora, T 20853, E; *Royal*, in centre, F, a/c but grubby; *Guaymas Inn*, 5½ km. N, air-conditioned rooms with shower, E.
    Motel *Bugambilia*, Padre Kino 712, T 45050, C. Two close to railway station.

Restaurants *Henry's Restaurant*, across the road from *Motel Encanto*, Blvd. Kino Norte, nice old house, good; *San César*, P. Elias Calle 71 Pnte., excellent chop sueys.

Tourist Office Blvd. Eusebio Kino 1000, T 51465/51.

Bus to Nogales US$3.80, 4 hrs.; 2nd class to Agua Prieta, 7 hrs., US$4; to Los

Mochis, 1st class, US$9, 2nd, US$8.50, 7½ hrs. through scrubland and wheat fields. Bus to Tijuana, US$14.50 1st class, 11 hrs, there can be long queues, especially near Christmas. Bus to Mazatlán 10-12 hrs., US$12 1st, US$11.50 2nd class. To Guaymas, US$1.60, 1½ hrs. The bus station is on the outskirts.

Train overnight to Mazatlán at 1945, arrives 0730, worth taking a sleeper (US$13).

Excursion A dry-weather road, 106 km., goes W to Bahía Kino, on the Gulf (bus US$1, from Autobuses de la Costa, Calle Plutarco, 1 block from Rosales). The Seri Indians, who used to live across El Canal del Infiernillo (Little Hell Strait) from the port on the mountainous Isla del Tiburón (Shark Island), have been displaced by the navy to the mainland, down a dirt road from Bahía Kino in a settlement at Punta Chueca (no east access). They come into Kino on Sat. and Sun. to sell their ironwood animal sculptures (non-traditional) and traditional basketware (not cheap). They may usually be found at the *Posada del Mar Hotel*. A fine Museo Regional de Arte Seri has opened in new Kino, Calle Puerto Peñasco, 3 blocks from the main beach road. **Camping** on the beaches is possible.

At Km. 1,867 (from Mexico City) the road reaches the Gulf at the port of *Guaymas* (200,000), on a lovely bay backed by desert mountains; excellent deep-sea fishing, and sea-food for the gourmet. Miramar beach, on Bocachibampo bay with its blue sea sprinkled with green islets, is the resort section. Water sports on May 10. The climate is ideal in winter but unpleasant in summer. The 18th century church of San Fernando is worth a visit; so also, outside the town, is the 17th century church of San José de Guaymas. Excursions to the cactus forests. Some 22 km. N of Guaymas is the Bahía San Carlos, very Americanized and touristy, where "Catch 22" was filmed; there is free camping on a good beach at the end of the runway made for the film; also good fishing. Both Miramar and San Carlos beaches are easily reached by bus. Nice little beach 1 km. past Miramar beach with pleasant cafés, at the end of F bus line. Airport.

Hotels *Club Méditerranée*, end of beach, T 60070. *Santa Rita*, Serdán and Calle 14, C with bath, a/c, clean, good; *Playa de Cortés*, on Bocachibampo bay, T 20121, A; *La Posada de San Carlos*, Bahía San Carlos, T 60015, A. *Leo's Inn* on Miramar beach, T 21337, C; *Ana*, Calle 25 No. 135, T 20593, near cathedral, a/c, C; *América*, Alemán (Calle 20) y Av. 18, T 21120, E, a/c, adequate. *Casa de Huéspedes La Colimense*, basic, rooms on the inside best, F, with fan, near bus station.

Motels *Flamingos*, Carretera Internacional, T 20960, C; *Malibu*, D, T 22244, Carretera Internacional N; *Bahía Trailer Court*, 6 kms. NW of town on Bahía San Carlos road and *Los Playibos*, motel/ restaurant/trailer park, 7 km. N on Highway 15 with pool and all facilities. Those who feel like avoiding high prices in Guaymas and can make Ciudad Obregón, 129 km. S, will find the *Costa de Oro* (see below).

Restaurant *Del Mar*, Aquiles Serdán and Calle 17, excellent seafood, expensive. *Cantón*, Serdán between 20 and 21, good Chinese. Generally, restaurants are overpriced.

Tourist Office Av. Serdán, lots of pamphlets.

Rail *Autovía* from Guaymas to Nogales leaves at 1000, 6 hrs., US$9, daily except

Sat.; book in advance.

Ferry Transbordadores sail from Guaymas to Santa Rosalía, Baja California, at 1100 every Sun., Tues. and Thur., and return on the same days at 2300, 7 hr. trip, but check in advance if this service is still operating, T 622-2324.

Buses 1st class bus to Hermosillo (1½ hrs., US$1.60); Mazatlán, frequent, 12 hrs., US$13; Tijuana, 2nd class, 18 hrs., US$19. To Culiacán, 9 hrs., US$7. Bus to Empalme will allow you to take the train at 1400 (very full at times) coming from Mexicali to Sufragio, to catch the Los Mochis-Chihuahua train the next morning (seats usually no problem).

From Guaymas to Mazatlán is 784 km. First comes **Ciudad Obregón** (*Motel Valle Grande*, M. Alemán y Tetabiate, T 40940; *Costa de Oro*, M. Alemán 210, T 41765, well-kept and pleasant; *Dora*, California 1016 Sur, D, CREA Youth Hostel, Laguna de Sainari s/n, C.P. 85000), mainly important (180,000 people) as the centre of an agricultural region. **Navajoa** (200,000 people) has the *Motel El Rancho* (T 20004) and *Motel del Río* (T 20331) and a trailer park in the N of town on Route 15; 52 km. E into the hills is the delightful old colonial town of **Alamos** (accommodation in short supply; *Los Portales Hotel*, T 80111, with beautiful frescoes, C, on plaza; *Somar*, on the road into Alamos, T 80125, Madero 110, E; *Enriques*, F, basic but O.K.) now declared a national monument. (Bus Navajoa-Alamos every hour on the ½ hr. from 0630, about US$0.30, until 1830, 45 mins—bus station can be reached from main bus station by going right out of the front door, again take first right and then walk six blocks to the terminal on the left.) It is set in a mining area fascinating for rock enthusiasts. About 10 mins. by bus from Alamos is Minas Nuevas, once an important source of silver, very photogenic, bus US$0.25. West of Navajoa, on Huatabampo bay, are the survivors of the Mayo Indians; their festivals are in May.

Los Mochis, in a sugar-cane area, is a fishing resort 25 km. from the sea with a US colony. A stairway leads up the hillside behind La Pérgola, a pleasant public park near the city reservoir, for an excellent view of Los Mochis. Km 1,636.5; 200,000 people.

Hotels Book well in advance, especially if arriving late at night. *Santa Anita*, A, Leyva y Hidalgo, T 20046, comfortable, clean dining room, noisy a/c, not very friendly or efficient, has own bus service to station; it is usually possible to change dollars. *Beltrán*, Hidalgo 281 Pte., T 20688, D, rec., has all travel time-tables; *Hidalgo*, opposite at No. 260 Pte., T 23456, E; *América*, D, Allende Sur 655, T 21355, clean, a/c, near bus station, has restaurant with good, cheap sandwiches; *Los Arcos*, Allende (round corner from Tres Estrellas terminal), E, a/c, clean, a bit dingy. *del Valle*, Guillermo Prieto y Independencia, T 2-01-05, F, a/c, bath, rec; *Lorena*, Prieto y Obregón, T 20958, fair value, a/c, D; *Fénix*, A. Flores 365 Sur, T 22623, D, safe, clean. *Montecarlo*, D, a/c, Independencia y Flores, T 21818. **Motel** *Santa Rosa*, López Mateos 1051 N, D.

Restaurants *El Farallón*, Flores and Obregón, good seafood and service; *El Vaquero* in *Hotel Montecarlo*, rec; *Los Globos*, near TNS bus station, reasonable. *Las Palmeras*, excellent, reasonably priced.

A railway trip to Chihuahua (**see page** 82) and back from Los Mochis station reached by "*peso*" taxi, US$4, 5 mins.; or regular bus from city centre shows you the spectacular scenery of the Sierra Madre and the

Urique (or Copper) Canyon. The *servicio estrella* leaves daily at 0700 (arrives 1905, US$20 with all meals, English-speaking hostess). Tickets can be bought at Flamingo Travel in *Hotel Santa Anita*, Leyva y Hidalgo (very helpful) the day before, avoiding the queue at the station but they will try to persuade you into taxis to the station (there is a bus), and into their preferred (expensive) hotels. Make sure that taxi prices when leaving the station are not per person, rip-offs reported. An ordinary train, US$6, 2nd class, leaves at 0700 (10 hours) for Chihuahua (this is the cheapest way to see the canyon—the train stops 15 minutes—in daylight; cold as you get to Creel, photographing possible. Train timetables bear little relation to actual departure times, so check at Los Mochis, those given here are of April, 1990. Sit on the right for views except when approaching Temoris, then return to the right until the first tunnel after Temoris, remain on the left for the rest of the journey. There is a time change (one hour forward) between Los Mochis and Creel. If you do not want to take the train all the way, go to Bahuichivo (simple hotel, F, a few shops), and return from there. Pick-ups go (5-hr. trip) to Urique (except Sun.) in the Urique Canyon (a bus from the *Misión Urique Canyon* meets the train in Bahuichivo). 2 simple hotels (F) in Urique.

Connection with the Nogales-Guadalajara train at **Sufragio**, 37 km. from Los Mochis (**see also page** 290). Fare to Mazaltán, US$3.85, 1st class (rec.), US$2 2nd.

Air To La Paz, Baja California Sur.

Bus Mexico City, US$24. Ciudad Obregón, US$6. Tijuana, US$18, several daily up to 24 hrs. Mazatlán US$7, 1st class, leaves 2100, arrives 0345; with Tres Estrellas de Oro or Transport Norte de Sonora. Nogales, 2nd class, US$14, 12 hrs. No reservations can be made for buses N or S at the terminal of Tres Estrellas de Oro and it is difficult to get on buses. Try instead Transportes de Pacífico, 3 blocks away and next to TNS terminal. First class bus to Guaymas 5½ hrs., US$5. To Tepic, Tres Estrellas de Oro, 1st class, US$9, 13 hrs. To Topolobampo, US$0.25, buses leave from lane behind Flamingo Travel.

An hour NE by train from Los Mochis is **El Fuerte** (120,000). This town has recently been renovated and has interesting colonial architecture. The station is a few miles from the town; taxis. *Hotel San Francisco*, good value. Good restaurants, nice plaza.

About half an hour's drive along a side road SW takes us from Los Mochis to **Topolobampo**, on the beautiful bay-and-lagoon-indented coast. It is difficult to find a beach unless one pays for a private launch. Now that a railway— take food with you—has been opened to Ojinaga (**see page** 81), Topolobampo is being developed as a deep-water port.

Hotels *Yacht Hotel*, modern, clean and good food, quiet, B, but seems to close for the winter; *Casa de Huéspedes* not rec.

Ferry Topolobampo-La Paz, Baja California Sur. Ferry leaves Topolobampo Mon., and Thur., 1000, arriving Pichilingüe (La Paz) 1800, book ticket before 1800 on previous day or before 0900 on day of travel. **See also page** 307.

Some 210 km. beyond Los Mochis (at Km. 1,429) is the capital of Sinaloa state, **Culiacán** (950,000 people), chief centre for winter vegetables.

No longer a colonial city, but attractive and prosperous; it has a university. The safe beaches of Altata are 30 minutes by dirt road.

Hotels *Executivo*, Madero y Obregón, T 39370, A. *Del Valle*, Solano 180, T 39026, C; *Beltrán*, E, clean, safe, quiet, was once a hospital with appropriate furnishings; *Louisiana*, F with bath and fan, in centre, clean and pleasant; *San Francisco*, Hidalgo 227, F, clean, friendly. **Motels**: *Los Caminos*, Carretera Internacional, C; *Los Tres Ríos*, 1 km. N of town on highway 15, trailer park, pool, resort style. *Pizzería Tivoli*, good, friendly.

Airport 10 km. from centre.

Transport Culiacán is suitable for connections to Los Mochis (**see page** 83 for trips to the Copper Canyon). Take one of the several daily Mexico City-Culiacán flights and then rent a plane (US$360 for five), hire a car (3 hrs.' drive), or take a bus. Whichever you do, try to arrive before the train at 2100, as hotel reservations are not always honoured. Bus to Tepic, 8¼ hrs., US$6.80; to Guaymas, 9 hrs., US$7.

Another 208 km. bring us to a roadside monument marking the Tropic of Cancer. Beyond, 13 km. is (Km. 1,089) **Mazatlán**, spread along a peninsula at the foot of the Sierra Madre. It is the largest Mexican port on the Pacific Ocean and the main industrial and commercial centre in the W (pop. 800,000). The beauty of its setting and its warm winters have made it a popular resort, but unfortunately with expansion it has lost some of its attraction. It overlooks Olas Altas (High Waves) bay, which has a very strong current. Tourism is now concentrated on Gaviota beach, which is solidly built up and where accommodation is expensive. On one side of the peninsula, the beach is fringed with groves of coconut palm; on the other a promenade overlooks a number of islands. There are more islands in the nearby lagoons, which teem with wild life. A promenade lined by hotels, with a long beach at its foot, curves round the bay; fine for watching the famous sunsets. The local Shrovetide carnival is almost as good as at Veracruz. The best beaches, 3 to 5 km. from the city, are easily reached by taxi. Boats ply between the shore and the island beaches. The lighthouse, on El Faro island, is 157 metres above sea-level.

Firmly rooted and extremely popular in the State of Sinaloa is a type of orchestra known as the Banda Sinaloense or Tamborera, which can be seen and heard playing "Chaparral" at almost any time of day or night in restaurants, dance halls, bars, at family parties or on the street. It usually has from 14 to 16 musicians: 4 saxophones, 4 trumpets, clarinets, tuba, 3-4 men on drums and other percussion instruments, including *maracas, guiro*, and loud, strong voices. It is unabashed, brutal music, loud and lively. One such Banda plays every afternoon at the *Chaparral* bar, opposite the Conasupo market near bus station.

This is one of the best places in Mexico to buy *huaraches* (leather sandals); seek out the "huarache-man" at one corner of the market.

Hotels Along the northern beach Sábalo-Camarón are: *Los Sábalos*, T 34455, Health Club facilities; *Playa Mazatlán*, T 35333, good atmosphere; *El Cid*, with *El Caracol* nightclub, T 33333; *Camino Real* (T 31111), *Oceano Palace*, (T 32222), *Holiday Inn* (T 32222, restort facilities) all in our A-L range, *Azteca Inn*,

T 34477, C. Along Av. del Mar beach are: *De Cima*, (T 17110), *Hacienda*, (T 27000), *El Dorado* (T 17418) all A; *Playamar*, C, with TV, air-conditioned; *Las Brisas*, T 30355, rec., C, with shower, swimming pool and on sea front, air-conditioned. Along Olas Altas beach are: *Freeman* (No. 79 Sur, T 12114) old, highrise; *Belmar*, T 20799, modernized but old, both C. Along Paseo Centenario are: *Olas Altas*, T 13192, D, efficiently run and clean, but fleas reported. Most of the others are in the downtown area away from the beach front: *Posada Colonial*, N of south docks, D, well-kept, good food; *Del Centro*, J.M. Canizales 705 Pte, T 21673, modern, D, behind main church; *Roma*, Av. Juan Carrasco 127, T 23685, very clean and friendly 2 blocks from beach, rec., E, with bath but some rooms noisy; *Zaragoza*, Zaragoza 18, old and pretty, D, with bath; *Posada familiar Sarita*, Mariano Escobedo, E, colonial, nr. beach; *Pensión María Luisa*, Mariano Escobedo, E, no fans, friendly but hot, quiet; *Tropicana*, Mariano Escobedo, D, a/c, shower, large rooms, rec.; *Lerma*, Simón Bolívar 5, near beach, D, friendly, simple, but quiet and cool; *Vialta*, Azueta 2006, three blocks from market, E, with bath, friendly, helpful; *Económico*, E, with bath and fan, noisy, dark but very clean, next to bus station, ½ km. from main beach; *The Sands*, D, pool, a/c, on beach, near bus station.

Although N of the city there are undeveloped beaches with free overnight camping, they are only rec. if you are in a group for security—travellers have warned against it: e.g. *Isla de la Piedra*, friendly, huts for US$1.50 or camping permitted if you have a meal there, good food. Beware of sandflies! At least 10 trailer parks on Playa del Norte/Zona Dorada and on towards the N, including *Casa Blanca Disco*, F, cheapest, on beach side, dirty. Much better is *La Posta*, ½ block off beach, with swimming pool and tent space, E, lots of shade. Big hotels rapidly expanding all along N beach seashore to Mármol.

Motels are strung all along the ocean front: *Las Palmas*, B; *Marley*, C; *Las Gaviotas*, B; *Azteca Inn*, C; *Del Sol*, C. On Highway 15: *Papagayo*, D. Downtown: *Maity*, E; *Mazatlán*, F. *Mar Rosa Trailer Park*, N of *Holiday Inn* on northern beach, US$8 for 1 or 2 plus car, hot water, safe, rec.

Restaurants *Doney's*, M. Escobedo 610, downtown, good home cooking; *El Bistro*, in craft centre in Zona Dorada, good steaks and seafood; *Shrimp Bucket* and *Señor Frog*, Olas Altas 11 and Av. del Mar, same owners, very famous, popular, good; *Lobster Trap*, Sábalo Camarón, good chicken(!); *Joncol's*, Flores 254, a/c, downtown, popular but deteriorated; *Bruno's*, Mariano Escobedo, good food and service, highly rec.; *Mamucas*, Bolívar 73, seafood expensive. *La Red*, Av. del Mar 112, reasonable lunches. *Pastelería y Cafetaría Panamá*, several branches for reasonable meals, pastries, coffee. *El Ostión Feliz*, Flores y Villa, seafood; *Pekin*, Juárez 4, good Chinese, inexpensive; *Pizza Hut*, Av. del Mar, good salads too; *Beach Boys Club*, on Malecón nr. fishermans' monument, good value meals, US owned; *Balneario Playa Norte*, Av. del Mar, nr. Monument, friendly, reasonable prices; *Balnearios Mazatlán* and *Miramar*, on Playa Norte, good cheap Mexican fare. *Casa del Naturista*, Zaragoza 809, sells good wholegrain bread. *Amadeus Video Tacos*, a/c, nice bar, occasional live music.

Sports Fishing is the main sport (sailfish, tarpon, marlin, etc.). Shrimp from the Gulf are sent, frozen, to all parts of Mexico. Its famous fishing tournament follows Acapulco's and precedes the one at Guaymas. In the mangrove swamps are egrets, flamingoes, pelicans, cranes, herons, and duck. Nearby at Camarones there is "parachute flying", drawn by motorboats. **N.B.** Always check with the locals whether swimming is safe, since there are strong rip currents in the Pacific which run out to sea and are extremely dangerous. There is a free Red Cross treatment station 9 blocks along the avenue opposite the Beach Man on the right. There are bull-fights at Mazatlán, US$4.50 for a general seat in the shade (*sombra*). Good view here, although you can pay up to US$15 to get seats in the first 7 rows—Sundays at 1600.

Tourist Office Av. Rodolfo T. Loaizo 100, Local N6; on road to northern beach, past *Señor Frog*. Also Av. Olas Altas 1300, Edificio Bancen, Col. Centro.

Bus Station at Centro Colonia, 10 mins. walk from beach or take yellow bus from centre marked "Insurgentes"; safe luggage store. Bus fare to Mexico City about US$13 (2nd class). Mexicali US$25, Pullman, 21 hrs. Guadalajara, with Transportes Norte de Sonora, several times a day, US$7 (10 hrs.); Tres Estrellas buses less good. To Chihuahua, US$16 1st class, 19 hrs. To crossroads for San Blas, US$3.75; Tepic US$4.25 (5¼ hrs., with Estrella Blanca, efficient, clean buses); bus (frequent) to Los Mochis (8 hrs.), US$7 with Transportes Norte de Sonora or Transportes del Pacífico. To Navajoa, US$5 1st class; 1st class Transportes del Norte bus to Durango, US$4.10, take an a.m. bus to see the scenery; Guaymas, 12 hrs., US$13, 2nd class. Bus to Rosario US$0.80, can then with difficulty catch bus to Caimanero beach, nearly deserted. Terminal Alamos, Av. Oeste Guerrero 402, 2 blocks from market, buses to Alamos every hour on the half hour.

Ferries La Paz (Baja California Sur), daily at 1700, 16-20 hrs. For fares, etc., see under La Paz, Baja California section. Allow plenty of time for booking and customs procedure. Quite a way from centre to dock (take bus marked "Playa Sur"). **N.B.** Ticket office for La Paz ferry opens 0830-1300 only, on day of departure, arrive before 0800, unclaimed reservations on sale at 1100. Don't expect to get vehicle space for same-day departure. The service is becoming increasingly unreliable. Ferry returns from La Paz also at 1700.

Rail Take Insurgentes bus out to Morelos railway station. Train to Guadalajara, 12 hrs., departs 0800, but is usually late, air-conditioned (if working), scenic trip with a variety of topography and agriculture. From Tepic it climbs gradually through the hills to 1,650 metres at Guadalajara, passing through some 30 or 40 tunnels. Best travel 1st class US$6 or pullman US$10.50; 2nd class dirty and uncomfortable, US$3, leaves before dawn. Buy tickets at agency in Pasaje Linguna in the Zona de Oro, close to Tourist Office or queue at 0730, seat numbers are not observed so sit in the first empty seat. Train to Tepic, special 1st US$3.50, 2nd class US$2.10, about 6 hrs. 1st class train fare to Mexico City, US$12.50.

Air Airport 26 km. from centre. Taxi, fixed fare US$6.60 airport-Mazatlan. Daily flights to La Paz and San José del Cabo (Baja California Sur), and the USA.

Excursions to Islas de Piedras, 30 km. of now littered beach. Take a small boat from S side of town from Armada (naval station near brewery), regular service, US$0.75, walk across island (10 mins.) to a clean beach where there is good surfing. Local *comedores* on beach provide primitive accommodation, or ask for permission to camp on the beach. Try smoked fish sold on a stick. Star Fleet boats may be rented at the sports fishing docks for a cruise round the Dos Hermanos rocks, where boobies and many other birds can be seen. A boat excursion on the *Yate Fiesta* cruises out at 1000 or 2000 (with dancing), from second last bus stop in the direction of Playa del Sur. Refreshments included, and you can see the wildlife in the day time; US$4.40. About 100 km. N of Mazatlán is a turn-off to the town of La Cruz, with two hotels: *Las Palmitas*, F, off the main street, quiet. Few tourists.

Twenty-four km. beyond Mazatlán, the Coast-to-Coast Highway to Durango (a spectacular stretch), Torreón, Monterrey and Matamoros turns off left at Villa Unión. Above Villa Unión, Santa Lucía has a small hotel, *Villa Blanca*, T 2-16-28. Heading E, the road reaches Concordia, a pleasant colonial town, then climbs the mountains past Copala, another mining ghost-town (basic hotel). Copala can be reached by tour bus from Mazatlán or by Auriga pick-up truck from Concordia. On this road there is a good German hotel with excellent restaurant. After reaching the high plateau the road passes through pine forests to Durango. The road to Tepic continues S from Villa Unión. At Rosario, 68 km. S of Mazatlán, the church is worth a visit. Before reaching Tepic both road and railway begin the long climb from the lowland level over the Sierra Madre to the basin of Jalisco, 1,500 metres above sea-level. Eleven km. short of Tepic a road on the right descends 900 metres to a pretty South Sea-type beach.

The resort of **San Blas** is 69 km. from Tepic and is overcrowded during US and Mexican summer holidays. It has an old Spanish fortress and a smelly harbour. In August it becomes very hot and there are many mosquitoes, but not on the beach 2 km. from the village (but there are other biting insects, so take repellent anyway); few tourists at this time or early in the year. The best beach is Playa de las Islas. Seven km. from San Blas (bus, taxi US$2 per car) is the beach of Matanchén, good swimming but many mosquitoes. 16 km. from San Blas is the beautiful Los Cocos beach (trailer park). **N.B.** Don't wander too far from public beach; tourists have warned against attacks and robberies.

Hotels *Marino Inn*, Bataillon, T 50340, a/c, friendly, pool, fair food, A; *Las Brisas*, Cuauhtémoc Sur 106, T 50112, very clean, B, highly rec., excellent restaurant; *Bucanero*, Juárez Poniente 75, T 50101, D with bath and fan, frequented by Americans, food good, pool, lizards abound, noisy discos 3 times a week and bar is open till 0100 with loud music; *Posada del Rey*, , very clean, swimming pool, excellent value, D, on Campeche, T 50123; *Posada de Morales* also has a swimming pool, more expensive, ½ block from *Posada del Rey*, T 50023, *Flamingos*, Juárez Poniente 105, E, clean, friendly; *Vallarta*, very basic with fan, 50 m. from beach, F; *María's*, fairly clean with cooking, washing and fridge facilities, F without bath, E with bath and fan; similar but better is *Hotel/Bungalows Posada*, E for bungalow, clean, pretty, good for long stay. No camping or sleeping permitted on beaches but several pay campsites available. *San Blas Motel*, near Zócalo, D, patio, fans, good value. Sometimes free camping possible behind *Playa Hermosa Hotel*, old house, only partly occupied, occupied rooms clean, 2 km from town, E. Trailer park at town beach. Many apartments for rent.

Restaurants *Tony's* and *La Isla* now said to be best. *La Familia*, try the merequetengue dishes, rec.; *Tropicana*, try its sopa marinera, fish soup; *La Diligencia*, on Calle Juárez near Zócalo, good food, especially fish, clean, friendly and cheap but slow service; *MacDonald* just off Zócalo. *Bar-Restaurant Torino*, steaks, seafood, pasta, wine by glass, very reasonable. Plenty of seafood restaurants on the beach; e.g. *Las Olas*, good and cheap.

Bank Banamex just off Zócalo, exchange 0830-1000 only. Comercial de San Blas on the main square will change money at 10% commission.

Bus To Tepic, 1st class, US$1.75, 3 a day, 2nd class, 5-6 a day, US$1, 1½ hrs. To Guadalajara, US$5, 1st class, US$3.90 2nd class, 8½ hrs.

It is possible to take a 4-hr. jungle trip in a boat (bus to launching point, US$0.50) to **La Tovara**, a small resort with fresh-water swimming hole and not much else, or walking, to do. Tour buses leave from the bridge

1 km. out of town and cost US$120 for canoe with six passengers. Official prices are posted and guides are reported to have combined against bargaining. There are coatis, raccoons, iguanas, turtles, boat-billed herons, egrets and parrots. Twilight tours enable naturalists to see pottos and, if very lucky, an ocelot. La Tovara is crowded at midday during the summer. A cheaper 1½-2 hr. cruise is also possible. When arranging your trip make sure you are told the length of journey and route in advance. You can take a bus from San Blas towards Santa Cruz (see below under Tepic) and get off at Matanchén beach (see above). From here, a boat for ½-day hire includes the best part of the jungle cruise from San Blas.

Quaint little towns just off the highway between Mazatlán and Tepic: Acaponeta (turnoff for Novillera beach), Rosario, Tuxpan and Santiago. The Mirador El Aguila is on Highway 15, 11 km. after the junction to San Blas; it overlooks a canyon where many birds can be seen in the morning and the late afternoon.

(Km. 807) **Tepic**, capital of Nayarit state, altitude 900 metres, population 200,000, founded in 1531 at the foot of the extinct volcano of Sangagüey. The Huichol and Cora Indians of the Sierra come to town in very picturesque dress; their craftwork—bags (carried only by men), scarves woven in colourful designs and necklaces (*chaquira*) of tiny beads and wall-hangings of brightly coloured wool—is available from souvenir shops, but best to let Indians approach you when they come to town. (These handicrafts are reported to be cheaper in Guadalajara, at the Casa de Artesanías.) There are many little squares, all filled with trees and flowers. The Cathedral, with two fine Gothic towers, in Plaza Principal, has been restored. Worth seeing are the Municipal Palace; the Casa de Amado Nervo (the poet and diplomat); the Regional Museum, Av. México 91 Norte (open 1000-1400 and 1700-2000 hrs., closed Mon.); and the Convento de la Cruz, on the summit of a hill close to the centre. The landscape around Tepic is wild and mountainous. Nearby are the Ingenio and Jala waterfalls, good places for picnics. The tombs in the cemetery are worth seeing.

Hotels *San Jorge*, Lerdo 124, T 21324, C, very comfortable, good value; *Ibarra*, Durango 297 Norte, T 23870, luxurious noisy rooms, C, with bath, and slightly spartan, cheaper, cooler rooms without bath, very clean. *Fray Junipero Serra*, Lerdo Poniente 23, T 22525, C, main square, a/c, good restaurant, friendly, good service; *Villa de las Rosas*, Insurgentes 100, T 31800, C, fans, friendly, noisy in front, good food, but not too clean; *Tepic*, E, with bath, Dr Martínez 438, T 31377, near bus station outside town, clean, friendly but noisy; *Mayo*, near bus station, E, clean and bright; *Nayarit*, E. Zapata 190 Pte. T 22183, E; *Corita*, Insurgentes 298, T 20477, modern, E, free parking in locked yard, good reasonable restaurant, attractive gardens; *Pensión Morales*, Insurgentes y Sánchez, 4 blocks from bus station, E, clean and friendly. *Pensión Marí*, 3 blocks off Zócalo, E, with hot water, friendly, clean, very good value. Others on Zócalo, E. *Juárez*, E, near Palacio de Gobierno, on Juárez 116, T 22112, clean room with bath, locks on room doors not very effective, limited parking in courtyard; *Altamirano*, Mina 13 Oriente, T 27131, near Palacio del Gobierno, E, noisy but good value; *Sarita*, Bravo 112 Poniente, T 21333, clean, good, E; *Mexico*, México 116 Nte, E.

Motels *La Loma*, Paseo la Loma 301 (swimming pool), T 32222, B, run down; *Cora Motel Apartamentos Koala*, La Laguna, Santa María del Oro, has units for up to 3 people with kitchen and bathroom, and snack bar, US$6.50 per unit. Fishing and waterskiing on nearby lagoon.

Restaurants Two restaurants in Tepic, both on the outskirts of town, sell carne en su jugo estilo Guadalajara, delicious meat and bacon stew with beans in a spicy sauce, served with stewed onions. *El Tripol*, in mall, near plaza, excellent vegetarian; *Danny O* ice cream shop next door. Restaurant in bus terminal, overpriced. The local huevos rancheros are extremely picante.

Transport Bus to San Blas from Central Camionera: TNS, US$1, 5 or 6 a day; Tres Estrellas three a day, US$1.75. To Guadalajara, US$3, 1st class, 4-4½ hrs.; Mazatlán, 4½ hrs., US$4.25 (2nd class); to Puerto Vallarta, US$2.55; Mexico City, US$10.50; Torreón, US$12. Culiacán, 8¼ hrs., US$6.80. Train to Guadalajara, US$1.75 (2nd class), US$4.50 (1st) leaves at 1130, arrives at 1800, sit on left-hand side for best views. Train to Mexicali, 22-27 hrs., special 1st class, a/c, US$18; to Nogales, 19-23 hrs., ditto, US$16. (Same train to Benjamín Hill, leaving Tepic 1400, then divides). Airport.

Time Change There is a time change, forward one hour, between Tepic and most places inland, such as Guadalajara.

Excursions One can visit Huichol villages only by air, as there are no real roads, takes at least two days. Flight to a village, US$10 return. To various beaches along the coast, some of them off the Nogales highway. About 5 km. from Tepic is an attractive lagoon, take the bus to Santa Mariá del Oro. A road runs through Compostela, a pleasant small town with an old church (1539) (1½ hrs. by bus from local bus station at Tepic), to **Santa Cruz**, about 37 km. from Tepic (rocky beach). 2½ hrs. ride by open-sided lorry, US$0.50, difficult to leave the town again, check for transport. No hotels, but accommodation at *Peter's Shop*, F, basic but pleasant and friendly. Simple food available, *Restaurant Belmar*, fish and rice, all reminiscent of the South Seas. (2 buses a day from San Blas to Santa Cruz, US$0.70.) From Compostela one can also catch an old bus to **Zacualpan**, 1½ hrs. over a very rough dirt road, to visit a small enclosed park with sculptures that have been found in the area, two blocks from main square. Gate to the park must be unlocked by caretaker: inside there is a small museum. Zacualpan is a pleasant village, knock on a door to ask for the caretaker. Ninety km. (1¼ hrs. by bus) from Tepic on the main road to Guadalajara is **Ixtlan del Río** (*Hotel Colonial*, E, Hidalgo 45 Pte, very friendly, rec; cheaper hotels round the Zócalo are *Roma* and *Turista*). Two km. out of town along this road are the ruins of a Toltec ceremonial centre. The main structure is the Temple of Quetzalcoatl, noted for its cruciform windows and circular shape. The journey from Tepic to Guadalajara can easily be broken at Ixtlan with a couple of hours' sightseeing; bus on to Guadalajara 3 hours, US$1.60. There are a few souvenir shops and a museum; harvest (maize) festival mid-September; nearby (15 km.) village of Jalán has festival mid-August. *Hotel Cambero*, F, from here the Ceboruco volcano can be reached in a day.

Other beaches between Santa Cruz and Puerto Vallarta include Rincón de los Guayabitos, which is being developed as a tourist resort with hotels, holiday village and trailer park; Chacala, lined with coconut palms and reached by an unsurfaced road through jungle; and Canalán, near Las Varas, reached only on foot, isolated and beautiful.

The next state S is Jalisco. The state's cultural life has been helped by an economy based on crafts, agriculture, and livestock, with fewer pockets of abject poverty than elsewhere in Mexico. Many villages have traditional skills such as pottery, blown glass, shoemaking, and a curious and beautiful form of filigree weaving in which miniature flower baskets, fruit and religious images are shaped from *chilte* (chicle, the raw substance from which chewing-gum is made). The state is the original home of Mexico's *mariachis*: roving musical groups dressed in the gala suits and *sombreros* of early 19th century rural gentry.

N.B. There is a time change between Nayarit and Jalisco; the latter is 6 hours behind GMT, the former, as will all the Pacific coast N of Jalisco, 7 hours behind.

Puerto Vallarta (population 100,000), is reached by plane from Tepic, Tijuana, Los Angeles and Mexico City. The town is divided by the River Cuale and on one side are the expensive hotels, many shops, the airport and the port where the ferry arrives from San Lucas. On the other side of the river are the bus terminal and some cheaper hotels. Latest reports indicate that every house in the old town has been turned into a tourist trap, speculation is rampant with hotels and timeshare apartments, goods are at "US prices and Mexican quality", and taxi drivers are rapacious. It offers aquatic sports, particularly fishing and hunting for sharks. From the public beach you can hire parachuting equipment to be pulled by motor-boat (US$10). The Malecón is the waterfront drive. The beach at Puerto Vallarta is dirty, but there are better ones about 8-10 km. south along the coast, e.g. Mismaloya (reached by bus 02, US$0.30). There is a paved road from Tepic to Puerto Vallarta, continuing down the coast to Barra de Navidad and Manzanillo with excellent *Hotel Careyes*, A, en route, and several cheaper ones, including *El Tecuán* (D) and *Hotel Tenacatita* (A) near the village of the same name (**see page 123**), and further to Zihuatanejo and Acapulco, and finally to Salina Cruz.

Hotels Puerto Vallarta is divided naturally into 3 sections: N of town are: ***Playa de Oro***, T 20348, A; ***Fiesta Americana***, T 22010, L; ***Las Palmas***, T 20650, A; ***Plaza Vallarta***, T 24448, A; ***Bugambilias Sheraton***, T 23000, L; ***Puerto Vallarta Holiday Inn***, Av. de las Garzas, T 21700, A-L. In town are: ***Buenaventura***, México 1301, T 23742, A; ***Rosita***, very pleasantly situated, 5 min. bus ride to beaches on other side of town, swimming pool, C; ***Cuatro Vientos***, Matamoros 520, T 20161, C, lots of stairs; ***Central***, E, off main square; ***Paraíso***, Paseo Díaz Ordaz, on the sea but stony beach, E. South of Río Cuale are: ***Camino Real***, T 20002, L; ***Garza Blanca***, Playa Palo María, T 21023; ***Oro Verde***, Gómez 111, T 215553, A, a/c, Swiss run, private beach, pool, rec. as clean, pleasant, friendly; ***Posada Río Cuale***, excellent food, Serdán 242, swimming pool, a/c, C; ***Fontana del Mar***, Diéguez 171, C, attractive; ***Molino del Agua***, Vallarta 130, T 21907, A, beautiful, beside the new bridge, clean, a/c, good service, pool, rec.; ***Playa los Arcos***, Olas Altas 380, T 2-3102, B, on beach near bus station, highly rec; ***Villa del Mar***, Cárdenas 444, E, good; ***Ana Liz***, Madero 428, 3 blocks from sea, E, clean, comfortable, secure, small rooms; ***Posada de Roger***, C, Badillo 237, T 20039, good value, near two main city beaches, beware of thieves, popular with students.

Playa de Bucerías, Carretera Tepic Km. 154, D. Several *casas de huéspedes* in town near bus companies' offices, e.g. *Lima*, F. Cheap apartments: *La Peña*, Rodríguez 174.

Camping 2 trailer parks, 2 km. from centre on main road to the airport, US$4 p.p., showers, good, but a lot of mosquitoes. *Chico's Paradise*, in the village of Mismaloya, is a restaurant with cascades forming fresh-water pools where one can swim. Also at fishing village of Yelapa: camp under shelters (*palapas*), about US$4 each.

Restaurants The *Mercado Restaurant* is good and very cheap. *Mismaloya Beach* restaurant, excellent, US$2-4 for dinner (8 km. S of Puerto Vallarta). *Ostión Feliz*, Libertad 177, excellent seafood. *El Coral*, Olas Altas, good breakfast and *comida corrida. Carlos O'Brians*, beautifully decorated, popular, young clientèle. *Gilmar*, a cheap, typical restaurant; *Tequila*, upstairs for good breakfast and a good view of what is going on; *Tony's Please*, Encino y Hidalgo, near bridge, good, reasonable food. Very good ice-cream and frozen yoghurt is sold along the Malecón and at *Bing's* near central plaza. Puerto Vallarta has an active night life, with many bars and discotheques.

Shopping Plaza Malecón, near *Hotel Río*, end of Malecón, has 28 curio shops, restaurant, music, etc.

Tourist Office In the government building on the main square, very helpful.

Buses By Sonora del Norte, Estrella Blanca and Autobuses del Pacífico, to Mexico City, 15-20 hrs. US$13. Puerto Vallarta to Guadalajara, US$4.75 1st class, 6 hrs.; to Manzanillo, US$3.55, midnight, Transportes Cihuatlan, Constitución y Francisco J. Madero.

Air Travel International airport 7 km. from centre.

Warning Those confined to wheelchairs are warned that Puerto Vallarta is a bad place, with its high kerbs and cobblestone streets.

Excursions To Yelapa, Indian village with waterfall, now commercialized; by boat US$5, or more cheaply from the Malecón at 1130 by the local boat. Stay with Mateo and Elenita, US$25 inc. breakfast, visit their waterfall.

Tequila (58 km. from Guadalajara), on the Tepic-Guadalajara road, is the main place where the famous Mexican drink is distilled, from the *maguey* cactus. Tours of Cuerva (free) and Sauza (small tip) distilleries off the highway. The Sauza distillery has a famous fresco illustrating the joys of drinking tequila. Half-way between Tequila and Guadalajara, in the mountains, is the British-run *Rancho Río Caliente*, 8 km. from the highway, a vegetarian thermal resort.

Guadalajara, Mexico's second city and capital of Jalisco state; altitude 1,650 metres, and slightly warmer than at the capital; population, 1,626,000 in 1980, but now reported as up to 4 million, and 573 km. from Mexico City, was founded in 1530. It used to be a fine, clean city, not unlike the towns of southern Spain, but pollution has now grown. Graceful colonial arcades, or *portales*, flank scores of old plazas and shaded parks. The climate is mild, dry and clear all through the year, although it can be thundery at night. A pedestrian mall, Plaza Tapatía, has been installed between the Cabañas Orphanage and the Degollado Theatre, crossing the Calzada Independencia, covering 16 square

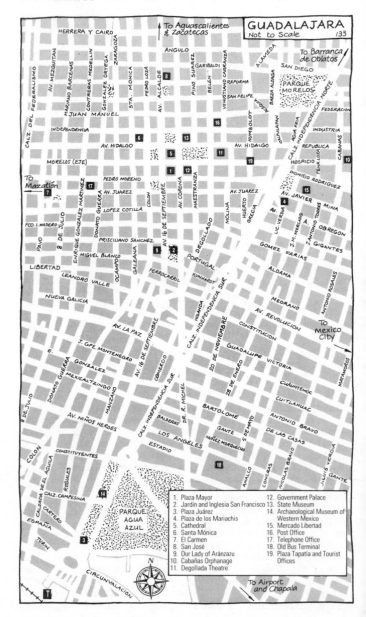

HERRERA Y CAIRO
ANGULO
To Barranca
de Oblatos
ZARAGOZA
AV. MEZQUITAN
MARIANO BARCENAS
CONTRERAS MEDELLIN
GONZALEZ ORTEGA
STA. MONICA
PEDRO LOZA
AV. ALCALDE
PINO SUAREZ
GARIBALDI
BELEN
VENUSTIANO CARRANZA
ALAMEDA
BAEZA AIZAGA
SAN DIEGO
PARQUE
MORELOS
CALZ. DEL FEDERALISMO
JUAN MANUEL
REFORMA
SAN FELIPE
ZALATIPAN
AGUA FRIA
FEDERACION
INDEPENDENCIA
HUMBOLDT
INDUSTRIA
CALZ. INDEPENDENCIA NORTE
REPUBLICA
CABANAS
To
Mazatlán
MORELOS (EJE)
AV. HIDALGO
AV. HIDALGO
HOSPICIO
PEÑA UIZA
DIONISIO RODRIGUEZ
PEDRO MORENO
AV. JUAREZ
AV. JUAREZ
AV. JAVIER
AV. VERDA
MINA
LOPEZ COTILLA
MOLINA
HUERTO
GRECIA
A. OBREGON
J.M. MERCADO
A. ANTONIO TORRES
FCO. I. MADERO
ENRIQUE GONZALEZ MARTINEZ
DONATO GUERRA
AV. CORONA
MAESTRANZA
COLON
AV. 16 DE SEPTIEMBRE
PRISCILIANO SANCHEZ
LIC. VERDA
J.H. GIGANTES
PAVO
DE JULIO
MIGUEL BLANCO
GALEANA
OCAMPO
DEGOLLADO
PORTUGAL
GOMEZ FARIAS
ALDAMA
LIBERTAD
LEANDRO VALLE
FERROCARRIL
KUNHARDT
MEDRANO
ANTONIO ROSALES
NUEVA GALICIA
HIDALGA
AV. REVOLUCION
To
Mexico
City
AV. LA PAZ
CALZ. INDEPENDENCIA SUR
20 DE NOVIEMBRE
CONSTITUCION
J. GPE. MONTENEGRO
GUADALUPE VICTORIA
E.
GONZALEZ
DONATO GUERRA
MEXICALTZINGO
AV. 16 DE SEPTIEMBRE
COMERCIO
MANZANO
25 DE ENERO
CUAUHTEMOC
MATAMOROS
AV. NIÑOS HEROES
CALZ. INDEPENDENCIA SUR
DR. R. MICHEL
BARTOLOME
CUITLAHUAC
ANTONIO BRAVO
DE JULIO
COLON
CONSTITUYENTES
REGULES
BALDERAS
GANTE
NUÑEZ MORQUECHO
LOS ANGELES
ESTADIO
DE LAS CASAS
5 BENITO
NICOLAS BRAVO
JULIUS VERDIA
CALZADA DE EL AGUILA
CALZ. CAMPESINA
CARTERO
ESPAÑA
TURIN
PARQUE
AGUA
AZUL
ANALCO
CONCHAS
GANTE
CIRCUNVALACION
To Airport
and Chapala

1. Plaza Mayor
2. Jardín and Inglesia San Francisco
3. Plaza Juárez
4. Plaza de los Mariachis
5. Cathedral
6. Santa Mónica
7. El Carmen
8. San José
9. Our Lady of Aránzazu
10. Cabañas Orphanage
11. Degollada Theatre
12. Government Palace
13. State Museum
14. Archaeological Museum of Western Mexico
15. Mercado Libertad
16. Post Office
17. Telephone Office
18. Old Bus Terminal
19. Plaza Tapatía and Tourist Offices

blocks. It has beautiful plants, fountains, statuary, a tourist office, and is designed in colonial style. The best shops are all found in or near the Plaza Mayor (Plaza de los Tres Poderes) and the Avenida Juárez. The Plaza del Sol shopping centre, with over 100 shops, is located at the S end of the city, while the equally modern Plaza Patria, with as many shops, is at the N end near the Zapopán suburb. The city is developing to the W across the Av. Chapultepec, there are many elegant buildings and shopping malls such as the Galeriá del Galzado, selling as the name implies, only shoes.

The Plaza Mayor is flanked by the Government Palace (1643) where in 1810 Hidalgo issued his first proclamation abolishing slavery (plaque). Orozco's great murals can be seen on the central staircase. In the main University of Guadalajara building, on Av. Juárez Tolsa, is the dome in which is portrayed man asleep, man meditating, and man creating, lie on your back or look in a mirror. Other works by this artist can be seen at the University's main Library, at Glorieta Normal, and at the massive Cabañas Orphanage near the Mercado de la Libertad (now known as Instituto Cultural Cabañas, housing, among other cultural attractions, Orozco's "Man of Fire"). The Orphanage is a beautiful building with 22 patios, which is floodlit at night (entry US$0.40). The contents of the former Orozco museum in Mexico City have also been transferred to Guadalajara. Between the Cabañas and the Mercado Libertad is a park, with a fine modern sculpture "The Stampede", by Jorge de la Peña (1982).

On the Plaza Mayor also is the Cathedral, begun in 1561, finished in 1618, in rather a medley of styles; there is no longer admission to the tower (the structure has been declared dangerous), where remarkable frescoes were recently discovered half-way up. There is a reputed Murillo Virgin inside (painted 1650), and the famous La Virgen del Carmen, painted by Miguel de Cabrera, a Zapotec Indian from Oaxaca. NE of the Cathedral is the State Museum (US$0.50, closed Mon.) in an old seminary (1700) with a good, prehistoric section (including the complete skeleton of a mammoth found in Jaliso) and interesting display of "hidden" tombs, excellent display of Colima and Jalisco terracotta figures, and possibly the finest display of colonial art in Mexico outside the Museo Virreinal in Mexico City (highly rec.). Two blocks E is the enormous and fantastically decorated Degollado Theatre (1866), half-price for students on Sats, University *ballet folklórico*, Sun. 1000, US$8, highly rec. There is an Archaeological Museum of Western Mexico on Plaza Juárez, open Mon.-Sat. 0900-1300 and 1600-1800, free. A school of crafts (ceramics, glass weaving, leatherwork) is on Alcalde and Avila Camacho; and there is also the Albarrán hunting museum, Paseo de los Parques 3530, Colinas de San Javier, Sat. and Sun. 1000-1400, with a collection of rare animals from all over the world.

The best churches are Santa Mónica (1718), with a richly carved façade; El Carmen, with a main altar surrounded by gilded Corinthian columns, San José, a 19th century church with a fine gilded rococo pulpit, San Miguel de Belén, enclosed in the Hospital Civil which contains three fine late 18th century *retablos*, and San Francisco (1550). To the N of this last church is the quite exquisite Jardín San Francisco, and to the W the old church of Our Lady of Aránzazu, with three fantastic churrigueresque altarpieces; in its shadow is a modern statue to teachers. María de Gracia, V. Carranza y Hidalgo, is beautiful. There are 3 universities (visit architectural faculty near Parque Mirador, 20 mins. by car from centre, or take bus 45 overlooking Barranca de Oblatos, a huge canyon), a Cultural Institute with contemporary arts displays and a film theatre (US$0.50), and a ticket office for Teatro Azul, and an open-air theatre, Auditorio Gonzalo Cunel. Other sights worth seeing are the Agua Azul park, now reported full of litter and swimming pools dirty; dances on Sun. at 1700, flower market, handicrafts shop; and the Parque Alcalde in the middle of the city. The markets, in particular the Libertad (San Juan de Dios) which has colourful items for souvenirs with lots of Michoacán crafts including Paracho guitars and Sahuayo hats, leather jackets, and delicious food upstairs on the 1st level (particularly goat meat, *birria*, also *cocada*), but expensive soft drinks (check prices before sitting down or you will be grossly overcharged as tourists), muggings have been reported, do not venture too far inside; the *tianguis* (Indian market) on Av. Guadalupe, Colonia Chapalita, on Fri. is of little interest to foreigners, bus 50 gets you there; the *tianguis* near the University Sports Centre on Calzada Tlaquepaque on Sundays; the Plaza de Los Mariachis, Obregón and Leonardo Vicario, near La Libertad; the Templo Expiatorio, with fine stained glass and intricate ceiling, gothic style, still unfinished after most of a century. There is a new, large park, zoological garden and planetarium just past the bullring going out on Av. Independencia.

Festivals 21 March commemorates Benito Juárez' birthday and everything is closed for the day. Ceremonies around his monument at the Agua Azul park. In June the virgin of Zapopán (see **Excursions** below), leaves her home to spend each night in a different church where fireworks are let off. The virgin has a new car each year but the engine is not started, men pull it through the streets with ropes, the streets are decorated. The climax is 12 October when the virgin leaves the Cathedral for home, there are great crowds along the route. At the end of October there is a great *fiesta* with concerts, bullfights, sports and exhibitions of handicrafts from all over Mexico. 28 October—20 December, *fiesta* in honour of the Virgin of Guadalupe; Av. Alcalde has stalls, music, fair etc. In December there is one at Parque Morelos and hand-made toys are a special feature.

Hotels Many in our price ranges B and up, including: *Fiesta Americana*, López Mateos at Minerva circle, T 253434, L; *Quinta Real*, Av. México y López Mateos, T 520000, small, A, good but slow restaurant; *Camino Real*, Vallarta 5005, T 478000, L, some way from the centre; *Francés*, Maestranza 35, T 131190, B; *Calinda Quality Inn Roma*, Juárez 170, T 148650, B; *El Tapatío*, Bld. Aeropuerto 3275, T 546050 (in Tlaquepaque, fine view of city), A; *Holiday Inn*, Av. López Mateos opp. Plaza del Sol, shopping centre, T 315566, L, restaurant, night club, etc., *Ana Isabel*, Javier Mina 184, D, central, TV, clean, very good value, tell them when you are checking out or room may be relet before you have gone. *Génova*, Juárez 123, T 137500, C, clean, good service, good restaurant, rec.; *Internacional*, Pedro Moreno 570, T 130330, D, clean, comfortable, safe, rec; *Universo*, López Cotilla 163, T 132825, D, somewhat run down; *Nueva Galicia*, D, older style, Av. Corona 610; T 132458, *Sevilla*, Prisciliano Sánchez 413, D, good, clean (4 blocks S of cathedral), owner speaks English, good restaurant (not always open).

Tres Estrellas, cheap, rooms on the street noisy, all rooms with bath, restaurant and garage, Calzada Independencia Sur 667 (restaurant closed in January), F. *Estación*, Calzada Independencia Sur 1297, T 190051, 2 blocks from train station, quiet, clean, safe, hot water, rec., station porters will carry luggage there US$0.50-1. There are cheap hotels along Calzada Independencia and in the two blocks N of the old bus station, Calle 28 de Enero and Calle 20 de Noviembre (where there is a small market, good for breakfasts) and the side streets (although rooms can sometimes be filthy, so check), many are said to have gone out of business since the long-distance bus station moved; they include *San José*, *San Carlos*, *Madrid*, *Señorial*, *Central*, *Cónsul*, *Monaco* (rooms on street very noisy), *Emperador de Occidente*, *Praga*, *Celta*, *Lincoln*, all E-F, all rec. *Reno*, Calle Independencia 482, E, clean, front rooms a bit noisy otherwise rec. *Calzada*, Calzada Independencia Sur, good value but loud TV and electronic games, F; *León*, Calzada Independencia Sur 557, D, clean, shower, ask for room at back. *Casa de Huéspedes Norteña*, Calle 28 de Enero, F, without bath, clean, room to wash clothes in patio. *Nayarit*, F, not very clean, some rooms better than others, Los Angeles 231Aa; *Pacífico*, Los Angeles 27, nice clean rooms, E.

Cheaper hotels in the centre, and near Mercado Libertad: *Hamilton*, E, clean and central, but cockroaches abound, tin doors, buses noisy from 0630, at Madero 381; *González*, behind Mercado Corona, 4 blocks W of cathedral, González Ortega 77, good value, E, often full, very friendly, highly rec.; *Continental*, and *Morales*, both on Calle Corona, E, rec. (but others of similar quality cheaper), often fully booked. *Posada San Pablo*, Madero 268, F, hot water, rec.; *Posada de la Plata*, López Cotilla y Ocho de Julio, in centre, E, large rooms, shower, clean, 2 rooms in poor condition, if offered ask to see another; *Maya*, López Cotilla 39, E with private bath, blankets, pleasant atmosphere, rec.; *Posada España*, López Cotillo, E with bath, nice courtyard, washing facilities, but extremely noisy, helpful manager; *Las Américas*, E, Calle Hidalgo, friendly and clean. *Janeiro*, Obregón 93, by market, clean, F, good value, clean; *México 70*, Javier Mina, opp. Mercado Libertad, E with bath, clean, rec.; *Azteca*, 1½ blocks from Mercado Libertad, clean, F.

Motels *Isabel*, Montenegro 1572, sector Hidalgo, T 26-26-30, C, pool; *Del Bosque*, L. Mateos Sur 265, T 214020, B; *Las Américas*, López Mateos Sur 2400, T 213857, opp. Plaza del Sol shopping centre, B, a/c, pool, good; *Posada del Sol*, López Mateos Sur 4205, T 210120/71, B. There are additional ones at the end of Vallarta: Vallarta 3305, T 155725, B; and along López Mateos near the edge of town, before the *periférico* road.

Youth Hostel CREA at Prolongación Alcalde 1360, Sector Hidalgo, T 24-62-65, away from centre, dirty, many mosquitoes. Bus from centre: Mezquitera, from bus terminal, No. 133, or No. 216 from Cathedral.

Restaurants *Gerardo*, on Calle La Paz, main dish about US$5, and *La Vianda*, just off López Mateos Sur by Plaza del Angel, are reported best. *La Concordia*, P. Moreno 1679, good seafood; *El Farol*, Pedro Moreno y Galeana, excellent dinner US$5; *El Tío Juan*, Independencia Norte 2246, local meat dishes including goat; Mexican specialities also at *Caballo Blanco*, López Mateos Sur 700; local country fare at *Ahualulco Campestre*, 20 de Noviembre 122A; *Jacques* (in Lafayette Park); *Guadalajara Grill*, López Mateos Sur, excellent meat and music; *El Tirol* on Duque de Rivas, Sector Hidalgo, excellent steak; *Café Makoka*, Martínez, just north of Hidalgo, excellent very early breakfasts; *Holiday Inn* does grills on Sun., 1300-1700. *Carnes Asadas Tolsa*, Tolsa 510 and Chapultepec 189, rec.

Bazar de la Salud, López Cotilla 608, good vegetarian shop; round the corner on Juárez is *La Naturaleza*, also vegetarian, both closed Sun. *Megga*, Prisciliano Sánchez 413, good bread and vegetarian food; *Zanahoria*, Av. Las Américas 538, for excellent, but expensive vegetarian food; good vegetarian buffet at *La Pileca*, US$1, Colonias 279, San Javier, open 1000-1730; *Los Caias*, Tepeyac 1156, vegetarian coffee shop and cultural centre.

Good but expensive Japanese restaurant, *Suchiro*. *Restaurant and Pastry Shop Suiza*, Vallarta 1519, good breakfast and coffee, rec.; *Don Tomasito*, Vidrio 1688 y Argentina, Jaliscan dishes, very good, unpretentious. *Café de la Parroquia*, Enrique González 25-2, good comidas (US$1.25) and breakfasts. *Agora*, in ex-Convento del Carmen, on Juárez, good for fish. *Madrid*, Juárez y Corona, good breakfast; *Mesón de Sancho Panza* on park where Calzada Federalismo and Av. Juárez bisect, good five-course meals and Mexican wines. *Las Banderillas* on Av. Alcalde, excellent roast meat, always open, try cerdo adobado (marinated pork) guacamole and cebollitas (onions). Cheap meals at *El Bordo*, Calle Independencia and at the *Fonda Vieja Mexicali* at No. 391 (Sur) of the same street. Many cheap restaurants in the streets near the bus stations, esp. in Calle de Los Angeles, and upstairs in the large market in centre. *Nino's*, Av. México and Manuel, reasonable and good; *Alpes*, Calle López Cotilla, German food, inexpensive. *Jeanine*, Plaza Lapatio, cheap very good meals; *Café Medoka*, nearby, very cheap Mexican food, popular with locals, service slow; *La Herradura*, Calle Estadio next to *Hotel Terminal* across from bus terminal, good carne asada. In Tlaquepaque, Dayton Herzog runs *El Restaurant sin Nombre*, on Fco. Madero, excellent food and drink out of doors, with singing waiters. In the cloister of La Merced is a fast food place, popular with young people; *La Chata* and *Gemma*, 2 chains serving Mexican food, are usually quite good (*Gemma* does Guadalajaran "lonches", tortas ahogadas). Delicious carne en su jugo from *Carnes Asadas El Tapatío* in Libertad or San Juan de Dios markets, or *Carnes Asadas Rigo's* in Corona market, Zaragoza y Independencia, US$2-2.50 with a refresco. Many bars serve snacks, botanas, with drinks between 1300 and 1500, free, e.g. *Pancho S.A.* (best) on Maestranza 179, several blocks from the Libertad market. Most of these bars are for men only, though. **N.B.** The bars in the centre are popular with the city's gay population.

Crafts Two glass factories at *Tlaquepaque* nearby where the blue, green, amber and amethyst blown-glass articles are made; visit the shop of Sergio Bustamante, who sells his own work: expensive but well worth a look, a stream runs through this colonial house. Also, the Casa de los Telares (Calle de Hidalgo 1378), where Indian textiles are woven on hand looms. Potters can be watched at work both in Guadalajara and at Tlaquepaque; you may find better bargains at Tonalá (pottery and ceramics), 15 km. SW of Guadalajara on the road to Mexico City, but no glass there; take bus 110, bumpy ½ hr. journey. Overall, Tlaquepaque is the cheapest and most varied source of the local crafts, with attractive shops set in old colonial villas; best buys: glass, papier mâché goods, leather (cheapest in Mexico), and ceramics. Casa de Artesanías, edge of Agua Azul park, high quality display (and sale) of handicrafts. There is another shop-cum-exhibition at the Instituto de Artesanía Jaliscense, México 54, extension of the Avenida Alcalde and Avila Camacho. Look out for leather belts with sewn-on tapestry. Parián is a covered commercial area with a whole variety of restaurants, music and handicraft shops, Calle Grecia, off Juárez. See also the Tienda Tlaquepaque, at Av. Juárez 267-B, in Tlaquepaque, T 35-56-63.

Car Rental Niños Héroes opp. *Sheraton*: Quick, Budget, National, Avis, Ford and Odin. Others scattered throughout the city.

Entertainment Folk dances every Sun. at 1000 in the Degollado Theatre; concerts and theatre in the ex-Convento del Carmen; concert every Thurs. and Sun. at 1900 in the Plaza de Armas, in front of the Palacio de Gobierno, free. Organ recitals in the Cathedral. *Peña Cuicalli*, Sector Juárez, López Cotilla 1225 with Atenas, opens 2000, small cover charge, food and drink available, fills up fast—local groups perform folk and protest songs. Music also at *La Peña* on Avenida Unión.

Sport Bullfights: October to March; football throughout year; *Charreadas* are held in mid-September at Unión de San Antonio; *Charreada* (cowboy show) near Agua Azul Park at Aceves Calindo Lienzo, Sun. at 1200. Baseball, April-Sept.; golf at: Santa Anita, 16 km. out on Morelia road, championship course; Rancho Contento, 10 km. out on Nogales road; San Isidro, 10 km. out on Saltillo road, noted for water hazards; Areas, 8 km. out on Chapala road.

Exchange Houses There are many *casas de cambio* on López Cotilla between Independencia and 16 de Septiembre. American Express, López Mateos Norte 430, open Sat. at 0930.

British Vice-Consul Mr S Cohen, Calz. González Gallo 1897, Apartado postal 32-94, T (91-36) 358295/358927.

Cultural Institutes US at Tolsa 300; British at Tomás V. Gómez 125, Sector Hidalgo, T 160268, closed between 1200 and 1600. Benjamin Franklin Library, Libertad 1492, US papers and magazines.

Spanish Classes Centro de Estudios para Extranjeros, Apto. Postal T 3392, lodging found with families, tuition, 5 weeks US$220 plus US$50 for registration.

Post Office V. Carranza, just behind Hall of Justice. **Telephone** from Teléfonos de México.

Laundromat Aldama 125, US$2 per load (walk along Independencia towards train station, turn left into Aldama).

Tourist Office Federal tourist office Paseo Degollado 44, Edif. Occidente, Plaza Tapatía, T 148665; state office Av. Juarez 638, opens after 1700, information on everything, maps, helpful. Instituto Nacional de Estadística, Geografía e Informática, Av. Alcalde 788, T 913614, for maps and information.

Rail Ticket office in town, López Cotilla 163. National Railways to Mexico City and Manzanillo. Mexico City-Guadalajara Tapatío (*servicio estrella*) leaves the capital 0840, arr. 0810, returns 2055, US$12.65 reclining seat, US$23.85 single sleeper, US$47.65 double. Colimense *servicio estrella* connects with Tapatío at 0900 for Manzanillo (7 hrs., US$7.80), 5½ hrs. to Colima. The ordinary train from Mexico City to Guadalajara leaves at 0930 and 1900 daily, 14-18 hrs., US$6.50 (1st class), US$3.85 (2nd class, which often sells out early; you need to be at the station 4 hours before the train leaves, to be sure of a seat). Train Guadalajara-Irapuato (US$1.70 2nd class) leaves at 0700, which connects there with the train to Mexico City from the north. Train to Mexicali, 0930 (*servicio estrella*), 28 hrs., ordinary 1200, 44 hrs. Daily trains to Los Reyes (change at Yurécuaro) and Manzanillo. Train to Mazatlán (book well in advance) 1st class and Pullman at 0910, US$3 and US$6 respectively. All classes on 1330 train, 2nd class US$2 (price difference really shows). Journey Guadalajara-Colima, US$1.40, 2nd class, 7 hours, worth taking because scenery between Ciudad Guzmán and Colima is spectacular. Train to Tepic leaves 0930, Primera Especial US$5.

Warning Do not accept cups of coffee at the station however friendly or insistent the offer is, they may be drugged. If possible avoid arriving at night.

Airport Miguel Hidalgo, 20 km. from town; fixed rate for 3 city zones and 3 classes of taxi: *especial, semi-especial* and colectivo—no tip necessary. Bus No. 71 from 1st class entrance at Terminal de Autobuses, US$0.20; VW buses, Calle Federalismo Sur No. 915, "servicio terrestre", US$2.50 p.p. Eight flights daily to and from Mexico City, 50 mins.

Bus New bus station near the El Alamo cloverleaf, 14 km from centre; minibus outside each building goes to centre, one block from San Francisco, US$0.15; taxi US$4.50. Bus No. 104 from Independencia, or colectivo from Av. Niños Heroes or Independencia Sur, US$0.20, also No. 275 along 16 de Septiembre; buses for people with luggage leave parking lot in front of the old bus terminal and go direct to the new terminal. It helps to know which company you wish to travel with as their offices are spread over a large area. Fixed price taxis, buy ticket at the bus terminal. To Uruapan, US$3, 2nd class, 6 hrs., with Estrella de Oro before 0900 and at 1500, with ADO, many departures, comfortable journey, 5 hrs., US$3, with Flecha Amarilla about 7 hrs.; departures every hour until midnight; with Norte de Sonora to Mazatlán, 9½ hrs., US$6; Ciudad Obregón, 15 hrs., US$13; Hermosillo, 19 hrs., US$17; Mexicali, 32 hrs., US$25; Tijuana, 36 hrs., US$28 and Ciudad Juárez, US$30, 1st class (15 hrs.) with Omnibus de México; Mexico City, US$7.70 1st class, US$6.80 2nd class, leave every hr., 8 hrs., much of road under repair; Nogales, US$15, 26 hrs.; Zihuatanejo, US$8, 12 hrs. (2nd class); Guanajuato 3 1st class, US$4.20, 2nd class hourly, US$4, 5 hrs. To Durango, US$6. To Morelia, every hour until midnight, 1st class US$6, 2nd US$4. Manzanillo, US$5, 6 hrs., Pátzcuaro, US$4, 4 a day, otherwise change at Quiroga, 6 hrs, a new road is being constructed, when open the journey will be cut by 1-1½ hrs. Interesting journey to Zacatecas, but Autobuses de México front window is half painted. To Querétaro, US$5, 7 hrs.; to Colima, US$3, 4 hrs.; to Chapala US$1. To Puerto Vallarta by Estrella Blanca, US$4.75, 6 hrs. To Nuevo Laredo with Transportes de Norte at 1800, express US$12.25, 13½ hrs. Local buses to anywhere in the city US$0.80.

The old central bus station, Los Angeles y 28 Enero, has re-opened serving towns within 100 km., this should cut time to reach Lake Chapala. Bus No. 222 goes to the old bus station.

Excursions 8 km. to the canyon of Barranca de Oblatos, 600 metres deep, reached by bus 42 and others from the market to end of line (admission US$0.05), with the Río Santiago cascading at the bottom (except in dry season). Guides to the bottom. Once described as a stupendous site; now reported made hideous by littering and sewage. See especially the Cola de Caballo waterfall and the Parque Mirador Dr All. Park crowded on Sunday; Balneario Los Comachos, a large swimming pool with diving boards set on one side of the Barranca de Oblatos, has many terraces with tables and chairs and barbecue pits under mango trees; drinks and snacks on sale; now descibed as dirty. Entry US$1.50. Also to Barranca de Huentitán, in the canyon of the River Lerma, access via the Mirador de Huentitán at the end of Calzada Independencia Norte, interesting flora, tremendous natural site, but also spoilt by litter. 1 hr. to the bottom (no guide needed) and the River Lerma which is straddled by the historic bridge of Huentitán. Buses to Huentitán: 42 "Jonilla Centro" from city centre; 44 "Sevilo C. Médico", stops 100 m. short. All buses cost US$0.05.

In a NW suburb of Guadalajara are the Basílica de Zapopán, with a miraculous image of Nuestra Señora on the main altar, given to the Indians in 1542, and a museum of Huichol Indian art (agricultural fair in Nov.). Zapopán is reached by taking the system of underground trolley buses, known as the *metro*, which also goes to Tlaquepaque, as far as the Avila Camacho station, then any bus marked Zapopán. En route for Tepic is the Bosque de Primavera, reached by town buses. Pine forests ideal for picnics, although increasingly littered; US$0.50 for a swim.

"From Guadalajara to Irapuato: via Tepatitlán (79 km, on the León road), a small unfinished market town with a *charro* centre, in an impressive setting with steep hills all around; Arandas has a curious neo-gothic church and a pleasant square with a white wrought-iron bandstand; the road then winds tightly up over a range of hills and then down into a long and heavily cultivated valley. Five-hour journey." writes Tim Connell.

Lake Chapala, 64 km. to the south-east, is near the town of Sayula from which D. H. Lawrence took the name when he wrote about Chapala in "The Plumed Serpent" (return 1st class bus fare to the lake US$2, every ½ hr, 1 hr. journey). There is an *Aldea India*, Indian settlement, on the Chapala road, with murals of the history of Jalisco.

Chapala town, on the northern shore of Lake Chapala (113 km. long, 24 to 32 wide), has thermal springs, several good and pricey hotels, 3 golf courses, helpful tourist office at Hidalgo 227, and is a popular resort particularly with moneyed North Americans. Watch women and children play a picture-card game called *Anachuac*. "The house in which Lawrence wrote his novel still stands at Zaragoza 307, although a second floor and some modernization have been added. The church that figures in the last pages of "The Plumed Serpent" still stands on the waterfront, its humble façade and interior now covered by a handsome veneer of carved stone," writes Robert Schmitz, of Chapala. The lake is set in beautiful scenery. There are boats of all kinds for hire, water-fowl shooting in autumn and winter, sailing, and the lake teems with freshwater fish. Not much swimming because the water isn't very clean. On the Fiesta de Francisco de Asís (Oct. 2-3) fireworks are displayed and excellent food served in the streets. Horses for hire on the beach, bargain.

Chagas disease was reported in the region round the Laguna de Sayula in 1989; see **Health Information** at the front of the book.

Hotels *Nido*, only one in town, D, clean, noisy, sparse furnishings, good restaurant, good swimming pool; *Chapala Haciendas*, Km. 40, Chapala-Guadalajara highway, D. Good discotheque, *Pantera Rosa*.

Ajijic, 7 km. to the W, a smaller, once Indian village, has an arty-crafty American colony. *Hotel Danza del Sol*, T 52505, B; *Posada Ajijic* is a pleasant place to stay, T 52523, from D, some rooms with fireplace, nice garden; *Las Casitas*, apartments, E (just outside Ajijic, at Carretera Puente 20). Try the *Teheban* bar for entertainment. Restaurant: *Italo*. The Way of the Cross and a Passion Play are given at Easter in a chapel high above the town. Bus from Chapala, US$0.45. Beyond Ajijic is the Indian town of **Jocotepec**, a sizeable agricultural centre (recently invaded by more cosmopolitan types) on the lake; there is a local *fiesta* on 11-18 January. Stay at *La Naranjita*, built 1828 as coaching inn, good food, and an art shop. *Hotel Olmedo*, E, opposite police chief's house. *Casa de huéspedes* on Calle Matamoros 83 (same street as bus station), E, with bath, modern facilities. *Ramón's Bar*, popular drinking place. Jocotepec can be reached from Ajijic or from the Mexico-Guadalajara highway. Bus Chapala-Jocotepec US$1, every hour in each direction. The Indians make famous black-and-white *sarapes*. Nearby is the *Motel El Pescador*. Between Ajijic and Jocotepec lies the small town of **San Juan Cosalá**, with thermal springs at *Balnearios y Suites Cosalá*, which has private rooms for bathing with large tiled baths. Sunbathing in private rooms also possible. Rooms to let at *Balneario Paraíso*, F. Bus service from Chapala.

About 130 km. S of Guadalajara off the road to Sayula and Ciudad Guzmán (*Hotel Flamingo*, nr. main square, D, excellent value, very modern, very clean, and quiet), is **Tapalpa**, very pretty indeed. 3½ hours' drive from Guadalajara. The bus has several detours into the hills to stop at small places such as Zacoalco (Sunday market) and Amacueca. The road up to Tapalpa is winding and climbs sharply; the air becomes noticeably cooler and the place is becoming increasingly popular as a place for weekend homes. The town itself, with only 11,000 inhabitants, shows ample signs of this influx of prosperity. There are two churches (one with a curious atrium) and an imposing flight of stone steps between them, laid out with fountains and ornamental lamps. Tapalpa is in cattle country; the rodeo is a popular sport at weekends.

The main street is lined with stalls, selling *sarapes* and other tourist goods on Sundays and fresh food the other days of the week. The more expensive restaurants have tables on balconies overlooking the square—the *Restaurante Posada Hacienda* (which has a US$1 cover charge) is well placed. Others are the *Buena Vista* (which also has rooms) and *La Cabaña*, and all are visited by the mariachis. Less grand is the *Hotel Tapalpa*, E, but clean and fairly cheap. Some rooms are for hire (*Bungalows Rosita*). The only local speciality is *ponche*, an improbable blend of tamarind and mescal which is sold in gallon jars and rec. only for the curious or foolhardy. If you are planning a day trip get your return ticket as soon as you arrive as the last bus back to Guadalajara (1800 on Sundays) is likely to be full.

Manzanillo has become an important port on the Pacific, since a spectacular 257-km. railway has been driven down the sharp slopes of the Sierra Madre through Colima. The road from Guadalajara is via Jal. 33 to Ciudad Guzmán and on to Manzanillo. Occupations for tourists at Manzanillo (population, 150,000) include deep-sea fishing, bathing, and walking in the hills. There is a bullring on the outskirts on the road to Colima. The best beach is the lovely crescent of Santiago, 8 km. N, but there are three others (San Pedrito beach is oily, convenient, refreshments available). Airport.

Hotels *Club Las Hadas*, L, a Moorish fantasy; *Roca del Mar*, Playa Azul, T 21990, vacation centre, A; *Las Brisas Vacation Club*, D, Av. L. Cárdenas, T 20306, some a/c, good restaurant; *La Posada*, Calz. L. Cárdenas 201, T 22404, A, US manager. On Plaza: *Savoy*, SW corner, big clean rooms with cold water, good views, F, rec. At Santiago beach: *Playa de Santiago*, T 30344, B, good but food expensive; *Parador Marbella*, D, including breakfast and dinner; *Anita*, D, built in 1940 it suffers from Mexican maintenance disease but is said to have a certain funky charm and it is clean and on the beach. At the port: *Colonial*, good restaurant, México 100, C, friendly; also *Colonial*, 10 de Mayo, E; *Flamingos*, 10 de Mayo y Madería, T 21037, E with bath, quite good; *Emperador*, Davalos 69, E, good value. *Medina*, México 133, E; *Pacífico*, E, with bath, also on Calle México. *Casa de Huéspades Posada Jardín*, Cuauhtémoc, reasonable, E; *Casa de Huéspedes Corona*, next to bus station, basic, clean, cold water. Camping at Miramar and Santiago beaches.

Tourist Office Juárez 244, 4th floor, helpful.

Transport Bus to Miramar, US$0.20, leaves from J. J. Alcaraz, "El Tajo". Autocamiones del Pacífico bus, 1st class to Guadalajara, US$4, 6 hrs. To Mexico City with Autobus de Occidente, 19 hrs., 2nd class, US$8.80. To Guadalajara, US$5, 6 hrs., less when the new road is completed; to Barra de Navidad, US$0.80, 1½ hrs.; to Colima, US$1.50; to Tijuana, bus US$48, 1st class, 36 hrs. Down coast to Lázaro Cárdenas and crossroads for Playa Azul (**see page** 212) by Autobus de Occidente or Galeana, US$4.50, 7 hrs. Bus terminal in Av. Hidalgo outside centre, local buses go there. Train to Guadalajara Colimense *servicio estrella* at 1300 (7 hrs., US$7.80) or daily at 0600, US$1.50. For minibus to the airport T 3-24-70, US$3.50 from the beach.

Another Route to Manzanillo Turn off Mexico City highway 35 km. S of Guadalajara and continue 270 km. S to Melaque bay and the village of **Barra de Navidad** (commercial but still pleasant; *Hotel Barra de Navidad*, with balcony on beach, D, or bungalows, US$6.60, where you can cook; *Delfín*, D, very clean, pool, hot water, highly rec; *Bosantes*, on beach, E with bath, clean, good value; at *Alice's Restaurant*, E, simple food; *Hotel Jalisco*, E, hot water, safe and clean; ask about camping on beach; fish restaurants e.g. *Antonio* on beach), where there is a monument to the Spanish ships which set out in 1648 to conquer the Philippines. Avoid oil spillages on beach. This road is paved. Pretty seaside villages near Barra de Navidad include La Manzanilla (*Posada del Cazador*) and **Tenacatita**, with perfect beach complete with palm huts, tropical fish among rocks. *Hotel* (no name) in village near beach, F, or you can sleep on the beach under a palm shelter— but beware mosquitoes. **Melaque** bay is one of the most beautiful on the Pacific coast but has become very commercialized. (Hotels, many, e.g. *Melaque*, too big and very noisy; *Club Náutico*, very pleasant, good value, small swimming pool, *Los Pelícanos*, cheap, good restaurant on beach; *San Nicolás*, E, beside Estrella Blanca bus station, noisy but clean; *Flamingo*, E, Vallarta 19, clean and friendly; *Bungalows Azteca*, 23 km. from Manzanillo airport, D for 4 at Calle Avante, San Patricio, T (333) 7-01-50, with kitchenette, pool, parking. Trailer park in village, just on beach, showers, US$3 p.p. The road, paved, goes on to Manzanillo. S of Manzanillo is **Tecomán**, (68,000) with delightful atmosphere. Unnamed *pensión* on the corner of the Zócalo, if you face the church it is on your left, F. Try the local deep-fried *tortillas* filled with cheese. The coast road (very dramatic) continues SE to Playa Azul, Lázaro Cárdenas, Zihuatanejo and Acapulco.

A beautiful hilly road runs from Manzanillo to **Colima**, (pop. 150,000) 96 km., capital of Colima state, at an altitude of 494 metres. Colima is a most charming and hospitable town with gothic arcade on main square and strange rebuilt gothic ruin on road beyond Cathedral. Museums: María Ahumada Museun of Western Cultures, Calzada Pedro Galván, in Casa de Cultura complex, Tues.-Sun. 0900-1300, 1600-1800; Museo de la Máscara, la Danza y el Arte Popular del Occidente, Calle 27 de Septiembre y Manuel Gallardo, folklore and handicrafts (items for sale—in the University Institute of Fine Arts); Museo de la Historia de Colima, on the Zócalo. For a change, go to Sr. Francisco Zaragoza's car spare parts business on Jardín Núñez; he has a large collection of dilapidated old cars, mostly US, all stored anyhow (some of his car parts look the same vintage). Public swimming pool in park on Calle Degollado. Airport.

Feria: November.

Hotels *Hotel América*, Morelos 162, T 20366, A, a/c, good restaurant, central, friendly; *Ceballos*, Torres Quintero 16, T 21354, E, main square, fine building but disappointing rooms, not very clean but good food in restaurant (pricey); *Gran Hotel*, pleasant rooms, Av. Rey Colimán 18, T 22526, near Jardín Núñez, D with bath, simple, clean, breakfast expensive; *Flamingos*, near Jardín Torres Quintero, not very clean, E; *Núñez*, Juárez 80 at Jardín Núñez, basic, dark, E with bath; *Hotel* un-named, Gabino Barreda 12, behind the Cathedral, F with bath, good value, rec; *San Cristóbal*, Reforma 98, T 20515, near centre, run down, E; *Galeana*, Medellín 142, F, near bus terminal, basic. Many *casas de huéspedes* near Jardín Núñez. *Rey de Colimán*, E, on continuation of Medellín on outskirts, large rooms; *Motel Costeño* on outskirts is rec. *Hotel Madero*, basic, F, may not have water.

Restaurants *La Fuente* in centre; *Palomas*, behind *Hotel Ceballos*, rec; *Café Colima* more expensive, but in a park; *Giovannis*, Constitucíon 58 El Norte, good pizzas and take away. Good yoghurt and wholemeal bread at *Centro de Nutrición Lakshmi*, Av. Madero 265.Try the local sweet cocada y miel (coconut and honey in blocks), sold in *dulcerías*.

Post Office, Av. Fco 1. Madero y Gral. Nuñez.

Tourist Office   Hidalgo near Jardín Torres Quintero, good, but no information on climbing local volcanoes.

Colima volcano (3,842 metres), one of the most exciting climbs in Mexico, which erupted with great loss of life in 1941, and of El Nevado (4,339 metres) are in the vicinity. They can be climbed by going to Ciudad Guzmán (formerly Zapotlán), and taking a bus to the village of Fresnito, from where it is 25 km. to the hut at 3,500 metres. At weekends it may be possible to hitch. From the hut it is a strenuous 3-4 hour hike to the top. Sr. Agustín Ibarra organises day trips to within a 2 hr. climb of the summit, US$90 for 4, or 3 ½ hr. horse ride to the refuge with a 3 hr. climb, US$50. It may be possible to hitch a lift down next day with the TV maintenance crew who work at the top. Sr. Ibarra provides accommodation in the village; otherwise you can camp behind the small restaurant, storing luggage there (no htoels). A few hotels (F) in Ciudad Guzmán; *Hotel del Sol (Posada Familiar)*, F. Bus, Ciudad Guzmán-Colima, Flecha Amarilla, US$1.40, 2 hrs. Taxi to station from centre US$0.60, train Colima-Ciudad Guzmán, US$0.55, 2nd class, 3 hrs., daily at 1035. Bus Ciudad Guzmán-Uruapan, change at Tamazula and Zamora (only one change of bus Colima-Uruapan). Train Colima-Guadalajara at 1445, US$5, including boxed lunch, for *primera especial* class; arrives Guadalajara 2000. Guadalajara-Manzanillo train stops at 1425.

Comalá is a pretty colonial village near Colima, worth a few hours' visit, bus US$0.10, 20 mins. every ½ hour.

Continuing to Mexico City   We go round the southern shores of Lake Chapala, and after 154 km. come to Jiquilpan (a road leads off, right,

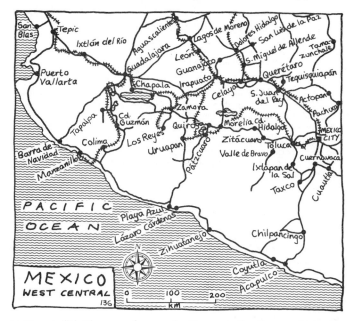

to Manzanillo). There are frescoes by Orozco in the library, which was formerly a church.

The State of Michoacán, where the Tarascan Indians live, is a country of deep woods, fine rivers and great lakes. Fruit, game, and fish are abundant. It has some of the most attractive towns and villages in the country. Visitors are attracted by the Tarascan customs, folklore, ways of life, craft skills (pottery, lacquer), music and dance. The dance is of first importance to them; it is usually performed to the music of wooden drum, flute and occasionally, a fiddle. Masks are often worn and the dance is part of a traditional ritual. The dances which most impress outsiders are the dance of Los Viejitos (Old Men; at Janitzio, 1 January); Los Sembradores (The Sowers; 2 February); Los Moros (The Moors; Lake Pátzcuaro region, *fiestas* and carnival); Los Negritos (Black Men; *fiestas* at Tzintzuntzán); Los Apaches (4 February, at the churches); Las Canacuas (the crown dance; Uruapan, on Corpus Christi). At the weddings of fisherfolk the couple dance inside a fish net. In the local *fandango* the woman has fruits in her hand, the man has a glass of *aguardiente* balanced on his head, and a sword.

Zamora (58 km. beyond Jiquilpan), with 135,000 people, is an agricultural centre founded in 1540. There is an interesting ruined gothic-style church in the centre, several other, fine churches, and a market on Calle Corregidora by the bus station. Nearby is tiny Lake Camecuaro, with boats for hire, restaurants and wandering musicians;

popular at holiday times.

Hotels *Fénix*, Madero Sur 401, T 20266, near bus station, C, clean, swimming pool, pleasant balconies; *Amalia*, Hidalgo 194, T 21327, E, pleasant; *Posada Marena*, simple, clean, E; other cheap *hospedajes* near market. **Motel** *Jérico*, A, Km. 3 on La Barca road just N of town, T 25252, swimming pool, restaurant.

On 40 km. is Carapán, from which a branch road runs 72 km. S through pine woods to **Uruapan** ("Place where flowers are plentiful"), a town of 250,000 set among streams, orchards and waterfalls at 1,610 metres in the Parque Nacional Barranca del Cupatitzio, cool at night. The most attractive of its three plazas is the Jardín de los Mártires, with the 16th century church facing it. In the *portales* or at the market can be bought the local lacquered bowls and trays, or the delicate woodwork of the Paracho craftsmen, Patamban green pottery and Capácuaro embroideries. Restored hospital, built by Fray Juan de San Miguel in the 16th century; now a ceramics museum. Adjoining it is a 16th-century chapel now converted into a craft shop. There is also a church of the same period, and a beautiful, tropical forest public park, Eduardo Ruiz, 1 km. from the centre, full of streams and waterfalls at the top of Calle Venustiana with a good handicraft shop at the entrance, selling wooden boxes and bracelets. Walk there or catch a bus at the Zócalo marked "El Parque". Airport.

Festivals In the first week of April the Zócalo is filled with pottery and Indians from all the surrounding villages. Around 16 September, in nearby village of San Juan, to celebrate the saving of an image of Christ from the San Juan church (see below) at the time of the Paricutín eruption. The two weeks either side of 15 September are *feria* in Uruapan, too.

Hotels *Victoria*, Cupatitzio 13, T 36700, B, good, quiet, restaurant and garage; *Hernández*, main square, T 21600, C, older, noisy; *Concordia* on main square has nice restaurant, C, T 30500; *El Tarasco*, Independencia 2, D, pool, lovely; *Oseguera*, main square, E, clean, hot water spasmodic; *Atzimba*, in street where the mariachis are waiting, E, modern, rec.; *Santa Fe*, Constitución 20, F, without bath, adequate, beside open-air food stalls; *Moderno*, main square, F, with bath, dark rooms; *Capri*, Portal Santos Degollado, by market, friendly, E. *Mirador*, Av. Ocampo 9 (on Zócalo), T 20473, E, hot water 0700-1000 and in p.m., rec.; *Económico*, F, 3 blocks from Zócalo, Calle N. Bravo 25; *Morelos*, Morelos 30, F with bath; *Mi Solar*, Juan Delgado 10, T 2-09-12, F, good value, rec.

Motels *Mansión del Cupatitzio*, on the road to Guadalajara, T 30333, pool, patio, restaurant, good souvenir shop, outstanding; *Pie de la Sierra*, on N outskirts, T 21510, C, good moderately-priced restaurant; *Paricutín*, Juárez 295, T 20303, D, well-maintained. *Las Cabañas*, Km. 1 Carretera a México, near the bus terminal, T 34777, clean, F, local bus until 2200.

Restaurants One with English menu near bus station at back of church, reasonably priced; *Oriental*, on the Plaza, near *Hotel Moderno*, clean, poor service. Locals eat at open-air food stalls under one roof at back of church, very picturesque. *Typ's*, Madero 16, is quite good, but expensive; *La Puesta del Sol*, supermarket, Juan Ayala, has good meals. *La Palma* behind Cathedral, good and cheap, student clientèle. Local speciality, dried meat, *cecina*.

Laundry Emilio Carranza 51.

Tourist Office close to main square, at 5 de Febrero 17 (T 20633), good map.

Train Two daily to Mexico City: *rápido* at 0635, first class tickets from *Hotel*

Victoria and Purepecha (*servicio estrella*) from Mexico City at 2200 (arr. 1010), returning 1915 (arr. 0720) reclining seat US$8.80, single sleeper US$14.55, double US$29.10.

Bus Bus station on the NE edge of town, necessary to get a city bus (US$0.07) into town, finishing at about 2100, or a taxi to the Plaza, US$0.90. To Mexico City, 9¼ hrs., 2nd class, Flecha Amarilla via Toluca leaves 0845 and then every hr., US$6.10, many stops; 1st class less frequent but quicker, US$7.50. Omnibus de México via night buses and Tres Estrellas morning departures. To Morelia, 2nd class (Flecha Amarilla) US$1.60 (2½ hrs.), nice ride. To Colima with Flecha Amarilla US$3.30, 5 hrs. and to Los Reyes, US$0.90, 1¼ hrs. with same company. To Zihuatanejo (Galeana–not rec.–or Occidente) 1st or 2nd class, several a day, 6½ hrs., US$3.50 (2nd) along winding, intermittently wooded road via Nueva Italia and Arteaga, which turns off just before Playa Azul at La Mira and on to Lázaro Cárdenas on the River Balsas. From there, frequent buses to Zihuatanejo (**see page** 210). Bus to Guadalajara, several companies, US$3, 2nd class, 6 hrs. Bus to Pátzcuaro, Flecha Amarilla every 20 mins. US$1.25, 1 hr; also with Galeana and Morelia.

Excursions Through coffee groves and orchards along the Cupatitzio (meaning Singing River) to the Zararacua Falls—heavily littered; restaurants at bus stop where you can hire a horse for US$2 to the falls. Good camping some 300 metres below the village under the shelter on the top of a rim, with a view down into the valley to the waterfall (1 km. away) and a small lake. A bus (marked Zararacua) will take you from the Zócalo at Uruapan to Zararacua, US$0.30, about every 40 mins. Parque Cholinde, 1.5 km. out of town, swimming pool, US$1.30; Colibrí Nurseries nearby. Balneario Caracha (frequent buses), alight at cross roads by sign, a delightful place, open daily with restaurant, hotel, several pools and beautiful gardens. Tingambato ruins are half way along road to Pátzcuaro, about 2 km. downhill from Tingambato town (pyramid and ball court).

The volcano of **Paricutín** is 64 km. from Uruapan; it started erupting in the field of a startled peasant on 20 February, 1943, became fiery and violent and rose to a height of 1,300 metres above the 2,200-metre-high region, and then died down after several years into a quiet grey mountain surrounded by a sea of cold lava. The church spires of San Juan, a buried Indian village, thrusting up through cold lava is a fantastic sight, (fizzy drinks on sale). If not taking an organized tour (with horses and guides), Paricutín is best reached by taking a "Los Reyes" bus over rough track to Angahuán, US$0.50 1½ hrs., 9 a day each way (from 0700 to 2000) with Galeana, but times erratic, then hire a horse or mule or walk (1 hr.). (Cars suitable for rough terrain can, we are told, also get there.) Sr. José Gómez in Angahuán has mules for hire, but he is expensive; Sr. Juan Rivera and Sr. Francisco Lázaro are recommended, but there are a host of other guides (it is definitely worthwhile to have a guide—essential for the volcano). Up to US$3 per mule or horse, US$1 for a guide—bargain—to San Juan, about 3 hours' journey there and back past a Tarascan village, and if you include also Paricutín the price is US$10 for 2, beware horses becoming frisky as they approach home again. Distance Angahuán–San Juan ruins, 3 km., an easy walk: go from the bus stop on the main road, then take right-hand road (with your back to the church) from the plaza, which will lead you to the new hostel, E, with restaurant, from where you can see the buried church. There is now also a hotel. To the peak of the volcano is 14 km. Walk westwards round the lava field, through an avocado plantation. Wear good walking shoes with thick soles as the lava is very rough and as sharp as glass; bear in mind the altitude too, as the return is uphill. Chris Kerfoot writes: One can continue on to the volcano itself; it takes about 7 hrs. there and back. The cone itself is rather small and to reach it, there is a stiff 30 min. climb from the base. A path goes around the tip of the crater, where activity has ceased. Take something to drink because it is pretty hot and dusty out on the plains. Best to leave Uruapan by 0800 so that you don't have to rush. Take sweater for evening. Last bus back to Uruapan at 1900 (but don't rely on it).

Past Angahuán and Peribán, after the volcano, over a terrible road is the little town of **Los Reyes**; good swim above the electricity generating plant in clear streams (take care not to get sucked down the feed pipe!). Hotels: *Arias* behind Cathedral, T 20792, D, best, clean, friendly; *Plaza*, not as good as *Arias* but nice, clean, D, on street facing Cathedral, T 20666; *Fénix*, E, clean, between bus station and plaza, T 20807; *Casa de Huéspedes*, clean, basic, F, lovely courtyard, a little further along the same road as *Villa Rica*, F, often no water; *Oasis*, with pool, Av. Morelos 229, good, E. Restaurant: *La Fogata*, in main square. Buses from Uruapan to Los Reyes go via Angahuán (so same frequency as above). Bus to Los Reyes from Guadalajara with Ciénaga de Chapala 4 a day, 14 hrs., US$2.80 2nd class. Train Guadalajara-Mexico City connects at Yurécuaro for Los Reyes, almost no wait, beautiful ride up fertile valley. Bus from Los Reyes, on Av. 5 de Mayo, to Angahuán, US$0.55, 1½-2 hrs.

Paracho, reached by bus from Pátzcuaro, is a quaint, very traditional Indian village of small wooden houses; in every other one craftsmen make guitars worth from US$10 to 1,000 according to the wood used. The town is virtually traffic free. Try local pancakes.

At Zacapu (Km. 400), see Franciscan church (1548). (Km. 357) **Quiroga**, where a road turns off right for Pátzcuaro, heart of the Tarascan Indian country. The town is named after Bishop Vasco de Quiroga, who was responsible for most of the Spanish building in the area and for teaching the Indians the various crafts they still practise: work in wool, leather, copper, ceramics and canework; many Indians, few tourists. Fair and craft exhibitions in December. Good place to buy cheap leather jackets—most shops in town sell them.

Hotels Three hotels on main street (Vasco de Quiroga), including *Quiroga* and *San Diego*, all E, p.p.

We pass through **Tzintzuntzan**, also touristy, the pre-conquest Tarascan capital; the fascinating ruins just above the town have almost been restored. In Calle Magdalena is a monastery built in 1533 but closed over 250 years ago, which has been restored, but its frescoes have deteriorated badly. The bells of its church, now burnt down, date from the 16th century; a guard will show you round the monastery. A

To Railway Station, Lake Pátzcuaro and Road to Morelia and Uruapan

AV LAS AMÉRICAS

1. Plaza Vasco de Quiroga
2. Plaza Bocanegra
3. Jardín de la Revolución
4. La Basílica/La Colegiata
5. La Compañía
6. El Sagrario
7. San Francisco
8. San Juan de Dios
9. El Humilladero
10. El Hospitalito
11. Museum of Popular Art/Colegio de San Nicolás
12. Casa de los Once Patios
13. Market
14. Post Office
15. Telephone Office

Hotels:
16. *Posada San Rafael*
17. *Gran*
18. *Misión San Manuel*
19. *Posada de la Salud*
20. *El Artillero*
21. *Posada de la Rosa*

PÁTZCUARO
Not to Scale   135

most interesting Passion play is given at Tzintzuntzan. Beautiful and extensive display of hand-painted pottery, very cheap but also brittle. (It is available in other markets in Mexico.) Good bargaining opportunities.

Pátzcuaro is 23 km. from Quiroga; altitude 2,110 metres (cold in the evenings); population 65,000, one of the most picturesque towns in Mexico, with narrow cobbled streets and deep overhanging eaves. It is built on Lake Pátzcuaro, about 50 km. in circumference, with Tarascan Indian villages on its shores and many islands. The Indians used to come by huge dugout canoes (but now seem to prefer the ferry) for the market, held in the main plaza, shaded by great trees.

There are several interesting buildings: the unfinished La Colegiata (1603), known locally as La Basílica, with its much venerated Virgin fashioned by an Indian from a paste made with cornstalk pith and said to have been found floating in a canoe (behind the Basílica there are remains of the precolumbian town and of a pyramid in the precincts of the Museum of Popular Art); the restored Jesuit church of La Compañía (and, almost opposite, the early 17th-century church of the Sagrario) at the top of Calle Portugal. Behind this street are two more ecclesiastical buildings: the Colegio Teresiano and the restored Templo del Santuario; on Calle Lerín is the old monastery, with a series of small patios. (Murals by Juan O'Gorman in the Library, formerly San Agustín.) On Calle Allende is the residence of the first Governor. On Calle Terán is the church of San Francisco; nearby is San Juan de Dios, on the corner of Calle Romero. Visit also the Plaza Vasco de Quiroga. Fifteen minutes' walk outside the town is the chapel of El Calvario, on the summit of Cerro del Calvario, a hill giving wide views; good views also from the old chapel of the Humilladero, above the cemetery on the old road to Morelia.

The very well arranged Museum of Popular Art is in the Colegio de San Nicolás (1540) entrance US\$0.40, English speaking, friendly guide: ask there for the Casa de los Once Patios, which contains the local tourist office and boutiques selling handicrafts. See also the attractive Jardín de la Revolución (F. Tena y Ponce de León) and, nearby, the old church of the Hospitalito. Excellent Fri. and also Sat. markets, often much cheaper than shops. Some stalls open daily on the main square, selling handicrafts, and there is a friendly handicraft shop on the road down to the lake, Vicky's, with interesting toys. There is a free medical clinic, English-speaking, on the outskirts of Pátzcuaro.

Fiestas 1-2 Nov.: Día de los Muertos (All Souls' Day), ceremony at midnight, 1 Nov., on Janitzio island, but mostly a tourist event, heavily commercialized; 6-9 Dec., Virgen de la Salud, when authentic Tarascan dances are performed in front of the *basílica*. There is an interesting *fiesta* on 12 December for the Virgin of Guadalupe; on 12 October, when Columbus discovered America, there is also a procession with the Virgin and lots of fireworks. Carnival in February when the Dance of the Moors is done.

Hotels All hotels fully-booked 4 weeks prior to Día de los Muertos. *Posada de don Vasco*, A, attractive, colonial-style hotel on Av. de las Américas (halfway between lake and town, T 20262), breakfast good, other meals poor; presents the Dance of the Old Men on Wed. and Sat. at 2100, no charge, non-residents welcome but drinks very expensive to compensate; also mariachi band. *Las Redes*, Av. Américas 6, T 21275, C, near lake, popular restaurant; *Posada La Basílica*, Arciga 6, T 21108, C, nice restaurant with good views, central; *Mesón del Cortijo*, Obregón, just off Américas, T 21295, C, rec., but often fully booked at weekends. *Los Escudos*, Portal Hidalgo 74, T 21290, C, colonial style; *Posada San Rafael*, Plaza Vasco de Quiroga, T 20770, D, clean, safe, very nice, restaurant, parking in courtyard; *Gran Hotel*, Portal Regules 6, on Plaza Bocanegra, T 20443, small rooms, C; *Mansión Iturbe*, Portal Morelos 59, restored mansion on main square, E; *Misión San Manuel*, Portal Aldama 12 on main square, T 21313, restaurant, highly rec., D; these are all central. *Posada Lagos*, Mendoza, E, clean; *Posada de la Salud*, Benigno Serrato, clean, quiet, pleasant, excellent value, some rooms with individual fireplaces, E; *Valmen*, Lloredo 34, T 45412-1161, E, with bath, charming colonial building but noisy. *El Artillero*, hot water, E, with bath, friendly, near Zócalo, Ibarra 22, T 21331 (discounts for long stays paid in advance). *Posada de la Rosa*, Portal Juárez 29 (Plaza Chica), E, hot water, rec.; next door is *Concordia*, F, good value, clean. *Casa de Huéspedes Pátzcuaro*, Ramos 9, F without bath. There are many *hospedajes* and hotels near the bus station.

Motels *Chalamu*, Pátzcuaro road Km. 20, trailer park too, T 20948, C; *San Felipe*, Cárdenas 321, T 21298, C, trailers; *San Carlos*, Muelle Col. Morelos, T 21359, C; *Pátzcuaro*, Av. de las Américas 506, T 20767 (Apartado Postal 206), 1 km. from centre, hot water, gardens, tennis, pleasant. *Trailer Park El Pozo*, on lakeside, hot showers a.m.

Camping Camping and caravan site at *Motel Pátzcuaro*, spotless, lush green grass, flowering trees, showers with hot water, toilets, tennis court and pool, cheap, 2 rooms to let, E.

Restaurants Most close early, it is difficult to get an evening meal. *El Patio*, on main square, clean, friendly, try pescado blanco (white fish), regional dish, it tends to be expensive; *El Munjo*, main square, reasonable food but slow service. *El Cayuco Café Cantante*, French owner, music Sat. and Sun., open 1600-2300. *Mansión Iturbe*, Portal Morelos 59, good, cheap, delicious coffee. *Hotel Escudos* restaurant, Plaza Quiroga, open till 2130, popular, very cheap, try Sopa Tarasca; *San Agustín*, Plaza Bocanegra, friendly, good donuts on sale outside in p.m. Make sure you don't get overcharged in restaurants—some display menus outside which bear no resemblance to the prices inside. *Gran Hotel*, filling comida corrida; good chicken and enchiladas over the market. Several interesting eating places by the jetty for Janitzio.

Tourist Office West portals of Plaza Vasco de Quiroga.

Transport New bus station out of town. To Mexico City, Tres Estrellas de Oro and Autobuses de Occidente— ADO (which also runs once a day from Pátzcuaro to Guadalajara; otherwise you change at Quiroga for Guadalajara)—1st (US$8.50) and 2nd class buses. Very enjoyable and cheaper, though slower, train ride around lake and plateau to Mexico City. Train leaves daily at 0655, from Mexico City to Pátzcuaro, arrives at 1920, beautiful views between Uruapan and Acámbaro (*fiesta*, 4 July), 1st class US$4. Train to Mexico City at 0905 (*rápido*) and 2000 (Pullman), sleeper US$16, 10 hrs. Take pullover. Trains to Uruapan: 0756, pullman; 1856, *rápido*; 1222, *normal* (slow, 2½ hrs., US$0.40 1st class).

Regular bus service to Morelia, 1 hr., US$1 with ADO and Flecha Amarilla (latter departs every ½ hr.). Buses to Guadalajara go through Zamora, with Occidental US$6.75 1st class, 6 hrs.; no trains to Guadalajara. Local buses from corner of market in town to lakeside.

Excursions Bus to lake (marked Lago) from corner of market. The best-known island is **Janitzio**, although it has become overrun by tourists and filled with cheap souvenir shops and beggars, which has made its local people hostile and the place lose its charm (45 mins. by motorboat, US$1.10 return, tickets from dock, including fishermen's show, most picturesque, but an unfortunate monument to Morelos crowning a hill). Winter is the best time for fishing in the somewhat fish-depleted lake, where Indians throw nets shaped like dragonflies. White fish from the lake was a delicacy, but the lake is now polluted, so beware (still plenty of places sell white fish). The Government is planning to improve the lake. On a lakeside estate is the Educational Centre for Community Development in Latin America, better known as Crefal (free films every Wed. at 1930). For a truly spectacular view of the lake, the islands and the surrounding countryside, walk to Cerro del Estribo; an ideal site for a quiet picnic. It is 1½ hrs. walk to the top from the centre of Pátzcuaro. Follow the cobbled road beyond El Calvario, don't take the dirt tracks off to the left. Cars go up in the afternoon, the best time for walking. No buses, 417 steps to the peak. The areas round Pátzcuaro are recommended for bird watching.

From Pátzcuaro one can also visit Tzintzuntzan and Quiroga by regular bus service. 30 minutes by local bus is **Ihuátzio** (US$0.15), on a peninsula 12 km. N of Pátzcuaro, 8 km. from Tzintzuntzan. This was the second most important Tarascan City; two pyramids are well-preserved and afford good views of the lake. No entrance fee to the site, but the caretaker expects a tip.

An excursion can be made into the hills to the village of Santa Clara del Cobre (fine old church), where hand-wrought copper vessels are made. (*Fiesta*: 12-15 August.) Nearby is the pretty Lake Zirahuen. Past Santa Clara, on the La Huacana road, after Ario de Rosales, one descends into the tropics; fine views all along this road, which ends at Churumuco. Pátzcuaro-Ario de Rosales-Nueva Italia-Uruapan-Pátzcuaro takes about 6 hrs., beautiful tropical countryside.

(Km. 314) *Morelia*, capital of Michoacán state, population 470,000, altitude 1,882 metres, is a rose-tinted city with attractive colonial buildings (their courtyards are their main feature), rather quiet, founded in 1541. The Cathedral (1640), is set between the two main plazas, with graceful towers and a fine façade, in what is called "sober baroque"; there are paintings by Juárez in the sacristy. Other important churches are the Virgin of Guadalupe (also known as San Diego) with a most ornate Pueblan interior, the modernized Iglesia de la Cruz, and the churches in the charming small Plaza de las Rosas and Plaza del Carmen. The oldest of Morelia's churches is the San Francisco of the Spanish Renaissance period, but lacking many of the decorative features of that style.

Even more interesting than the colonial churches are the many fine colonial secular buildings still standing. The revolutionary Morelos, Melchor Ocampo, and the two unfortunate Emperors of Mexico (Agustín de Iturbide and the Archduke Maximilian of Austria) are commemorated by plaques on their houses. The Colegio de San Nicolás (1540) is the oldest surviving institution of higher education in Latin America. (It has a summer school for foreign students.) The fine former Jesuit college, now called the Palacio Clavijero, contains government offices, with a helpful tourist office on the ground floor (corner of Madero Poniente y Nigromante). Also notable are the law school, in the former monastery of San Diego, next to the Guadalupe church; the Palacio de Gobierno (1732-70), facing the Cathedral; the Palacio Municipal; and the Palacio Federal. Visit also the churches of La Merced, with its lovely tower and strange, bulging *estípites* (inverted pyramidal supports), Capuchinas (Ortega y Montaño), which has some Churrigueresque *retablos*, and Santa María, on a hilltop S of the city.

Thursday and Sunday are market days: specialities are pottery, lacquer, woodcarving, jewellery, blankets, leather sandals; in this connection see the Casa de Artesanías de Michoacán, in the ex-Convento de San Francisco, next to the church of the same name; it is full of fine regional products for sale, not cheap. Shops close early. Free weekly concerts are held in the municipal theatre. At the E edge of the downtown area, on the road to Mexico City, are the 224 arches of a ruined aqueduct, built in 1788 (walk 11 blocks E from Cathedral along Av. Madero). Visit the Museo de Michoacán (archaeological remains), 3 blocks from the Cathedral, and the new Casa de la Cultura, Av. Morelos Norte, housed in the ex-Convento del Carmen, which has a good collection of masks from various regions, crucifixes; also at workshops

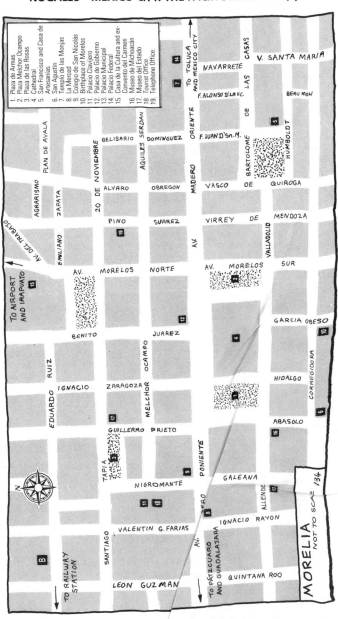

1. Plaza de Armas
2. Plaza Melchor Ocampo
3. Plaza de las Rosas
4. Cathedral
5. San Francisco and Casa de Artesanias
6. San Agustín
7. Templo de las Monjas
8. La Merced
9. Colegio de San Nicolás
10. Birthplace of Morelos
11. Palacio Clavijero
12. Palacio de Gobierno
13. Palacio Municipal
14. Palacio Federal
15. Casa de la Cultura and ex-Convento del Carmen
16. Museo Michoacán
17. Museo del Estado
18. Tourist Office.
19. Telephone Office.

MORELIA NOT TO SCALE 134

(nominal fee for US$1.55 for 12 weeks). The Museo de Estado has been opened in the house of Iturbide's wife (Casa de la Emperatriz), SE corner of Jardín de las Rosas. Both Banamex and Bancomer have their offices in magnificent old houses; the patio of the former is especially fine. Many good language schools. Fairly good zoo in Parque Juárez, S of the centre (25 mins. walk S along Galeana). Planetarium.

Hotels Some of the cheaper hotels may have water only in the morning; check. *Calinda Quality Inn*, A, Av. Acueducto, T 45969, colonial-style, modern. *Virrey de Mendoza*, Portal Matamoros, T 20633, A, superb old-style building, poor restaurant, service could be better, could be much cleaner, ask for room at front with balcony. Off the Plaza de Armas and much quieter is the *Posada de la Soledad*, Zaragoza and Ocampo, T 21888, fine courtyards, converted chapel as dining room, B, good value; *Catedral*, Zaragoza 37, T 30783, close to Plaza, spacious, C, rec.; *Casino*, main square, T 31003, C, clean, hot water, private bath; *Orozco*, Madero Poniente 507, central, cheerful, soft beds, clean, shower, F; *Posada San José*, Av. Obregón 226 beside Templo de San José, E, rooms like cells, clean; *Posada La Merced*, León Guzmán 50, E, a bit shabby, with bath. *Carmen*, E. Ruiz 673, T 21725, F, good value, but small rooms, overlooks the Casa de la Cultura, hot water; *del Matador*, same street No. 531, T 24649, D. Cheap hotels on Morelos Norte: *Colonial*, corner with 20 de Noviembre 15, T 21897, E, run down; *Casa de Huéspedes Lourdes*, Morelos Norte 340, 5 blocks E of bus station. *San Jorge*, Madero Poniente 719, T 24610, E with hot shower, clean; *Concordia*, Gómez Farías 328, T 23052, D; *Allende*, Allende 846, F with bath; *Señorial*, Santiago Tapía 543, F, also hourly rentals. Cheap *posadas* and *casas de huéspedes* tend to be uninviting.

On Santa María hill, S of the city, with glorious views, are hotels *Villa Montaña* (each room a house on its own, run by French aristocrats, very expensive but value for money), *Vista Bella* (T 20248) and *Villa San José* next door and much cheaper (C), reached only by car.

CREA youth hostel at corner of Oaxaca and Chiapas, T 33177, 1 km. SW of bus station (walk W to Calle Cuautla, then S along Cuautla to Oaxaca) F, p.p. Camping possible in a forest about 4 km. S of centre on unnumbered Pátzcuaro-signposted road.

Motels *Villa Centurión*, Morelos road, T 32272, C, good antiques, pool, TV; *Las Palmas*, Guadalajara road, also trailer park, E; *El Parador*, Highway 45, with trailer park, E.

Restaurants Superb food at the *Villa Montaña* hotel. *La Huacana*, García Obeso behind cathedral, regional, pleasant, mariachis; *Rey Sol*, rec. by locals; restaurant of local Woolworth's is in a 17th-century episcopal chapel. *Govinda*, vegetarian, Av. Morelos Nr 39, opp. cathedral, delicious lunch for US$1.20; *Quinta Sol*, Madero Oriente, 5 blocks E of Morelos, also vegetarian, both closed Sun. *Café Catedral* near Govinda has interesting clientele. Comidas corridas at the *Paraíso*, Madero Poniente 103 facing the cathedral, and at *El Viejo Paral*, Oriente and Quiroga, US$1. *Pizza Tony's*, Madero Ote 698; *Café Pindaro*, Morelos Norte 150, at No. 185, good fish; *Café yrte*, round corner from *Hotel Catedral*, coffee and drinks, good atmosphere. *Mona Lisa* café on Luis Moya, good drinks and sweets. Try stewed kid, best in cheaper restaurants.

The Mercado de Dulces, on Gómez Farías at W end of the Palacio Clavijero, is famous for fruit jams (*ates*), candies and *rompope* (a milk and egg nog).

Spanish Classes Centro Mexicano de Idiomas, Calz. Fray Antonio de San Miguel 173, intensive weekly classes.

Laundromat Lavandería Chapultepec Calle J. Ceballos 881.

Post Office in Palacio Federal is said to charge different rates from the rest of Mexico.

Tourist Office Nigromante 79, has local hotel information list and map, open 0900-2000 (closed Sun.). Also kiosk at bus terminal.

Rail Morelia-Mexico City at 2304 (Pullman), US$2.35 2nd class, US$3.90 1st, train starts at Uruapan. Slow train to capital at 1030.

Bus Terminal on Eduardo Ruiz, between Guzmán and Farías, many beggars, revolting toilets, has luggage office and tourist kiosk; 3 blocks W of plaza, then 3 N, timetables and services said to be chaotic. Many buses to Guanajuato, 6 hrs., US$2.20. Guadalajara, US$4. Uruapan, US$1.60 2nd class; Irapuato, US$1.80 2nd class, rough ride. Mexico City, 2nd class every hour or ADO (described as a tin can on wheels), every 20 mins., 6½ hrs., 4½ by *rápido*, US$4. Bus to Acapulco US$14, 15 hrs. Bus to Pátzcuaro every ½ hr., 1½ hrs., US$1. Also about 15 a day to Zihuatanejo on the coast, US$5.50.

Airport Daily flights to Mexico City.

Diversion Just after Morelia there is a good road to two villages on Lake Cuitzeo, the second largest in Mexico, but now completely dried up, an ecological disaster. At **Cuitzeo**, the first one (hotel, *Restaurant Esteban*, by post office), there is a fine Augustinian church and convent, a cloister, a huge open chapel, and good choir stalls in the sacristy. From here one can go to Valle de Santiago (*Hotel Posada de la Parroquia*, E), attractive mountain scenery. The second village, 23 km. to the N, **Yuriria**, has a large-scale Indian version of the splendid church and convent at Actopán (**see page** 68). (Before Yuriria is Moreleón, the clothing distribution centre of Mexico—buses empty here.) The road continues to Salamanca (hotel, appalling traffic), where one turns left for Irapuato or right for Celaya and Querétaro.

The road soon climbs through 50 km. of splendid mountain scenery: forests, waterfalls, and gorges, to the highest point at (Km. 253), Puerto Gartan, and Mil Cumbres (2,886 metres), with a magnificent view over mountain and valley, and then descends into a tropical valley. Between Morelia and Ciudad Hidalgo is Queréndaro, where the pavements are covered in *chiles* drying in the blazing sun, and all the shops are filled with large bags of *chiles* in the season.

Worth a glance are the façade of the 16th century church at **Ciudad Hidalgo** (km. 212, 100,000 people)—*Hotel Fuente*, E, some rooms have no keys, clean, showers, no water in the afternoon; *Restaurant Manolo*, inexpensive, good; and the old colonial bridge and church at **Tuxpan** (**Michoacan**) (km. 193; *Mara*, E, on main square, clean, hot water, wood stove; *Tuxpan*, noisy. At Km. 183 a side road runs, right, to the spa of **San José Purúa** at 1,800 metres, in a wild setting of mountain and gorge and woods. The radioactive thermal waters are strong. First-class hotel. Smaller, cheaper hotels lie on the road past the spa and in the town of Jungapeo.

Then comes **Zitácuaro**, a quiet and attractive place with a pleasant plaza and a good covered market. Bus to Mexico City, 3½ hrs.,US$1.80; to Guadalajara, 11 hrs., US$6, 409 km.

Hotels *Rancho San Cayetano*, 3 km. out on Huetamo road, T 31926, C, chalets, friendly, clean, highly rec.; *Salvador*, Hidalgo Pte. 7, T 31107, C, clean and pleasant; *Rosales del Valle*, Revolución Sur 56, T 31293, D-C, near bus station, fair, some rooms hired for very short stays; *Posada Michoacán*, E, main square, fairly clean: *Hotel Colón*, reasonable, fan, E, not very quiet, friendly management, can store luggage; *Florida*, E with bath, clean, garage US$0.50 a night; *El Turista* on main street, F with bath, restaurant.

A turning off the main road at Angangueo brings one to a unique site, the wintering grounds of the Monarch butterfly in **El Campanario Ecological Reserve**, above the village of El Rosario. It can be reached by taking an hourly local bus (labelled Angangueo) from Zitácuaro (Av. Santos Degollado Oriente) to Ocampo, 1 hr., and from Ocampo another local bus (1¼ hrs., 12 km.) to El Rosario. Entry to the reserve is about US$0.70; it has a small visitors' centre and several trails to see the myriads of large orange butterflies, which migrate every year from SE Canada and NE USA. The reserve can no doubt be reached from other towns nearby, such as Angangueo, Ciudad Hidalgo or Tuxpan, and Aguila Tours, Amsterdam 291-C, Col. Hipódromo Condesa, run tours from early December from Mexico City.

(Km. 86) A branch road, right, goes to the mountain resort of **Valle de Bravo**, a charming old town on the edge of an attractive artificial lake, with another Monarch butterfly wintering area nearby. This area gets the week-end crowd from Mexico City.

Hotels *Centro Vacacional ISSEMYM*, central, pool, restaurant, satisfactory, Independencia 404; *Refugio del Salto*, Fontana Brava, C; *Los Arcos* (C, but good) is several km. beyond, in pine woods, excellent restaurant. **Motels** *Avándaro*, Fraccionamiento Avándaro, C, pleasant.

If you want to avoid the Mil Cumbres pass take Route 126 from Morelia, via Queréndaro, then turn right 10 km. short of Zitácuaro and join Route 15 (to Toluca and Mexico City) at Huajumbaro. The road is at first flat then climbs and descends again to Maravatio (hotel) and then climbs steeply, towards **Tlalpujahua**, an old mining town with a museum, several churches, and cobblestoned streets, very picturesque among forests and hills. (*Casa de Huéspedes*). There are plenty of places to stop at on the way to Toluca.

(Km. 75) A road branches off to the volcano of Toluca (Nevado de Toluca; 4,583 metres, the fourth highest mountain in Mexico) and climbs to the deep blue lakes of the Sun and the Moon in its two craters, at about 4,270 metres, from which there is a wide and awe-inspiring view. During winter it is possible to ski on the slopes; 5 km. from the entrance is an *Albergue* (US$1) with food and cooking facilities. From here it is 10 km. to the entrance to the crater, where there is a smaller *albergue* (cooking facilities but no food, US$1.50). Trips to the volcano are very popular at weekends; no problem getting a lift to the lakes. If walking remember the entrance to the crater is on the far left side of the volcano. This route, the Mil Cumbres route, is by far the most difficult.

(Km. 64) **Toluca**, population 600,000, altitude 2,639 metres, about 4¾ hrs. from Morelia by bus, is the capital of the state of México. It is known mostly for its vivid Friday market—reportedly less colourful than it used to be— where Indians sell colourful woven baskets, *sarapes, rebozos,* pottery and embroidered goods (beware of pickpockets and handbag slashers). The new Market is at Calle Manuel Gómez Pedraza Oriente, open daily. As well as for textiles, the city is also famous for confectionery and for an alcoholic drink known as *moscos*. See the churches of the Tercer Orden and Vera Cruz, the convent of Carmen and the chapel of Santa María de Guadalupe, the new Cathedral, the Palacio de Gobierno, the Museo de Bellas Artes, the botanical garden, called the Cosmo Vitral because of its unique stained-glass decor, Chamber of Deputies, all in the centre of the city near, or on the Zócalo. Also the Museo de Arte Popular and Casa de las Artesanías, with an excellent display of local artistic products for sale, at the corner of Paseo Chamizal and Paseo Tollocán.

Hotels *San Carlos*, Madero 210, T 49422, D, remodelled, dirty, *Colonial*, Hidalgo Oriente 103, T 47066, E, small rooms, clean, TV, cheap food, rec.; *Morelia*, Hidalgo 615, F without bath, noisy; *Bravo*, Bravo 105, T 47196, E, near old bus terminal in centre; *Azteca*, Pino Suárez and Hidalgo, F, noisy, some rooms like cells, but clean; all the above are in the centre, not many cheap hotels. *Terminal*, adjoining bus terminal, T 57960, D.
  Motels *Del Rey Inn*, Mexico City road entrance, A, resort facilities.

Restaurants *Ostionería Escamilla*, Rayón Nte. 404, good fish; *San Francisco*, Villada 108, US$2 for 2; *Café L'Ambient*, Hidalgo 231 Pte.

Tourist Office Lerdo de Tejada Poniente 101, Edif. Plaza Toluca, 1° piso.

Transport To Mexico City, US$0.65. Bus to Pátzcuaro, 6 hrs., US$3.10, several daily; to Taxco, 4 buses a day, a spectacular journey. Many buses to Tenango de Arista (US$0.25, ½ hrs.), Tenancingo (US$1); also regular buses to Calixtlahuaca US$1.50 (1 hr.) from platform 7. Bus station away from centre. Train from Mexico City 2200, arr. 0025 (Pullman); returns 0509, arr. 0717.

Excursions From Toluca take a bus to the pyramids and Aztec seminary of *Calixtlahuaca*, 2 km. off the road to Ixtlahuaca; pyramids are to Quetzalcoatl (circular) and to Tlaloc; they are situated just behind the village, 10 mins. walk from the final bus-stop. Entry US$0.10.
  To reach the Toluca volcano (see above) take the first bus to Sultepec at about 0700. Leave the bus where the road to the radio station branches off, from there it is about 20 km. to the crater. There are 3 places to stay overnight, F, and a restaurant, but the trip can be done in one day.

Along a side road S of Toluca, or reached from it, are a number of most interesting "art and craft" producing villages, all with old churches. The first village is **Metepec**, the pottery-making centre of the valley, 1½ km. off the road to Tenango. The clay figurines made here—painted bright fuchsia, purple, green and gold— are unique. This is the source of the "trees of life and death", the gaudily-painted pottery sold in Mexico. Market is on Mon. Interesting convent. Also off the main highway near Tenango, turning right at La Marquesa, you will come to a sign pointing to Gualupita to the right; just beyond that is the town of **Santiago Tianpuistengo** (38,000). Good *cazuelas, metates,* baskets and *sarapes.*

Between July and early November displays of wild mushrooms for sale. Try *gordas* or *tlacoyos*, blue corn stuffed with a broad bean paste. If you are brave try *atepocates*; embryo frogs with tomato and chiles, boiled in maize leaves. Try restaurant *Mesón del Cid*, good regional food, go to kitchen to see choice. Try *sopa de hongos*, mushroom soup. Market day is Tuesday. The town is crowded at weekends.

The main road descends gradually to **Tenango de Arista** (Toluca-Tenango bus, US$0.25), where one can walk (20 mins.) to the ruins of **Teotenango** (Matlazinca culture, reminiscent of La Ciudadela at Teotihuacán, with 11 ball courts). There is an interesting museum by the ruins of Teotenango; entry to museum and ruins US$0.45; to enter go to the end of town on the right hand side. Restaurant in Tenango: *María Isabel*, cheap, good local food. 48 km. from Toluca the road descends abruptly through gorges to **Tenancingo**, still at 1,830 metres, but with a soft, warm all-the-year-round climate. Nearby is the magnificent 18th century Carmelite convent of El Santo Desierto, making beautiful *rebozos*. The townspeople themselves weave fine *rebozos* and the fruit wines are delicious and cheap. Market day is on Sun. Rec. hotels at Tenancingo are *Lazo*, with clean rooms in annex with shower, E, and *San Carlos*, F, good value. *Hotel Jardín* on main plaza, F, good value. There is a small waterfall near the bus station.

About 11 km. to the E over an improved road is **Malinalco**, from which a path winds up 1 km. to Malinalco ruins (Matlazinca culture, with Aztec additions), certainly one of the most remarkable pre-Hispanic ruins in Mexico, now partly excavated. Here is a fantastic rock-cut temple in the side of a mountain which conceals in its interior sculptures of eagle and jaguar effigies. Visit also the Augustinian convent to see the early frescoes. There is a *fiesta* in Malinalco on 6 January. (Camping. Two hotels, one expensive, one cheap. Ester at Ferretería La Provincia in Malinalco arranges accommodation, F, p.p. *La Salamandra*, on road to ruins, very good value; Swiss-run, open-air restaurant serves local trout, about US$2.50, superb, bring own supplies of beverages, bread, salad.) (Buses Tenancingo-Malinalco, 1 hr.) You can get to Malinalco from Mexico City or Toluca by taking a 2nd class bus to Chalma (see below); Malinalco is the next village along and can be reached by shared taxi for US$0.25 p.p. (Terminal in Mexico City, Central del Poniente, opp. Observatorio, ½ hr. frequency, at least two companies go there.) You can also go to Malinalco from Toluca by leaving the Toluca-Tenancingo road after San Pedro Zictepec, some distance N of Tenancingo, which is gravel surfaced and 28 km. long. Journey will take 45 mins. **Chalma** is a popular pilgrimage spot, and is also where you make connections if coming from Cuernavaca (take a Cuernavaca—Toluca bus to Santa Marta, then wait for a Toluca—Chalma bus).

On 32 km. from Tenancingo is **Ixtapan de la Sal**, a pleasant forest-surrounded leisure resort with medicinal hot springs. In the centre of this quiet whitewashed town is the municipal spa, adult admission US$0.55 (massage and facial US$1-4, 20 mins.). At the edge of town is Parque Los Trece Lagos. For the hedonist there are private "Roman" baths, for the stiff-limbed a medicinal hot-water pool, mud baths for the vain, an Olympic pool for swimmers, rowing boats and a water slide for the adventurous. The latter is 150 metres long (prohibited to those over 40) which can lead to plenty of bruises and some nasty clashes with any larger bodies hurtling around (US$1.55 entry, US$0.90 for 2 slides, US$2.20 for slides all day). "The Thirteen Lake Park" is privately run and has a train running around; there are numerous picnic spots. Market day: Sun. *Fiesta*: second Fri. in Lent.

Ixtapan de la Sal can also be reached in 2 hrs. by car from Mexico City on Route 55 (turn left off Toluca highway at La Marquesa). The road goes on to Taxco (see page 203).

Hotels *Ixtapan*, Nuevo Ixtapan, A, food and entertainment included; *Kiss (Villa Vergel)*, C; *Casablanca*, E; *María Isabel*, E, good; *Guadalajara*, F, with bath; *Casa Yuyi*, F with bath, clean; *Casa de Huéspedes Margarita*, Juárez, F, clean, rec; many others. Plenty of reasonable restaurants on Av. Benito Juárez, most close by 1900.

The basin of Toluca, the highest in the central region, is the first of a series of basins drained by the Río Lerma into the Pacific. To reach Mexico City from Toluca—64 km. by new dual carriageway—it is necessary to climb over the intervening mountain range. The centre of the basin is swampy. (Km. 50) Lerma is on the edge of the swamp, the source of the Lerma river. The road climbs, with backward views of the snow-capped Toluca volcano, to the summit at Las Cruces (km. 32; 3,164 metres). There is a good Bavarian restaurant, *La Escondida*, about 100 metres to the left of the Toluca-México road at 38 km., on a beautiful site. There are occasional great panoramic views of the City and the Valley of México during the descent.

MEXICO CITY (5)

Mexico City, the capital, altitude 2,240 metres, founded 1521, was built upon the remains of Tenochtitlan, the Aztec capital, covering some 200 square km. The Valley of México, the intermont basin in which it lies, is about 110 km. long by 30 km. wide. Rimming this valley is a sentinel-like chain of peaks of the Sierra Nevada mountains. Towards the SE tower two tall volcanoes, named for the warrior Popocatépetl and his beloved Ixtaccíhuatl, the Aztec princess who died rather than outlive him. Popocatépetl is 5,452 metres high, and Ixtaccíhuatl (Eestaseewatl) 5,286 metres. Both are snow-capped, but you need to get up early in the morning to see them from the city, because of the smog. To the S the crest of the Cordillera is capped by the wooded volcano of Ajusco.

About 20 million people (one in four of the total population) live in this city, which has over half the country's manufacturing employment, and much of the nation's industrial smog. The last-mentioned makes the eyes of the unaccustomed sore (contact-lens wearers take note).

The city suffers from a fever of demolition and rebuilding, especially since the heavy damage caused by the September 1985 earthquake. This was concentrated along the Paseo de la Reforma, Avenida Juárez, the Alameda, and various suburbs and residential districts. About 20,000 people are believed to have lost their lives, largely in multi-storey

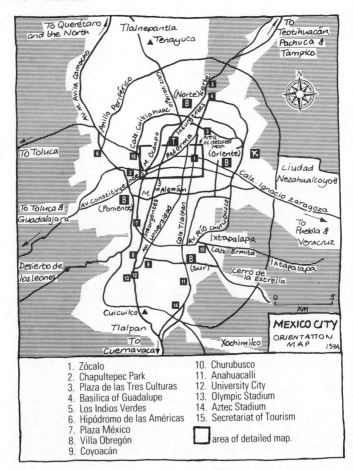

To Querétaro and the North
Tlalnepantla
▲ Tenayuca
To Teotihuacán, Pachuca & Tampico.
Av. Avila Camacho
Anillo Periférico
Calz.Vallejo
Calz. Cuitlahuac
(Norte) B
Insurgentes Norte
5
N
To Toluca
M. Ocampo
3 Area of detailed map.
Reforma
(Oriente)
B
15
1
Ciudad Nezahualcoyotl
2
B
Calz. Ignacio zaragoza
To Toluca & Guadalajara
Av. Constituyentes
(Poniente)
M. Alemán
To Puebla & Veracruz
7
Av. Insurgentes Sur
Calz. Tlalpan
Av. Río Churubusco
Ixtapalapa
Desierto de los Leones
8
9
10
Calz. Ermita
Ixtapalapa
13
12
B (Sur)
Cerro de la Estrella
11
14
0   5
Km
Cuicuilco ▲
Tlalpan
To Cuernavaca
Xochimilco

MEXICO CITY
ORIENTATION MAP 137A

1. Zócalo	10. Churubusco
2. Chapultepec Park	11. Anahuacalli
3. Plaza de las Tres Culturas	12. University City
4. Basilica of Guadalupe	13. Olympic Stadium
5. Los Indios Verdes	14. Aztec Stadium
6. Hipódromo de las Américas	15. Secretariat of Tourism
7. Plaza México	
8. Villa Obregón	☐ area of detailed map.
9. Coyoacán	

housing and government-controlled buildings, including Juárez hospital in which there were about 3,000 fatalities.

Mexico City has long burst its ancient boundaries and spread; the new residential suburbs are most imaginatively planned, though there are many appalling shanty-towns. Like all big centres it is faced with a fearsome traffic problem, despite the building of a new inner ring road. The noise can be deafening; Elizabeth Allen tells us that the definition of a split second in Mexico City is the amount of time between the traffic-lights going green and the first horn sounding. To relieve congestion eight underground railway lines are now operating. There is also a large traffic-free area E of the Zócalo. Mexico's architecture ranges from Spanish-Baroque to ultra-modern: it is, indeed, fast becoming a city of skyscrapers.

Because of the altitude the climate is mild and exhilarating save for a few days in mid-winter. The normal annual rainfall is 660 mm., and all of it falls— usually in the late afternoon—between May and October. Even in summer the temperature at night is rarely above 13°C, and in winter there can be sharp frosts. Despite this, central heating is not common.

Sightseeing in and around the city can easily take up ten days. The main places of interest are listed below.

You will find, as you explore the city, that you use two thoroughfares more than any others. The most famous is Paseo de la Reforma, with a tree-shaded, wide centre section and two side lanes; it runs somewhat diagonally NE from Chapultepec Park. At the Plaza de la Reforma it bends eastwards and becomes Avenida Juárez, still fairly wide but without side lanes. Beyond the Palacio de Bellas Artes this becomes Av. Madero, quite narrow, with one-way traffic. The other and longer thoroughfare is Av. Insurgentes, a diagonal north-south artery about 25 km. long. Reforma and Insurgentes bisect at a *plazuela* with a statue of Cuauhtémoc, the last of the Aztec emperors.

The Zócalo, the main square, or Plaza Mayor, centre of the oldest part barred to wheeled traffic 1000-1700 Mon.-Fri., is always alive with people, and often vivid with official ceremonies and celebrations. On the north side, on the site of the Great Teocalli or temple of the Aztecs, is

The Cathedral, the largest and oldest cathedral in Latin America, designed by Herrera, the architect of the Escorial in Spain, along with that in Puebla; first built 1525; rebuilding began 1573; consecrated 1667; finished 1813. Singularly harmonious, considering the many architects employed and time taken to build it. Restoration work has been completed. There is an underground crypt reached by stairs in the W wing of the main part of the building, open 0900-1330. Next to the Cathedral is the **Sagrario Metropolitano**, 1769, with fine churrigueresque façade. Behind the Cathedral at the corner of Av. Guatemala and Calle Seminario are the Aztec ruins of the **Templo Mayor** or *Teocalli*, which were found in 1978 when public works were being carried out. They are open to the public between 0900 and 1700 (a charge is made for taking pictures), a very worthwhile visit, especially since the Aztecs built a new temple every 52 years, and 7 have been identified on top of each other. The sculptured, dismembered body of the Aztec goddess of the moon, Coyolxauhqui, was found here. A **Museum** (**Museo Arqueológico del Sitio**) was opened in 1987 behind the temple, to house various sculptures found in the main pyramid of Tenochtitlán and six others, including the altar of stone of the moon goddess (recommended); at Seminario 4 y Guatemala, entrance in the corner of the Zócalo, open 0900-1800 daily except Mon., last tickets at 1700, entry US$0.40.

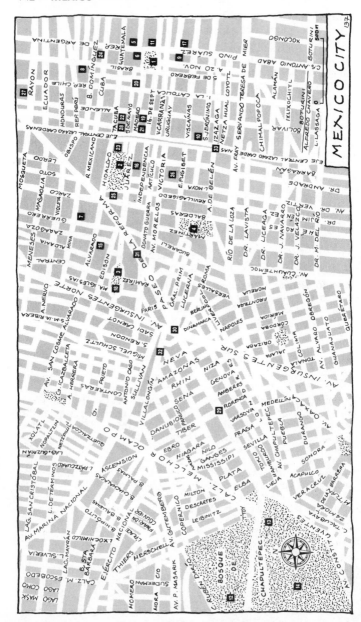

On the W side of the Zócalo are the Portales de los Mercaderes (Arcades of the Merchants), very busy since 1524. North of them, opposite the Cathedral, is

The Monte de Piedad (National Pawnshop) established in the 18th century and housed in a 16th-century building. Prices are government controlled and bargains are often found. Monthly auctions of unredeemed pledges.

The Palacio Nacional (National Palace) takes up the whole eastern side of the Zócalo. Built on the site of the Palace of Moctezuma and rebuilt in 1692 in colonial baroque, with its exterior faced in the red volcanic stone called *tezontle*; the top floor was added by President Calles in the 1920s. It houses various government departments and the Juárez museum (open Mon.-Fri., 1000-1800), free. Over the central door hangs the Liberty Bell, rung at 2300 on September 15 by the President, who gives the multitude the *Grito*—"Viva México!" The thronged frescoes around the staircase are by Diego Rivera (including *The History of Mexico*). Open daily; guides: ask them for the US$2 booklet on the frescoes. Other murals by Rivera can be seen at the Ministry of Education, four blocks N of Zócalo, on corner of Cuba and Argentina. In the Calle Moneda and adjoining the back of the Palace is the **Museo de las Culturas**, with interesting international archaeological and historical exhibits. Open 0930-1800; closed Suns. Also in Moneda are the site of the first university in the New World (building now dilapidated), the Archbishop's Palace, and the site of the New World's first printing press.

Wax Museum in a remarkable house at Londres 6, 1100-1900 daily.

Museo de Artes e Industrias Populares de México Av. Juárez 44, is reported to be less extensive than it was. Open Tues.-Sat. 1000-1400 and 1500-1800, shop 1000-1800 Mon.-Sat. Free. Operated by Instituto Nacional Indigenista (INI). It has well-arranged permanent exhibitions and the articles are for sale, although you may prefer to find cheaper goods at Ciudadela market (20% cheaper).

Supreme Court, opposite Palacio Nacional, on SE corner of the Zócalo, see frescoes by Orozco.

Mexico City: Key to map

1. Zócalo; 2. Alameda Central; 3. Plaza de la República; 4. Plaza Ciudadela and market; 5. Templo Mayor; 6. Cathedral; 7. San Fernando; 8. Santo Domingo; 9. Hospital de Jesus Nazareno; 10. Colegio de las Vizcaínas; 11. Palacio Nacional; 12. National Museum of Anthropology; 13. Museum of Modern Art; 14. Castle of Chapultepec; 15. San Carlos Museum; 16. Museum of Popular Arts and Industries; 17. Museum of the City of Mexico; 18. Museum and Monument of the Revolution; 19. Iturbide Palace; 20. Monte de Piedad; 21. Torre Latinoamericana and Casa de los Azulejos; 22. Palacio de la Minería and "El Caballito" statue; 23. Palacio de Bellas Artes; 24. Ministry of Education; 25. Pinacoteca Virreinal; 26. San Juan market; 27. Lagunilla market; 28. Main Post Office; 29. Independence Monument; 30. Monument to Cuauhtémoc; 31. Monument to Colombus; 32. La Madre Monument; 33. Salto del Agua fountain.

Palacio de Bellas Artes, a large, showy building, interesting for Art Deco lovers, houses a museum and a theatre, and a *cafeteria* at mezzanine level (light, average continental food at moderate prices). Open Tues.-Sun., 1100-1800. Its domes are lavishly decorated with coloured stone. The museum has old and contemporary paintings, prints, sculptures, and handicraft articles. The fresco by Rivera is a copy of the one rubbed out in disapproval at Radio City, New York, and there are spirited Riveras in the room of oils and water-colours. Other frescoes are by Orozco, Tamayo and Siqueiros. Daily, 1000-1730; Sun., 1000-1400. The most remarkable thing about the theatre is its glass curtain designed by Tiffany. It is solemnly raised and lowered before each performance of the Mexican Folklore Ballet. The Palace is listing badly, for it has sunk 4 metres since it was built. Operas are performed; there are orchestral concerts and performances by the superb Mexican Folklore Ballet on Wed., Sat. and Sun, 0930 and 2100—one must book in advance. Tickets from US$3 to US$10 (cheap balcony seats are good value as they provide a good vantage point to see formations from above). Tickets on sale from 1100. Cheap concerts at 1200 on Sun., and also at Teatro Hidalgo, behind Bellas Artes on Hidalgo, at the same time, book in advance.

Across the road, on the 41st floor of the **Torre Latinoamericana**, is a good restaurant and bar, *Cavalier*, with splendid views of the city, especially at sunset and after dark (entry fee US$3, cheaper to buy a drink at US$2.50). This great glass tower dominates the **Alameda Gardens**, once the Aztec market and later the place of execution for the Spanish Inquisition. Beneath the broken shade of eucalyptus, cypress and ragged palms, wide paths link fountains and heroic statues. (Much rebuilding going on in this area.)

On the northern side of the Alameda, on Av. Hidalgo, is the Jardín Morelos, flanked by two old churches: Santa Veracruz (1730) to the right and **San Juan de Dios** to the left. The latter has a richly carved baroque exterior; its image of San Antonio de Padua is visited by those who are broken-hearted for love. A new museum, the **Franz Mayer**, has been opened at the Hospital de San Juan de Dios (Hidalgo 45), next to the church, with fine exhibitions of European and Mexican decorative arts, paintings and sculpture, silver, pottery and furniture, also Mexican shawls and *sarapes* (open 1000-1700 except Mon., free on Sun.).

Escuela Nacional Preparatoria, N of Zócalo on Calle San Ildefonso, built 1749 as the Jesuit School of San Ildefonso in splendid baroque. There are some exciting frescoes by Orozco and (in the Anfiteatro Bolívar, which you will have to ask a guard to open up for you) by Diego Rivera and Fernando Leal.

Ministry of Education, on Argentina, 3 blocks from Zócalo, built 1922, contains frescoes by a number of painters. Here are Diego Rivera's masterpieces, painted between 1923 and 1930, illustrating the lives and sufferings of the common people.

Plaza Santo Domingo, two blocks N of the Cathedral, an intimate little plaza surrounded by fine colonial buildings: (a) a beautiful palace; (b) on the west side, the Arcades of Santo Domingo, where public scribes and owners of small hand-operated printing presses still carry on their business; (c) on the north side, the church of Santo Domingo, in Mexican baroque, 1737. Note the carving on the doors and façade; (d) the old School of Medicine, where the tribunals of the Inquisition were held (we are told that by standing on tiptoe in the men's room one can see—if tall enough—through the window into the prison cells of the Inquisition, which are not yet open to the public). There is a remarkable staircase in the patio, and striking Siqueiros murals above it. The nearby streets contain some fine examples of colonial architecture.

Two blocks E of Santo Domingo are the church and convent of **San Pedro y San Pablo** (1603), both massively built and now turned over to secular use. A block N is the public market of Abelardo L. Rodríguez, with striking mural decorations.

Church of Loreto, built 1816 and now tilting badly, but being restored, is on a square of the same name, surrounded by colonial buildings. Its façade is a remarkable example of "primitive" or "radical" neoclassicism.

La Santísima Trinidad (1677, remodelled 1755), to be seen for its fine towers and the rich carvings on its façade.

The Mercado Merced (metro Merced), said to be the largest market in all the Americas, dating back over 400 years. Its activities spread over several blocks. In the northern quarter of this market are the ruins of La Merced monastery; the fine 18th century patio is almost all that survives; the courtyard, on Avenida Uruguay, between Calle Talavera and Calle Jesús María, opposite No. 171, is nearly restored.

The oldest hospital in continental America, **Jesús Nazareno**, 20 de Noviembre 82, founded 1526 by Cortés, was remodelled in 1928, save for the patio and staircase. Cortés' bones have been kept since 1794 in the adjoining church, on the corner of Pino Suárez and República de El Salvador, diagonally opp. Museum of the City.

Avenida Madero leads from the Zócalo W to the Alameda. On it is **La Profesa** church, late 16th century, with a fine high altar and a leaning tower. The 18th century **Iturbide Palace**, Av. Madero 17, once the home of Emperor Agustín (1821-23), has been restored and has a clear plastic roof—wander around, it is now a bank head office. To the tourist the great sight of Av. Madero, however, is the **Casa de los Azulejos** (House of Tiles) at the Alameda end of the street. Now occupied by Sanborn's Restaurant, it was built in the 16th century, and is brilliantly faced with blue and white Puebla tiles. The staircase walls are covered with Orozco frescoes. (There are more Orozco frescoes at Biblioteca Iberoamericana on Cuba between 5 de Febrero and Argentina.) Over the way is the **Church of San Francisco**, founded in 1525 by the "Apostles of Mexico", the first 12 Franciscans to reach the country. It was by far the most important church in colonial days. Cortés' body rested here for some time, as did Iturbide's; the Viceroys attended the church.

Beyond San Francisco church, Eje Lázaro Cárdenas, formerly Calle

San Juan de Letrán, leads S towards **Las Vizcaínas**, at Plaza Las Vizcaínas, one block E, built in 1734 as a school for girls; some of it is still so used, but some of it has become slum tenements. In spite of neglect, it is still the best example of colonial secular baroque in the city. Not open to the public; permission to visit sometimes given.

Museo San Carlos, Puente de Alvarado 50 (metro Revolución), a 19th-century palace (open to visitors 1000 to 1700, closed Mon.), has fine Mexican colonial painting and a first-class collection of European paintings. The **Escuela Nacional de Artes Plásticas** at the corner of Academía and Calle Moneda, houses about 50 modern Mexican paintings. There is another picture gallery housing a collection of colonial paintings, the **Pinacoteca Virreinal**, in the former church of San Diego in Calle Dr. Mora, at the west end of the Alameda. (Cheap concerts on Thurs. at 2000.)

Moving eastwards along Av. Hidalgo, before the Palace of Fine Arts, on the right is the **Post Office**, built 1904.

North from the west side of the Post Office leads to the Calle Santa María la Redonda, at the end of which is **Plaza Santiago de Tlaltelolco**, next oldest Plaza to the Zócalo, heavily damaged in the 1985 earthquake. Here was the main market of the Aztecs, and on it, in 1524, the Franciscans built a huge church and convent. This is now the Plaza of the Three Cultures (Aztec, colonial and modern): (a) the Aztec ruins have been restored; (b) the magnificent baroque church of Santiago Tlaltelolco is now the focus of (c) the massive, multi-storey Nonoalco-Tlatelolco housing scheme, a garden city within a city, with pedestrian and wheeled traffic entirely separate.

About 4 blocks N of the Post Office off Eje Lázaro Cárdenas is **Plaza Garibaldi**, a must, especially on Saturday night, when up to 200 *mariachis* in their traditional costume of huge sombrero, tight silver-embroidered trousers, pistol and *sarape*, will play your favourite Mexican serenade for US$4. If you arrive by taxi you will be besieged. The whole square throbs with life and the packed bars are cheerful, though there is some danger from thieves and pickpockets, particularly after dark. The Lagunilla market is held about 4 blocks NE of the plaza, a hive of activity all week. Inexpensive nearby bar is *Guadalajara*: good drinks (but no soft drinks), dancing to *mariachi* band, entrance US$1, not dear. If very crowded, try *Tenampa*, somewhat dearer. On one side of Plaza Garibaldi is a gigantic eating hall, different stalls sell different courses, very entertaining.

Palacio de Minería, Calle Tacuba 9 (1797), is a fine old building, now restored, and once more level on its foundations. (Cheap concerts on Sun. at 1700, upstairs.) Moved from the Plaza de la Reforma to Plaza Manuel Tolsa opposite the Palacio is the great equestrian statue, "El Caballito", of King Charles IV cast in 1802; it weighs 26 tons and is the second-largest bronze casting in the world.

Museo Nacional de Arte, Tacuba 8, opp. Palacio de Minería, nr. main Post Office. Open Tues-Sun., 1000-1800; paintings, sculptures, objects from pre-hispanic times to modern artists. Entry US$0.20.

Along the S side of the Alameda, running E, is Av. Juárez, a fine street with a mixture of old and new buildings. Diego Rivera's "scandalous" fresco, "Sunday in the Alameda", has been removed from the earthquake-damaged Hotel del Prado and has been mounted in a new museum, **Museo Mural Diego Rivera**, on the N side of the new Parque de la Solidaridad (on the old Hotel Regis site) at Av. Juárez 77. A stroll down Calle Dolores, a busy and fascinating street, leads to the market of San Juan. The colonial church of Corpus Christi, on Av. Juárez, is now used to display and sell folk arts and crafts. The avenue ends at the small Plaza de la Reforma. At the corner of Juárez and Reforma is the National Lottery building. Drawings are held three times a week, at 2000: an interesting scene, open to the public. Beyond Plaza de la Reforma is the **Monumento a la Revolución**: a great copper dome, now rather tarnished, soaring above supporting columns set on the largest triumphal arches in the world. Beneath the monument is the **Museo Nacional de la Revolución**, dealing with the period 1867-1917, very interesting, lots of exhibits, videos (open Tues.-Sun., 1000-1700, free, but donation expected).

South of this area, on Plaza Ciudadela, is a large colonial building, **La Ciudadela**, dating from 1700. It has been used for all kinds of purposes but is now a library.

The wide and handsome but earthquake-damaged Paseo de la Reforma, 3 km. long, continues to Chapultepec Park: shops, offices, hotels, restaurants all the way. Along it are monuments to Columbus; to Cuauhtémoc and a 45-metre marble column to Independence, topped by the golden-winged figure of a woman, "El Angelito" to the Mexicans. Just before entering the park is the Salubridad (Health) Building. Rivera's frescoes in this building cannot be seen by the public, who can view only the stained-glass windows on the staircases.

Chapultepec Park, at the end of Paseo de la Reforma, with its thousands of ahuehuete trees, is beautiful but is becoming spoiled by constant littering (park closes at 1700). It contains a maze of pathways, a large lake, a marvellous botanical garden, shaded lawns, a zoo with giant pandas (free, closed Mon. and Tues.), a large amusement park (there is a section for children and another for adults) with huge roller-coasters (open Wed., Sat. and Sun., entry US$0.90, all rides free, except roller-coaster; on Sat. and Sun. only, US$0.22), bridle paths and polo grounds. Diego Rivera's famous fountain, the Fuente de Tlaloc, is near the children's amusement park. Just below the castle and a little to the left are the remains of the famous Arbol de Moctezuma, known locally as "El Sargento". This immense tree, which has a circumference of 14 metres and was about 60 metres high, has been cut off at a height of about 10 metres. In this park too, are the Don Quixote fountain, the Frog's fountain, the Niños Monument, and Monkey Island, a replica of Cacahuamilpa caves. In March there is a "Swan Lake" spectacle in the park. At the top of a hill in the park is Chapultepec Castle, with a view over Mexico Valley from its beautiful balconies, entry US$0.02. It has now become the **National Museum of History**, open 0900-1700. Its rooms were used by the Emperor Maximilian and the Empress Carlota during their brief reign. There is an unfinished mural by Siqueiros and a notable mural by O'Gorman on the theme of independence. Entrance US$0.20; US$0.12 on Sun. Halfway down the hill is the new **Gallery of Mexican History**. On Sun. mornings large numbers of people gather round the lake for open-air extension classes in a great variety of subjects (e.g. hairdressing, artificial flower-making, guitar-playing) organized by the University and open to all.

The crowning wonder of the park is the **Anthropological Museum** built by architect Pedro Ramírez Vásquez to house a vast collection illustrating pre-conquest Mexican culture. It has a 350-metre façade and an immense patio shaded by a gigantic concrete mushroom, 4,200 square metres—the world's largest concrete expanse supported by a single pillar. The largest exhibit (8½ metres high, weighing 167 tons) is the image of Tlaloc the rain god, removed—accompanied by protesting cloud bursts—from near the town of Texcoco to the museum. Open Tues.-Sat., 0900-1900 and Sun., 1000-1800. Only Mexican student cards accepted. Entrance is US$0.35 except Sun. (free), and holidays, when all museums charge US$0.10. Guides in English cost an additional US$0.20; ask for the parts you want to see as each tour only visits two of 23 halls; guided tours in Spanish free. Audio-visual introduction US$0.10. If you want to see everything, you need two days. Permission to photograph (no tripod or flash allowed) US$1.70 from entrance, if you are professionally interested, date must be fixed in advance; otherwise cameras not allowed. The most fanatical museum hater will enjoy this one, particularly the display of folk costumes upstairs. There is an excellent collection of English, French, German and Spanish books, especially guides to Mexican ruins, including maps. Cafeteria on site is good, reasonable prices.

Warning Be on the lookout for thieves in Chapultepec park, and especially in the underpass between Chapultepec metro and the Archaeological Museum. Sunday is the safest day.

There are five other museums in Chapultepec Park: the Tamayo Museum, and in the new section the museums of Natural History, Technology and **Modern Art** (US$0.50, students US$0.25). The last shows Mexican art only in two buildings, pleasantly set among trees with some sculptures in the grounds. The smaller building shows temporary exhibitions. The delightfully light architecture of the larger building is spoilt by a heavy, vulgar marble staircase, with a curious acoustic effect on the central landing under a translucent dome, which must have been unplanned; open 1100-1800 daily except Mon. The Gallery of Mexican History has dioramas, with tape-recorded explanations of Mexican history, and photographs of the 1910 Revolution. The **Tamayo Museum's** interior space is unusual in that you cannot tell which floor you are on or how many there are; usually displays Mexican artists, although international modern art is in its possession, situated between the Modern Art and Anthropology Museums, US$0.25 entry, ½ price to students with international card (only place in Mexico). The **Museum of Technology** is free; it is operated by the Federal Electricity Commission, has touchable exhibits which demonstrate electrical and energy principles. It is located beside the roller-coasters.

Natural History Museum In the Montana Rusa section of the Park, open 1000-1700, Tues to Sun. Entry 2 pesos.

Centro Cultural Contemporáneo, Campos Eliseos y Jorge Eliot, Polanco, has recently opened.

Further places of interest to tourists are as follows:

Museum of the City, on Av. Pino Suárez and República de El Salvador, shows the geology of the city and has life size figures in period costumes showing the history of different peoples before Cortés. In the attic above the museum is the studio of Joaquín Clausell, with walls covered with impressionist miniatures. Free admittance, Tues. to Thurs. Two blocks S on Misioneros from this museum is the **Anglican (Episcopal) Cathedral**, called the Cathedral of San José de Gracia. Built in 1642 as a Roman Catholic church, it was given by the Benito Juárez government to the Episcopal Mission in Mexico. Juárez himself often attended services in it.

Museo Nacional de las Culturas, Moneda 13, open 0930-1800, closed Sun. Exhibits of countries from all over the world and some historical information.

Museo de Arte Carrillo Gil, Av. Revolución esq. Los Leones, near San Angel; paintings by Orozco, Rivera, Siqueiros and others.

Instituto Nacional Indigenista, Av. Revolución 1297.

Escuela Nacional de Ingeniería, next to the main post office on Calle Tacuba, houses a permanent exhibition of meteorites found all over Mexico (up to 14 tonnes).

Museo Universitario del Chopo, E. G. Martínez 10, opp. metro San Cosme, nr. Insurgentes Norte. Contemporary international exhibitions (photography, art) in a church-like building. Saturday music market, records, cassettes, books, instruments, clothes traded and exchanged, particularly popular with young Mexicans.

Museo del Convento de Carmen, Av. Revolución 4, San Angel, open 1000-1700. **Museo Nacional de Culturas Populares**, Hidalgo 289, focuses on livelihoods in Mexico (open 0900-1600, Tues., Thurs., Sat.; 0900-2000, Weds. and Fri., and 1100-1700, Sun.)

Casasola Archive, Praga 16, in Zona Rosa, T 564-9214, amazing photos of the revolutionary period, reproduction for sale.

The **Siqueiros Polyforum**, on Insurgentes Sur, includes a handicraft shop, a museum of the evolution of man, and huge frescoes by Siqueiros, one of the largest in the world, inside the ovoid dome. Entrance to the frescoes US$1; *son et lumière* daily except Sun. at 1800 in English, 1600 and 1930 in Spanish. Next door is the former *Hotel de México* skyscraper, which is to become Mexico's World Trade Centre.

NB For details of other museums, far from the centre, see under Suburbs, **page 165**, and Teotihuacan, **page 170**.

Modern Buildings On Avenida Insurgentes Norte is a remarkable building by Alejandro Prieto: the Teatro de Los Insurgentes, a theatre and opera house seating 1,300 people. The main frontage on the Avenida consists of a high curved wall without windows. This wall is entirely covered with mosaic decoration, the work of Diego Rivera: appropriate figures, scenes, and portraits composed round the central motif of a gigantic pair of hands holding a mask, worth going a distance to see.

The most successful religious architecture in Mexico today is to be found in the churches put up by Enrique de la Mora and Félix Candela; a good example is the chapel they built in 1957 for the Missionaries of the Holy Spirit, in a garden behind high walls at Av. Universidad 1700. (An excellent Candela church, and easy to see, is the Church of La Medalla Milagrosa, just to the E of Avenida Universidad at the junction of Avenida División Norte, Metro station División del Norte.) "All the churches and chapels built by this team have such lightness and balance that they seem scarcely to rest on their foundations." One of the seminal works of one of Mexico's greatest modern architects, Luís Barragán, is at Los Clubes, Las Arboledas bus from Chapultepec bus station. See also the *objet trouvé* mural at the Diana cinema in the centre of the city, and Orozco's great thundercloud of composition, the "Apocalypse", at the Church of Jesús Nazareno. Both the *Camino Real Hotel* and the IBM technical centre were designed by Ricardo Legorreto; very well worth seeing. Consult Max Cetto's book on modern Mexican architecture. In this connection, University City (see next page) is also well worth a look.

The **Bull Ring** is said to be the largest in the world, and holds 60,000 spectators. Bull fights are held every Sunday at 1600 from October through March. The Bull Ring is in the Ciudad de los Deportes (City of Sports), Plaza México, reached by Av. de los Insurgentes. (A little to the W of where Los Insurgentes crosses Chapultepec, and on Av. Chapultepec itself between Calles Praga and Varsovia, are the remains of the old aqueduct built in 1779.) Besides the Bull Ring, the Sports City contains a football stadium holding 50,000 people, a boxing ring, a cinema, a *frontón* court for *jai-alai*, a swimming pool, restaurants, hotels, etc.

Sullivan Park (popularly known as Colonia Park or Jardín del Arte) is reached by going up Paseo de la Reforma to the intersection with Los Insurgentes, and then W two blocks between Calles Sullivan and Villalongín. Here, each Sunday afternoon, there is a display of paintings, engravings and sculptures near the monument to Motherhood, packed with sightseers and buyers; everything is for sale (beware of thieves).

Reino Aventura, S of the city near the Mall del Sur, amusement park for children along Disneyland lines, clean, orderly, popular with families.

The **Basilica of Guadalupe**, in the Gustavo A. Madero district, often called La Villa de Guadalupe, in the outer suburbs to the NE, is the most venerated shrine in Mexico, for it was here, in December 1531, that the Virgin appeared three times, in the guise of an Indian princess, to the Indian Juan Diego and imprinted her portrait on his cloak. The cloak is preserved, set in gold and protected by a 27-ton railing of silver, at the centre of the magnificent altar. A chapel stands over the well which gushed at the spot where the Virgin appeared. The great day here is December 12, the great night the night before. A huge, modern basilica has been built next door, impressive and worth visiting; it holds over 20,000 people. The original basilica is being converted into a museum and was closed in Dec. 1988. Mostly representations of the image on the cloak, but interesting painted tin plates offering thanks for cures, etc., from about 1860s. There are, in fact, about seven churches in the immediate neighbourhood, including one on the hill above; most of them are at crazy angles to each other and to the ground, because of subsidence; the subsoil is very soft. The Templo de los Capuchinos has been the subject of a remarkable feat of engineering in which one end has been raised 3.375 metres so that the building is now horizontal. There is a little platform from which to view this work. Buses marked La Villa go close to the site, or you can go by metro to La Villa (Line 6).

Festivals The largest is the Independence celebration on 15 September, when the President gives the *grito*: "Viva México" from the Palacio Nacional on the Zócalo at 2300, and rings the Liberty Bell (now, sadly, electronic!). This is followed by fireworks, and on 16 September (0900-1400) there are military and traditional regional parades in the Zócalo and surrounding streets.

Hotels Prices normally include 15% tax but not service, check in advance. The rates shown are for April 1990 (reductions often available); check if breakfast is included in the room price. Many hotels were destroyed or irreparably damaged by the 1985 earthquake, particularly in the following streets: Paseo de la Reforma, Av. Juárez, Calle Revillagigedo and Calle Luis Moya. Discounts in many hotels if booked through Wagon-Lits México. There are fair hotel reservation services at the railway station and at the airport; also services for more expensive hotels at bus stations.

The following paragraph lists, in alphabetical order, the hotels in our luxury price range: *Camino Real*, Mariano Escobedo 700, T 203-2121, L; *Crowne Plaza (Holiday Inn)*, Paseo de la Reforma 80, T 705-1515, L, with restaurants, bars, nightclubs, superior business facilities; *El Stouffer Presidente*, Campos Eliseos 218, T 250-7700, L-L+; *Fiesta Americana Aeropuerto*, Fundidora de Monterrey 89, L, includes health spa, T1-800-FIESTA 1; *Galería Plaza*, Hamburgo 195, T 211-0014, L; *Howard Johnson Gran Hotel de México* 16 de Septiembre 82 (Zócalo), T 510-4040, L, has an incredible foyer, 30's style; *Imperial*, Reforma 64, T 566-4879, L-L+, very good, restaurant, café, bar, 24-hr service, business facilities, etc; *Krystal*, Liverpool 155, T 211-0092, L. A new, rec. good hotel is the *Marco Polo*, Amberes 27, T 511-1839, in the Zona Rosa, L; *María Isabel Sheraton*, Paseo de la Reforma 325, T 207-3933, L-L+, Hotel and Towers (opp. Angel of Independence), all facilities; *Nikko*, Campos Eliseos 204, T 203-4020, L+; *Royal Zona Rosa*, Amberes 78, T 525-4858, L.

In our categories A and B are: *Aristos*, Paseo de la Reforma 276, T 211-0112, A; *Bristol*, Plaza Necaxa 17 (T 533-60-60), B, very good; *Century*, Liverpool 152, T 584-7111, A; the *Cortés*, Av. Hidalgo 85, T 518481, B, is the only baroque-style hotel in Mexico City, a former pilgrims' guest house, with a pleasant patio; *Diplomático*, Av. Insurgentes Sur 1105, T 563-6066, B; *Flamingos Plaza*, Av. Revolución 333, T 271-7044, A; *Genève Calinda*, Londres 130, T 211-0071, B, pleasant dining area. *María Cristina*, Lerma 31, T 566-9688, B; *Plaza Florencia*, Florencia 61, T 525-4800, A, in Zona Rosa.

Motels in the top price ranges include: *Holiday Inn*, Blvd. Aeropuerto 502, T

762-4088, L, with all facilities; *Dawn Motor Hotel*, Blvd. Avila Camacho 680, Naucalpan, T 373-2155, B; *Park Villa*, Gómez Pedraza 68 (near Chapultepec Park, T 515-5245, C.

Brasilia, excellent modern hotel, near Central del Norte bus station, D, on Av. Cien Metros 48-25, king size bed, TV, 24-hr. traffic jam in front; *Ejecutivo*, Viena 8, T 566-6422, C, staff helpful, rec.; *Hidalgo*, Sta. Veracruz 37, modern, good, C, good 5-course lunch. *Cancún*, Donato Guerra 24, C, safe, clean, rec. *Plaza Madrid*, Madrid 2, *Uxmal*, same entrance, D, with access to better *Madrid* facilities; *Fleming*, Revillagigedo 35, D, good value, central; *Prim*, Versalles 46, T 592-4600, C, clean, good in all respects; *Catedral*, Donceles 95, behind Cathedral, D, clean, spacious (but bed bugs); *Metropol*, Luis Moya 39, T 510-8660, D, touristy, good restaurant, good value, rec.; *Del Valle*, Independencia 35, T 521-8067, D, with bath, TV, clean; *Marlowe*, Independencia 17, T 521-9540, D, clean, helpful staff, but poor restaurant; *Mallorca*, Serapio Rendón 119, T 566-4833, D, clean, reasonable; *Gilbert*, Amado Nervo 37, Col. Buenavista, Mex. 4DF, T 547-92-80, D, good location but a bit spooky at night; *Pisa*, Insurgentes Norte 58, E, rec.; *Jardín Amazonas*, Río Amazonas 73 (T 533-59-50), C; *Regente*, París 9, T 566-8933, D, clean, friendly, noisy at front, restaurant; *Jena*, Jesús Terán 12, C, new, central, rec. (but not the travel agency on the premises). *Mayaland*, Maestro Antonio Caso 23, C, with bath, good value, rec.; *Polanco*, Edgar Poe 8, T 520-6040, near Chapultepec, dark, quiet, C, good restaurant; *Sevilla*, Serapio Rendón 126 and Sullivan, D, restaurant, garage, reasonable; *Avenida*, Lázaro Cárdenas 38, T 518-1007, (Bellas Artes metro), C with bath, hot water, safe, night porter. *Casa González*, Lerma y Sena (near British Embassy), D, full board, shower, English spoken by Sr. González, clean, quiet and friendly; *Atlanta*, corner of B. Domínguez and Allende, D, good, quiet, clean and friendly, rec.; *Marina*, opposite, is F, very good. *Isabel la Católica* (street of the same name, No. 63, T 518-12-13) is pleasant, popular, clean, central, quite good restaurant, D, with bath, luggage held, rooms on top floor with shared bathroom are cheaper; *Gillow*, 5 de Mayo e Isabel la Católica, T 518-1213, D, central, large, clean, many services, attractive.

We have been advised that the best of the cheaper hotels are in the old part of town between the Zócalo and the Alameda, and there are more N of the Plaza República. *Detroit*, Zaragoza 55, E, very central, clean, rec., has parking; *Savoy*, Zaragoza, F with shower, clean, good value; *Royalty*, Jesús Terán 21, E, clean, phone in room, highly rec.; *Yale*, Mosqueta 200 (near main railway station), E with bathroom, phone and TV, clean and friendly, rec.; *Suiza*, Aldama 99 in Guerrero district, near Delegación de Cuauhtémoc (near bus and railway stations), E, shower, clean, rec., except for noise; *Pontevedra*, Insurgentes Norte opp. railway station, E, clean, helpful, will store luggage; *Washington*, 5 de Mayo 54, E, clean, friendly, rec.; *Santander*, Arista 22, not far from railway station, E, with bath, good value and service, clean; *Monte Carlo*, Uruguay 69 (D. H. Lawrence's hotel), clean, friendly owner, E, with bath, good about storing luggage, car park inside the hotel premises—small fee, rooms in front noisy, recently renovated; *Concordia*, Uruguay 13, nr. Niño Perdido, excellent, E, lift, phone; *Ontario*, Uruguay 87, F, nice exterior but run-down rooms, telephone; on same street, one block away, *Roble*, Uruguay 109 y Pino Suárez, D, with shower, hot water, clean, phone and TV, good; *Carlton*, Ignacio Mariscal 32-bis, clean, safe, rec.; *Oxford*, Mariscal 67, E, very clean, radio and TV; *Casa de los Amigos*, Mariscal 132 (T 705-05-21), near train and bus station, F, use of kitchen, rec., max. 15-day stay, separation of sexes, run by Quakers, breakfast and laundry facilities, safe-keeping for luggage, advance booking recommended; *Danky*, Donato Guerra 10, E with bath, central, hot water, phone, clean, easy parking (T 546-9960/61), rec.; *República*, Cuba, E, a few blocks from Zócalo, central, clean, pleasant, but not all rooms have windows; *Cuba*, down from *República*, E, clean, good value;

Habana, República de Cuba 77, NW of Zócalo, D, good value; *San Pedro*, Mesones and Pino Suárez, F, clean and friendly, good value. *Congreso*, good, central, F, at Allende 18; *Jardines de Churubusco*, Calzada de Tlalpan 1885, nr. General Anaya metro, excellent value, F. Near Allende metro are *Rioja*, Av. 5 de Mayo 45, shared or private baths, fairly clean, nosiy at times, well placed, F, rec.; next door (No. 47) is *Canadá*, T 518-2106, D, good value, friendly and helpful; *York* on same street, F, cheaper for longer stays; *Florida*, Belisario Domínguez 57, E, TV, shower, clean, rec; *Galicia*, Honduras 11, good; *Galveston*, Insurgentes Sur 50, F, cheap, clean, safe; *Hospedaje Estadio* on Coahuila, nr. Insurgentes Sur, F, very clean; *América*, Buena Vista 4 (nr. Revolución metro), E, with bath, clean, good service, rec.; *Londres*, F, Buenavista 5, clean, friendly, occasionally noisy. *Lafayette*, Motolinia 40 and 16 de Septiembre in the Zona 1, E-D, with bath, and TV, clean, quiet (pedestrian precinct), but check rooms, there's a variety of sizes, watch your luggage; *Buenos Aires*, Motolinia, F, hot shower till 2200, friendly, noisy, cockroaches, will store luggage; *Lepanto*, Guerrero 90, E, set lunch, 6 courses, very good value, modern; *Ambasad*, E, with bath, telephone, TV room, clean, very good value, beside Pino Suárez metro; also nearby *Ambar*, San Jerónimo y Pino Suárez, E, shower, TV, phones in rooms, good service, highly rec.; *Encino*, Av. Insurgentes, 1 block from the railway station, E, clean, private bath; *Managua*, on Plaza de la Iglesia de San Fernando, near Hidalgo metro, D, with bath, phone, TV, good location, car park, very friendly, run down as is *Monaco* opposite, also D; *Cima*, Av. Alfonso Cevallo 12, 1 street from metro Moctezuma, convenient for Oriente bus terminal, F, clean, shower.

For longer stays, *Suites Quinta Palo Verde*, Cerro del Otate 20, Col. Romero de Terreros (Mexico 21 DF) T 554-35-75, C, pleasant, diplomatic residence turned guest house, near the University; run by a veterinary surgeon, Miguel Angel, very friendly, speaks English and German, but the dogs are sometimes noisy. *Suites Havre*, Havre 74, near Zona Rosa, rec. for longer stays, 56 suites with kitchen, phone and service, US$450 a month, US$150 a week. *Club Med* head office for Club Med and *Villas Arqueológicas* reservations, Calle Masaryk 183, Col. Polanco, México 11570, T 203-3086/3833, Telex 1763346.

Youth Hostels Asociación Mexicana de Albergues de la Juventud, Madero 6, Of. 314, México 1, D. F. Write for information. Mexico City SETEJ hostel at Cozumel 57, Colonia Roma, not far from Chapultepec Park (Sevilla metro, Line 1). Requires Mexican *and* IHS card, very basic, G, not rec. There is a similar organization, CREA, at Of. Oxtopulco No. 40, Col. Oxtopulco, casilla postal 04310, T 548-8740/8783. There is a CREA *albergue* (hostel) on Av. Insurgentes Sur y Camino Sta Teresa, Delegación Tlalpan, C.P. 14000, T 573-7740/655-1416, also accepts trailers. See also Setej, under **addresses** below. Agencia Nacional de Turismo Juvenil on Plaza Insurgentes.

Camp Sites Campo Escuela Nacional de Tantoco, Km. 29.5 on road Mexico-City to Toluca, T 512-2279, cabins and campsite; facilities also at CREA (see above). See also American Automobile Association's "Mexico by Motor". There is a trailer-park—15 km. N on road to Querétaro, Av. Hidalgo 11, Lago de Guadelupe, Cuantitlan, Izcali, T 873-2622, owner speaks English. Or try the parking lot of the Museum of Anthropology.

Restaurants All the best hotels have good restaurants.
Mexican food: Note the *Hotel Majestic's* Mexican breakfast, Sat. and Sun. till 1200, excellent, US$5.50, go to terrace on 7th floor, otherwise food mediocre. *San Angel Inn*, in San Angel, is excellent and very popular, so book well in advance (San Angel may be reached by bus from Chapultepec Park or by trolley bus from Metro Taxqueña). *El Caminero*, behind *María Isabel Sheraton Hotel*, is an excellent open-air taco restaurant; *Vero's*, Tolstoy 23, Col. Anzures, off Reforma and near Chapultepec Park, very reasonable corridas; many cheap

restaurants on Chapultepec, *Buffet Coyoacán*, on Allende, 50 metres from Frida Kahlo museum, fixed price (about US$4) for unlimited helpings. *Taquería Lobo Bobo*, Insurgentes Sur 2117, mushrooms a speciality; *Bellinghausen*, Londres y Niza (Mexican, not German); *Hostelería Santo Domingo*, Santo Domingo 72, 6 blocks from Cathedral, good food and service, the oldest restaurant in the city and one of the best; *La Plancha Azteca*, Río Lerma 54, good tacos and tortas, moderate prices; *Don Chon*, Regina, Aztec dishes, try mosquito larvae in wonderful piquant sauce; *Anderson's*, Reforma 400, very good atmosphere, reasonable, excellent local menu. *Fonda del Recuerdo* for excellent mole poblano, Bahía de las Palmas 39A, 17DF, with music. *Club de Periodistas de México*, F. Mata 8, near Calle 5 de Mayo, open to public, OK. More expensive but still good value, *Las Delicias*, Venezuela 41; *El Parador*, Niza 17, good local and international; *La Carreta Rosa*, Hamburgo 96B, good filling meals, reasonably priced; *Lory's de México*, Génova 73, and *La Calesa de Londres*, Londres 102, good meat at both. *Victor*, Ayuntamiento 169, near Buccarelli, metro Salto de Agua, very good value. A very old restaurant with interesting tile décor and not touristy is the *Café Tacuba*, Tacuba 28; it specializes in Mexican food, very good enchiladas.

International: *Ambassadeurs*, Paseo de la Reforma 12 (swank and high priced); *Del Lago*, in exciting modern building in Chapultepec Park, excellent; *Focolare*, Hamburgo 87 (swank and high priced); *Delmonico's*, Londres 87 and 16 de Septiembre, elegant; *Jena*, Morelos 110 (deservedly famous, à la carte, expensive); *Alex Cardini's*, Madrid 21, home of the Caesar Salad. *Le Gourmet*, Dakota 155, said to be most expensive restaurant in Mexico, and also said to be worth it! *El Refugio*, Liverpool 166, tourist-oriented, good desserts, check bill carefully.

US and other Latin American: *Shirley's*, Reforma 108, real American food, moderate prices, esp. the buffet after midday; *Sanborn's*, 36 locations (known as the foreigners' home-from-home: soda fountain, drugstore, restaurant, English language magazines, handicrafts, chocolates, etc., try their restaurant in the famous 16th century *Casa de los Azulejos*, the "house of tiles" at Av. Madero 17: famous dish is "chilaquiles Sanborns"); the *VIPS* chain in several locations offers plentiful food at moderate prices. Many US chain fast-food restaurants. *Rincón Gaucho*, Insurgentes Sur 1162, Argentine food.

Spanish: *La Cava*, Insurgentes Sur 2465 (excellent food and steaks, lavishly decorated as an old French tavern, moderate); *del Cid*, Humboldt 61, Castilian with medieval menu; *Mesón del Castellano*, Bolívar and Uruguay, good, plentiful and not too dear, excellent steaks; *Centro Catalán*, Bolívar 31, excellent paella (2nd floor). Many economical restaurants in Calle 5 de Mayo: *La Nueva Opera* there has Spanish and Mexican food. *Vasco*, Madero 6, 1st floor and *Español*, Calle López 60, good Spanish food, including roast kid. *Casa Regional Valenciana*, López 60, 3rd floor; *Mesón del Perro Andaluz*, Copenhague 26, very pleasant, US$5 for Spanish all-inclusive meal; *Centro Asturiano*, Orizaba and Puebla, Spanish.

Other European: French cuisine at *La Lorraine*, San Luís Potosí 132 (home style), *Les Moustaches*, Río Sena 88, and *La Madelon*, Río Plata 55, home style. *Napoleón*, French, and *Viena*, Viennese, in Plaza Popocatépetl; *Chalet Suizo*, Niza 37 (very popular with tourists, specializes in Swiss and German food, moderate); *Rivoli*, Hamburgo 123 (a gourmet's delight, high priced); *Café Konditori*, Génova 61, Danish open sandwiches; *Varsovia*, Paseo de la Reforma, Yugoslav food, very good value, also suitable for vegetarians. *La Pérgola*, Londres 107B, in the Zona Rosa, Italian; *La Casserole*, Insurgentes Sur near Núcleo Radio Mil building, French; *Rhin*, Av. Juárez, cheap, good, German décor. The *Piccadilly Pub*, Copenhague 23, serves British food at its best, especially steak and kidney pie, US$3; very popular with Mexicans and expatriates alike. Similar (and dearer), is *Sir Winston Churchill*, Avila Camacho 67.

Seafood: *La Marinera*, Liverpool 183, best seafood restaurant in Mexico City. Reasonable *ostionería* (oyster bar) at Bolívar 56, try Baja California Chablis. *El Nuevo Acapulco*, López 9 (excellent sea food, inexpensive).

Oriental and Middle Eastern: *Tibet-Hamz*, Av. Juárez 64 (Chinese restaurant specializing in Cantonese and Mexican national dishes, centrally located, nice atmosphere, moderate); *Ehden*, Correo Mayor 74, 1st floor, open Sun., authentic and reasonably priced Arab food; at Copenhague 20, *Ginza*, good Japanese. *Mr Lee*, Independencia 19-B, Chinese, seafood, good food, value and service; *Victoria*, Bolívar 41, cheap, good Chinese.

Vegetarian: *El Vegetariano*, Filomeno Mata 13, open 0800-2000, closed Sun., 4-course meal US$3.50; *Comedor Vegetariano No. 4*, Dolores 57, good lunch for US$1. *Chalet Vegetariano*, near Dr. Río de la Loza; *El Bosque*, Hamburgo 15 between Berlín and Dinamarca, rec. Vegetarian restaurant at Motolinia 31, near Madero, is open Mon.-Sat. 1300-1800, reasonably priced. *Yug*, Varsovia 3, excellent and cheap vegetarian, 4-course set lunch US$1.50 (it's worth queuing to get in). Wholewheat bread at *Pastelería Ideal* on 16 de Septiembre 14 (near Casa de Los Azulejos). Health food shop, *Alimentos Naturales*, close to metro Revolución, on P. Arriagal.

Cafés etc.: *El Buen Café*, Sonora 9, has chess sets to lend. *El Reloj*, 5 de Febrero 50, good comida and à la carte; *Pastelería Madrid*, 5 de Febrero 25, one block from *Hotel Isabel la Católica*, good pastries. Also on 5 de Febrero, *Café Blanca*, friendly, reasonably priced food, open till midnight. *Azteca*, Pino Suárez 68, good food. Good small restaurants in Uruguay, near *Monte Carlo Hotel*; the *Maple*, next to *Hotel Roble* at No. 109, has been rec. for its comida. Another centre for small restaurants is Pasaje Jacarandas, off Génova; *Llave de Oro* and many others. Cheap cafeterias in Calle Belisario Domínguez. Good breakfasts at *Coliseo*, Bolívar 28. *La Bombi*, corner of Tacuba and Brasil, rec. Typical, non-touristy snack-bar, *Poblanos*, at Heliópolis and Allende in the Tacuba area.

Bars *Opera Bar*, 5 de Mayo near Bellas Artes, good atmosphere, see Pancho Villa's bullet-hole in ceiling. *Bar Jardín*, in the *Hotel Reforma; El Colmenar*, Ejido y Eliseo; *El Morroco*, Club Marrakesh, Calle Florencia.

Cabarets and Night Clubs Every large hotel has one. *El Patio*, Atenas 9; *Passepartout*, Calle Hamburgo, *La Madelon*, Florencia 36; *Gitanerías*, Oaxaca 15, wild gypsy show; *Capri*, on the tourist guided route, to be avoided. *Hotel de Cortés* has Mexican Fiesta incl. meal Sat., entertainment. *El 77*, Calle Londres, Flamenco show. There are many discotheques in the better hotels and scattered throughout town.

Folk Music *Peña El Cóndor Pasa* is a cafeteria, open 1900-0100, closed on Tues., on Rafael Checal, San Angel; it has different folk-music groups every night; get there early. A fine place for light refreshments and music is the *Hostería del Bohemio*, formerly the San Hipólito monastery, near Reforma on Av. Hidalgo 107, metro Hidalgo. Look hard for the entrance: no sign, poetry and music every night from 1700 to 2200, light snacks and refreshments US$1, no cover charge.

Clubs *Sports* Reforma Athletic Club, Hacienda de los Morales, Lomas de Chapultepec; Churubusco Sports Club (golf, tennis, swimming); French Club in San Angel; British, Mexican, and Spanish boating clubs, in Xochimilco, near Mexico City; Polo Club in Lomas de Chapultepec. Club Suiza, Borja 840.

General American Legion, Lucerna 71; Spanish Club, Isabel la Católica 29; YMCA, Av. Ejército Nacional 253; YWCA, corner of Humboldt 62 and Artículo 123 (US$4.80 for single room with bath, good restaurant and laundry); Lions Club, Ures 13; Rotary Club, Londres 15; Automobile Club (Asociación Mexicana Automovilística-AMA), Av. Chapultepec 276; Women's International Club, Humboldt 47; University of Mexico, Paseo Reforma 150; Junior League Library,

Iturbide Building, Av. Madero.

Art Galleries *Arvil*, Cerrada Hamburgo 9, contemporary Mexican and international art; *Artmex*, Mexican Popular Gallery, Sabino 13; permanent exhibition of over 100 paintings of well-known Mexican artists, open 0900-1900. *Central Art Gallery Migrachi*, Av. Juárez 4, sculptures, drawings, also *Galería de Arte Migrachi*, on Génova 20. *Galería Lanai*, Hamburgo 151. *Galería Merkup*, Moliere 328. *Galerías Rubens*, Independencia 68. *Galería Tere Haas*, important contemporary artists, Génova 2-C. *Summa Artis*, Hotel Presidente Chapultepec, Campos Elíseos 218, contemporary Mexican art. *Val-Ray Gallery*, Reforma 412, Zona Rosa.

Shopping Mexico's "West End", the Zona Rosa (Pink Zone), where most of the fashionable shops and many restaurants are found, is bounded by the Paseo de la Reforma, Av. Chapultepec, Calle Florencia and Av. Insurgentes Sur. Note that most streets in the Zone are called after foreign cities—Londres, Liverpool, Hamburgo, Niza, Amberes (Antwerp), Génova, Copenhague, etc. The handicrafts section is between Liverpool and Hamburgo. There are also many handicraft shops on Av. Juárez. Mexican jewellery and hand-made silver can be bought everywhere. Among the good silver shops are *Sanborn's*, *Calpini*, *Prieto*, and *Vendome*. There are also good buys in perfumes, quality leather, and suede articles.

Markets San Juan market, Calle Ayuntamiento and Arandas, nr. Salto del Agua metro, good prices for handicrafts, especially leather goods (also cheap fruit); open 0930-1800. The Plaza Ciudadela market (Mercado Central de Artesanías, open 1100-1800 weekdays, Sun. 1100-1400), just off Balderas (metro Juárez), government-sponsored, reasonable and uncrowded, is cheaper, but not for leather, than San Juan; craftsmen from all Mexico have set up workshops here. Mercado Lagunilla on Calle Allende near Plaza de Sta. Cecilia (formerly Garibaldi) is mainly for domestic goods, open Sun. Market in Calle Londres (Zona Rosa) good for silver, but expensive. There is a market in every district selling pottery, glassware, textiles, *sarapes* and jewellery. Try also San Angel market, although expensive, many items are exclusive to it; good leather belts; open Sat. only from about 1100. Mexican tinware and lacquer are found everywhere. Copperware and more in market opp. airmail post office, Aldama 211. Fruit and veg market, Mercado Merced, Metro Merced. Buena Vista craft market, Aldama 187 y Degollado (nearest metro Guerrero), excellent quality. You can bargain in the markets and smaller shops.

   Government *artesanía* shop in basement of Siqueiros Polyforum, on Insurgentes Sur. Other sponsored shops: *Arts and Crafts of Michoacán and Querétaro*, Glorieta del Metro de Los Insurgentes, Locales 14 and 17 (T 525 01 37). *Tienda del Arte e Industrias Populares* at Juárez 44. Try also *Decorask*, Pino Suárez 28. *Fonart*, Fondo Nacional para el Fomento de las Artesanías, Av. Patriotismo 691, main office and branches at Av. Juárez 89, Londres 136 (Altos A) in the Zona Rosa, Londres 6 in Colonia Roma, Av. de la Paz 37 in San Angel, Insurgentes Sur 1630 and at Manuel Izaguirre 10 in Ciudad Satélite, with items from all over the country, rec. The Mercado de Artesanías Finas Indios Verdes is at Galería Reforma Norte S.A., F.G.Bocanegro 44 (corner of Reforma Norte, nr. Statue of Cuitlahuac, Tlatelolco); good prices and quality but no bargaining. There is an annual national craft fair in Mexico City, 1st week in Dec. Good selection of onyx articles at the *Brunner* shop, in Calle Dolores. *Victor*, at Av. Madero 10/305, 2nd floor, has genuine, and high quality craft articles. With the extension of the ring roads around the city, hypermarkets are being set up: there are two, *Perisur* at the extreme S end of the city (with Liverpool, Sears, Sanborn's and Palacio de Hierro), with quite futuristic designs, open Tues.-Fri. 1100-2000, Sat. 1100-2100; and *Plaza Satélite* at the extreme N end of the city (with Sumesa, Sears and Liverpool), open on Sunday. Luggage repairs (moderate prices) at Rinconada de

Jesús 15-G, opposite Museum of the City of Mexico on Pino Suárez, but opening times can be unreliable; better try the shop in Callejon del Parque del Conde off Pino Suárez opp. Hospital de Jesús church.

Handicrafts by Guatemalan refugees are available from the Secretaría de Ayuda a Refugiados Guatemaltecos, Apartado 18-858, T 523-2114 (please phone or write first). Address is Dr. Arce 25A, Colonia Doctores, near metro Hospital General.

Bookshops Many good ones, e.g. *American Book Store*, Madero 25, excellent selection of Penguins and Pelicans, low mark-up, stocks this *Handbook*; *Librería Inglés* opposite has English books; *Libros, Libros, Libros*, Monte Ararat 220, Lomas Barrilaco, T 540-47-78, hundreds of hardback and paperback English titles; a new shop in the Zócalo, at the entrance to the Templo Mayor, has a good selection of travel books and guides in many languages; *Librairie Française*, Reforma 250A, for French selection; *Librería Británica*, Av. de la Paz 23, San Angel; the British bookshop at Serapio Rendón 125 has a second-hand section where you can trade in old books (as long as they're neither even slightly damaged nor "highbrow") and buy new ones, but at poor rates; *Casa Libros*, Monte Athos 355 (Lomas), large stock of second-hand English book, the shop is staffed by volunteers, gifts of books welcome, all proceeds to the American Benevolent Society. *Librería Gandhi*, Calle Miguel Angel de Quevedo (metro Quevedo), art books, discs, tapes. *Libros y Discos*, Madero 1. The *Sanborn* chain has the largest selection of English-language paperbacks, art books and magazines in the country. Second-hand book market on Independencia just past junction with Eje Lázaro Cárdenas has some English books; also Puente de Alvarado, 100 m. from Hidalgo metro, and Dr Bernard 42, metro Niños Héroes.

Photography Kodak film (Ektachrome, not Kodachrome) is produced in Mexico and is not expensive. Small shops on República de Chile N of Tacuba are cheaper than larger ones S of Av. 5 de Mayo.

Traffic System The city has two ring roads, the Anillo Periférico around the city outskirts, and the Circuito Interior running within its circumference. In the centre, the system of Ejes Viales has been developed in recent years. It consists of a series of freeways laid out in a grid pattern, spreading from the Eje Central; the latter serves as a focal point for numbering (Eje 2 Poniente, Eje I Oriente etc.). Norte, Sur, Oriente, Poniente refer to the roads' position in relation to the Eje Central. The system is remarkably clear in its signposting with special symbols for telephones, information points, tram stops, etc. Beware of the tram lines—trams, buses, emergency services and plain simple folk in a hurry come down at high speed; and as often as not this lane goes against the normal flow of traffic! Bicycles are permitted to go the wrong way on all roads, which also "adds to the spice of life". **N.B.** Eje Lázaro Cárdenas used to be called Calle San Juan de Letrán. The transport police are reported to have become more helpful.

City Buses Buses have been coordinated into one system: odd numbers run North-South, evens East-West. Fares 100-300 pesos, exact fare only. There are 60 direct routes and 48 feeder (SARO) routes. We are informed that thieves and pickpockets haunt the buses plying along Reforma and Juárez. Be careful of your valuables! A most useful route for tourists (and well-known to thieves, so don't take anything you don't require immediately) is No. 76 which runs from Calle Uruguay (about the level of the Juárez Monument at Parque Alameda) along Paseo de la Reforma, beside Chapultepec Park. A new *Peribus* service goes round the entire Anillo Periférico (see Traffic System). The 100 bus line also insures its passengers: collection of insurance requires presentation of the ticket.

Taxis Taxis are fitted with taximeters, but they are not used when inflation changes prices, always ask in advance what a journey will cost. Cabs called by radio charge from the time of the call. Fixed-route taxis (VW Kombis) go back and forth on Reforma and its eastern extensions as far as the Zócalo, and on Insurgentes. Number of fingers held out indicates number of seats left. Fares about US$0.10, at driver's discretion. Wave down at special stops on kerb or even from kerb itself. Up to 17 fixed routes. No tip necessary. Fixed-route taxis have to be identified by a lime-green colour, rank taxis by coral and those with no fixed route by yellow.

Agree fares in advance, on basis of time and distance, outside the city. Taxis are very cheap, but the drivers often do not know where the street you want is; try and give the name of the intersection between two streets rather than a number, because the city's numbering can be erratic. When it is raining or dark you may have to agree to pay up to twice the normal amount. There are special tourist taxis, called "Turismo", which are dearer because they have English-speaking drivers, outside the main hotels: arrange the prices beforehand. VW taxis are very cheap, they should be tipped. Unmarked taxis may work out more expensive than marked ones. Hired cars with driver are dear.

Metro Maps of the network are usually available from ticket offices at big stations and tourist offices and are displayed at most stations since lines have been extended. There is a metro information service at Insurgentes station on Pink Line which dispenses maps and most interchange stations have information kiosks. (The *Atlas de Carreras*, US$1.65 has a map of Mexico City, its centre and the metro lines marked. Good metro and bus maps at the Anthropology Museum, US$1.25.) All the stations have a symbol, e.g. the grasshopper signifying Chapultepec. There are eight lines in service. 1 from Observatorio (by Chapultepec Park) to Pantitlán in the eastern suburbs. It goes under Av. Chapultepec and not far from the lower half of Paseo de la Reforma, the Mercado Merced, and 3 km. from the airport. 2, from Cuatro Caminos in the NW to the Zócalo and then S above ground to Taxqueña; 3, from Indios Verdes S to the University City (free bus service to Insurgentes); 4, from Santa Anita on the SE side to Martín Carrera in the NE; 5, from Pantitlán, via Terminal Aérea (which is close to gate A of the airport), crossing the green line at La Raza, up to Politécnico; 6, from El Rosario in the NW to Martín Carrera in the NE; 7, from El Rosario in the NW to Barranca del Muerto in the SW; 9 parallels 1 to the S, running from Tacubaya (where there are interesting paintings in the station) in the W to Pantitlán in the E. Trains are noiseless on rubber wheels. Music is played quietly at the stations. Tickets 300 pesos, buy several to avoid queuing, check train direction before entering turn-stile or you may have to pay again. If you want to use the metro often, you can buy an *abono*, 10,000 pesos (available on 1st or 15th of month), which allows you to use the whole system and the 100 bus for 15 days: remember in this case to use the blue entrances to the metro stations, or your *abono* will be lost. Originally a splendidly modern service (virtually impossible to get lost), it is still clean and efficient, although overcrowded at some times. Beware thieves, pickpockets and bag-slashers and women should avoid using the metro when alone between 0800-1000 and after 1630, severe attacks of "roving-hand syndrome" are common—between 1700 and 2100 men are separated from women and children at Pino Suárez, direction Zaragoza. Also beware: no heavy luggage permitted, maximum size 60 x 50 x 30 cms. (although at off-peak times the station security guard may allow you on with a back-pack if you carry it in your arms), but medium-sized rucksacks OK. At the Zócalo metro station there is a permanent exhibit about the metro, interesting. At Pino Suárez, station has been built around a small restored Aztec temple. **N.B.** Metro opens 0500 weekdays, 0700 on Sundays. Do not take photos or make sound-recordings in the metro without obtaining a permit and a uniformed escort from metro police, or you could be arrested. For lost property enquire at Oficina de Objetos Extraviados at Fray Servando on Line 4, T 768-81-75, open 0830-1600.

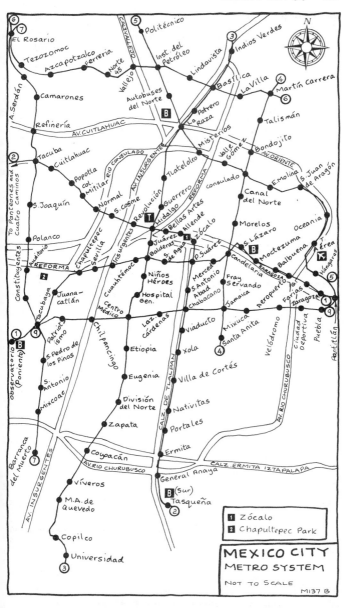

MEXICO CITY
METRO SYSTEM
NOT TO SCALE
M137 B

1 Zócalo
2 Chapultepec Park

Car Hire Agencies Budget Rent Auto, Reforma 60; Hertz, Revillagigedo 2; Avis, Medellín 14; VW, Av. Chapultepec 284-6; National Car Rental, Insurgentes Sur 1883; Auto Rent, Reforma Norte 604; quick service at Av. Chapultepec 168, T 533-5335 (762-9892 airport); Pamara, Hamburgo 135, T 525-5572—**N.B.** 200 km. free mileage; Odin, Balderas 24-A; and many local firms, which tend to be cheaper. It is generally cheaper to hire in the US or Europe.

Entertainments Theatres: Palacio de Bellas Artes (for ballet, songs, dances, also concerts 2-3 times a week), Fábregas, Lírico, Iris, Sullivan, Alarcón, Hidalgo, Urueta, San Rafael and Insurgentes in town and a cluster of theatres around the Auditorio Nacional in Chapultepec Park (check at Tourist Office for details of cheap programmes). Spectaculars (e.g. presidential inauguration) are often staged in the Auditorio Nacional itself. Also in Chapultepec Park is the Audiorama (behind the Castle on the Constituyentes side) where one may listen to recorded classical music in a small open ampitheatre in a charming wooded glade. A request book is provided, for the following day. There may be a free performance of a play in one of the parks by the Teatro Trashumante (Nomadic Theatre). Variety show nightly with singers, dancers, comedians, magicians and ventriloquists, very popular with locals, at Teatro la Blanquita, on Av. Lazaro Cárdenas Sur near Plaza Garibaldi. Especially rec., the Ballet Folklórico de México, at Palacio de Bellas Artes (**see page** 143). The Teatro de la Ciudad, Donceles 36 (T 510-2197 and 510-2942) has the Ballet Folklórico Nacional Aztlán. On Sundays there is afternoon bull-fighting in a vast ring (**see page** 150) and morning football at the stadium. The balloon sellers are everywhere.

Cinemas A number show non-Hollywood films in original language (Spanish sub-titles); check *Mexico City News* for details. Some recommended cinemas are: Ciné Latino, Av. Reforma between the statue of Cuauhtémoc and El Angel; Ciné Versalles, Versalles (side street off Av. Reforma, near statue of Cuauhtémoc); Ciné Electra, Río Guadalquivir (near El Angel); Ciné Diana, Av. Reforma, at the end where Parque Chapultepec starts; Ciné Palacio Chino, in the Chinese *barrio* S of Av. Juárez (also interesting for restaurants).

Football Sun. midday, Aztec and Olympic stadia (latter has a Rivera mural of the history of Mexican sport); also Thurs. (2100) and Sat. (1700).

Horse Races Hipódromo de las Américas, every Tues., Thurs., Sat. and Sun. almost all the year. Pari-mutuel betting (minimum bet US$0.40). Races begin at 1500, and may be watched from Jockey Club restaurant. Beautiful track with infield lagoons and flamingoes, and plenty of atmosphere. Free entry with a tourist card, just pay the tax.

Jai-Alai Events with the foremost players in the world every day except Friday at the Frontón México across from Monumento a la Revolución, at 1800. It seats 4,000, closed in 1989/90 because of strikes. Theoretically, jackets and ties are needed for admission. The people in the red caps are the *corredores*, who place the bets. Pari-mutuel betting. US$1.

Golf at Chapultepec Golf Club and Churubusco Country Club. These are private clubs, open to visitors only if accompanied by a member. Green fees are high (US$20 upwards).

Hiking Every weekend with the Alpino and Everest clubs. Club de Exploraciones de México, Juan A.Mateos 146, Col. Obrero, (Metro Chabacano), DF 06800, T 578-5730, 1930-2400 Wed. or Fri. organizes several walks in and around the city on Sats. and Suns., cheap equipment hire, slideshow Wed. Club Alpino Mexicano, Córdoba 234, Col. Roma (Metro Hospital General), T 574-9683, open Mon-Fri. 1030-2030, Sat. 1030-1530, small shop. **Mountain Rescue**, Socorro Alpino, Eje Lázaro Cárdenas 80-305, T 521-1813. Open after 1900 weekday evenings.

Swimming   Agua Caliente, Las Termas, Balneario Olímpico, Elba, Centro Deportivo Chapultepec and others.

Charreadas   (Cowboy displays), Rancho Grande de La Villa, at very top of Insurgentes Norte (nearest metro Indios Verdes, then walk N beyond bus station and keep asking), Sun. 1100-1500, US$1.30.

Exchange   Banks 0900-1330 (closed Sat.), there are long queues to change travellers' cheques at the few banks that accept them; Banco de Comercio (Bancomer, Visa agent), head office at Av. Universidad 1200, also Venustiano Carranza y Bolívar; Banco Nacional de México (Banamex), Calle Palmas, said to give best exchange rates (Banamex's offices nearby, at Av. Isabel la Católica 44, are in a converted baroque palace, ask the porter for a quick look into the magnificent patio; another worthwhile building is the bank's branch in the Casa Iturbide, where Agustín de Iturbide lived as emperor, at Madero 17 with Gante); Banco Internacional rec., they deal with Mastercard (Carnet) and Visa, also Banco Serfín, corner of 16 de Septiembre y Bolívar; Citibank, Av. Insurgente Sur, for Citicorp travellers' cheques. Apparently many banks carry the Eurocard symbol but do not in fact recognize the card. These include at least some of the branches of the Banco del Atlántico. American Express office at Reforma 234 will change cheques on Sats., 0930-1330, open Mon.-Fri. until 1800; *cambio* opposite *María Isabel Sheraton*, Paseo de la Reforma, between Niza and Génova, is open weekends; and many others. One can exchange into pesos at the airport from 0400 daily, but only US$500-worth back into dollars after you have passed through customs when leaving. *Casa de Cambio Alameda*, Londres 118, Zona Rosa, all main currencies negotiable. Impossible to exchange Guatemalan quetzales, Belizean dollars, and other "exotics".

Cultural Institutions   *American Community School of Mexico*, complete US curriculum to age of 12, Observatorio and Calle Sur 136, T 516-67-20; *American Chamber of Commerce*, Lucerna 78; *Benjamin Franklin Library*, Londres 116; *Anglo-Mexican Cultural Institute* (with British Council Library), Maestro Antonio Caso 127, T 566-61-44, keeps British newspapers; *Instituto Mexicano Norteamericano*, Hamburgo 115; 3-week intensive and painless courses in Spanish, US$150, 3 hrs. a day; free, excellent concerts, art exhibits, conversation club, reading-room, bulletin board advertising rooms. *Instituto Italiano* has the same courses, but less crowded. The Universidad Nacional Autónoma de México (Unam) offers cheap 6-week courses which include history lectures, US$300, 4 hrs. a day. *Goethe-Institut*, Tonalá 43 (metro Insurgentes), 0900-1300, 1600-1930; *Instituto Francés de la América Latina*, Nazas 43, free films every Thurs. at 2030.

Embassies and Consulates   Always check location of embassies and consulates; they tend to move frequently. Most take 24 hrs. for visas; check to make sure you have a visa and not just a receipt stamp.

   Guatemalan Embassy, Explanada 1025, Lomas de Chapultepec, 11000 México DF, T 520-27-94, a.m. only; tourist card costs US$1; visa issued on the spot, must be used within one month from date of issue, now costs US$10 payable only in US currency, no photo for UK passports; open 0900-1330; **Belizean Embassy**, Thiers, 152-B, Anzures, Delegación Miguel Hidalgo (metro Polanco), México DF, T 203-5642/5960, open 0900-1300 Mon.-Fri., visa US$10, takes a day; **Honduran Consulate**, Calle Alfonso Reyes 220, T 515-6689 (open 1000-1600), visas issued on the spot (no waiting) valid up to one year from date of issue US$3; **Salvadorean Embassy**, Paseo de las Palmas 1930, Lomas de Chapultepec, T 596-33-90 (colectivo Las Palmas from Reforma or from Auditorio metro); **Nicaraguan Consulate**, Nuevo León 144, nr. Parque España, 1st floor, visas for 30 days from date of issue, 2 photographs, US$11, one-day wait; embassy is at Sierra Villagran, Ahumada 36, T 553-9791; **Costa Rican Embassy**,

Río Póo 113, Col. Cuauhtémoc, T 525-7764 (metro Insurgentes); **Panamanian Embassy**, Cincinnati 40, Suite 402, Colonia Nápoles, T 563-9206; **Colombian Consulate**, Reforma 195, 3rd floor, will request visa from Bogotá by telegram (which you must pay for) and permission can take up to a month to come through.

USA Embassy, Reforma 305, Col. Cuauhtémoc, T 211-0042, open Mon.-Fri. 0830-1730; **Canadian Embassy**, Schiller 529 (corner Tres Picos), nr. Anthropological Museum; T 254-3288. **Australian Embassy**, Plaza Polanco Torre B, Jaime Balmes 11, 10th floor, Colonia Los Morales, T 395-6242/1292; **New Zealand Embassy**, Homero 229, 8th floor (metro Polanco), T 250-59-99.

British Embassy, Calle Río Lerma 71, T 511-4880 (Apartado 96 bis, Mexico 5), open Mon. and Thur. 0900-1400 and 1500-1800, Tues., Wed., Fri., 0900-1500; Consular Section at Calle Usumacinta 30, immediately behind main Embassy Building; reading room in main building; poste restante for 1 month, please address to Consular section, this is not an official service, just a valuable courtesy; **British Chamber of Commerce**, Río de la Plata 30, Col. Cuauhtémoc, T 211-56-54; **West German Embassy**, Byron 737, Colonia Rincón del Bosque, T 545-66-55; **French Embassy**, Havre 15, near the Cuauhtémoc Monument, T 533-13-61; **Netherlands Embassy**, Monte Urales 635-203 (near Fuente de Petróleos), T 540-7788; **Swedish Embassy**, Edificio Plaza Comermex, Blvd. M. Avila Camacho 1-6, T 540-63-93; **Danish Embassy**, Tres Picos 45, near Canadian ditto; **Finnish Embassy**, Monte Pelvoux 111, 4th floor, 11000, Mexico, D.F., T 540-6036; **Swiss Embassy**, Hamburgo 66, 5th floor. T 533-07-35, open 0900-1200 Mon.-Fri.; **Polish Embassy**, Cracovia 40, CP 01000, T 950-4700; **Israeli Embassy**, PO Box 25389; T 540-6340, Sierra Madre 215, open Mon.-Fri. 0900-1200.

Delegation Building Av. Central, the Ministry of Public Works is the place to report a theft; take a long book.

Official Translation English/Spanish, Virginia Mendoza Ríos, Av. Lagrange 103, 12th floor, US$10 per page.

Setej (Mexican Students' Union), Hamburgo 273, Zona Rosa, Metro Sevilla, only office to issue student card, which is required to buy a hostel card, T 514-42-13 or 511-66-91, deals with ISIS insurance. Student cards not available at Setej Youth Hostel on Calle Cozumel 57 (T 514-9230/4210).

English-Speaking Churches Roman Catholic—St. Patrick's, Calle Bondojito; Evangelical Union—Reforma 1870; Baptist—Capital City Baptist Church, Calle Sur 136; Lutheran—Church of the Good Shepherd, Palmas 1910; Christ Church, Monte Escandinavos 405, Lomas de Chapultepec; First Church of Christ Scientist— 21 Dante, Col. Anzures. Jewish—Beth Israel, Virreyes 1140.

American British Cowdray Hospital, or the ABC, to give it its popular name, on Observatorio past Calle Sur 136. T 277-5000 (emergency: 515-8359); very helpful.

Medical Services C. German, Calle Eucker No. 16-601, T 545-94-34. Dr. César Calva Pellicer (who speaks English, French and German), Copenhague 24, 3° piso, T 514-25-29. Dr Smythe, Campos Elíseos 81, T 545-78-61, rec. by US and Canadian Embassies. For any medical services you can also go to the Clínica Prensa, US$1.20 for consultation, subsidized medicines. Hospital de Jesús Nazareno, 20 de Noviembre 82, Spanish-speaking, friendly, US$4 to consult a doctor, drugs prescribed cheaply. It is a historical monument (**see page** 145). Most embassies have a list of recommended doctors and dentists who speak foreign languages.

Vaccination Centre Benjamín Hill 14, near metro Juanacatlán (Line 1), near Soviet Embassy. Open Mon.-Fri. 0830-1430, 1530-2030, avoid last half hour, also open on Sat. from 0830-1430; typhoid free (this is free all over Mexico), cholera and yellow fever (Tues. & Fri. only) US$2. For hepatitis shots you have to buy gamma globulin in a pharmacy (make sure it's been refrigerated) and then an injection there (cheap but not always clean) or at a doctor's surgery or the ABC Hospital (see above). Malaria prophylaxis and advice free from San Luis Potosí 199, 6th floor, Colonia Roma Norte, 0900-1400. Also from Dr Francisco Biagi, Paseo de las Palmas 403, T 524-96-40, highly recommended.

Pharmacies *Farmacia Homeopática*, Calle Mesones 111-B. Twenty-four hour pharmacy at *Farmacía Arrocha* off the Periférico next to Hospital de Seguro Social. *Sanborn's* chain and *El Fénix* discount pharmacies are the largest chains with the most complete selection.

Laundromats Laundry on Nápoles just off Av. Chapultepec, 3 kg. for US$2. Also on Río Danubio, between Lerma and Panuco and at Chapultepec and Toledo, nr. Sevilla metro. Lavandería Automática Atoyac, Atoyac 69, near Chapultepec Metro station, one block N of Reforma, corner C. Elba. Also at Parque España 14 and Antonio Caso 82, nr. British Council.

Post Office Tacuba, by San Juan Letrán, open for letters 0800-2400 Mon.-Fri., 0800-2000 Sat., and 0900-1600 Sun. For parcels open 0900-1500 Mon.-Fri. only; parcels larger than 2 kilograms not accepted and difficult to send things other than books, records and cassettes. Mail kept for only 10 days at poste restante window 3, rec. (**see page** 324). If they can't find your mail under the initial of your surname, ask under the initials of any other names you may happen to have.

International Post Office (Customs) Calle Aldama 218, Colonia Guerrero, near Guerrero metro, open until 1800—airmail only (only until 1400 for parcels). Surface parcels can be sent directly from Aduana Postal, Ceylan 468 (open 0900-1300, nearest metro La Raza, then EJ63 Norte buses 11 or 12 along Av. Cuitlahuac to Ceylan, or taxi—US$3).

Telephones The LADA system provides a range of useful services: Long distance— Dial 91 + town code + the number. There is a 25% discount between 1900 and 2200, and a 50% one between 2200 and 0700. International—Dial 95 for US and Canada. Discounts of 11%-34% are available depending on when you ring and where to. Dial 04 for exact information. Dial 98 for the rest of the world. Other services—92 person to person; 01 Directory enquiries; 02 Long distance; 03 Talking clock; 04 Ex-Directory; 05 Engineers; 09 International and Collect. Calls abroad can be made only from Parque Via 198 from 0800-2130, small office in José María Izazaga 20, near Salto de Agua metro, open until 1500 and at the International Airport.

 Chief Telegraph Office for internal telegrams, Palace of Communications and Transport, Av. Lazardo Gardena/Calzada Tacuba.

The **Mexican Secretariat of Tourism** is at Calle Masarik 172, between Hegel and Emerson, Colonia Polanco (reached by bus No. 32), T 250-85-55. Booking of hotels in other parts of the country possible here. The tourist office produces a telephone directory in English and French. There is another office at corner of Londres and Amberes, Zona Rosa. You may refer complaints here, or to the tourist police, in blue uniforms, who are reported to be very friendly. Articles from the various craft displays can be bought. Free maps not always available, but try Mexico City Chamber of Commerce, Reforma 42, which provides maps and brochures of the city; may otherwise be got from Department of Public Works; or buy in bookshops. Bus and metro maps available. Office hours: 0800-1900, closed Sat. and Sun. Information bureau outside Insurgentes metro station. Tourist information can be dialled between 0800 and 2000 (bilingual operator) on 250-01-23. Incidentally, museums are closed Mon., except Chapultepec Castle, which is open daily. A weekly magazine, *Tiempo Libre*, covers what's on in Mexico

City.

Maps Centro de Asesoría y Distribución de Información Estadística y Cartografía, Balderas 71 (mezzanine), México 1, D.F. T 585-70-55, ext. 287. Three times a year it publishes an *Inventario de Información Geográfica* with a list of all maps published. **Instituto Nacional de Estadística Geografía e Informática (INEGI)** sells maps and has information, branches throughout the country and in the Distrito Federal at Insurgentes Sur 795 p.b., Río Rhin 56 and at the airport, Local 61.

Travel Agencies *Corresponsales de Hoteles* will make reservations for high-category hotels in other Mexican towns, Av. Morelos 20, 7th floor, very friendly. *Trailways*, Londres 161, No. 48, T 525-20-50; *Hadad y Asociados Professionales de Viajes*, Miguel Noreña 39, Col. San José Insurgentes, C.P. 03900, T 523-7664/687-0488, arranges mileage tickets; *Wells Fargo & Co. Express*, Calle Niza 22; *Viajes Bojórquez*, Av. Juárez 98, very good tours arranged; *Thomas Cook*, about 11 branches, main office Av. Juárez 88; *Uniclam* agent in Mexico City is Srta. Rosa O'Hara, Río Pánuco 146, Apto 702, Col. Cuauhtémoc, T 525-53-93. *American Express*, Reforma 234 y Havre, T 533-03-80, open Mon.-Fri. 0900-1800, Sat. 0900-1300, charges US$3-4 for poste restante if you do not have their travellers' cheques and US$1 if no card or cheques are held for other services. Service slow and you must be firm if you want something. *Turistoria*, Insurgentes Centro 114, Room 209 (T 535-94-88) takes people to *fiestas* in different parts of the country, tours from ½ day to a few days—speaking Spanish an advantage. Recommended guide, Prof. Juan Cazares López, T 784-58-21, who can be found at the Templo Mayor museum on Sundays. Recommended guide/taxi driver: Raúl Méndez Guerrero, Frontera 80, Dpto. 6, T 536-88-97. For cheap tickets to Cuba, ask round agencies around Hamburgo.

Railways The central station is on Insurgentes Norte, junction Alzate with Mosqueta, nearest metro Revolución or Guerrero. For details of train services, see destinations in text. The *Servicio Estrella*, with reserved reclining seats in a/c cars, or single and double sleepers, all meals included, has been highly rec. Reservations T 547-3190/4114/5819; information T 547-1084/1097/6593.

International Airport, 13 km. from city. There are five access points: A. Aeroméxico arrivals; B. Departure for internal flights (US$4.50 tax); C. Internal arrivals; D. International departures (US$10 tax); E. International arrivals. The Instituto Nacional de Bellas Artes has a permanent exhibition hall and there is an interesting mural *La Conquista del Aire por el Hombre* by Juan O'Gorman. Telephone calls abroad from booth 19 (0600-2200) and booth 8 (0700-2300). Buy pesos opp. D and B, open 24 hrs. Near C is a post office, with telegraph and telex. Left luggage on 1st floor. Mexicana bookings in annex by C and Aeroméxico bookings and timetable booklets from near A. Opp. point E, cars are rented. Fixed-price taxis, buy tickets from a counter close to the luggage claim; about US$4 to Alameda, return by normal taxi more expensive, ring airport and arrange a pick-up. Telephone numbers of taxi companies can be found in the phone book. Journey about 20 mins. from town centre if there are no traffic jams. There are regular buses to the airport (e.g. No. 20, along N side of Alameda) but the drawback is that you have to take one to Calzada Ignacio Zaragoza and transfer to trolley bus at the Boulevard Puerto Aéreo (i.e. at metro station Aeropuerto). Buses to airport may be caught every 45 mins. until 0100 from outside *De Carlo Hotel*, Plaza República 35. It takes an hour from downtown and in the rush hour—most of the day—it is jam-packed. But you can take baggage if you can squeeze it in. See under "Metro" on how to get to airport cheaply, if you have no heavy luggage. The Mexican Hotel Association desk at the airport will call any hotel on its list and reserve a room for you, also has a collective taxi which will drop you at your hotel, but it does not open until 1000. For air freight contact the Agencia

Aduanales, Plazuelo Hermanos, Colima 114, Mon.-Fri. 0900-1700, US$5.76 per kilo.

Long-distance Buses   For details of bus services, see destinations in text. Buses to destinations in N. Mexico, including US borders, leave from **Central del Norte**. Avenida Cien Metros 4907 where there is also a tourist information kiosk (Spanish-speaking only, closed at 1630) which at times issues street plans and will make reservations for hotels. The bus station is on metro line 5 at Autobuses del Norte. City buses marked Cien Metros or Central del Norte go directly there. **Central del Sur**, at corner of Tlalpan 2205 across from metro Taxqueña (line 2), serves Cuernavaca, Acapulco, Zihuatanejo areas. Direct buses to centre (Donceles) from Central del Sur, and an express bus connects the Sur and Norte terminals. It is difficult to get tickets to the S, book as soon as possible; the terminal for the S is chaotic. The **Central del Poniente** is situated opposite the Observatorio station of line 1 of the metro, to serve the W of Mexico; check luggage in 30 mins before bus departure. You can go to the centre by bus from the "urbano" terminal outside the Poniente terminal (US$0.08). The **Central del Oriente**, known as TAPO, Calzada Ignacio Zaragoza, for buses to Veracruz, Yucatán and South East, incl. Oaxaca (it has a tourist information office open from 1000).

All bus terminals operate taxis with voucher system and there are long queues. It is much easier to pay the driver. However, make sure you don't part with the voucher until you're safely in the taxi. In the confusion some drivers move each other's cabs to get out of the line faster and may take your voucher and disappear. About US$2.20 to Zócalo area, US$3 to Zona Rosa.

Advance booking is rec. for all trips, and very early reservation if going to *fiestas* during Holy Week, etc. At Christmas, many Central American students return home via Tapachula and buses from Mexico City are booked solid for 2 weeks before, except for those lines which do not make reservations. You must go and queue at the bus stations; this can involve some long waits, sometimes 2-2½ hrs. Even if you are travelling, you may sometimes be required to buy a *boleto de andén* (platform ticket) at many bus stations.

Bus Companies: (tickets and bookings) Going N: Transportes del Norte, at Av. Insurgentes Centro 137, nr. Reforma (T 5460032 and 5355084); dep. from Central Norte. Omnibus de México, Insurgentes Norte 42, at Héroes Ferrocarrileros (T 5676756 and 5675858). Greyhound bus, Reforma 27, closed Sun.; information at Central Norte from 1100-1500, T 5678444 and 5678426. Going to Central States: Autobuses Anáhuac, Bernal Díaz 8 (T 5468382 and 5910533); Central Norte departures. Going NW: Tres Estrellas de Oro, Calzada de Niño Perdido 19A (T 5789888), Central Norte. Going NE: ADO, Av. Cien Metros 4967 (T 5678364 and 5678076). Going S (incl. Guatemala) Cristóbal Colón, Blvd. Gral Ignacio Zaragoza 38. T 5719128; from Central del Oriente; also ADO, Buenavista 9 (T 5660055 and 5467448). Going SW: Estrella de Oro, Calzada de Tlalpan 2205 (T 5498520 to 29).

Suburbs of Mexico City

Churubusco, 10 km. SE, reached from the Zócalo by Coyoacán or Tlalpan bus, or from General Anaya metro station, to see the picturesque and partly ruined convent (1762) at Gen. Anaya con 20 de Agosto, now become the Museo Nacional de las Intervenciones (open 0900-2100, closed Mon.). Seventeen rooms filled with mementoes, documents, proclamations and pictures recounting foreign invasions, incursions and occupations since independence. The site of the museum was chosen because it was the scene of a battle when the US Army marched into Mexico City in 1847. There is a golf course at the Churubusco Country

Club. Churubusco has the principal Mexican film studios. The new Olympic swimming pool is here. Near enough to Coyoacán (**see page 168**) to walk there.

Tlalpan, 6½ km. further out, or direct from Villa Obregón, (**see page 167**) a most picturesque old town on the slopes of Ajusco, an extinct volcano: colonial houses, gardens, and near the main square an early 16th century church with a fine altar and paintings by Cabrera. Reached by bus or trolley bus from the Taxqueña metro station. Two-and-a-half km. W is the village of Peña Pobre, near which, to the NE, is the Pyramid of **Cuicuilco**, believed to be the oldest in Mexico (archaeological museum on site, Insurgentes Sur Km. 16, intersection with Periférico, open 0800-1800, closed Mon.). The pyramid dates from the 5th or 6th century B.C.; it is over 100 metres in diameter but only 25 high. On the road from Mexico City to Cuicuilco there is a pre-classic burial area under the lava flow, at Copilco, which is closed to the public.

Another excursion can be made to ***Ajusco***, about 20 km. SW of Mexico City. Catch a bus from Estadio Azteca on Calzada Tlalpan direct to Ajusco (US$0.30). If you can find a way to the summit of the Volcán Ajusco, there are excellent views on a clear day (precise directions are very hard to come by). Foothills are also pleasant.

Xochimilco, to the SE, in the Valley of México. Take metro to Taxqueña (terminus), go to gate J and catch a colectivo No. 26 on platform L, or bus No. 140 (US$0.05) to the market. Turn left out of the station to catch the bus. The bus back leaves from the street left of the main church (don't believe taxi drivers who say there is no bus back). The bus stops some distance away beside the market (cheap fruit) in Xochimilco; bad signposting, but often tours from the *embarcaderos* will meet the buses and escort you to the boats. Otherwise keep to the right of the large church on the square, on Nuevo León, carry on until Violeta then turn right for 1 block and then turn left into Embarcadero. Xochimilco has a maze of canals, originally part of the canal system of Tenochtitlán, which wander round fruit and flower gardens. Punts adorned with flowers, poled by Indians, can be hired for about 1½ hrs for US$7-10 weekdays (one per "family", so arrange to join others beforehand) and US$0.25 at weekends only on "public" boats. Make sure you bargain hard before boarding and ensure you get all the time you paid for as many of the boats are punted by boys without watches. At the canal-side restaurants there is music and dancing. The canals are busy on Sundays, quiet midweek. There is a fine market on Saturday; Indians come from miles around. It has a 16th century fortified monastery, San Bernardo, built on Xochimilco's main square by the Franciscans in the 16th century, has escaped heavy-handed restoration. The main altar is a masterpiece of painting and sculpture. Only one hotel, basic, F. Many cheap souvenirs; fruit and flowers sold from boats in canals. Note that it is virtually impossible to get on to the Mexico City-Cuernavaca toll road from Xochimilco.

Ixtapalapa (2 good churches) is at the foot of the Cerro de Estrella, whose top is reached by a bad road or a path for a good view. One of the most spectacular of Mexican passion-plays begins at Ixtapalapa on Holy Thursday.

University City, world-famous, is 18 km. via Insurgentes Sur on the Cuernavaca highway. Perhaps the most notable building is the 10-storey library tower, by Juan O'Gorman, its outside walls iridescent with mosaics telling the story of scientific knowledge, from Aztec astronomy to molecular theory. The Administrative Building has a vast, mosaic-covered and semi-sculptured mural by Siqueiros. Across the highway is the Olympic Stadium, with seats for 80,000, in shape, colour, and situation a world's wonder. Diego Rivera has a sculpture-painting telling the story of Mexican sport. A new complex is being completed beyond the Ciudad Universitaria, including the newspaper library, Hemeroteca Nacional, Teatro Juan Ruiz de Alarcón, Sala Nezahuacoyotl (concerts etc.) and the Espacio Escultórico (sculptures). In the University museum there is an exhibition of traditional masks from all over Mexico. Beyond the Olympic Stadium is also a Botanical Garden which shows all the cactus species in Mexico (ask directions, it's a ½ hr. walk). The University of Mexico was founded in 1551. Bus (marked C.U., one passes along Eje Lázaro Cárdenas; also bus 17, marked Tlalpan, which runs the length of Insurgentes) gets you there, about 1 hr. journey. Another way to the university is on metro line 3 to Copilco station (10 mins. walk to University) or to Universidad station (15 mins. walk). At the University City there is a free bus going round the campus. The University offers cheap 6-week courses.

In the same direction as the University but further out is **Anahuacalli** (usually called the Diego Rivera Museum, open Tues.-Sun. 1000-1800, closed Holy Week). Here is a very fine collection of precolumbian sculpture and pottery, effectively displayed in a pseudo-Mayan tomb built for it by Diego Rivera. View of southern rim of mountains from the roof. Reached by bus from the Taxqueña metro station to Estadio Azteca, or take the bus marked División del Norte from outside Salto del Agua metro. Calle Museo crosses Div. del Norte.

Villa Obregón (popularly known as *San Angel*) 13 km. SW, has narrow, cobble-stone streets, many old homes, huge trees, and the charm of an era now largely past. See the triple domes of its church, covered with coloured tiles, and the former Carmen monastery, now a museum (open 1000-1700). See also the beautifully furnished and preserved old house, Casa del Risco, near the market, and the church of San Jacinto and its adjoining monastery. One of the more macabre sights of Mexico is the severed hand of Alvaro Obregón, preserved in a bottle inside his monument on the spot where he was assassinated in 1928. See also the Museo de Arte Carrillo Gil, Av. Revolución 1608, with excellent changing exhibits. In San Angel also, there is a *bazar sábado*, a splendid Saturday folk art and curiosity market, and the Parroquia, a Dominican convent church dating from 1566. Reach San Angel by bus from Chapultepec Park or by metro line 3 to M.A.Quevedo. Excellent restaurants: the *San Angel Inn* is first class. Desierto de los Leones (see below) is reached from Villa Obregón by a scenic road.

Coyoacán, an old and beautiful suburb adjoining Villa Obregón, and also reached via line 3, is the place from which Cortés launched his attack on Tenochtitlán. The Casa de Cortés, now the Municipal Hall, was built 244 years after the Conquest. The rose-coloured house at Francisco Sosa 383 is said to have been built by Alvarado. The San Juan Bautista church and the nearby Franciscan monastery are both early 16th century. Friday market. The Frida Kahlo Museum at Allende y Londres, preserved as lived in by Diego Rivera and Frida Kahlo, is fascinating and well worth an afternoon, reached by metro line 3 to Coyoacán then by Villa Coupe bus/colectivo or 20 mins. walk south. Drawings and paintings by both. Free guided tours Sat. and Sun. at 1100. Nearby, is the Jardín de la Cultura with large statue of Frida Kahlo, on Fernando Leal and Pacífico. Also nearby, Trotsky's house is open at 1100-1400 and 1500-1700, Tues.-Fri., and 1000-1600, Sat.-Sun. (students man it), as a museum at Viena 45 (with Morelos). The Museo Nacional de Culturas Populares, Hidalgo 289, should be seen: open Wed. and Fri. 0900-2000, Tues., Thurs. and Sat. 0900-1600, Sun. 1100-1700. The new market and the remarkable Chapel of Our Lady of Solitude are by Enrique de la Mora and Félix Candela. *El Coyote Flaco* is a good restaurant, as is *La Guadalupana*; night club *Peña Nahuatl*, fine folk singing and poetry readings.

The Pyramid of **Tenayuca**, 10 km. to the NW, is about 15 metres high and the best-preserved in Mexico. The Aztecs rebuilt this temple every 52 years; this one was last reconstructed about 1507; well worth seeing, for it is surrounded with serpents in masonry. The easiest way to get there by car from Mexico City centre is to go to Vallejo, 11 km. N of the intersection of Insurgentes Norte and Río Consulado. Admission US$0.08. By metro, take the line to the Central de Autobuses del Norte (**see page** 165), La Raza, and catch the bus there. By bus from Tlatelolco; ask driver and passengers to advise you on arrival as site is not easily visible. An excursion to Tula may go via Tenayuca. It is not far from the old town of **Tlalnepantla**: see the ancient convent (ask for the *catedral*) on the Plaza Gustavo Paz and the church (1583), which contains the first image, a Christ of Mercy, brought to the New World. Two-and-a-half km. to the N is the smaller pyramid of Santa Cecilia, interesting for its restored sanctuary.

Los Remedios, a small town 13 km. NW of Mexico City, has in its famous church an image, a foot high, adorned with jewels. See the old aqueduct, with a winding stair leading to the top. It can be reached by car or by taking the Los Remedios bus at Tacuba metro. Fiesta: 1 September to the climax 8 September.

At Tlatilco, NW of the city (just outside the city boundary on Querétaro road), pre-classic Olmec-influenced figurines can be seen.

Excursions from Mexico City

Desierto De Los Leones, a beautiful forest of pines and broad-leaved trees, made into a national park, can be reached from Mexico City (24 km.) by a fine scenic road through Villa Obregón. In the woods is an old Carmelite convent, around are numerous hermitages, inside are several subterranean passages and a secret hall with curious acoustic properties. Take a torch.

Take an hour's bus ride from Observatorio metro to La Venta and ask bus-driver where to get off for the path to the monastery (about 4 km.

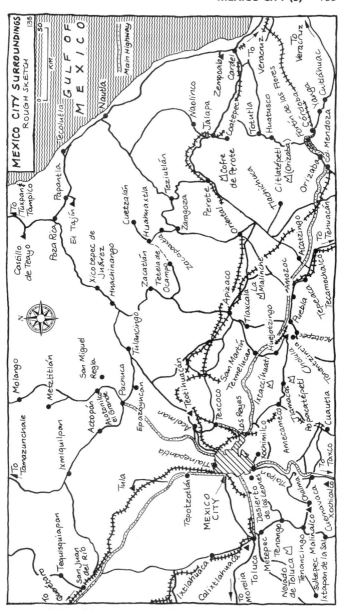

MEXICO CITY SURROUNDINGS
Rough Sketch

walk). One can either get there via the paved road or via the beautiful conifer-forest path, but the latter splits frequently so stick to what looks like the main path; or take the fire-break road below the row of shops and cheap restaurants near the main road. Food stalls abound, particularly at weekends when it is crowded. We have been advised that kidnap attempts have been made at Desierto de los Leones; do not let children wander out of sight. Do not leave valuables in your car, either. Many birds may be seen in the valley reached from the picnic area 6 km. S of La Venta on Route 15.

Acolman has the formidable fortress-like convent and church of San Agustín, dating from 1539-60, with much delicate detail on the façade and some interesting murals inside. Note the fine portal and the carved stone cross at the entrance to the atrium. Closed Fri. Reached by bus from Indios Verdes metro station, or from the Zócalo. It is 42 km. NE of the city.

Teotihuacan, 45 km. from Mexico City, has some of the most remarkable relics of an ancient civilization in the world. The old city is traceable over an area of 3½ by 6½ km. The Pyramid of the Sun (64 metres high, 213 metres square at the base) covers almost the same space as the Great Pyramid of Cheops in Egypt. The sides are terraced, and wide stairs lead to the summit; unfortunately its surface was restored in the wrong materials to wrong specifications around 1910. The Pyramid of the Moon, 1 km. away, is only half its size. There are temples of agriculture, of Tlaloc (the Rain God), of the Plumed Serpent, of Quetzalcoatl (Lord of Air and Wind), and the broad Highway of the Dead. There are subterranean buildings with large halls and coloured decorations, and many superimposed buildings of a later epoch. The pyramids, buildings, courts, etc., are now completely restored and well worth a visit. The Palace of Quetzalpapalotl, where the priests serving the sanctuaries of the Moon lived, has been restored together with its patio. Site open 0800-1700. (Entrance near the bus stop only opens at 1000 despite the sign; try entrance near the Pyramid of the Moon.) Entrance, US$0.25, US$0.10 per car, free on Sundays. Reckon on about 5-8 hrs to see the site properly, arrive early before the big tourist groups at 1100. Tetitla and Atetelco, two smaller sites to the W of the perimetral road, are worth seeing; they are about 1 km. N of the main entrance from the *autopista*; to get to them from the museum, exit W and walk right up to main road, turning left after crossing stream. NE exit from main site brings you to Tepantitlán, superb frescoes. There is a small museum. Easily reached from the bus station (bus shelter marked for Teotihuacan, platform J) at Indios Verdes metro station (green line 3) where the buses to and from Teotihuacan make a stop (US$0.75, 1½ hrs.), or from Terminal del Norte, Gate 8 (Autobuses del Norte metro), which takes 45 mins, US$0.70. Bus returns from Door 1 at Teotihuacan site, supposedly every ½ hr. *Son et lumière* display, costs US$4 per person (good *lumière*, not so good *son*); lasts 45 mins., 1900 in Spanish, 2015 in English (Oct.-June only) commentary. Shown between January and end-April; take blanket or rent one. You can ride back to town with one of the tourist buses for about US$2. Note that the site is more generally known as "Pirámides" than as "Teotihuacan". Train to Teotihuacan, 2 hrs., US$2.65. Tours to Teotihuacan, picking you up at your hotel, normally cost US$10 or so. Official guidebook on sale, US$0.90, gives a useful route to follow.

Hotel *Villas Arqueológicas*, C, pool (Apartado Postal 44 55800, San Juan Testihuacan, Edo. de México, T 6-09-09/6-02-44, Fax 6-09-28; in Mexico City, reservations at Club Med office). **Restaurants** around ruins reported high-priced and service slow.

Tepozotlán, about 43 km. NW of Mexico City just off the route to Querétaro, has a splendid Jesuit church in churrigueresque style. There are fine colonial paintings in the convent corridors. The old Jesuit monastery has been converted into a colonial art museum (Museo Nacional del Virreinato, open 1000-1700, closed Mon., entry US$0.40, US$0.20 Sun.) and tourist centre with restaurants.

Hotel San José, Zócalo, nice rooms, poor service and value; the *Hostería del Monasterio* has very good Mexican food and a band on Sun.; try their coffee with cinnamon. *Restaurant Artesanías*, opp. church, rec., cheap. Also good food at *Brookwell's Posada*. Bus from Tacuba metro station, US$0.50, 1 hr. ride. Many buses from Terminal del Norte pass the turn-off at "Caseta Tepozotlán" from where one can take a local bus or walk (30 mins.) to the town. (Do not confuse Tepozotlán with Tepoztlán, which is S of Mexico City, near Cuernavaca).

In the third week of December, *pastorelas*, or morality plays based on the temptation and salvation of Mexican pilgrims voyaging to Bethlehem, are held. Tickets are about US$10 and include a warming punch, the play, a procession and litanies, finishing with a meal, fireworks and music. Tickets from Viajes Roca, Neva 30, Col. Cuauhtémoc, Mexico City.

Another half-day excursion is to **Tula**, some 65 km., the most important Toltec site in Mexico; two ball courts, pyramids, a frieze in colour, and remarkable sculptures over 6 metres high have been uncovered. There are four huge warriors in black basalt on a pyramid, the great Atlantes anthropomorphic pillars. The museum is well worth visiting and there is a massive fortress-style church, dating from 1553, near the market. Admission to site and museum, US$0.45 weekdays, free Sun. and holidays. Multilingual guidebooks at entrance, fizzy drinks on sale. Site is open Tues.-Sun. 0930-1630 (museum open Wed.-Sun. till 1630). The town itself is dusty, however, with poor roads; *Restaurant la Cabaña*, on main square, local dishes, also *Nevería*, with good soup. If driving from Mexico City, take the turn for Actopán before entering Tula, then look for the Zona Arqueológica sign (and the great statues) on your left.

Transport 1½ hrs. by train from Buenavista station; leaves at 0735, returns at 2035, US$2 (excellent breakfast for US$0.65), but sometimes can be several hours late; it follows the line of the channel cut by Alvarado to drain the lakes of Mexico Valley, visible as a deep canyon (from station walk along track ½ hour to site). One can take bus back, which leaves earlier. It can also be reached by 1st class bus, "Valle de Mesquital", from Terminal del Norte, Avenida de los Cien Metros, goes to Tula in 1½-2 hrs.; US$1.70 each way, 30-min service; Tula bus terminal is 3 km. from the site (badly signposted, an alternative route is: 200m. to the Zócalo, to Calle Quetzalcoatl, to small bridge, sandy road to the right, and opening in the fence). Also bus or car from Actopán, on the Pan-American Highway (**see page** 68). Tula-Pachuca US$1.30; safe to leave belongings at bus station.

MEXICO CITY-VERACRUZ-MEXICO CITY (6)

By Road   A round tour by way of Cholula, Puebla, Tehuacán, Orizaba, Córdoba, Veracruz, Jalapa, Tlaxcala, and Alvarado. Paved all the way (no Pemex service station on road between Puebla and Orizaba, a distance of about 150 km.); total distance: 924 km., or 577 miles. A toll *autopista* (motorway) from Mexico City to Veracruz has been finished as far as Córdoba. From there on you take the regular highway.

Our description is a trip along the old road, which goes E along the Puebla road, past the airport and swimming pools, and some spectacular shanty-towns. At (Km. 19) Los Reyes, a road runs left into a valley containing the now almost completely drained Lake Texcoco, a valley early settled by the *conquistadores*. Along it we come to **Chapingo**, where there is a famous agricultural college with particularly fine frescoes by Rivera in the chapel. Next comes **Texcoco**, a good centre for visiting picturesque villages in the area. Bus from Mexico City, from Emiliano Zapata 92, near Candelaria metro station. Near Chapingo a road runs right to the lovely village of **Huexotla** (see the Aztec wall and the old church). Another road from Texcoco runs through the very beautiful public park of Molino de las Flores. From the old *hacienda* buildings, now in ruins, a road (right) runs up the hill of Tetzcotingo, near the top of which are the Baths of Netzahualcoyotl, the poet-prince. All the nearby villages are charming to stroll through. Another village worth visiting is (San Miguel de) **Chiconcuac** (road to San Andrés and left at its church), only 4 km. away. Here Texcoco *sarapes* are woven. Tues. is their market day and there is a rousing *fiesta* in honour of their patron saint on 29 September.

At Km. 29, Santa Bárbara, a road on the right leads to the small town of **Amecameca**, at 2,315 metres (pop. 57,000), 60 km. from Mexico City, Cristóbal Colón 1st class bus every hour, 1-1½ hrs'. journey, US$0.70, from the Central del Oriente; if hitching, take the Calzada Zaragoza, very dusty road. A road reaches the sanctuary of El Sacromonte, 90 metres above the town (magnificent views), a small and very beautiful church built round a cave in which once lived Fray Martín de Valencia, a *conquistador* who came to Mexico in 1524. It is, next to the shrine of Guadalupe, the most sacred place in Mexico and has a much venerated full-sized image of Santo Entierro weighing 1½ kg. only. Market day is Saturday. (On the way to Amecameca, see the restored 16th century convent and church at Chalco, and the fine church, convent and open-air chapel of the same period at Tlalmanalco.) Three hotels, E and F, close to Amecameca's main square, and rooms at the *San Carlos* restaurant on the main square, F, clean, good, modern, good food, but no hot water. Several eating-places and a food market.

Amecameca is at the foot of the twin volcanoes **Popocatépetl** ("smoking mountain") and Ixtaccíhuatl ("sleeping woman"); the saddle between them, reached by car via a paved road up to the Paso de Cortés (25 km. from Amecameca), gives particularly fine views. On Sats. a pickup truck leaves the plaza at Amecameca, US$1 p.p., for far up the mountain; also taxis for US$6-8. Just before the pass, cars (but not pedestrians) pay US$0.10 entry to the national park. The road on the other side of the pass to Cholula is very rough, steep and sandy, a very sturdy vehicle is needed.

Popocatépetl is not easy to climb. The best time to climb the volcanoes is between late October and early March when there are clear skies and no rain. From May to October the weather is good before noon; in the afternoons it is bad. Climbers are advised to spend at least a day at **Tlamacas** (3,950 metres) to acclimatize, reached from Paso de Cortés via the paved road which turns right (S), 5 km. on. It is also possible to take a taxi (or hitchhike from the turn-off 2 km. S of Amecameca, morning and early afternoon, best at weekends, no public transport) from Amecameca to Tlamacas, US$5, up to 5 people, 26 km. There are a few houses and a tourist hostel *Albergue de Tlamacas*, catering for day trippers from the capital, with cafeteria (open 0930-1900), limited and expensive food, and a restaurant which opens at weekends. You're not supposed to eat your own food within the hostel; sheets not provided; book in advance, US$1 a night in mixed dormitories (sleeping bag rec.); beautiful house in wooded enclosure, poor toilet facilities. 1½ km. below Tlamacas is a camping and picnic area. Minibuses charge US$2 p.p. and run only Sat. and Sun. (from the E to Tlamacas: a bus from Cholula goes as far as San Nicolás de los Ranchos—the remaining 10 km. to Paso de Cortés must be covered on foot or by hitching). From Tlamacas a path goes up to Las Cruces at 4,400 metres (where there was once a refuge) and the snowline; from there it is 3 hours (crampons and ice axe) to the rim of the crater and thence another hour's walk round the rim to the top. Equipment hire US$9 for boots, crampons and ice-axes at the hostel, or in Amecameca, but preferable to hire from Mountain Club in Mexico City. The Brigada de Rescate del Socorro Alpino de México, A.C., in Mexico City (Lázaro Cárdenas 80, T 521-1813) will provide information and free guides. If you wish to go to the top of Popacatépetl (5,400 metres) leave at 0400, as the ground is more solid early on (take warm clothes and a flashlight, and sunglasses for the snow-glare). Alternative routes from Paso de Cortés: straight down dirt road to reach eventually Puebla; or turn left (N) along another dirt road which leads past TV station for 12 km. to nearest parking to summit of Ixtaccíhuatl. From there you find various routes to summit (12-15 hrs. return) and 3-4 refuges to overnight (no furniture, bare floors, dirty).

To climb **Ixtaccíhuatl** take a taxi to La Jolla, from there follow the tracks up the grassy hill on the right. There are three huts between 4,600 and 5,000 metres, from the last hut it is 2½ hours to the top, over two glaciers, some rock climbing required.

Beyond Santa Bárbara the road climbs through pine forests to reach 3,196 metres about 63 km. from Mexico City, and then descends in a series of sharp bends to the quiet town of San Martín **Texmelucan**, Km. 91. The old Franciscan convent here has a beautifully decorated interior, and a former *hacienda* displays weaving and old machinery. Market day is Tuesday.

From here a side-road leads NE for 24 km. to the quaint old Indian town of Tlaxcala; a remarkable series of precolumbian frescoes are to be seen at the ruins of **Cacaxtla** near San Miguel de los Milagros, a steep 25-minute climb up from the main highway, between Texmelucan and Tlaxcala. The colours are still sharp and some of the figures are larger than life size. To protect the paintings from the sun they are only shown from 1000-1300 (closed Mon.), admission US$0.20; the whole site is now being roofed in. Then there is **Tlaxcala**, with its simple buildings washed in ochre, pink and yellow, capital of small Tlaxcala state whose wealthy ranchers breed fighting bulls, but whose landless peasantry is still poor. To see: the church of San Francisco, the oldest in Mexico (1521), from whose pulpit the first Christian sermon was preached in the New World—its severe façade conceals a most sumptuous interior; the extremely colourful murals (1966) depicting the indigenous story of Tlaxcala in the Palacio de Gobierno; and the ruins of the pyramid of San Esteban de Tizatlán, 5 km. outside the town. There is an hourly bus from the Central Camionera in Tlaxcala or take a city bus to La Garrita from which the ruins are a 15 min. walk. Most interesting relics are two sacrificial altars with original colour frescoes preserved under glass. The pictures tell the story of the wars with Aztecs and Chichimecs. The annual fair is held 29 Oct.-15 Nov. each year. Population 36,000. Altitude 2,240 metres. Frequent buses from Puebla, central bus station, 45 mins., US$0.40.

The **Sanctuary of Ocotlán** (1541), on a hill outside the town, described as "the most delicious building in the world", commands a view of valley and volcano. "Its two towers are of lozenge-shaped vermilion bricks set in white stucco, giving an effect of scarlet shagreen, while their upper storeys are dazzlingly white, with fretted cornices and salomonic pillars. . . . A pure-blooded Indian, Francisco Miguel, worked for 25 years on the interior, converting it into a kind of golden grotto."—Sacheverell Sitwell.

(Km. 106) **Huejotzingo** has the second-oldest church and monastery in Mexico, built 1529; now a museum. Market: Sat., Tues. Dramatic carnival on Shrove Tuesday, portraying the story of Agustín Lorenzo, a famous local bandit. *Hotel Colonial*, D, secure but poor value.

(Km. 122) **Cholula** is a small somnolent town (20,000 people, with the University of the Americas), but one of the strangest-looking in all Mexico. When Cortés arrived, this was a holy centre with 100,000 inhabitants and 400 shrines, or *teocallis*, grouped round the great pyramid of Quetzalcoatl, best photographed in the afternoon. In its day it was as influential as Teotihuacán. There used to be a series of pyramids built one atop another. When razing them, Cortés vowed to build a chapel for each of the *teocallis* destroyed, but in fact there are no more than about seventy. There is a very helpful tourist office opposite the main pyramid: Cholula map and guide book for US$1; the site is open 1000-1730.

Places to see are the excavated pyramid, admission US$0.45 on weekdays, US$0.23 on Sun. and holidays, guide US$2.25, it has 8 km.

of tunnels and some recently discovered frescoes inside, but only 1 km. of tunnel is open to the public, which gives an idea of superimposition. The entrance is on the main road into Cholula; the chapel of Los Remedios on top of it, for the view; the Franciscan fortress church of San Gabriel (1552), in the plaza (open 0600-1200, 1600-1900, Suns. 0600-1900); and next to it, the Capilla Real, which has 48 domes (open 1000-1200, 1530-1800, Suns. 0900-1800).

See also the Indian statuary and stucco work, newly repainted, of the 16th century church of Santa María de **Tonantzintla**, outside the town; the church is one of the most beautiful in Mexico (open 1000-1300, 1500-1700 daily, or get someone to open it for you for a small tip), and may also be reached by paved road from San Francisco **Acatepec** (see its 16th century church also, supposedly open 0900-1800 daily, but not always so) off the highway from Puebla to Cholula. Both these places are easily reached from Cholula or Puebla from 6 Poniente y 13 Norte, white bus, to Acatepec-Tonantzintla, 20 mins. Best light for photography after 1500. John Hemming says these two churches "should on no account be missed; they are resplendent with Poblano tiles and their interiors are a riot of Indian stucco-work and carving." Both churches, though exquisite, are tiny. Some visitors note that regular visiting hours are not strictly observed at Cholula, Acatepec, Tonantzintla and Huejotzingo.

One can visit Tonantzintla and Acatepec from Cholula main square with a "peso-taxi". Or one can take a bus from Cholula to Acatepec for US$0.25 from junction of Av. 5 and Av. Miguel Alemán (local bus to both places marked Chulipo). This is 2 blocks from Zócalo, which is 3 blocks from tourist office. You can walk back to Tonanzintla to see church, 1 km., and then take bus Tonanzintla-Puebla US$0.30.

Hotels in Cholula *Villa Arqueológica*, 2 Poniente 501, T 471966; *Los Sauces*, Km. 122, Carretera Federal Puebla-Cholula; *Motel de la Herradura*, Carr. Federal; *Trailer Park Las Américas*, 30 Oriente 602, F, hot showers, secure, rooms available also; *Cali Quetzalcoatl*, on Zócalo, T 471335, C, clean, expensive restaurant; *Hotel de las Américas*, 14 Oriente 6, T 470991, near pyramid, actually a motel, modern with rooms off galleries round paved courtyard (car park), small restaurant, clean, good value, D; *Reforma*, E, near main square, cheapest in town, rec. *Super Motel* on the road from Puebla as you enter town, each room with private garage, very secure, E. *Restaurant Choloyan*, also handicrafts, Av. Morelos, good, clean, friendly. Try "liquados" at market stalls, fruit and milk and 1 or 2 eggs as you wish; Mixote is a local dish of lamb or goat barbequed in a bag. Pure drinking water sold behind the public baths, cheaper to fill own receptacle, funnel needed.

Buses Second-class bus from Puebla to Cholula from 6 Poniente y 13 Norte, 9 km. on a new road, also colectivos to Cholula, US$0.15. From Mexico City, leave for Cholula from Terminal del Oriente with Estrella Roja, every 30 mins. 1st class buses to Mexico City every 10 minutes, US$1, 2½-3 hrs., 2nd class every 20 mins., a very scenic route through steep wooded hills. Good views of volcanoes.

Just before Puebla one comes to the superb church of **Tlaxcalantzingo**, with an extravagantly tiled façade, domes and tower. It is worth climbing up on the roof for photographs.

(Km. 134) *Puebla*, "The City of the Angels", one of Mexico's oldest and most famous cities and the capital of Puebla state, is at 2,060 metres. Unfortunately, its recent industrial growth—the population has risen to 836,000—is rapidly destroying its colonial appearance and filling it with smog, and the centre, though still beautifully colonial, is cursed with traffic jams, except in those shopping streets reserved for pedestrians. On the central arcaded plaza is a fine Cathedral, notable for its marble floors, onyx and marble statuary and gold leaf decoration (closed 1230-1530). There are statues flanking the altar which are said to be of an English king and a Scottish queen. The bell tower gives a grand view of the city and snow-capped volcanoes (open 1100-1200 only). There are 60 churches in all, many of their domes shining with the glazed tiles for which the city is famous.

In the Rosario chapel of the Church of Santo Domingo (1596-1659), the baroque displays a beauty of style and prodigality of form which served as an exemplar and inspiration for all later baroque in Mexico. There is a strong Indian flavour in Puebla's baroque; this can be seen in the churches of Tonantzintla and Acatepec (see above); it is not so evident, but it is still there, in the opulent decorative work in the Cathedral. Beyond the church, up towards the Fort of Loreto (see below), there is a spectacular view of volcanoes.

Other places well worth visiting are the churches of San Cristóbal (1687), with modern churrigueresque towers and Tonantzintla-like plasterwork inside; San José (18th century), with attractive tiled façade and decorated walls around the main doors, as well as beautiful altar pieces inside; the Congreso del Estado in Calle 5 Poniente, formerly the Consejo de Justicia, near the post office, is a converted 19th century Moorish style town house—the tiled entrance and courtyard are very attractive—it had a theatre inside (shown to visitors on request), and is now the seat of the state government; and the Museum of Santa Rosa has a priceless collection of 16th century Talavera tiles on its walls and ceilings. The Patio de los Azulejos should also be visited; it has fabulous tiled façades on the former almshouses for old retired priests of the order of San Felipe Neri; the colours and designs are beautiful; it is at 11 Poniente 110, with a tiny entrance which is hard to find unless one knows where to look. One of the most famous and oldest local churches is San Francisco, with a glorious tiled façade and a mummified saint in its side chapel; see also the pearl divers' chapel, given by the poor divers of Veracruz, the church thought it too great a sacrifice but the divers insisted. Since then they believe diving has not claimed a life. Santa Catalina, 3 Norte with 2 Poniente, has beautiful altarpieces; Nuestra Señora de la Luz, 14 Norte and 2 Oriente, has a good tiled façade and so has San Marcos at Av. Reforma and 9 Norte. The Maronite church of Belén on 7 Norte and 4 Poniente has a lovely old tiled façade and a beautifully tiled interior. Worth visiting is also the library of Bishop Palafox, by the tourist office, 5 Oriente No. 5, opposite the Cathedral.

Besides the churches, the fragile-looking and extravagantly ornamented Casa del Alfeñique (Sugar Candy House), a few blocks from the Cathedral is worth seeing (entry US$0.40). Nearby is Plaza y Mercado Parián, with onyx souvenir shops (6 Norte and 4 Oriente). Onyx figures

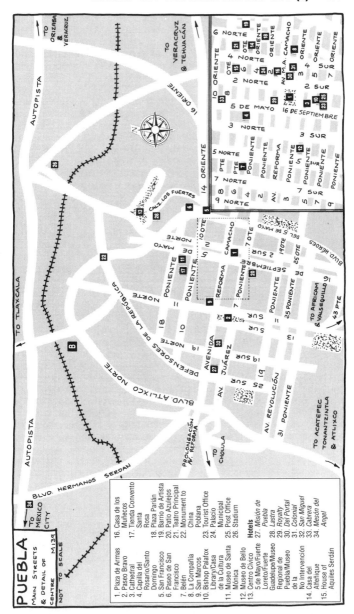

PUEBLA
MAIN STREETS
& DETAIL OF
CENTRE M 139
NOT TO SCALE

1. Plaza de Armas
2. Paseo Bravo
3. Cathedral
4. Capilla del
   Rosario/Santo
   Domingo
5. San Francisco
6. Paseo de San
   Francisco
7. Belén
8. La Compañia
9. San Marcos
10. Bishop Palafox
    Library/Casa
    de la Cultura
11. Museo de Santa
    Monica
12. Museo de Bello
13. Centro Cívico
14. Casa del
    Alfeñique
15. House of
    Aquiles Serdán
16. Casa de los
    Muñecos
17. Tienda Convento
    Santa
    Rosa
18. Plaza Parián
19. Barrio de Artista
20. Patio Azulejos
21. Teatro Principal
22. Monument to
    China
    Poblana
23. Tourist Office
24. Palacio
    Municipal
25. Post Office
26. Stadium

Hotels
27. *Misión de
    Puebla*
28. *Lastra*
29. *Royalty*
30. *Del Portal*
31. *Colonial*
32. *San Miguel*
33. *Cabrera*
34. *Mesón del
    Angel*

and chess sets are attractive and cheaper than elsewhere, but the *poblanos* are hard bargainers; another attractive buy is the very tiny glass animal figures. In the adjoining Barrio del Artista the artists' studios are near to *Hotel Latino*. Live music and refreshments at small *Café del Artista*. The University Arts Centre offers folk dances at various times, look for posters or enquire direct—free admission.

The Cinco de Mayo civic centre, with a stark statue of Benito Juárez, is, among other things, a regional centre of arts, crafts and folklore and has a very worthwhile Museo Regional de Puebla, open 1000-1700, Natural History Museum, auditorium, planetarium, fairgrounds and an open air theatre all nearby. In the same area, the forts of Guadalupe and Loreto have been restored; they were the scene of the Battle of Puebla, in which 2,000 Mexican troops defeated Maximilian's 6,000 European troops on 5 May, 1862 (although the French returned victorious ten days later). Inside the Fort of Loreto (excellent view of the city) is a small museum (Museo de la No Intervención) depicting the battle of 1862 (open 1000-1700, closed Mon.). 5 May is a holiday in Mexico.

Two other Museums: Museo de Bello—the house of the collector and connoisseur Bello—has good displays of Chinese porcelain and Talavera pottery, Av. 3 Poniente 302; the building is beautifully furnished (entry US$0.40, guided tours, closed Mon.). Museo de Santa Mónica (convent) at 18 Poniente 103, open 1000-1800, closed Mon.; generations of nuns hid there after the reform laws of 1857 made the convent illegal.

Also worth seeing are the church and monastery of El Carmen, with its strange façade and beautiful tile work; the Teatro Principal (1550), possibly the oldest in the Americas; the grand staircase of the 17th century Academia de las Bellas Artes and its exhibition of Mexican colonial painting; and the Jesuit church of La Compañía, where a plaque in the sacristy shows where China Poblana lies buried. This mythical figure, a Chinese princess captured by pirates and abducted to Mexico, is said to have taken to Christianity and good works and evolved a penitential dress for herself which has now become the regional costume; positively dazzling with flowered reds and greens and worn with a strong sparkle of bright beads. Also worth visiting is the house of Aquiles Serdán, a leader of the Revolution, preserved as it was during his lifetime. The tiled façade of the Casa de los Muñecos, 2 Norte No. 1 (corner of the main square) is famous for its caricatures in tiles of the enemies of the 17th century builder.

Festivals *Feria* in mid-April for two weeks.

Hotels *Lastra*, Calz. de Los Fuertes, T 351501, B; *Royalty*, Portal Hidalgo 8, T 424740, C, run down, central, quiet, restaurant good but expensive; *Misión de Puebla*, 5 Poniente 2522, A, delightful; *Del Portal*, Portal Morelos 205, T 460211, very good, but ask for room away from Zócalo side (noisy), restored colonial, D; *Colonial*, 4 Sur 105, old-fashioned and charming, has excellent restaurant and accepts American Express cards, ask for back room, D, with bath; *Imperial*, 4 Oriente 203, T 463825, D, basic, shower, noisy, parking; *Cabrera*, 10 Oriente 6, E, with shower and phone, clean, quiet in interior rooms, don't be put off by outward appearance of hardware store; *del Paseo*, 10 Sur No. 404, across Héroes, E, no entry from 2300-0600, but central, parking, hot water, quiet. *Latino*, 6 Norte 8, E, with bath, hot water, reasonable but noisy; *San Miguel*, 3 Poniente 721, clean and quiet, C; *San Agustín*, 3 Poniente 531, E, basic, clean, quiet; *Victoria*, near Zócalo, 3 Poniente 306, basic, E; *Jeresita* opposite, F for rooms on 4th floor, hot water, friendly, rec.; *Venecia*, 4 Poniente 716, F, without bath; *Casa de Huéspedes*, 3 Poniente 725, F; several basic *casas de huéspedes*, near market. Very cheap hotel (F), 2 blocks S of train station on 20 de Noviembre, big rooms, hot showers, clean, bus to town.

Motels *Mesón del Angel*, A, good, pool, gardens, Hermanos Serdán 141, T 482100, near first Puebla interchange on Mexico-Puebla motorway, possibly best in town. *Panamerican*, Reforma 2114, T 485466, D, restaurant, bar, rec.

Camping Possible on the extensive university grounds about 8 km. S of centre.

Food Specialities *Mole poblano* (meat or chicken with sauce of chiles, chocolate and coconut). Cheap mole at *Fonda la Mexicana*, 16 Sept. 706; best at *La Poblanita*, 10 Norte 1404-B, and *Fonda Sta. Clara*, 3 Poniente 307, good for local specialities. Also on Zócalo, at *Hostería de los Angeles*, but no dinner. Also good, *Iberia*, Portal Juárez. 101, 1st floor; *La Bola Roja*, 17 Sur 1305. Camotes (candied sweet potatoes) and dulces (sweets). Also nieves—drinks of alcohol, fruit and milk—worth trying, and excellent empanadas. Also noted are quesadillas— fried tortillas with cheese and herbs inside.

Other Restaurants *Monza's*, Calle Reforma, reasonable, good food. Cheap comidas at *Hermilo Nevados*, 2 Oriente 408, good value, rec. Many cheap places near main square with menus prominently displayed. *Hosteria del Virrey*, 11 Sur and 15 Poniente, live music and good atmosphere. *La Chiesa Veglia*, Swiss, good cheese fondue, attached to *Hotel San Pedro*, 2 Oriente, slow service. *Pizza Hadis*, 3 Norte between 3 Poniente y Reforma, cheap, good, friendly; *Antojitos Aries*, 5 Sur and 5 Poniente, serves a good, cheap comida corrida at lunchtime and à la carte menu for dinner, reasonable. *Librería Cafetería*, Reforma y 7 Norte, good coffee; *Super-Soya*, 5 de Mayo, good for fruit salads and juices; *Teorema* on Reforma and 7 Norte is a cold-store with a cafetería, good.

Shopping Craft shop sponsored by the authorities: *Tienda Convento Sta. Rosa*, Calle 3 Norte 1203, T 2-89-04. The famous Puebla tiles may be purchased from factories outside Puebla, or from *Fábrica de Azulejos la Guadalupana*, Av. 4 Poniente 911; *D. Aguilar*, 40 Poniente 106, opposite Convent of Sta. Mónica, and *Casa Rugerio*, 18 Poniente 111; *Margarita Guevara*, 20 Poniente 30.

Tourist Office 5 Oriente 3, Av. Juárez behind the Cathedral, T 46-09-28. Also 3 Sur 1501, 8th floor and at the bus station.

Roads and Buses A 4-lane highway, 70 mins., to Mexico City, toll US$1.30; ADO buses every 15 mins., seats bookable, 2 hrs., US$1.50; Mexico City-Puebla buses every 10 mins. but long queue; Estrella Roja from Central del Oriente. 2-lane highway to Orizaba, toll US$1.85. For the road from Puebla S through Oaxaca to Guatemala, **see page** 216. Bus to Oaxaca costs US$7 (9 hrs.). Bus to Veracruz 1st class, US$3.50. Bus to Jalapa (**see page** 193) ADO, 4 hrs. New CAPU bus terminal for all 1st and 2nd class buses N of city.

Rail Station is a long way from centre. Trains from Mexico City, 1st class US$2.30, US$1.35 2nd class to Puebla via Cuautla at 0704, a very slow (10-11 hrs.) Puebla train at 0815; train to Oaxaca (1st class), leaves Puebla 0640, US$3, 12 hours. The line weaves through cactus laden gorges recalling the Wild West. On clear days one gets a good view of Popocatépetl. A train from Mexico City leaves at 1730 and stops at 2230 at Puebla on its way to Oaxaca. Train Puebla-Jalapa leaves at 0910, US$1.25, 2nd class, takes 7-8 hrs. The ride to Jalapa is very enjoyable, excellent views, sit on left-hand side.

Excursions   Interesting day-trip to **Cuetzalán** market (via Tetela-Huahuaztla) which is held on Sun. in the Zócalo (3 hr walk up.). On 4 October each year dancers from local villages gather and *voladores* "fly" from the top of their pole. Nahua Indians sell cradles (*huacal*) for children; machetes and embroidered garments. Big clay dogs are made locally, unique stoves which hold big flat clay plates on which *tortillas* are baked and stews are cooked in big pots. Also available in nearby Huitzitlán. *Casa Elvira Mora*, Hidalgo 54, cheap, friendly place to stay in Cuetzalán. Women decorate their hair with skeins of wool. You can also go via Zaragoza, Zacapoaxtla and Apulco, where one can walk along a path, left of the road, to the fine 35-metre waterfall of La Gloria.

Direct buses from Puebla (Tezinteco line leaves 0830. Leaves Cuetzalán at 1520, back at Puebla at 2100. ADO has a night-bus, 1915 arrives 2245; returns 0700, arriving 1030. There are many buses to Zacapoaxtla with frequent connections for Cuetzalán.

15 km. S of Puebla lies Lake Valsequillo, with Africam, a zoo of free-roaming African animals. Entry US$1, open Mon.-Fri. 1000-1730, Sat., Sun. and holidays 0900-1800. Information from 11 Oriente, T 460888.

(Km. 151) **Amozoc**, where tooled leather goods and silver decorations on steel are made, both mostly as outfits for the *charros*, or Mexican cattlemen. Beyond Amozoc lies **Tepeaca** with its late 16th century monastery, well worth a visit; its weekly market is very extensive. An old Spanish tower or *rollo* (1580) stands between Tepeaca's main square and the Parroquia. Beyond Tepeaca, 57½ km. from Puebla, lies **Tecamachalco**: vast 16th century Franciscan monastery church with beautiful murals on the choir vault, in late medieval Flemish style, by a local Indian.

Beyond, the road leads to **Tehuacán** (population 113,000, altitude 1,676 metres), a charming town with a pleasant, sometimes cool, climate. It has some old churches. Water from the mineral springs is bottled and sent all over the country by Garci Crespo, San Lorenzo and Peñafiel, who also have baths at the spas where people come to bathe for health reasons (popular at weekends). From the small dam at Malpaso on the Río Grande an annual race is held for craft without motors as far as the village of Quiotepec. The central plaza is pleasant and shaded; the nights are cool. The government palace is decorated inside and out with murals. From Tehuacán there are two paved roads to Oaxaca: one, very scenic, through Teotitlán del Camino, and the other, longer but easier to drive, through Huajuapán (see page 225. Railway junction for Oaxaca and Veracruz; no passenger trains on line to Esperanza. Wild maize was first identified by an archaeologist at Coxcatlán Cave nearby. There is an airport.

Hotels *Hotel-Spa Peñafiel*, old "faded glory", reasonable, long term rates, resort facilities (use of pool US$0.90), warmly rec., just out of town, on the way to Puebla, T 20190; *México*, Reforma Norte and Independencia Poniente, one block from Zócalo, T 20019, garage, TV, restaurant, renovated colonial building, pool, quiet; *Iberia*, Independencia 211, T 21122, D, good; *Madrid*, 3 Sur 105, T 20272, opp. Municipal Library, E, comfortable, good value. Several *casas de*

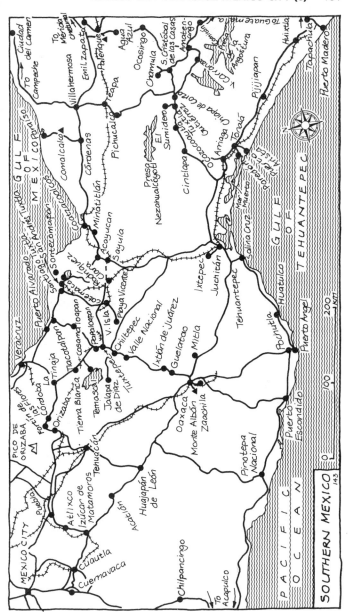

SOUTHERN MEXICO

huéspedes along Calle 3 (Norte and Sur) but low standards, and generally a shortage of decent cheap accommodation and restaurants. Cafés on Zócalo serve snacks and drinks, and some meals, but the main meal is served at midday in Tehuacán. Try **Restaurant Santander**, good and inexpensive, and **Peñafiel**, good. No good, cheap restaurants, but excellent taco stands.

Buses ADO bus station on Av. Independencia (Poniente). Bus direct to Mexico City, 3 hrs., US$2.40; to Oaxaca and the Gulf: Autobuses Unidos, 2nd class on Calle 2 Oriente with several buses daily to Mexico City and Oaxaca. Local bus to Huajuapan 3 hrs., US$2; from there, frequent buses to Oaxaca (4 hrs., US$2.50).

Teotitlán del Camino, en route to Oaxaca, is a glaringly bright town with a military base. Vehicles are stopped occasionally; make sure, if driving, that your papers are in order. From Teotitlán it is possible to drive into the hills, to the Indian town of Huautla de Jiménez, where the local Mazatec Indians consume the hallucinogenic "magic" mushrooms made famous by Dr. Timothy Leary. Huautla has "all four seasons of the year in each day; springlike mornings; wet, foggy afternoons; fresh, autumn evenings; and freezing nights." There are many police and military, with propaganda blaring from loud speakers. Drivers may be waved down by people in the road up to Huautla; do not stop for them, they may be robbers.

The road from Tehuacán to the coast soon begins to climb into the mountains. At Cumbres we reach 2,300 metres and a wide view: the silvered peak of Citlaltépetl (or Orizaba—**see page** 197) volcano to the E, the green valley of Orizaba below. In 10 km. we drop down, through steep curves, sometimes rather misty, to Acultzingo 830 metres below. The road joins the main toll road from Puebla to Orizaba at Ciudad Mendoza, where it has emerged from the descent through the Cumbres de Maltrata, which are usually misty and need to be driven with care and patience. (The toll road Puebla-Orizaba is a much safer drive than the route we have described.)

(Km. 317) **Orizaba**, the favourite resort of the Emperor Maximilian (population 115,000, altitude 1,283 metres), lost much of its charm in the 1973 earthquake, when the bullring, many houses and other buildings were lost, and is now heavily industrialized. In the distance is the majestic volcanic cone of Orizaba. The town developed because of the natural springs in the valley, some of which are used by the textile and paper industries and others are dammed to form small pools for bathing beside picnic areas; Nogales (restaurant) is the most popular, Ojo de Agua is another. The Cerro del Borrego, the hill above the Alameda park, is a favourite early-morning climb. The Zócalo at one time lost much of its area to permanent snack bars, but these have been removed. On the N side is the market, with a wide variety of local produce and local women in traditional dress, and the many-domed San Miguel church (1690-1729). There are several other quite good churches, and there is an Orozco mural in the Federal School on Av. Colón. The Palacio Municipal is the actual cast-iron Belgian pavilion brought piece by piece from France after the famous 19th century Paris Exhibition—an odd sight.

Hotels *Aries*, Oriente 6 No. 265, T 51116, C (nightclub on top floor). *Trueba*, Oriente 6 and Sur 11, T 42744, C, resort facilities. *De France*, Oriente 6 No. 186, T 52311, E and US$0.25 for parking in courtyard, clean, comfortable, shower, reasonable if uninspiring restaurant.

Restaurants *Romanchu* and *Paso Real*, on the main street, have excellent cuisine. Hare Krishna vegetarian restaurant, *Radha's*, on Sur 4 between Oriente 1 and 3, excellent. In the market, try the local morning snack, *memelita picadita*.

A road leaves Orizaba southwards, up into the mountains of Zongolica, a dry, poor and isolated region, cold and inhospitable, inhabited by various groups of Indians who speak Nahuatl, the language of the Aztecs. Zongolica village is a good place to buy *sarapes*; take early bus from Orizaba (ask for direct one) to get clear views of the mountains.

Beyond Orizaba the scenery is magnificent. The road descends to coffee and sugar-cane country and a tropical riot of flowers. It is very pleasant except when a northerly blows, or in the intolerable heat and mugginess of the wet season.

(Km. 331) **Fortín De Las Flores**, a small town devoted to growing flowers and exporting them. Sometimes Indian women sell choice blossoms in small baskets made of banana-tree bark. Near Fortín there is a viewpoint looking out over a dramatic gorge (entry free). The *autopista* from Orizaba to Córdoba passes over this deep valley on a concrete bridge.

Hotels *Ruiz Galindo*, now run down (swimming pool, over-elaborate for some tastes). *Posada la Loma*, T 30658, very attractive, moderately expensive. There are others, slightly cheaper, which also offer tropical gardens for relaxation.

Córdoba (population 126,000, altitude 923 metres), 8 km. on in the rich valley of the Río Seco, an old colonial city, is also crazy with flowers. Its Zócalo is spacious, leafy and elegant; three sides are arcaded; two of them are lined with tables. On the fourth is an imposing church with a chiming clock. There are several hotels in the Zócalo, which is alive and relaxed at night. In one of them, the *Hotel Zevallos*, Gen. Iturbide signed the Treaty of Córdoba in 1821, which was instrumental in freeing Mexico from Spanish colonial rule. There is a local museum at Calle 3, 303, open 1000-1300 and 1600-2000. Córdoba has the highest rainfall in Mexico, but at predictable times. The area grows coffee.

Hotels *Hostal de Borreña*, Calle 11 308, T 20777, modern, clean, really hot water, some traffic noise but good value, D. *Mansur*, Av. 1 y Calle 3, T 26600, on square, E, smart. Near the ADO terminal is *Palacio*, Av. 3 y Calle 2, T 22186; *Marina* (T 22600), *Iberia* (T 21301), *Trescado* (T 22366) and *Casa de Huéspedes Regis* are all on Avenida 2. *Casa de Huéspedes La Sin Rival* and *La Nueva Querétana* are at 511 and 508 of Avenida 4, respectively. *Los Reyes*, F, warmly rec.

The direct road from Córdoba to Veracruz is lined, in season, by stalls selling fruit and local honey between Yanga and Cuitláhuac. Yanga is a small village named after the leader of a group of escaped black slaves in colonial times. A slightly longer but far more attractive road goes from Córdoba northwards through Huatusco and Totutla, then swings E to Veracruz.

(Km. 476) **Veracruz**, the principal port of entry for Mexico (population approaching 1 million, according to latest local estimates) lies on a low alluvial plain bordering the Gulf coast. Cortés landed near here at Isla de Sacrificios, on 17 April, 1519. The first settlement was called Villa Rica de la Vera Cruz; its location was changed various times, including to La Antigua, now a pleasant little colonial town. The present site was established in 1599. The town is a mixture of the very old and the new; there are still many picturesque white-walled buildings and winding side-streets. In spite of the occasional chill north winds in winter, it is generally hot and has become a great holiday resort, and is reported touristy and noisy.

The heart of the city is Plaza Constitución (Zócalo); make at once for the traditional *La Parroquia* café, cool and tiled. (The newer café of the same name on the Malecón does not have the same atmosphere.) The square is white-paved, with attractive cast iron lampstands and benches, and surrounded by the cathedral, with an unusual cross, depicted with hands, the governor's palace and colonial-style hotels. The plaza comes alive in the evening at weekends: an impressive combination of the crush of people, colour and marimba music in the flood-lit setting. From 15 July to the end of August there is jazz in the Zócalo from 1900.

Culturally, Veracruz is a Caribbean city, home not only to the *jarocho* costume (predominantly white), but also to *jarocho* dance and music which features harps and guitars. The most famous dances, accompanied by the Conjunto Jarocho, are the *bamba* and *zapateado*, with much stamping and lashing of feet related to flamenco of Andalucía. Mexico's version of the Cuban *danzón* music and the indigenous *música tropical* add to the cultural richness. Many cultural events can be seen at the Instituto Veracruzano de Cultura, a few blocks from the Zócalo. At night the Malecón is very lively, and sometimes fire-eaters and other performers entertain the public. The Shrovetide carnival 7 weeks before Easter is said to be Mexico's finest, rivalling those of New Orleans, Brazil and Trinidad. At this time it is very difficult to find accommodation, or tickets for transportation.

The food is good, the fishing not bad, and the people lively and welcoming. The local craft is tortoiseshell jewellery adorned with silver, but remember that the import of tortoiseshell into the USA and many other countries is prohibited.

There are two buildings of great interest: the very fine 17th-century Palacio Municipal, on Plaza Constitución, with a splendid façade and courtyard, and the castle of San Juan de Ulúa (1565), on Gallega Island, now joined by road to the mainland; take bus marked Ulúa from Malecón Av. República. It failed to deter the buccaneers and later became a political prison. Mexico's "Robin Hood", Chucho el Roto, was imprisoned there, and escaped three times. (Entry US$0.45.) There is a city historical museum with a good collection of photographs, well displayed; it traces history from the Conquest to 1910; it is at Zaragoza 397. The Baluarte de Santiago, a small fort which once formed part of the city walls, is at Francisco Canal y Gómez Farias, open 0900-1800, Suns. and holidays, 1600-1900, closed Tues. On the southern arm of the harbour breakwater is a small aquarium (admission US$0.10).

Plazuela de la Campana, by Serdán and Zaragoza, is an attractive small square.

The beach along the waterfront, and the sea, are filthy. There is much pollution from the heavy shipping. Amber from Simojordis is sold on the town beach. A short bus ride from the fish market takes you to Mocambo beach, which has a good swimming bath (with restaurant and bar, admission US$0.40), beach restaurants, Caribbean-style beach huts and the water is quite a bit cleaner though still rather uninviting in colour. There are crabs and mosquitoes. The Gulf is even warmer than the Caribbean. The beach is crowded. At holiday time cars race up and down, there are loud radios, etc. There is little shade near the beach. There is a fine beach at Chachalacas, 30 km. N, not crowded (**see page 195**).

NB: Travellers are warned to be particularly wary of overcharging.

Hotels *Mocambo*, Boca del Río, T 371661, B, 8 km. out on Mocambo beach, 1930s palace, good service and food, highly rec.; *Emporio*, A, overpriced, with bath, swimming pool, inexpensive comida corrida, rather old-fashioned, on Paseo del Malecón (Insurgentes Veracruzanos y Xicoténcatl, T 320020), a block before the *Emporio* when approaching from the Zócalo is *Puerto Bello*, Avila Camacho 1263, T 310011, good, B; *Hostal de Cortés*, 3 star, convenient for clean beaches, Avila Camacho y de las Casas, T 320065; *Impala*, Orizaba 650, T 370169, D, with bath, cold water, mosquitoes but clean, near bus station; *Baluarte*, opp. the small fort of Baluarte, Canal 265, T 360844, D, good, clean, rec; *Colonial*, C, on Zócalo, T 320193, swimming pool, indoor parking, rec.; *Oriente*, on Zócalo, T 312440, D, secure parking, clean, friendly, balconies, good fans, some a/c, quiet, rec.; *Imperial*, on Zócalo, E, with bath; *Royalty*, E, nice and clean, Abasolo 34, T 361041, near beach, 20 min. walk from Zócalo, rec., but noisy as it caters mainly to student groups; *Cristóbal Colón*, Avila Camacho 681, T 823844, one block from *Royalty*, E, smaller, quieter, some rooms with sea-view balconies, clean; *Ortiz*, on Zócalo, E, family-owned, no hot water reported not clean; *La Paz*, Av. Díaz Mirón 1242, T 325399, nr. bus station, E, with bath, highly rec., cheap, clean and helpful; *Casa de Huéspedes Alvarez*, Abasolo 987, F, cold water, fan, clean, friendly. *Mar y Tierra*, Figueroa y Malecón, T 313866, F, good value, some rooms with balconies overlooking the harbour; *Central*, Mirón 1612, T 372222, E, clean, get room at back, esp. on 5th floor, laundry facilities; *Ruiz Milán*, D, Malecón, T 361862, good; *Príncipe*, Collado 195, F, some distance from centre, very clean with hot shower and toilet; many others in port area, reached by bus from the bus terminal. Two more on Miguel Lerdo, near the Portales: *Rías* and *Concha Dorada*.

CREA Youth Hostel, Paseo Doña Juana, Municipio de Ursulo Galván.

Trailer Parks Two at Mocambo, side by side, bus marked Boca del Río goes there from corner of Zaragoza and Serdán (but reported closed in 1990). Los Arcos has hot showers, laundry tubs, lighting and plugs, owner speaks English. The other is Los Arcos Fiesta; noisy from main beach road, but good and well supervised, esp. at night. Nearest supermarket is on the road into Veracruz at the modern shopping centre.

Restaurants The local gourmet speciality is *langosta loca* (mad lobster). *La Parroquia* (original) has fans, white tiled walls, cement floors and waiters in white jackets, overlooks town square; wonderful coffee, food not marvellous but place crowded in evenings. In the market for excellent fish, and opp. is an unnamed restaurant, good seafood, and *El Azteca de Cayetano*, Mario Molina 94, where mondongos de fruta (a selection of all the fruits in season) are prepared on one plate. Also on Molina, **Amparo** and **Santo Domingo**. **Torros** are the local drinks made of eggs, milk, fruit and alcohol—delicious and potent. **La Paella**, Plaza Constitución, has its name written into the concrete of the entrance floor, good comida corrida. **Pizza Palace**, Zamora, buffet 1200-1700, US$3; **Emir Cafeteria**, Independencia 1520, nr. F. Canal, good breakfast. There is a good local fish restaurant, **Olympica**, near the fish market in the street running parallel to Av. 16 de Septiembre, 2 blocks from the Zócalo. Recommended: **Pescadores**, for fish, Zaragoza y Morales (not evenings); and the steakhouse **Submarino Amarillo**, Malecón 472. Good shellfish at Boca del Río.

Exchange   Only Bancomer and Banamex, both on Independencia, change money; hotels are quicker and may use same rate—check at the desk.

Post Offices   Main post office by bridge to San Juan de Ulúa fortress, also at Palacio Federal, 5 de Mayo 4 Rayon, 0800-1900.

US Consular Agent   Mr Edwin L. Culp, Juárez 110.

Tourist Offices   Palacio Municipal on the Zócalo, T 32-99-42, helpful but no hotel price list; Federal office, T 32-16-13.

Airport   at Las Bajadas, 3 flights daily to the capital, T 37-04-17; Aeroméxico, Molina 138.

Rail   Rail to Mexico City: El Jarocho (servicio estrella) leaves Mexico City at 2115, arr. Veracruz 0700; leaves Veracruz 2130, arr. 0737, reserved seat US$7.80, single sleeper, US$25.50; ordinary trains at 0725 via Jalapa, at 0800 and 2130 via Córdoba, 1st class US$5.50 (US$7 reserved seat).

Buses   The majority of buses are booked solid for three days in advance throughout summer; at all times queues of up to 2 hrs. possible at Mexico City booking offices of bus companies (best company: ADO, Buenavista 9, Mexico City). Book outward journeys on arrival in Veracruz, as the bus station is some way out of town and there are often long queues. ADO terminal, Díaz Mirón y Jalapa, T 376790; Autobuses Unidos, Lafragua y Jalapa, T 372376. For local buses, get accurate information from the tourist office. Buses to the main bus station along Av. 5 de Mayo; marked ADO. Bus to Mexico City, US$4.30 (6 hrs.), via Jalapa, misses out Orizaba, Fortín and Córdoba; to Villahermosa US$12 (10 hrs.); to Puebla, US$3.50; to Oaxaca, ADO, 11 hrs., US$6; to Mérida US$18 (16 hrs.). Taxi to ADO terminal from centre US$1.20.

Connections with Guatemala   There are no through buses to Guatemala, but there are connecting services. Train leaves Veracruz 0915 daily for Ixtepec and Tapachula; 2nd class only; not recommended, no light for 30 hrs., so high likelihood of robbery. Take your own toiletries and food. No sleeping accommodation. The connecting railway from the border at Tecún Umán to Guatemala City is reported to have a service on Wed., Fri. and Sun. at 0700, but this is some way S of the Tapachula-Talismán crossing. Local bus services run Tapachula-border and border-Guatemala City; quicker than the much more mountainous route further N. Alternatively, take ADO bus to Oaxaca, then carry on to Tapachula (11½ hrs.) by bus. Another bus to frontier at Hidalgo, US$0.25. This route allows you to stop at intermediate points of your choice, but has few "comfort" stops. Buy bus tickets out of Veracruz well in advance.

Road very winding from Orizaba so take travel sickness tablets if necessary. Philippe Martin, of the Touring Club Suisse, writes: "The road from Veracruz to Oaxaca is spectacular but tiresome to drive and will take about a day. The road from Veracruz to La Tinaja and Tierra Blanca is good and fast although there are many lorries. From there to Miguel Alemán the road is bad, speed reasonable, still many lorries. The Tuxtepec area has lovely lowland, jungle areas, charming villages, and the traffic is sparser between Tuxtepec and Oaxaca, while there are no more gasoline stations. The road is very bad and winding and the fog only lifts after you leave the pines at 2,650 metres above sea level. After a descent and another pass at 2,600 metres you enter the bare mountainous zone of Oaxaca. Very few eating places between Tuxtepec and Oaxaca." This route is possible by bus but the Tuxtepec-Oaxaca stretch has been reported dangerous because of drug-traffickers.

Excursions   Isla de Sacrificios (see above), half an hour from the harbour, beautiful beach (trip US$2.20 return). Trips Sundays and holidays, every hour between 0900 and 1400. **Excursion to Zempoala (see page** 195), buses from ADO terminal ½ hr. each way, via Cardel, or less frequent direct 2nd class buses; a local bus from Cardel goes to La Antigua, US$0.15. On Sunday, to Mandinga for cheap fresh sea food (big prawns), and local entertainment.

The Papaloapan Region   At **Puerto Alvarado** (1½ hrs. S from Veracruz by bus, a modern, pleasant fishing port, *Hotel Lety*, E, reasonable but for grim plumbing system; *Hotel del Pastor*, F, avoid next-door restaurant; *María y Ileza*, E, quiet, clean; beware of small boys with pea-shooters in the plaza; fair/carnival 31 March-5 April), cross the Río Papaloapan (Butterfly River) by a toll bridge (US$0.50), go along Route 180 into the sugar-cane area around Lerdo de Tejada and Angel R. Cavada. At El Trópico a dirt road turns left to some quiet beaches such as Salinas and Roca Partida. Only at Easter are the beaches crowded: they are normally the preserve of fishermen using hand nets from small boats. In the dry season (Dec.-May) the road is passable around the coast to Sontecomapan.

At Tula, a little further along the main road, is a spectacular waterfall, El Salto de Tula; a restaurant is set beside the falls. The road then climbs up into the mountainous volcanic area of Los Tuxtlas, known as the Switzerland of Mexico for its mountains and perennial greenness.

Santiago Tuxtla, set on a river, is a small town of colonial origin. In the main square is the largest known Olmec head, carved in solid stone, and also a museum (open 0900-1500, Sat.-Sun. 0900-1200 and 1500-1800), containing examples of local tools, photos, items used in witchcraft (*brujería*), and the first sugar-cane press used in Mexico and another Olmec head. (*Hotel Castellanos*, on Plaza, D, cold shower, clean; *Morelos*, E, family run.)

The archaeological site of **Tres Zapotes** lies to the west; it is reached by leaving the paved road south towards Villa Isla and taking either the dirt road at Tres Caminos (signposted) in the dry season (a quagmire from May-Dec.), or in the wet season access can be slowly achieved by turning right at about km. 40, called Tibenal, and following the dirt road north to the site of the Museum which is open 0900-1700 hrs, entrance US$0.10. (If it is closed, the lady in the nearby shop has a key.) A bus from Santiago Tuxtla goes to the village of Tres Zapotes, the site is 1 km. walk. There is another Olmec head, also the largest carved stela ever found and stela fragments bearing the New World's oldest Long Count Date, equal to 31 B.C. Not far from Tres Zapotes are three other Olmec sites: Cerro de las Mesas, Laguna de los Cerros, and San Lorenzo Tenochtitlán.

Overlooking Santiago Tuxtla is the hillside restaurant *El Balcón*, which serves excellent langostino (crayfish) for US$4 and *horchata de coco*, a drink made from the flesh and milk of coconut.

15 km. beyond lies **San Andrés Tuxtla** (112,000), the largest town of the area, with narrow winding streets, by-passed by a ring road. This town is also colonial in style and has a well-stocked market with Oaxacan foods such at *totopos, carne enchilada*, and *tamales de elote* (hard tortillas, spicy meat, and cakes of maize-flour steamed on leaves). It is the terminus for trains (daily) from Rodríguez Clara to the south (**see page** 192) and it is the centre of the cigar trade. One factory beside the main road permits visitors to watch the process and will produce special orders of cigars (*puros*) marked with an individual's name in ½ hr.

Hotels *Catedral*, nr. Cathedral, F, very nice; *Figueroa, del Parque*, Madero 5, E, a/c, very clean, good restaurant; *Zamfer*, ½ block from Zócalo, E; *Casa de Huéspedes la Orizabana*, in the centre of town, F, without bath, clean hot water, friendly; *Ponce de León*, primitive, pleasant patio, F; Juárez, across from 2nd class bus station, F, clean, friendly. (Bus San Andrés Tuxtla-Villahermosa US$5.50, 6 hrs.)

Restaurants Near the the town centre is the restaurant *La Flor de Guadalajara*; it appears small from the outside but is large and pleasant inside, well rec.; sells *tepachue*, a drink made from pineapple, similar in flavour to cider, and *agua de Jamaica*.

At Sihuapan, 5 km. towards Catemaco, is a turning to the right on to a very bumpy dirt road which leads to the impressive waterfall of Salto de Eyipantla. Bridge toll payable at Comoapan, US$0.10, plenty of small boys offer their services as guides.

Catemaco is a pleasant little town (31,000 people) with large colonial church and picturesque situation on lake, 13 km. from San Andrés Tuxtla. Beware of thieves at all times. At weekends there is a stall selling handicrafts from Oaxaca, and boat trips out on the lakes to see the shrine where the Virgin appeared, the spa at Coyame and the Isla de Changos, and to make a necklace of lilies, are always available (about US$5). The town is noted for its *brujos* (sorcerers), although this is becoming more of a tourist attraction than a reality, and the Monte del Cerro Blanco to the north is the site of their annual reunion. Catemaco can be reached by bus from Veracruz, changing to a local bus at San Andrés Tuxtla; it is about 120 km. NW of Minatitlán (**see page** 245). Catemaco is synonymous throughout Mexico with picturesque, vulgar language.

Hotels *Catemaco*, T 30203, D, excellent food and swimming pool, and *Angel*, T 30411, a/c, satellite TV, similar prices; both on main square. *Motel Playa Azul*, 2 km. on road to Sontecomapan, T 30042, C, modern, a/c; in a nice setting, comfortable and shady, with water-skiing on lake, will allow trailers and use of showers. A number of hotels are situated at the lakeside; *La Finca*, T 30430, B, pool, attractive grounds; *Posada Komiapan* (swimming-pool and restaurant), very comfortable, D, T 30063; *Brujos*, F, fan, a/c, shower, nice clean rooms, balcony overlooking the lake; *Los Arcos*, T 30003, D, clean, fan, good value; *San Francisco*, Matamoros 26, F, basic.

Restaurants On the promenade are a number of good restaurants—*María*

José, best; *La Julita* (anguilla and tacholgolo), also lets rooms, E, pleasant, rec; *La Ola* (payiscadas, anguilla, tegogalso, carne de chango, and cesina) built almost entirely by the owner in the local natural materials, and *La Luna*, among others. Best value are those not directly on the lake e.g. *Los Sauces*, which serves mojarra.

The Gulf Coast may be reached from Catemaco along a dirt road (which can be washed out in winter). It is about 18 km. to Sontecomapan, crossing over the pass at Buena Vista and looking down to the Laguna where, it is said, Francis Drake sought refuge. The village of **Sontecomapan** (1,465 pop., *Hotel Sontecomapan*) lies on an entry to the Laguna and boats may be hired for the 20-min. ride out to the bar where the Laguna meets the sea (US$10 return). A large part of the Laguna is surrounded by mangrove swamp, and the sandy beaches, edged by cliffs, are almost deserted except for local fishermen and groups of pelicans. Two good restaurants in Sontecomapan. Beaches are accessible to those who enjoy isolation—such as Jicacal and Playa Hermosa. Jicacal can be reached by going straight on from the Catemaco-Sontecomapan road for 9 km. on a good dirt road to La Palma where there is a small bridge which is avoided by heavy vehicles; immediately after this take left fork (dirt road) for Monte Pío, a pretty location at the mouth of the river (basic rooms to let, F, and a restaurant), and watch out for a very small sign marked Playa Escondida; road impassable when wet, about 12 km., and then continuing for about 4 km. from there. Playa Jicacal is long and open, the first you see as you near the water. The track reaches a T-junction, on the right Jicacal, to the left to Playa Escondida, *Hotel*, F. It is not rec. to sleep on the beaches (assaults and robberies) although at Easter time many people from the nearby towns camp on the beaches.

At **Acayucán** (*Hotel Joalica*, Zaragoza 4, E; *Hotel Ritz*, F, adequate), 267 km. from Veracruz, turn right for Route 185 if you want to go across the Isthmus to Tehuantepec, Tuxtla Gutiérrez and Central America, but continue on Route 180 for Minatitlán, Coatzacoalcos and Villahermosa (Tabasco). The road across the Isthmus is straight but is not always fast to drive because of high winds (changing air systems from Pacific to Atlantic). Gasoline and food on sale at the half-way point, Palomares, where there is a paved road to Tuxtepec (**see page** 192), 2½ hours' drive. A few kilometres south of Palomares a gravelled road enters on the eastern side; this passes under an imposing gateway "La Puerta de Uxpanapa" where some 24,500 families are being settled on land reclaimed from the jungle. An hour's drive further south the road crosses the watershed and passes across the flat coastal plain to Juchitán (**see page** 229).

About 15 km. from Alvarado a new bridge replaces the old ferry-crossing at Buenavista over the Papaloapan River and the road heads southwards to the fishing village of **Tlacotalpan** where the Papaloapan and San Juan rivers meet. This town, regarded as the centre of Jarocho culture (an amalgam of Spanish, mainly from Seville, African and Indian cultures), has many picturesque streets with one-storey houses all fronted by stuccoed columns and arches painted in various bright pastel colours. Two churches in the Zócalo, and a Casa de las Artesanías on Chazaro, 1½ blocks from the Zócalo. The Museo Funster contains interesting local paintings and artefacts. There is a famous *fiesta* there on 31 January which is very much for locals rather than tourists (accommodation is impossible to find during *fiesta*).

Hotels and Restaurants   The *Viajero* and *Reforma*, D, hotels are good; so is the *Posada Doña Lala*, D with a/c and TV, restaurant expensive; *Jarocho*, E, seedy. Excellent *sopa de mariscos* and *jaiba a la tlacotalpina* (crab) at the *Restaurant La Flecha*.

Transport   Buses go to Veracruz via Alvarado (US$0.35, 45 mins.), to San Andrés, Tuxtla Gutiérrez, Santiago Tuxtla (US$1, 1½ hrs.) and Villahermosa.

Cosamaloapan, some 40 km. beyond Tlacotalpan (103,000 people), is the local market centre with a number of hotels, and the staging point for most bus lines from Veracruz, Orizaba and Oaxaca. One of the largest sugar mills in Mexico is situated just outside the town— Ingenio San Cristóbal—and there is a local airstrip. From Cosamaloapan to Papaloapan the banks on either side of the river are lined with fruit trees. Chacaltianguis, on the east bank of the river, reached by car ferry, has houses fronted by columns.

40 km. beyond Cosamaloapan is a ferry to **Otatitlán**, also on the east bank of the river (it leaves whenever there are sufficient passengers, US$0.08 the ride). The town, also known as El Sanctuario, dates back to early colonial times, its houses with tiled roofs supported by columns, but most interesting is the church. The padre maintains that the gold-patterned dome is the largest unsupported structure of its kind in Mexico, measuring 20 metres wide and 40 high. El Sanctuario has one of the three black wooden statues of Christ brought over from Spain for the son of Hernán Cortés. During the anti-clerical violence of the 1930s attempts to burn it failed, although the original head was cut off and now stands in a glass case. The first weekend in May is the saint's day and fair, for which pilgrims flock in from the *sierra* and from the Tuxtlas, many in local dress. (*Restaurant-Bar Pepe* serves delicious local, but unusual food; *Restaurant-Bar Ipiranga III* also offers excellent cooking; both by embarkation point.)

At **Papaloapan** on the eastern bank of the river, the main road from Orizaba to Rodríguez Clara crosses the main road from Alvarado to Oaxaca; the railway station has services to Yucatán and Chiapas, and to Orizaba or Veracruz. On the west bank is the bus terminal of Santa Cruz (almost under the railway bridge) where all second class buses stop. A passenger ferry may be taken from here to Papaloapan (US$0.08). Although Papaloapan is the route centre for the area the most convenient centre is Tuxtepec, 9 km. further south (see below).

The river basin drained by the Papaloapan and its tributaries covers some 47,000 sq. km.—about twice the size of the Netherlands—and is subject to a programme of regional development by the Comisión del Papaloapan, which includes the construction of two large dams to control the sometimes severe flooding of the lower basin. The lake formed behind Presidente Alemán dam at Temascal is scenically very attractive and boats may be hired to go to Mazatec Indian settlements on the islands or on the other side. There is also a daily ferry passing

round the lake. Soyaltepec is the closest settlement, situated high above
the water on an island, the peak crowned by a church. **Ixcatlan** lies on
a peninsula jutting into the lake on the SE side; it has one hotel and one
restaurant, as well as a large beer repository. Ixcatlan may also be
reached by dirt road from Tuxtepec, but it is less nerve-racking to take
a ferry.

Temascal (Sun. is the most active day) may be reached by taking Route
145 from Papaloapan through Gabino Barreda, Ciudad Alemán (no
facilities, centre of the Papaloapan Commission), Novara (petrol and 3
restaurants of varying prices, 1 air-conditioned), as far as La Granja
where the turn to Temascal is clearly marked. Route 145 continues
paved and straight past Tres Valles (cheap, good regional food; annual
fair mid-Nov.), and on to **Tierra Blanca** (hotels *Balun Canán*, cheap,
hot, F; *Principal*, E, own shower and fan, clean, just above bus station,
noisy; *Bimbis* restaurant by ADO bus station, good; shopping centre,
market, car repairs, e.g. Volkswagen agent). Mérida train from Tierra
Blanca leaves late although scheduled for 0530 (2nd class, US$2.90,
crowded, sleeper for 1—or two small people—US$11) stops at
Palenque, 15½ hrs. later. Train also stops at Ciudad Alemán on the way.
Route 145 passes under a sign saying "La Puerta del Papaloapan", to
join the main Orizaba-Veracruz road (Route 150) at **La Tinaja**, a
second-class bus junction, also gasoline, and restaurants (1
air-conditioned at service station). Papaloapan to La Tinaja takes about
1 hr., the road often has a lot of lorries and in the cane-cutting season
great care should be taken at night for carts travelling on the road
without lights. There are three railway crossings on the road, also poorly
marked, two near La Granja and one near Tierra Blanca. The tarmac is
often damaged in the wet season (June-Dec.).

From Papaloapan a paved road runs eastwards as far as Rodríguez Clara
(planned to continue to Sayula on the Trans-Isthmian road). This road
passes through the main pineapple-producing region of Mexico, which
has encouraged the development of towns such as **Loma Bonita** (local
airstrip, hotels, restaurants and gasoline) and **Villa Isla** (hotels, *La Choca*
restaurant good, railway station, ADO bus terminal, and centre for the
rich cattle-producing area that surrounds it).
  From Villa Isla a good dirt road runs south to **Playa Vicente** (6,974
pop.), another ranching town, located beside a wide river; excellent
crayfish may be eaten at the *Restaurant La Candileja*, while the café on
the central plaza serves tender steaks. Another dirt road leaves the Villa
Isla-Playa Vicente road for Abasolo del Valle (2,000 pop.), but only
reaches to within 7 km. The last few kms. can be impassable by vehicle
in the wet season. The town is set beside a lagoon and the houses are
surrounded by fruit trees (no hotels or restaurants). Gasoline can be
bought—ask at a shop who has some to sell.
  At the cross-roads of the Papaloapan-Sayula road about 80 km. from
Papaloapan, where the S turn is to Villa Isla, the N turn is a paved road
which in about ½ hour will take you past two turnings to Tres Zapotes
and up to Santiago Tuxtla.
  The road from Papaloapan continues E to a point just N of

Rodríguez Clara, which is reached by branching off S down a dirt road. This is a compact, thriving town, also with a railway station. There are 2 hotels, the better is in the centre of the town, *Hotel Roa*, E; *Restaurant Mexicana* rec. The railway line from Papaloapan is the only all-year means of transport to visit the villages and towns E of Rodríguez Clara.

Tuxtepec is the natural centre for a stay in the Papaloapan area. It is a small market town in the state of Oaxaca, some 9 km. south of Papaloapan (toll for Caracol bridge, US$0.40). Consequently the streets are alive every day in season with Indians who have come from surrounding villages to buy and sell, and there is a fascinating mixture of the music and exuberance of Veracruz with the food and handicrafts of Oaxaca. The town is built on a meander of the Santo Domingo River and a walk past the main shops in Calle Independencia will allow two halts at viewpoints for the river.

Hotels *El Rancho*, Avila Camacho 850, T 50641, restaurant, bar, evening entertainment, most expensive, accepts travellers' cheques as payment, rec.; *María de Lourdes*, Av. 5 de Mayo 1380, T (91-287)5-0410, E, hot water, clean, excellent car park, rec.; *Tuxtepec*, Matamoros 2, T 50944, good value; *Sacre*, also good, quiet, F; *Catedral*, Calle Guerrero, nr. Zócalo, F, very friendly, fan and shower; *Miramar*, E, look surprised and the price may be reduced, hot showers, fairly safe car park, with view of filthy river. Very good value is the *Avenida* in Independencia round the corner from ADO bus station, E, with bath and ventilator, basic, clean but restaurant below not very good value. *Posada del Sol*, basic and noisy, opp. Fletes y Pasajes bus station, F.

Restaurants *El Estero* across from the street from ADO (fish dishes and local cuisine excellent), *El Mino* (near Fletes y Pasajes bus terminal), *Mandinga* for fish dishes, *Queso Fundido* in Independencia. *Ostionería Pata-Pata*, on the street beside *Hotel Avenida*, good mojarra. *Ronda*, Calle Independencia, cheap and good; *La Mascota de Oro*, 20 de Noviembre 891, very friendly, cheap. Beer from the barrel can be bought from the bar next to the Palacio Municipal, and the best ices are found in *La Morida*.

Transport There are four bus terminals in town, clear street signs for each one. ADO bus services to Mexico City (Thurs., US$7), Veracruz and regular daily minibus (taking 5-6 hrs.) to Oaxaca leaving at 2230. AU (Autobuses Unidos, on Matamoros, ½ block from Libertad) daily to wide variety of destinations. AU to Oaxaca, US$4 2nd class, 8 hrs., slow, Buses Cuenca, direct route, US$2.70, ADO US$6.65. Fletes y Pasajes to local villages and Juchitán, and a 2nd class, wild journey to Oaxaca, 6 hrs.; Cristóbal Colón, which has its own terminal near the Cultural Centre, sometimes stop by the ADO office to find passengers for Chiapas or Mexico City. The Tuxtepec-Palomares road provides a short cut to the Transístmica; it passes through many newly cleared jungle areas. Bus to Acayucán, ADO, 4 hrs., US$1.50. There are scattered villages, the main halt being at María Lombardo (some 2 hrs. from Tuxtepec where food is sold); Zócalo is attractive. Gas station 4 km. further on at Cihualtepec junction, a village of Indians moved from the area flooded by the Temascal dam.

Excursions To Temascal to see the dam (see previous page); also a visit to the Indian villages of Ojitlán and Jalapa de Díaz (bus leaves from the end of Calle 20 de Noviembre, US$2.20, 2½ hrs.; hotel, F and food stores, good and cheaper *huipiles* from private houses) is well worth the ride; easily reached by car along semi-paved road and also by AU bus service (from Mercado Flores Magón, 20 de Noviembre y Blvd. Juárez, every hour on the half hour). The Chinantec Indians' handicrafts may be bought on enquiry; hotels non-existent and eating facilities limited but some superb scenery, luxuriant vegetation and little-visited area. Ojitlán is best visited on Sunday, market day, when the Chinanteca *huipiles* worn by the women are most likely to be seen. Part of the area will be flooded when the Cerro de Oro dam is finished and the lake will join that of Temascal. Heavily armed checkpoint on the road from Tuxtepec to Tierra Blanca (bus 1½ hrs., US$0.50), non-uniformed men, very officious, do not get caught with any suspicious goods.

The road from Tuxtepec south to Oaxaca (Route 175) is now well paved, and a spectacular route, cars need good brakes and it is reported to be difficult for caravans. Many people avoid it; it is said to have become dangerous for travellers because of drug plantations along its length. It takes about 5 hrs. to drive, up Valle Nacional. This valley, despite its horrific reputation as the "Valle de los Miserables" in the era of Porfirio Díaz, for political imprisonment and virtual slavery from which there was no escape, is astoundingly beautiful. The road follows the valley floor, on which are cattle pastures, fruit trees and a chain of small villages such as Chiltepec (very good bathing in the river), Jacatepec (reached by ferry over the river, produces rich honey and abounds in all varieties of fruit, there are no cars at all), Monte Flor (where swimming and picnicking are possible beside natural springs, but *very* cold water, and an archaeological site) and finally Valle Nacional. (Bus to Valle Nacional from Tuxtepec, 1½ hrs., basic hotel, restaurants, stores, and gasoline available; river swimming.) The road climbs up into the Sierra, getting cooler, and slopes more heavily covered with tropical forest, and there are panoramic views.

San Pedro Yolox lies some 20 minutes' drive W of this route down a dirt road; it is a peaceful Chinantec village clustered on the side of the mountain, while Llano de Flores is a huge grassy clearing in the pine forest with grazing animals and cool, scented air. Wood from these forests is cut for the paper factory in Tuxtepec. Ixtlán de Juárez has gasoline. While houses in the lowlands are made of wood with palm roofs, here the houses are of adobe or brick. From Guelatao (**see page 227**) it is about 1½ hours' drive, mainly downhill, to Oaxaca (**see page 217**), with the land becoming drier and the air warmer.

Veracruz to Mexico City By the road followed to Veracruz, the driving time from Mexico City is about 9 hrs. One can return to the capital by a shorter route through Jalapa which takes 6 hrs.; this was the old colonial route to the port, and is the route followed by the railway.

Jalapa (spelt Xalapa locally), capital of Veracruz state, 132 km. from the port, is in the *tierra templada*, at 1,425 metres. The weather is variable, hot with thunder storms, the clouds roll down off the mountains in the evening. There was a passion for renovation in the flamboyant gothic style during the first part of the 19th century. It is yet another "City of Flowers", with walled gardens, stone-built houses, wide avenues in the newer town and steep cobbled crooked streets in the old. The 18th century cathedral, with its sloping floor, has been recently restored. Population 213,000. Just outside, on the road to Mexico City, is an excellent, modern museum (opened Oct. 1986) showing archaeological treasures of the Olmec, Totonac and Huastec coastal cultures. The three colossal heads dating from the 2nd to the 5th centuries A.D., and displayed in the grounds of the museum, are Olmec (open 1000-1700, take the Foviste de Tejada bus). Jalapa has a University; you can take a pleasant stroll round the grounds, known as El Dique. Pico de Orizaba is visible from hotel roofs or Parque Juárez very early in the morning, before the haze develops. 2.5 km. along the Coatepec road are lush botanical gardens with a small museum.

Festival Feria de Primavera, mid-April.

Hotels Cheaper hotels are up the hill from the market, which itself is uphill from Parque Juárez (there is no Zócalo). Many hotels are overpriced; no price-lists displayed and not available at tourist office. *Xalapa*, Victoria y Bustamante, T 82222, L, good restaurant, excellent bookshop, changes travellers' cheques; *María Victoria*, Zaragoza 6, T 80268, B, good; *México*, Lucio 4, T 75030, D, clean, with shower, will change dollars; *Salmones*, Zaragoza 24, T 75435, D, restaurant, excellent view of Orizaba from the roof, rec. *Limón*, Revolución 8, ½ block up from Cathedral, F, tiled patio, laundry, rec.; *Amoro*, nr. market, F, no shower but public baths opp., very clean. *Hotel Suites*, by ADO bus station, E with bath, clean, not too friendly; *Continental*, on Enríquez, E, owner speaks some English, good lunches, friendly; *Plaza*, Enríquez, E, clean, safe, friendly, will store luggage, good view of Orizaba from the roof.

Restaurants *La Parroquia*, Zaragoza 18, rec., good strong coffee; *La Casona del Beaterío*, Zaragoza 20, good atmosphere; *La Barranquilla*, expensive but good; *Quinto Reyno*, Juárez 67 close to Zócalo, lunches only, excellent vegetarian with health-food shop, very good service. *Chino's*, on Enríquez, very friendly and pleasant; *Terraza*, opp. Parque Juárez, the cheapest breakfast in the centre; *Estancia*, opp. Barranquilla, good food; *Aladino*, Juárez, up from ADO, excellent Mexican food; *Pizzaría*, Ursulo Galván; *Enrico*, good value; *El Mayab*, next to *Hotel Regis*, for antojitos and good carne tampiqueña; *La Tasca*, a club, good music, rec. Health food shops, Ursulo Galván, nr. Juárez, good bread and yoghurt, another opp. the post office on Zamora, the famous Xalapeño chilli comes from this region.

Shopping Artesanía shop on Alfaro, more on Barcenas, turn off Enríquez into Madero, right again at the top, the owner of *El Tazín* on the corner speaks English.

Books Instituto de Antropología, Benito Juárez, has books in English and Spanish, student ID helps.

Moped Hire in Camacho US$4-6 per hour, Visa accepted.

Theatre Teatro del Estado, Av. Avila Camacho; good Ballet Folklórico Veracruzano and fair symphony orchestra.

Entertainments Centro de Recreación Xalapeño has exhibitions; live music and exhibitions in Ayora, underneath Parque Juárez; 10 pin bowling, Plaza Cristal, next to cinema. There are 2 cinemas next to *Hotel Xalapa*, off Camacho; 3-screen cinema in Plaza Cristal; cinemas in the centre tend to show soft porn and gore.

Exchange Houses *Casa de Cambio*, on right side of Zamora going down hill, English spoken. Banks are slow, money transferred from abroad comes via Mexico City, banks prefer to issue pesos, with persistence and tact it may be possible to obtain dollars. The liquor shop in Plaza Cristal will change dollars.

Laundromat 2 on Ursulo Galván, same day service.

Health Hospital, Nicolás Bravo, entrance in street on right. Dr Blásquez, Hidalgo, speaks English. There are 2 dentists on Ursulo Galván.

Communications Radio-telephone available opposite *Hotel María Victoria*; long distance phone in shop on Zaragoza, with a sign outside, others behind the government palace also in Zaragoza. Letters can be sent to the Lista de Correos in Calle Diego Leño, friendly post office, and another at the bottom of Zamora. There is a telegraph office next door where telegrams marked Lista de Correos are kept.

Travel Agents There are 4 on Camacho, the one nearest Parque Juárez is very helpful.

Tourist Office Av. Camacho, a long walk or short taxi ride. Look out for *Toma Nota*, free sheet advertising what is on, available from shop in front of *Hotel Salmones*.

Airport 15 km. SE, on Veracruz road.

Transport 2nd class bus station, Autobuses Unidos, uphill from Parque Juárez. 1st class buses (ADO) leave from the terminal 1 km. away. Frequent ADO service Jalapa-Veracruz. To Puebla, ADO, 4 hrs. To Villahermosa, ADO, 3 a day, 10 hrs. To Poza Rica, the coast road is faster, while the impressive route via Teziutlán requires a strong stomach for mountain curves. Railway station on outskirts, buses from near market to get there. Train to Mexico City at 1140, to Veracruz at 1530 (4 hrs.).

Excursions Hacienda Casa de Santa Anna, 20 minutes' drive, was taken over in the revolution and is now a museum with the original furniture, entrance free, no bags allowed in. To ruins of **Zempoala**, 65 km. N of Veracruz (hotel, *Chachalaca*, near sea, spotless, rec.), the coastal city which was conquered by Cortés and whose inhabitants became his allies. The ruins are interesting because of the round stones uniquely used in construction. (Entry US$0.40, small museum on site.) Take 2nd class bus to Zempoala via Cardel, which will let you off at the ruins, or take a taxi from the Plaza of Zempoala, US$1.20 return. You can also get there from Veracruz. To Texala waterfalls, some 15 km. away near the neighbouring town of Coatepec, famous for its ice-cream.

Tim Connell writes: "**Naolinco** is ½ hr. ride, 40 km. NE of Jalapa up a winding hilly road, *Restaurant La Fuente* serves local food; has nice garden. Las Cascadas, with a *mirador* to admire them from, are on the way into the town: two waterfalls, with various pools, tumble several thousand feet over steep wooded slopes. Flocks of *zopilotes* (buzzards) collect late in the afternoon, soaring high up into the thermals. Baños Carrizal: 8 km. off main road, 40 km. from Veracruz. **Chachalacas** is a beach with swimming pool and changing facilities in hotel of same name, US$0.70 adults. Thatched huts; local delicacies sold on beach, including *robalito* fish."

The coast road from Veracruz heads to Nautla 3 km. after which Route 131 branches inland to Teziutlán (see below). 42 km. up the coast from Nautla is **Tecolutla**, a very popular resort on the river of that name, toll bridge US$2.50.

Accommodation Hotels *Villas de Palmar*, B; *Playa*, E, good, *Tecolutla*, E, best, and *Marsol* (run down) are on the beach. *Posada Guadalupe* and *Casa de Huéspedes Malena* (F, pleasant rooms, clean) are on Avenida Carlos Prieto, near the river landing stage. Newer hotels, D, on road to Nautla. *Restaurant Paquita*, next to *Hotel Playa*, rec.

Some 40 km. inland from Tecolutla is **Papantla** (280,000 people) which is easily reached from Veracruz, 4 hrs., by ADO bus, US$4.80, good road, Jalapa, by ADO bus, US$2.60, 6 hrs., and Mexico City, via Poza Rica. Men and women come to market in the local costume and there are *voladores* at about 1100 on Sats. in the churchyard. Mariachi bands play in the *cervecerías* near Zócalo on Sundays. Papantla is also the centre of the vanilla-producing zone, and small figures and animals made in vanilla are for sale, as well as the essence.

Hotels *Tajín*, Calle Dr. Núñez 104, T 21064, restaurant and bar, D, reasonable; *Pulido*, Enríquez 205, modern, T 20036, but noisy, E, with bath, reported dirty, parking; *Papantla*, on Zócalo, E, very clean, hot showers, friendly; *Trujillo*, Calle 5 de Mayo 401, E, rooms with basin, but other facilities dirty, friendly. (It is better to stay in Papantla than in Poza Rica if you want to visit El Tajín.)

Restaurant *Las Brisas del Golfo*, Calle Dr. Núñez, reasonable and very good. *Sorrento*, Zócalo, good, cheap, rec.; cheap breakfasts at *Café Cathedral* on street above Cathedral.

Tourist Office   in municipal offices in the Zócalo; it is rarely open, mostly mornings.

About 12 km. away, in the forest, is **El Tajín**, the ruins of the capital of the Totonac culture (6th to 10th century AD) entry, US$0.30, ½ price on Sun. Guidebook US$1.25, available in Museum of Anthropology, Mexico City. At the centre of this vast complex is the Pyramid of El Tajín, whose 365 squared openings make it look like a vast beehive. Traditionally, on Corpus Christi, Totonac rain dancers erect a 30-metre mast with a rotating structure at the top. Four *voladores* (flyers) and a musician climb to the surmounting platform. There the musician dances to his own pipe and drum music, whilst the roped *voladores* throw themselves into space to make a dizzy spiral descent, sometimes head up, sometimes head down, to the ground. *Voladores* are now in attendance every day, most of the day, and fly if they think there are enough tourists. There are buses from both Poza Rica marked Martínez or San Andrés, US$0.50, frequent departures near market and Papantla; to reach Tajín from Papantla take a local bus to the crossroads of El Chote (½ hr.) then another local bus (direction Poza Rica) to the ruins (10 mins.); otherwise take a taxi. The tourist office near the Zócalo will show you bus schedules.

24 km. NW of Papantla is **Poza Rica**, an oil town, with paved streets, an old cramped wooden market and great temperament.

Hotels *Robert Prince*, Av. 6 Norte, 10 Oriente, T 25455, Col. Obrera, C; *Nuevo León*, Av. Colegio Militar, T 20528, opp. market, D, rooms quite spacious, fairly clean and quiet, rec. *Poza Rica*, 2 Norte, T 20134, D, fairly comfortable. *Fénix*, basic, E, opposite ADO bus station; *San Román*, 8 Norte 5, E; *Aurora*, Bolívar 4, basic but quiet and fairly clean, E; *Juárez*, Cortines y Bermúdez, E, average; *Madrid*, basic.

Bus All buses leave from new terminal about 1½ km. from centre (including about 100 a day to Mexico City, 5 hrs., US$5). To Veracruz, 4 hrs., US$6.25. To Pachuca, Estrella Blanca, 4½ hrs., US$2, change in Tulancingo. To Tecolutla (see below), US$1, 1¼ hrs.

From Poza Rica you can visit the Castillo de Teayo, a pyramid with the original sanctuary and interesting carvings on top, buses every ½ hr., change halfway. 25 km. along Route 8 is Barra de Cazones with a little developed, good beach.

On the coast, 55 km. from Poza Rica, 189 km. S of Tampico is **Tuxpan**, (*Veracruz*), tropical and humid, 12 km. from the sea on the River Tuxpan. Essentially a fishing town (shrimps a speciality), it is now decaying from what must have been a beautiful heyday. Interesting covered market, but beware of the bitter, over-ripe avocados; fruit sold on the quay. Beach about 2 km. E of town, reached by taxi or bus (marked "Playa"), at least 10 km. long. White sands; hire deckchairs under banana-leaf shelters for the day (US$2). Bus to Mexico City (Terminal del Norte), US$6, 6½ hrs. via Poza Rica. (*Hotel Florida*, Av. Juárez 23, B, clean, hot water; *Tuxpan*, OK, E; and others. Entertainment: *Hotel Teján*, over the river, south side, then about 1 km. towards the sea, very plush, good singers but US$6.50 cover charge; *Aeropolis* disco, dull, no beer.

The road towards the capital continues to climb to **Perote**, 53 km. from Jalapa. The San Carlos fort here, now a military prison, was built in 1770-77; there is a good view of Cofre de Perote volcano. A road branches N to **Teziutlán** (*Hotel Valdez*, hot water, car park, F), with a Friday market, where good *sarapes* are sold, a local fair, *La Entrega de Inanacatl*, is held in the 3rd week in June. The old convent at **Acatzingo**, 93 km. beyond Perote, is worth seeing. Another 10 km. and we join the road to Puebla and Mexico City.

Pico De Orizaba (Citlaltépetl) is the highest mountain in Mexico (5,760 metres). It is not too difficult to climb although acclimatization to altitude is advised and there are some crevasses to be negotiated. From Acatzingo one can go via a paved road to Tlachichuca (35 km, or you can take a bus from Puebla to Tlachichuca). Either contact Sr. Reyes who arranges trips in a four-wheel drive car up an appalling road to 2 huts on the mountain. He charges about US$80-100, including one night at his house (D full board). Alternatively, stay at *Hotel Margarita*, no sign, F, then, early in the morning hitch hike to the last village, Villa Hidalgo (about 15 km.). From there it's about 10 km. to the huts. Take the trail which goes straight through the forest, eventually to meet the dusty road. The huts, one small, one larger and colder, are at 4,200 metres (small charge at each). There is no hut custodian; it's usually fairly empty, except on Sat. night. No food or light, or wood; provide your own. Water close at hand, but no cooking facilities. Start from the hut at about 0500, first to reach the glacier at 4,700 metres, and then a little left to the rim. It's about 7-8 hrs. to the top; the ice is not too steep (about 35-40°), take crampons, if not for the ascent then for the descent which takes only 2½ hrs. At the weekend you're more likely to get a lift back to Tlachichuca.

MEXICO CITY-CUERNAVACA-TAXCO-ACAPULCO (7)

A 406-km. road, beginning as a 4-lane toll motorway, connects Mexico City with Acapulco. (The 4-lane ends at Iguala, 209 km. from Acapulco.) Driving time is about 6 hrs. The highest point, La Cima, 3,016 metres, is reached at km. 42. The road then spirals down through precipitous forests to (Km. 75):

Cuernavaca, capital of Morelos state (originally Tlahuica Indian territory); at 1,542 metres: 724 metres lower than Mexico City. Population 233,000 and growing (possibly now 400,000) because of new industrial area to the S. The temperature never exceeds 27°C nor falls below 10°C, and there is almost daily sunshine even during the rainy season. The city has always attracted visitors from the more rigorous highlands and can be overcrowded. The Spaniards captured it in 1521 and Cortés himself, following the custom of the Aztec nobility, lived there. The outskirts are dotted with ultra-modern walled homes and it is losing a lot of its charm as a result of rapid growth.

The Cathedral, finished in 1552, known as Iglesia de la Asunción, stands at one end of an enclosed garden. 17th-century murals were discovered during restoration; also, on the great doors, paintings said to have been done by an Oriental convert who arrived by a ship from the Philippines, relating the story of the persecution and crucifixion of 24 Japanese martyrs. The Sun. morning masses at 1100 are accompanied by a special *mariachi* band. *Mariachis* also perform on Sun. and Wed. evenings in the Cathedral. By the entrance to it stands the charming small church of the Tercera Orden (1529), whose quaint façade carved by Indian craftsmen contains a small figure suspected to be one of the only two known statues of Cortés in Mexico. (The other is a mounted statue near the entrance of the *Casino de la Selva* hotel.)

The palace Cortés built in 1531 for his second wife stands by the city's central tree-shaded plaza; on the rear balcony is a Diego Rivera mural depicting the conquest of Mexico. It was the seat of the State Legislature until 1967, when the new legislative building opposite was completed; it has now become the Regional Cuauhnahuac museum, showing everything from dinosaur remains to contemporary Indian culture (closed Thurs., as are other museums in Cuernavaca). The 18th century Borda Gardens, on Calle Morelos, were a favourite resort of Maximilian and Carlota, but have now more or less run wild (small fee). The weekend retreat of the ill-fated imperial couple, in the Acapantzingo district, is being restored. Other places worth seeing are the three plazas, Calle Guerrero, and, some distance from the main plaza, the new market buildings on different levels. The house of David Alfaro Siqueiros, the painter, is now a museum at Calle Venus 7 and contains lithographs and personal photographs. The very unusual Teopanzolco pyramid is to be found near the railway station. Remarkable frescoes have recently been found in the old Franciscan church of La Parroquia. There are occasional concerts at the San José open chapel. Many spas in surrounding area, at Cuautla, Xocitepec, Atrotomilco, Oaxtepec and others.

Hotels *Las Mañanitas*, Linares 107, T 12-4646, L (one of the best in Mexico), Mexican colonial style, many birds in lovely gardens, excellent food. *Hacienda de Cortés*, Atlacomulco suburb, 16th century sugar *hacienda*, magnificent genuine colonial architecture, garden, suites, pool, restaurant, A, access by car; *Posada Jacarandas*, Cuauhtémoc 805, T 15-7777, A, garden, restaurant, parking; *Presidente*, L, Narbo 58, T 13-3968; *Suites Paraíso*, Av. Domingo Diez 1100, T 13-3365, family accommodation, B; *Posada Xochiquetzal*, Francisco Leyva 200, T 12-0220, near Zócalo, restaurant, pool, garden, A. *Posada San Angelo*, Privada la Selva 100, T 14-1499, restaurant, gardens, pool, A; *Casino de la Selva*, A, Leandro Valle 26, T 12-4700, with huge mural by Siqueiros on the future of humanity from now till A.D. 3000, shops, restaurant, bars, gardens; *Hostería Las Quintas*, Av. las Quintas 107, T 12-8800, A, built in traditional Mexican style, owner has splendid collection of bonsai trees, restaurant, pool, magnificent setting, fine reputation; *Papagayo*, Motolinia 13, T 14-1711, 5 blocks from Zócalo, C, incl. breakfast and lunch or dinner, pool, gardens, clean, convenient, noisy, suitable for families, parking; *Hostería Peñalba*, Matamoros 204, T 12-4166, D, beautiful courtyard with exotic birds and a monkey, restaurant with famous Spanish food (long-term guests only), was once Zapata's H.Q. during the Revolution, very atmospheric and friendly but disappointing facilities, much insect life, rooms on street are very noisy; *Casa de Huéspedes*, Morelos Sur 702, good value, D including 3 good meals; for economy, *Roma*, Matamoros 405, T 12-0787, E, good value, with hot water 0700-0800 and shower. Probably cheapest is *Casa Blanca*, on Arista, 2 blocks from bus station, simple, F. Rooms from US$75 a month on Calle Degollado 104, quite clean, but heavy bus traffic outside; communal kitchen and bath. Furnished flat US$200 per month. Several cheaper hotels in Calle Aragón y León, rec. is *Colonia*, No. 104, T 12-0099, E, clean, friendly, secure; *El Buen Vecino*, Casa La Paz, Marilú, Francés, and *América*, E, noisy (couples only, but clean, basic; some rent rooms by the hour).

Motels *El Verano*, Zapata 602, T 17-0652, C; *Posada Cuernavaca*, Paseo del Conquistador, T 13-0800, view, restaurant, grounds, B; *Suites OK Motel* with *Restaurant Las Margaritas*, Zapata 71, T 13-1270, special student and long-term rates, apartments, trailer park; swimming pool and squash courts; *Torrell*, Jesús Preciado 414, nr. San Antón suburb, student discounts, E.

Camping *San Pablo*, Highway 95, D, 9 km. out of town, near the road, friendly; *Monasterio Benedito* on road to Tepoztlán, ½ hr. by bus to the centre, very quiet, hot showers, rec.

Restaurants *Las Mañanitas*, beautiful but expensive, Ricardo Linares 107; *Sumiya*, Barbara Hutton's oriental mountain-top retreat, in the suburbs, exquisite decor, must be seen; *Hostería Las Quintas*, Las Quintas 107, excellent; *Harry's Grill*, on Hidalgo, excellent Mexican food, good service and prices; *Los Arcos*, opp. post office in Zócalo, good, prices reasonable, foreigners meeting place in a.m., full at weekends. *Casa de Gardenias*, opp. Cortés' palace, open air, food at US$2 a dish; *Villa Roma* on Zócalo, good chilaquiles for breakfast, good service, pricier; *Château Renee*, Swiss-European cuisine, Atzingo 11, in woods above town. *Mister Grill*, entrance to town, steak house; *Eric Pup*, 2nd floor on main square, German-Mexican food; *Baalbek*, Netzahualcoyotl 300, gorgeous garden, best Lebanese food in town, expensive but worth it; *Vienés*, Lerdo de Tejada 4, German-Swiss food, very good; *La Parroquía*, main square, very popular, sidewalk café; *Madreterra del Oro*, in pretty patio near Cortés' palace, good vegetarian food. *Portal*, nearby, in Calle Galeana, has good cheap breakfasts. Mexican food at *Los Comales*, Morelos Sur 1321; *Hacienda Los Ocampo*, rec. for *mariachi* music, at 1400 the house-band plays, Av. Plan de

Ayala 310 and at No. 616 *Nuevo Comedor Pachuquilla; Mi Ranchito*, Domingo Diez 1518; vegetarian food at *La Remolada* on Matamoros, good, classical music; bar with live music at the *Parrilla Danesa* (guitar); Yucatán specialities at *Merendero Yucateco*, F. Villa 112.

Language Schools   There are about 12 Spanish courses on offer. These start from US$45 per week at the University, 4 hrs. daily; private schools charge US$80-125 a week, 5-6 hrs. a day and some schools also have a US$80-100 registration fee. The peak time for tuition is summer: at other times it may be possible to arrive and negotiate a reduction of up to 25%. There is a co-operative language centre, Cuauhnahuac, with Spanish courses, at 1414 Av. Morelos Sur. Intensive courses also at Instituto Panamericano, Morelos Sur 712 (nearest school to centre); Instituto de Idiomas y Culturas Latino Americanas, Dr. Manuel Mazari 100, Col. Miraval; Center for Bilingual Multicultural Studies, Apto. Postal 1520, T 17-05-33 or Los Angeles, LA, 213-851-3403; Instituto Fénix, Salto Chico 3, Col. Tlaltenango, T 13-17-43, which also has excursions and minor courses in politics, art and music; Cale, Nueva Tabachín, 22-A bis, Col. Tlaltenango, friendly; Cemanahuac, Calle San Juan 4, Las Palmas, claims high academic standards, field study, also weaving and pottery classes; Experiencia, which encompasses all these features, Registro Público 16, Colonia Burocrática; Cidoc, Av. Río Balsas 14, Colonia Vista Hermosa; Ideal, Privada Narcizo Mendoza 107, Col. Prodena, T 17-04-55; and Idel, Las Palmas 101, Colonia Jiguilpan. Staying with a local family will be arranged by a school and costs US$10-15 a day or US$100-250 a month incl. meals; check with individual schools, as this difference in price may apply even if you stay with the same family.

Telephones   Long-distance calls can be made at Farmacia Central, on the Zócalo.

Tourist Office   Av. Morelos Sur 900, very helpful, many maps also opp. cathedral, on 2nd floor of old office building (with gardens). For cultural activities, go for information to the university building behind the Cathedral on Morelos Sur.

Railway   Station on Calle Amacuzac; only passenger service is daily train to Iguala.

Buses   Terminal on Av. López Mateos, adjacent to main market. To Mexico City 0600-2200, every 15 mins.: Pullman de Morelos, US$1.20, is said to be the most comfortable and fastest, from Southern Bus Terminus, Mexico City; Estrella de Oro, 1st class, US$1.20, Flecha Roja, 2nd class, 2 hr. journey, US$0.65. To Acapulco, 6 hrs. with either. To Taxco, Flecha Roja, 2nd-class buses from Calle Morelos, US$0.80, 1½ hours, fairly comfortable, about every hour, or Estrella de Oro, 1st class, Las Palmas-Morelos Sur. Cuautla (**page** 216) via Yautepec every hour, 1 hr., interesting trip; go there for long-distance buses going South.

Warning Theft of luggage from waiting buses in Cuernavaca is rife; don't ever leave belongings unattended. Robberies have been reported on the non-toll mountain road to Taxco.

Excursions To the Chapultepec Park, W end of town, with boating facilities, small zoo, water gardens, small admission charge. To the potters' village of **San Antón**, perched above a waterfall, a little W of the town, where divers perform Sun. for small donations. To the charming suburb of **Acapantzingo**, S of the town, another retreat of Maximilian. To **Tepoztlán**—24 km.—at the foot of the spectacular **El Tepozteco national park**, picturesque steep cobbled streets, wild view, with Tepozteco pyramid high up in the mountains (US$0.30, open anytime between 0930 and 1030-1630, the climb is an hour long, and strenuous—the altitude at the top of the pyramid is 2,100 metres—but the view is magnificent) and a remarkable 16th century church and convent (entry US$0.45, site closes at 1630): the Virgin and Child stand upon a crescent moon above the elaborate plateresque portal, no tripod or flash allowed. Tepoztlán now sports a noticeably "hippy" population (*Posada del Tepozteco*, a very good inn, C, with swimming pool and excellent atmosphere; *Casa de Huéspedes Las Cabañas*, D, overpriced; budget travellers would do better to stay in Cuernavaca. *Restaurant Carmen*, S of convent, rec.). There is a small archaeological museum behind the church. This was the village studied by Robert Redfield and later by Oscar Lewis. Local bus from Cuernavaca Flecha Roja terminal takes 40 mins., US$0.40; bus to Mexico City, US$0.90.

Near Cuernavaca is Chalcatzingo, where there are interesting Olmec-style rock carvings. Near Jojutla is the old Franciscan convent of Tlaquiltenango (1540), frequent bus service. About 60 km. from Cuernavaca are the Malinoca pyramids, on a temple carved just before the Conquest from solid rock: interesting.

(Km. 100) **Alpuyeca**, whose church has good Indian murals. A road to the left runs to **Lake Tequesquitengo** (*Paraíso Ski Club*) and the lagoon and sulphur baths of Tehuixtla. Near the lake a popular resort—swimming, boating, water skiing and fishing—is *Hacienda Vista Hermosa* (A), Hernán Cortés' original *ingenio* (sugar mill), and several lakeside hotels (also at Jojutla, above). From Alpuyeca also a road runs right for 50 km. to the **Cacahuamilpa** caverns (known locally as "Las Grutas"); some of the largest caves in North America, open 1000 to 1700 (well lit); strange stalactite and stalagmite formations; steps lead down from near the entrance to the caverns to the double opening in the mountainside far below, from which an underground river emerges (entry, US$0.60, up to 1600).

Buses going to Cacahuamilpa from Cuernavaca leave every 20 mins. between 1000 and 1700 (1 hr.); they are usually overcrowded at weekends; enquire about schedules for local buses or buses from Taxco to Toluca, which stop there (from Taxco, 30 km., 40 minutes). Guided tours take you 2 km. inside; some excursions have gone 6 km.; the estimated maximum depth is 16 km.

At 15 km. is the right-hand turn to the **Xochicalco** ruins (36 km. SW of Cuernavaca), topped by a pyramid on the peak of a rocky hill, dedicated to the Plumed Serpent whose coils enfold the whole building and enclose fine carvings which represent priests. The site is large: needs 2-3 hrs. to see it properly.

Xochicalco was at its height between 650 and 900 AD. It is one of the oldest known fortresses in Middle America and a religious centre as well as an important trading point. The name means "place of flowers" although now the hilltops are barren. It was also the meeting place of northern and southern cultures and both calendar systems were correlated here. The sides of the pyramid are faced with andesite slabs, fitted invisibly without mortar. After the building was finished, reliefs 3-4 inches deep were carried into the stone as a frieze. There are interesting underground tunnels; one has a shaft to the sky and the centre of the cave. There are also ball courts, an avenue 18.5 metres wide and 46 m. long, remains of 20 large circles and of a palace and dwellings. Xochicalco is well worth the 4 km. walk from the bus stop; take a torch for the underground part to save employing a guide, entry US$0.10. (Flecha Roja bus to Xochicalco from terminal at Av. Morelos y Arista, marked Las Grutas, passes the turn-off to Xochicalco—same bus schedule as Cacahuamilpa, above.) Alternatively take bus from Cuernavaca to Cuentepec (infrequent), which passes by the entrance gate to Xochicalco ruins. This bus passes through Alpuyeca, which is also easily reached from Taxco by bus.

Leave the toll road at Amacuzac (Km. 121) and take the old road (39 km.) to **Taxco** (pop. 120,000), a colonial gem, with steep, twisting, cobbled streets and many picturesque buildings. The first silver shipped to Spain came from the mines of Taxco. A Frenchman, Borda, made and spent three fortunes here in the 18th century; he founded the present town and built the magnificent twin-towered, rose-coloured parish church of Santa Prisca which soars above everything but the mountains. Well worth a visit are the Casa Humboldt, where Baron von Humboldt once stayed, and the Casa Figueroa, the "House of Tears" (closed Sun.), so called because the colonial judge who owned it forced Indian labourers to work on it to pay their fines. Museo Guillermo Spratling, behind Santa Prisca, is a fascinating silver museum, entry US$0.20. Large paintings about Mexican history at the Post Office. The roof of every building is of red tile, every nook or corner in the place is a picture, and even the cobblestone road surfaces have patterns woven in them. It is now a national monument and all modern building is forbidden. Gas stations are outside the city limits. The plaza is 1,700 metres above sea-level. A good view is had from the Iglesia de Guadalupe. The climate is ideal, never any high winds (for it is protected by huge mountains immediately to the N); never cold and never hot, but sometimes foggy. The processions during Holy Week are spectacular. The most tourist-free part is up from the main street where the taxis can't go; day trippers fill the town in the early afternoon. Wear flat rubber-soled shoes to avoid slithering over the cobbles. Silverwork is a speciality and there are important lead and zinc mines.

Vendors will not bargain. Cheaper silver items can often be found in less touristy towns including Mexico City, but beware of mistaking the cheapish pretty jewellery, *alpaca*, which only contains 25% silver, for the real stuff. By law, real silver, defined as 0.925 pure, must be stamped somewhere on the item with the number 925. The downtown shops in general give better value than those on the highway, but they're still expensive. On the 2nd Sunday in December there is a national silversmiths' competition. Colourful produce market near the Zócalo.

N.B. All silver jewellers must be government-registered. Remember to look for the 925 stamp and, if the piece is large enough, it will also be stamped with the crest of an eagle, and initials of the jeweller. Where the small size of the item does not permit this, a certificate will be provided instead.

One of the most interesting of Mexican stone-age cultures, the Mezcala or Chontal, is based on the State of Guerrero in which Taxco lies. Its remarkable artefacts, of which there are many imitations, are almost surrealist. The culture remained virtually intact into historic times.

Hotels *De la Borda*, on left as you enter Taxco, largest, all facilities, A, great views, T 20225; dearest and best, *La Cumbre Soñada*, 1.5 km. or so towards Acapulco on a mountain top, colonial, exquisite, A. *La Hacienda del Solar*, Acapulco exit of town, T 20323, A, best restaurant in Taxco. *Rancho Taxco-Victoria*, Soto la Marina 15, walk to centre, A; *Posada Don Carlos*, Cerro de Bermeja 6, converted old mansion, restaurant, good view, C; *Los Arcos*, Juan Ruiz de Alarcón 2, T 20205, magnificently reconstructed 17th century ex-convent, charming, friendly, good restaurant, D; *Posada de los Castillo*, Alarcón 7, off

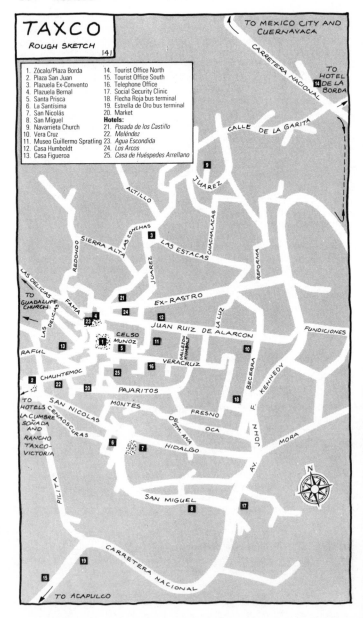

TAXCO
ROUGH SKETCH

1. Zócalo/Plaza Borda
2. Plaza San Juan
3. Plazuela Ex-Convento
4. Plazuela Bernal
5. Santa Prisca
6. La Santísima
7. San Nicolás
8. San Miguel
9. Navarrieta Church
10. Vera Cruz
11. Museo Guillermo Spratling
12. Casa Humboldt
13. Casa Figueroa
14. Tourist Office North
15. Tourist Office South
16. Telephone Office
17. Social Security Clinic
18. Flecha Roja bus terminal
19. Estrella de Oro bus terminal
20. Market

Hotels:
21. *Posada de los Castillo*
22. *Meléndez*
23. *Agua Escondida*
24. *Los Arcos*
25. *Casa de Huéspedes Arrellano*

main square, Mexican style, friendly, excellent value, D. *Meléndez*, T 20006, D, clean, no hot water, somewhat noisy as it is near market, good breakfast, other meals available; *Agua Escondida*, near Zócalo at Calle Guillermo Spratling 4, T 20726, C, with bath, nice view; *Posada de la Misión*, Cerro de la Misión 84, Juan O'Gorman mural, restaurant, good, pool, A; *Colina del Sol*, T 21091, E, clean, nice rooms, on the Kennedy Highway between Estrella de Oro and Flecha Roja terminals; the cheapest hotels are in this area. *Casa de Huéspedes Arellano*, Pajaritas 23, by Santa Prisca and Plaza Borda, E with bath (less without), clean, old beds, no soap or toilet paper.

Restaurants *La Ventana* of the *Hacienda del Solar* hotel, renowned. *Alarcón*, overlooking Zócalo, very good. *Sr. Costilla*, next to church on main square, good drinks and grilled ribs. *Cielito Lindo*, on Zócalo, good food, service and atmosphere; next door is *Papa's Bar*, a discotheque and a small pizza place in an arcade. *Paco's Bar*, at other end of square for drinks and people-watching. *Bora-Bora*, overlooks Zócalo, Guadalupe y Plaza Borda, good pizzas; *Pizzería Mario*, Plaza Borda, beautiful view over city; *Mi Taverna* next to the Post Office, excellent Italian food, friendly; *Concha Nuestra*, Plazuela San Juan, food and music excellent. *Mi Oficina*, straight up hill from where buses from Cuernavaca arrive. Good food at *Los Arcos* and *Victoria* hotels. Argentine *empanadas* at unnamed restaurant opp. Casa Humboldt, cheap, excellent breakfast. *Lonchería Liliana*, Juan Ruiz de Alarcón 13, rec.; *Pozolería Betty*, Mora 20 (below bus station), good food including the local beetle (jumil) sauce. Many small restaurants just near *Hotel Meléndez*. Good snacks in small shop on NW corner of Zócalo. Excellent comida corrida at *Santa Fe*, opp. *Hotel Sta. Prisca*.

Nightclub *La Jungla*, set in a jungle-like location (somewhat frightening 15-min. drive out of town), cover charge includes a show and dancing.

Buses Book onward tickets (e.g. to Acapulco) the day prior to departure. (Taxis meet all buses and take you to any hotel, approx. US$0.70.) Taxco is reached from Mexico City from the Central del Sur, Estrella de Oro, 1st class US$2.50, only two stops, quick, no overcrowding, five a day (3 hrs.); also five 2nd class, Flecha Roja, a day for US$2, up to 5 hrs. Buses to Cuernavaca; 1st class buses at 0900, 1600, 1800 and 2000 (Estrella de Oro), 2nd class hourly at a quarter to the hour, but can be erratic. Little 24-seaters, "Los Burritos", take you up the hill from the bus terminal on main road. Spectacular journey from Toluca, missing out Mexico City, 2nd class buses only, from Flecha Roja Terminal, change at Toluca for Morelia. To Acapulco 1st class, Estrella de Oro, US$4.75; 2nd class, Flecha Roja, US$2.50, 5 hrs.

Excursions Visit *Posada Don Carlos*, Bermeja 6, also Ventana de Taxco in *Hacienda del Solar* for view. "Combi" to Panorámica every 30 mins. from Plaza San Juan, US$0.10. About 20 km. out of Taxco a rodeo is held on Sat., guides available, admittance US$0.50. 12 km. from Taxco to Acuitlapán waterfalls, with colectivo or Flecha Roja bus; hire a horse to travel down 4 km. path to large clear pools for swimming. Taxis about US$4.50 per hour. To **Cacahuamilpa** for caverns, entrance US$0.80, 40 minutes. Buses from 0820 but service erratic, US$0.70, or take a long white taxi marked "Grutas" from opposite the bus station, US$1. To return, take bus from Toluca at junction, ½ km. from the caves. Visit the villages where *amate* pictures are painted (on display at Casa Humboldt and in the market). Xalitla is the most convenient as it is on the road to Acapulco, take 2nd class bus there. Other villages: Maxela, Ahuelicán, Ahuehuepán and San Juan, past Iguala and before the River Balsa.

Warning Travellers have stressed that people, especially women, should *not* wander alone in isolated places; there have been violent attacks, e.g. in Acuitlapán. In the town handbag snatchers and slashers operate.

The road descends. The heat grows. We join the main road again at Iguala, 36 km. beyond Taxco (*Hotel Central*, basic F; *Pasajero*, F; bus to Taxco US$0.50). Beyond the Mexcala river, the road passes for some 30 km. through the dramatic canyon of Zopilote to reach **Chilpancingo** (pop. 120,000, altitude 1,250 metres), capital of Guerrero state, at Km. 302. The colourful reed bags from the distant village of Chilapa are sold in the market. The Casa de las Artesanías for Guerrero is on the right-hand side of the main highway Mexico City—Acapulco. It has a particularly wide selection of lacquerware from Olinala. Its *fiesta* starts on December 16 and lasts a fortnight. It has a University. Hotel: *La Posada Meléndez*. Not far from Chilpancingo are Oxtotitlán and Juxtlahuaca, where Olmec cave paintings can be seen. The road goes down to Acapulco (about 420 km. from Mexico City). About 20 km. from the coast, a branch road goes to the NW of Acapulco; this is a preferable route for car drivers because it avoids the city chaos. It goes to a point between Pie de la Cuesta and Coyuca, is signed, and has a drugs control point at the junction.

Warning Avoid travelling by car at night in Guerrero, even on the Mexico City-Acapulco highway and coastal highway. Many military checkpoints on highway. *Guerrilleros* have been active in recent years, and there are also problems with highway robbers and stray animals.

Acapulco (population now thought to be over a million) is the most popular resort in Mexico, particularly in winter and spring. During Holy Week there is a flight from the capital every 3 mins. The town stretches for 16 km. in a series of bays and cliff coves and is invading the hills. The hotels, of which there are 250, are mostly perched high to catch the breeze, for between 1130 and 1630 the heat is sizzling; they are filled to overflowing in January and February. It has all the paraphernalia of a booming resort: smart shops, night clubs, red light district, golf club, touts and street vendors and now also air pollution. The famous beaches and expensive hotels are a different world from the littered streets, dirty hotels and crowded shops and buses which are only two minutes walk away. There are some twenty beaches, all with fine, golden sand; deckchairs on all beaches, US$0.50; parachute skiing in front of the larger hotels at US$7 for 5 mins. The two most popular are the sickle-curved and shielded Caleta, with its smooth water and now dirty sands, and the surf-pounded straight beach of Los Hornos. Take local bus to Pie de la Cuesta, 8 km. (now preferred by many budget travellers to Acapulco itself, but becoming commercialized), several bungalow-hotels and trailer parks (see below), nice lagoon and big beaches (warning: the surf is dangerous), where you drink *coco loco*—fortified coconut milk—and watch the sunset from a hammock. Beware at all times of thieves. One can swim, and fish, the year round. Best free map of Acapulco can be obtained from the desk clerk at *Tortuga Hotel*.

Acapulco in colonial times was the terminal for the Manila convoy.

Its main defence, Fort San Diego, where the last battle for Mexican independence was fought, in the middle of the city and is worth a visit. (Open 1000-1800, Tues. and Sun. only, free admission.)

Hotels can cost up to US\$200 a night double; cheaper for longer stays, but this also means less expensive hotels insist on a double rate even for 1 person and for a minimum period. In the off-season (May-November) you can negotiate lower prices even for a single for one night. For cheap hotels in Acapulco you can make reservations at the bus terminal in Mexico City.

The fabulous **Club Residencial de las Brisas**, L+, a hotel where the services match the astronomical price. (It begins at sea-level and reaches up the mountain slope in a series of detached villas and public rooms to a point 300 metres above sea-level. Each room has own or shared swimming pool. Guests use pink jeeps to travel to the dining-room and recreation areas.) **Acapulco Plaza** (**Holiday Inn**), Costera 123, T 59050, 3 towers, 2 pools, 5 bars, 4 restaurants, a city in itself, L-L+; **Exalaris Hyatt Regency**, next to naval base, and **Exalaris Hyatt Continental**, at Fuerte Diana, both with all services, L, T 42868 and 40909 respectively; **Villa Vera Raquet Club**, luxurious celebrity spot, L, T 40333; **Caleta**, Playa Caleta, T 39940, remodelled, A; **El Presidente**, Costera near Condesa beach, T 41700, A; **Elcano**, Costera near golf club, T 41950, A; and **Casa Blanca Tropical**, Cerro de la Pinzona, T 21217, C, with swimming pool, is rec.; **Condesa del Mar**, Costera at Condesa beach, T 42828, all facilities, A; **Acapulco Imperial**, Costera 251, T 41865, B; **Acapulco Tortuga** (T 48889), A, and **Romano's Le Club** (T 45332), both on Costera, many groups, A; **Maralisa**, Enrique El Esclavo, T 40976, B, smallish and elegant, Arab style, rec.; **Tropicano Best Western**, Costera 510, T 41100, C; **Maris**, Alemán y Magallanes, T 42800, B, very good; **Diana**, street beside Costera M. Alemán, B, a/c, clean, quiet, pool. The **Acapulco Princess Country Club**, part of the **Acapulco Princess**, 20 km. away on Revolcadero beach, is highly fashionable. **Vacaciones**, Costera Alemán 63, T 21637, Caleta zone E, good value. **Jungla**, Miguel Alemán 86, T 20255, E; **San Francisco**, Costera 219, T 20045, old part of town, friendly, good value, noisy in front, E; **Posada del Sol**, clean, friendly, on the beach, pool, good food, C, Playa del Coco opp. new convention centre, T 41010, thefts from safe-deposit reported; **Playa Hornos**, Calz. Pie de la Cuesta, T 33940, clean, friendly; **Playa Doral**, Hornos beach, C, a/c, pool, ask for front upper floors with balcony, good value; **Villa Lucía**, C, built around pretty swimming pool, with kitchens in rooms, mostly frequented by Mexicans, a/c, one block from sea and one block from **Ritz** (which is at Costera M. Alemán y Magallanes).

Most cheaper hotels are grouped around the Zócalo, especially Calles La Paz and Juárez; about 15 mins. from the 2nd class bus station (Flecha Roja) on Av. Cuauhtémoc. **Fiesta**, clean and nice, D, with bath, fan, 2 blocks NW from Zócalo, Azueta 16, T 20019; **Misión**, Felipe Valle 12, T 23643, E, very clean, colonial, close to Zócalo. **Casa García**, E, clean, cold shower, pleasant, 3 blocks SW of Zócalo; **Isabel**, La Paz y Valle, T 22191, E with fan, rec., near Zócalo; **Sacramento**, E. Carranza y Valle, E with bath and fan, no towel, soap or loo paper, friendly, noisy, OK, purified water, T 20821; **Añorve**, B, Juárez 17, T 22093, 2 blocks off Zócalo, clean, E, with bath; **Colimense**, E, J.M. Iglesias II, off Zócalo, T 22890, pleasant; **Santa Cecilia**, Francisco Madero 7, off Zócalo, E, with bath and fan, noisy, but otherwise fine. **California**, La Paz 12, T 22893, 1½ blocks W of Zócalo, D, good value, fan. Many cheap hotels on La Quebrada, basic but clean with fan and bathroom, including **El Faro** (No. 63, T 21365, clean, E), **Corral** (No. 56, T 20756, F, good value), **Casa de Huéspedes La Tía Conchita**, Guadalajara, **Casa de Huéspedes Aries** (E with bath, nice); **Amueblados Orozco**, near Quebrada, friendly, clean, E, with shower. Probably cheapest in town, **La Casa del Río**, 1½ blocks from the 2nd class bus terminal towards Los Hornos beach, cabins with stretchers and sheets; F; and **Betty**, Belisario Domínguez 4, 5 mins. from bus station, F with bath, fan, clean.

María Cristina's, E in bungalows for 4, clean and comfortable, shower and cooling facilities, at Pie de la Cuesta (Km. 11), near fresh water lagoon and sea; also there is *Villa Rosita*, E for bungalow and primitive accommodation next to *Restaurant Tres Marías*, F. Several other nice places at Pie de la Cuesta, E/D, in clean rooms with shower, *Quinta Karla, Quinta Blanca, Puesta del Sol*, expensive places for hammocks, *Quinta Dora Trailer Park*, E for hammock, managed by American, helpful.

The student organization Setej offers dormitory accommodation, F, if one has a valid international student card, at Centro Vacacional, Pie de la Cuesta, hours, 0700-2400. For longer (1 month plus) stays, try *Amueblados Etel*, Av. la Pinzona 92 (near Quebrada) for self-catering apartments, cheap off-season (before November), *Apartamentos Maraback*, Costera M. Alemán, D. The Tourist Bureau is helpful in finding a hotel in any price range.

Motels *Impala, Bali-Hai, Costera, La Joya, Monaco, Playa Suave, Villas del Sol* and *Gran Motel Acapulco* all along the Costera, B-C; *Ofelia, Victoria*, Cristóbal Colón, 1 block behind Costera, C.

Camping *Trailer Park El Coloso*, in La Sabana, small swimming pool, and *Trailer Park La Roca* on road from Puerto Márquez to La Sabana, both secure. *Estacionamiento Juanita* and *Quinta Dora* at Pie de la Cuesta (latter charges US$4 just to sling hammock), *Quinta Carla, Casa Blanca, U Kae Kim*, all US$50 a week upwards, but negotiable.

Restaurants There are a number of variously-priced restaurants along and opposite Condesa beach; many cheap restaurants cluster in the blocks surrounding the Zócalo, especially along Juárez; another group along the Caleta beach walkway; yet another group of mixed prices on the Costera opp. the *Acapulco Plaza Hotel. Antojitos Mayab*, Costera y Avilés, is a favourite for Mexican dishes; *Hong Kong*, near *Ritz Hotel* on Costera, best for Chinese food; *Madeira*, on the hill to *Hotel Las Brisas*, best fixed priced, elegant meal in town, delightful; *San Carlos*, Juárez (near Zócalo), fixed menu lunch, good; opp. is *100% Natural*, mostly vegetarian, other branches on Costera Miguel Alemán (opp. Hyatt Kingsgate), and up the hill from the yacht club. *Carlos and Charlie's*, opp. Condesa beach, 2nd floor, "fun place for the young at heart"; *Emmas*, next to *Playa Suave Motel*, local favourite for chicken; 250 more to select from.

Night Clubs There are dozens of discos including *Baby 'O, Magic, Tiffany's, UBQ*, etc. Every major hotel has at least one disco plus bars; *Discotheca Safari*, Av. Costera, free entry, 1 drink obligatory, good ambience; *El Fuerte*, famous Flamenco show; *La Perla*, renowned cliff divers, and at least 3 gay transvestite shows, plus a *Voladores de Papantla* pole dancers' show. Superb varied night-life always.

City Transport Taxis US$8 an hour. Several bus routes, with one running the full length of Costera Miguel Alemán linking the older part of town to the latest hotels, another operating to Caleta beach. Buses to Pie de la Cuesta, 8 km., US$0.15.

British Consul (Honorary) Mr D.B. Gore, MBE, *Hotel Las Brisas*, T (91-748) 46605.

Laundromat Tintorería Bik, 5 de Mayo.

Telephones Public offices will not take collect calls; try from a big hotel (ask around—there will be a surcharge).

Post Office Costera, 2 blocks S of Zócalo.

Tourist Information Costera Miguel Alemán at Hornos beach, helpful, but double-check details.

Buses Mexico City, 406 km., 6½ hours; de luxe air-conditioned express buses, US$8; ordinary bus, about US$6, all-day services from Estación Central de Autobuses del Sur by the Taxqueña metro station, with Estrella de Oro or Flecha Roja (part of Líneas Unidas del Sur). 1st class bus depot at Av. Cuauhtémoc 1490. Taxi to Zócalo, US$2; bus, US$0.12. To Oaxaca by continuation of the scenic highway from the beach and naval base at Icacas, 402 km.: 6 hrs. on main road, 264 km., of which 170 km. unpaved, 6 hrs. on rough dirt road through mountains by bus, change at Pinoteca Nacional; caught close to where highway from Mexico City joins the beach. Several 1st class buses (Estrella de Oro), 5 hrs., US$4.75 and 2nd class (Flecha Rosa) buses a day to Taxco at 1730, US$2.50. Bus to Puerto Escondido every hour on the half-hour from 0430-1630, plus one at 0200 and *directo* at 0915, 2nd class, Flecha Roja, seats bookable, advisable to do so the day before, 7½ hrs; also Transportes Gacela, 3 a day direct, 6½ hrs, US$6.

Air Services Airport, Plan de los Amales, 26 km. from Acapulco. Direct connections with New York, Philadelphia, Chicago, Dallas, Houston, Los Angeles and other US cities, by Mexican and U.S. carriers. Cancún, 4 hrs., via Mexico City. Guadalajara, 1 hr. 5 mins.; Mérida, via Mexico City, 3 hrs. 5 mins. Oaxaca, 1½ hrs. Villahermosa, 2 hrs. 50 mins. Mexico City, 50 mins. Transportación Aeropuerto taxi service charge return trip (*viaje redondo*) when you buy a ticket, so keep it and call for a taxi when required, US$6. Airport bus takes 1 hr., US$2 and *does* exist!

Excursions The lagoons can be explored by motor boats; one, Coyuca Lagoon, is over 110 km. long; strange birds, water hyacinths, tropical flowers. Daily, in the morning and after dark, amazing 40-metre dives into shallow water by boys can be watched from the Quebrada (US$1, 5 times a day, the first at 1300, the last, with torches, at 2200). There is a *jai-alai* palace. At Playa Icacos there is a marineland amusement park *Ci-Ci*, with a waterslide, pool with wave-machine and arena with performing dolphins and sea-lions, US$1.50. Pleasant boat trip across beach to Puerto Marqués, US$0.80 return; one can hire small sailing boats there, US$6.50 an hr. Bay cruises, 2½ hrs., from Muelle Yates, US$3, at 1100, 1630 and 2230. Visit island of La Roqueta, glass-bottomed boat, US$2.50 return, 2 hrs., overpriced. Parachute sailing (towed by motor boats), US$6.50 for a few minutes, several operators.

Coast NW of Acapulco

Between Acapulco and Zihuatanejo are Coyuca de Benítez, a lagoon with little islands 38 km. from Acapulco, also a market town selling exotic fruit, cheap hats and shoes. Pelicans fly by the lagoons, there are passing dolphins and plentiful sardines, and young boys seek turtle eggs. 1½ km. beyond Coyuca is a turn-off to **El Carrizal** (7½ km.), a village of some 2,000 people, a little paradise with a beautiful beach (many pelicans) with dangerous waves; *Hotel-Bungalows El Carrizal*, signed simply "Bungalows", E, new owner, swimming pool, access to lagoon, good restaurant opposite; more basic, *Aida*, E, friendly, rec., but little privacy, Mexican food (good fish). Shops will change dollars (e.g. Doña Joaquina's shoe shop, the video shop), and long-distance phone calls can be made from the *farmacia*. Frequent VW minibuses from Acapulco or Pie de la Cuesta, US$0.25. If driving, take Route 200, direction Zihuatanejo. A couple of km. SE of El Carrizal is El Morro on an unpaved road between the ocean and the lagoon. El Morro is a small fishing village (carp) reminiscent of African townships as it is constructed entirely of *palapa* (palm-leaf and wood). Every other house is a "fish-restaurant". San Jerónimo, 83 km. from Acapulco, has an 18th century parish church, you can make canoe trips up river to restaurants; Tecpan de Galeana, 108 km. from Acapulco, is a fishing village; there is a beach further on at Cayaquitos where a series of small rivers join the ocean and there is a large variety of birds and dense vegetation; three restaurants offer fish dishes, there is a reasonable modern hotel, *Club Papánoa*, with lovely views, and a camping site; and one can also visit the lovely bay of Papanda.

Zihuatanejo is a beautiful fishing port and expensive tourist resort 237 km. NW of Acapulco by the paved Route 200, which continues via Barra de Navidad along the Pacific coast to Puerto Vallarta (**see page** 112); 1st class bus from Acapulco, 4 hrs. (This road goes through coconut plantations where you can buy *tuba*, a drink made from coconut milk fermented on the tree, only slightly alcoholic.) There are 3 beaches: one in the natural harbour and one 20 min. walk from centre (Playa de la Ropa) with the *Sotavento* and other hotels, and some beach restaurants. Another is the Playa de la Madera. Las Gatas beach is secluded, a haven for aquatic sports and can be reached by boat from the centre (US$0.75 return) or a 20-min. walk from La Ropa beach over fishermen-frequented rocks. Watch out for coconuts falling off the trees! The chief attraction, apart from beaches, is clam fishing; there is also a small shark-processing factory. The desert islands off the coast may be visited. Difficult to find accommodation in March, and around Christmas/New Year.

Hotels   *Las Tres Marías*, very pleasant with large communal balconies overlooking town and harbour, D; *Villa del Sol*, Playa La Ropa, L; *Irma* (Playa la Madera), good hotel but not best location, A; *Catalina* and *Sotavento*, Playa la Ropa, A, same facilities. *Bungalows Capuli*, Playa la Ropa, C; *Sinar-Bahagra*, Playa La Ropa, very good value; *Posada Caracol, Bungalows Pacíficos*, on Playa de la Madera. Several other hotels along Playa Madera, try *Playa de la Madera*. Central hotels: *Posada Citlali*, C-D; *Avila*, Juan N. Alvarez 2, T 42010, B; *Zihuatanejo Centro*, C. *Casa Elvira* hotel-restaurant, E, in older part of town, very basic but clean, noisy from 0730, share bath, the restaurant is on the beach front (*the* place to watch the world go by), good and reasonable. *Safari*, T 42146, by bus station, expensive; *Casa La Playa*, similar to *Elvira*, E, but not as good; *Belmar*, all rooms face sea; *Casa Aurora*, and *Casa Bravo*, both E; *Imelda*, clean, rec., E.
    CREA Youth Hostel, Av. Paseo Zihuatanejo s/n, C.P. 40880.

Camping on Playa la Ropa (a long walk from town, but beautiful beach nearby), US$0.60 p.p. and US$0.60 per car; US$0.25 to sling hammock (friendly owners with ferocious dogs).

Restaurants On Playa la Ropa, cheap: *Elvi, La Perla*. In Zihuatanejo, *Mi Casita*, in town, rec.; *La Bocana*, favourite for seafood; *Cantamar*, downtown, "cute"; *Cabina del Capitán*, owned by an Englishman, good; *Don Juan*, downtown, English decor, fancy; *Coconuts*, downtown, "Hollywood tropical", nice but somewhat expensive garden restaurant; *Gitano's*, thatched roof beach spots, reasonable; *Kon Tiki*, road to Playa de la Ropa, pizzas and oriental, rec.; *Kapi Kofi*, downtown, a/c, breakfast. *Stall 27* at marketplace is very popular, cheap and good. Try local lobster for about US$10.

Night Clubs *Adán y Eva, Ibiza Disco, Chololo, Captain's Cabin, Joy Disco, Kan Kan.*

Car Hire Budget, N. Bravo y V. Guerrero, T 43040.

Skin Diving US$25 for one, US$35 for two, per day and hire of all equipment and guide from next to tourist office by town pier, lessons also offered. Off Playa de las Gatas is an underwater wall built by the Tarascan king Calzonzin, to keep the sharks away while he bathed; the wall is fairly massive and can be seen clearly while skin diving. Many fish too. US$1 a day for mask, snorkel and flippers.

Exchange Banca Serfín will change travellers' cheques without need to show passport; also lower commission than in banks in hotel district. Good rates at Mario's leather shop.

Language School Inter/Idiomas Cuauhtémoc 10—3rd floor.

Buses and Roads Four direct buses a day from Mexico City, Tres Estrellas de Oro, US$10, at Central del Sur (by Taxqueña metro station), a good 12 hrs. 5 times a day from Mexico City via Morelia, by Autobuses de Occidente. Estrella Roja del Sur not rec.: reckless drivers. Bus to Acapulco, US$6.50 1st, US$3.75 2nd class, 4 hrs, at least 20 times a day with Flecha Roja, very crowded and many stops; much better direct, a/c Hermengildo Galeana buses leave from the Estrella Blanca terminal, Acapulco US$3.25, they continue N to Lázaro Cárdenas where there is a connection to Manzanillo. To Manzanillo, at 2000 with Estrella de Oro, 16 hrs. To Guadalajara, US$8 overnight 2nd class, 12 hrs., frequent stops and people standing in the aisles, or with Autobuses de Occidente, US$11 at 1320 and 1720. To Morelia (**see page** 132) at least 15 a day, US$5.50 with Norte de Sonora; connections also to Michoacán at Lázaro Cárdenas (bus from Zihuatanejo US$1.50). To Puerto Escondido, US$4. There are through buses to Tijuana, US$37, 50 hrs. By road from Mexico City via the Toluca-Zihuatanejo highway (430 km.) or via the Acapulco-Zihuatanejo highway (405 km.).

Airport Ixtapa/Zihuatanejo international airport, 19 km. from town. Many flights from Mexico City and others from Mazatlán, Guadalajara, Oaxaca, Acapulco, Puerto Vallarta, Huatulco and, in the USA, Los Angeles, San Francisco, Houston, Dallas, Chicago and Philadelphia.

From Zihuatanejo one can drive 5 km. or take a bus (US$0.20) or taxi (US$2.50, colectivo, US$0.45) to **Ixtapa**, "where there are salt lakes". The resort, developed on a large scale, boasts 14 beaches: La Hermosa, Del Palmar, Don Juan de Dios, Don Juan, Don Rodrigo, Cuata, Quieta, Oliveiro, Linda, Larga, Carey, Pequeña, Cuachalate and Varadero. There are turtles, many species of shellfish and fish, and pelicans at El Morro de los Pericos, which can be seen by launch. There is an island a few metres off Quietas beach; boats go over at a cost of US$1.50. Ixtapa has ten large luxury hotels and a Club Méditerranée (all obtain food-supplies from Mexico City making food more expensive, as local supplies aren't guaranteed); a shopping complex, golf course, water-ski/parachute skiing and tennis courts. There are a yacht marina and an 18-hole golf club, Palma Real. Isla Grande is being developed as a nature park and leisure resort. **N.B.** The beach can be dangerous (strong undertow—small children should not be allowed in the sea unaccompanied). Also, there are crocodiles in the beautiful lagoons at the end of the beach.

Hotels All in L-A range: *Camino Real*, spectacular, in a small jungle; *Krystal* (highly rec., book in advance, T 42618), *Dorado Pacífico*, *Sheraton* (T 31858), with panoramic lift, *El Presidente*, A; *Aquamarina*; *Aristos*; *Holiday Inn* (P.O. Box 15, T 31186, resort facilities); *Riviera del Sol*. Taxi between centre and main hotels, US$2.

Restaurants Besides those in every hotel, there are *Montmartre*, *Villa Sakura*, *Villa de la Selva* (rec. for food and views, book in advance), *Baffone*, *Carlos y Charlie's*, *Hacienda de Ixtapa*, all more costly than in Zihuatanejo.

Nightclubs Every hotel without exception has at least one night club/disco and two bars.

Playa Azul, 350 km. NW of Acapulco (bus US$3.50) and 122 km. from Zihuatanejo, is a coconut-and-hammock resort frequented much more by Mexicans than foreigners, with a few large hotels. 40 km. of excellent deserted beaches N of Playa Azul. **N.B.:** Beware of the large waves at Playa Azul and of dangerous currents; always check with locals if particular beaches are safe.

Hotels *Playa Azul*, C, best value, good but expensive restaurant; *Costa de Oro*, E, clean, with fan, rec. *Posada Marilyn*, clean, run by La Mira schoolteacher, E, cold showers (hard to find; ask in main street). *Hospedaje Casa Silva*, E, very basic but adequate, restaurant around the corner and unnamed *hospedaje* opposite, F with shower. Many small fish restaurants along beach.

Transport Buses ply up and down the coast road, stopping at the road junction 4 km. from Plaza Azul. Colectivos take you between town and junction. *Lázaro Cárdenas* is the connecting point for buses from Uruapan, Manzanillo and Zihuatanejo (e.g. Galeana to Manzanillo 7¾ hrs. US$4.50; to Uruapán, US$3.50, 6½ hrs; Flecha Roja to Zihuatanejo). Avoid *Hotel Sam Sam* nr. terminal; go to 5 de Mayo for *Capri* or *Costa Azul*, both E with bath, several eating places.

Coast E of Acapulco

Highway 200, E from Acapulco along the coast, is paved all the way to Puerto Escondido; the stretch is known as the Costa Chica (there is a bridge missing about 55 km. from Acapulco, which necessitates a detour inland to Sabana Grande, when you turn off to Pinotepa). This road has been reported dangerous due to bandit hold ups of lone cars, check locally before driving this route. "From *Pinotepa* Nacional (*Hotel Carmona*, restaurant, good value but poor laundry service, F), you can visit the Mixtec Indian village of Pinotepa de Don Luis by *camioneta*. These leave from the side street next to the church in Pinotepa Nacional, taking a dirt road to Don Luis. The women there weave beautiful and increasingly rare sarong-like skirts (*chay-ay*), some of which are dyed from the purple of sea snails. Also, half-gourds incised with various designs and used both as caps and cups can be found. The *ferias* of Don Luis (January 20) and nearby San Juan Colorado (November 29-30) are worth attending for the dancing and availability of handicrafts." (Dale Bricker, Seattle)

Puerto Escondido is on a beautiful bay south of Oaxaca (population

25,000) and getting very touristy, good surfing. Palm trees line the beach, which is not too clean. The expansion of the SE end of town, "to make it the next Acapulco" (in the words of one developer) is well-advanced.

N.B. There can be dangerous waves, and the cross-currents are always dangerous; non-swimmers should not bathe except in the bay on which the town stands. Also, a breeze off the sea makes the sun seem less strong than it is—be careful. Do not stray too far along the beach; armed robbery by groups of 3-5 is becoming more and more frequent, take as little cash and valuables as possible, US$ sought after. Also at La Barra beach 10 km. away.

Hotels Very crowded during Holy Week; prices rise on 1 November because of the local Fiesta de Noviembre. Most hotels are on the beach, little air-conditioning. Many cheaper hotels have no hot water.

    Viva, most expensive; *Best Western Posada Real* (ex-*Bugambilias*), very pleasant, A, lovely gardens, pool, path to beach, attentive, a/c, good service, food included (à la carte, also lobster); *El Rincón del Pacífico*, D, very popular, always full, on beach, with restaurant, hot water, much stealing, not always friendly. *Virginia*, D, good views; *Mirador*, on highway into town with good views, D; *Loren*, D, clean, friendly, safe, rec.; *Real del Mar*, nr. bus station, D (cheaper for longer stays), bath, clean, nice view; *Paraíso Escondido*, noisy a/c, not on beach but with own swimming pool, management cool, but rec., C, colonial style; *Nayar*, D, big rooms, views, with bath and fan, restaurant, rec.; opposite is *Bungalows Barlovento*, C/D, very comfortable, highly rec. *Margeo*, Pérez Gazga, D, big rooms, good restaurant, friendly; *Alderete*, opp. bus station, E with private bath; *La Posada Económica*, one big dormitory, F, attached to restaurant, but also runs hotel across the road, ask for a room opp. the flat; good huachinango; *Alojamiento Las Cabañas* has dormitories with bunks, F, on main road (S side), friendly, very nice, food is good, you will be charged for all beds regardless of whether they are occupied, unless you share the cabin. *Cabañas Coco Beach*, in the town near the church, US$3 per cabin (6 or 7 available), family-run. *Bungalows Villa Marinero*, on beach, a bit run down, own cooking possible, friendly, D, restaurant a little dear but good. *Cabañas San Diego*, down a sand road just before bridge on road to Puerto Angel, F, safe, nice grounds but few facilities; *Cabañas Cortés*, F for small, basic huts or large, basic huts—in all cases, take mosquito nets.

Camping If camping, beware of clothes being stolen; 3 sites available. *Carrizalillo Trailer Park*, near old airport on W side of town, on cliff top with path leading down to secluded beach, swimming pool and bar, very pleasant, US$11 for 2 plus car. Campsite for vehicles, tents and hammocks on water front in centre of town, vehicles and tents accepted, swimming pool, US$2.20 p.p. Campsites *Las Palmas* (better), US$6 for 2 plus car, and *Neptuno*, same price (with cabins) next to each other on beach US$3.

Restaurants *Lolys*, cheap and good, try pescado a la parrilla, with sweet onion sauce, and lemon pie after; *Da Ugo*, good pizzas, popular. *Lisa's Restaurant*, nice location on beach but expensive and very poor service. Many restaurants on main street: *San Angel* for fish, *La Posada*, *Disco Macumba*. *Bananas* bar, good, satellite TV, ping-pong, chess, backgammon, Italian-run; *Sardinas*, good and cheap. Vegetarian at *Hotel Santa* Fe, on beach at end of bay. Good licuados at *Bambú Loco*, also fish. *La Estancia* is good but expensive. *Las Palapas*, good, it is just over the stream (sewer) on the right. *Pepe's*, great sandwiches. Food is good quality, but very expensive near the beach.

Shopping Small selection of foreign language books at *Papi's*, souvenir shop 3 doors from Mercado de Artesanías, buy or swap. Local crafts best not bought from vendors on the beach, but in the non-gringo part of town up the hill near where the buses stop.

Banks Bancomer, Banpeco, both open 0900-1330.

Health   Dr. Francisco Serrano Severiano, opp. Banpeco, speaks English, 0900-1300, 1700-2000.

Transport   Bus to Oaxaca, 5 or 6 a day, US$3, advertised as 7 hr. trip, but can take up to 17 hrs, very bad road and many accidents; also Estrella del Valle (1st class, from 2nd class terminal) and Auto Transportes Oaxaca-Pacífico, better, journey through spectacular cloud forest, goes via Pochutla, 10-18 hrs. (depending on roadworks)—leaves at 0700, 2nd class, 2300 1st class; all have bookable seats. Puerto Escondido-Pochutla, US$1.50, and on to Salina Cruz, US$3, Oaxaca-Pacífico company rec. The road to Salina Cruz is now paved (bus US$3.50, about 7 a day). It is now best to go from Oaxaca to Puerto Escondido by the road to Puerto Angel, turning off at Pochutla (see below). The direct highway to Oaxaca is being upgraded. Bus to Acapulco, 2nd class, Flecha Roja (near La Solteca terminal), 7½ hrs., not exciting. The 1030 bus stops for 2 hours' lunch at Pinotepa, book tickets at least one day in advance. First bus to Acapulco at 0400, hourly up to 2100 thereafter. Transportes Gacela run 3 direct buses a day to Acapulco at 1030, 1330 and 2300, only 2 short stops, US$6, 6½ hrs. The road is in bad condition. Transport to Puerto Angel from Puerto Escondido consists of VW bus or pick-up truck caught on main road, every hour, 1 hr. to Pochutla, then colectivo/bus.

Warning   Night buses have been robbed in this area, advisable to travel by day.

Flights   Airline offices will arrange VW bus to pick you up for your departure when you reconfirm or book your outward flight, US$0.75 p.p. Airport 10 minutes drive from town, orange juice and coffee sold; improvement programme under way. Puerto Escondido-Mexico City, with Mexicana daily, non-stop.

Also S of Oaxaca (240 km, paved road, but many curves) is **Puerto Angel**, a coffee port on the Pacific with a good safe beach, 69 km. from Puerto Escondido, with road connection but no direct buses; all services involve change at Pochutla. It is 8 hrs. by bus from Oaxaca, nine a day, US$3.50. There are check points, where you may be searched for drugs or guns, on the road to Salina Cruz via Sta Maria Huatulco.

Festival   Fiesta 1 October.

Hotels   Luxury hotel on a hill away from the beach, *Angel del Mar*, C, friendly, helpful, bookings not always honoured; for *cabañas* and hammock places ask at *Susanna's Restaurant*, near the football pitch; *Hotel Soraya*, E, fan, bath, very clean (changes dollars and travellers' cheques); *Anahi*, on road to *Angel del Mar*, F with fan, Indonesian-style wash basins; *Casa de Huéspedes Gladys*, just above *Soraya*, E, owner can prepare food, no hot water; *El Rincón Sabroso*, E, beautiful views, clean quiet, friendly, no hot water; *Casa de Huéspedes Gundi* (Gundi and Tomás López), clean, rooms (E) or hammocks (G), good value, snacks and breakfast (US$0.50-1.25). Similar is the *Pensión Puesta del Sol*, run by Harald and Maria Faerber, F (suite D), very friendly, English and German spoken, restaurant, on road to Playa Panteón, clean, rec. *Noah's Arc*, at the end of the beach, for the "flower-powered"; hammocks at *Gustavos*, F; *Posada Cañón de Vata*, on Playa Panteón, nice, very clean, D, lovely setting, but the beach is now reported to be covered in litter and dead fish, booked continuously; good restaurant *Capís* (has 5 rooms above). *Ma Bell* restaurant, good and cheap; many others. Cabins are being built by Roberto (speaks English) at Estacahuite, a beautiful, clean beach, 1 km. from town.

Services Long distance phone next to *Soraya*; for post office, exchange etc. go to Pochutla.

Three km. W is **Zipolite** beach (name means "the killing beach"—reached by taxi—US$3.50 for 4—or ½ hr. walk), can be dangerous for bathing, cabins and hammocks for rent, food available, "may be the last nude paradise in Mexico"—do not walk to the beach at night, packs of dogs have attacked people. The sea is said to be less dangerous at San Agustín, not a nudist beach. 45 mins. walk N is another beach and village with a turtle farm. Hammock spot and vegetarian restaurant *Shambhala* run by Gloria, an American woman. At the E end of the beach is *Lola's*, excellent food; there is a good *Panadería* on the road behind the beach, through the green gate. "About 25 km. from Zipolite (also known as Puerto Angelito) on a dirt road is a sign to Ventanilla beach; follow the rough track until you find a thatched ranch and ask for Hilario Reyes. The beach is long and empty and there are 2 lagoons with fresh water, a lost paradise", writes Janet Westgarth. There are no cabins: you need your own tent (or hammock/mosquito net). Ventanilla beach is also dangerous for bathing.

Restaurant *Suzy*, Playa Panteón, excellent seafood.

You can go to Salina Cruz from Puerto Angel via Pochutla: take bus or taxi (US$2) to **Pochutla** and catch half-hourly bus to Salina Cruz (US$3, 3½ hrs.), to which a new road is finished. Pochutla-Oaxaca (a safer route than Puerto Escondido-Oaxaca) six 1st class and five 2nd class buses a day, 7 hrs., US$3-4; San José del Pacífico is a pleasant stop on the way, with good restaurant. The bus service between Pochutla and Puerto Escondido (US$0.75) links with the bus to Puerto Angel. Minibus to Puerto Angel, US$0.25. At Pochutla there is a prison; you can buy black coral necklaces made by prisoners very cheaply.

West of Puerto Angel (50 km.) and 112 km. E of Salina Cruz, on the coast road, is the new resort of **Huatulco** being built on about 34,000 hectares around nine bays, for completion around 2020. Several 4- and 5-star hotels are open, including the *Sheraton*, L, (T 958-10055), *Posada Binniguenda* (4-star, B, 15 mins. by car and not on the beach) and the *Club Méditerranée* (5-star, reservations are cheaper when made at head office in Calle Masaryk, Mexico City); many to follow. The airport is open with daily, non-stop flights from Mexico City with Mexicana. Great care is to be taken to blend the resort into the landscape: about 80% of the total area is to be set aside as a nature reserve. The name means "place of the wood", which refers to a cross planted on the beach, legend tells, by Quetzalcóatl. After resisting efforts to pull it down, it was found to be only a few feet deep when dug up; small crosses were made from it

MEXICO CITY TO GUATEMALA (8)

The National Railway runs daily from Mexico City to Tapachula. Taxi to Talismán, on the Guatemalan border, for bus to Guatemala City (also accessible from Puebla). There is a new bridge which links Ciudad Hidalgo with Tecún-Umán (formerly Ayutla) in Guatemala. Cristóbal

Colón bus Mexico City-Guatemala City takes 23 hrs., with a change at the border to Rutas Lima. Mexico City-Tapachula, 20 hrs.

Note Motorists who know the area well advise that anyone driving from Mexico City to Tehuantepec should go via Orizaba-La Tinaja-Papaloapan-Tuxtepec-Palomares. This route is better than Veracruz-Acayucán and far preferable to the route which follows, via Matamoros and Oaxaca, if drivers are in a hurry. The reason is that between Oaxaca and Tehuantepec the road, although paved throughout and in good condition, serpentines unendingly over the Sierras. But as the Oaxaca route is far more interesting and spectacular we describe it below. For the alternative journey through the Papaloapan region, **see page** 187.

This road through southern Mexico is 1,355 km. long. It can be done in 3 or 4 days' driving time. There are bus services from Mexico City along the route through Oaxaca to Tehuantepec and on to the Guatemalan frontier through San Cristóbal de Las Casas to Ciudad Cuauhtémoc or through Arriaga to Tapachula. A road now runs (still rough in places) from Paso Hondo near Ciudad Cuauhtémoc via Comalapa and Porvenir to Huixtla on the S road, and from Porvenir to Revolución Mexicana.

From Cuernavaca to Oaxaca: take Route 160 via Yantepec to the semi-tropical town of **Cuautla** (94,000 people), with a popular sulphur spring (known as *aguas hediondas* or stinking waters) and bath, a crowded week-end resort for the capital. Tourist Cuautla is divided from locals' Cuautla by a wide river, and the locals have the best bargain: it is worth crossing the stream. From Cuautla go to Atotonilco by bus for a swim. There is a market in the narrow streets and alleyways around 5 de Mayo. The tourist office is opp. *Hotel Cuautla*, on Av. Obregón, satisfactory.

Hotels and Restaurants *Hotel Colón* in Cuautla is on the main square, E, good (opp. is excellent *Restaurante Manolo*, Guerrero 53); *Hotel del Sur*, F, rec.; *Hotel Madrid*, Los Bravos 27, F. *Jardín de Cuautla*, Dos de Mayo 94, nr. bus station, modern, clean, but bad traffic noise, pool, C; *Hotel España* in same street No. 22, E; cheap, clean and good hotel in a dirty barrio 1.5 km. S of city. CREA Youth Hostel, Unidad Deportiva, T 20218, C.P. 62040. Try the delicious *lacroyas* and *gorditas*, tortillas filled with beans and cheese. At least 2 good restaurants in main square. 11 km. from Cuautla, on road to Cuernavaca is the *Hacienda de Cocoyoc*, an old converted *hacienda* with a swimming pool backed by the mill aqueduct. Glorious gardens, 18-hole golf-course, tennis and riding, but isolated, A, AmEx not accepted, reservations at Centro Comercial El Relox, Local 44, Insurgentes Sur 2374, México 01000 D.F., T 550-7331.

Buses from Mexico City to Cuautla from Central del Oriente. Buses from Cuautla at Cristóbal Colón terminal, 5 de Mayo and Zavala, to Mexico City hourly; 2nd class buses to Cuernavaca hourly, 1 hr. US$0.65; to Oaxaca, US$5.80, there are only two 1st and two 2nd class Cristóbal Colón buses per day, try also Fletes y Pasajes 2nd class buses, or change twice, at Matamoros and Huajuapan. A road leads to Amecameca (**page** 172).

After Cuautla take Route 140 with long descent and then ascent to *Izúcar De Matamoros* 58,000 people (*Hotel Ocampo*, F, next to bus station, nice and clean), famous for its clay handicrafts, 16th-century convent of Santo Domingo, and two nearby spas, Los Amatitlanes (about 6 km. away) and Ojo de Carbón. A side road leads from Izúcar to Axochiapan (Morelos state), leading to a dirt road to the village of Jolalpan with the baroque church of Santa María (1553). Route 190 heads N from Izúcar to Puebla via Huaquechula (16th-century renaissance-cum-plateresque chapel) and *Atlixco* ("the place lying on the water"), with interesting baroque examples in the Chapel of the Third Order of St. Augustine and San Juan de Dios. There is an annual festival, the Atlixcayotl, on San Miguel hill (*Hotel Colonial* behind parish church, F, shared bath; nearby—20 mins.—are the curative springs of Axocopán). Thence to Acatepec (**page** 175) and, 30 km., Puebla. Route 190 S switchbacks to Tehuitzingo. Then fairly flat landscape to *Acatlán* (Hotels México, E, dirty, fleas; *Lux*, E; *Romano*, F) a friendly village where black and red clay figures, and palm and flower hats are made. Carry on to Petlalcingo (restaurant), then ascend to Huajuapan (**page** 225) and Tamazulapan (*Hotels México*, a highway, modern, E; *Santiago*, without sign on Zócalo, E; *Hidalgo*, behind church, F; restaurant). Road climbs slowly at first, then more steeply and eventually flattens to Nocluxtlán (*Hotel Sarita*, E).

The major route from Mexico City first runs generally eastwards to Puebla, where it turns S to wind through wooded mountains at altitudes of between 1,500 and 1,800 metres, emerging at last into the warm, red earth Oaxaca valley.

Oaxaca (population now thought to be over 300,000, altitude 1,546 metres) is 413 km. from Puebla, 531 km. from Mexico City. It is a very Indian town, of airy patios with graceful arcades, famous for its colourful market, its *sarapes*, crafts, dances and feast days. On Sat. Indians of the Zapotec and Mixtec groups come to market near the 2nd class bus station on the outskirts of town, which starts before 0800; prices are rising because of the city's great popularity with tourists.

The Zócalo with its arcades is the heart of the town; its bandstand has a nice little market underneath. Since the streets surrounding the sides of the Zócalo have been closed to traffic it has become very pleasant to sit there. In the daytime vendors sell food, in the evening their tourist wares and gardenias in the square. It is especially colourful on Sundays when Indian women weave and sell their wares.

On the Zócalo is the 17th century cathedral with a fine baroque façade, but the best sight, about 4 blocks from the square, is the church of Santo Domingo (reckoned by all to be beautiful) with its adjoining monastery, now the Regional Museum (see below). The church's gold leaf has to be seen to be believed. There is an extraordinary vaulted decoration under the raised choir, right on the reverse of the façade wall: a number of crowned heads appear on the branches of the genealogical tree of the family of Santo Domingo de Guzmán (died 1221), whose lineage was indirectly related to the royal houses of Castile and Portugal. By making a donation (say US$1) to the church you can get the lady at the bookstall to light up the various features after 1800. The Capilla del Rosario in the church is fully restored; no flash pictures are allowed.

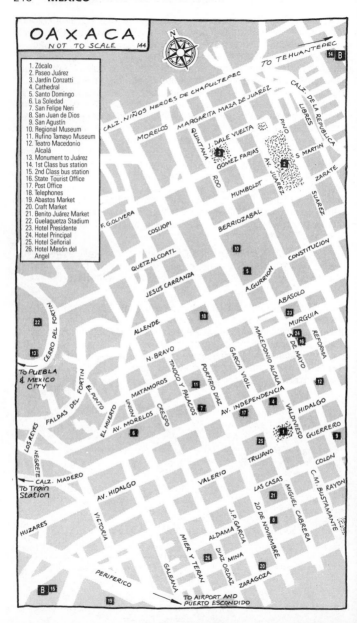

OAXACA
NOT TO SCALE 144

1. Zócalo
2. Paseo Juárez
3. Jardín Conzatti
4. Cathedral
5. Santo Domingo
6. La Soledad
7. San Felipe Neri
8. San Juan de Dios
9. San Agustín
10. Regional Museum
11. Rufino Tamayo Museum
12. Teatro Macedonio Alcalá
13. Monument to Juárez
14. 1st Class bus station
15. 2nd Class bus station
16. State Tourist Office
17. Post Office
18. Telephones
19. Abastos Market
20. Craft Market
21. Benito Juárez Market
22. Guelaguetza Stadium
23. Hotel Presidente
24. Hotel Principal
25. Hotel Señorial
26. Hotel Mesón del Angel

The massive 17th century church of La Soledad has fine colonial ironwork and sculpture (including an exquisite Virgen de la Soledad); there are elaborate altars at the church of San Felipe Neri, and Indian versions in paint of the conquest at San Juan de Dios; a museum of religious art behind the church is open in the morning. The church of San Agustín has a fine façade, with bas-relief of St. Augustine holding the City of God above adoring monks (apparently modelled on that of San Agustín in Mexico City, now the National Library).

The Regional Museum (entry US$0.50, US$0.25 on Sun., open Tues.-Sat. 1000-1800, Sun. 0900-1700, closed Mon.) has displays of regional costumes, and pottery, glass, alabaster, jewellery and other treasures from Monte Albán, whose jewellery is copied with surprising skill in several home workshops near Oaxaca. Museo Rufino Tamayo, Av. Morelos 503, has a beautiful display of precolumbian artefacts dating from 1250 BC to AD 1100 (1000-1400, 1600-1900, closed Tues.); entry for US$0.25. Teatro Macedonio Alcalá, 5 de Mayo with Independencia, beautifully restored theatre from Porfirio Díaz' time. Visit also the Street of the Little Arches, a picturesque, narrow, cobbled street with archways along the sides. There is a grand view from the amphitheatre on the Cerro de Fortín. The monument to Juárez is in the valley below. The house of the Maza family, for whom Bénito Juárez worked and whose daughter he married, still stands at Independencia 1306 (a plaque marks it). Similarly, a plaque marks the birthplace of Porfirio Díaz at the other end of Independencia, in a building which is now a kindergarten, near La Soledad. D. H. Lawrence wrote parts of "Mornings in Mexico" here, and revised "The Plumed Serpent"; the house he rented is in Pino Suárez, a block S of the Llano (the main park), NE corner. There is an observatory and planetarium on the hill NW of the town, two shows each evening, entrance US$0.20. Natural and man-made pools are fed by springs rising in Santiago Laollaga, free bathing, popular with Mexicans.

Specialities: black earthenware, tooled leather, blankets, ponchos, shawls, embroidered blouses, the drink *mescal*. The best *mescal* in the region is El Minero, made in Mitla. *Mescal* sours are good at the bar of *Misión Los Angeles*. The poor man's drink is *pulque*. Local *sarapes* are more varied and cheaper than in Mexico City. Buy at the market (which will come down a third) or at Casa Cervantes.

The Zapotec language is used by over 300,000 people in the State as a first or second language (about 20% of Oaxaca State population speaks only an Indian language). The Zapotec Indians, who weave fantastic toys of grass, have a dance, the *Jarabe Tlacolula Zandunga* danced by barefooted girls splendid in most becoming coifs, short, brightly coloured skirts and ribbons and long lace petticoats, while the men, all in white with gay handkerchiefs, dance opposite them with their hands behind their backs. Only women—from Tehuantepec or Juchitán—dance the slow and stately *Zandunga*, costumes gorgeously embroidered on velvet blouse, full skirts with white pleated and starched lace ruffles and *huipil*.

Festivals Carnival in February. Los Lunes del Cerro, on the first two Mondays after 16 July (the first is the more spontaneous, when Indian groups come to a hill outside the city to present the seven regional dances of the State in a great festival, also known as La Guelaguetza). Hotels book up early. Upper seats free, getting expensive near the front, be there 1½ hrs. in advance to get a good seat, tickets from Tourist Office. 2 Nov., the Day of the Dead, is a mixture of festivity and solemn commemoration; the decoration of family altars is carried to competitive extremes (competition in Calle 5 de Mayo between Santo Domingo and the Zócalo on 1 Nov.); traditional wares and foods, representing skulls, skeletons, coffins etc. are sold in the market. Ask before photographing. 6, 7, 8 Dec. with fine processions (Soledad), and 23 (Rábanos) with huge radishes carved in grotesque shapes sold for fake money; *buñuelos* are sold and eaten in the streets on this night, and the dishes ceremonially smashed after serving. Night of 24 Dec., a parade of floats (best seen from balcony of *Merendero El Tule* on the Zócalo; go for supper and get a window table). Posadas in San Felipe (5 km. N) and at Xoxo, to the S, the week before Christmas. Bands play in the Zócalo every evening except Sat., and there are regional folk dances twice a week.

Warning Travellers are being warned not to drive the direct road to Tehuantepec as violent robberies have occurred. Night buses should be avoided; check with the police on local conditions. Travellers have reported that men asserting they are local Indians sometimes get into conversation, especially near the Zócalo, invite you to a drink, order several things and then claim they have no money and leave the tourist to pay the bill! Beware pickpockets.

Hotels *El Presidente/Parador Santa Catalina*, Plazuela Bastida, magnificently restored convent circa 1690, true colonial with all services, street rooms noisy, restaurant greatly improved, L; *Calesa Real*, García Vigil 306, T 65544, modern colonial but many small dark rooms, good but expensive, *Los Arcos* restaurant, parking, central, slow service, B; *Margarita Courts*, at N entrance to city, good and reasonable, C; *Misión Oaxaca*, San Felipe del Agua, some way out, attractive, C; *Misión de Los Angeles*, Porfirio Díaz 102, T 51500, A, motel-style, 2 km. from centre, quiet and most attractive, with swimming pool, good food; *Victoria*, A, colonial house turned into hotel, bedrooms with showers built round the garden, good value, discount for elderly couples who book directly, up to 30%, many tour groups, but out of town (around 15-min. walk) at Km. 545 on Pan-American Highway, T 52633; *Hacienda La Noria*, Periférico con La Costa, T 67555, B, motel-type, pool, good and convenient; *Santo Tomás*, Abasolo 305, T 63800, clean, private shower, friendly, kitchen for use of guests, some comfort, washing facilities, D, quiet, rec.; *Francia*, 20 de Noviembre 212, T 64811, around enclosed courtyard, good food, popular, D; *Plazuela*, La Bastida 115, D, pleasant, friendly; *California*, Chapultepec 822, T 53628, near 1st class bus station, D, with bath, friendly, pleasant, restaurant; *Veracruz*, Chapultepec 1020, T 50511, next to ADO bus station, spotless, but poor value, D. *Del Bosque*, exit road to Mitla, T 52122, modern, restaurant, D; 2 blocks from the Zócalo at 5 de Mayo 208 is *Principal*, T 62535, D, colonial house, very clean, private shower with hot and cold water, English spoken, heavily booked (cockroaches too), not suitable for young, single women. *Vallarta*, Díaz Ordaz 309, T 64967, D, clean, good value, enclosed parking. *Señorial*, Portal de Flores 6, T 63933, will store luggage, suites or rooms, C, with bath, swimming pool, on main square, some rooms rather noisy, poor restaurant, will change travellers' cheques for guests; *Monte Albán*, D, Alameda de León 1, T 62777 friendly, opp. Cathedral; regular folk dance performances are given here at 2030, US$2.50, photography permitted; *Del Arbol*, Calzada Madero 131, T 64887, modern, comfortable, bath, D; *Ruiz*, Bustamente 103, T 63660, just off Zócalo, D, nice and clean, quiet, hot water only very early morning, don't leave valuables lying around, otherwise rec.;

María Luisa, J. García Tinoco 507, F, with bath, good, hot water a.m. only; *Roma*, J.P.García 504 and Aldama, F, fairly clean, a bit noisy (2 blocks from the market), reasonable; *Rivera*, one block from *Roma*, E. *Asunción*, Aldama and García, F, with bath, clean, nr. market; *Pombo*, Morelos 601 y 20 de Noviembre, near Zócalo, E, gringo hotel, beware of overcharging, hot shower, clean, rec.; *Central*, 20 de Noviembre 104, T 65971, E, private bathroom, hot water, good value but very noisy, fills up early; *Fortín*, Díaz Ordaz 312, nr. south side of main market, clean, some rooms good, others basic, noisy at ground floor level, F, with bath, hot water a.m. only; next door at 316 is *Díaz Ordaz*, F, clean and friendly, similar water problem; many others nearby; *Pasaje*, Mina 302, near market, in doubtful neighbourhood, E with bathrooms, parakeets in patio (Lorenzo is most entertaining), noisy, clean; *Yagul*, E, Mina 103 near market and Zócalo, use of kitchen on request, very clean; *Casa de Huéspedes Arnel*, two blocks to the right of ADO station, then three blocks right to Aldama 404, Col. Valatlaco, E, very clean and attractive, apartments also; *Chayo*, 20 de Noviembre 508, F, bath but no fan, clean, friendly and quiet with attractive patio, rec.; *Nacional*, same block, F, clean, quiet. There is also accommodation in private houses which rent rooms (*casas de huéspedes*); *Posada Las Palmas*, Av. Juárez 516, F, without bath, restaurant, rec.; *Casa de Huéspedes Farolito*, Calle de Las Casas 508, F, more expensive with bath. *Posada Margarita*, Calle Abasolo, 3 blocks from Zócalo, E, with bath, not clean, friendly. *Villa Alta*, Cabrera 303, T 62444, 4 blocks from Zócalo, friendly service, F, clean.

Villa María, Arteaga 410, 5 blocks from the Zócalo, pleasant modern well furnished apts., maid service if required, rec. On the road to Tehuantepec (Km. 9.8), *Hotel Posada Los Arcos*, Spanish-style motel at San Sebastián Totla, D.

N.B. Hotels near the corner of 20 de Noviembre and Mina are in the red light district. Many other cheap hotels in 400 block of Trujano.

Camping Oaxaca Trailer Park S of town off the road to Mitla at a sign marked "Infonavit" (corner of Calles Pinos and Violetas), US$7 for 1-2 persons, secure, clothes washing facilities not always available; bus "Carmen-Infonavit" from downtown.

Restaurants Most restaurants on the main square cater for tourists; several are deemed to be overpriced, also very slow service, up to 1½ hrs to get complete order. *Guelatao*, on main square, good for breakfast and snacks, cheap beer; *Portal*, next door, similar to *Guelatao* but better, local dishes US$1-1.50; *El Asador Vasco*, 2nd floor overlooking Zócalo, good food, main dish US$4-5; *Flor de Oaxaca*, Armenta y López 311, delicious hot chocolate; *Los Arcos*, García Vigil 306 under *Calesa Real* hotel, good but expensive. *Montebello*, good, at Trujano 307; *Colón*, Colón 111; *La Catedral*, corner of Gral. García Vigil and Morelos, 1 block from Cathedral, good for local specialities— steaks, good *tamales*, classical music. *Alameda*, J.P.García between Trujano and Hidalgo, excellent regional food, crowded Sun. *Flami*, on Trujano near Zócalo, good food.

Vegetarian: *Flor de Loto*, Av. Morelos 509, next to Rufino Tamayo museum, new (US$3 a meal); *Arco*, dearer, opp. ADO bus station, Niños Héroes de Chapultepec, US$4 for complete meal, loud music; *Comedor Piscis*, Hidalgo 119.

Gino's Pizza, pleasant café, inexpensive in Independencia, 500 block; *El Sol y la Luna*, on Murguia, good although not cheap, live music some nights, now open evenings only; *Café Fontana*, excellent, opp. *Hotel Presidente*; *Café ADO*, ADO Terminal; unmarked small restaurant in Calle Abasolo, between 212 and 218, cheap light meals, clean; *Colonial*, 20 de Noviembre, cheap comidas corridas, rec; *Las Chalotes*, Fiallo 116, French food, moderate prices. The best Oaxacan food is found in the *comedores familiares* such as *Clemente, Los Almendros, La Juchita*, but they are way out of town and could be difficult to get to; also try *El Bicho Pobre*, Tacubaya y Abasolo, local food, open 1330-1800, excellent value; *El Mesón*, good tacos, clean, quick service, on Hidalgo at NE corner of Zócalo; *Tropical Frutas*, Mina y J.P.García, excellent and cheap. *Café Tito*, near Zócalo on García Vigil, good value for breakfast; *Quickly*, clean, friendly, French, cheap, popular with students; *El Paisaje*, 20 de Noviembre, good, cheap chicken dishes; *El Hipocampo*, Hidalgo 505, cheap, good; *La Pinata*, Hidalgo (just E of Zócalo), good chicken in mole lunches; *La Bougainvillier*, M. F. Fiallo 116 y Hidalgo, good, clean, reasonable prices; *El Tecolote*, a few blocks from Zócalo, open air eating, good quesadillas and tacos; *Casa de Chocolate*, quiet, pleasant, on Av. Independencia, coffee and home-made cakes; *Cafetería Chips*, Trujano (in 1st block W of Zócalo), good coffee; *Cafetería Alex*, Díaz Ordaz y Trujano, good comida corrida, coffee and breakfasts; *El Patio*, 1 block from Zócalo, has mainly good fish and seafood dishes, moderate prices and good service. Cheap and clean café *Las Palmas* (near *Hotel Pasaje*) on 20 de Noviembre. Good *dulcería* (sweet shop) in the 2nd class bus station.

Shopping There are endless temptations such as green and black pottery, baskets and bags made from cane and rushes, embroidered shirts, skirts, and blankets; Saturdays are the best for buying woollen *sarapes* cheaply. A group of Zapotecs can be seen weaving on Zaragoza between 20 de Noviembre and Tinoco y Palacios on Saturday, selling wall hangings and *sarapes*. Also daily on Zaragoza and García, between 0800-2000, but more expensive than elsewhere. Unfortunately some of the woven products are of a different quality from the traditional product—more garish dyes and synthetic yarns are replacing some of the originals; but you can still find these if you shop around. *Aripo*, on García Vigil, cheaper and better than most, service good. *Artesanías Cocijo*, interesting collection of handicrafts, a little expensive, English spoken and will ship goods, García Vigil 212. *Pepe*, Avenida Hidalgo, for jewellery; cheap local crafts. Good for silver, *Plata Mexicana*, 20 de Noviembre 209-C. *Yalalag*, Alcalá 104, has good selection of jewellery, rugs and pottery, somewhat overpriced; cheapest and largest selection of pottery plus a variety of fabrics and sandals at *Productos Típicos de Oaxaca*, Av. Dr. B. Dominguez 602; city bus near ADO depot goes there. *Casa Aragón*, J. P. García 503, famous for knives and *machetes*; a large Mercaado Artesanal also on J.P. García. Fine cream and purple-black pottery (Zapotec and Mixtec designs) available at *Alfarería Jiménez*, Zaragoza 402; further along Zaragoza is a small straw market with all kinds of baskets and bags. Other potteries at Las Casas 614, makers of the Oaxacan daisy design, and Trujano 508, bold flower designs. Many excellent fixed-price bargains to be had at *El Gran Bazaar*, Av. Independencia. Large selection of cotton and wool. Bargain for up 50% reduction. The old market sells fruit, vegetables, meat and some handicrafts (good, cheap meals here); Mercado de Abastos, open daily, which sells mostly food and flowers next to the 2nd class bus station, where the old Saturday market has also moved and caters mainly to the tourist trade. Benito Juárez market, 20 de Noviembre y Las Casas, good tourist items, but bargain hard and watch the quality. Those disappointed with it should go to the Sunday market at Tlacolula.

Local Buses There is a bus marked "Circular" or "Circular Panteón" which connects the first class bus stations on the N of town with the Zócalo, the market, the 2nd class bus station and the railway station.

Entertainment *El Sol y la Luna*, good bar with music; *Guajiros*, Macedonia Alcalá, live music.

Exchange It's difficult to change travellers' cheques at weekends but if you get stuck try some of the more expensive restaurants in the Zócalo. Get to banks before they open, long queues form. Bancomer, 1 block from Zócalo, exchanges travellers' cheques, 0900-1330, on García Vigil. Banpais at corner of Zócalo has a better service, Amex office on Zócalo, very helpful. Good rates at *Casa de Cambio*, Abasolo 105, 0900-1400, 1600-2000 changes travellers' cheques. *Casa de cambio* at Armenta y López, nr. corner with Hidalgo, 0900-1230, 1600-1900, a.m. only Sat., poor rates.

Library English lending library with very good English books, a few French and Spanish, also English newspapers (*The News* from Mexico City), used books and magazines for sale, at Macedonio Alcalá 305—looks like an apartment block on a pedestrian street, a few blocks N of Zócalo (open Mon.-Fri., 1000-1300, 1600-1800). *The News* is also sold round the Zócalo by newsboys, from mid-morning.

Doctor Dr Victor Tenorio, Clínica de Carmen, Abasolo 215, T 6-26-12, close to centre (very good English); Dr Marco Antonio Callejo (English-speaking), Belisario Domínguez 115, T 53-492, surgery 0900-1300, 1700-2000.

Washing Self: Baños Reforma, Calle Reforma, US$4 for steam-bath for two, sauna for one, US$2. Clothes: E.L.A., Super Lavandería Automática, Antonio Roldán 114, Col. Olímpica, washes and irons. Another one at Francisco Zarco, off the Periférico, Super Lavandería Hidalgo on Calle 20 de Noviembre, 2½ blocks S of the market. All about US$2 for 7 lbs.

Travel Agents Tourist Information and Tours, García Vigil 110-B, T 62093, ½ block N of Zócalo, French, German and Danish spoken.

Tourist Office 5 de Mayo 200 y Morelos, free map, also on Miguel Cabrera 3½ blocks N of Zócalo. Tourist Police on Zócalo near Cathedral, friendly and helpful. Federal tourist office Matamoros 105 y García Vigil. Instituto Nacional de Estadística, Geografía e Informática, Calz. Porfirio Díaz 241A, for maps.

Railway Station on Calzada Madero at junction with Periférico, 15 min. walk from Zócalo. From Mexico City, 563 km., 17 hrs., take food, magnificent scenery, US$7 including food, 1st class special, US$4.50 1st class, US$3 2nd, at 1900 daily. To Mexico City daily at 1820, not always a sleeper, US$18 including food. Tickets must be bought the same day. Seats scarce in 2nd class, quite a scramble! El Oaxaqueño (*servicio estrella*) leaves Mexico City 1900, arr. 0930, leaves Oaxaca 1900, arr. 0920, reserved seat US$7.25, single sleeper US$19.25, double US$38.70. To Puebla 0710, 11 hrs., US$3. Derailments at times.

Buses 1st class terminal is NW of Zócalo on Calzada de Niños Héroes (no luggage office); 2nd class is W of Zócalo on Calz. Trujano, has left-luggage office. Beware of double-booking and short-changing, especially when obtaining tickets from drivers if you have not booked in advance. Cristóbal Colón to Mexico City, 10 hrs., about 8 a day, mostly evenings, US$8, 2nd class by Fletes y Pasajes, 9 hrs., comfortable; about 10 a day with ADO, 8 hrs., US$5, robberies have been reported on these buses. If buses to the capital are fully booked travel via Puebla. 1st class to Cuautla, US$6 (change there for Cuernavaca); Puebla (1st class, 9 hrs., 2nd class, 11 hrs., US$4, at 0800, 1200 and 1900 with Fletes y Pasajes); to Tuxtepec (1st class, 6 hrs., US$6.65 with ADO, road regarded as dangerous because of drug plantations), from same terminal, Cuenca goes by a more direct route 1st class US$2.70. To Veracruz, ADO, 2 a day from 1st class bus station, via Huajuapan, Tehuacán and Orizaba, 11 hrs., book early, or change as above, allow 16 hrs. Cristóbal Colón to Villahermosa, US$8.50, book well ahead, 13½ hrs., daily at 1700 and 2100. 1st class; San Cristóbal de Las Casas (US$8.75, at 0700, 12 hrs.) book 1-2 days in advance with C. Colón; and Tapachula, 11 hrs., US$9 (2200, Cristóbal Cólon). Also Fletes y Pasajes and Transportes Tuxtla (2nd class). Book well in advance as buses often come almost full from Mexico City. To Tuxtla Gutiérrez, 1st class, C. Colón, 3 a day, 9 hrs.; by 2nd class, 11 hrs., US$8 at 1030, 1730 and 2100. To Tehuantepec, scenic, 5 a day, 2nd class US$3, 5 hrs. To Ciudad Cuauhtémoc, US$9, 12 hrs. To Arriaga US$8, 5 a day. To Puerto Escondido, US$3, gruelling 13 hrs. journey (can be longer) at 1300, partly along dirt roads, interesting scenery. Night bus 5 hrs. faster. Probably better to go Oaxaca-Pochutla on new road, 7 hrs., US$3, six 1st-class buses a day, then change for Puerto Angel/Puerto Escondido. Oaxaca-Pacífico has good 2nd class buses (five a day to

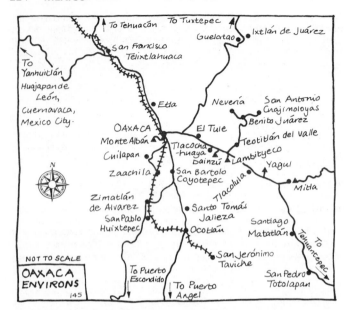

To Tehuacán / To Tuxtepec / Guelatao • Ixtlán de Juárez / San Francisco Telixtlahuaca / To Yanhuitlán / Huajapan de León, Cuernavaca, Mexico City. / • Etla / Nevería / San Antonio Cuajimoloyas / Benito Juárez / OAXACA / Monte Albán / El Tule / Teotitlán del Valle / Tlacocha-huaya / Lambityeco / Cuilapan / Dainzú / Zaachila / San Bartolo Coyotepec / Tlacolula / Yagul / Mitla / Zimatlán de Alvarez / Santo Tomás Jalieza / San Pablo Huixtepec / Ocotlán / Santiago Matatlán / To Tehuantepec / San Jerónimo Taviche / San Pedro Totolapan / To Puerto Escondido / To Puerto Angel / NOT TO SCALE / OAXACA ENVIRONS / 145

Pochutla, one a day to Puerto Angel arrives 0400, 9 a day to Puerto Escondido). Estrella del Valle run 1st class buses from 2nd class terminal, 8-10 hrs., at 0500 and 0730. Buses to most local villages go from this terminal, too.

Air Services The airport is about 8 km. S, direction Ocotepec. The airport taxis (*colectivos*) cost US$1.50 p.p. Book at Transportaciones Aeropuerto Oaxaca on the Alameda (T 67878) for collection at your hotel to be taken to airport. From Mexico City twice daily by Aeroméxico in less than an hr., or Mexicana three daily and Mon., Wed., Fri., at 1415; Tapachula flights with Aeroméxico, daily, 1110; Aeroméxico also flies daily to Huatulco. Aero Caribe flies to Villahermosa daily at 1500, 90 mins., US$100, continuing to Mérida and Cancún. Aerolibertad flies to Huatulco, Acapulco and Ixtapa/Zihuatanejo on Wed., Fri., and Sun., 0900 (the first two only also at 1315 Fri. and Sun.). Mexicana's flights to Guadalajara (daily), Mazatlán (daily), Puerto Vallarta (daily), Tampico (daily), Ciudad Juárez, Mexicali, and Monterrey all involve a connection in Mexico City; similarly its flights to Denver, Los Angeles, San Francisco, Chicago and Seattle (all daily except the last). Daily flights to Puerto Escondido, 40 mins. Aerovías Oaxaqueñas at 1100, returns at 0730 or 1200; Líneas Aéreas Oaxaqueñas fly at 1030 Mon.-Sat. and 0830 Sun. Costs US$40 one way, but all Puerto Escondido planes (DC-3s) break down frequently, and for several days, rough ride back if no plane, 9 hrs. at least. Once weekly flights also to Pochutla. Líneas Aéreas Oaxaqueñas office at Av. Hidalgo 503. T 65362, airport 61280. There is a Mexicana office next to *Hotel Señorial* on the Zócalo, helpful.

Excursions To *Monte Albán* (open 0800-1700) about 10 km. (20 mins.) uphill from Oaxaca, to see the pyramids, walls, terraces, tombs, staircases and sculptures of the ancient capital of the Zapotec culture. The place is radiantly colourful during some sunsets. Beware of fake "antique" sellers. Guide US$1. Take a torch. Autobuses Turísticos depart from behind *Hotel Mesón del Angel*, Mina nr. Díaz Ordaz (bus tickets available from hotel lobby) hourly on the half-hour from 0830 to 1330 fare US$1.70 return, last bus back at 1730; 2 hrs. at the site, allow not quite enough time to visit ruins before returning (you are allowed to come back on another tour on one ticket for an extra US$0.40 but you will not, of course, have a reserved seat for your return). To give yourself enough time, you can walk 4 km. downhill from the ruins to Colonia Monte Albán and get a city bus back from there. Good tours also from *Hotel El Presidente*, US$6 each with excellent guide. Entrance to ruins US$0.40, free on Sun. (and for students on request). Most people go in the morning, so it may be easier to catch the afternoon bus. A private museum in an old colonial house is worth visiting.

To the right, before getting to the ruins, is Tomb 7, where a fabulous treasure trove was found in 1932; most items are in the Regional Museum in the convent of Santo Domingo. The remarkable rectangular plaza, 300 by 200 metres, is rimmed by big ceremonial platforms: the Ball Court, and possibly a palace to the E, stairs rising to an unexcavated platform to the S, several platforms and temples to the W and one—known as Temple of the Dancers but in reality, probably a hospital—with bas-reliefs, glyphs and calendar signs (probably 5th century B.C.). A wide stairway leads to a platform on the N side. Most of the ruins visible are early 10th century, when the city was abandoned and became a burial place. Informative literature is available at the site. (Recommended literature is the Bloomgarden *Easy Guide* to Monte Albán or *Easy Guide* to Oaxaca covering the city and all the ruins in the valley, with maps. In major hotels or the bookshop at Guerrero 108, and all the ruins.) Restaurant on site, some food expensive, soup good.

A paved road leads to **Teotitlán Del Valle**, where Oaxaca *sarapes* are woven, which is now becoming rather touristy. If you knock at any door down the street, you will get them only a little cheaper than at the market, but there is greater variety. The best prices are to be had at the stores along the road as you come into town. (Make sure whether you are getting all-wool or mixture.) Buses leave every 2½ hrs. from 0800 from Miguel Cabrera nr. corner with Mina (US$0.30). *Juvenal Mendoza*, Buenavista 9, will make any design any size into a rug to order (daily at 1100). Opposite the turning for Teotitlán, turn right for **Dainzu**, another important ruin recently excavated. Its pyramid contains figures, probably ball players, similar to the Monte Albán dancers. The nearby site of **Lambytieco** is also well worth visiting, to see several fine and well-preserved stucco heads. Only 72 km. from Oaxaca is **Yanhuitlán**, with a beautiful 400-year-old church, part of a monastery. NW of Yanhuitlán is **Huajuapan De Leon**, with *Hotel García Peral*, on the Zócalo, good restaurant, *Hotel Casablanca*, Amatista 1, Col. Vista Hermosa, also good restaurant (just outside Huajuapan on the road to Oaxaca), and *Hotel Bella Vista*, E, and *Colón*, E, very good. 2nd class bus from Oaxaca to Huajuapan, four a day, US$1.75.

To Mitla, paved road, 42 km. from Oaxaca past (1) **El Tule** (12 km. from Oaxaca) which has what is reputed the world's largest tree, a savino

(*Taxodium Mucronatum*), estimated at 2,000 years old, 40 metres high, 42 metres round at base, weighing an estimated 550 tons, fed water by an elaborate pipe system, in churchyard (bus from Oaxaca, 2nd class bus station, every ½ hr., US$0.40, buy ticket on bus, sit on the left to see the Tule tree; bus El Tule-Mitla US$0.30); (2) **Tlacochahuaya**, 16th century church, vivid Indian murals, carpets and blouses sold in market nearby, admission US$0.45 to church; and (3) **Tlacolula** (*Hotel Glish Bal*, Zaragoza 3, F, reported clean), with a most interesting Sunday market and the renowned Capilla del Santo Cristo in the church, elaborate decorations and gruesome figures of saints (fiesta 9 October); can be reached by bus from Oaxaca, from the 2nd class bus station every 30 mins. but every 15 mins. on Sun., US$0.25. Taxi costs US$4 each to Mitla for 4 sharing, with time to take photographs at Tule and Mitla and to buy souvenirs at ruins. A band plays every evening in the plaza, take a sweater, cold wind most eves, starts at 1930. Tours (rather rushed) to Tule, Mitla and Tlacolula on Sunday from *Hotel Señorial*, US$5.50, in VW buses. Fletes y Pasajes bus from Oaxaca, 2nd class bus station, every 30 mins. to Mitla, 1 hour, US$0.50; the ruins are 10-min. walk across the village (from the bus stop).

From the main road a turn left leads 4 km. to **Mitla** (whose name means "place of the dead") where there are ruins of four great palaces among minor ones. Entry US$0.40 (Sun. free), open 0830-1800, literature available on site. See in particular the magnificent bas-reliefs, the sculptured designs in the Hall of Mosaics, the Hall of the Columns, and in the depths of a palace La Columna de la Muerte (Column of Death), which people embrace and measure what they can't reach with their fingers to know how many years they have left to live (rather hard on long-armed people); Indians gather on New Year's day to embrace it. There is a soberly decorated colonial church with three cupolas, and a rash of guides and pedlars. Beautiful traditional Indian clothes and other goods may be bought at the new permanent market. Also good *mescal*.

Accommodation *Hotel Mitla*, E, clean, local food (comida corrida, US$4.80). *Hotel La Zapoteca*, on road to ruins, E, newer and better than *Mitla*, cheaper food, good. The University of the Americas has a small guest-house, and runs the small Frissell museum in the Zócalo at Mitla, with very good and clean restaurant, *La Sorpresa*, in a patio (guesthouse and museum closed for renovation in 1990); restaurant opp. site, *Santa María*; *María Elena* restaurant 100 metres from site towards village, good comida corrida for US$0.90. The local technical college provides accommodation, showers and a bathroom; good shopping too.

Fletes y Pasajes buses and taxis from Oaxaca go to the ruins of **Yagul** (on the way to Mitla, ask to be put down at the turn-off to Yagul, entry, US$0.05), guided tours in English leave from *Mesón del Angel*, Mina, in Oaxaca, US$8, an outstandingly picturesque site where the ball courts and quarters of the priests are set in a landscape punctuated by candelabra cactus and agave. Yagul was a large Zapotec and Mixtec religious centre; the ball courts are perhaps the most perfect discovered to date; also fine tombs (take steep path from behind the ruins) and temples. You will have to walk some 2 km. from the bus stop to the site, and you can return the same way or walk 3 km. to Tlacolula to catch a bus (signposted). The 2 km.-long side road off the main road is paved.

Friday trips from Oaxaca to market at San Antonio Ocotlán on the road to Puerto Angel, with good prices for locally woven rugs and baskets, also excellent fruit and veg.; buses leave every 30 mins. for San Antonio from the co-operative bus station opposite Oaxaca Mercado de Abastos (½ hr. journey). Stop in San Bártolo Coyotepec to see black pottery (Doña Rosa's—she's been dead for years but her name survives—is a target for tours, but other families are just as good) and don't try to bargain (also red and green ceramics in the village), and in Santo Tomás Jalieza, where cotton textiles are made.

17 km. SW of Oaxaca is **Cuilapan**, where there is a vast unfinished 16th-century convent, now in ruins, with a famous nave and columns, and an "open chapel", whose roof collapsed in an earthquake. The last Zapotec princess was buried at Cuilapan. Reached by bus from Oaxaca from 2nd class bus station, take bus to Zaachila which leaves every 30 mins., then walk to unexcavated ruins in valley. **Zaachila** is a poor town, but there are ruins, with two Mixtec tombs, with owls in stucco work in the outer chamber and carved human figures with skulls for heads inside. Admission US$0.13, no restrictions on flash photography. There is an Indian market on Thursday.

To San Pablo de **Guelatao** (65 km. from Oaxaca), the birthplace of Benito Juárez. The town is located in the mountains NE of Oaxaca and can be reached by bus (3 hrs.) along a paved but tortuously winding road. There are a memorial and a museum to Juárez on the hillside within the village (entry, US$0.17), and a pleasant lake with a symbolic statue of a shepherd and his lambs.

There are 2 **national parks** in Oaxaca State: **Benito Juárez** in the municipality of Huayapan, some 5 km. from the capital, with pine forests, comprising 2,737 hectares; and the **Lagunas de Chacacahua** (14,187 hectares), including tropical vegetation and a 28-km. coastline on the Pacific, at Tututepec, 57 km. from Pinotepa Nacional.

We are approaching a more traditional part of Mexico; Tehuantepec isthmus and the mountains of Chiapas beyond, a land inhabited by Indians less influenced than elsewhere by the Spanish conquest. Only about 210 km. separate the Atlantic and the Pacific at the hot, heavily-jungled Isthmus of Tehuantepec, where the land does not rise more than 250 metres. There are a railway (to be renewed) and a Trans-Isthmian Highway between Coatzacoalcos and Salina Cruz, the terminal cities on the two oceans. Winds are very strong on and near the isthmus, because of the intermingling of Pacific and Caribbean weather systems. Drivers of high-sided vehicles must take great care.

N.B. In southern Mexico the word "Zócalo" is not often used for the main square of a town: "Plaza (Mayor)" is much more common.

Salina Cruz (43,000) is a booming and evil-smelling port with a naval base, extensive oil-storage installations and an oil refinery. Bathing is dangerous because of the heavy swell from Pacific breakers and also sharks. Beware of overcharging in the marketplace.

Hotels *Fuente*, E, bath, basic. *Río*, E, reasonable, nr. Cristóbal Colón bus station. Avoid the *Magda*, overpriced, unfriendly. *Posada del Jardín*, E.

Restaurant *Costa del Pacífico*, hires shower cabin, stores luggage.

Buses The 1130 bus from Salina Cruz to San Cristóbal comes from Oaxaca and is very often full (2nd class, US$5.50); take instead a 2nd class bus to Juchitán, then to Arriaga and from there to Tuxtla and San Cristóbal; a long route. To Coatzacoalcos, US$5, 6 hrs. Salina Cruz-Pochutla, US$3, 3½ hrs.; 2nd class to Puerto Esconido, 6 hrs., slow, US$3.50. Frequent buses to Tehuantepec, 30 mins., US$0.20. To Tapachula by Cristóbal Colón 2nd class, along the coast, 7½ hrs., 0740 and 2030, US$5. No luggage storage at bus station.

Ten km. to the S is a picturesque fishing village with La Ventosa beach which, as the name says, is windy. Buses go to the beach every 30 mins. from a corner of the main square. Accommodation: *La Posada de Rustrian*, overlooking the sea, E, with bath in new block, half in old block, poor value; unnamed *pensión*, F, on right of road before asphalt ends. Friendly family at the top of the dirt road coming from Salina Cruz (on the right) and 200 metres after the first path that leads down to the beach, rents hammocks, US$0.20 a night, fried fish US$1. *Champas*, or hammocks under thatch shelters by the beach, US$0.25-US$0.40 a night. The owners serve drinks and food (fish, shrimps, crabs just caught) from early morning on. Prices often high.

Warning Do not wander too far off along the beach as many people have been attacked and robbed. Do not sleep on the beach or in your car.

(Km. 804) ***Tehuantepec*** (population 25,000, altitude 150 metres) is 257 km. from Oaxaca and 21 km. inland from Salina Cruz. A colourful place, it is on the bend of a river around which most of its activities are centred and which makes it very humid. The plaza has arcades down one side, a market on the other, and many stands selling *agua fresca*, an iced fruit drink. Houses are low, in white or pastel shades. The Indians are mostly Zapotecs whose social organization was once matriarchal: the women are high-pressure saleswomen, with some Spanish blood; their hair is sometimes still braided and brightly ribboned and at times they wear embroidered costumes. The men for the most part work in the fields, as potters or weavers, or at the nearby oil refinery. Hammocks made in this area are of the best quality. The town is divided into 15 wards, and each holds a *fiesta*, the main one at the end of Holy Week, when the women wear their finest costumes and jewellery. There is another splendid *fiesta* in honour of St. John the Baptist on 22-25 June. January and February are good months for the ward *fiestas*. The people, especially the women, are reported to be hostile to foreigners, spitting and throwing things.

Hotels *Oasis* (central and good atmosphere), E, with bath and fan, near Plaza; *Posada Tehuanita*, E, central, rec.; *Donaji*, Juárez 10, fan, nr. market, E; *Posada Villa Real*, E, nice courtyard; *Casa de Huéspedes*, just off the main plaza, quiet, clean, basic, but reasonable, friendly, with lovely patio, F.

Restaurants *Café Colonial*, near the *Hotel Oasis*, and *Kike* under *Posada Colonial* have good comidas corridas for about US$4. Cheap food on top floor of market. The local quesadillas made of maize and cheese are delicious; sold at bus stops.

Warning The direct road to Oaxaca has been reported unsafe owing to violent robberies. Avoid night buses especially. Check conditions locally.

Bus There is now a bus station at N end of town. One bus a day to San Cristóbal at 1230, it may be full, standing is not allowed but the driver may accept a present and let you on (7½ hrs., US$6). To Coatzacoalcos at 0730, 9-10 hrs. Bus to Arriaga at 0600, 0800, 1800 to connect to Tonalá. To Tuxtla Gutiérrez, 1000 and 1500 (6 hrs.) 2nd class at 0130, and Tapachula. Bus to Tonalá (Cristóbal Colón) at 0030 and 0130. To Oaxaca, US$3, 5 hrs., with Fletes y Pasajes every 2 hours or so, or with Istmo at 1000 and 2200; to Salina Cruz, US$0.20. (**N.B.** Some buses from Salina Cruz do not stop at Tehuantepec.)

Train to Coatzacoalcos daily at 0700, about 11 hrs.

Excursions To neighbouring villages for *fiestas*. Near the town are the ruins of Criengola, apparently not very accessible.

27 km. beyond Tehuantepec on the road to Tuxtla Gutiérrez is **Juchitán** (*Hotel Don Alex*, F, clean, cheapest; *Hotel Casa Río*, has an Indian name, *Coty*, not posted, next to Casa Río shop, E, nr. market, clean; be prepared to bargain in cheap hotels), very old, Indian, with an extensive market, many *fiestas* and a special one on June 19 (2nd class bus Oaxaca-Juchitán, US$3.75, 6 hrs., frequent Juchitán-Tuxtla, 1st class, 4 hrs., US$3). Connect here with train from Veracruz to Tapachula, but Juchitán station is dangerous (at night wait for the train in Ixtepec). A road runs 6 km. N to **Ixtepec** (airport) (Hotels: *Panamericano*, noisy from railway station, F; *San Juan*, F, bath, acceptable; *Colón*) train Ixtepec-Coatzacoalcos at 0800. The Trans-Isthmian highway goes N from Juchitán, with a good hotel at Matías Romero, *Real del Istmo*, a/c, by the road, safe parking. At Las Cruces (restaurant), a road runs right to **Arriaga** (12,000 people; Hotels: *El Parador*, clean with swimming pool; *Juchitán*, E, with bathroom; *Colonial*, next to bus station, F, clean, friendly, quiet; *Restaurant Xochimilco* near bus stations), through **Tonalá**, formerly a very quiet town but now reported noisy and dirty, with a small museum; good market (bus Tonalá-Tapachula, 5 hrs., US$3; also buses to Tuxtla). At Huixtla, near Tapachula (*Casa de Huéspedes Regis*, Independencia Norte 23, F), there is a good market—no tourists—along the railway line. By Route 200 to **Tapachula** (144,000), a pleasant and neat, but expensive, hot commercial town (airport) and the Talismán bridge to Guatemala. Beyond Tonalá the road is mostly straight, smooth and fast. (North of Arriaga a road is now open paralleling the railway and by-passing Las Cruces, so avoiding dozens of sharp curves on a steep road.) This is by far the better road for travellers seeking the quickest way from Mexico City to Guatemala.

Tonalá Hotels *Galilea*, D, with bath, air-conditioned, good, basic cheap rooms on 1st floor, balconies, on main square, with good restaurants; **Casa de Huéspedes El Viajero**, Avenida Matamoros, near market, F, with bath, rough but OK; *Faro*, near Plaza, F; *Tonalá*, opposite museum, E; **Sta. Elena Restaurant**, at the S end of town, near Cristóbal Colón bus station on outskirts, good. On the Plaza, **Restaurant Nora**. Numerous Chinese-named restaurants; good breakfast at restaurants on Zócalo.

Tapachula Hotels In centre, *Posada Michel* and **Don Miguel**, both C; *Fénix*, 4 Av. Norte 19, T 50755, D; *San Francisco*, Av. Central Sur 94, 15 mins. from centre, good, air-conditioned, D; *Cinco de Mayo*, E with bath, not very clean, convenient for Talismán colectivos; *Casa de Huéspedes Mexicana*, 8a Avenida Norte, F, basic, with a little zoo in the courtyard. Many hotels along Avenidas 4, 6, 8 (near Plaza). *Pensión Mars* (Av. 4) has cheap comidas; *Tayopec*, F, friendly; *Motel Loma Real*, 1 km. N of city, D, operates as a 1st class hotel, use of swimming pool, cold showers. Good restaurant next to Cristóbal Colón terminal.

Laundromat There is a laundry, 1 hr. service, near Cristóbal Colón bus station, open Suns.

Exchange Avoid the crowds of streetwise little boys at the border; exchange is rather better in the town, bus station gives a good rate.

Travel Agent Viajes Tacaná, operated by Sr Adolfo Guerrero Chávez, 4a Av. Norte, No. 6, T 63502/63501/63245; trips to Izapa ruins, to mountains, beaches and can gain entry to museum when closed. Tourist office on main Plaza not recommended.

Into Guatemala 2nd class buses from Tapachula to the frontier at the Talismán bridge (8 km., open 24 hrs a day) take 50 mins.; they include Cristóbal Colón, which leaves at 1245 and 1600 (US$0.60), and Unión y Progreso near the market (1st class leave 0900 and 1100, US$0.80—stating "Col. Juárez" as its destination); no through buses. Kombi vans hourly or so from Unión y Progreso bus station, about US$1.20. Taxi Tapachula-Talismán, US$8, exit tax US$0.45. There is a *hospedaje* at the border. The Guatemalan customs post is 100 metres from the Mexican one. Exchange cash dollars for quetzales with men standing around customs on the Guatemalan side (but check rates before dealing with them, and haggle; there is no bank on the Guatemalan side). Crossing into Guatemala by car may take more than 2 hours. If you don't want your car sprayed inside it may cost you a couple of dollars. Guatemalan buses (Galgos) leave Talismán bridge at 0900 and 1100 and twice in p.m. for Guatemala City (6 hrs., entry tax 1 quetzal).

There are few buses between the Talismán bridge and Oaxaca or Mexico City (though they do exist); advisable therefore to travel to Tapachula for connection, delays can occur there also at peak times. Buses (Cristóbal Colón) from Tapachula to Mexico City, US$15, five a day, all p.m., take 8-12 hrs. to reach Oaxaca and same again to Mexico City. Bus to Oaxaca, 1800 may take 10 hrs. Buses from Mexico City all leave p.m. also; the 1545 and 1945 go on to Talismán. The train from Mexico City to Tapachula leaves daily at 2100, it costs US$12.50 1st class but takes 37 hours to complete the journey, changing at Veracruz (Veracruz-Tapachula, 30 hrs., 887 km., US$3.50 2nd class), stops to get food on the way. If travelling in the reverse direction, board train at Tapachula hours in advance of departure to get seats, and guard them. Tickets on sale in Tapachula only at 1630. Train departs daily at 1800 for connection to Mexico City but again requires change at Veracruz and tends to miss evening train to Mexico City. Best to stay overnight at Veracruz and catch morning train. Don't get off at Tierra Blanca to change to the Mérida-Mexico train; you arrive after it has gone. Hitch-hikers should note that there is little through international traffic at Talismán bridge. Tapachula—Salina Cruz, 9 hrs. with Flecha Roja, US$6.40.

Consulates It is possible (but very difficult for Canadians, we are told) to get a visa for El Salvador at the Salvadorean Consulate in Tapachula (Calle 2a Sur, No. 10) without any delay. There is a Guatemalan Consulate in Tapachula at 2 Calle Oriente and 7 Av. S., T 6-12-52, taxi from Colón terminal, US$0.75. (Open Mon.-Fri. 0800-1600; visa US$10, friendly and quick.)

Off the road between Tonalá and Tapachula are several fine-looking and undeveloped beaches (although waves are dangerous). *Puerto Arista* is now being built up and spoiled; bus from Tonalá every hour, 45 mins., US$0.25, taxi US$0.50—one hotel or hammocks on beach, US$0.85 a night (many sandflies), also several guest houses, US$24 a month, 3 or 4 restaurants (closed by 2000) with rooms to rent, e.g. *Restaurant Turquesa*; new small hotel/restaurant 3 blocks down on the right from where the road reaches the beach coming from Tonalá and turns right, next to bakery, no fan, basic, F. Buses also from Tonalá to Boca del Cielo further down the coast, which is good for bathing but has no accommodation, and similarly Cabeza del Toro. **Paredón**, on the huge lagoon Mar Muerto near Tonalá, has excellent seafood and one very basic guest house. One can take a local fishing boat out into the lagoon to swim; the shore stinks because fishermen clean fish on the beach among dogs and pigs. Served by frequent buses. En route for Tapachula one passes through Pijijiapan where there is the *Hotel Pijijilton*(!) next to the Cristóbal Colón bus station. Also **Puerto Madero**, 20 km. from Tapachula (bus US$0.80), worse than Puerto Arista, because built up and stench on beaches from rubbish being burned. Intense heat in summer. (*Hotel Puerto Madero*, accommodation in what are really remains of cement block room, F.) Water defences are being built. Many fish restaurants on beach.

45 km. (16 km. to turn-off) beyond Tapachula, on the way to Guatemala, is **Unión Juárez** (*Hotel Colonial*, E; *Restaurant Carmelita* on the square is modest with fair prices). Visit the ruins of **Izapa** (proto-classic stelae, small museum) on the way to Unión Juárez; the part of the site on the N is easily visible but a larger portion is on the S side of the highway, about 1 km. away, ask caretaker for guidance. These buildings influenced Kaminal Juyú near Guatemala City and are considered archaeologically important as a Proto-Mayan site. In Unión Juárez one can have one's papers stamped and proceed on foot via Talquián to the Guatemalan border at Sibinal. Take a guide.

A worthwhile and easy hike can be made up the Tacaná volcano (4,150 m.), which takes 2-3 days from Unión Juárez. Ask for the road to Chiquihuete, no cars. Jorge de León will guide you, or the Club Andinista at the Tapachula tourist office can help, on the Plaza Mayor.

Beyond Las Cruces we enter the mountainous Chiapas state, mostly peopled by Maya Indians whose extreme isolation has now been ended by air services and the two main highways. Chiapas ranks first in cacao production, second in coffee, bananas and mangoes, and cattle-grazing is important. Hardwoods are floated out down the rivers which flow into the Gulf.

Mike Shawcross writes: Anyone with a vehicle who has time to visit or is looking for a place to spend the night would find it well worth while to make a 4-km. detour. 50 km. beyond Las Cruces a gravel road leads north (left—last km. very rough) to the beautiful waterfall El Aguacero (small sign), which falls several hundred feet down the side of the Río La Venta canyon. There is a small car-park at the lip of the canyon. 798 steps lead down to the river and the base of the waterfall.

From Las Cruces to Tuxtla Gutiérrez, Route 190 carries on to

Cintalapa (restaurant) whence there is a steep climb up an escarpment. Carry on to Ocozocoautla (airport for Tuxtla, hotel, F), make a long ascent followed by descent to

(Km. 1,085) **Tuxtla Gutiérrez**, capital of Chiapas; pop.: 167,000; alt.: 522 metres, 301 km. (183 miles) from Tehuantepec. It is a hot, modern city with greatest interest to the tourist during the fair of Guadalupe, on December 12. The market is worth a look. There is a State Archaeological Museum with a fine collection of Mayan artefacts, open daily, at the E end of town, near the botanical garden (on a wooded hillside near the Teatro de la Ciudad—it has an orchid research station). There is a superb zoo some 3 km. S of town up a long hill (too far to walk), which contains only animals and birds from Chiapas, wild and in captivity. It has a respected reseach centre and is said to be the best zoo in Mexico, if not Latin America—good for birdwatchers too (open Tues.-Sun., 0830-1700, free; the buses "Zoológico" and "Cerro Hueco" from Calle 1a Oriente Sur, between Avs. 6a and 7a Sur Oriente, pass the entrance every 20 mins; taxi US$2.50 from centre.

The street system here is as follows: Avenidas run from E to W, Calles from N to S. The Avenidas are named according to whether they are N or S of the Avenida Central and change their names if they are E or W of the Calle Central. The number before Avenida or Calle means the distance from the "Central" measured in blocks.

Hotels *Bonampak*, Bld. Belisario Domínguez 180, T 32050, W end of town, the social centre, C, clean, good restaurant; *Flamboyant*, Bld. Belísario Domínguez 1081, T 29259/29311, comfortable, good swimming pool; *Gran Hotel Humberto*, Av. Central Pte. 180, T 22080, C; *Posada del Rey*, 2 Av. Norte Oriente 310, T 22911, C, a/c; *La Mansión*, 1 Poniente Norte 221, T 22151, D, a/c, bath; all centrally located. *Palace Inn*, Blvd. Belisario Domínguez (on highway just before bypass), T 24342, C, clean, pool, garden, good value; *Mar-Inn*, D, pleasant, clean, 2a Av. Norte Oriente 347, T 22715; *Balun Canan*, Av. Central Oriente 922, T 23848, D. Opp. Cristóbal Colón bus station are *María Teresa* (T 30102), E, and *Santo Domingo*, F with shower, good if you arrive late, but noisy; *Posada del Sol*, 1 block from Cristóbal Colón buses, F with hot shower, clean, friendly; *Posada Maya*, 4 Poniente Sur y 7 Sur Poniente, F p.p., clean, friendly; *Posada Muñiz*, near 2nd class bus station, not rec., but useful for early departures; *Santa Elena*, Oriente Sur 346, F, basic; *Canadá*, near market, F, without bath. CREA Youth Hostel, Calz. Angel Albino Corzo 1800, T 21201/33405, C.P. 29070, meals available.

Motels *La Hacienda*, trailer-park-hotel, Belisario Domínguez 1197, T 27832, E, Camping F, owner speaks English.

Restaurants *Los Cazadores*, good, regional, expensive; *Mina*, Av. Central Oriente 525, nr. bus station, good cheap *comidas*; *Parrilla La Cabaña*, excellent *tacos*, very clean; *Los Arcos*, Central Poniente 806, good international food; *Las Pichanchas*, pretty courtyard, *marimba* music between 1400-1700 and 2000-2300, on Av. 14 de Septiembre Oriente 837, worth trying; *Central*, on Plaza, reasonable; many others; *Las Calandrias*, 2a Av. Norte Poniente, 20 metres from Cristóbal Colón terminal, open 0700-2400, good and cheap. Coffee shop below *Hotel Serrano* serves excellent coffee.

Post Office on main square. International **phone** calls can be made from 1 Norte, 2 Oriente, directly behind post office, 0800-1500, 1700-2100 (1700-200 Sun.).

Travel Agency Carolina Tours, Sr José Narváez Valencia (manager), Av. Central Poniente 1138, T 2-42-81; reliable, recommended; also coffee shop at Av. Central Poniente 230.

Tourist Office Av. Central Poniente 1454, Col. Moctezuma, T 24535/25509.

Roads and Buses 35 km. E of Tuxtla, just past Chiapa de Corzo (see below), a road runs N, 294 km., to Villahermosa via Pichucalco (**see page** 249), paved all the way. Cristóbal Colón 1st class bus terminal is at 2 Av. Norte Poniente 268, Transportes Tuxtla 1st and 2nd class terminals are at 2 Av. Sur Oriente 712. Cristóbal Colón has buses daily to Villahermosa at 0620, 1300 and 1730, 8½ hrs., US$6; to Oaxaca at 1100 and 2245, 12 hrs., US$7; 4 a day to Mexico City, US$19, plus frequent buses to San Cristóbal de Las Casas, US$2, superb mountain journey. Tuxtla-Tapachula, US$5, 4 a day; one (1st class) to the Talismán bridge daily at 0300. Oaxaca Pacífico buses to Salina Cruz, from 1st class bus terminal. Take travel sickness tablets for Tuxtla-Oaxaca road if you suffer from queasiness. Transportes Tuxtla has 2nd class buses to Oaxaca, 5 a day, US$8, and 1st class buses to Pichucalco, 6 a day, US$4 (Pichucalco-Villahermosa and Villahermosa-Campeche (6 hrs.) have frequent services); to Villahermosa at 0500 and 1330, US$5; to Mérida at 1330, US$15. The scenery between Tuxtla and Mérida is very fine, and the road provides the best route between Chiapas and Yucatán. There are VW taxis at the bus station but they will not drive to the airport unless they have a full passenger load and may tout hotels before going there.

By Air The new airport for Tuxtla is way out at the next town of Ocozocoautla, a long drive to a mountain top. It is often shrouded in cloud and has crosswinds: there are times when aircraft do not leave for days! Good facilities, including restaurant. Tuxtla Gutiérrez to Tapachula, daily, 35 mins.; to Villahermosa daily, 25 mins.; to Veracruz, Mon. and Fri., 1 hr. 25 mins.; to Guadalajara and Monterrey almost daily via Mexico City with Mexicana; frequent to Mexico City, direct 1 hr. 15 mins. There is a 40 min. flight by Britten-Norman Islander to Palenque, very exciting, no reservations or tickets available. You must be at the airport before dawn, flights leave at about 0700, Sumidero canyon can be seen during flight.

Excursions Two vast artificial lakes made by dams are worth visiting: the Presa Netzahualcoyotl, or Mal Paso, 77 km. NW of Tuxtla, and La Angostura, SE of the city. Information from the tourist office. Mal Paso can also be visited from Cárdenas (**see page** 246). By paved road, which starts at zoo gates (23 km.), in excellent condition, to the rim of the tremendous ***Sumidero Canyon***, over 1,000 metres deep (tour US$30; taxi fare US$20 return; minibus daily from 1a Av. Norte Oriente 1121, go at 0900 and hope others turn up to share US$10 cost. To hire a boat for a 2-hr. trip, US$22.) Indian warriors unable to endure the Spanish conquest hurled themselves into the canyon rather than submit. At Cahuarte, 10 km. in the direction of San Cristóbal, it is possible to park by the river; boat trip into the Sumidero Canyon US$4. Excursions by air to Bonampak and Yaxchilán cheaper from San Cristóbal (see below). Transportes Tuxtla has a 1st class bus from Tuxtla to Palenque at US$6.50 one way, which leaves Tuxtla at 0500; 9-hr. journey via Pichucalco and Villahermosa.

Chiapa De Corzo (pop. 35,000), 15 km. on, a colonial town on a bluff overlooking the Grijalva river, is more interesting than Tuxtla: see a fine 16th century crown-shaped fountain, a church whose engraved altar is of solid silver, and famous craftsmen in gold and jewellery and lacquer work who travel the fairs. Painted and lacquered vessels made of pumpkins are a local speciality. There is a small lacquer museum. The *fiestas* here are outstanding: 20-23 January with a pageant on the river and another, early February. *Hotel Los Angeles*, on Plaza, F, only one; good seafood restaurants by the riverside. Plaza filled with bars playing jukeboxes. Chiapa de Corzo was a preclassic and proto-classic Maya site and shares features with early Maya sites in Guatemala; the ruins are behind the Nestlé plant, and some restored mounds are in a field near modern houses. Ask the householders' permission to climb over the fence as the ruins are on private property. Bus from Tuxtla Gutiérrez, 380 Calle 3C Oriente Sur; several buses a day (1 hr.) to San Cristóbal de Las Casas, US$1.

Mike Shawcross tells us: The waterfall at the Cueva de El Chorreadero is well worth a detour of 1 km. The road to the cave is 10 km. past Chiapa de Corzo, a few km. after you start the climb up into the mountains to get to San Cristóbal.

You can take a boat from Chiapa de Corzo from the river Grijalva, behind the Zócalo, into the Sumidero canyon, very impressive, US$25 per boat for a 2-hour trip (or US$5 p.p. if boat has 8 people), much wildlife to be seen.

(Km. 1,170) **San Cristóbal De Las Casas** (population 90,000), 85 km. beyond Tuxtla Gutiérrez, was founded in 1528 by Diego de Mazariegos and was the colonial capital of the region. It stands in a high mountain valley at 2,110 metres. It was named after Las Casas, protector of the Indians, its second bishop. There are many old churches; two of them cap the two hills which overlook the town. Santo Domingo, built in 1547, has a baroque façade, a gilt rococo interior and a famous carved wooden pulpit (see below). Museum in the Convent of Santo Domingo gives a very good history of San Cristóbal, and has a display of local costumes upstairs (open 0900-1400, Tues.-Sun.). There is a private museum of Indian dress and customs owned by Professor Moscosco, 16 de Septiembre, nr. Escuadrón. Other churches include San Nicolás, with an interesting façade, El Carmen, La Merced, and La Caridad (1715). From the Temple of Guadalupe there is a good view of the city and surrounding wooded hills. Behind the church is a crucifix made of licence plates. Various kinds of craftwork are sold in the new market, open daily, and in the Sunday markets of the local Indian villages. There is a small American colony. 25 July is *fiesta* day, when vehicles are taken uphill to be blessed by the Bishop. There is also a popular spring festival on Easter Sunday and the week after. There is a remarkable cemetery on the road to Tuxtla Gutiérrez, 2-3 km. from the centre of town. Caves near the town (reached by bus, entrance US$0.40) contain huge stalagmites and are lit for 800m.

Most Indian tribes here are members of the Tzotzil and Tzeltal groups. The Tenejapans wear black knee-length tunics; the Chamulans white wool tunics; and the Zinacantecos multicoloured outfits, with the ribbons on their hats signifying how many children they have. The Chamula and Tenejapa women's costumes are more colourful, and more often seen in town, than the men's.

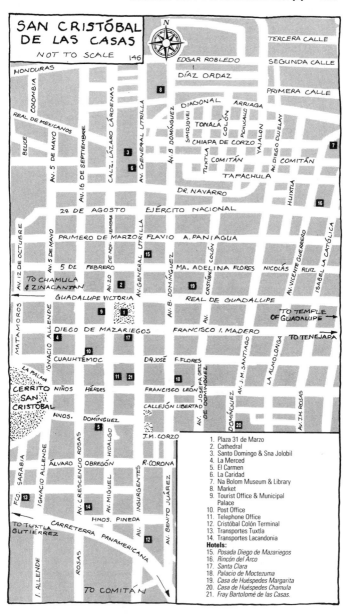

SAN CRISTÓBAL
DE LAS CASAS

NOT TO SCALE   146

N

1. Plaza 31 de Marzo
2. Cathedral
3. Santo Domingo & Sna Jolobil
4. La Merced
5. El Carmen
6. La Caridad
7. Na Bolom Museum & Library
8. Market
9. Tourist Office & Municipal Palace
10. Post Office
11. Telephone Office
12. Cristóbal Colón Terminal
13. Transportes Tuxtla
14. Transportes Lacandonia
Hotels:
15. *Posada Diego de Mazariegos*
16. *Rincón del Arco*
17. *Santa Clara*
18. *Palacio de Moctezuma*
19. *Casa de Huéspedes Margarita*
20. *Casa de Huéspedes Chamula*
21. *Fray Bartolomé de las Casas.*

N.B. Check on the situation before you visit the surrounding villages. Travellers are strongly warned not to wander around on their own, especially in the hills surrounding the town where churches are situated, as they could risk assault. Warnings can be seen in some places frequented by tourists. Heed the warning on photographing, casual clothing and courtesy (**see page** 241). Note also: international connections are difficult: only one public trunk telephone line; 30 mins.-2 hrs. wait.

Na Bolom, the house of the archaeologists Frans (died 1963) and Trudi Blom, has become a museum, open 1030-1230, 1600-1800, entrance US$1.15 (except Mon. and 7 July); address: Vicente Guerrero 33, and a beautiful individual guest house (previous reservation necessary, double room with 3 meals, US$46 a day), with good library, run by Mrs Trudi Blom. It is well worth visiting: beautifully displayed artefacts, pictures of Lacandón Indians, with information about their history and present way of life (in English), guided tour in English at 1630. Also only easily-obtainable map of Lacandón jungle. At 1600 sharp guides take you round display, rooms of beautiful old house, and garden. Entrance US$0.80. The Na Bolom library opens as follows: Mon., 1430-1800; Tues.-Sat., 0900-1300. We have been told that travellers can sometimes stay there free, in exchange for voluntary work.

Hotels Rooms for budget travellers are scarce, in the evening take what is available and change next day. *Motel Alcanfores*, on side of mountain W of city, two-bedroom bungalows (sleep 6), A; *Posada Diego de Mazariegos*, María A. Flores 2, T 8-06-21, 1 block N of Plaza, C, rec. reception at 5 de Febrero, restaurant and bar; *Parador Ciudad Real*, Diagonal Centenario 32, T 81886, W edge of city; *Bonampak*, Calzada México 5, T 8-16-21, C; *Rincón del Arco*, 8 blocks from centre, friendly, Ejército Nacional 66, T 81313, D, warmly rec., bar, restaurant, discotheque; *Molino de La Alborada*, Periférico Sur Km. 4, S of airstrip, T 80935, modern ranch-house and bungalows, D; *Santa Clara*, on Plaza, T 81140, C, colonial style, clean, good restaurant, rec.; *Palacio de Moctezuma*, Juárez 18, T 80352, colonial style, D, good Mexican food; *Posada Los Morales*, Ignacio Allende 17, E, cottages with open fires and hot showers, beautiful gardens, rec.; *Real del Valle*, Av. Guadalupe, next to Plaza, E, very clean, friendly, rec., washing facilities on roof, parking; *San Cristóbal*, Independencia near Plaza, E with bath, colonial style, renovated, pleasant; *Parador Mexicano*, Av. 5 de Mayo 38, T 81515, D, tennis court, quiet and pleasant; *Posada Capri*, Insurgentes 54, near Cristóbal Colón bus terminal, T 80015, D; 2 *Hoteles Mónica*, larger at Insurgentes 33, E, nice patio, restaurant, bar, rec., and smaller at 5 de Febrero 18 (T 81367), E (also have furnished bungalows to rent on road to San Juan Chamula); *Ciudad Real*, on Plaza, T 80187, clean, good value, good restaurant, attractive rooms, but noisy parrot talks a lot, D; *Molino de Las Casas*, small bungalows in spacious grounds near Pan-American Highway, D; *San Martín*, Calle Real de Guadalupe 16, T 80533, near Plaza, E, clean, good value, hot water, left-luggage, check you have enough blankets; *Maya Quetzal*, on Pan-American Highway, adjoining restaurant, E; *Fray Bartolomé de Las Casas*, Insurgentes and Niños Héroes, T 80932, D, with bath, nice rooms and patio, can be noisy, cold at night but extra blankets available; *Casa de Huéspedes Chamula*, Calle Julio M. Corzo, clean, hot showers, washing facilities, friendly, parking, noisy, E, rec.; *Pensión Ramos*, Cuauhtémoc 12, E with bath and hot water, small, rec. *Posada Insurgente*, Av. Insurgentes 5, clean, hot water, basic, but cheap F (bargain), one block from C.Colón station; *Casa de Huéspedes Margarita*, Real de Guadalupe 34, E in private room without bath, gringo hotel, spotless communal sleeping E, washing and toilets, clean, friendly, hot water, laundry possible, attractive restaurant serves breakfast and dinner, rather expensive, slow service, wholefood, horses and guides arranged for visits to nearby villages or caves in the mountains, US$16 incl. guides for 5 hrs; next door is *Posada Santiago*, E with private bath, clean, hot water, good cafeteria, rec.; *Posada Tepeyac*, one block from *Margarita*, friendly, clean, F; *Casa de Huéspedes Lupita*, Benito Juárez 12, F p.p., without shower; *Santo Domingo*, 28 de Agosto 4, 3 blocks from Zócalo, F, clean, hot showers, restaurant in same building; *Posada del Caudil*, Mexicanos, F, hot shower, clean, kitchen and washing facilities, good value; *Posada El Cerillo*, F, hot showers, washing facilities, not very clean but nice atmosphere, Av. B. Domínguez 27; *Jovel*, Flavio Av. Paniagua 28, T 8-17-34, F, new, clean, quiet, friendly, will store luggage, highly rec.; *Hueyzacatlan*, Insurgentes 55, F, clean, hot water, roof leaks in heavy rain, rec. at the price. *Baños Mercederos*, Calle 1° de Marzo 55, F, shared quarters (apparently Mexicans only), good cheap meals, steam baths ($0.80 extra). (*Baños Torres* next door has no rooms.) At No. 25 and No. 59 of the same street, pleasant rooms with families, quiet, clean, friendly, E, also good food. Several unmarked guest houses.

Camping *Rancho San Nicolás*, at end of Calle Francisco León, 1½ km. E of centre, beautiful, quiet location, is a trailer park (not secure for tent-camping), but do take warm blankets or clothing as the temperature drops greatly at night, hot showers, US$0.80 p.p., rooms available at same price, children free. *La Amistad* trailer park and campground is 27 km. from San Cristóbal (4 km. before Teopisca) on the Pan-American Highway towards Comitán. Hook-ups, hot showers, fresh vegetables. "White gas" available at small store on corner across from NE corner of main market (Chiwit).

Restaurants Restaurants close quite early. *El Fandango*, ex-*Olla Podrida*, US-run and frequented, international menu, rather expensive, slow service, handicrafts, English book exchange, Diego de Mazariegos 24. *El Mural*, Av. Crescencio Rojas, pleasant; *Yin Yang*, 28 de Agosto, outstanding food and decor, friendly service; *Café Torreón* in Plaza outside La Merced church. *La Plaza*, upstairs, SW corner of Plaza, clean. *La Parrilla*, Av. Belisario Domínguez 35, evenings only, good cheap grills. *Fulano*, on Flores near Plaza, excellent set meal. *El Patio*, next to *Posada Diego de Mazariegos*, try their coffee with liqueur, very exotic; *El Unicornio*, Av. Insurgentes 33a, is "gringo place", Italian food. *La Parroquia*, large and airy restaurant, on Guadalupe Victoria nr. 16 de Septiembre, the haunt of the local middle class. *Normita*, Av. Benito Juárez, good Mexican food, open 1300-1500 and for supper, owner plays guitar and his wife and daughter sing, billboard with cheap accommodation. *Tuluc*, Insurgentes 5 (owner changes money at good rate), good value, near Plaza; close by is *Rafaello*, Madero 9, modern, elegant, sells fine Indian weavings; also rec. are *La Peñita* and *Capri* on Insurgentes; *La Casa Blanca*, on Guadalupe, cheap; *Adelina y Martina*, 28 de Agosto, good, cheap, very friendly; *Cafetería San Cristóbal*, Dr José F. Flores near Plaza, very clean, good coffee, rec. *El Punto*, Domínguez y Madero, good pizza. *El Mesón Coleto*, Madero, good and cheap Mexico food; *El Langostino*, Madero 9, good seafood; *Los Arcos*, varied menu, on Madero. *Madre Tierra*, Insurgentes (opp. Franciscan church), Anglo-Mexican owned, European dishes, vegetarian specialities, wholemeal breads, pies, classical music, popular with travellers; *La Familia*, Av. Gen. Utrilla, vegetarian dishes, somewhat "hippie"; *El Trigal*, 1° de Marzo, restaurant and shop, vegetarian, good. Wholemeal bread at health-food shop marked with star-shape near post office; *Cafetería Macondo*, Madero 20, good tea and coffee, classical music and chess. Good cake at *Pan y Arte*, Ignacio Allende 5, amber jewellery for sale. Many others. San Cristóbal is not lively in the evenings: main meeting place is around ponche stall on Plaza.

Shopping Part of the ex-convent of Santo Domingo has been converted into a cooperative, *Sna Jolobil*, selling handicrafts from many Indian villages (best quality, so expensive; also concerts by local groups). For local goods try *Miscelánea Betty*, Gen. Utrilla 45, good value. A good place to buy handicrafts is at *Doña Paula*,

Calle Real de Guadalupe 25, just off the Plaza (there are craft shops all along the Guadalupe; the farther along, the cheaper) and *El Quetzal* for costumes from local villages. Beautiful handicrafts by Guatemalan refugees are sold in their place in the Seminario, Julio M.Corzo 16B, opposite *Casa de Huéspedes Chamula*; quality high and prices lower than in Guatemala. (If you want to visit the refugee camps, ask the Solidarity committee people in the Seminario). For jewellery at reasonable prices, try *Terra Amata*, Real de Guadalupe 5. (See also under Tenejapa, **page** 240). Main market is worth seeing as well. Bookshop *Soluna*, has good 2nd-hand stock and postcards. Bookshop, good, next to *Hotel San Martin* on Guadalupe.

Laundromat Lava Sec, Av. Rosas near Niños Héroes. Close to Plaza on Calle B. Domínguez, 5-hour service, 3 kg. for US$1.

Exchange *Restaurants Tuluc*, Insurgentes 5, *Unicornio*, Insurgentes 33A, or *Fulano* will change travellers' cheques at a reasonable rate if the three banks on the Plaza are closed (also into Guatemalan quetzales). *Casa Margarita* will change dollars. Banks (charge commission) are usually open for exchange between 1030 and 1200 only, check times; this leads to queues. *Casa de Cambio* in Lacantún travel agency, Francisco Madero 192, open daily except Sun., 0800-1730.

Language Schools Roberto Rivas Bastidas, Centro Bilingüe, Insurgentes 19, Int. 22, US$3 an hour for private lessons, rec. In the mornings, Mercedes organizes "non-touristic excursions for tourists who are different, in the villages", about US$7. Universidad Autónoma de Chiapas, Av. Hidalgo 1, Departamento de Lenguas, offers classes in English, French and Tzotzil.

Post Office Cuauhtémoc 13.

Tourist Office helpful, at the Palacio Municipal, W side of main Plaza, some English spoken. Ask here for accommodation in private house. Tours of local villages arranged for US$9 p.p. (ask for Mercedes—good guide). Maps of San Cristóbal US$0.35, also on sale at Kramsky, Diego de Mazariaga y 16 de Septiembre, behind Palacio Municipal.

Buses Beware of pickpockets at bus stations. From Mexico City direct, Cristóbal Colón at 1415, 1815, 2300. Cristóbal Colón 1st class bus to Oaxaca, about 12 hrs., at 1645 daily, book well in advance, monotonous trip, US$8.75. 622 km, robberies have been reported on these buses. To do the trip in daytime, you need to change at Tuxtla Gutiérrez (0745 Cristóbal Colón to Tuxtla, then 1100 on to Oaxaca); to Mexico City, via Tuxtepec, about 18 hrs., 1,169 km. at 2200, US$13; to Tapachula, 9 hrs., at 1200, US$6.25, 483 km.; to Puebla at 1400, US$11.25, 1,034 km.; to Tuxtla Gutiérrez, 1½ hrs., 10 a day, US$0.90. Book tickets as far in advance as possible—during Christmas and Holy Week buses are sometimes fully booked for 10 days or more.

Transportes Tuxtla has several 1st (US$2) and 2nd class (US$1.50) buses daily to Tuxtla Gutiérrez, and a 2nd class bus to Tapachula at 1330; to Tapachula via Motozintla: Transportes Tuxtla at 0800 and 0900, 5 hrs., then connections take about 3 hrs. to Tapachula. Cristóbal Colón has its own bus station on Insurgentes, 1st class; to Villahermosa, 6 hrs., US$4.50; to Arriaga, at 1200 via Tuxtla Gutiérrez, 235 km., US$2.55; to Coatzacoalcos at 0630, 576 km., US$6.25; to Orizaba 845 km.; to Chiapa de Corzo, 64 km., several daily. There is a new 210 km. paved road with fine views to Palenque; Lacandonia 2nd class bus to Palenque from 2nd class bus station on Calle Allende (where the 1st class bus station is also) at 0600 (arrives at 1200), US$2.50. First-class bus to Palenque, Trans. Tuxtla, 0600 and five others, 5 hrs., US$4.50, essential to book in advance. Same company's 2nd-class buses to Palenque, 0830 and 1600. Other buses leave one at Ocosingo, US$2, 4 hrs. Refunds of fares to Palenque when reaching Ocosingo are not rare, and you then have to make your own way. Transportes Tuxtla has a 1st class service to Palenque via Villahermosa, 0600, 9 hrs., US$8.50, and 2nd class at 0830, 1030 and 1530, but road to Villahermosa described as treacherous.

Into Guatemala Cristóbal Colón, S end of Av. Insurgentes (left luggage facilities open 0600-2000 exc. Sun. and holidays), clean station, direct 1st class buses to the Guatemalan border at Ciudad Cuauhtémoc, 170 km. every hour, 3½ hrs., US$3.25 (leave bus at border, not its final destination), plus US$0.30 to La Mesilla, 87 km., all tickets can be booked up to 4 days in advance (best is 0700 because it originates in San Cristóbal). Cristóbal Colón to Comitán (if you can't get a bus to the border, take one to Comitán and get a pick-up truck there—about US$1), 8 a day from 0700, US$2, 87 km (a beautiful, steep route). Transportes Tuxtla, S end of Av. Ignacio Allende, has several 1st and 2nd class buses, 4½ hrs., to the border daily, though these do not continue through to the Guatemalan customs post (3.7 km., uphill, taxi sometimes available, US$0.65 p.p., minimum 3 people). The 0800 Cristóbal Colón makes connections at the Guatemalan border at 1200 with El Cóndor for Huehuetenango and Guatemala City; 1200 bus from San Cristóbal is the last to make this connection. Note that it is cheaper to pay initially only to Huehuetenango and buy a ticket onwards from there (no change of bus necessary). Do not buy a ticket at the border until a bus leaves as some wait while others come and go. There is a Guatemalan consulate on the Mexican side of the border.

Air Services San Cristóbal no longer has an airport; it has been consumed by urban growth. The nearest airport is at Ocosingo (**see page** 249) about 50 km. along the Palenque road. To Tuxtla Gutiérrez Tues., Thurs., Sat. at 1345, 84 km. (Tuxtla is the major local airport for San Cristóbal **see page** 233). Regular daily flights, except Sundays, to Palenque, 0715 (some crashes); booking only at airport. Charter flights to see Lacanjá, Bonampak and Yaxchilán on the Usumacinta River, 7 hrs. in all (US$100 p.p. if plane is full, more if not). All with Aerochiapas at airport. Office in Real de Guadalupe has closed.

Excursions You are recommended to call at Na Bolom before visiting the villages, to get information on their cultures and seek advice on the reception you are likely to get. Photography is resisted by some Indians (see below) because they believe the camera steals their souls, and photographing their church is stealing the soul of God. Many Indians do not speak Spanish. On Sun. you can visit the villages of San Juan Chamula (horses can be hired near Na Bolom, to go here for a morning, at corner of Calle Comitán and Av. Vicente Guerrero, or from Julio González, who may be found at El Recoveco bookshop at 1900 each evening, or from *Casa de Huéspedes Margarita*, prices US$16-20 for horse and guide), Zinacantán and Tenejapa.

Zinacantán is reached by VW bus from market, US$0.20, ½ hr. journey, sometimes frequent stops while conductor lights rockets at roadside shrines. The men wear pink/red jackets with embroidery and tassels, the women a vivid pale blue shawl and navy skirts. At midday the women prepare a communal meal which the men eat in shifts. Main gathering place around church; the roof was recently destroyed by fire. Do *not* photograph anywhere or anything in Zinacantán.

You can catch a VW bus ride to *Chamula* every ½ hr., last at 1700, US$0.20 p.p. (or taxi, US$4) and visit the local church; a permit (US$0.40) is needed from the village (or the San Cristóbal) tourist office and photographing inside the church is absolutely forbidden. There are no pews but family groups sit or kneel on the floor, chanting, with rows of candles lit in front of them, each representing a member of the family and certain significance attached to the colours of the candles. The religion is centred around the "talking stones", and three idols and certain Christian saints. Pagan rituals held in small huts at the end of August. Pre-Lent festival ends with celebrants running through blazing harvest chaff. Just after Easter prayers are held, before the sowing season starts. Festivals in Chamula should *not* be photographed, if you wish to take other shots ask permission, people are not unpleasant, even if they refuse. The men wear grey, black or light pink tunics, the women bright blue blouses with colourful braid and navy or bright blue shawls. Good viewpoint of village and valley from hill SW of village: take road from SW corner of square, turn left towards ruined church then up flight of steps on left. Interesting walk from San Cristóbal to Chamula along the main road to a point one km. past the crossroads with the Periférico ring road (about 2½ km. from town centre); turn on to an old dirt road to the right—not sign-posted but 1st fork you come to between some farmhouses. Then back via the road through the village of Milpoleta, some 8 km. downhill, 5 hrs. for the journey round trip (allow 1 hr. for Chamula). Best not done in hot weather. Also, you can hike from Chamula to Zinacantán in 1½ hrs.: when leaving Chamula, take track straight ahead instead of turning left onto San Cristóbal road; turn left on small hill where school is (after 30 mins.) and follow a smaller trail through light forest. After an hour you reach the main road 200 m. before Zinacantán.

The Sun. market at **Tenejapa** (pleasant small *pensión*) is mainly fruit and vegetables, excellent woven items can be purchased from the weavers' cooperative near the church (and in San Cristóbal from the house at Calle 28 de Agosto 19). They also have a fine collection of old textiles in their regional ethnographic museum adjoining the handicraft shop. The cooperative can also arrange weaving classes. Buses leave from San Cristóbal market at 0700 and 1100 (1½ hr. journey), and colectivos every hour. We have been warned about threatening behaviour and violence in Tenejapa, but probably OK to visit in daytime if one behaves discreetly, ask permission to take pictures and expect to pay. Market thins out by noon.

Two other excursions can be made, by car or local bus, from San Cristóbal S on the Pan-American Highway (½ hr. by car) to **Amatenango Del Valle**, a Tzeltal village where the women make and fire pottery in their yards, and then SE (15 min. by car) to Aguacatenango, picturesque village at the foot of a mountain. Continue 1 hr. along road past Villa las Rosas (hotel) to **Venustiano Carranza**, women with fine costumes, extremely good view of the entire valley.

SE of San Cristóbal, 10 km., are the Grutas de San Cristóbal, caves with entrance (US$0.40) in a beautiful park, take the *camioneta* opposite *Madre Tierra* restaurant.

Get to outlying villages by bus or communal VW bus (both very packed); buses leave very early, and often don't return until next day, so you have to stay overnight; lorries are more frequent. To Zinacantán catch also VW bus from market. Buses from the market area to San Andrés Larrainzar (bus at 1000, 1100, 1400, overnight stay required, return at 0600) and Tenejapa. Transportes Fray

Bartolomé de Las Casas, behind Transportes Tuxtla, has buses to Chanal, Chenalhó (US$13 with taxi, return, one hr. stay), Pantelhó, Yajalón and villages en route to Ocosingo. Transportes Lacandonia on Av. Crescencio Rosas also go to the interior villages of Huistán, Oxchuc, Yajalón, on the way to Palenque, Pujiltic, La Mesilla and Venustiano Carranza. If you are in San Cristóbal for a limited period of time it is best to rent a car to see the villages.

Warning   Remember that locals are particularly sensitive to proper dress (i.e. neither men nor women should wear shorts, or revealing clothes) and manners; persistent begging should be countered with courteous, firm replies. It is best not to take cameras to villages: there are good postcards and photographs on sale. Drunkenness is quite open and at times forms part of the rituals—best not to take umbrage if accosted.

Follow the 170-km. paved road via Teopisca (*pensión*, F, comfortable), past **Comitán** (85 km.), a lively town of 55,000 people at 1,580 metres above sea level with a large, shady Plaza. Buses from San Cristóbal de la Casas with Cristóbal Colon, hourly, last bus back at 1900. Buses, kombis and pick-up trucks from Comitán run to the border at Ciudad Cuauhtémoc (not a town, despite its name; just a few buildings and a small restaurant with basic rooms).

Hotels in Comitán   Accommodation inferior in quality and almost twice the price of San Cristóbal. *Robert's*, 1 Av. Poniente Sur, T 20031, C, restaurant. *Los Lagos de Montebello*, T 20657, on Pan-American Highway, noisy but good, C; *Internacional*, D, Av. B. Domínguez 22, T 20112, near Plaza, decent restaurant. *Delfín*, on Plaza, E, fairly clean, as is *Hospedaje Santo Domingo*, Calle Central B. Juárez 45, E; *Ideal*, 2a Sur Oriente, clean, friendly, E, centrally located. *Casa de Huéspedes Río Escondido*, next to *Robert's*, F. *Posada Panamericana*, F, basic, and *Posada Maya*, F, both on 1 Av. Poniente Norte.

Restaurants   *Nevelandia*, clean, rec., and *Café Casa de La Cultura*, on the Plaza. *L'Uccello*, Italian, 1 Av. Poniente Norte, rec. *Cancún*, 2 Calle Sur Poniente. *Puerto Arturo* on Blvd. Dr. Belisario Domínquez is good. Several small *comedores* on the Plaza.

Exchange   Bancomer, on plaza will exchange Amex travellers' cheques.

Guatemalan Consulate   Open till 2000 at 2a Av. Norte Poniente 28; visa (if required) US$10, valid 1 year, multiple entry. Swiss citizens can obtain a free map of Guatemala from their Consulate.

Tourist Office   3a Norte Poniente, near 1a Poniente Norte, helpful.

A road branches off the Pan-American Highway 16 km. after Comitán to a very beautiful region of vari-coloured lakes, the **Lagunas De Montebello**. Off the road to Montebello, 30 km. from the Pan-American Highway, lie the ruins of **Chinkultic**, with temples, ballcourt, carved stone stelae and *cenote* (deep round lake) in beautiful surroundings; from the signpost they are about 3 km. along a dirt road and they close at 1600. Watch and ask for the very small sign and gate where road to ruins starts, worth visiting when passing.

Buses marked Tziscao to the Lagunas de Montebello (60 km. from Comitán, about 2 hrs.), via the Lagunas de Siete Colores (so-called because the oxides in the water give varieties of colours) leave frequently from 2 Av. Poniente Sur between 2 and 3 Calles, 4 blocks from Plaza in Comitán, the buses go as far as Laguna Bosque Azul; **Tziscao** is 9 km. along the road leading right from the park entrance, which is 3 km. before Bosque Azul; five buses a day Comitán-Tziscao, bumpy ride; the last bus back is at 1600 and connects with the 1900 bus to San Cristóbal. (US$0.90., VW Combis from Comitán bus station take half the time and cost only 10% more. The Bosque Azul area is now a reserve: there are, as well as picnic areas, an *Albergue Turístico* at Lake Tziscao (10 km., F, rooms for 4-6, no hot water, US$2.50 p.p., dirty kitchen facilities, camping US$1.60 per site incl. use of hotel facilities; boats for hire) two very basic food shops in the village, and there are small caves. The area is noted for its orchids and birdlife, including the famous *quetzal*; very crowded at weekends and holidays; better to stay at *Posada Las Orquídeas*, Km. 32, on the road to Montebello near Hidalgo and the ruins of Chinkultic, dormitory or cabin, F, family-run, very basic but friendly, small restaurant serving Mexican food. CREA Youth Hostel, Las Margaritas.

From Comitán the road winds down to the Guatemalan border at Ciudad Cuauhtémoc via La Trinitaria (restaurant but no hotel). Beyond the Guatemalan post at La Mesilla, the El Tapón section, a beautiful stretch, leads to Huehuetenango, 85 km. Allow 10 hours to reach Guatemala City by bus, not 6 as advised. This route is far more interesting than the one through Tapachula; the border crossing at Ciudad Cuauhtémoc is also reported as easier than that at Talismán. A tourist card for Guatemala can be obtained at the border, normally available for 30 days, renewable in Guatemala City, US$1. Holders of most European passports do not need visas (note that the British do), only tourist cards. Visas are also available at the border but buses do not wait for those who alight to obtain them. You pay US$0.45 to leave Mexico and 2 quetzales to enter Guatemala, and the border is open until 1900. Have your Mexican tourist card handy as it will be inspected at the Río San Gregorio, about 20 km. before the border. Don't change money with the Guatemalan customs officials: the rates they offer are worse than those given by bus drivers or in banks (and these are below the rates inside the country).

Buses are "de paso" from San Cristóbal so no advance booking is possible. The Cristóbal Colón bus leaves Comitán every hour for the border at Ciudad Cuauhtémoc, fare US$1.50. Frequent 2nd-class buses also by Transportes Tuxtla, US$1.10 (station at 4a Sur Poniente between 3a and 4a Poniente Sur). Another line leaves at 0745 for Ciudad Cuauhtémoc. From here take a taxi to the Guatemalan side and get your passport stamped to allow entry for a month. Cristóbal Colón (terminal on the Pan-American Highway) has 1st class buses to Mexico City at 0900, 1100 and 1600 (which leave the border 2½ hrs. earlier), fare US$24; to Oaxaca at 0700 and 1900, US$14; to Tuxtla Gutiérrez at 0600 and 1600, US$3.50, and to Tapachula (via Arriaga) at 1200 and 1800, US$9. Transportes Tuxtla, 3 Calle Norte Poniente and 1 Av. Poniente Norte, has 6 1st class (US$3.50) and 8 2nd class (US$3.40) buses daily to Tuxtla Gutiérrez; a bus to Tapachula, via Arriaga, at 1100, US$11; to Arriaga at 1215; and 7 buses daily to Motozintla (connections to Tapachula), US$3.30. There are colectivos running between the two border posts.

Airport Flights available from Comitán to Lacanjá, Bonampak, Yaxchilán, contact Capitán Pérez Esquinca, T Comitán 4-91.

Travellers report that the Lacandón Indians at Lacanjá are rude and threatening if one doesn't buy their tourist wares.

N.B. Entering Mexico from Guatemala, it is forbidden to bring in fruit and vegetables; rigorous checking at two checkpoints to avoid the spread of plant diseases.

YUCATAN PENINSULA (9)

The peninsula of Yucatán is a flat land of tangled scrub in the drier north-west, merging into exuberant jungle and tall trees in the wetter south-east. There are no surface streams. The underlying geological foundation is a horizontal bed of limestone in which rainwater has dissolved enormous caverns. Here and there their roofs have collapsed, disclosing deep holes or *cenotes* in the ground, filled with water. Today this water is raised to surface-level by wind-pumps: a typical feature of the landscape. It is hot during the day but cool after sunset. Humidity is often high. All round the peninsula are splendid beaches fringed with palm groves and forests of coconut palms. The best time for a visit is from October to March.

The people are divided into two groups: the pure-blooded Maya Indians, the minority, and the *mestizos*. The Maya women wear *huipiles*, or white cotton tunics (silk for *fiestas*) which may reach the ankles and are embroidered round the square neck and bottom hem. Ornaments are mostly gold. A few of the men still wear straight white cotton (occasionally silk) jackets and pants, often with gold or silver buttons, and when working protect this dress with aprons. Carnival is the year's most joyous occasion, with concerts, dances, processions. Yucatán's folk dance is the Jarana, the man dancing with his hands behind his back, the woman raising her skirts a little, and with interludes when they pretend to be bullfighting. During pauses in the music the man, in a high falsetto voice, sings *bambas* (compliments) to the woman.

The Maya are a courteous, gentle, strictly honest and scrupulously clean people. They drink little, except on feast days, speak Mayan, and profess Christianity laced with a more ancient nature worship. In Yucatán and Quintana Roo, the economy has long been dependent on the export of *henequén* (sisal), and chicle, but both are facing heavy competition from substitutes and tourism is becoming ever more important.

The early history and accomplishments of the Maya when they lived in Guatemala and Honduras before their mysterious trek northwards is given in the introduction to the book. They arrived in Yucatán about A.D. 600 and later rebuilt their cities, but along different lines, probably because of the arrival of Toltecs in the ninth and tenth centuries. Each city was autonomous, and in rivalry with other cities. Before the Spaniards arrived the Maya had developed a writing in which the hieroglyphic was somewhere between the pictograph and the letter. Bishop Landa collected their books, wrote a very poor summary, the *Relación de las Cosas de Yucatán*, and with Christian but unscholarlike zeal burnt all his priceless sources.

In 1511 some Spanish adventurers were shipwrecked on the coast. Two survived. One of them, Juan de Aguilar, taught a Maya girl Spanish. She became interpreter for Cortés after he had landed in 1519. The Spaniards found little to please them: no gold, no concentration of natives, but Mérida was founded in 1542 and the few natives handed over to the conquerors in *encomiendas*. The Spaniards found them difficult to exploit: even as late as 1847 there was a major revolt, mainly

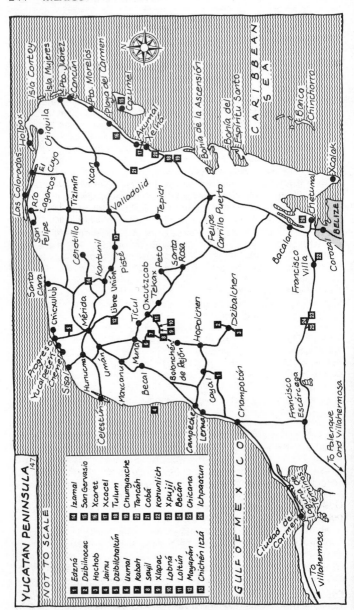

YUCATÁN PENINSULA 147

NOT TO SCALE

1 Edzná	**14** Izamal
2 Dzibilnocac	**15** San Gervasio
3 Hochob	**16** Xcaret
4 Jaina	**17** Xcacel
5 Dzibilchaltún	**18** Tulum
6 Uxmal	**19** Chunyaxche
7 Kabah	**20** Tancáh
8 Sayil	**21** Cobá
9 Xlapac	**22** Kohunlich
10 Labná	**23** Xpujil
11 Loltún	**24** Becán
12 Chichén Itzá	**25** Chicana
13 Mayapán	**26** Ichpaatun

arising from the inhuman conditions in the *henequén* plantations.

Many tourists come to Yucatán, mostly to see the ancient Maya sites and to stay at the new coastal resorts. The places which attract most visitors are Mérida, Palenque, Chichén Itzá and Uxmal. A good paved road (four ferries) runs from Coatzacoalcos through Villahermosa, Campeche and Mérida (Route 180). All the great archaeological sites except Palenque are on or just off this road and its continuation beyond Mérida. An inland road has been built from Villahermosa to Campeche to avoid the ferries; it gives easy access to Palenque. If time is limited, take a bus from Villahermosa to Chetumal via Francisco Escárcega, which can be done overnight as the journey is not very interesting (unless you want to see the Mayan ruins off this road—see pages 286). From Chetumal travel up the coast to Cancún, then across to Mérida. A train from Mexico City to Mérida goes through Palenque; Pullman passengers can make the whole trip without leaving the car in 2 nights. Route 307 from Puerto Juárez and Cancún to Chetumal is all paved and in very good condition. Air services from the USA and Mexico City are given under Mérida. Details of the direct road route, with buses, between Guatemala and Yucatán are given on **page 264**. The state of Quintana Roo is on the eastern side of the Yucatán Peninsula and has recently become the largest tourist area in Mexico with the development of the resort of Cancún, and the parallel growth of Isla Mujeres and Cozumel. Growth has been such, in both Yucatán and Quintana Roo, that there are insufficient buses at peak times, old 2nd class buses may be provided for 1st class tickets and 2nd class buses take far too many standing passengers. There is a lack of information services. Where beaches are unspoilt they often lack all amenities. Many hotels are spartan. **Warning** So many of the tourists coming to the coastal resorts know no Spanish that price hikes and short-changing have become very common there, making those places very expensive if one is not careful. In the peak, winter season, prices are increased anyway.

N.B.: Travellers have found that guards will not permit use of tripods for photography at sites.

Coatzacoalcos, 186,000 people, the Gulf Coast gateway for Yucatán, was 1½ km. from the mouth of its wide river, but now has expanded down to it. It is hot, frantic and lacking in culture, and there is not much to do save watch the river traffic (river too polluted for fishing and swimming—less than salubrious discos on the beach by the pier at the river-mouth; beach is dangerous at nights, do not sleep there or loiter). Ocean-going vessels go upriver for 39 km. to ***Minatitlán***, the oil and petrochemical centre (145,000 people; airport), whose huge oil refinery sends its products by pipeline to Salina Cruz on the Pacific (*Hotel Nacional*, on main street, F, fan, hot water, clean; *Plaza*; *Reforma*, close to ADO terminal). The road between the two towns carries very heavy industrial traffic. The offshore oil rigs are serviced from Coatzacoalcos. Sulphur is exported from the mines, 69 km. away.

Coatzacoalcos Hotels Very difficult as all hotels are used by oil workers. Don't spend the night on the street if you can't find lodging. Prices double those of hotels elsewhere. *Enríquez*, good, A; *Carilla*, F, with shower, basic. *Motel Colima* at km. 5, Carretera Ayucan-Coatzacoalcos, may have rooms if none in Coatzacoalcos; it is clean, in a quiet position, but does have a lot of red-light activity.

Restaurants Meals at *Gloria Café*; *Los Lopitos*, Hidalgo 615, good tamales and tostadas. Cheap restaurants on the top floor of the indoor market near the bus terminal. There is a 24-hr. restaurant in one of the streets just off the main Plaza, good empanadas with cream.

Bus to Mexico City, US$11; to Mérida US$12.25. To Veracruz (312 km, US$3.65, 7¼ hrs.), Ciudad del Carmen (US$7.35), Salina Cruz (US$2); to Minatitlán, to which taxis also ply. To Villahermosa, US$3.

Rail Railway station is 5 km. from town at Cuatro (for Mexico City and Mérida) at end of Puerto Libre bus route and on Playa Palma Sola route, smelly and dingy, the through train is swept out here; irregular bus services. Better walk about ½ km. to the main road and get a bus there, US$0.10. Train to Tehuantepec takes 13 hrs. (208 km.). Train to Mérida (at 1240). Train to Palenque, 1600. Coatzacoalcos-Campeche at 2030. Another station, in the city centre, serves Salina Cruz, small and dingy. The train to Salina Cruz leaves daily at 0700, costs US$2.50 for the 12 hr. journey 2nd class.

Air Services Minatitlán airport, 30 mins.

Cárdenas 116 km. from Coatzacoalcos and 48 km. from Villahermosa, is headquarters of the Comisión del Grijalva, which is encouraging regional development. Between Cárdenas and Villahermosa are many stalls selling all varieties of bananas, a speciality of the area, and the road passes through the Samaria oilfield. (From Chontalpa there is irregular transport to Raudales on the lake formed by the Netzahualcoyotl dam.) It is very hard to find accommodation in Cárdenas, *Hotel Xol-Ou*, cheapest, E, with bath, a/c, parking, clean, on main plaza.

Villahermosa, (pop. 275,000) capital of Tabasco state, is on the River Grijalva, navigable to the sea. It used to be a dirty town, but is now improving, though it is very hot and rainy. The cathedral, ruined in 1973, has been rebuilt. There is a warren of modern colonial-style pedestrian malls throughout the central area. The Centro de Investigaciones de las Culturas Olmecas is set in a new modern complex with a large public library, expensive restaurant, airline offices and souvenir shops, a few minutes' walk S out of town along the river bank. Three floors of well laid out displays of Mayan and Olmec artefacts, with an excellent bookshop. Entry US$0.40, open 0900-2000.

At the other side of town is Tabasco 2000, a futuristic mall/hotel/office area with an original statue of fishermen.

In 1925 an expedition discovered huge sculptured human and animal figures, urns and altars in almost impenetrable forest at La Venta, 96 km. from Villahermosa. Nothing to see there now: about 1950 the monuments were threatened with destruction by the discovery of oil nearby. The poet Carlos Pellicer got them hauled all the way to a woodland area near Villahermosa, now the **Parque Museo de La Venta**, Blvd. Adolfo Ruíz Cortines, with scattered lakes, next to a children's playground and almost opposite the old airport entrance.

There they are dispersed in various small clearings. The huge heads—one of them weighs 20 tons—are Olmec, a culture which flourished about 1150-150 B.C; this is an experience which should not be missed. Be sure to take insect-repellant for the visit. It takes 1 hr. to walk around, excellent guides, speak Spanish and English. *Son et lumière* Sun., Tues., Thur. 1900, Fri., and Sat., 1700 and 2015. There is also a zoo of lonely, dispirited and wretched creatures from the Tabasco jungle: monkeys, alligators, deer, wild pigs and birds. Open 0900-2000, entrance US$1, bus, marked "Gracitol", Villahermosa-La Venta from bus terminal US$0.40. Bus Circuito No. 1 from outside 2nd class bus terminal goes past Parque La Venta.

Villahermosa is heaving under pressure from the oil boom, which is why it is now such an expensive place. Buses to Mexico City are often booked up well in advance, as are hotel rooms, especially during the holiday season (May onwards). Overnight free parking (no facilities) in the Campo de Deportes. It is hard to find swimming facilities in Villahermosa: Ciudad Deportiva pool for cardholders only. There is a bull ring. Ash Wednesday is celebrated from 1500 to dusk by the throwing of water in balloon bombs and buckets at anyone who happens to be on the street.

Hotels   The price difference between a reasonable and a basic hotel can be negligible, so one might as well go for the former. Best is *Exalaris Hyatt*, Juárez 106, T 34444, all services, L; *Holiday Inn Tabasco Plaza*, Paseo Tabasco 1407, T 34400, A-L, 4 km. from centre, restaurant, bar, entertainment; *Maya-Tabasco*, on Paseo Tabasco, T 21111, all services, A; *Villahermosa Villa*, B, pool, excellent service, highly rec. in its price range; *Plaza Independencia*, Independencia 123, T 21299, C; *Don Carlos*, C, Madero 422, central, slightly faded parts being rebuilt, clean, helpful, good restaurant (accepts American Express card— one of the few that does) nearby parking; *Palma de Mallorca*, Madero 510, T 20144, D; many other hotels along Madero. *El Choco*, Merino 100, T 29444, C, friendly, clean, a/c, near ADO terminal; *Sureste*, one block from ADO bus station, D, a/c, small but clean and friendly; *Los Carlos*, Hnos. Basta-Zozoya 624, T 26409, E, a/c, hot water, from ADO terminal, cross main street, go 2 blocks then left 2 blocks; *Madero*, Madero 301, T 20516, E, hot water, good value, some rooms for 4 are cheaper; *María Dolores*, Aldama 104, a/c, D, hot showers, excellent restaurant (closed Sundays). *Oviedo*, Lerdo 303, good, E; *San Miguel*, Lerdo 315, T 21500, good value, but some rooms damp, no hot water p.m., E; *Tabasco*, Lerdo 317, T 20077, F, clean, constant hot water, rec; *Aurora*, Av. 27 de Febrero 623, F, basic, hot showers, E; *Sofia*, Zaragoza 408, T 26055, E, central, tolerable but overpriced, a/c. There is a CREA youth hostel at the Ciudad Deportiva, but it doesn't accept travellers arriving in the evening (4 km. SW of the bus station).

N.B. Tourists are often wiser to go directly to Palenque for accommodation; cheaper and no competition from business travellers. Villahermosa can be difficult for lone women: local men's aggressive behaviour said to be due to the effect of eating iguanas.

Camping   at the old airport, near Parque La Venta, mosquitoes.

Restaurants   *El Mural*, highly rec., 4-course lunch with drink included, US$4, dinner US$8, with band; *La Embajada*, good local food, suckling pig is the best, open for lunch only; a good restaurant at *Hotel Madam*, Madero 408, good breakfast; *La Rueda* serves good local specialities; the *Casino* for odd dishes like turtle steaks and dogfish; *Los Azulejos* serves good lunch for US$2.40; *Blanca*

Mariposa, near entrance to Parque La Venta, rec. Avoid the bad and expensive tourist eating places on and near the river front.

Local Transport Taxis now mainly on a fixed-route collective system (US$1 per stop), which can be a problem if you want to go somewhere else. You may have to wait a long time before a driver without fares agrees to take you.

Exchange American Express, Sáenz 222.

Postal Services DHL, parcel courier service, Paseo Tabasco.

Tourist Office in the 1st class bus station (English spoken) and another close to the La Venta park, at Paseo Grijalva and Paseo Tabasco, both good, closed 1300-1600.

Airport Daily services to Mexico City, Mérida, 1 hr. US$100, Oaxaca, Ciudad del Carmen, Minatitlán, Veracruz and Cancún, from airport 15 km. SE, out along the Palenque road, VW bus to town US$3 p.p., taxi US$7 for 2. Local flights to Palenque and Bonampak. Aeroméxico office, Blvd. Carlos Pellicer 511, T 24389; Mexicana, Av. 4 y Calle 13, Desarollo Urbano Tabasco 2000, or Mina y Paseo Tabasco, 2nd floor, T 35044 (airport T 21164).

Buses Bus station (ADO) with restaurant, but very uncomfortable owing to poor ventilation, 20 min.-walk to centre; no lockers for bags at ADO terminal, luggage may be left with Sra. Ana, in minute restaurant/shop at Pedro y Fuente 817, 100 metres from ADO terminal, reliable, open till 2000, cheap. Information office at this station with hotel lists. The booking system is complicated, infuriating and best avoided if possible: tickets can be difficult to obtain, even in low season. The 2nd class bus station is only 5 mins. walk from centre and 2½ blocks (15 mins. walk) from 1st class station: usually in disarray and it is difficult to get a ticket. Mind your belongings.

Several buses (1st class) to Mexico City, US$16, 12 hrs., direct bus leaves 1815 and 2015, expect to wait a few hours for Mexico City buses and at least ½ hr. in the ticket queue. To Jalapa with ADO, 3 a day, 10 hrs.; to Campeche, US$5 (6 hrs.); to Coatzacoalcos, US$2; to Tapachula, US$9, 14 hrs. Many buses to Mérida 8 hrs., US$8 (ADO at 0920, and others, cheaper) or go 2nd class from Palenque, **see page** 249) to San Cristóbal, US$4.50, 6 hrs.; also 2nd class bus with one change at Tuxtla, leaves 0800, arrives 2100, fine scenery but treacherous road. Cristóbal Colón from ADO terminal to Oaxaca via Coatzacoalcos and Tehuantepec at 0800 and 1900, 1st class, stops at about 7 places, US$10. Bus to Veracruz, US$7, 8 hrs.; to Chetumal, US$8.50, 10 hrs., but the road is now in a very bad state and it can take much longer, four buses. To Catazaja, US$2, 1½ hrs. To Palenque, US$2.50, 2½ hrs., leaves 0600, 0800, 1330 and 1630. Circuito Maya, US$2.60; 1st class 1000 (buy ticket day before) and 1700. To Emiliano Zapata and Tenosique (for Río San Pedro crossing into Guatemala—**see page** 265), buses 0700, 0800, 1330, 3-4 hrs.

Excursion NW of Villahermosa are the Maya ruins of *Comacalco*, reached by bus (3 a day by ADO, US$1.20, or local Zimillera bus, US$0.90 over dirt roads), then taxi US$2 or walk 3 km. The ruins are unique in Mexico because the palaces and pyramids are built of bricks, long and narrow like ancient Roman bricks, and not of stone. From Comacalco go to *Paraíso* near the coast, frequent buses from town to the beach 8 km. away. Interesting covered market, good cocoa. *Centro Turístico* beach hotel, D, clean, no hot water, food and drink expensive. Also Hotel *Hidalgo*, in centre, F, clean.

Further Travel If the Villahermosa-Mexico City bus is booked up, try taking the train from **Teapa** (buses run hourly between Teapa and Villahermosa on a paved road, 50 km), 1st class pullman fare, US$25. The dining car is good but very expensive. Check in rainy season whether bridges are OK. (It took one passenger 56 hrs. to travel some 950 km. after being diverted). Vendors ply the train with local foods and drinks. Journey 14 hrs. Teapa is a nice, clean little town with several cheap hotels (*Casa de Huéspedes Mija*, F, in the main street) and beautiful surroundings. The square is pleasant, and you can swim in the river or in the sulphur pool, El Azufre and cavern of Cocona (dear). From Teapa, Tapijulapa on the Chiapas border can be visited, beautiful views. Bus to Chiapa de Corzo at 0730, 7 hrs., US$4, lovely, mountainous landscape (**see page** 233).

80 km. SW of Villahermosa on Route 195 is **Pichucalco**, a very quiet town with some interesting tiles in the main Plaza. *Hotel México*, on left turn from bus station, E, with bath, fan, clean but musty, *Vila*, on Plaza, *Jardín*, F, noisy, *La Selva*. Buses almost every hour to Villahermosa, US$1.50.

Villahermosa to Guatemala by car is by route 195 and 190 to Ciudad Cuauhtémoc via San Cristóbal de Las Casas. Highway 195 is fully paved, but narrow and winding with landslides and washouts in the rainy season, high altitudes, beautiful scenery. If this route is impassable, travel back by route 180 to Acayucan, to 190, via 185 and go to Ciudad Cuauhtémoc or by route 200 to Tapachula.

From Villahermosa you can fly to Campeche, or sometimes by a small plane carrying 3 passengers, to Palenque, which can also be reached by the new paved road from Villahermosa to Campeche (no petrol stations until the Palenque turn-off; if you look like running out, turn left half-way for Macuspana, where there is one). This road has a turning at 117 km. from Villahermosa for Palenque, 26 km. away on a good paved but winding road. (If short of time you can fly Mérida-Villahermosa at 0655, hire car at Villahermosa airport, drive to Palenque and back with 3½ hrs. at ruins, and catch 2205 flight from Villahermosa to Mexico City.) Palenque can also be reached by paved road from San Cristóbal de Las Casas, a beautiful ride via **Ocosingo**, a not particularly attractive place (70,000 people) which has a local airport and many new hotels (two E, of which the best is on the main street across from the Plaza, *Central* on Plaza, F, shower, clean, verandah, and several others F) and clean restaurants. Road to ruins of **Toniná**, 12 km. away, is unpaved but marked with signs once you leave Ocosingo (jeep rec.); well worth visiting the ruins excavated by a French government team. Temples are in the Palenque style with internal sanctuaries in the back room. Stelae are in very diverse forms, as are wall panels, and some are in styles and in subject unknown at any other Mayan site. Ask guardian to show you second unrestored ballcourt and the sculpture kept at his house. (Take drinks with you; nothing available at the site.) Beside the Ocosingo-Toniná road is a marsh, frequented by thousands of swallows in January. The Agua Azul waterfalls (**see page** 254) are between Toniná and Palenque, on your left. The road to Palenque from San Cristóbal (Route 195) is now reported OK. Excellent road from Campeche, 5 hrs.' drive, only rough stretch about 1 hr. from Palenque;

toll bridge US$0.60.

Palenque, 143 km. from Villahermosa on a good, paved road (public transport difficult Sun.), is a splendid experience, with its series of Old Maya hilltop temples in remarkably good condition. It is best to visit the ruins early in the morning. The site is in a hot jungle clearing on a steep green hill overlooking the plain and crossed by a clear cascading brook (swimming allowed at pools downstream from the museum). Interesting wildlife, mainly birds, also includes howler monkeys and mosquitoes. The ruins are impressive indeed, particularly the Pyramid of the Inscriptions, easy to climb from the back, in the heart of which was discovered an intact funerary crypt with the Sarcophagus of the Sun God (you walk from the top of the pyramids into a staircase, descending to ground level, before having to walk up again, very humid; illuminated 1000-1600 only; take flashlight). Check time of opening of crypt. The temples around, with fantastic comb-like decorations on their intact roofs, and the sculptured wall panels, are undoubtedly the most exquisite achievement of the Maya. A path behind the Temple of Inscriptions leads through jungle to a small ruined temple—if you continue for 8 km. the path leads to a friendly village, the only means of access. A small museum at the ruins has some excellent classical Maya carvings (open 1000—more like 1100—to 1700). Entry to ruins, US$0.50 (Sun. free), charge for car parking. The site opens at 0800 and closes at 1700 (guide, up to 10 people). Beware of thieves at all times. The ruins are 8 km. from the town. A restaurant by the cascades serves a limited range of food, not rec. (stores luggage—compulsory on entering the ruins, no receipt—for US$0.25); shops quick to overcharge and souvenirs are dearer than elsewhere. 1-5 August is the Feria de Santo Domingo. The climate is hot and dry March—April, the coolest months are October to February. **Warning** The area is very malarial; make sure you're up-to-date with your tablets.

Fiesta Santo Domingo, first week in August.

Bus service from station to town, 5 km. goes to local bus stations, but unhelpful, be prepared to wait. Taxi from station to ruins US$1.35 p.p. with 4 people. Taxi, ruins to town US$1.20. Bus to the ruins from bus stations every 2 hrs. from 0600, 20 mins, US$0.25 until 1630. From the village to the ruins: either take a taxi, or a white VW minibus from Pemex station, or corner of Hidalgo and Allende, or the Plaza end of 5 de Mayo, or the Mayan head near bus terminals, US$0.20, 15 mins., from 0600-1800, every 15 mins. or so. It is convenient to stay at hotels near the Pemex service station, as they are also nearer the ruins and the bus stations.

Hotels (Prices treble around *fiesta* time.) *Misión Palenque*, far end of town in countryside, T 50241, complete resort, A, poor food. *Hotel La Cañada*, T 50102, very rustic but very clean, D, with fan, good value, lovely garden, good restaurant, noisy disco next door, the owner, Sr. Morales, is an expert on the ruins. *María de Sol*, next door, rooms cheap, excellent restaurant, highly rec.; *Motel Chan-Ka Inn*, at Km. 31, T 50014, closest to ruins, B, swimming pool fed from river, beautiful gardens, perfectly clean, restaurant overpriced; *Centro Turístico Tulijá*, T 50165, C, car park, convenient; hot water if you get them to turn it on; also bungalows, 10 km. from ruins, first as you enter town; reasonable restaurant; pool is dirty, book local flights here; *Hotel and Trailer Park Tulipanes*, Calle

Cañada 6, T 50201, C, basic, a/c, or fan, garage, pool, bar/restaurant next door; *Lacroix*, Hidalgo, next to church, E, will charge full room price for one or two, fan, no hot water, friendly, insects, good for motorcyclists; *Palenque*, 5 de Mayo 15, off Plaza, T 50103, E, with bath, a/c restaurant, vast, rambling menage, poor plumbing and service, has good rooms, pool, night-time robberies reported, usually through bathroom window, management unhelpful; long-distance telephone office here. *Casa de Pakal*, 1 block from Plaza, D, a/c, good but not very friendly; next door is *Misol-Ha*, at Juárez 14, T 50092, fan, with bath, E. *Santa Elena*, D, 2 blocks from ADO terminal, simple and quiet. *Kash'lan*, 5 de Mayo, T 5-03-09, D, with bath, clean, helpful owner; *Avenida*, Juárez 173, T 50116, opp. 2nd-class bus station above cinema, with restaurant, clean, large rooms, parking, D, but does not display price in rooms so ask for government list to check, no hot showers, some rooms with balcony. *Regional*, Hidalgo, 2 blocks from Plaza, E, 100 m. from bus station, no hot showers, but rec. otherwise. *Vaca Vieja*, 5 de Mayo 42, T 50377, 3 blocks from Plaza, popular with gringos, water shortages at times, D, cafeteria; *Pensión Charpito*, Av. 20 de Noviembre 15, E. *Posada Alicia*, Av. Manuel Velásquez Suárez, F, cheap, mixed reports, rooms on left as you enter are cooler; *Casa de Huéspedes*, Hidalgo, nr. Zócalo, E with bath, only cold water, some mosquitoes.

Camping *Trailer Park Mayabel*, a bit scruffy (lots of old-fashioned "hippies"), on road to ruins 2 km. before entrance (bus from town US$0.20) for caravans and tents, also for rent, US$1 for tent or to sling hammock, palmleaf huts, good restaurant; many ticks in long grass (we're told they avoid people who eat lots of garlic!) Watch your belongings. At night, around 0100, one can often hear the howler monkeys screaming in the jungle; quite eerie, there is a jungle trail to the ruins past waterfalls. Good swimming at *Balneario and Hotel Nututún*, 3 km. along Palenque-Ocosingo road, US$1 camping site per night, rather run down, no tent rentals, toilets and bath, disco bar, at restaurant with laughable service; and beautiful lake and waterfall open to the public for a small fee. Misol-Ha, 2 km. off same road at Km. 19, see below.

Restaurants *Maya*, on plaza, fair value; at moderately priced *Tarde*, or rough restaurant *El Jade* in town. Water is often hard to get. There is a good and friendly restaurant on Av. Juárez, *Français*, opp. *Hotel Avenida*, French owner, slow and rather expensive, less on offer than on menu, has tourist information. *El Rodeo*, on main street, does good breakfasts. *La Escondida*, 20 de Noviembre, 3 or 4 blocks from the Zócalo, good food, reasonable prices, English spoken; *Las Tinajas* 20 de Noviembre y Abasolo, good, family run, excellent food, reasonable prices; *Artemio*, Av. Hidalgo, nr. Plaza, reasonably-priced food. *Las Carmelitas*, good service, reasonably priced, at Av. Benito Juárez 77. *Chan Kah*, on Plaza, steak about US$3, good atmosphere; *Comedor La Terminada*, off the main street, good value. *Tertulia*, good steaks, rec. At Km. 0.5 on Hidalgo (road to ruins) is *La Selva*, expensive, live music at weekends. Good juice bar on Plaza in front of *Hotel Palenque*. Try the ice cream at *Holanda* in the centre. An anonymous reader writes that the best value restaurant has no name, it is on 5 de Mayo, 1 block beyond the Zócalo going towards ADO bus station.

N.B. We are told that the large influx of young "hippie-like" people has put off the locals, and visitors may be given misleading information. Also, the Federal police are very strict about tourist cards—*always* keep it with you, even when eating in your hotel. The penalty is searches and jail, with large fines. Visitors should respect the local customs and dress so as not to offend—men should wear footwear and always a shirt; women wearing shorts are unwelcome.

Exchange Exchange rate only comes through at 1030, then banks open until 1230. At weekends travellers' cheques will not be changed but the owner at Farmacia Central will change US$ at a reasonable rate.

Post Office Independencia, next block to Zócalo.

Laundromat Opposite ADO bus station.

Travel Agencies ATC Tours, Calle Allende y Juárez, local 6, T 50210, and Jiménez y 5 de Mayo (*Hotel Palenque*), run private tours to other Mayan sites (Bonampak, US$50 p.p., Yaxchilán, US$55 p.p.—US$85 to both, also flights, see below, Tikal, US$100, all min. 5 people), local attractions (Agua Azul, Mi Sol Ha waterfall), horseriding in the jungle, etc.

Tourist Office in the municipal offices on plaza, open 0900-1300 and 1700-2000 (maybe). Post Office in the same building, on left-hand side.

Buses All 3 bus companies have terminals at W end of Av. Juárez. Buy ticket to leave on arrival, buses are often full, very heavy ticket sales on 1 and 15 of each month when salaries are paid. 1st class bus to/from Mexico City, ADO, at 1800, 18 hrs., 1,006 km., US$20, insist when they say "no tickets". First-class bus to Villahermosa at 0800, 1200, 1600, 1700, 1800, 2½ hrs., US$2.50. 2nd class bus to Villahermosa at 0800 and 1200. ADO buses, seven a day, to Ciudad del Carmen, US$5.50. Bus 2nd class, to Campeche, US$5, 6 hrs., daily at 1700, overcrowded, arrive early. One direct bus a day from Campeche, leaves 0200, returns from Palenque 0730, US$2 (2nd), but if you wish to travel in the daytime there is a bus to *Emiliano Zapata* 0900 and 1400. *Hotel Ramos*, opp. bus station, F, reasonable restaurant, friendly. *San Agustín*, 5 de Mayo s/n, E, some a/c, clean and good value; at least 4 other hotels in town, F and E—one by the entrance to town near the Pemex station. No alcohol on Sun.

From Emiliano Zapata you can make connections to Campeche and Mérida but the bus from Palenque sets you down at the other end of Emiliano Zapata from the bus station: you will have to cross the town (minibus US$0.15). It might be easier to change at Catazaja to the Villahermosa-Campeche ADO bus, but this journey cannot be done all in daylight. Daily 1st class bus direct to Mérida at 1700 and 2300, US$8, 8 hrs, buy tickets at Agencia Tonina from 1930 the day before; 2nd class bus leaves from restaurant *La Quebrada*, round the corner from ADO, at 0100, 7 hrs. Bus to Mérida via Campeche with Líneas Unidas de Chiapas, leaves Palenque at 1700, daily. (566 km.), numbered seats book at least 24 hrs. in advance, US$8.50, 10 hrs., scheduled to arrive at Campeche 2300, arrives in Mérida in the middle of the night; same company runs 1st class bus at 1800 (another possibility is to take 0800 to Villahermosa or 0900 to Emiliano Zapata and travel on from there). (Also to Francisco Escárcega, 3 hrs, the road is in very poor condition). Daily San Cristóbal bus to Chetumal, leaves 0100 from *Restaurant Montes Azules*, Av. Juárez, or take ADO bus to Francisco Escárcega and change.

To San Cristóbal de Las Casas, good road throughout, 1st class buses at 0700 and 1030, US$4.50; five second class buses a day between 0730 and 2200 (6 hrs.), US$2.50 via Ocosingo, or 1230 via Pichucalco, 9 hrs.; via Villahermosa by 1st-class minibus, 8 hrs. or more, leaves at 0800 and 1230, US$6. Tuxtla Gutiérrez (no 1st class buses) 5 a day, 377 km., US$4.50, via San Cristóbal de Las Casas. The San Cristóbal-Villahermosa road has been described as "treacherous." Some buses go 63 km. past ruins to the crossroads leading to the beautiful Agua Azul waterfalls (see below).

Palenque-Flores, Guatemala: two routes, one via the Río San Pedro, the other via the Río Usumacinta (**see also page 254**) going to Chancalá with the 1200 bus and continuing by bus (evening or early morning) to Frontera Echeverría. From Echeverría boats go up the river in Guatemala, to Sayaxché. No direct bus Palenque-Tuxtepec, but can be done using 7 different buses, staying overnight at, say, Acayucan.

Trains There is one train daily from Mexico City at 2010, in theory (Tomasz

Cienkus of Poland writes that railways are not for amateurs) no sleeper, US$10 1st class, US$3.50 2nd (filthy toilets), up to 31 hrs. (book Palenque hotel in advance). Tickets on sale from Estación de Ferrocarril Buenavista on day of departure after a certain hour, no numbered seats; it is apparently impossible to buy 1st class tickets in Palenque for Mexico City but you pay 1st class because from Coatzacoalcos the carriages are treated as 1st class—this is accepted practice. Railway station for Palenque is 10 km. outside town (bus goes from in front of *Posada Alicia* at 2000). Taxi, railway station to Pemex service station US$1 for 2. The slow train from Campeche to Palenque leaves at 2030 (beware of thieves), arrives at 1100. *Rápido* train to Mérida at 2100 hrs., daily, usually late, takes about 11 hrs., keep your luggage with you, US$8, 1st (only one car, no sleeper) very comfortable, US$3, 2nd, dirty and smelly and no light, take a torch and insect repellant. Tickets on sale one hour before train arrives. The train may be crowded so it may be necessary to stand all the way. It is reported that the train is sometimes unreliable with delays of up to 11 hrs. **N.B.** If returning from Palenque to Mérida by train, bear in mind that in Dec. and Jan. it is nearly impossible to make reservations.

Air Travel Light aircraft Palenque-Ocosingo (for San Cristóbal) (watch for Agua Azul falls 5-10 mins into flight) with Aerochiapas, T 80037, 8 people, supposed to leave at 0715, but more like 0830, provided there isn't a better offer to fly into the jungle. Tickets either at airstrip (shed only), or from Arrendadora de Carros Ik, two doors away from *Restaurante Maya* (on Plaza) in Palenque town. Aviacsa flies from Palenque to Villahermosa and Tuxtla, T 50210. Transfer by bus to and from Villahermosa US$13.

Other Sites Flights from Palenque to **Bonampak** and **Yaxchilán** (refreshments), in light plane for 5, US$420 per plane, to both places, whole trip 6 hrs. Prices set, list available; Aviación de Chiapas at Av. Benito Juárez and Allende, open 0800-1330 and 1600-1800, Sat. 0800-1400, to Bonampak; book at airport, may be cheaper from Tenosique, best to visit in May—the driest month; Yaxchilán, which is still unexcavated and where there are more howler monkeys around than people, is said to be more interesting. Do not visit ruins at night, it is forbidden.

Day tours from Palenque by road for US$20 p.p., but private arrangements with a kombi driver to see both could well be better: Otolum, next to *Hotel Regional*, 2 days for US$0.60 p.p., minimum 4, without food; Coop Chambalu, Calle Allende, Palenque run all-day tours to Bonampak, leaving 0500, for US$220 for the whole bus, min. 6 passengers. However you go, take good boots and umbrella for jungle walking. Bonampak is 12 km. from Frontera Echeverría, sometimes known as Frontera Corozal (food, petrol and accommodation; you must register with the Migración office) and can be reached only on foot from the crossroads with the road to Echeverría and then with great difficulty (all maps are inaccurate, directions must be asked frequently). Beware of sandflies, black flies which cause river blindness, and mosquitoes— there is basic accommodation at the site, take hammock and mosquito net. Sturdy boots are needed for the 3½ hr. walk to the ruins. The workers are not to be trusted. There are many new tracks criss-crossing the Selva Lacandona (jungle), most going to Echeverría. It is reported that buses from the Palenque market at 0430 and 0700, link with a path that leads to Bonampak, bus travel hard, on unpaved roads.

A German traveller has reported on a journey from Flores (Guatemala) to Palenque along the **Pasión and Usumacinta rivers**. From Santa Elena to Sayaxché, bus 3 hrs., US$0.75; then private launch (4 hrs, US$60) or trading boat (2 days, US$2) to Pipiles at confluence of Pasión and Usuamacinta, or to Benemérito on the Mexican side of the Usumacinta. Bus on unmade road Benemérito-Palenque, at least 5 hrs., and need to pass Immigration just past bridge over Río Lancantún.

The Río Usumacinta, on the Chiapas border with Guatemala, is being dammed. Three dams are projected just downstream from Piedras Negras ruins. The ruins are accessible only by white water rafts, no road, no airstrip, unspoiled jungle (NW of Yaxchilán). Rafting trips run by Far Flung Adventures.

Agua Azul, a series of beautiful waterfalls aptly named for the blue water swirling over natural tufa dams on 7 km. of fast-flowing river, is a popular camping spot reached by a 4-km. paved road (in poor condition) from the junction with the paved road to San Cristóbal, 65 km. from Palenque. Best visited in dry season as in the rainy season the water is less blue and it is hard to swim because of the current (don't visit if it was raining the day before). It is extremely popular at holiday time. Several buses from Palenque daily, to crossroads leading to the waterfall, US$1.50, 2nd class (leaves at 1000 and 1130) 1½ hours. From the crossroads walk the 4 km. downhill to the falls. Back from the junction 1500-1600 with Transportes Maya buses. There are buses between San Cristóbal de Las Casas and Palenque (to 2nd class bus station, Transportes Maya) which will stop there, but on a number of others you must change at Temo, over 20 km. away, N of Ocosingo, which may require a fair wait. Between Palenque and Agua Azul are the *Misol-ha* waterfalls (entry, US$0.75). Entrance fee to this *ejidal* park US$0.50 on foot, more for cars, US$0.50 per tent for camping, parking a trailer or using a hammock. There are a few restaurants, *Internacional*, run by young people, rec., and many food stalls, also a *cabaña* for hammocks; if staying there, be very careful of your belongings; thefts have been reported. There is a good campsite, clean, popular and reliable, opposite the parking lot. 3 km. upstream is the Balcón Ahuau waterfall, good beach for sunbathing. Coop Chambalu, Calle Allende, Palenque run 5-hr. tours to Agua Azul and Misol-Ha for US$5.30, leaving 1000. Other minibuses from minibus terminal (nr. 4 Esquinas): they leave 0930-1000 from Palenque, returning from Agua Azul at 1300, stopping for a few minutes at Misol-Ha, US$4.60. Colectivos from Hidalgo y Allende, Palenque, for Agua Azul and Misol-Ha, 1000-1500, US$0.60.

Beware of ticks when camping in long grass, use kerosene to remove them (or eat raw garlic to repel them!). Watch out carefully for thieves; bring your own food, etc. Flies abound during the rainy season (June-November).

Travelling from Villahermosa to Campeche one can follow either the inland Highway 186, via Francisco Escárcega, with 2 toll bridges (cost US$1.35). There is marvellous birdlife on this route for 10-20 km. in the Río Chumpán area; take care stopping as there are no laybys. Or one can take the old coastal route, Highway 180, which takes 10 hours to drive and has 4 ferries (total cost for one car US$6.60). Fuel in Champotón, an attractive fishing town (pop. 20,000) where the coastal and inland roads converge.

Highway 186 (paved, but in very poor condition between Palenque and Francisco Escárcega), runs to **Francisco Escárcega** at the junction of the inland route to Campeche and the continuation of Highway 186 to Chetumal, on the Belize frontier. Off the latter road are interesting ruins (**see page** 286) at Chicana (145 km.), Becán (**page** 286, watch for very small sign—146 km.), and X-Puhil (153 km.).

Motel Ah Kim Pech, E, reasonable restaurant, nice rooms; good restaurant across from the motel; *Casa de Huéspedes Lolita* on Chetumal highway at E end of town, E, pleasant; *Hotel Bertha*, E, with bath, fairly clean; *Escárcega*, E, good value. Trailer park, 4 spaces, at *Las Gemelas Hotel*, behind Pemex station, not very clean, friendly. Restaurant at ADO terminal is hot, slow and overpriced. Also bank, market and motor repairs. Beside Highway 186, near Km. 231, W of Francisco Escárcega (near the turnoff for Candelaria) is a roosting spot for white ibis, known as Ojo de Agua. Bus Francisco Escárcega to Palenque at 0430, US$4.75, 3 hrs.; the town is on the Mexico City-Palenque-Mérida railway line. Only train leaves at 0300, crowded. Bus, Francisco Escárcega-Chetumal, 3½ hrs. No direct buses to Palenque; need to change from Villahermosa bus at Emiliano Zapata, but ask if your intended bus stops there.

Ciudad Del Carmen (pop. 145,000), on the coastal route, is hot, bursting at the seams since the oil boom, and spoilt by the new conditions. *Fiestas* at the end of July. There is a lot of shipbuilding here now and there are many trawlers in the harbour. The port is to be developed to become one of the biggest and most modern on the Mexican Gulf. The 3.2 km. Puente de la Unión, built in 1982, is considered the longest bridge in Mexico, linking Ciudad del Carmen with the mainland. There is a bull ring.

Hotels *Lli-re*, Calles 32 y 29, T 20588, near ADO station, best in centre, a/c, expensive restaurant, C; *Acuario*, Calle 51 No. 60, T 22547, a/c, comfortable, D; *Isla del Carmen*, Calle 20 No. 9, T 22350, a/c, restaurant, bar, parking, C; *Lino's*, Calle 31 No. 132, T 20738, a/c, pool, restaurant, C; three others on Calle 22. If you can't find accommodation, there are 3 buses between 2100 and 2200 to Campeche and Mérida. Ciudad del Carmen is renowned for its sea-food: giant prawns, clams, ceviche and baby hammerhead shark are all tasty.

Bus To Villahermosa at 1930, arriving 2300-0100; it depends how long one has to wait at the ferry. A connection can be made to Palenque at 2330 or 0400; slow but worthwhile trip. To Mérida 8 buses daily US$6, 9 hrs.

Campeche, capital of Campeche state (pop 220,000), is beautifully set on the western coast of Yucatán. It was the very first place at which the Spaniards landed in 1517. In the 17th century it was fortified against pirates; seven bastions of the old walls and an ancient fort (now rather dwarfed by two new big white hotels on the sea-front) near the crumbling cathedral remain. Some of the bastions house museums: Baluarte Soledad (N of the plaza), a small room of Mayan stelae, free (open Tues.-Sat., 0800-2000), Baluarte San Carlos (NW corner), museum of the fortifications (open Tues.-Sat. 0900-1300, 1600-2000, Sun. 0900-1300, free), Baluarte Santa Rosa (W side), Biblioteca

Histórica, open 0830-1400, 1600-1900. The Museo Regional is at Calle 59, No. 35, containing archaeology and history sections, open Mon.-Sat., 0900-2000, Sun. 0900-1300.

There are several 16th and 17th century churches. The most interesting are San Francisquito (16th century with wooden altars painted in vermilion and white), Jesús, San Juan de Dios, Guadalupe and Cristo Negro de San Román, and there is a historical museum on the Plaza (admission US$0.10). There is also a museum in the former church of San José, which changes its exhibits frequently, near the SW corner of the old town. The old houses are warmly coloured, but the town is now in a sad state of disrepair. The nearest beaches are Playa Bonita (which is no longer fit for swimming and is generally dirty, being next to oil storage tanks, but useful for car parking) and San Lorenzo. The people fish, trawl for shrimp, carve curios and make combs from tortoiseshell. The new market building is attractive. The bathing and fishing resort of Lerma is quite near; take a rickety bus marked Lerma or Playa Bonita; beach strewn with glass and other debris.

Hotels   In general, beware of overcharging. *Ramada Inn*, Av. Ruiz Cortines 51, T 62233, B/A (5 stars), on the waterfront; *Baluartes*, Av. Ruiz Cortines, T 63911, A, parking for campers, who can use the hotel washrooms, good meal US$2.40-3.20, waiters apt to short-change, pool; *López*, Calle 12, No. 189, T 63344, D, clean if a bit musty, with bath, better food; *Castelmar*, Calles 8 y 61, T 65186, colonial style, E, large rooms with bath, clean, friendly; *Cuauhtémoc*, F, clean (except downstairs rooms which are damp and smelly), with bath, in old house near the square (Calle 57). Several on Calle 10: *América*, No. 252, T 64588, D, hot water, clean, fans but hot, OK, and *Roma*, E, No. 254, T 63897 (often full) and nearby, on Calle 8, No. 257 *Reforma*, E, T 64464; *Colonial*, clean, good, Calle 14 No. 122, T 62222, not very friendly, D; *Autel El Viajero*, López Mateos 177, D, overcharges, but often only one left with space in the afternoon, T 65133; *Campeche*, Calle 57 No. 1, T 65183, E, basic but friendly.

35 km. S of Campeche is *Hotel Siho*, D, excellent, beautiful setting on Gulf coast, swimming and other facilities but expensive restaurant and nowhere else to eat nearby (bus to Sihoplaya from Campeche US$0.30). CREA Youth Hostel Av. Agustín Melgar s/n, Col. Buenavista, C.P. 24040, T 61802/62164, in the S suburbs, nr. University, bus from market US$0.12, clean and friendly. It is virtually impossible to get hotel rooms around the Mexican holiday period, starting May.

Camping   There is a trailer park with camping signposted in town. Can be reached by taking a Samula bus from the market place. Owner speaks English; US$1.50 p.p.

Restaurants   *Campeche*, good value; cafeteria next door sells good yoghurt and fruit juices; *Miramar* (good seafood, reasonable); *La Perla*, Calle 10 No. 329, good fish, busy and popular, venison, squid; locals' haunt, sometimes erratic service, off Plaza; *Lonchería Puga*, Calle 8 No. 53, open 0700, rec.; *Pizzería Gato Pardo*, corner of Calle 10 and 49, on Jardín San Martín, outside the wall, excellent pizzas, loud music. Two doors away, *La Cava*. It is hard to find reasonably-priced food before 1800; try the restaurant at the ADO terminal, or *La Parroquia*, Call 59 No. 9, open 24 hrs., good local atmosphere, friendly and clean, rec.

Shopping   Excellent cheap Panama hats (here they are called jipi hats, pronounced "hippie"). Handicrafts are generally cheaper than in Mérida. The new market (just outside the city wall) is worth a visit. Plenty of bargains here, especially Mexican and Mayan clothes, hats and shoes, fruit, vegetables; try ice-cream—though preferably from a shop rather than from a barrow. Some shops have slide film, ASA 100, 30 exp., US$7.40.

Tourist Information New centre near waterfront (Plaza Moch-Couch Turisplaza, Av. Ruiz Cortines), close to Palacio de Gobierno, good (open 0800-1430, 1600-2030, Mon.-Fri.).

Transport You can go to Mérida by rail, 4 hrs. or by road, 3 hrs., 252 km. (158 miles). First class buses go by the Via Corta, which does *not* pass through Uxmal, Kabah, etc. Take a really quite comfortable 2nd class bus from the same terminal, Via Larga, have 3 hours at Uxmal, and catch the next bus to Mérida, but don't buy a through ticket to Mérida; you'll have to pay again when you board the bus. Check bus times, as there are fewer in the afternoon. Bus Campeche-Mérida direct, US$3.30, 2nd class. Bus Campeche-Uxmal, US$3, 2nd class, 3 hrs., 5 a day (but none between 0900 and 1200). Buses along new inland road to Villahermosa; take posted times with a pinch of salt, 2nd class, 5 a day, US$7, 1st class US$8; 6½ hrs., 2300 bus comes from Mérida but empties during the night. Train Campeche-Palenque, 2nd class, US$2.50, 9½ hrs. Bus via Emiliano Zapata (2 hrs. before Villahermosa) to Palenque, change at Emiliano Zapata, **see page** 252. ADO bus to Mexico City, US$23. Train to Mexico City, 30 hrs., comfortable, US$19 1st class. Mexico City-Campeche train leaves at 2000 daily, very crowded in holiday times.

Excursions Two km. S. of Campeche is the 18th-century fort of San Miguel, containing museums and worth visiting for its archaeological pieces. Entry, US$0.15. Between Campeche and Champotón is Playa Seyba, a fishing village with good camping possibilities (but no facilities) N of the village. Eighty km. N of Campeche is Becal, centre of the panama hat trade. The hats are made in man-made limestone caves, whose coolness and dampness facilitate the weaving.

Maya Sites in Campeche State About 40 km. beyond Campeche on the road to Uxmal (**see page** 266), there is a deviation, right via China, along a white stone road for 20 km. (in bad condition) near Cayal to the pyramid of Edzná, (entry, US$0.22, bus from Campeche at 0800 but may leave hours later; possible to take 0800 bus to Cayal and hitch from there), but seemingly worth the trouble only for specialists. Restoration is in hand. SE of Edzná are Dzibilnocac and Hochob sites, with elaborately decorated temples and palaces. For these sites you need a car as the bus returns to Campeche almost at once after arrival at Dzibilnocac, and there is nowhere to stay. For those with a car, continue beyond Edzná on Route 261 to the very picturesque villages of Hopelchen and Bolonchen de Rejón.

Dzibalchen, for **_Hochob_** ruins, is on a road 40 km. from Hopelchen, may be reached by early morning bus from Campeche, 80 km., but again no return buses or accommodation guaranteed. At Hochob (famous for the temple wall, reproduced in the Anthopological Museum in Mexico City) there is another temple (with a serpent's-mouth entrance) about 30 mins. by car and foot from the well-known one: the guard will show you (for a consideration) after closing the main site in the evening. To get to Hochob, ask directions from church in Dzibalchen, which is run by Americans; basically you need to travel 12 km. on a dirt road to a village, Chenko, where the locals will show you the way; remember to bear left when the road forks, then the ruins (very

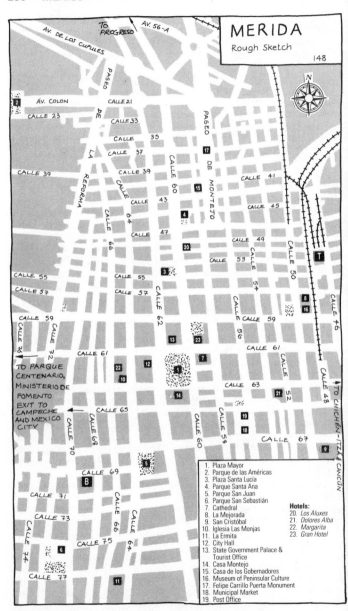

MERIDA
Rough Sketch
148

TO PROGRESO
AV. 56-A
AV. DE LOS CUPULES
PASEO DE LA REFORMA
AV. COLON
CALLE 21
CALLE 23
CALLE 33
CALLE 35
CALLE 37
CALLE 39
CALLE 39
CALLE 43
CALLE 47
CALLE 55
CALLE 57
CALLE 55
CALLE 57
CALLE 59
CALLE 59
CALLE 61
CALLE 61
TO PARQUE CENTENARIO, MINISTERIO DE FOMENTO
EXIT TO CAMPECHE AND MEXICO CITY
CALLE 65
CALLE 69
CALLE 71
CALLE 73
CALLE 75
CALLE 77
PASEO DE MONTEJO
CALLE 41
CALLE 45
CALLE 49
CALLE 59
CALLE 59
CALLE 61
CALLE 63
CALLE 67
CALLE 60
CALLE 62
CALLE 64
CALLE 66
CALLE 70
CALLE 72
CALLE 74
CALLE 50
CALLE 54
CALLE 56
CALLE 58
CALLE 46
CALLE 48
CALLE 52
TO CHICHEN-ITZA & CANCUN

1. Plaza Mayor
2. Parque de las Américas
3. Plaza Santa Lucía
4. Parque Santa Ana
5. Parque San Juan
6. Parque San Sebastián
7. Cathedral
8. La Mejorada
9. San Cristóbal
10. Iglesia Las Monjas
11. La Ermita
12. City Hall
13. State Government Palace & Tourist Office
14. Casa Montejo
15. Casa de los Gobernadores
16. Museum of Peninsular Culture
17. Felipe Carrillo Puerta Monument
18. Municipal Market
19. Post Office

Hotels:
20. *Los Aluxes*
21. *Dolores Alba*
22. *Margarita*
23. *Gran Hotel*

impressive and worth the walk, says Brad Krupsaw, of Silver Spring, Md.) are 1 km. after the fork on top of a hill.

Santa Teresa is a tiny village W of Hopelchen; turn off the main road S for ½ km.; very quiet and simple, excellent bakery with tall beamed ceiling and colourful tiled floor. There are Maya ruins on the islands of Jainu and Piedra, 3 hrs. by boat off the coast. Written official permission is required to visit as the islands are Federal property and guarded.

Mérida, capital of Yucatán state (pop. 700,000), suffers from pollution caused by heavy traffic, narrow streets and climatic conditions favouring smog-formation. It was founded in 1542 on the site of the Mayan city of Tihoo. Its centre is the Plaza Mayor, green and shady; its arcades have more than a touch of the Moorish style. It is surrounded by the severe twin-towered 16th century Cathedral, the City Hall, the State Government Palace, and the Casa Montejo, originally built in 1549 by the *conquistador* of the region, rebuilt around 1850 and now a branch of the Banco Nacional de México (Banamex), open to the public during banking hours. The Casa de los Gobernadores, on Paseo de Montejo, is an impressive building in the turn-of-the-century French style of the Porfirio Díaz era. A small museum well worth a visit, the Museo de Antropología e Historia, closed on Mon. (open 0800-1400 Sun., 0800-2000 all other days, US$0.35), opposite Centenario Park in an old prison on Av. Itzaes with Calle 59. In Centenario Park itself is a zoo; a popular place for family outings on Sunday. The Museum of Peninsular Culture, run by the Instituto Nacional Indigenista (INI), a contemporary crafts museum, is well worth visiting (good, inexpensive gift shop). There are several 16th and 17th century churches dotted about the city: La Mejorada, next to the Museum of Peninsular Culture (Calle 59 between 48 and 50) Tercera Orden, San Francisco and San Cristóbal. Along the narrow streets ply horse-drawn cabs of a curious local design. In all the city's parks you will find *confidenciales*, S-shaped stone seats in which people can sit side by side facing each other.

All the markets, and there are several, are interesting in the early morning. One can buy traditional crafts: a basket or *sombrero* of sisal, a filigree necklace (a good silver shop is next to *Hotel Panamericana*, Calles 50 and 52), also a good selection of Maya replicas. Tortoiseshell articles are also sold, but cannot be imported into most countries, as sea turtles are protected by international convention. The Mérida market is also particularly good for made-to-measure sandals of deerskin and tyre-soles, panama hats, and hammocks of all sizes and qualities. Some of the most typical products are the *guayabera*, a pleated and/or embroidered shirt worn universally, its equivalent for women, the *guayablusa*, and beautiful Mayan blouses and *huipiles*. In the Park of the Americas is an open-air theatre giving plays and concerts, and bands play in various plazas in the evenings; the Tourist Office has details. There are monuments to Felipe Carrillo Puerto, an agrarian labour leader prominent in the 1910 revolution. Redevelopment is rapid; many of the old houses are being pulled down. Mérida is a safe city in general (though be careful on Calle 58 and near the market), but the large influx of visitors in recent years is creating "mostly quiet hostility" towards them.

In Paseo de Montejo (part of Calle 62), together with many shops and restaurants, there are a few grand late 19th century houses. Calle 65 is the main shopping street and the Plaza Mayor is between Calles 61/63 and 60/62. Odd-number streets run E and W, even numbers N and S. In colonial times, painted or sculpted men or animals placed at intersections were used as symbols for the street: some still exist in the small towns of Yucatán. The houses are mostly of Spanish-Moorish type, painted in soft pastel tones, thick walls, flat roofs, massive doors, grilled windows, flowery patios. The water supply, once notorious, is improved. Begging and much molestation from car-washers, shoe-shiners and souvenir-peddlers. All streets are one-way. Free town map at tourist kiosk on the Plaza Mayor, or the Secretaría de Obras Públicas, almost opposite airport at Mérida (cheap bus from centre). Enquire at hotels about the house and garden tours run by the local society women for tourists to raise money for charity. Every Thursday evening there is free local music, dancing and poetry at 2100 in the Plaza Santa Lucía, two blocks from the Plaza Mayor (Calles 55 and 60), chairs provided. The Ermita, an 18th century chapel with beautiful grounds, is a lonely, deserted place 10-15 mins. from the centre.

In the State Government Palace, on the Plaza Mayor, there is a series of superb symbolic and historical paintings, finished 1978, by a local artist, Fernando Castro Pacheco. The Palace is open evenings and very well lit to display the paintings.

Fiesta Carnival on Tuesday before Ash Wednesday. Floats, dancers in regional costume, music and dancing around the Plaza and children dressed in animal suits. **N.B.** Banks closed Monday following carnival.

Hotels Cheaper hotels tend to be S of the main Plaza (odd streets numbered 63 and higher), near the market and especially the bus station (Calles 69 and 68). More expensive hotels are on the N side of the city and near the Paseo Montejo. *Los Aluxes*, Calle 60 No. 444, T 242199, delightful, pool, restaurants, A, very convenient, first class; *Calinda Panamericana*, Calle 59, No. 455, T 239111, good, expensive, with elaborate courtyard in the Porfirian style, very spacious and airy, with swimming pool, 5 blocks from centre, A; *Castellano*, Calle 57, No. 513, T 230100, modern, clean, friendly, pool, B-L A; *Holiday Inn*, Av. Colón and C.60, T 256877, L, all facilities, elegant but a long way from the centre; *Best Western María del Carmen*, A, Calle 63 y 68, No. 550, T 239133, breakfast reported poor; *Casa de Balam*, Calle 60, No. 488, A (Mayaland Resort, T in USA 305-344-6547/800-451-8891), a/c, close to centre, restaurant, bar, pool; *El Conquistador*, Paseo del Montejo 458, T 262155, A; *Governador*, Calle 59, No. 535, T 237133, B, a/c, big rooms, quite good; and others in our A and B price ranges.

Latino, Calle 66 and 63, T 213841, D, with fan and shower (water supply problems), friendly and clean; *Colón*, Calle 62, No. 483, T 234355, C, good value, pool; *Casa Bowen*, restored colonial house (inside better than out), corner of Calle 66, No. 521-B, and 65, rooms on the main street noisy, stores luggage, D, near ADO bus station, as is *Posada del Angel*, Calle 67, No. 535, between Calle 66 and 68, D, T 232754, clean, excellent value (don't bother with the restaurant next door); *México*, Calle 60, No. 525, T 19255, D, good restaurant, attractive; *Gran Hotel*, Calle 60 No. 496, T 17620, D, just off the Plaza, is clean, helpful, owner speaks English, Somerset Maugham atmosphere, Fidel Castro has stayed here frequently; *San Luis*, Calle 61, No. 534-68, T 17580, D, with fan and shower (and US$2.25 for noisy a/c), basic, friendly, patio pool, restaurant; *Rossana Pastora*, Calle 58, No. 563, T 11915, D, very clean, excellent value; *Príncipe Maya Airport Inn*, T 14050, C, noisy from night club, convenient for airport. *Montejo*, Calle 57 between 62 and 64, D (bargain), T 14590, clean, comfortable, convenient, rec.; *Casa Becil*, Calle 67 No. 550-C, entre 66 y 68, D, convenient for bus station, bath, hot water, clean, safe, popular; *América*, simple, private shower and toilet, noisy, will look after luggage, D, Calle 67, No. 500, between 58 and 60, T 15133, about 10 mins. from bus station and near centre, rec. *San Fernando*, opp. ADO bus terminal, D with fan and bath, clean; *Posada Toledo*, Calle 58, No. 487, T 3-16-90, C, good, central, in charming old house, has paperback exchange; *Flamingo*, Calle 58 and 59, T 17740, C, near Plaza, with private shower, swimming pool, noisy, so get room at the back, in poor condition; *Peninsular*, Calle 58, No. 519, T 236996, 1 block from post office and market, D, pool, a/c, clean, comfortable, convenient, friendly; *Reforma*, Calle 59, No. 508, D, swimming pool; *Parque*, Calle 60 No. 495, T17840, D, with bath and fan, clean, friendly, rec.; *Dolores Alba*, Calle 63 No. 464, T 13745, D, good, pool, clean, cool on 1st floor; *San Jorge*, across from ADO bus terminal, T 19054, D, clean, but take interior room as the street is noisy; *Mucuy*, Calle 57, No. 481, T 211037, between 56 and 58, T 211037, D, friendly, good, with shower, use of fridge, washing facilities, efficient, nice gardens, highly rec.

Casa de Huéspedes,E, Victorian showers, will keep luggage for small fee, mosquitoes, so take coils or net, pleasant and quiet except at front, Calle 62, No. 507, laundry expensive; *Del Mayab*, Calle 50, No. 536A, T 10909, E, with bath, reasonable, swimming pool and car park; *Alamo*, T 18058, E, with bath, clean, next to bus station, on Calle 68, rec., storage; *Trinidad Galeria*, 62 y 60, No. 464, E, old houses, lovely garden, good value, rec.; *Margarita*, Calle 66, No. 506 (with Calle 63), T 13213, E with shower, clean, friendly, rec.; *San José*, F, with bath, basic, restaurant, W of Plaza on Calle 63, one of the cheapest, will store luggage; another recommendation is *María Teresa*, Calle 64 No. 529 (between Calles 65 and 67), T 11039, clean, friendly, safe, central, E with bath. *Centenario*, E with bath, friendly, clean, safe on Calle 84, between 59 and 59A, T 3-25-32, *Farahón*, Calle 65, No. 468 y 59, E, above textile shop near Post Office, big rooms, not too clean, noisy; rooms on Calle 66 Norte, No. 386 (with private bath). *Hospedaje Casbillio*, Calle 56, between 53 and 55, clean and friendly.

Maya Paradise Trailer Park, rec., good pool, pick a site away from the water towers; right opp. the airport; *Trailer Park Rainbow*, Km. 8, on the road to Progreso, US$5 for one or two, hot showers.

Restaurants *Jaraneros Patio*, Montejo Circle, regional food and entertainment from 1600; *Pancho Villa's Follies*, very friendly, try *abalones*, owner speaks English, overpriced; and *Soberanis*, on Plaza with two branches elsewhere, serving delicious fish dishes, seafood cocktails highly rec., but expensive, one on Calle 60, No. 503 between 63 and 65 (slow service), and another on Calle 56, No. 504. *Los Almendros*, Calle 50A, No. 493 at Calle 59, in high-vaulted, whitewashed thatched barn, for Yucatán specialities, rec. but expensive, mind the peppers, esp. the green sauce! *Mesón del Mestizo* (Plaza Sta. Lucía), *Pórtico del Peregrino (Pop)*, Calle 57, between 60 and 62, excellent snacks, popular with foreigners, very charming; *Mesón del Quijote*, Calle 62 No. 519, cheap and excellent, try their fish dishes with garlic; the *Patio Español*, inside the *Gran Hotel*, well cooked and abundant food, local and Spanish specialities, moderate prices; *David*, Calle 62, No. 468A (Arab food—closes before 2100); *Café Alameda*, nr. Correos, Arab food, closes at 1900, cheap and good; *Santa Lucía*, Calle 60, good Arab food. *La Prosperidad*, Calle 53 and 56, good Yucateca food, live entertainment at lunchtime; *Yannig*, Calle 62, No. 480, best, cheapest French food. *Cedros de Lebanon*, Calle 59 No. 529, good family-style Arabic food. *El*

Mariachi Hacienda, Calle 60 No. 466, regional food, loud local music, dancing and cock-fighting, cover charge US$2. *El Faisán y El Venado*, Calle 59 No. 617, inexpensive, regional food, Mayan dance show, near zoo. *El Condado*, Calle 65 opp. Bazaar, good and cheap meals, highly rec. *La Carretera*, Calle 62 and 59, a little expensive but very good. Good food at *Flamingo*, Calle 51; *Leo's*, good value for meat dishes, pleasant, Calle 60, just N of Plaza Santa Lucía; *Pizzería Vito Corleone*, Calle 59 No. 508, near Plaza, good. *Restaurant Vegetariano y Pizza amanda Maya Gynza*, Calle 59 No. 507, between 60 and 62 (interior 6). good food and service; *La Pérgola*, warmly rec. (both drive-in and tables), at corner Calles 56A and 43, good veal dishes; also in Colonia Alemán at Calle 24 No. 289A. Cold sliced cooked venison (venado) is to be had in the Municipal Market. *Cafetería La Giralda El Rey*, in the shoe section of the market place, excellent coffee.

Good coffee in *Café Express*, on Calle 60, at Parque Hidalgo, good food, breakfast, traditional coffeehouse where locals meet; *Mil Tortas*, good cheap sandwiches, Calle 62 with 65 and 67; *Café Monebo*, Calle 65 between 58 and 60, good, popular, especially for breakfast. *Manos* (no sign outside), Calle 59 y 60 on Plazuela nr. El Méson, good place to hang out in the evening, friendly, music. *Café de Guaya*, Calle 60, between 53 and 55, vegetarian; *Naturalmente*, Calle 64, No. 48, vegetarian, rec.; banana bread and wholemeal rolls at *Pronat* health shop on Calle 59, No. 506 and good juice bar close by. *Jugos California*, good, expensive fruit juices, Calle 60, also in Calle 65 and at the main bus station; *Jugos de Caña*, Calle 62 between 57 and 59, very good; *Jugos Michoacán*, good milkshakes on Calle 57. *Dulcería Colón*, on Plaza Mayor, for excellent, if expensive, ices.

Shopping *Guayaberas: Kary*, Calle 64, No. 549 (between 67 and 69) opp. Parque San Juan, good prices; *Canul*, Calle 59, No. 496; *Genuina Yucateca*, Calle 50, No. 520. At *Mayalandia* on Calle 61, before Calle 48 archway, one can bargain. *Jack* in Calle 59, near Canul, makes *guayaberas* to measure in 4 hrs., expensive.

The best hammocks are the so-called 3-ply, but they are difficult to find, about US$20 (cheaper than in Campeche for cotton, US$7 for nylon). Never buy your first hammock from a street vendor and never bargain then accept a packaged hammock without checking the size and quality. The surest way to judge a good hammock is by weight: 1,500 grams (3.3 lbs) is a fine item, under 1 kg. (2.2 lbs) is junk (advises Alan Handleman, a U.S. expert). Also, the finer and thinner the strands of material, the more strands there will be, and the more comfortable the hammock. There are three sizes: single, matrimonial and family. Try *El Campesino*, Calle 58, No. 543 (between 69 and 71), Eustaquio Canul Cahum and family, rec. as helpful, reasonable, will let you watch the weaving; *Mayoreo de Mérida*, Calle 65, near Post Office; or *Claudia*, Calle 58 and 89 or *Francisco Asis*, Calles 65 and 52. *Jorge Razu*, Calle 56 No. 516B, rec.; also *La Poblana S.A.*, William Razu C., Calle 65 No. 492. (outside the market, where prices are cheaper but quality is lower), fixed prices, also good for huipil dresses and across the street by *El Tigre del 65*; bargain like mad if buying more than one.

Embroidered *huipil* blouses US$3-6. *El Arte Maya*, Calle 59 No. 498, between 58 and 60, fixed prices but fair, good for silver and typical clothing, speaks English, credit cards accepted. Good panama hats at *El Bombín* next to 511b (tailor's shop) on Calle 67, between 60 and 62. Also *Nipis Becal*, just by market. Clothes shopping is good along Calle 65 and in the García Rejón Bazaar, Cale 65 y Calle 60. Sr. Raúl Cervera Sauri has a reasonable souvenir shop on Calle 59, No. 501. *Uncle Sam's* on main square, run by retired American, reasonably priced hammocks, panama hats. Next door to restaurant *Los Almendros* on Calle 59 is the Cordamex (sisal products) outlet—don't go to the factory 8 km. from town as they won't sell there. Good buys in black coral jewellery and tortoiseshell (may not be imported into several countries—check) in the markets, particularly the

2-storey one on Calles 56 and 67. There is a big supermarket, *Blanco*, on Calle 67 and 52, well stocked.

Try Xtabentun, the liqueur made from sweet anise and honey since ancient Mayan times.

Cameras and Film Repairs on Calle 53/62. Mericolor, Calle 67 y 58, rec. for service and printing. Many processors around crossing of Calles 59 and 60.

Taxis We are warned that taxi drivers are particularly prone to overcharge by taking a long route, so always establish the journey and fare in advance. Taxi from centre to bus terminal, US$2.80. Taxis are hard to find on Sun. p.m.

Car Hire Car reservations should be booked well in advance wherever possible; there is a tendency to hand out cars which are in poor condition once the main stock has gone, so check locks, etc., on cheaper models before you leave town. Avis in *Hotel Mérida*; Hertz, Calle 55, No. 479; Budget, Calle 62, No. 588-3; Volkswagen, Calle 60, No. 486; Alquiladora de Autos Sureste, Calle 60, No. 481, and at airport; Mexico Rent-A-Car in the lobby of *Hotel del Parque*, Calle 60, No. 495, has good rates, new VW Beetles; Odin, Calle 59, No. 506-3. Turismo Planeta, Calle 59 y 60, collect rates from other agencies, they will offer a lower price, new cars.

Car Service Servicillos de Mérida Goodyear, very helpful and competent, owner speaks English, serves good coffee while you wait for your vehicle.

Exchange Banamex (passport necessary) in Casa de los Gobernadores on Plaza, at Tourist Office (Calles 57 y 60), and at Calles 56 y 59. Many banks on Calle 65, off the Plaza. Cash advance on credit cards possible only between 1000 and 1300. *Casa de Cambio*, Calle 56 No. 491 (between 57 and 59) open 0900-1700 Mon.-Sat., but bank's rates better. Jugos California on the main square may change dollars and travellers' cheques at good rates.

Post Office Calle 65, will accept parcels for sea mail. Generally crowded, use branches at airport (also for quick delivery) or on Calle 58, instead. Telegrams from Calle 56, between 65 and 65A, open 0800-2100.

International Calls Possible from central bus station, airport, the shop on the corner of Calles 59 and 64, or public telephones, but not from the main telephone exchange. No collect calls on Sat. or Sun.

British Vice Consul Major A. Dutton (retd), MBE, Calle 58 No. 450, T (91-992) 16799. Postal address Apdo. 89. US Consulate Paseo Montejo 453 y Av. Colón (T 255011). **Canadian Consulate** Calle 62, No. 309-D-19.

Immigration Office Calle 60 between 49 and 51 in Pasaje Camino Real, extension of stay easy and quick.

English-Speaking Doctor Dr. A. H. Puga Navarrete (also speaks French), Calle 13 No. 210, between Calles 26 and 28, Colonia García Gineres, T 25-07-09, open 1600-2000.

Laundry Calle 59 between Calles 72 and 74, at least 24 hrs. *Lavandería* on Calle 69, No. 541, 2 blocks from bus station, about US$2.80 a load. Self-service hard to find.

Tourist Office Corner of Calles 57 and 60, also corner of Calles 61 and 54, and on N side of Plaza Mayor in the Palacio de Gobierno. Has list of all hotel accommodation with prices and a list of tourist events. Organizes trips to Uxmal. Tourist information from Ministerio de Fomento, Calle 59 opp. Centenario park. Instituto Nacional de Estadística, Geografía e Informática, Paseo Montejo 442, Ed. Oasis, for maps and information.

Travel Agents Wagon-Lits (Cooks), helpful, Av. Colón 501 (Plaza Colón), T 554-11; **Yucatán Trails**, Calle 62, No. 482, is very helpful, run by Canadian, Denis Lafoy.

Trains Fees for red-capped porters posted at the station (Calles 48 and 57). From Mexico City at 2010. Only 2nd class available tickets have been refused to lone travellers on the ground that it is not safe. To Mexico City, 2nd class US$10.30, leaves Mérida at 2100 (37 hrs. but often more like 45 to 72); book ticket from 2000 on same day of departure at station, but queue much earlier. 2nd class not rec., dirty, live animals. Even though boarding not supposed to be before 1900, most people get on when train arrives, at 1830. No clean running water, lavatory dirty. Beggars get on at every stop; thieving. No food except for vendors at stations, stock up. Many stops up to Coatzacoalcos. Possible to break journey at Palenque but not on one ticket. Mérida-Palenque (on same train as to Mexico City), takes 12 hrs., US$8. 1st class also dirty and crowded, travelling time unpredictable, no *dormitorio* now available. Track recently improved, train rocks rather than jerks as it did, speed about 50 km. an hour. Air conditioning improves as you leave the station, but not spectacular. Fruit near station, bread and cheese a couple of streets away from station, better bought before leaving centre.

Mérida-Valladolid at 1510, 5 hrs., US$2. There are two picturesque narrow-gauge railway lines SE of Mérida—one to Sotuta and the other to Peto via Ticul and Oxcutzcab. One train on each line leaves daily at 1400 from Mérida, returns at 0400. The journey takes 5 hrs., covers 150 km., US$0.50 to Peto. You can return by bus from Oxcutzcab (**see also page 268**).

Buses Almost all buses except those to Progreso leave from terminal on Calle 69 between Calles 70 and 72. The station has lockers. To Mexico City, US$20, 24-28 hrs.; direct Pullman bus Mexico City 2200, 14 hrs to Coatzacoalcos, US$12. Bus to Veracruz, 2 a day, US$18, 16 hrs.; to Chetumal, see **Road to Belize** below. To Ciudad del Carmen 8 a day, 1st class, ADO, US$6, 9 hrs. Three buses to Tulum: at 0500, 1100 and 2300, 8 hrs., US$6.50, drops you off about ½ km. from the ruins. For buses to Uxmal and Chichén Itzá see under those places. Regular buses to Campeche (US$3, 4½ hrs.) also pass Uxmal. Last bus from Uxmal to Campeche (US$1.50, 3 hrs.) at 2315 is quite crowded. Buses to Puerto Juárez and Cancún (Autobuses de Oriente), every hr. 0600 to 2200, US$4.40 1st class, US$4 2nd, 4½ hrs. Make sure the driver knows you want Puerto Juárez, the bus does not always go there, especially at night. Buses to Progreso (US$0.50) passing the road to Dzibilchaltún (see next page), leave from the bus station on Calle 62, between Calle 65 and 67 every 15 mins. from 0500-2100. To Valladolid, US$1.80. Many buses daily to Villahermosa, US$8; one direct bus daily at 1330 via Villahermosa and Campeche to Tuxtla Gutiérrez, 16 hrs., US$10.40. Autotransportes del Sureste de Yucatán, at 0600.

Bus to Palenque and Tuxtla Gutiérrez with a connection to Guatemala leaves 2330 from ADO terminal, arrives 0830, US$13.50, 2nd class only, rather a grim proposition, better to travel in daytime, take Villahermosa bus to Catazaja-Playa, US$8.50, 8½ hrs., then minibus to Palenque US$0.80, ½ hr., or go to via Emiliano Zapata, 3 buses a day US$8, and local bus (see page 251). Buses to Celestún and Sisal from corner of Calle 50 and 67.

Route 261, Mérida-Francisco Escárcega, paved and in very good condition. Buses.

To Guatemala by public transport from Yucatán, take train from Mérida to Pichucalco (**see page 249**); it gets in about 1300. Take a small bus downtown and catch the bus to Tuxtla Gutiérrez. Road is slow, so it is probably quicker to cut across from Coatzacoalcos. Autotransportes del Sureste de Yucatán bus from Mérida to Tuxtla, via Palenque and Ocosingo to either San Cristóbal or Comitán; 2 or 3 changes of bus. Bus from Mérida direct to Tuxtla at 2330 hrs., then direct either Tuxtla-Ciudad Cuauhtémoc or to Tapachula; although the journey may not be as pretty, it saves changing.

Alternatively travel from Villahermosa by ADO bus (0700, 0800, 1330), 4 hrs., or from Emiliano Zapata hourly by ADO, or on the México-Mérida railway line to **Tenosique**, 1 hr. E by train from Palenque, or by colectivo to Catazaja (US$0.10), then bus (US$1.25, 3 a day). Bus also from Mexico City, ADO, 16½ hrs., arrives 0700 (*Hotel Garage*, E, a/c, on main square with restaurant, very clean; *Roma* on main street, E, bath, ask about cheaper rooms; *Azulejos*, Calle 26 No. 416, E with bath, dirty, hot water, friendly, opp. church, *Casa de Huéspedes La Valle*, Calle 19, G p.p., and others). For planes to Bonampak contact Sr. Quintero, T 20099. For overland trips ask at restaurant opp. new market, owner goes in his camioneta to Bonampak and Yaxchilán: negotiate price. From Tenosique (pleasant, friendly, money exchange at bookstore on street behind church and clothing shop Ortiz y Alvarez at Calle 28, 404), buses leave from Mercado Nuevo, Calles 28 and 50 (take bus "ADO-Centro" or walk 10 mins. from centre) at 0600, 0900, 1300 (one hour, US$0.50) to La Palma on the Río San Pedro, whence boats leave to El Naranjo (Guatemala) when the bus arrives. about 6½ hrs., US$12 (to check boat times, see Sr. Valenzuela, Calle 28, No. 142, Tenosique, or T 30811 Rural at the Río San Pedro). In La Palma, restaurant and exchange are poor value; Nicolás Valenzuela offers both services, and lodging. Make sure the boat takes you beyond the border, where there is a customs office. If you take the 0800 boat you can get to Flores in a day; if not you must stay at the border post (basic *hospedaje* and restaurant on Guatemalan side). From **El Naranjo** there is a new dirt road through the jungle to Flores; buses leave at 0300 and 1400 for Flores (US$3, 7 hrs.) or hitchhiking apparently possible. Beautiful trip. One can take a boat from La Palma (rather than San Pedro, which is more expensive) and go for US$2.50 to El Martillo.

Road to Belize: paved all the way to Chetumal. Bus Mérida-Chetumal US$7, 2nd class, 16 a day, takes 7 hrs. Bus station on corner of Calle 68 and 69.

By Air Mexicana office at Calle 58 and 61. From Calle 67 and 60 bus 79 goes to the airport, marked Aviación, US$0.10. Taxi US$4, voucher available from airport, you don't pay driver direct; colectivo US$2. Mexicana, T 248576/54/246633 (airport T 236986) and Aeroméxico both have about 6 flights to Mexico City daily, 1¾ hrs., Aeroméxico Miami-Mérida daily at 1955. (Mexicana daily 1450, 2 hrs., 5 mins.). Aero Caribe flies daily to Oaxaca, Cancún, 45 mins.; Cozumel, 45 mins.; Oaxaca, 3½ hrs.; Tuxtla Gutiérrez, 2½ hrs.; Villahermosa, 50 mins. (Aeroméxico leaves at 0645 and returns to Mérida at 2140, making it easier to visit Palenque in a rented car in a one-day tour). The airport is splendid. Mexicana to Cuba, Sun. and Sat., US$179 return, payable in pesos. A package tour (one week) Mérida-Havana-Mérida is available, US$238, including flight, good hotel, half-board (MAP), one excursion trip to *Tropicana Night Club*. For return to Mexico ask for details at Secretaría de Migración, Calle 60, No. 285. The smaller airlines tend to offer cheaper flights, on older aircraft. Food and drinks at the airport are very expensive.

Excursions North-west of Mérida is first Hunucma, like an oasis in the dry Yucatán, about ½ hr. from the Central Camionera bus station, US$0.30. Then about 52 km. (buses), is Sisal beach (frequent buses 0500-1700, from Calle 50, between Calle 65 and 67), with an impressive lighthouse (*Sisal del Mar Hotel Resort* due open in 1991, luxury accommodation, T in USA 800-451-0891 or 305-341-9173). West of Mérida regular buses (US$1.10) serve Celestún beach, a resort frequented by Meridans, with a huge lagoon with flamingoes; hire a boat (US$18 for one big enough for 6-8). Latest reports are that the place is very dirty, with many dead fish on the beach and the food in the restaurants cannot be trusted.

Halfway to Progreso turn right for the Maya ruins of *Dzibilchaltún*, open 0800-1700. This unique city, according to carbon dating, was founded as early as 1000 B.C. The most important building is the Temple of the Seven Dolls (partly restored); museum at entrance, where you can buy drinks. The Cenote Xlaca contains very clear water and is 44 metres deep; ruined church nearby. Buses from Mérida to Progreso pass the junction to the ruins, 8 km. from the main road, taxis wait at the bus stop; buses pass in either direction every 15 mins. Apparently one can swim in the *cenote*.

Progreso, the port 39 km. away, is reached by road or railway. Population 14,000; temperatures range from 27° to 35°C. Main export: *henequén*. It claims to have the longest stone-bridge pier in the world (it is being extended to 6 km.). The beach has been cleaned up, although latest reports say it is dirty again, and plenty of new hotels and houses have been built. It is very popular at holiday times (July-August).

Hotels On beach: *Tropical Suites*, E (more with kitchen), clean, rec.; *Hostal*, E, clean, big rooms; *Posada Linda*, E, clean, kitchen and balcony, rec. Free camping on the beach; huts for hammocks. Good **restaurants** and quite cheap are *Capitán Pescado*, and *Charlie's* expensive but good; *Soberanis; La Terraza*, variable results, expensive. Police permit free beach camping. Many homes, owned by Mexico City residents, available for rent, services included. Sr. A. Morán, at Calle 22 and 27 (speaks English) can arrange furnished accommodation (cheapest unfurnished). Good local market with lowest food prices in Yucatán, esp. seafood. You can buy fresh shrimps cheaply in the mornings on the beach. Bus, Progreso-Mérida US$0.50 every 15 mins. The beach front by the pier is devoted to cafés with seafood cocktails as their speciality. They also have little groups performing every weekend afternoon in summer; and the noise can be both spirited and deafening.

Boats can be hired to visit the reef of Los Alacranes where many ancient wrecks are visible in clear water.

The Progresso bus station is at Calle 19, between 80 and 82. A short bus journey (4 km.) W from Progreso are Puerto Yucalpetén and Chelem, a dusty resort. Balneario Yucalpetén has a beach with lovely shells, but also a large naval base. *Fiesta Inn* on the beach (A) and *Mayaland Club* (Mayaland Resorts, T in USA 800-4510-8891/305-341-9173), villa complex. Yacht marina, changing cabins, beach with gardens and swimming pool. Between the Balneario and Chelem there is a nice hotel of small Mayan-hut type bungalows, *Hotel Villanueva* (2 km. from village, hot rooms), and also *Costa Maya*, on Calle 29 y Carretera Costera, with restaurant. Fish restaurants in Chelem, *Las Palmas* and *El Cocalito*, reasonable, also other small restaurants. East of Progreso is another resort, Chicxulub, which is quite pleasant.

Uxmal is 74 km. from Mérida, 177 km. from Campeche, by a good paved road. If going by car, there is a new circular road round Mérida: follow the signs to Campeche, then Campeche via *ruinas*, then to Muna via Yaxcopoil (long stretch of road with no signposting). Muna-Yaxcopoil about 34 km. The Uxmal ruins are quite unlike those of Chichén-Itzá (see below), and cover comparatively little ground. Uxmal, the home of the Xiu tribe, was founded in 1007. Its finest buildings seem to have been built much later. See El Adivino (the Sorcerer, pyramid-shaped, topped by two temples with a splendid view); the Casa de las Monjas (House of Nuns), a quadrangle with 88 much adorned rooms; the Casa del Gobernador (House of the Governor), on three terraces, with well preserved fine sculptures; the Casa de las Tortugas (Turtle House) with six rooms; the Casa de las Palomas (House of Doves), probably the oldest; and the cemetery. Ruins open at 0800, close at 1700, entrance US$1.25 weekdays, free on Sundays. A new visitors' centre at entrance of ruins, houses a museum, souvenir shops and an expensive restaurant; also guide books here. There are caves which go in for about 100 metres near the main entrance (rather dull). Many iguanas (harmless) wandering about, watch out for occasional scorpions and snakes. There is a *son et lumière* display at the ruins nightly—English version (US$1.50) at 2100, Spanish version (US$1.05) 1900 (check for times), highly rec. (but bus leaves at 1400, arriving 1530, thus leaving you only 1½ hrs. to explore the ruins before the site closes). 2nd class bus from Mérida to Campeche ("Via Ruinas") passes Uxmal, US$0.90 one way, can buy tickets on bus, 1½ hr. journey, 2 hrs. just enough to see ruins. Bus stops just under ½ km. from entrance to ruins on main road, follow sign. Return from *Restaurant Bar Nicté-Ha* (open 1230-1900, expensive) across the road. From Mérida six 2nd-class buses a day. Return to Mérida after the show is only possible with tourist buses. After the Spanish show it may be possible to get a ride to Muna from where the last bus to Mérida leaves at 2200. (There may be spare seats for those without return tickets.) There is, however, a bus to Campeche at 2315. Good service with Yucatán Trails (**see page** 264). Taxi Mérida-Uxmal US$1.35. For best photographs early morning or late afternoon arrival is essential. Overnight parking for a van US$0.50.

Hotels *Hacienda Uxmal*, 100 metres from ruins, is quite good but very expensive (A, restaurant open 0800-2200), a/c, gardens, swimming pool. It has a less expensive dependency *Posada Uxmal*, B, meals in either part cost US$4.35 and US$6 depending on restaurant. From the *Hacienda Uxmal* jeeps visit the four ruins of Kabah, Sayil, X-Lapak and Labná (see below) daily, US$20 p.p., incl. box lunch. *Misión Uxmal*, A, 1-2 km. from ruins on Mérida road. Club Méditerranée *Villa Arqueológica*, A-B, beautiful, close to ruins, good, swimming pool. *Lapalapa*, A, including meals. New restaurant at ruins, good. **N.B.** There is no village at Uxmal, just the hotels. No camping allowed.

On the road from Uxmal to Mérida (with good restaurant, *Rancho*, a few km. from Uxmal) is **Muna** (15 km. from Uxmal, 62 from Mérida; delightful square and old church), with the nearest railway station to Uxmal. There is a new direct road (Highway 293) from Muna to Bacalar, Quintana Róo, just N of Chetumal.

By the main road a few km. S of Uxmal and often included in tours of the latter (about 5½ km. before the sign for Sayil), are the ruins of **Kabah** where there is a fascinating Palace of Masks, whose façade bears the image of Chac; mesmerically repeated over and over again about six hundred times. The style is classic Puuc. Watch out for snakes and spiders. Bus: Campeche-Kabah, US$0.30.

Further South of Uxmal, about half-way between Mérida and Campeche, a paved road branches off to the left to the *Sayil* ruins (5 km.), *Xlapak* (about 13 km.) and *Labná* (about 22 km.). The palace at Sayil (admission US$0.40) is a good 2 hrs.' walk from the main site. Labná has a most astonishing arch. Both Sayil and Labná are in low, shrubby bush country. From Labná, continue to immense galleries and caves of Bolonchen which are now illuminated (bus from Mérida).

If visiting Sayil, Xlapak and Labná, you can take a taxi from the village of Santa Elena at the turn-off (no hotels or restaurants), costing US$20 for 1-3 persons. By hire-car one can continue to Oxcutzcab (see below).

One can arrange to visit Kabah (20 mins.), Sayil (30 mins.), Xlapak (10 mins.) and Labná (30 mins.) with the J. González company Calle 59, No. 476, Mérida (T 10197, 19710, 10865), VW buses, daily round trip at 0900, US$13-20 (admission not included) including Uxmal (90 mins.), often price includes meal and sometimes *son et lumière*. Very tiring, especially since Uxmal last, but soft drinks available at sites. Entry cheaper on Sun. and holidays. Book preferably a day in advance. The ruins of Labná, Xlapak, Sayil, Kabah and Uxmal can also be reached by 2nd class bus from Mérida, 0800-1500, US$15 for the trip (tickets from inside bus terminal). This route allows 20 mins. each at Kabah, Sayil, Labná and Xlapak, but it's best to arrange your own return in order to spend sufficient time at Uxmal. One can connect with the 2nd class bus tours from Mérida from Campeche if one takes the 0600 bus to Kabah.

Recommended reading for the area: *The Maya*, by M. D. Coe (Pelican Books).

The road from Mérida (and also from Uxmal) to Chetumal is through Muna, *Ticul* (where pottery, hats and shoes are made; 3 hotels, *Sierra Sosa*, E, shower, fan, friendly; *San Miguel*, Calle 28 nr. Plaza, quiet, good value; *Los Almendros* restaurant, opp. Cinema Ideal, rec.), **Peto** (best avoided, via Tzucacab-Santa Rosa bypass, no restaurant) and Felipe Carrillo Puerto. Between Ticul and Peto is *Oxcutzcab*, with *San Carlos*, E, at W end of town, opp. Pemex station, on the road to Muna, fan, a little run-down. Hammocks provided, in some private houses, usually full, fluent Spanish needed to find them. Nearby, to the S, are the fantastic caverns and precolumbian vestiges at *Loltún* (supposedly extending for 8 km.). Caves are open Tues.-Sun., admission at 0930, 1130, 1330 and 1500 (US$0.25). Caretaker may admit tours on Mon., but no lighting. Take pickup or truck from the market going to Cooperativa (an agricultural town). For return, flag down a passing truck. Alternatively, take a taxi. Oxcutzcab is a good centre for catching buses to Chetumal, Muna, Mayapán and Mérida. It has a lot of character with a large market on the side of the Plaza and a church with a "two-dimensional" façade on the other side of the square. The area around Ticul and Oxcutzcab is intensively farmed with citrus fruits, papayas and mangos. Between Oxcutzcab and Peto is *Tekax* with restaurant *La Ermita* serving excellent Yucateca dishes at reasonable prices. From Tekax an unpaved but perfectly acceptable road leads to the ruins of Chacmultun. From the top one enjoys a beautiful view; there is a caretaker. All the towns between Muna and Peto have large old churches. Beyond Peto the scenery is scrub and swamp as far as the Belizean frontier.

Mayapán is a large, peaceful late Maya site easily visited by bus from

Mérida or from Oxcutzcab, beware of snakes at site; also two large pyramids in village of Acanceh en route. Before Acanceh, on the road to Mayapán, is a restaurant at Kanasin, *La Susana*, to which there are frequent buses. It is known especially for local delicacies like *sopa de lima*, *salbutes* and *panuchos*. Clean, excellent service and abundant helpings at reasonable prices. Between Acanceh and Mayapán is Tecóh, with the caverns of Dzab-Náh; you must take a guide as there are treacherous drops into *cenotes*.

Chichén-Itzá is 120 km. by a paved road running SE from Mérida. The scrub forest has been cleared from over 5 square km. of ruins. The city was founded in 432, and taken over by the Toltecs in the 10th century; the major buildings in the N half are Toltec. Dominating them is El Castillo, its top decorated by the symbol of Quetzalcoatl, and the balustrade of the 91 stairs up each of the four sides is decorated by a plumed, open-mouthed serpent. There is also an interior ascent to a chamber lit by electricity where the red-painted jaguar which probably served as the throne of the high priest burns bright, its eyes of jade, its fangs of flint (see below for entry times). There is a ball court with grandstand and towering walls each set with a projecting ring of stone high up; at eye-level is a relief showing the decapitation—death was the penalty for defeat—of the losing captain (wall paintings in the temple at the ball court are open 1500-1600, US$0.25, luggage store at entrance). El Castillo stands at the centre of the northern half of the site, and almost at right-angles to its northern face runs the sacred way to the Cenote Sagrado, the Well of Sacrifice. Into the Cenote Sagrado were thrown valuable propitiatory objects of all kinds, animals and human sacrifices. The well was first dredged by Edward H. Thompson, the U.S. Consul in Mérida, between 1904 and 1907; he accumulated a vast quantity of objects in pottery, jade, copper and gold. In 1962 the well was explored again by an expedition sponsored by the National Geographic Society and some 4,000 further artefacts were recovered, including beads, polished jade, lumps of copal resin, small bells, a statuette of rubber latex, another of wood, and a quantity of animal and human bones. The bottom of the well is paved with the ruins of a fallen temple. An other *cenote*, the Xtoloc Well, was probably used as a water supply. It requires at least one day to see the many pyramids, temples, ballcourts and palaces, all of them adorned with astonishing sculptures, and excavation and renovation is still going on.

Old Chichén, where the Mayan buildings of the earlier city are found, lies about ½ km. by path from the main clearing. The famous observatory (the only one known among the Maya ruins) is included in this group as is the Nunnery. A footpath to the right of the Nunnery takes one to the House of the Three Lintels after ½ hr. walking. It requires at least one day to see the many pyramids, temples, ballcourts and palaces, all of them adorned with astonishing sculptures, and excavation and renovation is still going on. Interesting birdlife can be seen around the ruins.

Entry to Chichén-Itzá, 0800-1700, US$1.20 (free Sun. and holidays); check at entrance for opening times of the various buildings. Best to arrive before 1030 when the mass of tourists arrives. Entry to see the jaguar in the substructure of El Castillo along an inside staircase at 1100-1500. Try to be among the first in as it is stuffy inside and queues form at busy times. Drinks and snacks available at entrance, also guidebooks, clean toilets. Also toilets on the way to old Chichén, and a drinks terrace with film supplies. The badly translated guide-book of José Díaz Bolio provides useful background comment; the little Bloomgarden booklet is also interesting; Panorama is the best. The Catholic church has walls built on a boulder and older foundations, and incorporates old Mayan stones, some with carvings (step to the side door); there are even two serpents over one of the doors. *Son et lumière* (US$1.30) at Chichén every evening, in Spanish at 1900, and then in English at 2100; said to be less good than at Uxmal. A tourist centre has been built at the entrance to the ruins with a restaurant, free cinema; luggage deposit US$0.40, open 0800-1700.

There are several tours daily to the Balancanchén caves, 3 km. E, just off the highway (caretaker turns lights on and off, answers questions in Spanish); minimum 3, maximum 15 persons. Worth the trip: there are archaeological objects, including offerings of pots and *metates* in a unique setting, except for the unavoidable *son et lumière* show; it is very damp, so dress accordingly. Open 0900-1100 and 1400-1600 on the hour, US$2, free Sun. (allow about ½ hr. for the 300-metre descent), closed Sat. and Sun. afternoons.

Hotels All are expensive for what they offer. The only two hotels close to the ruins are *Hacienda Chichén*, A, once owned by Edward Thompson with charming bungalows; *Villas Arqueológicas*, B, 1st class, pool, tennis. Both are on the other side of the fenced-off ruins from the bus stop; rather than walk through ruins take taxi (US$1-1.50). Others are further away: *Mayaland Hotel*, A-L, incl. breakfast and dinner, pool, but sometimes no water in it, no a/c, just noisy ceiling fans, but good service and friendly (T in USA 800-451-8891/305-341-9173); *Pirámide Inn*, B, with food, swimming pool, US satellite TV, well run, camping US$6 for 2 plus car; also *Pirámide Inn Trailer Court*, 1½ km. from ruins, camping, book swapping facility at desk, clean toilets and showers, lots of trees for hammock hanging (US$2 p.p. per night) and grass space for small tents, electricity and water outlets, US$1.30 p.p., noisy because close to main road, allows use of *Pirámide Inn* swimming pool, watch out for snakes and tarantulas; *Lapalapa Chichén*, B, with breakfast and dinner, a few km. from the ruins, excellent restaurant, modern, park with animals; *Dolores Alba*, small hotel (same family as in Mérida), 2½ km. on the road to Puerto Juárez (bus passes it), good and comfortable, D, with shower; has swimming pool and serves good, expensive meals, English spoken.
   Other hotels at *Pisté* about 2 km. before the ruins if coming from Mérida (taxi to ruins US$1.20): no accommodation under US$10, *Posada Novelo*, E, near *Pirámide Inn*, run by José Novelo who speaks English, restaurants nearby, not very good value, sanitation in poor condition. *Hotel Cunanchén*, on Plaza, prices negotiable with owner, not rec.; ask to see private *cenote*. *Posada del Paso*, E with shower, basic, but good, very friendly. A lot of traffic passes through at night, try to get a room at the back.
   There is a small pyramid in village opp. the *Hotel Misión Chichén Itzá*, A, not easily seen from the road; it has staircases with plumed serpents and a big statue facing N on top; close by is a huge plumed serpent, part coloured, almost forming a circle at least 20 metres long. There is no sign or public path, climb over

gate into scrubland, the serpent will be to right, pyramid to left (a traveller believes these to be the remains of a hotel built by a French concern in the 1940s; Ken Fishkin, Berkeley, CA, writes that they are both definitely fakes, unless the Maya discovered linoleum and Art Deco). Opposite *Hotel Misión*, between the snake and pyramid, an as yet, unnamed new hotel, D, clean, friendly, rec. Bank in Pisté, Banamex, open 0900-1300. Bus Pisté-Valladolid US$1.40.

Restaurants Mostly poor and overpriced in Chichén itself. *Hotel Restaurant Carrousel* (rooms E); *Las Redes*; *Nicte-Ha* opposite is cheaper and has chocolate milk shakes; *Fiesta* in Pisté, touristy but good.

Shopping Hammocks are sold by Mario Díaz (a most interesting character), excellent quality, huge, at his house ½ km. up the road forking to the left at the centre of the village. A few km. from Chichén is Ebtún, on the road to Valladolid. A sign says "Hammock sales and repairs": it is actually a small prison which turns out 1st class cotton or nylon hammocks—haggle with wardens and prisoners; there are no real bargains, but good quality.

Telephone International calls may be placed from Teléfonos de México, opposite *Hotel Xaybe*.

Transport If driving from Mérida, follow Calle 65 (off the Plaza) out as far as the dirt section, where you turn left, then right and right again at the main road, follow until hypermarket on left and make a left turn at the sign for Chichén-Itzá.

Chichén-Itzá is easily reached (but less easily during holiday periods) from Mérida by 1st (ADO) at 0845, US$3.20, bus station at Calle 69 between 68 and 70, and hourly 2nd class buses from 1000 (US$1.50 one way), bus station on Calle 50 between 65 and 67, about 1½ or 3 hours' journey; buses now take you direct to the ruins. Tours by 1st-class bus (0800, bus returns 1600) US$20 with dinner (take 0600 bus to avoid the crowds; no 1st class buses Sat. or Sun.). You can often also negotiate a fare with some of the VW buses that park in the lay-bys off the main road opp. the site entrance. 10 buses a day go to Cancún and Puerto Juárez, last at 1700, US$3.30. The first bus from Pisté to Puerto Juárez is at 0730, 3 hrs. Budget travellers going on from Mérida to Isla Mujeres or Cozumel should visit Chichén from Valladolid (see below). Buses from Valladolid go every hour to the site, the 0700 bus reaches the ruins at 0800 when they open, and you can return by standing on the road at the ruins and flagging down any bus going straight through. Bus Pisté—Tulum, US$3.

An interesting detour off the Chichén-Mérida highway is to turn in the direction of Yaxcaba at Libre Unión, after 3 km. turn on to a dirt road, singposted to cenote Xtojil, a beautiful cenote with a Mayan platform, which has well-preserved carvings and paintings.

On the way back, turn to the right at Kantunil (68 km. from Mérida) for a short excursion to the charming little town of *Izamal* (basic hotel on one of the two main squares, and a restaurant next door), to see the ruins of a great mausoleum known as Kinich-Kakmo pyramid, right at the centre of Izamal, with an excellent view of the town and surrounding *henequén* plantations from the top; a huge old convent, and the magnificent early Franciscan church, built on the ruins of a Mayan pyramid (1553). This church was founded by Fray Diego de Landa, the historian of the Spanish conquest of Mérida.

Train Mérida-Izamal leaves at 0600, returns 1500, US$0.30.

From Izamal one can go by the 1630 bus to *Cenotillo*, where there are several fine *cenotes* within easy walking distance from the town (avoid the one *in* town), especially Ucil, excellent for swimming, and La Unión. From Mérida, take 1530 train to Tunkas, and then bus to Cenotillo. Lovely train ride, US$0.20. Past Cenotillo is Espita and then a road forks left to Tizimín (see below).

The cemetery of Hoctun, on the Mérida-Chichén road, is also worth visiting, impossible to miss, there is an "Empire State Building" on the site. Take a bus from Mérida (last bus back 1700) to see extensive ruins at Aké, unique structure.

Beyond Chichén-Itzá, and easily reached from Mérida (bus, US$1.80) is *Valladolid* (pop. 70,000), a pleasant Mayan town with another large Franciscan church, on the paved road between Mérida and Puerto Juárez.

Hotels *María de la Luz*, Plaza Principal, T 6-20-71, good, dirty swimming pool (non-residents, US$0.50) and small night-club, poor restaurant, closes at 2230, D; *San Clemente*, Calle 41 and 42 No. 206 (T 62208), D, with air conditioning, has car park, swimming pool, opposite Cathedral, in centre of town. *Mesón del Marqués*, C, (T 62073), a/c, with bath, on square, with restaurant and shop (helpful for information), excellent value. *Oso Río*, on W side of Plaza, 2 blocks N, small, clean, friendly, E; quiet and excellent is *María Guadalupe*, Calle 44, No. 198, T 62068, D, with hot water, but uncertain water supply. *Lili*, Calle 44, E, hot shower, fan, basic, safe motorcycle parking, friendly; *Maya*, Calle 41, between 48 and 50, E, fan, clean, mosquitoes; *Mendoza*, Calle 39, No. 204C, good, clean, near bus station, E. *Alcócer*, E, with bath if you bargain, fairly clean. *Zaci*, Calle 44, C (D with fan rather than a/c), good. In *Mesón de Caminante*, 6 blocks W from bus station, hammocks US$0.80 a night, "noisy flophouse". **Restaurant** *Los Arcos*, near plaza, set lunch US$1.20; *Los Portales* on main square, very good, try local drink xtabentún. Excellent cheap restaurant next to *Hotel Lili*. Places serving comida on N side of Plaza. Good, cheap food stalls next to *Mesón del Marqués*.

Post Office Calle 43, between 38 and 40, almost opp. bus terminal, 1½ blocks S from square on E side (does not accept parcels for abroad); telegraph office, Calle 42, between 43 and 45, 1½ blocks S from square on W side.

Bank Bancomer on E side of square (to the right of church).

Buses To Chichén-Itzá, take Mérida bus, 2nd class, US$0.80, every 40 mins., from 0600-2100, 1 hr. ride (taxi US$15), also to Balancanchén caves; many buses go to Mérida, US$2.45, 2nd class US$2 (3 hrs.); and to Puerto Juárez, US$2.45, from 0800 and Cancún, 1st class, US$2.45 (2 hrs.). To Playa del Carmen at 0430 and 1300 (via Cobá and crossing 1 km. from Tulum) US$3 (3½ hrs.) also via Cancún, US$3.20 (4 hrs.); fare to Tulum, US$2.10, 2½ hrs.; to Chetumal, at 0600, 1100, 1500 and 2000, 2nd class US$4.20, 5 hrs. Many buses to Mérida. Taxi to Puerto Juárez (160 km.), US$31.10, takes seven passengers. N.B. beware of harassment by beggars at the bus station.

One can swim in the very clean electrically-lit *cenote* of Dzit-Nup, a huge cave with blue water (entry US$0.40, open until 1800, taxi, return plus wait, US$3 from Valladolid) outside Valladolid. Also lovely *cenote* at Zaci, with a restaurant and lighted promenades, 2 blocks N of *Hotel Don Luis*, but you cannot swim in it because of the algae. Road turns left from Puerto Juárez road a couple of blocks from main plaza.

A paved road heads N (buses) from Valladolid to *Tizimín*, a very pleasant town with a 16th-century church and convent, open squares and narrow streets, and a few hotels, E and F; it has a famous New Year *fiesta*. There is a good restaurant, *Tres Reyes*. There is also a local *cenote*, Kikib. The road continues N over the flat landscape to **Río Lagartos**, itself on a lagoon, where the Mayas extracted salt. (*Hotel Nefertiti*, E, hot shower, run down, fish restaurant.) There are a number of small eating-places. Swimming from island opposite Río Lagartos, where boats are moored. Bus from Río Lagartos to **San Felipe** (13 km.), can bathe in the sea; good cheap seafood at *El Payaso* restaurant. On a small island with ruins of a Maya pyramid, beware of rattlesnakes. One can also go from Río Lagartos to **Los Colorados** (15 km.) to swim and see the salt deposits with red, lilac and pink water. Boat trips (US$12, expensive, bargain the price before embarking) can be arranged in Río Lagartos to see the flamingoes (often only a few pairs, but apparently thousands in July) feeding in the lagoons E of Los Colorados. Not a lot else here, but if you are stuck for food, eat inexpensively at the *Casino* (ask locals). Road on to El Cuyo, rough and sandy, but passable. El Cuyo has a shark-fishing harbour. Fishermen cannot sell (co-op) but can barter fish—fry your shark steak with garlic, onions and lime juice.

Also N of Valladolid, turning off the road to Puerto Juárez after Xcan, is **Holbox Island**. Buses to Chiquilá for boats, 3 times a day. If you miss the ferry a fisherman will probably take you quite cheaply (say US$2). You can leave your car in care of the harbour master for a small charge; his house is E of the dock. Take water with you if possible. Totally unspoiled, take blankets and hammock (ask at fishermen's houses where you can put up), and lots of mosquito repellant. Best camping on beach E of village (N side of island). Fish expensive but bread very good. Wonderful shell-hunting. Five more uninhabited islands beyond Holbox. Beware of sharks and barracuda, though few nasty occurrences have been reported. Off the rough and mostly unpopulated bulge of the Yucatán coastline are several islands, once notorious for contraband. Beware of mosquitoes in the area.

N.B. The E coast of the Yucatán peninsula suffered damage from Hurricane Gilbert in September 1988.

The famous resort of **Cancún**, near the north-eastern tip of the Yucatán peninsula, is a thriving complex and town with skyscraper hotels, basically for the rich, and many smaller hotels with cheaper accommodation. Prices are higher on Cancún than elsewhere in Mexico because everything is brought in from miles outside. Hotels in Cancún town (or in Puerto Juárez, just 3 km. away) are much cheaper than on the beach and there are buses running every 5 minutes for US$0.05. There are many new developments for up to 30 km. outside Cancún, but local infrastructure is poor. The population is about 30,000, almost all dedicated to servicing the tourist industry. There is an archaeological museum next to the Convention Centre with local finds, which also houses the Ballet Folklórico shows in air-conditioned splendour. There are 3 supermarkets (one of them, Bodega El Teniente on Av. Tulum, is good place for changing US dollar cash or cheques) and 5 interconnecting shopping malls. Excursion to Isla Contoy daily, once a day, US$55, including boat, food and snorkelling equipment. The computer which is said to have selected the site seems to have failed in two respects: (a) there are sharks; (b) there are undercurrents. So swimming in the sea is discouraged on several beaches. See free publication, *Cancún Tips*, issued twice a year from Av. Tulum 29, Cancún, QR 77500, Mexico.

Hotels *Camino Real*; *Sheraton*, *Cancún Resort and Towers*, and *Pirámide de Sol*, all in the L+ range (P.O. Box 834, Cancún, T 31988); *Hyatt*, *Cancún Caribe* and *Exalaris Hyatt Regency*; *Holiday Inn Crowne Plaza* (L+, T 51022, all facilities), *Fiesta Americana* and *Krystal*. Slightly less expensive: *Aristos*, *Quality Inn*, *Club Lagoon Caribe*, *Viva* (B), *El Presidente* (L), *Miramar Misión*. Less expensive still: *Caribe Mar* and *Playa Blanca*. *Novotel*, near bus station, B and up, a/c, pool, rooms on street noisy, but other apartments quiet, clean, secure, cheapest good place. At the far end of the island is the *Club Méditerranée* with its customary facilities. Youth hostel, CREA, Km. 3.2 Blvd Zona Hotelera, T 31337, on the beach, dormitory style, 12 people per room, E (also possible to put up tent for US$4). Hotels in Cancún town: *América*, *Atlantis*; slightly less expensive: *Antillano*, *Batab*, *Carillo*, *Handall*, *Konvasser* (a Mayan, not German name), *María de Lourdes*, *Plaza Caribe*, *Plaza del Sol*, *Rivemar*, *Caribe Internacional*, *Soberanis*, *Villa Maya*, all C/D. Least expensive but acceptable still: *Arabe*, *Bonampak*, *Canto*, *Coral*, *Mar y Mar*, *Marufo*, *Villa Rossana*, *Yaxchilán*, and *La Carreta Guest House*. You'll be lucky to find anything below category E. Budget travellers can stay more cheaply in Puerto Juárez and spend the day on Cancún beach.

Camping is not permitted in Cancún town except next to the CREA youth hostel. It is otherwise restricted to a magnificent stretch of beach just past Puerto Juárez.

Restaurants There are about 200 restaurants apart from those connected with hotels. They range from hamburger stands to 5-star, gourmet places. The best buys are on the side streets of Cancún town, while the largest selection can be found on the main street, Av. Tulum. The best is said to be *100% Natural*, in front of *Hotel Caribe Internacional* on Yaxchilán; *Valladolid*, on Uxmal, is reasonable. The ones on the island are of slightly higher price and quality and are scattered along Blvd. Kukulkan, the main island drive, with a high concentration in the 5 shopping centres. The native Mexican restaurants in the workers' colonies are cheapest. Very popular is *El Establo* with *El Granero* disco, just off Av. Tulum on Claveles; *La Boom*, disco near the youth hostel, free entry before 2200.

Entertainment Crococun crocodile ranch, 30 km. on road to Playa del Carmen.

Exchange Banpais and *casa de cambio* next to *Novotel*, latter open Sun.

Car Hire Budget Rent-a-Car in Cancún has been rec. for good service.

Buses Local bus (Route No. 1), US$0.10 (taxis are exorbitant). Buses along the beach front are crowded with pickpockets. Within easy reach are Chichén-Itzá (bus, 3½ hrs., US$2.75), Tulum, and many lesser known Maya centres such as Cobá and Tablé. The road to Tulum is completely paved. Local bus to Puerto Juárez US$0.25, hourly between 0600-2300, taxi US$2. To Chetumal, US$6.45 1st class, 0800-1600 hourly, takes 5 hrs. To Tulum US$1.65, 4 daily 1st class, 5 daily 2nd class, walk 1 km. from bus stop. To Valladolid, US$2.45 1st, US$2 2nd class; To Mexico City, ADO, 1st class at 0615, 1215 and 1815, the road is bad, it can take 29 hrs. To Mérida, US$4.40 1st, US$4 2nd class, 4½ hrs.

Puerto Morelos (bus US$0.50), not far S of Cancún. It has 3 hotels, two expensive, one basic, *Amor*, E, near bus stop; also free camping. Popular with scuba divers and snorkellers, but beware of sharks.

Boat Services Expensive boats leave from the pier near *Calinda Quality Inn* in Cancún; go instead to Puerto Juárez.

Air Services Cancún (very expensive shops and restaurant), Cozumel and Isla Mujeres have airports. Aeroméxico, Av. Tulum 3, T 42758; Mexicana, Av. Cobá 39, T 411444; American Airlines, Aeropuerto, T 42947; United Airlines, Centro El Pavaín, T 42340. Mexicana has direct flights Mexico City-Cancún-Miami. From Cancún by Aeroméxico to Mérida, Monterrey, Mexico City, Houston (also Continental), and New York (also Continental and American). Continental also flies to New Orleans; United to Chicago (very limited service outside Dec.-April season). To Los Angeles daily with North West and Mexicana. Flights to Mexico City are heavily booked; try stand-by at the airport, or go instead to Mérida. Aero Quetzal to Guatemala City Tues. and Sat. 1130 (book well in advance, office in Mexico City—can also book this company's Guatemala City-Flores flights here). Lacsa flies Cancún-Costa Rica and on to Panama. Bookable only at *Hotel María de Lourdes*, closed during siesta-time. Nouvelles Frontières fly charter Zürich-Cancún, 66 Blvd. St. Michel, 75006 Paris, France. Many charters from North America. Taxi-buses from airport to Cancún town US$2. Irregular bus from Cancún to the airport four times a day. Ordinary taxi US$4.50-5.75.

Puerto Juárez is about 3 km. N of Cancún. *Hotel Caribel*, resort complex, C-B, with bath and fan; in the same price range is *San Marcos*; *Posada Zuemy*, 100 metres from bus terminal, on road to Cancún, D; *Isabel*, opp. ferry terminal, D, clean, very noisy, overpriced; *Palmeras* is E. *Restaurant Puerto Juárez* at bus terminal, friendly, good value. Camping/trailer park *Almirante de Gante*, hot showers, right on the beach, 4 km. from army camp and 1 km. from Punta Sam. *Cabañas Punta Sam*, clean, comfortable, on the beach, E with bath. Irregular bus service there, or hitchhike from Puerto Juárez. Check to see if restaurant is open evenings. No shops nearby. Take mosquito repellant.

Ferries Tourist kiosk, open 0900-1700, at passenger ferry to Isla Mujeres which leaves from the jetty opposite the bus terminal at Puerto Juárez 9 times a day; can be erratic and sometimes leaves early (US$0.75, 1 hr.). Also small boats, but these are much more expensive. Ferry from Punta Sam to Isla Mujeres, which takes cars (about 75), 5 km. by bus from Cancún via Puerto Juárez (facilities to store luggage), US$0.40 p.p. and US$1.20 per car; six times a day between 0830 and 2300, returning between 0715 and 2200 (45-min. journey). For early morning ferry from Isla Mujeres, tickets sold anytime from about 0615. Get there early as it is popular. The bus from Mérida (US$4) stops at the ferry and there are hourly buses from Puerto Juárez from 0500.

Buses go from Puerto Juárez and Cancún to Tulum (**see page** 280), Felipe Carrillo Puerto and Chetumal. Bus to Chetumal, 1st class US$7, 2nd class, US$4.80, 5 a day, 6 hrs. To Palenque 2nd class, US$4. To Chichén Itzá, 2nd class, 4 hrs., US$3.30. To Cancún US$0.25. All regular buses from Puerto Juárez stop at Tulum, US$2, 2 hrs. If driving from Puerto Juárez to Tulum, turn right by the Pemex station on to Route 307—it is badly signposted. On the whole it is better to catch outgoing buses in Cancún rather than in Puerto Juárez: there are more of them. You can travel to Emiliano Zapata (40 km. from Palenque) or Villahermosa in a day, taking a launch from Isla Mujeres at 0630, take 0800 bus from Cancún to Chetumal, take 1300 bus from Chetumal to Villahermosa (or later bus at 1430 to Tuxtla Gutiérrez) reach Emiliano Zapata at 1900, good hotels and restaurants; 2nd class buses hourly from E. Zapata to Plaza, at the crossing of the Palenque and Chetumal road.

Isla Mujeres (which got its name from the large number of female idols first found by the Spaniards) once epitomized the Caribbean island: long silver beaches (beware sandflies), palm trees and clean blue water at the N end (although the large *El Presidente* hotel spoils the view there) away from the beach pollution of the town, and the naval airstrip to the SW of the town. There are limestone (coral) cliffs and a rocky coast at the S end. A lagoon on the W side is now fouled up. The island is suffering from competition from Cancún and many hotels are run-down. Worse still, disease has destroyed practically all the palms which used to shade the houses and beach. New, disease-resistant varieties have been planted and it is hoped they will grow to maturity quickly. There was considerable damage from hurricane Gilbert, some of which is still visible. The main activity in the evening takes place in the square near the church, where there are also a supermarket and a cinema. Between December 1-8 there is a fiesta for the Virgin of the island, fireworks, dances until 0400 in the Plaza. If driving, respect speed limits, roads with new gravelling are tricky. The Civil Guard patrol the beaches at night.

At Garrafón beach, 7 km. (mind your belongings, entry US$1.50, and the same for a locker), there is a tropical fish reserve (fishing forbidden) on a small coral reef. Take snorkel (rental US$3 a day from shop opp. the ferry or outside entry to Park (need tourist card for security), but US$2 an hour at Park gate) and swim among a variety of multicoloured tropical fish—they aren't at all shy, but the coral is dead and not colourful. However, there can be more snorkellers than fish. Swim before 1100 when the music-boat from Cancún arrives. Worth walking on from here up a track to the lighthouse. (Taxi to Garrafón US$2.75; there is a bus which goes half-way there. Drinks at Garrafón cost twice as much as in town.) One can cycle down to the southern end of the island to the curious remains of a pirate's domain, called Casa de Mundaca, a nature reserve with giant turtles at El Chequero, and a little, ruined Mayan lighthouse or shrine of Ixtel. It is not signposted—mind you don't walk into the army firing range. Fine views. The island is best visited April to November, off-season (although one can holiday here the year round). The northern beach has dazzling white sand, so wear sunglasses. **N.B.** Travellers are warned that there is a very dangerous beach on the ocean side near the north with strong undertows and cross-currents; there have been numerous drownings. It is just behind the *Bojórquez Hotel*. Trip to unspoilt **Isla Contoy** (bird and wildlife sanctuary), US$30, two hours of fishing, snorkelling (equipment hire extra, US$2.50) and relaxing (see also under Cancún). Boats may not leave until full. An experienced diver, Erik Bernesson of Vaxtorp, Sweden, tells us that the underwater scene at Garrafón is much less interesting, and scuba diving more expensive, than at Cozumel or the Laguna Xelhá; Belize, he says, is even better.

There is public transport on Isla Mujeres, i.e. taxis at fixed prices, e.g. US$1.20 to N beach, and US$0.10 bus service. You can walk from one end of the island to the other in 2½ hrs. Worth hiring a bicycle (wonderfully rickety), by the hour, US$0.35, or US$2.50 a day (about US$7 deposit), or a Honda 50 hourly or for a day (US$15), to explore the island in about 2 hrs. Do check if there is any damage to the bicycle *before* you hire. Bicycles for hire from several hotels. Try Ciro's Motorrentor by *Hotel Caribe* for good motorbikes, US$16. You can rent skin and scuba diving equipment, together with guide, from Divers of Mexico, on the waterfront N of the public pier, a boat and equipment costs about US$40-50 p.p. for ½ day, check how many tanks of air are included and shop around. They can set up group excursions to the Cave of the Sleeping Sharks; English spoken. It is no cheaper to hire snorkel gear in town than on the beach. Deep sea fishing for 10 in a boat from *Aguamundo*. Diving is not in the class of Cozumel and Mexico Divers, with slapdash attitude to safety, not recommended.

Hotels At Christmas hotel prices are increased steeply and the island can heave with tourists, esp. in January. The island has several costly hotels and others, mainly in the D category, and food, especially fresh fruit, is generally expensive.

Reasonable hotels to stay at on Isla Mujeres are *Osorio*, D, Madero, 1 block from waterfront, clean, fan, with bath and hot water, rec., excellent bakery nearby. *Caribe Maya*, Madero 9, central, modern, fans, cockroaches and dirty loos, D; *Carmelina*, Guerrero 9, D, central with bath, clean, rec.; *El Paso*, Morelos 13, D, with bath, clean, facing the pier, 2nd floor; *Caracol*, Matamaros 5, T 20150, D, central, clean, good value; *Maria José*, Madero 25, T 20130, D, clean, fans, friendly, scooter hire; *Posada del Mar*, Alte. Rueda 15, T 20212, A (including meals) has pleasant drinks terrace but expensive drinks, restaurant for residents only; *Rocas del Caribe*, Madero 2, D, 100 metres from ocean, cool rooms, big balcony, clean, good service; *Isla Mujeres*, next to church, C/D, with bath, renovated, run by pleasant Englishman; *Berny*, Juárez y Abosolo, T 20025, C-D, with bath, good, long-distance calls possible, residents only, but does not even honour confirmed reservations if a deposit for one night's stay has not been made. *Las Palmas*, E, central, Guerrero 20, 2 blocks from N beach, good, clean; *Poc-Na Hostal*, F, is cheapest, dormitories, try for central section where there are fans, no bedding or mattresses, take insect repellant. Scrum for a cheap place after the arrival of the morning ferry. There is a trailer park on the island, with a restaurant. At S end of island is *Camping Los Indios* where you can put up your hammock. In town nobody seems to know (or want to know) about this place. **N.B.** If you arrive late, book into any hotel the first night and set out to find what you want by 0700-0800, when the first ferries leave the next morning.

Restaurants Many beach restaurants close just before sunset. *Ciro's*, beware of overcharging, unfriendly if asked for soft drinks; *Caracol*, good, slightly cheaper; *Super Tortas*, delicious sandwiches served by Jenny. *Villa del Mar*, rec., delicious but expensive. *Miriti*, opp. ferry, quite good value: *Rolandi's Pizza*, main shopping street, good breakfast, popular. At Garrafón Beach: *El Garrafón*, *El Garrafón de Castilla*, *French Marías*, all 3 cater for tour boats from Cancún, pricey lobster on magnificent tropical beach. *Gomar*, in town, expensive, possible to eat outside on verandah or in the colonial-style interior, popular; *Mano de Dios*, near the beach, probably cheapest on island, quite good. *Eric's*, 1 block inland, very good inexpensive Mexican snacks; *Tropicana*, 1 block from pier, simple, popular, cheap; *Cielito Lindo*, waterfront, open air, good service; *Peña*, overlooks beach good pizzas, nice atmosphere; *La Langosta*, 3 blocks S, good Mexican dishes, lovely view; *Bucanero*, downtown, steak, seafood, prime rib, classy for Islas Mujeres. *Sergio's* on main square, expensive, very good. *Dhaymaru*, inexpensive, good lentil soup; *Giltri*, in town, good value; *Cito* opp. *Ciro's*, best breakfast, good health food, rec. Small restaurants round market are good value; try the local Poc-Chuc (pork and vegetables) dish.

Opposite the restaurant *Gomar* is a souvenir shop that sells good stone Maya carvings (copies), macramé hangings and colourful wax crayon "Maya" prints. *El Paso Boutique*, opp. ferry, trades a small selection of English novels.

Paamul, about 90 km. S of Cancún, is a fine beach with chalets and campsites (recommended) on a bay, with good restaurant. Good snorkelling and diving. 2nd-class buses from Cancún and Playa del Carmen pass. Playa Aventuras is a huge beach resort 15 km. from Playa del Carmen. *Shangri-la Caribe* is another development, pool, diving equipment may be hired.

Playa Del Carmen is a fast growing tourist centre, with pleasant beaches (though there is litter, there are no sandflies) and many new hotels (but no camping) and restaurants. Swimming is not safe beyond the point (to the left facing Cozumel) where there is nude bathing. Apparently all atmosphere has now been lost. It is 68 km. or one hour by bus from Tulum (US$1), but also buses from Mérida, Cancún (US$1, 1 hr.) and Puerto Juárez. To Mérida 1st class buses go via Cancún, 1 hr., US$1, buy tickets 30 mins in advance, Valladolid, Chichén Itzá, US$3.75, Mérida US$5.50, at 0500, 1000, 1230, 1500, 1700 and 1930. From Mérida some buses co-ordinate with ferry to Cozumel, 2nd class buses 7 a day, 6 hrs. Campsite.

Hotels N of the town is *Blue Parrot*, on beach, with café, B, in bungalow, highly rec; *Las Molcas*, B, nr. beach, pool, luxurious, rec. About 6 km. outside are: At km. 297/8, before Playa del Carmen, *Cabañas Capitán Lafitte*, very good, pool, excellent cheap restaurant on barren beach, A; at km. 296 and similar, *El Marlín Azul*, A, swimming pool, better food; *Delfín*, C; *Posada Lily*, D, with shower, rec., 1 block from first class bus station; *Hotel Nuevo Amanecer*, C, very attractive, fans, mosquito nets, clean; *Yax-Ha* cabins, Calle 10 Norte, C-A (depending on size and season), excellent. *Sian Ka'an*, Calle Siyan Can, 100 m. from bus station, D, simple, clean, rec. By the T-junction on the outskirts, at Route 307, is reasonable *Hotel Maranatha*, with café next door for breakfast and *Doña Juanita's* restaurant (good, opp. Pemex station). Campsite and *cabañas* close to bus station, US$3-4 per tent, US$2 for hammocks, cabins E p.p. *"The Monastery"*, 1 block from *Cabaña Banaña*, D, better rates for longer stays, ask Sam, free use of kitchen and washing facilities, good restaurant with tame iguanas, English spoken, not fancy, but good. *Cabañas La Ruina*, on beach, E, cheapest, popular, rec.; *Costa del Mar*, on beach, pool. Lots of new places going up, none under US$10 a night. 8 km. from Playa del Carmen you can camp at Xcalacoco for US$2.50 a night (US$15 for cabins). CREA Youth Hostel, F, quite comfortable.

Restaurants *La Nena* and *Pizza Moluscas* (expensive, good service); *Balam*, good breakfasts; *Chac Mool*, good, reasonable, near airstrip. *Máscaras*, on beach, highly rec. *Lemons*, excellent; *Chateau Las Palmas*, across from school, good, especially breakfast.

Transport Ferry for Cozumel, US$2.20, 25 mins. journey, 12 a day from 0530-1930, returns between 0400 and 1800. There is also a slower ferry (45-50 minutes). Waterjet catamaran takes 40 mins. 0530-1930, to/from Playa del Carmen 0400-1830. Bus to Tulum and Chetumal (3½ hrs.), US$4.50 (several between 0530 and 2030); to Villahermosa (coming from Cancún) 1900, 13 hrs. US$10, ADO, seats can be booked in advance.

Cozumel island is not only a marvellous place for snorkelling and scuba diving, but is described as a "jewel of nature, possessing much endemic wildlife including pygmy species of coati and raccoon; the bird life has a distinctly Caribbean aspect and many endemic forms also"—Jeffrey L. White, Tucson, Ariz. A good map, including reef locations, is available from stores and shops. In the shops, dollars are preferred to pesos. It is reported to be becoming more and more a US holiday resort. Bicycles, motor bikes and cars can be hired, check safety. The best public beaches are some way from San Miguel town: in the N of the island they are sandy and wide, in the S narrower and rockier. All the main hotels are on the sheltered W coast. The E coast is rockier and has only one, rustic *Hotel Cupido*, more like bungalows. Swimming and diving on the unprotected side is very dangerous owing to ocean underflows.

The island is famous for the beauty of its underwater environment: snorkel 9 km. S of San Miguel de Cozumel at Parque Chankanaab, entrance US$2, restaurants expensive, hire facilities: equipment US$14 a day, good snorkelling for beginners but go early, or you will see only bodies and suntan lotion. The best reef for scuba-diving, and the second longest in the world, is Palacar, reached only by boat. Deportes Acuáticos Damián Piza on Calle 8 Norte, US$40 p.p. includes all equipment, 2 dives with diligent guide separated by a cooked lunch and sunbake on Playa San Francisco—fascinating. There are many diving agencies (Cozumel Divers recommended); the level of charging may vary between US$10 and US$40 a dive, including equipment, it is cheapest before mid-November. Restored ruins of Maya-Toltec period at San Gervasio (7 km. from Cozumel town, then 6 km. to the left).

Hotels (prices rise 50% around Christmas) *Maya Cozumel*, clean, friendly, pool, on Calle 5 Sur 4, T 20011, C; (there is also *Melia Mayan Cozumel*, 5 km. from airport, in the L-L+ bracket); *Aguilar*, 3 Sur 98, T 20307, C, pool, clean, central, a/c, rec.; *Marqués*, Lázaro Cárdenas 121, T 22998, C, rec; *Apartamentos Aguilar*, Calle 10, C, good value; *López*, Calle Sur 7-A, T 20108, C, hot showers, clean, main square, no meals; *Capitán Candela*, inland, pool, good value, D; *Blanquita*, 10-N, T 2-11-90, D, clean, friendly, owner speaks English, rents snorkelling gear and motor-scooters, rec. The cheapest hotels on the island, all D, are: *Yoli*, Calle 1 Sur 164 close to the Plaza, T 20024, with bath and fan; *Posada Edén*, Calle 2 Norte, 2 blocks (one N, one E) from Plaza; *Flores*, Adolfo Rosado Salas 7, T 20164, one block S of Plaza, ½ block E of waterfront, a little more expensive. First class (A-L) hotels include: *Cabañas del Caribe*, *Cozumel Caribe*, *El Cozumeleño*, *El Stouffer Presidente*, *La Ceiba*, *Fiesta Americana*. The first-class hotels on the island charge about US$50-150 d a day and all are directly on the rocky shore except the *Fiesta Americana*, which has a tunnel under the road to the beach.

Camping is not permitted although there are two suitable sites on the S shore. Try asking for permission at the army base.

Restaurants *Las Palmeras*, at the pier (people-watching spot), rec.; *Pizza Rolandi*, waterfront; *Grip's*, on waterfront, good; *Morgans*, main square, elegant; *Plaza Leza*, main square, excellent and reasonable; *La Choza*, Adolfo Rosales Salas 198, reasonable, rec; *Angelo's*, nearer the sea, more expensive, rec; *Karen's*, pizza cheap, good; *Gato Pardo*, good pizzas and try their "tequila slammers"; *Café del Puerto*, 2nd floor by pier, South Seas style; *Super Tortas Los Moros*, Av. Juárez and 10 Av. Norte, Mexican, popular; *Costa Brava*, good sea-food and breakfast, good value, rec. *Carlos and Charlie's* restaurant/bar, popular, 2nd floor on waterfront. *Tortas Denny*, Calle 1 Sur close to Plaza, good and reasonable; *Económico*, 10 Av. Norte between Calle 1 Sur and Calle Salas, friendly, good Mexican food.

Nightclubs *Joman's*, *Scaramouche*, *Grip's*, all downtown, as well as hotel nightclubs.

Air Services Cozumel-Mexico City via Mérida with Mexicana; Mexicana also flies to Dallas and Miami; Continental to Houston; American to New York/Newark; Aero Caribe to Cancún (several daily) and Chetumal.

Paved road on Cozumel but buses serve only the expensive hotels N of town; best to hire push-bike (quiet) when touring around the island so one can see wildlife—iguanas, turtles, birds—but if taking motorbike (Rentadora Cozumel not recommended) beware of policemen who take unguarded ones and then claim they were parked illegally; local police are strict and keen on fining so avoid illegal parking, U-turns, etc.

There are some Mayan ruins on the mainland, unrestored (the Pole ruins) at *Xcaret*, a turnoff left on Route 307 to Tulum, after Playa del Carmen. You can go to a hand-forged chain over a 2 km. bad road and pay whoever comes out of the house an entry fee and proceed down the road a few metres on foot. The ruins are near three linked *cenotes*, to their left; there are also lovely sea water lagoons—one can swim. Pole was the departure point for Mayan voyages to Cozumel. There is a roadside restaurant which despite its looks is very clean (accepts Visa).

Akumal, a luxury resort, is 20 km. N of Tulum, and reached easily by bus from there or from Playa del Carmen (30 mins.) Cove owned by Mexican Skin-Divers Society, 110 km. S from Puerto Juárez. *Hotel Club Akumal Caribe*, L, restaurant (there is a small supermarket nearby at Villas Mayas), poor service, overpriced, no entertainment, excellent beach, linked to two buildings separated by *Villas Mayas*, with coral reef only 100 metres offshore. Eat at restaurant marked *Comidas Económicas* outside the gate. In addition at *Villas Mayas*, bungalows A, with bath, comfortable, some with kitchens, on beach, snorkelling equipment for hire, US$6 per day, restaurant with poor service. Recommended as base for excursions to Xelhá, Tulum and Cobá. There is a small lagoon 3 km. N of Akumal, good snorkelling. Not far from Akumal are Chemuyil (*palapas*—thatched shelters for hammocks—US$2, plus US$1 for shower) and Xcacel beaches and campsites down new roads, with restaurants. Further south, about 8 km. N of Tulum, are the quiet, pleasant *Cabañas Los Arrecifes* on the beach, with cabins all prices from US$4 to US$30 a day, with good fish restaurant. Nearby turtles lay their eggs in July/August, and snorkelling on the nearby reef is good.

Tulum The Tulum ruins, Maya-Toltec, are 128 km. S of Cancún, 1 km. off the main road; they are 12th century, with city walls of white stone atop coastal cliffs (frescoes still visible on interior walls of temples). The temples were dedicated to the worship of the Falling God, or the Setting Sun, represented as a falling character over nearly all the West-facing doors (Cozumel was the home of the Rising Sun). The same idea is reflected in the buildings, which are wider at the top than at the bottom. Open 0800-1700, about 2 hrs. needed to view at leisure (entry US$0.50, half-price for students, Sun. free). Panorama guide book is interesting. Tulum is these days crowded with tourists (fewer p.m.).
  The village is not very large and has neither a bank nor post office

(nearest at Playa del Carmen or Felipe Carrillo Puerto); there are very few rooms to let so arrive early if you wish to stay, otherwise leave the bus at the ruins. Shops at the ruins are expensive and locals can be unfriendly. Beaches are beautiful but sometimes dirty, and there is thieving from beach camping spots and *cabañas*, so be careful. The ruins are just off the paved road, between Felipe Carrillo Puerto (98 km.) and Puerto Juárez (133 km.), and can also be visited by boat from Cozumel. The road from Tulum to Felipe Carrillo Puerto is paved. Service stations at Cancún, Tulum, Nuevo Xcan and Felipe Carrillo Puerto, but one only between Tulum and Cancún (140 km.).

There is a large car-park at the entrance to the ruins (here you can leave luggage), which is ringed by small shops (selling dresses, etc). and restaurants of which only one sells beer and liquor and closes at 1700. Soft drinks expensive, US$0.80. On the paved road to the right of the parking lot, along the coast, you will find a whole string of beach places with hammock and tent space and rooms with meals, F. Hammock space may also be rented in the village of Tulum, 2 km. from ruins (minibus to ruins at 0900,US$0.50); *Motel Crucero*, D; about 1½ km. from the ruins down the beach is *Santa Fe* where *cabañas* are rented for US$7.50, has a restaurant, good fish dinners, English, French and Italian spoken, basic toilets, OK but take precautions against theft; again along the beach nearby are *Cabañas El Mirador*, small, quiet, cabins US$10, no sanitation, and *El Paraíso*, very casual, scorpions found, agree rates in advance, electricity only from 1800 to 2100. Mosquito-net supplies are very limited so take good repellant lotion with you. Water at *El Mirador* and *Santa Fe* a bit smelly because well-water is used for washing and suds have spoiled it, but good water at a spot on the road between ruins and the path to the camp sites. Good restaurant at *Cabañas Don Armando*, E, no electricity, the best, good meeting place, between *Santa Fe* and *Paraíso*. One restaurant on the road and two restaurants next to the Navy camp, worth trying. Walk past the restaurants to the shops and main centre (15-20 mins.), where you can stock up on supplies which are cheaper than at the ruins. Continue on the road out of town past the village well and then some beehives, then take a well-worn path to the beach. *Pablo's House* (the village is 3 km. away from Pablo's), is cheaper with own hammocks, meals, no w.c. or showers, only a well, fairly basic, beware of over-charging. Watch your belongings. Trailer Park next door. *Chac Mul*, 5 km. S from ruins, wooden huts, D, good showers, restaurant, nice, relaxed. You can cook over open fires along the beach about ½ km. from the ruins, so take your own food. A new hotel, D, has been built at crossroads where buses stop to let people off for the ruins, and there is a restaurant there, which will hold luggage while you visit the site (US$0.40 per bag). *Hotel Posada Tulum*, 8 km. S of the ruins on the beach, D, has an expensive restaurant and is not served by public transport. About 6 km. from ruins are *Cabañas de Tulum*, D, also with restaurant, armies of cockroaches and scorpions; interesting fish in the cenote opposite, take taxi there (US$2), empty white beaches, no bus to ruins, cabins not clean, well built or well supplied, eat at *Anna y José*, rec. Many km. further S, *Rancho Retiro*, camping US$2, food and beer served, very relaxed atmosphere.

Parking or camping possible on beach S of lighthouse, whose keeper also rents huts along beach for US$1.20 a day, and at *Cabañas El Mirador*. Good swimming locally; divers bring in lobster from a coral reef about 400 metres offshore.

Bus from Tulum to Mérida, three daily via Puerto Morelos, US$6.50, 8 hrs, except Sun. when service is erratic; from Felipe Carrillo Puerto to Mérida via Muna, US$4, 4½ hrs. To Felipe Carrillo Puerto, 1 hr., US$1.50, few buses; to Chetumal, US$2.90, 4 hrs, it may be necessary to go to Playa del Carmen to get on (1st class from· village only, 4 a day before 1230); to Puerto Juárez, 2nd class; Cancún, US$1.65, 2 hrs.; to Playa del Carmen, 1 hr., US$1. To Cobá at 0600 and 1200, goes on to Valladolid (US$2.10, 2½ hrs.); at 1700 goes only to Cobá; bus to Cobá from Valladolid passes Xcan (no hotel but the owner of the shop where the road branches off to Cobá may offer you a room). (It is easier to reach Valladolid via Cancún than direct.)

N of Tulum (12 km.) at km. 245 (bus from Playa del Carmen, 45 mins.) is a beautiful clear lagoon, **Laguna Xelhá**, full of fish, but no fishing allowed as it is a national park (open 0800-1700), entry US$2, get a receipt if you want to leave and come back next day. Snorkelling gear can be rented at US$4.15 for a day, but it is often in poor repair; better to rent from your hotel. Arrive as early as possible to see fish (you need to dive down about a metre because above that level the water is cold and fresh with few fish; below it is the warm, fish-filled salt water) as later buses full of tourists arrive from Cancún, watch for sting-rays. Bungalows being built. Very expensive food. There is a marvellous jungle path to one of the lagoon bays. Xelhá ruins (known also as Los Basadres) are located across the road from the beach of the same name. You may have to jump the fence to visit. Small ruins of Ak are near Xelhá. N of Tulum, at Tancáh, are newly-discovered bright post-classical Maya murals but they are sometimes closed to the public.

There is a newly-laid road linking Tulum with the large but little-excavated city of Cobá (see below) with the turn-off to Cobá about 1½ km. along the main road in the direction of Chetumal, which joins the Valladolid-Puerto Juárez road at Xcan, thus greatly shortening the distance between Chichén-Itzá and Tulum.

The ruins of Chumyaxche, three pyramids (partly overgrown), on the left-hand side of the road to Felipe Carrillo Puerto, 18 km. S of Tulum, are worth a visit.

Cobá, the ancient political capital of the area, with the largest ruins (open 0900-1700, entry US$0.45), about 50 km. inland from Tulum, still unspoiled, is also being developed; an unusual feature is the network of ancient roads, known as *sacbes*.

Village is about 1 km. from ruins. Beware of ticks and snakes when rummaging through the brush. There is a lake where tucans may be seen very early. Swim in the laguna in the village; there are a pair of crocodiles in the one on the site, the male is called Victor in case anyone ever has to shout at him. 1½ km. from Cobá lies a huge pyramid called Nohoch-Mul. The entire archaeological zone encompasses about 6,500 structures and covers many square kilometres.

Lodging and Transport: *Villa Arqueológica* (Club Méditerranée), open to non members, clean and quiet, A, swimming pool, good food. Go via Valladolid, Chemax on Puerto Juárez road—or bus from Cancún or daily from Playa del Carmen via Tulum to crossroads 4 km. from Cobá. Bus, Cobá-Tulum, 1500. Few buses, but two daily to Valladolid at 0700 and 1200 (from Valladolid, 0430, 1315, US$1.50, 2 hrs.). Good, cheap restaurant in the village, *El Bocadito* (also has rooms, E), and little grocery store where you can buy soft drinks and safely leave your luggage.

At **Felipe Carrillo Puerto** Hotel Carrillo Puerto has been rec.; *El Faisán y El*

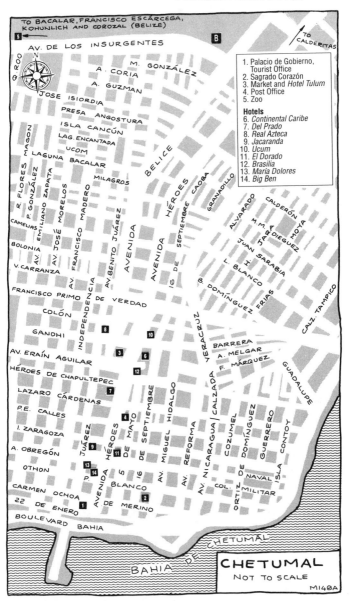

TO BACALAR, FRANCISCO ESCÁRCEGA, KOHUNLICH AND COROZAL (BELIZE)

TO CALDERITAS

1. Palacio de Gobierno, Tourist Office
2. Sagrado Corazón
3. Market and *Hotel Tulum*
4. Post Office
5. Zoo

Hotels
6. *Continental Caribe*
7. *Del Prado*
8. *Real Azteca*
9. *Jacaranda*
10. *Ucum*
11. *El Dorado*
12. *Brasilia*
13. *María Dolores*
14. *Big Ben*

CHETUMAL
NOT TO SCALE
M148A

Venado, D, with marble bathrooms; *Tulum*, E, with better restaurant; *San Ignacio*, nr. Pemex, F, good value; *Hotel Esquivel*, just off Plaza, F, not good, dirty, no locks on doors, noisy; *Restaurant Addy*, on main road, S of town, good, simple. South of Felipe Carrillo Puerto, on the road to Chetumal at Km. 8 and Km. 25, there are good trails leading East.

Chetumal, (pop. 120,000) the capital of the state of Quintana Roo, now being developed for tourism (albeit slowly), is a free port with clean wide streets, and a greatly improved waterfront with parks and trees. The State Congress building has a mural showing the history of Quintana Roo. Good for foreign foodstuffs—cheaper at covered market in outskirts than in centre. Some travellers have warned that there are many drunks roaming the streets; also many mosquitoes and high prices. Airport.

N.B. Now that Quintana Roo is no longer a territory but a state, it is illegal to sell cars and other imported goods there. Visas to Guatemala must be obtained in Chetumal (Consulate, Alvaro Obregón 342, US$10 and passport photo, for 30 days, one entry open, takes 10 minutes) because none in Belize. Hitching is difficult to the Belizean border. Cars with light-green licence plates are a form of taxi.

Hotels (accommodation may be a problem during the holiday season). *Continental Caribe*, Av. Héroes 171, T 21100, A; *Del Prado*, Héroes de Chapultepec, rather scruffy and poorly equipped, quiet, overpriced restaurant, A; *El Marqués*, Lázaro Cárdenas 121, T 22998, D, fan, a/c, hot water, restaurant, recommended; *Real Azteca*, Belice 186, T 20720, C, cheerful, friendly and clean, but no hot shower (top floor rooms best); *Jacaranda*, Av. Obregon 201, T 21455, D; *Ucum*, Gandhi 4, T 20711, E (no singles) with fan and bath, check that sheets are clean, good value; *El Dorado*, Av. 5 de Mayo 21, T 20316, D, hot water, a/c, overpriced (no restaurant); *María Dolores*, Alvaro Obregón, E, rec; *Brasilia*, Aguilar 186, T 20964, D, "cockroaches paradise"; *América*, E, on Juárez, 1 block from Héroes, basic, but friendly. *Luz María*, Carmen de Merino 204, T 20202, friendly but not very clean, E, owner speaks English; *Big Ben*, Héroes 48-A, T 20965, E, clean, pleasant and safe, but a bit overpriced; *Posada Colonial*, Benjamín Hill between Av. Héroes y Calle Librado y Rivera, E, basic but OK, closest to bus station (left to roundabout, left again for 200 m.); *Tulum*, Héroes 2, T 20518, above market, E, noise starts 0530, cheap. Plenty more. CREA Youth Hostel, F, corner Anaya y Obregón, T (91) 981-62164, C.P. 77000, hot water, clean, rec.

Camping at Zastal Yoo Canaab 13 km. from W junction to Calderitas, 26 spaces on beach, cold showers, mini store, friendly, US$8 for 2 plus car.

Restaurants bus station, clean and cheap, also one next door to *Hotel Ucum*, which is reasonable. Cheap snacks at *Lonchería Ivette* on Mahatma Gandhi 154. *La Charca de las Ranas Verdes*, opp. bandstand, cheap and good; *Sergio Pizza*, Obregón 182, good pizzas, good but expensive steak meals, a/c, good drinks too. Generally difficult to find restaurants Sunday night. *Caribe*, near park, with bandstand, near water, rec. *Viky* on Isla Cancún, ½ block W of the N side of the market, good local dishes, good value. *Cafetería Don Artur*, nr. market on Héroes, good value breakfasts; *Los Milagros*, Av. Zaragoza and 5 de Mayo, cheap breakfasts, OK. *Vaticano*, on the same street has good tamales. *Los de Colores*, Zaragoza and Juárez, good fish. Pleasant bar, *La Choza del Huinic*, at Av. Hidalgo 132. Try *Safari* roadhouse in Calderitas suburb for enterprising nightlife.

Shopping Shops are open from 0800-1300 and 1800-2000. For exchange, Banamex (0900-1330) on corner of Juárez and Obregón, may need to wait till

1100 for rates.

Garage Talleres Barrera, helpful, on Primo de Verdad; turn right off main street that passes market, then past the electrical plant.

Exchange Banks do not change quetzales into pesos.

Health Malaria prophylaxis available from Centro de Salud, opposite hospital (request tablets for "paludismo").

Tourist Information Av. Héroes, helpful. Turismo Maya at *Hotel Continental Caribe* will arrange flights in Belize, T 2-05-55.

Buses Bus station now 2-3 km. out of town at intersection of Insurgentes y Belice, clean facilities; taxi from town US$0.50. You can change pesos into Belize dollars both at bus station and at border. Many buses going to the border, US$0.15; taxi from Chetumal to border, 20 mins., US$4 for two. Buses are often all booked a day ahead so avoid unbooked connections. Autobuses del Caribe to Mexico City, 22 hrs., US$28, leave at 0900, 1300, 2000, 2230 daily via Villahermosa (US$7, 10 hrs., the road is bad and it can take longer); bus to Francisco Escárcega, 3½ hrs., US$3, 2nd class (2 in the morning, then at 1700, 1945 and 2100); from Chetumal to Palenque, better connections at Emiliano Zapata (bus to there at 0900, 1300, US$6) than Francisco Escárcega, more buses daily, but must take bus from E. Zapata to Catazaja, thence minibus or cheap taxi to Palenque Lacandonia has bus to San Cristóbal and Palenque at 2130, arrives back at 2000. Bus to Mérida, 16 a day, US$7 1st class, about 7 hrs. To Felipe Carrillo Puerto, US$1.75, 1½ hrs., many, on excellent road. To Cancún, 6 hrs., boring road, about 8 daily, between 0630 and 2400. To Tulum, five (2nd class) a day, 4 hrs., US$2.90. There are also buses to Veracruz, Campeche, Villahermosa, Córdoba, X-Pujil and Puerto Juárez. Green *colectivos* go along the coast US$9 to Cancún.

   To Belize Batty Bus and Venus Bus from bus terminal to Belize City (former each even hour, latter each odd hour), taking 3½ hrs. "express", otherwise 5 hrs. on new road, largely paved (0230, 0400 or 0600 Batty bus to make direct connection with Guatemalan frontier), US$3.50 in pesos, US dollars or Belize dollars. Be there in good time; they sometimes leave early if full. Bus Chetumal-Orange Walk, US$1.40. Money checked on entering Belize. Excess Mexican pesos are easily changed into Belizean dollars with men waiting just beyond customs on the Belize side. A list of nationalities who do *NOT* need a visa for Belize is given in the Belize **Information for Visitors** section. All others **must** have a visa in advance. The surest place to get one is in Mexico City at the Belize Embassy. There is an Honorary Consul (designate) in Chetumal, but you must phone him in advance to check that he is available and can perform this service: Sr Rafael Chávez, Av. Zaragoza 231, Altos 201, Chetumal, T (983) 20513.

   To hitch once inside Belize, it is best to take the *colectivo* from in front of the hospital (1 block from the bus station, ask) marked "Chetumal-Santa Elena", US$0.30. You can change US for Belizean dollar bills in the shops at the border, at a rather poor rate, this is not necessary as US$ are accepted in Belize. Note that on the Mexican side border guards can be rather offhand and indolent; money may help to remedy this. **N.B.** If travelling by car be at the border before 1500 to have your papers checked. On entering Belize you must purchase car insurance.

Excursions 6 Km. N of Chetumal are the stony beaches of Calderitas, bus US$0.12 or taxi, US$3.50, many fish restaurants. 16 km. N Laguna de los Milagros, a beautiful lagoon, and 34 km. N of Chetumal, on the road to Tulum (**page** 280), is Cenote Azul, over 70 metres deep, with an expensive waterside restaurant serving good regional food and a new and well-equipped trailer park (Apartado 88, Chetumal; other *cenotes* in area). About 3 km. N of Cenote Azul is the village of Bacalar (nice, but not special) on the Laguna de Siete Colores; swimming and skin-diving; minibus service from minibus terminal 2 blocks from the electricity generating plant in Chetumal, US$0.35. There is a Spanish fort there overlooking a shallow, clear, fresh water lagoon; hotel and good restaurants on the Laguna. *Buk-Halot*, D, and a cheap but comfortable *casa de huéspedes* near the fort on the park. Camping possible at the end of the road 100 metres from the lagoon, toilets and shower, US$0.10, but lagoon perfect for washing and swimming; Balneario Ejidal, with changing facilities and restaurant, rec; gasoline is sold in a side-street. N of Bacalar a direct road (Route 293) runs to Muna, on the road between Mérida and Uxmal. About 2 km. S of Bacalar (on left-hand side of the road going towards the village) is *Hotel Las Lagunas*, very good, swimming pool and opp. a sweet-water lake, C; restaurant is, however, overpriced. 30 km. S of Chetumal is Palmara, located along the Río Hondo, which borders Belize, swimming holes and restaurant.

From Chetumal one can visit the fascinating Mayan ruins that lie on the way to Francisco Escárcega. Buses leave at 0600 (2nd class) from Chetumal to Francisco Villa and Xpujil; there is no direct transport to Kohunlich, Becán and Chicana, so from Xpujil the following journey must be done privately. Just before Francisco Villa lie the ruins of **Kohunlich** (entry US$0.40), about 7 km. S to the main road, where there are fabulous masks (early classic, A.D. 250-500) set on the side of the main pyramid, still bearing red colouring; they are unique of their kind. Seven km. further on from **Xpujil**, 8th century A.D. (all that remains of one large pyramid, recently restored, beside the road), lies the large Maya site of **Becán**, shielded by the forest with wild animals still wandering among the ruins, surrounded by a water-less moat and a low wall, now collapsed, with vast temples and plazas and a decayed ball court. Two km. further on and 10 mins. down a paved road lies **Chicana**, with a superb late classic Maya temple with an ornate central door which has been formed in the shape of the open-fanged jaws of the plumed serpent. Free camping at both Becán and Chicana. Buses return from Xpujil at 1300 and 1700.

Across the bay from Chetumal, at the very tip of Quintana Roo is **Xcalak**, which may be reached from Chetumal by private launch (2 hrs.), or by a long, scenic (recent) unpaved road from Limones (3½ hrs., 120 km., suitable for passenger cars but needs skilled driver). Bus runs Fri. 1600 and Sun. 0600, returning Sat. a.m. and Sun. p.m. (details from Chetumal tourist office). Xcalak is a fishing village (250 pop.) with a few shops with beer and basic supplies and one hotel, F. Rent a boat and explore Chetumal Bay and Banco Chinchorro, unspoiled islands. N of Chetumal are also the unexcavated archaeological sites of Ichpaatun (13 km.), Oxtancah (14) and Nohochmul (20). Do *not* try to walk from Xcalak along the coast to San Pedro, Belize; the route is virtually impassable.

Maps of roads in Quintana Roo are obtainable in Chetumal at Junta Local de Caminos, Secretaría de Obras Públicas. The road from Chetumal through Tulum to Mérida (via Cancún) is paved.

BAJA CALIFORNIA

Baja California (Lower California) is that long narrow arm which dangles southwards from the US border between the Pacific and the Gulf of California for 1,300 km. It is divided administratively into the states of Baja California and Baja California Sur, with a one-hour time change at the state line. The average width is only 80 km. Rugged and almost uninhabited mountains split its tapering length. Only the southern tip gets enough rain: the northern half gets its small quota during the winter, the southern half during the summer. Most of the land is hot, parched deserts, but deserts of infinite variety and everchanging landscapes, clothed in a fascinating array of hardy vegetation. Most visitors find Baja a magical place of blue skies, fresh air, solitude and refuge from the rat race north of the border. Not only the northern regions near the US, but also the southern Cape zone is attracting increasing numbers of tourists. The US dollar is preferred in most places north of La Paz.

Stretching 1,704 km. from Tijuana to Cabo San Lucas, Highway 1 is in good repair, although slightly narrow and lacking hard shoulders. Service stations are placed at adequate intervals along it, but motorists should fill their tanks at every opportunity, particularly if venturing off the main roads. The same conditions apply for Highways 5 (Mexicali-San Felipe), 3 (Tecate-Ensenada-San Felipe road) and 2 (Tijuana-Mexicali-San Luís-Sonoita). Hitch-hiking is difficult, and there is very little public transport off the main highway. The local population has little time to spare for tourists; those from the USA may occasionally find them aloof, but in general the visitor experiences friendliness and hospitality.

There is no immigration check on the Mexican side of the border—the buffer zone for about 120 km. south of the frontier allows US citizens to travel without a tourist card. Immigration authorities are encountered at Mexicali and south of Maneadero (theoretically), at Quitovac, 28 km. south of Sonoita (Sonora) on Highway 2, and when boarding the ferries to cross the Gulf. Ferries ply from Pichilingüe (north of La Paz) and Santa Rosalía to various places on the mainland (see text). As a car needs an import permit, make sure you get to the ferry with lots of time and preferably with a reservation if going on the Pichilingüe-Mazatlán ferry. (See under La Paz below.)

Recommended guides The Automobile Club of Southern California's *Baja California*, which contains plenty of information and detailed driving logs for all of Baja's roads; *Baja California: A Travel Survival Kit*, Lonely Planet (1988); and *The Magnificent Peninsula*, by Jack Williams, which includes a km. by km. log to the highways as well as an enormous amount of background detail.

Maps There are only two really comprehensive maps—the road map published by the ACSC, which gives highly detailed road distances (but in miles) and conditions, and which is available only to AAA members; and International Travel Map (ITM) Production's *Baja California 1:1,000,000* (1989), which includes extra geographical and recreational detail on a topographic base. Many specialist maps and guides are available in book stores in Southern California. Both guidebooks and maps are sadly rare in Baja itself.

The Value Added Tax (IVA) is only 6% in Baja California compared with 15% on the mainland (although costs of food and accommodation are more expensive than the rest of Mexico, but less than in the USA). Tijuana, Ensenada and La Paz all have a good range of duty-free shopping. Stove fuel is impossible to find in Baja California Sur. Beware of overcharging on buses and make a note of departure times of buses in Tijuana or Ensenada when travelling S: between Ensenada and Santa Rosalía it is very difficult to obtain bus timetable information, even at bus stations. Don't ask for English menus if you can help it—prices often differ from the Spanish version. Always check change, overcharging is rife. Note also that hotels have widely divergent winter and summer rates; between June and November tariffs are normally lower than those given in the text below (especially in expensive places).

Cortés attempted to settle at La Paz in 1534 after one of his expeditions had become the first Europeans to set foot in Baja, but the land's sterile beauty disguised a chronic lack of food and water; this and sporadic Indian hostility forced the abandonment of most early attempts at settlement. Jesuit missionary fathers arrived at Loreto in 1697 and founded the first of their 20 missions. The Franciscans and then Dominicans took over when the Jesuits were expelled in 1767. The fathers were devoted and untiring in their efforts to convert the peninsula's three ethnic groups, but diseases introduced unknowingly by them and by ships calling along the coasts soon tragically decimated Indian numbers; some Indians remain today, but without tribal organization. Scattered about the Sierras are the remains of 30 of these well-meaning but lethal missions—some beautifully restored, others only eroded adobe foundations. Most are within easy reach from Highway 1, although 4-wheel drive is necessary for remoter sites such as San Pedro Mártir and Dolores del Sur.

Baja became part of Mexico after the signing of the peace treaty with the United States in 1848, ceded in exchange for Alta California. Battles were fought on the peninsula during the Mexican Revolution. Today's population of about 2.8 million has increased by two-thirds in the past decade through migration from Mexico's interior and Central Pacific coast. The development of agriculture, tourism, industry, migrant labour from California, and the opening of the Transpeninsular Highway has caused an upsurge of economic growth and consequently of prices, especially in areas favoured by tourists.

The Morelos dam on the upper reaches of the Colorado River has turned the Mexicali valley into a major agricultural area: 400,000 acres under irrigation to grow cotton and olives. The San Quintín Valley and the Magdalena Plain are other successful areas where crops have been wrenched from the desert. Industries are encouraged in all border regions by investment incentives; called *maquiladoras*, they are foreign-owned enterprises which import raw materials without duty, manufacture in Mexico and ship the products back to the United States.

Mexicali (pop. 850,000), capital of Baja California state, is not as geared to tourism as Tijuana and thus retains its busy, business-like border town flavour. It is a good place to stock up on supplies, cheap clothing and footware, and souvenirs.

The new Centro Cívico-Comercial, Calzada López Mateos, is an ambitious urban development comprising government offices, medical school, hospitals, bullring, bus station, cinemas, etc. The City Park, in the south-west sector, contains a zoo, picnic area and natural history museum (open Tues.-Fri. 0900-1700; weekend 0900-1800). University of Baja California's Regional Museum, Av. Reforma y Calle L; interesting exhibits illustrating Baja's archaeology, ethnography and missions (Tues.-Fri. 0900-1800; weekend 1000-1500, admission free). Galería de la Ciudad, Av. Obregón 1209, between Calles D y E, former state governor's residence, features work of Mexican painters, sculptors and photographers (Mon.-Fri. 0900-2000). There are *charreadas* (rodeos), held on Sundays during the April-October season, at two separate *charro* grounds on eastern and western outskirts of Mexicali—check times (T 568-2320).

Hotels *Holiday Inn*, L, Blvd. Benito Juárez 2220, T (656) 61300, a/c, best in town; *Lucerna*, B, Blvd. Juárez 2151, T 541000, a/c, meeting rooms, bar, nightclub; *Castel Calafía*, B, Calzada Justo Sierra 1495, T 682841, a/c, plain but comfortable, dining room; *Del Norte*, C, Calle Melgar y Av. Francisco Madero, T 540575, some a/c and TV, across from border crossing, pleasant. *Rivera*, near the railway station, a/c, best of the cheaper hotels; *Fortín de las Flores*, Av. Cristóbal Colón 612, T 524522; and *Las Fuentes*, Blvd. López Mateos 1655, T 571525, both with a/c and TV but noisy, tolerable if on a tight budget, D; *La Siesta*, D, Justo Sierra 899, T 541100, reasonable, coffee shop.

    Motels *Azteca de Oro*, D/E, Calle Industria 600, T 571433, opposite the station, a/c, TV, a bit scruffy but convenient. Others around town and in Calexico just across the border around East 4th St.

    Many good night clubs on Av. Justo Sierra, and on your left as you cross border, several blocks away.

Exchange All major banks: currency exchange is only from 0900-1330. *Casas de cambio* in Calexico give a slightly better rate. Several *cambios* on López Mateos.

Note The border crossing back into the U.S. is only from the end of Av. Cristóbal Colón (which parallels the frontier fence); Calzada López Mateos brings traffic into Mexico from Calexico.

Tourist Office State Tourism Office, Calle Comercio, between Reforma and Obregón ("Centro Cívico" bus); better is Tourist and Convention Bureau, Calzada López Mateos y Calle Camelias, helpful, English spoken, open Mon.-Fri. 0800-1900, Sat. 0900-1300. The Procuraduría de Protección al Turista, which provides legal assistance for visitors, is in the same building as the State Tourism office.

Airport 18 km. East, Blvd. Aviación; daily flights to Mexico City. Charter services.

Train The railway station to the S is about 3½ km. from the tourist area on the border and Calle 3 bus connects it with the nearby bus terminal. There is a passport desk at the station. The ticket information office closes at 1230 but there are timetables on the wall. The current Eurail guide gives through trains to Mexico City, if correct, this should reduce the times given. A special 1st class train, *servicio estrella*, leaves at 0900 daily for the capital, US$40, meals included, a/c, book in advance. Slow train (leaves 2000, 2nd class cars) to Guadalajara and Mexico City takes 57 hrs., there are reported to be rats in the carriages; fast train 44 hrs. (36 hrs. to Guadalajara) at 1000, has only sleepers and special 1st class (although at times it is as slow as the slow train owing to breakdowns), little price difference. Mexicali to Mazatlán, 23 hrs. Be sure to take your own food. If there are dining cars they can run out of food, when there are delays. Food and drink sold on station platforms. Make sure you are on the right car as some are disconnected—guards not always reliable, thieves especially active if lights are turned off. Thorough police luggage searches for drugs and guns possible. Toilets in each class are inefficient and therefore unpleasant. There is no air conditioning except in *dormitorio* cabins for 1-2 persons. Price difference between cabins and roomettes minimal, but cabin vastly preferable. 1st class seats are comfortable. Very hot and dusty in desert part of trip, though train is cleaned twice, cold at night between Los Mochis and Mexico City, take a blanket. Passengers not on sleeping cars on fast train change at Benjamín Hill to the train from Nogales which is often very full on arrival (on the slow train only the special 1st class car and the dining car are detached, the rest go all the way to Guadalajara). If you come from the N on the slow train and want to go to Chihuahua you'll arrive at 2005 at the junction, **Sufragio** (the fast train arrives at 0250). Pacífico train to Guadalajara, 0500 (18 hrs.) US$13, dirty, reported unsafe. For a hotel, go to San Blas, 5 mins. away by local bus, where there are 3 hotels: *Santa Lucía*, *San Marco*, both often full; *Pérez* dirty but adequate, F. If the next morning you are refused a ticket because the train is full, try getting in and getting a ticket on the train.

Bus Tijuana, 3 hrs., US$2.35 1st class, US$1.20 2nd class, sit on left for views at the Cantú Grade; San Felipe, 3 hrs., daily at 0800, 1200, 1600, 2000, US$1.50-2.00, Guadalajara, US$27. Mazatlán, US$25. Hermosillo, 10 hrs., US$9. Mexico City, US$36. Ensenada, US$3.75. Santa Rosalía, US$14. La Paz, daily 1630, 24 hrs., US$25. All trips leave from the new central bus station (Camionera Central) on Av. Independencia; four major bus companies have their offices here under one roof. Autotransportes Tres Estrellas de Oro serves both Baja and the mainland. Greyhound from Los Angeles to Calexico (901 Imperial Av.), US$30, 6 hrs. San Diego to Calexico via El Centro, US$18.65, 3 to 4 hours. The 1200 bus from San Diego connects with the Pullman bus to Mazatlán, US$25, 21 hrs. Local buses are cheap, about US$0.20. "Central Camionera" bus to Civic Centre and bus station.

Paved Highway 5 heads south from Mexicali 196 km. to San Felipe, passing at about Km. 34 the Cerro Prieto geothermal field. After passing the Río Hardy (one of the peninsula's few permanent rivers) and the Laguna Salada (Km. 72), a vast dry alkali flat unless turned into a muddy morass by rare falls of rain, the road continues straight across sandy desert until entering San Felipe around a tall, white, double-arched monument.

San Felipe is a pleasant, tranquil fishing and shrimping port on the Gulf of California with a population of about 9,000. Long a destination for devoted sportfishermen and a weekend retreat for North Americans, San Felipe is now experiencing a second discovery, with new trailer parks and the paving of many of the town's sandy streets. A new airport 8 km. south. San Felipe is protected from desert winds by the coastal mountains and is unbearably hot during the summer; in winter the climate is unsurpassed, and on weekends it can become overcrowded and noisy. A good view of the wide sandy beach can be had from the Virgin of Guadalupe shrine near the lighthouse.

Navy Day is celebrated on 1 June with a carnival, street dancing and boat races. Pasqual, "The Clam Man" and self-proclaimed "Official Greeter of San Felipe", can be found in a jumble of shacks by the main road as it enters town.

Hotels *Castel*, A, Av. Misión de Loreto 148, T 71282, a/c, 2 pools, tennis etc., best in town; *Vagabond Inn*, B, on same street, 3 km. south ot town, a/c, pool and beach; *Villa del Mar*, B/C, pool, volley ball court, restaurant; *Fiesta San Felipe*, C, 9 km. south on the airport road, isolated, every room has Gulf view, tennis, pool, restaurant. *Riviera*, C, 1 km. south on coastal bluff, T 71185, a/c, pool, spa, restaurant.

Motels *El Cortés*, B, on Av. Mar de Cortés, T 71055, beachside esplanade, a/c, pool, palapas on beach, launching ramp, disco, restaurant; *El Pescador*, D, T 71044, Mar de Cortés and Calzada Chetumal, a/c, modest but comfortable; *El Capitán*, C, Mar de Cortés 298, T 71303, a/c, some balconies, pool, lovely rancho-style building, hard beds but otherwise OK; *Chapala*, D, some a/c, free coffee, modest but adequate, on beachfront, T 71240.

Camping Many trailer parks and campgrounds in town and on coast to north and south, inc. *El Faro Beach and Trailer Park*, D, on the bay 18 km. south; *Ruben's*, *Playa Bonita*, *La Jolla*, *Playa de Laura*, *Mar del Sol*, and the more primitive Campo Peewee and Pete's Camp, both about 10 km. north. All from US$5-8 per night for two.

Tourist Office Mar de Cortés y Manzanillo, opp. *El Capitán Motel*, helpful, little handout material, open Tues.-Sun. 0900-1400 and 1600-1800.

The coastal road S of San Felipe has been paved as far as Puertecitos, a straggling settlement mainly of North American holiday homes. There is an airstrip, a simple grocery store, a Pemex station and the 8-room *Puertecitos Motel*. Fishing is good outside the shallow bay and there are several tidal hot springs at the south-east point. The road continues S along the coast (graded but rough in places; high-clearance vehicles rec.), leading to the tranquil Bahía San Luís Gonzaga, on which are the basic resorts of Papa Fernández and Alfonsinas; the beach here is pure sand, empty and silent. From here, the "new" road heads west over hills to meet Highway 1 near Laguna Chapala, 53 km. S of Cataviña, opening up a circular route through northern Baja California.

Highway 2 runs E from Mexicali through San Luis Río Colorado, Sonoita and Caborca to join the Pacific Highway at Santa Ana; **see page** 102.

The road from Mexicali W to Tijuana is fast and well surfaced, it runs across barren desert flats, below sea level and with organ-pipe cacti in abundance, until reaching the eastern escarpment of the peninsula's spine; it winds its way up the Cantú Grade to La Rumorosa, giving expansive, dramatic vistas of desert and mountain. La Rumorosa, sited high enough on a boulder-strewn plateau to receive a sprinkling of snow in winter, has a service station. There are three more Pemex stations along the highway before it reaches Tecate after 144 km.

Tecate is a quiet border town of 35,000, without a population centre on the US side. It is a pleasant place to break the journey, especially around the tree-shaded Parque Hidalgo. Brewing beer is an important local industry and the Tecate Brewery runs tours on the first three Saturdays of the month from 0800-1200 (Tecate and Carta Blanca are two of Mexico's most respected ales). The border crossing at Tecate is open 0700-2000 daily, non-US citizens can have their passports stamped here if they can find the office, otherwise it can be done at the bus terminal. *Motel El Dorado*, T 41102, C, a/c, central, comfortable; *Hotel Hacienda*, D, Av. Benito Juárez 861, T 41250, a/c, clean; *Hotel México*, F, Juárez 230, gloomy, rooms with and without baths, said to be a staging post for Mexicans waiting to cross the border illegally.

The highway continues west past the Rancho La Puerta, a spa and physical fitness resort, strictly for the rich, vegetarian meals, petrol station. Leaving the Rodríguez Reservoir behind, Highway 2 enters the industrial suburb of La Mesa and continues into Tijuana as a 4-lane boulevard, eventually to become Av. Revolución, one of the city's main shopping streets.

Tijuana (pop. 1,500,000), on the Pacific, is where 35 million people annually cross the border, fuelling the city's claim to be "the world's most visited city". It came to prominence with Prohibition in the United States in the 1920s when Hollywood stars and thirsty Americans flocked to the sleazy bars and enterprising nightlife of Tijuana and Mexicali. Today, tourism is the major industry; although countless bars and nightclubs still vie for the visitor's dollar, it is duty-free bargains, horse racing and inexpensive English-speaking dentists which attract many visitors. This area is much more expensive than further south, especially at weekends. Modern Tijuana is Mexico's fourth-largest city and one of the most prosperous.

Points of interest: Centro Cultural, Paseo de los Héroes y Av. Independencia (museum, handcraft shops, restaurant, concert hall, and the ultra-modern spherical Omnimax cinema, where three films are shown on a 180° screen: English performance at 1400 daily, US$4.50—Spanish version at 1800 costs only -US$0.70); Casa de la Cultura, a multi-arts cultural centre with a 600-seat theatre; the Cathedral of Nuestra Señora de Guadalupe, Calle 2. The Jai-Alai Palace (Palacio Frontón) is at Av. Revolución y Calle 7 (games begin at 2000 nightly except Weds.; spectators may bet on each game). Tijuana has two bullrings, the Plaza de Toros Monumental at Playas de Tijuana (the only one in the world built on the sea shore). A few metres away is an obelisk built into the border chain-link fence commemorating the Treaty of Guadalupe Hidalgo, 1848, which fixed the frontier between Mexico and the USA. El Toreo bullring is 3 km. east of downtown on Búlevard Agua Caliente; *corridas* alternate between the two venues May and September; Sun. at 1600 sharp. Tickets from US$4.50 (*sol*) to US$16 (sombra). Horse and dog racing is held at the Agua Caliente track, near the Tijuana Country Club; horse racing Sat. and Sun. from 1200; greyhound meetings Wed.-Mon. at 1945, Mon., Weds., Fri. at 1430. Admission US$0.50, reserved seats US$1. *Charreadas* take place each Sunday from May to Sept. at one of four grounds, free. Tourism office will give up-to-date information.

There is no passport check at the border, although US freeways funnelling eight lanes of traffic into three on the Mexican side means great congestion, particularly at weekends. A quieter alternative is the Otay Mesa crossing (open 0600-2200) 8 km. east of Tijuana, reached from the US side by SR-117. From the Mexican side it is harder to find: continue on the bypass from Highway 1-D to near the airport to "Garita de Otay" sign . Those visiting Tijuana for the day often find it easier to park on the San Ysidro side and walk across the footbridge to the city centre. Alternatively, the "San Diego Trolley" is an entertaining way to reach the border, taking visitors from downtown San Diego to "la línea" for US$1.50;

departures every 15 mins. between 0500 and 0100. There is a visitor information kiosk at the Trolley's southern terminus.

Hotels *Fiesta Americana Tijuana*, L, Blvd. Agua Caliente 4500, T 817000, heated pool, suites, etc., first rate; *Best Western Plaza de Oro*, A, Calle 2 y Av. Martinez, new, a/c, downtown; *Paraíso-Radisson*, A, Blvd Agua Caliente 1 at the Country Club, T 817200, pool, sauna, bar, a/c, etc.; *Lucerna*, A, Héroes y Av. Rodríguez in new Río Tijuana development, T 841000, a/c, pool, piano bar, popular with businessmen; *El Conquistador*, A/B, Blvd. Agua Caliente 700, T 817955, colonial style, a/c, pool, sauna, disco; *Palacio Azteca*, B, Highway 1 south, T 865301, a/c, modern, cocktail bar, extensively remodelled, in older, congested part of city; *Calinda Tijuana*, B, near the Paraíso-Radisson, a/c, pool, disco, convention centre; *Hotel Caesar*, B/C, Calle 5a y Av. Revolución, T 851606, a/c, restaurant, decorated with bullfight posters, unique character, good; *La Villa de Zaragoza*, C, behind the Jai-Alai *frontón*, a/c, comfortable; *Nelson*, C, Av. Revolución 502, T 854302, central, simple clean rooms, coffee shop; *París*, D/E, Calle 5a 1939, adequate, value-for-money budget hotel; *Hotel del Pardo*, D, Calle 5a y Niños Héroes, acceptable, noisy in parts; *Rey*, D, Calle 4a 2021, central, old but comfortable; *Adelita*, E, hot showers, clean, basic, Calle 4a 2770; *Machado*, E, restaurant, basic, reasonable, Calle 1 No. 1724; *San Jorge*, E, Av. Constitución 506, old but clean, basic; *Hotel del Mar*, E, Calle 1a 1448, opposite *Nelson*, central but in a poor section, communal bathroom, good budget hotel. Recommended along Calle Baja California are *Hotel Virrey*, E, and *Pensión Noche Buena*, F; nearby and as good are *Fénix*, Miguel Martínez 355, F; *Chula Vista*, Niños Héroes 380, F, and *Rivas*, on Constitución. *St. Francis*, Benito Juárez 2A, F, recommended, safe and pleasant area. CREA youth hostel T 832680/822760, far from centre, Vía Oriente y Puente Cuauhtémoc, Zona del Río, dirty, not rec., inexpensive cafeteria on premises, open 0700-2300.

Motels *La Misión*, C/D, in Playas de Tijuana near the bullring, T 806612, modern, a/c, restaurant, pool, popular with businessmen; *Padre Kino*, (T 864208), and *Golf*, (T 862021, both D), opposite each other on Blvd Agua Caliente, next to Tijuana Country Club, both OK, *Golf*, an older-type motel.

Restaurants *Capri*, cheap; *Tijuana Tilly's*, excellent meal, reasonably priced. Many more of every category imaginable.

Night Clubs recommended: *Flamingos*, S on old Ensenada road; *Chantecler*.

Shopping The Plaza Río Tijuana Shopping Centre, Paseo de Los Héroes, is a new retail development; opposite are the Plaza Fiesta and Plaza del Zapato malls, the latter specializing in footware! Nearby is the colourful public market. Downtown shopping area is Avs. Revolución and Constitución. Bargaining is expected at smaller shops, and everyone except bus drivers is happy to accept US currency.

Exchange Many banks, all dealing in foreign exchange. Better rate than *cambios* but less convenient. Countless *casas de cambio* throughout Tijuana open day and night; commission charged on dollars-for-pesos transactions at *cambios* in San Ysidro–beware!

US Consulate Calle Tapachula, between Agua Caliente racetrack and the Country Club. Mon.-Fri. 0800-1630. T (706) 681-7400.

Tourist Information State Tourism Secretariat, main office on Plaza Patria, Blvd. Agua Caliente, Mon.-Fri. 1000-1900. Branch offices at airport, first tollgate on Highway 1-D to Ensenada, and at the Chamber of Commerce, Calle 1 and Av. Revolución, English-speaking staff, helpful, Mon.-Fri. 0900-1400, 1600-1900; Sat. 0900-1300. Chamber of Commerce also offers rest rooms and first aid facilities to visitors. Procuraduría de Protección al Turista is in the Government Centre in the Río Tijuana development; 0800-1900.

Buses Local buses about US$0.20, taxis ask US$10, "Central Camionera" or "Buena Vista" buses to bus station, downtown buses to border depart from Calle 2a near Av. Revolución. New bus station is 5 km. SE of centre on the airport road at the end of Vía Oriente (at La Mesa). To Mexico City (every couple of hours) 1st class (Tres Estrellas de Oro), about 46 hours, US$34 (Transportes del Pacífico, similar fares and schedules). 2nd class (Transportes del Norte de Sonora), US$31. Other 1st class routes: Guadalajara, 36 hrs., US$27; Hermosillo, 11 hrs., US$10; Mazatlán, 29 hrs., US$21; 2nd class fares: Guadalajara US$24, Hermosillo US$9, Mazatlán US$19. By ABC line: Ensenada, about hourly 0500-2400, 1½ hrs., US$1.50; Mexicali, hourly from 0500-2200, US$2; San Quintín, 7 a day, US$2.75; Santa Rosalía, 1630, direct, US$10; La Paz, 0800, US$16; Tres Estrellas to La Paz, 1030, 1400, 1800, 2200; 24 hours, US$17.50. There are also many services east and south from the old bus station at Av. Madero and Calle 1a (Comercio); this is also the Greyhound depot for departures to San Diego and Los Angeles, every two hours (US$4 and US$18, about 1 hr. from San Diego). Tijuana is a major transportation centre and schedules are complex and extensive.

International Airport 5 km. east, 20 mins. from San Diego, CA; cheaper flights than from the US. Aero California, daily flights to Los Mochis, and to La Paz, Aquascalientes, Colima, Guadalajara, Los Cabos, and Mexico City. Mexicana: To Acapulco, Cancún, Ixtapa/Zihuatanejo, Mérida, Mexico City, Villahermosa and Zacatecas, but only La Paz and Zacatecas without a connection in Mexico City; direct jet services to La Paz, 1 hr. 45 mins; Aero México to the capital, many cities N of Mexico City and on the Pacific coast. Taxi to airport should cost US$2-3 but bargaining essential. Mexicoach run from San Diego to Tijuana airport for US$15, combination bus to Plaza La Jolla and taxi to airport.

A dramatic 106-km. toll road (Highway 1-D) leads along cliffs overhanging the Pacific to Ensenada; the toll is in three sections of US$0.65 each for cars; total for motorhomes US$4.26. This is the safest route between the two cities and 16 exit points allow access to a number of seaside developments and villages along the coast.

Largest is **Rosarito** (pop. 40,000), a drab resort strung out along the old highway, with numerous seafood restaurants, curio shops, etc. There is a fine swimming beach; horseriding along it is also popular. Many hotels and motels, including: *Quinta del Mar Resort Hotel*, A/B, pool, sauna, tennis, also condos and townhouses with kitchens (L, T 21145); *Motel Quinta Chico*, B,; *Motel Colonial*, B/C (T 21575); *Rene's Motel* (T 21020), D, plain but comfortable; *Motel La Prieta*, D. Best is the *Rosarito Beach Hotel*, B, which was one of the casinos which opened during Prohibition; its architecture and decoration is worth a look.

The coast as far as Cantamar is lightly built-up; there are several trailer parks and many restaurants specializing in local seafood. At Punta Salsipuedes, a *mirador* affords sweeping views of the rugged Pacific coast and the offshore Todos Santos Islands.

Ensenada (pop. 250,000) is Baja's third city and leading seaport. It is a delightful city on the northern shore of the Bahía de Todos Santos, whose blue waters sport many dolphins and underline the austere character of a landscape reduced to water, sky and scorched brown earth. Sport and commercial fishing, canning, wineries, olive groves and agriculture are the chief activities. Tourist activity concentrates along Av. López Mateos, where most of the hotels, restaurants and shops are located. The twin white towers of Nuestra Señora de Guadalupe, Calle 6a, are a prominent landmark; on the seafront boulevard is the new Plaza Cívica, a landscaped court containing large busts of Juárez, Hidalgo and Carranza. A splendid view over city and bay can be had from the road circling the Chapultepec Hills on the western edge of the business district. Steep but paved access is via the W extension of Calle 2a, two blocks from the bus station. The Bodegas de Santo Tomás is Mexico's premier winery, Av. Miramar and Calle 7; daily tours at 1100, 1300, 1500, US$1.50. *Charreadas* are held on summer weekends at the *charro* ground at Blancarte y Calle 2a. A weekend street market is held from 0700-1700 at Av. Riversoll y Calle 7a; the fish market at the bottom of Av. Macheros specializes in "fish tacos" (a fish finger wrapped in a taco!).

Hotels *Punta Morro Hotel Suites*, L, on coast 3 km. W of town, rooms have kitchens and fridges, 2 and 3-bedroom apartments available, pool; *Villa Marina*, A, Av. López Mateos y Blancarte, T 83321, heated pool, coffee shop; *San Nicolás Resort Hotel*, L, López Mateos y Av. Guadalupe, T 61901, a/c, suites, dining room, disco; *Las Rosas Hotel and Spa*, L, on Highway 1, 7 km. W of town, suites, spectacular ocean views, pool, sauna, restaurant; *La Pinta*, Av. Floresta y Blvd. Bucaneros (A on Fri.-Sat., B Sun.-Thurs.), TV, pool, restaurant; *Misión Santa Isabel*, A, López Mateos and Castillo, T 83616, pool, suites; *Bahía*, B/C, López Mateos, T 82101, balconies, suites, fridges, popular; *Plaza*, D, López Mateos 540, central, plain but clean, rooms facing street noisy. Several cheap hotels around Miramar and Calle 3, e.g. *Perla del Pacífico*, Av. Miramar 229, E, quite clean, hot water. Note that some of the larger hotels have different rates for summer and winter; cheaper tariffs are given above— check first! All hotels are filled in Ensenada on weekends, get in early.

Motels *Ensenada Travelodge*, Av. Blancarte 130, T 81601, a/c, heated pool, whirlpool, family rates available, restaurant; *Casa del Sol*, A, López Mateos 101, T 81570; *Cortés*, A, López Mateos 1089 y Castillo, T 82307; both part of Best Western chain, a/c, TV, pool, comfortable; *El Cid*, A on Fri.-Sat., B on Sun.-Thurs., Av. López Mateos 993, T 82401, Spanish-style building, a/c, fridges, suites available, dining room, lounge, disco; *Pancho*, Av. Alvarado 211, shabby but clean rooms, opposite the *charro* ground, cheapest habitable motel in town.

Restaurant *Domico's*, Av. Ruiz 283, also Chinese restaurants in same avenue; *Lonchería la Terminal*, opp. bus station, cheap and filling comida, good but basic.

Tourist Office Av. López Mateos y Espinoza, part of the Fonart artesan centre, Mon.-Sat. 0900-1900, accommodation literature; the Procuraduría is next door, same hours plus Sun. 0900-1600. Tourist and Convention Bureau, Lázaro Cárdenas y Miramar, Mon.-Sat. 0900-1900, Sun. 0900-1400, helpful; free copies of *Ensenada News and Views*, monthly English-language paper with information and adverts on northern Baja, Tijuana and Ensenada.

Airport 8 km. S; scheduled flights to Tijuana, Guerrero Negro, Cedros Island, La Paz, etc.

Highway 3 east to San Felipe leaves Ensenada at the Benito Juárez *glorieta* monument as the Calzada Cortés. 26 km. out of Ensenada, an 8-km. dirt road branches S for a steep descent to the basic resort of Agua Caliente (*Hotel Agua Caliente*, C, restaurant, bar, closed in winter; adjoining is a campground and large concrete pool heated to 38° by nearby hot springs; access road should not be attempted in wet weather).

At km. 39, a paved road leads off 3 km. to Ojos Negros, continuing E (graded, dry weather) into scrub-covered foothills. It soon climbs into the ponderosa pine forests of the Sierra de Juárez. 37 km. from Ojos Negros, the road enters the **Parque Nacional Constitución de 1857**. The jewel of the park is the small Laguna Hanson, a sparkling shallow lake surrounded by Jeffery pines; camping here is delightful, but note that the lake is reduced to a boggy marsh in dry seasons and that the area receives snow in mid-winter. A high-clearance vehicle is necessary for the continuation N out of the park to Highway 2 at El Cóndor 15 km. E of La Rumorosa.

At Km. 92½, Ejido Héroes de la Independencia, a graded dirt road runs 8 km. E to the ruins of Mission Santa Catarina, founded in 1797 and abandoned after a raid by the Yuman Indians in 1840; the Paipái women in the village often have attractive pottery for sale.

Highway 3 descends along the edge of a green valley to the rapidly developing town of Valle de Trinidad. A reasonable dirt road runs S into the **Parque Nacional Sierra San Pedro Mártir** and Mike's Sky Rancho (35 km.), a working ranch which offers motel-style accommodation, a pool, camping and guided trips into the surrounding mountains; rooms about US$8-10 per night, good meals.

After leaving the valley, the highway follows a canyon covered in dense stands of barrel cacti to the San Matías Pass between the Sierras Juárez and San Pedro Mártir which leads onto the desolate Valle de San Felipe. The highway turns E and emerges onto open desert hemmed in by arid mountains. 198½ km. from Ensenada it joins Highway 5 at the La Trinidad T-junction, 148 km. from Mexicali and 50 km. from San Felipe.

Highway 1 S from Ensenada passes turn-offs to several beach resorts. Just before the agricultural town of Maneadero, a paved highway runs 23 km. W onto the Punta Banda pensinsula, where you can see La Bufadora blowhole, one of the most powerful on the Pacific. Air sucked from a sea-level cave is expelled as high as 16 metres through a cleft in the cliffs. Concrete steps and viewing platform give easy access. Tourist stalls line the approach road and small boys try to charge US$1 for parking. This is one of the easiest side trips off the length of Highway 1.

N.B. Tourist cards and vehicle documents of those travelling south of Maneadero are supposed to be validated at the immigration checkpoint on the southern outskirts of the town; the roadside office, however, is not always in operation. If you are not stopped, just keep going.

Chaparal-clad slopes begin to close in on the highway as it winds it way south, passing through the small towns of Santo Tomás (*El Palomar Trailer Park*, campsite with swimming pool and dirty showers, nearby ruins of the Dominican Mission of 1791) and San Vicente (2 Pemex stations, cafés, tyre repairs, several stores), before reaching Colonet. This is a supply centre for surrounding ranches; several services. A dry weather dirt road runs 12 km. W to San Antonio del Mar: many camping spots amid high dunes fronting a beautiful beach renowned for surf fishing and clam-digging.

14 km. S of Colonet a reasonable graded road branches to San Telmo and climbs into the mountains. At 50 km. it reaches the Meling Ranch (also called San José), which offers resort accommodation for about 12 guests. 15 km. beyond San José the road enters the **Parque Nacional Sierra San Pedro Mártir** and climbs through forests to three astronomical observatories perched on the dramatic eastern escarpment of the central range. The view from here is one of the most extensive in North America: east to the Gulf, west to the Pacific, and south-east to the overwhelming granite mass of the Picacho del Diablo (3,096 m.), Baja's highest peak. The higher reaches of the park receive snow in winter. The observatories are not open to visitors.

109 km. from Ensenada **San Quintín**, a thriving market city (pop. 15,000) almost joined to Lázaro Cárdenas 5 km. south. There are service stations in both centres and San Quintín provides all services. Rising out of the peninsula west of San Quintín bay is a line of volcanic cinder cones, visible for many kilometres along the highway; the beaches to the south near Santa María are hugely popular with fishermen, campers and beachcombers.

Hotels *La Pinta*, A, isolated beachfront location 18 km. S of San Quintín then 5 km. W on paved road, a/c, TV, balconies, tennis, nearby airstrip; *Hada's Rooms*, E/F, just north of Benito Juárez army camp in Láraro Cárdenas, cheapest in town, shabby, basic, sometimes closed when water and electricity are cut off.
 Motels *Cielito Lindo*, C, 2 km. beyond the *La Pinta Hotel* on S shore of bay, restaurant, cafeteria, lounge (dancing Sat. nights), electricity Mon.-Sat. 0700-1100, 1500-2400, Sun. 0700-2400, modest but pleasant, last km. of access road unpaved, messy after rain; *Molino Viejo*, C, on site of old English mill—part of an early agricultural scheme, modest, on bay 6 km. of W of highway and S of Lázaro Cárdenas, rough access road, restaurant, bar, some kitchenettes, electricity 0800-0900, 1800-2200; *Ernesto's*, D, next door, rustic, overpriced, popular with fishermen, electricity 0700-2100; *Muelle Viejo*, D, between *Ernesto's* and the old English cemetery, restaurant, bad access road, hot showers, bay views; *Chávez*, D, on highway N of Lázaro Cárdenas, family-style, clean rooms, plain but good value.

Camping *Honey's RV Campground*, 15 km. S and 2 km. W on coast, toilets, showers, full hookups, beach access, US$5 per vehicle, great area for clam-digging. Trailer park attached to Cielito Lindo Motel, comfortable.

After leaving the San Quintín valley, bypassing Santa María (fuel), the Transpeninsular Highway (officially the Carretera Transpeninsular Benito Juárez) runs near the Pacific before darting inland at El Consuelo Ranch. It climbs over a barren spur from which there are fine views, then drops in a succession of tight curves into **El Rosario**, 58 km. from San Quintín: *Motel Rosario*, E, small, very clean. This small, agricultural community has a Pemex station, small supermarket, a basic museum, and meals, including Espinosa's famous lobster *burritos* and omelettes. 3 km. S is a ruined Dominican Mission, founded 1774 upstream, then moved to its present site in 1882; take the graded dirt road to Punta Baja, a bold headland on the coast, where there is a solar-powered lighthouse and fishing village.

Highway 1 makes a sharp 90° turn at El Rosario and begins to climb into the central plateau; gusty winds increase and astonishingly beautiful desertscapes gradually become populated with many varieties of cacti. Prominent are the stately *cardones*: most intriguing are the strange, twisted *cirios* growing to heights of 6 to 10 m.—they are unique to this portion of Baja California as far south as the Vizcaino Desert, and to a small area of Sonora state on the mainland. At Km. 62 a 5 km track branches S to the adobe remains of Misión San Fernando Velicatá, the only Franciscan mission in Baja, founded by Padre Serra in 1769. 5 km. further on, Rancho Santa Cecília offers meals and refreshments; over the road is an RV park with full hook-ups. The highway is now in the **Desierto Central de Baja California Natural Park** (as yet not officially recognised). About 26 km. north of Cataviña a strange region of huge boulders begins, some as big as houses; interspersed by cacti and crouching elephant trees, this area is one of the most picturesque on the peninsula.

Cataviña is only a dozen buildings, with a small grocery store/*Café La Enramada*, the only Pemex station on the 227-km. stretch from El Rosario to the Bahía de Los Angeles junction, and the attractive **La Pinta Hotel**, A, a/c, pool, bar, electricity 1800-2400, restaurant, tennis, 28 rooms. Attached to the **La Pinta** is the **Parque Natural Desierto Central de Baja California Trailer Park**, flush toilets, showers, restaurant, bar, US$3 per site. 2 km. S of Cataviña is Rancho Santa Inés, which has dormitory-style accommodation (E), meals and a paved airstrip.

Highway 1 continues south-east through an arid world of boulder-strewn mountains and dry salt lakes. At 53 km. the new graded road to the Bahía San Luís Gonzaga (see under San Felipe) branches off to the east. After skirting the dry bed of Laguna Chapala (natural landing strip at southern end when lake is totally dry), the Transpeninsular Highway arrives at the junction with the paved road east to Bahía de Los Angeles; café and gas station at junction, fuel supply sometimes unreliable, best to fill up at Cataviña to be safe.

Excursion The side road runs 68 km. through *cirios* and *datilillo* cactus-scapes and crosses the Sierra de la Asamblea to **Bahía De Los Angeles** (no public transport), a popular fishing town which, despite a lack of vegetation, is one of Baja's best-known beauty spots. The bay, sheltered by the forbidding slopes of Isla Angel de la Guarda (Baja's largest island), is a haven for boating. Facilities in town include: gas station, bakery, stores, two trailer parks and four restaurants, paved airstrip. **Villa Vita Motel**, B, modern, a/c, pool, jacuzzi, boat launch, trailer park, electricity 0700-1400, 1700-2000, bar, dining room; **Casa de Díaz**, C, 15 rooms, restaurant, grocery store, campground, boat rentals, clean, well-run, popular; **Guillermo's Trailer Park**, flush toilets, showers, restaurant, gift shop, boat ramp and rentals; **La Playa RV Park**, on beach, similar facilities and tariff (US$4 per site). La Gringa is a beautiful beach 13 km. north of town, many camping sites, pit toilets, rubbish bins, small fee.

Lynn and Walt Sutherland from Vancouver write: "Bahía de los Angeles (pop. 1,000) is worth a visit for its sea life. There are thousands of dolphins in the bay

June-December. Some stay all year. In July and August you can hear the whales breathe as you stand on shore. There are large colonies of seals and many exotic seabirds. Fishing is excellent. A boat and guide can be rented for US$40 a day; try Raúl, a local fisherman, who speaks English." Camping free and safe on beach.

The highway now runs due south through Villa Jesús María (gas station, store, cafés) to the 28th parallel, the state border between Baja California and Baja California Sur (soaring stylized eagle monument and *Hotel La Pinta*, A, a/c, pool, dining room, bar).

N.B. Advance clocks one hour to Mountain time when entering Baja California Sur, but note that Northern Baja observes Pacific Daylight Saving Time from first Sun. in April to last Sun. in October; time in both states and California is thus identical during the summer.

Guerrero Negro (9,000 people) is 3 km. beyond the state line and 4 km. W of the highway; 714 km. S of Tijuana, 414 from San Quintín, it is halfway point between the US border and La Paz. There are 2 gas stations, bank, hospital, cafés, stores, an airport with scheduled services (just north of the Eagle monument), and the headquarters of Exportadora de Sal, the world's largest salt-producing firm. Seawater is evaporated by the sun from thousands of salt ponds south of town; the salt is loaded at the works 11 km. SW of town and barged to a deepwater port on Cedros Island. From there ore carriers take it to the USA, Canada and Japan.

Hotel *Cuartos de Sánchez-Smith*, E/F, Calle Barrera, W end of town, basic rooms, some with showers, cheapest in town. **Motels** *El Morro*, D/E, on road into town from highway, modest, clean; *Las Dunas*, E, few doors from *El Morro*, modest, clean; *Gámez*, E, very basic, near city hall. **Camping** *Malarrimo Trailer Park*, on highway at junction to town, next to *Malarrimo Restaurant*, flush toilets, showers, bar US$4 per vehicle. Good restaurant at bus station.

Whale watching is the main attraction on nearby Laguna Ojo de Liebre, usually known as Scammon's Lagoon after the whaling captain who first entered in 1857. California Grey Whales mate and give birth between December and February, in several warm-water lagoons on central Baja's Pacific coast, some not departing until as late as May or June. They can be seen cavorting and sounding from the old salt wharf 10 km. NW of Guerrero Negro on the Estero San José, or from a designated "whale watching area" on the shore of Scammon's Lagoon 37 km. south of town, access road branches off Highway 1 8 km. east of junction (if going by public transport, leave bus at the turn off and hitch). Cars are charged US$3 to enter the park. Local personnel collect a small fee for camping at the watching area—this pays to keep it clean. The shores of Scammon's are part of the **Parque Natural de Ballena Gris**. Watch between 0700 and 0900 and again at 1700, saves hiring a boat (US$10 p.p.).

After Guerrero Negro the highway enters the grim Vizcaíno Desert. A paved but badly potholed road leads due east (42 km.) to El Arco, other abandoned mining areas and crossing to San Francisquito on its beautiful bay on the Gulf (77 km.), and to Santa Gertrudis Mission (1752), some of whose stone ruins have been restored; the chapel is still in use. It should be stressed that these minor Bajan roads require high-clearance, preferably 4x4, vehicles carrying adequate equipment and supplies, water and fuel. A new gravel road from Bahía de Los Angeles (135 km.) gives easier road access than from El Arco and opens up untouched stretches of the Gulf coast.

Vizcaíno Peninsula which thrusts into the Pacific south of Guerrero Negro is one of the remotest parts of Baja. Although part of the Vizcaíno Desert, the scenery of the peninsula is varied and interesting; isolated fishcamps dot the silent coast of beautiful coves and untrodden beaches. Until recently only the most hardy ventured into the region; now an improved dry-weather road cuts W through the peninsula to Bahía Tortugas and the rugged headland of Punta Eugenia. It leaves Highway 1 at Vizcaíno Junction (also called Fundolegal, Pemex station, café, market, pharmacy and auto parts store), 70 km. beyond Guerrero Negro and is paved for 8 km. to Ejido Díaz Ordaz. The new road passes Rancho San José (116 km.) and the easily-missed turnoff to Malarrimo Beach (where beachcombing is unparalled). After another bumpy 50 km. is **Bahía Tortugas**, a surprisingly large place (pop. 3,200) considering its remoteness. Many facilities including eating places, health clinic, gas station, airport with services to Cedros Island and Ensenada, and the small *Vera Cruz Motel*, D/E, restaurant, bar, very modest but the only accommodation on the peninsula apart from a trailer park at Campo René, 15 km. from Punta Abreojos. Two roads leave the Vizcaíno-Bahía Tortuga road for Bahía Asunción (pop. 1,600), which has the peninsula's only other gas station, then following the coast to Punta Prieta, La Bocana and Punta Abreojas (93 km.). A lonely road runs for 85 km. back to Highway 1, skirting the Sierra Santa Clara before crossing the salt marshes north of Laguna San Ignacio and reaching the main road 26 km. before San Ignacio.

The Highway continues SE on a new alignment still not shown on most maps and, 20 km. from Vizcaíno Junction, reaches the first of 23 microwave relay towers which follow Highway 1 almost to the Cape. They are closed to the public but make excellent landmarks and, in some cases, offer excellent views. 143 km. from Guerrero Negro is the turnoff for **San Ignacio** (pop. 2,200). Here the Jesuits built a mission in 1728 and planted the ancestors of the town's date palm groves. On the square is the beautifully-preserved mission church, completed by the Dominicans in 1786. The town is very attractive, with thatched-roof dwellings and pastel-coloured commercial buildings; there is limited shopping but several restaurants, service station, mechanical assistance and bank.

Hotel *La Pinta*, A, on road leading into town, a/c, pool, all facilities, built in mission style, attractive but overpriced; *Cuartos Glenda*, E, with shower, basic but cheapest in town, on highway E. **Motel** *La Posada*, D, on rise 2 blocks from zócalo, modest, fans, shower, good coffee shop, best value in town, helpful, worth bargaining.
   Camping *San Ignacio Transpeninsula Trailer Park*, Government-run, on Highway 1 behind Pemex station at the junction, full hookups, toilets, showers US$4 per site; two other basic campgrounds on road into San Ignacio, insects,

not recommended. West of the mission is La Candelaria, a beautiful palm-shaded camping spot on the edge of a pool—swimming in the middle of the Baja desert! *Loncheria Chalita*, on Zócalo, excellent value.

There are many cave painting sites around San Ignacio; colourful human and animal designs left by Baja's original inhabitants still defy reliable dating, or full understanding. To reach most requires a trek by mule over tortuous trails; Oscar Fischer, owner of the *La Posada Motel*, arranges excursions into the sierras (about US$10 per person to Santa Teresa cave). Most accessible is the cave at the Cuesta del Palmarito, 5 km. E of Rancho Santa Marta (50 NW of San Ignacio), filled with designs of humans with uplifted arms, in brown and black; a jeep and guide are required. A better road leads east from the first microwave station past Vizcaíno Junction up to San Francisco de la Sierra, where there are other paintings and petroglyphs in the vicinity.

Highway 1 leaves the green *arroyo* of San Ignacio and re-emerges into the arid central desert. To the north, the triple volcanic cones of Las Tres Vírgenes come into view, one of the most dramatic mountain scenes along this route. Dark brown lava flows on the flanks are evidence of relatively recent activity (eruption in 1746, smoke emission in 1857). The highest peak is 2,149 metres above the Gulf of California; the sole vegetation on the lunar-like landscape is the thick-skinned elephant trees.

72 km. from San Ignacio is **Santa Rosalía**, a bustling city of 14,500. It was built by the French El Boleo Copper Company in the 1880s, laid out in neat rows of wood frame houses, many with broad verandahs, which today give Santa Rosalía its distinctly un-Mexican appearance. Most of the mining ceased in 1953; the smelter, several smokestacks above the town and much of the original mining operation can be seen on the north of town. The port was one of the last used in the age of sail. The church of Santa Bárbara (Av. Revolución y Calle C, a block north of the main plaza), built of prefabricated galvanized iron for the 1889 Paris Worlds' Fair from a design by Eiffel, was shipped around the Horn to Baja. It arrived here by mistake! A car ferry leaves for Guaymas at 2300 on Tue, Thur. and Sun. from the small harbour (check in advance if still in operation). The tourist office is on the highway a kilometre S of the ferry terminal, opposite the service station.

Drivers should note that Santa Rosalía's streets are narrow and congested; larger vehicles should park along the highway or in the ferry dock parking lot. The Pemex station is conveniently located on the highway, unlike at Mulegé (see below), so larger RVs and rigs should fill up here.

Hotels *El Morro*, D, on Highway 2 km. S of town, T 20414, on bluff with Gulf views, modern, Spanish-style, a/c, bar, restaurant; *Francés*, Av. 11 de Julio on the North Mesa, T 20829, a/c, restaurant, bar, pool not always filled, D, historic 2-storey wooden French colonial building overlooking smelter and Gulf, photos of sailing vessels on walls. *Olvera*, D, on main plaza, 2nd floor, a/c, showers, clean, good value; *Real*, D, Av. Manuel Montoya near Calle A, similar to *Olvera*, rec; *Playa*, E, Av. La Playa between Calles B y Plaza, central, fans, bathrooms, good budget hotel; *Blanca y Negra*, E, basic but clean, Av. Libertad at end of Calle 3. *Panadería El Boleo*, widely noted for its delicious French breads and pastries.

Bus Bus station near tourist office and Pemex station 2 km. S of ferry terminal; stop for most Tijuana-La Paz buses, several per day.

Painted cave sites can be visited from the farming town of Santa Agueda, turnoff 8 km. south of Santa Rosalía then rough dirt road for 12 km. The fishing village of San Lucas, on a palm-fringed cove, is 14 km. south of Santa Rosalía; camping is good and popular on the beaches to north and south. *San Lucas RV Park*, on beach, full hookups, flush toilets, boat ramp, ice, restaurant, US$5 per vehicle. Offshore lies Isla San Marcos, with a gypsum mine at the south end.

Just beyond San Bruno is a reasonable dirt road to San José de Magdalena (15 km.), a picturesque farming village dating back to colonial days; ruined Dominican chapel, attractive thatched palm houses, flower gardens. An awful road leads on for 17 km. to Rancho San Isidro, from where the ruined Guadalupe Mission can be reached on horseback.

Mulegé, 61 km. south of Santa Rosalía, is another oasis community (pop. 5,000) whose river enters the gulf as a lushly-vegetated tidal lake. There are lovely beaches, good diving, snorkelling and boating in the Bahía Concepción. The old Federal territorial prison (La Cananea) is being converted into a museum. There is a good cheap fish restaurant 40 mins. walk along the river; the lighthouse, 10 mins. further on provides tremendous views and the sunsets are unforgetable. South of the bridge which carries the highway over the river is the restored Mission of Santa Rosalía de Mulegé, founded by the Jesuits in 1705; good lookout point above the mission over the town and its sea of palm trees. The bank will only change a minimum of US$100. **N.B.** the Pemex station is in the centre; not convenient for large vehicles, and a one-way system to contend with.

Hotels *Serenidad*, B, 4 km. E of town near the river mouth, a/c, pool, dining room, bar, banquet/mariachi band Wed. and Sat. nights, cottages, trailer park, T 20111; *Vista Hermosa*, B, opp. the *Serenidad*, a/c, pool, restaurant, bar; *Las Casitas*, C, Callejón de los Estudiantes y Av. Madero, central, a/c, showers, restaurant next door, shady garden patio, fishing trips arranged, pleasant older hotel, well-run; *Suites Rosita*, E, Av. Madero near main plaza, a/c, kitchenettes, clean and pleasant; *Terraza Motel*, E, Calles Zaragoza y Moctezuma, in business district, 35 rooms, rooftop bar, basic, clean; *Hacienda*, E, Calle Madero 3, next to *Suites Rosita*; *Casa Nachita*, F with fan, basic and pleasant, hot water in a.m.; next door is *Casa de Huéspedes Manuelita*, sloppily run but reasonably clean, E; *Restaurants Tandil* and *Las Casitas*; *Granny's Goodies*, good breads and pastries, good place for information.

Camping *The Orchid (Huerta Saucedo) RV Park*, on river south of town, partly shaded, off Highway 1, pool, boat ramp, fishing, up to US$10.50 for two; *Villa María Isabel RV Park*, on river and Highway east of *Orchid*, pool, recreation area, disposal station, American-style bakery, US$8.50 for two; *Jorge's del Río Trailer Park*, grassy, on river at E end of Highway bridge by unpaved road, US$7.50 per site; *Pancho's RV Park*, next to *María Isabel*, little shade, US$5 per day; *Oasis Río Baja RV Park*, on same stretch as those above, reasonable, US$6 per site. All the foregoing have full hookups, flush toilets, showers, etc. From here on down the Bahía Concepción coast and beyond are many *playas públicas* (*PP*); some have basic facilities, most are simple, natural camping spots on beautiful beaches where someone may or may not collect a fee. At Mulegé is the Playa Sombrerito at the hat-shaped hill (site of Mexican victory over US forces in 1847), restaurant and store nearby, US$1 per vehicle.

Beyond Mulegé the Highway climbs over a saddle and then runs along the shores of the bay for 50 km. This stretch is the most heavily-used camping and boating area on the Peninsula; the water is beautiful, swimming safe, camping excellent, varied marine life. Bahía Concepción and Playa Santispac are recommended, many small restaurants and *palapas* (shelters) for hire.

A new graded dirt road branches off Highway 1 to climb over the towering Sierra Giganta, whose desert vistas of flat-topped mesas and *cardón* cacti are straight out of the Wild West; it begins to deteriorate after the junction (20 km.) to San José de Comondú and limps another 37 km. into San Isidro after a spectacular drop into the La Purísima Valley. San Isidro has a population of 1,000 but little for the visitor; 5 km. down the valley is the more attractive oasis village of La Purísima (pop. 800). The road leads on southwards to Pozo Grande (52 km.) and Ciudad Insurgentes (85 km.), paved for the last 26 km. Two side roads off the San Isidro road lead down to the twin towns of San Miguel de Comondú and San José de Comondú (high-clearance vehicles are necessary); both oasis villages of 500 people each. One stone building remains of the mission moved to San José in 1737; the original bells are still at the church. A new graded road leads on to Pozo Grande and Ciudad Insurgentes.

Loreto (pop. 7,300), 1,125 km. from Tijuana, is one of the most historic places in Baja. Here settlement of the Peninsula began with Father Juan María Salvatierra's founding of the Mission of Nuestra Señora de Loreto on 25 October 1697. The Mission is on the Zócalo, the largest structure in town and perhaps the best-restored of all the Baja California mission buildings. It has a gilded altar. The museum beside the church is worth a visit: there are educational displays about the missions, Bajan history and historic horse and ranching equipment, book shop, open Tue.-Sat. 0900-1700. Inscription over the main door of the mission announces: "Mother of all the Missions of Lower and Upper California". Nestled between the slopes of the Sierra Giganta and the offshore Isla del Carmen, Loreto has experienced a tourist revival; fishing in the Gulf here is some of the best in Baja California.

Hotels *Oasis*, A, Calles de la Playa y Baja California, T 30112, on bay at S end of Loreto in palm grove, large rooms, pool, tennis, restaurant, bar, skiffs (pangas) for hire, fishing cruises arranged, pleasant and quiet, a/c; *La Pinta*, A/B, on Sea of Cortés 2 km. N of Zócalo, a/c, showers, pool, tennis, restaurant, bar, considered by many the best of the original "Presidente" paradores, 30 rooms, fishing boat hire, recommended; *Misión de Loreto*, C, Calle de la Playa y Juárez, T 30048, colonial-style with patio garden, a/c, pool, dining rooms, bar, fishing trips arranged, very comfortable, check for discounts; *La Siesta Bungalows*, C, small, manager owns the dive shop and can offer combined accommodation and diving trips; *Villa del Mar*, D, Colina Zaragoza, near sports centre, OK, restaurant, bar, pool, bargain rates, on beach; *Casa de Huéspedes San Martín*, E, Calle Benito Juárez 4, showers, renovated rooms, basic, but poor value. **Motel** *Salvatierra*,

E, Calle Salvatierra, on S approach to town, a/c, hot showers, clean, good value.

Camping *Ejido Loreto RV Park*, on beach a km. S of town, full hookups, toilets, showers, laundry, fishing and boat trips arranged, US$7.50 per site.

Airport International, 4 km. south; Aero California to La Paz, Los Angeles and Phoenix, Arizona.

Bus Bus station at Calle Salvatierra opposite intersection of Zapata; to La Paz 0800, 1000, 1400, 1500 daily, US$4.25; to Tijuana 1500, 1800, 2100, 2300, US$13, 17 hrs.

Just south of Loreto a rough road runs 37 km. through impressive canyon scenery to the village of San Javier, tucked in the bottom of a steep-walled valley; the settlement has only one store but the Mission of San Javier is one of the best-preserved in North America; it was founded by the Jesuits in 1699 and took 59 years to complete. The thick volcanic walls, Moorish ornamentation and bell tower are most impressive in so rugged and remote a location. Near San Javier is Piedras Pintas, close to Rancho Las Parras; there are eight prehistoric figures painted here in red, yellow and black.

The highway south of Loreto passes a picturesque stretch of coast. Fonatur, the government tourist development agency, is building a resort complex at *Nopoló*, (8 km.), which it hopes will one day rival its other resort developments at Cancún and Ixtapa. Campers have been driven out of Puerto Escondido except for the *Tripui Trailer Park*, claimed to be the best in Mexico. There are three lovely *PP*s between Loreto and Puerto Escondido; Notrí, Juncalito and Ligüí—palm-lined coves, which are a far cry from the bustle of the new resort developments nearby. Beyond Ligüí (36 km. south of Loreto) Highway 1 ascends the eastern escarpment of the Sierra Giganta before leaving the Gulf to strike out SW across the Peninsula again to Ciudad Constitución. It passes by Ciudad Insurgentes, a busy agricultural town of 13,000 with two service stations, banks, auto repairs, shops and cafés, then runs dead straight for 26 km. to **Ciudad Constitución**, which is the marketing centre for the Magdalena Plain agricultural development and has the largest population between Ensenada and La Paz (50,000). Although not a tourist town, it has extensive services of use to the visitor: department stores, restaurants, banks, public market, service stations, laundries, car repairs, hospital and airport (near Ciudad Insurgentes). Many businesses line Highway 1, which is divided and doubles as the palm-lined main street, with the first traffic lights since Ensenada, 1,158 km. away.

Hotels *Maribel*, D, Guadalupe Victoria y Highway 1, T 20155, 2 blocks S of San Carlos road junction, a/c, TV, restaurant, bar, suites available, clean, fine for overnight stop; *Casino*, D, a block E of the *Maribel* on same street, T 20754, quieter, 37 clean rooms, restaurant, bar; *El Arbolito*, E, shabby.

Camping *Campestre La Pila*, 2½ km. S on unpaved road off Highway 1, farmland setting, full hookups, toilets, showers, pool, laundry, groceries, tennis courts, ice, restaurant, bar, no hot water, US$10-13 for 4.

Excursion Deep artesian wells have made the desert of the Llano de Magdalena bloom with citrus groves and a chequerboard of neat farms growing cotton, wheat and vegetables; this produce is shipped out through the port of San Carlos, 58 km. to the west of Bahía Magdalena. Known to boaters as "Mag Bay", it is considered the finest natural harbour between San Francisco and Acapulco. Protected by mountains and sand spits, it provides the best boating on Baja's Pacific coast. Small craft can explore kilometres of mangrove-fringed inlets and view the grey whales who come here in the winter season. On the narrow S end of Magdalena Island is Puerto Magdalena, a lobstering village of 400. 7 km. away is a deepwater port at Punta Belcher, used for shipping out the phosphoric sand mined near Puerto López Mateos. On Santa Margarita Island are Puertos Alcatráz (a fish-canning community of 300) and Cortés (important naval base); neither is shown on the ACSC map.

Highway 1 continues its arrow-straight course south of Ciudad Constitución across the flat plain to the village of Santa Rita, where it makes a 45° turn E. 28 km. beyond Santa Rita, a road of dubious quality runs to the remote missions of San Luis Gonzaga (64 km.) and La Pasión (49 km.); it is planned to extend it to the ruins of Dolores del Sur (85 km.) on the Gulf of California, one of Baja's most inaccessible mission sites. There is a service station at the village of El Cien; meals and refreshments are available at the Rancho San Agustín, 24 km. beyond.

La Paz capital of Baja California Sur, is a fast-changing, but relaxed modern city (population 160,000), nestled at the southern end of La Paz Bay (where Europeans first set foot in Baja in 1533). Sunsets can be spectacular. Prices have risen as more tourists arrive to enjoy its winter climate, but free port status ensures that there are plenty of bargains (although some goods, like certain makes of camera, are cheaper to buy in the USA). Oyster beds attracted many settlers in the 17th C. but few survived long. The Jesuit mission, founded here in 1720, was abandoned 29 years later. La Paz became the territorial capital in 1829 after Loreto was wiped out by a hurricane. Although bursting with new construction, there are still many touches of colonial grace, arched doorways and flower-filled patios. The early afternoon *siesta* is still observed by many businesses, especially during summer.

Heart of La Paz is the Plaza Constitución, facing which are the Government Buildings and the graceful Cathedral of Nuestra Señora de la Paz, built in 1861-65 on or near the site of the original mission. The Post Office is a block NE at Revolución de 1910 y Constitución. The street grid is rectangular; westerly streets run into the Paseo Alvaro Obregón—the waterfront Malecón—where the commercial and tourist wharves back onto a tangle of streets just W of the main plaza; here are the banks, City Hall, Chinatown and many of the cheaper *pensiones*. The more expensive hotels are further SW. A must is the Museo Antropológico de Baja California Sur, Ignacio Altamirano y 5 de Mayo (4 blocks E of the Plaza), with an admirable display of peninsula anthropology, history and pre-history, folklore and geology. (The bookshop has a wide selection on Mexico and Baja. Open Tue.-Sat. 0900-1800; entry free.) A carved mural depicting the history of Mexico can be seen at the Palacio de Gobierno on Isabel La Católica, corner of Bravo. There are boat tours from the Tourist Wharf on the Malecón around the bay and to nearby islands like Espíritu Santo.

Hotels *Los Arcos*, A, Paseo Alvaro Obregón 498 at Allende, T 22744, a/c, pool, restaurant, coffee shop, across the Malecón from the beach, walking distance of centre, fishing trips arranged, excellent value; *Cabañas de los Arcos*, A, opposite with shared facilities, a/c, pool, slightly cheaper, T 22297; *La Posada*, A, on bay 3½ km. SW of centre, 5 blocks off Highway 1 on Colima, T 20653, a/c, pool, tennis, bar, restaurant, quiet and relaxing, recommended but away from the centre; *Gran Hotel Baja*, A, "the only high-rise structure south of Ensenada", so easy to find, T 23844, restaurant, bar, pool, disco, etc, on beach, trailer park adjacent; *Ramada La Paz*, B, 3 km. SW of centre, a/c, pool, beach, tennis, fishing, skin diving, 2 pools, disco, dining room; *El Morro*, B, 3½ km. NE on Palmira Beach, Moorish-style, a/c, TV, fridges, apartments with kitchenettes (1 bedroom US$40, 2 bedroom US$60), pool, restaurant, bar; *Misiones de La Paz*, A, on El Mogote sandspit, isolated, accessible by launch from Hotel La Posada, T 24021, a/c, showers, pool, restaurant, cocktail bar, quiet; *Palmira*, A, T 24000, 3½ km. NE of Pichilingüe road, a/c, pool, tennis, restaurant, disco, convention facilities, fishing trips arranged, popular with families; *La Perla*, on the water front, T 20777, C, clean, a/c, friendly, restaurant expensive; *El Presidente Sur*, A, 6½ km. NE at Caimancito Beach, T 26544, good location but furthest from town, a/c, pool, restaurant, bar, next door to Governor's mansion; *María Dolores Gardenias*, C, Aquíles Serdán y Vicente Guerrero, a/c, pool, restaurant (good), excellent value; *Hospedaje Marelí*, D/E, Aquíles Serdán 283 y Bravo, a/c, clean, 10 min. walk to Plaza Constitución, pleasant, recommended; *Clark*, D, a/c, with or without bathroom, ½ block from *Mareli* on Bravo, popular with families, best of the budget hotels, T 22569; *Pensión California*, E, Calle Degollado 209 near Madero, fan, shower, garden patio, basic but popular; similar is *Hostería del Convento*, E, Calle Madero 85, adequate; *Posada San Miguel*, E, Calle Belisario Domínguez Norte 45, near plaza, colonial-style, bathroom, clean, hot water morning and evening, OK; *Miriam*, Av. 16 de Septiembre, F p.p., cheapest; *Palencia*, E, Calle 16 de Septiembre nr. Francisco Madero, central, basic, fans, seedy, not recommended; *Cuartos Jalisco*, Belisario Domínguez 251, F, very basic. *Youth Hostel* on Carretera al Sur (Highway 1) near S end of Isabel La Católica, about 20 blocks from centre, dormitory bunk US$1.60 per night, open 0600-2300, good value, "8 de Octubre" bus from market.

Camping *El Cardón Trailer Park*, 4 km. SW on Highway 1, partly-shaded area away from beach, full facilities, US$11 for 2; *Aquamarina RV Park*, 3½ km. SW, 400 m. off Highway 1 at Calle Nayarit, on bay, nicely landscaped, all facilities, marina, boat ramp, fishing, scuba trips arranged, US$17 for 2; *La Paz Trailer Park*, 1½ km. S of town off Highway 1, access via Calle Colima, deluxe, nearest RV Park to La Paz, very comfortable, US$12 for 2. The ferretería across from the main city bus terminal sells white gas stove fuel (*gasolina blanca*). CCC Supermarket, opp. Palacio de Gobierno, is good for supplies.

Restaurants *Palapa Adriana*, on beachfront, open air, excellent service; *Antojitos*, next to *Pirámide* on 16 de Septiembre de 1810, friendly, good value. *La Tavola Pizza*, good value. Vegetarian restaurant *El Quinto*, Independencia y B. Domínguez, expensive (whole wheat bread is half the price at the *panadería* in the market place). Good *lonchería* and juice bars in the market.

Shopping A duty-free port (but see above). *Casa de las Artesanías de B.C.S*, Paseo Alvaro Obregón at Mijares, just N of Hotel Los Arcos, for souvenirs from all over Mexico; *Centro de Arte Regional*, Chiapas y Encinas (5 blocks E of Isabel La Católica), pottery workshop, reasonable prices; *Fortunato Silva*, Highway 1 (Abasolo) y Jalisco at S end of town, good quality woollen and hand-woven cotton garments and articles. Tourist shops are concentrated along the Malecón between the Tourist and Commercial Wharves.

Exchange Banks will not exchange travellers' cheques after 1100.

Immigration Second floor of large building on Paseo Alvaro Obregón, opp. the pier.

Tourist Office On Tourist Wharf at bottom of 16 de Septiembre, helpful, English spoken, open Mon.-Fri. 0800-1500, Sat. 0900-1300, 1400-1500, open till 1900 high season, will make hotel reservations, some literature and town maps.

Buses Local buses about US$0.20, depot at Revolución de 1910 y Degollado by the Public Market. Central Bus Station (Central Camionera): 5 de Febrero y Valentín Gómez Farías, about 16 blocks from centre, terminal for Tres Estrellas de Oro and Autotransportes Aguila; Autotransportes de La Paz leave from Public Market. Ciudad Constitución 13 departures a day, US$3; Loreto 3 per day, US$4.75; Guerrero Negro 6 per day, US$10; Ensenada US$18.50; Tijuana US$20, Mexicali US$22. To the Cape: San Antonio US$0.85, Miraflores US$2.10, San José del Cabo US$2.75, Cabo San Lucas US$3.10 (all 10 departures per day). Todos Santos, 6 per day, US$1.80; Cabo San Lucas via west loop US$3.

Air General Manuel Márquez de León International Airport, 11 km. SW on paved road off Highway 1. Taxi fare US$3-4, supposedly fixed, but bargain. Mexicana: to Tijuana non-stop, Mexico City; Aero México: to Culiacán, Guaymas, Mexico City, Puerto Vallarta, Tijuana (non-stop) and Guadalajara, also to Los Angeles, CA, and Tucson, Arizona. Aero California: to Los Mochis, daily 0800, US$30, with connection to Tijuana; city office at Malecón y Calle Bravo; also to Ciudad Obregón, Culiacán, Guadalajara, Hermosillo, Loreto, Los Cabos, Mazatlán, Mexico City, Tijuana and Los Angeles, CA.

Ferry Services Modern ferry terminal at Pichilingüe, 21 km. north on paved highway. Make reservations at town office (Ignacio Ramírez y Ejido, on NE edge of town), 3 days ahead if possible, or at Sematur in La Paz. Tourist cards must be valid, allow plenty of time (preferably before 1400) as there are long queues—trucks have loading priority. It should be noted that many motorists have had difficulty getting reservations or having them honoured; the ferry system (no longer government-owned) is becoming increasingly unreliable, infrequent and fares are rising alarmingly. Vehicles must have car permits, obtainable at ferry ports but best to get at Registro Federal de Vehículos in Tijuana; automobile clubs will provide information. Four classes of service: *salón* (unreserved reclining seat, not particularly comfortable), *turista* (roomette with with two bunks and a sink, sexes are segregated), *cabina* (bedroom with shower), *especial* (first class suite).

To Topolobampo Wed. and Sun., dep. 2000, arr. mainland 0400. Fares *salón*, US$5; *turista*, US$9; *cabina*, US$21; *especial*, US$28; motorcycle, US$16, cars and motorhomes also carried.

To Mazatlán Daily dep. 1700, arr. mainland 0900 next day (can take 20 hours); unclaimed cabins sold off to firstcomers one day in advance at 1500—chaotic queues; stand firm. Fares (Dec. 1989) *salón*, US$13.80; *turista*, US$15; *cabina*, US$30; *especial*, US$50; motorcycle US$16. Cars and motorhomes also carried. Children of 2-11 go half price. The deck gets wet during the night; toilets quickly get blocked, so make an early call. It has been reported that to be sure of a cabin you must book through a travel agent, prices are double. To get a tourist cabin, insist that you will share with strangers—a friendly chat may help. The queue for seats starts at 0630. Book cars 4 weeks in advance. On arrival, buses to Mazatlán may be full, ask about rides on the ferry.

Bus to ferry terminal from Medrita Travel Agency, Paseo Alvaro Obregón y Calle 5 de Mayo, frequent departures; from terminal, Calle Ejido (first on the left after leaving the ferry). Reasonable facilities at terminal but crowded; large parking lots—officials may permit RVs to stay overnight while awaiting ferry departures.

NB On all ferry crossings, delays can occur from September if there is bad weather, which could hold you up for 3 days; fog at the entrance to Topolobampo harbour is often a problem; mechanical breakdowns are not unknown! Keep a flexible schedule if travelling to the mainland.

Beaches Many, most popular on the Pichilingüe Peninsula. Going N from La Paz to ferry terminal on Highway 11; Palmira, Coromuel (popular with paceños), El Caimancito, Tesoro. Wind surfing and catamaran trips can be arranged on the main beach, if the English speaking owner likes you. Pichilingüe (bus at 0800 then hourly from 1000-1700, US$0.35 from station at Paseo Alvaro Obregón y Independencia), 100 m. N of ferry terminal is a *playa pública*, about US$1. Balandra (rubbish bins, *palapas*, US$2), Tecolote (same) and El Coyote (no water or facilities), reached by rough graded road after pavement ends at ferry terminal, ends at a gravel pit at Playa Cachimba (good surf fishing), 13 km. NE of Pichilingüe; beaches facing north are attractive but windy, some mosquitoes. El Comitán and El Mogote, are to SW of La Paz on bay, tranquil, no surf.

Excursions 17 km. W of La Paz a paved road branches NW off Highway 1 leading to the mining village of San Juan de la Costa, allowing a closer look at the rugged coastal section of the Sierra de la Giganta. Pavement ends after 25 km., road becomes wide, rolling, regularly graded; OK for large RVs to San Juan, which is a company town of neat-rowed houses; phosphorus is mined and loaded by conveyor and deep-water dock, to be shipped to processing plants for fertilizer production. After San Juan (45 km.), the road is passable for medium-size vehicles to Punta Coyote (90 km.), closely following the narrow space between mountains and coast; wonderful untouched camping spots. From Coyote to San Evaristo (27 km.) the track is poor—rugged vehicle recommended, travel time from Highway 1 about 4½ hours; San Evaristo is a sleepy fishing village on a delightful cove sheltered on the east by the Isla San José. Ideal boating area but as yet undiscovered. Visit the salt-drying operations near San Evaristo or on San José. This is a rewarding excursion for those with smaller, high-clearance vehicles (vans and pick-ups with shells) for the steep final 20 mile stretch.

State Highway 286 leads SE out of La Paz 45 km. to San Juan de Los Planes (pop. 1,350), a friendly town in a rich farming region. A fair road continues another 15 km. to the beautiful Ensenada del los Muertos, good fishing, swimming and "wild" camping. A further 11 km. is the headland of Punta Arena de la Ventana, with a magnificent view of the sterile slopes of Isla Cerralvo. (*Hotel Las Arenas*, L, resort overlooking Ventana Bay). 6 km. before Los Planes, a graded road leads to the Bahía de la Ventana and the small fishing villages of La Ventana and El Sargento; lovely beaches facing Cerralvo Island.

S of La Paz and its plain, the central mountain spine rises again into the wooded heights of the Sierra de la Laguna and bulges out into the "Cape Region", Baja's most touristically-developed area. The highway winds up to **El Triunfo**, a picturesque village (almost a ghost town); silver was discovered at nearby San Antonio in 1748 and at El Triunfo in 1862. The latter exploded with a population of 10,000 and was for a while the largest town in Baja. The mines closed in 1926 but small-scale mining has resumed in places. *Warning*: present-day miners are using arsenic in the old mine tailings; these areas are fenced and signed. There is a craft shop at the village entrance where young people make palm-leaf objects. 8 km. further on is the lovely mountain town and farming centre of San Antonio (gasoline, groceries, meals), which was founded in 1756 and served briefly as Baja's capital (1828-30) when Loreto was destroyed. 8 km. S of San Antonio was the site of Santa Ana, where silver was first discovered in 1748. It was from this vanished village that the Viceroy and Padre Junípero Serra planned the expedition to establish the chain of Franciscan missions in Alta California.

Highway 1 climbs sharply from the canyon and winds past a number of ancient mines, through the peaceful orchard-farming town of San Bartolo (groceries and meals) and down to the coastal flats around Los Barriles, a small town with fuel, meals and limited supplies. A number of resort hotels are situated near here along the beautiful Bahía de Palmas and at nearby Buena Vista; none is in the "budget" class but all are popular.

The Highway turns inland after Los Barriles (106 km. from La Paz). An "East Cape Loop" turns E off the Highway through La Rivera, following the coast to San José del Cabo. Off Cabo Pulmo, a beautiful headland, is the Northern Pacific's only living coral reef; fishing, diving and snorkelling are excellent (56 km. from Los Barriles). There are many camping spots along the beautiful beaches of this coast.

Santiago is a pleasant, historic little town (pop. 2,000) 3 km. off Highway 1. On the tree-lined main street are a Pemex station, café and stores grouped around the town plaza. A kilometre further W is the Parque Zoológico, the Cape's only zoo—modest but informative, free admission. The Jesuits built their 10th mission in Santiago in 1723 after transferring it from Los Barriles. The town was one of the sites of the Pericué Indian uprising of 1734. (**Hotel** *Palomar*, D, a/c, hot showers, restaurant, bar, on main street, modest, good meals).

3½ km. S of the Santiago turnoff Highway 1 crosses the Tropic of Cancer, marked by a large concrete sphere, and runs S down the fertile valley between the lofty Sierra de la Laguna (west) and the Sierra Santa Clara (east), to the Cabos International Airport (direct jet services to California, USA, and Mexico; modern terminal, parking and good transportation to San José del Cabo, 10 km. S).

San José del Cabo, the largest town south of La Paz, has a population of 10,000. Although founded in 1730, it is now essentially a modern town divided into two districts: the resort sectors and new Fonatur development on the beach, and the downtown zone to the north, with the government offices and many businesses grouped near the tranquil Parque Mijares, and numerous shops and restaurants along Calles Zaragoza and Doblado. The N end of Blvd Antonio Mijares has been turned into a "mini-gringoland ... which could have been transplanted from the Main St. of Disneyland" (Scott Wayne). San José also has two service stations, hospital, auto parts and mechanical repairs. The attractive church on the Plaza Mijares was built in 1940 on the final site of the mission of 1730; a tile mosaic over the entrance depicts the murder of Padre Tamaral by rebellious Indians in 1734. Most of the top hotels are located W of San José along the beaches or nearby *estéro*; the Fonatur development blocks access to much of the beach near town; best are Playas Nuevo Sol and California, about 3 km. from downtown. Unofficial camping is possible on those few not fronted by resort hotels.

Hotels *Palmilla*, L, one of the top resorts in Baja, 8 km. W at Punta Palmilla (outstanding surfing nearby), some a/c, showers, pool, beach, tennis, narrow access road, restaurant, bar, skin diving, fishing cruisers US$325 per day, skiffs US$125 (daily happy hour allows mere mortals to partake of margarita and appetizers for US$3 and see how royalty and film stars live!). *El Presidente*, L, T 20232, on lagoon S of town, a/c, all facilities, boat rentals, centrepiece of the Fonatur development at San José del Cabo; *Castel Cabo*, A, on beach off Paseo San José S of Town, T 20155, a/c, another Fonatur hotel; *Posada Real Cabo*, A, next door, a/c, colour TV, showers, pool, tennis, restaurant, bar, gift shop, fishing charters US$90 per day for 3; *Calinda Aquamarina-Comfort Inn*, A, next to Posada Real Cabo, T 20077, U.S. Comfort Inn chain, a/c, beach, pool, restaurant, bar, fishing, clean and comfortable; *Aston Cabo Regis Resort and Beach Club*, in hotel zone on Blvd Finisterra, a/c, colour TV, showers, kitchenettes, private balconies, pool, tennis, golf course, restaurant; *Nuevo Sol*, C, on beach S of intersection of Paseo San José and Highway 1, pool, restaurant, sports facilities, nicely-landscaped, acceptable and good beachside value; *Collí*, D, in town on Hidalgo above Budget Rent-a-Car, T 20052, fans, hot showers, 12 clean and adequate rooms; *Pagamar*, E, Obregón between Degollado y Guerrero 3½ blocks from plaza, fans, café, hot showers, clean, good value; *Ceci*, E, Zaragoza 22, 1 block W of plaza, T 20051, fans, hot showers, basic but clean, excellent value, central. CREA youth hostel, Domicilio Conocido Anikan s/n.

Motel *Brisa del Mar*, D, on Highway 1, 3 km. SW of town near Hotel Nuevo Sol, 10 rooms, restaurant, bar, pool, modest but comfortable, at rear of trailer park on outstanding beach.

Camping *Brisa Del Mar Trailer Park*, 100 RV sites in fenced area by great beach, full hookups, flush toilets, showers, pool, laundry, restaurant, bar, fishing trips arranged, US$6 for 2 plus car, popular, rec., good location ("unofficial" camping possible under *palapas* on beach).

Bus Bus station on Calle Manuel Doblado opp. hospital, about 7 blocks W of plaza. To Cabo San Lucas (Tres Estrellas) daily from 0700, US$0.60, ½ hr; to La Paz daily from 0630, US$3.10, 2 hrs.

Regrettably, many of the coastal views and natural camping spots on the 34 km. run from San José del Cabo to Cabo San Lucas are barred to visitors by beachfront developments. These include: *Hotel Cabo San Lucas*, L, *Twin Dolphin* (T 30140), L+, and *Calinda Cabo Baja-Qualilty Inn* (T 30045), L, part of Cabo Bello residential development. At km. 25, just after the *Twin Dolphin*, a dirt road leads off to Shipwreck Beach, with beachside camping area; there is a large ship rotting on the shore. 5 km. before Cabo a small concrete marker beside the highway heralds an excellent view of the famous Cape. The Highway enters Cabo San Lucas past a Pemex station and continues as Blvd Lázaro Cárdenas to the Zócalo (Guerrero y Madero) and the Kilómetro 0 marker.

Cabo San Lucas has grown rapidly in recent years from a sleepy fishing village (pop. 1,500 in 1970) to a bustling international resort with a permanent population of 8,500. There are trailer parks, many cafés and restaurants, condominiums, gift shops, discos and a marina to cater for the increasing flood of North Americans who come for the world-famous sportfishing or to find a retirement paradise. The town fronts a small harbour facing the rocky peninsula that forms the "Land's End" of Baja California. Francisco de Ulloa first rounded and named the

Cape in 1539. The sheltered bay became a watering point for the treasure ships from the Orient; pirates sheltered here too. Now it is on the cruise ship itinerary. A popular attraction is the government-sponsored regional arts centre, where distinctive black-coral jewellery is made and sold, located at the cruise liner dock. Post Office is at Morelos y Niños Héroes.

Hotels *Hacienda Beach Resort*, L, at N entrance to harbour, some a/c, showers, pool, tennis, yacht anchorage, various water sports, hunting, horseriding, restaurant, etc., claims the only area beach safe from strong Pacific swells; *Giggling Marlin Inn*, L, central on Blvd Marina y Matamoros, a/c, TV, showers, kitchenettes, jacuzzi, restaurant, bar, fishing trips arranged, lively drinking and poor food in attached cocktail bar; *Finisterra*, L, perched on promontory near Land's End, T 30000, a/c, TV, shower, pool, steps to beach, poolside bar with unsurpassed view, restaurant, entertainment, sportfishing cruisers US$295 per day; *Marina Sol Condominiums*, L:16 Oct-30 June, A: rest of year, on 16 de Septiembre, between Highway 1 and Bay, full hotel service in 3- and 7-storey buildings; *Solmar*, L, T 30022, the southernmost development in Baja California, a/c, showers, ocean view, pool, tennis, diving, restaurant, poolside bar, fishing cruisers US$275-295 per day, beach with heavy ocean surf; *Mar de Cortez*, B, on Highway 1 at Guerrero in town centre, T 30032, a/c, showers, pool, outdoor bar/restaurant, suites US$50; *Marina*, C, Blvd Marina y Guerrero, T 30030, central, a/c, restaurant, bar, can be noisy, pricey; *Casablanca*, E, Calle Revolución between Morelos y Leona Vicario, central, fan, shower, clean, cheapest in town.

  Motel *Los Cabos Inn*, C/D, Abasolo y 16 de Septiembre, central, 1 block from bus station, fans, showers, central, modest, good value.

Camping *El Arco Trailer Park*, 4 km. E on Highway 1, restaurant, US$8 per site; *El Faro Viejo Trailer Park*, 1½ km. NW at Matamoros y Morales, shade, laundry, ice, restaurant, bar, clean, out-of-town but good, US$6 for 2; *Vagabundos del Mar*, 3½ km. E on Highway 1, pool, laundry, good, US$15 for 2; *Cabo Cielo RV Park*, 3 km. E on Highway 1; *San Vicente Trailer Park*, 3 km. E on Highway 1, same as Cabo Cielo plus pool, both reasonably basic, rates unknown. All have full hookups, toilets and showers. Several *playas públicas* on coast E of town, inc. Cabo Real, 5 km., showers and restrooms, modest fee; "Barco Barrado" (Shipwreck Beach), 10 km., lovely beach, camping W of shipwreck, showers and restrooms, US$5 per night, popular with RVs.

Tourist Office next to ferry landing, town maps, Fonatur office. Many firms renting aquatic equipment and arranging boating excursions, etc; the beaches E of Cabo San Lucas offer endless opportunities for swimming, scuba diving and snorkelling. Boat trips to Lover's Beach about US$16 for 4; most hotels can arrange hire of skiffs to enable visits to the Arch and Land's End, about US$5-10 per hour.

Bus Bus station at 16 de Septiembre y Zaragoza, central, few facilities. To San José del Cabo, 8 departures a day, US$0.50. To La Paz 6 a day from 0630, US$4.75; Tijuana US$24, 1600 and 1800 daily via La Paz.

Ringed by pounding surf, columns of fluted rock enclose Lover's Beach (be careful if walking along the beach—huge waves sweep away several visitors each year), a romantic sandy cove with views out to the seal colonies on offshore islets. At the very tip of the Cabo is the distinctive natural arch ("el arco"); boats can be hired to see it close-up, but care is required because of the strong rips. At the harbour entrance is a pinnacle of rock—Pelican Rock—which is home to vast shoals of tropical fish; it is an ideal place for snorkelling and scuba diving or glass-bottomed boats may be rented at the harbourside.

Highway 19, the western loop of the Cape Region, was not paved until

1985 and the superb beaches of the west coast have yet to suffer the development and crowding of the east. The highway branches off Highway 1 just after San Pedro, 32 km. S of La Paz, and runs due south through a cactus-covered plain to **Todos Santos**, a quiet farming town of 4,000 only a few hundred metres N of the Tropic of Cancer. There is a Pemex station, cinema, stores, cafés, a bank, clinic and market, a museum—the Casa de la Cultura (Calles Topete y Pilar)—and **Misión de Todos Santos Inn**, C, historic brick building near town centre, showers, B&B, other meals available in dining room on request; **Hotel California**, C, Calle Juárez next to Pemex station a block N of Highway 19, fans, showers, pool, restaurant. **El Molino Trailer Park**, off Highway at S end of town, full hookups, flush toilets, showers, laundry, US$8 for 4, better value than the hotels!

Todos Santos was founded as a Jesuit mission in 1734; a church replacing the abandoned structure, built in 1840, stands opposite the Civic Plaza on Calle Juárez. The ruins of several old sugar mills can be seen around the town in the fertile valley. Fishing is also important.

2 km. away is the Pacific coast with some of the most beautiful beaches of the entire Peninsula. Nearest is Playa Punta Lobos, a popular picnic spot; better is the sandy cove at Playa Pedrito (4km SE). Backed by groves of Washingtonia fan palms and coconut palms, this is one of the loveliest camping spots anywhere. Opposite the access road junction is the Campo Experimental Forestal, a Botanical Garden with a well-labelled array of desert plants from all regions of Baja. Here too is the San Pedrito RV Park, an open area on the beach, full hookups, flush toilets, showers, pool, laundry, restaurant, bar, US$3 for tent, US$8 for RVs, one of the most beautifully-sited RV parks in Baja, very good value. 11 km. S of Todos Santos is El Pescadero, a fast-growing farming town with few facilities for visitors.

Excursion In the rugged interior E of Todos Santos is the **Parque Nacional Sierra de la Laguna** (under threat and not officially recognized). Crowning peak is the Picacho La Laguna (2,163 m.), beginning to attract a trickle of hikers to its "lost world" of pine and oak trees, doves and woodpeckers, grassy meadows and luxuriant flowers; there is nothing else like it in Baja. Trail is steep but straight forward; the panoramic view takes in La Paz and both the Gulf and Pacific. Cold at night. Best reached from Todos Santos by making local enquiries; 3-day guided pack trips are also offered by the Todos Santos Inn, US$325 per person.

7 km. S of El Pescadero is Los Cerritos RV Park on a wide sandy beach, 50 RV or tent sites but no hook-ups, flush toilets, US$3 per vehicle. Playa Los Cerritos is a playa pública; there are several camping areas but no facilities, US$1-2 per vehicle. The succession of rocky coves and empty beaches continues to Colonia Plutarco Elías Calles, a tiny farming village in the midst of a patchwork of orchards. The highway parallels the coast to Rancho El Migriño, then continues S along the coastal plain; there are no more camping spots as far as Cabo San Lucas. Many now prefer the West Loop to the main highway; it is 140 km. from the junction at San Pedro, thus cutting off about 50 km. and up to an hour's driving

time from the Transpeninsular Highway route.

INFORMATION FOR VISITORS

Documents A passport is necessary, but US and Canadian citizens need only show birth certificate (or for US, a naturalization certificate). Tourists need the free tourist card, which can be obtained from any Mexican Consulate or Tourist Commission office, at the Mexican airport on entry, from the offices or on the aircraft of airlines operating into Mexico; if you say you are in transit you may be charged US$8, with resulting paper work. N.B. Not all Mexican consuls in USA are aware of exact entry requirements; it is best to confirm details with airlines which fly to Mexico. Some nationalities, including West Germans, appear no longer to need a tourist card. Best to say you are going to an inland destination. (Airlines may issue cards only to citizens of West European countries, most Latin American countries—not Cuba, Chile or Haiti—the USA, Canada, Australia, Japan and the Philippines.) Also at border offices of the American Automobile Association (AAA), which offers this service to members and non-members. There is a multiple entry card valid for all visits within 6 months for US nationals. The normal validity for other nationals is 90 days, but sometimes only 30 days are granted at border crossings; insist you want more if wishing to stay longer.

Renewal of entry cards or visas must be done at Secretaría de Gobernación, Dirección General de Asuntos Jurídicos, Calle Francisco Del Paso, Metro San Lázaro, Mexico City (T 535-2718/5798), or in Guadalajara. There is also a helpful office at Room 78 in the International Airport. Take travellers' cheques as proof of finance. Best to collect visa, not have it forwarded by post. Travellers not carrying tourist cards need visas (Israelis and Finns need a visa), multiple entry not allowed, visa must be renewed before re-entry. Tourist cards are not required for cities close to the US border, such as Tijuana, Mexicali, etc. Businessmen who want to study the Mexican market or to appoint an agent should apply for the requisite visa and permit.

At border crossings make sure the immigration people don't con you to pay a dollar for the card or visa. It is free and the man typing it out is only doing his job. We would warn travellers that there have been several cases of tourist cards not being honoured, or a charge being imposed, or the validity being changed arbitrarily to 60 days or less. In this case, complaint should be made to the authorities in Mexico City. Some border stations do not issue tourist cards; you are therefore strongly advised, if travelling by land, to obtain a card before arriving at the border. Above all, do not lose your tourist card—you cannot leave the country without it and it takes at least a week to replace. If you want to return to Mexico after leaving there to visit Belize or Guatemala, remember that you will need a new visa/tourist card if yours is not marked for multiple entry.

At the land frontiers with Belize and Guatemala, you may be refused entry into Mexico if you have less than US$200 (or US$350 for each month of intended stay, up to a maximum of 180 days). This restriction does not officially apply to North American and European travellers, but we have heard that *everyone* entering Mexico from Belize needs a visa issued by the Mexican Consul in Belize City. (This is presumably an anti-drugs measure; check if still in force.) Persuasion, whether verbal or financial, can sometimes remedy this.

British business travellers are strongly advised to read *Hints to Exporters: Mexico*, obtainable from the Department of Trade, Export Services Division, Sanctuary Buildings, 16-20 Great Smith Street, London SW1P 3DB.

Airport Departure Tax US$10 on international flights; US$4.50 on internal flights.

N.B. VAT is payable on domestic plane tickets bought in Mexico.

How to Get There by Air Several airlines have regular flights from Europe to Mexico City. Air France from Paris via Houston, 4 times a week; Iberia from Madrid via Montreal; Aero México from Paris via Madrid and Miami; KLM from Amsterdam, one stop; Continental from Amsterdam via London (Gatwick) and Houston (with a change of plane in each), also from London (Gatwick), Delta with a change in Atlanta; Lufthansa from Frankfurt via Dallas. Aeroflot fly to Mexico City from Mosocw via Shannon and Havana, or via Luxembourg and Havana; the flight can be joined in Moscow, or in Shannon or Luxembourg, but it is *vital* to check that these services are in operation when you want to travel.

Mexico City from New York, under 4 hrs. (Delta, Aeroméxico, Pan Am, Continental, Mexicana); from Chicago, 4 hrs. (Mexicana and American Airlines); from Los Angeles, 3 hrs. with Mexicana ("Moonlight Express", cost about 60% of normal), also Aeroméxico, Lacsa, Delta, Continental, Pan Am, Avianca; from Houston, 2 hrs. (Aeroméxico as well as those mentioned above); from Washington, with United Airlines, Delta or Continental (via Houston). Other flights from the USA include: Philadelphia, Baltimore, San Antonio and Denver (Mexicana), Charlotte, Milwaukee, Memphis and Cincinnati (American), Dallas (many lines), Miami (American, Pan Am, Aeroméxico, Mexicana), San Francisco (Mexicana, Pan Am, United), Tucson (Aeroméxico), Seattle (Mexicana, United). Other flights from the USA to Mexican cities are given in the text. Japan Airlines twice weekly flight from Tokyo stops at Vancouver.

Flights from South and Central America: Aerolíneas Argentinas from Buenos Aires (twice a week via Lima), Aero-Perú also from Lima; Avensa from Caracas; Eucatoriana from Guayaquil and Quito; Avianca from Bogotá, also Varig en route from Rio and São Paulo (direct flights as well on Varig from Brazil); Aviateca and Mexicana from Guatemala City; Aeronica from Managua; Air Panama from Panama; Lacsa and Mexicana from San José, Costa Rica; TAN from Tegucigalpa and San Pedro Sula, Taca also from Tegucigalpa, who fly from San Salvador (as do Lacsa). Pan Am from San Juan, Puerto Rico.

To Cuba Return flight to Cuba, Sat. and Wed., with stop at Mérida if plane is not fully booked (Mexicana); Mexicana direct on Sun., Cubana Mon. and Fri. Cuba package tours US$285 for seven day all-inclusive stay and return flight from Mexico City or US$238 from Mérida. Ask around Hamburgo in Mexico City for cheap tickets: might pick them up for as little as US$120 or so. If you pay in dollars make sure the fact is noted on the ticket; if you pay in pesos and use the ticket later you may be surcharged if the peso price has risen meanwhile. Visas for Cuba available through Viñales Tours, Melchor Ocampo 469, Colonia Anzures, T 511-30-33; you have to show your return ticket for Cuba.

Overland Toronto to Mexico City, via Chicago-St. Louis-Dallas-San Antonio- Laredo-Monterrey, with Greyhound bus (74 hrs.) on a 15-day pass. Montreal-Laredo via New York, Washington, Atlanta, New Orleans, Houston and San Antonio, 60 hrs. Both Greyhound and Trailways provide services from Miami to the Mexican border and on to Mexico City. It's cheaper to make booking outside the US, but the information is hard to come by in Mexico City. Trailways in London, c/o Holiday Inn, Heathrow Airport, Stockley Rd., West Drayton, Middlesex, UB7 9NA. Los Angeles-Mexico City, 44 hrs.; New York-Mexico City, 70 hrs.; San Antonio-Mexico City, 20 hrs. If coming from the US it is usually cheaper to travel to the border and buy your ticket in the Mexican border town from the Mexican company. If going to the US it is worth checking Greyhound bus passes, cheap offers have been reported, check with Transportes del Norte or Wagon Lits offices in Mexico.

Customs Regulations The luggage of tourist-card holders is often passed unexamined. If flying into Mexico from South America, expect to be thoroughly searched (body and luggage) at the airport. US citizens can take in their own clothing and equipment without paying duty, but all valuable and non-US-made objects (diamonds, cameras, binoculars, typewriters, etc.), should be registered at the US Customs office or the port of exit so that duty will not be charged on returning. Radios and television sets must be registered and taken out when leaving. Tourists are allowed to take into Mexico duty-free 1 kg. of tobacco and 400 cigarettes (or 50 cigars), 2 bottles of liquor, US$80 worth of gifts and 12 rolls of film, also portable TV, radio, typewriter, camera, tent and bicycle. There are no restrictions on the import or export of money apart from gold but foreign gold coins are allowed into the US only if they are clearly made into jewellery (perforated or otherwise worked on). On return to the US a person may take from Mexico, free of duty, up to US$100 worth of merchandise for personal use or for personal gifts, every 31 days, if acquired merely as an incident of the trip. Alcoholic drinks may not be taken across the border from Mexico to California. Archaeological relics may not be taken out of Mexico. US tourists should remember that the US Endangered Species Act, 1973, prohibits importation into the States of products from endangered species, e.g. tortoise shell. The Department of the Interior issues a leaflet about this. Llama, alpaca, etc. items may be confiscated at the airport for fumigation and it will be necessary to return to the customs area on the Mexico City airport perimeter 2-3 days later to collect and pay for fumigation. Production of passport will be required and proof that goods are to be re-exported otherwise they may also be subject to import duties. Duty-free goods from Aeroboutiques at Mexico City, Mazatlán, Puerto Vallarta, Guadalajara, Monterrey, Mérida and Acapulco airports.

Travel in Mexico By Air Promotional packages for local tourism exist, with 30-40% discount, operated by hoteliers, restaurateurs, hauliers and Aeroméxico and Mexicana (the latter is more punctual). Their tickets are not interchangeable. Aeroméxico has all-inclusive travel (*VTI*) and journey-inclusive hotel (*VHI*) rates; the former includes 3 nights lodging, half-board and return flight, the latter transport and lodging only. Mexicana has similar arrangements with the initials *VIP* and *VHP* . Check whether you qualify for the dozen or so destinations. The two local airlines offer 15% discounts to foreigners for their domestic air services: 20% if the foreigners arrive on their own flights. Discounts must be claimed within one week of arrival.

Local Road Services There are three kinds of buses, first and second class, and local. Terminals for each are usually distinct, and may not be in one bus station. Buses in the country will not stop on curves—walk until you find a straight stretch. First-class buses assign you a seat and you may have to queue for 1-2 hrs. to get a ticket. It is not easy to choose which seat or to change it later. No standing, and you may have to wait for the next one (next day, perhaps) if all seats are taken. You *must* book in advance for buses travelling in the Yucatán Peninsula, especially around Christmas, but it is also advisable to book if going elsewhere. Bus seats are particulary hard to get during school holidays, around Easter and August and the 15 days up to New Year when many public servants take holidays in all resorts; transport from Mexico City is booked up a long time in advance and hotels are filled, too. In the north especially, try to travel from the starting-point of a route; buses are often full at the mid-point of their routes. Beware of "scalpers" who try to sell you a seat at a higher price, which you can usually get on a stand-by basis, when somebody doesn't turn up, at the regular price. Sometimes it helps to talk to the driver, who has two places to use at his discretion behind his seat (don't sit in these until invited). Lock your luggage to the rack with a cycle lock and chain. Stowing your luggage on the roof is not advisable on night buses since theft can occur.

First-class buses often have toilets and air-conditioning which does not work, but are nevertheless recommended for long-distance travelling. If going on an overnight bus, book seats at front as toilets get very smelly by morning. Second-class buses are often antiques (interesting, but frustrating when they break down) or may be brand new; the passengers are invariably more entertaining and courteous than in first-class buses. They call at towns and villages and go up side roads the first-class buses never touch. They stop quite as often for meals and toilets as their superiors do and—unlike the first-class buses—people get on and off so often that you may be able to obtain a seat after all. Seats are not bookable, except in Baja California. In general, it is a good idea to take food and drink with you on a long bus ride, as stops may depend on the driver and also a warm outer garment as air-conditioning on 1st class buses is often turned way down. First class fares are usually 10% dearer than 2nd class ones. Some companies give holders of an international student card a 50% discount on bus tickets; persistence may be required. There seem always to be many buses leaving in the early morning. Buses are sometimes called *camiones*, hence *central camionero* for bus station. A monthly bus guide is available for US$1 (year's subscription) from Guía de Autotransportes de México, Apartado 8929, México 1, D.F.

Rail Much of the passenger equipment in use dates from the forties or fifties, including a number of *autovías*. There are modern trains between Mexicali and Guadalajara in 36 hours, and overnight good Pullman trains between Mexico City and Monterrey, Guadalajara, Veracruz and Mérida. The *servicio estrella* services (see text for routes) provide good accommodation and all meals, and have been recommended. They have 1st class and 1st class special seats, the latter are much more comfortable and cost roughly ⅓ more than a bus, these trains are punctual. The railways claim that you can see more from a train than from any other form of transport; this may well be true, but trains tend to be slower than the buses (though cheaper; 2nd class is about one-third of 2nd-class bus fare; they can, however, be very crowded); they sometimes have comfortable sleeper cars with *alcobas* (better berths) and *camarines* (small sleepers). The special first class has air-conditioning and reclining seats and costs about 10% more than the regular 1st class, which costs about twice the 2nd class fare. Tickets are best booked at the stations: agencies tend to add a large commission and the tickets they issue sometimes turn out not to be valid. A condensed railway timetable may be obtained from the Mexican railways' office at 500 Fifth Ave. (Room 2623), New York, N.Y. 10036. (For extensive information about the Mexican railway network consult *Makens' Guide to Mexican Train Travel*, compiled by James C. Makens and published by Le Voyageur Publishing Co., 1319 Wentwood Drive, Irving, Texas 75061, at about US$6.)

If you should get caught during the holiday season try to book a 2nd class train, but this may involve queuing 12 hrs. or more if you want a seat. More first-class tickets are sold than the total number of first-class seats; first-class passengers are allowed on first, so you may still find a 2nd class seat. Some travellers have remarked that the last carriage of a 2nd class train is often half full of soldiers, who might deter would-be thieves from taking one's personal belongings if one shares their carriage. We have received a report of conductors turning out lights on night trains, enabling thieves to operate with impunity; take great care under these circumstances.

Automobiles These may be brought into Mexico on a Tourist Permit for 180 days. Entry and exit will be recorded in your passport. It takes 10 days to extend a permit, so ask for more time than you expect to need. Don't overstay—driving without an extension gets a US$50 fine for the first five days and then rises abruptly to *half the value of the car!* No fee is charged for the permit, and the AAA always writes "free" across the preliminary application form it gives its clients because, apparently, some Mexican border officials tend to forget this fact, take care of the permit, if lost there can be much delay and expense in order to leave the country. If you don't have proof of ownership (certificate or title of registration) you will need a notarized statement that you own the vehicle or drive with the permission of the owner. National or international driving licences are accepted; or you can get a Mexican licence at the International Airport, Mexico City, on presentation of visa/tourist card, signed statement of fitness and ability to drive, and local address. Your US car insurance does not cover you while driving in Mexico, but agencies on both sides of the border will sell you Mexican automobile insurance, so only buy 1-day US insurance if crossing the border. Sanborn's Mexican Insurance Service, with offices in Texas, New Mexico, Arizona and 6 Mexican cities, will provide insurance services (about US$3.20 a day, third party only) within Mexico and other parts of Latin America, and provide "Travelogs" for Mexico and Central America with useful tips. British AA members are reminded that there are ties with the AAA, which extends cover to the US and entitles AA members to free travel information including a very useful book and map on Mexico. Holders of 180-day tourist cards can keep their automobiles in Mexico for that time. Luggage is no longer inspected at the checkpoints along the road where tourist cards and/or car permits are examined.

Gasoline is either *extra*, unleaded, 87 octane, which is difficult to find outside Baja California, and *nova*, leaded, 80 octane. *Extra* is sold from silver pumps; *nova* from blue pumps; diesel from red pumps. There are dozens of minor swindles practised at filling stations. Make sure you are given full value when you tank up, that the pump is set to zero before your tank is filled, that both they and you know what money you've proffered, that your change is correct, that the pump is correctly calibrated, and that your filler cap is put back on. There is no legal surcharge for service at night, nor additional taxes: two more games frequently tried.

The Free Assistance Service of the Mexican Tourist Department's green jeeps ("*ángeles verdes*") patrol most of Mexico's main roads. The drivers speak English, are trained to give first aid and to make minor auto repairs and deal with flat tyres. They carry gasoline and have radio connection. All help is completely free. Gasoline at cost price. Parking: Multi-storey car parks are becoming more common but parking is often to be found right in city centres under the main square.

Car Rental is very expensive in Mexico, it is cheaper to arrange hire in the US or Europe.

Airport Taxis To avoid overcharging, the Government has taken control of taxi services from airports to cities and only those with government licences are allowed to carry passengers from the airport. Sometimes one does not pay the driver but purchases a ticket from a booth on leaving the airport. No further tipping is then required. The same system has been applied at bus stations but it is possible to pay the driver direct.

Motorbikes Grant and Susan Johnson, of Horizons Unlimited, Vancouver, tell us that motor-cycling is good in Mexico as most main roads are in fairly good condition and hotels are usually willing to allow the bike to be parked in a courtyard or patio.

All Japanese parts are sold only by one shop in Mexico City at extortionate prices (but parts and accessories are easily available in Guatemala at reasonable prices for those travelling there). Robert S. Kahn recommends Señor Romano's shop, Av. Revolución 1310, Mexico

City, for bike repairs. Sr. Romano, a Belgian-Mexican, speaks French and English. Some motorbike travellers have warned that particularly in Mexico City groups of plain clothes police in unmarked cars try to impound motorbikes by force of arms. Uniformed police are no help here.

Warnings When two cars converge on a narrow bridge from opposite directions, the driver who first flashes his lights has the right of way. Don't drive fast at night; farm and wild animals roam freely. In fact, it is advisable to drive as little as possible at night as robberies are on the increase especially in Guerrero and Oaxaca States. Some motorists report that it is better not to stop if you hit another car, as although Mexican insurance is proof of your ability to pay, both parties may sometimes be incarcerated until all claims are settled. "Sleeping policemen" or road bumps can be hazardous in towns and villages as often there are no warning signs; they are sometimes marked "*zona de topes*", or incorrectly marked as *vibradores*. In most instances, their distinguishing paint has worn away.

On the west coast, the Government has set up military checkpoints to look out for drug-smugglers and gun-runners, almost as far south as Puerto Angel. Papers will be checked at these points and your car searched. Reports have been received of payments being demanded for the return of passports, this is not legal practice. The degree of search is apparently linked to general appearance; young people travelling in VW vans can expect thorough searches all the way. Watch searchers carefully; sometimes they try to make off with tools, camping gear and the like, especially if there are two or more of them.

If you are stopped by police for an offence you have not committed and you know you are in the right, do not pay the "fine" on the spot. Take the number of the policeman from his cap, show him that you have his number and tell him that you will see his chief (*jefe*) at the tourist police headquarters instead. It is also advisable to go to the precinct station anyway whenever a fine is involved, to make sure it is genuine.

When entering Mexico from Belize by car point out to the authorities that you have a car with you, otherwise they may not note it and you could be arrested for illegally importing a car.

Tourists' cars cannot, *by law*, be sold in Mexico. This is very strictly applied. You may not leave the country without the car you entered in, except with written government permission with the car in bond.

Hitch-hiking is usually possible for single hikers, but apparently less easy for couples. The most difficult stretches are reported to be Acapulco-Puerto Escondido, Santa Cruz-Salina Cruz and Tulum-Chetumal.

Walking Walkers are advised to get *Backpacking in Mexico and Central America*, by Hilary Bradt and Rob Rachowiecki (new edition in preparation fo 1991). Do not walk at night on dark, deserted roads or streets.

Camping Most sites are called Trailer Parks, but tents are usually allowed. Beware of people stealing clothes, especially when you hang them up after washing. Paraffin oil (kerosene) for stoves is called *petróleo para lámparas* in Mexico; it is not a very good quality (dirty) and costs about US$0.03 per litre. It is available from an *expendio*, or *despacho de petróleo*, or from a *tlalalpería*, but not from gas stations. Gasolina Blanca may be bought in *ferreterías*, ironmongers, prices vary widely, also ask for Coleman fuel. Alcohol for heating the burner can be obtained from supermarkets. Repairs to stoves at Servis-Coliman at Plaza de San Juan 5, Mexico City.

Youth Hostels   21 CREA *albergues* exist in Mexico, mostly in small towns, and generally of poor quality. All US$2.00 with Youth Hostel card, US$2.50 without (except in Cancún—see text).

Hotels   Maximum rates are registered with the Government and advertised in the press. There are six rate zones: I: Guadalajara, Monterrey, Mexico City; II: Most seaside resorts, incl. Acapulco; III: Port zones, like Veracruz; IV: State of Yucatán, and several states surrounding the state of México; V: Most border zones, incl. the state of Baja California Sur; VI: The rest, including Chiapas. Rates are set on May 15 and December 15. Complaints about violations to be reported to the Department of Tourism, Presidente Masarik 172, Colonia Polanco, Mexico City. T 250-1964 and 250-8555. English is spoken at the best hotels. The Secretaría de Turismo publishes a *Directorio Nacional de Hospedaje*, with hotel listings (our category D and above), tourist information, maps of the capital of each state, good value at approx. US$6.50 for 680 pages.

Beware of "helpfuls" who try to find you a hotel, as prices quoted at the hotel desk rise to give them a commission. If backpacking, best for one of you to watch over luggage while the other goes to book a room and pay for it; some hotels are put off by backpacks. During peak season (November-April), it may be hard to find a room and clerks do not always check to see whether a room is vacant. Insist, or if desperate, provide a suitable tip. The week after Semana Santa is normally a holiday, so prices remain high, but resorts are not as crowded as the previous week. When using a lift, remember PB (*Planta Baja*) stands for ground floor. Discounts on hotel prices can often be arranged in the low season (May-October), but more difficult in Yucatán and Baja California. Rooms with double beds usually cheaper than those with 2 singles. Check out time from hotels is commonly 1400.

Motels and Auto-hotels, especially in central and south Mexico, are not usually places where guests stay the whole night (you can recognise them by curtains over the garage and red and green lights above the door to show if the room is free). If driving, and wishing to avoid a night on the road, they can be quite acceptable (clean, some have hot water, in the Yucatán they have a/c), and they tend to be cheaper than respectable establishments.

Food   Usual meals are a light breakfast, and a heavy lunch between 1400 and 1500. Dinner, between 1800 and 2000, is light. Many restaurants give foreigners the menu without the *comida corrida* (set meals), and so forcing them to order *à la carte* at double the price; watch this! Try to avoid eating in restaurants which don't post a menu. Meals cost about US$1-2 for breakfast, US$3-5 for lunch and US$4-10 for dinner (about US$7-17 a day on meals, depending on lavishness). In resort areas the posh hotels include breakfast and dinner in many cases. Check bills and change, even if service is included waiters may deduct a further tip from the change, they will hand it back if challenged.

What to Eat *Tamales*, or meat wrapped in maize and then banana leaves and boiled. Turkey, chicken and pork with exotic sauces—*mole de guajolote* and *mole poblano* (*chile* and chocolate sauce with grated coconut) are famous. *Tacos* (without *chiles*) and *enchiladas* (with all too many of them) are meat or chicken and beans rolled in *tortillas* (maize pancakes) and fried in oil; they are delicious. Try also spring onions with salt and lime juice in *taquerías*. Indian food is found everywhere: for instance, *tostadas* (toasted fried tortillas with chicken, beans and lettuce), or *gorditas*, fried, extra-thick tortillas with sauce and cheese. Black kidney beans (*frijoles*) appear in various dishes. Try *crepas de cuitlacoche*, best during rainy season—this consists of a pancake stuffed with maize fungus, which has a delicate mushroomy taste— very moreish. In the Pátzcuaro area ask for *budín de cuitlacoche*, with tomato, cream and *chiles*. Red snapper (*huachinango*), Veracruz style, is a famous fish dish, sautéd with *pimientos* and spices. Another excellent fish is the sea bass (*robalo*). Fruits include a vast assortment of tropical types—avocados, bananas, pineapples, *zapotes*, pomegranates, guavas, limes and *mangos de Manila*, which are delicious. Don't eat fruit unless you peel it yourself, and avoid raw vegetables. Try *higos rebanados* (delicious fresh sliced figs), *guacamole* (a mashed avocado seasoned with tomatoes, onions, coriander and *chiles*) and of course, *papaya*, or pawpaw. Mexico has various elaborate regional cuisines. Chinese restaurants, present in most towns, generally give clean and efficient service. Milk is only safe when in sealed containers marked *pasteurizado*. Fried eggs are known as *huevos estrellados*. On January 6, Epiphany, the traditional *rosca*, a ring-shaped sweet bread with dried fruit and little plastic baby Jesuses inside, is eaten. The person who finds a baby Jesus in his piece must make a crib and clothes for Him, and invite everyone present to a *fiesta* on 2 February, Candelaria.

Drink The beer (best brands: Bavaria, Bohemia, XXX, Superior and Tecate) is quite good. Negra Modelo is a dark beer, it has the same alcohol content as the other beers. Local wine, some of it of good quality, is cheap; try (Domecq, Casa Madero, Santo Tomás, etc.—the white sold in oyster restaurants *ostionerías*) is usually good. The native drinks are *tequila*, made mostly in Jalisco and potent, *pulque*, also powerful, and *mescal* from Oaxaca; all are distilled from cactus plants. Also available is the Spanish aniseed spirit, *anís*, which is made locally. Imported whiskies and brandies are expensive. Rum is cheap and good. Remember that drunkenness is detested in Mexico. There are always plenty of non-alcoholic soft drinks (*refrescos*)—try the *paletas*, safe and refreshing (those of Michoacán are everywhere)—and mineral water. Herbal teas, e.g. camomile, are available. There are few outdoor drinking places in Mexico except in tourist spots.

Tipping is more or less on a level of 10-15%; the equivalent of US$0.25 per bag for porters, the equivalent of US$0.20 for bell boys, theatre usherettes, and nothing for a taxi driver unless he gives some extra service. It is not necessary to tip the drivers of hired cars.

Security The number of assaults is rising, especially in Mexico City. Never carry valuables visibly or in easily picked pockets; leave passports, tickets and important documents in an hotel safety deposit. Underground pedestrian crossings are hiding places for thieves, take extra care at night. Cars are a prime target for theft. As with driving at night in the States of Guerrero and Oaxaca, avoid travelling by bus at night in these districts; if at all possible make journeys in day light. Also (and it is very sad having to write this), beware of getting too friendly with young gringos who seem to be living in Mexico permanently—unless, of course, they have jobs. Many of them stay in Mexico for the cheap drugs, and are not above robbery and assault to finance their habit. Couples, and even more, women on their own, should avoid lonely beaches.

Health The Social Security hospitals are restricted to members, but will take visitors in emergencies; they are more up to date than the Centros de Salud and Hospitales Civiles found in most centres, which are very cheap and open to everyone. There are many homeopathic physicians in all parts of Mexico. You are recommended to use bottled or mineral water for drinking, except in hotels which normally provide purified drinking water free. Tehuacán mineral water is sold all over Mexico; both plain and flavoured are first class. Water-sterilizing tablets can be bought at pharmacies. Raw salads and vegetables, and food sold on the streets and in cheap cafés, especially in Mexico City, may be dangerous. Advisable to vaccinate against typhoid, paratyphoid and poliomyelitis if visiting the low-lying tropical zones, where there is also some risk of malaria; advice and malaria pills from 6th floor, San Luis Potosí 199, Colonia Roma Norte, Mexico City, 0900-1400 (malaria pills are difficult or impossible to buy in chemists/pharmacies). Heavy eating and drinking of alcohol is unwise in the capital because of its altitude; so is overdoing it physically in the first few days. Some people experience nose-bleeds in Guadalajara and Mexico City because of pollution; they cease with fresh air. Locals recommend Imecol for "Montezuma's Revenge" (the very common diarrhoea).

Clothing People are usually smartly dressed in Mexico City. Women visitors should not wear shorts other than at the seaside, though trousers are quite OK. There is little central heating, so warm clothing is needed in winter. Four musts are good walking shoes, sun hats, dark glasses, and flip-flops for the hot sandy beaches. Women are always escorted, except in the main streets of the larger cities. Topless bathing is now accepted in parts of Baja California, but ask first, or do as others do. Men may need a jacket and tie in some restaurants. It is difficult to obtain shoes over US size 9 ½, but it is possible to have them made.

Hours of Business in Mexico City are extremely variable. The banks are open from 0900 to 1300 from Mon. to Fri. and (head offices only) 0900 to 1230 on Sat. Business offices usually open at 0900 or 1000 and close at 1300 or 1400. They reopen at 1400 or 1500, but senior executives may not return until much later, although they may then stay until after 1900. Other businesses, especially those on the outskirts of the city, and many Government offices, work from 0800 to 1400 or 1500 and then close for the rest of the day. Business hours in other parts of the country vary considerably according to the climate and local custom. In Monterrey they are roughly as in Britain.

National Holidays Sunday is a statutory holiday. Saturday is also observed as a holiday, except by the shops. There is no early-closing day. National holidays are as follows:
New Year (1 January), Constitution Day (5 February), Birthday of Benito Juárez (21 March), Maundy Thursday, Good Friday and Easter Saturday, Labour Day (1 May), Battle of Puebla (5 May), President's Annual Message (1 September), Independence Day (16 September), Discovery of America (12 October), Day of the Revolution (20 November), Christmas Day (25 December).

All Souls' Day 2 Nov. and Our Lady of Guadalupe 12 Dec., are not national holidays, but are widely celebrated.

Standard Time The same as US Central Standard Time, 6 hrs. behind GMT. In Sonora, Sinaloa, Nayarit and Baja California Sur, 7 hrs. behind GMT; and in Baja California Norte 8 hrs. behind GMT (but 7 hours behind GMT between 1 April and end October). The states north of the Tropic of Cancer have adopted a summer time (Zacatecas, León, Tamaulipas, Durango, Coahuila, Nuevo León, Chihuahua).

The **best season** for a business visit is from late January to May, but for pleasure between October and early April, when it hardly ever rains in most of the country. August is not a good time because it is a holiday month throughout Central America and most internal flights and other transport are heavily booked (also see above under **Travel in Mexico**).

Currency The monetary unit is the Mexican peso, divided into 100 centavos. Owing to the rapid inflation of the past few years both coins and notes are being reissued. The smallest note is for 500 pesos, then 1,000, 2,000, 5,000, 10,000, 20,000, and 50,000 pesos. Coins have all been changed from silver and bronze to strange alloys that have various colours. The tiny 5-peso piece is gold-coloured, as is the 100-peso coin. The 10-peso piece is octagonal; there is a small 20-peso coin as well as an older, larger one, similarly with the 50-peso coins. It is wise to check the number on coins. Local cheques are easier to cash in the issuing branch. There is a charge for cashing a cheque in a different city; if you can take someone along as a guarantor who has an account in the branch it helps.

Exchange In the border states such as Baja California Norte, the most-used currency is the US dollar, and the Mexican peso is often accepted by stores on the US side of the border. Travellers' cheques from any well-known bank can be cashed in most towns if drawn in US dollars; travellers' cheques in terms of sterling are harder to cash, and certainly not worth carrying outside Mexico City. The free rate of exchange changes daily and varies from bank to bank even though all are government-owned. Until the new day's rate is posted, at any time between 1000 and 1100, yesterday's rate prevails. Many banks, including in Mexico City, only change foreign currency during a limited period (often between 1000 and 1200), which should be remembered, especially on Fridays. Telegraphic transfer of funds *within* Mexico is not reliable. Beware of short-changing at all times. American Express, Mastercard and Visa are generally accepted in Mexico and cash is even obtainable with these credit cards at certain banks e.g. Bancomer or Banamex, commission of 6-8% may be charged, ask first. N.B. An American Express card issued in Mexico states "valid only in Mexico", and is used only for peso transactions. All other American Express cards are transacted in U.S. dollars even for employees living in Mexico. AmEx travellers' cheques are readily accepted.

Cost of Living The prices of accommodation and transport in this chapter can only be taken as representative. Both were increased in peso terms in 1989 and early 1990, but the depreciation of the peso against the dollar and inflation caused fluctuations in prices when converted into dollars by travellers. You are advised to check all local prices before booking. A survey in 1989 showed that, as a result of revaluation, the Mexican cost of living is only 8% lower than that of the U.S.A. and is the highest in Latin America. Owing to the housing shortage, high quality, seasonal tourist rentals have become expensive. Doctors and dentists provide good quality care at reasonable prices. Film is reasonably cheap.

Weights and Measures The metric system is compulsory.

Postal Services Rates are raised periodically in line with the peso's devaluation against the dollar but are reported to vary between towns. They are posted next to the windows where stamps are sold. Air mail letters to the US take about six days, and to the UK (US$0.25) via the US one to two weeks. Weight limit from the UK to Mexico: 22 lb., and 5 kg. in the reverse direction. About 3 months to Europe. Small parcel rate cheaper. Parcel counters often close earlier than other sections of the post office in Mexico. As for most of Latin America, send printed matter such as magazines registered. International parcels must be examined by the Customs at Aldama 218, Colonia Guerrero, near Revolución metro, open 0900-1400; or Correo Central at Calle Tacuba, open 0800-1300, window No. 48 from which only books or records can be sent; parcels with books in them must be less than 5 kg. (US$5 air mail to Europe per kg., US$1 surface mail to Europe per kg.) before posting. No more than 3 parcels may be sent at a time; maximum parcel size: 40 cm. X 60 cm.; registered letters received here. Surface parcels from Aduana Postal, Ceylán 468 (open 0800-1300, Mon.-Fri.); Colonia Cosmopólita. Take metro line 2 to Normal station, then a green colectivo No. 106. Bus No. 13 marked "Canal 13-Industrial Vallejo" also goes there. We have heard that the Customs Department at the airport hold up registered parcels coming in from abroad. Many travellers have also recommended that one should not use the post to send film or cherished objects as losses are frequent. A permit is needed from the Bellas Artes office to send paintings or drawings out of Mexico. Not all these services are obtainable outside Mexico City; delivery times in/from the interior may well be longer than those given above. Poste restante ("general delivery" in the US, *lista de correos* in Mexico) functions quite reliably, but you may have to ask under each of your names; mail is sent back after ten days. Address "*favor de retener hasta llegada*" on envelope. Within Mexico many businesses use 1st and 2nd class passenger buses to deliver letters and parcels. Each piece is signed for and must be collected at the destination. The service is considered quick and reliable.

Telephones Pay telephones take 1 peso coins, the coin should not drop until your call is made. Long distance calls from pay telephones must be made collect, follow local procedures, then dial 02 for calls inside Mexico and 09 for international calls, and be patient. Telephone service to USA, Canada and Europe. There is a heavy tax levied on all foreign long-distance calls originating and paid for in Mexico, so it is better to call collect from private phones, too (dial 09 and ask for operator). Calls to Britain are more expensive per min. from 0500 to 1700, but cheaper per min. from 1700 to 0500 and all day on Sun.

Telecommunications Telégrafos Nacionales maintains the national and international telegraph systems, separate from the Post Office. There is a special office at Balderas 14-18, just near corner of Colón, in Mexico City to deal with international traffic (open 0800-2300, Metro Hidalgo, exit Calle Basilio Badillo). There are three types of telegraph service: *extra urgente*, *urgente* and *ordinario*; they can only be prepaid, not sent collect. A telegram to Britain costs US$0.50 a word, and US$15 for 21 words including flat fee and taxes. Telex US$13-20 for 3 mins, will hold messages. There is a telegraph and telex service available at

Mexico City airport. Fax is now common in main post offices, US$5 per page.

Press The more important journals are in Mexico City. The most influential dailies are: *Excelsior, Novedades, El Día* (throughout Mexico), *Uno más Uno*; *The News* (in English, now available in all main cities); *El Universal (El Universal Gráfico)*; *La Jornada* (more to the left), *La Prensa*, a popular tabloid, has the largest circulation. *El Nacional* is the mouthpiece of the Government; *El Heraldo*; *Uno más Uno* publishes a supplement, *Tiempo Libre*, on Fridays, listing the week's cultural activities. There are influential weekly magazines *Proceso*, and *Siempre* . The political satirical weekly is *Los Agachados*.

Local Information All Mexican Government tourist agencies are now grouped in the Department of Tourism building at Avenida Masarik 172, near corner of Reforma. A few cities run municipal tourist offices to help travellers. The Mexican Automobile Association (AMA) is at Chapultepec 276, México, D.F.; they sell an indispensable road guide, with good maps and very useful lists of hotels, with current prices. The ANA (Asociación Nacional Automobilística) sells similar but not such good material; offices in Insurgentes (Metro Glorieta) and Av. Jalisco 27, México 18 D.F. For road conditions consult the AMA, which is quite reliable. A calendar of *fiestas* is published by *Mexico This Month*.

If you have any complaints about faulty goods or services, go to the Procuraduría Federal de Protección del Consumidor of which there is a branch in every city. Major cities, like Acapulco, also have a Procurador del Turista. The Tourist Office may also help with these, or criminal matters, while the Agente del Ministro Público (Federal or State District Attorney) will also deal with criminal complaints.

Maps The Mexican Government Tourist Highway map is available free of charge at tourist offices (when in stock). If driving from the USA you get a free map if you buy your insurance at Sanborn's in the border cities. The official map printers, Detenal, produce the only good large-scale maps of the country.

The Dirección General de Oceanografía in Calle Medellín 10, near Insurgentes underground station, sells excellent maps of the entire coastline of Mexico. Good detailed maps of states of Mexico and the country itself from Dirección General de Geografía y Meteorología, Av. Observatorio 192, México 18, D.F. T 515-15-27 (go to Observatorio underground station and up Calle Sur 114, then turn right a short distance down Av. Observatorio). Best road maps of Mexican states, free, on polite written request, from Ing. Daniel Díaz Díaz, Director General de Programación, Xola 1755, 8° Piso, México 12 D.F. Building is on the corner of Xola with Av. Universidad. Mapas Turísticos de México has Mexican (stocks Detenal maps) and world-maps, permanent exhibition at Río Rhin 29, Col. Cuauhtémoc, Mexico 5, T 566-2177. Maps also available from Instituto Nacional de Estadística, Geografía e Informática (INEGI), which has branches in Mexico City (**see page 164**) and in 40 other cities around the country. Good road maps of Mexican states also available from Sanborns at US$1.30. Pemex road atlas, US$2 in bookshops, has 20 pages of city maps.

Guidebooks Travellers wanting more information than we have space to provide, on archaeological sites for instance, would do well to use the widely available *Easy Guides* written by Richard Bloomgarden, with plans and good illustrations. *A Field Guide to Mexican Birds*, Peterson and Chalif, Houghton Mifflin, 1973, has been recommended. 2 books by Rudi Robins: *One-day Car Trips from Mexico City*, and *Weekend trips to Cities near Mexico City*.

Photographs The Instituto Nacional de Antropología e Historia (INAH), Córdoba 44, Colonia Roma, Mexico City, will grant teachers, archaeologists, etc. written permission to take any type of photograph at sites and museums, including photos which general public may not take. Also issue admission discounts.

Friends To meet interesting people, it is probably a good idea to visit the Casa de Cultura in any sizeable town.

We are most grateful to Sylvia Brooks for updating this chapter, to Kevin Healey (Melbourne, Vic.) for additional material on Baja California, and to the following travellers: Stan Anderton (Preston, Lancs), Michael Auer (Ottobrunn), Andrea Becker (Köln 80), R G M Bennett (British Forces, Belize), Salik Bernard Biais (Montmorency, France), Mike Boon (Calgary, Alberta), Dirk Von Braunmuehl (Bonn 1), Lucy Broadbent and Rick Palmer (Palmerston North, NZ), Remo Bulgheroni (Killroergen, Switz), Verena Burger and Christian Schmid (Hermingen, Switz), Jeremy Cameron (East Walton, Norfolk), Paul Carter (New Zealand) and Vivienne Mitchell (N Ireland), Pamela M Caunt and Robert B Brass (London N1), Tomasz Cienkus (Bogurzyn, Poland), Jim Cilek (Twin Falls, ID), Tim Connell (Ham, Surrey), Michel Courbiere (Villeurbanne, France), Bryan Crawford (Beauly, Inverness-shire), Jean Curtet (Geneva), M Davidson and K E Rowe (West Bletchley) for particularly useful information on Jalapa, Peter Driesch (Essen 1), Kate Edwards (Freeport, Grand Bahama), Ken Fishkin (Berkeley, CA), Olivier and Paloma Foro (St-Moritz), Véronique Gauais and Dominique Deghetto (Poitiers), Kurt and Linda Glaser (Toronto), Dan Golopentia (Seattle), Tony Gowers (Bristol), Lukas Grafakos (Papagou, Greece), Karl Gugler and Konstanze Mittendorfer (Vienna), Martin Gutzki (Aachen, W Ger), Rupert Hafner (Vienna), Alan Handleman (Hollywood, Fl), Jim Hardy (Waukesha, Wis), Wayne Harvey (South Australia), Beatrix Hausz and Lisa Sterzinger (Austria), Sylvio Hellemann (Bonn 2), Uli Herbert (Stuttgart 75), Ralf Hermann and Kathi Günter (Rheinfelden), Otto and Gaby Heuer-Oeschger (Lenzburg, Switz), Lee Higbie (Anchorage, Alaska), Dieter Hofmann (Witten Weiler, W Ger), Bob Horsfall and Judi Johnson (Auckland, NZ), Richard A Jacobsen (Bloomington, Minnesota), Allan Jensen and Vibeke Nageh (Munke-Bjergby, Dnmk), Tobias Kämpf (Rupperswil, Switz), Birgit Kastner and Hans Lindenthaler (Salzburg, Austria), Antony Kennedy and Danna Er-el (Israel), Carole King (Mexico), Rainer Kirchhefer (Kiel), Dr Joachim Kleinwächter (Hamburg 65), Sybille Klenk (Hamburg 60), H Klose (Cincinnati, OH), Rita Kränzlin (Luzern, Switz), Lucy, Ian and Laura Krause (Newcastle-upon-Tyne), Jirí Lambert (Göttingen, W Ger), Elizabeth Lancaster (Pudsey), Chris Larson (Oakleigh, Vic, Australia), Carl Loeber (San José, CR), Hubert Lugauer (Austria), Mika Määttänen (Tampere, Fin), Sasha Macmiadhachain (Swanage), A J M Markese (Managua), John McQueen (Glebe, NSW), Gino Meir (Israel), Patrick Meyer (Ammerschwihr, France), Cindy Miller (Vancouver, BC), Martha van Mil and Monica van Eysden ('s-Hertogenbosch, Neths), Matthias Müller (Berlin 31), Pierre J Musson (Stateline, NV), Stanley Nall (Viña del Mar), Stephen Newcomer (Centreville, Iowa), Hans van Nieuwkerk and Milou du Chatinier (Rotterdam), Eitan Nir (Beit Ha'emek, Israel) and Orit Sela (Cabri), Jim O'Brien (Orinda, CA), Bryan F O'Leary (Redondo Beach, CA), Julia Peet and Nicole Fry (Worthing), Marian and Peter Phelan (Dee Why, NSW), Shauna Picard (Victoria, Australia), Andreas Poth (Kiel 1), Winfried Maier-Revoredo (Winnenden, W Ger), George M Ridenour (Albuquerque, NM), Marilyn and BB Rietner (Rockville, MD), Paul Saunders (Toronto), Chr Scherlenzky (Bendorf, W Ger), Isabelle and Heinz Scholl-Kalt (Zürich), Dr J W F Scrimgeour (Thunder Bay, Ontario), Matthew Shugart (San Diego, CA), Jörg Singer (Bonn 1), Bob Snyder (Norwich, Ontario), J Stener (Hognan, Switz), The Loving Team (London), Marian Temple (Mérida, Mexico), Volker Tiemann (Berlin 33), Heinz Trautwein (Winnenden), Urs Waeber (Oberägeri, Switz), Markus Weder (Binningen, Switz), Barbara White (Broxbourne), Urs Wigger (Menznau, Switz), Dolores Williams (Foster City, CA), Emma Williams (Teddington) and Paul Newman (Dublin), Petra Witteler (Frankfurt), Meg Worley (Maryville, TE), Margy Levine Young (Lexington, MA) and Robert A Zimmerman (Teaneck, NJ).

CENTRAL AMERICA

CENTRAL AMERICA comprises the seven small countries of Panama, Costa Rica, Nicaragua, Honduras, El Salvador, Guatemala and Belize (formerly British Honduras). Together they occupy 544,700 square km., which is less than the size of Texas. The total population of Central America in 1989 was about 28 million and it is increasing by 2.7% each year.

The degree of development in these countries differs sharply. Costa Rica and Panama have the highest standard of living, with two of the highest rates of literacy in all Latin America. At the other end of the scale, Honduras and Nicaragua have the lowest standards of living.

Geographically, these countries have much in common, but there are sharp differences in the racial composition and traditions of their peoples. Costa Ricans are mostly white, Guatemalans are largely Amerindian or *mestizo*; Hondurans, Nicaraguans and Salvadoreans are almost entirely *mestizo*. Panama has perhaps the most racially varied population, with a large white group. Most of these countries also have a black element, the largest being found in Panama and Nicaragua.

Early, Post-Conquest History   At the time of the coming of the Spaniards there were several isolated groups of Indians dotted over the Central American area: they were mostly shifting cultivators or nomadic hunters and fishermen. A few places only were occupied by sedentary agriculturists: what remained of the Maya (see **Pre-Conquest History**) in the highlands of Guatemala; a group on the south-western shores of Lakes Managua and Nicaragua; and another in the highlands of Costa Rica. The Spanish conquerors were attracted by precious metals, or native sedentary farmers who could be christianized and exploited. There were few of either, and comparatively few Spaniards settled in Central America.

It was only during his fourth voyage, in 1502, that Columbus reached the mainland of Central America; he landed in Panama, which he called Veragua, and founded the town of Santa María de Belén. In 1508 Alonso de Ojeda received a grant of land on the Pearl Coast east of Panama, and in 1509 he founded the town of San Sebastián, later moved to a new site called Santa María la Antigua del Darién. In 1513 the governor of the colony at Darién was Vasco Núñez de Balboa. Taking 190 men he crossed the isthmus in 18 days and caught the first glimpse of the Pacific; he claimed it and all neighbouring lands in the name of the King of Spain. But from the following year, when Pedrarias replaced him as Governor, Balboa fell on evil days, and he was executed by Pedrarias in 1519. That same year Pedrarias crossed the isthmus and founded the town of Panamá on the Pacific side. It was in April 1519, too, that Cortés began his conquest of Mexico.

Central America was explored from these two nodal points of Panama and Mexico. Cortés' lieutenant, Alvarado, had conquered as far south as San Salvador by 1523. Meanwhile Pedrarias was sending forces into Panama and Costa Rica: the latter was abandoned, for the natives were hostile, but was finally colonized from Mexico City when the rest of Central America had been taken. In 1522-24 Andrés Niño and Gil Gonzales Dávila invaded Nicaragua and Honduras. Many towns were founded by these forces from Panama: León, Granada, Trujillo and others. Spanish forces from the north and south sometimes met and fought bitterly. The gentle Bartolomé de Las Casas, the "apostle of the Indies", was active as a Dominican missionary in Central America in the 1530s.

Settlement   The groups of Spanish settlers were few and widely scattered, and this is the fundamental reason for the political fragmentation of Central America today. Panama was ruled from Bogotá, but the rest of Central America was subordinate to the Viceroyalty at Mexico City, with Antigua Guatemala as an Audiencia for the area until 1773, thereafter Guatemala City. Panama was of paramount importance for colonial Spanish America for its strategic position, and for the trade passing across the isthmus to and from the southern colonies. The other provinces were of comparatively little value.

The comparatively small number of Spaniards intermarried freely with the local Indians, accounting for the predominance of *mestizos* in Central America today. In Guatemala, where there were the most Indians, intermarriage affected fewer of the natives, and over half the population today is pure Indian. On the Meseta Central of Costa Rica, the Indians were all but wiped out by disease; today, as a consequence of this great disaster, there is a buoyant community of over 2 million whites, with little Indian admixture, in the highlands. Blacks predominate all along the Caribbean coasts of Central America; they were not brought in by the colonists as slaves, but by the railway builders and banana planters of the nineteenth century and the canal cutters of the twentieth, as cheap labour.

Independence and Federation   On 5 November 1811, José Matías Delgado, a priest and jurist born in San Salvador, organized a revolt in conjunction with another priest, Manuel José Arce. They proclaimed the independence of El Salvador, but the Audiencia at Guatemala City quickly suppressed the revolt and took Delgado prisoner.

It was the revolution of 1820 in Spain itself that precipitated the independence of Central America. When on 24 February 1821, the Mexican general Iturbide announced his Plan of Iguala for an independent Mexico, the Central American *criollos* decided to follow his example, and a declaration of independence, drafted by José Cecilio del Valle, was announced in Guatemala City on 15 September 1821. Iturbide invited the provinces of Central America to join with him, and on 5 January 1822, Central America was declared annexed to Mexico. Delgado refused to accept this decree, and Iturbide, who had now assumed the title of Emperor Agustín the First, sent an army south under Vicente Filísola to enforce it in the regions under Delgado's influence. Filísola had completed his task when he heard of Iturbide's abdication, and at once convened a general congress of the Central American provinces. It met on 24 June 1823, and established the Provincias Unidas del Centro de América. The Mexican republic acknowledged their independence on 1 August 1824, and Filísola's soldiers were withdrawn.

The congress, presided over by Delgado, appointed a provisional governing *junta* which promulgated a constitution modelled on that of the United States on 22 November 1824. The Province of Chiapas was not included in the Federation, for it had already adhered to Mexico in 1821. No federal capital was chosen, but Guatemala City, by force of tradition, soon became the seat of government.

Breakdown of Federation The first President under the new constitution was Manuel José Arce, a liberal. One of his first acts was to abolish slavery. El Salvador, protesting that he had exceeded his powers, rose in December, 1826. Honduras, Nicaragua, and Costa Rica joined the revolt, and in 1828 General Francisco Morazán, in charge of the army of Honduras, defeated the federal forces, entered San Salvador and marched against Guatemala City. He captured the city on 13 April 1829, and established that contradiction in terms: a liberal dictatorship. Many conservative leaders were expelled and church and monastic properties confiscated. Morazán himself became president of the Federation in 1830. He was a man of considerable ability; he ruled with a strong hand, encouraged education, fostered trade and industry, opened the country to immigrants, and reorganized the administration. In 1835 the capital was moved to San Salvador.

These reforms antagonized the conservatives and there were several risings. The most serious revolt was among the Indians of Guatemala, led by Rafael Carrera, an illiterate *mestizo* conservative and a born leader. Years of continuous warfare followed, during the course of which the Federation withered away. As a result, the federal congress passed an act which allowed each province to assume what government it chose, but the idea of a federation was not quite dead. As a result, Morazán became President of El Salvador. Carrera, who was by then in control of Guatemala, defeated Morazán in battle and forced him to leave the country. But in 1842, Morazán overthrew Braulio Carrillo, then dictator of Costa Rica, and became president himself. At once he set about rebuilding the Federation, but was defeated by the united forces of the other states, and shot on 15 September 1842. With him perished any practical hope of Central American political union.

The Separate States Costa Rica, with its mainly white population, is a country apart, and Panama was Colombian territory until 1903. The history of the four remaining republics since the breakdown of federation has been tempestuous in the extreme. In each the ruling class was divided into pro-clerical conservatives and anti-clerical liberals, with constant changes of power. Each was weak, and tried repeatedly to buttress its weakness by alliances with others, which invariably broke up because one of the allies sought a position of mastery. The wars were rarely over boundaries; they were mainly ideological wars between conservatives and liberals, or wars motivated by inflamed nationalism. Nicaragua, for instance, was riven internally for most of the period by the mutual hatreds of the Conservatives of Granada and the Liberals of León, and there were repeated conflicts between the Caribbean and interior parts of Honduras.

Of the four republics, Guatemala was certainly the strongest and in some ways the most stable. While the other states were skittling their presidents like so many ninepins, Guatemala was ruled by a succession of strong dictators: Rafael Carrera (1844-1865), Justo Rufino Barrios (1873-1885), Manuel Cabrera (1898-1920), and Jorge Ubico (1931-44). These were separated by intervals of constitutional government, anarchy, or attempts at dictatorship which failed. Few presidents handed over power voluntarily to their successors; most of them were forcibly removed or assassinated.

Despite the permutations and combinations of external and civil war there has been a recurrent desire to reestablish some form of *la gran patria centroamericana*. Throughout the 19th century, and far into the 20th, there have been ambitious projects for political federation, usually involving El Salvador, Honduras and Nicaragua; none of them lasted more than a few years. There have also been unsuccessful attempts to reestablish union by force, such as those of Barrios of Guatemala in 1885 and Zelaya of Nicaragua in 1907.

During colonial times the area suffered from great poverty; trade with the mother country was confined to small amounts of silver and gold, cacao and sugar, and cochineal and indigo. During the present century the great banana plantations of the Caribbean, the growing coffee and cotton trade and industrialization have brought some prosperity, but its benefits have, except in Costa Rica and Panama, been garnered mostly by a relatively small landowning class and the middle classes of the cities. Nicaragua is now a case apart, with extensive and radical reforms carried out by a left-leaning revolutionary government, but protracted warfare and mistakes in economic management have left the country still extremely poor. Poverty, the fate of the great majority, has brought about closer economic cooperation between the five republics, and in 1960 they established the Central American Common Market (CACM). Surprisingly, the Common Market appeared to be a great success until 1968, when integration fostered national antagonisms, and there was a growing conviction in Honduras and Nicaragua, which were doing least well out of integration, that they were being exploited by the others. In 1969 the "Football War" broke out between El Salvador and Honduras, basically because of a dispute about illicit emigration by Salvadoreans into Honduras, and relations between the two were not normalized until 1980. Despite the handicaps to economic and political integration imposed by nationalist feeling and ideological differences, hopes for improvement were revived in 1987 when the Central American Peace Plan, drawn up by President Oscar Arias Sánchez of Costa Rica, was signed by the Presidents of Guatemala, El Salvador, Honduras, Nicaragua and Costa Rica. The plan proposed formulae to end the civil strife in individual countries, but with the exception of Nicaragua, there has been little progress.

We are most grateful to Peter Pollard for updating the Central America section. For help with material for the revision we should like to thank: Dr Palmer Acheson (Montreal), Dr Barry D. Adam (Windsor, Ontario), Lindsay Adam (Forest Row, W. Sussex), Tam Agosti-Gisler (Anchorage, Alaska), Dr J.R.J. Van Asperen De Boer (Amsterdam), Michael Auer (Ottobrunn), Aurelian Lis (Richmond, Surrey), Maarten Beeris (San Pedro de Atacama), R.G.M. Bennett (British Forces, Belize), Erik Bernesson (Båstad, Swe.), Dirk Von Braunmuehl (Bonn 1), Binka Le Breton (Muriaé, Minas Gerais), Remo Bulgheroni (Killroergen, Switz.), Dawn and Anthony Cameron (Monroe, NY), Jeremy Cameron (East Walton, Norfolk), Paul Carter (New Zealand) and Vivienne Mitchell (N Ireland), Mark Cherkas (Collaroy Plateau, NSW), Jim Cilek (Twin Falls, ID), Michel Courbiere (Villeurbanne, France), W. Curtis Cowan (Nashville), Bryan Crawford (Beauly, Inverness-shire), Tricia Dixon (Nottingham), Peter Driesch (Essen 1), Marsha Feeney (Fulford, York), Ken Fishkin (Berkeley, CA), Monika Friedhoff and Ignaz Utz (Frankfurt and Biel, Switz.), Rüdiger and Renate Funk (Laubach 1, W. Ger.), Tony Gowers (Bristol), Karl Gugler and Konstanze Mittendorfer (Vienna), Jason T. Hafemeister (San Luis Obispo, CA), Jim Hardy (Waukesha, Wis), Wayne Harvey (South Australia), Kevin Healey (Melbourne, Vic.), Dr Paul Heaton (London NW6), O. Helf (Kelowna, BC), Sylvio Hellemann (Bonn 2), Uli Herbert (Stuttgart 75), Bill Hite (Forest, VA), Dieter Hofmann (Witten Weiler, W. Ger.), Trond S. Høgh (Westby, Norway), Tobias Kämpf (Rupperswil, Switz.), Rainer Kirchhefer (Kiel), Dr Joachim Kleinwächter (Hamburg 65), Rita Kränzlin (Luzern, Switz.), Jirí Lambert (Göttingen, W. Ger.), Elizabeth Lancaster (Pudsey), Chris Larson (Oakleigh, Vic, Australia), Bernhard Lauss (Wels, Austria), John Lewis (London NW2), Hubert Lugauer (Austria), Mika Määttänen (Tampere, Fin.), Sasha Macmiadhachain (Swanage), A.J.M. Markese (Managua), Barbara McAuley (Sydney, Aus.), Anne McLauchlan (San Salvador), David McNally (Consett, Co. Durham), John McQueen (Glebe, NSW), Gino Meir (Israel), Patrick Meyer (Ammerschwihr, France), Cindy Miller (Vancouver, BC), Martha van Mil and Monica van Eysden ('s-Hertogenbosch, Neths.), Matthias Müller (Berlin 31), Pierre J. Musson (Stateline, NV), Stanley Nall (Viña del Mar), Hans van Nieuwkerk and Milou du Chatinier (Rotterdam), Eitan Nir (Beit Ha'emek, Israel) and Orit Sela (Cabri), Harrie Nouwens (Eindhoven, Neths.), Jim O'Brien (Orinda, CA), Peter Ovenden (Geneva), Marian and Peter Phelan (Dee Why, NSW), Klaus Reuter (München 40), Winfried Maier-Revoredo (Winnenden, W. Ger.), Dennis Rogers (Port Orford, OR), Marvin and Pat Rosen (New York), Piero Scaruffi (Redwood City, CA), Andrea Schneiber (Herborn, W. Ger.), Andrea Schneiber (Herborn, W. Ger.), Isabelle and Heinz Scholl-Kalt (Zürich), Matthew Shugart (San Diego, CA), Irene Singer and Leonel Lurua (Buenos Aires), Bob Snyder (Norwich, Ontario), Sietse Steensha (Perth, WA), Hans and Ina Stoffregen (Celle, W. Ger.), R.W. Le Sueur (Jersey), The Loving Team (London), Richard D. Tucker (Amsterdam), Allan Wearden (Blackburn, Lancs.), Barbara White (Broxbourne), Dolores Williams (Foster City, CA), Emma Williams (Teddington) and Paul Newman (Dublin) and Jacqueline P.M. Williams (London SW1).

Travellers who have made particularly valuable contributions to updating individual Central American country sections are listed at the ends of the sections concerned.

GUATEMALA

INTRODUCTION

GUATEMALA (108,889 square km., 8.93 million people), is the most populous of the Central American republics and the only one which is largely Indian in language and culture. It still has large areas of unoccupied land, especially in the north; only about two-thirds is populated. Two-thirds of it is mountainous and 38% forested. It has coastlines on the Pacific (240 km.), and on the Caribbean (110 km.).

A lowland ribbon, nowhere more than 50 km. wide, runs the whole length of the Pacific shore. Cotton, sugar, bananas and maize are the chief crops of this lowland, particularly in the Department of Escuintla. There is some stock raising as well. Summer rain is heavy and the lowland carries scrub forest.

From this plain the highlands rise sharply to heights of between 2,500 and 3,000 metres and stretch some 240 km. to the N before sinking into the northern lowlands. A string of volcanoes juts boldly above the southern highlands along the Pacific. There are intermont basins at from 1,500 to 2,500 metres in this volcanic area. Most of the people of Guatemala live in these basins, drained by short rivers into the Pacific and by longer ones into the Atlantic. One basin W of the capital has no apparent outlet and here, ringed by volcanoes, is the splendid Lake Atitlán. The southern highlands are covered with lush

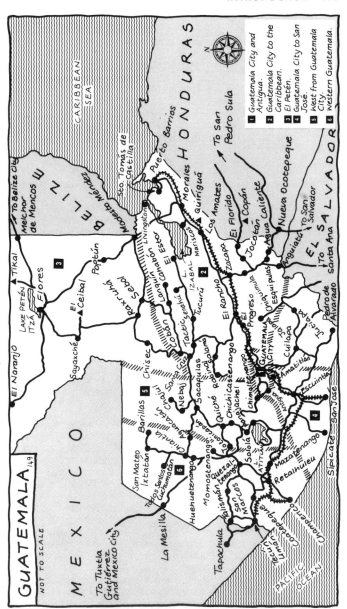

GUATEMALA

NOT TO SCALE

1 Guatemala City and Antigua.
2 Guatemala City to the Caribbean.
3 El Petén.
4 Guatemala City to San José.
5 West from Guatemala City.
6 Western Guatemala.

vegetation over a volcanic subsoil. This clears away in the central highlands, exposing the crystalline rock of the E-W running ranges. This area is lower but more rugged, with sharp-faced ridges and deep ravines modifying into gentle slopes and occasional valley lowlands as it loses height and approaches the Caribbean coastal levels and the flatlands of El Petén.

The lower slopes of these highlands, from about 600 to 1,500 metres, are planted with coffee. Coffee plantations make almost a complete belt around them. Above 1,500 metres is given over to wheat and the main subsistence crops of maize and beans. Deforestation is becoming a serious problem. Where rainfall is low there are savannas, where water for irrigation is now drawn from wells and these areas are being reclaimed for pasture and fruit growing.

Two large rivers flow down to the Caribbean Gulf of Honduras from the highlands: one is the Río Motagua, 400 km. long, rising among the southern volcanoes; the other, further N, is the Río Polochic, 298 km. long, which drains into Lake Izabal and the Bay of Amatique. There are large areas of lowland in the lower reaches of both rivers, which are navigable for considerable distances; this was the great banana zone.

To the NW, bordering on Belize and Mexico, in the peninsula of Yucatán, lies the low, undulating tableland of El Petén, 36,300 square km. of almost undeveloped wilderness covered with dense hardwood forest. Deep in this tangled rain-forest lie the ruins of Maya cities such as Tikal and Uaxactún. In the Department of Petén, almost one-third of the national territory, there are only 209,000 people. In some parts there is natural grassland, with woods and streams, suitable for cattle, and large scale tree-felling has begun in the south and east of El Petén.

Climate, which depends upon altitude, varies greatly. Most of the population lives at between 900 and 2,500 metres, where the climate is healthy and of an even springlike warmth—warm days and cool nights. The pronounced rainy season in the highlands is from May to October; the dry from November to April.

History   For early history see the introductory chapter to Central America. Cochineal and indigo were the great exports until 1857, when both were wiped out by competition from synthetic dyes. The vacuum was filled by cacao, followed by coffee and bananas, and essential oils. The upland soil and climate are particularly favourable to coffee.

Only coffee of the Bourbon variety is planted below 600 metres, and until 1906, when bananas were first planted there, the low-lying *tierra caliente* had been used mostly for cane and cattle raising. The first plantations of the United Fruit Company were at the mouth of the Motagua, near Puerto Barrios, then little more than a village. Blacks from Jamaica were brought in to work them. The plantations expanded until they covered most of the *tierra caliente* in the NE—along the lower Motagua and around Lake Izabal.

In the 1930s, however, the plantations were struck by disease and the Company began planting bananas in the Pacific lowlands; they are railed across country to the Caribbean ports. There are still substantial plantations at Bananera, 58 km. inland from Puerto Barrios, though some of the old banana land is used for cotton and *abacá* (manila hemp).

Jorge Ubico, an efficient but brutal dictator who came to power in 1931, was deposed in 1944. After some confusion, Juan José Arévalo was elected President and set out to accomplish a social revolution, paying particular attention to education and labour problems. He survived several conspiracies and finished his term of six years. Jacobo Arbenz became President in 1950, and the pace of reform was quickened. His Agrarian Reform Law, dividing large estates expropriated without adequate compensation among the numerous landless peasantry, aroused opposition from landowners. In June 1954, Colonel Carlos Castillo Armas, backed by interested parties and with the encouragement of the United States, led a successful insurrection and became President. For the following 29 years the army and its right-wing supporters suppressed left-wing efforts, both constitutional and violent, to restore the gains made under Arévalo and Arbenz; many thousands of people, mostly leftists, were killed during this period. In August 1983 General Oscar Mejía Víctores took power; he permitted a Constituent Assembly to be elected in 1984. This Constituent Assembly drew up a new constitution and worked out a timetable for a return to democratic rule. Presidential elections were held in December 1985. The victor was Vinicio Cerezo Arévalo of the Christian Democrat party (DC), who took office in January 1986. The Christian Democrats won 51 of the 100 seats in the National Congress. The return to elected government has not as yet greatly reduced the influence of the armed forces, narrowed the huge gap between rich and poor, or brought to an end the civil war being fought in parts of the country (the Arias Peace Plan notwithstanding). The stability of the civilian government was not assured and several military coup attempts were made. Violence increased again in 1989 and the President blamed right wing groups for trying to destabilize his government, while admitting that the security forces were involved in a wave of kidnappings and murders of students.

The People   About 55% of the population are classed as Amerindian, while 42% are ladino and only 3% black or white. Birth rate: 37.9 per 1,000; infant mortality, 53.6 (1988); population growth: 2.9%; urban growth: 3.5%. Some 65% of the people live at elevations above 1,000 metres in 30% of the total territory; only 35% live at lower elevations in 70% of the total territory.

Culture   When the Spaniards arrived from Mexico City in 1523 they found little precious metal: only some silver at Huehuetenango. Those who stayed settled in the intermont basins of the southern highlands around Antigua and Guatemala City and intermarried with the groups of native subsistence farmers living there. This was the basis of the present *mestizo* population living in the cities and towns as well as in all parts of the southern highlands and in the flatlands along the Pacific coast; the indigenous population—more than half the total—is still at its most dense in the western highlands and Alta Verapaz. They form two distinct cultures: the almost self-supporting indigenous system in the highlands, and the *ladino* commercial economy in the lowlands. At first sight the two seem to have much in common, for the Indian regional economy is also monetary, but a gulf opens between the two systems when it is realized that to an Indian trade is seen as a social act, not done out of need, and certainly not from any impulse to grow rich.

The scenery of the Indian regions W of the capital is superb and full of colour. In the towns and villages are colonial churches, some half ruined by earthquakes but often with splendid interiors. The Indians speak some 20 languages and 100 or more dialects. The coming of the Spaniards transformed their outer lives: they sing old Spanish songs, and their religion is a compound of image-worshipping paganism and the outward forms of Catholicism, but their inner natures remain largely untouched.

Their markets and *fiestas* are of outstanding interest. The often crowded markets are quiet and restrained: no voice raised, no gesture made, no anxiety to buy or sell; but the *fiestas* are a riot of noise, a confusion of processions, usually carrying saints, and the whole punctuated by grand firework displays and masked dancers. The chief *fiesta* is always for a town's particular patron saint, but all the main Catholic festivals and Christmas are celebrated to some extent everywhere.

Indian dress is unique and attractive, little changed from the time the Spaniards arrived: the colourful head-dresses, *huipiles* (tunics) and skirts of the women, the often richly patterned sashes and kerchiefs, the hatbands and tassels of the men. It varies greatly, often from village to village. Unfortunately a new outfit is costly, the Indians are poor, and denims are cheap. While men are adopting western dress in many villages, women are slower to change. As a result of the increase in cotton-growing and the problems of land distribution (see below), many Indians are now moving from the highlands to the *ladino* lowland cotton areas; other Indians come to the southern plains as seasonal labourers whilst retaining their costumes, languages and customs and returning to the highlands each year to tend their own crops.

N.B. The word *ladino*, used all over Central America but most commonly in Guatemala, applies to any person with a "Latin" culture, speaking Spanish and wearing normal Western clothes, though he may be pure Amerindian by descent. The opposite of *ladino* is *indigena*; the definition is cultural, not racial.

The Economy The equitable distribution of occupied land is a pressing problem. The Agrarian Census of 1950 disclosed that 70% of the cultivable land was in the hands of 2% of the landowners, 20% in the hands of 22%, and 10% in the hands of 76%—these figures corresponding to the large, medium and small landowners. A quarter of the land held by the small owners was sub-let to peasants who owned none at all. There were 531,636 farms according to the 1979 census, of which 288,083 (54%) were of less than 1.4 hectares, 180,385 (34%) were of under 7 hectares, while 482 (less than 1%) were of more than 900 hectares. Between 1955 and 1982, 665,000 hectares were redistributed (compared with 884,000 between 1952 and 1954, but it was estimated that in 1982 there were 420,000 landless agricultural workers. A peaceful movement of *campesinos* (farm labourers) was formed in 1986 to speed land distribution.

In international trade the accent is still heavily on agriculture, which accounts for some 65% of total exports. Coffee is the largest export item, followed by bananas and cotton, but sugar, soya, sorghum and cardamom are also important crops. There has been an attempt to diversify agricultural exports with tobacco, vegetables, fruit and ornamental plants, and beef exports are increasing.

The industrial sector has been growing steadily; the main activities, apart from food and drink production, include rubber, textiles, paper and pharmaceuticals. Chemicals, furniture, petroleum products, electrical components and building materials are also produced. Local industries, encouraged by tax remissions and tariff barriers, are gradually eliminating the need for imported consumer goods. Guatemala's exports (mostly industrial) to the other Central American countries account for about 25% of its total exports.

Petroleum has been discovered at Las Tortugas and Rubelsanto in the Department of Alta Verapaz. The Rubelsanto find is estimated to have proven and probable reserves of 27.3 m barrels, with production from this field and from West Chinajá running at 6,600 bpd. A pipeline to transport oil from Rubelsanto to the port of Santo Tomás de Castilla has been completed. Exploration is continuing in both the Rubelsanto area and in the nearby department of El Petén. New wells, for prospects are good, are at Yalpemech, Xan and Caribe. Offshore exploration has so far been unsuccessful. In order to lessen imports of petroleum, five hydroelectricity projects have been developed. Aguacapa (90 Mw) and Chixoy (300 Mw) are already completed and could satisfy electricity needs until the 1990s.

Guatemala's poor growth record in first half of the 1980s was attributable to the world recession bringing low agricultural commodity prices, particularly for coffee, and political instability both at home and in neighbouring Central American countries. The return to democracy and economic restructuring brought confidence and higher rates of growth as inflows of foreign funds were renewed. Other factors improving the balance of payments included moderate imports, rising exports, a rebound in tourism and selective debt rescheduling arrangements. An attempt at economic liberalization in 1989, involving the floating of the exchange rate, was reined in in 1990. The Government reintroduced control over the rate after it fell sharply, causing a surge in inflation. Measures were announced to reduce liquidity and curb the fiscal deficit by raising tax income, although two previous efforts to increase taxes were followed by military coup attempts and had to be diluted.

Government Guatemala is a Republic with a single legislative house with 100 seats, 75 elected directly and 25 by proportional representation. The Head of State and of government is the President. The country is administratively divided into 22 Departments. The Governor of each is appointed by the President, whose term is for 5 years. The latest constitution was dated May 1985.

Religion   There is no official religion but about 75% consider themselves Roman Catholic. The other 25% are Protestant, mostly affiliated to evangelical churches.

Education   53% of the population aged 25 and over have had no formal schooling; 37% of the men and 53% of the women are illiterate.

Communications   There are 18,000 km. of roads, 2,880 of which are paved. The only public-service railway links the Caribbean seaboard with the Pacific, running from Puerto Barrios up the Motagua valley to Guatemala City and on to the port of San José. From Santa María a branch line runs W through Mazatenango to the port of Champerico and the Mexican frontier. From Zacapa, half-way from Puerto Barrios to the capital, a branch line runs S to San Salvador (no passenger services). There are 867 km. of public service railways and 290 km. of plantation lines.

The quetzal, a rare bird of the Trogon family, is the national emblem. A stuffed specimen is perched on the national coat of arms in the Presidential Palace's ceremonial hall and others are at the Natural History Museums in Guatemala City, Quezaltenango, the Camino Real Hotel in Guatemala City and in the Historical Exhibit below the National Library. (Live ones may be seen, if you are very lucky, in the Biotopo on the Guatemala City-Cobán road, or in heavily forested highlands.)
   Cecon (Centro de Estudios Conservacionistas) and Inguat are setting up Conservation Areas (Biotopos) for the protection of Guatemalan wildlife (the quetzal, the manatee, the jaguar, etc.); 3 have been opened (see text), more are planned. Those interested should see Thor Janson's book *Animales de Centroamérica en Peligro*.

Note   Conditions in the northern departments of Huehuetenango, Quiché, Alta Verapaz and El Petén in Chimaltenango, San Marcos and south of Lake Atitlán should be checked prior to travelling because of sporadic guerrilla and military activities. This applies particularly if you intend to travel at night. Chichicastenango and Tikal, however, are safe. Nevertheless, do not necessarily be alarmed by "gunfire" which is much more likely to be fireworks etc., a national pastime, especially early in the morning.

GUATEMALA CITY AND ANTIGUA (1)

Guatemala City, at 1,500 metres, was founded by decree of Charles III of Spain in 1776 to serve as capital after earthquake damage to the earlier capital, Antigua, in 1773. The city lies on a plateau in the Sierra Madre. The lofty ranges of these green mountains almost overhang the capital. To the S looms a group of volcanoes. Population, 1,500,000.
   The climate is temperate, with little variation around the year. The average annual temperature is about 18°C, with a monthly average high of 20° in May and a low of 16° in December-January. Daily temperatures range from a low of 7°C at night to a high of about 29° at midday. The

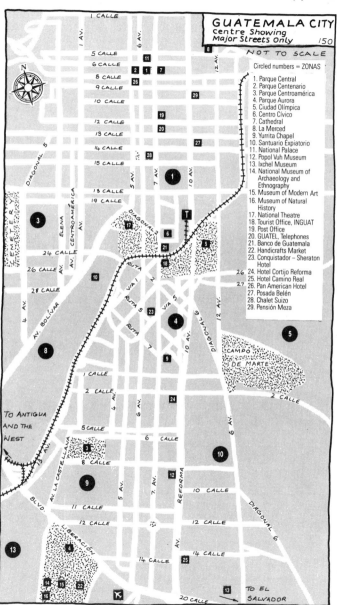

GUATEMALA CITY
centre Showing
Major Streets Only 150

NOT TO SCALE

Circled numbers = ZONAS

1. Parque Central
2. Parque Centenario
3. Parque Centroamérica
4. Parque Aurora
5. Ciudad Olímpica
6. Centro Cívico
7. Cathedral
8. La Merced
9. Yurrita Chapel
10. Santuario Expiatorio
11. National Palace
12. Popol Vuh Museum
13. Ixchel Museum
14. National Museum of Archaeology and Ethnography
15. Museum of Modern Art
16. Museum of Natural History
17. National Theatre
18. Tourist Office, INGUAT
19. Post Office
20. GUATEL, Telephones
21. Banco de Guatemala
22. Handicrafts Market
23. Conquistador – Sheraton Hotel
24. Hotel Cortijo Reforma
25. Hotel Camino Real
26. Pan American Hotel
27. Posada Belén
28. Chalet Suizo
29. Pensión Meza

rainy seasons are from late April to June (light), September to October, with an Indian summer (*canicula*) in July and August; the rain is heaviest in early September. It averages about 1,270 mm. a year, and sunshine is plentiful. The city has a serious smog problem.

The city was almost completely destroyed by earthquakes in 1917-18 and rebuilt in modern fashion or in copied colonial; it was further damaged by earthquake in 1976. A plaza called Parque Central lies at its heart: it is intersected by the N-S running 6 Avenida, the main shopping street. The eastern half has a floodlit fountain; on the west side is Parque Centenario, with an acoustic shell in cement used for open-air concerts and public meetings. To the E of the plaza is the Cathedral; to the W are the National Library and the Banco del Ejército; to the N the large Palacio Nacional. Behind the Palacio Nacional, built of light green stone, is the Presidential Mansion.

Guatemala City is large. Any address not in Zona 1—and it is absolutely essential to quote Zone numbers in addresses—is probably some way from the centre. Addresses themselves, being purely numerical, are easy to find. 19 C, 4-83 is on 19 Calle between 4 and 5 Avenidas.

Many of the hotels and boarding houses are in the main shopping quarter between 2 and 11 Avenidas and between 6 and 18 Calles, Zona 1. The railway station is in the southern part of Zona 1, at 10 Av., 18C, facing the Plaza named for Justo Rufino Barrios, to whom there is a fine bronze statue on Av. las Américas, Zona 13, in the southern part of the city. To see the finest residential district go S down 7 Avenida to Ruta 6, which runs diagonally in front of Edificio El Triángulo, past the Yurrita chapel (Zona 4), into the wide tree-lined Avenida La Reforma. Just south are the Botanical Gardens (open Mon.-Fri., 0800-1200, 1400-1800) and the Natural History Museum of the University of San Carlos at Calle Mariscal Cruz 1-56, Zona 10 (same hours as the Botanical Gardens). Admission free. Parque El Obelisco (also known as Próceres or Independencia), with the obelisk to Guatemalan independence, is at the S end of the Avenida. La Aurora international airport, the Zoo (free, newer areas show greater concern for the animals' well-being), the Observatory, the Archaeological and the Modern Art Museums and racetrack are in Parque Aurora, Zona 13, in the southern part of the city.

There is a magnificent view all the way to Lake Amatitlán from Parque de Berlín at the S end of Av. las Américas, the continuation of Av. La Reforma, though some recent poor quality building has spoilt the foreground.

In the northern part (Zona 2) is the fine **Parque Minerva**, where there is a huge relief map of the country made in 1905 to a horizontal scale of 1 in 10,000 and a vertical scale of 1 in 2,000 (open 0800-1700). Buses 1 (from Av. 5, Zona 1) and 18 run to the park, where there are basketball and baseball courts, swimming pool (filled at weekends only, and then used for washing!), bar and restaurant and a children's playground (it is reported to be unsafe for women at night).

The most notable public buildings built 1920-44 after the 1917 earthquake are the National Palace (the guards have keys and may show you round the rooms of state), the Police Headquarters, the Chamber of Deputies and the Post Office. The modern civic centre includes the City Hall, the Supreme Court, the Ministry of Finance, the Banco de Guatemala, the mortgage bank, the social-security commission and the tourist board.

The National Theatre dominates the hilltop of the W side of the Civic Centre. An old Spanish fortress provides a backdrop to the Open Air Theatre adjoining the blue and white mosaic-covered National Theatre; open Mon.-Fri. (unaccompanied tours not permitted in the grounds).

On the W outskirts in Zona 7 are the Mayan ruins of Kaminal Juyú (Valley of Death). About 200 mounds have been examined by the Archaeological Museum and the Carnegie Institute. The area is mainly unexcavated, but there are three excavated areas open to the public, and a sculpture shed.

Churches

Cathedral Begun 1782, finished 1815, damaged by the 1976 e2arthquake. Paintings and statues from ruined Antigua. Solid silver and sacramental reliquary in the E side chapel of Sagrario. Next to the Cathedral is the colonial mansion of the Archbishop.

Cerro del Carmen A copy of a hermitage destroyed in 1917-18, containing a famous image of the Virgen del Carmen, situated on a hill with views of the city, was also severely damaged in 1976.

La Merced (11 Av. and 5 C, Zona 1), dedicated in 1813, which has beautiful altars, organ and pulpit from Antigua as well as jewellery, art treasures and fine statues, also damaged in 1976.

Santo Domingo church (12 Av. and 10 C, Zona 1), 1782-1807, is a striking yellow colour, reconstructed after 1917, image of Nuestra Señora del Rosario and sculptures.

Santuario Expiatorio (26 C and 2 Av., Zona 1) holds 3,000 people; colourful, exciting modern architecture by a young Salvadorean architect who had not qualified when he built it. Part of the complex (church, school and auditorium) is in the shape of a fish.

Las Capuchinas (10 Av. and 10 C, Zona 1) was another victim of the earthquake. It has a very fine St. Anthony altarpiece, and other pieces from Antigua.

Santa Rosa (10 Av. and 8 C, Zona 1) was used for 26 years as the cathedral until the present building was ready. Altarpieces again from Antigua (except above the main altar). Now damaged.

San Francisco (6 Av. and 13 C, Zona 1) has a sculpture of the Sacred Head, originally from Extremadura. Interesting museum with paintings at the back, though in poor condition.

Capilla de Yurrita (Ruta 6 and Vía 8, Zona 4), built in 1928 on the lines of a Russian Orthodox church as a private chapel. It has been described as an example of "opulent 19th century bizarreness and over-ripe extravagance." There are many wood carvings.

Carmen El Bajo (8 Av. and 10 C, Zona 1) built in the late 18th century; façade severely damaged in 1976.

Festival 7 December, Devil's Day, hundreds of street fires are lit, any old rubbish burnt so the smell is awful, but it's spectacular.

Warning Thieves and handbag snatchers operate openly around 7 Av. and 18 C (18 C., between 4 Av. and 8 Av. is bad all the way). Do not park on the street, either day or night, or your car may well be broken into. There are plenty of lock-up garages and parking lots (*estacionamientos*).

Hotels (Av.=Avenida; C.=Calle). More Expensive. Zona 1: *Pan American*, 9 C. 5-63, B, central and rec. as quiet and comfortable, TV and baths with plugs, try to avoid rooms on the main road side, restaurant with good and reasonably-priced food, parking; *Ritz Continental*, 6 Av. "A" 10-13, C; *Maya Excelsior*, 7 Av. 12-46, D, crowded, noisy and commercial but comfortable rooms, good service and recommended restaurant, now rebuilt after a fire in 1987.

Zona 2: *La Gran Vía*, Av. Simeón Cañas 7-23, C, fully-equipped apartments.

Zona 4: *Conquistador-Sheraton*, Vía 5, 4-68, T 364691, L, luxurious, good; *Motel Plaza*, Vía 7, 6-16, D, outdoor pool, squash court, satisfactory.

Zona 9: *Cortijo Reforma*, Av. La Reforma 2-18, A, rec.; *El Dorado Americana*, 7 Av. 15-45, B; *Villa Española*, 2 C., 7-51, T 65417, restaurant, bar, parking, colonial atmosphere, C, rec.

Zona 10: *Camino Real*, Av. La Reforma and 14 C., A; *Guatemala Fiesta*, 1 Av. 13-22, A; *Residencial Reforma* (*Casa Grande*), Av. La Reforma 7-67, T 310907, near American Embassy, C; *Alameda Guest House*, 4 Av. 14-10, C.

Medium price, all in Zona 1 unless otherwise stated: *Posada Belén*, 13 C. 'A' 10-30, with bath in a colonial-style house, C, quiet, good laundry service, friendly, Francesca and René Sanchinelli speak English, highly rec., good dining room (T 29226, 534530, 513478); *Hogar del Turista*, 11 C. 10-43, E, clean, friendly, highly rec.; *Casa Real*, next door to *Hogar del Turista*, D, clean, quiet; *Brasilia*, 2 Av. 4-20, D, with bath (10% discount if staying a week or more); *Colonial*, 7 Av. 14-19, D, reasonable restaurant, quiet and rec., although ground floor rooms are small and poorly ventilated, ask for 2nd floor; *Lessing House*, 12 C. 4-35, E, small, clean, friendly, rec.; *San Juan*, 16 C. 2-51, E, with bath, clean, quiet, convenient; *International Boarding House*, next door, a little cheaper; *Posada Real*, 12 C. 6-21, E, OK, but beware overcharging; *Hernani*, 15 C. 6-56, E, no restaurant, clean, friendly, safe to leave luggage while travelling, the Spanish owner is severe in manner but noble in spirit! *Maya Quiché*, 10 Av. y 12 C., very friendly, many families use it, good restaurant attached.

Inexpensive, all in Zona 1 unless otherwise stated: *Ritz*, 6 Av. 9-28, 2nd. floor, E, central, hot water, German owner, speaks English, very helpful; *El Virrey*, 5 Av. 13-52, F, meals US$1.25; *El Virrey 3*, 7 Av. 15-46, F, communal baths, upstairs no water, but cheaper; *13 Calle Inn*, 13 C. 9-08, 2nd. floor, F, clean; *Spring*, 8 Av. 12-65, E, with shower and hot water, cheaper without, quaint, good breakfasts, rec.; *Bristol*, 15 C. 7-36, F, shared bath, pleasant, back rooms are brighter; *Bilbao*, 8 Av. 15 C., F, clean, some English spoken, shared showers, good toilets; *San Diego*, 15 C. 7-37, E, with bath (cheap breakfast and meals, annex opp., F, good value, full by 1000); *Diligencia*, 14C, 7-36, F, reasonable but unfriendly; *CentroAmérica*, 9 Av. 16-38, E, with 3 meals, US$1 extra with bath, clean, bright; next door is *Albergue*, F, courtyard, friendly, very basic but pleasant except for bathrooms; *Capri*, 9 Av. 15-63, F, with shower, a bit noisy, clean, hot water, rec.; *Chalet Suizo*, 14 C. 6-82, E, with or without shower, (US$2.25 for extra bed) popular, often crowded, friendly, locked luggage store US$0.10/day, but theft has been reported; *Fénix*, 7 Av. 16-81, F, some rooms with bath, clean, safe, corner rooms noisy, good meals US$1.25 and 1.50, breakfast available; *Pensión Meza*, 10 C. 10-17, F, popular, helpful staff, hot electric showers, noisy, inhabited mainly by young travellers, good place to arrange travel with others (1990), basic, beware of petty theft; *Meza Annex*, 13 C., 10 Av. 'A', G; *Hostal Biskaia*, 8 Av. No. 16-14, F, hot shower a.m. only, very pleasant, safe, will store luggage, couples preferred, but live music till midnight next door, Basque owners; *Ajau*, F, 8 Av. 15-62, convenient for El Petén and El Salvador buses; on 7 Av. *Santa Ana No. 2*, G, hot water, friendly; *Tranquilidad*, 14 C. 9-59, F, without shower, quiet, hot water, poor service; *Karen Inn*, 17 C. 8-58, F, reasonable; *Pensión San Antonio*, 19 C. between 8 and 9 Av. (near Rutas Orientales), G, or F in new block (rooms with bath, good). *Venecia*, 4 Av. 'A', 6-90, Zona 4, very comfortable, E, with bath, reasonable meals.

Youth Hostel Information AGAJ, Edificio Inguat, Nivel 2, Centro Cívico, T 311333/47.

N.B. The water supply in hotels tends to be spasmodic, and water for showering is often unobtainable between 1000-1800. Hotels are often full at holiday times, e.g. Easter, Christmas, when visitors from other countries and the interior come to shop. At the cheaper hotels it is not always possible to get single rooms. Hotels charge a 10% room tax. There are many other cheap *pensiones* near bus and railway stations and market; those between Calles 14 and 18 are not very salubrious.

Camping For campsites within easy access of Guatemala City **see page** 379 under Amatitlán. Parking is available free at the Airport from 1900-0700. Camping-gas cartridges not hard to find (they are stocked at Almacén Orval, 11 C. y 8 Av., Zona 1).

Restaurants (Restaurants at hotels. Food prices vary less than quality.) In the capital, the tourist can easily find everything from the simple national cuisine (black beans, rice, meat, chicken, soup, avocado, cooked bananas—plátanos—and tortillas with everything) to French, Chinese, Italian and German food (and pastries). A simple, but nourishing, three-course meal can be had for US$1 at any *comedor*. For local food served in 14 different "menus", try *Los Antojitos*, 15 C. 6-28, Zona 1, with music, though a bit pricey. Fashionable places, such as *Hola* (French and Italian), Av. Las Américas, Zona 14, *Romanello* (Italian), 1 Av. 13-38, Zona 10, *El Parador*, 4 Av. y C. Montúfar, Zona 9, excellent platos típicos; *Estro Armonico* (French), Vía 4, 4-36, Zona 4, *Puerto Barrios* (seafood), 7 Av. 10-65, Zona 9, or *Grischun* (Swiss), 14 Av. 15-36, Zona 10, charge on average US$10 for a three-course meal. Wine and other alcoholic drinks are expensive, beer good and inexpensive. *Peña de los Charrangos*, 6 Av. 13-62, Zona 9, reasonable prices, live music weekends; also with music, *Arrin Cuan*, 5 Av. 3-27, Zona 1, serving food from Cobán; *Palo Alto*, 14C, 4 Av. Zona 10, superb but dear. *Mediterráneo*, 7 Av. 3-31, Zona 9, Italian/Spanish with nice garden, good food; *El Rodeo*, 7 Av. 14-84, Zona 9, excellent steaks, good value. Fast food is available in all parts of the city, and is relatively safe; e.g. *Picadilly*, 6 Av., C.12, good; *Las Cebollines*, several locations in Zona 1, Mexican, inexpensive, good. *El Gran Pavo*, 13 C. 4-41, Zona 1, good regional Mexican, well patronised, rec. A rec. pizza chain is *A Guy from Italy* (in Zona 1, 12 C. 6-33 and 5 Av. 5-70). Rec. vegetarian restaurants: *El Arbol de la Vida*, Ed. Reforma Montúfar, 12 C. y Av. Reforma, Zona 9; and *Comida de Vegetales* chain, several branches, also take-away.

The best cafeterias for pies, pastries and chocolates (German, Austrian and Swiss styles) are *Zurich*, 4 Av. 12-09, Zona 10; *Los Alpes*, 10 C. 1-09, Zona 10; *Jensen*, 14 C. 0-53, Zona 1. *Café Austria*, 12 C. between Avs. 6 y 7, less than one block up from the main post office in Zona 1, excellent coffee and authentic Dresden stollen. The *Pastelería Lins* chain (4 or 5 in Zona 1) has been rec. *American Doughnuts*, 5 Av. 11-47, Zona 1, and several other branches in the capital. (With thanks to Rainer Gruss of Guatemala City, and other travellers' recommendations.)

Clubs The American Club (introductions can be arranged for temporary membership). Lions Club. Rotary Club. Von Humboldt (German). Italian Club.

Shopping The Central Market was destroyed in the 1976 earthquake but a new one has been opened, behind the Cathedral, from 7 to 9 Av., 8 C., Zona 1; one floor is dedicated to native textiles and crafts, and there is a large, cheap basketware section on the lower floor. Apart from the Mercado Terminal in Zona 4 (large, watch your belongings), there is the Mercado del Sur, 6 Av. 19-21, Zona

1, primarily a food market though it has a section for popular handicrafts. There is also a new *artesanía* market in Parque Aurora, near the airport, where marimba music is played, and which is strictly for tourists. *La Placita* by the Church of Guadalupe at 18 C. and 5 Av. is good for conventional clothes, leather suitcases, etc. Silverware is cheaper at the market than anywhere else in Guatemala City, but we are told that a better place for silverware is Cobán. The market is, however, rec. for all local products. Bargaining is necessary at all markets in Guatemala. Also, *4 Ahau*, 11 C.4-53, Zona 1, very good for *huipiles*, other textiles, and crafts and antiques; hand-woven textiles from *Miranda* factory, 8 Av. 30-90, Zona 8; *El Patio*, 12 C. 3-57, Zona 1; *Rodas Antiques*, 5 Av. 8-42, Zona 1 and *Barrientos Antigüedades*, 10 C. 4-64, Zona 1, have high priced silver and antiques. *Mayatex*, 12 C. 4-46, good choice, wholesale prices. *Maya Exports*, 7 Av. 10-55, credit cards accepted. Opposite is *Sombol*, Av. Reforma 14-14 and Calle 7-80, good for handicrafts, dresses and blouses. *La Momosteca* has a stall in Plaza Barrios and a shop at 7 Av. 14-48, Zona 1, and sells both textiles and silver. Pasaje Rubio, 9 C. near 6 Av., is good for antique silver charms and coins. Shop hours 0830-1230, 1500-1930 weekdays; may open all day on Sats.

Bookshops   *Arnel*, Edificio El Centro No. 108, 9 C.y 7 Av., Zona 1, excellent selection including German magazines and newspapers (T 24631); *Geminis*, 6 Av. 7-24, Zona 9 (good selection); both have new English books; *La Plazuela*, 12C. 6-14, Zona 9, large selection of 2nd hand books (very poor resale value, better to buy); *Vista Hermosa*, 2 C. 18-48, Zona 15, (English, German, Spanish); *El Palacio de las Revistas*, 9 Av. 10-14, Zona 1, and 7 Av. 7-16, Zona 4, has limited selection of magazines and US newspapers. *Don Quijote*, Av. Reforma y 14 C., Zona 10 (in Galería), good selection in Spanish. Museo Popol Vuh bookshop, Av. La Reforma 8-60, Zona 9, has a good selection of books on precolumbian art, crafts and natural history; also bookshop of *Camino Real* hotel. Bookshops also at *Conquistador-Sheraton*, Museo Ixchel, and the airport. *Librería Bremen*, Pasaje Rubio, 6 Av. between 8 C. and 9 C., Zona 1, has material in German plus old books on Guatemala. Instituto Guatemalteco Americano (IGA), Ruta 1 and Vía 4, Zona 4 (also library).

Car Rental   *Hertz*, 19 C. 7-07, Zona 1, T 510202, US$190 per week for Toyota Starlet + US$10 per day insurance and 7% tax; *Avis*, 12 C. 2-73, Zona 9, T 316990, US$205 all inclusive, unlimited mileage for a week, Nissan March, but US$162 if reserved in advance in N America; *Budget*, Av. Reforma y 15 C., Zona 9, T 316546; *National*, 14 C. 1-42, Zona 10, T 680175; *Dollar*, 6 Av. "A" 10-13, Zona 1, T 23446 (at *Hotel Ritz*, rates as for Avis); *Tikal*, 2 C. 6-56, Zona 10, T 316490; *Ambassador*, 6 Av. 9-31, Zona 1, T 85987; *Tabarini*, 2 C. "A" 7-30, Zona 10, T 316108, airport T 314755 (have Toyota Land Cruisers); *Rental*, 11 C. 2-18, Zona 9, T 341416, good rates, also motorbikes. *Tally*, 7 Av. 14-74, Zona 1, T 514113 (have Nissan and Mitsubishi pick-ups).Check carefully the state of the car when you hire. You may be charged for damage already there. The lowest rates offered are US$25 per day, 100 km. free, but these vehicles are not always available. Local cars are usually cheaper than those at international companies; if you book ahead from abroad with the latter, take care that they do not offer you a vehicle which is not available. If you wish to drive to Copán, you must check that this is permissible; Tabarini and Hertz do allow their cars to cross the border. Insurance rate (extra) varies from US$4-6 a day.

Local Buses   in town, US$0.05 per journey. Not many before 0600 or after 2000.

Taxis   are from US$0.50 for a short run to US$3 for a long run inside the city. Hourly rates are from US$4 to US$5. Taxis of the Azules, Concordia and Palace companies rec. Agree fares in advance; no meters. Taxis always available in Parque Central and Parque Concordia (6 Av. and 15 C., Zona 1) and at the Trébol (the main crossroads outside city if coming from Pacific or Highlands by bus, convenient for airport).

Traffic Traffic lights operate only between 0800 and 2100; at all other times Avenidas have priority over Calles (except in Zona 10, where this rule varies).

Night Clubs *La Quebrada*, 6 Av. 4-60, Zona 4; *Plaza Inn, Motel Plaza*, Vía 7, 6-16, Zona 4; *Brasilia* in *Hotel Ritz Continental*. Discothèques: *After Eight*, Ed. Galerías España, Zona 9; *Kahlúa*, 1 Av. 13-21, Zona 10; *Manhattan*, 7 Av. opp. *Hotel El Dorado*, Zona 9; *El Optimista*, Av. La Reforma 12-01, Zona 10; *La Petite Discothèque*, La Manzana, Ruta 4, 4-76, Zona 4. *El Establo*, Av. La Reforma 11-83, Zona 10, is a bar with excellent music. *Pandora's Box*, Ruta 3-38, Zona 4, popular.
     Guatemala (with southern Mexico) is the home of marimba music (see **Music** in the Introduction). The marimba is a type of xylophone played with drum sticks by from one to nine players. Up country the sounding boxes are differently sized gourds, the *marimbas de tecomates*. The city ones are marvels of fine cabinet work.

Theatres National Theatre. Teatro Gadem, 8 Av. 12-15, Zona 1; Antiguo Paraninfo de la Universidad, 2 Av. 12-30, Zona 1; Teatro Universidad Popular, 10 C. 10-32, Zona 1; Teatro Artistas Unidos, 3 Av. 18-57, Zona 1. Occasional plays in English, and many other cultural events, at Instituto Guatemalteco Americano (IGA), Ruta 1 and Vía 4, Zona 4. List of current offerings outside Teatro del Puente, 7 Av. 0-40, Zona 4, and in local English-language publications and city newspapers.

Cinemas are numerous and often show films in English with Spanish subtitles. Sound is often bad, but then the locals are reading the subtitles! Prices are US$2. Alianza Francesa, 4 Av. 12-39, free film shows on Mon., Wed. and Sat. evenings; other activities on other evenings, rec.

Concerts Concerts of the Philharmonic Orchestra take place in the Teatro Nacional, Civic Centre, 24 Calle, Zona 1. During the rainy season at the Conservatorio Nacional, 5 C. and 3 Av., Zona 1, and occasionally in the Banco de Guatemala.

Sports There is an 18 hole golf course at the Guatemala Country Club, 8 km. from the city, and a 9 hole course at the Mayan Club. The Guatemala Lawn Tennis Club and the Mayan Club are the chief centres for tennis.

Swimming Pools Apart from those at the Parque Minerva (**page** 372) there are pools at Ciudad Olímpica, 7 C., 12 Av., Zona 5 (monthly membership only, US$2.50 a month— photograph required; you may be allowed in for a single swim); Piscina Ciudad Vieja, Zona 15; Baños del Sur, 13 C. "A" 7-34, Zona 1, has hot baths for US$0.50, saunas for US$1.50. Try the hotels and the campsites near Amatitlán also.

Bowling Ten-pin variety and billiards at Bolerama, Ruta 3, 0-61, Zona 4, 2 blocks from *Conquistador-Sheraton* hotel.

Museums **The National Museum of Archaeology and Ethnology**, Salón 5, Parque Aurora, Zona 13, contains stelae from Piedras Negras and typical Guatemalan costumes, and good models of Tikal, Quiriguá and Zaculeu, and other Maya items. (Open 0900-1600, Tues.-Sun.) Admission US$0.40, Sun. free for Guatemalans only. Contains sculpture (including stelae, murals, etc.), ceramics, textiles, and a collection of masks. Its excellent jade collection is closed at weekends.
     The Museum of Modern Arts, Salon 6, Parque Aurora, Zona 13, "modest, enjoyable collection". Open Tues.-Fri., 0900-1600, Sat. 0900-1200, 1400-1600, US$0.12.
     Museum of Natural History, collection of stuffed birds and animals as well

as butterflies, geological specimens etc., in Parque Aurora, 7 Av. 6-81, Zona 13; open Tues.-Sun., 0900-1600, free.

National Museum of Arts and Industry, 10 Av. 10-72, Zona 1, small exhibition of popular ceramics, textiles, silversmiths' work etc. Hours Tues.-Fri. 0900-1530, Sat. and Sun. 1000-1200, 1400-1600 (US$0.12).

Museo Ixchel del Traje Indígena, 4 Av. 16-27, Zona 10, has a collection of over 4,000 examples of Indian costumes. Open Mon.-Sat., 0900-1730, entrance US$1.20, students US$0.40; get off bus at Av. La Reforma and 16 C.

Popol Vuh Museum of Archaeology, Edificio Galerías Reforma, Av. La Reforma 8-60, Zona 9 (6th floor, T 318921). Extensive collection of precolumbian and colonial artefacts. Has a replica of the Dresden Codex, one of only 3 Maya parchment manuscripts in existence. Open Mon.-Sat., 0900-1730. Admission US$1.20 (students US$0.40, children US$0.10-20). US$5 charge to take photographs. The research library of FLAAR (**see page** 348) is on long-term loan to the Popol Vuh Museum.

National Museum of History, 9 C. 9-70, Zona 1 (Tues.-Sun. 0830-1600), US$0.12, historical documents, and objects from independence onward; and colonial furniture and arms.

Fray Francisco Vásquez Museum, 13C. 6-34, Zona 1, 18th century paintings, Mon.-Fri. 0900-1800.

N.B. Each museum has a sign in 4 languages to the effect that "The Constitution and Laws of Guatemala prohibit the exportation from the country of any antique object, either precolumbian or colonial". The USA in fact prohibits the import of such items and penalties are severe.

Exchange Lloyds Bank International (8 Av. 10-67, Zona 1); agencies at Plazuela 11 de Marzo, 7 Av. 4-87, Zona 4; Autovía Mixco 4-39, Zona 11 and C. Marti 14-57, Zona 6. Open weekdays, 0900-1500. Banco de Guatemala (7 Av. and 22 C., Zona 1) open Mon.-Thurs. 0830-1400, Fri. 0830-1430, will change foreign cash and travellers' cheques after 1000. Banks now change US dollars into quetzales at the free rate. Bank of America cashes its own cheques into dollars for Q0.03 per dollar. There is a bank open 7 days a week at the airport, weekdays 0730-1830, Sat., Sun. and holidays 0800-1100, 1500-1800 (only place to change foreign banknotes—but not quetzales back into foreign currencies). When shut, try airport police or porters who may be able/willing to change US$ cash for quetzales. All banks mentioned above cash travellers' cheques, although some travellers have experienced difficulties. Try also the Banco Industrial (which sometimes advances quetzales on Visa cards, on Av. 7, nr. Central Post Office), Banco Internacional, or Bandesa, 9 C. between 9 and 10 Avs., Zona 1. American Express at Banco del Café, Av. La Reforma, 9-00, Zona 9 (bus 2 or 14 from centre), T 311463, open 0830-1530, 1500 on Fri.

The legal street exchange for cash and cheques may be found on 7 Av., 12-14 C. near the Post Office (Zona 1), although it is better to go direct to the exchange offices to avoid paying the street dealers' commission (for example, in the basement of the big shopping centre between 6 and 7 Av. behind the car park, opp. Post Office). Good place for exchange, *Le Point* shoe shop, C. 14 between 4 and 5 Avs. When changing travellers' cheques, always keep the receipt. Be careful when changing money on the street; never go alone. Quetzales may be bought with Visa or Mastercard in the basement of 7 Av., 6-22, Zona 9 (open until 2000, Mon.-Fri.).

Spanish Classes Instituto Guatemalteco Americano (IGA) offers 6-week courses, 2 hours a day, for US$60. Several other schools in the city.

Embassies and Consulates Addresses change frequently.

USA, Av. La Reforma 7-01, Zona 10 (T 311541-55). **Canada,** Galería España, 7 Av. and 12 C., Zona 9. **Mexico**, Consulate, 13 C. 7-30, Zona 9 (closes 1430 for tourist cards). **El Salvador,** 12 C. 5-43, Zona 9, T 629385, 0800-1400, for visa take passport photo, letter of recommendation, visa costs US$20 and you will be charged for telex to San Salvador, may take a week. **Honduras,** 16 C. 8-27, Zona 10. **Nicaragua,** 10 Av. 14-72, Zona 10 (open Mon.-Fri. 0900-1300, visas in 1-2 weeks). **Costa Rica,** Edificio Galerías Reforma Oficina 320, Av. Reforma, 8-60, Zona 9, T 325768. **Panama,** Edificio Maya, Vía 5, 7 Av., Suite 717, Zona 4 (T 325001/320763).

Argentina, 2 Av. 11-04, Zona 10. **Bolivia,** 12 Av. 15-37, Zona 10. **Brazil,** 18 C. 2-22, Zona 14, T 37-09-49. **Colombia,** Edificio Gemini 10, 12 C., 1 Av., Zona 10, unhelpful, T 320603/4. **Chile,** 13 C. 7-85, Zona 10. **Ecuador,** Diagonal 6, 13-08, Zona 10 (T 316119). **Paraguay,** 7 Av. 7-78 (8th floor), Zona 4. **Peru,** 2 Av. 9-48, Zona 9 (T 318409). **Uruguay,** 20 C. 8-00, Zona 10. **Venezuela,** 8 C. 0-56, Zona 9.

Israel, 13 Av. 14.07, Zona 10 (T 371303). **Japan,** Ruta 6, 8-19, Zona 4. **South Africa,** 10 Av. 30-57, Zona 5 (T 62890).

Austria, Trade Council, 6 Av. 20-25, Zona 10; Consulate, 6 Av. 11-00 (T 64314, 0900-1100). **Belgium,** Av. La Reforma 13-70 (2nd floor), Zona 9. **Denmark,** 7 Av. 20-36 (Apartment 1, 2nd floor), Zona 1. **Finland,** 10 C. 6-47, Zona 1. **France,** 14 C. 5-52, Zona 9, T 66-336. **West Germany,** 6 Av. 20-25, Edificio Plaza Marítima 2nd floor, Zona 10, T 370028, 370031, open 0900-1200 (bus 14 goes there). **Netherlands,** Consulate General, 12 C.11-91, Edificio La Curaçao, Zona 9, 4th floor, T 313505 (open 0900-1200). **Italy,** 8 C. 3-14, Zona 10. **Norway,** 6 Av. 7-02, Zona 9. **Portugal,** 5 Av. 12-60, Zona 9. **Spain,** 10 C. 6-20, Zona 9. **Sweden,** 8 Av. 15-07, Zona 10, T 680621. **Switzerland,** Edif. Seguros Universales, 4 C. 7-73, Zona 9 (T 65726, 31-3725); **British Embassy,** Ed. Centro Financiero, Torre 2, 7th floor, 7 Av. 5-10, Zona 4 (T 321601/02/04/06).

Immigration Office 12 C and 8 Av., Zona 1 (for extensions of visas, take photo to "Inspectoria").

Central Post Office 7 Av., 12 C., Zona 1. Ground floor for overseas parcel service, at the back (allow plenty of time). Watch your belongings when standing in queues here. This is the only post office in country from which parcels over 2 kg. (other than books) can be sent abroad. Poste restante keeps mail for 2 months (US$0.03 per letter). Open Mon.-Fri. 0800-1630. Free marimba concert at post office every Fri. at 1500. Alternative: American Express, for its customers only.

Telecommunications Empresa Guatemalteca de Telecomunicaciones (Guatel), 7 Av. 12-39 Zona 1 for international calls; 24-hr national and international telephone service. Local telegrams from central post office.

Non-Catholic Churches Episcopalian Church of St. James, Av. Castellana 40-08, Zona 8, and the Union Church of Guatemala (Plazuela España, Zona 9). Sun. morning service in English at the first: 0930; at the second: 1100.

Synagogues 7 Av. 13-51, Zona 9. Service at 0930 Sat.

Health Centro Médico Hospital, 6 Av. 3-47, Zona 10, private, but reasonably priced, all senior doctors speak English; very helpful. Dr Mariano A. Guerrero, 5 Av. 3-09, Zona 1, German-speaking, understands English (US$10 for treatment). Dr. Manuel Cáceres, 6 Av. 8-92, Zona 9, 1600-1800, speaks English and German. Dentists: Dr Freddy Lewin, Centro Médico, 6 Av. 3-69, Zona 10, T 325153 (German, English), Dr Bernal Herrera, 6 C. 1-50, Zona 1, T 518249 (English, Japanese).

Laundromats Lava-Centro Servimatic, Ruta 6, 7-53, Zona 4 (opposite Edificio El Triángulo) sometimes has hot water; Express (dry cleaners), 7 Av. 3-49, Zona 4; El Siglo (dry cleaners), 7 Av. 3-50, Zona 4, 11 Av. 16-35, Zona 1, and 12 C. 1-55, Zona 9. 4 Av., just up from 13 C., Zona 1. Dry cleaner also at Vía 2, 4-04, Zona

4, open Mon.-Fri., 0730-1830.

Car Insurance for Mexico Granai y Townson, 7 Av. 1-82, Zona 4.

Car Repairs Christian Kindel, 47 Calle 16-02, Zona 12. Honda **motorcycle** parts from F.A. Honda, Av. Bolívar 31-00, Zona 3; general manager and chief mechanic are German, former speaks English. In Guatemala City, parts available for most motorcycles.

Camera Repairs Sertecof Panamericana, 10 C. 9-68, Zona 1, Edif. Rosanza, Of. 105, T 537-533, 537-613, expensive but work guaranteed 3 months.

Tourist Information Inguat, 7 Av. 1-17, Zona 4 (Centro Cívico); T 311333/47. Very friendly. Hotel lists, will ring hotels, but tends to have information only on the more expensive ones. Open Mon.-Fri. 0830-1800, Sat. 0830-1200, accurate map of city, other maps, information, major tourist attractions and will book tours. Information on nature from Inafor, 7 Av. 13 C. Zona 9, T 325064.

Travellers wishing to get to know Guatemala should contact Yvonne Martínez, 11 Avenida, 25-04, Zona 12, who very kindly offers to provide information and a meeting place for young visitors.

Maps Maps can also be bought from the Instituto Geográfico Nacional, Av. Las Américas 5-76, Zona 13, open 0800-1600 Mon. to Fri., closed Sat. and Sun.; some of the more detailed maps can only be obtained by post, and permission must be obtained from the Ministry of Defence before buying maps of "sensitive areas". Those that cannot be bought may be copied by hand from the book containing all the 1:50,000 and 1:250,000 maps of the country. Also good map of city on back of map of country, from Hertz at airport when in stock.

Travel Agents *Clark Tours*, 6 Av. y Vía 7, no exchange, in Edificio El Triángulo, Zona 4, very helpful, tours to Copán, Quiriguá, etc; *Setsa Travel*, 8 Av., 14-11, very helpful, tours arranged to Tikal, Copán, car hire; *Aire, Mar y Tierra*, Plaza Marítima, 20 C. y 6 Av., Zona 10, and Ed. Herrera, 5 Av. y 12 C., Zona 1; *Tourama*, Av. La Reforma 15-25, Zona 10, both rec., German and English spoken. *Servicios Turísticos del Petén*, 3 C. 10-58, Zona 10, trips to Flores and Tikal (owns *Hotel Maya Internacional*, Flores).

Archaeological Tours Anyone interested in genuine archaeological (or botanical, ornithological and zoological) expeditions should contact **Foundation for Latin American Anthropological Research (FLAAR)**, 6355 Green Valley Circle, No. 213, Culver City, CA 90230 and Apartado Postal 1276, Guatemala City. (There is no Guatemalan research centre; the foundation's library is on long-term loan to the Popol Vuh Museum.) This organization runs trips to well-known and almost unknown areas of interest (including Yaxchilán, Piedras Negras, Toniná, Comalcalco, El Tajín, Xochicalco, and all of Yucatán, Campeche and Quintana Roo, and the archaeology of Belize). FLAAR, formerly EPANS, has published *Tikal, Copán Travel Guide*, by Nicholas Hellmuth, on all the Mayan sites in Central America and Mexico. It costs US$25 (available from the Popol Vuh museum, the museum at Tikal, and from California address above) and gives useful tips on how to get to each of the sites. Turismo Kim'Arrin, Edificio Maya, Office No. 103, Vía 5, 4-50, Zona 4, and Panamundo Guatemala Travel Service also arrange tours to Maya sites.

Airline Agents Local airlines: Aviateca, 10 Calle 6-30, Zona 1, and at airport; Aeroquetzal, at airport, fly to Flores and Cancún, Aerovías (T 81463/316935), for Flores and Belize City, Tapsa for Flores: these 3 have offices at Av. Hincapié and 18 C., Zona 13 at the national part of the airport. In Edificio El Triángulo, 7 Av. and Ruta 6, Zona 4, are offices of Copa and Avianca. SAM, Av. Reforma 12-01, Zona 10. Agencia de Viajes Mundial, 5 Av. 12-44, Zona 1, is very good. PanAm, 6 Av. 11-43, Zona 1 (reconfirmations, T 821817), Iberia (Ed. Galerías Reforma,

Av. La Reforma, 8 C., Zona 9), Mexicana, KLM (20 C. and Av. 6, Zona 10—bus 2, black or 14 from Av. 10, Zona 1, open 0900-1700) and the Central American airlines all have offices, so has Lufthansa, Plaza Marítima, 6 Av. 20-25, Zona 10.

Airport At La Aurora, 8 km. S; restaurant with cheap "meal of the day" (more appetizing than it looks); all prices marked up in the shops. Taxi to town, US$2.50 one way, US$5 return (airport tourist office supplies official taxi-fare chits—drivers may try to charge new arrivals US$8 to town). Nos. 5 (in black not red) 6 and 20 buses from 8 Av., Zona 1, and the Zona 4, 4 Av., 1 C, bus terminal, run the ½ hour's journey between airport and centre (US$0.05). (Bus 20 runs from Centro Cívico to Aeropuerto Local.) There is also a bus to 7 Av., C. 18 (US$0.08 at night). Domestic flights to Flores (**see page** 371 leave from a separate terminal at La Aurora. All other domestic flights must be chartered. N.B. The airport is closed from 2100-0400, so you cannot stay the night there.

Rail Guatemalan Railways to Puerto Barrios, 0645, Mon., Wed., Fri. 1300, US$1.50 (an excellent, if slow, opportunity to get a first impression of the country, trains are usually delayed). Return Tues., Thurs., Sat. Trains to Tecún Umán (290 km.) 0700 Tues., Thurs. and Sat., arr. 1900, US$1.40 via Escuintla (arr. 1300) and Retalhuleu (arr. 1500). No cooked meals are served in trains, although sandwiches and light refreshments, iced beer and soft drinks can be bought at inflated prices. Station at 18 C. 9 and 10 Av., Zona 1, on east side of Plaza Barrios (T 83031/39). No passenger connections to El Salvador, nor from Escuintla to the Pacific port of San José.

Buses Note Information on interior bus services is available at Inguat, see Tourist Information above. To Flores (for Tikal and Belize), Fuente del Norte, 17 C. 8-46, Zona 1, 5 a day before 0900, book the day before, first on the list is first on the bus, express bus US$12.50, 12 hrs., others, US$5 or so, take up to 20 hrs., take food. The route goes over dreadful roads via Morales and Modesto Méndez; La Pinita runs via Sayaxché "no timescale". To Huehuetenango, Rápidos Zaculeu, 9 C. 11-42, Zona 1, 0600 and 1500, 1st class, El Cóndor (5 a day, US$2.60), Los Halcones, Av. 15-27, Zona 1 (reliable, reserved seats) 0700, 1400. To Quezaltenango, Marquensita, 21 C. 1-56, Zona 1, 0430 and 0630, US$2, Rutas Lima, 4 a day, US$2; Galgos, 5 a day, rec., US$2.25. To Panajachel, Rebuli, 20 C. 3-42, Zona 1, terminal C.1 and A. 2-36, Zona 9, take city bus No. 17, hourly 0500-1600, US$1.25 (3 hrs., 1st class), To Chichicastenango, Reyna de Utatlán, bus terminal, throughout the day, US$1.50 (3½ hrs.). To Puerto Barrios, Litegua, 15 C., 10-40 Av., Zona 1, hourly 0600-1700, US$6, 6 hrs. (good sandwiches sold on bus); Fuente del Norte, Unión Pacífica y Las Patojas, 9 Av., 18-38, Zona 1 (Zona 4 terminal), 4 a day, US$2.50. To Esquipulas, via Chiquimula, Rutas Orientales, 19 C, 8-18, Zona 1, every ½ hr., 0400-1800, 4 hrs. (US$2.65 "Pullman"). Transportes Guerra to Chiquimula, US$1.25, 3½ hrs., 0700 (Rutas Orientales, US$2.15 pullman, 3 hrs.). To Santa Cruz del Quiché, via Los Encuentros and Chichicastenango, Reyna de Utatlán, Zona 4 bus terminal, 0600 to 1600, 4 hrs., US$1.60. To Cobán (US$2.45) and San Pedro Carchá (US$2.75), Escobar-Monja Blanca about 15 a day, arrive early in the morning and book a seat on the first available bus; take a Cobán bus for the Biotopo del Quetzal, US$1.90.

The Zona 4 bus terminal between 1-4 Av. and 7-9 C. serves the Occidente (West), the Costa Sur (Pacific coastal plain) and El Salvador. The area of 19 C. 8-9 Av. Zona 1, next to the Plaza Barrios market, contains many bus offices and is the departure point for the Oriente (East), the Caribbean zone, Pacific coast area toward the Mexican border and the north, to Flores and Tikal. Direct bus to Flores daily at 2300, be there at 0900 the same day to get a ticket to a numbered seat, cost about US$10. First class buses often depart from company offices in the south-central section of Zona 1.

International buses To San Salvador: Inter-Futuro Express, 8 Av. 15-69, Zona

1, daily at 0600, 5 hrs., US$2.50 (not rec.; may desert you at the border). With this service one arrives in San Salvador early enough to catch a bus to the El Salvador-Honduras border. (Don't trust phone reservations.) Mermex, 20 C. 6-39, Zona 1, T 539952, twice daily; Transportes Centroamérica, 9 Av. 15-06, Zona 1, T 23432 (minibus service to hotel on request), daily, 0730 after all passengers have been collected. Melva, 4 Av. 1-20, Zona 9, 2 buses daily from 0800, US$2.50, Pezzarossi 6 departures daily, 6 hrs.; both rec., own terminal in Zona 4 (office at 4 Av. 1 C., Zona 9, at edge of bus station at 4 Av. 7 C., reserve the day before if you can—all except Pezzarossi go also to Santa Ana). To Honduras avoiding El Salvador, take bus to Esquipulas (see below), then minibus to border. To Mexico: Moreliana (from bus terminal) to Talismán, US$2.50, from 0530 to 1600, also to Tecún Umán; Galgos, 7 Av. 19-44, and Rutas Lima, 8 C. 3-63, both Zona 1, have several buses daily to Talismán, US$3.25, connections with Cristóbal Colón bus line— rebookings at the border may be necessary (local buses to Talismán take 7 hrs., involve 3 changes, and cost US$2.50). El Cóndor, 2 Av. 19 C., Zona 1, has several buses daily to La Mesilla, connections with Cristóbal Colón. Unión Pacífica, 9 Av. 18-38, Zona 1, go to El Carmen and Tecún Umán; at both one can get connections to Tapachula, 0630, 0845, 1245 daily. No Guatemalan bus goes into Mexico. Through tickets to Mexico City are available, but don't be tempted to buy one; purchase tickets as you go along because of poor connections and full buses from the border into Mexico.

To Antigua, the shortest route is 45 km. via San Lucas Sacatepéquez (**see page** 358) by paved double-lane highway passing (25 km. out) El Mirador (1,830 metres), with fine view of the capital. Road then rises to 2,130 metres and gradually drops to 1,520 metres at Antigua.

Antigua was the capital city until it was heavily damaged by earthquake in 1773. Population today: 30,000. Founded in 1543, after destruction of a still earlier capital, Ciudad Vieja, it grew to be the finest city in Central America, with a population of 60,000, numerous great churches, a University (1680), a printing press (founded 1660), and famous sculptors, painters, writers and craftsmen. Centre of the city is the Parque Central, the old Plaza Real, where bullfights and markets were held. The Cathedral (1534) is to the E, the Palace of the Captains-General to the S (1769), the Municipal Palace (Cabildo) to the N (all have been repaired since the 1976 earthquake) and an arcade of shops to the west. Alvarado was buried in the Cathedral, but whereabouts is not known. All the ruined buildings, though built over a period of three centuries, are difficult to date by eye, partly because of the massive, almost romanesque architecture against earthquakes: cloisters of the convent of Capuchinas (1736), for example, look 12th century, with immensely thick round pillars (entrance, US$0.12). The most interesting ruins (apart from those mentioned) are of the monastery of San Francisco, the convent of Santa Clara (1723-34, entrance US$0.12), El Carmen, San Agustín (the last two may only be viewed from outside), La Compañia de Jesús (being restored with a Unesco grant), Santa Cruz, Escuela de Cristo church, La Recolección (1703-17) off the road, set among coffee groves, Colegio y Hermita de San Jerónimo (Real Aduana), open every day except Mon., 0800-1700, La Merced (being restored, said to have largest fountain in the New World), the Hospital (badly damaged by 1976 earthquake, and no longer functioning), and the Museum. Other ruins, such as Santa Isabel,

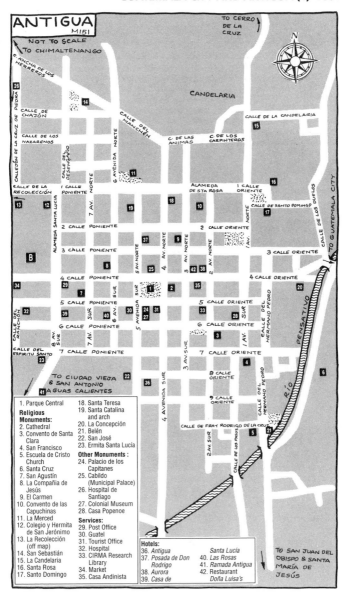

ANTIGUA
M151
NOT TO SCALE
TO CHIMALTENANGO

TO CERRO DE LA CRUZ

CANDELARIA

1. Parque Central
Religious Monuments:
2. Cathedral
3. Convento de Santa Clara
4. San Francisco
5. Escuela de Cristo Church
6. Santa Cruz
7. San Agustín
8. La Compañia de Jesús
9. El Carmen
10. Convento de las Capuchinas
11. La Merced
12. Colegio y Hermita de San Jerónimo
13. La Recolección (off map)
14. San Sebastián
15. La Candelaria
16. Santa Rosa
17. Santo Domingo
18. Santa Teresa
19. Santa Catalina and arch
20. La Concepción
21. Belén
22. San José
23. Ermita Santa Lucía
Other Monuments:
24. Palacio de los Capitanes
25. Cabildo (Municipal Palace)
26. Hospital de Santiago
27. Colonial Museum
28. Casa Popenoe
Services:
29. Post Office
30. Guatel
31. Tourist Office
32. Hospital
33. CIRMA Research Library
34. Market
35. Casa Andinista

Hotels:
36. Antigua
37. Posada de Don Rodrigo
38. Aurora
39. Casa de
Santa Lucía
40. Las Rosas
41. Ramada Antigua
42. Restaurant Doña Luisa's

TO CIUDAD VIEJA & SAN ANTONIO
AGUAS CALIENTES

TO SAN JUAN DEL OBISPO & SANTA MARÍA DE JESÚS

San Cristóbal, El Calvario and San Gaspar Vivar, all south of the town, are well worth visiting. Many sculptures, paintings and altars have been removed to Guatemala City. The Casa Popenoe, 1 Av. Sur, between 5 and 6 C. Oriente, is a restored colonial house with a few original 16th-century parts (the kitchen, herb garden), and contains many old objects from Spain and Guatemala; guided tours only, 1400-1600, Mon. to Sat. (it's still a private house), entry US$0.25.

Antigua is so restored that only convents and churches are in ruins, and San Francisco church has been rebuilt. The old cobblestones are being replaced in the original pattern. Indian women sit in their colourful costumes amid the ruins and in the Parque Central. Most picturesque. Good views from the Cerro de la Cruz, 40 mins'. walk N of town (beware of theft).

This is certainly the cultural centre of Guatemala as shown by the sections on museums and shopping below. Indigenous music can be heard everywhere, and the Marimba Antigua plays Bach and Mozart.

Orientation Agua volcano is due S of the city and the market is to the W. Avenidas are numbered upwards running from East (Oriente) to West (Poniente), and Calles upwards from Norte to Sur. Avenidas are Norte or Sur and Calles Oriente or Poniente in relation to the central Plaza; however, unlike Guatemala City, house numbers do not give one any clue towards how far from the central Plaza a place is. There are authorized guides whose tours of Antigua and surroundings are good value.

Fiestas Holy Week. The most important and colourful processions are those leaving La Merced at 1500 on Palm Sunday and 0800 on Good Friday, and Escuela de Cristo and the Church of San Felipe de Jesús (in the suburbs) at 1630 on Good Friday. Bright carpets, made of dyed sawdust and flowers, are laid on the route. The litter bearers wear purple until 1500 on Good Friday afternoon, and black afterwards. Only the litter bearing Christ and His Cross passes over the carpets, which are thereby destroyed. Holy Week in Antigua is claimed to be one of the finest in the New World. Also 21-26 July and 31 Oct.-2 Nov. (All Saints and All Souls, in and around Antigua).

Hotels In the better hotels, advance reservations are advised for weekends and Dec.-April. *Antigua* (best), 5 Av. Sur and 8 Calle (4 blocks S of Parque), L-A, beautiful gardens, pool (see **Bathing** below); *Ramada Antigua*, 9 C. Poniente and Carretera Ciudad Vieja, T 9-320011-5, Fax 9-320237, L, pool (see below), riding, tennis courts, discotheque, sauna; *Posada de Don Rodrigo*, 5 Av. Norte 17, B, very agreeable, good food, in colonial house (Casa de los Leones), rec., marimba music p.m.; *Aurora*, 4 C. Oriente 16, C, breakfast available, the oldest hotel in the city, quieter rooms face the patio, beautiful gardens, expensive; *El Rosario*, 5 Av. Sur and 9 C., D, pleasant apartment lodge motel complex in a coffee and orange farm round the corner from the *Antigua*, small pool, proprietress speaks English and will tell you all about the area, house-keeping apartments by the month US$150-160, not as secure as it claims; *El Descanso*, 5 Av. Norte 9, 2nd floor, F, with private bath, clean, pleasant; *Casa de Santa Lucía*, Alameda de Santa Lucía 5, near bus terminal, highly rec., F (no singles), with bath, hot water (better in the upstairs rooms), good value; close by, *Hospedaje El Pasaje*, Alameda de Santa Lucía 3, F, clean, quiet, friendly, washing facilities, will store luggage for US$0.50, good view of volcanoes from roof, rec.; *Posada Colonial*, 2 C. Poniente 2, picturesque, F, with or without bath, cheaper rates for longer stays, clean (beware of dog); *Las Rosas*, 6 Av. Sur 8, F, clean, comfortable, hot water; *Santa Clara*, 2 Av. Sur 20, C/D, 8 rooms, 4 with private bath, hot water, very clean, Doña María Panedes, the owner very helpful; *Posada El Refugio*, 4 C. Poniente 28, F, with bath, or full board, G, without, showers, no hot water, serves good cheap meals, popular, cooking facilities; *Posada La Antigüeñita*, 2 C. Poniente, F, very basic; *Angélica Jiménez*, 1 C. Poniente 14A, offers accommodation and meals, cheap, clean; *Posada de Doña Angelina*, 4 C. Poniente 33, F, with shower, G without (rooms in new part more expensive, D, but good), near market. *Placido*, Calle del Desengaño, 7 blocks from Parque Central, F, good, not all rooms have hot water, beautiful courtyard, cooking facilities, rec. *Pensión El Arco*, 5 Av. N. between 1 and 2 C. Poniente, F, clean, shared bath, hot shower, quiet, good value; *Posada Landivar*, C. 5, close to bus station, E, very clean, safe, hot water all the time, rec. Rooms, from about US$50 per month, and houses, from about US$150 per month, are sometimes advertised in the Tourist Office and in Doña Luisa's café. Rec. is Familia Juárez Méndez, 5 Av. Norte 33. For room rental also contact sculptor José Tinoco (speaks English), 7 Av. Norte No. 64; for weekly stays Juan Cuéllar (fire chief) at *Zeus* or *Madison Rock* stores, 4 C. Poniente 23, or Candelaria 38, US$50 for room and board. *Martha*, 2 Av. Sur 53, US$48 for two, including meals, for a week. The buses are often met by men who ask to show you around the unmarked *pensiones* for a tip of about US$0.25. Good accommodation in Jocotenango, 15 mins.' walk, 5 mins. in kombi (on road to Chimaltenango), Doña Marina's, 13 Calle 1-69, Colonia los Llanos. During Holy Week hotel prices are generally double.

Camping at Texaco opposite *Ramada Hotel*.

Restaurants In several of the more expensive hotels. *El Sereno*, 6 C. Poniente 30 (T 0320-073), well-prepared meals in beautifully-reconstructed colonial-style house, open 1200-1500, 1830-2200 Wed. Sun. highly rec., reservations advised, especially Sun. lunch (children under 8 not served), chamber music recitals often on Mon. and Tues., art exhibitions, handicrafts and old books on display and for sale. *Panadería y Pastelería Doña Luisa Xicotencatl* ("*Doña Luisa's*"), 4 C. Oriente 12, 1½ blocks E of the Plaza, cable TV, a popular meeting place, serves superb pies and bread, breakfasts, chile con carne, etc.; *Café de las Américas*, 4 C. Oriente (a few blocks E of *Doña Luisa's*), best cakes and chocolates in town, though others claim *La Cenicienta* next to *Fonda de la Calle Real* on Av. 5 Norte, takes that honour e.g. cinnamon roll, New York cheesecake, etc. Near Plaza are *La Estrella*, 5 C. Poniente No. 6, Chinese and other food, rec., *Café Flor*, Mexican food, and *El Churrasco*, steakhouse, 4 C. Poniente. *Welten*, 4 C. Oriente 21; *El Mesón Panza Verde*, 5 Av. Sur 19, both expensive (latter has 4 excellent rooms to let, D range). *El Oasis*, 7 Av. Norte, new. *Zen* (Japanese), closed Weds. after 1200, 3 Av. Sur, No. 3, popular, rec., has mail service for travellers; *Govinda*, 7 Av. No. 2, 2 blocks W of Parque Central, good vegetarian; *Fonda de la Calle Real*, 5 Av. Norte No.5, speciality is queso fundido, guitar trio on Sun. evenings, good, reasonable prices; *Quesos y Vino*, 5 Av. Norte 31A, Italian food; *El Capuchino*, 6 Av., between C.5 and 6, excellent Italian food and salads, try the garlic spaghetti, friendly English-speaking owner; *Angeletti*, 5 C. Poniente 18 also good Italian; *Emilio*, on 4 C. Poniente, and *Gran Muralla* opposite, both sell reasonable Chinese food; *Casa de Café Ana*, adjoining *El Rosario* lodge, serves all meals, and sells fine ice-cream, closed Weds.; *San Carlos*, on main square, sells good set meals; *Martedino*, 4 C. Poniente 18, pizzas; *Café Jardín*, on W side of main square, nice atmosphere; *Café Mistral* (close to *Doña Luisa's*), for licuados, juices and snacks. *Comedor Veracruz* in the market, good; *Asjemenou*, also near market in C.5, Dutch, rec.; *Lina*, near market on Alameda de Santa Lucía, serves good, cheap meals; *El Prado*, in San Felipe, 2 km., limited menu, good food, pleasant atmosphere. *Pastelería Okrassa*, 6 Av., C. 1-2, for meat and fruit pies. *Panificadora Colombia*, 4 C. Poniente 34, close to bus terminal, good breakfasts.

Bars *Mío Cid*, 3 Av. Sur, Canadian owned, good food and music, meeting place for foreigners. *Moscas y Miel*, 2 blocks from Zócalo, lively.

Market There is an extensive daily market, particularly on Mon., Thurs. and Sat. (best) next to the bus terminal at end of 4 Calle Poniente, W of Alameda Santa Lucía. Good handmade textiles, pottery and silver.

Shopping Mercado de Artesanías is at 7 Av. between 4 and 3 Calles. *Casa de Artes* for traditional textiles and handicrafts, antiques, jewellery, etc. 4 Av. Sur. *Casa de los Gigantes* for textiles and handicrafts and Concha's Footloom, both opposite San Francisco Church. *Fábrica de Tejidos Maya*, 1 Av. Norte, C. 1-2, makes and sells good cheap textiles, wall hangings, etc. The *Utatlán* cooperative on 5 Av. Norte specializes in good handicrafts and antiques (expensive). Doña María Gordillo's sweet (candy) shop on 4 C. Oriente is famous throughout the country. There are many other stores selling textiles, handicrafts, antiques, silver and jade on 5 Av. Norte and 4 C. Oriente (*Ixchel* on 4 C. Oriente sells blankets from Momostenango). *Galería Klaske*, 3 C. Poniente. A number of jade-carving factories may be visited, e.g. *Jades*, S.A., 4 C. Oriente 34, open 0900-1830, *La Casa del Jade*, 4 C. Oriente 3 or *J.C. Hernández*, 2 Av. Sur, 77, *San José*, Calzada Santa Lucía N, No. 23 A. Jade is sold on the Parque Central on Sats. more cheaply. Painted ceramics can be obtained from private houses in 1 Av. del Chajón (C. San Sebastián) near C. Ancha, and glazed pottery from the *Fábrica Montiel*, N of Calle Ancha on the old road to San Felipe. Near San Felipe is the silver factory where much of the silver ornaments sold in Antigua and Guatemala City are made. Various local handicrafts at *Hecht House* in the same area. Ceramic birds at handicrafts shop in the *Posada de Don Rodrigo* (see under Hotels above). *Calzado Fase*, 6 Av. Norte 61, makes made-to-measure leather boots.

Bookshops *Casa Andinista*, 4 C. Oriente 5A, sells books in Spanish and English (including the *Mexico and Central American* and the *South American Handbooks*), photographs, posters, rubbings, maps (easier than the Instituto Geográfico in Guatemala City), postcards, cards, weavings from Ixil Triangle, camping gear for rent (opp. *Doña Luisa's*, which sells *Time* and *Newsweek*), has photocopying machine, repeatedly recommended. *Un Poco de Todo*, on W side of Plaza, sells English language books, postcards, maps. *Librería Pensativo*, 5 Av. Norte 29, good for books in Spanish about Central America. *Librería Marquense*, 6 C. Poniente between 5 and 6 Av.

Car Rental Avis, 5 Av. Norte between the square and the arch.

Bike and Horse Hire Bicycles (US$1/hour, US$5/day) and motorcycles (US$50 for 3 days) for hire in 6 Av. Sur No. 8, also mountain bikes in 5 Av. Sur, US$1 per hour. Horses from Günter Wamsu, Alameda Santa Lucía No. 7 (opp. bus station), starting at US$8 for 2 hours.

Bathing Non-residents may use the pool at the *Hotel Antigua* for a charge of US$2.20, you may be obliged to have a buffet meal as well (US$45/month); also, at *Ramada Antigua* for US$2 a day, US$35 a month. Both hotels have special Sunday prices of US$3.75 for buffet lunch, swimming and marimba band (the *Ramada* also has children's shows). At the latter, weekly and monthly rates for use of sports facilities can be negotiated. Warm mineral springs (public pool and private cubicles) at San Lorenzo El Tejar: Chimaltenango bus to San Luis Las Carretas (about 8 km.) then 212 km. walk to "Balneario". Public saunas US$0.75, massage US$2.50, health foods, medicinal herbs in Jocotenango, 2 km. N.

Sports Karate school: Bie Sensei (Danish), 3rd degree black belt gives hour long lessons.

Museums Colonial museum in the old University of San Carlos Borromeo (1680), facing Cathedral, includes colonial sculptures and paintings. US$0.12 to get into museum (open 0900-1200, 1400-1800) and other ruins around the town. Museo de Santiago in municipal offices to N of Plaza, contains replica of 1660 printing press (original is in Guatemala City), old documents, collection of 16th-18th-century books (1500 volumes in library, open afternoons), and representations of the colonial way of life, and the Museo de Armas weapons collection. Open Mon.-Fri. 0900-1600, Sat. and Sun. 0900-1200, 1400-1600. Admission US$0.12 (free Sundays). Also small museum in Convento de Capuchinas. Museum of Indian Music, K'ojam, Calle de Recoletos 55, next to churchyard behind market, good collection of traditional musical instruments, slide shows on music and culture, open 0830-1230, 1400-1700 Mon.-Sat., US$0.50.

Cinemas Los Capitanes on 5 Av. Sur. Showings several days a week. English films with Spanish subtitles often shown, US$0.80.

Concerts Music festival in November, excellent. The Alianza Francesa, 3 C. Oriente 19, has French music on Fridays between 1600 and 2000, also French newspapers. Concerts also at Capuchinas convent and *El Sereno* restaurant (see above).

Exchange Lloyds Bank International, 4 C. Oriente 2 on NE corner of Plaza, Mon.-Fri. 0900-1500; Banco del Agro, N side of Plaza, same times but is also open Sat.; Banco de Guatemala, W side of Plaza, Mon.-Thurs. 0830-1400, Fri. 0830-1430. Banco Industrial, 5 Av. Sur 4, near Plaza, gives cash on Visa credit card at 10% less than usual exchange rate. Branch of Banco del Agro, Alameda Santa Lucía y 5 C., near Post Office, open 0900-1800, Mon.-Sat. Try also *Roly* hairdresser, 4 Av. Sur 1, good rates. US dollars not obtainable. May exchange personal cheques for quetzales.

Spanish Language Schools There are about 32 in all, consequently Antigua is full of foreigners learning Spanish. Those of which we have received favourable reports are: Proyecto Lingüístico Francisco Marroquín, 4 Av. Sur 4, T 320-406, Apartado 237, Antigua. This school provides up to 7 hrs. individual tuition a day and places students with local families. The fee for one week incl. 7 hrs. study, board and lodging is Q250 (it is more expensive than the other schools). Maya, 5 C. Poniente 20, fees, Q165 for first week, reduction of Q10 for each consecutive week up to 4 (6 hr. day)—must be paid in advance; Nahual, 5 Av. Norte 31, rates from Q145 for 4 hrs. per day for a week upwards; Tecún Umán, 6 C. Poniente 34, individual tuition, rec. (rates from US$250-400 per month, depending on number of hours per day); Español Dinámico; Jiménez, near La Merced, 1 C. Poniente 41, small, 5 teachers, US$70 a week staying with family. Cooperativa de Lengua Española Antigua, rec.; contact Vinicio Muñoz, Colonia Candelaria 9; Instituto Antigüeño de Español, 1 C. Poniente No. 33, Mario Valle García, small, friendly, US$44.50 for 5 days, 4 hrs. a day; US$25.50 for board and lodging with family. El Quetzal, 5 Av. Sur 11, US$50 per week, 6 hrs. per day, accommodation with a family costs an additional US$20 per week (20% of profits go to local hospital); Arcoiris, 7 Av. Norte 2. Marco Tulio's Centro Lingüístico Antigua, 6 Av. Norte 25 (T 320-388) has received mixed reports, US$65 for 5 days, tuition and lodging (recommended you pay the family that you stay with direct). The Professional Spanish Language School, 7 Av. Norte 82, T 320-161, opened in early 1989 under the directorship of Roberto King, author of *Spanish, An Easy Way*; the school offers individual tuition for 2, 4 or 6 hrs. a day for any number of weeks, with a change of teacher each week so that students get used to different tones and rhythms of speech (profits go to the Shawcross Aid Programme for Highland Indians). Also new is the Amigos del Mundo run by Daniel Ramírez Ríos, the volcano guide, 6 Av. Norte 34. Highly rec. private teacher, Julia Solís, 5 C. Poniente 36, another is María Elena Estrada, *La Cenicienta*, 5 Av. Norte 7. Also check advertisements in Doña Luisa's and the Tourist Office (Director helpful) for private lessons (about US$1 per hour). There are guides who take students around all the schools and charge a commission; avoid them if you don't want this extra cost. If you have time, it is a good idea to shop around.

Laundromat 5 Av. Sur 24.

Post Office, Telephone, Cables Post Office at Alameda Santa Lucía and 4 C., near market (local cables from here); *lista de correos* keeps letters for a month. Boxes of books up to 5 kg. can be sent from the post office, but other packages weighing more than 2 kg. must be posted from Guatemala City (do not seal parcels before going to the capital). The Pink Box (52 Av. Norte No. 14, near the main square) advertizes fast, secure shipping of all parcels, but we have received numerous unfavourable reports. International cables in Guatel building, SW corner of main square. Telephone service is poor from Antigua.

Research Library The Centro de Investigaciones Regionales de Mesoamérica (Cirma), 5 C. Oriente 5, offers good facilities for graduate students and professional scholars of Middle American history, anthropology and archaeology.

Public Library On E side of Plaza, open evenings only. The Banco de Guatemala library, on W side of Plaza, is open to the public, Mon.-Fri. 1000-1200, 1400-1900.

Doctor Dr. Julio R. Aceituno, 2 C. Poniente, No. 7, T 0320-512, speaks English; Dr. Joel Alvarado, 4 C. Poniente 23, keeps regular hours and a quick cure for dysentery.

Tourist Office E corner of Palace of the Captains-General, S side of Plaza, is helpful (street plan available, US$0.10); English and a little German spoken. Open: 0900-1600 (7 days a week). The tourist office can arrange guides for visits to monuments for between US$3 and US$6 per day. Ask here for campsite details (there are no caravan parks).

Guide Book *Antigua, Guatemala, City and Area Guide*, by Mike Shawcross.

Travel Agent Agencia de Viajes above art gallery on W side of the main square. Connection Travel, at *Ramada Antigua*, rec.

Buses Half-hourly from Guatemala City, from 0700 to 1900, US$0.40, 45 mins, from Av. Bolívar, 32 Calle, Zona 3 and from 15 C. and 4 Av. Zona 1 (at least 10 bus lines). Buses to Guatemala City leave from Alameda Santa Lucía near the market, with the same time and schedules as buses to Antigua. To Chimaltenango, on the Pan-American Highway, hourly, US$0.25, for connections to Los Encuentros (for Lake Atitlán and Chichicastenango), Cuatro Caminos (for Quezaltenango) and Huehuetenango (for the Mexican border). It is possible to get to Chichicastenango and back by bus in a day. To Escuintla, US$0.45. Buses and minibuses also to nearby villages.

Buses Inter-Hotel y Turismo run a transfer service (1 hr.) from Antigua to La Aurora airport for US$10, at 0440 and 1500, starting at *Ramada*, calling at *Antigua Hotel*, *Posada Don Rodrigo*, *Doña Luisa's* and *Hotel Aurora*; for tickets T 320011/15. Tickets available at *Doña Luisa's* and Casa Andinista. Direct buses to Panajachel from Inter-Hotel y Turismo on Tues., Thur. and Sun. Taxi to Guatemala City US$20, same rate to airport.

Excursions To ***Ciudad Vieja***, 5½ km. SW at the foot of Agua volcano. In 1541, after days of torrential rain, an immense mud-slide came down the mountain and overwhelmed the city. Alvarado's widow, newly elected Governor after his death, was among the drowned; you can see the ruins of the first town hall. Today it is a mere village (***Hospedaje Shigualita***, cheap, at S end of village), but with a handsome church, founded 1534, one of the oldest in Central America. *Fiesta*: December

5-9. Small early market, busiest Sundays; bus US$0.10. At **San Juan del Obispo**, not far, is the restored palace of Francisco Marroquín, first bishop of Guatemala, now a convent. The parish church has some fine 16th century images.

Behind San Juan del Obispo, on side of Agua volcano, is the charming village of **Santa María de Jesús**, with a beautiful view of Antigua. In the early morning, there are good views of all 3 volcanoes 2 km. back down the road towards Antigua. Beautiful *huipiles* are made and sold in the houses. Frequent buses from Antigua on main market days, US$0.10 (Mon., Thurs., Sat.); last bus returns at 1700. *Fiesta* on 10 Jan., accommodation at *municipalidad* for US$0.30; *Hospedaje y Comedor El Oasis* on road to Antigua has clean, pleasant rooms, F; *San José*, F, basic and noisy.

About 9 km. SE of Antigua (bus service, US$0.10) is **San Antonio Aguas Calientes**, a village with many small shops selling locally made textiles. Carmelo and Zoila Guarán give weaving lessons for US$1 per hr., as do Rafaela Godínez, very experienced, and Felipa López Zamora, on the way to the church, 30 metres from bus station (bring your own food and she will cook it with you), US$2 daily. *Fiestas*: first Sunday in January; 13 June; 1 November.

Volcanoes The three nearby volcanoes provide incomparable views of the surrounding countryside and are best climbed on a clear night with a full moon or with a very early morning start. Altitude takes its toll and plenty of time should be allowed for the ascents. Plenty of water must be carried and the summits are cold. Descents take from a third to a half of the ascent time. There have been reports of robberies on the volcanoes (taking a guide reduces the risk). Tourist Office in Antigua helpful. Enquire there about conditions (both human and natural) before setting out. There is a volcano-climbing club: Club de Andinismo, Chicag, Volcano Tours, Daniel Ramírez Ríos, 6 Av. Norte, No. 34, Antigua; members are informative, enthusiastic, will act as guides for a small fee, and Daniel speaks English.

Agua Volcano 3,760 metres, the easiest of the three (or the least difficult as one traveller described it!), is climbed from Santa María de Jesús (directions to start of ascent in village). Crater (with football field) with small shelter (dirty) and 5 antennae at top. Fine views of Volcán de Fuego; 3 to 5 hours' climb, two hours down. To get the best views before the clouds cover the summit, it is best to stay at the radio station at the top. Bus from Antigua to Santa María de Jesús at 0500 (irregular) allows you to climb the volcano and return to Antigua in one day. Guided tours on Sats., return Sun., US$6; information from *Zen* restaurant.

Acatenango Volcano 3,976 metres. The best trail (west of the one shown on the 1:50,000 topographic map) heads south at La Soledad (15 km. west of Ciudad Vieja on Route 10) 300 metres before the road (Route 5) turns right to Acatenango (good *pensión*, G, with good cheap meals). A small plateau, La Meseta on maps, known locally as El Conejón, provides a good camping site two-thirds of the way up (3-4 hrs.). From here it is a further 3-4 hrs. harder going to the top. There is a shelter on the col between the 2 summits. Excellent views of the nearby (lower) active crater of Fuego. To reach Acatenango, take a bus heading for Yepocapa or Acatenango (village) and get off at Soledad, or from Antigua to San Miguel Dueñas, and then hitch to Soledad. Alternatively, take an early bus to Ciudad Vieja from where you can hitch to Finca Concepción Calderas (bus Ciudad Vieja-Calderas 0645 Sat. only), then 1 hr. walk to La Soledad. Be sure to take the correct track going down (no water on the way up, hut at top in reasonable repair).

Fuego Volcano 3,763 metres, for experienced hikers only. Can be climbed either via Volcán de Acatenango (sleeping on the col between the two volcanoes), up to 12 hrs. hiking, or from Finca Capetillo in village of Alotenango (south of Ciudad Vieja), 9 km. from Antigua. One hour to reach base of mountain, then 7 hrs. ascent with an elevation gain of 2,400 metres. A very hard walk, both up and down, and easy to lose the trail. Steep, loose cinder slopes, very tedious in many places. Danger of eruptions and sulphur fumes. The deep active crater however is an awesome sight.

At the village of San Felipe (US$0.05 by bus, or 15 min. walk from Antigua) is a figure of Christ which people from all over Latin America come to see. *Restaurant El Prado* is rec. There is a small silver workshop which is worth visiting. Robbery in the village reported.

Three Indian villages N of Guatemala City are easily reached by bus. At Chinautla (9½ km.), the village women turn out hand-made pottery. Eight km. beyond is another small village, San Antonio las Flores: good walking to a small lake (70 mins.) for bathing. Santo Domingo Xenacoj can be reached by bus from the Zona 4 terminal, Guatemala City. It has a fine old church and produces good *huipiles*.

At **San Lucas Sacatepéquez**, the Fábrica de Alfombras Típicas Kakchikel at Km. 29½, Carretera Roosevelt (usually known as the Pan-American Highway) will make rugs for you. Restaurants: *La Parrilla, La Cabaña, Nim-Guaa, La Diligencia*, and *El Ganadero*, all good for steaks; *Delicias del Mar* for seafood. 5 km. beyond San Lucas is Santiago Sacatepéquez, whose *fiesta* on Nov. 1 is characterized by colourful kite-flying.

A most interesting short trip by car or bus from the capital is to **San Pedro Sacatepéquez**, 22½ km. NW. Good view over Guatemala valley and mountains to the N. Its inhabitants, having rebuilt their village after the 1976 earthquake, are returning to the weaving for which the village was renowned before the disaster. The Cooperative (a member of Artexco, the Federation of Artisans' Cooperatives) is San José Caben. Bus from Guatemala City, Zona 4 bus terminal, US$0.20, 1 hr.; bus to Rabinal, 5½ hrs., a beautiful, occasionally heart-stopping ride. *Hotel Samaritano*, near Plaza, F with bath, clean, hot shower. *Fiestas*: Carnival before Lent; 29 June (rather rough, much drinking) and great ceremony on 15 March when passing the Image of Christ from one officeholder to the next, and in honour of the same image in May.

6½ km. beyond, through flower-growing area, is San Juan Sacatepéquez, where textiles are also made. *Hospedaje* under construction 1989.

San Raimundo beyond is a friendly town. Buses go N through Rabinal to Cobán (see page 361).

28 km. N of San Juan Sacatepéquez is **Mixco Viejo**, the excavated site of a post-classic Mayan fortress, which spans 14 hilltops, including 12 groups of pyramids, but was badly damaged by the earthquake. It was the 16th century capital of the Pokomam Maya; there are a few buses a day from the Zona 4 bus terminal in Guatemala City, departures at

1000 and 1700. The bus goes to Pachalum; ask to be dropped at the entrance. A new bridge now enables you to drive to the site.

The village of **Rabinal** was founded in 1537 by Las Casas as the first of his "peaceful conquest" demonstrations to Emperor Charles V. It has a handsome 16th century church (under reconstruction), Sun. market interesting; brightly lacquered gourds, beautiful *huipiles* and embroidered napkins, all very cheap. The local pottery is exceptional. Local festival on 16 Feb. with mask dancers. (*Pensión Motagua*, F, friendly, has bar attached, not rec. for women travelling alone. *Hospedaje Caballero*, F without bath, nearby. *Restaurant El Cevichazo* has good food).

The town of **Salamá** can be reached from the capital direct, or from San Juan Sacatepéquez and Rabinal through San Miguel Chicaj along another road which offers stunning views (Rabinal-Salamá US$0.50, takes 1-1½ hours). Its church contains carved gilt altarpieces. Market day is Monday; worth a visit. *Hotel Tezulutlán*, best, E with bath, cheaper without, good restaurant but service a bit slow, 7 Av. Zona 1, just off plaza; *Pensión Verapaz*, 3 C. 8-26 and *Hospedaje Juárez*, 5 C. 8-98, both F p.p. with bath, cheaper without.

Another popular excursion is to the still active **Pacaya** volcano (last major eruption January 1987). Tours are available for US$8. It can be reached by private vehicle, the road from Antigua is unpaved, but not suitable for ordinary cars. Alternatively take a bus from the central bus station in Zona 4 to **San Vicente de Pacaya** (US$0.35); then one must walk to San Francisco (1½ hrs.), and walk up 1 hr. to the TV station at the first ridge. In early 1988 it was not possible to go to the old cone (2 hrs.) above the active cone because of the continuing eruptions, which could be seen clearly from the first ridge. Check the situation in advance in San Francisco for both climbing and camping (if safe, take torch, warm clothing and a handkerchief to filter dust and fumes). A few buses go to both villages from the turn-off on the Guatemala City-Escuintla road. Last bus back from San Vicente is at 1630. There is also a bus from Palín (**see page** 380), US$0.15. If you miss the last bus back to Palín or San Vicente, you can stay overnight with Luis the Mexican in San Francisco (a good guide), or you can sleep in the porch at the school in El Cedro, the village below San Francisco, or in a house at the entrance to San Vicente (US$1), or with other locals. An Austrian traveller (1989) recommended leaving San Francisco at 0500 for the sunrise near the cone. "An unforgettable experience in a magical world." He was offered coffee, tortillas and beans on his return by his hosts of the previous night. **Warning**: There have been several reports of armed robbery and equipment being stolen from campsites on the slopes of Pacaya volcano.

GUATEMALA CITY TO SAN SALVADOR

The paved Pan-American Highway through Fraijanes, Barberena and Cuilapa keeps to the crest of the ridges most of the way to the border, 166 km. Beyond Cuilapa it crosses the Río de los Esclavos by a bridge first built in the 16th century. Fifty km. on is **Jutiapa** (population 9,200, a pleasant, lively town with a big food market in Zona 3; at least 6 hotels/*hospedajes* nearby, e.g. *Catagüe*, G p.p., *España*, *Posada Belén*, *Pensión Gloria*). Beyond, it goes through the villages of Progreso and Asunción Mita, where another road runs to Lake Güija. Before reaching the border at Cristóbal it dips and skirts the shores (right) of Lake Atescatempa, an irregular sheet of water with several islands and set in heavy forest. From the border to San Salvador is 100 km.

A right turn after Cuilapa towards Chiquimulilla (road No. 16, with old trees on either side, some with orchids in them) leads after 20 km. to a sign to Ixpaco. A 2-3 km. steep, difficult and narrow road (no problem in a jeep) goes to the Laguna de Ixpaco, an impressive, greenish-yellow lake, boiling in some places, emitting sulphurous fumes, set in dense forest. There is a bus service.

The quickest way of getting to San Salvador is to take a paved highway which cuts off right from this route at Molino, beyond the Esclavos bridge. This cut-off goes through El Oratorio and Valle Nuevo to Ahuachapán and San Salvador. (Try *Motel Martha*, 15 km. from frontier on Guatemalan side, F, excellent breakfast, swimming pool.) A third paved road, in less good condition, runs from Guatemala City through Escuintla and Guazacapán to the border bridge over the Río Paz at La Hachadura, then through the coastal plain to Sonsonate and on to San Salvador, 290 km. in all; this road gives excellent views of the volcanoes. At Pedro de Alvarado (formerly Pijije) there are several *hospedajes* (all G, basic). If stuck at La Hachadura (the last bus for Sonsonate leaves at 1800), you can get food at the service station restaurant and there is a very basic *hospedaje*, G, nearby—not recommended for lone women.

5 km. W of Guazacapán, at Taxisco, is a turn-off to the coast and the Nature Reserve of Monterrico (operated by the University of San Carlos and Inguat); it combines estuarine and coastal ecosystems with a great variety of waterbirds, turtles, mangroves and other aquatic plants. It is also on the migratory routes of North and South American birds.

GUATEMALA CITY TO THE CARIBBEAN (2)

From the SE corner of Guatemala City (Zona 10) the Pan-American Highway leads out toward the Salvadorean border. After a few kilometres a turning to San José Pinula leads to a paved winding branch road, 203 km. long through fine scenery to Mataquescuintla, Jalapa, San Pedro Pinula, San Luis Jilotepeque, and Ipala to Chiquimula (**see page** 364). It was the route to the great shrine at Esquipulas, but visitors now use the Atlantic Highway to Río Hondo and the new road to Honduras past Zacapa (**see page** 363) and Chiquimula.

Jalapa, capital of Jalapa Department, 114 km. from Guatemala City, is set in an attractive valley at 1,380 metres. The capital can also be reached by bus to Jalapa station on Guatemalan Railway and thence by train, but this route takes longer. Population 42,000.

Hotel *Pensión Casa del Viajero*, F.

The Atlantic Highway from Guatemala City to the Caribbean port of Puerto Barrios (Route CA9) is fully paved and gives access to the Honduran border, Cobán and the Petén. Note that the distances between filling stations are greater than in other parts of the country. Along the way is Sanarate (*Hotel Las Vegas*), El Progreso (also known as Guastatoya—*Hotel Guastatoya*, E, bath, swimming pool, relaxed, friendly), Teculután (one hotel), and Santa Cruz (for some reason a whole clutch of hotels). Shortly after Santa Cruz is Río Hondo and the turn off for the new road to Esquipulas and the Honduran border.

The branch road to Cobán is at El Rancho, Km. 85, between El Progreso and Teculután; this is a better alternative to the route through Rabinal and Salamá (**see page 359**).

Between Cobán and Guatemala City at Km. 163, 4 km. S of Purulhá and 53 km. from Cobán, is the **Biotopo del Quetzal**, a reserve established by San Carlos university for the preservation of the quetzal bird and its cloud-forest habitat; camping (free, good, lots of mosquitoes) and beautiful trails in the jungle. (Bus Cobán-Purulhá, US$0.50; from Guatemala City, take a Cobán bus and ask to be let out at the Biotopo; more difficult to get a bus back to the capital; bus El Rancho-Biotopo, US$0.80, 1 hr.).

Mike Shawcross writes: "I saw my first quetzal late in 1980, and consider the sighting a highlight of all my time here; it really is an incredibly beautiful bird. A series of trails, taking up to 3 hrs. to cover on foot, lead more than 300 metres up the mountainside. At Km. 156 is the new hotel and restaurant *Posada Montaña del Quetzal*, E, highly rec., café, bar, swimming pool, gardens (T 31-41-81 in Guatemala City for reservations, book in advance, especially at weekends)." Free camping at entrance. 100 metres N of the entrance to the Biotopo is the *Hospedaje Los Ranchos*, F in 10-bed cabins, fairly basic, limited restaurant; they allow you to cook your own food in the kitchen. The *Hospedaje* is a good place to see the bird. The *farmacía* at Purulhá has rooms to let, F. *Comedor San Antonio* in Purulhá, simple meals. Electricity is a problem, a torch is handy in this area.

Tactic, on the main Guatemala City-Cobán road, is famous for beautiful *huipiles* and for its "living well", in which the water becomes agitated as one approaches. (Ask for the Pozo Vivo; it is along a path which starts opposite the gas station on the main road—now reported dirty and disappointing.) Colonial church with Byzantine-influenced paintings, well worth a visit. *Fiesta* 3rd week in August. (*Hotel Sulmy*, G, nice, clean, meals, US$0.75; *Pensión Central*, G, clean, hot showers, cheap meals; and *Hospedaje Pocompchi*, less good, G.) Doña Rogelia sells *huipiles* made in the surrounding area, and the silversmith near her shop will make silver buttons etc. to order. Market days are Thursday and Sunday (very few people now wear traditional costume). To the W of Tactic is **San Cristóbal Verapaz**, which has a large colonial church with interesting altar silver and statue of San Joaquín (*Pensión Central* and *Pensión Torres*, both G). The lake is popular for fishing and swimming. Markets: Tuesday and Sunday; festival July 21-26. From Tactic the road (paved) runs 25 km. N to Cobán, past Santa Cruz Verapaz, which has a fine old 16th century church and a festival 1-4 May.

Cobán, capital of Alta Verapaz Department, is the centre of a rich coffee district. Population 59,307, altitude 1,320 metres, climate semi-tropical. Road S to El Rancho (buses), on Guatemalan Railway and the highway to Guatemala City. Founded by Apostle of the Indies, Las Casas, in 1544.

See church of El Calvario (1559), now completely renovated, original façade still intact. Daily market (local costume no longer in evidence). *Fiestas*: Holy Week (which is said to be fascinating) and 3 August (procession of saints with brass bands, pagan deer dancers and people enjoying themselves), followed by a folklore festival, 22-28 August.

Hotels *La Posada*, 1 C., 4-12, D, full board available, reasonable; *Central*, 1 C., 1-79, F, very clean, with hot shower, good restaurant entered through *Café San Jorge*; *Oxib Peck*, 1 C., 12-11, F, with bath; *Hospedaje Maya*, opp. Ciné Norte, F, hot showers, friendly, rec.; *Valenciana*, G (you can sleep on the balcony for US$0.50), basic; *Chipi-Chipi*, G, clean, dark and noisy, hot water in morning, but how can you pass up the name?; *El Carmen*, on main square, G, clean; *La Paz*, 6 Av. 2-19, F, with extension which is rec.; *Monterrey*, next door, G, rec.; *Pensión Familiar*, Diagonal 4, 3-36, Zona 2, 1 block N of Parque Central, G, warm water, fairly basic, friendly; nameless *pensión* at 1-12 Av. Estado (near *Hotel La Paz*), clean. Accommodation is hard to find in August.

Restaurants *La Posada* (address above), rec.; *Comedores Chinita*, *El Refugio* (Parque Central, good comidas corridas), *Café Norte* (good fast food), and *Las Delicias* serve meals for less than US$1; *Restaurant Chapín*, good.

Electric Current 110 volts. It has been recommended not to use standard electrical appliances in Cobán as the voltage is variable.

Buses from Guatemala City: US$2.45. Transportes Escobar-Monja Blanca, 8 Av. 15-16, Zona 1 (hourly till 1700, 4 hrs.). The bus from El Estor takes 9 hrs., 3 services a day (0600, 0800, 1000). Return buses leave at 0400 and 0800. The trip from the capital via Rabinal, along an old dirt road, takes about 12 hrs. (change buses in Salamá). Cobán can also be reached from Sacapulas and Quiché (**page 392**) and from Huehuetenango (**page 400**). There are also buses from Flores via Sayaxché and Sebol.

Excursions Near Cobán is the old colonial church of San Juan Chamelco, well worth a visit. *San Pedro Carchá* (5 km. east of Cobán, bus US$0.10, 15 mins. frequent; *Hotel Shanghai*, F; *Delgado*, G; *Pensión Central*, G, cheap, basic, dirty, serves good meals—all close at 2200) used to be famous for its pottery, textiles and wooden masks, and silver, but only the pottery seems to be available at the Tuesday market. Small local museum displays examples of local crafts. Truck to Sebol (**see page 377**), 7 hrs., US$1.20. Good swimming and walks at Balneario Las Islas, just outside the village, well signposted; crowded at weekends, good camping.

From Cobán a rough road runs 70 km. to *Lanquín* cave, in which the Lanquín river rises. If you want to visit the cave ask at the police station in the village (2 km.) to turn the lights on (this costs US$5, however many, or few, people in the group, though the amount may vary); the entrance fee is US$0.50 (a guide costs US$2.50). The bats flying out at dusk is impressive. The cave is very slippery, so wear appropriate shoes and take a torch for additional lighting. Outside the cave you can swim in the deep, wide river, and camp or sling a hammock under a large shelter. From Lanquín one can visit the natural bridge of *Semuc Champey* stretching 60 metres across the Cahabón gorge, 10 very hard km. walk, up to 4 hrs., along a new road which runs to the footbridge over the river, 20 minutes from Semuc Champey. At the end of the road, which is very steep in places, is a car park (quite a few cars, lifts possible). A steep track heads down to the new bridge half-way along the road (the route is not signposted so ask frequently for the shortest route). The natural bridge has water on top of it as well as below, and the point where the river Cahabón goes underground is spectacular. One can swim in the pools on top of the bridge. At Semuc Champey is a place where you can camp. If planning to return to Lanquín the same day, start early to avoid the midday heat. At Lanquín there is *Hospedaje Mary*, pleasant, G, cheap, basic, and small restaurants and *Hospedaje La Divina Providencia*, G, probably better, with a cheap restaurant. The church has fine images and some lovely silver. Bus from Cobán at 0530, 4 hrs., US$0.75 including breakfast stop en route; returns at 0700; also to and from San Pedro Carchá, 0530 (you can try hitching from San Pedro Carchá, from the fumigation post, where all trucks stop, to the turn-off to Lanquín, then 12 km. walk—very little traffic). There are buses at 0500 and 0730 from **Lanquín to Pajal** (12 km., 1 hr., US$0.30) from where one can go to **Sebol**, US$0.75, 5½ hrs. (**page 377**); Pajal is just a shop. Pick-up Lanquín-Sebol, US$1.

From Tactic, a reasonable and very beautiful unpaved road runs down the Polochic valley to El Estor, quite easy to hitch (**see page** 370). Tamahú (12 km.) and Tucurú (28 km.) produce fine *huipiles*; market days are Thurs. and Sat. and there are interesting images in the Tucurú church. 47 km. beyond Tucurú is a turnoff to **Senahú**, (the journey from Cobán takes 8 hrs., Autotransportes Valenciano, departures from Cobán at 1030, US$1.25, particularly crowded on Sundays, difficult to hitch to Senahú). Climb to the cemetery for good views. (*Pensiones* at Senahú: *González*, G, good meals for US$0.60, at entrance to village, *Gladys*, near main square, G, meals for US$0.55, and another in centre, G with full board, rec.). Walking in the Senahú district is magnificent. It is possible to cross the mountains to the village of Cahabón (24 km. E of Lanquín), which will take a full day, or, if you can get a lift to Finca Volcán, only 6 hrs. (either way is quicker than by road). Beyond the turn-off to Senahú, the road continues to Telemán (bus from Senahú at 0300), **Panzós** (pick-up from Telemán; guest house; bus to El Estor p.m. and Cahaboncito (6 km. from Panzós). Here you can either carry on to El Estor, or take an appalling road (ave. speed 10 kmph) to Cahabón and Lanquín. Trucks take this road, passing the turning at about 0800, on Fri. and Sun., and possibly Thurs., otherwise no traffic (the alternative is to go back to Cobán and go from there to Lanquín).

To the W of Cobán is Nebaj which can be reached by taking the Huehuetenango bus to Sacapulas (preferable to ride on the roof) and either hitching from there or waiting for the bus from Quiché. **See pages 394 and 402** for places en route to Sacapulas, Nebaj and Huehuetenango.

At Km. 126 on the Atlantic Highway is the *Motel Longarone*, C, with bungalows and a/c, good service, pool, in a delightful setting. At **Río Hondo**, 138 km. from Guatemala City there is *Hotel Hawaii*, F, helpful, rather individual idea of door locks, clean except for resident cockroaches. Also *Motel Río*. From here a paved road runs S to **Zacapa**. Population 15,000, altitude 187 metres. Sulphur springs for rheumatic sufferers at Baños de Agua Caliente, well worth a visit (closed on Mon.); tobacco grown. It is an attractive town with a colourful market, 148 km. from Guatemala City. Climate hot and dry. *Fiestas*: 29 June, 1-9 Dec. 30 April-1 May, small local ceremony. Just outside the town is

Estanzuela (minibus, US$0.30), a village whose museum houses a complete skeleton of a prehistoric monster.

Hotels *Wong*, F, with bath; *De León*, F; next to station is *Ferrocarril*, D; other *pensiones* (basic) opposite; *Pensión Central*, opposite market, F, clean, friendly, very good, delightful setting, rec. *Posada Doña María*, E of Zacapa at Km. 181 on road to Puerto Barrios, F, with bath, rec.

Restaurant *Comedor Lee*, 50 metres from *Pensión Central*, good rice, friendly Chinese owners.

Exchange Banco Granai y Townson, near central market, changes travellers' cheques.

Transport Bus from Guatemala City to Zacapa, US$1.25 with Rutas Orientales, every ½ hr., 3½ hrs. Train to Quiriguá and on to Puerto Barrios 1330, Tues., Thurs., Sat., usually late.

From Zacapa the paved road runs S to Chiquimula and Esquipulas. **Chiquimula** (21 km.), capital of its Department, population 42,000, has a colonial character; see church ruined by 1765 earthquake. Daily market. The town has a historic ceiba tree. A road, 203 km., runs W through splendid scenery to the capital (**see page** 392). *Fiestas*: 12-18 August, Virgen del Tránsito, 12 December.

Hotels *Posada Perla del Oriente*, few blocks from centre, restaurant, E, pool, rec.; *Pensión Hernández*, F, rec., good cheap food; next door is *España*, G; *Chiquimuja*, E, with bath, good quality, casual; *Hospedaje Río Jordan*, between main plaza and bus station, F/E without or with bath, pleasant owners; *Casa de Viajeros*, G, basic but clean; *Dária*, 8 Av., 4-40, ½ block from main square, F, with or without bath, rec. *El Chino* and *Pollo Frito* for a good meal. The town's water supply is often cut off.

Exchange possible at Banco de Guatemala, corner of main square, Mon.-Fri. 0830-1400, or at Almacén Nuevo Cantón on the Plaza, will change quetzales into lempiras.

Bus from Zacapa US$0.12, from Quiriguá, US$0.55, and from Cobán via El Rancho (where a change must be made) US$1.65.

At Vado Hondo (10 km.) on the road to Esquipulas, 51 km. from Chiquimula, a good-quality dirt road branches E to the great Mayan ruins of Copán (see Honduras section, **page** 501). It goes through the small town of **Jocotán** (*Pensión Ramírez*, G, showers, pleasant, very friendly, good local food from *comedor*; *Pensión Sagastume*, bus will stop outside, good meals on request; meals at the bakery; exchange at *farmacia*, with 10% commission, *fiesta* 25 July) which has hot springs 4 km. from town, and to the border at **El Florido**, where there is now a good bridge. From El Florido to Copán there is a 14-km. dirt road. The drive to Copán (by car) takes 4-5 hrs. from Guatemala City, or 2 from Vado Hondo, including the frontier crossing.

To Copán There is a through bus from Chiquimula to El Florido at 0600 and 1100 (Transportes Vilma, US$1, 2½ hrs.). At 0900, 1430, 1730 a bus goes as far as Jocotán (no connection to border on last bus). Bus Jocotán to the border, US$0.50, taxi, US$5. Transportes Rutas Orientales buses from 19 C. 8-18, Zona 1, Guatemala City run to Chiquimula from 0530, hourly (US$1.50, US$2 Pullman), any before 0730 should make this connection, but if you take the 1100 bus to the border, you won't get to Copán until 1530, and the ruins close at 1600. Also Transportes Guerra from Guatemala City to Chiquimula. There is a Vilma bus from Zacapa to the border at 0530, US$1, which will enable you to spend 2-3 hours at Copán and return the same day. From the border to Copán there are minibuses, US$1 (leave when full—if no minibus, it may be possible to hire a pick-up for US$15 to take you to the ruins and collect you later to go back to the border if only staying one day). Those travelling by bus will find that it is impossible to visit Copán from Guatemala City and return in one day. It is best to spend the night in Copán village. Bus to border at 0800, which is met by a pick-up truck to Jocotán (last bus from Copán to El Florido 1300 for connecting bus from Jocotán to Chiquimula at 1700). Through bus border-Chiquimula 0900 and 1400. Last bus Chiquimula-Guatemala City at 1800. Taxi Chiquimula to the border, US$10 (there may be colectivos for US$2); Chiquimula to Copán and back in same day, US$20. This way is much cheaper than package tours from Guatemala City (to Copán as much as US$150 round trip), but going by local bus needs plenty of time. You can sometimes get a lift to Guatemala City with tourist agency guides whose minibuses are not full—cost about US$2. Travel agents do a one-day tour from Guatemala City to Copán and back, for about US$35 p.p. You may also be able to hitch a ride from the border to Copán for US$1.

If you are coming in to Guatemala at this point you must carry a visa or tourist card as there are often no facilities for obtaining one. There is no transport from the border after 1700. If returning to Guatemala remember that you must have a new visa or tourist card (**see page** 407, **Documents**). However the Guatemalan border official will give a 72-hr. exit pass to visit Copán, stapled into passport (this avoids having to get a new visa or tourist card to reenter), but if you try to reenter at a different border post, the pass may not be recognized. If you do have any undue difficulties at this crossing, ask to speak to the *delegado*. Make sure that the customs official stamps your papers. You have to pay all exit and entry taxes: Q5 to leave Guatemala, and a Q5 (re)entry charge, plus a 10 lempiras entry/exit charge for Honduras. Crossing the border by car takes ½-1 hr.; altogether you need 11 stamps, 5 in Guatemala, 6 in Honduras, and you have to pay for practically every one. Leaving Guatemala costs US$38 (mostly for car), returning to Guatemala costs US$7.50 (ask for a receipt, or bargain); it is all very civil, but the vehicle will be sprayed (make sure none of the disinfectant gets inside). Unfortunately the border officials of the two countries do not keep the same hours: Guatemalan hours are 0800-1200, 1400-1800; Honduran hours 0800-2100. If you leave Guatemala outside business hours there is an extra charge of US$0.50.

To visit the Mayan ruins of El Petén, take a bus from Chiquimula to Río Hondo (US$0.35, 1 hr.) to connect with the 0730 bus from Guatemala City to Flores which leaves Río Hondo at 1030, cost US$3.

The main road continues south from Vado Hondo to San Jacinto and Quezaltepeque (no hotel, but a *comedor* one km. towards Esquipulas has rooms). Thence to Padre Miguel where you turn east to **Esquipulas** (population: 7,500), a typical market town in semi-lowland. However, at the end of its 1½-km. shabby street is a magnificent white basilica, one of the finest colonial churches in the Americas. In it is a black Christ carved by Quirio Catano in 1594 which draws pilgrims from all Central America, especially on 27-30 January and during Lent and Holy Week. The image was first placed in a local church in 1595, but was moved in 1758 to the present building. The old quarter near the Municipal Building is worth a visit.

The Benedictine monks who look after the shrine are from Louisiana and therefore speak English. They show visitors over their lovely garden and their extensive library.

Hotels Plenty of hotels, *pensiones* and *comedores* all over town. Near the basilica are **Payaquí**, E p.p., hot water, swimming pool; *Los Angeles*, E; *El Angel*, E with bath, cold water; **Pensión Casa Norman**, F, nice rooms with bath; *Pensión Santa Elena*, F, behind market; near the Rutas Orientales bus stop, **Santa Rosa** (1 block opposite), E, hot water; *San Francisco*, F; *París*, 10 C., 1 Av., G. 2 km. south on road to Honduras is **Posada del Cristo Negro**, C p.p., motel style, swimming pool, restaurant, good.

Honduran Consulate in the lobby of the *Hotel Payaquí*, very helpful.

Transport Buses from the capital every 30 mins. US$2.65 (4-5 hrs), Rutas Orientales and Rutas Guatesqui. The road goes on to Atulapa, on the Honduran border (minibuses when full, US$0.25-40, plus US$0.25 across border), and continues to the Honduran town of Nueva Ocotopeque and S to San Salvador.

El Salvador may be reached from Guatemala City by leaving the Esquipulas bus at the Padre Miguel junction, from where colectivos run to Anguiatú on the border, or from Esquipulas by taking the road to Concepción Las Minas and then on to Anguiatú. From there a good road goes to Metapán.

Part of the Department of Chiquimula falls within the International Biosphere "La Fraternidad", a reserve of cloud forest and its surroundings in the Montecristo range. The reserve will be administered jointly by Guatemala, Honduras and El Salvador.

Quiriguá is about 4 km. from some remarkable Mayan Old Empire remains: temple, carved stelae, etc. In 1975 a stone sun-god statue was unearthed here. The tallest stone is over 8 metres high. Many of the stelae are now in a beautiful park (but all have shelters which makes photography difficult), where refreshments are served. Open 0800-1800.

From the main highway to the ruins, ride on the back of a motorbike, US$0.50, walk or take a taxi. *Hotel Royal*, F, with bath, clean, mosquito netting on all windows, good meals US$1.60; camping in car park of the ruins, US$0.50. Reached by road from Guatemala City to Los Amates, then a 3½-km. dirt road (ask to be put down at the "ruinas de Quiriguá", 10 km. after Los Amates), Velázquez bus at 0700, US$1.25, 3½ hrs. If driving the road branches off the Atlantic Highway at Km. 207. Train to Zacapa, 1030, Wed., Fri., Sun. Take insect-repellant. The best reference book is S. G. Morley's *Guide Book to Ruins of Quiriguá*, which should be obtained before going to the ruins.

Puerto Barrios, on the Caribbean (population 23,000), 297 km. from the capital by the Atlantic Highway (toll, free for motorcycles) and with rail connections also, has now been largely superseded as a port by Santo Tomás. It is the capital of the Department of Izabal. The beach of Escobar on the northern peninsula is recommended. Toll, US$0.25. The launch to Livingston leaves from here, and one can take a boat to Puerto Modesto Méndez, on the Sarstún river.

Hotels *Del Norte*, 7 C. and 2 Av., "rickety old wooden structure" on sea front, E (rooms 5 and 7 have bath), a timeless classic, clean, rec., will change US$ cash at good rate, huge breakfasts, mainly seafood dinners, US$2.50 (but not every night), being renovated 1989-1990; *San Marcos*, 7 C. 7 Av. 63, F, with bath, 3 good meals, US$4.25; *El Dorado*, 13 C. between 6 and 7 Av., F, with bath, clean, friendly; *Europa*, 8 Av., 8 and 9 C., new, clean, F, with bath, restaurant; *Español*, 13 C. between 5 and 6 Av., E with bath, clean, friendly; *Caribeña*, 4 Av., between

10 and 11 C., F, rec., close to boat and bus terminals; *Hotel Xelajú*, 9 C. between 6 and 7 Av., G, clean, friendly, by market and bus station, noisy; *Pensión Xelajú*, 8 Av., between 9 and 10 C., quiet, clean, G. There are other cheap hotels on 7 and 8 Calles between 6 and 8 Avenidas (e.g. *Canadá*, 6 C., between 6 and 7 Av., F), and on and near 9 Calle towards the sea.

Restaurants Most hotels. *Cafesama*, 8 C., and 6 Av., open 24 hours. reasonable. *Ranchón La Bahía*, reasonable prices but watch the bill; *Guana Chapi*, on 9 C. near landing stage for Livingston ferry, very cheap and good. *Copos* and *Frosty* ice-cream parlours, 8 C. between 6 and 7 Av., both good and clean; *Frutiland*, good juices, sandwiches. Numerous others, undistinguished, in centre and on 9 Calle.

Market In block bounded by 8 and 9 C. and 6 and 7 Av. Footwear is cheap.

Exchange Lloyds Bank, 7 C. and 2/3 Av., open 0900-1500, Mon.-Fri. (will not cash American Express travellers' cheques). Banco de Guatemala on seafront, opens and closes ½ hr. earlier (will cash Amex cheques). Quinto store in the market place changes money.

Post Office 3 Av. and 7 C., behind Bandegua building.

Cables/Telephones Guatel, 10 C. and 8 Av.

Buses to capital, 6 hrs., US$6, first class, Litegua office, 6 Av., 9-10 C, hourly, first at 0100, last at 1600. Fuente del Norte, 17 C. 8-46, runs a regular service; Unión Pacífica y Las Patojas has 4 2nd-class buses a day to capital, and one semi-pullman a day, with luggage on top, to Pacific coast (US$5). Bus to El Rancho (turn-off) for Biotopo del Quetzal and Cobán, US$2.40, 4 hrs.

Train to Guatemala City Tues., Thur., Sat. 0700, arr. 1900. Fare US$1.50 single. Apparently a passenger coach is sometimes coupled to freight trains to the capital, with a fare of US$0.25, but it would be as quick to walk all the way.

Ferry to Belize Government passenger boat to Punta Gorda, Belize, Tues. and Fri. 0830, from Puerto Barrios, US$5; return same days at about 1400. It seems that seats for this boat are no longer sold in Livingston. **N.B.** There are immigration offices in both Livingston (Calle 9, near landing) and Puerto Barrios: to avoid confusion, get your exit and entry stamp in Puerto Barrios (if Livingston is no longer on the ferry route); immigration tries to charge Q10 entry, which is not necessary, only Q3 at customs—be warned. There is a service on Sat. and Sun.

On the possibility of crossing from Guatemala to Honduras in this region, Piero Scaruffi of Redwood City, CA, writes: If you want to go from Puerto Barrios (Guatemala) to nearby Puerto Cortés (Honduras) there is no boat and no road, but there is a way. It's a one-day trip (guaranteed), even if you have luggage and need frequent stops. You leave around 0600 from the market of Puerto Barrios on the bus to Entre Ríos. At the terminal in Entre Ríos you can either take the mini-train (if any is running) or, much better, take just what everybody else is taking: the small 4-wheel railway maintenance vehicles (it costs less than US$1). The railway ends at Finca Chinoq, where you have to walk to the river and hire a boat to take you to El Cinchado (US$3 or so). Mind: the locals go to Capao, but there is no immigration there; the only legal way to cross the border is through El Cinchado. The boat leaves you at the immigration. Get an exit stamp (wait a few minutes if the office is closed) and ask for directions to walk to Corinto. It's a three hour walk in the middle of nowhere and under hot sunshine. You will get lost because the trail disappears pretty soon. Look for the tree trunks they use as bridges between the canals; they follow the trail. Alternatively, wait for a local to show up. One hour of walk leads you to a village called Jimeritos, where you can rest and buy drinks and fruit. From there the trail is much better but there are many forks; you should meet considerably more people as all around are farms and plantations, and thus all you have to do is ask for directions. Two more hours of good walking get you to Corinto, which is in Honduras. You can sleep at *Victorio's* for about US$3 or get on a camioneta going to Cuyamel (offer US$1 for the ride). Gorgeous scenery on the way (hills, jungle, pueblos, streams). Road is unpaved and there are no bridges. From Cuyamel you may catch a bus to Puerto Cortés. There are immigration offices in Puerto Cortés (closed weekends) where you can get your entry stamp. The trip is not recommended if the sky is overcast: storms are sudden and wild. Going the other way is slightly more complicated, but you can still do it in one day.

Other correspondents have stressed that this "Jungle Trail" is only possible in the driest of weather; there seems to be disagreement on the trail's safety (both from the terrain and robbers), so seek local advice. The nearest car crossing is at Copán or Esquipulas.

Santo Tomás de Castilla, a few km. S of Puerto Barrios on Santo Tomás bay, is now the country's largest and most efficient port on the Caribbean. It handles 77% of the exports and half the imports as well as 20% of El Salvador's imports and 10% of its exports. Cruise ships put into Santo Tomás. Apart from *Hotel Puerto Libre* (see below), no good hotel or eating place as yet, and no shops, and nothing to do save sea bathing; the sea and beach are none too clean.

Hotel *Puerto Libre*, 25 rooms, at highway fork for Santo Tomás and Puerto Barrios, D, a/c and bath, TV, phone for international calls, restaurant and bar, swimming pool.

Shipping It is possible to ship a car to New Orleans: the cost depends on size of car.

Transport To Guatemala City one has either to take a local bus to Puerto Barrios to connect with the train, or to Puerto Barrios or the highway fork by the *Hotel Puerto Libre* to catch the Pullman bus.

Puerto Barrios to Río Dulce Launch to **Livingston** (22½ km.), at the mouth of the Río Dulce, leaves daily, 0700, 1000, and 1700 taking 1½ hours; arrive 1 hour in advance to ensure a seat, cost US$0.40 (private dugout, US$4-8). (Launch returns at 0500, 0800, 1300, 1700.) Tickets from the office at the end of Calle 9, 5 minutes walk to wharf where the boat leaves. Very quiet, now there is little trade save some export of famous Verapaz coffee from Cobán, and bananas. Population: 3,030, mostly blacks of Jamaican origin, a few English-speaking. The beach is reported to be dirty; many young travellers congregate here. Beach discotheques at the weekend are popular. Some hotels will change travellers' cheques, as will the Chinese shop. No phone service between 1900 and 0700.

Warning Don't stroll on the beach after dark, or in daylight at the Siete Altares end as there is a serious risk of rape and robbery.

Hotels at Livingston: *Tucán Dugú*, A (Fri.-Sun., less in week—all rooms with bath), sea view, swimming pool (US$4 for non-residents), restaurant, bars, laundry service, mini zoo, to book, T 0-481-572/588, or Guatemala City 321259, Telex 5139; *Minerva*, F, restaurant good for breakfast, clean; *Casa Rosada*, 300 metres first left from dock, 5 thatched cabins for 2-3 persons each on the beach, E, breakfast and bar, boat trips to Río Dulce (US$10) or just for swimming can be arranged, rec., call Guatel in Livingston for reservations, hotel will call back,

American owner, Jean Swanson. *African Place* (also known as *Río Dulce*), main street 300 m. from dock, F with bath, clean, pleasant, restaurant, left on paved road at top of hill; *Caribe*, 100 metres first left from dock, F with bath, cheaper rooms without, noisy but good. *Flamingo*, Playa de París D-823, E, with garden, clean, comfortable cottages, safe, German owner (we have been told that coloureds are not welcome). Camping is said to be good around Livingston. Beware of theft from hotel rooms.

Restaurants *El Malecón*, 100 metres from dock, on right, reasonable. *African Place*, reasonable and friendly, Spanish owner. *Café Margoth*, rec. *La Cabaña*, good but a little pricey. Good meals can be obtained in private houses. *Comedor Coni*, clean, good, cheap. **N.B.** Coconut bread, although delicious, can cause constipation.

Río Blanco beach can be reached by *cayuco*, and Los Siete Altares, beautiful waterfalls and pools during the rainy season, some 6 km. from town on foot (well recommended), or by *cayuco*. Beware of theft when leaving belongings to climb the falls. Also paddle up the Río Dulce gorge. *Cayucos* can be hired near Texaco station, US$2.50 per day.

Boats Puerto Barrios-Livingston-Río Dulce, US$6 one way (it will not leave Puerto Barrios if there aren't enough passengers; it should arrive at Livingston about 0900). Return from Río Dulce to Livingston at 1400. One can get the mail boat from Livingston up to the new bridge at Río Dulce at 0930, Tues. and Fri. (0600 in the other direction) but schedules subject to change, US$4. Boats may be hired for Livingston-Río Dulce trip for about US$45, allowing you to stop where you please. Take food and drink along with you.

Near **Río Dulce**, 23 km. upstream at entrance to Lake Izabal (site of new bridge, toll US$1), is *Turicentro Marimonte*, 500 metres to right at Shell station, C for bungalows (phone Guatemala City 324493/334511 for reservations), restaurant, pool, mixed reports; camping site US$3, use of showers and pool; *Izabal Tropical*, C in bungalow, new, over the bridge look for sign in the village, 4 km. to hotel on lake shore (it is 1 km. from Castillo San Felipe), charming setting, rec.; *Marilú*, El Relleno on N side, F with bath, but rooms are sheds full of holes, uncertain water supply, no electricity late p.m., beware of overcharging; *Hospedaje* at Río Dulce bus stop is not rec. (dirty, unsafe, F). The US-owned *Catamaran*, B (taxes extra), in bungalows, pool, meals about US$2, is reached by outboard canoe (US$1.50 from Río Dulce, 2 km. or 10 mins. downstream, phone 324-829, Guatemala City, for reservations). *Hotel Del Río*, a few km. downstream, B, incl. 3 meals—subject to change during your stay even (Guatemala City 310-016 for reservations). There are yachting facilities at Río Dulce. In the Río Dulce there are hot springs at Aguas Calientes; unfortunately there is no beach so you have to swim to them from a boat.

At the entrance to Lake Izabal, 2 km. upstream, is the old Spanish fort of San Felipe in an attractive setting (boat from El Relleno, Río Dulce—below the new bridge—US$2.50 return for one, US$0.50 p.p. in groups; it is a 5 km. walk, practically impossible after rain). (*Hotel Don Humberto*, at San Felipe, E; also basic *pensión*, G.) Lake Izabal is a habitat for the manatee (sea cow). A reserve, the **Biotopo del Manatí**, has been set up halfway between San Felipe and Livingston at El Golfete. It covers 135 sq. km., with both a land and an aquatic trail. (The Park, like the Biotopo del Quetzal, is run by Centro de Estudios Conservacionistas—Cecon—and Inguat.). Sr. Cambell and others in Livingston run boat trips to the reserve (and up rivers) for about US$25 for 6 people—bargain. The likeliest way to see manatees is to hire a rowing boat and allow plenty of time; the animals are allergic to the noise of motor boats. On the NW shore is *El Estor*—its name dates back to the days when the British living in the Atlantic area got their provisions from a store situated at this spot—where nickel-mining began in 1978 but was suspended after the oil crisis of 1982 because the process depended on cheap sources of energy. The mine is still closed. One can hire a boat from Río Dulce to El Estor for about US$60, which can be alternatively reached by taking two buses to Mariscos on the south side of Lake Izabal, then crossing on the afternoon boat (1300) to El Estor, to which there is no direct road. *Hotel Vista del Lago*, 6 Av., 1-13, E, owned by Oscar Paz who will take you fishing; *Hotel Los Almendros*, F, rec.; *Hospedaje El Milagro* G, and *Santa Clara*, G (friendly), others at similar prices. Also restaurants (*Rancho Mery*, fish and beer only, big helpings, delicious; a very good one at ferry point for Mariscos).

A ferry leaves El Estor at 0600 for Mariscos (US$1, 1 hr. 50 mins., returns 1300) from where there are buses to **Bananera** (officially called **Morales**) US$0.60 and Puerto Barrios, US$1; from Bananera there are buses to the Río Dulce crossing (road paved, 30 km.), Puerto Barrios and the Petén (US$3.50, 10 hrs. to Flores; return buses from Río Dulce to Bananera start at 0600; train to Guatemala City is supposed to leave at 0915). At Bananera, *Hospedaje Liberia, Simon's*, both G and basic but OK. *Cauca* (dory) trips can be arranged to Livingston, via San Felipe, from Mariscos, 5 hrs., US$18 for 3 people. At **Mariscos**, *Hospedaje Karilinda*, G (per room, regardless of number of occupants), rec., good food; *Cafetería/Hospedaje Los Almendros*, G, good. For the routes from El Estor to Cobán via either Panzós and Tactic, or Cahabón and Lanquín, see page 363.

EL PETEN: THE MAYA CENTRES AND THE JUNGLE (3)

El Petén Department in the far N, which was so impenetrable that its inhabitants, the Itzáes, were not conquered by the Spaniards until 1697, is now reached by road either from Km. 245, opposite Morales, on the Atlantic Highway, or from Cobán, through Sebol and Sayaxché, or by air. The local products are chicle and timber (the tropical forest south of Flores is being rapidly destroyed)—and mosquitoes in the rainy season; take plenty of repellant, and re-apply frequently.

Driving from Guatemala City or from Puerto Barrios, the road from the Atlantic Highway is paved to Modesto Méndez. Never drive at night. Some drivers suggest driving in front of a truck and, if you break down, do so across the road, then you will be assured of assistance. Alternatively after rain, it is advisable to follow a truck, and do not hurry. A new bridge has been built over the Sarstún River, then 215 km. on a road which is narrow and winding in stretches, otherwise broad, dusty and potholed. Despite the first, paved 40 km. it takes 7 hrs. to drive.

N.B. Since Tikal is a "must" on the visitor's itinerary, there are many tourists at Flores and the ruins. Demand has outstripped supply, prices are therefore high and quality of service often poor. Sadly less desirable characters have collected here, theft is common, and watch out for rip-offs. Tikal, however, will not disappoint you.

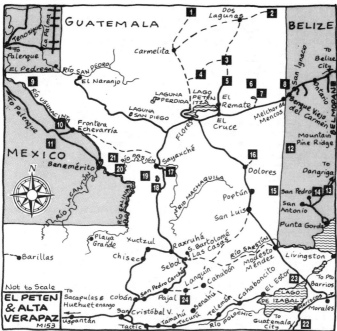

1. El Mirador; 2. Río Azul; 3. Uaxactún; 4. El Zotz; 5. Tikal; 6. Nakum; 7. Yaxhá; 8. Xunantunich; 9. Piedras Negras; 10. Yaxchilán; 11. Bonampak; 12. Caracol; 13. Nimli Punit; 14. Lubaantun; 15. Naj Tunich cave; 16. Ixcún; 17. El Ceibal; 18. Aguateca; 19. Dos Pilas; 20. Altar de los Sacrificios; 21. Itzán; 22. Quiriguá. Others: 23. Castillo de San Felipe; 24. Semuc Champey; NB ———— = major roads, not necessarily paved or all-weather; – – – – = other roads.

Flores, the Department's capital, lies in the heart of the Petén forests, and is built on an island in the middle of Lake Petén Itzá. It is linked by a causeway with Santa Elena (airport). Its population is 5,000. From Flores the ruins of Tikal and other Maya cities can be reached. (For description of Maya culture **see the Introduction to this book**). There is a collection of stelae, altars, etc., from Naranjo and other remote Maya sites, in a park W of the airport; no labels or guide book. *Fiesta*: 1-14 January.

Hotels in Flores: *Yum Kax*, D, with bath and a/c, comfortable, but noisy, restaurant not rec.; *El Itzá*, F, basic, no hot water (the owner is a good doctor); *Petén*, T 0811-392, E with cold water, D with hot, clean, rec., breakfast a little extra, helpful travel agency (will change travellers' cheques), will store luggage; *Petén Anexo* (formerly *Santana*), F, algae growing in shower, uncomfortable beds; *Pensión Universal*, near Banco de Guatemala, down an alley towards the water, F, pricey, cold shower, friendly, washing facilities; *Tziqui Na Ha*, near airport, C, a/c, new, pool; *El Jade*, F, clean, basic, just by the dyke leading to Flores, thieving reported; *Savannah*, D, huge rooms, good service, manager from

Belize.

At Santa Elena; *Maya Internacional*, E + tax, tepid water, beautifully situated, good restaurant, used by package tours from the capital; *Diplomático*, F with shower, basic; *Monja Blanca*, E; *Ahauna-Ula*, G, good restaurant; *San Juan* at the Pinita bus stop and Aviateca office, G without bath, F with, noisy, uncooperative, fleas at least, conveniently placed but not rec. for a multitude of reasons; *Don Quixote*, across the street, E, clean, friendly and good restaurant, will store luggage. *Villa Maya*, 5 km. from Santa Elena airport on road to Tikal, nice setting, helpful, B (not inc. taxes), rec.

Restaurants *El Jacal*, on road to left of causeway, good regional dishes; *Gran Jaguar*, pleasant, very good, rec.; *La Jungla*, reasonably priced, rec.; opposite is *Arco Iris*, simple but friendly, owner, Francisco, is very helpful; *Restaurant Típico*. *The Mirrors of the Lake*, due open 1990, run by Englishman Randolph Wiliams.

At Santa Elena, *El Rodeo*, 2 C. y 5 Av., excellent, reasonable prices; *Cafetería Oriental* is said to be good and cheap, as is *Comedor Los Angeles*. Santa Elena market, well-stocked, 2 blocks from *Hotel San Juan*, just off Guatel road.

Laundry Lavandería Fénix with dryer.

Dugouts can be hired to paddle yourself around the lake (US$0.50 per hour from Don Rosso, house before *Hotel Petén*). You can swim from "Radio Petén" island, the small island which used to have a radio mast on it, US$0.12 by boat, though there are signs of increasing water contamination. Petenito (La Guitarra) island in the lake is being developed for tourism (known as "Paraíso Escondido"); there is a small zoo of local animals, birds and reptiles, 3 water toboggan slides, and plant-lined walks, rec., but popular at weekends. Dugout to island, US$3 p.p. Boat tours of the whole lake cost about US$10 per boat, calling at these islands, a lookout on a Mayan ruin and *Gringo Perdido* (see page 375); whatever you may request, the zoo will almost certainly be included in the itinerary.

San Benito, a US$0.05 (US$0.10 after 1800) ride across the lake, has some small restaurants (e.g. *Santa Teresita*), which are cheaper but less inviting than those in Flores. *San Juan*, G, clean; *Hotel Rey*, G, friendly, untidy, noisy; *Hotel Miraflores*, F, good, private showers. A dirty village. Regular launch service from San Benito across the lake to San Andrés (US$0.12) and San José (US$0.15) on NW shore. *Hospedaje El Reposo Maya*, at San Andrés, G.

Car Hire at airport, mostly Suzuki jeeps; Jade agency is recommended.

Exchange Flores is the only place in the Petén where one can reliably change travellers' cheques. Banco de Guatemala open Mon.-Thur. 0830-1400, Fri. 0830-1430. Banks close December 24-January 1. The major hotels change cash and travellers' cheques.

Airport 4 companies fly from Guatemala City to Flores: Aviateca, Aerovías, Aeroquetzal and Tapsa, US$84 return. The schedules appear to change frequently, but all but Aviateca fly daily about 0700; Aviateca flies Fri. and Sun. at 1600. If returning from Flores by plane, reconfirm flight on arrival; flights back leave between 1600 and 1700, but check. Don't buy air tickets at *Hotel San Juan*; they add on all sorts of extras, but they do have a free minibus from airport to hotel. You must have passport (or identity documents) to pass through Santa Elena airport: all bags will be searched and all fruit confiscated. Taxi airport-Flores, US$0.80 p.p., or *San Juan* bus to Santa Elena village then walk. Airport to Flores is 3 km.

Buses The Flores bus terminal is in Santa Elena, a 10-min. walk from Flores (taxi, US$0.40 by day, US$0.80 at night). Daily Fuente del Norte buses leave Guatemala City in the early morning for the 13-22 hr. run via Morales-Río Dulce-Puerto Modesto Méndez to Flores, US$12.50 one way for express service with reserved seat, take food; other cheaper, slower services at around US$5; return buses to Guatemala City at 0500, 1100, 2100 from centre of Santa Elena ("the first 6 hours are terrifying, a virtual rollercoaster: book early if you want a front seat!"); Pinita to Guatemala City from *Hotel San Juan 1* (don't believe them if they tell you Pinita is the only company to the capital), 1100, not as good. Bus Flores to Río Dulce, US$3.50, Fuente del Norte, 8 hrs. Bus between Flores and Quiriguá (**see page** 366), US$5, 11 hrs. In the rainy season the trip can take as much as 28 hrs., and in all weathers it is very uncomfortable and crowded (flights warmly rec.).

Maya ruins fans wishing to economize can travel to Copán by bus from Flores to Río Hondo, then from Río Hondo to Chiquimula, then from Chiquimula to El Florido (**see page** 364) and finally from there to Copán. La Pinita also has a service to Flores from Guatemala City via Sebol, El Pato and Sayaxché, see below.

Those who wish to break the journey could get off the bus and spend a night in Morales, Río Dulce, San Luis (*Pensión San Antonio*, G, nice; *Comedor Oriente*, cheap, good) or Poptún. **Poptún** is 100 km. from Flores; 5 minibuses a day from Flores, US$2 or take Fuente del Norte bus, US$1.15, 4 hrs; bus Poptún-Guatemala City at 0900, 11 hrs., US$6, long and bumpy; take this bus also for Cobán, alight at the turn-off to Sebol, 5 km. before Modesto Méndez, hitch to Fray Bartolomé de las Casas (**see page** 377), then take 0500 bus to Cobán. *Pensión Isabelita*, F, clean, rec. but no electricity at night; *Pensión Gabriel*, G. Also at certain times of the year delicious mangoes are on sale in this area. Good view of the town from Cerro de la Cruz, a 15-minute walk from the market.

3 km. S of Poptún is *Finca Ixobel*, a working farm owned by Mike and Carole DeVine; here one may camp for US$1 p.p., rec. ("a paradise"). There are shelters, tree houses, showers, free firewood, swimming, farm produce for sale; family-style meals available, and there is a small guest house, F, travellers' cheques exchanged; they have a restaurant-bar (also called *Ixobel*, excellent too, with two unforgettable parrots and *hospedaje* next door) in the centre of Poptún where the buses stop. Two cave expeditions are organized. Unfortunately, the 3-day mule hike to the Cueva de las Inscripciones (Naj Tunich), once used by Maya, has been suspended after vandals in 1989 rubbed off some of the marvellous glyphs. The cave is now closed.

24 km. N of Poptún, 8 km. NE of Dolores, is the small Maya site of Ixcún, unexcavated, with a number of monuments (some carved), and a natural hill topped by the remains of ancient structures. The access road is impassable in the rainy season.

In 1982, the **Cerro Cahui Conservation Park** was opened on the northern shore of Lake Petén Itzá; this is a lowland jungle area where one can see 3 species of monkeys, deer, jaguar, peccary, some 450 species of birds; run by Cecon and Inguat.

Tikal The great Maya ruins of vast temples and public buildings are reached by plane to Santa Elena, from where buses run (see below). Tikal lasted from the 4th century A.D. until the tenth. An overall impression of the ruins (a national park) may be gained in 4-5 hrs., but you need two days to see everything. Guides are available near the Plaza Mayor. A Land Rover trip through the ruins costs US$2.50. Marvellous place for seeing animal and bird life of the jungle. There is a secluded part, called "El Mundo Perdido", in which wildlife can be seen. *Birds of Tikal* book available at the museum. Wildlife includes spider monkeys, howler monkeys (re-established after being hit by disease), three species of toucan (most prominent being the "Banana Bill"), deer, foxes and many other birds and insects. Mosquitoes can be a real problem even during the day if straying away from open spaces.

To visit Tikal you can take package tours from Guatemala City, but due to tourist demand these are now expensive, say US$200 for 3 days/2 nights with not necessarily much time to see the ruins. A one day air trip can cost US$150, the plane fare alone, US$107. Buses are detailed below. If you wish to drive, you will need a sturdy vehicle though not 4-wheel drive. From Santa Elena, it is now possible to visit Tikal in a day: take 0600 minibus arrive by 0700, return at 1300, allowing 6 hrs. at the site. You may hitch back with a tourist bus 1 hr. later if it is not full. Tour from *Hotel Maya Internacional* in Santa Elena: dep. 0800, return 1600, transport only US$3.50 p.p., guided tour US$18 (time may be reduced to accommodate people catching flights). *Hotel Petén* also runs tours from 0600-1700.

Hotels Note: It is advisable to book a hotel room or camping space as soon as you arrive—in high seasons, book in advance. **Jaguar Inn**, B, full board, triple room D (without board: E), will provide picnic lunch at US$1.30. Its electricity supply is the most reliable (1800-2200); will store luggage, very friendly though you may share your room with bugs and lizards. Tents can be hired at about US$5, to use in their campground. *Tikal Inn*, B in rooms (1 to 4 people) and B for up to four in a bungalow, cheap accommodation without electricity also available, meals said to be good (US$1 for dinner); *Posada de la Selva* (Jungle Lodge—reservations may be made at Edificio Villa Real, 6 Av., in the capital although this is not recommended as you have to pay for one night in advance and the booking is likely to get lost somewhere down the line), from E p.p. (communal shower) to D with bath, new bungalows have been built, full board available (food fair, but service slow, some reports have been unfavourable; roofs of cheapest accommodation leak badly) has its own campsite with toilets and cold shower facilities where you can sling your hammock for US$2.50 and rent hammocks for about US$2. Some mosquito nets for rent but better take your own. Jungle Lodge's Tikal tours (US$5) have been rec.; runs bus to meet incoming flights, US$2.50 one way. Three comedores, *Comedor Tikal*, *Corazón de Jesús*, and (best) *Imperio Maya* (opens 0530). Economical travellers are best advised to bring their own food (but not fruit, which will be confiscated), and especially drink. Everyone should take drinking water.

Wear light cotton clothes, a broad-brimmed hat and take plenty of insect repellant. The nights can be cold, however; at least one warm garment or sleeping bag is advisable. There is one campsite (US$1.85), by the airstrip, good, rents small hammocks for US$3.70, very popular. Mosquito netting is rec. Take your own water as supply is very variable, sometimes rationed, sometimes unlimited, depending on season. Bathing is possible in a pond at the far end of the airstrip (check first). Beware of chiggers in the grass. Soft drinks are available near the Plaza Mayor and Temple IV (US$0.25). No banking services available. Ruins (open 0600-1730) charge US$1.85, and museum US$0.75 (open Mon.-Fri. 0900-1700, Sat. and Sun. 0900-1600). Extended passes to see the ruins at sunrise/sunset (until 2100) are easy to obtain from the Inspectoría office on the slope by the path to the ruins (especially good for seeing animals). It is best to visit the ruins after 1400 (fewer tourists). Also recommended to see the wildlife around Temple 3 between sunrise and 0800. There is officially nowhere to store luggage at Tikal while you are visiting the ruins but you may be able to persuade the Inspector's office to help. Recommended guide book (Spanish or English) is *Tikal*, by W. R. Coe, with essential map though somewhat out of date, price US$11 in the capital, US$7.50 at Casa Andinista, Antigua, or slightly more at the Tikal Museum. Without a guide book, a guide is essential (Clarence has been rec.), as outlying structures can otherwise easily be missed. Take a torch, electricity at Tikal is only available 1800-2200 and then is intermittent.

Warning There are increasing numbers of bats in Tikal, and anyone bitten must seek medical aid right away. This means an immediate return to Guatemala City and a visit to the Centro de Salud, 9 C. between Av. 2 and 3 for treatment, including tetanus shots if necessary. The treatment is free.

Buses leave Santa Elena for Tikal from *Hotel San Juan* daily at 0630 and 1300, US$1.30 one way (63 km., 2½-3 hrs. on good paved road). Buses return at 0600 and 1300 (Pinita). Several hotels, including *San Juan* and *Petén*, run minibuses to Tikal for US$4 return (singles available), leaving between 0600 and 1000, returning between 1300 and 1700, 1 hr.; reservations should be made day before. *Jungle Lodge* minibus from Tikal at 1400. Minibuses meet Guatemala City-Flores flights to take visitors to Tikal. Taxi to Tikal costs US$16 (per vehicle), or US$24 waiting for return.

Note Heavy rains and flooding can close the roads between Tikal and Flores, but apart from 50 km. the road is generally good.

To Belize There are 4 buses daily from Flores to **Melchor de Mencos** (US$1.50) on the border (take the 0500 Pinita bus from the market—it's usually full when it reaches *Hotel San Juan 1* at 0530—they promise to wake you up, but don't count on it, to be sure of making a connection in San Ignacio for Belize City). *Hotel San Juan* runs a minibus to the border for US$5, and does a through trip to the Belize/Mexico border. Pinita bus can be caught at El Cruce if coming from Tikal, though by then, it may be full. The 0630 or 1300 bus from Tikal gives you a 1 hr. wait at El Cruce (US$0.50) for the Flores-Melchor de Mencos bus, one leaves El Cruce at 1500 (El Cruce-Melchor de Mencos, 4 hrs., US$1). Pinita bus to Flores leaves Melchor de Mencos 4 times a day (first at 0300—best for Tikal connection is the last at 0800), with a 2-4 hr. wait at El Cruce for the bus to Flores, argue price; to Tikal (some Flores-Tikal buses do not stop for passengers at El Cruce; it may be easier to get a ride in a taxi). Journey takes about 3 hrs. and the bus tours town, including the border, for passengers. Pick-up Melchor de Mencos-Flores, US$3.85; taxi from the border to Flores, argue price; to Tikal, US$35 for up to 6 passengers. About 3 km. from El Cruce on the Tikal road, if one turns off to the left along the north shore of Lake Petén-Itzá, is El Gringo Perdido, with a restaurant, cabins, C, camping (US$1.20 a night) and good swimming in the lake, meals available at US$1.25. Canoes (US$4 per day), mountain bikes, horses and guides are available. Good walking. It is almost at the entrance to the Cerro Cahui Conservation Park (see above). The road from El Remate to *El Gringo Perdido* is often flooded. For onward connections, it is best to take a taxi from the border to San Ignacio (Cayo), US$10. From there you can catch a bus to Belize City. Hitching is not easy as there is little traffic on these roads. Taxis to Belize City can be hired, about US$10 p.p. Banco de Guatemala at the border, when open, gives better rates than money changers; also black market in Belizean dollars. If driving from Flores/Tikal to Belize, be prepared for police checks (watch out for drugs being "planted" in your vehicle) and take spare fuel. **N.B.** If you need a visa to enter either Belize (other than transit) or Mexico, it is safer to get it before crossing from Guatemala at this point though you may be able to get one at the border for US$5. You can also fly from Flores to Belize City by Aeroquetzal, US$46 one way.

Hotels at Melchor de Mencos: *Maya*, G (sells bus tickets and acts as bus stop, small rooms); *Zacaleu*, G, clean, good value, shared toilets/showers; *Mayab*, F, clean, comfortable, shared showers and toilets, hot water, rec., safe parking. Tienda Unica will change travellers' cheques, but at a poor rate. *Restaurant Damarco*, very good, US$1 for meal, usually closed in evening; *La Chinita*, 1 block from *Maya*, good dinner under US$2.

To Mexico From Flores or Tikal to Chetumal in a day is possible if the 0500 bus Flores—Melchor de Mencos, or 0630 from Tikal (change at El Cruce) connects with a bus at 0920 from the border to Belize City, from where you can take an afternoon bus to Chetumal. 72-hour transit visas for Belize can be obtained at the border, but make sure you have all necessary documentation for Mexico before leaving Belize City.

A rough, unpaved road runs 160 km. to **El Naranjo** on the San Pedro River—a centre for oil exploration, unfriendly—near the Mexican border. There is a big army base there. There are daily buses from Santa Elena at 0500 and 1230 from *Hotel San Juan* (US$3, 5½ hrs. at least; bus from El Naranjo to Flores at 0300 and 1300). At *Posada San Pedro*, G, basic (under same ownership as *Maya Internacional* in Santa Elena) there is information, group travel, guides, and arrangements for travel as far as Palenque; reservations can be made through travel agencies in Guatemala City. One other basic hotel, also G; the restaurant by the dugouts is expensive, others in town better value. Also bungalows in El Naranjo, which has an immigration office. If you take the midday bus from Flores, next morning, go to immigration and have your passport stamped (if not travelling alone, make sure everyone gets a stamp). From El Naranjo, daily boats leave at 0700 and sometime after 1100 (on arrival of the 0500 Flores bus), for La Palma in Mexico (US$8, 4 hrs.), from where buses go to Tenosique and on to Palenque. Return from La Palma to El Naranjo at 1400. Bus La Palma-Tenosique at 1700; it is not possible to go Palenque the same day. Mexican tourist cards can be obtained at the border. Expect thorough searches on both sides of the border.

A third route to Mexico is to take a bus from Santa Elena to Sayaxché (see below), then take a boat down the Río de la Pasión to the military post at Pipiles (exit stamps given here) or to the town of Benemérito on the Río Usumacinta (trading boat US$2, 2 days; private launch US$60, 4 hrs.). If stuck at Pipiles, a farmer who lives 800 metres upstream may take you to Benemérito in his launch. At Benemérito, a shop near the river lets out rooms at the back, no electricity, water from well. From Benemérito, buses go at 0600, 0700 and 0800 to immigration just past the Río Lacantún (or hitch in a truck); unpaved road, 6-9 hours by bus Benemérito-Palenque (more in the wet). Allow 7 days Flores-Palenque; get Mexican tourist card in advance to avoid offering bribes at border. Take also hammock, mosquito net, food and insect repellant; there are no hotels between Sayaxché and Palenque and dollars cannot be exchanged. Yaxchilán and Bonampak in Mexico can be visited from the road Benemérito-Palenque.

Sayaxché is a good centre for visiting the Petén, whether your interest is in the wild life or the Maya ruins.

The *Hotel Guayacán*, known locally as *Hotel de Godoy* after the owner Julio

Godoy, is a good source of information on the area, F, beware of theft, expensive food and drink, on S bank of river, close to ferry; *Hotel la Montana*, G, has its own separate restaurant (at which Julián Mariona Morán is very informative); *Hotel Mayapán*, S bank near ferry, F, no water or electricity after 2200; or *Hotel Sayaxché*, G, basic, dirty, food not bad. *Comedor Delphi*, opposite market, good. If travelling south, stock up with fruit in the market. No money-changing facilities. Viajes Don Pedro runs launches to El Ceibal, Petexbatún and Aguateca, 4 hrs., and 2-day trips to Yaxchilán.

There are buses to and from Guatemala City via Sebol, and to and from Santa Elena, Flores, 0600, 1300 (US$0.80, 3 hrs.); La Pinita has a through bus, Guatemala City-Flores, via Sayaxché (no transport south in the rainy season).

On 24 August, all-night mass is celebrated in **Sebol** (free food at 0100) with games played on the church lawn in the daylight hours. 10 km. from Sebol (no accommodation) is **Fray Bartolomé de Las Casas** (*Hospedaje Ralíos*, F, shared bath, OK, and 2 others; restaurants), a pleasant village which has a *fiesta* (parade and rodeo) on 1 May. A rough dirt road links Sebol with Sayaxché via **Raxruhá** (*Pensión Aguas Verdes*, G, basic, pleasant; good *pensión* nr. bridge, G p.p., *comedor* opp.; many *comedores*, e.g. *El Ganadero*, quite good) and El Pato (2 *comedores* and 1 basic *pensión*, G).

Besides the direct Guatemala City-Sebol-Sayaxché-Flores bus, local transport connects most of these towns: Sayaxché-Raxruhá, by pick-up only, 0600, 0900, 1100, 1300, 4 hrs., US$2.60, bad road, also bus Del Rocío runs Flores-Sayaxché-Chinajá-Raxruhá-Sebol starting early (0400) and midday (1230) in both directions; El Pato-Raxruhá (minibus 0500 daily); Raxruhá-Sebol, occasional bus, US$0.40, pick-up more common, US$0.75 (very bad road, 2 hrs. for 25 km.) or El Pato-Sebol; Fray B. de Las Casas-Cobán, 0500, 9 hrs., US$1.50 (Cobán-Sebol at 0530). You can also go from Lanquín to Sayaxché via Pajal, Las Casas, Sebol and Raxruhá (**see page** 362) (not rec. as a 1-day journey, better to rest in Raxruhá).

From Sebol, there is an 0300 bus to Poptún (**see page** 373), via Fray Bartolomé de Las Casas and San Luis (on the Morales-Río Dulce-Poptún-Flores road). This route is impassable in the rainy season. From San Luis there is an 0630 bus to Flores, stopping at Poptún (4½ hrs.). It is easy to get a ride on one of the many trucks which run on all these routes.

Up the Río de la Pasión from Sayaxché is **El Ceibal**, where the ruins were excavated by Peabody Museum and Harvard. Some of the best preserved *stelae* in Guatemala are found in a jungle setting. There is now a difficult road linking Sayaxché with El Ceibal—impassable in the wet (leave bus at El Paraíso on the main road—local pick-up from Sayaxché US$0.20.—then walk to the ruins, a further 12 km., 1½ hrs.) so the trip can be made either by road or by river (launch hire US$25, 2 hrs.—*pensión* G). You can sling a hammock at El Ceibal and use the guard's fire for making coffee if you ask politely—a mosquito net is advisable, and take repellant for walking in the jungle surroundings. From Sayaxché the ruins of the Altar de Sacrificios at the confluence of the Ríos de la Pasión and Usumacinta can also be reached. Further down the Usumacinta river is Yaxchilán, just over the border in Mexico (temples still standing, with sculptures and carved lintels—**see page** 224). Still further down the Usumacinta in the west of Petén department is **Piedras Negras**, with little standing architecture, and most sculpture removed to the National Museum in Guatemala City (imagination needed), which can be reached by special rafts suitable for light rapids, at some considerable expense (can be arranged through FLAAR, **see page** 348). The Usumacinta river has been dammed by Mexico below Piedras Negras; so no longer are river trips possible.

The Río de la Pasión is a good route to visit other, more recently discovered Maya ruins. From Laguna Petexbatún (16 km.), a fisherman's paradise, which can be reached by outboard canoe from Sayaxché (US$10 or more for 6 people and luggage) excursions can be made to unexcavated ruins: these include Arroyo de la Piedra (a small site with a number of mounds and stelae, between Sayaxché and Dos Pilas), **Dos Pilas** itself (many well-preserved stelae), **Aguateca** (excursion over only known Maya bridge and down into huge chasm) and **Itzán**—discovered in 1968. Lagoon fishing includes 150-lb. tarpon, snoek and local varieties. Many interesting birds, including toucan and *guacamayo*. On W side of Laguna Petexbatún is the *Posada del Mundo Maya*, set in a jungle wilderness. Rooms F (E incl. 3 meals). Camping US$0.50 per day. Hire of hammock US$0.50 per day. Meals US$1.25 each. Jungle guides can be hired for US$1.50-2.50 per day.

(On the foregoing information, Mr. John Streather comments that the ruins are spread over a large area and that the non-specialist could well content himself with seeing El Ceibal and, possibly, Dos Pilas.)

About 30 km. from Flores, on the road towards the Belize border, is Lake Yaxhá. On the northern shore is the site of **Yaxhá**, the third-largest known classic Maya site in the country, accessible by causeway (little excavation has yet been done). In the lake is the site of Topoxte. (The island is accessible by boat.) The site is unique since it flourished between the 12th and 14th centuries, long after the abandonment of all other classic centres. Twenty km. further north lies **Nakum**, with standing Maya buildings. It is possible to drive part of the way (dry season, April-May) only, or else to walk, but since there are numerous forks in the track, it is essential to hire a guide (no overland transport or flights in the off-season).

The largest Maya site in the country is at **El Mirador**, 36 km. direct from Carmelita, very many more by jungle trail from Flores (a 2-4 day trek—a guide is essential, take plenty of food; only possible by 4-wheel drive in dry season). The larger of the two huge pyramids, called La Danta, is probably the largest pyramid in the world. There are paintings and other treasures; guards at the site will show you around if no one else is on hand. Camping is possible. Tom Courtenay-Clack (of New York City) writes: Permission, in the form of a letter from the Governor of El Petén, is required. He is to be found at the FYDEP complex on the mainland near Flores. Free water purification tablets for the trip can be obtained at the pharmacy of the army barracks by the airport. Drive or hitch-hike to Carmelita (no bus service); a hard 35 km. that can take 5 hrs.—after rain four-wheel drive, a winch and shovel are necessary. At Carmelita, ask around for space to sling your hammock or camp. Also ask for guides who go with mules to El Mirador (Victor is rec.; the one who lives next to the doctor is not, he doesn't take mules and is unreliable): US$40 with mule. Allow 2 days each way unless you want a forced march. Take water, food, hammocks, mosquito nets, tents and torches; cooking gear is not essential because guides will make a fire and the guards may let you use their kitchen if you're polite (they also appreciate gifts, e.g. a giant can of peaches).

25 km. north of Tikal is **Uaxactún**, which has a stuccoed temple with serpent head decoration. Uaxactún is one of the longest-occupied Maya sites. There is a direct bus from Flores (same times as for Tikal), US$2 return. The hardy might consider walking the 24 km. through the jungle from Tikal, as the dirt road is impassable to vehicles from June to February, but December to April it can be driven by a standard vehicle (1¼ hrs.). Guides ask about US$8 for a 2-day trip from *Posada de la Selva* in Tikal. Tour from *Hotel Maya Internacional*, US$40 for transport, guide and lunch. No *pensiones*, but the signalman at the airfield will let you sling your hammock in his home for US$0.25. Nearby is **El Zotz**, another large site, reachable by a reasonable dirt road. In the far north of El Petén is **Río Azul**, which has impressive early tomb murals and Early Classic standing architecture (under investigation each dry season). The road to Río Azul goes via Dos Lagunas, beyond which it is very bad, 2-3 days from Tikal by 4-wheel drive (the army sometimes restricts travel north of Dos Lagunas). All the sites are accessible by jeeps and FLAAR runs tours to them in the dry season.

GUATEMALA CITY TO SAN JOSE (4)

Amatitlán is 37 km. by rail and 27 by road SW of the capital, on Lake Amatitlán, 12 by 4 km. (but diminishing in size as a result of sedimentation in the Río Villalobos which drains into it—caused by deforestation). Fishing and boating; bathing is not advisable, as the water has become seriously contaminated. Sunday boat trips cost US$1, or less, for 45 mins.; beware of people offering boat trips which last no more than 10 minutes. Very popular and colourful at weekends. The thermal springs on the lake side, with groves of trees and coffee plantations, feed pools which *are* safe to bathe in. The lake is surrounded by picturesque chalets with lawns to the water's edge. Altitude 1,240 metres, population 12,225. Grand view from the United Nations Park, 2½ km. N, above Amatitlán. A road goes round the lake; a branch runs to the slopes of Pacaya volcano, US$0.15 by bus (**see page** 359). The town has two famous ceiba trees; one is in Parque Morazán. Buses from Guatemala City (every ½-hr. US$0.20) go right to the lakeside.

Fiesta Santa Cruz, 2-3 May.

Hotels *Blanquita*, on the road to Guatemala City, D room with bath; *Rocareña*, E, pay in advance as prices may go up overnight, unfriendly; *Pensión Karla*, F, clean, friendly, family-run; *Amatitlán*, three blocks from *Karla*, F, parking inside, clean, friendly but noisy; *Hospedaje y Comedor Kati*, F, clean, pleasant dining room.

There are many **restaurants** near the lake—take care with local fish because of water pollution.

Camping The by-road to the UN Park (turning at 19½ km. from Guatemala City) ends at camping sites and shelters; it is rather steep and narrow for caravan trailers. View, US$0.12 entrance fee. On the main highway S of Amatitlán, accessible by any bus going to Palín, Escuintla or beyond, is Automariscos (km. 33.5, T (0)330479), English-speaking owner, electric and water hook-ups, large warm swimming pool (thermal), hot jacuzzi, baby pool, good toilets, entry US$1, restaurant. A second, next door in the direction of Escuintla, is La Red, which has swimming pools fed by volcanic springs (US$0.60 each); restaurant/bar and good toilet facilities (camping US$1). Bus, Guatemala City to any of these 3, US$0.25.

Road continues S to the Pacific port of San José through Palín; rail continues W to Tecún Umán.

Palín, 14½ km. from Amatitlán, has a Sunday Indian market in a square under an enormous ceiba tree. Grand views to E, of Pacaya, to NW, of Agua volcano, to W, of Pacific lowland. Power plant at Michatoya falls below town. Road runs NW to Antigua through Santa María de Jesús (**see page** 357). See old Franciscan church (1560). *Fiestas*: 8 December, first Sunday January, 3 June, and movable feasts of Holy Trinity and Sacred Heart. Textiles here are exceptional, but are becoming hard to find. *Pensión Señorial*, G, basic.

Escuintla, 18 km. from Palín on the road to San José, is a market town in a rich tropical valley at 335 metres. Population 62,500. Famous for its medicinal baths and fruits. There is a large market on Sunday, and a daily market over 2 blocks. Marimbas frequently play in the central plaza, the local banana bread is worth trying and *basitas*, real fruit ice-lollies. Agua volcano looms to the N. Road N to Antigua. Beyond Escuintla a railway branches W at the station of Santa María to Mexico.

The Pacific Highway to the Mexican border at Tecún Umán (paved all the way, 200 km.) and E to El Salvador (first 25 km. bad, then only fair) runs through Escuintla. As a route to Mexico, it is shorter, faster and easier to drive, but much less picturesque, than the El Tapón route to the N. There is a meat packing plant. *Fiesta*: 8 (holiday) to 12 December. Many buses to the capital (US$0.38, Veloz Porteño) also direct to Antigua at 0730 and 1500, US$0.50 (poor road).

Hotels (each with acceptable restaurant) *Motel Sarita*, Km. 59, CA2 road, E; *Motel Texas*, Km. 59, CA9 road, E. *La Castilia*, near market, G, basic, clean; *Campo Real*, 10 C. behind market, F, with fan, very clean, pleasant owners; *Mansión La Paz* and *Pensión Marina*, both G, on Calle 10; *Hospedaje Comodidad*, near market, G; *Shing Chi Rest*, G.
   Restaurant Deliciosas Tony, meals for US$0.75; also several Chinese restaurants.

Exchange Lloyds Bank (agency) 7 Calle 3-09, Zona 1. Open 0830-1200, 1400-1600.

The Department of Escuintla, between the Pacific and the chain of volcanoes, is the richest in the country, producing 80% of the sugar, 20% of the coffee, 85% of the cotton, and 70% of the cattle of the whole country.

Between Escuintla and Santa Lucía **Cotzumalguapa** is **La Democracia** (7 km. off the Pacific Highway), where sculptures found on the Monte Alto and Costa Brava estates (*fincas*) are displayed. These are believed to date from 400 BC or earlier and have magnetic navels or temples. Visit the Museo del Pueblo on the main square. At Cotzumalguapa, a friendly town, is the 9th century site of Bilbao (or Cotzumalguapa), which shows Teotihuacán and Veracruz influences. El Baúl, a pre-classic monument (stelae) which dates back to the Izapan civilization (see the Introduction to this book), is 6 km. from Cotzumalguapa: cross bridge, keep left and follow the road to the timberyard where numerous interesting stelae are displayed. From this early art, the classic Maya art developed. El Castillo, between Bilbao and El Baúl, has some small sculptures dating back to Maya times. On the Las Ilusiones and Finca Pantaleón estates are ruined temples, pyramids and sculptures, and there are other stelae to be found in the area. More detailed information and a map can be obtained from FLAAR in Guatemala City (**page** 348).

Hotels at Cotzumalguapa: *El Camino*, E; *Galeano, El Carmen*, both G. Hotel at La Democracia, *El Reposo*, F. Buses from the Zona 4 terminal in the capital run to both places.

San José, 52 km. beyond Escuintla, 109 km. by road from the capital (fully paved, bus US$1.50, Reyna del Pacífico), is the country's second largest port; it handles nearly half the imports. Population 8,000. Hot climate. Fishing, swimming, though beware the strong undercurrent. *Fiesta*: 19 March, when town is crowded and hotel accommodation difficult to get. Interesting trip can be taken through Chiquimulilla canal by launch from the old Spanish port of **Iztapa**, now a bathing resort a short distance to the E. At Iztapa you can camp on the beach (dirty). By road you need to cross the canal by ferry which takes cars.

Hotels at San José *Casetas San Jorge*, F p.p.: *Viñas del Mar*, on the beach, E, with bath, run down, unfriendly; *Turicentro El Coquito*, D, on the road to Escuintla; *Motel La Roca*, at km. 71, F; *Veracruz* (Calle Principal), G, clean. *Posada Roma Linda*, G, extra for sheet); no shower, basic, good fish meals with family. At Iztapa *Santa María*, E with swimming pool; basic *hospedaje*, F. **Restaurant** *Papillon*, on the beach, serves cacerolas (fish and shrimp soup), also has rooms, E.

Bus San José-Guatemala City hourly from 0600; from Iztapa to San José US$0.12. To Escuintla, US$0.50. Reyna del Pacífico to the capital, US$1.25.

Beyond San José is the smart resort of **Likin**, which fronts on both the Chiquimulilla canal and the Pacific. (Hotel: *Turicentro Likin*, C, per bungalow, clean, a/c, transfer by boat to hotel, secure parking, acceptable restaurant.) Further on is the less expensive resort of **Monterrico**, best approached from Taxisco on the main lowland route to El Salvador. It is a small black sand resort (beach shoes advisable). Stay at *Beach Hotel* run by ex Peace Corps girl, Nancy, F, excellent seafood, good surfing but busy at weekends.

WEST FROM GUATEMALA CITY (5)

The Pacific Highway goes W from Guatemala City to Tapachula in Mexico. The Pan-American Highway (fully paved) cuts off NW at San Cristóbal Totonicapán and goes into Chiapas by the El Tapón, or Selegua, canyon. This is a far more interesting route, with fine scenery. A railway also runs through south-western Guatemala from Guatemala City to the Mexican frontier.

Some 6½ km. W of the capital a road (right) leads to San Pedro Sacatepéquez (**see page** 358) and Cobán (**see page** 361). Our road twists upwards steeply, giving grand views, with a branch to Mixco (16½ km. from Guatemala City). About 14 km. beyond, at San Lucas Sacatepéquez, the road to Antigua turns sharp left. **Sumpango**, which is a little over 19 km. beyond this turn-off, has a Sun. market, and *huipiles* can be bought from private houses; they are of all colours but preponderantly red, as it is believed to ward off the evil eye. Good font in church. At **Chimaltenango**, another road runs left, 20 km., to Antigua; this road is served by a shuttle-bus (US$0.25 or US$0.40 in minibus), so Antigua can be included in the Guatemala-Chichicastenango circuit. Chimaltenango is the capital of its Department. *Pensión La Predilecta*, G, pleasant rooms with bath, rooms without bath not so nice, poor water supply, unfriendly, tends to overcharge, rebuilt since the earthquake. Good restaurant nearby: *La Marylena*. Widows' cooperative selling weavings to support widows and orphans of the disappeared: contact Margarita de Similax, Segunda Calle 8-72, Chimaltenango. Excellent views at 1,790 metres, from which water flows one side to the Atlantic, the other side to the Pacific. Thermal swimming pool at San Lorenzo El Tejar, which can be reached by bus from Chimaltenango. *Fiesta*: 18-20 January. Buses to Antigua pass the famous park of Los Aposentos, 3 km. (lake and swimming pool). Bus to Panajachel, US$1.20. At **San Andrés Itzapa** (2 km. off Antigua road, 4 km. from Chimaltenango) there is a very interesting chapel to Maximon (San Simón) which is well worth a visit. Shops by the chapel sell prayer pamphlets and pre-packaged offerings.

A side-road runs 21 km. N to San Martín **Jilotepeque** over deep *barrancas*; markets on Sun., Thurs. Bus from Chimaltenango, US$0.50. *Fiesta*: November 11. Fine weaving. Striking *huipiles* worn by the women. Ten km. beyond Chimaltenango is Zaragoza, former Spanish penal settlement, and beyond that (right) a road (13 km.) leads N to the interesting village of **Comalapa**: markets 1000-1430, Mon.-Tues. bright with Indian costumes. Fine old church of San Juan Bautista (1564). *Fiestas*: 24 June, 8, 12 Dec.

There are several local artists working in Comalapa; no studios, so best to ask where you can see their work (Artexco cooperative, *Figura Antigua*). There is a *pensión* here, G.

Six km. beyond Zaragoza the road divides. The southern branch, the old Pan-American Highway, goes through Patzicía and Patzún to Lake Atitlán (see below), then N to Los Encuentros. The northern branch, the new Pan-American Highway, much faster, goes past Tecpán and over the Chichoy pass, also to Los Encuentros. From Los Encuentros there is only the one road W to San Cristóbal Totonicapán, where the new road swings NW through El Tapón and La Mesilla to Ciudad Cuauhtémoc, the Mexican border settlement; and the old route goes W through Quezaltenango and San Marcos to Tapachula, in Mexico.

The northern road to Los Encuentros: from the fork the Pan-American Highway runs 19 km. to near **Tecpán**, which is slightly off the road at 2,287 metres. It has a particularly fine church: silver altars, carved wooden pillars, odd images, a wonderful ceiling which was severely damaged by the 1976 earthquake. The church is being slowly restored: the ceiling is missing and much of its adornment is either not in evidence, or moved to a church next door. The women wear most striking costumes. Market: Thursdays. *Fiestas*: 3 May (Santa Cruz), 1-8 October, and 8 December. *Hotel Iximché; Restaurant de la Montaña*, 1 km after the road to Tecpán; the owner of *Zapatería La Mejor* has a guest house, G. Also *Restaurante Katok*, on the highway, good *parrillados*, but expensive. Buses from Guatemala City (Zona 4 terminal), 2¼ hrs., every hour; easy daytrip from Panajachel.

Near Tecpán are the very important Mayan ruins of **Iximché**, once capital and court of the Cakchiqueles, 5 km. of unpaved road from Tecpán, open 0900-1600 (admission US$0.20). Iximché was the first capital of Guatemala after its conquest by the Spaniards; followed in turn by Ciudad Vieja, Antigua and Guatemala City. There is a museum at the site.

Beyond Tecpán the road swings up a spectacular 400 metres to the summit of the Chichoy pass. The pass is often covered in fog or rain but on clear days there are striking views. Some 14 km. from Tecpán, at km. 101, is the *Café Chichoy*, with cheap accommodation (rec.); 58 km. from the fork is Los Encuentros (and the road to Chichicastenango) and 3 km. further on the new northern road joins the old southern one from Sololá. 12 km. before Los Encuentros is a new road to Godínez (see below); buses may now run along it, but it's worth taking if in a car; the paved road down to the lake has many small potholes.

Sololá, at 2,113 metres, 11 km. from the junction, has superb views across Lake Atitlán. Population 4,000. Fine Tuesday and Friday markets, to which many of the Indians go. Good selection of used *huipiles*. Note costumes of men. Great *fiesta* around 15 August; good place to photograph Indians (discretely). Hot shower 500 metres from market on Panajachel road, behind Texaco station, US$0.18.

Tightly woven woollen bags are sold here: far superior to the usual type of tourist bags. Prices are high because of nearness of tourist centres of Panajachel and Chichicastenango.

Hotels *Tzoloj-yá*, near main square, F, hot shower, good, comfortable; *Letona*, G, communal, cheap food, not clean, outdoor washing facilities, not rec.; *Posada Santa Elena*, G; *Pensión Paty*, on road to Panajachel, very basic, G. Also good cheap restaurant, *Santa Rosa; Flipper* store near market sells food all day.

Bus to Chichicastenango US$0.35, 2 hrs. Bus to Panajachel, US$0.25, or 1½-2 hour walk; to Chimaltenango, US$1. Colectivo to Los Encuentros, US$0.15.

From Sololá the old Pan-American Highway drops 550 metres in 8 km. to Panajachel: grand views on the way. Take the bus up (US$0.25, they stop early in the evening), but quite easy to walk down (the views are superb), either direct by the road or via San Jorge La Laguna. The walk is highly recommended (you also miss the unnerving bus ride down!). You can return to Panajachel from San Jorge along the lake, if you take the southern road from the plaza, go through the woods and down to the flats. Ask permission at the house on the lake shore to follow the trail; a 3-hour walk.

The southern road from Zaragoza to Los Encuentros (much more difficult than the northern, with a very poor surface, steep hills and hairpin bends, bus, US$0.35) goes through **Patzicía**, a small Indian village founded 1545 (no accommodation). Market on Wed. and Sat. *Fiesta* for the patron, Santiago, on 23-26 July. The famous church, which had a fine altar and beautiful silver, was destroyed by the 1976 earthquake; some of the silver is now in the temporary church. Fourteen km. beyond is the small town of **Patzún**; its famous church, dating from 1570, was severely damaged; it is still standing, but is not open to the public. Sun. market, which is famous for the silk (and wool) embroidered napkins worn by the women to church, and for woven *fajas* and striped red cotton cloth. *Fiesta*: 17-21 May (San Bernardino). Lodgings at the tobacco shop, G, or near market in unnamed *pensión*.

Road (very bad, with many robberies) descends, then climbs to Godínez, 19 km. W of Patzún, where there is a good place for meals (no bus Patzún-Godínez). A branch road runs S to village of San Lucas Tolimán and continues to Santiago Atitlán; both can be reached by a lake boat from Panajachel. The high plateau, with vast wheat and maize fields, now breaks off suddenly as though pared by a knife. From a viewpoint here, there is an incomparable view of Lake Atitlán, 600 metres below; beyond it rise three 3,000-metre-high volcano cones, Tolimán, Atitlán and San Pedro, to the W. The very picturesque village of San Antonio Palopó is right underneath you, on slopes leading to the water. It is about 12 km. from the viewpoint to Panajachel. For the first 6 km. you are close to the rim of the old crater and at the point where the road plunges down to the lakeside is **San Andrés Semetebaj** with a beautiful ruined early 17th century church. Market on Tuesdays. The road from Panajachel to Patzún "is really adventurous, but fascinating on a bike." (Matthias Müller, Berlin).

Occasional guerrilla activity and armed robbery have been reported in this area.

Lake Atitlán, 147 km. from the capital via the northern road and Los Encuentros, 116 km. via the southern road and Patzún, and 1,562 metres above sea-level, about 7-10 km. across and 18 km. long, is one of the most beautiful and colourful lakes in the world. It changes colour constantly—lapis lazuli, emerald, azure—and is shut in by purple mountains and olive green hills. Over a dozen villages on its shores, some named after the Apostles, house three tribes with distinct languages, costumes and cultures. The lake was the only place in the world where the *poc*, a large flightless water grebe, could be seen (**see page** 389). Beware of robbers (armed) at the lake.

Six hotels are actually on the lakeshore: *Atitlán, Visión Azul, Monterrey, Del Lago, Playa Linda* and *Tzanjuyu*. Apart from them, visitors to the lake stay at or near **Panajachel**, 1 km. from the lake; the main attraction is the scenery. (Visitors planning to travel round the lake should be warned that the only bank is here.) The town is a popular tourist resort and inhabited by many *gringos* ("Gringotenango"). The main tourist season is the second half of November to February. There is water-skiing (at weekends), private boating (kayaks for hire) and swimming in fresh clear water (but the beach is dirty). Good market on Sun. mornings, especially for embroidery; you are expected to bargain (despite the amount of tourism, prices are reasonable). Visit La Galería (near *Rancho Grande Hotel*), where Nan Cuz, an Indian painter, sells her pictures which evoke the spirit of village life. The village church, originally built in 1567, was restored, only to be badly damaged by the 1976 earthquake. *Fiesta*: 2-6 Oct.

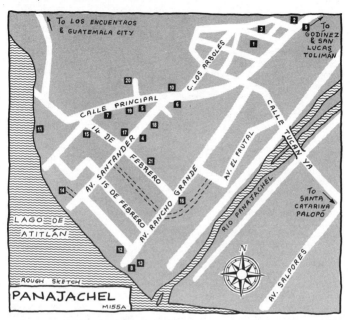

Panajachel: Key to map

1. Church; 2. Market; 3. Post Office; 4. Guatel; 5. Tourist Office; 6. Bank; 7. Texaco Station; 8. Public beach, boats; 9. Main bus stop; 10. Bus stop; 11. *Hotel Tzanjuyu* and mail boat pier; 12. *Hotel del Lago*; 13. *Hotel Playa Linda*; 14. *Hotel Monterrey*; 15. *Cacique Inn*; 16. *Hotel Rancho Grande*; 17. *Hotel Regis*; 18. *Hospedaje Santander*; 19. *Fonda del Sol*; 20. *Rooms Santa Elena*; 21. *The Last Resort*.

WILL YOU HELP US?

We do all we can to get our facts right in **The Mexico & Central American Handbook.** Each chapter is thoroughly revised each year, but the territory covered is vast, and our eyes cannot be everywhere.

Your information may be far more up-to-date than ours. If your letter reaches us early enough in the year it will be used in the next edition, but write whenever you want to, for all your letters are used sooner or later.

 Thank you very much indeed for you help.

Hotels *Del Lago*, luxury hotel on lakeshore, A, pool, rec.; *Atitlán*, A (but check beforehand), 3 meals US$10 (breakfast is very good, less choice at other 2 meals), 1 km. W of centre on lake, excellent; *Tzanjuyu*, C, 3 meals US$10, a bit disappointing, balconies and private beach; *Monterrey*, E, discounts for longer stay, 3 meals US$9, restaurant fair; *El Aguacatal*, near *Hotel del Lago*, has bungalows, C, for 4, T 0621482; *Turicentro Los Geranios*, also near *Hotel del Lago*, has fully-equipped new bungalows which sleep 6, B, on Sat. and Sun., C, on other days, outdoor pool; *Bungalows Guayacán*, beautifully located among coffee bushes 700 metres from centre on road to Santa Catarina Palopó, D; *Rancho Grande*, cottages in charming setting, 4 blocks from beach, popular for long stay, good, simple food, D, includes breakfast, rec.; *Cacique Inn*, C (full board available), swimming pool, garden, English spoken, good food, rec.; *Regis*, D, well-kept house, variable rooms, also apartments, garden, friendly, rec.; *Primavera*, D, new, clean, a bit overpriced, expensive restaurant serves German food; *Playa Linda*, above public beach, D, slow service in restaurant; *Visión Azul*, near *Hotel Atitlán*, D, friendly staff, good meals but grubby pool, hot water in evenings; *Mini Motel Riva Bella*, bungalows, E, with bath, rec.; *Galindo*, on main street, D, with bath, dirty, thin walls, check for bedbugs, nice garden and good set meal, US$3.50; *Fonda del Sol*, on main street, E, with bath, occasional hot water, or F without, noisy but comfortable; *Mayan Palace*, on main street, E, with shower, clean; *Maya Kanek*, E, good, clean, friendly; *Del Camino*, next to Texaco, E with bath, clean, comfortable; *Cabaña Country Club*, Av. Rancho Grande, G, clean; *Del Viajero*, on main street, F, basic; *Viajero Annex*, F, camping US$0.75 p.p.; *Panajachel*, near market, simple, F, hot water rarely, clean, lots of other travellers; *Rooms Santa Elena* (N of main road), G, with bedding, beds uncomfortable, cheaper without, all facilities charged extra, friendly, clean, rec.; has annex (off Guatel road) which is OK; 2nd-hand English books on sale. There are a number of cheap *pensiones* on same road to the beach as Guatel building, including *Santander*, F, clean, friendly, lovely garden, rec.; *Villa Martita*, F, friendly, rec.; *Hospedaje Ramos*, close to lake shore, F, run by an Indian family, friendly, safe, but going downhill, not helped by loud music from nearby cafés; nearby *Bungalows El Rosario*, E, safe, clean, run by Indian family, hot water 0700-1100; *Hospedaje García*, same street as *Last Resort*, G p.p., reasonable; opp. *Galería*, G, clean, hot showers extra; *Hospedaje Zulema*, near *Hotel del Lago*, F, clean, hot showers, rec.; *Hospedaje Mi Chosita*, just beyond *Last Resort*, F, clean, friendly, family atmosphere; *Pensión Londres*, G, basic, friendly owner; *Mario's Rooms*, F, T 621313, with garden, clean, hard beds (try to pick your room), laundry, hot showers US$0.20 (sheets US$0.35, good breakfast US$0.55), *Vista Hermosa*, on road to *Monterrey*, basic, but very pleasant family, hot showers, G. For long stay, ask around for houses to rent; available at all prices from US$10-75 a month, but almost impossible to find in November and December. Break ins and robberies of tourist houses are not uncommon. The water supply is generally bad, with water usually only available 0630-1100.

Camping No problem, but campsites (US$0.50 p.p.) are dirty. Camping on the lakeshore is currently allowed in a designated area.

Restaurants Many of the higher priced hotels have restaurants open to the public, as does *Fonda del Sol* (large varied menu, reasonable prices, rec.). *Casa Blanca* on main street, a bit expensive, but good, German owned; next door is *La Fontana*, where main streets meet, good, Italian, but expensive. *The Last Resort*, on left after Guatel building, "gringo bar", good breakfast, bar (open 1800). *El Patio*, same street as Guatel, good food, very good breakfast, often crowded; *Blue Bird*, on side street to market, excellent, specials rec. US$0.75, good yoghurt and fruit salad (closed Thursdays); *Doña Rosita*, next door, simple but good. *El Cisne*, opposite *Hotel del Lago*, good cheap set meals; also nearby *Tres Hermanas*, good pies, slow service. *Brisas del Lago*, good meals at reasonable prices, on lake shore; a number of others on beach front, e.g. *El Pescador* for fish (good bass). *El Paraíso*, large meals, inc. vegetarian, in lane, off main street to lake. *Atitlán Fiesta* near market. On the street to the market are a number of vegetarian restaurants: *Comedor Hsieh*, nearest to market, great variety of dishes inc. vegetarian, rec.; *Casa de Pays* (pie shop, also known as *La Zanahoria*), good food, good value, clean and friendly (shows English language videos in evening US$0.60). *El Unico Deli*, coffee shop, dear, but nice food including bagels and cream cheese, good coffee; *Xocomil*, good scene, also vegetarian food, pasta cheap and good; *Canapé Tearoom*, speciality smoked chicken. *Copo's*, opposite Texaco station, has ice-cream. Go to *Panadería San Martín* at 1500 for fresh brown and banana bread; *Pizza Hot*, US run, excellent pizzas and banana pie, newspapers to read; pizzas also at *Yax Che*. On Guatel road: *Villa Martita*, rec., good ice cream, and *Ranchón Típico Atitlán*. *El Bistro*, Swiss-owned, "overpriced, bland food", near beach on same road as Guatel; *Restaurant Sicodélico*, next to *Rooms Santander*, is pleasant and good value (good yoghurt and *crêpes*); next door is *Amigos*, US-run, very good. The yoghurt dishes at *Mario's* restaurant are highly rec., but slow service, his crêpes filled with yoghurt and fruit are rec. *Jebel* (same management as *Blue Bird*), good yoghurt, avocado omelette, rec. *Munchies*, good snacks, chocolates and cakes.

Entertainment *Posada del Pintor*, bar and restaurant, beer and steaks, owners are a Swiss couple; *Shell Station Bar*, on site of old gas station, often has live music and dancing, and films on TV *Past Ten* discotheque, open till 0400, Q3 entry. Opp. *Hotel del Lago*, *Circus Bar*, good live music; *The Last Resort*, bar and restaurant, popular, table tennis, foreign magazines; next door, *Los Techos*, above *Cakchiquel* restaurant, English language films on video twice daily. *Video Bar*, on the Guatel road, has US cable TV, US news nightly at 1800, and video films, entry US$1.

Shops Many small stores selling local handicrafts including *Tomás Xon*, on Guatel road, and *Mundo Real* which has jewellery and authentic weaving (they also buy, sell and swap used books), and *Caramba*, both on main street. Also on road to San Andrés Semetebaj is the *Idol's House*, an antique shop where you must bargain. (Indians sell their wares cheaply on the lakeside.)

Bicycle Hire US$2-3 a day.

Health There are good clinics at Santiago Atitlán and San Lucas Tolimán, which specialize in treating dysentery. Amoebic dysentery and hepatitis are less common than in the past. Treatment free, so a donation is appropriate. Fleas endemic. Take care to treat bites in case of infection.

Exchange Bank open Mon.-Thurs. 0900-1500. Fri. to 1530. Exchange after 1000. Prefers to change smaller denomination travellers' cheques (if at all). Better rates at Toro Pinto exchange office (0900-1800) opp. Texaco station. The barber's shop near the bank will change travellers' cheques.

Post Office Will not arrange for parcels to be sent, or received, from abroad.

Tourist Office Open Wed.- Sun., 0800-1200 and 1400-1800, Mon. 0800-1200, Tues. closed; has maps. (Sells flight tickets for Flores.)

Bus Rebuli, first class to Guatemala City, 3 hrs. US$1.50; several to the capital daily. There are direct buses to Los Encuentros on the Pan-American Highway (US$0.40). To Chichicastenango direct, supposedly 3 before 0900 and on Sun. at 0730 (US$1), but more reliable to go to Los Encuentros, where you can change for other buses to Guatemala City, Chichicastenango, or Quezaltenango. Direct bus to Quezaltenango 0600. There are direct buses to Cuatro Caminos, US$0.50 (**see page 395**) from 0530, for connections to Totonicapán, Quezaltenango, Huehuetenango, etc. (No buses from Los Encuentros to Panajachel after 1830). Bus to Chimaltenango (for Antigua), US$1.20. Tourist bus to Antigua, Tues., Thur.,

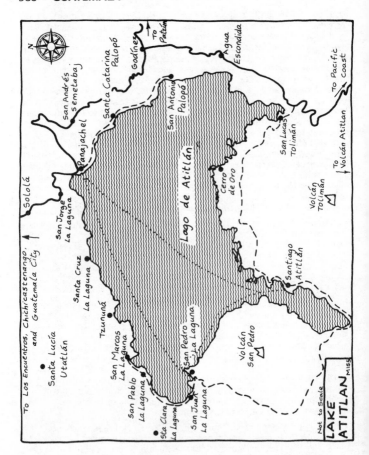

WILL YOU HELP US?

We do all we can to get our facts right in **The Mexico & Central American Handbook.** Each chapter is thoroughly revised each year, but the territory covered is vast, and our eyes cannot be everywhere.

Your information may be far more up-to-date than ours. If your letter reaches us early enough in the year it will be used in the next edition, but write whenever you want to, for all your letters are used sooner or later.

 Thank you very much indeed for you help.

Sun. 1200, US$10. Bus to Sololá, US$0.25. Best to wait for buses by the market, not by the Guatel road to the lake.

Excursions To **Santiago Atitlán** by mail boat from the pier at the *Hotel Tzanjuyu* at 0845 and 1135 daily (check at hotel for times of services), US$1.25 single (for which you may have to compete), US$2 return, 1-1½ hrs., back to Panajachel at 1200 and 1700. This service is not very reliable. From the beach, many between 0900-0930, returning between 1200 and 1700, US$1 single. By bus to San Lucas Tolimán, and from there by bus, US$0.65. The road is very rough for private cars after San Lucas. The women wear fine costumes and the men wear striped, half-length embroidered trousers. There is an Artexco cooperative: *Flor del Lago*. There is a daily market, best on Friday, *Fiesta*: 5 June and 25 July. The Franciscan church dates back to 1568. Nearby were the ruins of the fortified Tzutuhil capital on the Cerro de Chuitinamit (nothing now to see). *Pensión Rosita*, near the church, F, dirty. *Hospedaje Chi-Nim-Ya*, F, problematic water supply (good café opposite). Houses can be rented, but be extremely careful to check for, and protect against, scorpions and poisonous spiders in the wooden frames. *Santa Rita* restaurant good and cheap. Bus to Guatemala City, US$1.50 (5 a day, first at 0300). Buses back to Panajachel at 0600, 2 hrs. 16 km. rough dirt road from San Lucas Tolimán (OK for private cars in dry season) then paved to Panajachel via Godínez.

2 km. N of Santiago Atitlán is the **Parque Nacional Atitlán** which had a small reserve for the *poc*, the Atitlán grebe. According to the British Royal Society for the Protection of Birds, the *poc* is now extinct because of replacement by, or hybridization with, the pied-billed grebe, which it closely resembled. Safe camping, take food and water; the guards may put you up in their cabin. Also in the reserve is a tame *pavo del cacho* (a big black bird with a red horn on its head). To get there, go by canoe from Santiago (US$0.65), with the reserve workers, or on foot, about ½ hr. on the San Lucas Tolimán road, but ask directions.

At **San Lucas Tolimán**, on the southern tip of the lake, there is cheap accommodation at *Pensión Las Conchitas*, G p.p. in 4-bedded rooms (good vegetarian food and yoghurt, parking), and *Hospedaje El Exito*, G, all rooms single, good value, clean. *Pensión Central*, E with private bath, F without, hot water, meals US$1, opened in 1989; *Cafetería Santa Ana*, shop and café, will put you up for Q3, clean. Restaurants: *Comedor Victoria*, Guatemalan food; *Café Tolimán*, home made yoghurt and local dishes, rec.; *Restaurant El Buen Gusto*, varied menu. Motor boats can be hired for US$9.25 per hour. There is a market on Tues., Fri., and Sun. From San Lucas the cones of Atitlán, 3,535 metres, and Tolimán, 3,158 metres, can be climbed. Warm clothing and sleeping gear are essential, as the climb takes 2 days (less if you are very fit); maps are not available at present, ask in hotels for advice on routes and safety vis à vis guerrilla activity. Bus to San Lucas from Panajachel at 0630 and 1600 daily, 1 hr., US$0.50. A bus leaves San Lucas to Panajachel, 0700 and 1800; to Santiago, hourly between 0900 and 1800, 1 hr., returning hourly between 0300 and 1300. Bus San Lucas to Quezaltenango, US$1.50, 0430 and 0600. Between Santiago and San Lucas is Cerro de Oro, a small village on the lake.

Ferries leave from *Hotel Tzanjuyu* at Panajachel for **San Pedro La Laguna**, daily at 0400, Tues., Fri. and Sun. at 1500, returning at 0630 on Mon., Wed., Sat., and at 1630 daily (US$0.75 one way). There is a ferry from Santiago to San Pedro at 1200 and 1700 (45 mins., US$0.75) locals pay less (ferry to Santiago at 0700 and 0800). N.B. There are two landing stages in San Pedro. 0300 bus to Guatemala City, US$1.50, 7 hrs. San Pedro is at the foot of the San Pedro volcano, which can be climbed in 4-5 hrs., 3 hrs. down, not difficult except for route finding through the coffee plantations and heavy cover. A guide is therefore advisable, Florencio was recommended in 1988 by the *Pensión Chuazanahi*, cost Q15. Go early for the view, because after 1000 the top is usually smothered in cloud.Canoes are made here (hire, US$0.50 a day) and a visit to the rug-making cooperative on the beach is of interest. Backstrap weaving is taught at some places, about US$0.50 per day. Try Rosa Cruz, past the "Colonel's Place", turn right up the hill. Market days Thurs. and Sun. (better). Dugouts can be hired for US$0.50 per day.

There are many *pensiones*, including two on the public beach, at about US$0.50. (*Pensión Balneario*, G, good, *Pensión Chuazanahi*, G (known as the Colonel's Place), bedding US$0.50 p.p., boating and swimming, you can sling your hammock for US$1, reasonable meals, friendly staff; next door is *Tikaal*, G, wooden cabins; rooms also at the *Blue House* down road beside *Chuazanahi*, G; *Johanna*, near landing stage for Panajachel mail boat, G, nice rooms without bath, cold water only, friendly, also *cafetería*; all are basic; houses can be rented on a weekly basis for US$2.50). Good food is available at *Restaurant Chez Michel*, for US$0.75 (some French spoken), good, cheap but slow, turn right from landing stage along beach road, past *Pensión Chuazanahi*; *La Carolina*; good food but slow service at *Comedor Ranchón*, opp. **Chuazanahi**. Buy banana bread from the *Panadería El Buen Gusto*, near centre of town; *Restaurant Rosalinda* reported very good; *Tulipán* has wide variety and vegetarian dishes. Village café, meals US$0.30.

From San Pablo (on the way to San Pedro) you can walk to San Marcos and Santa Cruz (a difficult track), where there is a 16th century church, you can get beautiful views of the lake and volcanoes in the early morning light. Sisal bags and hammocks are made at San Pablo. If hiking around the lake, the only hotel between San Pedro and Panajachel is the bungalow accommodation of Wolfgang Kallab and Annegret Kallab-Welzel in Santa Cruz, E (Aptdo. Postal 39, Panajachel), with small restaurant, excellent food, very friendly, highly rec. (they sell weavings from the Ixil Triangle); boat to Panajachel about 1300, or 2½ hrs.' walk.

Warning Not a safe area for women to go walking alone; rape is not uncommon. Beware of theft, including of clothes hanging out to dry, in the Lake Atitlán area. Also beware of overcharging on private boats crossing the lake: practices include doubling the price half-way across and if you don't agree, out you get.

Santa Catarina Palopó is within walking distance of Panajachel (about 2 hrs., path goes through many tiny farms, very friendly and pleasant; truck US$0.12). The town has an attractive adobe church. Reed mats are made here, and you can buy *huipiles* (beautiful, green, blue and yellow) and men's shirts. Must bargain for articles. New hotel, *Villa Catarina*, A, nice setting. Houses can be rented here. From Santa Catarina you can walk to the Mirador of Godínez for views, but the path is very steeply uphill for quite a while.

San Antonio Palopó (3 km. beyond Santa Catarina), 1 hr. walk, has another splendid church; it lies at the head of the lake in an amphitheatre formed by the mountains behind. The village is noted for the costumes and headdresses of the men, and *huipiles* and shirts are cheaper than in Santa Catarina. You will be charged for photography—whether you take pictures or not. Fiesta: June 14. The Artexco cooperative is called by the name of the village. *Hotel Casa de don Félix* (or *Casa del Lago*), superb views and good bathing, E, only a few rooms but gradually being expanded, good restaurant; you can stay in private houses (e.g. Don Tiedera nr. the Post Office) or rent rooms (take sleeping bag). A good hike is to take the bus from Panajachel to Godínez, walk down from there to San Antonio Palopó (1 hr.) and then along the new road back to Panajachel via Santa Catarina Palopó (3 hrs.).

You can walk on round the lake from San Antonio, but you must eventually climb up to the road at Agua Escondida then back down again to within 2 km. of San Lucas Tolimán.

Los Encuentros The old and new Pan-American Highways rejoin 11 km. from Sololá. 3 km. E is Los Encuentros, the junction of the Pan-American Highway and the road 18 km. NE to Chichicastenango. Altitude 2,579 metres. (Very poor accommodation available, G, if you miss a bus connection, easy to do as they are all full.)

Chichicastenango (also known as Santo Tomás) is the hub of the Maya-Quiché highlands, and is very popular with tourists. Altitude 2,071 metres, and nights cold. About 1,000 *ladinos* in the town, but 20,000 Indians live in the hills nearby and flood the town, almost empty on other days, for the Thursday and Sunday markets. The town is built around a large square plaza of 180 metres a side, with two churches facing one another: Santo Tomás parish church and Calvario. Santo Tomás is now open again to visitors, although restoration work is still going on; photography is not allowed, and visitors are asked to be discreet and enter by a side door. Groups burn incense and light candles on steps and platform before entering. Inside, from door to high altar, stretch rows of glimmering candles, Indians kneeling beside them. Later they offer copal candles and flower-petals to the "Idolo", a black image of Pascual Abaj, a Maya god, on a hilltop 1½ km. SW of the plaza (beware of armed robbery on the way), boys act as guides for US$1; be very respectful at the ceremony and do not take photographs. Next to the church are the cloisters of the Dominican monastery (1542) where the famous Popol Vuh manuscript of Maya mythology was found and translated into Spanish in 1690; Father Rossbach's jade collection can be seen in the municipal museum on the main square and is well worth a visit (open 0800-1200, closed Mon.), and so is the house of a mask-maker on the way up to the "Idolo", who rents masks and costumes to the dancers and will show visitors the path to the idol. This is a little difficult to find even then, and clear instructions should be obtained before setting out.

Derivation of town's name: *chichicaste*—a prickly purple plant like a nettle, which grows profusely—and *tenango*, place of. The town itself is charming: winding streets of white houses roofed with bright red tiles wandering over a little knoll in the centre of a cup-shaped valley surrounded by high mountains. Fine views from every street corner. The costumes are particularly splendid: the men's is a short-waisted embroidered jacket and knee breeches of black cloth, a gay woven sash and an embroidered kerchief round the head. The cost of this outfit, over US$200, means that fewer and fewer men are in fact wearing it. Women wear *huipiles* with red embroidery against black or brown and skirts with dark blue stripes. The Sun. market is more colourful than the one on Thurs.: more Indians, brighter costumes and dancing to marimba bands, but it certainly becomes very touristy after the buses arrive from Guatemala City (bargains may be had after 1530 when the tourist buses depart). In fact the markets begin, and are better, on the previous p.m. You must bargain hard. Good value handicrafts at Cooperativo Santo Tomás, opp. *Mayan Inn* on market place.

Fiestas Santo Tomás, 17-21 December: processions, dances, marimba music (well worth a visit—very crowded); Holy Week; 1 November; 20 January; 19 March; 24 June (shepherds). There is also a *fiesta* at the end of May.

Hotels *Mayan Inn*, B, seen better days, breakfast, US$2, bar, marimba music, laundry service; *Santo Tomás*, A with beautiful colonial furnishings (a museum in itself), often full at weekends, very good, friendly service, helpful owner (Sr. Magermans), good restaurant (set meals US$6) and bar, marimba music p.m., same day laundry, nice patio, meals US$2.50; nearby *El Salvador*, 10 C. 4-47, 2 blocks from main square, F with sheets and bath (G without), friendly, noisy; *Maya Lodge*, 6 C. 4-08, E with bath and up, with breakfast, mixed reports; *Martita*, F, with bath and sheets (G without either); *Pensión Chigüilá*, 5 Av. 5-24, clean, good, D, with bath and breakfast, F without, meals another US$3.85 (some rooms have fireplaces, wood costs US$0.90 a day extra), rec. *Pensión-Restaurant Katokok*, F, without sheets, serves good meals; *Posada San Antonio*, F (less without sheets), good but basic. *Pensión Girón*, F (G without sheets), opp. vegetable market, good, ample parking. Local boys will show you other cheap lodgings, G.

Restaurants   At hotels; *Tapena*, 5 Av. 5-21, clean, a bit expensive; *Las Marimbitas; El Samaritano* (reasonable). Good café opposite *Pensión Chigüilá*, meal for US$3. *El Torito*, under the *Pensión Girón*, good; *Eben Ezer*, good breakfasts; *Txiquan Tinamil*, 5 Av. y 6 C., near *Pensión Chigüilá*, good. *Cantina Claveles*, US$0.35 for a good meal. There is a bakery attached.

Exchange   Banks do not change money at holiday times; *Mayan Inn* will exchange cash, *Santo Tomás* cheques and cash at those times.

Buses   Rutas Lima bus leaves Guatemala City four times daily for Quezaltenango, connecting at Los Encuentros for Panajachel (US$0.35) and Chichicastenango. The slower Reyna de Utatlán bus from the capital, 4 hrs. (Zona 4 Terminal) costs only US$1.50, several daily. For return, take local bus (US$0.35) to Los Encuentros where you can pick up another for the capital. One direct bus to Panajachel (2 hrs.) on Sun. at 1330 from *Hotel Santo Tomás*, US$1, and others in week (supposedly—better go to Los Encuentros). For Antigua, change at Chimaltenango until 1730, after that at San Lucas Sacatepéquez until 2000 (or taxi from Chimaltenango, US$5). Beware of overcharging on buses in the Panajachel/Chichicastenango area. To Huehuetenango, via Los Encuentros, US$1.75. 2 weekly buses Chichicastenango-Nebaj, US$1, may have to change at Sacapulas, otherwise take a bus to Quiché and change there.

The Quiché Region (see note on page 338.) 19 km. N by road from Chichicastenango is Santa Cruz del **Quiché**, a quaint town at 2,000 metres, colourful market on Sun. and Thurs. There are few tourists here and prices are consequently reasonable. Good selection of local cloth. Quiché's speciality is palm hats, which are made and worn in the area, best quality and prices from shop facing the bus terminal. Population 7,750. Remains 3 km. away of palaces of former Quiché capital, Gumarcaj, sometimes spelt Kumarkaah and known also as Utatlán, destroyed by Spaniards; the ruins consist of adobe mounds, their chief attraction being the setting. They can be reached on foot (¾-hr. walk W along 10 Calle from bus station) open 0700-1800, entry US$0.20. There are two subterranean burial chambers (take a torch) still used by the Indians for worship; small but interesting museum at the entrance. *Fiestas*: about 14-20 August (but varies around Assumption), 3 May. Serious earthquake damage.

Hotels   are reluctant to open doors late at night. *San Pascual*, 7 C. 0-43, F, with usually hot showers, clean, quiet, locked parking; *Hospedaje Hermano Pedro*, F, friendly, clean, private shower, close to bus terminal so arrive early; *Posada Calle Real*, 2 Av. 7-36, parking, F, clean, friendly, rec.; *Pensión Santa Clara*, G, hot water, plus US$0.50 for good meals; *Centroamérica*, G without bath, very basic; *Tropical*, 1 Av. 9 C., G. Basic accommodation near bus terminal.

Restaurants *Lago Azul*, 2 Av. 6-45, quite good, pricey; *Musicafé* and one next to it, with bookshop, reasonable; most are dirty.

Thermal baths at Pachitac, 4 km. away, and beside the market building.

Electric Current 220 volts.

Bicycle Hire 4 Av. y 5C., Zona 1 or 4 Av. y 2 C., Zona 5.

Cinema 3 Av. y 6 C.

Exchange Banco de Guatemala, 3 C. y 2 Av.

Post Office on 3 C., Zona 5; **Guatel**, on 1 Av. Zona 5.

Buses Terminal at 10 C. y 1 Av. Reyna de Utatlán from Guatemala City (US$1.60). ½ hr. from Chichicastenango, US$0.30, every ½ hr. from *Pensión Chigüilá*. To Nebaj, 2 or 3 a day between 0800 and 1000, US$1.25, 5 hrs.; a rough but breathtaking trip (may leave early if full). At 1000, 1130 and 1330 to Uspantán, 5 hrs., US$1.25. Bus to Joyabaj, 0930 daily, US$0.50, 1½ hrs. 0300 bus Uspantán to Cobán and San Pedro Carchá, about 5 hrs., the best part is done in darkness. If going to Momostenango for the market, take the bus at 0400 as the 0800 one arrives too late (6 hr. journey).

There is a paved road E from Quiché to (8 km.) Santo Tomás Chiche, a picturesque village with a fine rarely-visited Indian Sat. market (*fiesta*, 21-28 December). Buses and vans (US$0.25) run from Quiché. (There is also a road to this village from Chichicastenango. Although it is a short-cut, it is rough and should be attempted in dry weather only, and even then only in a sturdy vehicle.)

On 32 km. from Chiche is **Zacualpa**, where beautiful woollen bags are woven. There is an unnamed *pensión* near the square; on the square itself is a private house which has cheap rooms and meals. (Mosquito coils are a must.) Market: Sun., Thurs. Church with remarkably fine façade. Two shops opposite each other on the road into town sell weavings, good prices. On another 11 km. is **Joyabaj**, where women weave fascinating *huipiles*; there is nowhere to stay, but the mayor may have some ideas. This was a stopping place on the old route from Mexico to Antigua. During *fiesta* week (the second in August) Joyabaj has a *palo volador*—two men dangle from a 20-metre pole while the ropes they are attached to unravel to the ground. The villages of San Pedro and San Juan Sacatepéquez (**see page** 358) can be reached from Joyabaj by a dry-season road suitable only for strong vehicles. The scenery en route is spectacular (Joyita bus, Guatemala City 3-4 Av. 7-9 C. Zona 4, to Joyabaj, US$1.50).

A road goes N from Quiché, 48 km., to **Sacapulas**, 1,220 metres, at the foot of the Cuchumatanes mountains, highest in the country. Bus from Quiché, at 0930, very crowded, US$1, 3 hrs. for rough journey; 6 buses to Quiché, but all early morning. Bus to Huehuetenango via Aguacatán (see below), at 0500, 4½ hrs, road can be closed in rainy season. Remains of bridge over Río Negro built by Las Casas. Primitive salt extraction. Market under large ceiba trees on Thursday and Sunday. The only *pensión* is *Comedor Gloris* near the bridge (G), which is a basic, cheap flea circus, with poor meals, US$0.65, best avoided; *Comedor Bartolomé* nearby, better. British travellers have been made very welcome at *Comedor Central* near the market. Colonial church with surprising treasures inside, built 1554, and there are communal hot springs.

The road E to Cobán from Sacapulas is one of the most beautiful, if rough, mountain roads in all Guatemala, with magnificent scenery in the narrow valleys. Truck to Cobán, 5 daily a.m., US$1.25, 5 hrs. There is no direct bus to Cobán; instead, take one of the three Quiché-Uspantán buses (passing Sacapulas at about 1230, 1400, 1600) to Uspantán, *fiesta* 6-10 May (US$0.60) stay the night at the *Viajero* (3 blocks E of Plaza, basic, G, clean, pleasant), then take early morning bus (0300-0400, you can spend the night on the bus before it leaves) or hitch-hike to Cobán. (Truck Uspantán-San Cristóbal Verapaz, US$1.25.) Buses to Quiché at 0530, 0700, 1530. A morning bus starts at 0200 in Quiché, with a change at Cunén (*fiesta* 5-7 February, with dancing with silver deer masks, especially interesting at night; *Tienda y Comedor Rech Kanah María*, next to church, good; ask at *farmacia* where to stay). The road W of Sacapulas, through Aguacatán, to Huehuetenango is also beautiful, but tough on the driver who has little time to admire the scenery.

Branching off this road, about 13 km. N of Sacapulas, is a spectacular road to the village of Nebaj (see below). It is easy enough to get by truck to Nebaj (US$0.50) and there are buses from Quiché. It is not so easy to get to the other two villages of the Ixil Triangle, Chajul and Cotzal, though there is a bus to Chajul occasionally, and a small, basic *pensión* there, as well as a small *comedor*. Cotzal is now reported to have a *hospedaje*. There are no lodging or restaurant facilities in other small villages and it is very difficult to specify what transport facilities are in fact available in this area as trucks and the occasional pick-up or commercial van (probably the best bet—ask, especially in *Las Tres Hermanas*, Nebaj) are affected by road and weather conditions. For this reason, be prepared to have to spend the night in villages, even though there may be no accommodation. Chajul has a pilgrimage to Christ of Golgotha on the second Friday in Lent, beginning the Wednesday before (the image is escorted by "Romans" in blue police uniforms!) Also hunting with blowpipes. Chajul has market Tues. and Fri. In Cotzal it is possible to stay in the monastery, market Sat. A short walk up the river between Chajul and Nebaj, look for an attractive waterfall.

Nebaj has *Las Tres Hermanas*, G (friendly, full of character, but very basic), good food available for about US$0.50; *Las Gemelitas*, nice, basic, G without bath, rec.; *Little Corner Hostel*, near *Las Genelitas*; *Ixil Hotel*, just before entering town. Alternatively you can get a room in a private house for slightly less. *El Rincón*, G, woodstove provides hot water, dinner for US$1, rec.; from *Comedor de Olimpia Irene Moreno* next door, 1 block S from square, painted blue-green, good. There is also an army camp. *Huipiles* may be bought from María Santiago Chel (central market) or Juana Marcos Solís (Cantón Simacol), who gives weaving lessons from 1 day to 6 months. This village has a very good Sun. market (also on Thurs.). Nebaj has a *fiesta* on 15 August. There are magnificent walks from Nebaj along the river or in the surrounding hills. Although the weather is not very good at this altitude, the views of the Cuchumatanes mountains are spectacular. From Nebaj, bus to Sacapulas and Quiché 0100, 0300, and on Sun. 0800, 2½ hrs. to Sacapulas (US$0.60), a further 3 to Quiché (service times unreliable).

There is good walking West of Nebaj, and the roads are better in this direction than to Chajul and Cotzal since there a number of "model villages" resettled by the government. These include Acul (1½ hrs. walking up-and-down from Nebaj, starting 2 blocks from *Las Tres Hermanas*, or 2½ hrs. walking along the road); there is a good cheese farm 1 km. before the village; Tzalbal, 2½ hrs. walking; Salquil Grande, 26 km. NW of Nebaj (several hours walk); La Pista, where the airstrip is. None has accommodation or restaurants; there is no public transport, only pick-ups; ask for advice at *Las Tres Hermanas*, Agustín will act as guide. Las Violetas, 15 mins. walk from the centre of Nebaj, is a squatters' village where people who have come down from the mountains live when they arrive in Nebaj.

WESTERN GUATEMALA (6)

The stretch of Pan-American Highway between Los Encuentros and San Cristóbal Totonicapán runs past **Nahualá**, at 2,470 metres, a most interesting Indian village where *metates*, or stones on which maize is ground to make *tortillas*, are made. The inhabitants wear distinctive costumes, and are considered by other Indians to be somewhat hostile. Good church. Market on Thursdays and Sundays, at which finely embroidered cuffs and collars are sold, also very popular *huipiles*, but check the colours, many run. No accommodation except perhaps with Indian families at a small cost. *Fiesta* (Santa Catalina) on 25 November. Population 1,369.

There is another all-weather road a little to the N and 16 km. longer, from Los Encuentros to San Cristóbal Totonicapán. In 40 km. it reaches Totonicapán.

Totonicapán, 14½ km. E of Cuatro Caminos (see below), is the capital of its Department, at 2,500 metres. Population 52,000, almost all Indian. There are sulphur baths, but they are dirty and crowded. Market (mind out for pickpockets) considered by Guatemalans to be one of the cheapest, and certainly very colourful, on Tues. (small), and Sat. (the main market noted for ceramics and cloth-very good); annual fair 26-30 September; *fiestas* on 29 September and 25 July. The school of handicrafts in the centre of town is well worth a visit. *Chuimekená* cooperative is at 9 Av. between C. 1 and 2, Zona Palín. Frequent buses to Quezaltenango along a paved road (fine scenery), US$0.35, and there are buses from Quiché at 0400 and 0500 daily on a little-travelled but spectacular route (bus returns at 1030, US$1, 4 hrs). Bus to Los Encuentros, US$1.50.

Hotels On 4 Calle: *Pensión Rosario*, G, basic and dirty; *Hospedaje San Miguel*, 2 blocks from town square, F, clean, comfortable.

San Cristóbal Totonicapán, 1 km. from the **Cuatro Caminos** road junction (Pan-American Highway, with the roads to Quezaltenango, Totonicapán, Los Encuentros and Huehuetenango; *Hotel y Restaurant Reforma*, F, T 066-1438) has a huge church, built by Franciscan friars, of which the roof has recently been renovated. The silver lamps, altars and screens, all hand-hammered, and Venetian glass altars are worth seeing. Noted for textiles (and *huipiles* in particular) sold all over Guatemala; they are cheap here because the town is off the main tourist circuit. Also well known for ceramics. Market, Sunday, on the other side of the river from the church (only 2 blocks away), spreading along many streets. Annual fair, 20-26 July. Altitude 2,340 metres, population 3,186. Two hotels. Bus service to Quezaltenango.

Excursion Two km. W of the Cuatro Caminos junction a road runs N to San Francisco El Alto (3 km.) and Momostenango (19 km.). **San Francisco El Alto**, at 2,640 metres (also reached by a new paved road 5 km. W of Cuatro Caminos, at Km. 151), stands in the mountain cold, above the great valley in which lie Totonicapán, San Cristóbal and Quezaltenango. Church of metropolitan magnificence. Crammed market on Friday; Indians buying woollen blankets for resale throughout country, and fascinating cattle market. An excellent place for buying woven and embroidered textiles of good quality, but beware of pickpockets. Colourful New Year's Day celebrations. It is a pleasant walk from San Francisco down to the valley floor, then along the river to San Cristóbal. There is a bus from Totonicapán at 0800 on Fri. Bus from Quezaltenango on Fri., 20 mins., from market terminus, US$0.35 (go early if you wish to avoid staying overnight).

Hotel *Hospedaje Central San Francisco de Asís* on main street near market, G. *Vista Hermosa*, F, clean, hot water. Good *comedor* opposite.

Momostenango, at 2,220 metres, is the chief blanket-weaving centre. Indians can be seen beating the blankets on stones to shrink them. The Feast of the Uajxaquip Vats (pronounced "washakip") is celebrated by 30,000 Indians every 260 days by the ancient Mayan calendar. Frequent masked dances also. Momostenango means "place of the altars", and there are many on the outskirts but they are not worth looking for; there is, however, a hilltop image of a Mayan god, similar to the one outside Chichicastenango. There are said to be 300 medicine-men practising in the town; their insignia of office is a little bag containing beans and quartz crystals. Outside town are three sets of *riscos*: eroded columns of sandstone with embedded quartz particles, which are worth visiting. The most striking are the least accessible, in the hills to the N of the town. The town is quiet except on Wed. and Sun., the market days (the latter being larger, and interesting for weaving; also try Tienda Manuel del Jesús Agancel, 1 Av., 1-50, Zona 4; on non-market days, ask for weavers' houses). It has a spring-fed swimming pool; also a sulphur bath (5 in all) at Palo Grande, near town; the water is black, but worth experiencing. Bus service from Cuatro Caminos (US$0.35) and Quezaltenango, US$0.45 (mornings only).

Accommodation *Hospedaje Roxane*, G, bad; *Hospedaje Paclom*, G, basic, hot water, cheap meals, rec. *Comedor Tonia*, friendly, cheap.

At San Cristóbal the old and the new routes of the Pan-American Highway, which joined at Los Encuentros, part again. The new route to the Mexican border at Ciudad Cuauhtémoc (not a town, despite its name: just a few buildings) goes NW, by-passing Huehuetenango before entering the Selegua canyon stretch, known as El Tapón, now in very good condition. The old route, running W to Tapachula, in Mexico, reaches, 5 km. from San Cristóbal, the small *ladino* town of

Salcajá, where jaspé skirt material has been woven since 1861. Yarn is tied and dyed, then untied and warps stretched around telephone poles along the road or along the riverside. Many small home weavers will sell the lengths—5 or 8 *varas*—depending on whether the skirt is to be wrapped or pleated. The finest, of imported English yarn, cost US$40. The Artexco cooperative is *San Luis*, Calle Capitán Juan de León y Cardona, Zona 2. Market, Tues.; it is early, as in all country towns. The church of San Jacinto behind the market is 16th century and also worth a visit. (Good restaurant, *Cafesama*.) The taxi rate is US$2.50-3 per hour. Several minibuses a day from new commercial centre, 10 Av. and 8 C.

Quezaltenango (commonly known as Xela, pronounced "shella"), 14½ km. SW of Cuatro Caminos, over 100,000 people, is the most important city in western Guatemala. Altitude 2,335 metres, and climate decidedly cool and damp (particularly November to April, and there is no heating anywhere). Set among a group of high mountains and volcanoes, one of which, Santiaguito, the lower cone of Santa María (which can be easily climbed), destroyed the city in 1902 and is still active sometimes. A modern city, but with narrow colonial-looking streets and a magnificent plaza (between 11 and 12 Av. and 4 and 7 Calle). Especially interesting is the stately but quaint Municipal Theatre (14 Av. and 1 C.). There is a modern gothic-style church, the Sagrado Corazón, on the Parque Juárez near the market; other churches include San Juan de Dios on 14 Av. and La Transfiguración, from which there is a good view. The cathedral is modern with a 17th-century façade. A National Artisan Park has been built but is almost abandoned; there are a textile museum, warehouses, a craft school, showrooms, shop and restaurant. Festivals 30 March-5 April,12-18 Sept. and Holy Week (very interesting). There is a museum on the S side of the Parque Central, open Mon.-Fri., 0900-1700 (closed in December). A good centre for buses to all parts of the Indian highlands. Airfield. Tourist cards for Mexico can be obtained from the Mexican consulate at the *Pensión Bonifaz,* open 0800-1200 Mon.-Fri. (free for US and most European tourists, although French citizens need a visa which costs US$18). (All addresses given are in Zona 1, unless otherwise stated.)

Hotels At Easter, 12-18 September and Christmas, rooms need to be booked well in advance. *Pensión Bonifaz*, 4 C. 10-50, C (not inc. tax), 3 meals US$7, good restaurant (really not a *pensión* but an excellent hotel), clean, comfortable, US cable TV in all rooms, central heating, quiet, lounge with fireplace (good for taking afternoon coffee); *Del Campo*, at city limits (4 km.) at turn-off to Retalhuleu, on road to Cuatro Caminos, C, good meals (European and Chinese), rec.; *Los Alpes*, 4 km. from centre in Zona 3, Swiss-owned, private bath, rec.; *Centroamérica Inn*, Boulevard Minerva 14-09, Zona 3, D; *Modelo*, 14 Av. 'A', 2-31, D, good, with good restaurant; *Gran Hotel Americano*, 14 Av. 3-47, Zona 1, E/F, "tourists" pay more than "travellers"—(so look like a traveller!), good, friendly, restaurant, TV; *Kiktem-Ja*, 13 Av. 7-18, E, all with bath, rec.; *Radar 99*, 13 Av. near C. 4, F with bath and hot water, cheaper without bath, friendly; *Canadá*, 4 C. 12-22, F, helpful, reasonable value; *Casa del Viajero*, 10 Av. 9-17, F, with bath, hot water, limited but good restaurant, English-speaking manager, parking (US$0.30 extra), mixed reports; *Pensión El Quijote*, G, no hot water, clean, near *Casa del Viajero*; *Pensión Altense*, 9 C. and 9 Av., F with bath (cheaper without), new part rec., meals US$0.75, good, hot water extra; *Regia*, 9 Av., 10 C., G, clean, narrow rooms; *El Aguila*, 12 Av. and 3 C., F, friendly, hot

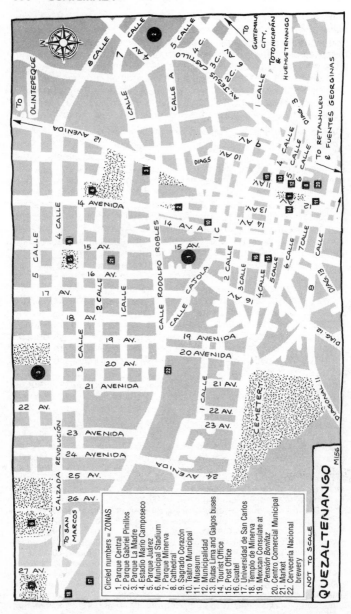

Circled numbers = ZONAS
1. Parque Central
2. Parque Gabriel Pinillos
3. Parque La Madre
4. Estadio Mario Camposeco
5. Parque Juárez
6. Municipal Stadium
7. Parque Minerva
8. Cathedral
9. Sagrado Corazón
10. Teatro Municipal
11. Museum
12. Municipalidad
13. Rutas Lima and Galgos buses
14. Tourist Office
15. Post Office
16. Guatel
17. Universidad de San Carlos
18. Templo de Minerva
19. Mexican Consulate at *Pensión Bonifaz*
20. Centro Comercial Municipal
21. Market
22. Cervecería Nacional brewery

QUEZALTENANGO

NOT TO SCALE

MI56

water extra; **Pensión Nicolás**, Av. 12, 3-16, very basic, no bath, G, parking; **Residencial**, nearby, F, good.

Restaurants *Bikini*, 10 C., behind municipal offices, Chinese restaurant next to **Hotel Canadá**; **Kopetin**, 1 block from **Hotel Canadá**, friendly, good, meat and seafood dishes; **Maruc**, near brewery, good but expensive; **Taberna de Don Rodrigo**, 14 Av. 2-42, hamburgers and beer, cakes and coffee; **Pizza Ricca**, 14 Av. y 3 C., good; **Café Marzia**, 14 Av. y 3 C., pleasant; **Delicadezas La Polonesa**, 14 Av. 'A' 4-71, snacks, cold meats, sausage, etc.; **Comidas Típicas** 9 C. and 9 Av., good local food, cheap, friendly; **Ut's Hua**, Av. 12 y C. 3, typical food, less good; **La Rueda**, by University in Zona 3, good steaks, somewhat expensive; **Buena Vista** on square, reasonable; **El Portalito**, Av. 12 just above the square, good, cheap; **Coffee Center**, 4 C. 13-3, good cheap meals and coffee; **Pollo Chivo**, US$1 for chicken meals; **Pollos 24 Horas**, 13 Av. y 6 C., for bad but early food; **Hotel Modelo** restaurant (open earlier than most others); **La Oropendola**, 3 C., good light meals; **Bombonier**, 14 Av. 2-20, new, snacks, excellent pastries and ice-cream. **El Señor Sol**, 9 Av. 6-12, Zona 1, cheap, clean, friendly service, vegetarian.

Shopping *Artexco*, the National Federation of Artisans' Cooperatives, has its headquarters at 7 Av. 15-97, Zona 5, and at Local No. 12, Centro Comercial Municipal, very good value. For local items better to try the markets of which there are 4: main market at Templo de Minerva at Western edge of town (take local bus, US$0.04), has craft section; at the SE corner of Parque Centro América (central park) is a shopping centre with craft stalls on the upper levels, food, clothes, etc. below; another market at 2 C. y 16 Av., Zona 3, S of Parque Benito Juárez. Fine small boutique selling local handicrafts, handmade textiles and traditional costumes of excellent quality in *Los Mangos* restaurant. *Curiosidades La Chivita* makes up locally produced woollen blankets into jackets.

Cinemas Cadore, 13 Av. and 7 C., Roma, 14 Av. 'A' and Calle 'A'; from US$0.15.

Exchange Many banks on the central plaza. Banco de Guatemala, W side, Mon.-Thurs. 0830-1400, Fri. to 1430, Sat. 0830-1400.

Spanish Language Schools KIN (a cooperative); another cooperative, English Club and International Language School, 3 Calle, 15-16, Zona 1, rec., also offers Maya classes. International School of Spanish, 8a. Avenida 6-33, Zona 1, Aptdo Postal 265 (T 061-4784), cost for 5 hrs': tuition, room and 3 meals a day: 2 weeks US$195, 3 weeks, US$285, 4 weeks, US$375. Proyecto Lingüístico Xelajú, 1 C, 16-87, Zona 1, T 2631. Instituto Central America (ICA), 1 Calle 16-93, Zona 1, T 6786, cost US$100 per week, rec. (in USA: 900 Frances Way No. 339, Richardson, TX 75081, T 214-699-0935).

Laundry Minimax, Av. 14, No. C-47, 0730-1930, US$3, wash and dry.

Communications Post and Telegraph Office, 15 Av. and 4 Calle, Telephone (Guatel) 15 Av. 'A' and 4 Calle.

Tourist Office SW corner of the Plaza, Mon.-Fri., 0900-1200, 1430-1700. Helpful. Free maps of city. Ask here for the Club de Andinismo for information on mountain climbing in the area.

Buses Rutas Lima, 4 a day to Guatemala City (US$2, 3½ hours). The 0800 bus has connections to Chichicastenango, Panajachel and Sololá (US$1.50, 2½ hrs.). Galgos, near La Rotonda, 1st class buses to Guatemala City, 5 a day (US$2.25, 4 hrs; will carry bicycles.). For Antigua, change at Chimaltenango (Galgos, US$2). Rutas Lima to Huehuetenango 0500 and 1530, US$0.75; to frontier at La Mesilla, 0500, US$2.25 (cheaper if change at Huehuetenango); to frontier at Talismán bridge 0500 via Tecún Umán (US$2.25, 5 hrs.). Rutas Lima to San Pedro (**see page**

404) at 1200. Regular buses from 10 Av., 8 C. to Cuatro Caminos US$0.75 (where buses for Guatemala City and Huehuetenango stop on the highway; bus Guatemala City-Cuatro Caminos, US$1.65), Totonicapán, 1 hr. (US$0.35) San Francisco El Alto (US$0.35) and Momostenango (0600, US$0.45). Also many second class buses to many parts of the country from Zona 3 market (13 Av. 4 C. "A"), e.g. Transportes Velásquez to Huehuetenango, US$0.65; to Malacatán, US$1.25; to Los Encuentros, US$1.20; to Chichicastenango, US$0.65, 1200, 2 hrs.; to Zunil, US$0.30; also to La Mesilla at 0800.

Excursions Many places of interest around on roads N to Huehuetenango, W to San Marcos and Mexico, S to Ocós and Champerico. Six km. SE is **Almolonga**, which is noted for its fine 16th-century church and beautiful costumes, especially skirts, which are hard to buy. There is also an interesting vegetable market. *Fiesta* 29 June. Good swimming pool (entrance, US$0.25). About 1 km. further on are the thermal baths of Cirilo Flores (US$0.50 for large pool, US$1 to soak for an hour, hot, soothing water but heavily used— frequently cleaned) and El Recreo (entrance, US$0.30); bus from Quezaltenango, US$0.15. The Fuentes Georginas hot springs, 15 km. from Quezaltenango, are mentioned under Zunil (**page** 406). Take picnic or barbecue equipment, but it might be best to avoid Sundays when the Guatemalans descend on the springs. There are also hot steam baths at Los Vahos, reached by a dirt road to the right (3 km.) on the outskirts of town on the road to Almolonga; a taxi will take you there and back with a one-hour wait for US$1.50. El Baúl, a hill to the E, may be reached by winding road, or direct trail to the top where there is a cross (visible from the city), monument to Tecún Umán. To reach the Santa María volcano take bus to Llano del Piñal (every 30 mins. or when full from the Shell station on Av. 9; last bus back from Llano del Piñal leaves at 1830). Get off at cross roads and follow dirt road until it sweeps up to the right, where you should take the footpath on left (marked with paint for some distance); bear right at the saddle where another path comes in from left—look carefully, it is easily missed. A rough 4½-hr. climb (1,435 metres) but worth it for the superb views of the Pacific and to watch the still active crater, Santiaguito, on the Pacific side. The volcano can also be reached from Retalhuleu (**see page** 406) by bus to Palajunoz, from where it is also a 4½-hr. climb.

According to folklore, at Olintepeque, an Indian town 6 km. from Quezaltenango (on a road parallel to the main road, ½ day's good walk, but not open to vehicles), the greatest battle of the conquest was fought, and Alvarado slew King Tecún Umán in single combat. Its river is still known as Xequizel, the river of blood. Market, Tuesday; *fiestas*, June 24, August 29 (beware of theft). The local idol, San Pascual Baillón, has its own little church. The direct road climbs 18 km. to San Carlos Sija, at 2,642 metres, with wide views. The Spanish strain is still noticeable amongst the inhabitants, most of whom are tall and fair. A climb through conifers for another 10 km. to Cumbre del Aire, with grand views behind of volcanoes, and ahead of Cuchumatanes mountains. Another 25 km. to the junction with the Pan-American Highway.

From Cuatro Caminos the Pan-American Highway climbs for several km. before dropping down past the *ladino* town of Malacatancito (48 km.) and swinging NW through the **Selegua (El Tapón) gap** to Mexico.

A 6½ km. spur from this road leads to **Huehuetenango**, a mining centre in farming country, with Indians from remote mountain fastnesses coming in for the daily market, and particularly Thurs. and Sun. Fair, 12-18 July. Racecourse. Population, 20,000; altitude, 1,905 metres. The Honorary Mexican Consul at the Farmacia del Cid (5 Av. and 4 C.) will provide you with a Mexican visa or tourist card for US$1; Huehuetenango is the last town before the La Mesilla border post, on the Pan-American Highway into Mexico. It is also a good town for the serious Spanish language student: there is very little English spoken here, and good language schools.

Hotels *Centro Turístico Pino Montano*, at Km. 259 on the Pan-American Highway, 2 km. past the fork to Huehuetenango on the way to La Mesilla, a bit run down; *Zaculeu*, attractive hotel but poor food in restaurant, 5 Av., 1-14, Zona 1, E, clean; *Gran Shinula*, 4 C., E with bath, negotiate for cheaper rate, restaurant; *Mary*, 2 C. 3-52, Zona 1, F with bath, cheaper without, rec.; *Pensión Astoria*, 4 Av., N of Plaza, F, good meals; *Palacio*, 2 C. 5-49, E, incl. 3 meals; *Central*, 5 Av., 1-33, G, communal baths, basic, meals available, washing facilities, dark and depressing, but cheap; *Auto Hotel Vásquez*, 2 C. 6-67, 2 blocks W of Plaza, F, with bath, clean; *Maya*, 3 Av., 3-55, F, with bath, hot water, clean, good value; *Hospedaje El Viajero*, 2 C., 5-20 Zona 1, G, basic but friendly. There are a number of cheap *pensiones* on 1 Av., by the market, including *Pensión San Román*, G, basic, friendly, convenient for bus stations; near market, *Tikal* 2, G, friendly, hot shower extra; *Tikal*, G (reasonably clean), *San Antonio*, next door, G, and *Centroamericana*, 1 Av., 4-85, G. N.B. The cheap *hospedajes* (F and under) are not rec. for single women.

Camping at Zaculeu ruins, or further on the same road at the riverside.

Restaurants All hotel restaurants are open to the public. *Los Alpes*, 2 C., good; *Superlyckoss*, 2 C., quite good; *L'Emperador*, 2 Av. near 2 C., excellent; *Las Magnolias*, 4 C. and 6 Av. are best of the central restaurants; *Cafetería Las Palmeras*, very good, close to Plaza; *Pizza Hogarena*, 6 Av. between 4C and 5C, rec.; *Damasco*, 4 Av., N of Plaza; *Taberna del Conquistador*, ½ km. S of town, peaceful location; *Snoopy's Helados*. *Tienda Santa Marta*, 6 C. is good café; *Rico Mac Pollo*, 3 Av., for chicken; numerous cheap *comedores* on E side of market including *Ideal*, and W side of Plaza; *Doña Estercita's*, 6 Av. 2-6, coffee and pastries, rec.; *Ebony*, 2 C. near market, cheap and good, rec.

Shopping Artexco, Local No. 10, Centro Comercial Xinabajul. In the Huehuetenango area are two Artexco cooperatives: *La Jacaltequita*, at Jacaltenango, and *La Guadalupana*, at San Miguel Acatán.

Cinema Lili on 3 Calle, W of Plaza, often has films in English.

Swimming Pool Known as Brasilia, entry US$0.50, 12 hr. walk SE of town.

Exchange Banco de Guatemala, 4 C. and 5 Av., Mon.-Thurs., 0830-1400, Fri., 0830-1430, will exchange Mexican pesos for quetzales. Several local banks, some open Sat. a.m. All change travellers' cheques. Try also the hairdresser near Banco Café for good rates for pesos. *Cambio* at bus station, touts will find you.

Spanish Language Schools Most operate in the summer months only. Casa Xelajú, Aptdo. Postal 302, 6 C., 7-42, Zona 1, runs classes all year, accommodation, meals, laundry with family, individual tuition, 5 hrs., a day, films, seminars, field trips included. Fundación XXIII, 6 Av. 6-126, Zona 1, T 0-641478, repeatedly recommended, cost is US$100 for the first week, then declining for each succeeding week.

Post and Phones Guatel and Post Office are on 2 C. across the street from *Hotel Mary*.

Buses To Guatemala City (about 5 hrs.): US$2.60. Los Halcones, 7 Av., 3-62, Zona 1, 0700, 1400, reliable; Rápidos Zaculeu, 3 Av. 5-25, 0600 and 1500, good service; El Cóndor, 5 a day. To Zaculeu, Los Flamingos, S side of market, 0445. To La Mesilla: (2 hrs.), buses hourly, US$0.50; US$0.75 Pullman); Los Verdes, 1 Av. 1-34, 0500 and 1330, US$0.50; Osiris, 1 Av. and 3 C., 0430, 1030, 1230,

US$0.50; López, 4 C. 2-39, 0630, US$0.50. To Cuatro Caminos, for Quezaltenango, Momostenango and Totonicapán, US$0.50; to Los Encuentros, for Lake Atitlán and Chichicastenango, US$1.50; to Sacapulas, US$0.75, 1200 (Rutas Zaculeu, returns 0600); to Nentón, Cuilco and other outlying villages, enquire on 1 Av. near market. Beware of touts at the bus station who tell you, as you arrive from the border, that the last bus to wherever you want to go is about to leave; it's probably not true.

Car Insurance for Mexico and Guatemala can be arranged at Granai & Townson, next door to Mexican Consulate (see above).

Ruins of **Zaculeu**, old capital of the Mam tribe, pyramids, a ball court and a few other structures, completely reconstructed, concrete stepped forms, devoid of any ornamentation (museum), 5 km. NW on top of a rise ringed by river and *barrancas* (admission US$0.50, open 0800-1800). Yellow Alex bus runs at 1030, 1330 and 1530 as long as at least 5 people are going (fare US$0.05) and regular minibuses (US$0.15) to the ruins from *Hotel Maya*. It is possible to walk to the ruins in about 60 mins. The going for both vehicles and pedestrians can get very poor after rain.

The views are fine on the road which runs between Huehuetenango and Sacapulas. **Aguacatán** at 1,670 metres is 26 km. E of Huehuetenango, 36 km. from Sacapulas (*Pensión La Paz*, G; unsigned *Hospedaje*, 2 blocks E of market and 1 North, G). Aguacatán has an interesting market on Sunday (beginning Saturday night) and Thursday (excellent peanuts). The women wear beautiful costumes and head-dresses.

The source of the Río San Juan is about 2 km. past the centre of Aguacatán town (signposted); there is a small admission charge to the park, which is a delightful place for a freezing cold swim. Camping is permitted. Los Verdes, 1 Av. 2-34, Huehuetenango has buses to Aguacatán at 1300 (last return bus at 1500), US$0.50, and buses for **Sacapulas**, Quiché, Nebaj and Cobán pass through the village. There are jeeps, Huehuetenango-Aguacatán. Zaculeu, 1 Av. 2-53, to Sacapulas, 1400, 2 hrs. US$1 (truck at 1630, arrives 2000, US$1), and from the same place Alegres Mañanitas has a bus to Quiché at 0415. Bus to Chichicastenango from Aguacatán 0400, very crowded, or take a truck. The Campo Alegre company has buses to Nebaj from the *Hospedaje San José*, 1 Av. and 4 C.'A', and buses for Cobán leave from the same area.

Chiantla, 5 km. N of Huehuetenango, has a great pilgrimage to the silver Virgin of La Candelaria on 2 February. Another *fiesta* on 8 September. The church is well worth a visit. Daily market, largest on Sun. Buses leave regularly from 1 Av. and 1 Calle. Road runs N 117 km. to **San Mateo Ixtatán**, at 2,530 metres, in the Cuchumatanes mountains. The *huipiles* made there are unique and are much cheaper than in Huehuetenango. The road passes through San Juan Ixcoy, Soloma (*Nuevo Hotel Río Lindo*, D-E with bath, hot water, parking, rec.; *Mansión Katty* rec.; *Hospedaje San Ignacio*), and Santa Eulalia (*Hospedaje El Cisne*, G). San Mateo itself (very basic *pensión*, G, bring own sheets or sleeping bag) is a colourful town, with an interesting old church and black salt mines nearby. There are some impressive ruins on the outskirts of the town. Bus from Huehuetenango to San Juan Ixcoy,

Soloma, Santa Eulalia, San Mateo Ixtatán and Barillas leaves at 0200, very crowded, be early and get your name high up on the list as passengers are called in order. The bus returns to Huehuetenango from San Mateo (at least 5 hrs.) at 1330, but it is advised to take two days over the trip. Solomerita buses (1 Av. and 2 C.) run as far as Soloma, at 0500 and 1300. 5 km. beyond the turn off to Todos Santos Cuchumatán the road becomes rough, narrow and steep.

After San Mateo the road runs 27 km. E to Barillas (several cheap *pensiones*, *Terraza* rec., G): a fine scenic route. Some 13 km. N of Chiantla is a viewpoint with magnificent views over mountain and valley.

The village of **Todos Santos Cuchumatán** (*Hospedaje Tres Olguitas*, G, friendly, basic, cheap meals; *Hospedaje La Paz*, F, better, but fleas and cold, enclosed parking, shared showers; *Katy* is the better of the two cheap *comedores*) is very interesting (2,481 metres); some of Guatemala's best weaving is done there, and fine *huipiles* may be bought in the cooperative on the main street and possibly at the makers' huts. There are also embroidered cuffs and collars for men's shirts, and colourful crotcheted bags made by the men. There is an Artexco cooperative, *Estrella de Occidente*. A fair selection of old woven items can be bought from a small house behind the church. The Sat. market is fascinating. One can learn backstrap weaving here; a rec. teacher is Srta. Santa Jiménez J. *Fiesta*: 1 Nov., characterized by a horse race in which riders race between two points, having a drink at each turn until they fall off. Bus from Huehuetenango at 1100 and 1300, 2½ hrs., US$0.65, crowded on Fri. (return at 0500 and 1200). Sat. bus at 1100 arrives after market has finished, and there is no afternoon return. The drive is spectacular, ascending to 4,381 metres (according to the sign), but much of the land has been overgrazed and there is much soil erosion.

From Todos Santos, one can walk to San Juan Atitán, 5 hrs. (more interesting costumes; Artexco cooperative *Atiteca* and from there the highway, 1 day's walk). Also, walk to San Martín (3 hrs.), or Santiago Chimaltenango (7 hrs., stay in school, ask at Municipalidad; the Artexco cooperative here is *Flor de Pascua*), then to San Pedro Necta, and on to the Pan-American Highway for bus back to Huehuetenango. **N.B.** Remember the warning on violence in this region.

The Pan-American Highway runs W from Huehuetenango to La Mesilla, the Guatemalan border post, and on 3.7 km. to Ciudad Cuauhtémoc (just a few buildings), the Mexican border point, a very good and interesting route. Rooms at Ciudad Cuauhtémoc and La Mesilla (both very basic); best to avoid having to stay at either, by leaving Huehuetenango early. Coming into Guatemala, the peso-quetzal rate is better than the dollar-quetzal rate (don't change dollars until Huehuetenango or, better still, Guatemala City). The Guatemalan authorities charge Q3 exit tax. Outside the hours of 0800-1200, 1400-1800, an extra US$0.50 is charged. A US$0.20 "bridge tax" (!) may also be demanded. Mexican visas are obtainable at the border. From Ciudad Cuauhtémoc, Cristóbal Colón and Transportes Tuxtla buses go to Comitán and San Cristóbal de Las Casas. There is a taxi, US$0.40 p.p., between the border posts during the day; Mexican officials charge exorbitant fees for transport between the border posts.

At the border, in La Mesilla, is *Hospedaje La Gasolinera*; in La Democracia, 6 km. from La Mesilla, is an unsigned *mesón*, 1 block N of the market, basic, clean, G.

Buses from La Mesilla to Huehuetenango US$0.50 or US$0.75 (first class). Express buses go to Guatemala City. Change at Los Encuentros for Lake Atitlán and Chichicastenango, and at Chimaltenango or San Lucas for Antigua.

Quezaltenango W to Mexico Eighteen km. to San Juan Ostuncalco, at 2,530 metres, noted for good twice-weekly market and beautiful sashes worn by men. *Fiesta*, Virgen de la Candelaria, 2 Feb. See below for road S to Pacific town of Ocós. The road, which is paved, switchbacks 60 km. down valleys and over pine-clad mountains to a plateau looking over the valley in which are San Pedro and San Marcos, also known as La Unión. Interesting town hall, known as the Maya Palace. **San Marcos**, at 2,350 metres, is 2 km. or so beyond San Pedro. **San Pedro** (full name San Pedro Sacatopéquez, same name as the town near Guatemala City) has a huge market every Thursday. Its Sunday market is less interesting. The Indian women wear golden-purple skirts. Tajumulco volcano, 4,200 metres (the highest in Central America), can be reached by taking the road from San Marcos to San Sebastián; after the latter, several km. on is the summit of a pass at which a junction to the right goes to Tacana, and to the left is the start of the ascent of Tajumulco, about 5 hours' climb. Once you have reached the ridge on Tajumulco, turn right along the top of it; there are two peaks, the higher is on the right. The one on the left is used for shamanistic rituals; people are not very friendly, so do not climb alone. Tacana volcano may be climbed from Sibinal village. About 15 km. W of San Marcos the road begins its descent from 2,500 metres to the lowlands. In 53 km. to **Malacatán** it drops to 366 metres, one of the toughest stretches in Central America—even for 4-wheel drive vehicles. It is a tiring ride with continuous bends, but the scenery is attractive.

Hotels At San Marcos: *Pérez*, with good dining room, G, meals US$0.50; *Palacio*, G, without bath; *Pensión Minerva*, G, basic. At San Pedro: *El Valle*, G, said to be good. *Bagod*, G. At Malacatán: *América*, F, lunch, US$1, good; *Pensión Santa Lucía*, G; *Hospedaje Santa Emilia*, G; *Hospedaje La Predilecta*, G; *Hospedaje Rodríguez*, G, good.

The international bridge over the Suchiate river at Talismán into Mexico is 18 km. W of Malacatán. Beyond the bridge the road goes on to Tapachula; most of the motor traffic from Mexico comes down this road.

There is a Mexican consular service at the border, and at Malacatán (closed after 1300). Travelling by bus to Mexico is quicker from Quezaltenango than from San Marcos. Most traffic seems to go via Coatepeque and Quezaltenango and not via San Marcos; the former road is longer but is reported very good. From Quezaltenango to Tapachula there is one direct bus to the border in the early morning (Rutas Lima, US$2). Otherwise take 1200 Rutas Lima bus from Quezaltenango to San Pedro; from bus terminal on 4 Av. in San Pedro, frequent local buses from 0430 to 1630 to Malacatán, from where colectivos will get you to the border with ease, arriving Tapachula about 1800. Or take bus from Quezaltenango to Retalhuleu, 1½ hrs., US$0.55, then another to the border, 2 hrs., US$1.85. From the border to Quezaltenango, go via Retalhuleu (take Galgos bus from the border). Beware of overcharging on buses from the border to Quezaltenango. Bus Talismán-Guatemala City, US$3.25, 6½ hrs. because of checkpoints.

Quezaltenango to Ocós After San Juan Ostuncalco (see above) S for 1½ km. to **Concepción Chiquirichapa**, one of the wealthiest villages in the country. It has a small market early every Thursday morning. 5½ km. to **San Martín** (sometimes known as Chile Verde; this village appears in Miguel Angel Asturias' *Mulata de Tal*), in a windy, cold gash in the mountains. *Huipiles* and shirts from the cottage up behind the church. Accommodation next door to the Centro de Salud (ask at the Centro), US$0.50. Food in *comedor* opposite church, US$0.20. Indians speak a dialect of Mam not understood by other Maya tribes, having been separated from them during the Quiché invasion of the Guatemalan highlands. The men wear very striking costumes. *Fiesta*, 11 November (lasts 5 days). Ceremonies of witchdoctor initiation held on 2 May at nearby Lake Chicabel, in crater of volcano. The walk to the lake from San Martín takes about 2 hrs; there are two paths. The last bus to Quezaltenango leaves at 1900. Road descends to lowlands. From Colomba a road branches S (28 km.) to Retalhuleu: the road to Ocós runs 21 km. W from Colomba to **Coatepeque**, at 700 metres, with a population of 13,657; one of the richest coffee zones in the country; also maize, sugar-cane and bananas, and cattle. Fair, 10-15 March.

Hotels at Coatepeque: *Europa*, 6 C., 4-01, E; *Virginia*, at km. 220, E; *Beachli*, 6 C., 5-35, E; *Posada Santander*, 6 C., 6-43, F. Bus from Quezaltenango, US$0.38.

Both railway and paved Pacific Highway go to **Tecún Umán**, 34 km. W, on the Mexican frontier, separated by the Suchiate river from the Mexican town of Suchiate. This is an alternative crossing point to the Talismán bridge and many buses run to it from Guatemala. It is quite a quick border crossing. Buses run from the Mexican side of the border to Tapachula, ½ hr., cheap (beware of overcharging). Be warned, however, that you have to walk across a very long bridge (toll, US$0.20) over the river between the two border posts. For a small fee, boys will help you with your luggage. The bus to the capital costs US$3.25. Colectivo from Coatepeque, US$0.50. Trains to Guatemala City, Wed., Fri. and Sun., depart 0700, arrive 1800, US$1.40. Road N to Malacatán for international road bridge into Mexico. Population 4,250. Hotels: *La Perla; Pensión Rosita*.

Ocós, a small port now closed to shipping, is served by a 22-km. road S from Tecún Umán. Across the river from Ocós is **Tilapa**, a small resort; buses from Coatepeque and ferries from Ocós (*Pensión Teddy*, G, friendly, but said to have deteriorated). The swimming is good, but both here and at Ocós there are sharks, so stay close to the shore.

Quezaltenango to Champerico, via Retalhuleu: a 53-km. link between the old Pan-American Highway and Pacific Highway, paved all the way. A toll (Quezaltenango-Retalhuleu, US$0.25) is collected. The first town (11 km.) is **Cantel**, which has the largest textile factory in the country. There are three Artexco cooperatives: *Ixchel*, at Xecán; *Monja*

Blanca, Barrio Centenario Antiguo; *Copavic*, a cooperative of glassblowers. Market, Sunday; *fiestas*, 15 August and a passion play at Easter.

Nine km. from Quezaltenango is **Zunil**, picturesquely located in canyon of Samalá river. Market, Mon., Fri. for vegetables (beware pickpockets); *fiesta*, 25 November, and a very colourful procession on Palm Sunday. Striking church, inside and out. The local idol is San Simón, described by a traveller as a plastic tailor's dummy, dressed in ski wear: ski hat, scarf, gloves and sunglasses; the statue is lodged in a 2-storey green house on the left uphill from the main plaza. Behind the church is a cooperative (*Santa Ana*, a member of Artexco) which sells beautiful *huipiles*, and shirt and skirt materials. Zunil mountain, on which are the thermal baths of Fuentes Georginas to the E (entrance US$0.50; rooms for night with individual hot spring baths, E), in attractive surroundings. They can be reached either by walking the 8 km., uphill (300 metres' ascent; take right fork after 4 km.) to south of Zunil, a beautiful route, or by truck (US$2.50 to hire). Alternatively, take the bus from Quezaltenango to Mazatenango, but get out at the sign to Fuentes Georginas. The springs are 13 km. from Almolonga (**see page** 400).

The road descends through Santa María de Jesús (large hydro-electric station) to **San Felipe**, at 760 metres, 35 km. from Zunil. Tropical jungle fruits. Spur line to Mulua, on Guatemalan Railways. Beyond, 3 km., is San Martín, with a branch road to Mazatenango. The thermal baths of Aguas Amargas are also on Zunil mountain, below Fuentes Georginas; they are reached by a road E before Santa María de Jesús is reached. **N.B.** The main road by-passes San Felipe, which has a one-way road system (delays of up to 1½ hrs. if you go through the town).

Mazatenango, 18 km. from San Martín, is chief town of the Costa Grande zone. Altitude 380 metres, population 21,000. Chitalón airfield 3 km. away. The Pacific Highway passes through. Road paved to Quezaltenango.

Hotels *Jumay*, G; *Alba*, E; *La Gran Tasca*, F; *Roma*, F; *Costa Rica*, G; *Pensión Mejía*, G, without bath. **Motel** *Texas*.

SW 11 km. from San Martín is **Retalhuleu**, at 240 metres, a town of 42,000 people on the Pacific Highway and on Guatemalan Railways to border with Mexico. It serves a large number of coffee and sugar estates. *Fiesta*, 6-12 December.

Hotels *Astor, Modelo*, both on 5 C. and 4 Av, and both F; *Pacífico*, G, next to new market; *Posada de Don José*, 3 Av. "A", 5-14, E. **Motel** *La Colonia* (swimming pool), 1½ km. to the N, is good, E.

Trains to the capital on Wed., Fri. and Sun. at 0900.

N.B. Retalhuleu is normally referred to as "Reu", both in conversation and on bus signs.

Champerico, 43 km. SW of Retalhuleu by a paved road, once the third most important port in the country, is little used now. Population 4,500. Good beach, though the sand is black and there is a strong undercurrent; good fishing. There is a municipal fresh water swimming pool US$0.50.

Hotels *Martita*, F, without private bath; *Miramar*, F, both with restaurants; *Posada del Mar*, E on outskirts of town; *Hospedaje Recinos*, G, and *Hospedaje Buenos Aires*, G, are both very basic.

Post Office two blocks behind *Hotel Martita*, in direction of port.

Buses Last bus to Quezaltenango departs at 1700. Every 30 mins. to Retalhuleu. Direct bus to Guatemala City, 0300 and 0600, 4-5 hrs.

INFORMATION FOR VISITORS

Documents Necessary, a passport and a tourist card, issued free by the airlines or at the border (best to get it in advance, though), or a visa issued before arrival, for those entering overland. This type of visa is free. A very few nationalities need a visa in every instance and this has to be paid for. Among those that an obligatory visa are Canada, Ireland and Australia (valid for 30 days, US$10, one passport photo required, must be used within 30 days), but check carefully with airlines, travel agencies etc., experiences vary. It is advised that identification should always be carried. Tourist cards are valid for 30 days from day of issue, then 6 months from entry into Guatemala (they allow the tourist to leave the country and return once provided that the time outside Guatemala is not more than 30 days). They must be renewed in Guatemala City after 30 days at the Migración office, on the corner of 12 C. and 8 Av., Zona 1, open weekdays 0800-1630. This office extends visas and renews tourist cards on application (before noon) for 30 days at a time (up to 90 days maximum)—takes 1 day. Renewing a visa takes one day (but you will have to insist), costs US$10, fingerprints and photograph required, and you may not be given the full 90 days. Those wishing to make more than one visit should try to get a multiple-entry visa (there are, apparently, no multiple-entry tourist cards). Multiple entry visas are free for US citizens and are valid for five years (very useful if travelling back and forth across the El Salvador and Honduras borders). If experiencing obstruction in renewing a visa, it is easier to leave the country for 3 days and then come back.

If you wish to stay longer than 90 days, you must have a Guatemalan guarantor whose financial resources must be vouched for. Visitors staying less than 30 days, and holders of tourist cards, do not need an exit permit, which costs US$2.50.

Although not officially required, some airlines may not allow you to board a flight to Guatemala without an outward ticket (e.g. SAM in Colombia).

Taxes There is a 17% ticket tax, single or return, on all international tickets sold in Guatemala. A stamp tax of 2% is payable on single, return, baggage tickets and exchange vouchers issued in Guatemala and paid for in or out of the country. A US$5 tourism tax is levied on all tickets sold in Guatemala to Guatemalan residents for travel abroad. There is also a US$7 (Q20) airport departure tax, and an entry tax of Q1/US$1 and a departure tax of Q3/US$3 if travelling overland. An additional US$0.50 is charged outside official working hours (0800-1200, 1400-1800—borders are open 24 hours). However these taxes vary from one border crossing to another, entry or departure, to as much as Q25 (entry from Ahuachapán, El Salvador). Bribery is rife at border crossings; the Government is trying to eliminate overcharging for tourist cards and entry and exit taxes. Always ask for a receipt and, if you have time and the language ability, do not give in to corrupt officials.

By Air From London, fly British Airways, Pan Am, Continental or Virgin Atlantic to Miami, and Aviateca, American and Pan Am fly from Miami daily to Guatemala City. Other carriers from the USA: from Miami: Taca (via San Salvador), Lacsa (via San José); from Houston: Aviateca, Continental, Taca (via San Salvador); from New Orleans: Aviateca, Taca (via San Salvador); from Los Angeles: Pan Am, Aviateca (3 times a week), Taca, Lacsa, Mexicana; from San Francisco: Pan Am, Taca (via Los Angeles and San Salvador), Continental (via Houston); from New York: Lacsa, American. From Europe, KLM fly to Guatemala from Amsterdam (via Netherlands Antilles, and San José); Iberia from Madrid via Santo Domingo and Panama.

Carriers from Central America/Caribbean: from San Salvador: Taca, Copa, Pan Am. From Tegucigalpa: Taca, Sahsa. From San Pedro Sula: Taca (via San Salvador). From Mexico: Aviateca, Mexicana. From Cancún: Aeroquetzal. From Belize: Taca (via San Salvador), Aerovías (Tues., Fri., Sat. and Sun. at 0700 Guatemala City-Flores, 1400 Flores-Belize City). From Managua: Copa, Aeronica, Aviateca. From San José: Aviateca, Lacsa, SAM, Copa, Mexicana. From Panama: Copa, KLM, Iberia, Taca (via San Salvador). From Kingston (Jamaica): Copa (via Panama). From San Andrés: SAM. Carriers from South America: flight connections through Panama/San José, e.g. Barranquilla (Lacsa), Caracas (Copa), Medellín (Copa), Cartagena (Copa) etc. **N.B.** You will have to have an outward ticket from Colombia to be allowed a visa (though worth checking with Colombian embassy first); round trip tickets Guatemala-Colombia are stamped "Refundable only in Guatemala", but it is possible either to sell the return part on San Andrés island—at a discount—or to change it to an alternative destination. There are no direct flights to Peru or Ecuador; connections via Panama or Colombia. Probably the cheapest way to fly from Central America to South America is via San Andrés Island by SAM and thence to Colombia. Cost (mid 1989) US$137, with stopover in San José, Costa Rica. Round-trips Miami-Guatemala are good value, and useful if one does not want to visit other Central American countries. MCOs are not sold in Guatemala.

Customs You are allowed to take in, free of duty, personal effects and articles for your own use, 2 bottles of spirit and 80 cigarettes or 100 grams of tobacco. Once every 6 months you can take in, free, dutiable items worth US$100. Temporary visitors can take in any amount in quetzales or foreign currencies; they may not, however, take out more than they brought in. The local equivalent of US$100 per person may be reconverted into US dollars on departure at the airport, provided a ticket for immediate departure is shown.

Road Travel Tourists can get an entry permit from the customs to take their cars into Guatemala for 30 days (US$10 or Q10), renewable at the Aduana, 10 C. 13-92, Zona 1. There is an exit tax for cars of US$1.50, and to take a car across the Mexico-Guatemala border costs US$5.50. There is also a charge of US$2.50 when the whole car is fumigated on entry. Spare tyres for cars and motorcycles must be listed in the vehicle entry permit, otherwise they are liable to confiscation. It is better not to import and sell foreign cars in Guatemala as import taxes are very high.

The paved roads are very bad in places and generally poor, and the dirt roads are often very bad. Identification should be carried at all times. Stopping is compulsory: if driving your own vehicle, watch out for the "ALTO" sign. When driving, keep at least 200 metres in front of, or behind, army vehicles; their drivers are concerned about attacks on military personnel. Police may impound your licence if you are stopped for an infraction which can take some time to redeem. To avoid this, a tip of say US$5 will help. Another suggestion is to take one or more International Driving Licences as well as your national licence.

Gasoline costs US$1.10 "normal", US$1.15 "extra" for the U.S. gallon. All Japanese motorbike parts and accessories are available at decent prices in Guatemala, better than anywhere else in Central America.

Hired cars may not always be taken into neighbouring countries (none is allowed into Mexico); rental companies that do allow their vehicles to cross borders charge US$7-10 for the permits and paperwork. Credit cards or cash are accepted for car rental. Tourists involved in traffic accidents will have to pay whether the guilty party or not. If someone is injured or killed, the foreigner will have to pay all damages. Car insurance can be arranged at **Granai & Townson**, 7 Av. 1-82, Zona 4, Guatemala City, T 61361. They will also sell you insurance for all Central America.

Most **buses** are in a poor state of repair and breakdowns can be expected; they are always overloaded. Although recent government legislation has reduced problems of overcrowding, it is still difficult to get on buses in mid route. The correct fare should be posted up; if not, ask your neighbours.

Note Many long names on bus destination boards are abbreviated: Guate = Guatemala City, Chichi = Chichicastenango, Xela = Xelajú = Quezaltenango, Toto = Totonicapán, etc. Buses in the W and N are called *camionetas*. Regarding pronunciation, "X" is pronounced "sh" in Guatemala, as in Yucatán.

Railways The railways operate from Atlantic to Pacific and to the Mexican border. Service is neither luxurious nor reliable but very cheap and less crowded than buses.

Hitchhiking is comparatively easy, but increasingly risky, especially for single women, also beware of theft of luggage, especially in trucks. The only way to retrieve "lost" luggage is by telling the police the vehicle registration number.

Walkers should get a copy of *Backpacking in Mexico and Central America* by Hilary Bradt and Rob Rachowiecki (new edition due 1991). **N.B**. If walking in the Quiché, Huehuetenango or Totonicapán regions, a letter of permission from the army or civil defence in the main town is not obligatory. It is wise to check on conditions before setting out, but the authorities may be reluctant to let you venture into outlying areas.

Hotels The tourist office in Guatemala City will deal with complaints about overcharging if you can produce bills etc. Room rates should be posted in all registered hotels. Hotel rooms are subject to 7% sales tax and 10% tourism tax. Most budget hotels do not supply toilet paper, soap or towels. Busiest seasons, when hotels in main tourist centres are heavily booked, are Easter, December and the European summer holiday (July-August).

Tipping Hotel staff: bell boys, US$0.25 for light luggage, US$0.50 for heavy. Chamber maids at discretion. Restaurants: 10%, minimum US$0.25. Taxi drivers: none. Airport porters: US$0.25 per piece of luggage. Cloakroom attendants and cinema usherettes are not tipped.

Shopping Woven goods are normally cheapest bought in the town of origin, or possibly even cheaper at big markets held nearby. Try to avoid middlemen and buy direct from the weaver or from a member-cooperative of Artexco, to be found in all main towns. Guatemalan coffee is highly recommended, although the best is exported.

Kerosene is called "Gas corriente", and is good quality, US$0.80 per U.S. gallon; sold only in gas stations.

Film is very expensive, and film for transparencies is very hard to find (it is available at 9 Calle, 6-88, Zona 1, Guatemala City, US$15 for 36 exposures).

Health Guatemala is healthy enough if precautions are taken about drinking-water, milk, uncooked vegetables and peeled fruits; carelessness on this point is likely to lead to amoebic dysentery, which is endemic. In Guatemala City the Bella Aurora, and Centro Médico hospitals are good. Herrera Llerandi is a good private hospital. Most small towns have clinics. At the public hospitals you may have an examination for a nominal fee, but drugs are expensive. There is an immunization centre at Centro de Salud No. 1, 9 C., 2-64, Zona 1, Guatemala City (no yellow fever vaccinations). In the high places avoid excessive exertion. If going to the Maya sites and the jungle areas, prophylaxis against malaria is strongly advised; there may also be a yellow fever risk.

Clothing Men and women should wear dark clothes in the evening. Trousers are OK for women. It is illegal to bring in, or wear, military-style clothing and equipment; such items will be confiscated.

Hours of Business Business and commercial offices are open from 0800-1200, and 1400-1800 except Saturdays. Shops: 0800-1200, 1400-1800, but 0800-1200 on Saturday. Banks in Guatemala City: 0900-1500. In the interior banks tend to open earlier in the morning and close for lunch, and be open later. Government offices open 0700-1530.

British Business Travellers should read "Hints to Exporters: Guatemala", obtainable from Dept. of Trade, Export Services Division, Sanctuary Buildings, 16-20 Great Smith St., London SW1P 3DB.

Public Holidays 1 January; 6 January: Epiphany, Holy Week (4 days); 1 May: Labour Day; 30 June; 15 August (Guatemala City only); 15 September:

Independence Day; 12 October: Discovery of America; 20 October: Revolution Day; 1 November: All Saints; 24 Dec.: Christmas Eve: from noon.; 25 Dec.: Christmas Day.; 31 Dec. (from noon).

12 October and Christmas Eve are not business holidays. During Holy Week, bus fares may be doubled.

Although specific dates are given for *fiestas* there is often about a week of jollification beforehand.

Time   Guatemalan time is 6 hours behind GMT; 5 hours during Summer Time (May-August).

Currency   The unit is the *quetzal*, divided into 100 centavos. There are coins of 25, 10, 5 and 1 centavos. The paper currency is for 50 centavos and 1, 5, 10, 20, 50 and 100 quetzales. If you have money sent to Guatemala, you will only be given half in US dollars. In January 1985, the Banco de Guatemala authorized the establishment of exchange houses, effectively legalizing the black market. The black market disappeared in November 1989 when the exchange rate was freed. It fell initially from Q2.75 to the US$ to Q4 by March 1990. Miami airport is sometimes a good place to buy quetzales at favourable rates. **Warning**: Torn notes are not always accepted, so avoid accepting them yourself if possible. There is often a shortage of small change.

Weights and Measures   The metric system is obligatory on all Customs documents: specific duties are levied on the basis of weight, usually gross kilograms. United States measures are widely used in commerce; most foodstuffs are sold by the pound. The metric tonne of 1,000 kg. is generally used; so is the US gallon. Old Spanish measures are often used; e.g. *vara* (32.9 inches), *caballeria* (111.51 acres), *manzana* (1.727 acres), *arroba* (25 lbs.), and *quintal* (101.43 lbs.). Altitudes of towns are often measured in feet.

Electric Current   Generally 110 volts AC, 60 cycles, but for variations see under individual towns.

Posts and Telecommunications   Urgent telegrams are charged double the ordinary rate. Sea mail from Europe takes about 40 days. Airmail to Europe takes 6-12 days (letters cost 60 centavos for first 5 grammes, 15 centavos for each additional 5 g). Telephone calls to other countries can be made any day at any time; to Europe, these are slightly cheaper between 1900 and 0700 (personal calls to Europe cost about Q77.50 for minimum 3 mins. including 7% VAT, plus Q16.05 for each extra minute; station to station calls to Europe Q54). In 1990 the charges listed in the telephone book were quoted in US dollars at an exchange rate of Q2.78 = US$1. The cost of overseas calls will therefore fluctuate according to the current exchange rate. Collect calls may be made only to Central America, Mexico, USA (including Alaska), Italy, Spain, Sweden and Japan. All telephone services and the international cable service are in the hands of Guatel, but local telegrams are dealt with at the post office.

Mail to the US and Canada on average takes twice as long as to Europe. Airmail parcel service to the US is reliable (4-14 days); 2-3 months by boat. Parcels sent abroad must be checked before being wrapped for sending; take unsealed package, tape and string to office 119 at the Central Post Office between 0800 and 1530. Parcels by air to Europe cost about US$16/kg.; a good service. Note, though, that parcels over 2 kg. may only be sent abroad from Guatemala City (except 5 kg. of books from Antigua); in all other cities, packets under 2 kg. must be sent registered abroad. Mail from Mexico is specially slow. **N.B.** The Lista de Correos charges US$0.03 per letter received. Correos y Telégrafos, 7 Av. 12 C.,

Zona 1; Guatel next door. Also, no letters may be included in parcels: they will be removed.

Press The main newspapers are *Prensa Libre* and *El Gráfico* in the morning; *La Hora* in the afternoon (best). *Siglo Uno* is a new paper. Weekly magazine *La Crónica* is worth reading, recommended.

Information Instituto Guatemalteco de Turismo (Inguat), 7 Av. 1-17, Zona 4, Guatemala, provides bus timetables, hotel and camping lists and road maps. Tourist information is provided at the Mexican border for those entering Guatemala. Recommended reading: Paul Glassman's *Guatemala Guide*, and *Guatemala for You* by Barbara Balchin de Koose. Maps include Belize as Guatemalan territory. Roads marked in the Petén are inaccurate.

If you would be interested to volunteer to help in local children's homes, write to: Casa Guatemala, 14 C. 10-63, Zona 1, Guatemala City, or Casa Alianza, Apartado Postal 400, Antigua, Guatemala.

For information on Guatemala we are deeply grateful to Mike Shawcross (Antigua) and to the following travellers: Salik Bernard Biais (Montmorency, France), David Burford (Templestowe, Victoria), Peter Caesar (Bogotá), Tomasz Cienkus (Bogurzyn, Poland), Jean Curtet (Geneva), Philip J. Dunn (Gloucester, MA), Kate Edwards (Freeport, Grand Bahama), Edward F. Fischer (Birmingham, AL), Petra Franke (Gundelsheim, W. Ger.), Véronique Gauais and Dominique Deghetto (Poitiers), Martin Gutzki (Aachen, W. Ger.), Beatrice Hanimann (Switz.), Beatrix Hausz and Lisa Sterzinger (Austria), Etai Heled, Ronit Glazer, (Kibbutz Hokuk, Israel) and Ami and Sary Saranga (Menahamia, Israel), Johan Hindahl (Oslo), Ursula Hochuli (Switz.) and Vincent Choblet (Paris), Birgit Kastner and Hans Lindenthaler (Salzburg, Austria), Sybille Klenk (Hamburg 60), H. Klose (Cincinnati, OH), Sherril Labovich (Montreal, Canada), Diane St. Marie (Seattle, WA), Richard Mathews (Bisbee, AZ), Kerstin Meyer (Nürnberg 40) and Anne Nyffenegger (Wabern, Switz.), Mette Nordaw and Claus Jørgensen (Lyngby, Dnmk.), Shauna Picard (Victoria, Australia), Andreas Poth (Kiel 1), Kai Reikko (Turku, Finland), Andreas and Bettina Schlitt (Berlin 51), Otto Schneeberger (Zürich), Markus Weder (Binningen, Switz.) and Boris and Steen Zeichner (Denmark).

BELIZE

INTRODUCTION

BELIZE, formerly known as British Honduras, borders on Mexico and Guatemala, and has a land area of about 8,900 square miles, including numerous small islands. Its greatest length (N-S) is 174 miles and its greatest width (E-W) is 68 miles. Forests occupy some 65% of the area.

The coastlands are low and swampy with much mangrove, many salt and fresh water lagoons and some sandy beaches. In the north the land is low and flat, but in the south-west there is a heavily forested mountain massif with a general elevation of between 2,000 and 3,000 ft. In the eastern part are the Maya Mountains, not yet wholly explored, and the Cockscomb Range which rises to a height of 3,681 ft. at Victoria Peak. To the west are some 250 square miles of the Mountain Pine Ridge, with large open spaces and some of the best scenery in the country.

From 10 to 40 miles off the coast an almost continuous, 150-mile line of reefs and cayes (meaning islands, pronounced "keys") provides shelter from the Caribbean and forms the longest coral reef in the Western Hemisphere (the second-longest barrier reef in the world). Most of the cayes are quite tiny, but some have been developed as tourist resorts. Many have beautiful sandy beaches with clear, clean water, where swimming and diving are excellent. (However, on the windward side of inhabited islands, domestic sewage is washed back on to the beaches, and some beaches are affected by tar.)

The most fertile areas of the country are in the northern foothills of the Maya Mountains: citrus fruit is grown in the Stann Creek valley, while in the valley of the Mopan, or upper Belize river, cattle raising and mixed farming are successful. The northern area of the country has long proved suitable for sugar cane production. In the south bananas and mangoes are cultivated. The lower valley of the Belize river is a rice-growing area as well as being used for mixed farming and citrus cultivation.

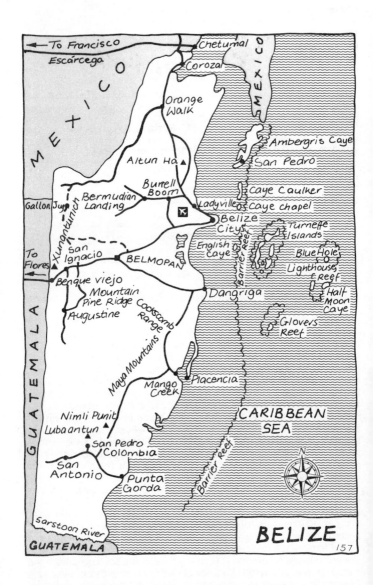

To Francisco Escárcega

M E X I C O

Chetumal

Corozal

Orange Walk

M E X I C O

MEXICO

Ambergris Caye

San Pedro

Altun Ha

Burrell Boom

Bermudian Landing

Gallon Jug

Xunantunich

Ladyville

Belize City

Caye Caulker

Caye Chapel

Turneffe Islands

San Ignacio

To Flores

BELMOPAN

English Caye

Blue Hole

Lighthouse Reef

Benque Viejo

Mountain Pine Ridge

Cockscomb Range

Dangriga

Half Moon Caye

Augustine

G U A T E M A L A

Maya Mountains

Glovers Reef

Barrier Reef

Mango Creek

Placencia

Nimli Punit

Lubaantun

CARIBBEAN SEA

N

San Pedro Colombia

San Antonio

Punta Gorda

Barrier Reef

Sarstoon River

GUATEMALA

BELIZE

157

Climate Shade temperature is not often over 90°F (32°C) on the coast, even in the hotter months of February to May. Inland, in the W, day temperatures can exceed 100°F (38°C), but the nights are cooler. Between November and February there are cold spells during which the temperature at Belize City may fall to 55°F (13°C). However humidity is normally high making it "sticky" most of the time in the lowlands.

There are sharp annual variations of rainfall—there is even an occasional drought—but the average at Belize City is 65 inches, with about 50 inches in the N and a great increase to 170 inches in the S. Hurricanes can threaten the country from June to November, but there have been only four in the past thirty years. An efficient warning system has been established and there are hurricane shelters in most towns and large villages.

History Deep in the forests of the centre and S are many ruins of the Old Maya empire, which flourished here and in neighbouring Guatemala from the 4th to the 9th century and then somewhat mysteriously emigrated to Yucatán. It has been estimated that the population then was ten times what it is now.

The first settlers were Englishmen and their black slaves from Jamaica who came about 1640 to cut logwood, then the source of textile dyes. The British Government made no claim to the territory but tried to secure the protection of the wood-cutters by treaties with Spain. Even after 1798, when a strong Spanish force was decisively beaten off at St. George's Cay, the British Government still failed to claim the territory, though the settlers maintained that it had now become British by conquest.

When they achieved independence from Spain in 1821, both Guatemala and Mexico laid claim to sovereignty over Belize as successors to Spain, but these claims were rejected by Britain. Long before 1821, in defiance of Spain, the British settlers had established themselves as far south as the river Sarstoon, the present southern boundary. Independent Guatemala claimed that these settlers were trespassing and that Belize was a province of the new republic. By the middle of the 19th century Guatemalan fears of an attack by the United States led to a *rapprochement* with Britain. In 1859, a Convention was signed by which Guatemala recognized the boundaries of Belize while, by Article 7, the United Kingdom undertook to contribute to the cost of a road from Guatemala City to the sea "near the settlement of Belize"; an undertaking which was never carried out.

Heartened by what it considered a final solution of the dispute, Great Britain declared Belize, still officially a settlement, a Colony in 1862, and a Crown Colony nine years later. Mexico, by treaty, renounced any claims it had on Belize in 1893, but Guatemala, which never ratified the 1859 agreement, renews its claims periodically.

Belize became independent on 21 September, 1981, following a United Nations declaration to that effect. Guatemala refused to recognize the independent state, but in 1986, President Cerezo of Guatemala announced an intention to drop his country's claim to Belize. A British military force has been maintained in Belize since independence. Dr. Minita Gordon was named Governor-General of the new state in 1981. Mr. George Price, of the People's United Party, who had been reelected continuously as Prime Minister since internal self-government was instituted in 1964, was defeated by Mr Manuel Esquivel, of the United Democratic Party, in general elections held in December 1984 (the first since independence). General elections took place in 1989 and Mr. George Price was returned as Prime Minister. The People's United Party won a 15 seat to 13 majority, which was increased by a defection to 16-12 in 1990.

The People   The population is estimated at 180,000. About 40% of them are of mixed ancestry, the so-called Creoles, a term widely used in the Caribbean. They predominate in Belize City and along the coast, and on the navigable rivers. 33% of the population are mestizo; 7% are Indians, mostly Mayas, who predominate in the north between the Hondo and New rivers and in the extreme south and west. About 8% of the population are Garifuna (Black Caribs), descendants of the Black Caribs deported from St. Vincent in 1797; they have a distinct language, and can be found in the villages and towns along the southern coast. The remainder are of unmixed European ancestry (the majority Mennonites, who speak a German dialect, and are friendly and helpful) and a rapidly growing group of North Americans. Birth rate (1985), 40.1 per 1,000; death rate, 4.0; annual population growth, 2.8%; adult literacy 90%. Free elementary education is available to all, and all the towns have secondary schools.

English is the official language, although about 75% speak mostly "Creole" English. Spanish is the mother tongue for about 15%. About 30% are bilingual, and 10% trilingual. Spanish is widely spoken in the northern and western areas.

The Economy   Belize's central problem is how to become self-sufficient in food: imports of food are still some 25% of the total imports. Necessity is forcing the people to grow food for themselves and this is gathering pace. One difficulty is that the territory is seriously under-populated and much skilled labour emigrates. Three immigrant Mennonite communities have already increased farm production, and new legislation provides for the development of lands not utilized by private landowners.

Agriculture is by far the most important sector of the Belizean economy, employing more than half the population, and bringing in 65% of the country's total foreign exchange earnings. The main export crops, in order of importance, are sugar, citrus and bananas. Maize, beans, cocoa and rice are grown, and attempts are also being made to increase the cattle herd. Poultry, eggs and honey grew significantly during the 1980s.

Timber is extracted during the first six months of the year. Forest products were for a long time the country's most important export, but their relative importance has fallen. Fish products are exported, though some of the traditional grounds have been overfished and restrictions necessary for conservation are enforced.

The Government is encouraging the development of tourist facilities.

There is also some light industry and manufacturing now contributes about 12% of gdp. The value of clothing exports has risen to 20% of total exports, making garments the second most important export item after sugar. Oil was discovered, near the Mexican border, in 1981; the search for oil is being intensified.

The slowing down of economic growth at the beginning of the 1980s was attributable to decline in the sugar industry and pressures on Belize's international accounts. Prudent financial policies in the mid-1980s led to the elimination of external debt arrears and the increase of foreign exchange reserves. In the second half of the 1980s gdp grew at an average of over 5% a year.

Government Belize is a constitutional monarchy; the British monarch is the chief of state, represented by a Governor-General. The head of government is the Prime Minister. There is a National Assembly, with a House of Representatives of 28 members elected by universal adult suffrage, and a Senate of 8: 5 appointed by the advice of the Prime Minister, 2 on the advice of the Leader of the Opposition, 1 by the Governor-General after consultation. General elections are held at intervals of not more than 5 years.

Communications Formerly the only means of inland communication were the rivers, with sea links between the coastal towns and settlements. The Belize river can be navigated by light motor boats, with enclosed propellers, to near the Guatemalan border in most seasons of the year, but this route is no longer used commercially because of the many rapids. The Hondo River and the New River are both navigable for small boats for 100 miles or so. Although boats continue to serve the sugar industry in the north, the use of waterborne transport is much diminished.

Some 400 miles of all-weather roads, with bus and truck services, connect the eight towns in the country. There are road links with Chetumal, the Mexican border town, and the Guatemalan border town of Melchor de Mencos.

The road system has been upgraded in the interests of tourism. There are no railways in Belize.

Nature Conservation has become a high priority, with nature reserves sponsored by the Belize Audubon Society, the Government and various international agencies. "Nature tourism" is Belize's fastest growing industry. The reserves (some of which are described below) are: Half Moon Caye, Cockscomb Basin Wildlife Sanctuary (the world's only jaguar reserve), Crooked Tree Wildlife Sanctuary (swamp forests and lagoons with wildfowl), Community Baboon Sanctuary, Blue Hole National Park and Guanacaste Park. All information from the Belize Audubon Society, 49 Southern Foreshore, Belize City, T (02) 7369. A private reserve is the Shipstern Butterfly Farm, near Sarteneja in the N (Paul and Zoe Walker, P.O. Box 1158, Belize City).

N.B. A wildlife protection Act was introduced in 1982, which forbids the sale, exchange or dealings in wildlife, or parts thereof, for profit; the import, export, hunting or collection of wildlife is not allowed without a permit; only those doing scientific research or for educational purposes are eligible for exporting or collecting permits. Also prohibited are removing or exporting black coral, picking orchids, exporting turtle or turtle products, and spear fishing in certain areas or while wearing scuba gear.

BELMOPAN AND BELIZE CITY

Belmopan is the new capital; the seat of government was moved there from Belize City in August 1970. It is 50 miles inland to the west, near the junction of the Western Highway and the Hummingbird Highway to Dangriga (Stann Creek Town)—very scenic. It has a National Assembly building (which is open to the public), two blocks of government offices (which are copies of Mayan architecture), police headquarters, a public works department, a hospital, over 700 houses for civil servants, a non-governmental residential district to encourage expansion, and a market. The Department of Archaeology in the government plaza has a vault containing specimens of the country's artefacts, as there is no museum to house them. Guided tours are offered on Mon., Wed. and Fri. (prior appointment advisable). The city can be seen in a couple of hours (break Belize City-San Ignacio bus journey, storing luggage safely at Batty Bus terminal). A recent addition is the civic centre. The Western Highway from Belize City is now good (one hour's drive), continuing to San Ignacio, and an airfield has been completed.

Hotels and Restaurants *Belmopan Convention Hotel*, Bliss Parade (opp. bus stop and market), A-L, a/c, hot water, swimming pool, restaurant, bars; *Circle A Lodgings*, 35/37 Half Moon Avenue, C-B, a/c and fans available, despite sign, friendly, breakfast is extra, dinner also served, and bath (laundry BZ$3.75); *Bull Frog Hotel*, 23/25 Half Moon Avenue, D-B, a/c, restaurant, laundry (these 2 are a 15-minute walk S of the market through the Parliament complex). There are two restaurants (*Caladium*, next to market, limited fare, moderately priced, small portions; *Bullfrog*, good, reasonably priced); there is a *comedor* at the back of the market, which is very clean. Local food is sold by vendors, 2 stands in front sell ice cream (closed Sat. and Sun.), fruit and vegetable market open daily, limited produce available Sun. Shops close 1200-1400. No cafés open Sun.

Buses Batty Bus service to San Ignacio, 45 mins.—1 hr., BZ$1.50 (28 miles), daily every hour between 1430 and 1730, plus Sun. 1330. Novello's hourly between 1100 and 1700 Mon.-Sat. (to 1500 on Sun.) to San Ignacio and Benque Viejo. Buses to Dangriga, Punta Gorda, see under Belize City. Bus to Belize City, 1 hr., BZ$2.75, Mon.-Sat. 0800, 0930, 1030, 1130, Sun. hourly between 0800 and 1200.

Exchange Barclays Bank International (0800-1300, Mon.-Fri., and 1500-1800 Fri.). Visa transactions, no commission (but see under Belize City, below).

British High Commission. Office in Belmopan (P.O. Box 91, T 2146/7). Officially "visits" Belize City, 11 Marks Street, T 45108, Monday mornings, 0900-1100.

Excursion At Mile 41 on the Western Highway is the small but excellent **Belize Zoo** (The Place), open daily 1000-1700, BZ$5, many local species, tours, T-shirts, postcards on sale. At the junction of Belmopan road and the Western Highway is the **Guanacaste Park**, which is along the Belize River: 4.8 km. of trails, birds and a large guanacaste tree which shelters a large collection of epiphytes including orchids. Bird watching rewarding, especially in the winter months with the arrival of North American migrants. Good bathing nearby.

Belize City is the old capital and chief town. Most of the houses are built of wood, with galvanized iron roofs; they stand for the most part on piles about seven feet above the ground, which is often swampy and flooded. Ground-floor rooms are used as kitchens, or for storage. A sewerage system has been installed, and the water is reported safe to drink, though bottled water may be a wise precaution. Humidity is high, but the summer heat is tempered by the NE trades. The population—42,000—is just over a quarter of the total population, with the African strain predominating. The Anglican Cathedral and Government House nearby are interesting; both were built in the early 19th century. In the days before the foundation of the Crown Colony the kings of the Mosquito Coast were crowned in the Cathedral. In the Cathedral, note the 19th century memorial plaques which give a harrowing account of early death from "country fever" and other tropical diseases. There is an attractive memorial park on the sea front.

Coming in by sea, after passing the barrier reef, Belize City is approached by a narrow, tortuous channel. This and the chain of mangrove cayes give shelter to what would otherwise be an open roadstead.

Belize is the nearest adequate port to the State of Quintana Roo (Mexico), and re-exports mahogany from that area.

Note Hurricane Hattie swept a 10-ft. tidal wave into the town on October 31, 1961, and caused much damage and loss of life. Hattieville, 16 miles from Belize City on the road to Cayo, originally a temporary settlement for the homeless after the hurricane, still has from 2,000 to 3,000 people. In 1978, Hurricane Greta caused extensive damage.

Warning Take good care of your possessions. Cars should only be left in guarded carparks (such as Budget Store in N. Front St., BZ$10 a night; cars can enter at any time—no sleeping in parked vehicles allowed—but can only be collected between 0800-1630). Do not trust the many self-appointed "guides" who also sell hotel rooms, boat trips to the Cayes, drugs, etc. Local advice is not even to say "no"; just shake your head and wag your finger if approached by a stranger. Street money changers are not to be trusted either. The Government is making every effort to improve the security in the city in the interests of tourism; nevertheless, do not walk in any side street, day or night, nor in any main street at night. You are best advised to take a taxi. No jewellery or watches should be worn.

The whole city closes down on Sunday except for a few shops open on Sunday morning, e.g. Brodies in the centre of town.

Hotels All hotels are subject to 5% government tax. *Fort George Hotel*, 2 Marine Parade (P.O.Box 321, T 77400, Telex 220), has much the same tariff as luxury Caribbean hotels, and rooms are air-conditioned, L, helpful staff, reservations must be made, safe parking, good restaurant, good pool (non-residents may use pool for BZ$5). Other hotels: *Villa*, 13 Cork St., L, a/c, TV, good restaurant, bar; *Bellevue*, 5 Southern Foreshore (T 2290), A, including 2 meals, a/c, and private bath, nice bar with live music Fri. and Sat. nights, good entertainment; *El Centro*, 4 Bishop St., B (T 2413), a/c, restaurant, good (damaged by fire); *Venus*, Magazine Rd., at Venus Bus Station, D; *Bliss*, 1 Water Lane (T 3310), B with a/c, C without, rooms without a/c have ceiling fans, and

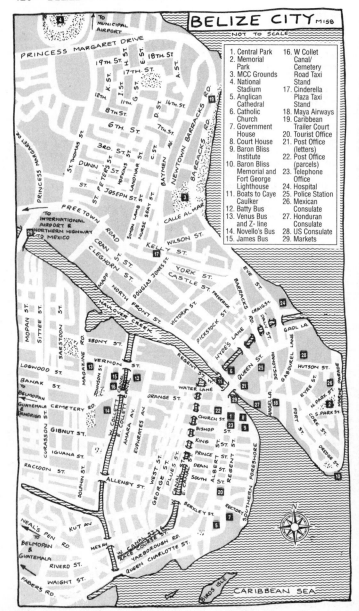

BELIZE CITY M158

NOT TO SCALE

1. Central Park
2. Memorial Park
3. MCC Grounds
4. National Stadium
5. Anglican Cathedral
6. Catholic Church
7. Government House
8. Court House
9. Baron Bliss Institute
10. Baron Bliss Memorial and Fort George Lighthouse
11. Boats to Caye Caulker
12. Batty Bus
13. Venus Bus and Z- line
14. Novello's Bus
15. James Bus
16. W Collet Canal/ Cemetery Road Taxi Stand
17. Cinderella Plaza Taxi Stand
18. Maya Airways
19. Caribbean Trailer Court
20. Tourist Office
21. Post Office (letters)
22. Post Office (parcels)
23. Telephone Office
24. Hospital
25. Police Station
26. Mexican Consulate
27. Honduran Consulate
28. US Consulate
29. Markets

are quieter and lighter, private bath, clean, safe; *Mopan*, 55 Regent Street (T 3356), B, with bath, breakfast, a/c, very clean, in historic house, has restaurant and bar (owners Tom and Jean Shaw), a bit overpriced and relies overmuch on its past reputation; *Belize Guest House*, 2 Hutson St., T 77569, B, nice balcony, helpful owner, rec.; *4 Fort Street* (address as name), C, charming, excellent but expensive restaurant, rec.; *Mom's Hotel and Restaurant* (formerly *Mom's Triangle Bar*), 11 Handyside St., P.O. Box 332, C, restaurant very popular, rec.; *Glenthorne Manor*, 27 Barracks Rd. (T 4-4212), C, with or without bath, colonial-style, meals available, highly rec.; *International Airport Hotel*, at Ladyville, 9 miles on Northern Highway, 1½ miles from airport, B, restaurant and bar; *Chateau Caribbean*, 6 Marine Parade (T 2813), from D to A, a/c, with bar, rec., restaurant and discotheque, parking, rec.; *Golden Dragon*, 29 Queen St., D, with bath and a/c, cheaper rooms with bath and fan, cheaper still without bath, hot water, good, clean but noisy; *Simon Quan's "Luxury" Hotel*, 24-26 Queen St. (T 4-5793), E with fan, and D, private shower, hot water, a/c, unattractive building; *North Front Street Guest House*, T (02) 77595, 1 block N of Post Office, 15 mins. walk from Batty bus station, 124 North Front St., E, no hot water, fan, book exchange, TV, clean, friendly, good fish dinners, laundry, French spoken, good information; keep windows closed at night and be sure to lock your door; *Riverview*, 25 Regent St. West, E, basic; *Mar's Riverside Resort*, 44 Regent St. West, F, no fan, friendly, basic; *Bon Aventure*, Pickstock and Front Sts., E, dirty but helpful, Spanish spoken, good meals at reasonable prices, safe to store luggage here; *Marin Travel Lodge*, 6 Craig St., E, good, fans, shared hot showers, clean, safe, laundry facilities; *Golden Star Guest House*, 114 New Rd., D, fan, clean, shower, simple, facilities leave something to be desired, not very friendly; *Freddie's*, 86 Eve St., E, with shower and toilet, fan, hot water, clean, very nice; *Han's Guest House*, 53 Queen St., E, little or no English spoken by Chinese owners, basic, noisy but clean; *Sea Side Guest House*, 3 Prince Street, T 78339, E, comfortable, quiet, very helpful owners, German spoken, meals, highly rec.

Camping In the city is the *Caribbean Trailer Court*, at the end of Eve St., caravan park with 2 dilapidated showers and toilet, cold drinks available; some supervision, but no fence, beware of thieves; BZ$3 p.p., BZ$5 per car plus BZ$2 per extra person. Caribbean Charter Service, Mile 5 North Highway, short and long stay trailer parking and camp site. Camping on the beaches, in forest reserves, or in any other public place is not allowed. **N.B.** Camping Gaz is not available in Belize and there are no campsites for tents.

Restaurants *Golden Dragon*, Queen St., good, reasonably priced; *Four Fort Street* (at that address), near Memorial Park, nice atmosphere, sit out on the verandah, run by two ladies, desserts a speciality; *Macy's*, 18 Bishop Street (T 3419), rec. for well-prepared local game, different fixed menu daily, charming host; *Barracks Restaurant and Bar*, 136 Barracks Rd.; *Grill*, Barracks Green (a short taxi ride), new, rec; *DIT's*, King St., good, cheap; *Caribbean*, 36 Regent St., creole and Chinese; *Hong Kong*, 50 Queen St., Chinese, reasonably priced; *China Village*, 46 Regent St., lunch specials; *Shek Kei*, 80 Freetown Rd., Chinese, good; *Ding Ho*, North Front St., good Chinese, try their "special" dishes; other Chinese (try): *Yin Kee*, 64 Freetown Rd., *Taiwan*, 93 Cemetery Rd., *New Chon Saan*, 55 Euphrates Av., take away. *Edward Quan Fried Chicken*, New Rd., take away, good. *King's*, St Thomas St., good value; *Big Daddy's*, Pickstock St. (2 blocks from N Front St.), good, vegetarian food available, eat in or take-away, rec.; *H & L Burgers*, 4 locations; *Play Boy Restaurant*, King St., good sandwiches; *Pizza House*, King St., closed Mon., inexpensive, good also for juices and shakes. For fried chicken, look for a red door on Albert St., half a block down from Church St., by Central Park. No sign. Ask for "two dollar chicken" (or "three dollars" if you are really hungry). *Blue Bird*, Albert St., cheap fruit juices; *Admiral*

Burnaby's Coffee Shop, Regent St.; *Babb's Saloon*, Queen and Eve Sts., good pastries, meat pies, juices, friendly.

Bars Lots of bars some with juke boxes and poolrooms. *Privateer*, Mile 4½ on Northern Highway, on seafront, expensive drinks but you can sit outside. Try the local drink, anise and peppermint, known as "A and P"; also the powerful "Old Belizeno" rum. The local beer, Belikin, is good, as is the "stout", strong and free of gas.

Clubs and Discos *The Pub*, North Front St., bar and disco, admission charged, taped music, frequented by British soldiers; *The Big Apple*, same street, live music at weekends; *Bellevue Hotel* has live music at weekends, respectable, rec. The *Old Louisville Democratic Bar*, though rec. by Richard West of *The Spectator*, has been described as dangerous by a woman visitor. *Legends*, new (1989), up market disco on Queen St.

Shopping Handicrafts, woodcarvings, straw items, are all good buys. Try the gift/souvenir at Caribbean Charter Services, Mile 5, North Highway (see below); *Cottage Industries*, 26 Albert Street. *The Book Centre*, close to bridge and Catholic church, very good. *Belize Bookshop*, Regent St. (opp. *Mopan Hotel*), sells Trade & Travel Publications' *Handbooks* (also available in some expensive hotels). Zericote (or Xericote) wood carvings can be bought in Belize City, for example at *Brodies Department Store*, which also sells postcards, the *Fort George Hotel*, or from Egbert Peyrefitte, 11a Cemetery Road. Such wood carvings are the best buy, but to find a carver rather than buy the tourist fare in shops, ask a taxi driver. (At the Art Centre, near Government House, the wood sculpture of Charles Gabb, who introduced carving into Belize, can be seen.)

Taxis have green licence plates (drivers must also have identification card); within Belize, BZ$3 for one person; for 2 or more passengers, BZ$2 p.p. There is a taxi stand on the corner of Collet Canal Street and Cemetery Road. Outside Belize City, BZ$2 per mile, regardless of number of passengers. Check fare before setting off. No meters. No tips necessary.

Car Hire Caribbean Charter Service (see below under **Tourist Information**); Pancho's, 18th St., T 02-2813; National, near airport, T 025-2114. Smith & Sons, 125C Cemetery Road, T 02-3779; Elija Sutherland, 127 Neal Pen Road, T 02-3582; S & L Tours, 69 West Collet Canal, T 02-3062. Rates US$50/day; some offer tours. Land Rovers at about BZ$90 a day (BZ$400 deposit, no credit cards) at Belize. It is impossible to hire a car with insurance.

Exchange All banks have facilities to arrange cash advance on Visa card (if you want US dollars, you may be sent to get permission from the Central Bank, US$200 maximum in cash, the remainder in cheques—you may also be asked for proof that you are leaving the country). The Belize Bank is particularly efficient and modern; also Barclays Bank International, with some country branches. Bank of Nova Scotia. Banking hours: 0800-1300 Mon.-Thurs., 0800-1200, 1500-1800 Fri. It is easy to have money telexed to Belize City. Guatemalan quetzales are very difficult to obtain. American Express at Global Travel, 41 Albert Street (T 7185/7363/4). All banks charge 2% commission. Money changers at Batty Bus terminal just before departure of bus to Chetumal (the only place to change Mexican pesos). The black market is not recommended.

Baron Bliss Institute Maya remains (3 stelae), and public library.

Churches There are an Anglican Cathedral, a Catholic Cathedral, a Methodist and a Presbyterian church. The Baptist Church on Queen St. is interesting for the sermons (very vivid).

Cinemas Two, Palace and Majestic, films and prices change according to popularity. Majestic stages sporting events from time to time.

Consulates Mexico, 20 North Park St. (open 0900-1230, Mon.-Fri.; if going to Mexico and requiring a visa, get it here, not at the border, tourist card given on the spot, visa ready by afternoon); **Honduras**, Front St., above *The Pub*; **El Salvador**, 11 Handyside St.; **Panama**, Cork St. No Guatemalan Consulate; Guatemalan visas must be obtained in Chetumal (Calle Alvaro Obregón 342), Mexico. **USA**, 20 Gabourel Lane; **Canada**, South Foreshore; **Belgium**, Eve St.; **Norway and the Netherlands**, 22 Regent St.

Post Office Letters, Queen St. and N. Front St.; parcels, Church St. Letters held for one month. Beautiful stamps sold.

International Telecommunications Telegraph, telephone, telex services, Belizean Telecommunications Ltd, Church Street just off Central Park.

Tourist Information Belize Tourist Bureau, 53 Regent Street, Belize, P.O. Box 325, T 02-77213 (open 0800-1200, 1300-1700 Mon.-Thurs., and till 1630 Fri.), provides complete bus schedule with a map of Belize City, as well as list of hotels and their prices. Also has a list of recommended taxi guides and tour operators, and free publications on the country and its Mayan ruins, practical and informative. Excellent maps of the country for BZ$4 (or US$3 including postage). Mon.-Fri. 0800-1200, 1300-1700. Suggested reading is *Hey Dad, this is Belize*, by Emory King, a collection of anecdotes, available in bookshops. Maps (BZ$6), books on Belizean fauna etc. available at Angelus Press, Queen St.

Caribbean Charter Services, Mile 5 North Highway, P.O.Box 752, Belize City, T (011-501-2) 4-5841, Telex 263 Rebco Bz. is a tourist information centre with good maps of Belize City (BZ$6) and of the country. Also agency for boat charters, inland resorts and other facilities including excellent guarded car and boat park and tent sites. Car hire at good rates; open 7 days a week, 0700-1800 in tourist season. The owners (Americans George and Ruha'mah Baguette) operate M.V.s *Princess, Toucan, Jaguar, Le 'Beau* and *Hickatee* for fishing, diving and sightseeing trips to the Cayes.

Tours S and L Guided Tours, 69 W. Collet Canal, recommended group travel in Land Rovers; International Zoological Expeditions, 210 Washington Street, Sherborn, MA 01770, USA, offer guided trips to the rainforests and coral reefs of Belize. Personalized Services (Beth La Croix), P.O. Box 1158, Belize City, T (011-501) 2331, rec. Cunningham Tours, T 7-8016 or (agent) 4-5841, have been highly recommended.

Transport There are bus services to the main towns. To Chetumal, Mexico (**see page** 284), several daily each way between 0400 and 1800 (there is an express Batty Bus at 0600 stopping at Orange Walk and Corozal only), BZ$7, 3-4 hrs., with 2 companies: Batty Bus, 54 East Collet Canal, T 2025, and Venus, Magazine Rd., T 3354. Batty Bus to Belmopan and San Ignacio, 4 hrs., BZ$3.75, Mon.-Sat. 0630, 0800, 0900, 1000, Sun. 0630, 0730, 0830, 0930, 1030. The 0630 bus goes on to Melchor de Mencos, Guatemala. To San Ignacio and Benque Viejo via Belmopan, Novello's, West Collet Canal, BZ$4.25 to Benque, every two hours Mon.-Sat., 1100 to 1700 (to 1600 on Sun.). To Dangriga, via Belmopan and the Hummingbird Highway. Z-line, from Venus bus station, daily, 1000, 1100, 1500, 1600, plus Mon. 0600, US$8 to Dangriga (the 1000 bus connects with the 1530 Z-line bus to Punta Gorda); James Bus Line, Pound Yard Bridge (Collet Canal), unreliable, slow, 9-12 hrs., BZ$19, to Punta Gorda via Dangriga and Mango Creek, Tues., Wed., Fri. 0600, Mon., Sat. 0900. Within the city the fare is BZ$1. Take a taxi to town from the bus stations at night.

Airport There is a 10-mile tarmac road to the Belize International Airport; collective taxi BZ$25; make sure your taxi is legitimate. Any bus going up the

Northern Highway passes the airport junction (BZ$1), then 1½ mile walk. There is a municipal airstrip for local flights, taxi from the city, BZ$5. To Corozal, 30 mins., BZ$62; to Punta Gorda, BZ$60; to San Pedro, BZ$35; Caye Chapel, BZ$25; Dangriga, BZ$36 (one way fares).

Airline Offices Taca (Belize Global Travel), Albert St.; Sahsa/TAN, just off Queen St. Maya Airways, 6 Fort St., T 02-77215. American and Continental Airlines now also fly to Belize. Tropic Air, T 02-45671.

Shipping The only boat to Guatemala goes from Punta Gorda. Obtain all necessary exit stamps and visas before sailing (remember, nearest Guatemalan consulate is in Chetumal). For Dangriga and Punta Gorda boats must be chartered. To Puerto Cortés, Honduras, BZ$720, 2-4 days, for 8 people.

Excursions Bargain with local drivers for a visit to Tikal ruins, in Guatemala (**page 373**). Mr. Richard Smith has his own station waggon. There are buses from Belize to the Guatemalan border; for connections to Flores **see page 431** under Benque Viejo.

The Maya remains of **Altun Ha**, 31 miles N of Belize City and 3 miles off the old Northern Highway, are worth a visit (insect repellent necessary); they are deserted after 1800 hours. Since there is so little transport on this road, hitching is not rec., best to go in a private vehicle. A vehicle does leave Belize City in the early afternoon, but does not return until 0500 next day; camping not permitted at the site. No accommodation in nearby villages. Tourist Board provides a good booklet on the ruins for BZ$2, and a guide book for BZ$12 (possibly out of print now). The largest piece of worked Maya jade ever found, a head of the Sun God weighing 9½ pounds, was found here in 1968. It is now in a bank vault in Belize City.

Fishing The rivers abound with tarpon and snoek. The sea provides game fish such as sailfish, marlin, wahoo, barracuda and tuna. On the flats, the most exciting fish for light tackle—the bonefish—are found in great abundance. Check with the local experts on which fish are in season. In addition to the restrictions on turtle and coral extraction noted above under **Nature Conservation**, the following regulations apply: no person may take, buy or sell crawfish (lobster) between 15 March and 14 July, shrimp from 15 April to 14 August, or conch between 1 July and 30 September.

Skin Diving The shores are protected by the longest barrier reef in the Western Hemisphere. Old wrecks and other underwater treasures are protected by law and cannot be removed. Spear fishing, as a sport, is discouraged in the interests of conservation. The beautiful coral formation is a great attraction for scuba diving. Boats can only be hired for diving, fishing or sightseeing if they are licensed for the specific purpose by the government. This is intended to ensure that tourists travel on safe, reliable vessels and also to prevent the proliferation of self-appointed guides.

THE CAYES

The Cayes off the coast are most attractive. They are used by holiday campers from February to May and in August. From many of the holiday villas stretch pens or "crawls" to protect the bather from sharks or barracudas, and to keep the water clean.

There are 212 square miles of cayes. St. George's Caye, 9 miles NE of Belize, was once the capital and was the scene of the battle in 1798 which established British possession. The larger ones are Turneffe Island and Ambergris, Caulker, and English Cayes. Fishermen live on some cayes, coconuts are grown on others, but many are uninhabited swamps. The smaller cayes do not have much shade, so be careful if you go bathing on them. Sandflies infest some cayes (e.g. Caulker), the sandfly season is December to beginning of February; mosquito season June, July, sometimes October. On Big Caye Bokel, at the southern end of the Turneffe group, are 3 "Caribbean Lodges" for big-spending fishermen and skin-divers, each holding 12 guests (*Turneffe Island Lodge*, bar, restaurant, diving and snorkelling trips, very good; *Turneffe Island Flats*, less expensive). Caye Chapel has a large hotel and a private airstrip, and Caye Caulker several guest rooms and hotels.

Travel by boat to and between the islands is becoming increasingly regulated and the new licensing requirements will probably drive the cheaper boats out of business. In general, it is easier to arrange travel between the islands once there, than from Belize City. All authorized boats leave from the Shell station on North Front Street. Cargo boats are no longer allowed to carry passengers, too many have capsized with tourists on board, causing loss of life.

On Caye Chapel is the *Pyramid Island Resort*, A without a/c, L with, American or European Plan available, diving packages, air transfers to Belize City (P.O.Box 192, Belize City, T 4-4409). Caye Chapel is free of sandflies and mosquitoes and there are several beaches, cleaned daily. 40 mins. by boat from Belize City. There is also a landing strip used by army helicopters and Maya Airlines.

Ambergris Caye This island, with its village of San Pedro, is being rapidly developed as a tourist resort and is expensive. Snorkelling at *Amigo* costs BZ$20.

Accommodation and Food *Ramon's Reef Resort*, a diving and beach resort, US$85 p.p. per day for double room, all meals and all diving, highly recommended even for non-divers (fishing, swimming, boating, snorkelling), very efficient. Hotels: *San Pedro Holiday Hotel*, L, including meals; *Journey's End*, P.O. Box 13, T (501) 026-2173, L, resort facilities including diving; *Conch Shell Inn*, on beach B; *Coral Beach*, A, incl. meals; *Royal Palm*, A-L; *San Pedrano*, C without, to A with meals; *El Pescador*, on Punta Arena beach, L, a/c; facilities for sailing, diving etc. *Tomas Hotel*, D (more if reserved in advance) with bath, clean, trips to reef; *Spindrift Hotel*, has been rec., B, 30 rooms, 4 apartments, trips up the Belize River, a/c, comfortable, restaurant. *Rosie's*, D, friendly, clean, airy rooms overlooking sea; *Lily's*, C, nice rooms with sea view, fan, clean, friendly, T 026-2059; *Yoli's*, C with bath, clean, rec. There are other expensive hotels, several in the BZ$20-45 range, and some basic hotels. *Big Daddy's Disco*, rec. The *San Pedro Grill* is a good place to meet other travellers and swap information on boats, etc. Other eating places are: *Elvi's Kitchen*, reasonable prices; *Lily's Restaurant*, best seafood in town; *Pier Restaurant*, Italian/Swiss, expensive; *The Hut*, Mexican, friendly. At Coral Beach, the Forman, Gómez, González and Paz families provide rooms and meals for BZ$18 each. At Sea Breeze, the Paz and Núñez families offer the same accommodation at the same price.

In the same building complex as the *Spindrift* is a branch of the Atlantic Bank, a post office and a chemist.

Transport Several flights daily to and from Belize City with Tropic, Island and Maya Air, BZ$35 one way, BZ$60 return. Universal Travel at San Pedro airfield helpful. They can arrange charter flights to Corozal. Boat from Shell station, Belize City, BZ$20, non-stop. Leaves at 1300, returns from Holiday Pier, San Pedro, at

0700, daily. Boats, irregular, between Ambergris and Caye Caulker, no set fare. Bikes can be rented at *Sands Hotel* for BZ$4/hour. One cannot in practice walk N along the beach from San Pedro to Xcalak, Mexico.

Caye Caulker   A lobster-fishing island, which used to be relatively unspoilt, but the number of tourists is now increasing and the shoreline has become dirty (some services are reported to have deteriorated, and theft and unpleasantness from some mainlanders who go to the caye with tourists occurs). There are no beaches, but you can swim at the channel ("cut") or off one of the many piers. A reef museum has opened with enlarged photos of reef fish, free for school parties, tourists are asked for a US$2 donation to help expansion.

Hotels   *Tom's Hotel*, E, with fan, basic, clean, friendly, excellent value, laundry service US$5, barbeque, rec. Tom's boat trips cost BZ$7. *Mira Mar*, E p.p., bargain if staying longer, helpful owner Melvin Badillo, he owns liquor store, his family runs a pastry shop and grocery store; *Shirley's Guest House*, E, south end of village, very relaxing; *Reef Hotel*, C (formerly *Martínez Caribbean Inn*), under new management since 1989, small rooms, basic, but reasonable for the caye; *Edits*, F per bed in room (whether occupied or not), good; *Marin*, F, with bath, rec. (the proprietor, John Marin, will take you out for a snorkelling trip on the reef for BZ$10), *Riva's Guest House*, E, basic accommodation. Their reef trips in an attractive schooner are the longest; snorkelling equipment hire, BZ$3; *Daisy's* (or *Deisy's*), E with shower, toilet and fan, reductions for longer stays, cash travellers' cheques, good. *Vega's Far Inn* rents 7 rooms, all doubles, E with ceiling fan and fresh linen, flush toilets and showers (limited hot water) shared with camping ground, which is guarded, has drinking water, hot water, clean toilets, barbecue, can rent out camping gear (camping costs BZ$5.30), but aggressive owners. *Ignacio Beach Huts*, small huts or hammocks just outside town, E for a hut for 3-4, rec., camping space (Ignacio's reef trips cost BZ$4 and he has equipment; he is principally a lobster fisherman); *Rainbow Hotel*, on the beach, 10 small bungalows, D, with shower. Beach houses can also be rented for BZ$100-300 a month. Camping on the beach is forbidden.

Restaurant   For dinner, seek out Mrs. Rodríguez, who serves meals at 1700/1730 for around BZ$10 for 2, very good (limited accommodation available). *Melvin's*, excellent lobster meals (opp. *Riva's*); *Tropical Paradise* for excellent seafood. Cakes and pastries can be bought at houses displaying the sign, rec. are *Daisy's, Jessie's* (open 0830-1300, 1500-1700, behind *Riva's*); *Emma*, on path to co-op, sells delicious lobster pies, and chocolate-coconut pies. Many private houses serve food.

International telephone connections available on Caye Caulker. The island also

boasts two book swaps. Good nightlife at the *Black Coral* disco, very busy Fri. and Sat.

Transport Boats leave from behind Jan's Shell Station on North Front Street, for Caye Caulker, at about 0930 daily except Sun. (BZ$12 p.p., payable only on arrival at Caye Caulker—otherwise you'll be swindled), BZ$24 return, 45 mins. one way (boats depend on weather and number of passengers), return boats at 0700 (if booked in advance at *Edit's Hotel*, BZ$10). Jerry Pacheco's *Blue Wave*, Emilio Novelo's *Ocean Star* and "Chocolate's" *Soledad* are the currently authorized boats.

Reef trips (see also above, under Hotels), BZ$6-8 each for 3-7 hours as long as there are 3 or more in a group. Protect against sunburn on reef trips. Mervin, a local man, is reliable for snorkelling trips, he will also take you to Belize City. Also Gamoosa, who will spend all day with you on the reef (BZ$10 for a day's snorkelling, BZ$20 for a trip to San Pedro; his boat leaves at about 1100) and then invite you to his house to eat the fish and lobster you have caught, prepared deliciously by his wife; she also offers a healthy breakfast of banana, yoghurt, granola and honey for BZ$3.50. Also recommended is Alfonso Rosardo, a Mexican, reef trips for up to 6 people, 5-6 hrs., BZ$9, sometimes offers meals at his house afterwards. Also recommended is Lawrence (next to *Riva's Guest House*) and Obdulio, BZ$6 p.p. for 3 hr trip (or BZ$40 for a full day's fishing, inclusive). Lobster fishing and diving for conch is also possible. Mask, snorkel and fins for BZ$3-6 (for instance at the post office). Wind-surfing equipment hire: BZ$8 an hour, BZ$20 ½ day, BZ$40 a day, lessons, BZ$10 exc. equipment. Frank and Janie Bounting (P.O.Box 667, T 44307, ext. 143 mainland side, past the football pitch) charge US$55 for 2 scuba dives, day and night, good value; they also offer a 3-day PADI certificate course, recommended. For sailing charters, Jim and Dorothy of "Sea-ing is Belizing", who also run scuba trips to Goff's Caye Park and the Turneffe Islands (5-10 days). There is a sailing school, charging BZ$60 for a 5-hr., solo beginner's course. It may be possible to hire a boat for 6-8 people to Chetumal. There are also boats leaving for Honduras from Caye Caulker, but be sure to get exit stamps and other documentation in Belize City first.

English Caye, 12 miles off Belize City, is beautiful, with no facilities; take a day trip only. It is part of the reef so you can snorkel right off the beach.

Half Moon Caye at Lighthouse Reef, 45 miles E of Belize City, is the site of the **Red-Footed Booby Sanctuary**, a national reserve. Besides the booby, which is unusual in that almost all the individuals have the white colour phase (normally they are dull brown), magnificent frigate birds nest on the island. The seabirds nest on the western side, which has dense vegetation (the eastern side is covered mainly in coconut palms). Of the 98 other bird species recorded on Half Moon Caye, 77 are migrants. Iguana, the wish willy (smaller than the iguana) and the *anolis allisoni* lizard inhabit the caye, and hawksbill and loggerhead turtles lay their eggs on the beaches. The Belize Audubon Society, 49 Southern Foreshore, maintains the sanctuary; there is a lookout tower and trail. A lighthouse on the caye gives fine views of the reef. Around sunset you can watch the boobies from the lookout as they return from fishing. They land beside their waiting mates at the rate of about 50 a minute. They seem totally unbothered by humans.

There are no facilities; take all food, drink and fuel. On arrival you must register with the warden near the lighthouse (the warden will provide maps and tell you where you can camp).

In Lighthouse Reef is the **Blue Hole**, an almost circular sinkhole with depths exceeding 400 feet. It was studied by Jacques Cousteau in 1984. Stalagmites and stalactites can be found in the underwater cave. Scuba diving is outstanding at Lighthouse Reef, including two walls which descend almost vertically from 30-40 feet to several thousand.

Bobby takes passengers by sailing boat from Caye Caulker to Half Moon Caye and the Blue Hole for US$25 p.p. including food (bring your own tent and sleeping bag). To charter a motor boat in Belize City costs about US$50 p.p. if 10 people are going (6 hour journey). Bill Hinkis, in San Pedro Town, Ambergris Caye, offers three-day sailing cruises to Lighthouse Reef for US$150 (you provide food, ice and fuel). Bill and his boat *Yanira* can be found beside the lagoon off Back Street, just north of the football field. Other sailing vessels charge US$150-250 per day.

NORTH AND WEST BELIZE

Two main roads penetrate the country from Belize City: one to the N and other to the W. The Northern Highway is well paved to the Mexican border. Fifteen miles on there is a turning left to **Bermudian Landing**, a small Creole village 25 miles from Belize City (beyond Burrell Boom), where there is a local wild life museum and the **Community Baboon Sanctuary** nearby, with baboons and black howler monkeys. Trails in and around the reserve. Boats can be hired from the warden for river trips to see monkeys and birds. Booklet (US$3, excellent) from the Audubon Society, 49 Southern Foreshore. The warden, Fallet Young, will also arrange accommodation locally, T 44405. Bus from Belize City about midday; return 0530.

The Northern Highway continues to Sand Hill where a road turns off to the NW to the Crooked Tree Lagoons, an exceptionally rich area for birds. Ask for information at the Audubon Society. North of Sand Hill the road forks, the quicker route heading direct to Orange Walk, the older road looping N then NW, passing near Altun Ha. The new highway runs to (66 miles) Orange Walk, centre of a district where about 17,000 Creoles, Mennonites and Maya Indians get their living from timber, sugar planting and general agriculture. In the Orange Walk District is a large Old Maya ceremonial site, **Nohochtunich**; enormous masonry slabs were used in a stairway up one of the pyramids.

The population of **Orange Walk**, a bustling agricultural centre, is 8,500. A toll bridge (BZ$1) now spans the New River. Spanish is the predominant language. It is a centre for refugees from other parts of Central America. Despite government action against drug-trafficking in this area, travellers still describe it as "a dodgy little town after dark."

Hotels *Chula Vista Hotel*, at gas station just outside town, safe, clean, helpful owner, D. *Mi Amor*, 19 Belize-Corozal road, E with shared bath, and more expensive rooms, noisy from short-stay activity, restaurant; *Jane's*, Market Lane, E; *La Nueva Ola*, 73 Otro Benque Rd., E; *Paradise* restaurant, very expensive; *Rocky's Restaurant*, rather dear; *Julie's*, nr. police station, good, inexpensive creole cooking; similarly at *Baker's*. Several Chinese restaurants.

Exchange Bank of Nova Scotia; same hours as Belize City (**see page** 422).

Bus All Chetumal buses pass Orange Walk Town (hourly); Belize-Orange Walk, BZ$3.50.

A road heads W from Orange Walk, then turns S, parallel first to the Mexican border, then the Guatemalan (where it becomes unmade). At Gallon Jug on this part is *Chan Chich*, a jungle tourism lodge built around a small Maya ruin; recommended (flights to Chan Chich can be chartered).

The Northern Highway continues to Corozal (96 miles from Belize) then for 8 miles to the Mexican frontier, where a bridge across the Río Hondo connects with Chetumal. Border crossing formalities are relatively relaxed. Driving time, Belize-frontier, 3 hours, Belize City-Chetumal, 4 hrs. including the border stop. (Taxi, BZ$8 Corozal-border, BZ$17 Corozal-Chetumal, bus, Belize City-Chetumal BZ$7). One can no longer acquire a tourist card at the border; you must get one at the Mexican Consulate in Belize City. If entering Belize for only a few days, you can ask the Mexican officials to save your tourist card for you (but don't depend on it). If you want a new tourist card for a full 30 days you must get it in Belize City. It is possible to buy pesos at the border with either US or Belizean dollars (outside office hours, try the shops; rates at the border are on a par with those in the Yucatán). If coming from Mexico it is best to get rid of pesos at the border. Bargain for good rates of exchange at the border (there is a small bank near customs, so compare rates), better here than with money changers in Orange Walk Town or Corozal.

Corozal, with a population of 7,000, was the centre of the sugar industry. Like Orange Walk Town it is economically depressed because the local sugar factory has been closed; there has been a greater dependence on marijuana as a result. Corozal is much the safer place. It is open to the sea with a pleasant waterfront.

Hotels At Consejo Shore, *Adventure*, C with no meals, to L full board, 7 miles from town, bar and restaurant (no public transport); *Maya*, South End, E; *Nestor's Hotel*, 125, 5th Av. South (T 04-2354), E with bath and fan, very good value, refrescos available, very helpful owner (Jake); *Capri*, 14 Fourth Ave., run down, E. Two motels: *Caribbean*, South End, C, basic, restaurant with great cheeseburgers; *Tony's*, South End also, D (C, with a/c), clean but unfriendly, restaurant overpriced. Other restaurants: *Club Campesino*, decent bar, good fried chicken after 1800; *Rexo*, North 5th St., Chinese; also Chinese: *Bumpers* (rec.); *King of Kings*; *Hong Kong*.

Camping *Caribbean* Motel and Trailer Park, on Barracks Road, camping possible but not very safe, (US$2 p.p.), shaded sites, good restaurant, beach.

Exchange Barclays Bank International, Bank of Nova Scotia, open same hours as Belize City (**see page** 422).

Buses There are 15 buses a day from Belize to Corozal by Venus Bus, Magazine Road, and Batty Bus, 54 East Collet Canal, 3½-5 hrs., BZ$6. Both continue to Chetumal where there is a new bus terminal on the outskirts of town; because of the frequency, there is no need to take a colectivo to the Mexican border unless travelling at unusual hours (BZ$5). The increased frequency of buses to Chetumal and the number of money changers cater for Belizeans shopping cheaply in Mexico—very popular, book early. Through tickets can be bought from Corozal to San Ignacio (see below), via Belize City, but you must get a new seat number at the Batty Bus counter in Belize City. For those coming from Mexico who are more interested in Tikal than Belize, Batty Buses leaving Chetumal at 0230, 0400 or 0600 go straight to the Guatemalan border.

Excursion 8 miles N of Corozal, on the road to Chetumal, is 4 Miles Lagoon, about ¼ mile off the road (buses will drop you there). Clean swimming, better than Corozal bay, some food and drinks available; it is often crowded at weekends.

The Western Highway runs from Belize City to Belmopan and on through savanna, pine ridge and high canopied forest to **San Ignacio** (capital of Cayo District, 72 miles) and the Guatemalan frontier. About 60 miles along this road is Ontario Village. There is camping space and a trailer to rent, hot showers. San Ignacio, known locally as Cayo, has a population of about 5,600. It stands at 200-250 feet, with a pleasant climate, and is a good base for excursions into the Mountain Pine Ridge, some 120 square miles of well-watered, undulating country rising to 3,000 feet. High waterfalls and attractive river scenery, picnic sites, bathing places are features. You can camp at Augustine, seek information from rangers. (Bus to Belize City, Mon.-Fri., 1330, 1530, plus 1230 on Mon., Sat., and Sun., 1300, 1400, 1500, 1600 BZ$3.75, with Batty Bus; also Novello's, 4 daily Mon.-Sat., 1030 on Sun.)

Hotels and Restaurants *Central*, 24 Burns Ave., E with bath, clean, friendly, rec., breakfast possible; *Hi-Et Hotel*, 12 West St., E, noisy, no fans, low partition walls, clothes washing permitted; *Belmoral*, D, showers, fan, a bit noisy; *San Ignacio Hotel*, on road to Benque Viejo, C, with bath, fan, hot water, clean, helpful staff, swimming pool, excellent restaurant, highly rec., disco at weekends, bar opens at 1000 (good place for meeting British soldiers); around the corner is *Piache Hotel*, 18 Buena Vista Rd., E-D in either thatched cottages with bath or room without bath, cold water, basic, bar in p.m. Doña Elvira Espat serves good meals at her house (inc. breakfast), advance notice required, good, friendly with a wealth of local information (no sign, corner of Galvez Street and Bullet Tree Road). *La Fuente*, Eve St. and West St., good juices and pastries; *The Place*, small pastry shop on Burns Ave., good; *Maxim's*, Bullet Tree Rd. and Far West St., Chinese, good food, poor service. George, at the *Club Shangrila*, makes a good cup of tea, and offers assistance of all sorts. Also highly informative is Bob at *Eva's Bar*, Burns Ave. (good, inexpensive local dishes). *Farmers Emporium*, Burns Ave., a shop selling wholewheat bread, raisins, juices, fresh milk. Fruit and vegetable market every Sat. a.m. Note that all shops and businesses close 1700-1900.

Exchange Venus Stores, 23 Burns Ave. (09-2186) or changers in the town square give better rates of exchange for cash (inc. quetzales) and travellers' cheques than you can get at the border with Guatemala.

Tours Jungle View Tours, No. 26 18th St., San Ignacio, T 092-2012, recommended. Local taxis which offer tours of Mountain Pine Ridge in the wet season probably won't get very far; also, taking a tour to Xunantunich is not really necessary. Mountain Equestrian Trails, Mile 8, Mtn. Pine Ridge Rd., Central Farm P.O., Cayo District, Fax 092-2060 T (011-501) 82-3180 for international reservations, 082-3180 for local reservations and 092-2197 for transport, offers ½-day or full-day adventure tours on horseback in western Belize, "Turf" and "Turf and Surf" packages, and other expeditions accommodation in *Casa Cielo Resort Hotel* (owners Jim and Marguerite Bevis). Ask at *Eva's Bar* for information on canoe trips up the river with Tony, wildlife, small rapids, 6 hours, BZ$20, good value. Also ask there about a trip with Chris Heckert, a German, who will take you to the Maya ruins at Caracol, about 30 miles (as the crow flies), South through the jungle (group of 8, US$300).

The British Army's Holdfast camp is about 12 miles from the border.

San Ignacio is on the eastern branch of the Old, or Belize River, known as the Macal, navigable almost to the Guatemalan frontier. The river journey of 121 miles from Belize, broken by many rapids, needs considerable ingenuity to negotiate the numerous "runs".

Places to Stay *Chaa Creek Cottages*, on the Macal River, 5 miles upstream from San Ignacio, has rooms from B (b. and b.), to L (all meals), set on a working farm in pleasant countryside, highly rec. Trips on the river, to Xunantunich, to Tikal, to Mountain Pine Ridge, to Caracol, nature walks and jungle safaris organized; also joint vacations arranged with *Rum Point Inn*, Placencia. If coming by road, turn off the Benque road at Chial; hotel will collect you by boat from San Ignacio (US$25 for 4), or from international airport (US$90); reservations P.O. Box 53, San Ignacio, T 092-2037.

Nabitunich Cottages, turn off the Benque road 1½ miles beyond Chial, offers spectacular views of Xunantunich and another, unexcavated Maya ruin, jungle trails, horse riding, canoeing; book through agent, P.O. Box 752, Belize City, T 4-5841.

Maya Mountain Lodge (Bart and Suzi Mickler), also on the Macal River, ¾ mile from San Ignacio at 9 Cristo Rey Road (taxi from town US$2.50, C-B, most welcoming, highly rec., special weekly and monthly rates and for families, **also discounts on lodging** (50%) and food (20%) to backpackers with Trade & Travel Publications' *Handbooks*, T 092-2164 (The Farm Store), P.O. Box 46, San Ignacio, restaurant, laundry, postal service, swimming, hiking, riding, canoeing, fishing. Explore Belize Tours in the region and beyond; also "Parrot's Perch" social and educational area with resident naturalist and ornithologist.

Jungle View Campground, 2½ miles on Mountain Pine Ridge road (leave Western Highway at the community of Santa Elena, near Hawksworth Bridge), popular, Maya and American-run, US$7.50 for 2 including car. Local tours and to Tikal. *Barton's Creek* is a Mennonite community, from which one can buy produce. Five miles away is *Georgeville*, where one can try the Mennonites' ice cream and cheese. **N.B.** Between January and June, the risk of fire in the reserve is very great, please take extra care; camp fires are strictly prohibited.

El Indio Perdido, a farm/guest house (rec.), is 1½ miles N of the Western Highway (turn-off 5 miles from San Ignacio, 2 from Benque Viejo), D with shared shower, C with shower, B with private bath, meals US$3-7.50; activities include swimming, boating (US$5-15), riding (US$5-15), walking, trips to Xunantunich, Tikal (Sats.), the Caves and Mountain Pine Ridge. The farm is on the Mopan River, near Xunantunich (but is not open all the time). Address: Colette Gross, Benque Viejo del Carmen, Cayo District, Belize, T 092-2025 or VHF 8450.

Nine miles up-river from San Ignacio is **Benque Viejo del Carmen**, near the Guatemalan frontier (road not sealed, very dusty in the dry season). Population, 2,500. Visas and tourist cards can be obtained at the border. Exchange rates for buying quetzales are better either in the central square in San Ignacio or the Banco de Guatemala on the Guatemalan side of the border (travellers' cheques changed) than with the Belizean money changers at the border.

Hotels *Okis*, George St., E, and *Hotel Maya*, E, 11 George St., opposite the bus station, are the least bad. (Hotels on Guatemalan side of the border are better.)

Meals at *Riverside Restaurant*, on main square; *Restaurant Los Angeles*, Church St.; *Hawaii*, on main street, rec.; or at one of picturesque huts.

Three miles away, at **Xunantunich**, now freed from heavy bush, there are Classic Maya remains in beautiful surroundings. The views from the roof of the spectacular main temple (reportedly the highest man-made structure in Belize) are magnificent. (A leaflet on the area is available from the Archaeological Dept. for BZ$0.25.) Xunantunich can be reached by walking along the Cayo road for about 10 mins. until you reach the landing stage for a ferry; this will take you across the river (US$0.25 p.p., does not run 1200-1400, last one at 1630), then there is a strenuous 1½ hr. walk uphill, not rec. for cars; motorcyclists may find the hill impossible after rain; taxi from San Ignacio, BZ$3. On the far side turn right for Xunantunich (open 0800-1700, entry, BZ$3).

Opposite the ferry, a 2 km. walk brings you to a farm run by an American couple where you can stay in the middle of the wilderness.

South of San Ignacio is the rediscovered Maya city of **Caracol**, "six times the size of ancient Rome in the classic period".

Transport Novello's run daily buses from Belize City to Benque Viejo; frequent buses from San Ignacio to Benque Viejo, taxi BZ$20, or colectivo from central square, BZ$3 (or BZ$3 to Melchor de Mencos in Guatemala, 30 minutes). To Guatemala from Benque Viejo by taxi, BZ$3 or BZ$1 by colectivo. Free passage of border only weekdays (or if your stay in Belize was 24 hours or less), 0800-1200 and 1400-1700; at other times a fee is charged (US$1). The bridge over the Río Mopán has been rebuilt. On far side someone will carry the luggage to Melchor de Mencos (hotels, and money change possible—see page 375), where there is a landing strip (flights to Flores). There is also a road (very rough) on to Santa Elena, for Flores (a bus leaves the border for Flores at 1130, US$1.50, or 4 daily buses from Melchor de Mencos, 3½ hrs., US$1.50, leave Belize City before 0930 to catch the 1400 bus); it is only possible to get to Tikal by bus by asking the driver of the border-Flores bus to let you off at the road junction (El Cruce), where you can get a connecting bus to Tikal (**see page** 375). Taxi from the border to Tikal, US$35 (takes 6); to Flores, US$7.50.

SOUTHERN BELIZE

Some 48 miles from Belize City, near Belmopan, the narrow 52-mile Hummingbird Highway branches off SE from the Western Highway, through beautiful jungle scenery to **Dangriga** (chief town of the Stann Creek District), some 105 miles from Belize City and 1¾-2½ hours drive from Belmopan. En route, near Over the Top Camp, is the Blue Hole, an azure blue swimming hole where the water comes out of a cave and re-enters another 100 feet away. Make sure you protect your car and belongings while swimming, 2 miles SW of Blue Hole are St Hernan's Caves, ½ mile off the road along a dirt track. You can walk for more than half a mile underground: torch essential. Dangriga's population is 2,500. In this, the most fertile area in the country, are grown citrus fruits, bananas, cassava, and general food crops. The town is on the seashore, and has an airstrip and cinema. Houses built of wood, on piles. Mosquitoes and sand flies are a nuisance.

Local Holiday 18-19 Nov., Garifuna, or Settlement Day, re-enacting the landing of the Black Caribs in 1823. Dancing all night and next day; very popular. All transport to Dangriga is booked up a week in advance and hotel rooms impossible to find.

Hotels *Riverside*, 135 Commerce St., D, not always clean, *Pelican Beach*, outside town (P.O. Box 14), on the beach, L, with private bath and a/c; both have good restaurants. *Cameleon*, 119 Commerce St., E, good and friendly (close by, towards the bridge) is an excellent Chinese restaurant. Cheaper lodgings in *Catalina*, 37 Cedar St., E, its only merit is that it is cheap. Also you can stay in private homes (basic), e.g. Miss Caroline's. There is a cooperative which runs a place to pitch a tent or sling a hammock. Unfurnished houses are rented out for BZ$40-60 a month.

Restaurants *Ten kitchen*, next to Z-line bus office, good. At Mile 25.5 on the Hummingbird Highway, N of Dangriga, is *Hummingbird Café*, owned by Ron and Louise Lines (Canadians—mailing address P.O. Box 120, Belmopan); excellent meals and very helpful. *Starlight*, Chinese, cheapish.

Entertainment Listen for local music "Punta Rock", a unique Garifuna/African based Carib sound. A local band, the Turtles, maintain a Punta museum in town.

Exchange Bank of Nova Scotia; Barclays Bank International. Same hours as Belize City. (See page 422.)

Bus from Belize City, Z Line, Magazine Street, daily at 1000, 1100, 1500 and 1600, plus 0600 Mon., returning daily 0500, 0600, 0900, 1000, Sun. at 0900, 1000, 1500, BZ$8, 4 hrs. (buy ticket in advance to reserve seat), or truck, BZ$2. Two buses daily to Punta Gorda, one is the James Line bus from Belize City and the other, Z line, at 1530, 4-5 hrs., BZ$8.50 (very crowded), stops at Independence, near Mango Creek.

Dangriga and Mango Creek (for Placentia) are connected by the Southern Highway. 20 miles south of Dangriga is **Kendal** with some Maya ruins nearby. Turning inland at Maya Center some 5 miles further on is the 150 square mile **Jaguar Wildlife Sanctuary**, 6 miles into the Cockscomb Range. There is a visitor centre with a number of guided jungle trails. Spectacular wildlife of all kinds including jaguar, though you are not likely to see them. Camping (BZ$3 p.p.) or clean cabin with cooking facilities (BZ$12). Potable water available but you must bring your own food. Nearest shop at Maya Center on the Highway. You can also climb Victoria Peak (3,675 ft), a 2-3 day hike.

Turning east towards the Caribbean near Kendal leads down the Sittee River to a new centre being created by Jim and Dot Waters near Possom Point Biological Station. Jungle surroundings, birdwatching, canoeing. Dot will cook for you, but as yet accommodation is primitive.

Further down the Southern Highway watch for the sign for Maya Beach. 9 miles leads to Riversdale, then down a spit of land to Maya Beach. *Tropical Lodge* BZ$120 per day, full board, camping BZ$5, hot showers. Run by Ted and Peggy Williams, remote, good place to relax, or enjoy the Caribbean.

Placencia, a quiet, unspoilt little resort 30 miles S of Dangriga, reached by dugout, BZ$10 each way, 3 hrs., or, now that the road from Dangriga is finished, by bus (leaves Dangriga at 1530, 1½ hrs., BZ$7). Maya Airways fly 3 times a day Belize City-Dangriga-Placencia/Big Creek (dugout Placencia-Big Creek arranged at *Sonny's*; flight tickets are sold at Placencia's new post office), BZ$63 one way. Big Creek, on the mainland opposite Placentia is 3 miles from Mango Creek (see below).

Accommodation (note that rooms may be hard to find in p.m., e.g. after arrival of the bus from Dangriga) *E-Lee Placencia*, E, full board BZ$15 extra (single meals available), creole cooking, run by Dalton Eiley and Jim Lee; they offer reef fishing, snorkelling, excursions to the jungle, Pine Ridge, Mayan ruins and into the mountains. If arriving by air at Big Creek, first contact Hubert Eiley, 3 Richard Sidewalk, Belize City (T 3567) who will arrange for a boat to take you to Placencia; *Ran's Travel Lodge*, E, shared shower, toilet, friendly, fresh coconut bread baked next door (1000-1100); *Maya Beach Tropical Lodge*, C no meals—L full board (P.O. Box 23, Dangriga); *Placencia Cove*, A, and *Rum Point Inn* (L, latter T 06-2017); *Kitty's Place*, T 06-2027, beach apartment BZ$90 per day, BZ$270 per week, rooms BZ$40, camping BZ$10, with hot showers; *Hilltop*, F; Miss Jackson rents rooms, E-F, BZ$7 for 3 meals (book in advance if non-resident), cooking facilities, friendly (contact Bill, an American, here, for trips to the reef); Mrs. Leslie at the Post Office rents houses at BZ$40 per day (4-6 people, fridge and cooker); she also has hammock space for 3, BZ$5 per night (noisy); Mrs Leslie's son Charles makes all arrangements for the boat to Puerto Cortés, Honduras (see below), and occasionally changes travellers' cheques; he also organizes trips to the reef, etc. Mr. Clive rents 2 houses, one at BZ$4.50, one at BZ$5 p.p. per day; Mr. Zabari's house (rented by Mr. Leslie), BZ$20 per day, 3 large rooms, all facilities. Rooms for rent behind *Galley* restaurant, very basic but cheap, friendly owner. Camping on the beach or under the coconut palms.

Restaurants *The Galley*, rec., especially the seaweed punch, order meals 2-3 hrs. in advance, information on fishing and snorkelling; *Jennie's*—ask here for lodgings at *Seaspray*, F, without bath, good value, by post office; *Jene's*, a bit of cool luxury and excellent food. *Jayl's*, opposite, Bill (and his family) will feed you well and cheaply. *The Stone Crab* (sign nr. volleyball court), good seafood; and *Sonny's*; at least 5 shops (fresh fruit and vegetables supplied to *The Market* once a week, mostly sold out the same day), a video-cassette movie theatre, four bars (*Cosy's* is rec., disco every night, good hamburgers), the fishing cooperative, open Mon.-Sat., a.m., sells fish cheaply, and supplies the town's electricity.

There is a police station. The people are very friendly and excursions can be made to the coral reef, 16 km. off-shore (US$75-100 for 6 people). The only telephone is at the Post Office (good source of information on boats). Nearest bank in Mango Creek (Bank of Nova Scotia) open Fri. only 0900-1200, but shops and market change travellers' cheques. Visa extensions obtainable in Mango Creek.

Mango Creek is a banana exporting port, 30 miles (40 by road) S of Dangriga. Bus Belize City-Mango Creek, Southern Transport, James Bus Service, from Pound Yard Bridge, Tues., Wed., Fri. at 0600, Mon., Sat. at 0900; return Sun., Fri. at 1300, Sun., Tues., Thurs. 0600. BZ$13 (insect-repellant imperative). 1000 Z-line bus from Belize City to Dangriga connects with another Z-line bus to Mango Creek, 2 hrs, BZ$5. Hotel above *People's Restaurant*, F; food better at the white house with green shutters behind it (book 2 hrs. in advance if possible); *Hello Hotel* (at Independence) run by Antonio Zabaneh at the shop where the Z-line bus stops, E, clean, comfortable, helpful.

Motorized canoe from Mango Creek to Puerto Cortés, Honduras, no fixed schedule, but mostly Thurs.-Sun. (Antonio Zabaneh at his store—phone 06-2011— knows when boats will arrive), US$50 one way, 7-9 hrs. (rubber protective sheeting is provided—hang on to it, usually not enough to go round, nor lifejackets—but you will still get wet unless wearing waterproofs, or just a swimming costume on hot days; it can be dangerous in rough weather). Remember to get an exit stamp (preferably in Belize City), obtainable at the police station in Mango Creek, not Placentia (the BZ$20 departure tax demanded here is not official). Glover's Reef, about 45 miles off Dangriga, is an atoll with beautiful diving, cottages for rent (BZ$10-25 p.p., bring own food); boats BZ$40-80.

The Southern Highway runs 100 miles from Dangriga S, past Mango Creek, then turns sharp left to the coast. Shortly before this there is a bridge across the Rio Grande at Big Fall (mile 83—the waterfall here is worth seeing). Behind the grocery store is a warm pool where you can swim, camp, hang a hammock. At the end of the road you come to **Punta Gorda**, port of the Toledo District (the road is unpaved, but good all-weather surface). Population 2,500. Rainfall is exceptionally heavy: over 170 inches. The coast, which is some 10 feet above sea-level, is fringed with coconut palms. The main products are beans, rice, cattle and pigs.

Hotels *St. Charles Inn*, C, with or without bath, good; *Foster's*, 19 Main St., E; *Wahima*, on waterfront, E, small rooms, basic, but clean and safe, owner is local school teacher, friendly and informative. You can flag down the 0500 bus to Belize in front of hotel—buy ticket the night before; *Nature's Way Guest House*, D, 65 Front Street, not too clean but good breakfast, will arrange tours; *Lux Drive Inn*, 17 Front St., D with bath, often full, cockroaches, noisy, damp; *Mahung's Hotel*, 11 Main St., E, cockroaches, not rec.; *Mira Mar*, 95 Front St., C-A, overpriced, noisy disco, restaurant not rec. If you arrive too late to find a hotel, try asking around for Ched (a friendly American), who has a house to rent near the church, BZ$30, only one bed but plenty of space to sling hammocks, clean, quiet, cold shower. *Kowloon Restaurant*, rec. The town has a cinema.

Bus from Belize, 9-12 hrs., BZ$19, daily except Thurs. and Sun. (times as for Mango Creek); returns (Z-line) 0500 daily (James Bus Service) Sun., Fri. 1300, Sun., Tues., Thurs. 0600, with a 1700 bus on Fri. for passengers from Guatemala ferry. To Dangriga, Z-line daily at 0530, arriving in time to catch 1000 bus to Belize City.

Air Daily flights to Big Creek, Dangriga, Belize City and if requested to International airport.

Ferry to Guatemala The ferry has superseded the dugout passages to Livingston and Puerto Barrios, Tues. and Fri. at 1400-1500, 4½ hrs. to Puerto Barrios, ticket must be purchased before 1400, costs BZ$11 (US$5.50) or Q6 (US$2.50); the Tuesday boat tends to be faster, perhaps because there is more demand for the Friday boat (queuing for tickets starts at 0800, sales not till 0930) and it is therefore heavier. Rough trip. Ferry ticket agent is on Middle Main Street (open a.m. only, in a shop 2 blocks from *Hotel Mira Mar*); he will insist that you have a visa for Guatemala. If you do not need a visa, insist on being sold a ticket without one; if you do need a visa, the nearest place to obtain one is Chetumal, Mexico. Police station for exit stamp is near the ticket office. Leaving Belize City by 0600 bus on Tues., Wed. or Fri., theoretically you can be in Guatemala on the same day, but with changes of bus in Dangriga and delays it is usually impossible; besides it's a tiring journey (to make sure, fly to Punta Gorda). In the other direction, two days are needed. If the ferry is not running the day you wish to travel, or is full, small boats are still available. Beware however of unsafe, unseaworthy craft. The weather can be treacherous, and you and your luggage will certainly get wet. Ferry favours Guatemalans and Beliceños, not much you can do about it! Jerry, an American, charges BZ$30 on his boat from Punta Gorda to Livingston if the ferry is not going to call there (and it appears now that it does not).

As there are few places to change Belizean dollars into quetzales in Guatemala, try Vernon's or other grocery stores in Punta Gorda (travellers' cheques or cash). Don't expect much of a rate in Guatemala: BZ1 to Q1 is standard.

About 9 miles N of Punta Gorda, about ¾ mile off the Southern

Highway, is the Maya site of Nimli Punit.

There is a road inland to two villages in the foothills of the Maya mountains; **San Antonio** (21 miles), with Maya ruins of mainly scientific interest (*Hotel Indita Bonita*, with *comedor*, good, clean; picturesque accommodation at Tacho's, BZ\$2; may be allowed use of an army hut); medical centre here. About 3 miles along the road to San Antonio is a branch to **San Pedro Colombia**, a Kekchi village. (Kekchi is a sub-tribe of Maya speaking a distinct language.) The Maya and Kekchi women wear picturesque costumes. There are many religious celebrations, at their most intense (mixed with general gaiety) on San Luis Rey day (5 August). There is a place to stay, run by Hawaiians. No bus; pick-up vans for hire in Dangriga, or get a ride in a truck from the market or rice co-operative's mill in Punta Gorda (one leaves early p.m.); alternatively, go to the road junction, known as Dump, where the northern branch goes to Independence/Mango Creek, the other to San Antonio, 6 miles, either hitch or walk. Transport daily from San Antonio to Punta Gorda at 0500, 0530 punctually; if going to Dangriga, take the 0500, get out at Dump to catch 0530 Z-line bus going N.

Turn left, just after crossing the new bridge at San Pedro Colombia, for one mile to reach the Maya remains of **Lubaantun**, excavated by Cambridge University in 1970 and found to date from the 8th to 9th centuries A.D., late in the Maya culture and therefore unique. According to latest reports, however, the site is fast reverting to jungle. Local food at a hut and swimming in a river nearby. If hiking in the jungle in this area, there are plenty of logging trails and hunters' tracks, but do not go alone.

Beyond San Antonio, a dirt road leads to Santa Cruz and Pueblo Viejo, both attractive villages. There is reported to be a trail on to the Guatemalan border and in theory you would end up on the road between Modesto Méndez and Poptún, but it is doubtful if this would appeal to the authorities.

INFORMATION FOR VISITORS

Documents All nationalities need passports, as well as sufficient funds and, officially, an onward ticket. Visas are usually not required from nationals of the UK, some Commonwealth countries (citizens of India do need a visa), USA, Canada, Belgium, Finland, Denmark, France, Greece, Italy, Leichtenstein, Luxemburg, Mexico, The Netherlands, Norway, Panama, Sweden, Turkey, Uruguay, Venezuela and Switzerland. Visas can be obtained from the Belizean Consulate in Chetumal, Mexico, for US\$10 (may also be charged the price of a telex to Mexico City, US\$40)—note that in May 1990 this post had not been confirmed; if the consul is unavailable, you must apply for a visa in Mexico City. Visas may not be purchased at the border. Free transit visas are available at borders (for 24 or 48 hours). It is possible that a visa may not be required if you have an onward ticket, but check all details at a Consulate before arriving at the border. Those going to other countries after leaving Belize should get any necessary visas in their home country. Visitors are initially granted 30 days' stay in Belize; this may be extended every 30 days up to 6 months at the Immigration Office, Barrack Rd., Belize City. At the end of 6 months, visitors must leave the country for at least 24 hours. Visitors must not engage in any type of employment, paid or unpaid, without first securing a work permit from the Department of Labour; if caught, the penalty for both the employer and the employee is severe. Travellers should note that the border guards seem to have complete power to refuse entry to people whose looks they do not like. Backpackers will be turned back unless all documents are in order; if you need a visa, you must have it to hand on arrival. There have also been reports that tourists carrying less than US$30 for each day of intended stay have been refused entry.

Motorists should carry their own driving licence and certificate of vehicle ownership. Third party insurance is mandatory, and can be purchased at any border (about BZ$35 a week). There may be no one to collect it after 1900. Valid International Driving Licences are accepted in place of Belize driving permits. BZ$5 exit fee for car.

Departure tax of BZ$20 on leaving from the international airport, but not for transit passengers who have spent less than 24 hrs. in the country. There is a land departure tax of BZ$2 except for those who have spent less than 24 hrs. in the country and for children under 12.

How to get there   There is no regular sea passenger service (but see under Belize City). There is a first-class airport, 10 miles from Belize, served by American, TAN Airlines and Taca International from Miami (reached by British Airways, Pan Am, Continental or Virgin Atlantic). Other US points served: New Orleans, (Sahsa, Taca), Houston (both by Continental, Taca, Sahsa) and Los Angeles (Taca). Also daily flights to San Pedro Sula (Sahsa), Tegucigalpa (TAN and Sahsa) San Salvador, San José, and Panama (all Taca). Sahsa has connections to Managua via Tegucigalpa. Tropic Air flies to Cancún (Mexico). Daily flights to Flores (Guatemala) and Guatemala City by Aerovías (Taca also flies daily to Guatemala City). West Caribbean Airlines flies daily to La Ceiba and Roatán, Honduras.

Customs   Clothing and articles for personal use are allowed in without payment of duty, but a deposit may be required to cover the duty payable on typewriters, dictaphones, cameras and radios. The duty, if claimed, is refunded when the visitor leaves the country. Import allowances are: 200 cigarettes or ½ lb. of tobacco; 20 fluid ozs. of alcohol; 1 bottle of perfume. Visitors can take in any amount of other currencies. No fruit or vegetables may be brought into Belize; searches are very thorough. Also drink any Mexican beer you have with you before crossing the border.

Sellers of cars must pay duty (if the buyer pays it, he may be able to bargain with the customs official), but prices are quite good particularly in Orange Walk (ask taxi drivers in Belize City). Also, O. Perez & Sons, 59 West Canal Str., Belize City may be able to help.

Internal Transport   Traffic drives on the right. When making a left turn, it is the driver's responsibility to ensure clearance of both oncoming traffic and vehicles behind; generally, drivers pull over to the far right, allow traffic from behind to pass, then make the left turn. Many accidents are caused by failure to observe this procedure. All major roads have been, or are being, improved.

Maya Airways flies daily to each of the main towns (see under Belize City) and offers charter rates to all local airstrips of which there are 25. 5 other companies have charters from Belize City to outlying districts. (Belize Aero Company, T 44102; Cari Bee Air Service, T 44253; Flight Service Ltd, T 7049; National Air Service, T 3727; Tropical Air Service, T 7049; Island Air Service). Charter rates: Cessna 3-seater, BZ$240; 4/5-seater, BZ$320; 9-seater, US$560.

Passenger transport between the main towns is by colectivo or bus, and trucks also carry passengers to many isolated destinations, although they are no longer allowed to carry passengers to places served by buses. Enquire at market place in Belize City. By law, buses are not allowed to carry standing passengers; some companies are stricter than others. Hitch hiking is very difficult as there is little traffic.

Food   For the cheapest meals, order rice. It will often come with beans, banana or plantain, or chicken.

Health   Europeans leading a normal life and taking common precautions find the climate pleasant and healthy. Malaria was reportedly under control, but once again precautions against the disease are essential. Also carry mosquito repellent. Dengue fever exists in Belize. Inoculation against yellow fever and tetanus is advisable but not obligatory. No case of either has been reported in years. Out-patients' medical attention is free of charge. Myo' On Clinic Ltd, Belize City (central, off Queen St.) has been recommended, but it charges for its services.

Clothing   The business dress for men is a short-sleeved cotton or poplin shirt or *guayabera* (ties not often worn) and trousers of some tropical weight material. Formal wear may include ties and jackets, but long-sleeved embroidered *guayaberas* are commoner. Women should not wear shorts in the cities and towns; acceptable only on the cayes and at resorts.

Hours of Business   Retail shops are open 0800-1200, 1300-1600 and Fri. 1900-2100, with a half day from 1200 on Wed. Small shops open additionally most late afternoons and evenings, and some on Sundays 0800-1000.

Government and commercial office hrs. are 0800-1200 and 1300-1600 Mon. to Fri.

Public Holidays   1 January: New Year's Day; 9 March: Baron Bliss Day; Good Friday and Saturday. Easter Monday; 1 May: Labour Day; 24 May: Commonwealth Day; 10 Sept: St George's Caye Day; 21 Sept: Belize Independence Day; 12 Oct: Pan American Day (Corozal and Orange Walk); 19 Nov: Garifuna Settlement Day; 25 December: Christmas Day; 26 December: Boxing Day.

Warning   Most services throughout the country close down Good Friday to Easter Monday: banks close at 1130 on the Thursday, buses run limited services Holy Saturday to Easter Monday, and boats to the Cayes are available. St. George's Caye Day celebrations in September start 2 or 3 days in advance and require a lot of energy.

Official time   is 6 hrs. behind GMT.

The **monetary unit** is the Belizean dollar, stabilized at BZ$2=US$1.

Currency notes (Monetary Authority of Belize) are issued in the denominations of 100, 50, 20, 10, 5, 2 and 1 dollars, and coinage of 1 dollar, 50, 25, 10, 5 and 1 cent is in use. Notes marked Government of Belize, or Government of British Honduras, are only redeemable at a bank; all notes should be marked Central Bank of Belize. The American expressions Quarter (25c.), Dime (10c.) and Nickel (5c.) are common, although 25c. is sometimes referred to as a shilling. US dollars are accepted in many places. There is a 2% charge for cashing travellers' cheques. Belize Bank gives cash on Visa and Mastercard (but see under **Exchange**, Belize City, above). Good rates for Mexican pesos in Belize. Best rates of exchange at the borders.

The **Cost of Living** is high.

Weights and measures Imperial and US standard weights and measures. The US gallon is used for gasoline and motor oil.

Electricity 110/220 volts single phase, 60 cycles for domestic supply.

Telephone and Cable There is a direct-dialling system between the major towns and to Mexico and USA. Belize Telecommunications Ltd., open 0730-2100 Mon.-Sat., closed Suns. and holidays, has an international telephone, telegraph and telex service. To make an international call from Belize costs far less than from neighbouring countries. BZ$18 for 3 min. to UK and Europe (a deposit of BZ$30 required first); BZ$15.75 to most of USA and Canada; BZ$10.50 to Florida and US South-East; BZ$8 per min. to Australia. Collect calls to USA, Canada, Australia and UK only.

Airmail Postage to UK 4-5 days. BZ$0.75 for a letter, BZ$0.45 for a postcard; BZ$0.60 for a letter to U.S.A, BZ$0.25 for a post card. Parcels: BZ$1.25 per half-kilo to Europe, BZ$0.75 per half-kilo to USA. The service to Europe and USA has been praised.

Press Belize: *Belize Times*; *Amandala, People's Pulse, Reporter* (weekly).

Language English is the official language, but Spanish is widely spoken. Belize Broadcasting Network (BBN) devotes about 40 per cent of its air-time to the Spanish language. A Low German dialect is spoken by the Mennonite settlers, and Mayan languages and Garifuna are spoken by ethnic groups.

We are most grateful to Trevor Petch (London N7), David Burford (Templestowe, Victoria), Otto and Gaby Heuer-Oeschger (Lenzburg, Switz.), Stig Hartvig Nielsen (Viborg, Dnmk.), Helmut Scheider (Berlin 21), Marian Temple (Mérida, Mexico) and Urs Waeber (Oberägeri, Switz.).

EL SALVADOR

INTRODUCTION

EL SALVADOR is the smallest, most densely populated, most industrialized and most integrated of the Central American republics. Its intermont basins are a good deal lower than those of Guatemala, rising to little more than 600 metres at the capital, San Salvador. Across this upland and surmounting it run two more or less parallel rows of volcanoes, 14 of which are over 900 metres. The highest are Santa Ana (2,365 metres), San Vicente (2,182), San Miguel (2,129), and San Salvador (1,893). One important result of this volcanic activity is that the highlands are covered with a deep layer of ash and lava which forms a porous soil ideal for coffee planting.

The total area of El Salvador is 21,040 square km. Guatemala is to the W, Honduras to the N and E, and the Pacific coastline to the S is 321 km. or so.

Lowlands lie to the N and S of the high backbone. In the S, on the Pacific coast, the lowlands of Guatemala are continued to just E of Acajutla; beyond are lava promontories till we reach another 30-km. belt of lowlands where the 325 km. long Río Lempa flows into the sea. The northern lowlands are in the wide depression along the course of the Río Lempa, buttressed S by the highlands of El Salvador, and N by the basalt cliffs edging the highlands of Honduras. The highest point in El Salvador, Cerro El Pital (2,730 metres) is part of the mountain range bordering on Honduras. After 160 km. the Lempa cuts through the southern uplands to reach the Pacific; the depression is prolonged SE till it reaches the Gulf of Fonseca.

Climate El Salvador is fortunate in that its temperatures are not excessively high. Along the coast and in the lowlands it is certainly hot and humid, but the average for San Salvador is 23°C with a range of only about 3°. March, April, May are the hottest months; December,

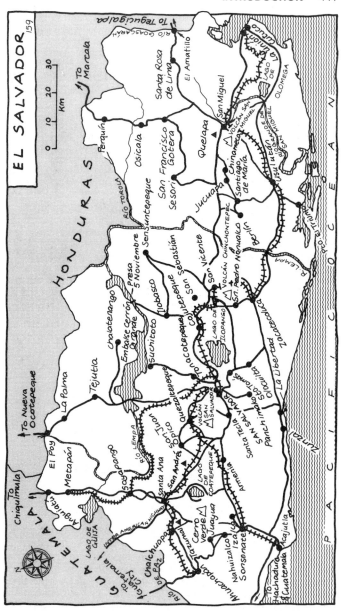

January, February the coolest. There is one rainy season, from May to October, with April and November being transitional periods; there are only light rains for the rest of the year: the average is about 1,830 mm. Occasionally, in December and March there is a spell of continuously rainy weather, the *temporal*, which may last from two or three days to as many weeks. The pleasantest months are from November to January. From time to time the water shortage can become acute.

History The dictator who came to power in 1931, General Maximiliano Hernández Martínez, was responsible for the massacre of thousands of peasants in 1932 in confrontations between the authorities and trade unions. Although Hernández was overthrown in 1944 by popular pressure and general strikes, the military did not relinquish power. Through a series of coups, the army kept control, at the same time maintaining the status quo of the oligarchy which owned most of the land and production.

On October 16, 1979, the President, General Carlos Humberto Romero, was overthrown in a military coup and replaced by a reformist civilian-military junta. In December 1980 a civilian member of the Junta, the Christian Democrat Sr. José Napoleón Duarte, was appointed President (he was elected to the post in May 1984). A decline in popular support and the founding of an opposition front, the Frente Democrático Revolucionario (FDR), and attempted reforms to shift power away from the landowning and banking families, increased political tension to the proportions of civil war. In addition to the deaths caused by confrontation between the army and guerrillas, 40,000 non-combatants were killed between 1979 and 1984, mostly by right-wing death squads. Among the casualities was Archbishop Oscar Romero, who was shot while saying mass in March 1980. The leftist guerrilla forces (the Farabundo Martí National Liberation Front—FMLN) maintained their strength, but neither exploratory meetings between the guerrillas and President Duarte (the FDR and FMLN have consistently boycotted elections), nor the president's signing of the Central American Peace Plan (drawn up by President Arias of Costa Rica, in August 1987) brought any positive results.

The war continued in stalemate until 1989, by which time an estimated 70,000 had been killed. The Christian Democrats' inability to end the conflict, either by victory or agreement, to reverse the economic decline, or to rebuild after the 1986 earthquake led to a resurgence of support for the right-wing Nationalist Republican Alliance (Arena). After 1986 Arena gained support at both congressional and municipal level. In the 1988 congressional elections Arena won 30 seats against 23 for the Christian Democrats. The Arena candidate, Alfredo Cristiani, won comfortably the presidential elections held in March 1989, taking office in June.

In January 1990 the FMLN agreed to peace talks with the government under the mediation of the UN Secretary General. In April the two sides signed a seven-point document providing for a ceasefire, moves toward full democracy, respect for human rights and legalization of the guerrillas as a political party. A truce would be dependant upon progress in the talks, to start the following month. The FMLN aimed to become a registered party before the 1991 congressional elections.

The People The population is far more homogeneous than that of Guatemala. The reason for this is that El Salvador lay comparatively isolated from the main stream of conquest, and it had neither the precious metals nor the agriculturally active Indians that acted as magnets for the Spaniards. The small number of Spanish settlers intermarried with the Indians to form a group of mestizos herding cattle in the valley of the Lempa and growing subsistence crops in the highlands. There were only about half a million people as late as 1879, but soon afterwards coffee was planted in the highlands; easy access to the coast made this crop profitable. The population grew quickly and the prosperity of the coffee planters fertilized the whole economy, but the internal pressure of population has led to the occupation of all the available land. Several hundred thousand Salvadoreans have emigrated to neighbouring republics because of the shortage of land and the concentration of landownership, and more lately because of the civil war.

Of the total population, 5,138,000 million in 1989, some 20% are regarded as ethnic Indians, although the traditional Indian culture has almost completely vanished. Other estimates put the percentage of pure Indians as low as 5.3%. Less than 5% are of unmixed white ancestry; the rest are *mestizos*. Birth rate: 36; death rate, 10.4 per 1,000; infant mortality, 57 per 1,000 live births. Annual growth rate 1.3% (1980-88); urban growth: 2.4%; and 48.2% live in the towns. Expectation of life at birth, 57 years.

With a population of 242 to the square km., El Salvador is the most densely peopled country on the American mainland. Health and sanitation outside the capital and some of the towns leave much to be desired, and progress has been very limited in the past few years because of the violence.

The Economy Agriculture is the dominant sector of the economy, accounting for 75% of export earnings as well as employing some 40% of the population. Coffee and cotton are the most important crops, but attempts have been made at diversification and now sugar and maize are becoming increasingly important as foreign exchange earners. Land ownership has been unevenly distributed with a few wealthy families owning most of the land, while the majority of agricultural workers merely lived at subsistence level; this led to serious political and social instability despite attempts at agrarian reform by successive governments, of which the latest (and most determined) was in 1980.

With the expansion of the industrial sector in the 1960s and 1970s, there was a rapid growth in the middle and industrial working classes. The most important industry is textiles: others include shoes, furniture, chemicals and fertilizers, pharmaceuticals, cosmetics, construction materials, cement (and asbestos cement), food and drink processing, rubber goods. A small quantity of petroleum products, including asphalt, is also produced. Exports of manufactured goods, mostly to other Central American countries, account for some 24% of foreign exchange earnings.

There are small deposits of various minerals: gold, silver, copper, iron ore, sulphur, mercury, lead, zinc, salt and lime. There is a gold and silver mine at San Cristóbal in the Department of Morazán. In 1975 a geothermal power plant came into operation at Ahuachapán, with capacity of 30 mw. The plant was expanded by 60 mw in 1978. Hydraulic resources are also being exploited as a means of generating power and thermal plants have been shut down, thus affording an even greater saving in oil import costs.

The country's agricultural and industrial production, and consequently its exporting capability, have been severely curtailed by political unrest. In 1986 further economic and social damage was caused by an earthquake; damage to housing and government property alone was estimated at US$311m, while the total, including destruction and disruption of businesses was put at US$2bn. El Salvador is heavily dependent upon aid from the USA to finance its budget. Total US assistance was estimated at over US$4 bn in the 1980s. In 1989 the new government outlined a national rescue plan to provide jobs, food and low cost housing to those most in need. Efforts were also made to put order into public finances, reduce inflation and encourage exports. However, the lack of foreign exchange reserves remained a serious constraint and El Salvador was declared ineligible for World Bank lending after arrears exceeded limits.

Government   Legislative power is vested in a unicameral Legislative Assembly, which has 60 seats and is elected for a three-year term. The head of state and government is the president, who holds office for five years. The country is divided into 14 departments.

Education and Religion   The illiteracy rate is 32%. Education is free if given by the Government, and obligatory. There are 14 universities, one national and the others private or church-affiliated, and a National School of Agriculture. Roman Catholicism is the prevailing religion.

Note   At the time of writing it is safe to travel around the country, to the beaches, lakes and mountains, particularly in the West and South West. However, care is advised when travelling to North, East and South East, in departments such as Chalatenango, Morazán, La Unión, Cabañas and Usulután. Tourists are not numerous at present; the Salvadoreans will be glad to see you (see also the comments in the **Information for Visitors**, in the **Note** after **Documents**).

SAN SALVADOR AND ENVIRONS

San Salvador, the capital, is in an intermont basin at 680 metres, on the Río Acelhuate in the Valle de las Hamacas and with a ring of mountains round it; the population is 460,000. It was founded by Pedro de Alvarado in 1525, but not where it now stands. The city was destroyed by earthquake in 1854, so the present capital is a modern city, most of its architecture conditioned by its liability to seismic shocks. However, in the earthquake of October 10, 1986, many buildings collapsed; over 1,000 people died. As a result, many government offices and public services have been temporarily relocated until reconstruction has been completed. Even in 1989, the centre was still in a very bad condition, with many people not yet returned to proper housing. The climate is semi-tropical and healthy, the water supply pure. Days are often hot, but the temperature drops in the late afternoon and nights are always pleasantly mild. Since it is in a hollow, the city has a smog problem, caused mainly by traffic pollution.

Four broad streets meet at the centre: Av. Cuscatlán and its continuation Av. España run S to N, Calle Delgado and its continuation Calle Arce from E to W. This principle is retained throughout: all the *avenidas* run N to S and the *calles* E to W. The even-numbered *avenidas* are E of the central *avenidas*, odd numbers W; N of the central *calles* they are dubbed Norte; S of the central *calles* Sur. The even-numbered *calles* are S of the two central *calles*, the odd numbers N. E of the central *avenidas* they are dubbed Oriente, W of the central *avenidas* Poniente. It takes a little time to get used to this system.

Nearly all the more important buildings are near the main intersection. On the E side of Av. Cuscatlán is Plaza Barrios, the heart of the city. A fine equestrian statue looks W towards the Renaissance-style National Palace (1904-11). To the N is the new cathedral which is, however, unfinished. To the E of Plaza Barrios, on Calle Delgado, is the National Theatre (the exterior has been magnificently restored and is now open). If we walk along 2a Calle Oriente we come on the right to the Parque Libertad; in its centre is a flamboyant monument to Liberty looking E towards the rebuilt church of El Rosario where José Matías Delgado, father of the independence movement, lies buried. The Archbishop's Palace is next door. The big building on the S side of the square is the Municipal Palace. Not far away to the SE (on 10a Av. Sur) is another rebuilt church, La Merced, from whose bell-tower went out Father Delgado's tocsin call to independence in 1811.
    Across Calle Delgado, opposite the theatre, is Plaza Morazán, with a monument to General Morazán. Calle Arce runs W to the Hospital Rosales, in its own gardens. SW of the Hospital, along Av. Roosevelt, is the National Stadium. On the way to the Hospital, if you turn S opposite the great church of El Sagrado Corazón de Jesús, you come after one block to Parque Bolívar, with the national printing office to the S, and the Department of Health to the N.

N.B. The city centre is considered unsafe after dark. In general, robberies, particularly on crowded city buses, have increased of late; pickpocketing and bag slashing are common. Women are advised not to wear expensive jewellery on the street.

Festivals At the edge of the city (to the N along Avenida España and W along 9a Calle Poniente) is the Campo de Marte, a large and popular park where the Palacio de Deportes has been built, and through which runs the Avenida Juan Pablo II. During Holy Week, and the fortnight preceding 6 August, is held the Fiesta of the Saviour ("El Salvador"). As a climax colourful floats wind up the Campo de Marte. On 5 August, an ancient image of the Saviour is borne before

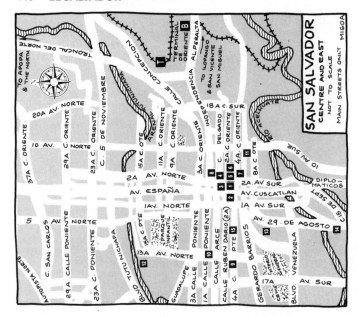

a large procession; there are church services on the 6th, Feast of the Transfiguration. On 12 December. Day of the Indian, there are processions honouring the Virgin of Guadalupe in El Salvador (take bus 101 to the Basilica of Guadalupe, half-way to Santa Tecla, to see colourful processions).

Hotels Prices are without meals unless otherwise stated. Hotel tax: 10%.

El Salvador Sheraton (not part of the Sheraton chain), 89a Av. Norte on the slopes of a volcano on the outskirts, A, outdoor pool; *Presidente*, San Benito, A, pool, garden, very pleasant, good buffets (US$8); *Siesta*, on Autopista Sur, off Pan-American Highway, west of the city, C. *Novo*, 61 Av. N (in cul-de-sac), rooms with bath and kitchen US$650/month (shorter periods possible), mini swimming pool, garden, pleasant; *Alameda*, 43a Av. Sur and Alameda Roosevelt, C; *Camino Real*, Blvd. de los Héroes, A (journalists and businessmen); *Escalón Apartments*, 3689 Paseo General Escalón at Av. 71 Sur, US$300 per month double. *Panamerican*, 8 Av. Sur 113, E, with cold shower, closes early (but knock on door), meals from US$2 and parking space, rec. *American Guest House*, 17 Av. N 119, C, friendly, helpful; *Ritz Continental*, 7a Av. Sur 219, D-C; *Terraza*, 85 Av. Sur, Calle Padre Aguilar, C-B; *The Boarding House*, 6 Av. y 10 Calle Poniente, 425 Colonia Flor Blanca, C including bath and breakfast.

Florida Guest House, Blvd. Los Héroes y Pasaje Los Almendros 115, D, T 26-1858, all rooms with bath, proprietor speaks English; *Casa Austria*, 1a C. Poniente 3843 (between 73 and 75 Av.), small, quiet, family atmosphere, D, rec., English- and German-speaking owner; *Family Guest Home*, 1a C. Poniente Bis 925, D, safe, clean, expensive meals available; *Hospedaje Izalco*, Calle Concepción 666, E; *Imperial*, Calle Concepción 659, friendly, serves reasonable meals and has car park, E, with toilet and shower, can be noisy.

Custodio, 10a Av. Sur 109, F, without bath, basic, clean and friendly but noisy;

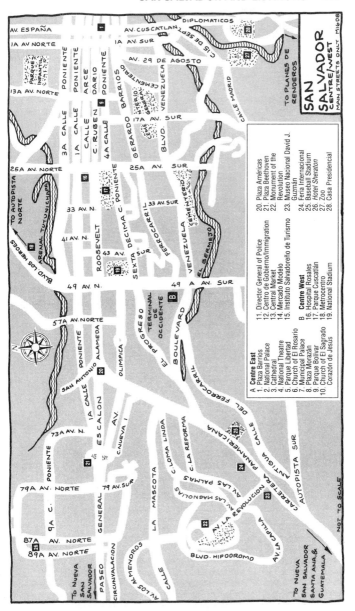

SAN SALVADOR CENTRE/WEST
MAIN STREETS ONLY M16-08J

A Centre East
1. Plaza Barrios
2. National Palace
3. Cathedral
4. National Theatre
5. Parque Libertad
6. Church of El Rosario
7. Municipal Palace
8. Plaza Morazán
9. Parque Bolívar
10. Church of El Sagrado Corazón de Jesús

11. Director General of Police
12. Centro de Gobierno/Immigration
13. Central Market
14. Mercado Modelo
15. Instituto Salvadoreño de Turismo

B Centre West
16. Hospital Rosales
17. Parque Cuscatlán
18. Metrocentro
19. National Stadium

20. Plaza Américas
21. Plaza Beethoven
22. Monument of the Revolution
23. Museo Nacional David J. Guzmán
24. Feria Internacional
25. Baseball Stadium
26. *Hotel Sheraton*
27. Zoo
28. Casa Presidencial

NOT TO SCALE

Bruno, 1 Calle Oriente, between 8 and 10 Av., F with bath, cheaper without, not very clean, quite safe (but not a safe area of town); *Hospedaje España*, 12 Av. Norte 123, F, near the *Bruno* and better. *San Carlos*, Calle Concepción 121, E with bath, early morning call, cold drinks available, good; *León*, Av. 10, Calle Delgado, F, friendly, poor water supply, safe, parking; *Hospedaje Yucatán*, Calle Concepción 673, F with bath, basic, friendly, noisy; excellent restaurant (*Rosita*—vegetarian food good) downstairs; on Blvd. Venezuela west of Occidente bus terminal is *Occidental*, clean, friendly.

Motels *Boulevard*, E, with shower, very clean, with parking, 2 km. from centre, but good bus service. Several motels on all main roads leading out of the capital.

Restaurants At hotels. All close between 2000 and 2100. *Siete Mares*, Paseo Escalón, very good seafood; *Diligencia* (for good steaks) and *El Bodegón* (Spanish style) both on Paseo Escalón, are excellent; also on Paseo Escalón: *La Ponderosa* (famous for steaks with *chirimol*, near Plaza Beethoven), *Le Mar* (seafoods), *Beto's* (Italian), *Pip's Carymar* (also in Santa Tecla—good, cheap typical food), *Rancho Alegre* (cheap, also opp. Metrocentro shopping mall), and tacos and pupusas at Redondel Masferrer, good view over city, lively atmosphere, mariachis, but be alert at night for fights and drug dealing on the less well-lit side of the Redondel. *Texas Meats*, Calle La Mascota, good for steaks; *Doña Mercedes*, Blvd. Los Héroes, 3 blocks north of Metrocentro, is another good steakhouse. *München*, Av. Roosevelt, German; opp. is *China Palace*, excellent value (oldest Chinese restaurant in San Salvador); *Romano*, Av. Roosevelt 45 y 47 Av., *El Café Don Pedro* (drive-in in Av. Roosevelt); *Pupusería Margot*, opp. Estado Mayor on the road to Santa Tecla, good. *Rosal*, El Mirador, near *Sheraton*, Italian, good; *Pizza Capri*, Italian-owned, behind *Hotel Camino Real*.

Restaurants in the Zona Rosa, Blvd. Hipódromo, are generally very good, but expensive. These include: *Marcelino's*, *Mediterráneo* (good ceviche), *La Ola*, *Chili's*, *Paradise* (all popular); *Basilea/Schäffer's*, also in Zona Rosa, restaurant and excellent cakes, nice garden atmosphere. Branches of *MacDonalds* and *Biggest* (hamburgers, fast food); *Pollo Campero* (branches throughout the city, good); *Don Paro's*, Calle Arce is especially good for breakfast; *Café Don Alberto*, Calle Arce y 15 Av. Sur, good and cheap.

Vegetarian restaurants: *La Zanahoria*, Calle Arce 1199; *Govinda's*, 51 Av. Norte No. 147, Colonia Flor Blanca, T 23-2468, take Bus 44 (a bit hard to find but worth it); *Kalpataru*, 100 m. N of Redondel Masferrer, nice atmosphere; *El Tao*, 21 Av. Norte y Calle Arce, and Centro de Gobierno, 19 Calle Poniente; *Actoteatro*, 1 Calle Poniente (between 15 and 13 Av. N), good atmosphere, patio, music, good buffet lunch, cheap, central. Good pupusas at a cave restaurant in Puerta del Diablo. Good cheap *comedores* in Occidente bus terminal. *Victoria*, bakery, good for pastries. The food market, one of the biggest and cleanest in Latin America, has many stalls selling cheap food. *Pops*, near *Bruno Hotel* on 1 Calle Oriente and Av. 4, is a good ice-cream parlour; there is another branch on Escalón, near the British Club (and at Metrocentro). Coffee shops: *Shaw's*, chocolates and coffee; *Flashback*, Blvd. Hipódromo (Zona Rosa), good coffee.

Clubs Club Salvadoreño, admits foreigners, owns a fine Country Club on Lake Ilopango called Corinto (with a golf course), and has a seaside branch at Km.43 on the coast road, near La Libertad, much frequented during the dry season, November to April. The Automobile Club of El Salvador has a chalet for bathing at La Libertad. British Club (Paseo Escalón 4714—approx), has British newspapers and swimming pool. (Temporary visitors' cards if introduced by a member.) The Country Club Campestre (Paseo Escalón), admits foreigners with cards only. Club Náutico, at the Estero de Jaltepeque, famous for its mud boat races.

Shopping Mercado Cuartel, crafts market, 8 Av. Norte, 1a C. Oriente, a few blocks E of the National Theatre. One can buy towels here with various Maya designs. A large new shopping precinct with ample parking (Metrocentro) is on Boulevard Los Héroes, NW of city centre. Metrocentro and the Zona Rosa have handicraft shops, but at least twice as dear as Mercado Cuartel.

Bookshops at the Universidad Centroamericana (UCA) and Universidad de El Salvador (UES); *Nuevo Mundo*, 67 Av. Sur 144; *Clásicos Roxsil*, 6 Av. Sur 1-6, Santa Tecla. A few English books at *Librería Quixaje*, Calle Arce, and a few at *Shaw's* chocolate shop, 1 block past Parque Beethoven on Paseo Escalón.

Local Buses Flat fare of US$0.06 or US$0.12 (fares shown on bus).

Taxis Plenty (all yellow), none has a meter, ask fare before getting in. Fares: from centre to outskirts or *Hotel El Salvador Sheraton*, US$3; central runs, US$2. Double fare after dark. Taxis from Acontaxis (T 223361, 223268, 223294), Acomet (T 259114, 259576), Acosat (T 244015) and Dos Pinos (T 222321).

Car Hire Rentals from Avis, 42 Av. Sur 137, nr. *Hotel Alameda*; Budget, 85 Av. Sur 220, in the front of *Hotel Terraza*; Hertz, Calle Los Andes behind *Hotel Camino Real*.

Night Clubs All leading hotels have their own night club. *Mario's* on Blvd. Hipódromo, Zona Rosa, with good live music; *Faces on the Top*, double-disco, Calle El Mirador, near *Sheraton*. *Club M*, also near *Sheraton*. *Memories*, Paseo General Escalón; *Luzeiro*, Calle El Mirador; *My Place*, Paseo General Escalón and 83 Av. Norte.

Entertainments Many cinemas, with Cinerama at the Grand Majestic (best quality cinemas cost US$2, films in English with sub-titles), or ballet and plays at the National Theatre of Fine Arts, and music or plays at the Cámara Theatre.

Sports Bowling at Bolerama Jardín and Club Salvadoreño. Football is played at the Stadium on Sun. and Thurs. according to programme at the Cuscatlán and Flor Blanca Stadiums. Motor racing at new El Jabalí autodrome on lava fields near Quezaltepeque. Basketball, tennis, international swimming, fishing, target shooting, wrestling, boxing and boat and sailing boat races, but in private clubs only.

Museums Museo Nacional David J. Guzmán, 1 block W of Feria Internacional on Av. de la Revolución, has a small but good archaeological exhibition. Open Tues.-Sun. 0900-1200 and 1400-1700. Natural History Museum, end of C. Los Viveros, Col. Nicaragua, Wed.-Sun. 0930-1630.

Exchange Citibank, Edificio SISA, 2nd floor near El Salvador del Mundo; and national banks. Open 0900-1300, 1345-1500; some banks have a late night counter until 1900. Banks charge 1 colón for changing money and cheques; cashing travellers' cheques involves lengthy paperwork. Credomatic, for obtaining funds with either Visa or Mastercard, Edificio Cidema, Alameda Roosevelt y Calle 51, 5% commission. Foreign currency is difficult to obtain. Black market can be found outside the Centro Gobierno, near the Post Office, and on the W side of Parque Infantil for dollars cash, travellers' cheques and quetzales (safe).

Embassies **Guatemalan**, 15 Av. Norte 135 y C. Arce (0900-1200). **Honduran**, 7 C. Poniente y 83 Av. Norte, T 78-9524; **Nicaraguan**, 9 Calle Poniente y 89 Av. Norte; **Belizean**, 15C. Poniente 4415 (½ block behind *Sheraton*, T 23-5271, 0830-1200); **Mexican**, Paseo Gral. Escalón 3832 (T 24-0162, 0900-1400); **Panamanian**, Col. San Francisco, C. Los Bambúes y Av. Bugambilia 21, T 98 0773.

US, 25 Av. Norte, 1230, in front of Fuente Luminosa, T 267100. **British**, Paseo

General Escalón 4828, T 240473. **Dutch**, Of. La Curazao, Edif. Lotisa 2° piso, Final C. La Mascota y Av. Masferrer (T 23-4000, 0800-1200, 1330-1630). **West German**, 3a C. Poniente 3832, Col. Escalón (T 23-6173, 0800-1400). **French**, 1a C. Poniente 3718 y 73 Av. Norte, Col. Escalón (T 23-0728, 0900-1200). **Swiss**, closed, but Chancellery, Edif. Centroamericano, 3rd floor Alameda Roosevelt 3107, T 23-47-87.

Immigration Department　In the Ministry of Interior Building, Centro de Gobierno, T 226700/227573, open Mon.-Fri. 0800-1600.

Complaints　Director General of Police, 6a Calle Oriente. T 71-4422.

Post Office　At 11 Av. Norte y 5 C. Poniente; branches at Almacenes Simón, Librería Hispanoamérica, Centro Comercial Gigante (Col. Escalón), Supermercados Todo's Escalón, Mercado Central Local No. 3, Mercado Modelo, 1st floor above PHL stationer on Plaza Morazán. Open Mon.-Fri. 0730-1730, Sat. 0730-1600. *Lista de correos*, Mon.-Fri. 0800-1200, 1430-1700.

Churches　Anglican Centre (St. John's Episcopal Church), 63 Av. Sur and Av. Olímpica, services on Sun., 0900 in English, 1000 in Spanish; American Union Church, C. 4 off Calle La Mascota, has services in English on Sun., at 1000, and also has a gift shop (local crafts and textiles) and an English paperback library (both open Weds. and Sat.). Synagogue, 23a Av. Norte 215.

International Industrial Fair, held in November, every two years (even dates), in Calle Santa Tecla, near the Monument of the Revolution. Site is also used for other functions such as the traditional August fair.

Tourist Office　Instituto Salvadoreño de Turismo, Calle Rubén Darío 619. T 22-8000 (Mon.-Fri. 0800-1600, Sat. 0800-1200, closed Sun.). They will advise on the security situation in the country. They give away a map of the country and city, but the Texaco and Esso maps (obtainable from their respective service stations) are more accurate. The office is very helpful. Also "Advice to Tour Guides", a rec. booklet. Good map of the country (about US$6) is available from the Instituto Nacional de Geografía, Av. Juan Bertis, 59 and Librería La Ibérica, 1 Calle Oriente, 127. The tourist office at the International airport is open 0800-1630 all year round except Dec. 25 and Jan. 1, T 39-9454, 39-9464.

Tourist Agents　*El Salvador Travel Service*, 23 Av. Sur 201. *Avia*, 1a Calle Poniente, at junction with 73a Av. Norte in Colonia Escalón, are rec. Tour operators include: *Alpha Tours*, Alameda Roosevelt y 55 Av. Norte, T 24-6928; *Joanesa*, 41 Av. Sur 518, T 22-1920; *Rinsa*, 67 Av. Sur, Pas. 2-3 E-69, T 24-4863; and others.

Airport　The new international airport at Comalapa is 44 km. from San Salvador, near Costa del Sol beach, reached by 4-lane highway. Acacya minibus to airport from 3 C. Poniente and Av. Norte in front of Shell gas station, T 71-4937, 0600, 0700, 1200, 1500 (be there 15 min. before), US$3 one way (leave from airport when full, on right as you go out). Taxi Acacya US$18 one way. The prices in the gift shops at the airport are exorbitant; there is a post office at the tourist office.
　The old airport is at Ilopango, 13 km. away. It is primarily used by the air force. However, from Ilopango small planes fly to San Miguel (30 mins., good, US$25), Usulután, Santa Rosa de Lima and La Unión; tickets from the civilian traffic offices (TAES, Taxis Aéreos El Salvador, or Gutiérrez Flying Service). No regular internal air lines but charter flights are easily arranged.

Rail　There are no passenger services.

Long-Distance Buses　Terminal del Occidente, down an alleyway off Boulevard Venezuela, opposite No. 2963 (dangerous area; take city buses 4, 27 or 34). Most international buses pass through if not starting from here. **To Guatemala**: About 12 buses a day to Guatemala City (5 hrs.). Single, US$3. From Terminal del

Occidente: Melva y Pezzarossi (T 24-2953) 8 a day between 0500 and 1430 (be at terminal ½ hr. before departure); Centroamérica (T 24-4258), 0600—home pick-up at 0530, US$7; Taca (T 24-3236), 0930; El Cóndor (T 24-6548), 0530, 0800, 1330; Transsesmer (T 24-1965), 1300; Futuro Express (13 Av. Sur y Pasaje Alcaine, T 22-4272) run a home pick-up service at 0530, US$6; Mermex (Ed. Corfinca Local 3, 11 Av. Sur y Pasaje Costa Rica, T 22-1258), 0600 at office, or 0700 at Terminal del Occidente. El Cóndor also runs daily from Terminal del Occidente to Talismán, on Mexico-Guatemala border, 0700 and 1000, US$7.

To Tegucigalpa: No through service at present. Take local services to El Amatillo. The only way to Managua and further S is by taking frequent local buses beyond San Miguel or Santa Rosa from Terminal Oriente, end of Av. Peralta (take city buses 7, 33 or 29): hourly, first at 0400, then to the border, thence to Choluteca and on to Nicaragua.

N.B. The Honorary British Consul in El Salvador advises, "If buses are running regularly, the route is probably reasonably safe." Bus routes most frequently attacked by guerrillas are the Troncal del Norte to Chalatenango and El Poy and the eastern Pan-American Highway between San Vicente and San Miguel, and San Miguel and Goascarán.

A good **sightseeing tour** of from 2 to 3 hrs. by car is along Av. Cuscatlán, past the Zoo (which though small, is quiet and attractive—open Wed.-Sun. 0930-1630) and the Casa Presidencial and up to the new residential district in the mountain range of Planes de Renderos. This place, reached by bus 12 from the centre, is crowned by the beautiful Balboa Park (good view of city from El Mirador at foot of Park). From the park a scenic road runs to the summit of Cerro Chulo, from which the view, seen through the Puerta del Diablo (Devil's Door), is even better. The Door consists of two enormous vertical rocks which frame a magnificent view of the San Vicente volcano. At the foot of Cerro Chulo is Panchimalco (see below). There are local buses (12, US$0.20 and 17, and 12 minibus marked "Mil Cumbres") to Puerta del Diablo about every hour. There are reports that mugging is increasingly common at Cerro Chulo; it is unsafe to make the trip alone. The Teleférico on the hill overlooking the city and Lake Ilopango has good views, cafeterias and a children's funfair. Reached by 9 bus from centre, US$1.60. Open Fri., Sat., Sun. only, 0900-1900.

For a quick "taste" of San Salvador, Taca airlines take passengers in transit through San Salvador to the *Sheraton Hotel* from the airport, provide a free lunch, and a room for US$5 (this generally applies to flights between Managua/San José and Tegucigalpa/Guatemala City, which involve an 8-hour wait in El Salvador for connecting Taca flights).

Excursions can be made by road to Panchimalco and Lake Ilopango; to the crater of San Salvador volcano; and to the volcano of Izalco (1,910 metres) and the near-by park of Atecosol, and Cerro Verde (**see Sonsonate, page** 459); to the garden park of Ichanmichen (**see Zacatecoluca, page** 458); to Lake Coatepeque (lunch at *Hotel del Lago*) and to Cerro Verde in 90 minutes. The excavated site of San Andrés, on the estate of the same name, 32 km. west of San Salvador, is unimpressive (take bus 201 from Terminal del Occidente). Bus 495 from the Terminal del Occidente goes to Costa El Sol, a developing seaside resort (**see page** 458). Sihuatehuacán and the pyramid of Tazumal (page

462) are reached by bus 202. There are swimming pools at Los Chorros (bus 79 from Calle Ruben Darío—see below). Buses from the Oriente terminal go to Quezaltepeque, near which is La Toma, a popular inland resort, to Amapulapa, where there are gardens and a swimming pool, and to Lake Apastepeque (**see page 455**).

Panchimalco is 14½ km. S by a paved road. Around it live the Pancho Indians, pure-blooded descendants of the original Pipil tribes; a few have retained more or less their old traditions and dress. Streets of low adobe houses thread their way among huge boulders at the foot of Cerro Chulo (rolled down the hill to repel the Spaniards, according to local legend). A very fine baroque colonial church with splendid woodcarvings in the interior and a bell incised with the cypher and titles of the Holy Roman Emperor Charles V. An ancient ceiba tree shades the market place (disappointing market). Bus 17 from Mercado Central at 12 Calle Poniente, San Salvador, every 45 min., US$0.30, 1½ hrs.

Lake Ilopango A 4-lane highway, the Ilopango Boulevard, runs E for 14½ km. from San Salvador to Ilopango airport, quite near Lake Ilopango, 15 km. by 8, in the crater of an old volcano, well worth a visit. Pre-Conquest Indians used to propitiate the harvest gods by drowning four virgins here each year. There are a number of lakeside cafés and bathing clubs, some of which hire dug-outs by the hr. *Hotel Vistalgo*, D. A number of private chalets make access to the lake difficult, except at clubs and the Turicentro. Bus 15, marked Apulo, runs from the bus stop on 2a Av. Norte y Plaza Morazán to the lake (via the airport), 70 minutes, US$0.30. Entrance to the Turicentro camping site costs US$0.18 and is rec; plenty of hammock hanging opportunities; showers and swimming facilities. The water is reported to be polluted and it is busy at weekends.

Santa Tecla, also known as Nueva San Salvador, 13 km. W of the capital by the Pan-American Highway, is 240 metres higher and much cooler, in a coffee-growing district. Population, 63,400. (*Hospedaje*, no name, Calle Daniel Hernández y 6 Av., 3 blocks from Parque San Martín, G, good, safe, will store luggage.) The huge crater of San Salvador volcano (known as Boquerón by the locals)—1½ km. wide and 543 metres deep—can be reached from Santa Tecla, road starts 1 block E of Plaza Central, going due N (very rough). Bus (101) leaves 3 Av. Norte, near the junction with Calle Ruben Darío, San Salvador, every ten mins. for Santa Tecla (US$0.12). There is a bus (103) from there to Boquerón hourly, last one back at 1500 (US$0.30) and from there you must walk the last 1½ km. to the crater. A walk clockwise round the crater takes about 2 hrs.; the first half is easy, the second half rough (the path is used by soldiers and guerrillas). The views are magnificent. The inner slopes of the crater are covered with trees, and at the bottom is a smaller cone left by the eruption of 1917. The path down into the crater starts at the westernmost of a row of antennae studding the rim, 45 mins. down (don't miss the turn straight down after 10 mins. at an inconspicuous junction with a big, upright slab of rock 20 metres below), 1 hr. up. There are a number of army checkpoints on the way to the summit. A road further North leads also to San Salvador volcano through extensive coffee plantations. Santa Tecla, has a training school for factory technicians, set up with British funds and technical help.

At **Los Chorros**, in a natural gorge 6 km. N of Santa Tecla, there is a beautiful landscaping of 4 pools below some waterfalls. The first pool is shallow, and bathers can stand under the cascades, but there is good swimming in the other three. Visit at night for the lighting effects. Entry, US$0.15. Car park fee: US$0.40. Camping is allowed, US$1 for two people. There is a trailer park at Los Chorros, with restaurant and showers.

Just before Santa Tecla is reached, a branch road turns S for 24 km. to **La Libertad**, 37 km. from San Salvador, now only a fishing port. Population 22,800. It is also a popular seaside resort during the dry season, with good fishing and surf bathing, but watch out for undercurrents and sharks. The beaches are black volcanic sand; they are dirty but the surf is magnificent (watch your belongings). (The Automobile Club and the Club Salvadoreño have beach chalets.) Bus 102 from San Salvador leaves from 4 Calle Poniente, 17 Av. Sur, US$0.62. Bus from Santa Tecla, US$0.30.

The Costa del Bálsamo (the Balsam Coast), stretching between La Libertad and Acajutla (**see page** 459), is now rather a myth, but on the steep slopes of the departments of Sonsonate and La Libertad, scattered balsam trees are still tapped. The pain-relieving balsam, once a large export, has almost disappeared. Bus along the coast to Sonsonate at 0600 and 1300, about 4 hrs.

Hotels   Hotels charge for 12 hrs. only. Many in C range, overpriced. *Don Rodrigo*, C; *Don Lito*, D; *Nuevo Amanecer*, 1 C. Poniente No. 24-1, F, safe, clean, rec. *Posada Familiar*, F, basic, shared bath; *Pensión Peace and Love*, F, very basic and friendly; *Bar Gringo* on the beach front lets rooms, F, so does the *Miramar* restaurant (E, negotiable); *Rik*, opposite *Punta Roca* restaurant, F, clean, friendly. **Motel** *Siboney*, nearby, good.

Restaurant   Food is good in the town, especially at *Punta Roca* (American-owned, by Don Bobby), try the shrimp soup, and *Altamar* for seafood. *Pupusería*, specializes in snacks, rec. *Los Mariscos*, good, reasonable prices, popular, closed Mons. *The Fisherman's Club*, excellent seafood, bar, swimming pool, tennis court, private beach, entry fee US$2. Cheap restaurants near the pier; also cheap food in the market.

Excursions   To the large village of Jicalapa, on high rockland above the sea, for its magnificent festival on St. Ursula's day (October 21). 8 km. to the west is *Zunzal*, which has superb surf (*Hospedaje El Pacífico*, F, 1 km. towards La Libertad; buses 102 and 192, from La Libertad. 15 km. away is the *Atami Beach Club*, with pool, private beach, restaurant, 2 bars, gardens, a beautiful place; tourists may enter for US$2, and stay the night for US$11, food, prices are reasonable. Bus to San Diego beach (from road parallel to La Libertad beach), US$1, ½ hourly, nice but deserted. To the Salto y Cueva Los Mangos: walk along the 2 km. trail almost opposite *Motel Siboney* to a 60 m. waterfall; a little further downstream is the Salto San Antonio (50 m.), best reached by bus 287 from La Libertad to San Antonio quarry (just before San Diego beach), then walking 1 km. upstream. Generally the coast road to Acajutla is very scenic with rocky bays and remote black sand beaches for bathing, but take great care with the sea which can be dangerous.

EASTERN EL SALVADOR

E to La Unión/Cutuco   There are two roads to the port of La Unión/Cutuco on the Gulf of Fonseca: (i) the Pan-American Highway, 185 km., through Cojutepeque, San Vicente (road being repaved either side of this city), the 15 de Septiembre dam (since the destruction of the Cuscatlán bridge) and San Miguel; (ii) the Coastal Highway, also paved, running through Santo Tomás, Olocuilta, Zacatecoluca, and Usulután. The roads have frequently been cut by guerrilla action against bridges (most rivers are now crossed by Bailey bridges or dry fords).

By Pan-American Highway   Some 5 km. from the capital a dry-weather highway branches N to Tonocatepeque, Suchitoto, and Chalatenango.

Tonocatepeque, 13 km. from the capital, is an attractive small town on the high plateau, in an agricultural setting but with a small textile industry. There has been some archaeological exploration of the town's original site, 5 km. away.

Suchitoto is quite near the Lempa River, and the Cerrón Grande reservoir, under which is the old road to Chalatenango. The new road to Chalatenango branches right off the Troncal del Norte beyond the Cerrón Grande (**see below and page 464**). There has been much guerrilla and counter-insurgency activity in this northern area: visitors are advised to take care.

Continuing along the Pan-American Highway: a short branch road (about 2 km. beyond the airport) leads off right to the W shores of Lake Ilopango. The first town is ***Cojutepeque***, capital of Cuscatlán Department, 34 km. from San Salvador, reached by bus 113 from Oriente terminal in San Salvador, US$0.75. Population 31,300. Lake Ilopango is to the SW. Good weekly market. The town is famous for cigars, smoked sausages and tongues, and its annual fair on 29 August has fruits and sweets, saddlery, leather goods, pottery and headwear on sale from neighbouring villages, and sisal hammocks, ropes, bags and hats from the small factories of Cacaopera (Dept. of Morazán).

Hotels *Turista*, 5 C. Oriente 130, F; *Hospedaje Viajero*, 1 block E of *Turista*, F (also hourly rentals); *Motel Edén*, E, with shower; *Comedor Toyita*, good value.

Cerro de las Pavas, a conical hill near Cojutepeque, dominates Lake Ilopango and gives splendid views of wide valleys and tall mountains. Its shrine of Our Lady of Fátima draws many pilgrims.

Excursion   From San Rafael Cedros, 6 km. E of Cojutepeque, a 16-km. paved road N to Ilobasco has a branch road E to Sensuntepeque at about Km. 13. *Ilobasco* has 48,100 people, many of them workers in clay; its decorated pottery is now mass-produced and has lost much of its charm. The area around, devoted to cattle, coffee, sugar and indigo, is exceptionally beautiful. Annual fair: September 29. An all-weather road leads from Ilobasco to the great dam and hydroelectric station of Cinco de Noviembre at the Chorrera del Guayabo, on the Lempa River. Bus to Cojutepeque. Another road with fine views leads to the Cerrón Grande dam and hydroelectric plant; good excursion by bus or truck. Permission is given in normal times to enter the dam area and one can climb the hill with the Antel repeater on top for a view of the whole lake created by the dam. The whole Lempa valley is now a security zone and there has been much guerrilla activity there.

Four km. further S along the Pan-American Highway at San Domingo (km. 44 from San Salvador) an unpaved road leads in 5 km. to **San Sebastián** where colourfully patterned hammocks and bedspreads are made. You can watch them being woven on complex looms of wood and string, and can buy from the loom. The 110 bus from the Oriente terminal runs from San Salvador to San Sebastián (US$1.50). There are also buses from Cojutepeque.

Sensuntepeque, 35 km. E of Ilobasco, is a pleasant town at 900 metres, in the hills S of the Lempa valley. It is the capital of Cabañas Department, once a great source of indigo. There are some interesting ceremonies during its fair on 4 December, the day of its patroness, Santa Bárbara. It can be reached from the Pan-American Highway from near San Vicente. Population: 45,000.

N.B. San Vicente and San Miguel have been the centres of intense guerrilla activity in Eastern El Salvador and consequently there is a strong military presence.

San Vicente, 61 km. from the capital, is a little SE of the Highway on the Río Alcahuapa, at the foot of the double-peaked Chinchontepec volcano, with very fine views of the Jiboa valley as it is approached. Population: 56,800. Its pride and gem is El Pilar (1762-69), most original church in the country. It was here that the **Indian chief, Anastasio Aquino**, took the crown from the statue of San José and crowned himself King of the Nonualcos during the Indian rebellion of 1833. In its main square is the *tempesque* tree under which the city's foundation charter was drawn up. Bus 116 from Oriente terminal, San Salvador. Carnival day: 1 November.

Hotels *Pensión Vicentina*, E. Better is *Casa Romero*, which is near the bridge but has no sign, so ask for directions, E; good meals for US$0.80, parking available, *Hospedaje Viajero*, F; *Hospedaje Rivoly*, E, good food.

Excursions Two km. E of the town is the Balneario Amapulapa, one of a number of recreational centres developed by the National Tourist Board. There are three pools at different levels in a wooded setting. Small entry and parking charges. Reached by bus 174 from San Vicente. **Lake Apastepeque**, near San Vicente off the Pan-American Highway, is small but picturesque.

The Highway (in poor condition after San Vincente) used to cross the Río Lempa by the 411-metre-long Cuscatlán suspension bridge (destroyed by guerrillas in 1983). It now crosses the 15 de Septiembre dam at the San Lorenzo hydroelectric plant, and goes on to

San Miguel, 136 km. from San Salvador, capital of its Department, founded in 1530 at the foot of the volcanoes of San Miguel (Chaparastique—which erupted in 1976, and Chinameca). It has some very good parks and a bare 18th century cathedral. Some silver and gold are mined. It is an important distributing centre. Population, about 250,000. Bus 301 from Oriente terminal, San Salvador (US$1.40, return every ½ hr. from 0500 to 1630). Fiesta of the Virgen de la Paz: 20

November. There is a charming church with statues and fountains in its gardens about 16 km. away at Chinameca.

Hotels Very few in centre, most on the entrance roads: *Trópico Inn*, C, clean, comfortable, reasonable restaurant; *Hispanoamericano*, 6A Av. Norte B, F, with toilet and shower, air-conditioned (cheaper in older rooms without a/c); *Motel Milián* (pool), D, rec., good food; *China House*, D, clean, friendly; *Central*, G, English spoken; *Pension Lux*, C. 4 Oriente, 6 Av. Oriente, G, reasonable. *Pensión El Carmen*, F; *San Luis*, G, clean and quiet. *Hospedaje Argueta*, 4C. Oriente y 6-8 Av., G p.p.; also *El Faro*, *Primavera*, *Santa Fe*. Plenty of cheap places near the bus station.

Restaurants *La Puerta del Sol*, 3 Av. Sur, 4C. Poniente, good variety; *El Gran Tejano*, 4C. Poniente near cathedral, great steaks; *Chetino's Pizzería*, 5 C. Poniente, near Centro Médico; *Bati Club Carlitos*, 12 Av. Norte.

Exchange Local banks. Open: 0830-1200, 1430-1800.

From San Miguel a good paved road runs S to the Pacific Highway. Go S along it for 12 km., where a dirt road leads to Playa El Cuco (**see page** 458). Bus 320 from San Miguel, US$1. The climate in this area is good. A mainly paved, reasonable road goes to San Jorge and Usulután: leave the Pan-American Highway 5 km. W of San Miguel. The road goes through hills and coffee plantations with superb views of San Miguel volcano. Accessible only by private car from San Miguel is **Laguna de Alegría** in a crater of an extinct volcano and fed by both hot and cold springs; good swimming. To the N are the Indian ruins of **Quelapa** (bus 326), but there is not much to see.

San Francisco Gotera, the capital of Morazán Department, can be reached from the Oriente terminal in San Salvador, or from San Miguel. It is the last stop for foreigners on Route 7 to the Honduran border (Upper Morazán has been completely controlled by the FMLN and the road is closed). 2 places to stay: *Hospedaje San Francisco*, Av. Morazán 23, nice garden and hammocks, F; *Motel Arco Iris*, next door. Beyond San Francisco, the road runs to Jocaitique (there is a bus) from where an unpaved road climbs into the mountains through pine forests to Sabanetas, near the Honduran border. Accommodation at both Jocaitique and Sabanetas. (This trip is not possible while guerrilla activity continues.) 22 km. NE of San Francisco is Corinto with two caves nearby of precolombian interest including wall paintings. Enquire if it is possible to visit and if a military permit is required.

It is another 42 km. from San Miguel to the port of La Unión/Cutuco. Before it gets there the Pan-American Highway turns N for the Goascarán bridge to Honduras. Bus San Miguel-Goascarán, US$0.80, 2½ hrs. (may be disrupted by guerrillas). There is a tourist office at the border (El Amatillo)—border closes 1700.

To save time when travelling eastwards, take the Ruta Militar NE through (34 km.) Santa Rosa de Lima to the Goascarán bridge on the border with Honduras, 56 km. (There are plenty of money changers, accepting all Central American currencies and travellers' cheques, but beware of short-changing on Nicaraguan and Costa Rican currencies.)

Santa Rosa de Lima (27,300 people) is a charming little place with a wonderful colonial church, set in the hills. There are gold and silver mines. Don't miss the excellent *sopa de apretadores* (crab soup, the best in El Salvador), near the town centre—everyone knows the place. *Hospedaje Mundial*, nr. market, F, basic, friendly; *Hospedaje Florida*, Ruta Militar, F, clean, friendly, their crab soup is recommended, too. Unnamed *comedor* on the Pan American Highway, good and cheap. Buses to the Honduran border half-hourly.

La Unión/Cutuco, on the Gulf of Fonseca, is the only port in El Salvador except Acajutla at which ships can berth. Population, 43,000. The port handles half the country's trade. The whole coast is a military zone. Bus 304 from Oriente terminal, San Salvador.

Hotels *Centroamérica*, C, with fan, more with a/c; *Miramar*, G, good; *Hospedaje Annex Santa Marta*, F, with shower and fan, not bad; opposite, a bit further away from square is a hotel, F, friendly, noisy, basic, but OK; *San Carlos*, opposite railway station, E, good meals available; *Hospedaje Santa Rosa*.

Restaurant *La Patia*—fish; *Comedores Gallego* and *Rosita* rec. *Comedor Tere*, Av. General Menéndez 2.2, fairly good.

Exchange at *Cafetín Brisas del Mar*, 3 Av. Norte y 3 Calle Oriente. Black market sometimes in centre.

Customs 3 Av. Norte 3.9; **Immigration** at 3 Calle Oriente 2.8.

Ferry There is no longer a ferry to Puntarenas (Costa Rica). It may be possible to take a cargo boat to Costa Rica; ask the captains in Cutuco. It is not possible for foreigners to travel by boat to Potosí (Nicaragua). There is reportedly a boat to Honduras, but it is easier to go by land.

Buses Terminal is at 3 Calle Poniente (block 3); to San Salvador, US$1.75, 4 hrs., many daily, direct or via San Miguel, one passes the harbour at 0300. Bus to Honduran border at El Amatillo, No. 353, US$0.50.

Excursions To Conchagua to see one of the few old colonial churches in the country; Conchagua volcano can also be climbed and a hard walk will be rewarded by superb views over San Miguel volcano (good bus service). One can take an early morning boat to the islands in the Gulf of Fonseca: to Zacatillo (about 1 hr.) and Meanguera (more), where there are many secluded little beaches. Take plenty of provisions, as afternoon boats can be uncertain and one may have to spend the night in a fishing hut. To El Tamarindo (bus 383, US$0.25, service not good so best start early), a small, attractive fishing village with beautiful white beaches. No accommodation, but the place is popular and huts to sling a hammock are US$2 a day. Check if the military will allow excursions to the coast. Also from La Unión, the ruins of Los Llanitos can be visited.

By Coastal Highway This is the second road route, running through the southern cotton lands. It begins on a 4-lane motorway to Comalapa airport at Cuscatlán. The first place of any importance after leaving the capital (13 km.) Santo Tomás. There are Indian ruins at Cushululitán, a short distance N.

Beyond, a new road to the E, rising to 1,000 metres, runs S of Lake Ilopango to join the Pan-American Highway beyond Cojutepeque.

Ten km. on from Santo Tomás is **Olocuilta**, an old town with a colourful market on Sunday under a great tree. Good church. (Both Santo Tomás and Olocuilta can be reached by bus 133 from San Salvador.) From the airport, the road becomes a 2-lane toll-road, going E across the Río Jiboa to

Zacatecoluca, capital of La Paz Department, 56 km. from San Salvador by road and 19 km. S of San Vicente. Bus 133 from Occidente terminal, San Salvador. José Simeón Cañas, who abolished slavery in Central America, was born here. Population, 81,000.

Hotels *América*, E. *Hospedajes América* and *Popular* clean, E. *Comedor Margoth* (beware high charging).

Near the town is the garden park of Ichanmichen ("the place of the little fish"). It is crossed by canals and decorated with pools: there is, in fact, an attractive swimming pool. It is very hot but there is plenty of shade.

Between Olocuilta and Zacatecoluca, a road branches N to the small towns of San Pedro Nonualco and Santa María Ostuma (with an interesting colonial church and a famous *fiesta* on February 2); both are worth visiting, but not easy to get to. Bus 135 from Terminal del Occidente goes to San Pedro. If you get off this bus at the turn off to San Sebastián Arriba, you can walk to the Peñón del Tacuazín (or del Indio Aquino), 480 metres above sea level, which is 4½ km. N of Santiago Nonualco. A cave at its summit was used as a refuge by Anastasio Aquino (**see page** 455), before his execution in April 1833.

A branch road to the S before Zacatecoluca leads to the Playa **Costa El Sol** on the Pacific, being developed as a tourist resort. There are extensive black sand beaches and several luxury hotels already open: *Tesoro Beach*, A-L, apartment style rooms, swimming pool, 9-hole golf course; *Izalco Cabaña Club*, A-L, 30 rooms, pool, seafood a speciality; *Pacific Paradise* (75 rooms).

Both road and railway cross the wide Lempa River by the Puente de Oro (Golden Bridge) at San Marcos. (The road bridge has been destroyed; cars use the railway bridge.) A branch road (right) leads to tiny Puerto El Triunfo on the Bay of Jiquilisco, with a large shrimp-freezing plant. About 110 km. from the capital is

Usulután, capital of its Department. Population, 69,000. Bus 302 from San Salvador.

Hotels *Hotel and Restaurant España*, on main square, rec., nice patio, bar and discotheque. *Millions*, D; *Motel Usulután*, D; *Central*, E.

A road branches NE from Usulután, some 45 km. to San Miguel (**see page** 455) On this road is Lake Jocotal, a national nature reserve supported by the World Wildlife Fund, which can be visited by arrangement with the warden.

The Coastal Highway goes direct from Usulután to La Unión/Cutuco.

12 km. from junction for San Miguel there is a turn to the right leading in 7 km. to **Playa El Cuco**, a popular beach with several places to stay (E/F), near the bus station (buses to San Miguel). *Hotel Cucolindo*, 1 km. along the coast, F, basic, cold water, mosquitos. Nearby is the *Trópico Club* with several cabins, run by the *Trópico Inn* in San Miguel which can provide information. Another popular beach, El Tamarindo, is reached by another right turn off the road to La Unión, *Cabañas* for rent. Boat from El Tamarindo across the bay leads to a short cut to La Unión.

WESTERN EL SALVADOR

The route from the capital S to La Libertad has already been given. Both a paved road and the railway connect San Salvador with Sonsonate and the port of Acajutla. The road goes W through Santa Tecla (**see page** 452) to Sonsonate, and then S to the port. 6 km. W of Santa Tecla on the main road is Los Chorros (see under Santa Tecla); 3½ km. beyond, the Pan-American Highway (good) runs NW past Lake Coatepeque to Santa Ana.

Acajutla, Salvador's main port serving the western and central areas, is 85 km. from San Salvador (bus 207 from Occidente terminal, US$2.80), 58 km. from Santa Ana (it is 8 km. S of the Coastal Highway). It handles about 40% of the coffee exports and is a popular seaside resort (good surfing) during the summer, though not an attractive town. Population: 36,000.

Hotels *California*, E. *Brisas del Mar*, F. Good, cheap *pensión* at back of La Campana store.

The nearby beaches at Metalio and Barra de Santiago are rec., but Los Cobanos is dirty, expensive and unsafe.

Sonsonate, 19 km. N on the road to the capital (64 km.) produces sugar, tobacco, rice, tropical fruits, hides and balsam. An important market is held each Sun. Sonsonate is in the chief cattle-raising region. Population: 60,900. It was founded in 1552. The beautiful El Pilar church is strongly reminiscent of the church of El Pilar in San Vicente. The Cathedral has many of the cupolas (the largest covered with white porcelain) which serve as a protection against earthquakes. The old church of San Antonio del Monte, just outside the city, draws pilgrims from afar. Capital to Sonsonate by bus 205, US$1.50, 90 mins. In the northern outskirts of the city there is a waterfall on the Sensunapán river. Legend has it that an Indian princess drowned there, and on the anniversary of her death a gold casket appears below the falls.

Hotels *Sonsonate*, 6 Av. Norte with Calle Obispo Marroquín, D, with a/c, meals available; *Orbe*, D; *Centroamericano*, near centre, E; *Florida*, beside bus terminal, G, basic, manager speaks English; *Castro*, 3 blocks from Parque, G, good, safe, friendly; *Hospedaje Taplán*, near bus station, G, basic; *del Viajero*, opposite bus station, F, dirty, very basic; *El Brasil*, 4 Av. Norte, F, basic, clean and friendly.

Restaurants *Milkbar; Comedor Santa Cecilia*.

Roads N to Santa Ana, 39 km., a beautiful journey through high, cool coffee country, with volcanoes in view; NW to Ahuachapán, 40 km., and on to Guatemala (road paved from Ahuachapán through Apaneca and passes through some spectacular scenery); S and W to the Guatemalan frontier points of La Hachadura and Ciudad Pedro de Alvarado at the bridge over the Río Paz. Border crossing is straightforward, but if in a private vehicle requires a lot of paperwork (about 2 hrs.). Many buses ply between La Hachadura and Sonsonate, US$0.60 to Ahuachapán, US$0.50, 4 hrs.

At the foot of Izalco volcano, 8 km. from Sonsonate, is the town of **Izalco** (population 43,000), which has resulted from the gradual merging of the *ladino* village of Dolores Izalco and the Indian village of Asunción Izalco. Festivals, 8 to 15 August and during the Feast of St. John the Baptist from 17 to 24 June. Near Izalco, on the slopes, is the spacious swimming pool of Atecozol, in the middle of a beautiful park with a restaurant. The park is shaded by huge mahogany trees, palms, aromatic balsam trees and *amates*. There is a battlemented tower; a monument to Tlaloc, god of the rain; another to Atonatl, the Indian who, on this spot, shot the arrow which lamed the *conquistador* Pedro de Alvarado; and a statue to the toad found jumping on the spot where water was found. Izalco village and Izalco volcano are not directly connected by road. A paved road branches from the highway 14 km. from the turning for Izalco village (about 22 km. from Sonsonate) and goes up towards Lake Coatepeque (see below); when you reach the summit, an all-weather road branches for **Cerro Verde** with its fine views down into the Izalco crater. A camping ground and car park at 1,980 metres overlook the crater. The camping is good, ask the warden if you need basics for preparing meals. To climb Izalco: a path leads off the road (signposted) just below the car park on Cerro Verde. In 20-30 minutes descend to the saddle between Cerro Verde and Izalco, then 1-1½ hrs. up (rather steep, but manageable). A spectacular view from top. For a quick descent, find a rivulet of soft volcanic sand and half-slide, half-walk down in 15 mins., then 45 mins. to 1 hr. back up the saddle. This "cinder running" needs care, strong shoes and a thought for those below. You are probably also aiding erosion. Cerro Verde can be very busy at weekends.

The fine *Hotel Montaña* (C) at the top of Cerro Verde was originally built so that the international set could watch Izalco in eruption; unfortunately, the eruptions stopped just as the hotel was completed. Good food is provided at fairly reasonable prices. There is a US$0.25 charge for parking, but none for camping, although permission must be obtained first from the Departamento de Bienestar, Ministerio de Trabajo in San Bartolo on the outskirts of San Salvador. There is a bus (No. 248) twice daily from Santa Ana to a junction 14 km. from the top of Cerro Verde (US$1). From Sonsonate to the turn-off for Cerro Verde costs US$0.30; from there it is easy to hitch a lift (tip expected).

The road to Cerro Verde has fine views of Lake Coatepeque; ¾ of the way to Cerro Verde, a track branches off to the right to Finca San Blas (also can be reached on foot from Cerro Verde car park, 20 mins.). From there it is a 1 hr. walk straight up Santa Ana volcano. There are four craters inside one another; the newest crater has a lake and fuming columns of sulphur clouds. You can walk around the edge and down on to the ledge formed by the third crater (beware of the fumes). The main paved road goes on to the lakeshore.

In the Sonsonate district are a number of waterfalls and other sites of natural beauty: near the village of Santo Domingo de Guzmán (bus 246 from Sonsonate) are the falls of El Escuco, Tepechapa and La Quebrada, all within walking distance of Santo Domingo and each other. Near Caluco (which has a colonial church and a ruined Dominican church, bus 432 from Sonsonate) are Las Victorias Falls, just past the Atecozol Turicentro, with 2 caves above the falls, the meeting of hot and cold streams at Los Encuentros to form the Shuteca/Aguas Calientes river, and La

Chapina pool and springs. Bus 219 goes to Cuisnahuat, from where it is 2 km. S to the Río Apancoyo, or 4 km. N to Peñón El Escalón (covered in balsam trees) and El Istucal Cave, at the foot of the Escalón hill, where Indian rites are celebrated in November.

Between Sonsonate and Ahuachapán (see below) is the Indian village of **Nahuizalco**. The older women still wear the *refajo* (a doubled length of cloth of tie-dyed threads worn over a wrap-round skirt), and various crafts are still carried on, although use of the Indian language is dying out. Beyond is Jauyúa, with Los Chorros de la Calera 2 km. N (bus 205 from Sonsonate). From San Pedro Puxtla (bus 246) you can visit the Tequendama Falls on the Sihuapán river. (Details on these and other sites from the Instituto Salvadoreño de Turismo.)

The Pan-American Highway runs through Santa Tecla to Santa Ana. A new dual carriageway road parallels the old Pan-American Highway, bypassing Santa Ana; toll: US$0.40. (Keep your ticket if turning off to Coatepeque, as it serves for the return.) The road, with turnoffs for Sonsonate and Ahuachapán, carries on to San Cristóbal on the Guatemalan frontier.

There is an archaeological site at San Andrés, half-way between Santa Tecla and Coatepeque. Exhibits from it and from Tazumal are at the National Museum.

Some 13 km. short of Santa Ana a short branch road leads (left) to **Lake Coatepeque**, a favourite week-end resort with good sailing, swimming, and fishing near the foot of Santa Ana volcano. There are good hotels, restaurants, and lodging houses. The surroundings are exceptionally beautiful. (Bus 201 from San Salvador to Santa Ana, where one changes to a 220 (hourly) for the lake, or take a bus from San Salvador to El Congo on Pan-American Highway, US$1, then another to the lake, US$0.20.) Cerro Verde is easily reached in 90 mins. by good roads through impressive scenery.

Tourists are put up free in cabins with mattresses and showers at Balneario Los Obreros (a resort for workers). When you reach the lake shore from the rim of the crater follow the road a little. Permission to stay must be obtained from the Departamento de Bienestar, Ministerio de Trabajo, in San Bartolo on the outskirts of San Salvador. Restaurant and supervised swimming. Otherwise, water difficult to reach because of the number of weekend homes.

Hotels Hotels charge per 12 hrs. *Del Lago* (try the crab soup), D, overpriced; *Torremolino*, E, noisy, unfriendly (*Comedor Janet* opposite is good); *Lido*, E.

Santa Ana, 55 km. from San Salvador and capital of its Department, is the second largest city in the country (bus 201 from Terminal del Occidente, San Salvador). The intermont basin in which it lies at 656 metres on the NE slopes of Santa Ana volcano is exceptionally fertile. Coffee is the great crop, with sugar-cane a good second. The city is the business centre of western El Salvador. There are some fine buildings, particularly the classical theatre, the neo-gothic cathedral, and several other churches, especially El Calvario, in colonial style. Population: 208,322.

Hotels *La Libertad*, near cathedral, C with bath, good meals for about US$2; *Roosevelt*, E, good meals for US$1.60; *Florida*, room with bath, E, rec., serves excellent meals for US$2; *Internacional-Inn*, 25 C. Poniente y 10 Av. Sur, E with bath, TV, not the most conventional of hotels; *Hospedaje Carao*, Av. José Matías

Delgado, F, with bath, basic, quite clean; *Pensión Lux*, on Parque Colón. *Colonial*, F, 8 Av. Norte 2, clean, helpful, good breakfasts for less than US$1, a little noisy; *Hospedaje Livingston*, 10 Av. Sur, 29, F, with bath, clean, friendly, good value; *Pensión Monterrey*, 10 Av. Sur, 9-11, F, without bathroom, and *Hospedaje El Santaneco*, F, without bath, basic, on same street. 3 *hospedajes* S of Parque Colón, G.

Restaurants are expensive so it is best to eat in *comedores*, or at the market in front of the cathedral. The best recommended restaurant is *Kiyomi*, 4 Av. Sur between 3 and 5C., good food and service, clean, reasonable prices. Everything closes at about 1900.

Exchange Local banks. Open 0830-1200, 1430-1700. Black market around the banks (called Wall Street by the locals!).

The border with Guatemala is 30 km. by paved road from Santa Ana (the fastest road link from San Salvador to Guatemala City is via the Santa Ana bypass, then to Ahuachapán and on to the border at Las Chinamas—tourist office here). Buses (Melva) leave from the *Pensión Lux* on the east side of Parque Colón for Guatemala City, US$3, 5½ hrs. including meal and border stops. Also Inter Futuro Express, Transportes Centroamérica, and Mermex, US$5, unreliable. Alternatively there are local buses to the border for US$0.30; they leave from the market. Bus 406 from the capital (Terminal del Occidente), goes direct to the frontier at Las Chinamas.

Excursions To Lake Coatepeque, 19 km. (220 bus to *Hotel del Lago* US$0.40). *Chalchuapa*, 16 km. from Santa Ana, on the road to Ahuachapán, population 34,865, is at 640 metres. President Barrios of Guatemala was killed in battle here in 1885, when trying to reunite Central America by force. There is some good colonial-style domestic building; the church of Santiago is particularly striking. See the small but picturesque lake; the very interesting church, almost the only one in El Salvador which shows strong indigenous influences, and the **Tazumal** ruin next to the cemetary in Chalchuapa, built about A.D. 980 by the Pipil Indians but with its 14-step pyramid now, alas, restored in concrete. The site has been occupied since 5000 B.C. and in the simple museum are the artefacts found in the mud under the lake. There are very interesting bowls used for burning incense, intricately decorated with animal designs. The ruin, which is open 0900-1200 and 1300-1730, closed on Mondays, is free of entry and only 5 minutes' walk from the main road. Minibus (No. 218) from Santa Ana, 20 mins., US$0.30. On the west of the town is the El Trapiche swimming pool. Bus 51 or 55 goes to **Turicentro Sihuatehuacán**, on city outskirts; US$0.13 admission to pools, café, park, etc.

Hotel at Chalchuapa: *Gloria*, E.

Guatemalan consul in Chalchuapa (Av. Club de Leones Norte, between Primero and Calle Ramón Flores—unmarked blue house, knock for attention).

Ahuachapán, capital of its Department, is 35 km. from Santa Ana, at 753 metres. Population, 63,500. It is a quiet town with low and simple houses, but an important distribution centre. Coffee is the great product. Like many places in the area, it draws the mineral water for its bath-house from some hot springs near the falls of Malacatiupán, near-by. Power is from the falls of Atehuezián on the Río Molino, which cascade prettily down the mountain-side. See also the *ausoles*—geysers of boiling mud with plumes of steam and strong whiffs of sulphur, which have been harnessed to produce electric power. A road runs NW through the treeless Llano del Espino, with its small lake, and across the

Río Paz into Guatemala. Ahuachapán is 116 km. from the capital by bus 202 from San Salvador (US$2.75). Buses direct to the border, US$0.80.

The *ausoles* are interesting—an area of ground which is warm to the touch. They are used for generating electricity; only the smallest remains uncovered by drums and pipes. One can take a bus from Ahuachapán to El Barro, take a taxi or walk the 5 km. to the area. Permission to visit the power station can be obtained from the barracks on the hill overlooking the town as the site is guarded by the Army.

Hotel *Astoria*, E; *La Ahuachapaneca* guest house, E; *Hospedaje San Juan*, E. One can get good meals at *Restaurant El Paseo*. *Pastelería María*, good cakes and biscuits.

Between Ahuachapán and Sonsonate are two small lakes, Laguna Verde and Apaneca, whose crater-like walls are profusely covered in tropical forest, in the Cordillera de Apaneca, part of the narrow highland belt running SE of Ahuachapán; they are popular with tourists. It is possible to swim in the former, but the latter is too shallow and reedy. Local buses run some distance away, leaving one with a fairly long walk. Laguna Verde can also be reached by road via Cantón Tulapa, from a turn off on the CA-8 road east of Apaneca. S of here is the Cascada del Río Cauta (take bus 216 from Ahuachapán towards Jujutla, alight 3 km. after the turn-off to Apaneca, then walk along trail for 300 m.). 9 km. W of Ahuachapán near the village of Los Toles is the Tehuasilla falls, where the El Molino river falls 75 metres.

Metapán (32 km. N of Santa Ana) is about 10 km. NE of Lake Güija. Its colonial baroque cathedral is one of the very few to have survived in the country. The altarpieces have some very good silver work (the silver is from local mines) and the façade is splendid. Lots of easy walks with good views to the lake. There are many lime kilns and a huge cement plant. Population: 51,800.

Hotels *Gallo de Oro*, G; *Ferrocarril*, G. Restaurant *Rincón del Pelon*, best in town, helpful, friendly.

A mountain track from Metapán gives access to **Montecristo National Nature Reserve**, El Salvador's last remaining cloud forest. There is an abundance of protected wildlife; permits to visit have to be obtained in San Salvador (and are not given during the breeding season, thought to be Feb. to May). This now forms part of El Trifinio, or the International Biosphere "La Fraternidad", administered jointly by Guatemala, Honduras and El Salvador. Near the top of Cerro Montecristo (2,418 m.), which is the point where the three frontiers meet, there is an orchid garden, with over 100 species (best time to see them in flower is early Spring), an apple orchard and a camping ground in the forest. A 4-wheel drive vehicle is essential to get there; allow 2 hrs. from Metapán. For information and permission to visit, contact Dr. Adonis Moreira, Director, Centro de Recursos Naturales, Cantón El Matazano, Soyapango, T 270484..

A good paved road runs from Metapán to the Guatemalan frontier.

Lake Güija, on the Guatemalan border, 16 km. by 8, is very beautiful and dotted with small islands, but it is not easy to reach. A new dam at the lake's outlet generates electricity for the western part of the country.

NORTHERN EL SALVADOR

There has been much guerrilla and counter-insurgency activity in the northern areas; visitors have to pass through an "internal border" before the Río Lempa bridge on the Troncal del Norte, where "official El Salvador" meets "FMLN El Salvador". If the region is not safe, foreigners will not be allowed beyond this point, but usually there is no problem or danger.

The Troncal del Norte is paved throughout, and runs due North through Apopa (junction with a good road to Quezaltepeque) and Aguilares to the western extremity of the Cerrón Grande reservoir. A branch to the right skirts the northern side of the reservoir to Chalatenango, capital of the department of the same name. **Chalatenango**, 55 km. from San Salvador, is a delightful little town with an annual fair and *fiesta* on 24 June. (Bus 125 from Oriente terminal, San Salvador, US$0.55.) Population, 30,000. It is the centre of an important region of traditional livestock farms. Good market. 2 *hospedajes*: *El Nuevo Amanecer*, F, good views of the Cathedral from the 2nd floor; one unnamed, G. If walking in the countryside, you may meet FMLN guerrillas who are interested in meeting foreigners, but you also run the risk of meeting army patrols who may arrest you.

The main road continues north through Tejutla to **La Palma**, a charming village set in pine clad mountains, and well worth a visit. It is famous for its local crafts, particularly the brightly-painted wood carvings and hand-embroidered tapestries. There are a number of workshops in La Palma where the craftsmen can be seen at work and purchases made. (The products are also sold in San Salvador.) Buses run from San Salvador to La Palma (No. 119, US$1).

The road continues north to the frontier at El Poy, for western Honduras (at least 5 buses a day—No. 119—from Terminal del Oriente in San Salvador, frequent military checks, 3-4 hrs. in all). 2 km. before El Poy is *Hotel Cayahuanca*, F, clean, friendly. Travellers' cheques exchanged at El Poy. Exit tax 3 colones, plus a 5 colones "tourist tax" (stamp affixed to passport—don't try to leave without it, you will be turned back).

INFORMATION FOR VISITORS

Documents   A passport is necessary for nationals of all countries. Citizens of most countries require a visa; those that do *not* need visas are: West Germany, Austria, Belgium, Spain, Finland, UK, Italy, Norway, Switzerland, Luxemburg, Japan, Mexico, Guatemala, Honduras, Costa Rica and Colombia. This is subject to change and it is best to apply in your own country. Visas cost US$20/£8 and take 48 hrs. at a consulate, or up to a week in bordering countries, for a stay of only 8 days, or sometimes, 15 days. Visas can be renewed for up to 30 days at Immigration at the Centro de Gobierno in San Salvador, next to the ANTEL office, T 226700/227573, at cost of US$2.48. We understand that visas are not available for East European visitors, and in late 1989 travellers reported being allowed to stay only 15 days.

Travellers doing business directly in the country must get an ordinary (non-immigrant) visa and visit the Immigration Bureau (Centro de Gobierno) within 48 hours of arrival and get a permit to stay for 30 days. It costs US$4. They must get an exit permit from the same place, at the same price, before they leave the country. Business travellers are sometimes assessed for income tax during their stay. Border formalities tend to be relatively brief, although thorough searches are common. A baggage charge of 2 colones is made at borders. There is an entrance tax of, and an exit tax of 6 colones. There are restrictions on entry by citizens of Belize and Cuba.

"Hints to Exporters: El Salvador" can be obtained from Dept. of Trade, Export Services Division, Sanctuary Buildings, 16-20 Great Smith Street, London SW1P 3DB.

Note   After many years of semi-civil war, much in El Salvador is run-down, does not work and is disorganized, in addition, poverty abounds. Visitors should take this into account. However, tourists do help and are welcome (although U.S. citizens should not emphasize their nationality). Contrary to the advice for many other countries, look like a tourist, but don't point your camera in the wrong direction.

Do not try to enter El Salvador carrying literature that may be regarded as subversive or left-wing, for example books from Nicaragua, or by Russian authors. At best, it will be confiscated, or you may be refused entry. Furthermore, it is advisable not to say that Nicaragua is on your itinerary (this restriction may change in 1990, following the change of Nicaraguan government). Army-style clothing will also be confiscated. It is wise not to camp out, but generally travellers report no problems; keep well away from politics and be prepared for plenty of police checks and body searches on buses (the officers are polite, if respected).

If driving through the eastern part of the country e.g. on the Panamerican or Coastal Highways, do not drive up close to army vehicles. If you can travel in pairs, it is safer; solo travellers are considered suspicious. Dangerous areas are closed by the army but safe conduct passes, issued by the General Staff in San Salvador may be available. Make careful enquiries on where you may not go; several travellers have told us of interrogations and arrests because they did not have military passes.

Taxes   There is a 10% tax on international air tickets bought in El Salvador and a US$1 boarding tax. There is also an airport tax of US$9 if staying more than 6 hours. MCO tickets can be bought.

How to get there   From London: To Miami with Pan Am, Continental, British Airways or Virgin Atlantic, thence to San Salvador with American or Taca (direct). Other connecting cities in the USA with flights to San Salvador are: Houston (Continental, Taca), New Orleans (Taca), Los Angeles (Pan Am, Taca, Lacsa), San Francisco (Pan Am, Taca), New York and Orlando (Continental, via Houston, or, for New York, Miami). Taca flies to all Central American capitals, except Managua, to San Pedro Sula and to Mexico City (also served by Lacsa). Copa flies to the other Central American capitals, except Belize City and Tegucigalpa (which is served by Sahsa). Pan Am flies to Guatemala City, Lacsa to San José and Copa to Panama, with connection to Kingston (Jamaica). From Europe, San Salvador can be reached with Taca connecting flights from Guatemala City, to which Iberia and KLM fly (both twice a week). Alternatively, go to Miami and connect from there. Connections for South America through San José or Panama.

Customs All personal luggage and goods up to a value of US$100 are allowed in free of duty. Also allowed in free: 1 kg. of tobacco products, or 100 cigars or 600 cigarettes, and 2 bottles of liqueur. There are no restrictions on export or import of any currency except that of Nicaragua (again this may have changed in 1990). All animal products are prohibited from importation, with the exception of boned, sterilized and hermetically sealed meat products. Fruits are inspected carefully and destroyed if necessary. Hide, skins and woollen goods will be fumigated against disease. Animals must be free of parasites, fully inoculated and have a vetinary certificate and import permit.

Internal Transport Buses are good (if sometimes crowded). San Salvador has plenty of taxis. Hitchhiking is comparatively easy. There are no longer any rail passenger services.

Motoring At the border, after producing a driving licence and proof of ownership, you are given a permit to stay for 15 days at the Customs Office and Police Department. This can be extended at the Dirección General de la Renta Aduanas, near the Terminal de Oriente in San Salvador. In any case the formalities for bringing in a car involve considerable paperwork. There is a 4.50 colones charge for compulsory tyre fumigation. There is also a 2-colón quarantine charge and a 5-colón transit fee for cars. Insurance is not compulsory in El Salvador, but you should arrange cover. A good map, both of republic and of capital, can be obtained from Texaco or Esso, or from the Tourist Institute. Petrol costs 7.50 colones a US gallon.

Food Try *pupusas*, stuffed *tortillas* in 3 varieties (*chicharrón*—pork; *queso*—cheese; *revueltas*), typical, tasty and cheap; also *garobo* (iguana) and *cusuco* (tatou—armadillo). They are sold at many street stalls and in fact are better there than in restaurants. On Sat. and Sun. nights local people congregate in *pupuserías*.

Tips at hotels and restaurants: 10%, but 15% for small bills. Nothing for taxi drivers except when hired for the day; airport porters, "boinas rojas", US$1 a bag; haircut, US$0.20, not obligatory.

Health The gastro-enteric diseases are the most common. Visitors should take care over what they eat during the first few weeks and should drink *agua cristal* (bottled water). Specifics against malaria should be taken if a night is spent on the coast. Warning of dengue fever has been reported from that part of the main road running north from San Salvador between Suchitoto and Tejutla and elsewhere, where a large area of land has been flooded for the Cerrón Grande dam. The San Salvador milk supply is good.

Clothing White suits and white dinner jackets are not worn.

The **best months** for a business visit are from February to May, when there is least rainfall and most business. August is the holiday season. Business is centralized in the capital, but it is as well to visit Santa Ana and San Miguel.

Hours of Business 0800-1200 and 1400-1800 Mon. to Fri.; 0800-1200 Sat. Banks in San Salvador 0900-1300, 1345-1500 Mon. to Fri.; different hours for other towns given in text. Government offices: 0800-1600 Mon. to Fri.

Public Holidays The usual ones are 1 January, Holy Week (3 days, government 10 days), 14, 17 April, 1 May, 10 May, Corpus Christi (half day), 5-6 August, 15 September, 12 October, 2 and 5 November (half-day), 24 December (half-day), and Christmas Day. Govenment offices are also often closed on religious holidays. Little business in weeks ending Easter week, the first week of August, and the Christmas-New Year period. Banks are closed for balance 29, 30 June, and 30, 31 December.

Time in El Salvador is 6 hrs. behind GMT.

Currency The unit is the colón (¢), divided into 100 centavos. Banknotes of 1, 2, 5, 10, 25 and 100 colones are used, and there are nickel coins for the fractional amounts. The colón is often called a peso. Black market trading is done in the street, but banks may give better rates. Either is preferable to the border, where rates can be much lower. Credit card payment are subject to 5% commission and are charged at the official rate. When leaving El Salvador, one may only change US$40-worth of colones back into dollars on presentation of boarding pass and passport at the airport bank. Money sent to El Salvador will be paid out in colones only. **N.B.** Change all colones before entering Guatemala or Honduras, where they are not accepted or changed anywhere (except at borders).

Warning Prices in El Salvador are sometimes quoted in US dollars. Make sure which currency is being used.

The **metric system** of weights and measures is used alongside certain local units such as the *vara* (836 millimetres, 32.9 inches), *manzana* (7,000 square metres, or 1.67 acres), the *libra* (0.454 kilogramme, about 1 English pound), and the *quintal* of 100 *libras*. Some US weights and measures are also used. US gallons are used for gasoline and quarts for oil.

Electric Current 110 volts, 60 cycles, A.C. (plugs are American, 2 flat pin style).

Posts and Telecommunications Air mail to Europe takes up to one month; from Europe about 15 days, from the USA, 1 week. The correct address for any letter to the capital is "San Salvador, El Salvador, Central America". The main post office is at the Centro de Gobierno.

The charge for a local telephone call is ¢0.10 for 3 mins. A private telephone call or telex to Europe costs US$20 for first 3 minutes, US$5 per extra minute (if made from the state telecommunications company, Antel, Centro de Gobierno, Calle Rubén Darío y 5 Av. Sur). Calls made from hotels cost US$6-7 per minute. Direct dialling is available to Europe, USA (US$2 per min.) and other parts of the world. No collect calls to Europe.

Radio Inc. communicates with all parts of the world through local stations. Public telex at Antel. British businessmen can use the telex system at the Embassy.

Press In San Salvador: *Diario de Hoy*, *La Prensa Gráfica*, and *Diario Latino* every day, including Sunday, *El Mundo*, afternoon paper, but not on Sunday. There are provincial newspapers in Santa Ana, San Miguel and elsewhere. Weekly bilingual newspaper (English and Spanish, right wing), *El Salvador News Gazette*, available from most hotels which take foreigners. *Semana*, weekly magazine for El Salvador and Central America (liberal).

Most of the 39 radio stations cover the whole country, and all accept advertisements. There are 3 commercial television stations, all with national coverage, and two government-run information channels.

Local Information can be got from the National Tourist Institute, Calle Rubén Darío 619, San Salvador. The Tourist Institute provides a small map of the country with the main beaches and the 15 "Turicentros" marked on it.

Language Spanish, but English is widely understood. Spanish should be used for letters, catalogues, etc.

We are most grateful for Salvadorean information to A. Halbach (Geneva 19), D.M. Spranger (Geneva, Switz.), S.L. Wyatt, and to other travellers whose names are listed in the general Central America section.

WILL YOU HELP US?

We do all we can to get our facts right in **The Mexico & Central American Handbook.** Each chapter is thoroughly revised each year, but the territory covered is vast, and our eyes cannot be everywhere. A new highway or airport is built; a hotel, a restaurant, a cabaret dies; another, a good one is born; a building we describe is pulled down, a street renamed. Names and addresses of good hotels and restaurants for "budget-minded" travellers are always very welcome. We would especially like to receive diagrams of walks, national parks and other interesting areas to use as source material for the Handbook and other forthcoming titles.

Your information may be far more up-to-date than ours. If your letter reaches us early enough in the year it will be used in the next edition, but write whenever you want to, for all your letters are used sooner or later.

Thank you very much indeed for you help.

Trade & Travel Publications Limited
6 Riverside Court
Riverside Road
Lower Bristol Road
Bath BA2 3DZ. England

HONDURAS

INTRODUCTION

HONDURAS is larger than all the other Central American republics except Nicaragua, but has a smaller population than El Salvador, less than a fifth its size. Bordered by Nicaragua, Guatemala, and El Salvador, it has an area of 112,088 square km.—rather less than England. It has a narrow Pacific coastal strip, 124 km. long, on the Gulf of Fonseca, but its northern coast on the Caribbean is some 640 km. long.

Much of the country is mountainous: a rough plateau covered with volcanic ash and lava in the S, rising to peaks such as Cerro de las Minas in the Celaque range (2,849 metres), but with some intermont basins at between 900 and 1,400 metres. The volcanic detritus disappears to the N, revealing saw-toothed ranges which approach the coast at an angle; the one in the extreme NW, along the border with Guatemala, disappears under the sea and shows itself again in the Bay Islands. At most places in the N there is only a narrow shelf of lowland between the sea and the sharp upthrust of the mountains, but along two rivers—the Aguán in the NE, and the Ulúa in the NW—long fingers of marshy lowland stretch inland between the ranges. The Ulúa lowland is particularly important; it is about 40 km. wide and stretches southwards for 100 km. From its southern limit a deep gash continues across the highland to the Gulf of Fonseca, on the Pacific. The distance

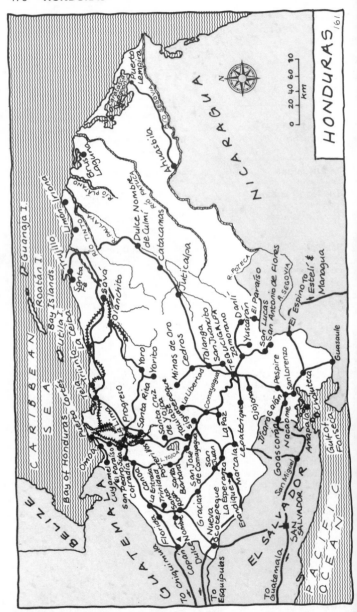

between the Caribbean and the Pacific along this trough is 280 km.; the altitude at the divide between the Río Comayagua, running into the Ulúa and the Caribbean, and the streams flowing into the Pacific, is only 950 metres. In this trough lies Comayagua, the old colonial capital. The lowlands along the Gulf of Fonseca are narrower than they are along the Caribbean; there is no major thrust inland as along the Ulúa.

The prevailing winds are from the E, and the Caribbean coast has a high rainfall and is covered with deep tropical forest. The intermont basins, the valleys, and the slopes sheltered from the prevailing winds bear oak and pine down to as low as 600 metres. Timber is almost the only fuel available. In the drier areas, N and E of Tegucigalpa, there are extensive treeless savannas.

The Spaniards, arriving in the early 16th century, found groups of Indians of the Maya and other cultures. Pushing E from Guatemala City they came upon silver in the SE, and in 1578 founded Tegucigalpa near the mines. The yield was comparatively poor, but enough to attract a thin stream of immigrants. Settlement during the ensuing century was mostly along the trail from Guatemala City: at Gracias, La Esperanza and Comayagua. Gradually these settlements spread over the S and W, and this, with the N coast, is where the bulk of the population lives today. The Spaniards and their descendants ignored the northern littoral and the Ulúa lowlands, but during the 19th century US companies, depending largely on black workers from the British West Indies and Belize, developed the northern lowlands as a great banana-growing area. Today the second largest concentration of population per square mile is in the Department of Cortés, which extends northwards from Lake Yojoa towards the Caribbean; it includes the major portion of the river basins of Ulúa and Chamelecón, also known as the Sula valley: the most important agricultural area in the country, with San Pedro Sula as its commercial centre and Puerto Cortés as its seaport. The Atlantic littoral consumes two-thirds of the country's imports, and ships the bananas which are half the country's exports.

Even today, land under some form of cultivation is only 16% of the total, while meadows and pastures make up 30% of total land use; 33% of Honduras is forest. Rugged terrain makes large areas unsuitable for any kind of agriculture. Nevertheless, there are undeveloped agricultural potentials in the flat and almost unpopulated lands of the coastal plain E of Tela to Trujillo and Puerto Castilla, in the Aguán valley southward and in the region NE of Juticalpa. The area further to the NE, known as the Mosquitia plain, is largely unexploited and little is known of its potential.

Climate Rain is frequent on the Caribbean littoral during the whole year; the heaviest occurs from September to December inclusive. In Tegucigalpa the dry season is normally from November to April inclusive. The coolest months are December and January but if a traveller visits the Caribbean littoral he should avoid these months because heavy rains impede travel; the best months for this area are April and May, though very hot.

History For Honduras' early history, see the introductory chapter to

Central America. Honduras was largely neglected by Spain and its colonists, who concentrated on their trading partners further north or south. The resulting disparity in levels of development between Honduras and its regional neighbours caused problems after independence in 1821. Harsh partisan battles among provincial leaders resulted in the collapse of the Central American Federation in 1838. The national hero, General Francisco Morazán, was a leader in unsuccessful attempts to maintain the Federation and the restoration of Central American unity was the main aim of foreign policy until 1922.

Honduras has had a succession of military and civilian rulers and there have been 300 internal rebellions, civil wars and changes of government since independence, most of them in the 20th century. Political instability has led to a lack of investment in economic infrastructure and sociopolitical integration, making Honduras one of the poorest countries in the Western Hemisphere. It earned its nickname of the "Banana Republic" in the first part of the 20th century following the founding of a company in 1899 by the Vaccaro brothers of New Orleans which eventually became the Standard Fruit Company and which was to make bananas the major export crop of Honduras. The United Fruit Company of Boston was also founded in 1899 and in 1929 was merged with the Cuyamel Fruit Company of Samuel Zemurray, who controlled the largest fruit interests in Honduras. United Fruit (UFCo), known as El Pulpo (the octopus), emerged as a major political influence in the region with strong links with several dictatorships.

The 1929 Great Depression caused great hardship in the export-oriented economies of the region and in Honduras it brought the rise of another authoritarian régime. Tiburcio Carías Andino was elected in 1932 but though his ties with foreign companies and other neighbouring dictators he was able to hold on to power until renewed turbulence began in 1948 and he voluntarily withdrew from power in 1949. The two political parties, the Liberals and the Nationals, came under the control of provincial military leaders and after two more authoritarian Nationalist governments and a general strike in 1954 by radical labour unions on the north coast, young military reformists staged a palace coup in 1955. They installed a provisional junta and allowed elections for a constituent assembly in 1957. The assembly was led by the Liberal Party, which appointed Dr Ramón Villeda Morales as President, and transformed itself into a national legislature for six years. A newly created military academy graduated its first class in 1960 and the armed forces began to professionalize its leadership in conjunction with the civilian economic establishment. Conservative officers, nervous of a Cuban-style revolution, preempted elections in 1963 in a bloody coup which deposed Dr Villeda, exiled Liberal Party members and took control of the national police, which they organized into special security forces.

In 1969, Honduras and El Salvador were drawn into a bizarre episode known as the "Football War", which took its name from its origin in a disputed decision in the third qualifying round of the World Cup. Its root cause, however, was the social tension aroused by migrating workers from overcrowded El Salvador to Honduras. In 13 days, 2,000 people were killed before a ceasefire was arranged by the Organization of American States. A peace treaty was not signed, though, until 1980, and the dispute provoked Honduras to withdraw from the Central American Common Market (CACM), which helped to hasten its demise.

The armed forces, led chiefly by General López Arellano and his protegés in the National Party, dominated government until 1982. López initiated land reform, but despite Liberal policies, his régime was brought down in the mid-1970s by corruption scandals involving misuse of hurricane aid funds and bribes from the United Brands Company. His successors increased the size and power of the security forces and created the largest air force in Central America, while slowly preparing for a return to civilian rule. A constituent assembly was elected in 1980 and general elections in 1981. A constitution was promulgated in 1982 and President Roberto Suazo Córdoba, of the Liberal Party, assumed power. During this period, Honduras cooperated closely with the USA on political and military issues, particularly in moves to isolate Nicaragua's left wing government, and became host to some 12,000 right wing Nicaraguan contra rebels. It was less willing to take a similar stand against the FMLN left wing guerrillas in El Salvador for fear of renewing border tensions. In 1986 the first peaceful transfer of power between civilian presidents for 30 years took place when José Azcona Hoya (Liberal) won the elections. Close relations with the USA were maintained in the 1980s, Honduras had the largest Peace Corps Mission in the world, non-governmental and international voluntary agencies proliferated and the government became increasingly dependent upon US aid to finance its budget.

In 1989 general elections were won by the right wing Rafael Leonardo Callejas Romero (National Party), who was inaugurated for a four-year term on 27 January 1990. In the National Assembly, the National Party won 71 seats, the Liberals 55 and the Innovation and Unity Party (Pinu) two seats. Under the terms of the Central American Peace Plan, the contra forces were to be demobilized and disarmed by June 1990, but at the time of writing there were still several thousands of contras and other refugees on Honduran soil.

Population There are very few pure-blooded Indians, and fewer (less than 1%) of pure Spanish ancestry. The largest proportion of Indian blood is found from Santa Rosa de Copán westwards to the border with Guatemala (Chorti is still spoken in this region). The population is 90% *mestizo*, and was estimated at 4.9 million in 1989; death rate 10.1 per 1,000; birth, 44; annual population growth: 3.5%; urban growth, 6.0%, but only 43.1% are urban. Some 53% are peasants or agricultural labourers, with a relatively low standard of living.

The Economy Honduras has traditionally been the poorest economy in Central America with one of the lowest income rates per head in all Latin America although the war in Nicaragua depressed income levels there below even those of Honduras (see Economic Indicators, page 676). Unemployment is about 25% of the working population, owing to low investment, and poor harvests and labour disputes in the agricultural sector. Inflation has dealt less severely with Honduras than with some other Central American countries: the rate has been less than 10% a year in the 1980's.

About 75% of the population live by the land: coffee and bananas are the main export crops. Cotton, once important, is now far less so. Tobacco, maize, beans, rice and sugar are grown mostly for domestic use but small quantities are sometimes exported. Cattle raising is important and exports of both meat and livestock are growing. Some 33% of the land is forested and timber is the third leading export; it is to become more important as the development of forestry reserves in the Department of Olancho is carried out. This project includes the installation of a vast paper and pulp complex and is expected to have a considerable impact on the whole economy, once implemented.

Honduras has considerable reserves of silver, gold, lead, zinc, tin, iron, copper, coal and antimony, but only silver, gold, lead and zinc are mined and exported. Considerable offshore exploration for petroleum is in progress. There is an oil refinery at Puerto Cortés and exports of petroleum derivatives are becoming significant. The US$600m. hydroelectric scheme at El Cajón was expected greatly to reduce the country's oil bill.

Local industries are small, turning out a wide range of consumer goods, besides being engaged in the processing of timber and agricultural products. The more important products are furniture, textiles, footwear, chemicals, cement and rubber.

Honduras' total external debt amounts to some US$3.2bn, over three times merchandise exports. From 1982 the government held negotiations to reschedule its debt with commercial banks but failed to sign any agreement. Arrears mounted and in 1989 the negotiating committee disbanded to allow banks individually to recover their debts as best they could. In 1990 a new economic package was introduced with emergency spending cuts and revenue raising measures designed to reduce the fiscal deficit. The lempira was allowed to float freely against the US dollar in a legalization of the black market rate where the currency was trading at L4=US$1 compared with the official rate since 1926 of L2=US$1. The new President thereby attempted a rapprochement with the international financial community; Honduras had previously been declared ineligible to borrow from the IMF, the World Bank and the Inter-American Development Bank, while US aid had been cut by 30%. Negotiations with the multilateral agencies were expected to lead to the clearing of arrears and the implementation of economic support programmes.

Government Honduras is a multi party republic. The Legislature consists of a single 134-seat Chamber. Deputies are elected by a proportional vote. Executive authority rests with a President, directly elected for 4 years. No President may serve two terms in succession. The National Assembly elects members of the Supreme Court, which, together with the Court of Appeal, Justices of the Peace and lesser tribunals, constitute the judiciary. The Constitution was revised by a Constituent Assembly elected in April 1980. The country is divided into 18 departments, each with an administrative centre.

Communications The railways are in the N, and since 1975 the 595 km. in operation belong to the Ferrocarril Nacional de Honduras.

A light aeroplane is the only way of getting to large areas of the country, but the road system has improved rapidly in recent years. Total road length is now 17,431 km., of which 12% are paved. The main paved roads are the Northern Highway linking Tegucigalpa, San Pedro Sula and Puerto Cortés; the road W from Puerto Cortés along the North Coast, through Omoa, to the Guatemalan frontier (although one bridge is missing, necessitating 2 hrs. travel on foot); the highway from Tegucigalpa to Olancho, passing through Juticalpa and Catacamas; the Pan-American Highway in the SW between El Salvador and Nicaragua, and the Southern Highway which runs to it from Tegucigalpa; the North Coast Highway joining San Pedro Sula with Progreso, Tela and La Ceiba, and on to Trujillo; the Western Highway linking San Pedro Sula with Santa Rosa de Copán, Nueva Ocotepeque and the Guatemalan and Salvadorean frontiers, with a branch from La Entrada to Copán ruins; the Carretera del Occidente, from Lake Yojoa to Santa Bárbara, and the stretch from La Paz to Marcala in the Department of La Paz; the road linking Choluteca on the Pan-American Highway with the Nicaraguan frontier at Guasaule; and the Eastern Highway linking Tegucigalpa, Danlí, El Paraíso and Las Manos (Nicaraguan frontier). Travel is still by foot and mule in many areas. Tegucigalpa, La Ceiba and San Pedro Sula all have international airports. More details in the text below.

Religion and Education Education is compulsory, but half the rural children do not go to school. 40.3% of the population are illiterate. 34% of the population over the age of 25 have no formal schooling. The National University is centred in Tegucigalpa though it also has departments in San Pedro Sula and La Ceiba. Also in Tegucigalpa is the Universidad José Cecilio del Valle; there is also a university in San Pedro Sula. The majority of the population is Catholic, but there is complete freedom of religion.

TEGUCIGALPA

Tegucigalpa, the capital, a city of over 800,000 inhabitants, stands in an intermont basin at an altitude of 975 metres. No railway serves it. It was founded as a mining camp in 1578: the miners found their first gold where the N end of the Soberanía bridge now is. The name means "silver hill" in the original Indian tongue. It did not become the capital until 1880. On three sides it is surrounded by sharp, high peaks. It comprises two towns: the almost flat Comayagüela and the hilly Tegucigalpa built at the foot and up the slopes of El Picacho. A steeply banked river, the Choluteca, divides the two towns, now united administratively as the Distrito Central. Tegucigalpa has not been subjected to any disaster by fire or earthquake, being off the main earthquake fault line, so retains many traditional features. Many of the stuccoed houses, with a single heavily barred entrance leading to a central patio, are attractively coloured. However, the old low skyline of the city has now been punctuated by several modern tall buildings.

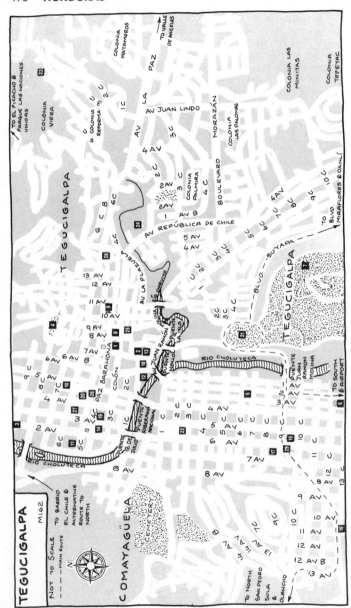

TEGUCIGALPA

M162

Not to Scale
— Main Route
--- Alternative Route to North

TEGUCIGALPA

TEGUCIGALPA

COMAYAGÜELA

TO VALLE DE ANGELES

COLONIA MATAMOROS

LA PAZ

COLONIA VIERA

TO EL PICACHO & PARQUE LAS NACIONES UNIDAS

LA COLONIA REFORMA

AV JUAN LINDO

MORAZÁN

COLONIA LAS PALOMAS

COLONIA LAS MINITAS

COLONIA TEPEYAC

4 AV

2 AV

COLONIA PALMIRA

BOULEVARD

AV REPÚBLICA DE CHILE

5 C

4 AV

TO BLVD MIRAFLORES & DANLÍ

BLVD. SUTAPA

13 AV
12 AV

11 AV

10 AV

9 AV
8 AV

7 AV

6 AV

AV LA PLAZUELA

PAZ BARAHONA

COLÓN

JUAN RAMÓN MOLINA

PUENTE LA ISLA

RÍO CHOLUTECA

PUENTE JUAN RAMÓN MOLINA

RÍO CHOLUTECA

PUENTE SOBERANÍA NACIONAL

PUENTE 12 DE JULIO

4 AV

5 AV

6 AV

7 AV

8 AV

TO SOUTH TO AIRPORT

CEMETERY

TO NORTH SAN PEDRO SULA & OLANCHO

9 AV

10 AV

11 AV

12 AV

12 AV B

13 AV

TO BARRIO EL CHILE & ALTERNATIVE ROUTE TO NORTH

N

Its altitude gives it a reliable climate: temperate during the rainy season from May to November; warm, with cool nights, in March and April, and cool and dry, with very cool nights, in December to February, although hot breezes can make the atmosphere oppressive. The annual mean temperature is about 74°F (23°C).

The Carretera del Sur (Southern Highway), which brings in travellers from the S and from Toncontín Airport, 6½ km. from Plaza Morazán, runs through Comayagüela into Tegucigalpa. It goes past the obelisk set up to commemorate a hundred years of Central American independence, and the Escuela Nacional de Bellas Artes, with a decorated Mayan corridor and temporary exhibitions of contemporary paintings and crafts.

Crossing the river from Comayagüela by the colonial Mallol bridge, on the left is the Presidential Palace (1919). Calle Bolívar runs through the area containing the Congress building and the former site of the University, founded in 1847. Calle Bolívar leads to the main square, Plaza Morazán (commonly known as Parque Central). On the eastern side of the square are the City Hall, and the domed and double-towered Cathedral built in the late 18th century. (See the beautiful gilt colonial altarpiece, the fine examples of Spanish colonial art, the cloisters and, in Holy Week, the magnificent ceremony of the Descent from the Cross).

Av. Paz Barahona, running through the northern side of the square, is a key avenue. On it to the E is the church of San Francisco, with its clangorous bells, and (on 3a Calle, called Av. Colón) the old Spanish Mint (1770), now the national printing works. If, from Plaza Morazán, we go along Av. Paz Barahona westwards towards the river, by turning right along 4 Av. we come to the 18th century church of Virgen de los Dolores. Two blocks N and 3 blocks W of the church is Parque Concordia with copies of Maya sculpture and temples (open only Sun. and holidays, but people climb the fence anyway).

Back on Av. Paz Barahona and further W are the Ministerial Palace, the National Theatre, with a rather grand interior (1915) and, across the square, the beautiful old church of El Calvario. Crossing the bridge of 12 de Julio (quite near the theatre) one can visit Comayagüela's market of San Isidro, which is interesting.

In Colonia Palmira, Tegucigalpa, is the Boulevard Morazán, an elegant shopping and business complex, with restaurants, cafeterias, discotheques, etc. (worth a visit on Fri. or Sat. evening). You can get a fine view of the city from the Peace Monument on Juana Laínez hill,

Tegucigalpa: Key to map

1. Plaza Morazán/Parque Central; 2. Plaza La Merced; 3. Parque Concordia; 4. Parque Leona; 5. Parque La Libertad; 6. Parque El Obelisco; 7. Juana Lainez/Monumento a La Paz; 8. Cathedral; 9. Iglesia San Francisco; 10. Virgen de los Dolores; 11. El Calvario; 12. Presidential Palace; 13. Congress & Tourist Office; 14. National Theatre Manuel Bonilla; 15. Ciné Centenario; 16. Hedman Alas buses; 17. El Ray buses; 18. Banco Central; 19. Post Office; 20. Hondutel; 21. National Stadium; 22. San Isidro Market; 23. San Pablo Market; Hotels; 24. *Honduras Maya*; 25. *Prado*; 26. *Marichal*; 27. *Boston*; 28. *Granada*; 29. *Centenario*.

near the football stadium.

One is always conscious, in Tegucigalpa, of the summit of El Picacho looming up to the N (at the top is a zoo of mostly indigenous animals, open Thurs.-Sun., US$0.25). From Plaza Morazán go up Calle 7a and the Calle de la Leona to Parque Leona, a handsome small park with a railed walk overlooking the city. Higher still is the reservoir in El Picacho, also known as the United Nations Park, which can be reached by number 9 bus from behind Los Dolores church (in front of Farmacia Santa Bárbara), Sun. only, US$0.15; camping is allowed here. Parque La Libertad in Comayagüela (where one can find cheap enjoyable entertainment in the evening) is also pleasant.

N.B. If you have anything stolen, report it to Dirección General de Investigación Nacional, DIN, ½ block N of Los Dolores church.

Fair at Comayagüela Fair of La Concepción, 7 to 24 December.

Hotels in Tegucigalpa: *Honduras Maya*, Av. República de Chile, Colonia Palmira, T 32-31-91, L, rooms and apartments, casino, swimming pool (US$2.50), bars (the main bar is relaxed and you get appetizers with every alcoholic drink, US TV channels), cafeterias (*Black Jack's Snack Bar*, at Casino Royal, *Cafeteria 2000*), restaurant (*El Candelero*), conference hall, view over the city (only from uppermost rooms); *Alameda*, Blvd. Suyapa (some distance from centre), A, comfortable, pool, good restaurant *Le Chalet* (T 32-69-20). **Downtown**: *La Ronda*, 6 Av, 11 C., 5 blocks from cathedral (T 37-8151/55), a/c, TV, rec., A/B, cafeteria (*Rondalla*) and night club; *Plaza*, in Av. Paz Barahona (T 37-0182/84), A; *Papagallo* restaurant. *Prado*, Av. Cervantes, 7 y 8 Av., A/B, *La Posada* restaurant; *Istmania*, 5 Av., 7 and 8 Calle (T 37-1638/39, 37-1460) near Church of Los Dolores, A-B, *Versalles* restaurant; *Marichal*, 5 Av., 5 Calle, D/E (T 37-00-69) (ask for a back room), noisy, clean, centrally located; *Nuevo Boston*, Av. Jérez No. 313, T 37-9411, D, hot water, central, clean, laundry, run by an ex-truck driver from Missouri, constant (free) coffee and biscuits available, highly rec.; *MacArthur*, 7 Av., 1225, D/E, good, reasonably-priced restaurant; *Nuevo Hotel MacArthur*, C, expensive, 8C., 4 y 5 Av., under same management; *Iberia*, Peatonal Los Dolores, D, hot showers, clean, noisy, T 37-92-67, no meals; *San Francisco*, Av. Cervantes, D, fan, TV, restaurant, bar, T 37-71-01; *Imperial* (opposite *Istmania*) E, with or without bath (but make sure there is water before paying for a bath!), good value, Chinese run, above their restaurant, cockroaches; *Fortuna*, 5 Av., near Los Dolores church, E with or without bath; *Excelsior*, Av. República de Chile, at foot of hill leading to *Honduras Maya* (2 blocks away), E, good room with private bath, hot water, popular; *Granada*, Av. Gutemberg 1401, Barrio Guanacaste, E (hot water on 2nd floor only), good, table tennis, T 37-23-81, annex 1½ blocks uphill, turn right at sign for Cinés Tauro and Aries, also E (but a bit more than old building), better beds, hot water in all rooms.

Comayagüela is convenient for buses to the North and West and there are many cheap *pensiones* and rooms. It is noisier and dirtier than Tegucigalpa, and many establishments are unsuitable for travellers: *Ritz*, 4a C., and 5 Av., E-D, cold shower, clean but noisy; *Centenario*, 6 Av., 9-10 Calles, E-D (T 37-1050), rec.; *Real de Oro*, Av. Cabañas, 11 and 12 C., D/E, clean, friendly; *Hotelito West*, 10C., 6 and 7 Av., F, towels and soap, shared hot showers, very friendly, change travellers' cheques, rec.; *Regis*, 4a Av., 1 and 2 Calle, E, rec., clean, friendly; *París*, C.4 between 3 and 4 Avs., F for single with bath, café, cheap, good meals, family style; *San Pedro*, 9 Calle, 6 Av., D with bath, E without or with private cold shower, popular, clean, restaurant; *Jupiter*, 5 Av., Calles 5 and 6, 509, E-D, clean and comfortable; *Moderna*, 7a Av., 3a-4a Calle, F, good service; *Ticamaya No. 1*, 6 Av., 9 Calle, D, quiet, restaurant, open to non-residents, breakfast from 0600;

Ticamaya No. 2, 7a Av., Calle 4 and 5, E, clean, friendly, noisy, restaurant below; *Anexo Ticamaya*, Calle 8, Av. 6-7, G p.p.; *Teleño*, 7 Av., F, clean, friendly; there are 5 *Hospedajes El Nilo*, No. 4 is clean, but the rest are to be avoided; *Royal*, 7 Av., nr. market, F, noisy but cheap; *Hotel Richard No. 1*, 4a Calle, 6 and 7 Av., F/E, "laundry" on roof; *Hotel Richard Nos. 2, 3, 4* and *5* on 5a Calle, all between 5 and 7 Av., fewer facilities, all F, with or without bath. *Hospedaje Familiar*, 6 Av., No. 812, F, clean, noisy.

A 7% sales tax is added to hotel bills.

Restaurants A meal in a good restaurant costs between US$4-7; for hotel restaurants, see above. International food: *El Arriero*, Av. República de Chile, near *Honduras Maya*, good steaks and seafood; *Kloster* and *Bugalow*, Blvd. Morazán; *Marbella*, 6 C., 3-4 Av., central, good for breakfast, has cornflakes! Seafood: *Hungry Fisherman*, Av. República de Chile 209, Col. Palmira. Italian: *Café Allegro*, Av. República de Chile 360-B, Colonia Palmira, excellent coffee, "Time" magazine, international atmosphere, HQ of International Hash House Harriers, owner Jorge provides good information, welcoming, rec. (*Mexico and Central American/South American Handbook* sold here); *Roma*, near Av. Rep. de Chile, Col. Palmira, rec.; pizzerias: *Tito*, Callejón Los Dolores, and Blvd. Morazán, Col. Palmira, both branches rec.; *Pizza Deli*, Blvd. Morazán; *Vicente*, near *Honduras Maya*, try the "medio metro" pizza. Spanish: *Mesón de Castilla*, Av. Rep. de Chile 1802, Col. Palmira; next door is *Tapas*, one of the nicest bars in town; *Don Quixote*, Callejón La Vega, eat outdoors, good value, rec; *Rincón Español*, Blvd. Morazán. French: *Jardín de París*, Blvd. Morazán, highly rec. *Waldschenke* (*Posada del Bosque*), Cerro El Trigo, El Hatillo, Tegucigalpa, 2½ km. from church to the right, Swiss run, open Sat. and Sun. only, ecological orientation. Latin American: *Taco Loco*, Blvd Morazán, food Mexican fast food; *Gauchos*, Av. de La Paz, near US Embassy. Chinese: *La Gran Muralla*, Barrio Guanacaste, good; *Pekín*, 3 C. No.525, Barrio San Rafael, 1 block from *Hotel Maya*; *Mei-Mei*, Pasaje Midence Soto, central, rec.; *Cafetería Koc Wa*, clean, friendly and efficient; *Ley-Hsen*, Pasaje Fiallos Soto; *Seoul*, Blvd. Morazán, Korean. Meat: *El Patio 2*, Blvd. Morazán, good value for the hungry; *La Granja*, and *Jack's Steak House*, same street, also burgers and American style sandwiches. 2 *Burger Hots*, 2 C. north of Parque La Merced, and Centro Comercial Los Castaños. *Café y Librería El Paradiso*, Av. Paz Barahona, 6 blocks E of Parque Central, popular gringo place; *Don Pepe's Terraza*, near Bancahsa, downtown, cheap, noisy orchestra but typical Honduran atmosphere. *Café de Pie*, Edificio Fiallos Soto, downtown; *Duncan Maya*, 2 blocks from *Hotel Iberia*, good for breakfast; *Al Natural*, behind Cathedral, nice garden atmosphere; *Restaurante Vegetariano*, Calle Cervantes; *Pops*, ice cream. *Dunkin Donuts*, several outlets. *Pastelería Francesa*, opp. French embassy, rec. Many cheap restaurants on 2 Av., Comayagüela and near market. Fried chicken is sold at small lunch counters all over Honduras, providing an excellent, cheap meal.

Market Mercado Colón or San Isidro, Avenida 6 at Calle 1, Comayagüela; many things for sale; food available. Saturday is busiest day. Good supermarkets: La Colonia, Sucasa, Plaza Más x Menos.

Souvenir Shops Candú, opp. *Hotel Maya*, and in Av. República de Chile; *Cármon Honduras Quality Art and Handicrafts*, 1½ blocks S of *Hotel Maya* on Av. República de Chile, 338, Col. Palmira, Tegucigalpa; *Amano*, at begining of Blvd. Morazán, good quality.

Bookshops *Book Village*, Centro Comercial Los Castaños, Blvd. Morazán, English books, both new and secondhand, for sale or exchange. *Librería Panamericana*, 6a Av., 2a Calle, stocks English books and magazines, expensive. For books in Spanish on Honduras and Central America, *Editorial Guaymuras*, Av. Miguel Cervantes 1055. Secondhand bookstalls in Mercado San Isidro (6 Av. y 2

Calle, Comayagüela), good value. There is an English weekly called *Tegucigalpa This Week*; to submit news and ads. write to: Aptdo 1312, Tegucigalpa, T 315821.

Pharmacy *Farmacia Rosna*, in pedestrian mall off Parque Central, T 370605, English spoken, rec. *Regis Palmira*, Ed. Ciicsa, Av. República de Panamá, Col. Palmira; *El Castaño*, Blvd. Morazán.

Car Rentals Car rentals Avis, T 32-00-88; Toyota, Col. El Prado, T 33-52-10; at Toncontín airport: Molinari, T 33-13-07, Blitz, Budget, T 33-51-70, National, T 33-49-62. Main companies in *Hotel Honduras Maya*.

Car Repairs Metal Mecánica, 1 block S of Av. de los Próceres, Colonia Lara.

Taxis About US$1 p.p. (no reduction for sharing, but bargaining possible); more after 2200, but cheaper (US$0.50) on designated routes e.g. Milaflores to centre.

Local buses Cost US$0.06, stops are official but unmarked.

Cinemas Plaza 1, 2 and 3 in Centro Comercial Plaza Miraflores; Regis and Real at Centro Comercial Centroamérica, Blvd. Miraflores; Alfa and Omega in Av. de La Paz (all have good US films). In city centre, double cinemas Lido and Palace, Clamer and Variedades. Tauro and Aries, Av. Gutemberg, Barrio Guanacaste opposite *Hotel Granada*.

Entertainment *Casino Royal* in *Hotel Honduras Maya*, all types of gambling. In front of the National University is a *peña*, where people dance and sing; also a discotheque *El Portal*, piano bar, Colonia Lomas del Guijarro, live music, national and international artists. *Backstreet Pub*, Av. Rep. de Uruguay in Colonia Alameda, bar/disco, good atmosphere, no cover except when live music. Boulevard Morazán has plenty of choice in night life.

Museum Museo Nacional Villa Roy, in home of a former President, has an exhibition of archaeological finds. It is situated on a hilltop above the beautiful Parque Concordia (entry US$0.50, open 0830-1530, closed Mon.—due to be moved to the old university building on Parque Merced).

Exchange Banco de Londres (Lloyds Bank) 4a Calle y 5a Av. Tegucigalpa. Open 0900-1500; closed Sat. Banco Atlántida, 5C. in front of Plaza Morazán; Banco de Honduras (Citibank), Edif. Midence Soto, Tegucigalpa; Banco de Ahorro Hondureño, 5C. in front of Plaza Morazán; Banco Ficensa, Blvd. Morazán, does Visa advances. All accept American Express travellers' cheques, and cash travellers' cheques which are accredited to them, but not for US$. Visa cash advances and travellers' cheques, Credomatic de Honduras, Blvd. Morazán. American Express: main office Av. República de Chile, opp. *Honduras Maya*, Colonia Palmira; agency at Transmundo Tours, Calle 5a, Costado Norte Ministerios, usually redirect you to main office, otherwise good. Black market (very little difference from bank rate) outside *Hotel Plaza*, at bus stations, in the Maison Blanc office opp. Supermarket Más x Menos, US$ cash much better rate.

Institutes Alliance Française, end of 4 Av., Barrio Abajo, cultural events Fri. p.m., French films Wed. 1730, T 37-04-45; Centro Cultural Alemán, 8 Av., Calle La Fuente, German newspapers to read, cultural events, T 37-15-55; Instituto Hondureño de Cultura Interamericana (IHCI), Calle Real de Comayagüela has an English library and cultural events, T 37-75-39. **School** American and Elvel School, on US lines with US staff.

Embassies **El Salvador**, Colonia San Carlos—one block from Blvd. Morazán, friendly, helpful; **Guatemala**, Colonia Lomas de Tepeyac, higher up than Nicaraguan Embassy, Mon.-Fri., 0900-1300; **Nicaragua**, Colonia Lomas del Tepeyac (T 324290), 10 blocks SE of Blvd. Morazán (take "Alameda" bus from above La Isla recreation centre, which is across the Río Chiquito from Av. Juan

Ramón Molina, before the National Stadium, alight 1 block above "Planificación de familia", walk left up side street and turn up 4th street on right, a dirt road, with the consulate on a steep hillside on the right, or walk up Av. Juan Lindo and keep straight on up for 20 mins. to climb a dirt track which passes the consulate on right—bear left for Guatemalan Consulate), 0800-1200, visa takes 5-10 days; has to be used within 4 weeks of issue; **Costa Rica**, Colonia Palmira, Primera Calle Casa 704, T 32-1054 (Near Mas x Menos supermarket); **Mexico**, 3 Av., 2 C. No. 1277, Col. Palmira.

USA, Av. La Paz (0800-1100, Mon.-Fri.—take any bus from Parque Central in direction "San Felipe", T 32-31-20); **Canada**, Edificio Comercial Los Castaños, piso 6, Blvd. Morazán; **Jamaican** consul, Mr George Schofield, **Hotel Boston**, Calle Jérez.

UK (also **Belize**), Edificio Palmira, 3rd floor, opp. *Hotel Honduras Maya* (Apartado Postal 290, T 325429); **West Germany**, Ed. Paysen, Blvd. Morazán. **France**, Av. Juan Lindo 416, Colonia Palmira. **Spain**, Col. Matamoros 103; **Israel**, Ed. Palmira, 5th floor, T 222529/324232, opp. *Hotel Maya*; **Italy**, Col. Reforma; **Netherlands** (also **Portugal**), Lomas del Mayab; **Switzerland**, consul at Oficina de Cosude (Cooperación Suiza al Desarrollo), T 328261 (emergencies only).

To get to Colonia Palmira where most Embassies are, take buses marked "San Miguel" and "Lomas". Take "San Felipe" bus from Central Park for the following consulates: Costa Rica, USA and El Salvador.

Immigration Dirección General de Migración, on Calle Jérez, Tegucigalpa.

Laundry Lavaflex, Calle la Salud y Blvd. José C. del Valle, open daily (bus, direction Prado). Lavandería Maya, corner of Paseo Rep. Argentina and Calzada Maifar, nr. *Honduras Maya*, 0700-1900, Mon.-Sat.

Churches Episcopal Anglican (Col. Florencia—take Suyapa bus) and Union Church, Colonia Lomas del Guijarro, with services in English. Catholic mass in English at the chapel of Instituto San Francisco at 1000 every Sunday.

Peace Corps on Av. República de Chile, up hill past *Hotel Honduras Maya*; open Mon.-Fri. 0800-1600.

Post Office Av. Miguel de Cervantes y Calle Morelos, 4 blocks from Parque Central. *Lista de Correos* (Poste Restante) mail held for 1 month. Books should be packed separately from clothes etc.

Telephone, Telex Hondutel, Calle 5 and Av. 4, Tegucigalpa, has several direct AT&T lines to USA, no waiting.

Tour Operators *Trek Honduras*, Edificio Midence Soto 217, downtown, tours of the city, Bay Islands, Copán, San Pedro Sula, Valle de Angeles and Santa Lucía. Mundirama, Ed. Ciicsa, Av. República de Chile, 100 m. S of *Hotel Maya*. *Explore Honduras Tour Service*, Ed. Med'cast, 2nd level, Blvd. Morazán, T 311003, Copán and Bay Islands; *Centro Americana de Turismo*, in front of the E side of the parking lot of the National Stadium, Barrio Morazán, Tegucigalpa, T 310911, specializing in Hondruas; *Gloria Tours* across from N side of Parque Central in Casa Colonial, information centre and tour operator.

Tourist Office Under Congress Building (Plaza La Merced), opp. Banco Central, also at Tocontín airport. Provides lists of hotels and sells posters, postcards (cheaper than elsewhere) and slides. Information on cultural events around the country from Teatro Manuel Bonilla, better than at regional tourist offices. The best map of the country is produced by the Instituto Geográfico Nacional and may be bought from the Institute on production of passport and map request, typed, in triplicate (it is a long process, involving a trip to the Treasury). Some hotels sell these for double the price, but no paperwork. Open weekdays 0730-1200, 1230-1530. Texaco also do a good map of the country, available at

Texaco stations.

National Parks   The Asociación Hondureña de Ecología (Aptdo. T-250, Toncontín, Tegucigalpa, office in Centro Comercial Centroamérica, Nivel 2, T 32-90-18) has drawn up a list of over 70 natural reserves in Honduras which it hopes will be developed as national parks or reserves, and 56 plant, animal, bird and aquatic species in danger. Its book *Areas silvestres de Honduras* gives all details (US$7.50). It also publishes *Ecosistemas terrestres de Honduras* (US$3.50) and *Mamíferos silvestres de Honduras* (US$6); *Aves de Honduras* was due for publication in 1989. The parks system is in its infancy, but all support and interest is most welcome. Parks in existence are La Tigra, outside Tegucigalpa (see next page), and the Biosphere of the Río Plátano **(see page** 515). Under development since 1987 are Mount Celaque **(page** 506), Cusuco **(page** 498) and Pico Bonito **(page** 489—these 3 parks will have visitors' centres, hiking trails and primitive camping), and the following have been designated national parks by the government: Montecristo-Trifinio **(see page** 501), Cerro Azul (Copán), Santa Bárbara, Azul Meambar (Cortés and Comayagua), Pico Pijol (Yoro), Montaña de Yoro, Agalta (Olancho) and Montaña Comayagua. Some of these sites have Peace Corps Volunteers, who would be a good source of information.

Motorists   Tegucigalpa is appallingly badly signposted and is a nightmare for motorists. Motorists leaving Tegucigalpa for San Pedro Sula or Olancho can avoid the congestion of Comayagüela market by driving N down to Barrio Abajo, crossing the river to Barrio Chile and taking the motorway up the mountainside, to turn right to Olancho, or left to rejoin the northern outlet to San Pedro Sula (at the second intersection, turn right for the old, winding route, go straight on for the new, fast route).

Airport   Toncontín, 6½ km. from the centre. Checking-in takes a long time; restaurant, souvenir shop. Buses to airport from Comayagüela, Loarque Rutas No. 1 and No. 11, on 4a Av. between 6 and 7 Calle, or opp. Ciné Palace in downtown Tegucigalpa; into town US$0.10, 20 mins. from left-hand side outside the airport; yellow cabs, US$6, smaller colectivo taxis, US$3.20.

Airlines   For national flights: Aero Servicios, Toncontín airport, T 33-12-69 (private); TAN/Sahsa, Toncontín, T 33-10-10, in town, T 37-86-74. SAMi, T 33-85-49, for daily flights to Puerto Lempira/Mocorón. Sosa Aerolíneas fly to La Ceiba, Mosquitia and the Bay islands; Isleña flies from Tegucigalpa to La Ceiba at 1400. Taca International, Blvd. Morazán, T 32-08-08; Pan Am and Lacsa, Ed. San Miguel, Barrio La Plazuela, T 37-01-57; Alitalia, Centro Comercial Los Castaños, Blvd. Morazán, T 32-18-82; Iberia, Ed. Palmira, opp. *Honduras Maya*, T 31-52-53; KLM, Edificio Ciicsa, Av. República de Chile, Col. Palmira; Lufthansa, Ed. Midence Soto, 5 piso, No.503, T 37-69-00.

Buses   To San Pedro Sula on Northern Highway; 4½ hrs. (6 companies including Sáenz, 12 Calle, 7 and 8 Av., El Rey, Av. 6, Calle 9, Comayagüela, Hedmán Alas, 13-14C., 11 Av., Comayagüela, T 377143, 7 a day, and Norteño, all charge US$2.50, except Hedmán Alas, US$3, excellent, first bus leaves at 0630, then 6 more at intervals to 1730. Mi Esperanza, Av. 6, Calle 23 or 26, Comayagüela, to Choluteca, 3 hrs., US$1.90, 0400 onwards. To La Esperanza, Empresa Joelito, 4 Calle No. 834, Comayagüela, 8 hrs, US$2.60. To Comayagua, US$1.10, Transportes Catrachos, Comayagüela, every 30 mins., 1½-2 hrs.

For travellers leaving Tegucigalpa, take the "Villa Adela" (now named Tiloarque but still known as "Villa Adela") bus in Av. Máximo Jérez, by Cine Pálace, and alight in Comayagüela at Cine Centenario (Av. 6a) for nearby Empresa Aurora buses (for Olancho) and El Rey buses (for San Pedro Sula or Olancho); 3 blocks S is Ciné Lux, near which are Empresas Unidas and Maribel for Siguatepeque (to town centre, US$0.50 cheaper but 1 hr. slower than San Pedro Sula buses which drop you on the main road, a US$0.50 taxi ride from Siguatepeque). By the Mamachepa market is the Norteño bus line for San Pedro Sula; also nearby are buses for Nacaome and El Amatillo frontier with El Salvador. "Villa Adela" bus continues to Mi Esperanza bus terminal (for Choluteca and Nicaraguan frontier). Take a "Belén", "Garnisal" or "Santa Fe" bus from Tegucigalpa for the hill ascending Belén (9a Calle) for Hedman Alas buses to San Pedro Sula and for Comayagua buses (to town centre, cheaper but slower than main line buses to San Pedro Sula which drop passengers on main road, a taxi ride away from the centre).

International Buses To Nicaragua, take bus to San Marcos de Colón, then taxi or local bus to El Espino on border. To San Marcos. 4 a day from 0730, and direct to frontier at 0400, US$2.60, 4 hrs. (0730, 0900 buses to San Marcos best for onward connections). To Guatemala, go to San Pedro Sula and take either Impala or Congolón to Nueva Ocotepeque and the frontier at Agua Caliente, or take the route via Copán (**see page** 502). To San Salvador, direct bus to border at El Amatillo, US$2.50, 3 hrs., several daily; alternatively from San Pedro Sula via Nueva Ocotepeque and El Poy.

Excursions Eight km. NE to the church at Suyapa, which attracts pilgrims to its wooden figure of the Virgin, a tiny image about 8 cm. high set into the altar. Excursions to Copán (1 hr. by air, US$295 for a plane taking 5 passengers), visits to **the Agricultural School at Zamorano**, and sight-seeing tours of Tegucigalpa and Comayagüela are arranged by several tour operators. It is about a ½ hour drive to **Valle de Angeles**, 6,635 people 1,310 metres on a plain on La Tigra mountain, surrounded by pine forests which help to keep its climate cool the year round. There are old mines, many walks possible in the forests, picnic areas, swimming pool, crowded on Sundays, *Hotel y Restaurante Posada del Angel*, rec., moderate prices; *Hotel San Francisco*, F; *Comedor La Abejita*, rec.; several others. Hospital de los Adventistas, in the valley, a modern clinic, sells vegetables and handicrafts; there are many handicraft shops in town—a visit to the Artisans' School is recommended. Continue to San Juan de Flores (also called Cantarranas) and San Juancito, an old mining town. (Bus to Valle de Angeles hourly, US$0.40, leaves from Av. de los Próceres, around the service station—take a Colonia 21 de Octubre bus from Parque Central to Mercado San Pablo in Barrio El Manchen, 10 mins.; to San Juan de Flores 1000, 1230, 1530.) On the way to Valle de Angeles take a right turn off to visit the quaint old mining village of **Santa Lucía** (4,230 people), perched precariously on a steep mountainside overlooking the wide valley with Tegucigalpa below. The town has a beautiful colonial church with a Christ given by King Philip II of Spain in 1592; there is a festival in the 2nd and 3rd weeks of January. There is a charming legend of the Black Christ which the authorities ordered to be taken down to Tegucigalpa when Santa Lucía lost its former importance as a mining centre. Every step it was carried away from Santa Lucía it became heavier. When impossible to carry it further, they turned round and by the time they were back to Santa Lucía, it was as light as a feather. Delightful walk down old mule trail across pine-clad ridges to the city (1½ hrs.). Bus to Santa Lucía from Mercado San Pablo, US$0.30. Weekend tours to Valle de Angeles and Santa Lucía leave from Av. La Paz, Tegucigalpa, opp. Ciné Presidente.

There are bracing climbs to the heights of Picacho; take right fork at summit to El Hatillo and on 24 km. to visit the rain forest (small buses from north of Parque Herrera, Tegucigalpa). To San Juancito (*Hospedaje Don Jacinto*; simple meals in the village), above which is **La Tigra** rain forest, a National Park (a stiff, 1-hr. uphill walk to park offices and trail, Sendero Bosque Nublado); a few quetzal birds survive here, but do not leave paths when walking as there are precipitous drops; highest point 2,290 m. and a spectacular 100 m. waterfall (Cascada de la Gloria) which falls on a vast igneous rock. There is accommodation on a first come, first served basis (no problem on weekdays, can be cold at night), and a restaurant. Bus leaves from San Pablo market, Tegucigalpa, from 1000, 1½ hrs., US$0.75 for San Juancito; passes turn-off to Santa Lucía and goes through Valle de Angeles.

From Parque Herrera a bus at 1200 goes to the village of El Peleguín; a delightful 40-min. walk down the pineclad mountainside leads to El Chimbo (meals at *pulpería* or shop—ask anyone the way), then take bus either to Valle de Angeles or Tegucigalpa.

At km. 17 on Zamorano road (at summit of range overlooking Suyapa church) take dirt road left to TV tower. From here a delightful 2-hour walk over forested ridges leads to Santa Lucía. At km. 24 on Zamorano road, climb the highest peak through the Uyuca rain forest, information from Pan-American Agricultural School at Zamorano from their office in the Edificio Guillén in Tegucigalpa. The school has rooms for visitors. On the NW flank of Uyuca is the picturesque village of Tatumbla.

A half-hour drive from Tegucigalpa to **Ojojona**, another quaint old village (6,670 people); turn right 24 km. down Southern Highway. The village's pottery is interesting (but selection reported to be poor). There is a small museum. The Galeria de Arte, open on Sunday, 0900-1500, is owned by the noted landscape painter Carlos Garay. *Fiesta* 18-20 Jan. There are 3 well preserved colonial churches in Ojojona (notice the fine paintings), plus two more in nearby Santa Ana which is passed on the way from Tegucigalpa. Ojojona is completely unspoiled; *Pensión Joxone*, comfortable; *comedor*. (Bus every 15-30 mins. from Calle 4, No. 825, Comayagüela, US$0.40, 1 hr.) From another location, buses go to Lepaterique ("place of the jaguar"), another colonial village, over an hour's drive through rugged, forested terrain. Distant view of Pacific on fine days from heights above village.

Minas de Oro, on a forested tableland at about 1,060 metres, is a centre for walking in wooded mountains, 3-hrs. bus ride with Transportes Díaz-Donavil, 10 Av. 11 C. Barrio Belén, Comayagüela at 0630 and 1300 (US$1.90). It is a picturesque old mining town, 73 km. N of Talanga, which is on the Olancho highway. Several *pensiones*, incl. *Los Pinares* (F, meals US$1) and *Hospedaje Mi Esperanza* (F, clean, basic). Robert Millar writes: Climb Cerro Grande (beware of snakes); walk to Malacatán mountain and Minas de San Antonio; follow old mule trail to San José Potrerillos. Strenuous climb, 3 hrs., over forested mountain range to lovely old colonial village of **Esquías**, with church, *cabildo* (town hall), tree-shaded plaza; bus from Esquías to Tegucigalpa (irregular), otherwise hitch from Minas de Oro or Comayagua (via

Rancho Grande). Also nearby are the villages of San Luis, San José del Potrero, and Victoria and the Montana de la Flor, in a remote area, inhabited by the Xicaques tribe. Bus Minas de Oro-Comayagua (daily) passes through **Cedros**, one of Honduras' earliest settlements, dating from Pedro de Alvarado's mining operations of 1536. It is an outstanding colonial mining town, with cobbled streets, perched high on an eminence, amid forests. The festival of El Señor del Buen Fin takes place in the first two weeks of January.

Swimming at thermal springs of Balneario San Francisco Támara; 32 km., along road to San Pedro Sula, turn off right 8 km. N of Támara. **Parque Aurora**, midway between Tegucigalpa (about 50 km. N) and Comayagua, has a small zoo and picnic area among pine-covered hills, a lake with rowing boats (hire US$1 per hour), a snack bar and lovely scenery. Camping US$0.50 p.p.; admission US$0.75. Food supplies nearby.

THE NORTH COAST

Puerto Cortés, at the mouth of the Ulúa river, is 58 km. by road and rail from San Pedro Sula, 333 from Tegucigalpa, and only two days' voyage from New Orleans. About half of Honduran trade passes through it. The climate is hot, tempered by sea breezes; many beautiful palm-fringed beaches nearby; rainfall, 2,921 mm. It has a small oil refinery, and a free zone was opened in 1978. Population 60,500. Festival, in August, including "Noche Veneciana" on 3rd Saturday.

Hotels *Playa*, on outskirts, hotel complex, good fish dishes in restaurant; *Costa Azul*, new on beach, first class; *International Mr. Ggeerr*, Barrio El Centro, B, hot water, a/c, bar, video, satellite TV, rec.; *Hotel-restaurante Costa Mar*, Playas de la Coca Cola, T 55-15-39/55-13-67, new, pleasant. *Los Piratas*, F, basic but friendly; *Tuck-San*, on the plaza, F, large rooms, cold water, a bit run down; *Colón*, F, basic, noisy, in red-light district; *Formosa*, F, dirty, but good food. Other hotels in the F range: *Puntarenas*, *Motagua*, *Las Vegas* and *La Cascada*.

Restaurants *Café Vienna*, on Parque, good, reasonably priced; *Chun Wah*, on Parque, good, big comidas; *Restaurant-Cafe Kalúa* in centre of town. *Restaurant Formosa*, expensive, but good. *La Roca*, Av. Ferrocarril; *Príncipe Maya* on road to Omoa.

Shops There are two souvenir shops in the customs house at the entrance to the National Port Authority, which sell hand-embroidered clothes. A shop on the main street sells mahogany wood carvings and the market in the town centre is quite interesting.

Exchange Banco de Londres (agency), 2a Av. y 3a Calle; Banco Atlántida and other local banks. Banco de Comercio cashes travellers' cheques. Banco de Occidente, Calle Principal; Bancahsa, 2 Av. 2 Calle. Open 0800-1130, 1330-1600; Sats. 0800-1100. El Puesto de Tenis, near plaza, behind the market, changes money.

Protestant Church Anglican/Episcopal.

Travel Agencies *Cortés* and *Trans Mundo*.

Rail Daily train departs 0815 to San Pedro Sula and Potrerillos, 95 km., 1.067 metres gauge. Two daily trains to Tela, change at La Junta, one at 0700 (US$1, second class, US$1.75 first). Timetables change—check if you wish to travel.

Road To San Pedro Sula and Potrerillos and on to the capital. Bus service hourly to San Pedro Sula, US$0.75, 45 mins., Citul and Impala lines.

Shipping See **Introduction and Hints** for schedule of Harrison Line's *Author* which calls here. A *goleta* (canoe) leaves Pueblo Nuevo, Puerto Cortés, for Mango Creek, Belize, normally twice a week, US$20, 7 hrs., no fixed schedule; can be dangerous in rough weather. Remember to get your exit stamp. The Immigration Office is near the Plaza Central (it is not noted for its efficiency—exit stamps cost US$2.50-US$5, depending on the official). If entering Puerto Cortés by boat, one must go to Immigration immediately. Passports are sometimes collected at the dock and you must go later to Immigration to get them; you must pay US$1 entry fee, make sure that you have the stamp. This is the only official payment; if asked for more, demand a receipt.

Excursions W to Tulián, along the bay, for picnics and freshwater bathing. Minibuses (US$0.35 each way) ply along the tropical shoreline past Tulián W to **Omoa** (or 3-hr. walk—15 km. from Puerto Cortés), with its restored 18th century castle (a popular site, admission, US$0.25). There is a paved road through Omoa, continuing to the Guatemalan border at Corinto, but the road stops there and there is no way through by car to Puerto Barrios. For a description of the crossing on foot, "The Jungle Trail", **see page 367**. At Omoa you can stay at *Hospedaje Puerto Grande*, but rooms are boxlike and sanitation unspeakable. The alternatives are going back to Puerto Cortés or going on further to Chivana, where there is the *Acantilados del Caribe* (*Caribbean Cliff Marine Club*), B, good food, nice atmosphere. Near Omoa are waterfalls (Los Chorros) and good hiking in attractive scenery both along the coast and inland. Restaurants include *Pancho*, *Champa Julita* and *Wahoo*, good seafood.

Other buses go E to beaches of coconut palms and white sands at Travesía, Baja Mar, etc., which are beautiful, and unspoilt. Café at Travesía, but none at Baja Mar. The black fishing communities are very friendly. Beware of sunburn, and mosquitoes at dusk. From November to May, because of tourist ships arriving two or three times a week, there are tours to La Lima to visit the banana plantations, trips to Copán to visit the Maya ruins and tourist parties at the Ustaris Hacienda.

Tela, another important banana port some 50 km. to the E, is reached from Puerto Cortés by sea, rail, road, or from San Pedro Sula by rail and by bus service via El Progreso. It is pleasantly laid out, with a magnificent sandy beach (not as safe as it used to be); there is a pleasant walk along the beach to Ensenada (a café and not much else). Population 67,890. *Fiesta*: San Antonio in June.

Hotels *Villas Telamar*, a complex of wooden bungalows, set on a palm-fringed beach, rooms B, villas from A, restaurant, bar, golf club, swimming pool, service disappointing; *Paradise Hotel*, in a palm grove about 3 km. W of Tela, beside magnificent beach, cabins, C-B, restaurant, insecure; *Tela*, Calle El Comercio, E, good, with restaurant, rec; *Daniels*, good value for budget traveller, noisy dance nights; *La Playa*, E (singles more), latest reports poor, contaminated water and vermin, not rec; next door is *Atlántida* (D, with a/c, E without, both on western end of beach), not good value; *Mar Azul*, on same street, E with fan and bath, rec. *Miramar*, E, fans, helpful, looks good. The *hospedaje* owned by Doña Sara is quite good, Calle Leonicio D. Herrera (on beach, east end of town), E with bath, F without, has 3 good cabins priced according to number of occupants; *Hotel Robert*, F, unfriendly and water erratic but in red light district, noisy, close to bus and railway stations. Plenty of cheap *hospedajes* near railway station, e.g. *Valencia*, rec. (on R-hand side of tracks as you arrive). *Gina Boarding House*,

E, with bath and fan, parking. *Pensión Muñoz* on eastern beachfront, F, meals extra, basic; *Pensión Iris*, both budget. During Easter week, the town is packed; room rates double and advance booking is essential. *Nuevo Puerto Rico* under construction on eastern end of beach, to be finished early 1991; restaurant open, will be in E/D range, with bath, a/c, TV.

Camping at municipal site next to beach, US$1. Also possible, but not safely, on beach.

Restaurant *Northern Lights* (*Luces del Norte*), Canadian owned (Slim Jim and Mercedes), one block towards beach from Parque Central, excellent value, very popular, also free English book exchange; *César's*, on the beach, serves good food; also *Sherwood's*, attractive. *Los Angeles*, on main street, Chinese, run by Hong Kong owners, good. *Tiburón Playero*, on eastern beach, good for a drink and watching the sea, food not so good. *Maribú Inn*, opp. Colegio San Antonio. Across the bridge in Tela West (or New Tela) are many bars and cafeterías—a selection: *Oso Polar* (nice patio), *Paco's*, *MacDonalds* (not the international chain), *Don Moncho*, *Burgher Hut*, *Maraby*.

Exchange Banco Atlántida, Bancahsa, Banadesa.

Hondutel and Post Office both on 4 Av. N.E.

Protestant Church Anglican.

Buses Cati or Tupsa lines from San Pedro Sula to El Progreso (US$0.45) where you must change to go on to Tela (3 hrs. in all) and La Ceiba (last bus at 1900). Bus from Tela to El Progreso every 30 mins., US$0.95; to La Ceiba, 2½ hrs., US$1.35.

Rail The National Railways 1.067-metre gauge line W to Puerto Cortés; two trains per day US$1 2nd class, 4 hrs. A branch of this line runs south along the eastern bank of the Ulúa River to Progreso and Potrerillos. Train to San Pedro Sula with change at Baracoa, at 1345 (in theory) 4¼ hrs.: Mon. and Thurs. direct to Baracoa, other days change at La Junta to Puerto Cortés train. Fare to San Pedro Sula, US$1.50 1st class, US$0.70 2nd. Timetables change, check if you want to travel.

Excursions To the tropical experimental farm at Lancetilla (established 1926), 5 km. inland; open Tues.-Fri., 0730-1530; Sat., Sun. and holidays 0830-1600, admission US$0.50. *Hospedaje* (*Turicentro Lancetilla*, E, a/c) and *comedor*, full at weekends, and camping facilities. Either take employees' bus from town centre at 0700, or local bus to entrance from where tours run frequently the 4 km. to the botanical gardens (first at 0900, last at 1400, 1 hr. tour). Ask for Víctor Gámez for a good guided tour.

Local buses and trucks from the corner just E of the market go E to the Black Carib village of *Triunfo*, site of the first Spanish settlement on the mainland, in a beautiful bay, in which a sea battle between Cristóbal de Olid and Francisco de las Casas (2 of Cortés' lieutenants) was fought in 1524. Bus to Triunfo, US$0.40 (about 5 km.- if no return bus, walk to main road where buses pass). Also, W to the Carib villages of Tornabé and San Juan (4 km. W of *Villas Telamar*), worth a visit, beautiful food (fish cooked in coconut oil). 5 km. W of Tela is *Paradise Cabins*, restaurant, but dilapidated; beautiful palm grove on beach. Further NW, along palm-fringed beaches and blue lagoons, is Punta Sal, a lovely place. To get there you need a motor boat though it is possible to walk to the lake (Laguna de los Micos) and cross to the sand spit if the water level is low (dry season).

El Progreso, on the Río Ulúa, an important agricultural and commercial centre (no longer just a banana town) is less than an hour's drive on the paved highway SE of San Pedro Sula en route to Tela. Population, about 106,550. Local *fiesta*: La Virgen de Las Mercedes, third week of

September. Visit the Santa Elizabeth handicraft centre, where women are taught wood carving.

Hotel *Municipal*, Calle de Comercio, E to C with a/c and bath, clean, comfortable restaurant. *Plaza Victoria*, 2 Av. Sur, opp. Migración, E and up, pool, good; *Honduras*, F p.p. with bath, run down, meals US$1.25; *Imperador*, attractive, F with bath; *Rubí*, moderate; *Las Vegas*; other cheap *pensiones*.

Restaurants *Maya*, 1 Av., 4-5 C.; *La Posta*, Calle del Comercio.

Exchange   Bancahsa, Banco Atlántida, Banco del Comercio, Banco Sogerín, Banadesa, Banffaa.

20 minutes from El Progreso is Balneario las Minas, a 10-metre waterfall. The Santuario de Arena Blanca in the village of the same name, south of El Progreso on the road to Tegucigalpa, has a festival on 13 January in honour of the Black Christ of Esquipulas. The temple has baroque and modern architecture, with trees and gardens.

The highway is paved 25 km. S of El Progreso to Santa Rita; if one continues towards the San Pedro Sula-Tegucigalpa highway, one avoids San Pedro Sula when travelling from the N Coast to the capital. The highway is paved from Santa Rita to Yoro. **(See also page 509.)** 10 km. S. of El Progreso on the paved highway to Yoro or Santa Rita, at the village of Las Minas, is El Chorro (1 km. off the highway), a charming waterfall and natural swimming pool. A rugged hike can be made into the mountains and on to El Negrito from here.

La Ceiba, the country's busiest port for the export of bananas and pineapples, is 100 km. E of Tela, from which it is reached by sea or road. The capital of Atlántida Department, it stands on the narrow coastal plain between the Caribbean and the rugged Nombre de Dios mountain range, crowned by the spectacular Pico Bonito (2,435 metres—see below). The climate is hot, but tempered by sea winds. There are some fine beaches nearby (La Barra and Miramar are the most popular), though some are dirty. Beyond La Ceiba is the old colonial village of Jutiapa. The Bay Islands are usually visited from La Ceiba. Population 80,160. *Fiesta*, Feria Isidra (National Carnival), third week in May; main day is the 3rd Saturday of the month (live music from dusk till dawn).

Hotels *Gran Hotel París*, C, some rooms cheaper, a/c, faded, cafetería (*Le Petit Café*, definitely not rec.), swimming pool (open to non-residents for US$2), parking; *Partenos Beach* (Greek-owned, family apartments), swimming pool, restaurant, T 43-04-04; *Colonial*, on beach 20 mins. from La Ceiba, 5-star, a/c, sauna, pool, cable TV, nice atmosphere; *Ceiba*, Av. San Isidro, 5 C., D with fan and bath, C with bath and a/c, restaurant and bar; next door is *Iberia*, D, a/c, clean, quiet, comfortable, ample hot water, good value; one block down from the *Iberia* is *Dorita*, D with bath, friendly, clean. *San Carlos*, D, a bit dirty and noisy but has colourful cafetería where Bay islanders assemble Monday mornings for boat trip to Utila. *Los Angeles*, Av. La República, F, pleasant staff, good value, but cockroaches; *Príncipe*, 7 Calle, E, with bath, better than average; *La Isla*, opp. bus station, F, nice rooms, fans, clean; *El Paso*, Av. La República, E, OK; *Royal*, same Av., 2-3 C., E; *Pensión Tegucigalpa*, F, very small rooms, poor beds. Many cheap hotels beside railway line leading from central plaza to pier: *Arias*, F without bath, good value, but short of water. **Camping** at the airport for US$0.20.

Restaurants *Atlántico*, Av. 14 de Julio; *Deportivo*, Blvd. Las Américas; *Ricardo's* (American-owned), very good food, garden setting and a/c tables, highly rec. **Mini Café** (near **Pensión Tegucigalpa**), reasonable, helpful owner; **Imperial Palace**, one block from Central Park, large Chinese menu, seafood, churrasco, good; **Toto**, Av. San Isidro, one block south of main square, good pizzería. **Pizzería Italiana**, reasonable. Numerous small, cheap eating places.

Rent a Car   Molinari.

Discotheques   Leonardo's; D'Lido; Black and White; Scaramouche; all popular.

Exchange   Banco de Londres, Av. San Isidro y 10a Calle; Banco Atlántida; Bancahsa, 9 C., Av. San Isidro; Bancahorro, Av. San Isidro, 7 C.; Banco Sogerín, Av. San Isidro. Open 0830-1130, 1330-1600; Sats. 0800-1200.

Non-Catholic Churches   Anglican, Methodist, Mennonite, Evangelist and Jehovah's Witnesses, among others.

Travel Agents   Hondutours, Laffitte, Trans Mundo.

Tourist Office   Calle 1, 2 blocks east of the pier.

Buses   Most leave from a central terminal, 8 blocks west from centre (taxi US$0.50). Regular bus service to San Pedro Sula, US$2.45 (7 a day from 0530, 3 hrs.). Alternatively, take bus to Tela (2 hrs.), then another to El Progreso, then another to San Pedro Sula, cost in all US$2.35, but much slower. To Trujillo, 4 hrs., US$3.75; to Olanchito, US$1, 3 hrs.; also regular buses to Sonaguera, Tocoa, Jutiapa, Balfate, Isletas and Iriona and San Esteban.

Airport   Golosón, with direct jet services to Miami and New Orleans as well as internal destinations. Sahsa flies to Tegucigalpa, also flights to Roatán, Utila, and Guanaja (Bay Is.). To Puerto Lempira, Isleña (Ed. Hermanos Kawas, T 42-01-79), Tues. and Sun., booked up 2-3 weeks ahead (T 42-26-83). Taxi to town US$6 per car, share with other passengers, also buses.

The **Pico Bonito** national park (674 sq. km.) is the largest of the 11 new parks designated in 1987. It has deep tropical hardwood forests which shelter, among other things, jaguars and three species of monkey, deep canyons and tumbling streams and waterfalls (including Las Gemelas which fall vertically some 200 metres). Access is limited to the fringes of the range, and to the Río Cangrejal, which cuts through a gentler section, and which is bordered by the old, unpaved road to Olanchito from La Ceiba. As of 1987, Pico Bonito itself (2,433 m) had only been climbed by four expeditions, the shortest of which took nine days. The preferred route is along the Río Bonito, starting 10 km. from La Ceiba, and from there up a ridge which climbs all the way to the summit. Expertise in rock climbing is not necessary, but several steep pitches do require a rope for safety; good physical condition is a necessity. Poisonous snakes, including the fer-de-lance (barba amarilla) will probably be encountered en route.

A Peace Corps volunteer stationed in La Ceiba is working on the development of Pico Bonito national park and would be a good source of advice on access. Alternatively go to Cohdefor in La Ceiba. Maps at US$2 should also be available. (Leon Kolankiewicz)

32 km. west of La Ceiba between the Cuero and Salado rivers, near the coast, is a superb wildlife refuge which has a great variety of flora and fauna, with a large population of local and migratory birds. It extends for 12,300 hectares of swamp and forest. To get there from La Ceiba, go to La Unión where the railway goes to Río Salado. From there you can take speed boats or canoes (quieter), or walk the

Sendero El Coco to Barra de El Zacate. Good fishing; visitors' centre, camping area, fresh water.

Other excursions from La Ceiba: Jutiapa, a colonial town with a pleasant church; El Bejuco waterfall, E of La Ceiba in the village of Las Mangas, 80 metres high with a round, deep pool in dense jungle, access to the old Olanchito-Yoro road.

A roundabout railway and a direct, paved road run from La Ceiba to **Olanchito**, a prosperous but hot and ugly town (called La Ciudad Cívica) in the Agúan valley in the hills to the SE. It was founded, according to tradition, by a few stragglers who escaped from the destruction of Olancho el Viejo, between Juticalpa and Catacamas, then a wealthy town. They brought with them the crown made of hides which the image of the Virgin still wears in the church of Olanchito. Population: 12,200. Festival: 2nd week of September, Semana Cívica.

Hotels *Colonial*, Calle del Presidio; *Valle Aguán y Chabelito*, E.

Restaurants *Bar/restaurant Uchapa, La Gavilla, Helados Castillo*.

Exchange El Ahorro Hondureño.

Bus To La Ceiba, 2½ hrs., US$1 via Jutiapa and Savá (Cotol 7 times a day; Cotrail); to Trujillo, 3 hrs., US$3.75 via Tocoa and Savá (Cotol).

Trujillo, 90 km. to the east again, is a port and former capital. The population is 23,760. The town was founded in 1525 (the oldest in Honduras) by Juan de Medina; Hernán Cortés arrived there after his famous march overland from Yucatán in pursuit of his usurping lieutenant, Olid. It was near here that William Walker (see under Nicaragua) was shot in 1860 (a commemorative stone marks the spot); the old cemetery where he is buried is interesting, giving an idea of where early residents came from. El Castillo (Santa Bárbara), a ruined Spanish fortress overlooking the Bay, is worth a visit. Ask the caretaker to show the relics found there. Good beaches are on the peninsula. Take a bus from Central Park towards Puerto Castilla and ask the driver to let you off at the beach. To the S, and E to the Río Segovia, lies a huge territory of jungled swamps and mountains lived in by a few Indians and timber men (**see page** 514). Nearby is Guaymoreto lagoon, which has a bird island (Isla de Pájaros) and monkeys. Flying in is best—Lansa has flights to La Ceiba, but no longer scheduled. The town can be reached by bus from San Pedro Sula, Tela and La Ceiba now that a road (paved, through Savá, Tocoa, to Corocito) has been built from La Ceiba (a dull journey, 2½ hrs. via Tocoa, 3 direct buses early a.m. from Trujillo, US$3.75). There is a direct road along the coast taking 3 hours but liable to flooding in the wet season. Public transport also to San Esteban and Juticalpa (pick-up from plaza 0730, US$10, all day ride—**see page** 513). In this area, many people speak English, so if answered in English, do not continue in Spanish.

Local holiday: San Juan Bautista in June, with participation from surrounding Garifuna (Black Carib) settlements.

Hotels *Villa Brinkley* (known locally as Miss Jean's) T 44-44-44, B, private beach, swimming pool, good view, mixed reports; *Colonial*, D with bath, near plaza, opp. El Castillo, good; *El Castillo*, has overpriced restaurant; *Central*, E, with bath, basic, no water during the day, not rec. (*Rubens Restaurant*, good, in the hotel). *Emperador*, E, small but comfortable rooms, friendly; *Imperial*, E, basic, noisy; *Trujillo*, G, fan, clean sheets daily, good value.

Restaurants *Bucaneer*, on main plaza, a/c, video, a bit expensive; *Granada*, good standard meals, breakfasts and snacks. Excellent seafood at *Cocopando*, set in a coconut grove on western beach (room for rent); *Comedor Albita*, near telephone office, good. Also good food in the market. Many fish restaurants along the beach; *pan de coco*, delicious, is baked almost daily. "Punta" band and dancing at the *Río Cristales*.

Exchange Banco Atlántida.

There are interesting villages of Black Caribs (Garifuna) at Santa Fe, 10 km. W of Trujillo (US$1 by bus), San Antonio and eastwards at Limón. At Puerto Castilla near Trujillo, Columbus landed in 1502 and the first mass on Central American soil was said. It is a meat-packing station and active shrimping centre; a new port is being built. A military training centre operates here. The beach between the port and the spit of land that forms Trujillo Bay is deserted. There are some pleasant beaches around the magnificent Bay. Twenty minutes' walk from Trujillo plaza is Riveras de Pedregal (known as *la piscina*), a series of swimming pools filled from the Río Cristales. The owner, Sr. Rufino Galán, has a collection of precolumbian, colonial and modern artefacts and curios. The pools are usually open at weekends and holidays, but not during the Nov.-Feb. rainy season. Close-by, wreckage of a US C-80 aircraft which crashed in 1985.

THE BAY ISLANDS

The Hog Islands (Cayos Cochinos), with lovely primeval hardwood forests, are 17 km. NE of La Ceiba (two small islands and thirteen palm-fringed cays): privately owned with reserved accommodation at Cayos del Sol. On the Isla de Cochino Grande is a dive resort; very beautiful. The owner of the largest island, Bobby Griffith, permits camping, especially if you can give him a news magazine or two. Take a bus from the stop 1 block from La Ceiba market to Nueva Armenia (US$2), then try to hitch on a dugout, or charter one (about US$10).

The *Bay Islands* (Islas de la Bahía) lie in an arc which curves NE away from a point 32 km. N of La Ceiba. The three main islands are Utila, Roatán, and Guanaja. At the eastern end of Roatán are three small ones: Morat, Santa Elena, and Barbareta; there are other islets and 65 cays. Their total population is 21,550. The main industry is fishing, mostly shellfish, with fleets based at French Harbour. Boat-building is a dying industry. Apart from fish, trade is mostly in coconuts, bananas and plantains. There are some blacks and Black Caribs; the majority are fair-skinned people originally of British stock and still English-speaking. The culture is very un-Latin American. Columbus anchored here in 1502, on his fourth voyage. In the 18th century the islands were bases for English, French and Dutch buccaneers. They were in British hands for over a century but were finally ceded to Honduras in 1859. The government schools teach in Spanish, and the population is bi-lingual. The islands are very beautiful, but beware of the strong sun (the locals bathe in T-shirts) and sand gnats and other insects, especially away from the resorts.

The underwater environment is rich and extensive; reefs surround the islands, often within swimming distance of the shore. Caves and caverns are a common feature, with a wide variety of sponges and the best collection of pillar coral in the Caribbean. The islands are destined to become a major diving centre within a few years. It is difficult to arrange diving independently (i.e. without staying at a resort), although Bay Islands Divers give instruction to PADI certification level; prices start at US$195 for individually structured courses. T 22-75-56 in Tegucigalpa and ask for Bobby, or leave a message. See also below.

Utila (population 1,515) is only 32 km. from La Ceiba and is low lying, with only one hill. On it there are caves to which you can hike. One of the caves is reputed locally to have been a hideout for Henry Morgan. There is some evidence of Paya Indian culture. The main town is known locally as East Harbour. Utila is the cheapest of the islands to visit. Take plenty of insect repellant in the rainy season, sandflies are a menace. Do not pick coconuts, even in the remotest places; you may well be fined. Sunbathing and swimming are not particularly good. Snorkelling and diving equipment for hire; a popular snorkelling spot is by the airport.

A 40-minute boat ride from East Harbour are the Cays, a chain of small islands populated by fisherfolk off the S coast of Utila. On the main Cay, a few families live; they are very friendly to foreigners, but there is nowhere to put a tent. 3 islands further out is Water Cay where you can camp, sling a hammock or, in emergency, sleep in the house of the caretaker; take food and fresh water. It is a coconut island with "white holes" (sandy areas with wonderful hot bathing in the afternoon) and some of the most beautiful underwater reefs in the world. To hire a *dony* (big motorized canoe) costs US$30 for four; many boatmen go and will collect you in the evening, rec. You can hike to Pumpkin Hill where there are some fresh water caves.

Hotels and restaurants on Utila *Trudy's*, 3 minutes from airport, C, dear, E without bath, comfortable, good meals, US satellite TV, diving equipment and boats for hire. *Grant's Cabins*, US$15 for 4 people, cooking facilities, good value. Nearby is the *Manhattan Restaurant*, cheap, good, clean, chocolate and spice cake rec. Good, reasonable food from *Yellow Light Restaurant* (who organizes good picnics on the Cays, US$2 p.p. and US$1.50 for food, "unforgettable"). *Big Mama's Restaurant*, good seafood at reasonable prices. *Monkey Tail Inn*, F, quite good, cooking facilities, water all the time (beyond the *Bucket of Blood Bar*, the owner of which is Mr Woods, a mine of information on the history of Utila and the Cays). There are plenty of houses and rooms for rent, from US$2.50 a person: e.g. at Willis Bodden, US$12 for 3 people (runs a boat trip to the Cays, US$25).

Ronald Janssen (the Dutchman who owns Cross Creek), has scuba diving equipment for hire, US$30 if four people go (T 45-31-34). Divers should visit Günther, an Austrian with lots of local information. He supplies scuba equipment.

There is a bank for changing dollars, but dollars are accepted, a post office and a good clinic. The discotheque is very busy on Saturdays. Local crafts include wood-carving (see Marc Coburn, called Tom).

Transport Isleña and Sosa fly from La Ceiba for US$15 one way. The first has two regular flights, at 0600 and 1600, except Sunday. Check all flight times in advance. Sometimes air fares are reduced if there is competition from a boat. No need to take a taxi from Utila airport to town; US$2 for 300 metres.

A boat leaves every Tuesday around 1100. The *Caribbean Pearl* usually sails to Utila from La Ceiba on Mon., US$4 single, 3 hrs., and returns overnight to Puerto Cortés (bunks available), US$5, times posted in main street. Take food and torch. Captain Juni Cooper sails from La Ceiba to Utila from Mon. p.m. to Tues. a.m., US$4 for the 2½-3 hr. trip. He sails to Roatán a day or so later. From Utila to Roatán he charges US$5, 3½ hrs., irregular sailings. Two boats a week between Puerto Cortés and Utila, no regular schedule, US$10, continuing to Roatán. Fishing boats from La Ceiba charge US$10 to Utila.

It is a few hours' sail to **Roatán**, the largest of the islands (population 10,245). The capital of the department, Roatán (locally known as Coxen's Hole), is on the south-western shore. Port Royal, towards the eastern end of the island, and famous in the annals of buccaneering, is now almost deserted. Archaeologists have been busy on the islands but their findings are very confusing.

From Coxen's Hole it is 2 hours' walk to Sandy Bay, or US$1 by bus; airport employees try to charge US$12, beware: it should only be US$2 from airport. West End, on the opposite coast, can be reached by a stiff walk over the hills (3 hours, bus US$1.50). There are many buses on the unmade roads, but those that charge US$1-1.50 on set routes daily at nightfall or on Sunday charge US$10 for express journeys. Frequent bus service from Coxen's Hole to French Harbour (US$1.50), with its shrimping and lobster fleet. At Brick Bay, just before French Harbour, the Caribbean Sailing Club has a modern hotel (A with breakfast) and rents a fleet of 30 sailing boats for US$200 per day. From French Harbour to Oak Ridge by bus, on a rough road, is US$1.50; Oak Ridge, situated on a cay (US$0.50 crossing in dory), is built around a deep inlet. Hire a boat for an hour's sail up the coast to Port Royal (also reached by good road from Oak Ridge); old British gun emplacements on Fort Cay. No bus from Port Royal to Oak Ridge, and it's a tough 3-hr. walk. Note the Black Carib village of Punta Gorda on the north coast (probably the first non-Indian settlement on the islands). Beaches excellent but Roatán is expensive, twice as dear as the mainland.

Hotels on Roatán At West End, *Roberts Hill*, D, with meals, diving, etc., friendly, good value; *Lost Paradise* C, full board (D without), delicious meals, snorkelling equipment, transport back to airport; owner Tyll Sass (US phone 813-593-1259); *Sarina's*, F, reasonable rooms, meals around US$2.50. There is no food to be bought at West End, but a new restaurant (1990) is open near *Roberts Hill*, good seafood, no sandflies, owned by Foster Diaz, his wife Laverne is the cook; *Chino's* restaurant serves local meals and seafood, T 45-1314.

At Sandy Bay, *Anthony's Key Resort*, L (US$75 full board), glorious situation, launch and diving facilities (US$20, US$40 non-residents); *Pirate's Den*, D-A, full board, poor service, beware of overcharging (well named); *Bamboo Inn*, D, clean and good (nice restaurant next door, reasonable prices); *Quinn's*, reasonable.

At French Harbour, *Coral Reef Inn*, E-D; *Caribinn*, D; *French Harbour Yacht Club*, B, ocean-view rooms, cable TV in every room, reasonable rates, good food, friendly, T 45-14-78; *Buccaneer Inn*, C-A; *Fantasy Island Beach Resort*, 80 rooms, luxurious on a cay, C-A; *Hotelito*, E, sometimes no water, in the village; unnamed hotel just before *Buccaneer Inn*, E with fan, very good value.

At Brick Bay: *Island Garden*, good European-run guest house (contact Michael Free, Fax Hondutel 45-62-06), airport transfers, full board available, snorkelling, sailing, scuba diving US$20 p.p. per dive; *Romeo's Resort Dive and Yacht Club*, C up, good.

At Oak Ridge, *Reef House Resort*, B-L, inc. meals and boats, though sometimes closed for lack of water. *San José Hotel*, D, clean, pleasant, good value, good food, English-speaking owner, Louise Solórzano; *Gran Hotel Ronnie*, cafeteria nearby; *Clear View Hotel*, B.

At Port Royal, *Camp Bay Resort*, A; *Roatán Lodge*, Port Royal, L, accommodation in cabins, hosts Brian and Lisa Blancher provide scuba diving and snorkelling expeditions; *Miss Merlee's Guest House*.

At Coxen's Hole: *Elizabethan Inn*, luxury; *Central*, E, basic but rec., run by a doctor; *Coral*, E, Peace Corps favourite, basic; *Airport View*, C (D without bath or a/c); *Cay View*, C (E without bath or a/c); *Comedor Isleña*, good, cheap and *Cafetería El Punto*.

There are other, cheaper, places to stay, for example, Miss Effie's (near *Anthony's Key Resort*) and houses to let (at West End, Half Moon Bay, or Punta Gorda). *Sunrise*, hotel and dive shop, excellent value, offers packages which include a welcome drink, 3 good meals a day (seafood), hot water, laundry, daily trips to Baily's Cay, picnics at West Bay, scuba courses and equipment rental.

At Coxen's Hole are a post office, tourist information, travel agencies, a supermarket and souvenir shops. Banco Atlántida in French Harbour.

Barbareta Beach Club on Barbareta Island; excellent diving, but expensive. The adjacent Pigeon Cays are ideal for snorkelling, shallow scuba, picnics. There are stone artefacts on the island, and you can hike in the hills to caves which may have been inhabited by Paya Indians. The island was once owned by the descendants of Henry Morgan. The island, plus its neighbours Santa Elena and Morat, are part of the proposed Barbareta National Marine Park.

Transport Take a plane to Coxen's Hole (airport is 20 mins. walk from town, taxi US$1.50) and launch up coast to French Harbour and Oak Ridge. Flights to La Ceiba, Tegucigalpa and San Pedro Sula (US$25) with Sahsa or Isleña, several daily. Sahsa flies frequently to Guanaja. Some direct flights to Miama (TAN), Houston and New Orleans (Sahsa) and Belize City (Western Caribbean Airlines). Roatán airport has been extended to take jets.

Boats go irregularly from Puerto Cortés to Roatán, US$5 plus US$0.50 dock charge for tourists. Boats most days at 1400 for La Ceiba, US$20. *Caribbean Pearl* sails irregularly from Puerto Cortés, via Utila, to Roatán; also fishing boats for US$10 p.p. Charter sailing yacht *Lusanda*, US$900 for 4 people for 4 nights/3 days, with transport to and from La Ceiba by air.

Columbus called *Guanaja*, the easternmost of the group, the Island of Pines, and the tree is still abundant. The island was declared a forest reserve in 1961, and is now designated a national marine park also. Good (but sweaty) clambering on the island gives splendid views of the jungle and the sea. Several attractive waterfalls. The locals call the island Bonacca. Much of Guanaja town, covering a small cay off the coast, is built on stilts above sea water: hence its nick-name, the "Venice of Honduras". The island's population is about 4,000. Bathing is made somewhat unpleasant by the many sandflies. These and mosquitos cannot be escaped on the island, all the beaches are infected (olive oil will help to ward off sandflies and doubles as sun protection). The cays are better, including Guanaja town. South West Cay is specially recommended.

Hotels on Guanaja *Alexander*, C new (1990), good, T 45-43-26, C, or US$100 in 3-bed, 3-bathroom apartment. *Bayman Bay Club* (beautiful location) and

Posada del Sol (on an outlying cay), both A-L with launch trips, diving gear for rent, first class; *Miller*, D-C (cheaper without a/c or bath); *Harry Carter*, E-D, but "passed-it", ask for a fan, all the a/c is broken down, clean however. *Rosaino*, C, with bath and a/c. *Club Guanaja Este*, A, full board, many aquatic activities, and horseriding and hiking, reservations and information P.O. Box 40541, Cincinnati, Ohio 45240 or travel agents. *Casa Sobre El Mar*, on Bound Key, T 45-41-80 (31-05-95 in Tegucigalpa), offers all-inclusive packages for US$75 per person.

Restaurants *Harbour Light*, through *Mountain View* discotheque, good food reasonably priced for the island; *The Nest*, good eating in the evening; *Glenda's*, good standard meals for under US$1, small sandwiches.

There are 3 banks.

Transport An airport on Bonacca Island, boat to Guanaja, US$1; Sahsa has two flights most days to San Pedro Fula via Roatán and La Ceiba leaving at 0600 and 1320. Other non-scheduled flights available.

The *Suyapa* sails between Guanaja, La Ceiba and Puerto Cortés. The *Miss Sheila* also does the same run and goes on to George Town (Grand Cayman). Cable Doly Zapata, Guanaja, for monthly sailing dates to Grand Cayman (US$75 one way). Irregular sailings from Guanaja to Trujillo, twice a week, 5 hrs., US$10. Irregular but frequent sailings in lobster boats for next to nothing to Puerto Lempira in Caratasco Lagoon, Mosquitia, or more likely, only as far as the Río Plátano (**see page 514**).

SAN PEDRO SULA

San Pedro Sula, 58 km. S of Puerto Cortés by road and railway (76m. above sea level), the second largest city in Honduras, is a centre for the banana, coffee, sugar and timber trades, a focal distributing point for northern and western Honduras with good road links, and the most industrialized centre in the country. Its business community is mainly of Arab origin. It is considered the fastest growing city between Mexico and Colombia. The population is 319,740.

The city was founded by Pedro de Alvarado on 27 June 1536 but there are no old buildings of interest. The large neo-colonial-style cathedral, started in 1949, is now completed. San Pedro Sula is situated in the lush and fertile valley of the Ulúa (Sula) river, beneath the forested slopes of the Merendón mountains and, though pleasant in the cooler season from October to March, reaches very high temperatures in the summer months with considerable humidity levels.

The higher and cooler suburb of Bella Vista with its fine views over the city affords relief from the intense heat of the town centre. The cafeteria and foyer swimming pool of *Hotel Sula* provide a cool haven for visitors. The city's main festival, San Pedro, is in the last days of June.

Hotels *Gran Hotel Sula* (the best), 1 C., 3 and 4 Av., C-A, pool, restaurant (upstairs, very good, reasonably priced) and café (for authentic American breakfast), also good, 24-hr. service; *Copantl Sula*, very modern, A in Col. Las Mesetas, free bus to city centre, Telex IT5584; *Bolívar*, 2a C., 2 Av., N.O., D/A, cabins beside pool, with a/c, restaurant, run down but elegant; *San Pedro*, 3 C., and 2 Av., S.O., F-D, with bath and a/c, also cheaper rooms, popular, inexpensive restaurant; *Manhattan*, 7 Av. 3-4 C., E-D, with a/c; *Terraza*, C with a/c, E without, dining room rather dark and grimy, friendly staff, 6 Av., 4-5 Calle S.O.;

Colombia, 3 Calle, 5-6 Av., E/D, with a/c, E without; *Colombia Annex*, a few blocks away, E without bath, run down, pricey; *San Juan*, 6 C., 6 Av. S.O., F, modern building, nothing special but good value; *Moderno*, 7 Av., 5-6 C., E, opp. Empresa el Rey buses, very basic; *Brisas del Occidente*, a 5-storey building on Av. 5, E, with fan (F without bath), friendly, comfortable, rec. (do not confuse with nearby *Brisas de Copán*, a dive which rents rooms by the hour); *Palmira*, 6 Av., 6 C., E, good (there are 2 *Palmiras* in same street; they and the *Brisas*, are nr. Av. Los Leones, not the best area late at night); *Siesta*, 2 Av. S.E., 7 C. (T 522650), E, cheaper without bath, clean, safe, rec., but noisy; *Monte Cristo*, 2 Av. 7C., F, clean, fan, safe; *París*, near bus station for Puerto Cortés, F, shared bath, clean but noisy. Cheap hotels between bus terminals and downtown market. 5 km. south, on the road to Tegucigalpa, is *Tropical*, a good stopping place for motorists.

Restaurants *Touché*, good food, but expensive and slow service; *Le Petit France*, French, good but expensive; *La Espuela*, Av. Circunvalación N.O., good grilled meats; *La Cascada*, Centro Comercial La Carreta, Av. Circunvalación N.O., rec.; *Don Udo's*, in *Hotel Suites Los Andes*, same Avenida, restaurant and café-bar; *Lucky*, on main square, Chinese, large portions, good; *Motel Vitanza* and *Mesón Español* (near *Hotel Manhattan*), good typical dishes available; *Madrid* on Plaza, good; *Pizza Don Corleone*, several throughout the city; *Italia*, near *Gran Hotel Sula*, good; *Vicente* and *Nápoli* restaurants, centre of town, Italian, reasonable; *Salón Marte*, near market, good, cheap light meals in evening; *José y Pepe's*. Av. Circunvalacion S.O., Mexican; *La Estancia*, 2 C., 9 y 10 Av. N.O., behind Supertiendas Prisa, Uruguayan; *Chalet Suizo*, Av. Circunvalación S.O. specialities with an authentic touch; *Popeye's Chicken and Biscuits*, in front of Cervecería Hondureña on road to Puerto Cortés; *La Cesta*, good for chicken; *Pizza Hut* at W end of Blvd. Morazán; *Taos*, good ice cream; *Pops* and *Ka-Boom* for ice cream. Many good fried chicken stands in market.

Shopping Excellent wood and leather products are sold at CDI, in the old US Consulate building. Large artesan market 6 blocks NW of Central Park; typical Honduran and some Guatemalan handicrafts at good prices (bargain).

Taxis Cheap; ask the price first and bargain if necessary (US$1-1.50 per journey).

Discotheques *Fondo del Recuerdo* and *Sancho Panza*, good; *Don Quijote*; *San Fernando* (small). *Scaramouches*, popular.

Theatre The Círculo Teatral Sampedrano puts on plays at the Centro Cultural Sampedrano, 3 Calle N.O., No. 20, which also has an art gallery and an English and Spanish library. There are five air-conditioned cinemas.

Exchange Banco de Londres at 4a Av. S.O. 26, between 3a and 4a Calle; Banco Atlántida; Banco de Honduras (Citibank); Banco de Ahorro Hondureño, has a beautiful mural in its head office, 5 Av., 4 Calle S.O. Bancahsa, 5 Av., S.O., No. 46; and all other local banks. Open 0830-1500, closed Sat. Black market at *Hotel Gran Sula*. Rates are better in some shops; they will also accept travellers' cheques.

Consulates Belize, Sr. Antonio E. Canahuati, Edif. Plásticos Sula, Km. 5, T 52-61-91, open 0800-1100, 1300-1600. Guatemalan, 8 C., 5-6 Av. No. 38. Swiss, 19-20 Av. S.O. No. 152, Barrio Río de Piedras, T 52-54-95. British, Terminales de Puerto Cortés, Aptdo. 298, T 542600.

Schools and Institutes La Escuela Internacional (English-speaking), on US lines with US and some British staff. Alianza Francesa, Ed. Bermúdez, 5 Calle S.O. No. 38, T 53-11-78, has a library, French films on Wed., and cultural events on Fri.

Churches Episcopal Church, round corner from Sports Stadium, English service, Sun., 1000. High Mass on Suns., 1030, at Orthodox church at Río Piedras is picturesque and colourful.

Telephone, Telex and Cables from Hondutel.

Tourist Office SECTUR, Edificio Inmosa, 4C N.O. 3-4 Av. and at airport, road maps US$1.50.

Airport Ramón Villeda Morales, 13 km. from city centre, US$7.50 p.p. by taxi; US$3 by colectivo. Buses do not go to the airport terminal itself; you have to walk the final 1½ km. from the La Lima road (bus to this point, US$0.30). Flights to Tegucigalpa (35 mins.) 4 times daily. Twice daily to La Ceiba and to Belize. Direct flights every day to Guatemala, New Orleans and Miami. Irregular flights to other Honduran cities and to the Copán ruins.

Buses To Tegucigalpa, 4-4½ hrs., 250 km. by paved road. Main bus services with comfortable coaches and terminals in the town centre are Hedmán Alas, 7-8 Av. N.O., 3 C., Casa 51, T 531361, 7 per day 0630 to 1730 4 hrs (US$3), which is the best, and Transportes Sáenz (Av. 9 y 10, C.9 y Av. S.O.), El Rey, Av. 7, Calle 5 y 6 (all US$2.50), last bus at 1900. Small friendly buses run by El Norteño. Other services operate with less comfortable buses. The road to Puerto Cortés is paved; a pleasant 1-hr. journey down the lush river valley. Buses run N to Puerto Cortés (Empresa Impala, 2 Av., 4-5 C., several each hour, or Citul, US$0.75), E to La Lima, El Progreso (US$0.60), Tela and La Ceiba (Tupsa, 2 Av. N., 5-6 Calle, 12 a day, from 0530, US$2.45, 2½-3 hrs.), S to Lake Yojoa and Tegucigalpa, and SW to Santa Rosa and then through the Department of Ocotepeque with its magnificent mountain scenery to the Guatemalan border (US$3.40 to the border by bus). Transportes Impala, 2 Av., 4-5 Calle S.O. No. 23, has 6 buses a every other day to Nueva Ocotepeque and Agua Caliente on the Guatemalan border (first at 0330, last 1500), on alternate days Congolón runs this route, terminal US$0.75 from centre; Empresa Torito and Transportes Copanecos go to Santa Rosa de Copán every 30 mins. from 0445 to 1715 US$1.80 (6 y 7 Avs., 6 C.S.O., T 54-19-54/53-49-30, and 6 C., 4-5 Av. S.O., respectively, latter's terminal is US$0.75 taxi ride from centre). Take these buses to La Entrada for connection to Copán. Journey some 3-4 hrs. Road paved all the way.

Train To Tela at 0625 changing at Baracoa, US$1.50 1st class, US$0.70 2nd. Also to Puerto Cortés. Check timetables if you wish to travel.

Excursions One can take a taxi up the mountain behind the city for US$1-1.50; good view, a restaurant, and interesting vegetation on the way up. Lake Ticamaya, near Choloma, is worth visiting between June and December. The head office of the former United Brands subsidiary is at **La Lima** (45,000 inhabitants), 15 km. to the E by road (bus frequent, US$0.25), where the banana estate and processing plants can be seen. There is a club (golf, tennis, swimming) which takes members from outside. A little to the E, near the Ulúa river, is Travesía (not the Travesía near Puerto Cortés, which can also be reached for a day out at the beach), where Mayan pottery remains have been found, but no ruins as such. Buses run E to El Progreso and on N to Tela on the coast, and to La Ceiba. (The train to Tela goes via Baracoa at 1500, 3 hrs.) A bus from 2 Av. goes to Las Vegas-El Mochito mine where there is a cheap *pensión* (F) and walks along W side of Lake El Rincón.

The waterfall at Pulhapanzak is on the Río Lindo, off the main San Pedro Sula-Tegucigalpa road; by car it's a 1½ hr. drive, longer by bus. Take a Mochito bus from San Pedro Sula (hourly 0500-1700) and alight at the sign to the falls, US$0.95. Alternatively stay on the bus to Cañaveral (take identification because there is a power plant here), and walk back along the Río Lindo, 3-4 hours past interesting rock formations and small falls. The waterfall (42 metres) is beautiful in, or just after the rainy season, and in sunshine there is a rainbow at the falls. There is a picnic area and a small overpriced restaurant, but the site does get crowded at weekends and holidays; there is a small admission charge (US$0.50).

Leave early for this trip. Return buses leave only up to mid afternoon. *Pensión* at Peña Blanca, 4 km. from the falls.

Twenty km. west of San Pedro Sula, the cloud forest national park of **Cusuco** is under development (access by dirt road from Cofradía, on the road to Santa Rosa de Copán).

COPAN AND WESTERN HONDURAS

The Western Highway (171 km.) runs from San Pedro Sula SW along the Río Chamelecón to Canoa (from where there is a paved road S to Santa Bárbara) and Santa Rosa de Copán; it goes on to San Salvador. **Santa Bárbara** (23,000 inhabitants) is 32 km. W of Lake Yojoa, in hot lowlands. Panama hats and other goods of *junco* palm are made in this pleasant town. In the vicinity the ruined colonial city of Tencoa has recently been rediscovered. The road goes on paved to join the Northern Highway S of Lake Yojoa.

Hotels *Herrera*, *Santa Marta*, both on La Independencia, F; *Hospedaje Rodríguez*, F, with bath, rec.; *Boarding House Moderno*, Barrio Arriba, T 64-22-03, E, with hot shower, reasonable dining room.

Restaurants *Brasero*, the best, Barrio El Centro; *El Maxim*, Av. La Independencia, Barrio El Centro; *Comedor Estudiantina*, for good, cheap, basic meal.

Cinema Galaxia.

Exchange Banco Atlántida.

Bus from Tegucigalpa, Tues., Thurs., Sat. at 0600, return Mon., Wed., Fri., at 0500, US$3, 6 hrs. with Transportes Junqueños (passing through remote villages in beautiful mountain scenery); from San Pedro Sula, 2 hrs., US$1.90, 7 a day between 0500 and 1630.

A branch road from the road to Santa Bárbara goes to **San Luis**, a coffee town in beautiful scenery. *Hospedaje San José*, F, clean, friendly; *Hospedaje San Isidro*. Several *comedores*. Bus from San Pedro Sula, US$2.50, twice daily. (Electricity 1800-2130 only.) Near Santa Bárbara is Ilama (7,000 people) with one of the best small colonial churches in Honduras (no accommodation).

In the Department of Santa Bárbara is an area known as El Resumidero, in which are the Quezapaya mountain, and six others over 1,400 metres, and a number of caves (Pencaligüe, Los Platanares, El Quiscamote, and others). From Santa Bárbara, go to El Níspero and thence to El Quiscamote; or go to San Vicente Centenario (thermal springs nearby), and on to San Nicolás, Atima, Berlín, and La Unión, all of which have thermal waters, fossils, petrified wood and evidence of volcanic activity.

Santa Rosa de Copán, 153 km. by road from San Pedro Sula, is the centre of a rich agricultural and cattle-raising area. Altitude 1,160 metres, population 28,865. One of the most attractive towns set in some of the best scenery in Hondruas. Much maize and tobacco is grown in the area. Tobacco factory near the *Hotel Elvir* sometimes arranges tours; large selection of cigars for sale. Excellent *sombreros de junco* (Panama hats) are made here. Santa Rosa is a colonial town with delightful narrow cobbled streets. The central plaza and church are perched on a hilltop. It holds a festival to Santa Rosa de Lima from 21

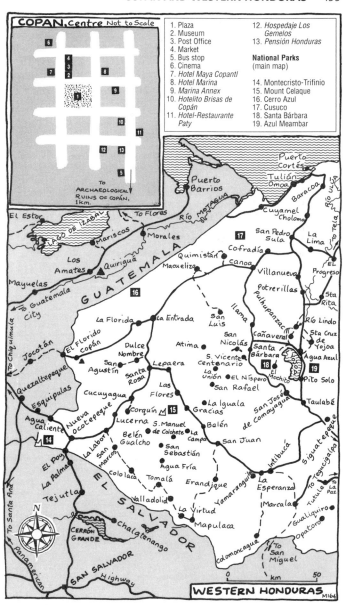

COPAN. Centre Not to Scale

1. Plaza
2. Museum
3. Post Office
4. Market
5. Bus stop
6. Cinema
7. *Hotel Maya Copantl*
8. *Hotel Marina*
9. *Marina Annex*
10. *Hotelito Brisas de Copán*
11. *Hotel-Restaurante Paty*
12. *Hospedaje Los Gemelos*
13. *Pensión Honduras*

National Parks
(main map)

14. Montecristo-Trifinio
15. Mount Celaque
16. Cerro Azul
17. Cusuco
18. Santa Bárbara
19. Azul Meambar

To ARCHAEOLOGICAL RUINS OF COPÁN, 1km.

WESTERN HONDURAS

to 31 August.

Hotels *Elvir* (the best), Calle Real Centenario O, 2 Av. O, D, all rooms have own bath, good meals in cafeteria or restaurant; nearby: *Hotel Maya* (not to be confused with *Hospedaje* Maya, see below), 1 C. N.O. y 3 Av. N.O., F, *Continental*, F with bath, friendly management; *Rosario*, 3 Av. N.E. No. 139, E with bath, F without; next door is *Hospedaje Guillén*, F, No. 193; *Hospedaje Santa Rosa*, 3 Av. N.E. No. 119, F, simple, clean; *Copán*, 3 Av. N.E. y 4 C. N.E., E with bath, hot water, F without, clean, and next door; *Hospedaje Maya*, F. *Hospedaje Calle Real*, Real Centenario y 6 Av., F, clean, quiet, friendly, sometimes water failures, good cheap meals; *Hispano*, on main square, 1 C. N.E. y 1 Av. N.E., F; *Hospedaje Santa Eduvigis*, 2 Av. N.O. y 1 C. N.O., F, with reasonable restaurant; *Erick*, 1 C. N.E. No. 362, E with bath. *Mayaland*, opp. bus station on Carretera Internacional, E p.p., parking, restaurant, but noisy and hostile management; *El Rey*, also opp. bus terminal, F p.p., rooms with bath, restaurant, parking.

Restaurants *Danubio Azul*, 1 Av. S.E., No. 040, 1 block from Plaza; *Las Haciendas*, 1 Av. S.E., varied menu, filling comida corriente, rec.; *El Patio*, next door, varied menu, good; *El Pollo Dorado*, two blocks N of *Hotel Elvir*, excellent baleadas; *El Pollito Copaneco*, good chicken dinners, on the main square next to Banco Atlántida; *Miraflores* in Col. Miraflores.

Discotheques *Tiffany's* and *Nuevo Ovni*, both near centre.

Exchange Banco de Occidente and Atlántida, both on main plaza. Banadesa, Calle Real. Bancahsa.

Travel Agent Cramer Tours.

Bus from Santa Rosa to Tegucigalpa via San Pedro Sula leaves at 0400 from main square, US$3.40, 7-8 hrs. 4 buses daily to Gracias 0930, 1130, 1300, 1600, 2½ hrs., US$1.50. To San Pedro Sula, US$1.80, 4 hrs. every 30 mins. (Empresa Torito, and Transportes Copanecos), bus to La Entrada, 1 hr., US$0.50. Frequent service S to Nueva Ocotepeque (US$1.50, 3 hrs.). Local bus from bus station (on Carretera Internacional, below town) to centre ("El Urbano"), US$0.10, very slow, goes all around the houses; taxi US$0.50.

Excursions Robert Millar writes: There is a bus from Santa Rosa at 1000 and 1400, west to the small town of Dulce Nombre de Copán (US$0.55). Hardy hikers can continue west through forested mountains to stay at the primitive village of San Agustín (take hammock or sleeping bag), continuing next day to emerge a few kms. from Copán ruins. From Santa Rosa there is a 3-hr. bus ride to Lepaera (17,775 inhabitants, cheap, simple *pensión* and *comedores*) perched on a lovely mountainside (also reached from Gracias). One can scale the peak or descend on foot by an old mule trail heading back to Santa Rosa, crossing the river on a swingbridge (*hamaca*), then hitch-hiking.
　　Numerous daily buses go to Corquín (US$0.75, 2 hrs.)—2 good *pensiones*, one with a charming garden. From here take a rough, dusty, 2½-hr. ride in a pick-up truck (US$0.75) to Belén Gualcho, 1,850 metres up in mountains, amid coffee plantations. There are 3 simple *pensiones* (F, cheap meals); it is a fine centre for walking in the dense rain forests of the Celaque mountains; colourful Sunday Indian market. A steep descent east from Belén by mule trail leads in 5 hrs. to San Manuel de Colohuete, with a magnificent colonial church whose façade is sculpted with figures of saints. There is an equally fine colonial church 5 hrs. to the south-west at San Sebastián, continuing then by mule trail via the heights of Agua Fría to reach the bus route near the frontier at Tomalá. Alternatively, one can walk 5 hrs. east from San Manuel to La Campa (colonial church) where there is irregular transport to Gracias.

There are buses from Santa Rosa to Mapalaca and villages bordering El Salvador.

From San Pedro Sula there are regular buses via Santa Rosa south to **Nueva Ocotepeque** (6 hrs., US$3.40); road is well paved. From Nueva Ocotepeque, buses to San Pedro Sula stop at La Entrada (US$1.70), first at 0030, for connections to Copán. There are splendid mountain views. The Salvadorean border S of Nueva Ocotepeque is open again. Colectivos to El Poy on border, US$0.50, and several buses daily from El Poy to San Salvador. You can cross into Guatemala at Atulapa, just after Agua Caliente (tourist office here, one *hospedaje*, bargain). There are several buses a day from San Pedro Sula to Agua Caliente, first at 0300 (e.g. Congolón, Impala; US$3.50, 6-7 hrs.; money changers get on the bus between Nueva Ocotepeque and the border, poor rates; the Honduran and Guatemalan migration offices are about 2 km. apart, minibuses do the trip for US$0.30). Minibuses then go to Esquipulas (US$0.25), from where first class buses run to Guatemala City. You can get into El Salvador via Esquipulas, Guatemala (**see page** 364). About 25 km. before Nueva Ocotepeque (at the junction to San Marcos Ocotepeque) there is a police checkpoint. Make sure all documents are in order and to hand. There are Guatemalan consuls in San Pedro Sula and Nueva Ocotepeque (hours 0800-1100, 1400-1600, Mon.—Fri., one photo required for visa, US$10); it is preferable to get a visa at them than at the border. There is an old colonial church, La Vieja (or La Antigua) between Nueva Ocotepeque and the border. The **Montecristo national park** forms part of the Trifinio/ La Fraternidad project, administered jointly by Honduras, Guatemala and El Salvador.

Hotels in Nueva Ocotepeque *Sandoval*, TV, café, hot water; *Ocotepeque*, F (by Transportes Impala); restaurant *La Cabaña*. *Gran*, F-D is at the junction of the roads for El Salvador (South) and Guatemala (West) nearby, at Sinuapa.

The magnificent Maya ruins of **Copán** are 225 km. by air from Tegucigalpa or 186 by air from San Pedro Sula (also a paved road), and 1 km. from the pleasant village, called Copán Ruinas (population 22,185). The road from San Pedro Sula runs SW for 125 km. to La Entrada, where it forks left for Santa Rosa and right for an attractive 60 km. road through deep green scenery to Copán. The regular bus is recommended rather than the dangerous minibus service.

La Entrada is a hot, dusty little town (*Hotel Central*, E, OK; *Hospedaje Copaneco*, 1 Av. No. 228, F; *Hospedajes Alexandra, Mejía; Hotel Tegucigalpa; Hospedaje María*, F, clean, good, limited food also; eat in the market or at the bus station, or at *Comedor Isis*, excellent). There is a small archaeological museum on main street next to Banco Atlántida (US$0.50). This bank won't cash travellers' cheques, but Banco Sogerín will. A few km. beyond is the small town of Florida (24,100 inhabitants, primitive accommodation). The owner of the gas station here will advise archaeologists about the many Maya ruins between Florida and Copán. There are a number of hilltop stelae between the border and Copán. At Jihua, 3 km. to the left from Km. 4 from La Entrada, is a restored colonial church.

There is a signposted path beside the road from the village of Copán to the ruins, passing stelae en route (1 km., no need to take a minibus). It is advisable to get to the ruins (open 0800-1600) as early as possible, or late in the day (though it takes a full day to see them properly); this way you will miss the guided tours. There is a cafeteria by the entrance to the ruins, and also a shop. Guided tours available all year. There is a tourist office in the Parque Arqueológico, next to the shop, where luggage can be left for no charge (clean toilets here, too). Entry to ruins US$1.50 and museum (on town square open 0800-1600) with photographs of the excavation work, a maquette of the site and explanations of the glyphs, US$0.50 for foreigners.

When Stephens and Catherwood examined the ruins in 1839, they were engulfed in jungle. In the 1930s the Carnegie Institute cleared the ground and rebuilt the Great Stairway, and since then they have been maintained by the Government. Some of the most complex carvings are found on the 21 stelae, or 3-metre columns of stones on which the passage of time was originally believed to be recorded, and which are still in their original sites among the buildings. Under each stela is a vault; some have been excavated. The stelae are deeply incised and carved with faces and figures and animals. They are royal portraits with inscriptions recording deeds and lineage of those portrayed as well as dates of birth, marriage(s) and death. (Some of the finest examples of sculpture in the round from Copán are now in the British Museum or at Boston.) Ball courts were revealed during excavation, and one of them has been fully restored. The Hieroglyphic Stairway (now covered for protection) leads up a pyramid, with mythical creatures rearing from the steps; the upper level supported a temple. Its other sides are still under excavation.

The last stela was set up in Copán between A.D. 800 and 820, after less than five centuries of civilized existence. That no further developments took place is attributed by one theory to revolt by the common people against an increasingly distanced nobility and priesthood, rather than outside invaders. The nearby river has been diverted to prevent it encroaching on the site when in flood. 1 km. from the main ruins (in the opposite direction from the village) is an area called Las Sepulturas, a residential area where ceramics dating back to 1000 BC have been found. A tomb from the site is on display in the museum (entry US$0.50). Also near the ruins is a nature trail through the jungle to the minor ball court (called Sendero Natural); take mosquito repellant if you intend to stand still. (See general account of Maya history in the Introduction to this book.)

How to get there One can charter flights from Tegucigalpa and Guatemala City. There are also regular buses (Copanecos, Impala or Torito lines) from San Pedro Sula to La Entrada, US$1.50 (2 hrs.); from La Entrada to Copán, US$1.50 by bus, US$2.25 by minibus (2½-3 hrs.), from 0600 hourly (or when full) till 1600, stops at entrance to ruins. For minibus from village to La Entrada, see below. If going by bus from San Pedro Sula, and returning, it is impossible to see Copán in one day. But if going on to Guatemala, one can take the 0445 San Pedro-La Entrada bus, 0600 La Entrada-Copán, arriving 0900, then the 1300 bus from Copán to the border; minibus Copán-border or vice-versa, leave when full, first at 0710 outside *Paty* US$0.75, but not on Sundays. Etumi bus from San Pedro Sula direct to Copán, at 1030 and 1300, 5-6 hrs. Direct bus also from 6 Av. S. O. y 7 C. S. O., at 1100 daily, US$1.90, 5-6 hrs. Return to San Pedro Sula direct at 0400 and 0500. 3 early a.m. buses from Copán to Santa Rosa, 4 hrs., US$1.90. To return to San Pedro Sula, minibuses will collect you from your hotel and take you to La Entrada, from where buses go to San Pedro Sula.

Copán can also be reached by road from Guatemala City. The Honduran immigration office is now at the border; one can get exit stamps there. For the most direct route from Guatemala, **see page** 364.

To enter (or return to) Guatemala an alternative route is via Nueva Ocotepeque (see above and **page** 365 for transit into Guatemala); every 40 mins. a bus leaves Copán for La Entrada (US$1.50, 2½-3 hrs., longer in rain), last bus at 1630. From there, there are several buses a day to Santa Rosa (US$0.75, 1 hr.). Buses run from Santa Rosa to Nueva Ocotepeque.

Exit tax from Guatemala is Q3, entry to Honduras US$2.50. If you are leaving Honduras make sure to get your passport stamped at the police check point just outside Copán on the road to the border. The nearest Guatemalan consulate is in San Pedro Sula, so if you need a visa, you must get one there.

Hotels in Copán: *Maya Copantl*, E, with bath, restaurant; *Marina*, on the Plaza, E, with bath, hot water, meals US$3, breakfast US$1.50, cheaper annex, F, excellent value (but rooms on street noisy); *Hotelito Brisas de Copán*, F p.p. without bath, quiet, rec.; *Hospedaje Los Gemelos*, F, without bath, nice, good value, use of kitchen on request, rec; *Hotelito Peña*, F, clean, friendly, showers. *Pensión Honduras*, G, food available, clean, friendly, good; *Hotel-Restaurante Paty*, friendly, under the same ownership as one of the minibus companies, has good meals (a bit dear) and 10 clean rooms, G p.p. without bath, E in newer rooms with bath. *Paty* and *Honduras* are noisy from buses after 0400. *Restaurant El Sesteo*, opposite *Brisas de Copán*, reasonable. *Comedor Isabel* near the plaza, good, cheap; *La Llama del Bosque*, 2 blocks W of central Plaza. *Tunkul*, opened 1989, properietors Honduran/American, good. Good meals at the market. There is a cinema (films at 1930, daily except Tues. and Wed.), which leaves much to be desired. Horses for hire near the square, US$1 per day (if you look around and bargain).

Travellers' cheques may be changed at the bank (0830-1200, 1400-1600, Mon.-Fri., 0800-1100 Sat.). Guatemalan currency is rarely accepted at Copán; it is possible to change quetzales near where buses leave for the border. Change dollars at the better hotels. Post office next to museum; stamps sold at corner shop opposite. There is a service station at Copán.

SAN PEDRO SULA TO TEGUCIGALPA

Potrerillos (*Hotel Alvarez*), the railhead, is 37 km. S of San Pedro Sula. From Potrerillos the paved Northern Highway (288 km.) climbs some 37 km. from the hot lowlands to **Lake Yojoa**, 600 metres high, 22½ km. long and 10 km. wide, splendidly set among mountains. To the W rise the Jicaque mountains; to the E some lower hills, with Los Naranjos and other villages along the shores or set back towards the hills. Pumas, bears and jaguars range the forests and pine-clad slopes. The road follows the eastern margin to the lake's southern tip at Pito Solo, where sailing boats and motor boats can be hired. The road is mostly out of sight of the lake: the side-road to the lake itself is not signposted and can be easily overlooked. (Bus to Lake from San Pedro Sula, US$1.15, 1½ hrs.; bus from Lake to Tegucigalpa, US$2.25, 3½ hrs.).

Accommodation   *Restaurante y Balneario Los Remos* has cabins and camping facilities at southern end of the lake, C and up, beautiful setting, good food, no beach but pool, boat trips; *Motel Agua Azul* (at N end of lake), B, meals for non-residents; facilities for swimming and boating; bus waits at junction with the main road to take people to the hotel. *Comedores* on the road beside the lake serve the bass that is caught there. Buses between Tegucigalpa and San Pedro stop to let passengers off at *Los Remos*, and at Peñas Blancas, 5 km. from the turning for *Agua Azul*. At Peña Blanca Córtez on N side of Lake is *Comedor El Cruce*, very good home cooking. 10 km. N of the lake is the turn off for the village of Santa Cruz de Yojoa, and at 24 km. is the El Cajón hydroelectric project (to visit the dam, apply at least 10 days in advance by phone—22-21-77, or in writing to Oficina de Relaciones Públicas de la ENEE, 1 Av., Edificio Valle-Aguiluz, Comayagüela, D.C.) Accommodation can be booked at El Mochito mine of the American Pacific Holdings Company, near Lake Yojoa.

El Cajón hydroelectric dam (226 metres high) has formed a 94 square km. lake, which lies between the departments of Cortés, Yoro and Comayagua. The dam is 22 km. from Santa Cruz de Yojoa.

Thirty-two km. beyond Pito Solo is **Siguatepeque**, a town (population 39,165) with a cool climate. It is the site of the Escuela Nacional de Ciencias Forestales and, being exactly half-way between Tegucigalpa and San Pedro Sula, a collection point for the produce of Intibucá, La Paz and Lempira departments. The beautiful Cerro and Bosque de Calanterique, behind the Evangelical Hospital, is ¾ hour's walk from town centre. There are two central squares; most of the hotels and two cinemas are around one of them. *Hotel Gómez* is between the two.

Hotels and Restaurants   *Hotel Internacional Gómez*, T 73-21-26, E with bath, clean, use of kitchen on request; *Boarding House Central*, F, reasonable; *Versalles*, F; both have restaurants; *Mi Hotel*, 1 km. from main road, E, with bath, parking, restaurant. *Cafetería Ideal*, hamburgers and light lunches; *China Palace*, Chinese and international; *Pizzería y Restaurante Fiallos*, clean, varied menu, or eat in the market; on the Northern Highway there are several restaurants, best are *Nuevo* and *Antiguo Bethania*, good, abundant, inexpensive meals.

Exchange   Bancahsa, Banco Atlántida, Banco de Occidente.

Bus   to San Pedro Sula, ½ hourly, US$1.90; Tegucigalpa with Empresas Unidas or Maribel, US$1.50, 3 hrs. (Tegucigalpa-San Pedro Sula buses do not go into town, but leave passengers at junction 2 km. from town, easy to hitch); to Comayagua, Transpinares, US$0.50, 45 mins.

From Siguatepeque, a road (rebuilt, but it will not be paved for some time) goes through lovely forested mountainous country, SW via Jesús de Otoro (two basic *hospedajes*) to **La Esperanza** (98 km.). Capital of Intibucá Department, at 1,485 metres, this old colonial town is set in a pleasant valley. It has an attractive church in front of the park, and soldiers in a toy-like fort. There is a grotto carved out of the mountainside W of the town centre, a site of religious festivals. Good views. Market: Sun., at which Lenca Indians from nearby villages sell wares and food, including *junco* blankets. Nearby is Yaramanguila, an Indian village. The area is excellent for walking in forested hills, with lakes and waterfalls. In Dec.-Jan. it is very cold.

Hotels   There are simple but pleasant *pensiones*, e.g. *Hospedaje Mina*, F, adequate, 1 block E of market, food available; *Hotel Solis*, 1 block E of market, E (hot water extra), restaurant, rec.; *Rosario*, F, basic, on road to Siguatepeque; *San Cristóbal*, F; *San José*, 4 Av. Gen. Vásquez No. C-0005, F; *La Esperanza*, F, basic, clean, friendly, good meals; *Pensión Mejía Paz Batres*, 1 block W of Plaza, E with bath, F without, hot water, overpriced; *San José*, in same building as Farmacia La Esperanza, 2 blocks S of Plaza, F; *Hotel y Comedor San Antonio*, F; *La Rey*, clean and friendly, F.

Bus from La Esperanza to Tegucigalpa 0500 (Cobramil, also to San Pedro Sula) and 0530 (Joelito, 5½ hrs., US$2.60), to Siguatepeque 0700, 0900, last at 1000, US$1.75, 3 hrs.; bus, La Esperanza, Siguatepeque, Comayagua at 0600, buses from La Esperanza to the Salvadorean border; bus stops by market.

An unpaved road, bus 2 hrs. at 0800, runs from La Esperanza E to *Marcala* (1,300 metres—population 10,770), Department of La Paz (a paved road has been completed to La Paz). The Marcala region is one of the finest coffee-producing areas of Honduras. Cosude (Cooperación Suiza al Desarrollo) has different projects in the area, includung support to Lenca Indian ceramic production. There are caves nearby on Musula mountain, the Cueva de las Animas in Guamizales and Cueva de El Gigante in La Estanzuela with a high waterfall close by. Transport goes to La Florida (stay with priest, who has a collection of Indian artefacts) where there is good walking to Indian village of Opatoro and climbing Cerro Guajiquiro. *Fiesta* in honour of San Miguel Arcángel, last week of September.

Hotels *Medina* the most comfortable, modern with bath, F-E; *Ideal*; *Hospedaje Margoth*; *Hotel y Cafetería La Sureña*, all F-E. *Motel Montana*, E. Plenty of *comedores*; *Darwin*, excellent.

Buses Daily bus to Tegucigalpa (0400, US$2.65), via La Paz (bus from Tegucigalpa at 1000, except Sun., Empresa Lila, 4-5 Av., 7 C., No. 418 Comayagüela, opp. Hispano cinema); bus to La Paz only, 0800, 2 hrs.

NW from La Esperanza a very bad road runs to Santa Rosa de Copán (see above). There are a number of settlements including San Juan del Caite (with two *hospedajes*, helpful people and a Peace Corps worker). This is the turn-off for Erandique. The largest town on this road is *Gracias* (population 19,380). It is one of the oldest and most historic settlements in the country, dominated by the highest mountains in Honduras, Montañas de Celaque. There are 3 colonial churches, San Sebastián, Las Mercedes, San Marcos (a fourth, Santa Lucía, is 2½ km. SW of Gracias), and a restored fort, with two fine Spanish cannon, on a hill in the outskirts (the fort is being converted into a museum which will probably house military historical exhibits currently in Omoa). Some 5 km. from Gracias swim in hot, communal thermal pools in the forest, Agua Caliente (1 hrs. walk by a path, 1 hr. 20 mins. by the road, ask anyone, rec.).

Gracias was the centre from which Montejo, thrice Governor of Honduras, put down the great Indian revolt of 1537-38. Cáceres, his lieutenant, besieging Lempira the Indian leader in his impregnable mountain-top fortress at Cerquín, finally lured him out under a flag of truce, ambushed him and treacherously killed him. When the Audiencia de los Confines was formed in 1544 Gracias became for a time the administrative centre of Central America.

From Gracias buses go through coffee plantations to San Rafael (makeshift accommodation) from where one can walk to El Níspero (*pensión*) and catch a bus to Santa Bárbara. A strenuous 6-hr. hike east from Gracias by mule trail through a wilderness of forest and mountain leads to La Iguala, a tiny village attractively set between 2 rivers, magnificent colonial church. Irregular transport from/to Gracias.

It takes a whole day to climb the summit of Mount Celaque (2,849 metres, the highest point in Honduras) from Gracias. The trail begins from behind the visitors' centre being prepared for the Celaque National Park; it is recommended to carry a compass for the last part as it is hard to keep one's bearings in the dense cloud forest canopy (the most impressive in Honduras). Packhorses, and possibly a guide, may be hired from the Villa Verde community ½ hr. below the visitors' centre (animals cannot climb the last half of the trip). It is worthwhile just walking up to the visitors' centre, but the completion of trails higher up should make for beautiful hiking. Quetzales were seen near the summit by botanists in 1989.

For all information, contact Enrique López or Roy Romero at the Cohdefor (forestry) office just off the square in Gracias; or ask for the Peace Corps volunteer working on the project.

Hotels in Gracias *Erick*, hospedaje and shop, 1 block from square, opp. Escuela Normal in same street as bus office, F p.p., rec.; *Herrera*, G, clean, basic; *Hospedaje San Antonio*, on main street, N edge of town, F, good, clean; *Pensión Girón*, 2 Av. No. 76, F, basic; *Iris*, 2 Av. 40, opp. San Sebastián church, E, with restaurant and disco. Many *comedores* and cafeterias. *Comedor Elizabeth*. *La Nasa*, at bottom of the hill, O.K.; *Odiseo 2000*, one block from plaza, good, cheap, friendly; excellent *tacos* ½ block from main square.

Exchange Banco de Occidente, changes money.

Hondutel and Post Office 1 block S of square.

Buses One post bus per day to La Esperanza, wakes you at your hotel (0300, in theory); bus La Esperanza-Gracias at 1400 daily, US$1.75, 7 hrs. An alternative to La Esperanza is to take the daily 0530 bus to San Juan (collects you from your hotel), get off at El Crucero checkpoint (3 hrs.), 1 km. from San Juan, then hitch (police at the checkpoint will help), or rides can be taken on pick-up trucks for US$1.50; a plane trip costs US$8. There is also a bus service from Gracias to Santa Rosa de Copán, US$1.50, 0430, 0700, 1030, 1530, 2½ hrs. (**see page 498**); beautiful journey through majestic scenery. Cotral office is 1 block N of Plaza. A new road is under construction between Siguatepeque, La Esperanza, Gracias and Santa Rosa de Copán; it is due for completion in 1991.

South West from Gracias, up in the Celaque mountains is Belén Gualcho, with an impressive church and picturesque market on Sundays. There is also a route in from San Pedro de Copán near Cucuyagua on the highway between Santa Rosa and Nueva Ocotepeque.

Alban Johnson of Sandy Bay, Tasmania, and Jorge Valle-Aguiluz write: Roughly half way between Gracias and La Esperanza is San Juan del Caite (see above), from where a rough track runs 45 km. S to *Erandique* (*Pensiones*, of Reginaldo Muñoz, and Doña Bárbara Cruz, F; meals at the house of Doña María Felix de Inestroza, 2 other *comedores*). Set high in pine-clad mountains not far from the border with El Salvador, Erandique is a friendly town, and very beautiful. Lempira was born nearby, and was killed a few km. away. The third weekend in January is the local *fiesta* of San Sebastián. Best time to visit is at the weekend. Each of the three *barrios* has a nice colonial church. For the visitor there are lakes, rivers, waterfalls, springs and bathing ponds; you need to ask around. Nearby is San Antonio where fine opals are mined and may be purchased. There is only one road in the area, and it is impassable from July to October; transport to the many hamlets in the surrounding mountains is on foot or by horse (beware, it is very easy to get lost on the multitude of tracks). Despite what people say, there are minibuses to Erandique, but most people go by truck from Gracias or La Esperanza (US$2.25, very dusty).

Thirty-two km. beyond Siguatepeque the road dips into the rich Comayagua plain, part of the gap in the mountains which stretches from the Ulúa lowlands to the Gulf of Fonseca. In this plain lies

Comayagua, a colonial town of 59,535 people at about 300 metres, 1½ hrs.' drive N from the capital. It was founded on 7 December 1537 as Villa Santa María de Comayagua, on the site of an Indian village by Alonzo de Cáceres, Francisco de Montejo's lieutenant. On 3 September 1543, it was designated the Seat of the Audiencia de los Confines by King Felipe II of Spain. President Marco Aurelio Soto transferred the capital to Tegucigalpa in 1880. There are many old colonial buildings: the former University, the first in Central America, founded in 1632, closed in 1842 (it was located in the Casa Cural, Bishop's Palace, where the bishops have lived since 1558); the Cathedral (1685-1715—the clock in the tower comes from the Alhambra in Granada, donated by King Felipe II); the churches of La Merced (1550-58) and La Caridad (1730); San Francisco (1574); San Sebastián (1575). San Juan de Dios (1590, destroyed by earthquake in 1750), the church where the Inquisition sat, is now the site of the Santa Teresa Hospital. El Carmen was built in 1785. The most interesting building is the Cathedral in the Central Park, with its square plain tower and its decorated façade with sculpted figures of the saints, which contains some of the finest examples of colonial art in Honduras. The clock in the tower was originally made over 800 years ago in Spain; it was given to Comayagua by Philip II in 1582. At first it was in La Merced when that was the Cathedral, but moved to the new Cathedral in 1715. There are two colonial plazas shaded by trees and shrubs. A stone portal and a portion of the façade of Casa Real (the viceroy's residence) survives. It was built 1739-41, but was damaged by an earthquake in 1750 and destroyed by tremors in 1856. The army still uses a quaint old fortress built when Comayagua was the capital. There is a lively market area.

There are two museums nearby: the ecclesiastical museum (a small contribution is expected) and the anthropological museum (housed in the former presidential palace) with Indian artefacts (closed Monday). The latter is the less interesting of the two.

The US military base (recently renamed Soto Cano Airbase) at Palmerola, 8 km. from Comayagua, exerts a strong socio-economic and cultural influence over the entire Comayagua Valley, and the city itself. The base has English-language radio and TV stations.

Hotels *Halston*; *Norimax*, a/c, restaurant; *Libertad*, on Parque Central, F, much choice of room size, noisy, clean, but nothing to write home about; *Libertad Annex*, F with bath, cheaper without, as good as main hotel; *Emperador*, E-D, good but overpriced, a/c, cable TV, cafeteria, on the boulevard; *Imperial*, Barrio Torondón, E with bath and fan, attractive, parking; *Hospedaje Terminal*, E; *Boulevard*, F, small, clean, economic, dark rooms; *Motel Quan*, 8 C. N.O., 3 y 4 Av., excellent, E, with private bath, popular; *Quan Annex*, E; *Motel Puma*, off the same Boulevard, garage parking, hot water, E with bath (catering for short-stay clientèle).

Camping possible 2 km. N of town, beside the stream; beware of sandfleas.

Restaurants   Central Park is surrounded by restaurants and fast food establishments. *Casa Vieja*, near new cinema, good but overpriced; *China*, 3 blocks W of Plaza, good, but beware of the overpriced "tourist" menu; *Gran Muralla* on park, Chinese and international food, good; *Restaurant Central* (good, not the cheapest), *Sayvic* and *Flipper* in the central park serve ice cream, tacos, etc.; *Tuanis Burger Shop*, Calle de Comercio; *Pájaro Rojo* on main boulevard, expensive, food good; *Urbano's*, private house, 4 blocks SW of façade of the Cathedral, excellent meals and value). *Cafetería Central* (not to be confused with *Restaurant* on central park), *Palmeras*, S side of Central Park; some food in the market. In the Centro Turístico Comayagua is a restaurant, bar, disco, and swimming pool; good for cooling off and relaxing; Calle del Estadio Hispano, Barrio Arriba.

Exchange   Banco Atlántida, Banco de Occidente, Bancahsa, Bancahorro, Banco Sogerín.

Bus   To Tegucigalpa, US$1.10, every 45 mins., 2 hrs. (Catrachos—or walk 1¼ km. to highway and catch a quicker San Pedro Sula-Tegucigalpa bus); to Siguatepeque, US$0.40 with Transpinares. To San Pedro Sula, either catch a bus on the highway or go to Siguatepeque and change buses there.

Excursion   To the coffee town of La Libertad (hourly bus, 2 hrs., US$0.75), several *hospedajes* and *comedores*; a friendly place. Before La Libertad is Jamalteca (1½ hrs. by bus US$0.50), from where it is a 40-minute walk to a large, deep pool into which drops a 10 metre waterfall surrounded by lush vegetation. Here you can swim, picnic or camp, but it is on private property and a pass must be obtained from the owner (ask at Supermercado Carol in Comayagua). Best to avoid weekends, when the owners' friends are there.

A paved road runs S of Comayagua to *La Paz*, capital of its Department in the western part of the Comayagua valley. Population: 19,900. From the new church of the Virgen del Perpetuo Socorro, on the hill, there is a fine view of the town, the Palmerola military base, and the Comayagua Valley. A short road runs E from La Paz to Villa San Antonio on the highway to Tegucigalpa. 5 km. from La Paz is Ajuterique, which has a fine colonial church. Bus from Comayagua, Cotrapal (opp. Iglesia La Merced), every hour from 0600, passing Ajuterique (colonial church) and Lejamaní. Lila bus from the capital, from opp. Hispano cinema in Comayagüela. Colectivo from main N-S highway to La Paz, US$2..

Hotels   in La Paz: all F: *Córdoba* (with restaurant), *Pensión San Francisco* (cheaper, but nicer). *Hotelito Ali* (5 rooms), eat at *Ali's Restaurant* food and lodging excellent.

Exchange Bancahsa, Banco Atlántida, Banadesa.

A paved road runs SW from La Paz to Marcala (**see page** 505, frequent buses 2 hrs.). Along this road lies **Tutule**, the marketplace for the Indians of Guajiquiro (one of the few pure Indian communities in Honduras). Market: Thurs. and Sun. There are two minibus services a day from Marcala (US$1).

We are grateful to Robert Millar for the following description of the road from **San Pedro Sula to Tegucigalpa**: 46 km. S of San Pedro there is a paved road leading E through banana plantations to Santa Rita, thence either E to Yoro, or N to Progreso and Tela, thus enabling travellers between Tegucigalpa and the North Coast greatly to shorten their route by avoiding San Pedro Sula. An unpaved road right, at Caracol, leads up to Ojo de Agua (a pretty bathing spot), then on to El Mochito, Honduras' most important mining centre. This same turnoff at Caracol, marked "Río Lindo", also leads to Peña Blanca and Pulhapanzak with some unexcavated ceremonial mounds adjacent. On the northern shore of Lake Yojoa (**see page** 503) a paved road skirts the lake for 5 km. and a further 11 km. (unpaved) to Pulhapanzak. The main highway S skirts the eastern shore of the lake. 16 km. S of the lake at Taulabé is the turnoff northwest of a road (being paved) to Santa Bárbara (**see page** 498).

1 km. S of Taulabé uphill on the highway South are the caves of Taulabé (illuminated and with guides, open daily). The road now ascends an enormous forested escarpment of the continental divide to reach cool, forested highlands around Siguatepeque (**see page** 504). Proceeding S, the highway descends to the vast hot valley of Comayagua, skirting the old capital of Honduras with its colonial churches. At the southern end of the valley the road ascends another forested mountainous escarpment. After about 5 km. climb a track leading off to the left (ask for directions), with about half-an-hour's climb on foot to a tableland and natural fortress of Tenampua where Indians put up their last resistance to the *conquistadores*, even after the death of Lempira. Visitors last century rated Tenampua of equal importance archaeologically with Copán, but sadly it has now been looted of its treasures, except for an interesting wall and entrance portal.

The road continues its ascent through lovely forested heights to Zambrano and Parque Aurora (**see page** 485)—this spot would be perfect for camping and for caravans, which need to avoid the narrow streets and congestion of Tegucigalpa. The road then descends to the vast intermont basin of Támara; a turning right at the village leads to San Matías waterfall, another delightful area for walking in cool forested mountains. There is another entry to San Matías when the road S has once more climbed about 9 km. north-east of the capital.

FROM TEGUCIGALPA TO THE PACIFIC

A paved road runs S from the capital through fine scenery. Just off the highway is Sabanagrande, with an interesting colonial church (1809, Nuestra Señora del Rosario "Apa Kun Ka", the place of water for washing); *fiesta* La Virgen de Candelaria, 1-11 February. Further S is **Pespire**, a picturesque colonial village with a beautiful church. At **Jícaro Galán** (92 km.) the road joins the Pan-American Highway, which enters Honduras from El Salvador over the Santa Clara bridge at Goascarán and runs through **Nacaome**, where there is a 16th-century colonial church (5 *hospedajes*; *Intercontinental* in centre, basic but friendly, F), to Jícaro Galán (40 km.). A temporary pass can be purchased in Honduras for US$1.50 for a visit to the Salvadorean village of El Amatillo for an hour or so (many Hondurans cross to purchase household goods and clothes; towels are the best buy. Bus Tegucigalpa—El Amatillo, US$1.90, 4 hrs.). This border is very relaxed, with good rates of exchange with money changers. Border closes 1700 (one cheap *hospedaje* on the Honduran side). On the Pacific coast nearby is **San Lorenzo**, on the shores of the Gulf of Fonseca (21,025 people). The climate on the Pacific littoral is very hot, but healthy.

Hotels The only good modern hotel is the *Miramar* at San Lorenzo, 26 rooms, 4 air-conditioned, E. Also *Paramount*, E, and *Hospedaje Perla del Pacífico*, F, very basic. There are hotels of a sort at Goascarán (pop.: 2,190), Nacaome (pop. 4,474). At Jícaro Galán (pop.: 3,007) is *Oasis Colonial*, B, and an unnamed, basic guesthouse. Restaurants at all these places.

Frequent service of small *busitos* from Tegucigalpa to San Lorenzo (US$1) and to Choluteca (US$1.50).

The Pacific port of **Amapala** (7,925 people), on Tigre Island, has been replaced by Puerto de Henecán in San Lorenzo, reached by a 3.5 km. road which leaves the Pan-American Highway on the eastern edge of San Lorenzo. Amapala has a naval base, but otherwise it is "a charming, decaying backwater". Fishermen will take you—but not by motor launch— to San Lorenzo at a low charge: the trip takes half a day. It is possible to charter boats to La Unión in El Salvador. There is an airport, and a plane for the capital (35 mins.) can be chartered. The deep-sea fishing in the gulf is good. There is a passable bathing beach. *Hotel Playa Blanca Sur*, cabins, bar, restaurant, private beach, transportation, etc.; *Hotel Internacional* on the harbour, F, very basic; *Tino's Restaurant*, owned by Sr. Tino Monterrosa who has recently opened two bungalows (US$25 for 4, rooms at D); he also arranges fishing trips. Swimming at beautiful Playa Grande, 30 mins. walk from Amapala. The 1,000 metre volcano on the island may be climbed, best to start at 0500.

There is a daily direct bus service between Tegucigalpa and Tigre Island, except on Sunday, with Transportes CHE; leaving Tegucigalpa at 1130, 3-4 hrs. A new 31 km. road leaves the Pan-American Highway 2 km. W of San Lorenzo, signed to Coyolito (buses San Lorenzo-Coyolito). It passes through scrub and mangrove swamps before crossing a causeway to a hilly island, around which it winds to the jetty at Coyolito (no facilities). Motorized dugouts and a small car ferry cross to Amapala. Return journey starts at 0400 from Tigre Island.

The Pan-American Highway runs SE from Jícaro Galán past Choluteca and San Marcos de Colón to the Nicaraguan border at El Espino, on the Río Negro, 111 km., and NW from Jícaro Galán to the Salvadorean border at Goascarán, 40 km.: a total of 151 km. in Honduras.

Choluteca, 34 km. from San Lorenzo in the plain of Choluteca, has a population of 87,889, expanding rapidly. Coffee, cotton and cattle are the local industries. The town was one of the earliest foundations in Honduras (1535) and has still a colonial centre. The church of La Merced (1643) is now the Casa de la Cultura. The local feast day, of the Virgen de la Concepción, is December 8. The climate is very hot; there is much poverty here.

Hotels *Pierre*, Av. Valle y C. Williams, T 82-0676, C, with bath (ants in the taps) and a/c, D, with fan, central, free protected parking, cafeteria, very central, credit cards accepted, rec; *Lisboa*, Av. Rosa (by Transportes Mi Esperanza), E (some with bath), rec., laundry facilities, clean, good restaurant; *Pacífico*, also near Mi Esperanza terminal, outside the city, clean, quiet, E, breakfast US$1.50; *Tomalag*, moderately priced with bath and fan; *La Fuente*, Carretera Panamericana, C, with bath, rec., swimming pool, a/c, meals; *Rosita*, E, with bath, basic, friendly, good food; *Camino* Real, road to Guasaule, D, good steaks in restaurant, rec; *San Carlos*, F with shower, pleasant, Paz Barahona 757, Barrio El Centro; *Hibueras*, F, with bath and fan, clean, purified water, *comedor* attached, Av. Bojorque; *Motel Fraternidad*, E, on Panamericana. Local specialities are the drinks *posole* and *horchata de morro*.

Banco de Honduras is close to market, as are Post Office (US$0.15 per letter for post restante; telephone collect calls to Spain, Italy, USA only) and Banco Atlántida. Travel agency Trans Mundo. Good rates of exchange on the black market at Choluteca bus station (a fascinating place!). There is also a black market in Jícaro Galán. The Texaco service station, which is known as *Gringa Patricia's*, is very helpful in case of car trouble. Laundry, groceries and propane on sale. The campsite here is run by a Canadian, Elvin; shaded camping, showers, swimming pool, peaceful, pleasant, safe water supply, US$1. Mosquito repellant or netting may be needed.

Bus or taxi to El Espino (Nicaraguan border) from Choluteca, US$1.15, 1 hr., 0700. Mi Esperanza buses regularly to Tegucigalpa (US$1.90); bus station is 5 blocks from market. Taxis will wait at the border post as you go through the formalities and then take you into Nicaragua.

An hour's drive from Choluteca over an excellent road leads to Cedeño beach, very basic accommodation (inc. *Hotel Coco*) and poor meals—US$2 tp sleep on a dirt floor with cockroaches in beach shacks, US$3.75 for a basic room. A lovely though primitive spot, but becoming spoilt; avoid public holiday and weekend crowds. In the dry season, there is little fresh water, often none for bathing. Spectacular views and sunsets over the Gulf of Fonseca S to Nicaragua and W to El Salvador, with the volcanic islands in the bay. Turning for Cedeño is 13 km. W of Choluteca. Hourly bus from Choluteca, US$0.75 (1¼ hrs.). A turn off leads from Choluteca- Cedeño road to Ratón beach, much more pleasant than Cedeño, bus from Choluteca 0400, returns early next morning.

Beyond Choluteca is a long climb to **San Marcos de Colón**, 915 metres in the hills (a clean, tidy town of 9,570 people with plenty of eating places). 3 *pensiones* in San Marcos: *Colonial*, E, friendly, clean; a shabby *hospedaje* next door, F; *Hospedaje Flores*, F, friendly, clean, cell-like rooms, washing facilities, breakfast and typical dinner, good, exchange. Bus from Choluteca at 0700, US$0.75, 1½ hrs., one bus back at 1130; bus from Tegucigalpa, Mi Esperanza, 6 Av. 23 or 26 C., Comayagüela (office in San Marcos near Parque Central), from 0730. 6 km. beyond San Marcos the road enters Nicaragua at El Espino—a ghost town—(altitude 890 metres); immigration is 100 metres from the border. Taxis/minibuses run from Choluteca to the border. Entry and exit tax in Honduras, US$2.50, but on Sat. and Sun. officials may try to charge extra: ask for a receipt and/or bargain. Border closes between 1600 and 0800 (open till 1700 on the Nicaraguan side). Exchange is easy at the border for dollars, córdobas, Costa Rican colones, even Salvadorean colones, but the rate for buying córdobas is better on the Nicaraguan side, where you are obliged to change US$25 (cash or travellers' cheques) if in transit—under 24 hrs., or US$60 if staying longer in Nicaragua. Border formalities tedious at El Espino, do not allow yourself to show irritation at the Honduran officals' personal questions. Officials on the Nicaraguan side are more friendly. Americans and Europeans travelling N through Central America are advised to check with their embassies in San José, Costa Rica, to see if there are any restrictions on entering Honduras from Nicaragua. **N.B.** After floods in May 1982, the border bridge at Guasaule was washed away and the road Choluteca-Chinandega (Nicaragua) is closed.

EAST OF TEGUCIGALPA

A good paved road runs E from Tegucigalpa to Danlí, 121 km. away, in the Department of El Paraíso. Some 40 km. along, in the Zamorano valley (**see page** 483), is the Pan-American Agricultural School run for all students of the Americas with US help: it has a fine collection of tropical flowers. At Zamorano turn off up a narrow winding road for about 5 km. to the picturesque old mining village of **San Antonio de Oriente**, much favoured by Honduran painters such as Velásquez (it has a beautiful church). A little further along, an unpaved road branches S to **Yuscarán**, in rolling pine-land country at 1,070 metres (*Hospedaje Monserrat*, F, good value). The climate here is semi-tropical. Yuscarán was an important mining centre in colonial days and is a picturesque, typically Spanish colonial village, with cobbled streets and houses on a steep hillside. The Yuscarán distillery is considered by many to produce the best *aguardiente* in Honduras (tours possible). Cardomom plantations are being developed here. The Montserrat mountain which looms over Yuscarán is riddled with mines; the disused Guavias mine is about 4 km. along the road to Agua Fría, 10 km. to the SE by a steep, narrow, twisting and very picturesque road. Population, 9,270. For information, ask the lady who owns the *comedor* opposite the church in Yuscarán. From Zamorano, a road goes to Güinope (one hotel, F, several *comedores*) famed for its oranges and jam. Good walking in the area.

Danlí (100,800 people), a pleasant town, grows sugar for making *aguardiente* and is a centre of the tobacco industry. There are 7 cigar factories; visit the Honduras-América S.A. factory (opposite Ciné Aladino) and purchase export quality cigars at good prices. Museo Municipal in the municipality on the park. Its *fiesta* at the last weekend of August (Fiesta del Maíz, with cultural and sporting events, all-night street party on the Saturday) is very crowded with people from Tegucigalpa. One road continues from Danlí to Santa María, crossing a mountain range with panoramic views. Another goes S to **El Paraíso** (124 km. from the capital, hourly bus, US$1.80, 2 hrs.; 27,291 people), from which a connecting paved road links with the Nicaraguan road network at Las Manos/Ocotal. This is the better of the two routes from Tegucigalpa to the Nicaraguan border.

Hotels at Danlí Centro Turístico Granada with **Gran Hotel Granada**, bar, restaurant and swimming pool; *La Esperanza*, Gabriela Mistral, E, adjoining restaurant; *Danlí*, Calle del Carral, F without bath, good; *Las Vegas*, next to bus terminal, F, restaurant, washing facilities, parking; *Apolo*, del Canal, E, with bath; *Maya Ejecutivo*, C, with bath; *Regis*, F, with bath, basic; *Xalli*, F with bath, cheap, basic. **Restaurants**: *Pepy Lu's*, very good food at reasonable prices; *Rancho's Típico* nr. *Hotel Danlí*, excellent; *McBeth's*, snackbar, good ice cream. *Nan-kin 2*, Chinese. *Rodeo*, good food and service.

Hotels at El Paraíso *Eva*, E; *Florida*, F; *Recreo*, F. None recommended, lacking most basic facilities. Better stay in Danlí, 20 minutes away by good road.

Exchange in both towns, Bancahsa, Banco Atlántida, Banadesa, and other local banks.

Buses To Danlí, from near Mercado Jacaleapa, Colonia Kennedy, Tegucigalpa, 2 hrs., US$1.50, Emtra Oriente, Comayagüela, runs at 0830, 0910, 1230 and 1630 to El Paraíso, 2½ hrs., US$1.95; buses from El Paraíso to Las Manos.

From Danlí to the north is Cerro San Cristóbal; to the south Piedra de Apagüizto and the beautiful Lago San Julián.

NORTH-EAST OF TEGUCIGALPA

The Carretera de Olancho runs from the capital to the Río Guayape, 143 km., and continues another 50 km. to **Juticalpa** (capital of Olancho department), at 820 metres above sea-level in a rich agricultural area, herding cattle and growing cereals and sugar-cane. There is a gravel road N to Olanchito and a paved road NE through the cattle land of Catacamas, continuing to the coast at Cabo Camarón. A road is now completed from Catacamas through Dulce Nombre de Culmi, San Esteban, El Carbón and Durango to Trujillo. Paving started in 1989 on the Culmi-San Esteban section. Population 74,000. Airfield.

Hotels at Juticalpa *Antúñez*, Barrio El Centro, D with bath, E without; *El Paso*; *Las Vegas*, E; *Boarding House Honduras*, F. **Restaurants** *Danny's* and *El Centro*.

Catacamas, 210 km. from Tegucigalpa, is in the Río Guayape valley, at the foot of the Agalta Mountains in the Department of Olancho. It is an agricultural and cattle-raising district with the National School of Agriculture (ENA) in town, and El Sembrador school, which offers room and board. The Río Guayape (named after an Indian dress, *guayapis*) is famous for the gold nuggets found in it. During the hot months, the banks near the bridge are a popular bathing place, at Paso del Burro on the way to San Pedro Catacamas. From February to May you can taste the *vino de coyal*, extracted from a palm (a hole is made at the top of the trunk and the sap which flows out is drunk neat). With sugar added it becomes alcoholic (*chicha*), so strong it is called *pata de burro* (mule kick). *Fiesta* St Francis of Assisi, 4 October. Near Catacamas is the Río Talgua with interesting caves; worth a visit.

Hotels and Restaurants *Central*, *Juan Carlos* for lodging; *Los Castaños*, *El Rodeo* for food.

Bus Líneas Terrestres Aurora from Tegucigalpa to Juticalpa and Catacamas.

There is an adventurous bus service from Juticalpa to Trujillo (see page 490), via San Francisco de la Paz and San Esteban (*Hotel San Esteban*, F, expensive but clean; *Hospedaje Henríquez*), the last part being on a good, unpaved road; it passes through interesting scenery. The road is being paved; it passes through San Jerónimo, the setting of Paul Theroux's *The Mosquito Coast.*

Bus Tegucigalpa to Juticalpa/Catacamas, Empresa Aurora (8C. 615, Av. Morazán) 8 times a day, 3½ hrs. to Catacamas, US$2.75. Bus Catacamas-Dulce Nombre de Culmi (see below), 3 hrs., US$1.35, several daily; bus Juticalpa-San Esteban from opp. Aurora bus terminal at 1200, 6 hrs., US$2.25, very difficult in rainy season. Pick-up Juticalpa-Trujillo, US$7.50, whole day's journey.

The route by road from Tegucigalpa to Trujillo is 413 km. via Talanga, San Diego (restaurant *El Arriero*), Los Limones and Juticalpa (fill up with fuel here as there is none available until Trujillo). After Juticalpa, take the turn off, where the paved road ends, to San Francisco de la Paz. Beyond San Francisco is Gualaco, which has an interesting colonial church; from here to San Esteban you pass Agalta mountain and some of the highest points in Honduras, and the waterfalls on the Babilonia river. The road from San Esteban to Bonito Oriental (via El Carbón, a mahogany collection point with Paya Indian communities in the vicinity) is being paved. The final 38 km. from Bonito Oriental to Trujillo are paved, through Corocito. The alternative from Juticalpa via Catacamas is mentioned above.

Mosquitia is the name given to the region in the far NE of the country, which is forested, swampy and almost uninhabited, but well worth visiting. Apart from the one road that stretches 100 km. from Puerto Lempira to Leymus and a further 100 km. to Ahuasbila, both on the Río Coco, there are no roads in the Honduran Mosquitia. The Government has still to build the last stage of the Tegucigalpa-Puerto Lempira road, between Catacamas. Osmán Paz (private pilot) flies twice a week (may be contacted through Glenda at World Relief, Tegucigalpa, T 327667/326139/324578). The UN High Commission for Refugees (called ACNUR in Honduras) has daily flights (usually full); it is a good place to get information on flights, and if going to Mocorón a permit from ACNUR is essential (T Tegucigalpa 321995). Isleña flies from Tegucigalpa to Coyoles in Atlántida and to Mocorón/Puerto Lempira in Mosquitia. SAMi flies between Tegucigalpa and Mosquitia. Coastal vessels leave several times a week from La Ceiba to Brus Laguna and Puerto Lempira and back (2-3 day journey), carrying passengers and cargo. There are also refugee boats which are quicker. Essential equipment: torch.

Communication between Honduras and Nicaragua is not possible in Mosquitia but the Río Coco border area was reported safe to visit in 1988, but as well as an ACNUR permit, one must also be obtained from the army battalion outside Mocorón. This village is largely populated by refugees (*Chaly's,* accommodation F p.p., basic, meals for US$1.25, agent for Osmán Paz; ACNUR will find lodging for those staying a long time). Rus Rus may be visited with difficulty (in terms of getting permits and transport—any vehicle will give a lift); a beautiful, quiet village (accommodation at Friends of America hospital's house; meals from *Capi's* next door, ask Friends about transport out).

Robert Millar writes (with additional information from Grace Osakoda of Hawaii): Numerous large cayucos (canoes) with outboard motors cross the large **Caratasco Lagoon from Cauquira to Puerto Lempira** for about US$2.50. *Pensión Modelo*, F (good, friendly, electricity 1800-2230), and inferior *Pensión Santa Teresita*, F, at **Puerto Lempira**; *La Perla* restaurant, next to dock, fish meals US$1.75; *Restaurant Quinto Patio*, good breakfasts and information on refugee boats; generous meals at Doña Marina's for US$1.25 (Isleña flight tickets for La Ceiba may be bought here; Lansa tickets at *La Perla*). Contact helpful Reverend Stanley for almost daily flights in tiny Moravian mission plane to the Evangelical hospital at Ahuas; a 15-minute (US$15) scenic flight above Caratasco Lagoon and grassy, pine-covered savannas to **Ahuas**, one hour's walk from the Patuca River (fabled for gold). *Hospedaje y Comedor Suyapa*, F, basic, no electricity, meals, US$1.25; mosquito repellant and coils absolutely essential here. Irregular *cayucos* sail down to **Brus Laguna** (Brewer's Lagoon) for US$2.50, at one mouth of the Patuco River, or US$12.50 (15-mins.) scenic flight in the mission plane. George Goff rents rooms (good but basic, no electricity, F,) and has meals for US$1, he speaks English and runs the Lansa agency (flights to La Ceiba—he will also help with mission-plane flights). Behind his house is a *hospedaje* being built by the "Medio-Francés" (who speaks English, German, French, "Scandinavian" and Spanish); he plans to operate tours. Meals with Sarah de Eden, but plague of mosquitoes for all but 5 months of the year (winter and spring). Two tiny hilly islands near the entrance to the wide lagoon were hideouts where pirates once lurked. It is better to fly direct from Ahuas for US$15 via Brus and the mouth of the **Plátano River** to mosquito-free **Cocobila** (Belén), picturesquely situated on a sandspit between the ocean and huge, sweetwater Ibans Lagoon. (Nicaraguan refugee settlements S of here may be visited). Excellent meals (US$1.25) with Miss Erlinda, and room with Alfonso Molina who has a motor boat for **Paplaya** at the mouth of the Río Negro or Sico (bad mosquitoes), or walk the distance in over two hours along the beach. Malaria is endemic in this area; take anti-malaria precautions. Room and meals with Doña Juana de Woods at Paplaya. Boats to La Ceiba (US$11), or up the Río Sico (US$5) to Sico. Paplaya is the western terminal of the Honduran Mosquitia. Plátano village at the mouth of the Río Plátano can be reached by lobster boat from Guanaja or by the supply ships from La Ceiba to Brus Laguna (in all cases *cayucos* take passengers from ship to shore); Plátano-Brus Laguna, 1½ hrs., US$2.50, Plátano-La Ceiba, US$17.50.

The **Río Plátano Preserve** was established by the U.N. and the Honduran government in 1980 to protect the outstanding natural and cultural resources of Río Plátano valley and environs. The tropical jungles that still cloak the landscape here shelter a number of endangered birds, mammals, and fish, among them scarlet macaws and harpy eagles, jaguars and tapirs, and the cuyamel, a prized food fish going extinct throughout Honduras. In addition, there are a number of archaeological sites about which little is known, and the fabled lost White City of the Maya is said to be hidden somewhere in the thick jungles of the Plátano headwaters.

Miskito and Paya (who call themselves "Pech") Indians living along the lower Plátano cultivate yuca, bananas, rice, corn, and beans, as well as hunting and fishing. The upper (southern) portion of the Plátano watershed was virgin jungle until quite recently, but is being quickly populated by *mestizo* immigrants from the poverty-stricken south of Honduras. These new residents are cutting down the forest to plant crops, hunting wildlife mercilessly, and using homemade dynamite in a very destructive form of fishing. Given the pressure the Preserve is under, it is recommended to visit it sooner rather than later.

To get there, you can fly or take one of the boats that periodically leave from La Ceiba and Trujillo to either Palacios, Cocobila, Belén or Barra Río Plátano, the main villages in the vicinity of the river mouth. Expect to pay perhaps US$15-20 for passage from Ceiba. There are, however, regular daily commercial flights on Sosa and Isleña from La Ceiba to Belén, for US$40. From Belén to the Biosphere headquartes in Kuri it is a 45 min. walk or 10 min. ride (US$2). The staff are friendly and can probably put you up for the night free. They can also help you contract with a *tuk-tuk* (motorized dug-out canoe) to carry you upriver as far as Las Marías, the Miskito-Pech village that is the limit of upstream settlement. The cost is about US$70 one way, regardless of the number of passengers (up to 6) and takes 6-8 hours (3-4 downstream).

Once in Las Marías, it is possible to contract villagers for trips upstream in a *pipante*. This is a shallow dugout canoe manoeuvered with poles called *palancas* and paddles (*canaletes*): remarkably graceful. Each *pipante* can carry up to two passengers and their gear, plus three villagers who pole it upstream. The cost per day to rent *pipante* and crew is about US$12.50 per passenger (negotiable).

The rainy season is from June-December: it is harder to advance upriver then.

Palacios, situated in the next lagoon west of Paplaya, is mosquito-free; cannons are relics of an old English fort. Room for US$2.50 with Felix Marmol and meals for US$1. Lansa's Wednesday 6-seater plane (often booked up) flies for US$28 to La Ceiba or East to Brus/Puerto Lempira. When sea is calm, irregular sailings of the *Baltimore* or *Douglas*, US$11, go to La Ceiba. One can also cross the lagoon by *cayuco* (US$0.50) from Palacios to Black Carib village of Batalla, from which it is 112 km. W along beach to Limón where, in dry months March to May, there are buses to Tocoa, Trujillo and La Ceiba. The beach route is gruelling, past *morenales*, or Black Carib villages (honest, friendly) of Tocamacho (Reverend Donald Grable is a godsend to benighted travellers), Sangrelaya (Catholic mission), Siraboya (dry weather walk from here across forested mountain to Sico River, and downriver to Sico village); further W along the beach to Iriona Casuna and interminable stretch of 48 km. along the beach to Limón (this stretch is now inadvisable because of recent murders and robberies when crossing the beautiful forested headland at Farellones). One can take a picturesque *cayuco* trip from Paplaya up the Río Sico for US$4-5 to Sico village (possible food and meals with Edmund Jones—insist on paying him). A strenuous 32 km. walk from Sico (only in dry months from March to May) up forested Río Paulaya Valley to stay with Ray Jones, who has mined gold here for 60 years (insist on paying him too). One can also descend the Paulaya River from Dulce Nombre de Culmi, Olancho (*Hospedaje Tania*, G, very basic, on main street; several *comedores* on main square), 34 km. in the pick-up of "el Indio", then on foot or muleback over the Cerro de Will, staying en route with the *campesinos*, arriving in about three days at Mr. Ray's. (Local police say there is a footpath in the dry season from Dulce Nombre de Culmi to San Esteban). For notes on Nicaraguan Mosquitia see page 551.

INFORMATION FOR VISITORS

Documents Visa not required, nor tourist card, for nationals of West European countries (except Ireland, France, Austria, and Portugal) and Japan. Citizens of Canada, the USA, Australia, New Zealand require a visa and a tourist card which can be bought from Honduran consulates for US$2-3. Holders of the card must show proof of nationality. The price of a visa seems to vary per nationality, and according to where bought. At present visas are apparently not available for East European visitors.

Practice varies as to whether a visa can be bought at the border. For this reason it is imperative to check entry requirements in advance at a consulate. (For instance, Canadians do not officially require visas, but may have trouble without one.) 2-day transit visas costing US$5, for any travellers it seems, are given at the El Florida border for visiting Copán, but you must leave at the same point and your right of return to Guatemala is not guaranteed, especially if your Guatemalan visa is valid for one journey only.

Officials at land borders and airports allow only 30 days for visitors, regardless of arrangements made prior to arrival. Make sure border officials fill in your entry papers correctly and in accordance with your wishes. Extensions of 30 days are easy to obtain (up to a maximum of 6 months' stay, cost US$5). There are immigration offices for extensions at Tela, La Ceiba, San Pedro Sula, Santa Rosa de Copán, Siguatepeque, La Paz and Comayagua, and all are more helpful than the Tegucigalpa office. A valid International Certificate of Vaccination against smallpox is required only from visitors coming from the Indian subcontinent, Indonesia and the countries of southern Africa. A ticket out of the country is necessary for air travellers (if coming from USA, you won't be allowed on the plane without one); onward tickets must be bought outside the country. Proof of adequate funds is normally asked for at land borders. An entry and exit tax is charged to all but travellers in transit, US$2.50 each (and sometimes requested in dollars, though most recent (1990) information is of no exit tax). An additional US$1 "baggage inspection charge" is levied on bus passengers. Customs charge US$3.50 for "special Sunday service". It is advisable always to carry means of identification, since spot-checks have increased. Charges for motorists appear to be: on entry, US$2 for provisional permission from the police to drive in Honduras, US$1 (official minimum) for car papers, US$1 baggage inspection; on exit, US$1 to return permission, US$1 to have papers stamped and US$2 more for registration, etc. You can be fined if you do not have two reflecting triangles in your car. Be prepared for hassle from police and military, keep cameras and valuables hidden while driving. Bicycles are regarded as vehicles but are not subject to entrance taxes. No fresh food is allowed to cross the border and the interiors of cars are fumigated (US$2 on entry, with receipt). There is a fair amount of bribery at border crossings.

N.B. To enter, you must *not* have in your passport a stamp from a communist country (i.e. with which Honduras does not have diplomatic relations; this includes India); there is no official regulation concerning this, it is left to the individual judgement of border officials and therefore treatment may vary according to entry point. If going on to Nicaragua and needing a visa, do *not* get it before Tegucigalpa, otherwise you may have to pay US$25-40 for custodial transit through Honduras. This means a civil guard will accompany you (at your expense) until you cross into Nicaragua. You may be allowed this option if you have a communist country visa in your passport—see above. If coming from Nicaragua, all literature and maps concerning that country, even Nicaraguan produce, will be confiscated; if you have spent more than a month in Nicaragua you may not be allowed into Honduras (this regulation may be altered following the changes in the Nicaraguan government in 1990). There have been cases of tourists being deported for carrying left-wing literature.

Taxes There is an airport tax and hospital tax of 3% on all tickets sold for domestic journeys, and a 10% tax on airline tickets for international journeys. There is an airport departure tax of US$10 and a customs tax of US$3 (neither charged if in transit less than 9 hrs.). Note that the border offices close at 1700, not 1800 as in most other countries; there is an extra fee charged after that time.

How to get there From London: British Airways, Pan Am, Continental or Virgin Atlantic to Miami, then American Airlines or TAN to Tegucigalpa. Also from Miami, Taca via San Salvador; to Tegucigalpa from New Orleans and Houston with Sahsa and Taca (via San Salvador); Lacsa flies to San Pedro Sula from New York, New Orleans, Los Angeles and Cancún. Sahsa flies from Tegucigalpa to all Central American capitals, and to San Andrés Island; Lacsa flies to San José from San Pedro Sula direct; TAN flies to Mexico City and Belize City direct while Taca flies to Mexico City and Guatemala as well as to San Salvador. Aerovías de Guatemala flies between San Pedro Sula and Guatemala City. Connections with Curaçao are made at Guatemala City (KLM/Taca). From Europe: Iberia twice weekly to Guatemala City, connecting with Sahsa; KLM have the same connection; alternatively, fly to Miami and on from there.

N.B. If you are flying from Honduras to a country that requires an onward ticket, Sahsa will not let you board their planes without it. If you are flying TAN from Miami to Tegucigalpa, be warned that your luggage may be left behind in the USA arriving or more days later (1990).

Customs There are no Customs duties on personal effects; 200 cigarettes or 100 cigars, or ½ kg. of tobacco, and 2 quarts of spirit are allowed in free.

Internal Flights There are airstrips in the larger and smaller towns. Sahsa, Aero Servicios, SAMi and Isleña have daily services between Tegucigalpa, San Pedro Sula, La Ceiba, and the Caribbean coastal towns and islands.

Internal Land Transport Buses tend to start early in the day; very few leave late afternoon or evening, which may make onward connections difficult. Hitch-hiking is relatively easy. If hiring a car, make sure it has the correct papers, and emergency triangles which are required by law. **N.B.** There are frequent police searches on entry or exit from towns and villages. You must stop at Puestos de Tránsito, indicated by "Alto Repórtese" signs (usually in smaller letters than the Coca Cola or other *refresco* advert on the sign).

Food Cheapest, meals are the *comida corriente* or (sometimes better prepared and dearer) the *comida típica*; these usually contain some of the following: beans, rice, meat, avocado, egg, cabbage salad, cheese, *plátanos*, potatoes or yuca, and always tortillas. Pork is not rec. as pigs are often raised on highly insanitary swill. *Carne asada* from street vendors, charcoal roasted and served with grated cabbage between tortillas is good, though rarely sanitarily prepared. *Tajadas* are crisp, fried *plátano* chips topped with grated cabbage and sometimes meat; *nacatamales* are ground, dry maize mixed with meat and seasoning, boiled in banana leaves. *Baleadas* are soft flour tortillas filled with beans and various combinations of butter, egg, cheese and cabbage. Good, filling and always cheap, whether on the street, in *comedores* or restaurants. *Pupusas* are thick corn tortillas filled with chicharrón (pork sausage), or cheese, served as snacks with beer. *Tapado* is a north coast fish stew with plantain, bananas and coconut milk. *Pinchos* are meat, poultry, or shrimp kebabs. *Sopa de mondongo* (tripe soup) is very common.

Cheap fish is best found on the beaches at Trujillo and Cedeño and on the shores of Lake Yojoa. While on the north coast, look for *pan de coco* (coconut bread) made by *garifuna* (Black Carib) women.

Drink Soft drinks are called *refrescos*, or *frescos*, the name also given to fresh fruit blended with water; *licuados* are fruit blended with milk. *Horchata* is rice water and cinnamon. Coffee is thick and sweet. There are 4 brands of beer, Port Royal Export, Nacional, Imperial and Salvavidas (more malty than the other 3).

Tipping Normally 10% of bill.

Shopping The best articles are those in wood: straw baskets, hats, etc., are also highly rec. Leather is cheaper than in El Salvador and Nicaragua, but not so cheap as in Colombia. The coffee is good. Note that film is expensive.

Health Dysentery and stomach parasites are common and malaria is endemic in coastal regions, where a prophylactic regime should be undertaken and mosquito nets carried. Inoculate against typhoid and tetanus. Drinking water is definitely not safe; drink bottled water, if you can find it. Otherwise boil or sterilise water. Salads and raw vegetables must be sterilized under personal supervision. There are hospitals at Tegucigalpa and all the larger towns. Excellent ointments for curing the all-too-prevalent tropical skin complaints are Scabisan (Mexican) and Betnovate (Glaxo).

Hours of Business Mon. to Fri.: 0900-1200; 1400-1800. Sat.: 0800-1200, and some open in the afternoon. Banks in Tegucigalpa 0900-1500; 0800-1100 only along the N coast on Sat. In San Pedro Sula and along the N coast most places open and close half an hour earlier in the morning and afternoon than in Tegucigalpa. Post Offices: Mon.-Fri. 0700-2000, Sat. 0800-1200.

Clothing Western; suits optional for most businessmen; on the north coast, which is much hotter and damper, dress is less formal. Laundering is undertaken by most hotels.

British business travellers planning a visit should get a copy of "Hints to Exporters: Honduras", on application to Dept. of Trade, Export Services Division, Sanctuary Buildings, 16/20 Great Smith Street, London SW1P 3DB.

Public Holidays Most of the feast days of the Roman Catholic religion and also 1 January: New Year's Day.; 14 April: Day of the Americas; Holy Week: Thurs., Fri., and Sat., before Easter Sunday; 1 May: Labour Day; 15 September: Independence Day; 3 October: Francisco Morazán; 12 October: Discovery of America; 21 October: Army Day.

Official Time 6 hours behind GMT.

Currency The unit is a lempira. It is divided into 100 centavos. There are copper coins of 1 and 2 centavos and nickel or silver coins of 5, 10, 20, and 50 centavos. US visitors will find that many coins are exactly the same size and material as US coins of equivalent value; hence the 20 centavos is a "dime". A *real* is 12½ centavos (there are no coins of this value, but the term is much used). Bank notes are for 1, 2, 5, 10, 20, 50 and 100 lempiras. Any amount of any currency can be taken in or out.

Note With the floating of the lempira against the dollar in 1990, Honduras has become a much cheaper country for visitors travelling with US dollars. If no further changes are made to the exchange rate régime, accommodation and transport prices may be less than shown in the book, in dollar terms.

Weights and Measures The metric system of weights is official and should be used. Land is measured in *varas* (838 mm.) and *manzanas* (0.7 hectare).

Electric Current generally 110 volts. US-type flat-pin plugs.

Air Mail takes 4 to 7 days to Europe and the same for New York. Airmail costs 85 centavos for a letter to N America (1 lempira to Europe), 60 centavos for a postcard (80 centavos to Europe); aerograms (not easy to find), 75 centavos.

Telephones Hondutel provides international telephone and telex services from stations at Tegucigalpa, San Pedro Sula, Puerto Cortés, Tela, La Ceiba, Comayagua, Siguatepeque, Santa Rosa de Copán, Danlí, Choluteca, Juticalpa, La Paz, La Lima, El Progreso, Valle de Angeles, El Paraíso, Catacamas and Marcala.
    Telephone service between Honduras and Britain costs about L40 for a 3-min. call; calls to USA L22 for 3 mins. Collect calls to N America and Europe can be made from Hondutel office in Tegucigalpa.

Media The principal **newspapers** in Tegucigalpa are *El Heraldo* and *La Tribuna*. In San Pedro Sula: *El Tiempo* and *La Prensa* (circulation about 45,000). None is of very high quality.
    There are 6 television channels and 167 broadcasting stations.

Language Spanish, but English is spoken in the N, in the Bay Islands, by West Indian settlers on the Caribbean coast, and is understood in most of the big business houses. Trade literature and correspondence should be in Spanish.

We are most grateful to Jorge Valle-Aguiluz (Tegucigalpa), for a complete revision of the Honduras chapter, Linda Casey (Okemos, Michigan), James Fraser Darling and Richard Tucker (UK and USA), Ronald Janssen (Utila), Thomas A. Kelley Jr. (Northampton, MA), Robert Millar (Tela) for more useful comments and updatings and Tyll V. Sass (Roatán); also to other travellers whose names are listed in the general Central America section.

WILL YOU HELP US?

We do all we can to get our facts right in **The Mexico & Central American Handbook.** Each chapter is thoroughly revised each year, but the territory covered is vast, and our eyes cannot be everywhere.

Your information may be far more up-to-date than ours. If your letter reaches us early enough in the year it will be used in the next edition, but write whenever you want to, for all your letters are used sooner or later.

Thank you very much indeed for you help.

Trade & Travel Publications Limited
6 Riverside Court
Riverside Road
Lower Bristol Road
Bath BA2 3DZ. England

NICARAGUA

INTRODUCTION

NICARAGUA (128,000 square km.), the same size as England and Wales, is the largest Central American republic. It has 541 km. of coast on the Caribbean and 352 km. on the Pacific. Costa Rica is to the S, Honduras to the N. Only 8% of the whole country, out of a possible 28%, is in economic use.

There are three well-marked regions. (1) A large triangular-shaped central mountain land whose apex rests almost on the southern border with Costa Rica; the prevailing moisture-laden NE winds drench its eastern slopes, which are deeply forested with oak and pine on the drier, cooler heights. (2) A wide belt of eastern lowland through which a number of rivers flow from the mountains into the Atlantic. (3) The belt of lowland which runs from the Gulf of Fonseca, on the Pacific, to the Costa Rican border south of Lake Nicaragua. Out of it, to the E, rise the lava cliffs of the mountains to a height of from 1,500 to 2,100 metres. Peninsulas of high land jut out here and there into the lowland, which is from 65 to 80 km. wide along the Pacific.

In this plain are two large sheets of water. The capital, Managua, is on the shores of Lake Managua, 52 km. long, 15 to 25 wide, and 39 metres above sea-level. The river Tipitapa drains it into Lake Nicaragua, 148 km. long, about 55 km. at its widest, and 32 metres above the sea; Granada is on its shores. Launches ply on the Río San Juan which drains it into the Caribbean.

Through the Pacific lowland runs a row of volcanoes. The northernmost is the truncated zone of Cosegüina, overlooking the Gulf of Fonseca; then the smoking San Cristóbal, the highest of them all; a number of smaller volcanoes, of which Cerro Negro was built up during its last eruption in 1971; and the famous Momotombo, which normally smokes a little and now has a geothermal power station at its foot.

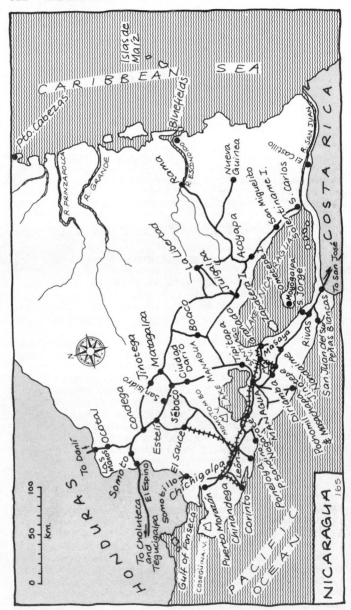

NICARAGUA

165

Around Managua, even in the city centre, there are small craters, but none is active. Further south is the twin cone of Masaya/Santiago, which stopped smoking in late 1986. In Lake Nicaragua is the beautiful Concepción, the second highest, on the Isla de Ometepe, on which also stands the extinct Las Maderas. The volcanic chain continues northwest into El Salvador and to the south into Costa Rica. The volcanic ash makes rich soil for crops.

Climate The wet, warm winds off the Caribbean pour heavy rain on the Atlantic coastal zone, especially in the southern basin of the San Juan river, with more than six metres annually. While the dry season on the Atlantic coast is only short and not wholly dry, the Pacific dry season, or summer (November to April), becomes very dusty, especially when the winds begin to blow in February. There is a wide range of climates. According to altitude, average annual temperatures vary between 15°C and 35°C. Mid-day temperatures at Managua range from 30° to 36°C, but readings of 38° are not uncommon from March to May, or of 40° in January and February in the West. It can get quite cold, especially after rain, in the Caribbean lowlands. Maximum daily humidity ranges from 90% to 100%.

History The Spanish *conquistadores* reached the lowland from Panama as early as 1519. On the south-western shores of Lake Nicaragua they found an area comparatively densely settled by peaceful Indians, who lavished gold ornaments on them. Five years later another expedition founded colonies at Granada and León, but the flow of gold soon stopped and most of the Spaniards moved elsewhere. In 1570 both colonies were put under the jurisdiction of Guatemala. The local administrative centre was not rich Granada, with its profitable crops of sugar, cocoa, and indigo, but impoverished León, then barely able to subsist on its crops of maize, beans and rice. This reversal of the Spanish policy of choosing the most successful settlement as capital was due to the ease with which León could be reached from the Pacific. In 1858 Managua was chosen as a new capital as a compromise, following violent rivalry between Granada and León.

For more on Nicaragua's early history, see the introductory chapter to Central America. The country became an independent state in 1838. The famous (or infamous) filibustering expedition of William Walker is often referred to in the text. William Walker (1824-1860) was born in Nashville, Tennessee, graduated at the University in 1838, studied medicine at Edinburgh and Heidelberg, was granted his M.D. in 1843, and then studied law and was called to the bar. On 5 October, 1853, he sailed with a filibustering force to conquer Mexican territory, declared Lower California and Sonora an independent republic and was then driven out. In May 1855, with 56 followers armed with a new type of rifle, he sailed for Nicaragua, where Liberal Party leaders had invited him to help them in their struggle against the Conservatives. In October he seized a steamer on Lake Nicaragua belonging to the Accessory Transit Company, an American corporation controlled by Cornelius Vanderbilt, He was then able to surprise and capture Granada and make himself master of Nicaragua as Commander of the Forces. Two officials decided to use him to get control of the Transit Company; it was seized and handed over to his friends. A new Government was formed and in June 1856 Walker was elected President. On 22 September, to gain support from the southern states in America he suspended the Nicaraguan laws against slavery. His government was formally recognized by the US that year. A coalition of Central American states, backed by Cornelius Vanderbilt, fought against him, but he was able to hold his own until May 1857, when he surrendered to the US Navy to avoid capture. In November 1857, he sailed from Mobile with another expedition, but soon after landing near Greytown, Nicaragua, he was arrested and returned to the US. In 1860 he sailed again from Mobile and landed in Honduras. There he was taken prisoner by Captain Salmon, of the British Navy, and handed over to the Honduran authorities, who tried and executed him on 12 September, 1860. Walker's own book, *The War in Nicaragua*, is a fascinating document.

In 1909, US Marines assisted Nicaraguan Conservative leaders in an uprising to overthrow the Liberal president, José Santos Zelaya. In 1911 the United States pledged help in securing a loan to be guaranteed through the control of Nicaraguan customs by an American board. In 1912 the United States sent marines into Nicaragua to enforce the control. Apart from short intervals, they stayed there until 1933. During the last five years of occupation, nationalists under General César Augusto Sandino waged relentless guerrilla war against the US Marines. American forces were finally withdrawn in 1933, when President Franklin Roosevelt announced the "Good Neighbour" policy, pledging non-intervention. An American-trained force, the Nicaraguan National Guard, was left behind, commanded by Anastasio Somoza García. Somoza's men assassinated General Sandino in February 1934 and Somoza himself took over the presidency in 1936. From 1932, with brief intervals, Nicaraguan affairs were dominated by General Anastasio Somoza until he was assassinated in 1956. His two sons both served a presidential term and the younger, Gen. Anastasio Somoza Debayle, dominated the country from 1963 until his deposition in 1979; he was later assassinated in Paraguay.

The 1978-79 revolution against the Somoza government by the Sandinista guerrilla organization (loosely allied to a broad opposition movement) resulted in extensive damage and many casualties (estimated at over 30,000) in certain parts of the country, especially in Managua, Estelí, León, Masaya, Chinandega and Corinto. After heavy fighting General Somoza resigned on 17 July, 1979 and the Government was taken over by a Junta representing the Sandinista guerrillas and their civilian allies. Real power was exercised by nine Sandinista *comandantes* whose chief short-term aim was reconstruction. A 47-member Council of State formally came into being in May, 1980; supporters of the Frente Sandinista de Liberación Nacional had a majority. Elections were held on 4 November, 1984 for an augmented National Constituent Assembly with 96 seats; the Sandinista Liberation Front won 61 seats, and Daniel Ortega Saavedra, who had headed the Junta, was elected president. The Democratic Conservatives won 14 seats, the Independent Liberals 9 seats and the Popular Social Christians

6 (the Socialists, Communists and Marxists/Leninists won 2 seats each). The failure of the Sandinista government to meet the demands of a right-wing grouping, the Democratic Coordinating Board (CDN), led to this coalition boycotting the elections and to the US administration condemning the poll as a "sham".

Despite substantial official and private US support, anti-Sandinista guerrillas (the "contras") could boast no significant success in their war against the Government. In 1988, the Sandinistas and the contras met for the first time to discuss the implementation of the Central American Peace Plan drawn up by President Oscar Arias Sánchez of Costa Rica, and signed in August 1987. To comply with the Plan, the Nicaraguan government made a number of political concessions. By 1989 the contras, lacking funds and with diminished numbers, following a stream of desertions, appeared to be a spent force; some participated in general elections held on 25 February 1990. The Sandinista government brought major improvements in health and education, but the demands of the war against the contras and a complete US trade embargo did great damage to the economy as a whole. The electorate's desire for a higher standard of living was reflected in the outcome of the elections, when the US-supported candidate of the free market National Opposition Union (UNO), Mrs Violeta Chamorro, won 55.2% of the vote, compared with 40.8% for President Ortega. The 14-party alliance, UNO, won 52 seats in the National Assembly, the FSLN 38 and the Social Christian Party one seat. Mrs Chamorro, widow of the proprietor of *La Prensa*, who was murdered by General Somoza's forces in 1978, took office on 25 April 1990. The USA was under considerable pressure to provide substantial aid for the alliance it created and promoted. The contras began disarming on 25 April and were to demobilize completely by 10 June. However, progress was in doubt when several commanders refused to order their troops to disarm following the announcement by President Chamorro that General Humberto Ortega would continue temporarily as head of the armed forces. In a separate agreement with the Sandinistas, it had been decided that he should stay until the contra demobilization, and a parallel reduction of the armed forces, was completed.

Note While the information given in this chapter was valid at the time of going to press, we expect imminent changes following the elections of 1990. These may affect availability of goods in shops, transport fares, exchange procedures, working on brigades, visa requirements and border formalities.

The People Population density is low: 31.1 persons to the square km., as compared with El Salvador's 244.2. An odd feature for a country so slightly industrialized is that 60% of its people live in towns and urban population growth is 4.5% a year. Nine in ten of the 3.75m people of Nicaragua live and work in the lowland between the Pacific and the western shores of Lake Nicaragua, the south-western shore of Lake Managua, and the south-western sides of the row of volcanoes. It is only of late years that settlers have taken to coffee-growing and cattle-rearing in the highlands at Matagalpa and Jinotega. Elsewhere the highlands, save for an occasional mining camp, are very thinly settled.

The densely forested eastern lowlands fronting the Caribbean were neglected, because of the heavy rainfall and their consequent unhealthiness, until the British settled several colonies of Jamaicans in the 18th century at Bluefields and San Juan del Norte (Greytown). But early this century the United Fruit Company of America (now United Brands) opened banana plantations inland from Puerto Cabezas, worked by blacks from Jamaica. Other companies followed suit along the coast, but the bananas were later attacked by Panama disease and exports today are small. Along the Mosquito coast there are still English-speaking communities in which African, or mixed African and indigenous, blood predominates. Besides the *mestizo* intermixtures of Spanish and Indian blood (69%), there are pure blacks (8%), pure Indians (4%), and mixtures of the two (mostly along the Atlantic coast). A small proportion is of pure Spanish and European blood. Death rate is 8.0 per 1,000; birth rate, 41.8; infant mortality, 61.7; life expectancy, 60 years males, 62 years females. Annual population growth: 3.4%.

The Economy Nicaragua's economy showed a fairly stable average annual growth rate over the two decades up to 1977, despite sharp fluctuations from year to year as agricultural production and world commodity prices varied. The economy is based on agriculture, principal export items being cotton, coffee, sugar, beef, seafood and bananas. The Government encouraged a diversification of exports, and exports of tobacco and other agricultural products gained in importance. At present agriculture constitutes 24% of gdp but employs 33% of the labour force and is responsible for by far the largest proportion of exports. Land reform was actively undertaken by the Sandinistas. Agricultural land under permanent cultivation is only 11% of the total, although pasture lands account for 44%. A third of the land is forested. In the 1970s substantial industrialization developed, mainly through foreign investment. Main industries are food processing (sugar, meat, shrimps), textiles, wood, chemical and mineral products. There are few mineral resources in Nicaragua; although gold, copper and silver are mined, they are of little importance to the overall economy.

Since the late 1970s gdp has fallen, starting with a decline of 29% in 1979, although there have been a few years of growth. The huge variations have been caused by guerrilla insurgency, the US trade embargo, fluctuations in Central American Common Market trade, floods, drought and changing commodity prices. Growth has usually been led by agriculture when weather, international prices and political conditions have been favourable.

Inflation, which had been traditionally low, has been a problem since the 1972 earthquake; it rose to 84% in 1979 as a result of the civil war, moderating to an average of 30% in 1980-84. As an effect of insurgency requiring heavy budget spending on defence and other difficulties, the rate shot up to an estimated 750% in 1986, 1,200% in 1987 and 24,000% in 1988, while the public sector deficit rose to 27% of gnp. In 1988 a new currency was introduced as part of an anti-inflation package which realigned prices of the dollar and basic goods, but neither this nor subsequent economic packages succeeded in eliminating inflation. Nicaragua is dependent upon foreign aid, which averaged US$600m a year in 1980-89, of which the USSR is believed to have granted nearly half. The EEC and Canada were the other major donors. There have been no new investment projects for several years. Nicaragua's foreign debt, including arrears, amounts to some US$7.6bn, but reduced foreign exchange earnings in the mid-1980s (partly because of the US blockade) made it impossible for the Government to service the debt.

In 1990 the US-supported Government of Pres. Violeta Chamorro took office amid great optimism that the economy could be revived on the back of renewed trade with the USA. Trade sanctions were lifted and the US Congress was asked to provide US$300m in aid immediately, to be followed by a further US$200m. Other countries were also asked for substantial aid. These funds were to be used to resume debt service to the IMF and multilateral development agencies, for economic restructuring, for agricultural, oil and medical supplies, to rebuild bridges, schools, roads and hospitals and repatriate and resettle the contra rebel forces and other refugees. However disbursement took longer than hoped and the new administration operated in extremely straightened circumstances.

Government A new Constitution was approved by the 96-member National Constituent Assembly in 1986 and signed into effect on 9 January 1987. Legislative power is vested in a unicameral, directly elected National Assembly of 960 representatives, each with an alternate representative, with a six-year term. In addition, unelected presidential and vice presidential candidates become representatives and alternates respectively if they receive a certain percentage of the votes. Executive power is vested in the President, assisted by a Vice President and an appointed Cabinet. The Presidential term is six years.

Ports and Communications The main Pacific ports are Corinto, San Juan del Sur and Puerto Sandino. The two main Atlantic ports are Puerto Cabezas and Bluefields. The **roads** have been greatly extended and improved. The Pan-American Highway from the Honduran border to the borders of Costa Rica (384 km.), is paved the whole way and so is the shorter international road to the Honduran frontier via Chinandega (though the frontier here is closed); the new road between Managua and Rama (for Bluefields) is almost all paved and in good condition. There are now 14,997 km. of road, 1,650 paved and 1,300 km. all-weather. There is only one **railway**, the Ferrocarril del Pacífico, 349 km. long, single track, with a gauge of 1.067 metres.

Religion and Education Roman Catholicism is the prevailing religion, but there are Episcopal, Baptist, Methodist and other Protestant churches. Illiteracy has been reduced by a determined government campaign: 88% of the population, it is estimated, can now read and write. Higher education at the Universidad Nacional Autónoma de Nicaragua at León, with 3 faculties at Managua, and the private Jesuit

Universidad Centroamericana (UCA) at Managua is good (with strong Sandinista links). There are two, separate Universidades Nacionales Autónomas de Nicaragua (UNAN).

MANAGUA

Managua, the nation's capital and commercial centre since 1858, is on the southern shores of Lake Managua, at an altitude of between 40 and 150 metres. It is 45 km. from the Pacific, but 140 km. from the main port, Corinto, though a new port, Puerto Sandino (formerly Puerto Somoza), is only 70 km. away. Managua was destroyed by earthquake in March 1931, and part of it swept by fire five years later; it was completely rebuilt as an up-to-date capital and commercial city (population 850,000) but the centre was again completely destroyed, apart from a few modern buildings, by another earthquake in December 1972. There was further severe damage during the Revolution of 1978-79.

The Sandinista Government decided that the old centre should be rebuilt, adding parks and recreational facilities (one such has opened E of Avenida Central, the tourist office is located here), although it is anticipated that this project will take years to complete. Present-day Managua has no centre as such, but rather consists of a series of commercial developments in what used to be the outskirts of the old city. No street names are in evidence, and the overall effect can be disconcerting. Directions are given according to landmarks; in place of cardinal points, the following are used: Al Lago (N), Arriba (E), Al Sur (S), Abajo (W). (**N.B.** This applies to the whole country, even where there are street names or numbers, Nicaraguans give direction by landmarks).

The principal commercial areas of Managua are now situated on the Masaya road and the two bypass roads S of the city. These centres contain a wide variety of shops, modern cinemas and discotheques.

In the old centre of Managua, one can still see examples of colonial architecture in the Palace of the Heroes of the Revolution (previously the National Palace) and the Cathedral. The Cathedral is open, although its interior is in ruins, and its exterior cracked. These buildings are situated on the Parque Central and provide a striking contrast with the modern Ruben Darío theatre on the lake shore (good plays and musical events, entry US$1.50; also Teatro Experimental) and the Banco de América building in the background. At the Iglesia Santa María de los Angeles a Catholic/secular mass is held each Sunday at 1730 (very popular).

Fiesta Santo Domingo is the patron saint of Managua. His festival is held at El Malecón from 1 to 10 August: church ceremonies, horse racing, bull-fights, cock-fights, a lively carnival; proceeds to the General Hospital. 1 August (half day) and 10 August are local holidays.

Hotels Hotel bills must be paid in US dollars, except where indicated. Several hotels have been built along the highway that bypasses the old part of the city, but there is still a shortage. Try to choose a central hotel (i.e. near *Intercontinental* or Plaza España) since transport to the outskirts is so difficult. There are, however, 2 good hotels close to the airport, *Camino Real*, A, shuttle

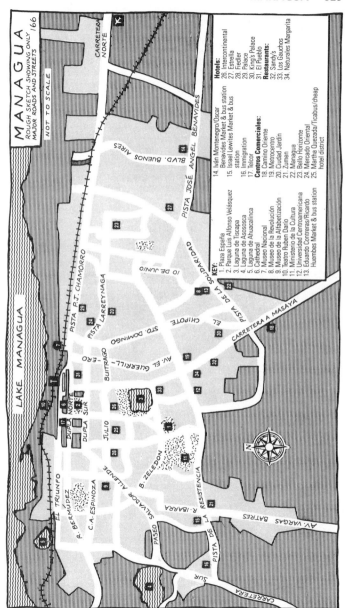

MANAGUA
ROUGH SKETCH SHOWING ONLY
MAJOR ROADS AND STREETS /66

NOT TO SCALE

LAKE MANAGUA

KEY:
1. Plaza España
2. Parque Luis Alfonso Velásquez
3. Laguna de Tiscapa
4. Laguna de Asososca
5. Laguna de Ahuacalinca
6. Cathedral
7. Museo Nacional
8. Museo de la Revolución
9. Museo de la Alfabetización
10. Teatro Rubén Darío
11. Ministerio de la Cultura
12. Universidad Centroamericana
13. Huembes Market & bus station
14. Iván Montenegro/Oscar Benavides Market & bus station
15. Israel Lewites Market & bus station
16. Immigration
17. Telcor

Centros Comerciales:
18. Camino Oriente
19. Metrocentro
20. Ciudad Jardín
21. Zumen
22. Managua
23. Bello Horizonte
24. Mercado Oriental
25. Martha Quezada/Ticabus/cheap hotel district

Hotels:
26. Intercontinental
27. Estrella
28. Fiedler
29. Palace
30. King's Palace
31. El Pueblo

Restaurants:
32. Sandy's
33. Los Gauchos
34. Naturales Margarita

bus to the airport free, no English spoken, restaurant, live music; and *Las Mercedes*, B, good food, pleasant hotel, opp. airport, swimming pool, local phone calls can be made here when airport office is shut. There is regular water rationing and most hotels do not have large enough water tanks. The government stipulates a small additional charge for rooms with a telephone (whether used or not).

Intercontinental, just N of Calle Colón, L, service poor, sauna, use of swimming pool for non-residents on Sunday, US$3, do not take photographs in vicinity as it is surrounded by military areas; *Casa Serrano*, 3 streets N of Sears (T 2-52-64), C b. and b., a/c, pleasant, friendly; *Las Cabañas*, B, nr. Plaza 19 de Julio, good, with pool and decent restaurant next door; *Casa San Juan*, D, shared bath and private bath, clean; *Ticomo* at Km. 81/2, Carretera Sur, has parking facilities, rents apartments, a/c, with maid service and kitchenette, C, breakfast extra, good for longer stay; *Estrella*, Pista de la Solidaridad, A, a/c, swimming pool, with breakfast, long way from centre, book in advance as it's very popular; *Casa de Fiedler*, 8a Calle Sur-Oeste 1320, C, with bath and a/c or fan, comfortable, good breakfasts; *Palace*, Av. Pedro A. Flores, C, with a/c and bath, comfortable, helpful, TV lounge, quiet and good value; at Km. 3.5 on Carretera Sur is *Hotel D'Lido*, C + 10%, use of swimming pool by non-residents, US$1; *Tres Laureles*, C with bath, fan, clean, rec.; *El Colibrí*, single-storey, thatched, clean, with shower, good value if travelling alone, food, often fully-booked, E p.p., 4 blocks from *Intercontinental*; *Colón*, near Sirca bus terminal and road to Masaya, D, with bath and fan, a bit run down, secure, good restaurant.

For accommodation in our E range or below: *El Pueblo*, in the old centre, F with bath, run down, friendly, laundry, cockroaches, breakfast available (accepts córdobas) *Hospedaje Oriental*, nr. Mercado Oriental, F, clean; *Royal*, near railway station, F (payable in córdobas), shared shower and toilet, nice family, always full; *Sultana* (basic) E, noisy, clean, rec., if full, staff will arrange for you to stay at *Mi Siesta* on the other side of town (E with bath and a/c, F no a/c), good, friendly, laundry facilities; *Mascote* also accepts córdobas, F, opp. Mercado Huembes, not very clean, often full; *Hospedaje Fuente*, 2 blocks behind this hotel, F (córdobas accepted), friendly, safe.

Many cheap hotels W of *Intercontinental Hotel* in the Barrio Martha Quezada and nr. the Ciné Dorado; most have very thin walls and are therefore noisy. This district, which also has a number of good eating places, is where many gringos congregate and is known as "gringolandia"; *Casa de Huéspedes Santos*, on street leading to *Intercontinental Hotel*, F, shared rooms, basic, friendly, clean; one block away on same street is *Hospedaje Meza* (T 22046), G p.p., very basic and dirty, TV, friendly, popular; *Hospedaje Quintana*, from Ticabus, 1 block "al Jago", then 1/2 a block "abajo", F p.p., large rooms with fan, shared shower (cold), laundry, friendly, clean, meals available, good value; *Casa de Huéspedes Gladys*, in same area, F; *Hospedaje Carlos* 2 blocks W of Ciné Dorado, F, good value, clean, good *comedor* on opposite corner; *Pensión Norma*, F, shared rooms, basic, friendly, popular (excellent pancakes, breakfast, lunch on nearest corner to this *pensión*; *Hospedaje Meléndez*, near *Comedor Sara*, G, will accept córdobas, use of kitchen, no privacy. *El Dorado*, 8 blocks from *Intercontinental*, F, clean, basic, safe but noisy (good breakfast next door); *El Chepito*, close to *Hotel D'Lido* (see above), G, with bath, basic but friendly, safe, much "passing trade". Many others in same area, e.g. *Azul* (blue doors, no sign), east of Lewites terminal; nearby is *El Portal*, F, shower, cheap.

Camping 181/2 km. from the centre, W of Managua on Route 12, 21/2 km. after the junction with Ruta 2.

Restaurants The *Hotel Intercontinental* serves enormous breakfasts (0600-1100) for US$5 (plus 20% tax and service), and an excellent lunch between 1200 and 1500, US$6 for as much as you want, open to non-residents (best to dress smartly). Bill is made out in US dollars, major credit cards accepted.

In the *Intercontinental*/Plaza España/Barrio Martha Quezada area: *Antojitos*, opp. *Intercontinental*, Mexican, a bit overpriced, interesting photos of Managua pre-earthquake, good food and good portions, and garden (open at 1200); a good piano bar next door; *Costa Brava*, N of Plaza España, excellent seafood. Also near Plaza España, *Plaza*, moderate prices, Earl Grey tea, nice ice cream, casata, Australian owner and Thai cook. *La Terraza*, 300m N of Plaza España, good; *Pizza Boom*, Plaza España; *Yierba Buena*, Pista Benjamín Zeledón, 2 blocks E of Plaza España, open 1700-2400 except Sun., coffee house, good recorded music and chocolate cake; 2 good *sorbeterías* on the street N of Plaza España. 3 blocks towards the lake from *Intercontinental*, a thatched-roof restaurant run by Salvadorean refugees, good, handicrafts shop nearby, information on cooperatives in Estelí region. *Comedores Sara* and *Victoria*, cheap, popular with gringos; other cheap *comedores* in the area. Near *Comedor Sara* is *Cepitios*, good food, reasonable prices, nice atmosphere, *Eskimo* ice cream, W of *Intercontinental* and 2 opp. Ciné Dorado (you can eat at the factory at Km.3 on Carretera Sur). *El Bambu*, 400 m. west of *Intercontinental* and in the same block as the Ticabus terminal, good variety of vegetarian breakfast, good value, from 0700 to 1100.

Also on Carretera Sur: *The Lobster's Inn* (Km. 5.5), good for guess what; *Los Ranchos* (Km. 3); *El Tucán* (Km. 7.5), rec., and another at Km. 8.5.

On Carretera a Masaya: *La Carreta* (Km. 12), rec.; *Lacmiel* (Km.4.5), good value, real ice cream; *El Chaguite*, just S of Pista de la Resistencia; *Los Gauchos*, steaks; *El Coliseo* (Km.8), Italian; *Pizza Deli* (Km.6); *La Marseillaise*, Colonia Los Robles, French, excellent. *Sandy's* is the bad local version of MacDonalds, one on Carretera a Masaya, about Km. 5, and 2 other branches. Vegetarian: *Soya Restaurant*, just off the Carretera on Pista de la Resistencia; *Naturales Margarita*, several blocks towards lake from casa de cambio, also does other dishes, good refrescos (closed Tues.).

Other recommendations: Cheap meals at Mercado Huembes, but look to see what you're getting first. *Mirador Tiscapa*, overlooking Laguna Tiscapa, good food, slow service, live music 2000-2400 (0200 Sat., closed Wed.); health food bakery near Tiscapa (E from *Intercontinental*, turn R at drycleaners, after 2 blocks turn L, bread sales at 1100, get ticket at 1000, max. 4 loaves p.p.). In Bello Horizonte, *La Botija*, and pizza bars on La Rotonda. In Camino Oriente entertainment centre, *El Ternero* and *La Fonda* (also has a *Sandy's*—see above, cinemas, discos and bowling alley). *El Rincón Español*, Av. Monumental, old Managua, Spanish; *Los Nopales*, good food and service; *Faisán Dorado*, Ciudad Jardín L-3. If you can find it, try the local fish, guapote, excellent eating. Cheap places close by 2100.

Shopping Some handicrafts (goldwork, embroidery, etc.) are available in the Centro Comercial Managua; good general shopping here and at Mercado Huembes (also called Eduardo Contreras), for crafts (some are disappointed by the selection at Huembes), both on Pista de la Solidaridad (buses 110 or 119). Good shopping also at Metrocentro, Pista de la Resistencia. Best bookshops at the Centro Sandinista de Trabajadores, Ho Chi Minh Way, and in the Centro Antonio Valdivieso, Calle José Martí, near *Mirador Tiscapa* (also sells records), and at the Centro Comercial Managua. Most ordinary shops are in private houses without signs. Dollartienda (formerly Diplotienda), opp. *Los Gauchos* restaurant on Carretera a Masaya, offers Western-style goods, take your passport, accepts dollars and travellers' cheques if to value of purchase (another Dollartienda is under construction). At the Mercado Oriental you can get just about anything, on the black market.

Local Transport Bus service in Managua is cheap and as good as can be expected under the circumstances. They operate on tokens, widely available at shops or tables near bus stops. All buses are packed. Last services begin their routes at 2200; buses are frequent but it is difficult to fathom their routes. Beware of pickpockets on the crowded urban buses particularly those on tourist routes (e.g. No. 119). A map from the Tourist Office (poor), and a couple of days riding the buses will help you orient yourself. Taxis can be flagged down along the street, but they run mostly on set routes, so you have to know where you're going and what the price should be. Most taxis are colectivos, bargain on those that aren't (fares range from US$0.40-US$1.50). One pays per zone.

Car Hire Hertz, Avis and Budget. Rates are US$25 per day plus US$0.25 per km.— only foreign exchange or credit cards accepted; special weekend rates available. Vimsa, Km. 31/2 Carretera Sur, US$122 per week + US$0.15 per kilometre + 10% insurance and 10% tax, córdobas accepted. Given the poor public transport and the decentralized layout of Managua, renting a car is often the best way to get around. Alternatively hire a taxi for long-distance trips, about US$1.50-2 per hour for the car; for journeys out of Managua, taxis need a special permit from an office opp. *Hotel Intercontinental* (opens 0930).

Cycle Hire Bicycles for US$3 per day (dollar cash) from "Bicycles not Bombs" near Statue Montoya.

Entertainment Discotheques: *Lobo Jack*, *La Nueva Managua*, *Frisco Disco*, *Casa Blanca*, *Pantera Rosa*. 2 discos, cinemas, restaurants in Camino Oriente centre (bus 119 or 117). Live music is offered at *La Vista*, *Torre Blanca*, *Tiffany's Saloon* and *El Arroyito*. Plaza 19 de Julio, Pista de la Resistencia opp. Universidad Centroamericana, two live bands, crowded, festive, great dancing. Jazz club at *Cafetería de la ASTC* in El Carmen, from 2000, inexpensive, good food. **Ballet** Ballet Tepenahuatl, folkloric dances in the ruins of the *Gran Hotel*.

Cinemas Most films in English with Spanish sub-titles (US$0.50). Cinemateca, on Av. Bolívar (behind Cine González), Government theatre with good programmes (only US$0.20 on Sun. a.m.).

Sport Baseball—between Plaza de España and Plaza 19 de Julio on Sunday mornings (the national game), a good seat US$0.20. Also there are basketball, cockfighting and bullfighting (but no kill), swimming, sailing, tennis, golf.

Museums The National Museum is near the lakeshore, to the E of the railway station (closed Sun.). Museo de la Alfabetización (closed Mon.) near Parque Las Palmas in W section of city commemorates the Sandinista Government's literacy programme. Museum of the Revolution, behind bus station near Mercado Eduardo Contreras; fascinating collection of photographs, weapons and documents from 1880s to the struggle against the Somozas (open Tues.-Sat., 0900-1200, 1400-1700; admission free). Centro Cultural Ruinas del Gran Hotel, near Palacio Nacional, permanent display of "revolutionary" art and visiting exhibitions; small cafetería (expect to have to deposit your bag at the door).

Exchange Banco Central de Nicaragua, Km. 7, Carretera del Sur (not for exchange). Local banks all nationalized in July 1979. Banco Nicaragüense del Interior y Comercio at Plaza España changes both bank notes and travellers' cheques. *Casas de cambio* behind Ed. Oscar Pérez Cazar at Km. 4.5 on road to Masaya, opp. *Sandy's* restaurant (Bus 119), takes Master Card, open 0900-1200, 1400-1600; at terminal for Granada buses, several in Ciudad Jardín; much quicker than banks (ask taxi drivers). If stuck buy postcards or a snack at the *Intercontinental* with a travellers' cheque and change will be given in córdobas, but normally the hotel only changes dollars for residents. It is advisable to change money in Managua as it is very difficult elsewhere. Cred-o-matic, Camino Oriente on Carretera a Masaya. The illegal "black" market offers far better rates of exchange. Otherwise change money at the official parallel rate in banks and *casas* *de cambio* (this is not the same as the official rate, at which government business is conducted). Beware of short-changing. (**See page** 557.)

Spanish Classes and thorough introduction to Nicaragua: Casa Nicaragüense de Español, Km. 11.5 Carretera Sur; accommodation with families. Universidad Centroamericana has Spanish courses which are cheaper, but with larger classes.

Embassies **Panamanian** Consulate, near UCA, Plaza 19 de Julio; **Costa Rican**, Pista Benjamín Zeledón, nr. Plaza España, 1 block to the south. **Honduran** Consulate, Carretera del Sur, Km. 15, Colonia Barcelona, open Mon.-Fri., 0800-1400 (bus 118 from **Hotel Intercontinental**); **Guatemalan**, just after Km. 11 on Masaya road, visa US$10 (for British citizens, cash only), fast service. 0900-1200 only.
    USA, Km. 41/2 Carretera del Sur (T 23881); **Canadian Consul**, 208 C del Triunfo, Fuente Plazoleta Telcor Central, T 24541.
    British, El Reparto, "Los Robles", Primera Etapa, Entrada Principal de la Carretera a Masaya, Cuarta Casa a la mano derecha, T 70034, Telex 2166, Apdo Aéreo 169, it is located on a R-turn off Carretera a Masaya; Honorary **British Consul** at Viajes Griffiths, No. C8, Centro Comercial San Francisco, T 72365/74785; letters to Apdo. Postal 13, Managua; **French**, Km. 12 Carretera del Sur, T 26210/27011; **Dutch**, from *Hotel Bolonia*, 2 blocks towards the lake, Aptdo. Postal 529; **Swiss**, in emergency, at Hungarian Consul, T 74173; **Swedish**, from Plaza España, 1 block W (Abajo), 2 blocks to the Lake, 1/2 block W (Abajo), Apartado Postal 2307, T 60085; **Danish** Cosulate General, Iglesia del Carmen, 2 cuadros al Oeste No. 1610, T 23189; **W. German**, off Plaza España.

Immigration Pista de la Resistencia, approx. 1 km. from Km. 7 Carretera del Sur, bus No. 118, open till 1400.

Customs Km. 5 Carretera del Norte, bus No. 108.

General Post Office 3 blocks W of Palacio Nacional and Cathedral, 0700-1600 (closed Sat. p.m.). Separate entrance and exit. Wide selection of beautiful stamps. Poste Restante (Lista de Correos) keeps mail for 1 month.

Cables Telcor, same building as Post Office. Mercado Roberto Huembes (Eduardo Contreras), on bus route 109 from *Hotel Intercontinental*.

Tourist Information Inturismo 2 blocks E of *Hotel Intercontinental*, enter by side door. Standard information available. Maps of Managua (almost up-to-date), with insets of León and Granada and whole country on reverse, US$5 (paid in dollars, no change given). Inturismo will help with finding accommodation with families, with full board. Post cards for sale at Tourist Office, Ministry of Culture, Mercado Huembes and *Intercontinental Hotel* (more expensive); also at Tarjetas Gordión. Nica-tours Turnica, Av. 11 S.O., 2 mins. from Plaza España, sells maps of Managua and of the country.

Airlines Around Plaza España: Sahsa, Aeronica (international flights; internal information at airport), Aeroflot, Iberia (MCOs only), KLM (300 metres E.); in Colonia Los Robles (Carretera a Masaya), Copa, Taca, Cubana (E of Plaza 19 de Julio, turn right on road opp. *Restaurant Lacmiel*, T 73976). Foreigners have to pay in dollars for all flight tickets.

Airport César Augusto Sandino, 12 km. E of city, near the lake. Take bus 105, very crowded so may be better to take a taxi, US$5 from main road, US$12 from terminal, or Taxis Unidos (a bit more expensive), regardless of number of passengers. Be early for international flights since formalities can take 2 hours. X-ray machines reported not safe for film. Internal flights to Puerto Cabezas, Bluefields and the Corn Islands with Aeronica (only 6 seats reserved for tourists, so book early, flights are cancelled frequently, US$30 one way to Bluefields).

Rail Station behind the Cathedral; to Granada (45 km.), via Masaya, 0800, 1330 and 1730 (1 hr. 25 mins., US$0.60), to Masaya one a.m., one p.m. Trains on the continuation to Jinotepe, Masatepe, San Marcos and Diriamba run only a few times a year for tourists. Trains daily to León (90 km.) at 0730, 1100 and 1800, 3 hrs., US$0.15; change there for the branch line to El Sauce (90 km.) and Río Grande. The León-Chinandega-Corinto section of the Pacific Railway has been out of service since 1982. Be 30 minutes early to get seats. Always very dusty in the dry season, and there are no windows to close.

Buses The Comandante Casimir Sotelo bus station by the Mercado Roberto Huembes (Mercado Eduardo Contreras), on Pista de la Solidaridad, is for Granada, Masaya, Estelí, Somoto, Matagalpa, etc., and all destinations in the N. Take bus 109, which runs past *Hotel Intercontinental* and terminates near railway station, or bus 118 and alight at San Juan Bosco church and walk 2 blocks. Bus to Granada, Ruta 4, 0530-2200, every 10 minutes, US$0.20, 1 hr. (luggage extra). To Masaya, US$0.12. To Somoto, 0430, 7½ hrs., US$0.50. To Ocotal US$2 (with Lestram). To Estelí US$0.60, every 20 mins, 3 hrs. For León, Corinto and Pacific Coast, Chinandega and Rivas, the terminal is beside Mercado Israel Lewites, Pista de la Resistencia, on SW side of city (bus 118). To get from the first to the second, take bus 109, then change at *Intercontinental* to bus 118. Bus to León, US$0.15, 1½ hrs., or take Interlocal taxi from bus station, 1½ hrs., US$3; to Rivas, 3 hrs., US$0.80, hourly or so from 0520, to Peñas Blancas on Costa Rican border, 3½-4 hrs., US$1; to Chinandega, 3 hrs., US$0.80. Buses to Boaco, Juigalpa and Rama leave from the Mercado Oscar Benavides/Ivan Montenegro, on Pista José Angel Benavides, in the east of the city. Buses tend to be very full; children scramble on board first, grab seats and "sell" them to passengers. Possible (and safer) to sit on your luggage than put it on the roof. You may have to pay extra for your baggage.

International Buses Look in *El Nuevo Diario* for buses running to San Salvador, Tegucigalpa and Guatemala City. Ticabus to San José and Panama (Tues., Thurs., Sat., US$25 single, US$40 to Panama City, US$ only), and to Honduras and Guatemala (US$35 return to Guatemala City, 36 hrs., singles not sold, return section valid for 3 days only); terminal is in Barrio Martha Quezada. Sirca Express leaves 0600 Mon., Wed., and Fri. or Sat. for Costa Rica (office near *Sandy's* restaurant, taxi for 0600 departure very expensive, US$5). Sirca Bus to San José, US$12, 12-15 hrs. (inc. 4-6 at border); Sirca office and terminal in Altamira, Av. Eduardo Delgado, behind Plaza de Compras, T 73833/75726. A very cheap way (US$4) of travelling to San José is to take a bus Managua-Rivas, then colectivo to border and another between the border posts, then take local bus to San José; takes 15 hrs. altogether. International buses are always booked-up many days in advance and tickets will not be sold until all passport/visa documentation is complete.

Tours of city by private car, 1 or 3 persons, about US$10. All-day tour to Granada and León, US$30. A 2-day round trip by bus and riverboat from Managua to Bluefields costs US$50. Bus tours are available Managua –Tegucigalpa – Copán –Guatemala City for US$28. All tours run by Turnica must be paid in US dollars. Few tours of the country are available.

Excursions There are several volcanic-crater lakes in the environs of Managua, some of which have become centres of residential development and also have swimming, boating, fishing and picnicking facilities for the public. Among the more attractive of these lakes is Laguna de Xiloá, situated about 16 km. from Managua just off the new road to Léon. At Xiloá a private aquatic club (El Náutico) has recently opened; here boats can be rented; bathing possible. On Sat. and Sun., the only days when buses run, Xiloá gets very crowded, but it is quiet during the week, when you must walk there. You can camp there. Take bus 113 to Piedracitas for bus to Xiloá; admission US$0.50. Other lakes within a 45-min. drive of Managua are the Laguna de Apoyo and Laguna de Masaya (**see page** 546 **and** 545), situated respectively at Kms. 35 and 15 on the Masaya road.

The Huellas de Acahualinca are Managua's only site of archaeological interest. These are prehistoric animal and human footprints which have been preserved in tufa, located close to the old centre of town, near the lakeshore at the end of the South Highway. Bus No. 102 passes the site, on which there is also a small museum which exhibits a variety of prehistoric artefacts.

A 10-km. drive down Carretera Sur—this is the Pan-American Highway— through the residential section of Las Piedrecitas passes the US Ambassador's residence to Laguna de Asososca, another small lake (the city's reservoir) in the wooded crater of an old volcano. Piedrecitas Park is to one side of the lake: there is a beautiful 3½-km. ride, playgrounds for children, a café, and splendid view of Lake Managua, two smaller lakes—Asososca and Xiloá—and of Momotombo volcano. Beyond again is the little Laguna de Nejapa (medicinal waters). The Pan-American Highway to Costa Rica passes through Casa Colorada (hotel), 26 km. from Managua, at 900 metres, with commanding views of both the Pacific and of Lake Managua, and a delightful climate (but no trees because of poisonous gases from Santiago volcano, **see page** 544).

Boats can be hired on the shores of Lake Managua for visiting the still-smoking Momotombo and the shore villages (**see also page** 540). At its foot lies León Viejo, which was destroyed in 1609 and is now being excavated. It was in the Cathedral here that Pedrarias and his wife were buried. Near the large volcano is a smaller one, Momotombito. A fine drive skirts the shores of the lake. Do not swim in Lake Managua, as it is polluted in places.

Beaches There are several beaches on the Pacific coast, about an hour's drive from Managua. The nearest are **Pochomil and Masachapa** (54 km. from Managua, side by side, regular bus service from terminal in Israel Lewites market) and Casares (69 km. from Managua, dirty, thorns on beach; one hotel—*Casino Casares*, clean, simple—and 2 restaurants). A few km. from Casares is La Boquita, visited by turtles from Aug. to Nov. Because of their proximity to the capital, these are very popular during the season (Jan.-April) and tend to be somewhat crowded. Out of season, except at weekends, Pochomil is deserted (don't sleep on the beach, mosquitoes will eat you alive); it is clean and being developed as a tourist centre with hotels and restaurants. Only hotel at present, *Baja Mar*, B with a/c, C without, basic, not worth the money though they do accept córdobas. Masachapa is cheaper but dirtier; hotels on beach, G (but *Terraza* not rec.); *Hotel Summer* on the main street to the beach, E, restaurant, fair; *Hotel Rex*, very very basic, G. Very slow bus journey from Managua. A visit to the broad, sandy El Velero beach (turn off at Km. 60 on the old road to León and then follow signs) is recommended despite the US$3.50 entrance charge. All facilities controlled by the INSSBI, for the benefit of state employees, and at weekends is fully booked for weeks in advance. You may be able to rent a cabin (F for 2) in the week, pay extra for sheet and pillows. You can eat in the restaurant (*Pirata Cojo*), at the INSSBI cafeteria (bring your own utensils, buy meal ticket in advance, or take your own food). However, the beach itself is beautiful, and the sea is ideal for both surfing and swimming. El Tránsito is a beautiful, undeveloped Pacific beach; bus from Managua at 1300 (from end of No. 107 bus route behind Ciné México), return at 0600 or 0700. Good cheap meals from Sra Pérez on the beach (possible accommodation); *Restaurant Yolanda*; beach flats for 4-6 people normally available mid-week at N end (Centro Vacacional de Trabajadores, good value).

MANAGUA TO HONDURAS

The Pan-American Highway runs from Managua to Honduras (214 km.) and is paved the whole way. Also paved is the branch road to Matagalpa and Jinotega. The border crossings with Honduras on the more easterly route, through Somoto and by road from Ocotal via Las Manos to Danlí, are open, but the more westerly Chinandega-Río Guasaule-Choluteca link is closed.

The first stretch of 21 km. to Tipitapa is along the southern edge of Lake Managua. **Tipitapa**, on the SE shore of the lake, is a tourist resort with hot sulphur baths, a casino, a colourful market, and a *fiesta* of El Señor de Esquipulas on 13-16 January. Swimming in El Trapice park, US$0.50.

Hotel *Aguas Calientes*, G with shower.

Restaurant *Salón Silvia*, unpretentious. Slightly cheaper, but good, is the a/c restaurant attached to the thermal baths. *Entre Ríos*, helpful, looks like the best in town.

Bus from Managua (minibus), US$0.20. Bus to Estelí, US$1.

The Pan-American Highway goes N through Tipitapa to Sébaco, 105 km. Fourteen km. before reaching Sébaco is Ciudad Darío (off the main road, turning N of town, is not signposted), where the poet Ruben Darío was born; you can see the house, which is maintained as a museum. There is no hotel in Ciudad Darío, but in Sébaco there is *Hotel Valle*. East of the Highway is Esquipula, 100 km. from Managua, 2½ hrs. by bus, a good place for hiking, fishing, riding; *Hotel Oscar Morales*, G, clean, shower, friendly.

From Sébaco a 24-km. branch road leads (right) to **Matagalpa** at 678 metres, in the best walking country in Nicaragua, population 70,000. Matagalpa has an old church, but it is about the only colonial style building left; the town has developed rapidly in recent years. It was badly damaged in the Revolution, but is undergoing reconstruction, retaining much of its original character. The birthplace of Carlos Fonseca is now a museum, 1 block E of the more southerly of the 2 main squares; off the northerly square (with the Cathedral) is a Galería de los Héroes y Mártires; N of the Cathedral is the Centro Popular de la Cultura, with murals on the outside. The town is safe, but visitors can expect frequent police checks. There is a small zoo in the northern suburbs along the river. The main occupation is coffee planting and there are cattle ranges; the chief industry is the Nestlé powdered-milk plant. A 32-km. road runs from Matagalpa to the Tuma valley. 24 September, Día de La Merced, is a local holiday.

Hotels *Selva Negra*, at 1,200 m., 10 km. on road to Jinotega, D (pay in US$), good, as is the restaurant (reserve in advance at weekends by telegram); *Soza*, opp. river, E, basic; *Ideal*, E, with bath, same range without (but C for those not on a work brigade), better rooms are upstairs, good but expensive restaurant; *Bermúdez*, reasonably clean, friendly, no meals; *Hospedaje Plaza*, on main plaza, G, clean, quiet; on other side of square, *Hospedaje Colonial*, G, basic; round, brick hostel with communal rooms, nr. *Hotel Bermúdez*, no sign, basic, inexpensive.

Restaurants *Comedor San Martín*, main street, good breakfasts; *San Diego*, opp. cinema near plaza, good; *Comedor* in park near church (built with assistance from Tilburg, Neth.), rec.; *Comedor Vicky*, S of cathedral, good breakfast and lunch (closed p.m.); *Sorbetería* 1 block E of square with Fonseca quotes, on a corner, rec.; *Chinatown*, Chinese, 1 block E, 1 block N of plaza; *Lanchería Marcia*, opp. fire station, excellent value lunch; *Los Pinchitos Morenos*, near the centre, good and cheap. *Pizzas Don Diego*, next to *Bermúdez Hotel*.

Shopping Mercado del Norte, close to northern highway; Mercado del Oeste, 2 blocks W of *Royal Bar*; Dollartienda to open. Bookshop: Fundacíon Manolo Morales, 1 block N, ½ block E of plaza, Spanish editions of international literature and stamps. Look for fine black pottery made in a local cooperative.

Exchange Banco Nacional de Desarrollo.

Buses every half hour to Managua, 127 km., take 2½ hrs. (US$0.50) (express at 1100 and 1500, queue from 0900). Buses for the local area leave from Guanuco, a long way from the centre in the E suburbs.

There is a fine 34-km. highway from Matagalpa to **Jinotega**, and on another 80 km. (unpaved), via the picturesque villages of San Rafael del Norte and Yalí, to join the main highway at Condega, 51 km. from the Honduran border *Hotel Primavera*, G p.p., nothing special, but plumbing works. Jinotega (altitude 1,004 metres) is served by buses from Managua and Matagalpa. Population 20,000; famous images in church. The Somoza jail has been converted into a youth centre. Excellent coffee grown here and in Matagalpa. Road (18 km.) to El Tuma power station; another to Estelí, through La Concordia, unpaved, picturesque, but very little transport from La Concordia to Estelí.

The 134-km. section from Sébaco to the border at El Espino is through sharp hills with steep climbs and descents, but reasonably well banked and smooth.

A road (very poor in places) leads off the Pan-American Highway 10 km. N of Sébaco, near San Isidoro, to join the Pacific Highway near León (110 km.). This is an attractive alternative route to Managua through the Chinandega cotton growing area, past the spectacular chain of volcanoes running W from Lake Managua, and through León. (Bus Estelí-San Isidoro, US$0.20, San Isidoro-León, 2½ hrs., US$0.80). On this road, 12 km. N of the intersection with the Chinandega-León road, is San Jacinto; 200 metres to the west of the road is a field of steaming, bubbling mud holes (approach carefully, the ground may give, and scald your legs).

The Pan-American Highway goes through **Estelí** (606 metres), a rapidly developing departmental capital of about 20,000 people (heavily damaged during the Revolution of 1978-79). It is the site of prehistoric carved stone figures (in park in front of tourist information office). Worth visiting are the Casa de Cultura (fiestas, meetings, exhibitions), Galería de los Héroes y Mártires on next corner (mementoes of those killed defending the Revolution, wonderful paintings on the outside walls)—to reach these two, stand in main square with church behind you, take street in the opposite direction from the fire station —and the Salvadorean cooperative, take Av. Bolívar from Cathedral Plaza towards bus station—some crafts, café with posters all over the walls, good. The Ministry of Health Information Centre, on Gran Vía Bolívar, 4 blocks from Plaza, is involved with projects to revive traditional medicine and healing; it offers advice on a wide range of herbal remedies. Also ask at the Reforma Agraria Office (above Banco de América) if you wish to see any local farming cooperatives. The Amnlae women's centre has social and educational projects which are interesting to visit and which may welcome volunteers. Tourist information at Cathedral Plaza.

Hotels *Mesón*, 1 block N of Cathedral and plaza, D with shower, clean, restaurant; *Hospedaje El Chepito*, clean, friendly, G; *Mariela*, G behind bus station, clean, safe, washing facilities, C, accepts córdobas; *Bolívar*, unmarked, 2 blocks S on main street from *Restaurant La Plancha*, G; *Nicarao*, 1 block closer to main square from *Bolívar*, clean, fresh-smelling, accepts córdobas, with shower, restaurant, good service; *3 hospedajes* on Av. Bolívar, all G: *Xilanem*, one block N of main square, clean, noisy, G; *Nahuali* nearby, good, pricey, E, but good food; *La Florida* (not rec., but has space for car), *Juárez*, F, near bus station, very basic, parking inside gates; *Barlop*, Av. Bolívar, 5 blocks from main square, 12 rooms, 6 of which good, 6 basic, former have showers, T (071) 2486, E, good, friendly; *Galo*, Nicaragua y Central, F, accepts córdobas.

Restaurant Opp. *Sorbetería Estelí*, is La Plancha; *El Mesero*, on street which joins main street at hospital, opp. an open field (from Texaco 1 "abajo", "al Norte"), popular and very good despite appearance. *Chupis* ice cream, next to *El Faisán* restaurant on Calle Bolívar (latter promotes use of soya); about 3 blocks N of park on same street *Panadería España*, good but pricey. *Casa de la Amistad*, Salvadorean cafetería, 50 m. W of main square.

Shopping 2 small markets, one N, one S of Cathedral Plaza. Dollartienda.

Spanish Classes Nuevo Instituto de Centro América (NICA), 5-week programme of Spanish tuition and courses on Nicaragua, including meetings with people, volunteer work, visits to cooperatives, etc. Apply at least a month in advance; charge is 5% of your annual income, or minimum US$950. All accommodation is with local families. Details from NICA, PO Box 1409, Cambridge MA 02238, USA, or Apartado Postal 50, Estelí.

Exchange Banco Nacional de Desarrollo.

Buses Leave from the market S of central plaza. For León, change at San Isidro; for Honduras change at Somoto or Ocotal.

Bathing near Estelí at Puente La Sirena, 200 metres off the road to Condega, or Salta Estanzuela, 5 km. S of Estelí, a waterfall of 25 metres, with a deep pool at the bottom, surrounded by trees and flowers (inc. orchids—only worth it in the rainy season), at least 5 km. off the Managua road, four-wheel drive recommended. Take the dirt road, starting ½ km. S of Estelí on Pan-American Highway, through San Nicolás.

A new gravel road from Estelí runs to Achuapa and El Sauce (**see page**

543); there is a poor, direct road Estelí-El Sauce. North of Achuapa, an unmade road continues through San Juan de Limay (one *hospedaje*), an *artesanía*, and marble town, and Pueblo Nuevo (2 basic *hospedajes*), near which is an archaeological site. From here the road goes on to join the Pan-American Highway a few km. E of Somoto.

The Highway then goes to Condega (5,000 people) and to **Somoto** (7,000 people), centre of pitch-pine industry, thence to El Espino (20 km.), a ghost town 5 km. from Honduran border at La Playa. The Nicaraguan passport control and customs are at El Espino in the ruined customs house, 100 metres from the Honduran border. Minibuses run between Somoto and the border (US$0.20, plus US$0.40 per bag), and 3 or 4 buses daily between Somoto and Estelí (US$0.40); Somoto-Managua, 5 hrs., US$0.50 plus extra for luggage, 0400 and 0600 only (private car Somoto-Managua, US$25). You may have a better chance of a seat if you change at Estelí. The border opens at 0800 on each side, Nicaraguan side closes at 1630, and 1200-1300 for lunch (if you arrive at the border after 1630, there is no public transport back to Somoto after about 1700 and nowhere to stay in El Espino). (There is a food bar on the Nicaraguan side but several cafés on the Honduran side.) Take care: you may be advised during the day that the buses have broken down and you should take a taxi. Sure enough within a short distance, the bus passes going the other way!

Hotels in Somoto *Panamericano*, on main square, G, but new section being built will be more expensive, landlord helpful, speaks English, rec; *Baghan*, F, clean, friendly, helpful; *Internacional*, 1 block from central plaza, F, clean and basic. **Restaurant**: *Victoria*, serves good food.

Just before reaching Somoto a road leads off from Yalagüina right (18 km.) to *Ocotal*, a clean, cool, whitewashed town of 3,863 people at 600 metres on a sandy plain (well worth a visit). It is near the Honduran border, to which a road runs N (bus marked Las Manos); this border is open again; bus Ocotal-Somoto, US$0.20. Close by, at San Albino, there are many gold mines and gold is washed in the river Coco (bus only from Ciudad Sandino—formerly Jícaro, 50 km. from Ocotal). Friendly, helpful Tourist Office 2 blocks from main square, opposite the market. Bus Estelí-Ocotal, US$0.70, 2 hrs., beautiful views; Ocotal-Managua, 0630, US$1.70.

Hotels at Ocotal *El Portal*, G, reasonable; *El Castillo*, G, basic, quiet; *Segovia*, cheap, basic, OK; *Pensión Centroamericana*, G, not as dirty as most others. For eating, *Restaurant La Cabaña*; *El Deportivo*, excellent value comida corriente, friendly; *Brasilia*, very good, ask for directions; *Café Capri* is best for refrescos.

Exchange Banco Nacional de Desarrollo.

MANAGUA TO CORINTO

The first city of note along the railway is León, 88 km. from Managua, reached in 2¼ hrs. The Pacific Highway between Managua and Corinto (140 km.) follows the shore of Lake Managua and goes on to Chinandega; it has been continued to Corinto and to the Honduran border (border bridge destroyed by floods early in 1982, and frontier crossing closed). The old, paved road to León crosses the Sierra de Managua, offering fine views of the lake (it is no longer than the Pacific Highway, but is very bad in places).

About 60 km. down the new road to León lies the village of La Paz Centro (road to here newly paved; *Hospedaje El Caminante*, close to Highway, basic, friendly, G, cheap). It is from here that one can gain access to the volcano **Momotombo**, which dominates the Managua skyline from the West.

One now has to have a permit from Empresa Nacional de Luz y Fuerza in Managua to climb Momotombo; they have built a geothermal power station on the volcano's slopes; alternatively ask police in León Viejo for a permit (very difficult to get).

León, with a population of 130,000, was founded by Hernández de Córdoba in 1524 at León Viejo, 32 km. from its present site, at the foot of Momotombo. It was destroyed by earthquake on 31 December, 1609 (the ruins can be reached by boat from Managua), and the city moved to its present site the next year. It was the capital from its foundation until Managua replaced it in 1858; it is still the "intellectual" capital, with a university (founded 1804), religious colleges, the largest cathedral in Central America, and several colonial churches. It is said that Managua became the capital, although at the time it was only an Indian settlement, because it was half-way between violently Liberal León and equally violently Conservative Granada.

The city has a traditional air, its colonial charm unmatched elsewhere in Nicaragua: narrow streets, roofs tiled in red, low adobe houses and time-worn buildings everywhere. The old Plaza de Armas, in front of the Cathedral, is now Parque Jérez, but is usually referred to as Parque Central; it contains a statue of General Jérez, a mid-19th century Liberal leader.

The Cathedral, begun in 1746 and not completed for 100 years, is an enormous building. It has a famous shrine, 145 cm. high, covered by white topazes from India given by Philip II of Spain, which is kept in a safe in the vestry, and the bishop holds the key; a very fine ivory Christ; the consecrated Altar of Sacrifices and the Choir of Córdoba; the great Christ of Esquipulas, a colonial work in bronze whose cross is of very fine silver; and statues of the 12 Apostles. At the foot of one of these statues is the tomb of Ruben Darío, the 19th-century Nicaraguan poet, and one of the greatest in Latin America, guarded by a sorrowing lion.

The western end of the city is the oldest, and here is the oldest of all the churches: the parish church of Subtiava (1530) where Las Casas, the Apostle of the Indies, preached on several occasions. It has a fine façade, the best colonial altar in the country and an interesting representation of the sun ("El Sol") revered by the Indians. Near the Subtiava church are a small town museum (entrance free) and the ruins of the parish church of Vera Cruz, now crumbling. Other churches well worth visiting include El Calvario (beautifully decorated ceiling), La Recolección (fine façade), La Merced, San Felipe, Zaragoza, San Francisco and El Laborío. There is a pleasant walk S across the bridge, past the church of Guadalupe, to the cemetery. The house of Ruben

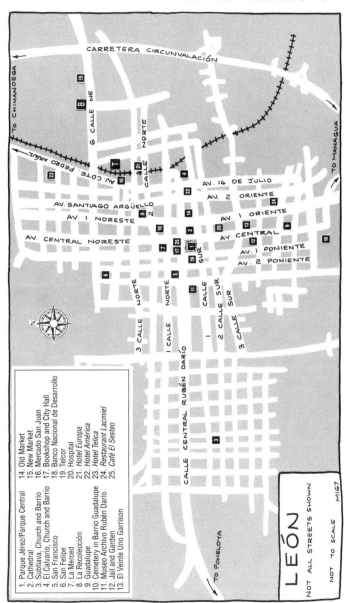

1. Parque Jérez/Parque Central
2. Cathedral
3. Subtiava, Church and Barrio
4. El Calvario, Church and Barrio
5. San Francisco
6. San Felipe
7. La Merced
8. La Recolección
9. Guadalupe
10. Cemetery in Barrio Guadalupe
11. Museo Archivo Rubén Darío
12. Jail and Garden
13. El Veinte Uno Garrison
14. Old Market
15. New Market
16. Mercado San Juan
17. Bookshop and City Hall
18. Banco Nacional de Desarrollo
19. Telcor
20. Hospital
21. *Hotel Europa*
22. *Hotel América*
23. *Hotel Telica*
24. *Restaurant Lacmiel*
25. *Café El Sesteo*

LEÓN

NOT ALL STREETS SHOWN

NOT TO SCALE

M167

Darío, the famous "Four Corners" in Calle Ruben Darío, is now the Museo-Archivo Ruben Darío; he died in 1916 in another house in the NW sector marked with a plaque. The Holy Week ceremonies are outstanding. Visit the Casa de Cultura in the suburb of Subtiava. A plaque marks the spot in the centre of the city where the first President Somoza was assassinated in 1956 by poet Rigoberto López Pérez.

León was the centre of heavy fighting during the 1978-79 Revolution; much of the damage has still to be repaired (a public works programme was promised in 1988), but there are also many monuments from that time in the city (descriptions of León's fight against the Somoza régime can be found in *Fire from the Mountain: The Making of a Sandinista* by Omar Cabezas). Visitors can see El Fortín, the ruined last stronghold of the Somocista national guard (a commemorative march goes there each July, from the Cathedral, go W about 10 blocks, then S, best in early a.m.); El Veinte Uno, the national guard's 21st garrison, also ruined, with the jail around the corner converted into a garden (3 blocks S of cathedral); statue of Luisa Amanda Espinoza, the first woman member of the FSLN to die (in 1970), after whom the women's organization (AMNLAE) is named (7-8 blocks N of market behind Cathedral, in Barrio San Felipe); 2 blocks W of La Merced church is the Centro Popular de la Cultura (frequent exhibitions and events); Galería de Héroes y Mártires, a museum just W of main square. In the blocks N of the Cathedral is a commemorative park with portraits of Sandino, Carlos Fonseca and Jérez.

Local Holidays 20 June (Liberation by Sandinistas), 24 September, 1 November (All Saints' Day).

Hotels *Europa*, 2 blocks S of railway station, best, E (córdobas accepted), with bath, F without, excellent, good breakfasts (US$0.35), but makes a fuss about unmarried couples; *América*, Av. Santiago Argüello, 2 blocks E of central market, F, with bath and fan, clean and friendly, restaurant (good breakfast), also secure garage nearby; *Telica*, F with shower, clean, good breakfast, 4 blocks N of railway station; *Hospedaje de la Primavera*, Calle 9N, 3½ blocks W of railway station, F with shower, pleasant but women travelling alone should take one of the more expensive rooms close to reception as drunken men are a problem here, also has rats. Several cheap *pensiones* near the railway station.

Restaurants *La Cueva del León*, good seafood and steaks, two blocks N of Parque Jérez, slow service; *El Filete*, 4 blocks N of Parque Jérez, good fish, pricey; *Los Angeles* and *Dragón de Oro* (Chinese), ½ block N of Parque Jérez; *Gringo* café, *El Sesteo*, on plaza; *La Casa Vieja*, 1 ½ blocks N of San Francisco church, pleasant bar, good quality snacks, good value, highly rec.; *El Barcito*, NW of Parque Central, popular, soft drinks, milk shakes, slow service; *Central*, Calle 4 Norte, good comida corriente. *Marisquería Sol y Mar*, 1 block from main square, good seafood but expensive; *Metropolitano*, 1 block W of Post Office, good steaks. *Capricornio*, nr. Central University, good comida corriente, interesting atmosphere; good value comida corriente at *Comedores Emu* (nr. La Recolección church) and *La Cucaracha* (1 block S of *Hotel América* on opp. side of street, no sign); *Sacuanjoche*, Calle Darío several blocks W of Cathedral, expensive but good; *Lacmiel*, 5 blocks S of Cathedral, good food, live music, open air, rec.; *Los Pescaditos*, nr. Subtiava church, excellent for fish at reasonable prices. Excellent ice cream parlour 1 block N of central square.

Shopping The old market (dirty) is in the centre, and the new market is at the bus terminal, 5-6 blocks E of railway station. Also Mercado San Juan. Good bookshop next to city hall at Parque Jérez. Dollartienda.

Cinemas 3 in centre. 2 discotheques at weekends.

Exchange Banco Nacional de Desarrollo, 1 block N of Cathedral.

Post Office and Telephones Telcor, Parque Central, opposite Cathedral. Phone calls abroad possible. Small Telcor office on Darío, on road to Subtiava, about 10 blocks from main plaza, open till 2200, less crowded.

Buses From bus station at new market: Managua-León, Route 12, 1½ hrs., US$0.15 (fight for a ticket and place). Colectivo, US$3; to Chinandega and Corinto hourly between 0500 and 1900. For Estelí, take a bus to San Isidro, 3 hrs., US$0.80, then catch a bus going N from Managua or Matagalpa.

Train Managua-León, US$0.15, 2-3 hrs.; train from León to Managua departs 0430 (good views of Momotombo at sunrise) 0900, 1540; rough, dusty (in dry season), colourful, real experience! Trip gives good view of lakes and volcanoes. A branch railway runs to Malpaisillo (unnamed *hospedaje* at village entrance, 4 rooms, basic, G) and *El Sauce*, 90 km., 3-4 hrs., once or twice a day, where there is a large 19th century church, and a riotous fair in February (*Hospedaje Diana*, G, clean, basic; *Hospedaje Viajero*, noisy, dirty; *Restaurant Mi Rancho* and others). Regular trucks to Estelí, on a very rough road.

There is a road (20 km.) to the sandy Pacific beach at **Poneloya** (large waves, strong currents, extremely dangerous). (*Hotel Lacayo*, basic, unfriendly, G, meals, beware of insects at night, bring coils; good fish restaurant down the road.) The place is pretty run down and all the houses of wealthy León families are locked up. It only comes alive during Semana Santa, at which time it gets crowded. Camping possible on the beach. Bus 101 from centre of León (US$0.25, 50 mins., last at 1700) finishes at Las Peñitas at the S end of Poneloya beach (swimming much safer here; several small restaurants).

Chinandega is about 35 km. beyond León. Population 37,000. This is one of the main cotton-growing districts, and also grows bananas and sugar cane. Horse-drawn cabs for hire, and a crocodile in the fountain in the main square. Not far away, at Chichigalpa, is Ingenio San Antonio, the largest sugar mill in Nicaragua, with a railway to its own port on the Pacific. From Managua, by road, 3 hrs., US$0.80. Hourly buses to Managua from main square from 0500. From León, 1 hr. by bus, US$0.15. Local holiday: 26 July .

Hotels *Glomar*, F (shower extra), friendly, safe, may be closed Sun. p.m., owner (Filio) will change dollars; *Salón Carlos*, F, with breakfast, share shower; *Pensión Cortés*, S of Parque Central, G, basic. *Pensión Urbina*, G, basic; *Hospedaje Aguirre*, G. On the road to Honduran border, *Cosigüina*, 50 rooms, 2 restaurants, shops, cinema and discotheque.

Restaurants *Corona de Oro*, Chinese, 1½ blocks E of Parque Central, T 3511;

Central Palace, same street; *Caprax Pizza*, one block E of Parque Central.

Exchange Banco Nacional de Desarrollo.

Post Office in new building opp. *Caprax Pizza*.

A road runs NE to Puerto Morazán. This passes through the village of El Viejo (US$0.20 by bus from Chinandega, 5 km.) where there is an old church. (Restaurant: *El Retoño*, on main street, N of market; bars close to market.) Puerto Morazán (hotel), 26 km. from Chinandega (bus at 1030 and 1600, 1½ hrs., US$0.20), is a modern town on a navigable river running into the Gulf of Fonseca. From Chinandega there is a bus at 1400 daily to Potosí, at least 3 hrs., US$0.40 (return 0330). *Comedor Adela*, 24-hr. service, cheap. You can sling your hammock at the *comedor* 150 metres past immigration for US$0.50. Ask Héctor for permission to stay in the fishing cooperative. The fishermen are very friendly. The passenger ferry from Potosí to La Unión (El Salvador) has been suspended.

It is a 4-hour hike to the cone of Cosigüina volcano. On 23 January, 1835, one of the biggest eruptions in history blew off most of the cone, reducing it from 3,000 metres to its present height of 870 metres. Michael Tesch and Leone Thiele of Cape Paterson, Australia, tell us: There are beautiful views of the lake inside the cone and over the islands of Honduras and El Salvador. There is plenty of wildlife in the area, including poisonous snakes, so take a machete. There are pleasant black sand beaches; the sea, although the colour of *café con leche*, is clean. In the centre of the village are warm thermal springs in which the population relaxes each afternoon.

From Chinandega a paved road goes to the Honduran border at Somotillo, on the Río Guasaule, where it is continued by an equally good road to Choluteca, Honduras. **N.B.** The bridge over the Río Guasaule was washed away in floods in May 1982 and the bridge over the Río Negro was destroyed by guerrillas in the same year. The border here was closed at the time of going to press (1990).

Jiquilillo beach, 42 km. from Chinandega, is reached by a mostly-paved road branching off the El Viejo-Potosí road. It lies on a long peninsula; small restaurants (e.g. *Fany*) and lodgings.

Corinto, 21 km. from Chinandega, is the main port of entry, and the only port at which vessels of any considerable size can berth. About 60% of the country's commerce passes through it. The town itself is on a sandy island, Punto Icaco, connected with the mainland by long railway and road bridges. There are beautiful old wooden buildings with verandahs, especially by the port, but photography near the port is forbidden. (Entry to the port is barred to all except those with a permit.) Population: 10,000. On the Corinto-Chinandega road is Paseo Cavallo beach (*Restaurante Buen Vecino*).

Hotel *Hospedaje Luvy*, G, fan, dirty bathrooms, 2 blocks from plaza.
Restaurants *Meléndez*, on main square, good but pricey; *El Imperial*, evenings only; cheapest meals in market, but not rec.

MANAGUA TO GRANADA

There are two routes, one by rail and one by a 61 km. paved road with a fast bus service; both run through Masaya.

Santiago Volcano The entrance to **Masaya National Park** is at km. 23. The road is paved up to the crater (6 km.). The volcano is double-crested, but half (Masaya) is dormant. The other crater

(Santiago) collapsed in late 1986, and the resulting pall of sulphurous smoke made the soil in a broad belt to the Pacific uncultivable. There is a beautiful picnic area half-way up and a fine but expensive restaurant (next door is a good science museum, entrance US$0.10). Take something to drink. There is no public transport, although you can alight from the Managua-Masaya bus at Km. 23. Park rangers may give you a lift. Luggage may be left at the gate lodge safely. Drivers have to pay US$1 in córdobas, to get their cars in; pedestrians 1 centavo. The Park is open 0900-1700 (closed Monday). Look for the green parrots in the Masaya crater.

Masaya (population 70,000), 30 km. SE of Managua, is the centre of a rich agricultural area growing tobacco. Small **Laguna de Masaya** (at the foot of Masaya volcano, water too polluted for swimming), and Santiago volcano are near the town. Interesting Indian handicrafts and a gorgeous *fiesta* on 30 September, for its patron, San Jerónimo (Indian dances and local costumes). Another important pilgrimage is 16 March, the Virgen de Masaya and the Cristo de Milagros of Nindirí (see below) are taken down to the lake, whose waters are blessed. Ceremony leaves the church at 1500. The market (Sunday at railway station) is reportedly commercialized now, but the selection and quality are good, especially for snake-, iguana-, and alligator-skin items. There is a new Centro de Artesanías, near the hospital and overlooking Laguna de Masaya, but the choice is not as wide as the market (closed Sun.). Nearby is *Taller de Tapices Luis* where brightly coloured straw mats can be bought more cheaply than in the market. Doña Luisa (near church) sells good woven articles. Masaya is also the centre for Nicaraguan rocking chairs. The Cooperativo Teófilo Alemán has a good selection at around US$35. The best place for Indian craft work is Monimbo (visit the church of Magdalena here), and 15 minutes from Masaya is Villa Nindirí, which has a rich museum and an old church with some even older images. There are horse-drawn carriages, some very pretty and well-kept. Statue of Sandino. A branch railway runs SW to Jinotepe and Diriamba in the small highland between the two lakes. The town suffered severely in the Revolution of 1978-79. Visit the Museo de Héroes y Mártires.

Hotels *Motel El Nido*, D, expensive, not too good. *Regis*, Sergio Delgado (main street), F, clean, basic, breakfast (other meals if ordered), helpful owner; *Victoria*, G; *Rex*, G, dark, dirty but friendly, near the church; *Cailagua* (Km. 29.5, Carretera a Granada), clean, F with bath (cold water), good, very friendly, meals available (but breakfast only by arrangement), reasonably priced. *Pensiones* are hard to find, and dirty when you've found them.

Restaurants *Chema*, Arturo Velazques, no sign (except *Nueva Bar*), very good food, service and value; *El Jade*, near 2nd market, good Chinese food. *Alegría*, nr. main square, good, not expensive, good pizzas; *El Arabe* at station; *Mini 16*, W end of town, nr. hospital. *Pochil*, near park, good food, ask for vegetarian dishes. *Cafetín Verdí*, in central park, good atmosphere, snacks, ice cream.

Exchange Banco Nacional de Desarrollo.

Doctor Dr. Freddy Cárdenas Ortega, near bus terminal rec. gynaecologist.

Transport from Managua, 2 trains daily, Managua-Masaya, 1½ hrs. (0800, 1300, return 0930, 1430); tourist trains to Jinotepe occasionally. By car to

Managua, ½ hr.; taxi, US$10; bus every 10 mins., US$0.12; bus and train to Granada, US$0.15. Entering Masaya by bus, do not wait for the end of the line as there are no hotels near the market terminal.

Excursions   Just outside Masaya, on the road from Managua, is an old fortress, Coyotepe, also called La Fortillera. It was once a torture centre, and is now deserted, eerie "with a Marie Celeste feel to it" (take a torch). Near the Masaya Lake, S of the town there are caves with prehistoric figures on the walls; ask around for a guide.

To Niquinohomo, Sandino's birthplace: the house where Sandino lived from the age of 12 with his father and his father's family is a museum, open Sunday 0900-1300, Tues.-Sat. 0900-1200, 1400-1700. The house is opposite the church in the main square.

James N. Maas writes: Take a bus from Masaya (or Granada) to San Juan de Oriente, a colonial village with an interesting school of pottery (products are for sale). It is a short walk to neighbouring Catarina, and a 1 km. walk uphill to El Mirador, with a wonderful view of **Laguna de Apoyo** (very clean, quiet during week but busy at weekends—swimming, drinking, drowning—entrance fee US$0.20; get out of bus at Km. 38 on Managua-Granada road, walk 1½ hrs. or hitch—easy at weekends), Granada and Volcán Mombacho in the distance. Follow the Jinotepe branch railway down to Masaya.

Another 18 km. by road and rail is **_Granada_**, on Lake Nicaragua, the terminus of the railway from the port of Corinto (190 km.). It is the third city of the republic, with a population of 45,200, and was founded by Hernández de Córdoba in 1524 at the foot of Mombacho volcano. The rich city was three times attacked by British and French pirates coming up the San Juan and Escalante rivers, and much of old Granada was burnt by filibuster William Walker in 1856, but it still has many beautiful buildings and has faithfully preserved its Castilian traditions. The Cathedral has been rebuilt in neo-classical style; also of interest are the church of La Merced (1781-3), the church of Jalteva in the outskirts, and the fortress-church of San Francisco: its chapel of María Auxiliadora, where Las Casas, Apostle of the Indies, often preached, is hung with Indian lace and needlework. Horse-drawn cabs are for hire (bargain over the price), there are many oxcarts and a fine cemetery. The lake beach is popular, but dirty; huge camp ground, children's playground, bars, cafés; marimba bands stroll the beach and play a song for you for a small charge. The vegetation of the islands in the lake is unusual and different, so are the Indian idols found there on display in the Instituto Nacional del Oriente, next door to the San Francisco church; most of the idols come from one of two larger islands, Isla Zapatera; worth visiting. (The Instituto is a school; teachers will open the door for you.) See below on how to get to the islands.

Fiestas   Holy Week: Assumption of the Virgin, 14-30 August; and Christmas (masked and costumed mummers).

Hotels   *Alhambra*, Parque Central, T 2035, pleasant, comfortable rooms with bath, B (dollars only), large restaurant serves good food, often has good, live music, parked cars guarded by nightwatchman; *Granada*, Calle La Calzada (opp. Guadalupe church), B, luxury, swimming pool, a/c, breakfast only served, very good, only US$ accepted, T 2974. *Pensión Cabrera*, Calle Calzada, F without bath, not always clean, pleasant; opposite and of same standard is *Pensión Vargas*, G, basic, mixed reports; These three hotels are on the road from the main square to the wharf. *Esfinge*, opposite market, G even with private shower. *Pensión Cigarro*, G (short stay, thieves). There is a shortage of hotels and restaurants in Granada (do not arrive after 2100 at the latest).

Restaurants *Pingüín*, good, expensive; *Drive Inn El Ancla*, opp. *Hotel Granada*, clean, rec.; *Interamericano*, road to Masaya next to Esso, clean, dear. *La Cabaña Amarilla*, on lakeshore. *Asia*, rec., a/c, good food, steaks and fish in particular, friendly, dollars changed; *Chupi's Ice Cream Parlour*. A tourist complex on the lakeside (S of Plaza España) includes 2 expensive restaurants and bars (you can walk there from the cathedral). 1 km. further along the beach are 3 restaurants which have launch trips for US$2.50 p.p. for an hour to some of the islands (not Sun.). Good breakfasts at the market.

Shopping Dollartienda near *Hotel Alhambra*.

Exchange Banco Navional de Desarrollo.

Post Office, telephones Telcor in moorish building on Parque Central, left of Cathedral.

Buses leave from an area 200 metres beyond the market, except those going S (e.g. to Rivas) which leave from a "fenced lot uptown". Many fast minibuses to Managua, US$0.20, 1 hr. (these do not stop in Masaya). Bus to Nandaime, US$0.25. Bus to Masaya, US$0.15, 15 mins. Express bus to Rivas, 1130, 1½ hrs., US$2, other, slower buses every ½ hr., US$0.20. To Costa Rican border: if you ask around the Cathedral you may find someone to drive you to the border for US$10: note, taxis are not allowed out of town. Sirca Bus from Granada or Masaya to San José 3 times a week: you must purchase your ticket in advance from the Sirca office, 1½ blocks from the square. Bus leaves 0730 Mon., Wed. and Fri. Tica from Granada to San José.

Rail To Managua, via Masaya, 3 a day, US$0.60, journey times vary from 1hr. 25 mins., to 2 hrs. 5 mins.; ½-¾ hr. to Masaya, US$0.15. The "train" is basically a dusty tramcar.

Lake Nicaragua, the "Gran Lago", 148 km. long by 55 at its widest, is a fresh-water lake abounding in salt-water fish, which swim up the San Juan river from the sea and later return. It is said to include sharks, though none has been seen for some years; some say because Somoza had them fished out. Terrapins can be seen sunning themselves on the rocks and there are many interesting birds. There are about 310 small islands, Las Isletas (most of them inhabited), which can be visited either by hired boats or motor launches, from *La Cabaña Amarilla*, about 3 km. along the beach from Granada (turn right at the wharf, taxi from city centre, US$0.40), for US$1 p.p. for 1½ hrs. Alternatively, take the morning bus from Granada to Puerto de Aseses, or Asese, a few km. further S (pleasant restaurant with fine view) and hire boats or take organised trips, e.g. to Zapatera and El Muerto, for US$15 p.p. including lunch and fruit, or to Ometepe, Solentiname, San Carlos and the Río San Juan. Call Casa de Gobierno in Granada, T 4513.

The largest island, Ometepe (population 20,000), has two volcanoes, one of them a perfect cone rising to 1,610 metres. There are two villages on the island: *Moyogalpa* (population 4,500) and Alta Gracia, which are connected by bus (1 hr. US$1.50). Boat from Granada to Alta Gracia, US$2, 4½ rough hrs., the public service is on Tues. and Thurs., at 1000 and Sat. at 1300; returning the following days. Boat Moyogalpa-Granada, Sun. a.m. Moyogalpa is pleasanter than Alta

Gracia (which has several unnamed *hospedajes* of varying quality—take your own toilet paper); *Pensión Aly*, opp. Esso, friendly, clean, helpful and *Pensión Moyogalpa*, both G, very noisy, cheap. Cheaper, *Pensión Jade*. Cock-fights in Moyogalpa on Sunday afternoons. One can stroll to the base of Volcán Concepción for good views of the lake and the company of howler monkeys (*congos*). To climb the volcano you need permission from the police who will give information on paths. Very steep near summit, 10 hrs. round trip.

Moyogalpa can be reached from **San Jorge** on the lake's SW shore; boats at 1100 and 1500, US$0.65, returning at 0600 and 1350, 1¼ hrs., schedules can be checked at the Tourist Board in Managua (1330 boat is too late for last bus Rivas-Granada). *Hotel Nicarao*, left off the Rivas-San Jorge road, F, basic meals, friendly. From San Jorge a road runs through Rivas (bus service every 10 mins., US$0.12, 30 mins.) to the port of San Juan del Sur. The Río San Juan, running through deep jungles, drains the lake from the eastern end into the Caribbean at San Juan del Norte. Launches ply down the river irregularly from the lakeside town of **San Carlos** (15-20,000 people) at the SE corner of the Lake. Much of the town was destroyed by fire in 1984, but some rebuilding has been done. Several boats run from Granada to San Carlos: three slow passenger/cargo boats leave on Mon., Wed. and Fri. at 1400, taking 15-20 hrs.; they start the return journey next day. Fare is US$4 (plus US$1.20 for a hammock— be early; tickets from near the pier). Two fast boats a week leave Granada, 8 hrs. returning next day, costing US$15 (a noisy trip, anything left on deck will get wet). Tickets must be bought from the office by *Hotel Granada*, open at 0800 but be there earlier. The slower boats stop at San Miguelito (pop. 8,000, one primitive *pensión*). (Bus Granada-San Miguelito, Mon., Tues., Wed., Thurs. 0830 from the pier, 8 hrs.)

At San Carlos are the ruins of a fortress built for defence against pirates (*Restaurant Río San Juan*, good meals, rooms for rent, G, dirty, noisy; also *San Carlos* and 2 more basic *pensiones*; vacancies hard to find; exchange at Banco Nacional de Desarrollo). Some 6 hrs. down river (9 hrs. back, US$1) are the ruins of another Spanish fort, Castillo Viejo (*Pensión Merlot*, G, no sign). This is the furthest point down the Río San Juan that non-military travellers are allowed to go (a permit needed nonetheless).

Boats also run from San Carlos to the **Solentiname Islands** in the Lake. A special permit used to be required to visit this area, but this should not now be necessary, **see page 556. The only hotel on the islands is** *Hotel Isla Solentiname*, on San Fernando island, safe, acceptable but basic (you wash in the lake), cost including meals D (at official rate); on Mancarrón island, the largest, is a library and an interesting church. Ernesto Cardenal (the poet and former Minister of Education) lived and worked here. The islands are home to many renowned primitive painters and are pleasant to hike around.

About 40 km. S of San Carlos, on the Río Frío, is Los Chiles, over the border in Costa Rica (**see also page** 587). Until 1988, no foreigners were allowed into this area, but some reports say it is possible now to cross into Costa Rica from San Carlos. Check with the police in advance for the latest position.

Warning The lake is dirty in some places, so swim in it with care. Swimming is possible in nearby Laguna de Apoyo (**see page** 546).

MANAGUA TO COSTA RICA

The Pan-American Highway, in good condition, has bus services all the way to San José de Costa Rica (148 km.). The road runs into the Sierra de Managua, reaching 900 metres at Casa Colorada, 26 km. from Managua. Further on, at El Crucero, a paved branch road goes through the Sierra S to the Pacific bathing beaches of Pochomil and Masachapa (**see page** 535). The Highway continues through the beautiful scenery of the Sierras to **Diriamba**, 42 km. from Managua, at 760 metres, in a coffee-growing district. Population 26,500. Hotel: *Diriangén*, G with bath. Good fish at restaurant *2 de Junio*. Its great *fiesta* is on 20 January. There is a 32-km. dirt road direct to Masachapa (no buses), and another NE to Masaya, on the Managua-Granada highway. Being on a through route, it is impossible to get on buses to Managua or Rivas.

Five km. beyond Diriamba is **Jinotepe**, capital of the coffee-growing district of Carazo, joined also by railway with Diriamba and Masaya. It has a fine neo-classical church with modern stained glass windows from Irún, in Spain. The *fiesta* in honour of St. James the Greater is on 24-26 July. Altitude 760 metres; population 17,600; *Hospedaje San Carlos*, G, no sign, ask around for it; local holiday, 25 July. Banco Nacional de Desarrollo for exchange.

From **Nandaime**, 21 km. from Jinotepe, altitude 130 metres, a paved road runs N to Granada (bus US$0.25). Nandaime has two interesting churches, El Calvario and La Parroquia (1859-72). About 45 km. beyond Nandaime (US$0.40 by bus) is **Rivas**, a town of 21,000 people. The Costa Rican national hero, the drummer Juan Santamaría, sacrificed his life here in 1856 when setting fire to a building captured by the filibuster William Walker and his men. The town has a lovely old church. In the dome of the Basilica, see the fresco of the sea battle against the ships of Protestantism and Communism. Rivas is a good stopping place (rather than Managua) if in transit by land through Nicaragua. The road from the lake port of San Jorge joins this road at Rivas; 11 km. beyond Rivas, at La Virgen on the shore of Lake Nicaragua, it branches S to San Juan del Sur.

Hotels *Nicaragua*, on street behind bank on main square, (accepts córdobas), E, clean, well-equipped, but does not supply toilet paper, soap or towels, good restaurant but pricey (cinema next door); **Pensión Primavera**, F, basic; *El Coco*, G, near where bus from frontier stops, basic, friendly, comedor with vegetarian food; *Hospedaje El Mesón*, basic; *Hospedaje Delicia*, on main Managua-border road, G, basic and dirty, friendly; several on Highway, *Hospedaje Lidia*, near Texaco, F, clean, noisy, family-run. (At the Texaco station, Lenín, who speaks English, is very helpful.) *Restaurant Chop Suey* on Parque Central; *Rinconcito Salvadoreño*, on Parque Central, open air, charming. *Restaurant El Ranchito*, near *Hotel El Coco*, friendly, serves delicious chicken and churrasco.

Exchange Banco Nacional de Desarrollo.

Buses to the frontier: every 2 hrs.: 0545 and 0700 good for connections for buses to San José (US$0.20, 1 hr.) (taxis available, about US$8), or try to get on the Sirca bus which stops at the Sirca office about 0830, Mon., Wed. and Fri. or Sat. (N.B. Tica bus stops in Rivas, but only to let people off). Bus to Managua, from 0400 (last one 1700), 3 hrs., US$0.80; taxi, US$25. One fast bus to Granada, US$2; other, slower buses, frequent. Regular bus to San Jorge on Lake Nicaragua (taxi to San Jorge, US$0.40).

San Juan del Sur is 34 km. from Rivas (regular minibus from market, crowded, 45 mins., US$0.20), 93 from Granada. There are roads from Managua (a 2½-hr. drive) and Granada. Population 4,750. It has a beautiful bay with a sandy beach and some rocky caves reached by walking round the point past the harbour. (The caves are close to a military complex and you may not be allowed to get there.) Best beaches (Playa del Coco, Playa del Tamarindo) are 15 km. away on the road to Ostional. Sunsets here have to be seen to be believed. Check tides with officials at the Customs Office, who will give permission to park motor-caravans and trailers on the wharves if you ask them nicely.

These vehicles may also be parked on Marsella beach, about 5 km. from San Juan; coming S, turn right on entering San Juan, by shrimp-packing plant.

Hotels *Barlovento*, Government-owned on hill above town, B p.p., restaurant, accepts only US$ for room bill but meals can be paid for in córdobas, tax free shop (US$ only) for toiletries, radios etc. *Estrella*, on Pacific, F, with balconies overlooking the sea, breakfast extra, partitioned walls, take mosquito net, toilet facilities outside, rooms must be shared as they fill up; *Irazú*, one block from beach, some rooms with bath, very run down; *Buengusto*, opposite, F, OK. *Hospedaje Casa No. 28*, 40 metres from beach, near minibus stop for Rivas, G p.p., shared showers, mosquitos, kitchen and laundry facilities, clean, rec; 2 other *casas de huéspedes* near market. *Gallo de Oro*, ½ km. north of town, G, very basic but friendly and cheapest around.

Restaurants *Salón Siria*, good; good *panadería* one block from beach. Good cafés along the beach for breakfast and drinks; the beach front restaurants all serve good fish. Lobster and prawns are specialities. Breakfast and lunch in market. Food in the evening from a stall in street running W from the market; *Lago Azul*, good fish restaurant at N end of bay beyond the river; *Rancho Miravalle*, good for fish.

Exchange Banco Nacional de Desarrollo.

Post Office 2 blocks S along the front from *Hotel Estrella*.

The road reaches the Costa Rican boundary at Peñas Blancas, 37 km. beyond Rivas (no gasoline for sale between border and Rivas; no hotels at the border). It is easy to exchange money on the Costa Rican side of the border, which is closed from 1200-1300 and 1800-0800. Nicaraguan side closes 1200-1300 and 1600-0800. It is 3½-4 hrs. by bus to Managua, 4 to San José, but through journeys are longer because of slow border formalities (last bus to Liberia, 1715). Minibuses run the 4 km. from the Nicaraguan border offices at Sapoá to the Costa Rican border posts every 20 mins., US$1.20, otherwise you must walk or hitch. When the Tica or Sirca bus passes through, the queues are long; if not on a Tica or Sirca bus, arrive at border before 0800 to miss the queues. This border presents no problems for motorists, but remember that it is compulsory to buy insurance in Costa Rica (**see page** 612).

THE CARIBBEAN COAST

The Autonomous Atlantic Region was given the status of a self-governing region in 1987. These tropical lowlands have heavy rainfall between May and December. The economy is based on timber, fishing and mining.

The area, together with about half the coastal area of Honduras, was never colonized by Spain. From 1687 to 1894 it was a British Protectorate known as the Miskito kingdom. It was populated then, as now, by Miskito Indians. Today there is also strong African influence which has its roots in the black labourers brought in by the British to work the plantations and in Jamaican immigration. Other groups are Sumu, Rama and Garifuna, as well as Spanish-speaking *mestizos*. English is widely spoken. The Sandinista revolution, like most other political developments in the Spanish-speaking part of Nicaragua, was met with mistrust, and many Indians engaged in fighting for self-determination. About half the Miskito population fled as refugees to Honduras, but most returned after 1985 when a greater understanding grew between the Sandinista government and the people of the East Coast.

Note During most of the 1980s movement was restricted for tourists to the urban centres. In early 1990 much of the area was still under military control, so if intending to travel overland, check conditions in advance. Permits are no longer needed; see page 556.

At San Benito, 35 km. from Managua on the Pan American Highway going north, the Atlantic Highway branches E, paved all the way to Rama on the Río Escondido, or Bluefields River. Shortly after Teustepe, a paved road goes NE to Boaco. A turn-off, unpaved, goes to Santa Lucía, a village inside a crater, with a women's handicraft shop. **Boaco** (15,000 people) has several *hospedajes* and its specialities are white cheese and cream. From Boaco, unpaved roads go N to Muy Muy and Matagalpa, and S to Comoapa (4,000 people). The Atlantic Highway continues through **Juigalpa** (30,000 people; 139 km. from Managua). Here is one of the best museums in Nicaragua, with a collection of idols resembling those at San Agustín, Colombia. Lodging at *Hotel Mayales*, (unsigned) close to Cathedral, best of a bad lot; *Hospedaje Central*, basic and noisy; *Hospedaje Angelita* the same; the hospedaje in *Comedor San Martín* is unfriendly; better is *Presillas* (Km. 269), unnamed, beside *Comedor González*; all G p.p. Small zoo in the valley below town. A gravel road goes to La Libertad, a goldmining town at 600 metres (4,000 people, *hospedaje*), and on to Santo Domingo. 25 km. S of Juigalpa an unpaved road turns off to Acoyapa (7 km., 5,000 people, *hospedaje*), El Morrito, San Miguelito and San Carlos on Lake Nicaragua (**see page** 547).

The main road goes S to Santo Tomás (10,000 people, several *hospedajes*) and smaller villages (including La Gateada, turn-off to Nuevo Güinea, centre of cacao production), to Cara de Mono (*hospedaje*), on the Río Mico, and finally to **Rama**, (pop. 12,000), 290 km. from Managua. The town was badly hit by Hurricane Joan in October 1988 when the river rose 16 metres above normal height. *Hospedaje Ramada Inn* seems to be the best; Hotels *Amy* and *Johanna* both F, neither has showers, *Amy* cleaner and quieter, near main jetty.

From Managua to Bluefields Take a bus from Mercado Ivan Montenegro/Oscar Benavides, Managua to Rama along the now-completed road (in poor condition near Rama), 6-7 hrs., leaves 0300, to connect with boat to Bluefields at 1100, Sat. or Sun., Tues., Thurs. (check days—both legs US$2, book 24 hrs. in advance). Take your own food and drink. Trip downriver takes 6 hrs. On other days 4 or 5 buses from Managua and a fast boat can be hired for US$17 or hitch on a fishing boat. Return from Bluefields: boat at 0500, bus to Managua 1300 (combined tickets available, ticket office at Encab, nr. dock). Or take your car and park it in the compound at the Chinaman's store at Rama (opposite *Hotel Amy*) for US$0.50 a day. Buses back to Managua leave Rama from 0300 onwards.

On the "Bluefields Express", David McNally of Consett, Co. Durham, writes: "Some two hundred people, assorted animals and goods crowd the deck. Only two men share the luxury of the roof space, one carries a rocket launcher, the other a machine gun.

The journey passes through the sparsely populated eastern half of Nicaragua, a beautiful, yet eerie landscape devastated by Hurricane Joan in 1988. The river is wide and fast flowing; the forest begins at the banks and stretches back into the distance. An hour into the trip the branches are bare, the trees thin, a blasted landscape. Although remarkably little human life was lost, homes and buildings were blown, or washed away. The mangled remains of boats appear in the trees, the skipper pilots the "Express" around a sunken wreck and suddenly, unbelievably, a huge container ship high on the bank, as if in dry dock, looms above us".

Bluefields, the most important of Nicaragua's 3 Caribbean ports, gets its name from the Dutch pirate Abraham Blaauwveld. It stands on a lagoon behind the bluff at the mouth of the Bluefields river (Río Escondido), which is navigable as far as Rama (96 km.). In May there is a week-long local festival, Mayo-Ya!, with elements of the British Maypole tradition and local music, poetry and dancing. Bananas, cabinet woods, frozen fish, shrimps and lobsters were the main exports until the hurricane in 1988 (see below). Population 17,700.

Tragically, in October 1988, Hurricane Joan detroyed virtually all of Bluefields, but the rebirth is well underway. Information on the region can be found at the Cidca office. Local bands practice above the Ivan Dixon Cultural Centre, beside the library. There are several bars, a couple of reggae clubs, *comedores* and restaurants (2 with a/c), and a Dollartienda. Prices are about the same as in Managua. The atmosphere is relaxed and friendly.

Hotels *Costa Sur*, C p.p., *Cuato*, damaged by the Hurricane, no running water, not rec. (yet); *El Dorado*, may offer floor space to late arrivals; *Marda Maus*. *Café Central* provides accommodation, has colour TV. Everywhere can be full if you arrive late, or are last off the ferry.

Flights Aeronica daily from Managua (except Sunday), US$30 one way (dollars only), and on to the Corn Islands, US$15; check schedules in advance.

Boats From the main wharf small boats leave irregularly for coastal villages such as Orinoco and Tasbapounie (*hospedaje* run by Mr. Leonard Richard Brent); food may be scarce in all settlements. A boat leaves most days around 0600 to Laguna de Perlas (Pearl Lagoon) 80 km. north of Bluefields 3-6 hours, US$5. The lagoon itself is some 50 km. long with Indian villages round its shores. At the village of Pearl Lagoon there is a newly established hostel, *Miss Ingrid's*, very friendly, stay with the entertaining family. Larger vessels may be available for transport to Puerto Cabezas, but it is not possible to travel south since the area south of Bluefields and east of San Carlos is a military zone. El Bluff is another military zone across the lagoon from Bluefields. It is accessible by ferry (15 mins. US$0.50) from a small wharf behind the market, but no photography allowed.

Corn Islands (Islas del Maíz), in the Caribbean opposite Bluefields, are two small beautiful islands fringed with white coral and slender coconut trees, though sadly many on the larger island were blown down by the hurricane. The smaller island escaped serious damage; it can be visited by boat from the larger island, but there are no facilities for the tourist. The larger is a popular Nicaraguan holiday resort; its surfing and bathing facilities make it ideal for tourists (best months March and April). For fishing (barracuda, etc.), contact Ernie Jenkie (about US$5/hour). If you climb the mountain, wear long trousers, as there are many ticks. The language of the islands is English. The local coconut oil industry has been devastated by Hurricane Joan, but lobsters provide much prosperity.

Passenger-carrying cargo boats leave Bluefields for the Corn Islands from the docks of Copesnica, N of town, around a small bay and past the ruined church. Depart 0500, with a stop in El Bluff where foreigners must register with the police, US$3 one way. The water around Bluefields is dirty, muddy brown, soon becoming a clear, sparkling blue. Boats back to Bluefields leave from Will Bowers Wharf; tickets available in advance from nearby office. There are no regular sailings. It is possible to hitch a lift on a fishing boat, enquire at Inpesca at the port. Air services daily (except Sun. and may change throughout the year), US$15 one way to Bluefields, US$30 to Managua; book well in advance and book return immediately on arrival. Also, check your reservation continually; there is a waiting list and your chances depend on the size of the plane (either 22-or 26-seater).

Hotels and Restaurants There are 4 hotels: *Hospedaje Miramar* is rec., serves meals; *Hospedaje Playa Coco*, also serves meals; two others; one can find rooms for about US$2 (rec. is Miss Florence's house—*Casa Blanca*—at Playa Coco). The chief problem in all the hotels is rats, which may not be dangerous, but neither are they pleasant. *Comedor Blackstone*; *Mini* Café; ice cream parlour; several bars and reggae clubs. Ask around for where meals are available. Try banana porridge and sorrel drink (red, and ginger-flavoured). There is a severe shortage of food, water and most drinks (except rum). Main market area is near Will Bowers Wharf. Dollars are widely used and there is a dollartienda. In general, the islands are expensive. Bank for exchange is 30 mins. walk from Will Bowers Wharf, near the Promar lobster fleet offices.

The best beach for swimming is Long Beach on Long Bay; walk across the island from Playa Coco.

San Juan del Norte on the Costa Rican border has been destroyed and is now a military base.

Puerto Cabezas (Bilwi in local language) is N of the Río Grande. Population: 22,000. There are air services daily (except Thur. and Sun.) at 0800 from Managua (US$95 return). Permit needed. Aeronica flies from Bluefields on Thurs.; there are occasional cargo boats from Bluefields. The port is run down and heavily militarized; visitors are not allowed outside the town without special invitation. There are severe food shortages. At Bocana is a nice beach with a fresh water lagoon behind.

Hotels and Restaurants *Hospedaje Rivera* is better than *Descanso del Viajero* which is filthy and full of mosquitoes. Several restaurants: *Atlántico* (best); Doña Sergia opposite does good, cheap meals; *Ma Weh*; *Linda Vista*. 3 lively discos, the best being *Scorpio* and *Blue Beach*.

Exchange Banco Nacional de Desarrollo.

Note There is no access to the Honduran border, nor to the mining towns of Rosita, Siuna and Bonanza.

INFORMATION FOR VISITORS

Documents Visitors must have a passport with 6 months validity (at least), and proof of US$200 (or equivalent in córdobas) in cash or cheques for their stay in the country (according to the Nicaraguan Consulate in London—but see below). No visa is required by nationals of Central American countries, USA, Belgium, Denmark, Finland, Ireland, Liechtenstein, Luxembourg, Netherlands, Norway, Spain, Sweden, Switzerland or the United Kingdom for a 90-day stay. **N.B.** Visa rules are changing frequently, check before you travel. Citizens of all other countries need a visa, which should be bought before arriving at the border, is valid for arrival within 30 days, and for a stay of up to 30 days; it costs US$25; 6 months validity on passport, 2 passport photographs and an onward ticket are required. Visas can take 24 hrs. to be processed. Extensions are difficult to obtain. W. Germans can obtain visas (DM 70) from Generalkonsulät von Nicaragua, 2 Hamburg, P.O. Box 32 33 54, or in Central America. Ensure that your visa runs from the day you enter the country, not from the day of issue: ask the Generalkonsulät to give a written statement, in Spanish, to this effect. Commercial travellers should carry a document from their firm accrediting them as such. Only those visitors who have no tourist cards and require visas for entry need an exit permit. 72-hour transit visas cost US$20, from embassies, but apparently not at borders. A transit visa, obtained at a land border, cannot be converted into a full visa within the country. An air ticket can be cashed if not used, especially if issued by a large company, but bus tickets are sometimes difficult to encash. It is reported, however, that the Nicaraguan Embassy in a neighbouring country is empowered to authorize entry without the outward ticket, if the traveller has enough money to buy the ticket. Also, if you have a visa to visit another Central American country, you are unlikely to be asked to show an outward ticket (this applies to all Central American countries: be two visas ahead!). An exit stamp costing US$10 is required for visitors who have stayed over 30 days in the country.

In 1983, a regulation was introduced stating that all visitors, whether arriving by air or land, *must* change US$60 (cash or travellers cheques if you insist) into córdobas at the official rate (US$25 for transit-visa holders, but *only* if you remain in Nicaragua less than 24 hours). Check what you are given for your US$60, some travellers report being cheated by as much as 10%. If turned back from Honduras or Costa Rica for any reason, get your Nicaraguan exit stamp cancelled, not a new entry stamp, otherwise you will have to change another US$60. Motorists and motorcyclists must pay US$20 in cash on arrival at the border (bicyclists pay US$2); allow plenty of time for border facilities (especially when coming from Honduras)—average is 4 hours—because vehicles not cleared by 1630 are held at customs overnight. Also, the last transport into Nicaragua (to Somoto) leaves at 1700. There is nowhere to stay at the border. Make sure you get all the correct stamps on arrival, or you will encounter all sorts of problems once inside the country. You will also be asked on arrival to show that you have US$200 to cover your stay in Nicaragua and fill in a declaration on the amount of money and valuables you are bringing in. Hotel bills must be paid in dollars in Managua and a few more expensive places elsewhere. You get a better rate changing córdobas back into US$ in Costa Rica than in Honduras.

Warning Nicaraguan customs and border formalities can take up to 8 hours (but sometimes much less).

Taxes All passengers have to pay a sales tax of US$5 on all tickets issued in and paid for in Nicaragua; a transport tax of 1% on all tickets issued in Nicaragua to any destination; and an airport tax of US$10 on all departing passengers (except on Aeroflot and Cubana flights).

Air Services From London: British Airways, Virgin Atlantic, Continental or Pan Am to Miami and connect to Lacsa, or Aviateca (via Guatemala City). Aeronica flies to Mexico City direct, Guatemala City, San José and Panama City; Sahsa flies to Tegucigalpa, and Copa flies to Guatemala City, San José, San Salvador and Panama. From Europe, with Iberia to Managua on Wed., or connect with KLM in San José. Aeronica (twice) and Cubana (once a week) fly to Havana (to fly to Havana you need an onward ticket). Aeroflot fly to Nicaragua from Moscow via Shannon and Havana, or via Luxembourg and Havana, but it is *vital* to check that these services are in operation when you want to travel. All flight tickets purchased by non-residents must be paid in US dollars.

Customs Duty-free import of ½ kg. of tobacco products, 3 litres of alcoholic drinks and 1 large bottle (or 3 small bottles) of perfume is permitted.

Internal Transport Hitchhiking is widely accepted, but not easy because so many people do it and there is little traffic—offer to pay ("pedir un ride"), even with military vehicles. Local buses are the cheapest in Central America, but are extremely crowded owing to a lack of vehicles and fuel. Baggage that is loaded on to the roof or in the luggage compartment is charged for, usually twice the rate for passengers.

Motoring Low octane gasoline costs US$1 a US gallon (shortages frequent, take extra fuel with you), diesel, US$0.80. Cars will be fumigated on entry, for which there is a US$2 charge. For motorcyclists, the wearing of crash helmets is compulsory. Service stations close at 1700-1800. Beware when driving at night, the national shortage of spare parts means that many cars have no lights. Your car may be broken into if unattended and not in secure place.

Food There is still a food shortage in some parts of the country, and it can be difficult to find items such as eggs and rice outside Managua. Sugar and salt are rationed to one packet each per purchase. Note the government-owned *Colectivo de Soja* which encourages the use of soya as an alternative source of protein; vegetarian restaurants of this chain in Masaya, Managua, Granada and Estelí. Nicaraguan "pizzas" are not much like the real thing.

Tipping in Nicaragua: 10% of bill in hotels and restaurants (many restaurants add 10% service and 15% tax to bills); US$0.50 per bag for porters; no tip for taxi drivers.

Security Visitors to Nicaragua must carry their passports (or a photocopy) with them at all times. Border officials do not like army-type clothing on travellers, and may confiscate green or khaki rucksacks (backpacks), parkas, canteens. They also inspect all luggage thoroughly on entering and leaving Nicaragua. Do not photograph any military personnel or installations.

Pickpocketing and bagslashing has increased greatly in Managua, especially in crowded places, and on buses throughout the country.

Until mid 1989 all the border zones and the Atlantic Coast were "special regions" (i.e., fighting is possible) and permits were required by tourists wishing to visit. Even before the 1990 elections, permits were no longer required, and with significant political changes since April 1990, it is impossible to predict the situation for 1991. Check with Inturismo, hotels, Aeronica (for Bluefields and Puerto Cabezas) for up to date information.

Health The usual tropical precautions about food and drink. Tap water is probably all right in Managua, but avoid uncooked vegetables and peeled fruit. Intestinal parasites abound; if requiring treatment, take a stool sample to a government laboratory before going to a doctor. Malaria risk especially in the wet season; take regular prophylaxis. Medicines are in very short supply and you are strongly advised to bring anything you may need with you. Treatment in Centros de Salud, medical laboratories and dispensaries is free, though we have reports that visitors may have to pay. Dengue fever was reported in late 1989 in Masaya. Private dentists are better-equipped than those in the national health service (but no better trained).

Clothing Dress is informal; business men often shed jackets and wear sports shirts, but shorts are never worn. The wearing of trousers is perfectly OK for women. The dry season runs from December to May, and the wettest months are usually June and October. Best time for a business visit: from March to June, but December and January are the pleasantest months.

Hours of Business 0800-1200, 1430-1730 or 1800. Banks: 0830-1200, 1400-1600, but 0830-1130 on Sat. Government offices are not normally open on Sat. in Managua, or in the afternoon anywhere.

Much detailed commercial information is given in "Hints to Exporters: Nicaragua", obtainable on application to the Dept. of Trade, Export Services Division, Sanctuary Buildings, 16-20 Great Smith Street, London SW1P 3DB.

Public Holidays 1 January: New Year's Day. March or April: Thursday of Holy Week and Good Friday. 1 May: Labour Day. 19 July: Revolution of 1979. 14 September: Battle of San Jacinto. 15 September: Independence Day. 2 November: All Souls' Day (Día de los Muertos). 7 and 8 December: Immaculate Conception (Purísima). 25 December: Christmas Day.

Businesses, shops and restaurants all close for most of Holy Week; many companies also close down during the Christmas-New Year period. Holidays which fall on a Sunday are taken the following Monday. Local holidays are given under the towns.

Standard Time Six hours behind GMT.

Currency The unit is the new córdoba (C$), divided into 100 centavos. A new currency the córdoba oro, was scheduled for introduction in July, 1990.

Exchange controls are fairly stringent. The **black market** for exchange, which is illegal and therefore dangerous, can be found with difficulty in Managua, in **Ciudad Jardín**, or in Granada. Safer is the official parallel rate, which banks and *casas de cambio* use. Visa card is hardly accepted anywhere (in banks only), but Master Card is used and, to a lesser extent, Cred-o-Matic and Diners Club.

Remember, when changing money at the border, that hotel bills in Managua, and in larger hotels outside, are in most cases charged in dollars; so do not overstock with córdobas.

Cost of living It is reported that the availability of goods in 1990 was improving, although you may have to search in various establishments (if not dollartiendas) for what you need. There were, however, great fluctuations in prices month by month, depending on whether the rate of devaluation matched the rate of inflation. As a rough guide a *comida corrida* costs about US$1-2 outside Managua, more in the capital; a beer US$0.50, a coke US$0.30 and a newspaper US$0.20.

Weights and Measures The metric system is official, but in domestic trade local terms are in use; for example, the *medio*, which equals a peck (2 dry gallons), and the *fanega*, of 24 *medios*. These are not used in foreign trade. The principal local weight is the *arroba*=25 lb. and the *quintal* of 101.417 English lb. Random variety of other measures in use include US gallon for petrol, US quart and pint for liquids; *vara* (33 ins.) for short distances and the lb. for certain weights.

Voltage 110 volts AC, 60 cycles.

Postal Services Airmail to Europe takes 2-4 weeks (letter rate US$0.05); from Europe 7-10 days.

Telegraph and Telephone lines are owned by the Government (Telcor). Rather unreliable automatic telephone services between Managua, León, Chinandega and Corinto. A few public telephones in Managua of the Brazilian "big-ear" type (they take 1 córdoba coins). There are wireless transmitting stations at Managua, Bluefields and Cabo Gracias a Dios, and private stations at Puerto Cabezas, El Gallo, and Río Grande.

Telephone calls from Managua to Europe: in any major town at the Telcor office, open 0700-2200. International phone calls are usually paid in córdobas, but dollars may be asked for in Managua; calls are very cheap in dollar terms, e.g. US$1 per minute to US. You may have to wait a long time for a line, except for early in the morning on weekdays. Collect calls to the USA are easy ("a pagarse allá"), also possible to Europe.

Press Managua: *La Prensa* (pro-government), *El Nuevo Diario*. *La Barricada*, official organ of the Sandinista Front (has a fortnightly international edition). León: *El Centroamericano*. *La Gaceta* is the official gazette. *Ya Veremos*, monthly, covering international subjects. *Revista Conservadora* is the best monthly magazine. Other magazines: *Semana Cómica*, weekly satirical. *Envío* (monthly, English and Spanish editions, Jesuit); *Pensamiento Propio* (current affairs, monthly); *Soberanía* (Nicaraguan affairs, Spanish/English bilingual). *El Pez y la Serpiente* is a monthly magazine devoted to the arts, poetry and literature.

Working in Nicaragua Volunteer work in Nicaragua is a good way of meeting the people. After the 1990 elections, it was not clear if the practice of accepting foreigners on work brigades would continue. It seemed to depend on which political party dominated the local council (in León, for example, the FSLN won and was keen that overseas volunteers should stay, but this is generally not the case). To discover the current situation, contact non-governmental organizations in your home country (e.g. the Catholic Institute of International Relations—CIIR—in the U.K.), twin town/sister-city organizations and national solidarity campaigns (NSC, 23 Bevenden St., London N1 6BH; Dutch Nicaragua Komitee, Aptdo Postal 1922, Managua). If you wish to help with harvests, go to Matagalpa for coffee, León for cotton, or Chinandega for sugar cane. Another option is to teach English, since there is a great shortage of teachers of the language. In all cases, a letter of introduction from an appropriate political or professional organization at home is a good idea.

In addition to those travellers listed in the general Central America section we should like to thank the following for new information on Nicaragua: Lynn Clark (Toronto), Marcel Kersten (Roosendaal, Neth.), Julie Millar, Martin Mowforth (Tavistock), Catherine Rogers (Oxford) and P. Zilhmann (Basel).

COSTA RICA

INTRODUCTION

COSTA RICA is the smallest but one—El Salvador—of the Central American republics. Its area is 51,100 square km. Only Panama has fewer inhabitants, but it is known throughout Latin America as the continent's purest democracy. In November 1989, Costa Rica celebrated its centenary of democracy. The Army was abolished in 1949, though it should be stressed that there is a very efficient-looking khaki-clad Civil Guard. Costa Rica has the highest standard of living in Central America, the fastest population growth and the greatest degree of economic and social advance.

Costa Rica lies between Nicaragua and Panama, with coastlines on both the Caribbean (212 km.) and the Pacific (1,016 km.). The distance between sea and sea is from 119 to 282 km. A low, thin line of hills between Lake Nicaragua and the Pacific is prolonged into northern Costa Rica, broadening and rising into high and rugged mountains in the centre and S. The highest peak, Chirripó Grande, SE of the capital, reaches 3,820 metres. Within these highlands are certain structural depressions; one of them, the Meseta Central, is of paramount importance. To the SW this basin is rimmed by the comb of the Cordillera; at the foot of its slopes, inside the basin, are the present capital, San José, and the old capital, Cartago. NE of these cities about 30 km. away, four volcano cones rise from a massive common pedestal. From NW to SE these are Poás (2,704 metres), Barba (2,906 metres), Irazú (3,432 metres), and Turrialba (3,339 metres). Irazú and Poás are intermittently active. Between the Cordillera and the volcanoes is the

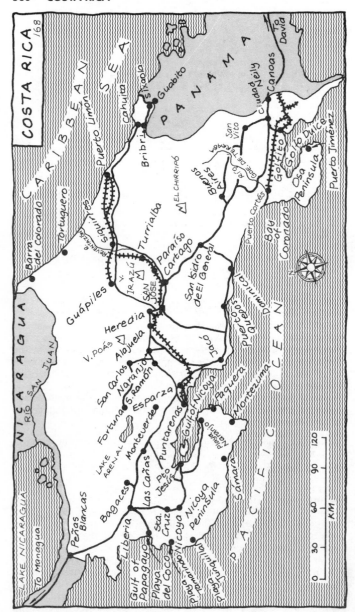

Meseta Central: an area of 5,200 square km. at an altitude of between 900 and 1,800 metres, where two-thirds of the population live. The north-eastern part of the basin is drained by the Reventazón through turbulent gorges into the Caribbean; the Río Grande drains the western part of it into the Pacific.

There are lowlands on both coasts. The Nicaraguan lowland along the Río San Juan is continued into Costa Rica, wide and sparsely inhabited as far as Puerto Limón. A great deal of this land, particularly near the coast, is swampy; SE of Puerto Limón the swamps continue as far as Panama in a narrow belt of lowland between sea and mountain.

The Gulf of Nicoya, on the Pacific side, thrusts some 65 km. inland; its waters separate the mountains of the mainland from the 900-metre high mountains of the narrow Nicoya Peninsula. From a little to the S of the mouth of the Río Grande de Tárcoles, a lowland savanna stretches NW past the port of Puntarenas and along the whole north-eastern shore of the Gulf towards Nicaragua.

Below the Río Grande the savanna is pinched out by mountains, but there are other banana-growing lowlands to the S. Small quantities of African palm and cacao are now being grown in these lowlands. In the far S there are swampy lowlands again at the base of the Peninsula of Osa and between the Golfo Dulce and the borders of Panama. Here there are 12,000 hectares planted to bananas. The Río General runs through a southern structural depression almost as large as the Meseta Central.

Climate   Altitude, as elsewhere in Central America, determines the climate, but the *tierra templada* and the *tierra fría* start at about 300 metres lower on the Pacific than on the Atlantic side. The Pacific side is the drier, with patches of savanna among the deciduous forest; the Atlantic side has heavy rainfall— 300 days a year of it—and is covered far up the slopes with tropical forest: about a third of Costa Rica is forested.

The climate varies from the heat and humidity of the Caribbean and Atlantic lowlands to warm temperate on the Meseta Central and chilly temperate at the greater heights. On the Cordillera Talamanca, the average temperature is below 16°C. There are dry and wet seasons: the dry runs from December to April, the wet from May to November, when the rainfall in the Meseta Central averages 1,950 mm. and roads are often bogged down. The hottest months are March and April. Between December and April is the best time to visit.

History   Costa Rica was discovered in September 1502, during Columbus' last voyage. Rumours of vast gold treasures (which never materialized) led to the name of Costa Rica (the Rich Coast). The Spaniards settled in the Meseta Central, where there were some thousands of sedentary Indian farmers (whose numbers were soon greatly diminished by the diseases brought by the settlers). Cartago was founded in 1563 by Juan Vásquez de Coronado, but there was no expansion until 145 years later, when a small number left Cartago for the valleys of Aserrí and Escazú. They founded Heredia in 1717, and San José in 1737. Alajuela, not far from San José, was founded in 1782. The settlers were growing in numbers (many farmers emigrated from northern Spain) but were still poor and raising subsistence crops only. Independence from Spain was declared in 1821 whereupon Costa Rica, with the rest of Central America, immediately became part of Mexico. This led to a civil war, during which, two years later, the capital was moved from Cartago to San José. After independence, the government sought anxiously for some product which could be exported and taxed for revenue. It was found in coffee, introduced from Cuba in 1808, which Costa Rica was the first of the Central American countries to grow. The Government offered free land to coffee growers, thus building up a peasant landowning class. In 1825 there was a trickle of exports, carried on mule-back to the ports. By 1846 there were ox-cart roads to Puntarenas. By 1850 there was a large flow of coffee to overseas markets: it was greatly increased by the opening of a railway from San José and Cartago to Puerto Limón along the valley of the Reventazón in 1890.

From 1850, coffee prosperity began to affect the country profoundly: the birth rate grew, land for coffee was free, and the peasant settlements started spreading, first down the Río Reventazón as far as Turrialba; then up the slopes of the volcanoes, then down the new railway from San José to the old Pacific port of Puntarenas.

Bananas were first introduced in 1878; Costa Rica was the first Central American republic to grow them. Labour was brought in from Jamaica to clear the forest and work the plantations. The industry grew and in 1913, the peak year, the Caribbean coastlands provided 11 million bunches for export, but the spread of disease lowered the exports progressively. The United Fruit Company then turned its attentions to the Pacific littoral especially in the S around the port of Golfito. However, although some of the Caribbean plantations were turned over to cacao, *abacá* (Manilla hemp) and African palm, the region has regained its ascendancy over the Pacific littoral as a banana producer (the Standard Fruit Company is an important redeveloper of the region).

Costa Rica's long tradition of democracy begain in 1889 and has continued to the present day with only a few lapses. In 1917 the elected president Alfredo González, was ousted by Federico Tinoco, who held power until 1919, when a counter revolution and subsequent elections brought Julio Acosta to the presidency. Democratic and orderly government followed until the campaign of 1948 when violent protests and a general strike surrounded disputed results. A month of fighting broke out after the Legislative Assembly annulled the elections, leading to the abolition of the constitution and a junta being installed, led by José Figueres Ferrer. In 1949 a constituent assembly drew up a new constitution and abolished the army. The junta stepped down and Otilio Ulate Blanco, one of the candidates of the previous year, was inaugurated. In 1952, Figueres, a socialist, founded the Partido de Liberación Nacional (PLN), and was elected President in 1953. He dominated politics for the next two decades, serving as President in 1953-58 and 1970-74. The PLN introduced social welfare programmes and nationalization policies, while the intervening conservative governments encouraged private enterprise. The PLN was again in

power from 1974-78 (Daniel Oduber Quirós) and 1982-86 (Luis Alberto Monge). In 1986 the PLN candidate, Oscar Arias Sánchez was elected with 52.3% of the vote and the PLN won 29 of the 57 seats in the Legislative Assembly.

President Arias moved immediately to assemble proposals for a peace pact in Central America and concentrated greatly on foreign policy initiatives. Diplomatic relations were restored with Nicaragua, efforts were made to expel contras resident in Costa Rica and the country's official proclamation of neutrality, made in 1983, was reinforced. The Central American Peace Plan, signed by the five Central American presidents in Guatemala in 1987, earned Arias the Nobel Peace Prize, although progress in implementing its recommendations was slow.

In the general elections held in February 1990, Rafael Angel Calderón Fournier, a conservative lawyer and candidate for the Social Christian Unity Party (PUSC), won a narrow victory with 51% of the vote, over President Arias' handpicked candidate of the PLN. Calderón, the son of a former president who was one of the candidates in the 1948 disputed elections, had previously stood for election in 1982 and 1986. The PUSC won 29 seats in the Legislative Assembly, against 25 for the PLN, and won the majority of the 81 municipal councils. Smaller parties won only three seats, despite proportional representation.

The People Population in 1989 was 2.94 million—a density of 58 to the square kilometre. In all provinces save Limón over 98% are whites and *mestizos* but in Limón 33.2% are blacks and 3.1% indigenous Indians, of whom only 5,000 survive in the whole country. Although officially protected, the living conditions of the indigenous Indians are very poor. But even in Limón the percentage of blacks is falling: it was 57.1 in 1927. Many of them speak Jamaican English as their native tongue. Much of the Caribbean coastland, more especially in the N, remains unoccupied. On the Pacific coastlands a white minority owns the land on the *hacienda* system rejected in the uplands. About 46% of the people are *mestizos*. The population has risen sharply in the mountainous Peninsula of Nicoya, which is an important source of coffee, maize, rice and beans.

Some 51% are urban. Population growth rate is 2.8%; urban growth rate 4.3%. Contact with the rural population is easy: the people are friendly and enjoy talking. (The national adjective, *costarricense*, is rather a mouthful: the universal short form is "tico/a".)

The Economy The country's economy is based on the export of coffee, bananas, meat, sugar and cocoa. The Meseta Central with its volcanic soil is the coffee-growing area: here too are grown the staple crops: beans, maize, potatoes and sugar cane, and the dairy farming is both efficient and lucrative. Some 12% of the land area is planted to crops, 45% to pasture and 32% is forested. The country's timber industry is very small and its resources have yet to be commercially utilized.

High growth in the industrial sector has led to considerable economic diversification, and manufacturing accounts for about 22% of gdp, compared with 19% in the case of agriculture. Industry is largely concerned with food processing but there is also some production of chemicals (including fertilizers—also exported), plastics, tyres, etc. Current major industrial projects include aluminium processing, a petrochemical plant at Moín, and a tuna-fish processing plant at Golfito.

There are small deposits of manganese, mercury, gold and silver, but only the last two are worked. Deposits of iron ore are estimated at 400m. tons and sulphur deposits at 11m. tons. Considerable bauxite deposits have been found but have not yet been developed. In 1980, the Arenal hydroelectric plant was opened; when operating at full capacity it can supply 98% of the country's electricity needs. The Government is presently involved in developing the Corobicí and other hydroelectric complexes as well as improving the port of Caldera on the Pacific coast and encouraging manufacturing. Oil companies are interested in offshore concessions in the Pacific. There is an oil refinery at Puerto Limón.

Despite several IMF-supported austerity programmes, the Costa Rican economy still suffers from large public sector deficits, partly because of a high level of government spending on social welfare. The country is burdened with a large foreign debt, which including accumulated arrears, amounts to US$5bn and is one of the highest per capita in the developing world. In the late 1980s, Costa Rica turned to the IMF and the World Bank for help in adjusting its economy. It was one of the first countries to take advantage of a US-sponsored, debt reduction proposal. An agreement was negotiated with commercial bank creditors in 1989-90, to be supported by funds from official creditors.

Government Legislative power is vested in a Legislative Assembly of 57 deputies, elected by proportional representation for four years. Executive authority is in the hands of the President, elected for the same term by popular vote. Men and women over 18 have the right to vote. Voting is secret, direct and free. Judicial power is exercised by the Supreme Court of Justice.

Communications Costa Rica has a total of 35,313 km. of roads of which 14% are paved. The route of the Pan-American Highway (now wholly paved) is described on **page** 593. A new highway has recently been built from San José to Caldera, a new port on the Gulf of Nicoya which has replaced Puntarenas as the principal Pacific port, and another has been completed from San José via Guápiles and Siquirres to Puerto Limón. Also a new road is being built to improve access to the Pacific beaches, from Playas de Jacó to Puerto Quepos and Puerto Cortés. All 4-lane roads into San José are toll roads (US$0.03-0.10). There are 1,286 km., all of 1.067-metre gauge; 967 km. are plantation lines—336 km. of the Northern Railway and 631 km. of the United Brands Company. The formerly British-owned Northern (Atlantic) Railway has 525 km.: its main line is between Puerto Limón and San José (166 km.), and it has a branch line (21 km.) between San José and Alajuela. The government-owned Ferrocarril Eléctrico al Pacífico between San José and Puntarenas has 132 km. of track; this line has been lengthened by the new branch to Caldera. New track has been laid in the Río Frío banana plantation zone; these trains are electric. Plans exist for electrification of the entire Atlantic railway.

Religion and Education Roman Catholicism is the official religion and over 90% of the population are Roman Catholic, the remainder being mostly Protestant. Educational standards are high: only 8.3% of the economically active population over the age of 25 have no formal schooling. Consequently literacy is high; 92.6% of the population aged 15 and lower is literate.

National Parks Tourists will particularly enjoy the many well-kept and well-guarded national parks and nature reserves which protect some samples of the extraordinarily varied Costa Rican ecosystems. Some of the last patches of dry tropical forest, for instance, can be found in the Santa Rosa National Park, and other parks protect the unique cloud forest.

The first step is to visit the **Servicio de Parques Nacionales (SPN)** in San José (Calle 17 y Av. 9; write in advance to Apartado 10094, or T 33-50-55), to get permits if necessary. To contact park personnel by radio link, T 33-54-73, or 23-69-63, but good Spanish is a help.

Bird watchers and butterfly lovers have long flocked to Costa Rica to see some of the 850 or so species of birds (the whole of the United States counts only about 800 species) and untold varieties of butterflies. All of these can be best seen in the parks, together with monkeys, deer, coyotes, armadillos, anteaters, turtles, coatimundis, raccoons, snakes, wild pigs, and, more rarely, wild cats and tapirs. Bird lists can be purchased in San José from the Organization for Tropical Studies is 4½ blocks west of Colegio Lincoln, in front of the Bodega del Banco Central. Take the Florida or Llorente bus from Calle 2; they will have a breakdown by park. You can also get plant and butterfly lists from them, and other valuable natural history information as well. Good field guides are Petersen, *Birds of Mexico* and *Birds of North America*; Stiles/Skutch, *Guide to the Birds of Costa Rica*; Ridgely, *Birds of Panama*; Golden Guide, *Birds of North America*; Daniel H.Janzel, *Costa Rican Natural History*; Philip J. de Vries, *Butterflies of Costa Rica*. Cheap maps and all information for the parks are available at the CIDA office of the SPN in Parque Bolívar (the zoo), Av. 11 just E of Calle 7, open Mon.-Fri., 0800-1530 (on Mon. ask zoo guard to let you in as zoo grounds are closed Mon.). The map annex to the SPN office in San José has all the parks marked in the excellent Instituto Geográfico maps, and the latter can be purchased at various places.

Nature guides can be found at The Bookshop in San José, and there is also available an illustrated book, *The National Parks of Costa Rica*, by Mario A. Boza (1986), which gives a good impression of what the different parks are like.

Although the National Parks and other privately owned reserves are a main tourist attraction, many are in remote areas and not easy to get to on public transportation. For those on tight budgets, try making up a party with others and sharing taxis or hiring a car. Descriptions of the individual parks, and how to get there, will be found in the text.

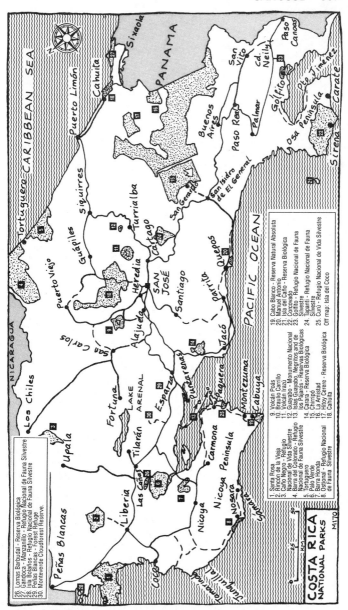

COSTA RICA
NATIONAL PARKS

M170

1. Santa Rosa
2. Rincón de la Vieja
3. Caño Negro - Refugio Nacional de Fauna Silvestre
4. Barra del Colorado - Refugio Nacional de Fauna Silvestre
5. Tortuguero
6. Palo Verde
7. Barra Honda
8. Ostional - Refugio Nacional de Fauna Silvestre
9. Volcán Poás
10. Braulio Carrillo
11. Volcán Irazú
12. Guayabo - Monumento Nacional
13. Isla Guayabo, Negritos and de los Pájaros - Reservas Biológicas
14. Carara - Reserva Biológica
15. Chirripó
16. La Amistad
17. Hitoy Cerere - Reserva Biológica
18. Cahuita
19. Cabo Blanco - Reserva Natural Absoluta
20. Manuel Antonio
21. Isla del Caño - Reserva Biológica
22. Corcovado
23. Golfito - Refugio Nacional de Fauna Silvestre
24. Tapantí - Refugio Nacional de Fauna Silvestre
25. Curú - Refugio Nacional de Vida Silvestre
Off map: Isla del Coco

26. Lomas Barbudal - Reserva Biológica
27. Gandoca - Manzanillo - Refugio Nacional de Fauna Silvestre
28. Islas Bolaños - Refugio Nacional de Fauna Silvestre
29. Peñas Blancas - Forest Refuge
30. Monteverde Cloudforest Reserve.

SAN JOSE

San José, with a population estimated at over one million, stands in a broad, fertile valley at an altitude of 1,150 metres, which produces coffee and sugar-cane. It was founded in 1737 and is a pleasant mixture of traditional Spanish and modern. The climate is excellent, though the evenings can be chilly. The lowest and highest temperatures run from 15° to 26°C. Slight earthquake shocks are frequent. Rainy season: May to November. Other months are dry.

Streets cross one another at right-angles. Avenidas run E-W; the Calles N-S. The three main street are Av. Central, Av. 2 and the intersecting Calle Central: the business centre is here. The best shops are along Av. Central. It is best not to take a car into San José between 0700 and 2000; traffic is very heavy. Many of the narrow streets are heavily polluted with exhaust fumes. Seven blocks of the Av. Central, from Banco Central running east to Plaza de la Cultura, are closed to traffic.

Avenidas to the N of Av. Central are given odd numbers; those to the S even numbers. Calles to the W of Calle Central are even-numbered; those to the E odd-numbered. The Instituto Costarricense de Turismo has an excellent map of the city, marking all the important sights and business houses. **N.B.** Few buildings have numbers, so find out the nearest cross-street when getting directions (200 metres means 2 blocks).

Sightseeing Many of the most interesting public buildings are near the intersection of Avenida Central and Calle Central. The Teatro Nacional (1897)—marble staircases, statuary, frescoes and foyer decorated in gold with Venetian plate mirrors—is just off Av. Central, on Calle 3 (US$0.75 to look around). Functions (ballet, concerts, etc.) take place most Tuesdays; it is closed on Sundays. It has a good coffee bar. Nearby is Plaza de la Cultura, Av. Central, C. 3/5. The Palacio Nacional (Av. Central, Calle 15) is where the Legislative Assembly meets; any visitor can attend the debates. Along Calle Central is Parque Central, with a bandstand in the middle among trees (bands play on Sun. mornings). To the E of the park is the Cathedral; to the N are the Raventos and Palace theatres, interesting; to the S are the Rex Theatre and a branch of the Banco Nacional. N of Av. Central, on Calle 2, is the Unión Club, the principal social centre of the country. Opposite it is the General Post and Telegraph Office. The National Museum, with a good collection of precolumbian antiquities, is in the reconstructed Vista Buena barracks, E along Av. Central (open 0900 to 1700; closed Mons.). Facing it is the new Plaza de la Democracia, constructed to mark the November 1989 centenary of Costa Rican democracy. Two blocks N of the National Museum is Parque Nacional, with a grandiloquent bronze monument representing the five Central American republics ousting the filibuster William Walker (see Nicaraguan chapter) and the abolition of slavery in Central America. There is also a statue donated by the Sandinista Government of Nicaragua to the people of Costa Rica. To the N of the park is the National Library.

Still further N is Parque Bolívar, now turned into a recreation area, with zoo (sloths in the trees), entrance, US$0.30. Along Av. 3, to the W of Parque Nacional, are the four gardens of Parque Morazán, with another bandstand at the centre. On Sun. there is an art market here. A little to the NE, Parque España—cool, quiet, and intimate—has for neighbours the Casa Amarilla (Yellow House), seat of the Ministry of Foreign Affairs, and the Edificio Metálico, which houses several of the main schools. In the park opposite the church of La Merced is a huge carved granite ball brought from the archaeological site at Palmar Norte.

The attractive Paseo Colón continues the Av. Central W to the former La Sabana airport (now developed as a sports centre, which is worth visiting) with a colonial-style building with frescoes of Costa Rican life in the Salón Dorado, on the upper floor. Further W is La Sabana, which has the National Stadium, seating 20,000 spectators at (mainly) football matches, basketball, volleyball and tennis courts, a running track, lake and swimming pool.

Local Holiday 28 to 31 December. Festivities last from 18 December, with dances, horse shows and much confetti-throwing in the crowded streets. Also parades during Easter week in the streets.

Warning Pickpockets are on the increase in San José, especially in the centre, in the market and on buses—the same applies throughout the country; be careful. We have also received reports of travellers (in particular backpackers) being detained or harassed by the police in a drive against illegal immigration, although few explanations are given. You must carry your passport (or a photocopy) with you at all times and make sure your papers are in order. To report theft: Policia Judicial-Detectives, Av. 6, C. 17/19.

Hotels

	Address	Tel	US$ Price Single	Stars Double	
Alameda	C.12 Av.Ctl	23-63-33	22	26-28	1
Ambassador	C.26 P.Colón	21-81-55	35	45	2
L'Ambiance	C.13 Av.9-11	22-67-02	40	50	-
Amstel*	C.7/Av.1	22-46-22	30	37	2
Aurola Holiday Inn†	C.5 Av.5	33-72-33	95	105	4
Balmoral	C.7 Av.Ctl	22-50-22	42	51	3
Bougainvillea †‡	Barrio Tournon	33-66-22	40-50	45-55	3
Cariari †‡	Near Airport	39-00-22	99	110	4
Club Paso Fino ‡	Santa Ana	49-14-66	18	25	-
Corobici ‡	Sabana Norte	32-81-22	85	95	3
Gran Hotel Costa Rica	C.3 Av.2	21-40-00	42	57	3
D'Galahi ‡	San Pedro	34-17-43	20-25	25-30	2
Diplomat	C.6 Av.Ctl-2	21-81-33	32	36	1
Doral	C. 6-8 Av. 4	33-50-69	17	27	-
Dunn	Bo. Amon	22-32-32	45	45	-
Europa †	C.Ctl Av.3-5	22-11-22	36-51	47-62	3
Suites Royal Dutch	C.4 Av.Ctl-2	22-10-66	41-43	54	2
Royal Garden	C.Ctl. Av.2	57-00-23	32	38	1
Sheraton Herradura †‡	Near Airport	39-00-33	100	110	4
Santo Tomás	C. 3-5 Av. 7	55-04-48	50	65-90	-
Irazú †‡	La Uruca	32-48-11	45-60	55-72	3
La Gran Vía	C.3 Av.Ctl	22-77-37	29	38	2
Posada Pegasus ‡	S.Antonio de Escazú	28-41-96	16-18	20-24	2
Plaza	C.2 Av.Ctl 2	2-55-33	20	30	1

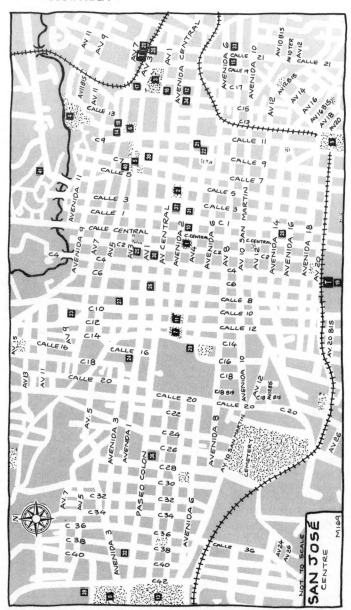

SAN JOSÉ
CENTRE
NOT TO SCALE
M169

	Address	Tel	US$ Price	Stars
			Single Double	
President	C.7-9 Av.Ctl	22-30-22	50 60	2
Talamanca	C.8-10 Av.	33-50-33	25 29	1
Tara Resort †‡	S. Antonio de Escazú	38-96-51	68 100	-
Torremolinos †	C.40 Av.5	22-52-66	55 60	3
Tennis Club ‡	Sabana Sur	32-12-66	40 45	2

Apartotels (With kitchen etc.)

	Address	Tel	Single	Double	Stars
Apartotel San José	C.17 Av.2	22-04-55	32	38	1
Apartotel Los Yoses †‡	Los Yoses	25-00-33	28-36	32-40	2
Apartotel Conquistador†‡	Los Yoses	25-30-22	23	28	1
Apartotel Castilla	C.24 Av.2-4	22-21-13	27	32	2
Apartotel Lamm§	C.15 Av.1	21-49-20	26	29	1
Apartotel Ramgo‡	Sabana Sur	32-38-23	25	33	1
Apartotel María Alexandra‡	Escazú	28-15-07	40	40	1
Apartotel Napoleon	C.40 Av.5	23-32-52	34	38	1
Apartotel Villas de Cariari	Cariari	39-26-22	75-95 per day	900 per month	2
Apartotel Res. de Golf‡	Cariari	39-10-20	80 per day	1200 per month	3

* Food recommended, book in advance   †Swimming pool

‡Out of town   §10% discount given for monthly stays

These rates are per day, without food and exclusive of 13.3% tax (March 1990). A deposit is recommended, especially in high season, Dec.-April, to guarantee reservations.

The **Gran Hotel Costa Rica** has good food, friendly English-speaking staff, rooms noisy unless you have a room over the central courtyard, rec. The **Ambassador** is rec., clean, modern, TV and phone in rooms, travel agency next door, restaurants and cinemas opposite, noisy, but friendly, heavily booked; **Bougainvillea** (rooms facing the street are noisy from traffic) and **Amstel** also rec.; **Irazú**, rec., hotel will organise excursions and visits. The **Herradura Sheraton**, on the other hand, has had some unfavourable reports, about reliability in particular. **Talamanca**, very friendly, good breakfast, try their rum punch.

Don Carlos, C. 9, Av. 7/9, T 21-67-07, 2-star, B with bath and breakfast, clean, comfortable, convenient; **Pico Blanco Inn**, B, T 28-19-08, San Antonio de Escazú, all rooms with balconies and views of Central Valley, several cottages,

San José: Key to map

1. Parque Central; 2. Plaza de la Cultura, Teatro Nacional, Gold Museum and Tourist Information Office; 3. Parque Nacional; 4. Parque Bolívar; 5. Parque Morazán; 6. Parque España; 7. Parque La Merced; 8. La Sabana; 9. Plaza González Víquez; 10. Cathedral; 11. Iglesia La Merced; 12. Museo Nacional; 13. Museo de Arte Costarricense; 14. Jade Museum; 15. Museo de Criminología; 16. Asamblea Legislativa; 17. Biblioteca Nacional; 18. Casa Amarilla (Ministry of Foreign Affairs); 19. Train station for Puntarenas (Pacific Railway); 20. Train station for Puerto Limón (Northern Railway); 21. Sirca Bus; 22. Tica Bus; 23. Buses for Puntarenas; 24. Coca Cola bus station; 25. Post Office and Telegraph Office; 26. Mercado Central; 27. Mercado de Borbón; 28. Clínica Bíblica; 29. Ministerio de Salud; 30. Banco Central; 31. Banco Anglo Costarricense; 32. Centro Colón (embassies, etc); 33. Migración; 34. Plaza de la Democracia; 35. Buses to Limón; HOTELS; 36. Ambassador; 37. Gran Hotel Costa Rica; 38. Amstel; 39. Corobici; 40. Aurola Holiday Inn; 41. Bougainvillea.

English owner, restaurant with English Pub—Costa Rican flavour; *Park*, C. 2/4, Av. 4, B, clean, with bar (T 21-69-44); *Ritz*, C. Central, Av. 8 and 10, T 224103, D with bath and hot water, friendly, manager helpful, free coffee, good breakfast, 2nd-hand book exchange, clothes washing facilities, a bit run down but rec.; *Pensión Centro Continental*, Av. 8-10, C. Central (T 33-17-31), E without bath, Japanese hospitality, clean, friendly, laundry, helpful, coffee available, rec.; *Bellavista*, Av. Central, C.19/21, T 23-00-95, E, friendly and helpful, with bath, clean, opposite *Dennies* restaurant; *Boston*, C. Central, Av. 8 (T 21-05-63), E, with or without bath, good, very friendly, but noisy; *Galilea*, Av. Central, C.13, T 33-69-25, D, friendly, hot showers, run by Dutch lady, English and German also spoken, rec.; *Roma*, C. 14, Av. Central and 1, T 23-21-79, uphill from Alajuela bus station, E, clean, safe, good value but windowless rooms; *Johnson*, C. 8, Av. Central (T 23-76-33), D, clean, restaurant and bar, good value, popular with Peace Corps; *Napoleón*, C. 6, Av. 3-5 (T 21-06-94), E, bath, friendly, small rooms, run down; *Marlyn*, C.4, Av. 7-9, F, hot showers, safe, parking for motorcycles; *Residencial Balboa*, Av. 10, C. 6, F, safe, cold shower, thin walls, basic, cheap; *Aurora*, Av. 4, C.8, F, good value, hot shower, clean, friendly, rec. *Príncipe*, Av. 6 y C. 2, F with bath, clean, hot water, noisy on street side.

Pensiones are: *Araica*, Av. 2 No. 1125, T 22-52-33, F without bath, clean, dark, thin walls, friendly; *Americana*, C. 2, Av. 2, F, without bath, clean, friendly, luggage store, washing facilities, rec; *Reforma Hilton*, C. 11, No. 105, E with bath, T 21-97-05, restaurant; *Moreno*, C. 12, Av. 6-8, T 21-71-36, E with bath. *Astoria*, Av. 7, No. 749, T 21-21-74, F, clean, hot showers, uncomfortable beds, thin walls, noisy; *Managua*, C. 8, Av. 1/3, F, small rooms, cold showers, rec.; *Boruca*, C. 14, Av. 1/3, T 23-00-16, F without bath, clean, laundry service, popular with Peace Corps, restaurant; *Musoc*, C. 16, Av. 3/5 (T 22-94-37), E, with private bath (F without), very clean, hot water, luggage stored, near to (and somewhat noisy because of) bus stations, but rec.; *San José*, C. 14 and Av. 5, E, with shower, clean, friendly, near bus station; *Asia*, C. 11 No. 63N (between Avs. Central and 1), T 23-38-93, E, clean, friendly, but paper-thin walls, lots of noise from rapid turnover, hot showers, Chinese-run, English spoken; *América*, Av. 7, C. 4, F, clean, good value, but also some hourly guests; *Corobicí*, Av. 1, between C. 10 and 12, F, cold showers, run down; *Pensión Otoya*, C. Central, Av. 5-7 (T 21-39-25) F, pleasant, popular with foreigners, English spoken; *Pensión Familiar* (also called *Hotel Delca*), Av. 6, C. 6-8, F, bath, clean, good value; *Rialto*, Av. 5 and C. 2, E, hot showers, some report it dirty, run down, cockroaches, noisy, others good value.

Near Tica Bus terminal are: *Illimani*, C. 9/11, Av. 2, T 22-06-07, F, friendly, will change money; *Avenida* 2, Av. 2, C. 9-11, F, clean, friendly, shared hot showers; *Nicaragua*, Av. 2, No. 1167, F, clean, friendly, safe to leave luggage, partitioned rooms. *Ticalinda No. 1*, Av. 2, No. 553 (unsigned), F, friendly, noisy, very dirty, little privacy, cheap laundry, good information, "gringo" place, often full, next door is the *Esmeralda Mariachi Palace* which operates all night except Sunday. There are several hotels near the various markets, such as the *España*, Av. 3/5, C. 8, F, run by a Spanish family; *Comerciante* annex (C. 10, Av. 3/5) and *Valencia* (C. 8, Av. 1, T 21-33-47, in F range) which are quite clean. Cheaper hotels usually have only wooden partitions for walls, so they are noisy. Also, they often rent only by the hour. **N.B.** Hotels in the red light district, C. 6, Avs. 1-5, near Mercado Central, charge on average US$10d with toilet and shower for a night.

Toruma Youth Hostel, T 24-40-85, Av. Central between Calles 31 and 33, spacious, kitchen, clean, rec., hot water not always available, F p.p. more expensive for those who do not hold International Student Identity Card (which can be purchased here); music, free for guests, on Fri. and Sat. nights; a good place for meeting other travellers to arrange group travel (ask for Fred Morris, editor of *Meso America* journal). Youth hostel information: Recaj, P.O. Box restaurant, club house, bars, pool, disco, T 68-07-84).

A number of beaches are reached by unpaved roads from the Nicoya-Liberia road. They can be reached by bus from the Liberia bus station. **Playa Junquillal** is reached by taking a bus from Liberia to Santa Cruz (on the Nicoya road), then bus at 1000 or 1415 from Guillermo Sánchez store to Paraíso (US$0.80), from where it is a 4 km. walk to Playa Junquillal, or take a car from one of the *cantinas* (*Hotel Antumalal*, B with bath, pool, T 68-05-06; *Villa Serena*, C, T 68-07-37; *Junquillal*, F, nice, friendly, good food; *Tortuga Inn*, 2 rooms for rent, F, restaurant, all meals, US$1/3, tent, and hammock space, run by Californian Bill Lauer who has plenty of information for travellers, also riding, fishing, hiking, surfing—and beautiful sunsets) glorious camping and a good beach.

Another good beach is **Playa Tamarindo**, which has an airport (plane Mon., Wed., Fri., US$18, to San José), and is served by several buses from Liberia. *Hotel Tamarindo Diria*, A with bath, T 68-06-52, excellent but overpriced; *Pozo Azul*, cabins, D (all rooms), cooking facilities, clean, good; two small *pensiones: Cabinas Zullymar*, D, rec., friendly bats (free, protected camping nearby), and *Dolis Bar*, E, basic. *Tamarindo Diria* has a good restaurant and there are several bars and a good restaurant, next to *Zullymar*. *Boutique New York*, good French clothing and waffles. The beaches go on for many km. (one, to the left is covered in small shells).

At Playa Flamingo (white sand) are *The Presidential Suites*, L (T 68-06-20/-04-44), *Villas Flamingo*, B, T 68-09-60; *Centro Vacacional Playa Bahia Flamingo*, A, T 68-09-76; *Club Flamingo*, L, T 33-80-56; *Flamingo Beach Condo Rentals* and *Club Playa Flamingo*, L, T 68-06-20. At Playa Potrero (black sand), *Hotel Potrero*, D, T 68-06-69; bus from Santa Cruz at 1030 and 1430. Playa Conchal: *Hotel Cóndor Club*, A, T 68-09-20. Playa Brasilito: *Hotel Las Palmas*, A, T 68-09-32. Good camping is reported at a beach 2 km. N of Brasilito. Playa Pan de Azúcar: *Hotel Sugar Beach*, A, 7 km. N. of Playa Flamingo. Playa Ocotal: *Hotel El Ocotal*, L, T 67-02-30. At **Playa Hermosa** is Playa Hermosa Cabinas, run by an American couple, C, T 67-01-36, clean, good reasonably-priced food; also cheaper cabins (F p.p.); 3 small restaurants on the beach. Also *Condovac La Costa*, L (T 67-02-67), luxury bungalows; *Condo hotel Costa Alegre*, B, T 67-02-18; *Complejo Turístico Los Corales*, L, T 67-02-55; cheaper places at the other end of the beach . Walking either to the left or the right you can find isolated beaches with crystal-clear water.

Popular (but noisy) is **Playa del Coco** in an attractive islet-scattered bay hemmed in by rocky headlands; to reach it one should leave the bus at Comunidad. There are bars, restaurants and one or two motels along the sandy beach: *Cabinas Chale*, D; *Flor de Itabo*, A, T 67-00-11/67-02-92, Fax 67-00-03, a/c rooms, 5 bungalows, restaurant, pool, horse-riding, excursions, specialists in big-game fishing; *Casino Playa del Coco*, E with bath and cockroaches; *Luna Tica* D, T 67-01-27, also has a dormitory (friendly, clean), both usually full at weekends. Bus to San José 0800 (Arata company), US$4, 4 hrs., bus from San José (Calle 14, Av.1-3) at 1000 and from Liberia at 1230 (US$0.50).

At **Playa de Panamá** is *Los Bananos*, cabins, restaurant and bar, D with bath, friendly, English spoken, good hiking, swimming, horseriding can be arranged, rec. (address is Apdo. 137, Liberia, Guanacaste); *Cabinas Vallejo*, F, with bath; camping possible on beach, a few basic fish restaurants, one *pulpería*—a peaceful place. Buy food inland in **Santa Cruz**, NW of Nicoya. Hotels in Santa Cruz: *Palenque Diria*, D, bath, restaurant; *Sharatoga*, D, bath (T 68-00-11); *Agente Viajero*, E, T 68-02-39. Cheap *pensiones*, G and basic: *Anatolia*, good value; *Santa Cruz*, *Isabel*. La Tortillera tortilla factory is an excellent place to eat. Bus San José-Santa Cruz, 0730 direct, US$2.80; bus Santa Cruz-Tamarindo at 1500,

10227, 1000 San José, T 22-33-69. Students are taken in as guests in private houses at low rates.

Trailer Park *Belén*, in San Antonio de Belén, 2 km. W of intersection at Cariari and San Antonio, 4 km. from airport, US$60/month, US$4/day, American-owned, shade, hot showers, laundry, good bus service to San José.

Restaurants Apart from the hotels, the best ones are the *Bastille*, French type (limited choice), on Paseo Colón; *Ile de France*, C. 7, Av. Central and 2 (T 22-42-41), good French chef; next door is *La Hacienda Steak House*, expensive but good; *Salón París*, Av. 3, C.1/3, rec.; *La Tranquera* (parking space) on the highway to Cartago at Curridabat, 6-8 km. E of San José, serves good steaks and other foods (orchestra for dancing at weekends). On N side of old La Sabana airport on Av. 3 and about C. 50 are two good restaurants, *El Chicote* (country-style; good grills) and *El Molino*. *Los Anonos*, in Escazú area, grills; also *Il Tula*, very good, same area; *Las Cascadas de Pavas*, 3 km. from centre, very good. *El Chalet Suizo*, Av. 1, C. 5-7 (T 223118), good food and service, international. *La Flecha*, Centro Colón Building, Paseo Colón, superb; *Lobster Inn*, Paseo Colón, C. 24, seafood, large choice, expensive; *La Casa de los Mariscos*, Los Yoses; *Italiano*, Carretera a Sabanilla, 1 block N. of Av. Central; *Goya*, Av. 1, C. 5/7, Spanish food (in the centre). *Casa de España*, in Bank of America, C. 1, good lunches; *Masia de Triquell*, Av. 2, Calle 38/40, Barra 1, Catalan, warmly rec. *Piccolo Roma*, Av. 2, Calle 24, highly rec.; *Los Lechones*, Av. 6, C. 11 and 13, good food, live music Fri. and Sat., reasonable prices; *Antojitos*, on Paseo Colón and in Centro Comercial Cocorí (road to suburb of San Pedro), serves excellent Mexican food at moderate prices; *La Perla* (name on doormat), C. Central y Av. 2, 24 hr., rec.; *El Balcón de Europa*, Av. Central y C.1, Italian, good, especially the cheeses; *San Remo*, C. 2, Av. 5-7, also Italian, friendly service, good value, frequently rec.

Chinese: *Kuang Chaou* on C. 11 between Av. Central and Av. 2; *Kiam Kon*, C.Central and Av. Central-2, good, large helpings; *Kaw Wah*, Av. 2, C. 5-7, rec.; *Fortuna*, Av. 6, C. 2-4; *Lung Mun* on Av. 1, between C. 5 and 7, reasonably priced. Also rec., *Fu Su Lu*, C. 7, Av. 2, Chinese, Korean, very good; *Tin Hao*, Av. 10, C. 4, T 21-11-63, good; and *Kam King*, Av. 10, C.19-21.

Japanese: *Jardín Jade*, Av. 4, C. 6-8, good value.

Vegetarian: *La Mazorca*, in San Pedro, near University of Costa Rica (Rodrigo Facio site), vegetarian and health foods; *Macrobiótica*, C. 11, Av. 6-8, health shop selling good bread; *Shakti*, Av. 8, C. 13, excellent; *Don Sol*, Av. 7b No. 1347, excellent 3 course lunch US$1.60, run by integral yoga society (open only for lunch); *Vishnu*, C. 3, Av. 1, good plato del día US$1.50, try their soya cheese sandwiches and ice cream.

McDonald's, Av. Central, C. 4, near Banco Central, opp. Plaza de la Cultura, and in Sabana, and Guadalupe, for hamburgers; *Kentucky Fried Chicken*, Paseo Colón, Calle 32, also Av. 2, C. 6, and Av. 3, C. 2, and Los Yoses, Av. Central; *Pollo Obay*, Av. 10, 6 C., good fried chicken; *La Fánega*, in San Pedro, for excellent hamburgers, folk music some nights; *Orléans*, also in San Pedro, serves crêpes; *Churrería Manolo*, Av. Central, C. Central and 2, good sandwiches and hot chocolate; *Don Taco*, Av. 1, C. 2, Mexican food in MacDonald's style; *José Taco*, Av. 1, C.3-5, Mexican fast food, plato del día US$1.50; *Corona de Oro*, Av. 3, excellent value midday meals; *Pastel de Pollo*, C. 2, Av. 6-8, excellent pies; *Comedor* beneath "Dorado" sign, C. 8, Av. 4-6, very cheap; *Las Condes*, Av. Central/1, C. 11, inexpensive; *Café H.B.*, C.2, Av. 5 for breakfast; *Lido Bar*, C.2, Av. 3., for casado. *Soda Malagaly*, Av. Central, C.23, nr. Youth Hostel, good, cheap; *Soda Coliseo*, Av. 3, C.10-12, next to Alajuela bus station, rec.; *Soda Póas*, Av. 7, C. 3-5, good value; *Soda Amon*, C.7, Av. 7-9, good, cheap casados; *Soda Nini*, Av. 3, C. 2-4, cheap; *La Geishita*, C. Central, Av. 14, cheap casado; *Soda Maly*, Av. 4, C. 2-4, Chinese and tico, good; *Soda Puntarenas*, C. 12, Av.

7-9, good for light meals and breakfast, open 0500-2200, useful for buses to Puntarenas and Puerto Viejo Sarapiquí which leave from there.

Restaurants are decidedly expensive in San José; the budget traveller is advised to stick to the bars W of C. 8, i.e. in even-numbered Calles with a number larger than 8. Food bars in restaurants in the Mercado Central (C.6/8) are good for breakfast and lunch, high standards of sanitation. At lunchtime cheaper restaurants offer a set meal called a casado, US$1-1.50, which is good value; e.g. in the snack bars in the *Galería* complex, Av. Central-2, C. 5-7. Try *Chicharronera Nacional*, Av. 1, C.10/12, very popular, or *Popular*, Av. 3, C.6/8, good casado.

Ice cream, confectionery, etc.: *Helados Rena*, C.8, Av. Central, excellent; also *Helados Boni*, C. Central, Av. 6-8, home-made ice cream; *Pops*, near Banco Central, and other outlets, for ice cream (excellent); also for ice cream *Mölnpik*, Av. Central, C. Central. *Las Cuartetes*, 2 C., 1 block N of Post Office, excellent pastries and expresso; *Spoon*, Av. Central, C. 5-7, good coffee and pastries; *Fudge*, Centro Comercial Los Lagos, Escazú, coffee and pastries; *Heladería Italiano*, excellent ice cream; *El ABC*, Av. Central between Calles 11 and 9, self-service, good, clean, cheap. *La Selecta* bakeries rec.; *Le Croissant*, Av. Central, C.33, good French bakery. *Café del Teatro*, reasonably priced, belle époque interior, popular meeting place for poets and writers.

Bars Good places to have a drink include *Key Largo*, Av. 3, C. 7, a bar with live music, expensive; *El Cuartel de la Boca del Monte*, Av. 1, C.21-23, rec., nice atmosphere.

Shopping Market on Av. Central, Calles 6/8, open 0630-1800 (Sun. 0630-1200), good leather suitcases and wood. Mercado Borbón, Avs. 3/5, Calles 8/10, fruit and vegetables in abundance. More and more *artesanía* shops are opening, e.g. *Mercanapi* (C. 11, Av. 1) and *Mercado Nacional de Artesanía* (C. 11, Av. 4), and others on Av. Central, C. 1 and 3. La Casona, a market of small *artesanía* shops, Av. Central-1, C. Central. In Moravia (8 km. from centre) *El Caballo Blanco*, T 35-67-97, workshops alongside, and *H.H.H.* are good for leather work. The leather rocking chairs (which dismantle for export) found in some *artesanía* shops are cheaper in Sarchí. Coffee is good value and has an excellent flavour (although the best quality is exported). *Automercados* are good supermarkets in several locations (e.g. C.3, Av. 3). *Cosiña de Leña*, new shopping centre (good regional food available).

Bookshops *The Bookshop*, Av. 1, Calle 1 and 3 (T 21-68-47), good selection of English language books (double US prices), also in Pavas, opp. new American Embassy; *Universal*, Av. Central, Calles Central and 1, for Spanish books and maps. Lehmann, Av. Central and C. 3, maps, Spanish, a few English and German books; *Librería Italiana/Francesa*, C. 3, Av. Central/1, English, French, Italian books, German magazines; *Staufer*, nr. Centro Comercial, Los Yoses, also in San Rafael de Escazú and Plaza del Sol shopping mall in Curridabat, English and German books; *Apple*, Barrio California; Airport shop; *Casey's*, C. Central between Av. 7 and 9, second-hand books and book exchange (1 new for 2 old), English only, good.

Photography 1 hr. colour processing available at all IFSA (Kodak) branches (15% discount for ISTC cardholders), poor reports received. Fuji processing in 1 hr. at Universal stores. Minor camera repairs undertaken. Camera repairs, Taller de Equipos Fotográficos, 120 metres E of kiosk Parque Morazán, Av. 3, C. 3-5, 2nd floor, T 23-11-46 (Canon authorized workshop). Film prices are well above those of Europe.

Buses Bus fares in San José: large buses: US$0.10, small: US$0.15 from the centre outwards. Hand baggage in reasonable quantities is not charged, but no trunks of any kind are taken.

Taxis Minimum fare US$0.60 for first km. Taxis are red and now have electronic meters (called "Marías"); make sure they are used.

Car Rentals Check your vehicle carefully as the rental company will try to claim for the smallest of "damages". International driver's licence and credit card generally required. Insurance costs US$10 per day extra; basic prices: compact car US$17 (plus US$0.17/km.), or US$31 free km.; jeep costs US$31 plus US$0.33/km plus insurance, or US$54 free km. Microbus, 9 persons, US$33.50 plus US$0.33/km., insurance or US$60 unlimited. There is a 3-day minimum for free km.; no cars under 1300 cc available for rent. Budget, C. 30, Paseo Colón (T 23-32-84, typical charge US$158 per week, no km. charge, US$10 per day insurance + 6% service charge for Subaru Justy (early 1990); Avis, Sabana Norte (T 32-99-22); Dollar, C. Central, Av. 9 (T 33-33-39); Hertz, C. 38, Pasceo Colón, National, C. 36, Av. 7 (T33-40-44); and many local ones (Elegante has branches throughout the country, rec.). Various companies at airport, including Ada, T 41-12-60, Budget, T 41-44-44, Santos, T 41-30-44, Hertz, T 41-00-97. You can often obtain lower rentals by making reservations before arrival with the major companies.

Night Clubs *Grill La Orquídea* at the *Hotel Balmoral*; *Les Moustaches* in Centro Colón, Paseo Colón, C. 38, expensive. Many restaurants and bars with varying styles of music at El Pueblo centre on road to San Francisco (take "Calle Blancos" bus from C. 1, Av. 5-7, alight 500 m. after river); also 3 discos here, *Cocoloco*, *Infinito* and *La Plaza* (very luxurious and expensive). Discos in the centre: *Kamakiri*, on the way to Tibas; *Top One* (US rock music); *La Rueda* (for the over 30's). Other nice, less expensive dance spots downtown: *El Túnel del Tiempo*, *Talamanca* and *Disco Salsa 54*. *La Torre*, C. 7 between Av. Central and Av. 1, popular gay disco. Night spots W of Calle 8 are in the red light district.

Theatres All are closed on Monday. Teatro Nacional, Av. 2, C. 3/5 (rec. for both the productions and the bar/café), behind it is La Plaza de la Cultura, a large complex. Teatro Carpa, outdoor, alternative; plays, films, C. 9, opp. Parque Morazán. Teatro Tiempo (also called Sala Arlequín), C. 13 between Av. 2 and Central. Compañía Nacional de Teatro. Teatro del Angel, Av. Central, between C. 13 and 15. 3 modern dance companies. All good.

Cinemas Many excellent modern cinemas showing latest releases. Prices, US$1.40. See *La Nación* for films and times.

Swimming Pools The best is at Ojo de Agua, 5 minutes from the airport, 15 minutes from San José. It is open up to 1700 hours; direct bus from Parque Carrillo, Av. 2, C. 14, US$0.65 or take bus to Alajuela via San Antonio de Belén. There is also a pool in La Sabana (at western end of Paseo Colón), entrance US$3, open 1200-1400, about 2 km. from the city centre. Open air pool at Plaza González Víquez (south-eastern section of city).

Museums Museo Nacional, Calle 17, Av. Central and 2, very interesting, partly under reconstruction, open Tues.-Sun., 0900-1700; replicas of precolumbian jewellery may be bought at reasonable prices (entrance, US$0.25). **Gold Museum** in the Plaza de la Cultura complex adjoining the Teatro Nacional, Av. Central, C.3/5, excellent, open Tues.-Sun. 1000-1700, free 1½-hr. bilingual guided tour available (get ticket in advance); **Museo de Arte Costarricense** at the end of Paseo Colón, Calle 42, in La Sabana park in the old airport building (Tues.-Sun 1000-1700, US$0.20). In the INS building, Av. 7, C. 9/11, is the **Jade Museu** on the 11th floor (Mon.-Fri., 0900-1500), with jade carvings, very interesting "must", and a beautiful view over the city. **Museo de Ciencias Natur** Colegio La Salle, Mon.-Fri., 0730-1500; US$0.10 (in the grounds of the Mi

of Agriculture; take "Estadio Sabana" bus from Av. 2, C.2/ Central to the gate).
Entomology Museum, in basement of Musical Arts building of the University of
Costa Rica in San Pedro. Mon.—Fri. 1300-1700, to check times T 25-55-55,
extension 318, many beautiful insects, only museum of its kind in Central
America. **Museo Criminológico**, 2nd floor, Supreme Court Building, Av. 6, C.
17-19, Mon. Wed. and Fri. 1300-1500 "pretty grisly"; **Postal Telegraphic and
Philatelic Museum**, 2nd floor main Post Office, Mon.-Fri., 0800-1500; **Museum
of National Press**, Imprenta Nacional, La Uruca, open Mon.-Fri. 1000-1500.

Zoo There is a small zoo in Parque Simón Bolívar (Av. 11, just E of C.7), near INS
building. Entrance US$0.40, open 0830-1530, Tues.-Fri., 0900-1600, Sat. Go
down C. 11 about 3 blocks from Av. 7; not very satisfactory—lack of variety and
small cages for large cats.

Exchange Opening times: Mon.-Fri., 0900-1500 Banco Nacional, head office,
Av. 3, C. 2/4; Banco de Costa Rica, Av. Central, C. 4., changes travellers' cheques
for colones and for dollars, but must present a ticket out of Costa Rica—take
passport. Banco de San José, C. Central, Av. 3-5. Money can be sent through
Banco de San José or Banco de Costa Rica at 4% commission. Banco Anglo
Costarricense, Av. 2 near Teatro Nacional, very good service for travellers' cheques.
Credit card (Visa, Mastercharge) holders can obtain cash advances from Banco
de San José in colones; minimum cash advance: US$50 equivalent. Banco Crédito
Agrícola de Cartago, 9 branches, also makes advances on Visa, no limits. Since
August 1986, banks may charge whatever commission they please on foreign
exchange transactions and other services: shop around for the best deal. Dollars
are available at banks but a commission is payable when cashing any cheque and
there is a maximum limit of US$50-worth (in some cases, much paperwork and
at least 1-hr. wait involved; you have to show your ticket out of the country and
the dollars can only be obtained when you are leaving; in others, it's
straightfoward, no paperwork or onward ticket required, e.g. Banco Banex, Av.
1, C. 2, 2% commission, minimum US$10). All *casas de cambio* have been closed
down, and exchange transactions on the street, the centre for which is the corner
of Av. 2, C.2 (beware fake notes), are now illegal, though still reported active,
10% better rates. Most hotels will change dollars (cash or travellers' cheques) into
colones, but only for guests; hotels cannot sell dollars, however.

Libraries Centro Cultural Costarricense Norteamericano (Calle Negritos—good
films, plays, art exhibitions and English-language library), University of Costa Rica
(in San Pedro suburb), and National Library (opp. Parque Nacional; has art and
photography exhibitions), all entry free. Alianza Franco Costarricense, Av. 7, C.
5, French newspapers, French films every Thursday evening, friendly.

Language Schools Conversa, Apartado No. 17, Centro Colón (T 21-76-49), 12 monthly programmes. Centro Cultural Costarricense Norteamericano, C. Negritos, T 25-93-47; Instituto Lengua Española, San Francisco suburb, T 26-92-22. Instituto de Idiomas, Av. 3, C. 3-5, Edif. Victoria, piso 3, T 23-96-62, Spanish lessons and lodging with Costa Rican families. Intensa, C. 33, Av. 5-7, Barrio Escalante, T 25-60-09, P.O. Box 8110, 1000 San José.

British School San Pedro, Av. Central, C. 33 (T 34-22-66).

Embassies and Consulates Nicaraguan, Av. Central, Calles C.25-27, Mon.-Fri., 24-hr. wait for visa (in some cases, 2 weeks, apply elsewhere); **Panamanian,** La Granja (100 metres S of Banco Popular), San Pedro district (T 25-34-01), none further south; **Honduran,** Av. 5, C. 1, T 22-21-45; **Salvadorean,** Los Yoses, opposite Venezuelan Embassy; **Guatemalan,** Embassy and Consulate, 250 metres, carretera a Pavas from Sabana Oeste (T 31-66-45/54), visa given on the spot, US$10 in some cases (dollars only—see Guatemala **Information for Visitors**); **Mexican,** Consulate, Av. 7, C. 13-15, T 22-54-85, open 0800-1000, 1400-1500. **Belizean,** Curridabat (T 53-96-26).
  Argentine, Av.6, C.21-25 (T 21-34-38); **Bolivian,** C. 19 and 21, Av. 2, T 33-62-44; **Brazilian,** Av. 2, C. 24, T 23-15-44. **Colombian,** corner Av. 5 and C. 5, La Viña building, 2nd floor, T 21-07-25 (Mon.-Fri. 0800-1230) issues free tourist cards for Colombia, but onward ticket must be shown and 2 photos provided. **Ecuadorean,** Av. 2, C. 19-21, T 23-62-81; **Paraguayan,** Los Yoses (T 25-28-02). **Peruvian,** Los Yoses (T 25-91-45); **Uruguayan,** C 2, Av. 1 T 23-25-12, **Chilean** Barrio Dent, T 24-42-43, **Venezuelan,** C. 37-37, Av. 2, consulate open Mon.-Fri. 0900-1230, T 25-13-35, visa takes 48 hrs.
  US, Consulate: Av. 3, C. 1, 2nd floor, T 22-55-66, open Mon.-Fri. 0800-1130, 1230-1500, a new embassy is now open (T20-39-39) in the western suburb of Pavas. **Canadian,** Av. Central, C. 3, Cronos Building, 6th floor, Aptdo 10303 (T 55-35-22, plans to move to Sabana Norte), **Japanese,** Bo. Rohrmoser, T 32-12-55. **Israeli** C 2, Av 2-4, T 21-64-44.
  British, Centro Colón, 11th floor, end of Paseo Colón with C. 38 (Apartado 10056), T 21-55-66 (also serves Nicaragua); **West German,** Sabana Oeste, Aptdo 4017, T 32-55-33; **Swiss,** Paseo Colón, Centro Colón, 4th floor, Calles 34/36, T 21-48-29; **French,** Curridabat, 200 metres S, 25 metres W of Indor Club, T 25-07-33. **Belgian,** C. 35-37, Av. 3, T 25-62-55; **Dutch,** Los Yoses, C.35-37, Aptdo 10285, Mon.-Fri. 0900-1200, T 34-09-49; **Italian,** C. 29, Av. 8-10, T 34-23-46; **Spanish,** Paseo Colón, C. 32, T 21-19-33; **Danish,** Sabana Este (T 22-13-07); **Finnish,** Centro Colón Building, Paseo Colón, T 55-25-15, **Norwegian,** Centro Colón, 10th floor, T 57-14-14.

Immigration Irazemi Building, C. 21, Av. 6-8; you need to go here for exit visas, extensions, etc. If they are busy, you could queue all day. Better to find a travel agent who can obtain what you need for a fee, say US$5.

Churches Protestant, in English: The Good Shepherd, Av. 4, Calles 3-5 (Anglican), Union Church, Moravia; free bus service from downtown hotels; times and locations given in Friday *Tico Times*. International Baptist Church, in San Pedro, 150 metres N from Banco Anglo Costarricense corner, on San Pedro or Periférico bus route, English services at 0900 on Sun., Sunday school at 1100, nursery provided, Chinese services at 1100 on Sun. Cariari Christian Fellowship, Costa Rican Academy, Cariari, phone 25-52-18 to check location. Sun. 1630; Escazú Christian Fellowship (Country Day School campus), Sun. 1800; Victory Christian Centre (125 metres W of Tennis Club, Sabana Sur), Sun. 1000. Roman Catholic services in English at *Sheraton Herradura* Hotel, 1600 every Sun. Centro de los Amigos para la Paz, Quaker, English books, US periodicals, information, T 21-03-02.

Post Office Av. 1 and 3, C. 2; charges 8 colones for receiving letters (*Lista de Correos*).

Telephone and Cable Services Internal telegrams from main post office. Cable abroad from Compañia Radiográfica Internacional de Costa Rica, Av. 5, C. 1, 0730-1000. Collect telephone calls can be made from special booths, though latest information suggests you can use most phone booths. English speaking operators are available. See also under **Information for Visitors**.

Hospitals and Inoculations Social Security Hospitals have good reputations (free to social security members, few members of staff speak English), free ambulance service run by volunteers: Dr Calderón Guardia (T 22-41-33), San Juan de Dios (T 22-01-66), México (T 32-61-22). The Clínica Bíblica C. 1, Av. 14, (T 23-64-22) and Americana (C. Central-1, Av. 14 (T 22-10-10) have both rec.; both offer 24-hr. emergency service at reasonable charges and have staff who speak English; better than the large hospitals, where queues are long. Bíblica also has addresses for emergencies it cannot handle. Yellow fever inoculation, Ministerio de Salud (Av.4, C.16), Departamento de Enfermedades Epidémicos, Dr. Rodrígo Jiménez Monge, or at his private clinic, C.5, Av.4, T 21-66-58. Free malaria pills also from Ministerio de Salud, from information desk in office to left of ministry. Dermatologist: Dr. Elias Bonilla Dib, C. Central, Av. 7/9, T 212025.

Dentist Clínica Dental Dr. Francisco Cordero Guilarte, T 323645, Sabana Oeste, opposite Colegio La Salle. Take bus marked Sabana Estadio. Dra. Fresia Hidalgo, corner C. 10, Av. 15, 1400-1800, English spoken, reasonable prices, rec. (T 22-16-53).

Laundromat Washing and dry cleaning at Centro Comercial San José 2000, 0730-2000, US$3.75 for large load. Sixaola, branches throughout San José, 2-hr. dry cleaning available, expensive. Doña Anna, Av. 20, C. 13, cheap and fast. Martinizing, US franchise, at Curridabat, Sabana Norte and Escazú, rec. Lava-matic Doña Anna, C. 13, Av. 16, US$3.50 wash and dry.

Travel Agencies *Swiss Travel Service*, in *Hotel Corobici*, T (506) 31-40-55, P.O.Box 7-1970, Fax 31-30-30, with branches in *Hotels Sheraton, Irazú, Cariari, Amstel* and *Balmoral*, large agency, good guides, much cruise business, railway excursions, warmly rec. *Panorama Tours*, C. 9, Av. Central/1, P.O. Box 7323, Greyhound agent; *Viajes Rodan*, Calle 1, 75 yards (*varas*) S of American Embassy. French-speaking owner. *American Express*, TAM, only open Mon.-Fri., Edif. Alde, 4th floor, Calle 1, Av. Central/1, good domestic service, not so good for travel outside Costa Rica. *Mundo Acuático*, 200 metres N of *Mas X Menos*, San Pedro, rents snorkelling gear. *Tursa, Gran Hotel Costa Rica*, T 336194/214000, all types of tour offered. Those specialising in naturalist tours include: *Costa Rica Expeditions*, Av. 3, C. Central/2 including white water rafting etc. (P.O. Box 6941),

T 23-99-75; *Explore Costa Rica* (Pavas near US Embassy); *Horizontes*, 2nd floor Edificio Crystal, Av. 1, C. 1-3; and *Tikal*, Av. 2, C 9-11, rec.

Tourist Office Instituto Costarricense de Turismo, information office: below Plaza de la Cultura, C. 5, Av. Central/2, T 23-1733, ext. 277, and 22-1090 (Mon.-Fri. 0900-1700, 0900-1300 Sat., closed Sun.). Also at Juan Santamaría airport (very helpful) and borders. Head office is at Av. 4, C. 3/5 (open at 0900). Excellent service. Free guide: *Gran Pequeño Guía de San José*, good. **Otec, youth and student travel office** and cheap lodgings, C. 3, Av. 1-3, T 22-08-66, for ISTC and FIYTO members (has discount booklet for shops, hotels, restaurants; ask also about discounts on fares; no discounts on international flights in Dec.-Jan. high season, though). The Instituto Geográfico, Av. 20, C. 9/11 at Ministry of Public Works and Transport, supplies very good topographical maps for walkers (which can easily be bought at Librerías Universal and Lehmann). The national park service (SPN, office: Calle 17, Av. 9) can provide very interesting material on the flora and fauna of the parks, brochure with descriptions and how to reach the parks, US$0.50 from its CIDA information office in the zoo grounds at the N end of Av. 11 (**see page 566**). American Express office has good, free maps of San José. New up-to-date maps are available at most bookstores. **N.B.** It is much cheaper to take tours aimed at the local rather than the tourist market.

Airports The Juan Santamaría international airport is at El Coco, 16 km. from San José by motorway (5 km. from Alajuela). Minibus from Av. 2, C. 10/12, or Av. 2, C. 12/14, every 10 mins., US$0.30, or by Alajuela bus via the motorway from C. 14, Av. 5 and 7. Taxi to airport, US$10 (can be less if ordered in advance); Sansa runs its own bus service to the airport. Taxis run all night from the main square to the airport and for early flights, you can reserve a taxi from any San José hotel the night before. All taxi companies run a 24-hour service. Bank at the airport open 0800-1600; at other times try car rental desks, or the restaurant cash desk. X-ray machines reported unsafe for film. Light aircraft use the Tobias Bolaños airport at Pavas, about 5 km. W of San José.

Airlines Addresses (and telephone numbers) of major airlines: Copa, Av. 5, C. 1-3 (23-70-33); SAM, Av. 5, C.1-3 (33-30-66); Lacsa, Av. 5, C. 1 (31-00-33); Aeronica, Ed. Cristal, Av.1, C. 1-3 (23-02-26); Sansa, Paseo Colón, C.24 (21-94-14); Sahsa, Av. C. 1-3 (21-55-61); Taca, Av. 3, C. 1 (22-17-90); Mexicana, Av. 2-4, C. 1 (22-17-11); Varig, Av. 5, C. 3-5 (57-00-94); Viasa, Av. 5, C. 1 (23-34-11); TWA, Av. 1-Central, C.2 (22-13-32); Pan Am, Av. 7, C. 5-7, (21-89-55); Eastern, Paseo Colón, next to *Ambassador Hotel*, C. 26, T 22-56-55 (to cash an MCO takes 6 weeks, must be sent to Miami); British Airways, Paseo Colón (23-56-48); Iberia, Paseo Colón, C.40 (21-33-11); KLM, Av. Central, C. 1 (21-30-81); Lufthansa, Av. 3-5, C. 5 (22-73-11); Air France, Av. 1, C. 4-6 (22-88-11); Swiss Air, Av. 1-3. C. Central (21-66-13). Singapore Airlines, Av. 1, C. 3-5 (55-35-55). Lloyd Aéreo Boliviano, Av. 2, C. 2-4, upstairs; American, opposite *Hotel Corobici*, Sabana Grande Este (55-19-11); Aviateca, Av. 3, C. 1, (33-83-90); Lan Chile, *Hotel Torremolinos* (57-02-80); Alitalia, Av. Central/2, C. 1, (22-60-09); Aeroperú, Av. 5, C. 1-3, (23-70-33).

Internal Flights Sansa operate internal flights throughout the country at reasonable prices from Juan Santamaría airport, Mon.-Sat. only. Check-in is at Sansa office on Paseo Colón at C.24 one hour before departure (free bus to and from airport); reservations here, or from Super Viajes. Check schedules on 21-94-14 or 33-32-58, Fax 55-21-76. If you made reservations before arriving in Costa Rica, confirm and collect tickets as soon as possible after arrival. Book ahead, especially for the beaches. In February and March, planes can be fully booked 3 weeks ahead.

Flights operate Tues., Thurs. and Sat. to Barra del Colorado (US$12), Golfito Mon.-Sat. (US$15) Quepos Mon.-Sat. 2 flights daily (US$9), Coto 47, Palmar Sur,

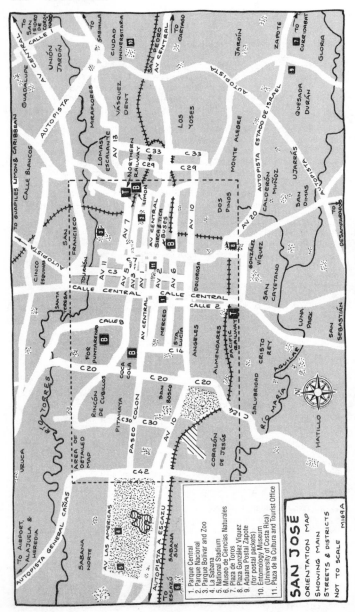

SAN JOSÉ

ORIENTATION MAP

SHOWING MAIN

STREETS & DISTRICTS

NOT TO SCALE

1. Parque Central
2. Parque Nacional
3. Parque Bolívar and Zoo
4. La Sabana
5. National Stadium
6. Museo de Ciencias Naturales
7. Plaza de Toros
8. Plaza González Víquez
9. Aduana Postal Zapote
   (for postal packets)
10. Entomology Museum
    (University of Costa Rica)
11. Plaza de la Cultura and Tourist Office

Mon., Wed. and Fri. (US$12 and US$15 respectively), Tamarindo and Sámara on Mon., Wed. and Fri. (both US$18), Nosara, Mon., Wed., and Fri., (US$18). Extra Tues., Thur., Sat. flights to Barra del Colorado, Coto 47, Golfito and Quepos (may be seasonal). Sansa Vacatones, T 21-94-14, offer 1-3 night packages including flight and accommodation at Manuel Antonio, Sámara, Nosara and Tamarindo. Hustler Tours offer San José—Quepos daily flights from Tobias Bolaños airport at Pavas, west of San José, US$30, T 37-54-00 or 37-49-00; Quepos, T 77-05-05.

Railway Services On the NE side of Parque Nacional is the main station of the Northern Railway to the Atlantic port of Limón, Av. 3, C. 21 (T 26-00-11). The main station of the Ferrocarril Eléctrico al Pacífico to the Pacific ports of Puntarenas and Caldera is in the extreme S of the city C. 2, Av. 20, T 26-00-11 (take bus marked Paso Ancho). The two 1.067-metre gauge lines are connected. The trains are slow, noisy and dusty, but comfortable; rec. for beautiful views.

There is one train a day from San José to Puerto Limón (156 km., the "jungle train") at 1000, ticket office opens at 0900; train from Limón to San José at 0600. Journey takes about 7-8 hrs. to Limón (on a good day) and 9 back. Fare: US$3. Train times should be checked in advance: the timetable varies. Light refreshments are served on all trains except the local service, which operates once a day between San José, Heredia and Alajuela on the Northern Railway. A luxury, 1st class coach may be taken to Puerto Limón for US$65 (bookable through Swiss Travel Service).

The journey to Limón is one of the most beautiful railway journeys anywhere. On the way to Limón, sit on the right-hand side. From the continental divide near Cartago the line follows the narrow, wooded Reventazón valley down past Turrialba and Siquirres (2 hrs. from Limón). One can shorten the journey by transferring to a bus at Siquirres. The 40 km. of line in the lowlands near Limón cost 4,000 lives during building in the 1870s, mostly from yellow fever. The last 16 km. into Limón run along the seashore, amid groves of coconut palms. Train splits at Siquirres, front half to Puerto Limón, rear to Guápiles. Beware of robberies on trains after dark and in the crush while boarding. There is some advantage in travelling by bus, San José to Limón and returning by train. You are more likely to see the whole trip by daylight, and clouds and rain are more likely later in the day.

Between San José and Puntarenas there are two trains daily, this also is a very scenic journey; from Puntarenas to San José (116 km.) leaving at 0600 and 1600 and from San José to Puntarenas leaving at 0600 and 1500 (the timetable changes sometimes). Journey takes about 4 hrs. Fastest trains (*directo*) 3 hrs. Fare US$1 one way. Last return train on Sundays is overcrowded. Passengers can buy light refreshments at wayside stations and stops. There are also services to the new port of Caldera.

Buses There are services to most towns. *Cartago*, every 15 mins., 0500-2300, *Turrialba* buses start from the Parque Nacional. *Puntarenas* every hour from 0600 to 1900 (US$1.55), Av. 7-9, Calle 12. *Heredia*, every 30 mins., Av. 5, Calle 1. Minibuses from Av. 6, C. 14. *Alajuela* (including airport), 30 mins. (US$0.30) Av. 2, Calle 12-14 every 15 mins., to Sarchí, change at Alajuela, to Poás Volcano, change at Alajuela's central park where bus leaves, Sun. only, 0830. *Quepos*, from Coca Cola bus station, Calle 16, Av. 1-3, 4 buses daily, 3 hours, US$2.75. Direct bus to Manuel Antonio, 0600, 1200, US$4.50, 3½ hrs., from Coca Cola station. Many buses for nearby towns and others to the west of San José leave from the main Coca Cola bus station or the streets nearby (eg: *Santa Ana, Escazú, Acosta, Puriscal, Santa María Dota, San Marcos, San Ramón*). *Escazú* minibuses from Av. 6, Calle 14; buses from front of Coca Cola terminal. *San Isidro de El General*, regular buses, near Coca Cola. *Liberia, Nicoya, Sta. Cruz, Cañas* buses, Empresa Alfaro, Coca Cola bus station. *Grecia*, bus Calle 6, Av. 5-7. *San Carlos* bus at Coca Cola terminal. *Guápiles*, Calle 2, Av. 7-9. *Monteverde* (Mon.-Thurs. 1430, Sat.-Sun. 0630, Express, US$3.40) and *Puerto Viejo*, by Puntarenas terminal, Av.

7-9, Calle 12. *Siquirres*, Av. Ctl, Calle 11-13. *Limón*, hourly service, 0600-1800, 2½ hours, good views, leaving on time, you may buy ticket the day before, US$2, Calle 19-21, Av. 3 Transportes Unidos/ Coop Limón. *Paso Canoas* (Panamanian border), 4 daily (US$5.25), *Golfito, Ciudad Neily* (Zona Sur) buses, Tracopa, Calle 2-4, Av. 18 (21-42-14). Direct to *Sixaola* (via Puerto Viejo, Cahuita and Bribri), C.1 Central, Av.11, 0600 and 1630, 5 hrs., US$4.60. *Jacó Beach* 0730, 1530 from Coca Cola terminal US$1.80. *La Cruz, Peñas Blancas*, 0445, 0750, 1300, 1615 from C. 16, Av. 3, Trapala or Pulmitan US$2.75. *San Vito*, Coto Brus, 0730, 1530 from C. 14-16, Av. 5 US$3.45.

Minibuses run on most routes to nearby towns offering better service, never crowded like the regular buses. Fares about US$0.20-0.25.

International Buses Sirca (Av. 2, Calle 11, T 22-55-41) runs a scheduled service along the Pan-American Highway from San José to Peñas Blancas, on the Nicaraguan frontier, and on to Managua (US$7), dep. 0500 (Wed., Fri., Sun.; schedules appear to change frequently), reports of unreliability with this company (book on Fri. for following week). Tica buses run to David, Panama City and Managua; the terminal is at Calle 9-11 and Av. 2 (T 21-89-54). It is here that all refund claims have to be made (have to be collected in person). Ticabus to Managua leaves at 0700, Mon., Wed., Fri., US$15.30. The Ticabus journey from San José to Panama City (with at least 3 hrs. at the border) US$36 (at official exchange rate and much cheaper than in Panama), leaves at 0400 or 2000 daily (check in advance) 19 hrs. (book at least 3 days in advance); by Ticabus to David, US$18. To get a Panamanian tourist card one must buy a return ticket. Tracopa, opposite Pacific railway station on C.2/4, Av.18 (T 21-42-14), goes as far as David, US$7.70 (buses daily at 0730, 9 hrs.); fare to border US$6; book in advance. A bus to Changuinola via the Sixaola-Guabito border post leaves San José at 1000 daily, from outside the *Hotel Cocori*, Calle 16, Av. 3, US$5 payable on board in colones, best to arrive 1 hr. before departure; the bus takes the splendidly scenic, fast new road through the Braulio Carillo National Park to Guápiles and Siquirres and is the quickest route to Limón. The journey from San José to Changuinola takes 6-7 hrs.

Excursions San José is a good centre for excursions into the beautiful Meseta Central. The excursions to the Orosí valley and volcano of Irazú are given under Cartago. Poás volcano (described on **page** 592) can be visited from Alajuela. Enquire first about the likely weather when planning a visit to Poás or Irazú. To reach Barba take a bus to San José de las Montañas (**see page** 591). A road runs NE of San José to (11 km.) San Isidro de Coronado, a popular summer resort (bus from Terminal Coronado, Av. 7, C. Central and 1); its *fiesta* on 15 February. Those interested in medical research can visit the Instituto Clodomiro Picado snake farm, open Mon.-Fri. 0800-1600 (snake feeding, Fri. only 1330-1600), take Dulce Nombre de Coronado bus from C.3, Av. 5/7, 30 mins., or San Antonio Coronado bus to end of line and walk 200 metres downhill. They also sell snake-bite scrum. The road goes on through fine countryside to Las Nubes (32 km.), a country village which commands a great view of Irazú. For horseback excursions, *Finca Ob-la-dí Ob-la-dá*, 17 km. W of San José, Villa Colón, offers 1-day and longer trips (1-day trip, including transport from your hotel, lunch and all tack, costs US$59). Call 55-07-91 for a one day luxury yacht cruise on the *Fantasia* to Tortuga island in the Gulf of Nicoya, Wed.-Sat.-Sun., from San José US$65 inc. lunch. Calypso Island Cruise offers one day tours in the Gulf of Nicoya from San José, Wed.-Fri.-Sun., US$69 inc. lunch, T 55-30-22.

FROM SAN JOSE TO THE ATLANTIC COAST

Cartago, 22½ km. from San José, stands at 1,439 metres at the foot of the Irazú volcanic peak and is encircled by mountains. It was founded in 1563 and was the capital until 1823. It has a population of only 30,000, though the neighbourhood is densely populated. Earthquakes destroyed it in 1841 and 1910, and it has been severely shaken on other occasions. That is why there are no old buildings, though some have been rebuilt in colonial style.

The most interesting church is the Basilica, rebuilt 1926 in Byzantine style, of Nuestra Señora de Los Angeles, the Patroness of Costa Rica; it houses La Negrita, under 15 cm. high, an Indian image of the Virgin which draws pilgrims from all over Central America because of great healing powers attributed to it. The feast day is August 2, when the image is carried in procession to other churches in Cartago and there are celebrations thoughout Costa Rica. In the Basilica is an extraordinary collection of very finely- made silver and gold images, no larger than 3 cm. high, of various parts of the human anatomy, presumably offered in the hope of being healed. Worth seeing is the old parish church (La Parroquia), ruined by the 1910 earthquake and now converted into a delightful garden retreat with flowers, fish and humming birds. There is an impressive procession on Good Friday.

Hotels *Casa Blanca* in Barrio Asís, E, *Pensión El Brumoso*, C.5, Av. 6-8, F, *Vanecia*, F, clean, are among the very few NOT in the red light district; *Familiar Las Arcadas*, at railway station, F (rents rooms hourly late into the night). *Pensión La Provincia*, F, safer than most, rec.

Restaurants *Salón París*, very good food; *Ambientes* in front of La Parroquia, is also very good; *City Garden*, Av. 4, C. 2-4; *Puerta del Sol*, in front of the Basilica. *Pizza Hut*, opp. La Parroquia ruins. Restaurants, among other places, are closed on the Thursday and Friday of Holy Week, so take your own food.

Shopping Bookshop at Librería Cartago, C.1, Av. 2-4. High quality Costa Rican clothes at Boutique Belinni International, in front of post office. There is a market facing the train station. The main **post office** is at C.1, Av. 2-4, near the park.

Buses The main terminal is at Av. 4, C.2-4, but buses to most destinations, including Turrialba, make a stop at the Cartago ruins on Av. 3.

Excursions Best is by a road (40 km., paved) to the crater of *Irazú* (3,432 metres). Michael J. Brisco of Cambridge writes: Irazú crater is a half-mile cube dug out of the earth, and all around is desolate grey sand, with little wildlife other than the ubiquitous Volcano Junco, a bird like a dunnock, and the few plants which survive in this desert. The phrase "it's like the surface of the moon" describes Irazú quite well. Entrance to Irazú in season, US$0.10, out of season free. There is a small museum. Cartago buses to Irazú from 1 block N of Cartago ruins at 0700 and 1300 on Mon. and Thurs. and 0700 on Sun. (but check in advance if bus is running), 1¾ hrs. up, the first bus arrives long before the tour buses and private cars, but returns after about 30 minutes, so you must either hitch down, or wait until the afternoon bus goes down at about 1500, US$2 return; taxi is US$24 return (it is very difficult to get taxis to return for you in the morning if you have stayed at the crater overnight). Since it can be difficult to find a hotel in Cartago that is not rented hourly (and therefore very expensive for a full night) it may be easier to take one of the guided tours leaving from San José, about US$20; tours to Irazú and Orosi valley US$28-30. The clouds come down early, obscuring the view. Alternatively you can take a bus from Cartago to Sanatorio. Ask the driver at the crossroads just outside the village. From there you walk to the summit. 16 km.; on the way up are the *Hotel Montana* (D, not very helpful, no keys to rooms),

Hotel Gestoria Irazú, F, T 53-08-27, and the *Bar-Restaurant Linda Vista*. 1½ km. from the crater a road leads to Laguna Verde and a camping site; the road is paved, but steep beyond the Laguna. If driving from San José, take the road signed "Plantel M.O.P.T. Cartago, 3 kms.", just after Río Taras, which goes directly to Irazú, avoiding Cartago. The walk down, on a dirt road through Pinchas, is also rec. On Sat. and Mon. a bus goes from Cartago to San Juan, 12 km. from the summit (0630 and 1300); *Hotel Gran Irazú*, E, comfortable, clean.

National Park rules forbid visitors to walk around the crater: on the tourist track on the North side is a "Prohibido pasar" sign, which can be passed only at your own risk, there are some very dangerous drops, and the rim is cracking (we advise obeying the rules). There is an easier walk on the southerly side, which ends before the high crest; J. Douglas Porteous of the University of Victoria, B.C., writes: "Stupendous views: you look down on mountain tops, clouds, light aircraft. Wear good shoes and a hat, the sun is strong. Those with sensitive skins should consider face cream if the sulphur fumes are heavy. By 1300 (sometimes by even 0900 or 1000) clouds have enveloped the lower peaks and are beginning to close in on Irazú; time to eat your picnic on the far side of the crater before returning to the tourist side."

Mike Marlowe, of Blacksburg, Virginia, writes: "In the afternoon the mountain top is buried in fog and mist or drizzle, but the ride up in the mist can be magical, for the mountainside is half-displaced in time. There are new jeeps and tractors, but the herds of cattle are small, the fields are quilt-work, handcarts and oxcarts are to be seen under the fretworked porches of well-kept frame houses. The land is fertile, the pace is slow, the air is clean. It is a very attractive mixture of old and new. Irazú is a strange mountain, well worth the two-plus hours' bus ride up."

Aguas Calientes is 4 km. SE of Cartago and 90 metres lower. Its *balneario* (warm water swimming pool) is a good place for picnics. 4 km. from Cartago on the road to Paraíso is the *Jardín Lancaster* orchid garden (run by the University of Costa Rica), 10 mins.' walk from the main road (ask bus driver to let you out at Campo Ayala—Cartago-Paraíso bus); the best display is in April. Although off the beaten track, the gardens are definitely worth a visit; open 0830-1530, entry usually at 30 minutes past each hour, US$0.50. 1 km. further on is Parque Doña Ana (La Expresión), a lake with picnic area, basketball courts, exercise track and bird watching, open 0900-1700, US$0.50. Get off bus at Cementario in Paraíso and walk 1 km. south.

Ujarrás (ruins of a colonial church and village) is 6½ km. E of Cartago by a road which goes from Paraíso through a beautiful valley to the small town of **Orosi**, in the enchanting Orosi valley, down which flows the tumultuous Reventazón (*Hotel Río*, C, T 73-31-28, two pools, and *Restaurant Río Palomo*). Bus from Cartago, US$0.15. Here are magnificent views of the valley, a 17th century mission with colonial treasures, and just outside the town two *balnearios* (bathing, US$1.60) and restaurants serving good meals at fair prices. The *miradores* of Ujarrás and Orosi both offer excellent views of the Reventazón valley. There are buses from Cartago to all these places. A beautiful one-day drive from Cartago is to Orosi, then to Ujarrás, and on to Cachi where there is a dam with artificial lake (very popular with residents of San José, Charrarra buses from 1 block N of Cartago ruins, several daily). The Charrarra tourist complex, with a good restaurant, swimming pool, boat rides on the Orosi river and walks, can be reached by direct bus on Sun., otherwise ½-hr. walk from Ujarrás.

12 km. beyond Orosi is the Tapanti Wildlife Refuge (**Refugio Nacional de Vida Silvestre Tapanti**, run by the Forest Service), on the headwaters of the Reventazón. It is a 4,700 hectare reserve of mainly cloud forest and pre-montaine humid forest with 211 species of birds recorded, including the quetzal which nests in late spring and can be found on the western slopes near the entry point. Jaguar and ocelot are found in the reserve as well as monkeys, orchids and ferns. There

are picnic areas, a nature centre with slide shows (ask to see them) and good swimming in the dry season (Nov.-June), and trout fishing (1 April to 31 October). Open daily 0600-1600, US$0.10. From June to Nov.-Dec. it rains every afternoon. To get there take 0600 bus from Cartago to Orosi which goes to Puricil by 0700, then walk (5 km.), or take any other Cartago-Orosi bus to Río Macho and walk 9 km. to the refuge, or take a taxi from Orosi (ask for Julio who, for US$7 round trip, will take 6 passengers). We are told there is now (Dec 1989) nowhere to stay in or near Tapanti.

The Turrialba volcano may be visited from Cartago by a bus to the village of Pacayas, where horses may be hired to take you to the top (fine view and a guesthouse).

Turrialba (57 km. from San José, 40,000 people, altitude 625 metres), on the railway between Cartago and Puerto Limón, has the Centro Agronómico Tropical de Investigación y Enseñanza (CATIE) and many fine coffee farms. CATIE covers more than 2,000 acres of this ecologically diverse zone, has one of the largest tropical fruit collections in the world and houses an important library on tropical agriculture; visitors welcome. The railway runs down to Limón on a narrow ledge poised between mountains on the left and the river on the right.

Hotels *Wagelia*, Entrada de Turrialba (T 56-15-96), D with bath, best; *Albergue La Calzada*, F; *Central*, F with restaurant, no bath; *Interamericano*, F with bath (all opp. railway station); *Pensión Primavera*, F, 1 block away; opp. is *Restaurant Kingston*, reasonable food but a bit expensive. About 22 km. from Turrialba is the naturalists' and birdwatchers' lodge, *Albergue de Montaña Naturalista*, A, with bath, gourmet meal, horse riding, transfers from San José and airport, 6 rooms only so reservations essential—write P.O. Box 6951, 1000S San José; 7-14 night programmes organized for birdwatchers and naturalists.

From Turrialba you can get to the village of Moravia del Chirripó, where guides and horses can be hired for an excursion into the jungled, trackless area of the Talamanca Indians, where there are legends of lost goldfields (bus from Turrialba takes 4 hrs., only certain in dry season; in wet season go to Suiza and get out at Gran d'Oro, from where it's one hr. walk—no accommodation in Moravia, stay put at *pulpería* in Gran d'Oro). About 19 km. N of Turrialba, near **Guayabo**, an Indian ceremonial centre has been excavated and there are clear signs of its paved streets and stone-lined water-channels. Archaeological site open 0800-1600 weekends and holidays. This area is now a National Monument, and the site dates from the period AD 1000 to 1400. There are buses most days (check times) from Turrialba (US$0.45) to Guayabo (*Albergue y Restaurant La Calzada*, E, T 56-04-65) from where it is a 1½ hour walk to the site (several buses each day pass the turn-off to Guayabo, the town is a 2-hr. walk uphill). It is possible to camp at the park (water and toilets, but no food); entry US$0.30. Further along this road (1½ hours' drive) is Santa Cruz, from which the Turrialba volcano can be reached. Bus from Cartago to Turrialba, 1 hr., US$0.60.

Going NE from Turrialba, the main road follows the River Reventazón down to Siquirres. On this road is Parones with *Albergue Mirador Pochotel*, D, T 56-01-11.

Puerto Limón, on a palm-fringed shore backed by mountains, is the country's most important port. It was built on the site of an ancient Indian village, Cariari, where Columbus landed on his fourth and last voyage. Much of the population is black. Visitors should see the palm promenade and tropical flowers of the Parque Vargas (where nine Hoffman's two-toed sloths live in the trees); also in Parque Vargas is a botanical display, a shrine to sailors and fishermen and a bandstand with concerts 3 times a week. The nightlife is good, particularly for Caribbean music and dancing. A new highway to the capital (190 km.) has been built. Population 49,600. Some 2.8 million bunches of bananas are exported each year. New docks were recently completed. Moín, just outside Puerto Limón, has docks for tankers, container and ro-ro ships, and is also the departure point for barges to Tortuguero and Barra del Colorado (8 hrs.).

Warning Beware of theft at night, and remember it is a port as well as a tourist town.

Hotels *Maribu Caribe*, A, T 58-45-43, bungalow accommodation, swimming pool; *Acón*, C. 3, Av. 3, T 58-10-10, C with bath, a/c, clean, safe, good restaurant, discotheque *Aquarius*; *Puerto*, C. 7, Av. 5/6, D, a/c, restaurant, bar; *Lincoln*, Av. 5, Calle 2-3, E, with bath, dirty and run down; *Venus*, Av. 5 near Lincoln, F, beach view; *Tete*, C.4-5, Av. 3 (T 58-11-22), C with bath, but cheaper possibly available; *Internacional*, Av. 5, C. 2-3, T 58-04-34, D; *Pensión Los Angeles*, Calle 6-7, Av. 7, F, with bath, cheap, average; *Fung*, E, by market, modern; *Palace*, also near market, E, small, basic, plants, chairs on balcony, rec; *Miami*, C. 4-5, Av. 2, T 58-04-90, E, back rooms quieter, a/c, Chinese food in restaurant; *Internacional*, C. 2-3, Av. 5, T 58-04-34, E, quite good; *Park*, C. 1-2, Av. 3, T 58-34-76, F, sea facing rooms quiet and cool, rooms not clean but restaurant OK; *Gran Hotel Los Angeles*, C. 4, Av. 2-3, T 58-20-68, E; *Caribe*, C. 1-3, Av. 2, T 58-01-38, E; *Galaxy*, Av. 2, next to market, T 58-28-28, F, share bath, clean, friendly; *Pensión Hotel Costa Rica*, 1½ blocks E of central park, F, small rooms, noisy; *Pensión El Sauce*, one block from main square, F, reasonably clean; *Paraíso*, C. 5, Av. 5-6, F, no bath, clean, noisy; *Hong Kong*, on main street, F, clean but noisy; *Nuevo Oriental*, F, nice, cold showers; *Centro*, E, clean, basic, noisy, cold showers; *Pensión Dorita*, C. 3-4, Av. 4, fairly clean, friendly, basic, reported no blacks accommodated, close to bus stop for Cahuita; *Ng*, C. 3, Av. 5, T 58-21-34, F with bath. *Balmoral*, near market, G, basic; *Caballo Blanco*, 2 blocks from market coming from railway station, F, basic, quite clean but noisy; *Linda Vista*, Parque Vargas, F, basic, friendly, noisy.
    On the road to nearby Portete, *Las Olas*, C, a/c, bath, with pool and sauna, set on rocks in the sea (buses every 1½ hr.), own water supply, no protection against insects, expensive restaurant; in Portete *Matama*, Playa Bonita, T 53-65-28, B, recently refurbished, bath, a/c, restaurant, tennis, pool, boats for rent to Tortuguero; *Cabinas Getsemaní*, cabins, C, bath, a/c, restaurant, pleasant (T 58-11-23).

Restaurants Several Chinese restaurants. *Park Hotel*, C.1-2, Av.3, does good meals, US$2.25; *American Café Springfield* (try the tortuga). *Restaurant La Chucheca* serves good comidas and breakfast. *La Hacienda*, for steaks, cheap. *Soda/Restaurant Mares*, on main square, clean; *Soda/Restaurant Roxie*, opp. hospital, some way out of town, good value casado. *Tienda Toda*, good, near market; *Harbour Restaurant*, good value meal of the day. *Mölnpik* for good ice cream; *Milk Bar La Negra Mendoza* at the central market has good milk shakes and snacks. Casados in market in the day, outside it at night. Cheap food at the corners of the Central Park.

Swimming Japdeva, the harbour authority, has a 25-metre pool open to the public for a small fee in the harbour area.

Exchange Banco Nacional de Costa Rica, and also Banco Anglo Costarricense (open Sat. a.m.) next to Limón-San José bus terminal.

Post Office out of town (take "Pueblo Nuevo" bus). **Cables** Radiográfica maintain offices in Limón.

Protestant Church Baptist, with services in English.

Hospital Social Security Hospital.

Rail One train daily to San José, 0700, US$3 (sit on left); the new station is on the edge of town (bus from centre, US$0.03).

Buses Town bus service is irregular and crowded. Service to San José with Transportes Unidos del Atlántico, every hour on the hour between 0500-1700; leave from the street between central plaza and Parque Vargas (ignore the old signs for the departure point), US$2, 3-4 hrs. To Cartago, US$1.50.

The Atlantic Coast The Río San Juan forms the border between Costa Rica and Nicaragua; the frontier (which was closed in 1981 but may now be open again) is not in mid-river but on the Costa Rican bank. *Los Chiles* has cheap accommodation (F range) and restaurants; the principal traffic is on the river, but a road has been built to Los Chiles (bus to Quesada, US$1). English is spoken widely along the coast.

Northward from Limón, past *Siquirres* (a clean, friendly town: hotels include *Colerón, Wilson, Idamar, Garza, Cocal* and *Vidal*, all E), trains run to *Guápiles*, centre of the new Río Frío banana region. One flight daily from San José to Río Frío. The new San José-Limón highway passes Guápiles, only 1 hr. from the capital. Standard Fruit have built about 75 km. of new railway lines on from Guápiles.

Hotels *Keng Wa* and *As de Oro* (with bath, both E; *Hugo Sánchez Cheng, Cariari* and *Alfaro* (with bath, above noisy bar), all F; *Hospedaje Guápiles*, F, good—T 71-61-79.

6½ km. N of Limón is *Moín*, with a pleasant beach and *Hostal Moín* (F, T 58-24-36, 15 mins. from railway and docks—runs 24-hr. service), buses run every 40 minutes from 0600-1740, ½ hr., US$0.10. From Moín one can go to *Tortuguero*, a 52,129-acre National Park protecting the Atlantic green turtle egg-laying grounds and the Caribbean lowland rain forest inland. The turtles lay their eggs at night from July to September (the eggs start hatching in the second week of September), but before going to watch, contact the National Park administration, or the scientists at Casa Verde (very helpful), Km. 0.6, for instructions, otherwise you may disturb the protected turtles (take a torch if going at night). No permission is needed to enter the park, though enquire if you wish to go to the beach at night. At the Southern end is *Parismina*, where you can stay at the *Tarpon Lodge*, L, including meals, boat and guide. Further north is the settlement of Tortuguero itself. There are several hotels: *Tortuga Lodge*, A, T 71-68-61 (owner Costa Rican Expeditions, packages available from San José, B); *Mawamba Lodge*, T 33-99-64, B, comfortable, fans, restaurant, canal and egg-laying turtles in front of property; *Ilan Ilan*, B, T 55-20-31; *Jungla Lodge*, B, T 33-01-55; *Cabinas Tortuguero Tatane*, D; *Sabina's Cabañas*, E, clean, some cabinas with separate bathroom, good food is limited, but better at *Miss Juni's* with Mona Lisa painting (book in advance) and at *Tío Leo's*. Don't dally on arrival if you want cheap accommodation. The main tours are Mawamba Boats, 3 days/2 nights, US$165, daily, private launch so you can stop en route, with launch tour of National Park included, accommodation at *Mawamba Lodge*, T 33-99-64, or Limón 58-49-15, P.O. Box 10050 San José, and Miss Caribe, US$100 inclusive, T 33-01-55. Colorado Prince Boat, 3 day/2 night package, Tues., Fri., Sun. US$125, T 55-30-31. OTEC (**see page** 579) runs 3-day, 2-night tours for US$90 with student card, US$125 without. Out of "turtle season" Tortuguero is popular for family outings, with nice food but poorly arranged tours into the forest.

Park rangers are friendly and make trips into the jungle waterways; particularly recommended for viewing tropical rain forest wildlife (birds, crocodiles, tapirs, jaguars, ocelots, peccaries, anteaters, manatees, sloths, monkeys, gars); their trips are quite short, about US$2 p.p. for 3-4 hr. trip. Canoe and guide can be rented for US$3 p.p. per hour. There are several boats for rent from Tortuguero, ask at the *pulpería*. Take insect repellant against the ferocious mosquitoes, ticks and chiggers. From Moín, a regular boat goes to Tortuguero, Thurs., 0800, Sat., 0900, (check these times), returning Fri., 0600 and Sun., 1000, US$6 one way, 7 hrs. (locals are always given preference, ask one to get tickets for you; the boat is noisy and often out of order, take protection against rain). You can hire a boat for between US$120-200 (US$20-25 p.p. in a group) each way, but take care the boat is in good condition. Other boats (every 2 days or so) go to Barra del Colorado and take 9 hrs. through the natural canals to Tortuguero. If excursion boats have a spare seat you may be allowed on. Generally it is getting more difficult to "do it yourself", but it is still possible, ask around the boat owners. Official tours and tourist guides with accommodation included are now normal. A road is under construction from Guápiles.

Michael J. Brisco writes: "The canals pass many small settlements, and for many of them the barge is their only means of communication. The canals are part artificial, part natural; they were originally narrow lagoons running parallel to the sea, separated from it by ¾ km. of land. Now all the lagoons are linked, and it is possible to sail as far as **Barra del Colorado**, in the extreme NE of Costa Rica, 25 km. beyond Tortuguero." There is a plan to link the Parque Nacional Tortuguero with the Barra del Colorado into a continuous National Park area. The area is world famous for fishing. The passenger launch from Moín to Tortuguero continues to Barra del Colorado on Thurs., returning early Fri. a.m. There is a luxury hotel lodge operated by Swiss Travel Service; *Río Colorado Lodge*, C p.p. inc. 3 meals and fishing with guide, reservations rec., T 71-88-92; *Isla de Pesca*, D with bath (T 32-82-19); *Hotel Pesca Casa Mar*, A, with bath (T 41-28-20); *Cabinas New Tropical Tarpon* with bath (T 27-04-73). You can hire a canoe and guide for about US$2.50 per hour p.p., minimum 4, excellent way to see wildlife including crocodiles, ask for Damma. Flight San José-Barra del Colorado with Sansa Tues., Thurs. and Sat., 0600 (returns 0645), US$12 one-way.

Southward from Limón, travellers can catch a train to Penshurst or can drive; the road is paved. Here the road branches to Valle de Estrella, a large Standard Fruit banana plantation; camping is easy in the hills and there are plenty of rivers for swimming. Small buses leave Limón (C. 4, Av. 6) for Valle de Estrella/Pandora at 7 a day from 0500, at 2-hourly intervals, last at 1800, 1½ hrs. (returning from Pandora at similar times).

From Penshurst it is 11½ km. to **Cahuita**; this stretch of the road is paved to the edge of Cahuita. There is a bus service direct from San José (Av.11, C.1-Central), 0600 and 1430, 4 hrs., returning 0930, US$3, and from Puerto Limón, in front of Radio Casino (0500, 1000, 1300, 1700, return 0600, 1000, 1200, 1730, US$0.60, 1-3 hrs., both continuing on paved road to Bribri, two basic *residencias*, and on to Sixaola on the Panamanian border (US$1, 2 hrs.). The Cahuita National Park has a narrow strip of beach (1,067 hectares) and a unique coral reef off shore, sadly being damaged by agricultural chemicals etc. from the rivers. An old Spanish wrecked ship may be seen, although the water can be very cloudy at times (both can be reached without a boat; take snorkelling equipment, but the undercurrent is strong and wear shoes if you go on the reef). The Park extends from Cahuita town to Puerto Vargas further SE. Best access to the Park is from Puerto Vargas where there are the Park headquarters, a nature trail, camping facilities, drinking water, toilets (take the bus to Km. 5, then turn left at the sign; the road from the Cahuita-Bribri road to Puerto Vargas is muddy; take a torch if walking it after dark). The length of the beach can be walked in 2 hrs., passing endless coconut palms and interesting tropical forest, through which there is also a path, including fording the shallow Perezoso River, which is brown with tannin. It is hot and humid, but a wide range of fauna can be seen, including howler monkeys, white face monkeys, coatimundis, snakes, butterflies and hermit crabs. Over 500 species of fish inhabit the surrounding waters. Reef tours avilable. No permission is necessary from SNP to enter the Park.

The bus drops you at the crossing of the 2 main roads in Cahuita. On the street parallel to the sea, towards the Park entrance are *Cabinas Vaz*, E, friendly, cold shower, some fans, T 58-15-15 ext. 218, and *Hotel Cahuita*, D, friendly, French Canadian owner, expensive restaurant, T 58-15-15 ext. 201 (opp. is *Soda Sol y Mar*, rec.). *Cabinas Surfside*, E, T 58-15-15 Ext 246 run by David Buchanan and Anna, both speak English, rec. A little road from the bus stop goes straight to the seafront, passing *Cabinas Palmer*, E (T 58-15-15, ext. 243), clean, helpful, but noisy; carry on to the sea, and on left is *Jenny's Cabinas* (same phone, but ext. 256), E, clothes washing area, Canadian owned, rustic, basic, running water, rec. On the road from Limón to Cahuita, Km. 22, is *Club Campestre Cahuita*, C with bath, fans, swimming pool, T 55-61-76, isolated and difficult to get to Cahuita National Park from here. For cheaper rooms, walk 15 mins. N to Playa Negra: *Pepe's Place*, pleasant owner, but beware of theft; *Grant's Cabins*, F, good water service, Señorita Letty Grant (North American), blue house on right of track to black beach, rents rooms (F) and *cabañas*, clean, nice, friendly; *El Atlántico*, next to football ground, nice gardens, E with bath, fan, mosquito screen, pleasant, free safe parking for cars and motorcycles (also known as Canadian Jean's (French) rec.); *Cabinas Black Beach*, E, clean and well situated; *Samwell's*, F, clean, friendly, rec; *Brigitte's*, E, friendly, quiet, Swiss run. There are also empty rooms to let, so take a hammock or sleeping bag. Camping: US$0.25 p.p., good facilities but no meals. *Daisy's Café*, for breakfast and dinner, 100 metres past ball ground, good view of beach, good service, also book exchange and snorkelling equipment hire, very expensive. Other restaurants: *Sands*, cheap, *Tipico*, good, Winston is very helpful but not always accurate. *Miss Edith*, delicious Caribbean food, nice people, good value, many recommendations in 1989 and 1990, though don't expect quick service; *Sol y Mar*, good value, ask for Chepe who speaks English and is fun to talk to, rec.

On public holidays Cahuita is very crowded; the remainder of the year it is a favourite resort of backpackers (don't bathe or sun-bathe naked). Money can be changed in the store in same building as *Bar Vaz*. Tony Mora runs glass-bottomed boats over the coral reef. Also horses can be hired, but ensure they are in good shape. The National Park services have warned against muggings in the park at night, if walking the path take a torch. Some of the jungle has been cleared for safety. Also beware of theft on the beach, and drug pushers who may be undercover police.

The beaches at **Puerto Viejo (Limón)**, 13 km. from Cahuita, unpaved (bus from San José—en route to Sixaola—4½ hrs., US$3, ½ hr. from Cahuita), are also worth a visit. Hotels: *Rafa's*, dearest; *Apartamentos Antigua Bohío*, E, modern, best of the budget places; *Maritza*, E, clean, friendly, English spoken; *Cabinas Manuel León*, F with bath, T 58-08-54; *Cabinas Chimiruí*, North edge of town, F, thatched huts, horseriding.; *Standford's Disco*, lively nightlife; *Banbú*, next door, good food; *Soda Tamara*, open 0600-2100, local homemade snacks. Note that water can be scarce in Puerto Viejo. You need to bring towels, insect repellant and a torch.

It is possible to walk along the beach from Puerto Viejo to Cahuita in one day; there is a bus, US$0.45. Take road from Cahuita to Hone Creek where one road (dirt) goes to Puerto Viejo and another (paved) to Bribri, one of the villages at the foot of the Talamanca range, which has been declared an Indian Reserve. Halfway between Hove Creek and Puerto Viejo is *Violeta's Pulpería*. Turn off here to the coast for *Cabinas Black Sands*, a bamboo, laurel wood and thatch cabin of Bri-Bri Indian design. Space can be rented at US$4 p.p.

From Limón, Aerovías Talamaqueñas Indígenas fly cheaply to Amubri in the Reserve (there is a *Casa de Huéspedes* run by nuns in Amubri). Villages such as Bribri, Chase, Bratsi, Shiroles and San José Cabécar can be reached by bus from Cahuita. (For a good introduction to the Talamanca mountains, read *Mamita Yunai* by Fallas, or *What Happen* by Palmer.) Continuing S from Cahuita is **Sixaola**, on the border with Panama. 2 hotels just before the bridge: *Central*, Chinese run with good restaurant, and *Pensión Doris*, F. There are no banks in Sixaola, but it may be possible to change money in one of the shops before the bridge. A narrow-gauge railway runs to Almirante (Panama) from Guabito, on the Panamanian side (shops will accept colones). Remember to advance watches by 1 hr. on entering Panama. If crossing to Panama take the earliest bus possible to Sixaola (**see page** 646). Direct Sixaola-San José bus, 5 hrs., US$3 (T Sixaola 58-15-72), 0600 and 1430; also 4 a day to Puerto Limón via Cahuita.

THE NORTH AND THE NW PACIFIC COAST

A paved road and a railway run from the capital to the two other main towns of the Meseta: Heredia and Alajuela.

Heredia, capital of its province, 10 km. from San José, is a great coffee and cattle centre. Altitude 1,137 metres, population 30,000. It looks a little like the towns of southern Spain: church towers above red-tiled roofs, iron grilles at the windows, and bright gardens set among whitewashed adobe and stone walls. The main church was built in 1797. There is a statue to the poet Aquileo Echeverría (1866-1909). The Tourist Institute will arrange a visit to a coffee *finca*. One of the largest coffee "beneficios" is La Meseta; the bus from Heredia to Santa Bárbara will drop you at the gate and you can ask for a guided tour.

Hotels *Bougainville de Santo Domingo*, A, spectacular mountain setting; *Herediana*, E, Calle 6; *Colonial*, C.4-6, Av.4, G; *El Verano*, C.4, Av.6, F; *Rosa Blanca* at Santa Bárbara de Heredia, T 39-93-92, L. **Restaurant**: *Pizza Hut* in the centre of town.

North from Heredia, through beautiful mountain scenery, a road leads to the town of **Puerto Viejo de Sarapiquí** once an important port on the River Sarapiquí, where launches can be taken via the Colorado river to the Canales de Tortuguero and Moín, about 10 km. by road and rail from Puerto Limón. There is good fishing on the River Sarapiquí. *(Cabinas Monteverde*, T 71-69-01, ext. 236, F with bath, but reported dirty; Hotels *El Antiguo*—ext 205—and *Santa Marta*, both G; *pensiones Las Brisas* and *González*, both F, latter above hardware store (ferretería), not signed, *Pip's* restaurant, good. There is a spectacular waterfall near here. There is a bus service from San José, C. 12, Avs. 7-9, via Heredia, US$2.50, at 0630 and 1400, returning at 0730 and 1230. Buses from Puerto Viejo to Río Frío and San Carlos. Nearby is *Selva Verde Naturalists' Lodge*: two lodges on 500 acres of virgin rainforest reserve—*Creek Lodge*, shared bathrooms, inclusive of meals, B. *River Lodge*, with private bathroom, A, T 71-64-59. At Las Horquetas de Sarapiquí is *Rara Avis*, a rustic lodge in a 1,500 acre forest reserve owned by ecologist Amos Bien. This admirable experiment in educating visitors about rainforest conservation takes small groups, led by biologists. You must be prepared for rough and muddy trails. Clean bunks, 3 meals and guides US$35 per day, T 53-08-44. Also in the neighbourhood is the Organization of Tropical Studies station at *Finca La Selva* on the Río Sarapiquí. To visit, phone in advance to book, T 71-68-97 or San José OTS office 40-50-33. Visitors are provided with maps of the superb primary rain forest and a bunk in a co-ed dormitory; rates are US$70 a day inc. all meals for ordinary visitors, US$35 for students, researchers or interested journalists (proof required). Day entry, with lunch included, US$15. High rates for tourists help to support the scientists. Try to avoid the rainy season. To get there by car, take Route 9 from San José, 2 hours' driving; park at the suspension bridge then walk. Buses run from Puerto Viejo. The river flows into the San Juan, which forms the northern border of Costa Rica. River trips on the Sarapiquí and on the Río Sucio are beautiful (US$15 for 2 hrs.). In the mountains near Heredia is **San José de la Montaña** (hotels with beautiful views across the Meseta Central: *El Pórtico*, T 37-60-22, rec., *Cabinas Montaña Cypresal*, T 37-44-66, *Cabinas Las Ardillas*, T 37-60-22, all D with bath). At Monte de la Cruz is *Hotel Chalet Tirol*, B, T 39-70-70.

Braulio Carrillo National Park. This large park was created to protect the high rain forest north of San José from the impact of the new San José-Guápiles-Puerto Limón highway. It extends for 44,000 hectares with five different types of forest. Wildlife includes many species of birds, jaguar, ocelot and Baird's tapir. Various travel agencies offer naturalist tours, approx. US$65 from San José. The park also includes Barva Volcano, 2,906 metres. The latter is only accessible from Heredia, there is no entrance from the new highway; take a bus to **San José de la Montaña**; from there it is 4 hrs.' walk to Sacramento, but some buses continue towards Sacramento, halving the walk time (otherwise walk, hitchhike, or arrange a ride with the park director). Ranger station nearby, from which 3 km. of easy climb to the top. Good views; no permit needed here. Jungle Trails (T 55-34-86) offers day trips from San José to Barva Volcano. Easter Week is a good choice. A recommended trail is the "Sendero Botella" in the rain forest (information at the Ranger Station), with waterfall en route. The views down the Patria River canyon are impressive. Bird watchers will also get their fill. The park is also widely known among (illegal) birdcatchers. Alternatively, you can take one of many buses to San Jerónimo de Moravia (1 hr. from San José).

Alajuela, 13 km. beyond Heredia (5 km. from Juan Santamaría international airport), capital of its province, stands at 952 metres, and is a midsummer resort for people from the capital. It is famous for its flowers and its market days (Sat. market is good value for food); an interesting craft cooperative produces pictures in relief metalwork; the unusual church of La Agonía in the E part of town has murals done from life. The national hero, Juan Santamaría, the drummer who fired the building at Rivas (Nicaragua) in which Walker's filibusters were entrenched in 1856, is commemorated by a monument. The Museo Histórico Juan Santamaría (Tues.-Sun. 1000-1700) tells the story of this war, confusingly. Just outside the town is the Ojo de Agua swimming pool (good restaurant) in beautiful surroundings: a popular bathing and boating resort. Entrance, US$0.60 p.p., plus US$0.80 per vehicle. The gushing spring which feeds the pool also supplies water for Puntarenas. Population 28,700.

Festival Fiesta de la Maíz in La Garita off the Pan-American Highway, near the Recope fuel depot.

Hotels *Alajuela*, C. 2, Av. Central and 2 (T 41-12-41), E, with shower, clean, friendly (best to book in advance). *El Real*, C.8, Av.1-Central, clean, F, opp. bus terminal; *Moderno*, same street but other side of railway, "modern" is an overstatement, but basic and clean; *El Americano*, at Turrucares (T 48-71-92), F with bath. *Chico*, hourly rentals till 2100, but cheapest, G p.p.

Restaurants *El Cencerro*, on Parque Central, good meat, especially steaks; *Pizza Hut*, central; *La Jarra*, near Alajuela hotel, good cheap meals in pleasant surroundings.

Language School Centro Lingüistico Latinoamericano, Apartado 151, T 41-02-61, recommended (located in San Antonio).

Excursion From Alajuela a paved road runs to 2,704-metre volcano **Poás** (57 km. by road from San José). In the National Park of Poás (5,600 hectares), the still-smoking volcano is set in beautiful tropical forest. The crater is 1½ km. across (said to be the second largest in the world). Within part of its sharp-sided walls is a lake of very hot water. In another area geysers may throw steam 600 metres or so. One km. away is a still, forest-fringed lake in another crater. A 30-min. jungle trail to the crater starts from the car park. **Clouds often hang low over the crater** after 1000 permitting little to be seen. Entrance to Park, US$0.40. The volcano can be reached by car from San José. Typical tour prices from San José US$20 for Poás volcano tour in morning, or the volcano and Sardú US$30. Make sure you arrive at the volcano before the clouds. On Sunday there is a regular excursion bus from the main square of Alajuela right up to the crater, leaving at 0830, connecting with bus from San José (from Av.2, C.12-14); be there early for a seat, extra buses run if necessary, the area gets very crowded, US$3 return. The bus waits at the top with ample time to see everything (clouds permitting), returning at 1500. Daily bus Alajuela-Poasito 1200 (US$1). From Poasito hitch a lift as it is a 10 km. walk. The visitors' centre offers shelter, electricity outlets and good water even when closed (hours claim to be Mon.-Fri. 0800-1200, 1300-1500, Sat., Sun. and holidays 0800-1600); further up the road are good toilets. There is a restaurant near the parking area. If you spend the night there, a ranger might take you down to the water's edge on a clear night to watch and listen to the dome. The volcano is very crowded on Sun., go in the week if possible. The park has abundant birdlife and has the only true dwarf cloudforest in Costa Rica. Trails are well marked.

Hotel *Country Club Monte del Mago*, Carrillo de Poas (T 61-24-10), D with bath, swimming pool, restaurant. **Campsite** Trailer park nearby, with hookups: the *Inca*.

Beyond Alajuela the Pan-American Highway divides into a toll highway and a *vía libre*, which is the old road. Though it is rough, the latter passes through attractive countryside and the towns of Naranjo (*Pensión Naranjo*, greenhouse on corner 200 m. W of fuel station at entrance to village, very basic, G p.p.) Sarchí and Grecia.

San Carlos, also known as Ciudad Quesada, lies 48 km. from the Pan-American Highway and can be reached by a road which branches off the highway near Naranjo. It is the main town of the lowland cattle and farming region. Between San Carlos and the Highway is the mountain town of Zarcero, known for its beautiful park and church. There are buses every hour from San José (US$2.50).

San Carlos Hotels *El Tucán Country Club*, B, 8 km. from San Carlos towards Agnas Zarcas, thermal pools, sauna, T 46-18-22; *Balneario Carlos*, E with bath, swimming pool (T 46-07-47); *La Central*, T 46-03-01, E, with bath, restaurant; *Conquistador*, E with bath; *El Retiro*, T 46-04-03, E with bath, clean and comfortable, but noisy; *Lily, Cristal, Diana, Ugalde, París, Los Fernandos*, all F; *La Terminal*, G.

1 hour from San Carlos by bus (US$0.60) is **Venecia** (3½ hrs., US$2.50 by bus from San José); one hotel, F, clean, friendly. Nearby is Ciudad Cutris, precolumbian tumuli (a good road goes to within 2 km. of Cutris, from there walk or take 4-wheel drive vehicle; get a permit to visit from the *finca* owner). A reasonable paved road goes from San Carlos to *La Fortuna* (bus at 1300 and 1645, 3½ hrs. US$1.50). At the base is a thermal pool with bar/restaurant (*Balneario Tabacón*; plans are underway to build cabins). Free camping is encouraged at the site, which is 10 km. from La Fortuna on the road to Tilarán (at night you can see red hot lava bursting out into the night sky). Buses from San Carlos or Tilarán daily (limited service Tues. and Wed.); several cheap hotels in La Fortuna (*Pensión San Bosco*, E with bath; *La Central*, F, quiet, cold showers, friendly, but beware rats; *Restaurant El Jardín*, good food, public phone with international access). Nearby is *Arenal Lodge*, A, T 46-18-81 offers fishing, horses.

Arenal volcano can be reached by taking the road S for 20 km. (buses every 1-2 hrs. from San Carlos, or at 0800 from *Hotel Central*, La Fortuna); here are the lake and dam for hydroelectric power and irrigation. Hot baths near the dam. Full day tours from San José, arranged by Costa Rica Sun Tours, T 55-35-18, US$65. The volcano can be climbed, but is very dangerous because it is active with flying white-hot rock, jets of steam and explosive noises (two tourists were reportedly killed in the attempt in 1989). The S side of Lake Arenal is very difficult to drive, with many fords; the longer N side is paved for all but 3 km. From San Carlos there are buses to Tilarán at 0800 and 1600 near the western end of the lake, and a Youth Hostel 9 km. from the dam, 1½ km. from Nuevo Arenal, E including breakfast T 60-50-08. Buses also go to the Río Frío district and to towns on the San Carlos and Sarapiquí rivers including Puerto Viejo de Sarapiquí, see above.

The Pan-American Highway to the Nicaraguan border, 332 km., completely paved and good. From San José it leads past El Coco airport, Heredia and Alajuela, on a a new dual-carriageway section, to San Ramón (see below).

At **Sarchí** one may visit the factory that produces the traditional painted ox-carts, which are almost a national emblem. Also, hand-made cowhide rocking chairs and wooden products may be purchased at Fábricas de Carretas; there are many shops at the roadside (prices are lower than those in San José). Travel agents in San José charge US$20 or more; Tuasa buses every 15 mins. from Alajuela bus station. The pink-painted church in Sarchí is especially attractive at sunset. **Grecia** is the centre for the pineapple-growing area (*Cabaña Los Cipreses*, D per cabin; *Complejo Trailer y Cabinas Los Trapiches*; *Pensión Quirós*, G with bath). Two very attractive towns in this region are **San Ramón** (76 km. from San José—*Hotel Nuevo Jardín*, E, with bath, hot water; *El Viajero*, F; *Restaurant Tropical*) and, 7 km beyond, Palmares (one hotel). (The people in this region are friendly and like talking to foreigners.) Further on along the Pan American highway is **Esparza**, an attractive town with *Hotel Castanuelas*, T 63-51-05, E, a/c, quiet, cooler alternative to Puntarenas; *Pensión Cordoba*, F p.p., clean and modern.

The stretch of the Highway between San Ramón and Esparza (34 km.) includes the sharp fall of 800 metres from the Meseta Central. (Beware of fog on this stretch if driving or cycling.) Beyond Esparza there is a left turn at Barranca for Puntarenas, 15 km.

Puntarenas (population 50,000) is on a 5-km. spit of land thrusting out into Nicoya Gulf and enclosing the Estero lagoon. It is hot (mean temperature 27°C), the beaches are dirty, and are crowded on Suns. There is a new public swimming pool on the end of the point (US$0.35 entrance). Good surfing off the headland. Across the gulf are the mountains of the Nicoya Peninsula. In the gulf are several islands, the Islas Negritos, to which there are passenger launches. The chief products around Puntarenas are bananas, rice, cattle, and coconuts. Puntarenas is connected with San José by a road (1½ hrs,. by hourly buses), and a railway (116 km.; 4 hrs., **see page** 581). It is being replaced as the country's main Pacific port by Caldera.

Hotels *Tioga*, Barrio El Carmen (T 61-02-71), beachfront and C. 9, C with bath, including continental breakfast, swimming pool, very good indeed. *Colonial*, Calle 72-74, Av. Central, C, a/c, swimming pool, with breakfast, T 61-18-33, very friendly, comfortable, some distance from the centre of town but highly rec; *Porto Bello*, Calle 68 y 70, Av. Central, next door, B with bath, a/c, pool, quiet, clean, gardens, excellent food, helpful Italian owner, T 61-13-22; *Cavesas*, Av. 1, C. 2-4, E, clean, very good value; *Ayo Can*, C.2, Av. 1-3, E, a little noisy but clean; *Cayuga*, Calle 4, Av. Central, E, with shower, a/c, restaurant, dirty, run down. *Yacht Club*, T 61-07-84, at Cocal, caters for members of foreign yacht clubs. Others are *Las Brisas*, on the waterfront, C.31-33, Av. 4, C, good restaurant, swimmimg pool; *Chorotega*, Calle 3, Av. 3, E, with bath and fan, clean, central, rec. (one block east of river); *Viking*, C. 32, Av. 2, new, on the beach, D; *Imperial*, on the waterfront by jetty, round corner from bus station for San José, E, clean front rooms, some single rooms are tatty; *Río*, Av. 3, C. Central/2, near market, Chinese owners, F, with shower, basic and noisy, but clean and friendly; *Cabinas Thelma*, very good, friendly (ask at Holman Bar, Calle 7). Many *cabinas* on Av. 2. *Cabinas Los Jorón*, C. 25, 7 blocks from ferry, T 61-04-67, D, roomy, fridge, a/c, restaurant, rec; *Las Hamacas* on waterfront, E, T 61-03-98, nice rooms but noisy. Apartments for rent from Jacob Puister, Contigua Casino, Central, 2° piso, T 61-02-46, US$37 for 2 weeks. *Cabinas Orlando* at San Isidro de Puntarenas, with bath and kitchen, D; *Villa del Roble*, by the sea 18 km. E (T 63-04-47), B, 5 rooms, quiet, charming; *Río Mar Hotel* at Barranca, 15 km. from Puntarenas, D with bath, restaurant, good, pricey. Accommodation difficult to find Dec.-April, especially at weekends.

Restaurants Next to *Hotel Tioga* is *Aloha Restaurant* (good). *Mariscos Kahite Blanco*, downtown, excellent seafood. A number of Chinese restaurants on the main street (e.g. *Mandarín*, good value). Good food from market stalls, e.g. sopa de carne. *Fonda Brisas del Pacífico*, near wharf, good value casado. There is a lively night life in the cheaper bars. On the beach, *Bierstube*, good for sandwiches, hamburgers and spaghetti. Recommended bars: *Pier 14*, near wharf, good pizza and hamburgers made by Captain Ed from Mobile (Alabama) and his wife; *Yate Bar*, friendly, English-speaking owner (no girls at either).

Cables ICE and Radiográfica.

Warning Thieves abound on the beach.

Crossing to Nicoya Peninsula (see page 599) is by ferry to Salinero and by launch to Paquera. (see page 600) To Playa Naranjo (Salinero), US$1 p.p., US$7 per car, 1½ hrs., crossings Mon.-Fri. 0700 and 1600, returning 0900 and 1800; Sat. and Sun. 0700, 1100 and 1600, returning 0900, 1400 and 1800 (T 61-10-69). Snacks and drinks are sold on the ferry. Buses meet the ferry for Coyote, Bejuco, Nicoya and Jicaral. Launches to Paquera (for Cóbano, Playa Montezuma, etc.) daily 0600, 1500, returning at 0800 and 1800, 2 hrs., US$1.25. Take bus "Barrio Carmen" from centre for ferry.

Isla San Lucás is a prison island, but you may visit its beautiful beaches on Sunday. The prisoners are friendly and sell arts and crafts very cheaply. You can buy them or exchange them for items such as toothpaste, soap, etc. There is a shop selling refreshments. Launch leaves Puntarenas Sun. 0900, but arrives by 0800; returns 1500, US$1.50.

Isla Jesuita, in Gulf of Nicoya has an hotel: *Hotel Isla Jesuita*, lodge and cottages, hammocks reached by hotel's boat or public launch from Puntarenas. Package rates from San José, also arrangements can be made in the US T 800-327-9408.

On the San José-Puntarenas railway, near the new port of Caldera, is **Mata de Limón**, which has a beach. It is on a lagoon surrounded by mangroves, peaceful. Bus from Puntarenas market every hour (marked to Caldera); train back to Puntarenas passes through at about 1615. Hotels: *Casablanca*, C. 2-4, Av. 14, T 22-29-21, E, full board available, or cabins; *Manglares*, near train stop, E, reasonable, good restaurant; excellent bar/restaurant next to railway booking office. South of the village (care when crossing wooden bridge at night, missing planks!) there are several basic places to stay, all basic, F, but acceptable: *Viña del Mar*, *Villas Fanny*, *Villas América*. Good fishing nearby.

Monteverde The site of the 10,500 hectare private Monteverde Cloudforest reserve (managed by the Tropical Science Centre) is mainly primary cloud forest. It contains over 400 species of birds (including the resplendent quetzal, best seen between January and May, which are the dry months, especially near the start of the Nuboso trail, three-wattled bellbird and bare-necked umbrellabird), over 100 species of mammals (including monkeys, baird's tapir, jaguar, margay and ocelot), reptiles, amphibians (including the entire range of the golden toad). The reserve includes an estimated 2,500 species of plants and more than 6,000 species of insects.

Reserve entrance fee US$5 (students with ID US$3); discounted 3-day pass US$12 (students US$7.20) and 7-day pass US$29.75 (students US$17.85). Various checklists, postcards, gifts and T-shirts are on sale. Reserve office opens 0700 daily. Protective rainwear and boots are a must, especially in rainy season. The best months are January to May, especially February, March and April. From January 1991 the total number of visitors in the reserve at any one time will be limited. The entrance is at 1,500 metres, but the maximum altitude in the reserve is over 1,800 metres. Mean temperature is between 16 and 18°C and average annual rainfaull is 3,000 mm. The weather changes quickly, and wind and humidity often made the air feel cooler. Shelter facilities throughout the reserve cost US$2.50, bring sleeping bag. Rubber boots can be rented at hotels. Trail walks take from 2 to 6 hours. Limited camping at the entrance; dormitory-style accommodation at reserve, *Albergue Reserva Biológica de Monteverde*, T 61-2655, G, kitchen facilities.

Natural History walks with biologist guides, every morning, US$12, 4-hours; reserve in advance at the office or your hotel. Free maps of reserve at the entrance. An experienced guide is Gary Diller (Apdo 10165, 1000 San José T 61-0903); he charges US$20 p.p. (min. US$50) for private tours, 3-4 hrs.

Donations to the reserve can be made at the reserve office or Tropical Science Centre (Apdo. 8-3870, 1000 San José, T 25-2649 or 53-3308) at El Higerón, 100 mts sur, y 125 mts este, Barrio La Granja, San Pedro. The Monteverde Conservation League (Apdo. 10165—1000 San José, T 61-2953) opp. Monteverde Gas Station, open 0830-1600, is purchasing additional land for the reserve and welcomes donations. There is a plan to prepare a trail northwards to the Arenal volcano.

Hotels   *Hotel de Montaña Monteverde*, T 61-1846, B, is just before Monteverde Gas Station on right, rec., restaurant, private bathroom, 4 suites, horses for hire (US$7/hour), views of Nicoya, excellent, birdwatching on 15 acre reserve; transportation from San José available; *Belmar*, T 61-1001, B, 300m from Monteverde Gas Station, Swiss-Chalet style, beautiful views of Nicoya, restaurant, good, transportation from San José available; *Fonda Vela*, T 61-2551, B, nearest to Reserve, 40 mins. walk, on a 20 hectare farm, private bathroom, horses for hire; *Heliconia*, T 61-1009, B, 100 m before *Hotel de Montaña Monteverde*, private bathroom, restaurant; *Pensión Quetzal*, T 61-0955, C p.p. full-board, some rooms with bathroom, 3 new cabins, American-run, very popular, located next to Sendero Bajo Tigre Trail, between Monteverde and Reserve; *Pensión Flor Mar*, T 61-09-09, c p.p. full-board, located between Reserve and Monteverde, helpful, American owner, but expensive; *Monteverde Inn*, T 61-2756, D, 100 m before *Hotel de Montaña Monteverde*, private bathroom, full board, good value; *Pensión Tucán*, F, with restaurant, showers, basic, but friendly management, T 61-10-07.

The settlement at Monteverde was founded by American Quakers in the 1950's; it is essentially a group of dairy farms and a cheese factory run by a cooperative. Excellent cheeses of various types can be bought, also fresh milk and *cajeta* (a butterscotch spread) are sold. The Quakers have an English Library at Monteverde. Service Station in Monteverde. Casem, a cooperative gift shop, is located just outside Monteverde on the road to reserve. It sells embroidered shirts, T-shirts, wooden and woven articles and baskets. *Restaurant El Bosque*, next to Casem Shop. From Monteverde to the reserve is a minimum 45 mins. walk. Stable "The Star" has horses for hire. Near *Pensión Quetzal*, The Monteverde Conservation League has Sendero Bajo Tigre trail (open 0600-1600, US$1.20).

Buses   A direct bus, Monteverde Express, runs from San José (4 hrs., US$3.40) Mon.-Thurs. 1430, Sat.-Sun. 0630, returning Tues.-Thurs. 0630, Fri.-Sun. 1500. Be early. A bus from Puntarenas to Santa Elena (2½ hrs. US$1.20) about 4 km. from Monteverde, leaves daily 1415, returning 0600. Taxis available between Santa Elena and Monteverde. By car, follow the Pan-American highway north from San José to Río Lagarto. Turn right just before the river, and continue for about 40 km. on gravel road (allow 2½ hrs.). Check that your car rental agreement allows you to visit Monteverde.

Santa Elena 4 km. before Monteverde, has several *pensiones*: *Pensión Santa Elena*, T 61-1151, E, pleasant, clean, good food; *Pensión de Franklyn Vargas* (F) with shower, clean; *Pensión Iman*, inexpensive, clean. Banco Nacional will change travellers' cheques.

50 km. north of Barranca on the main road is **Las Cañas**. (5 buses daily from Coca Cola terminal, San José. Hotels: *Cañas*, C. 2, Av. 1, E with bath; *El Corral*, C. 4, Av. Central, E with bath; *Guillén*, C. Central, Av. 2, F; also *Luz* and others; a good restaurant is *Rincón Corobicí*, clean and pleasant.) From there are buses to **Tilarán** (and from San José, 0730, 4 hrs.). (Hotels *Grecia*, F with shower, cheaper without, *Central*, F; *Cabinas El Sueño*, both 1 block from bus station, and other *Cabinas* including *Cabinas Mary* T 69-54-70, small pleasant rooms upstairs recommended; *Cabinas Narabit*, T 69-53-93, E, south of church; *Cabinas Central*, F, T 69-53-63, good value, and *Cabinas El Sueño*, D, T 69-53-47, rooms round central patio, friendly, rec.) Two buses leave each afternoon for Arenal on the N side of the lake formed by the new Arenal dam (check return times if you want to go back same day).

North of the lake, near the Nicaraguan border are the villages of the Guatuso Indians. Upala and Caño Negro. There is now a direct bus from San José to Upala (from Av. 5, C. 14 at 1445, 4 hrs., US$2.80), where there are the *Hotel Rigo*, *Hotel Upala*, T 47-01-69, *Pensión Isabela*, *Pensión Buena Vista*, basic, F, food available.

5 km. N of Las Cañas is a very good campsite and hotel, *La Pacífica*, on Pan-American Highway 4 km. N, D, T 69-00-50, Swiss-run, with restaurant, cottages, cabins, pool, small zoo, medical service, workshop, spare parts, and rafting down the Río Bebedero to the Gulf. There is free camping along the river.

Also on the Nicoya Peninsula, is the **Palo Verde National Park**, over 5,700 hectares of marshes with many water birds. Indeed, in the Laguna Foohas, over 50,000 birds are considered resident. Research Station, operated by OTS, T 40-50-33, has accommodation facilities, ordinary visitors US$35 with meals, students, researchers, US$30. Day visits with lunch, US$15. Make advance reservations. Get there from Cañas by bus to Bebedero, or turn off the Pan-American Highway at Bagaces, half way between Cañas and Liberia, no public transport. The bird santuary is 10 km. beyond the camping site.

The Pan-American Highway runs for 198 km. from Las Cañas to the Nicaraguan border. It passes through the lowhills of **Guanacaste** Province, which includes the Peninsula of Nicoya and the lowlands at the head of the gulf. The Province, with its capital at Liberia, has a distinctive people, way of life, flora and fauna. The smallholdings of the highlands give way here to large *haciendas* and great cattle estates. Maize, rice, cotton, beans and fruit are other products, and there is manganese at Playa Real. The rivers teem with fish; there are all kinds of wildlife in the uplands.

The people are open-handed, hospitable, fond of the pleasures of life: music, dancing (the Punto Guanacasteco has been officially declared the typical national dance), and merry-making (cattle and jollity often go together). There are many *fiestas* in January and February in the various towns and villages, which are well worth seeing. Rainfall is moderate: 1,000 to 2,000 mm. a year, but there is a long dry season which makes irrigation important, but the lowlands are deep in mud during the rainy season.

Liberia (pop.: 13,700) is a neat, clean, cattle town with a church in the most modern style and a small meticulous market (119 km. from Esparza, 79 from Peñas Blancas). A well paved branch road leads SW into the Nicoya Peninsula. There is a tourist office in the Oficina de Viajes del Norte.

Hotels *La Siesta*, Calle 4, Av. 4-6, D with bath, clean, swimming pool, helpful owner who speaks English; *Las Espuelas*, 2 km. South, C, expensive but good, swimming pool, American Express accepted (T 66-01-44); *La Ronda* (T 66-04-17), E with bath, restaurant; *El Sitio*, just off highway on road to Nicoya, C, bath, a/c, good; *Intercontinental*, D, new, good; *Bramadero Motel*, C, not all rooms have bath, open air restaurant and bar but somewhat noisy, swimming pool; *Liberia*, 50 metres from main square, F with shower (less without), noisy, reasonable; *Margarita*, F, basic but OK, friendly; *Boyeros* (also has swimming pool) D, bath, restaurant; *Oriental*, F, bath, restaurant (Chinese), rec; *Motel Delfín*, 5 km. N of Liberia on the Pan-American Highway, E, with bath, run down, large swimming pool.

Good Chinese **restaurants**: *Cuatro Mares* (just off main square), *Cantón*, *Shan Ghai*, *Elegante* restaurant opp. *Hotel Liberia*, big meals. On the west side of the Plaza is *Soda Las Finajas*, which specializes in *refrescos*.

There is also a photographic studio.

Bus Liberia-Peñas Blancas, US$1.25, usually very crowded at 0900, very few between late a.m. and late p.m., third and last bus Peñas Blancas-Liberia at 1700. Regular buses Liberia-San José, 7 a day, 4 hrs., US$2.30. Bus Peñas Blancas-San José, Tracopa, 1030 and 1500, from San José—Coca Cola terminal—at 0445 and 0745, 6 hrs, US$2.50.

The last town before the border is La Cruz, with eating places and 3 small hotels (*El Faro*, F, clean), lovely views over the bay. At nearby Ciruelas de Miramar, there is a good restaurant; *Palenque Garabito*; try their fried yucca. At Peñas Blancas there are a duty-free shop, a bank which changes travellers' cheques and a black market. There is a good bar and restaurant adjoining the Costa Rican immigration offices; a good map of Costa Rica is available from the tourist office at the border (the desk opposite the counter where one pays entry tax). It's a 5 km. walk from Costa Rican immigration to the Nicaraguan side of the border. The Costa Rican border offices and the Nicaraguan border are closed 1200-1300. Crossing to Nicaragua can be a slow process (up to 6 hrs.). If you have no outward ticket for Costa Rica, you can buy a cheap bus ticket back to Nicaragua at the border (valid for 1 year). For documents and other requirements, see under **Information for visitors—Documents**.

37 km. north of Liberia, about half-way to the Nicaraguan border, is the **Santa Rosa National Park** (entry US$0.35; camping US$0.55). Together with the Murciélago Annex, which lies north of the developed park, it preserves some of the last dry tropical forests in Costa Rica, and shelters abundant and relatively easy-to-see wildlife. They are also attempting to reforest some of the cattle ranches of the area (helped by the fact that cattle have not been profitable in recent years). During the dry season, the animals depend on the water holes, and are thus easy to find (except at the end of the season when the holes dry up). Santa Rosa National Park (49,500 hectares) is easy of access from San José, as it lies west of the Pan-American Highway, about one hour north of Liberia. Any bus going to Peñas Blancas (from Liberia, US$0.80, 1½ hrs.) on the Nicaraguan border will drop you right at the entrance at a cost of US$0.35, ½ hour. There is a pleasant campground about 7 km. from the entrance with giant strangler figs that shade your tent from the stupendously hot sun, and very adequate sanitary facilities, picnic tables, and so forth. Bring your own food; a tent is useful—essential in the wet season. You may be able to sleep on the verandah of one of the scientists' houses. Bring a mosquito net and insect repellant against gnats. If the water is

not running, ask at Administration. Take care, there are plenty of poisonous snakes. In the park is the Santa Rosa *hacienda* (*Casona*), at the start of the nature trail and close to the camp. There the patriots repelled the invasion of the filibuster Walker, who had entrenched himself in the main building.

Michael Tesch and Leone Thiele of Cape Paterson, Australia, write "Playa Naranjo (3 hrs.' walk or more) and Playa Nancite (about the same distance from the entrance) are major nesting sites of Leatherback and Ridley sea turtles. The main nesting season is between August and October (although stragglers are seen up to January regularly) when flotillas of up to 10,000 Ridley turtles arrive at night on the seven kilometre long Playa Nancite. Females clumsily lurch up the beach, scoop out a 2-foot hole, deposit and bury an average of 100 ping-pong-ball sized eggs before returning exhausted to the sea." Playa Nancite is a restricted access beach; you need a written permit to stay there free, otherwise, US$1 per day to camp, or US$1.50 in dormitories. Permits from SPN in San José, and the Park Administration building at Santa Rosa.

Rincón de la Vieja National Park (14,000 hectares, NE of Liberia) was created to preserve the area around the Volcán Rincón de la Vieja, including dry tropical forest and various geothermal curiosities: mudpots, hot sulphur springs, hot springs of various other kinds. The ridge of which the volcano is the highest peak can be seen from a wide area around Liberia; it is often enshrouded in clouds. The area is cool at night and subjected to strong, gusty winds and violent rains; in the day it can be very hot, although always windy. These fluctuations mark all of the continental divide, of which the ridge is a part. To get there: a bumpy 2-hr. ride from Liberia in a truck leaving at irregular hours; alternatively, inquire when the park's truck will visit Liberia; a frequent occurrence. If you take your own transport you will need four-wheel drive. You can stay for free in an old, spacious, refurbished *hacienda* 2 km. inside the park. Bring your own food and bedding. From the old *hacienda* you can hike to the boiling mudpots and come back in the same day; the sulphur springs are on a different trail and only 1 hr. away. Lots of birds including toucans, parrots, and also howler monkeys and coatimundi. Horses can be rented from the park for US$0.60 per hour. The climb to the volcano requires camping near the top (need a tent) in order to ascend early in the morning before the clouds come in. Permission required from the SPN for visiting the park. Warning: millions of tiny ticks can be picked up in a short time of strolling in the apparently innocuous grass. Bring masking tape and a flashlight for those midnight tick hunts.

From San José to **Nicoya**, one can go via Liberia; or one can take the Pan-American Highway to a point between Puntarenas and Cañas, at a sign to Río Tempisque ferry. After crossing on this ferry (hourly 0600-1800, US$0.50) one can drive to Nicoya. A third route is: San José to Puntarenas, then take the Salinero ferry across the Gulf of Nicoya to Playa Naranjo (see below). Buses ply along the road from Playa Naranjo (due W across the Gulf from Puntarenas) through Carmona to Nicoya (40 km. unpaved, 30 km. paved road, crowded), US$1.25, 2¼ hrs. and to Sámara, US$1.30. At Nicoya there are connections for Liberia (US$1.30, 2 hrs., US$6 from Playa Naranjo) on the Pan-American Highway. All the beaches on the Nicoya Peninsula are accessible by road in the dry season.

Nicoya, on the Peninsula, is a pleasant little town distinguished by possessing the country's second-oldest church. 5 buses a day to San José, and to nearby towns. Daily buses to Liberia.

Hotels At Nicoya: *Curime*, D with bath, restaurant; *Las Tinajas*, near bus station, E with bath, modern, clean, good value; *Chorotega*, E with bath (F without), very good; *Jenny*, E with bath, T 68-50-50, a/c, towels and soap, even TV, spotless, rec.; *La Elegancia*, F, with bath; *Ali*, F, dirty, avoid; *Pensión Venecia*, opp. old church, F, considered good for the price. *Cabinas Loma Bonita*, behind hospital, E/F, T 68-52-69, fans, bar, shaded parking. A good restaurant is *Chop Suey* (Chinese). *Restaurant Jade*, 1½ blocks behind church, being remodelled 1989, one of the few authentic Chinese restaurants in Costa Rica.

Beaches on the Nicoya Peninsula At Playa Naranjo is *Oasis del Pacífico*, B, a/c, bath; *El Paso*, E, T 61-26-10, and at Playa Nandayure are *El Banco*, F, and *Hotel San Marcos*, F. On the Gulf of Nicoya is Jicaral (*Hotel Guamale*, F with bath, restaurant). The beaches of Tambor and Montezuma can be reached by car from Nicoya (and bus, except there is no bus connection between Naranjo and Paquera) or by launch from Puntarenas to Paquera, 1½ hrs., US$1.25 (daily 0600 and 1500); Cóbano, near Montezuma, can be reached by bus from Paquera ferry terminal, 1½ hrs., US$1.25, and buses meet the launches from Puntarenas (not the ferry), US$1.50; *La Hacienda* at Tambor, B, T 61-28-80, built around a cattle farm, excellent, good restaurant; *Dos Lagartos*, E, T 61-11-22; *Tangomar*, L, T 61-27-98, 3 km. from Tambor. The beach is 14 km. long, grey sand, rolling surf, 1½ hrs. on a boneshaking road from ferry; *Hotel Playa de Tambor* at Tambor, C (other *pensiones*, F). North of Playa Tambor is the **Curu National Wildlife Refuge**. Only 84 hectares, but 5 different habitats exist here with 110 species of birds. From Cóbano it is a ½-hr. ride by taxi (US$2.50 up to 5 passengers, or hitch) to **Montezuma**, a small village on the sea. *Montezuma Pacific* and *Casa Blanca*, C; *Hotel Montezuma*, E, T 61-24-72, large rooms, clean, own shower (cold), *Cabinas Mar y Cielo*, D, both with restaurants, the latter has cabins for up to 8; several restaurants, a grocery shops, vegetarian car comes to Montezuma; *Hospedaje Arenas*, E; *Lucie*, E, rec; *Cabinas Karen*, F, 2 rooms in small, cosy clean cottage in the village, plus 3 one-room beach front cottages in Karen's 170 acres private nature reserve, which has lots of wild monkeys etc; Doña Marta next door has the key. Doña Karen, who lives 1½ km. N, is Danish, speaks English, is very friendly. She and her late husband established Costa Rica's first national park; the income from renting rooms goes towards the upkeep of her nature reserve. After her death it will be a national park too. Next door to the *Cabinas Karen* there is a restaurant, good food, fresh fruit and yoghurt, owned by Dutch/americans. At night they show movies (book exchange). There are beautiful walks along the beach, sometimes sandy, sometimes rocky, always lined with trees. Close to the village, 20 mins. up the Montezuma river, is a beautiful, huge waterfall with a big, natural swimming pool (it's beyond a smaller waterfall). Horses for hire from the hotels, but carefully inspect that the horses are fit and not overworked, for the sake of the horses too! 11 km. from Montezuma is the **Cabo Blanco Reserve** (1,172 hectares). Marine birds include frigate birds, pelicans and redfooted boobies. There are also monkeys, anteaters, kinkajou and collared peccary. Bathing in the sea or under small waterfall. Open 0700-1600, jeep from Montezuma US$16, but can take up to 7.

The beach at *Sámara*, 37 km. from Nicoya, is recommended as probably the safest major bathing beach in Costa Rica. Tourists are spoiling this, and other beautiful beaches, by leaving litter. Bus from Nicoya, US$1.15, 2 hrs., twice daily (bad road, poor bus). Sansa operates flights Mon.-Wed. Fri. US$18 from San José. *Brisas*, A, T 68-08-76, with a/c, pool, expensive restaurant, German-owned; *Cabinas Milena*, F, clean, safe, restaurant; *Cabinas Los Almendros*, on beach, E, restaurant, disco Sat.; *Cabinas Punto Sámara*, E. Camping on the beach possible. North of Sámara is Nosara (one bus daily from Nicoya, US$2, 2 hrs., 31 km. and three flights a week from San José), with 2 beaches, Guiones, which is safe for swimming, and Peladas; a colony of North Americans has formed the Nosara Association, to protect its wildlife and forests, and prevent exploitation. There is the *Hotel Playa de Nosara* (B, T 68-04-95), expensive restaurant, *Pensión Estancia Nosara*, F, and a condominium. 12 km. S of Nosara is *Hotel Villaggio La Guaria Morada*, at Punta Guiones de Garza, L, a luxury beach hotel (30 bungalows, Italian

US$0.85; Santa Cruz-Nicoya, US$0.30.

Barra Honda National Park Small park in the North of the Nicoya Peninsula (2,295 hectares). No permit required. Created to protect some caves (in particular Terciopelo) on a *mesa* and small remainders of dry tropical forest at the *mesa's* foot. First go to Nicoya (frequent buses from Liberia, or take the Tempisque ferry if you come from San José). There are several buses a day to Quebrada Honda, a settlement one hour's walk away. The park office is there at Barra Honda, at the foot of the *mesa*, and there are two different trails to the top; two hour's hiking. Also noteworthy are the *cascadas*, bizarre limestone fountains built by sedimentation on a seasonal riverbed. You'll need a guide to get here, as the trails are hopelessly muddled by cowpaths; arrange in advance for the visit to the cave. A full visit requires harnesses, ropes and guides, US$2 p.p. Avoid coming in the rainy season (May to November), but the dry season is exceedingly hot in the open fields. Bring your own food from Nicoya.

THE SOUTH PACIFIC COAST

S of San José one can visit Aserrí, a village with a beautiful white church; further along the same road is the *Mirador Ram Luna*, a restaurant with a fine panoramic view. At the end of the road is San Ignacio de Acosta, again with a good church containing life-size Nativity figures.

Some 155 km. S of San José, in Puntarenas province, is Puerto **Quepos**, built by United Brands as a banana exporting port, but now falling apart. The banana plantations were overwhelmed by Panama disease in the mid 1950s. The road is beautiful and paved until beyond Santiago; the last hour goes through United Brands' palm oil plantations (between Santiago and the plantations is difficult on a motorbike because of the loose surface). There are 4 buses a day from the capital, book a day in advance, 3 hrs., US$2.50; from Quepos there are buses W along the coast to Puntarenas, 3 hrs., US$2.50. There is one daily a.m. flight and an afternoon flight Mon. to Sat. (Sansa, US$9) to the international airport, 20 mins. Book in advance, San José T 33-03-97, Quepos, T 77-01-61. Also, Hustler Tours run flights (see under San José, Internal Flights).

Accommodation and Food *Hotel Kamuk*, Quepos Centre T 77-01-25; *Hotel Pedro Miguel*, D, T 77-00-35; *Hotel Viña del Mar*, D, T 77-00-77, with bath, fan, restaurant, but generally run down; *Hotel Quepos*, T 77-02-74, E with bath, rec., budget hotel; *Linda Vista*, F with bath, OK but noisy; *Luna*, E with bath. *América*, G p.p., basic, clean; *Ramus*, T 77-02-45, in the centre of town, E with bath, fan, bar; *Ceciliano*, D with WC and shower, T 77-01-92, in centre, family run, quiet; *Majestic*, F, dirty, not rec. Accommodation is impossible to find on Sats., Dec.-April. The *Jardín Cervecero Los Arcos* sells good food; *Rancho Restaurant*, French food, expensive but nice for a splurge; *El Gran Escape*, central, good food, cheap, slow service; *Soda Nido* and *Restaurant Ana*, cheap casados. *Soda Nahomi*, inexpensive.

A few km. E of Quepos (½ hr.) lie the 3 beautiful beaches, perhaps the best in Costa Rica, of **Manuel Antonio** which have been declared a National Park (entrance US$1, good hiking in the area, especially the path (steep in places) round the Punta Catedral between two beaches, the Espadilla Sur and the Manuel Antonio; camping, US$0.25 p.p., beware of theft); the beach on which the hotels stand has dangerous rip tides, the 2 inside the park are safest (all littered and may be crowded at weekends). The Park is of 490 hectares with swamps as well as beaches, and a rich variety of bird life. Plenty of snakes, lizards and white faced monkeys can be seen. No permit is needed to enter. A paved road runs from Quepos to Manuel Antonio and to a pleasant beach at Dominical, which has simple cabins for rent. There is a regular bus service from Quepos, 6 a day (US$0.25; taxi, US$2.50), and three buses a day from San José, 3½ hrs (0600, 1200, 1900), US$4.50. Minibuses meet flights at Quepos airport, US$1.25.

Accommodation *La Quinta*, B, T 77-04-34, balconies, screens, fans, quiet, highly rec; *La Arboleda Beach and Mountain Hotel*, 8 hectare wood, 400m. from National Park entrance, B-D, cabins 2-3 persons, bath, fan, restaurant, but beware snakes, crabs and monkeys in the yard at night, T 77-04-14; *El Lirio*, A, T 77-04-03; *Hotel Manuel Antonio*, D, no hot water, restaurant, good breakfast, rec.; *Hotel Plinio*, D, T 77-00-55; *Cabinas Ramírez* (T 77-05-10), E, without bath, food and bar, friendly, generous owners, contact Sr. Ramírez (hammocks and camping free), guests can help with cooking in exchange; *Cabinas Espadillas*, B, T 77-04-16, new 1989, fan, very clean, helpful, 10 mins. walk from beach; *Divisamar*, A, T 77-03-71; *Vela-Bar*, B with private bath, large rooms, fans, safes, good restaurant, 150 m. from beach, organizes fishing and other trips, also has a fully-equipped house to rent (77-04-13, or write to Rosa, Apt. 13 Quepos); *Manuel Antonio Cabinas*, E without bath in house behind beach, F p.p. in small dirty rooms at back, no hot water, or D-C for family cabin on beach, gets very damp in rainy season; *Costa Linda*, T 77-03-04, also listed as a Youth Hostel, cheapest, F, quite noisy; very basic rooms behind *Soda El Grano de Oro*; *Karahue*, B, T 77-01-70, friendly, clean; *Los Almendros*, good fish restaurant, has rooms for 1-4 people, C, quiet, pleasant. On beach, just S of *Ramírez*, is a shop renting surf boards, selling drinks and light meals, has a collection of English novels to read in the bar. Also, *Hotel Mariposa*, T 77-03-55, 3 km. from Manuel Antonio on way to Quepos, L+, exclusive (no guests allowed under 15), but non-residents may use restaurant, good meals (book in advance), and swimming pool for US$1 in USA, calld 800-223-6510; nearby are the cabins of John and Mavis Beisanz (T 49-15-07), also expensive but very good; *Byblos*, A, T 77-04-11, good but expensive French restaurant. Also nearby is *Vela Bar* (and restaurant) good but not cheap and *Barba Roja* restaurant/bar, US-style, popular, not cheap (closed Sept.- Nov.). Cheapest restaurant is *Mar y Sombra*, *casado especial* for US$2.50 is good. Take a torch when walking on roads at night; there are snakes, reportedly poisonous.

SW of San José is the Santa Ana valley, which includes the popular weekend centre of Lagos de Lindora. The road (being paved) goes on through lovely scenery to Puriscal and Puerto Quepos. Before Quepos, at Parrita, is a fine beach, Playa Palma; Hotels *El Nopal* (F) and *Memo* (E, with bath). W of Parrita is the beach at Esterillos Este (*Hotel El Delfín*, B, T 71-16-40, swimming pool, all rooms with breezy balcony, secluded, good restaurant, considered by many as one of the most delightful beach hotels in Costa Rica; other *cabinas*). Further NW is the beach at **Jacó** (with many small pebbles and rip tides, 50 km. from Quepos, paved), which now has a good hotel *Jaco's Beach*, B; *Cabinas Tanyeri*, B, T 42-09-77, modern, attractive landscaping, pool, excellent value for groups; *Coral*, D, 64-30-67, on beach S of town, 2 pools, hammocks, German spoken, warmly rec; *El Jardín*, D with bath, pool, other hotels and many *cabinas*, including *Antonio* (E), *Cabinas Heredia*, E with bath, and *Cabinas Las Brisas*, D, T 64-30-87, attractive grounds, on beach. N. American owner, specially rec.

Jacó can be reached from San José (bus service, from Coca Cola terminal, 1500 daily plus 0845 at weekends, US$1.60) by taking the highway via Alajuela and turning off at Atenas to Orotina and the Río Tárcoles (bridge) and then on to Jacó. Between Orotina and Jacó is the **Carara Biological Reserve**, 4,700 hectares with abundant wildlife—scarlet macaws, whitefaced monkeys, coatimundis and crocodiles. San José travel agencies offer tours at approx US$60. Atenas, accommodation: *Villa Tranquilidad*, C, T 46-54-60, bed and breakfast, bath, swimming pool; Orotina, excursion: Finca Los Angeles offer one day nature tour on horseback US$65 from Orotina through the mountains to the beach, T 24-58-28.

A coastal road has been built from Esparta (on the Pan-American Highway) through Orotina, Jacó, Quepos, Playa Dominical and thence inland to San Isidro de El General. Paving and bridges were completed in 1989 for the coastal section. Playa Dominical is long and quiet but suitable for swimming only at low tide and even then can be dangerous. *Cabinas Costa Brava*, S of village, E, restaurant, basic but friendly. There is better swimming 4 km. S at Punta Dominical (no transport); *Cabinas Punta Dominical*, D, T 71-08-66, restaurant, fishing, horseriding, good value for seekers of solitude.

To get to the Panamanian border from Puerto Quepos take the direct bus to San Isidro de El General at 0430 and 1330 daily from the cinema (5-5½ hrs.), hard ride on the unpaved coastal section, landslides can make the paved section (from Dominical) hazardous. Motorists can do a round trip from San José via San Isidro de El General and the Pacific Coast in a day in the dry season. (Turn-off on the coast road to San Isdro is near Baru).

Isla del Coco is a thickly-wooded island and National Park of 24 square km., 320 km. off the Peninsula of Osa, in the S. It has a 2-man outpost. Contact Michael Kaye of Costa Rican Expeditions for reasonably priced tours; also Otec in San José, **see page** 579. Arrangements for reaching it by chartered boat can be made in Puntarenas, after a permit has been got from the Government, or you can now take a luxury "adventure" cruise on the *Okeanos Agressor*, 10 days, two sailings a month, T 32-05-72 ext. 60. It was at one time a refuge for pirates, who are supposed to have buried great treasure there, though none has been found by the 500 expeditions which have sought it. Treasure seekers make an initial cash payment, agree to share any treasure found with the Government, and are supervised by Costa Rican police. The offshore waters are a fisherman's paradise.

SAN JOSE TO THE PANAMA BORDER

The Pan-American Highway to the Panama border runs 352 km. from San José (frequent rockslides during rainy season). First to Cartago (toll road, US$0.10), and southwards over the mountains between Cartago and San Isidro de El General (124 km.). (This is a spectacular journey. The climate is ideal for orchids.) At Cartago begins the ascent of Cerro

Buena Vista, a climb of 1,830 metres to the continental divide at 3,490 metres; this is the highest spot on the Highway (with an interesting *páramo* ecosystem). Those unaccustomed to high altitude should beware of mountain sickness brought on by a too rapid ascent—see **Health Information, page** 3734. For 16 km. it follows the crest of the Talamanca ridge, with views, on clear days, of the Pacific 50 km. away, and even of the Atlantic, over 80 km. away.

5½ km. S. of the highest point (at Km. 95, 3,335 metres, temperatures below zero at night) is *Hotel Georgina*, E, a bit primitive but good food; before you get there a side road leads off to the peaceful mountain villages of **Santa María de Dota** (*Hotel Santa María*, E with bath; *Hotel Marieuse*, F, without bath, T 74-11-76, very friendly, run by an elderly lady, Doña Elsie) and San Marcos de Tarrazú (Hotels: *Marilú*, F, restaurant; *Continental*, E with bath; *Zacateca*, F with bath). Santa María is quiet, and beautifully situated; it is in a good area for walking, and 8 km. away is a small lake where many waterbirds nest. Nearby is San Gerardo de Dota; *Cabinas Chacón*, D, T 71-17-32, good chance of seeing quetzales on the property, and there is trout fishing in the Río Savegre. From Santa María one can hike (10 hrs.) to the Pacific coast of the Puerto Quepos district, or go by road (3 hrs. in a 4-wheel drive vehicle). The road then drops down into **San Isidro de El General**, 702 metres above sea-level in a fertile valley in the centre of a coffee and cattle district. The town is growing fast.

Hotels and Restaurants *Del Sur*, 10 km. S of town, D with bath, comfortable, swimming pool, tennis, good restaurant; *Amaneli*, with restaurant, and *Manhattan*, both E with bath; *Central*, next to *Amaneli*; *Lala*, G, p.p. cheap, shared bath, poor ventilation; *Iguazu*, modern; *Hotel Balboa* in the centre, F, bath; *Hotel Chirripó*, E with bath, near bus office, modern, clean, good; *Pension Jerusalén*, opp. market; *El Jardín* hotel, F (good value), and good restaurant (especially the breakfast); *Astoria*, not rec; *Restaurant Wu Fu* is good, as are *Kong Kong*, across the park from *Hotel Chirripó*, and *Soda El Parque*, one block from Parque Central, reasonable prices; *Restaurant El Tenedor*, not bad.

Club de Montañismo Kabata (part of Asociación Costarricense de Conservación de la Naturaleza) meets 1st and 3rd Fri. of each month at 1900, 25 metres from main square, sign on 2nd floor balcony next to dentist.

From San Isidro de El General one can go to the highest mountain in Costa Rica, Cerro El Chirripó (3,820 metres) in the middle of the **Chirripó** National Park (at 50,150 hectares, the second largest), including the highest peaks of Costa Rica and a considerable portion of cloud forest. Splendid views from the mountaintops; interesting alpine environment on the high plateau, with lakes of glacial origin and very diverse flora and fauna.

At San Isidro de El General, get food and take the Pueblo Nuevo bus to San Gerardo (0500 or 1400; be early; it leaves from the West side of the central plaza, but enquire carefully or you may miss it). Highly interesting trip up the Chirripó River valley; San Gerardo is situated in a cool, pleasant landscape at the confluence of two rivers. You can stay at the small shop opposite the football pitch and buy (limited) food there. You can camp at or near the park office, 500 metres further up the road from the bus stop. Check in first and pay US$0.30. Horses can be rented. There is a hot spring 1 km. from San Gerardo. Start in the early morning for the 8- to-10-hr. hike. The first shelter, where the horses will take you, is barely adequate and located in a windy spot; the second, 40 min. away, is better built, larger, and more convenient for reaching Cerro Chirripó the next morning before the clouds come in. There are three huts 1½ hours from the top. Stay in the yellow one, wood stove, toilet, shower. Two other peaks can be reached from these huts, Crestones, 45 mins., and Ventisqueres, 1½ hours. Plan for at least two nights on the mountain, and bring warm sleeping bags and clothing. It can be hot in the daytime, though. In the rainy season trails up the plateau are uncomfortably slippery and muddy, and fog obscures the views. These are stiff walks, but no technical climbing is called for. Time your descent to catch the 1530 bus to San Isidro. Permission from SPN necessary for this park.

Also, in this central area of Costa Rica, there are many rivers running NE to the Caribbean that are good for white water rafting, especially July to December e.g. Pacuare, Chirripó and Reventazón. Enquire at Costa Rica Expeditions, Calle Central, Av. 3, San José.

At Km. 197 (from San José) is Buenos Aires, with *Cabinas Mary*, 500 m. from centre, F, quiet clean, *Cabinas La Redonda Familiares*, close to the Pan-American Highway and a *Hotel y Restaurante* 50 m. W of the market. At Palmar Norte (Km. 257) are *Hotel y Cabinas Casa Amarilla*, cabin E, room F with fan; also *Quebrada*, noisy and basic, *El Puente Hotel y Restaurante*, and *Xinia*. At **Palmar Sur** (gas station), 99 km. from the Panamanian border, a banana plantation has stone spheres, 1½ metres in diameter and accurate within 5 mm., which can also be seen in other places in Costa Rica. They are of precolumbian Indian manufacture, but their use is a matter of conjecture; among recent theories are that they were made to represent the planets of the solar system, or that they were border markers. Flights San José-Palmar Sur on Mon., Wed., Sat., US$12.

Near the border is the town of **San Vito**, built by Italian immigrants among denuded hills; it is a prosperous but undistinguished town. *Hotel Pitier*, 2 blocks off main street, new, clean, E with bath; *Las Mirlas* in same range; and *El Ceibo*, without bath, E, T 77-30-25, good restaurant . Tracopa bus from San José, 0630 daily, book previous day. Hotels also in the nearby village of Cañas Gordas. At Las Cruces there is a botanical garden run by an American couple, in an old coffee plantation, 8 km. from San Vito. It consists of 50 hectares of tropical plants, orchids, other epiphytes, and tropical trees. Many birdwatchers come here. It is possible to spend the night here if you arrange first with the Organization of Tropical Studies in San José (cost around US$40 a night with food, students/researchers US$30, day visits with lunch US$15, T 77-32-78). Buses to Ciudad Neily (see below) 0700, 1730, or easy to hitch; from San Vito at 0530 and 0700; return buses pass Las Cruces at 1510.

Thirty-three km. N of the border a road (26 km.) branches S at Río Claro (several *pensiones*) to **Golfito**, the former banana port (fuel available at the junction on the Pan-American Highway). Many of the banana plantations have been turned over to oil palm, others are diseased, so much of Golfito's business has disappeared. Golfito is really two towns—the banana company community and the town itself—about 2½ km. apart. (Hotels: *Costa Rica Surf*, D; *Delfina*, G; *Golfito*, E with bath; *Las Gaviotas*, C, with excellent restaurant on waterfront; *El Refugio*, T 75-04-49; *El Uno*, above restaurant of same name, G, basic, friendly.) About 6 km. (1½ hr. walk) from Golfito is the Playa de Cacao and Captain Tom's place, where you can sling your hammock or camp for US$5 a day (he also has accommodation: boat, caravan or shed—the cheapest—and sells pricey drinks), but take your own food as local shopping is poor. A taxi boat from Golfito will take you there for US$0.50 (1½ km.), or you can drive (if it hasn't rained too heavily) along an inland road, starting at the left of the police station in Golfito, and left again a few km. later. Also nearby is Playa Zancudo where you can stay in cabins at *Sol y Mar*, E, run by Bob and Monika Hara who speak German and English. To get there contact staff of Yacht Club at the entrance of Golfito and ask to radiophone to Zancudo, 750056; well recommended. 0630 bus from San José (US$3.50) with Tracopa; from San Isidro de El General, take 0730 bus to Río Claro and wait for bus coming from Ciudad Neily. Daily flights San José-Golfito, US$15. Bus Golfito-Paso Canoas, US$0.70. South of Golfito, at Punta Blanco is *Tiskita Lodge*, A, T 55-35-18, a 400-acre property with excellent birdwatching. Charter flights from San José possible.

At the southern end of the country is the ***Osa Peninsula***, reached by public boat from Golfito. A boat leaves at 0700 and 1200 for ***Puerto Jiménez***, the only town on the Peninsula (1 hr., US$1; returning 0500 and 1000, all times subject to the tide). At the same time a smaller boat leaves for Rincón (boat is called *Rincón*, 4 hrs., US$1.75). Accommodation in Puerto Jiménez: best is *Cabinas Los Manglares*, small, cold showers, D, restaurant, T 78-50-02 for reservation; *Cabinas Brisas del Mar*, F with bath (T 78-50-12); *Pensión Quintero*, G p.p., clean, good value. Also on the Peninsula: Estación Biológica Marenco (information, P.O. Box 4025, San José, T 21-15-94). Plenty of deserted beaches (tide goes out a long way, plenty of sandflies at high tide). Puerto Jiménez is full of North Americans because of the gold mines near Carate on the Pacific coast and elsewhere on the Peninsula. Several buses a day to Dos Brazos to see the gold mines; ask for the road which goes uphill, beyond town, for the mines. Last bus back from Dos Brazos at 1530 (often late). Rubber boots advisable as a precaution against poisonous snakes (see below). To reach Puerto Jiménez from the Pan-American Highway (70 km.), turn right at the restaurant about 30 km. S of Palmar Sur; the road is newly paved to Rincón, therafter best tackled with four-wheeled drive as a few rivers have to be forded (high clearance essential). They are working on bridges (March 1989). Bus Puerto Jiménez-Ciudad Neily 0500 and 1400, 3½ hrs., US$2.50. There is a police checkpoint 47 km. from the Pan-American Highway. Trucks, called "taxis" run daily between Puerto Jiménez and La Palma (several, 1 hr., US$1.50); from the small settlement of La Palma an all-weather road goes to Rincón.

From Agujitas boats go to the ***Corcovado National Park***. Including the Isla del Caño, it comprises 86,000 hectares, making it the largest park in the system. It consists largely of tropical rainforests, and it includes swamps, miles of empty beaches, and some cleared areas now growing back. It is located at the western end of the Osa Peninsula, on the Pacific Ocean. The SPN plane will fly you in (Wednesdays US$47 round trip) if they have room. Reserve well in advance. You may also arrange to eat meals and lodge at Sirena (where the plane leaves you). Double check that you have ordered food, if you do not take your own. There is a reasonable fee for these services; lodging is US$1.20, in the open and relatively cool attic of the main building at Sirena; bring mosquito netting. Another suggestion is vitamin B1 pills (called "tiamina"). Mosquitos detest the smell and leave you alone. There is however occasionally trouble between gold prospectors and the park guards. If it is dangerous for visitors you will not be allowed into those parts.

From Sirena you can walk north along the coast to the shelter at Llorona (adequate; plenty of water—waterfalls, in fact), from which there is a trail to the interior with another shelter at the end. From Llorona you can proceed north through a forest trail and then along the beach to the station at San Pedrillo on the edge of the park. You can stay here, camping or under roof, and eat with the friendly rangers, who love company. From San Pedrillo you can take the park boat (not cheap) to Isla del Caño, a lovely park outpost with 2 men. New tourist facilities at Bahía Drake, close to Isla del Caño include: *La Paloma Jungle Lodge*, L with bath, meals, T 39-29-11. *Drake Bay Wilderness Camp*, B with meals per person, pleasant family atmosphere, canoeing, ocean fishing, horse riding facilities, large reductions for children, rec., T 71-74-36; *Cabinas Isla Fantasma*, E. Continue north to the village of Agujitas (*Cabinas Sir Francis Drake*, B with bath per person, meals, T 71-24-36), outside the park. Frequent trips with the park boat from San Pedrillo to Agujitas. From Agujitas you can get a boat (road under construction) to Sierpe on the Sierpe River (4 hrs.; perhaps 2 boats a week; boat from Sierpe to Bahía Drake, 1½ hrs., US$60 return p.p.); Sierpe is connected by bus with the town of Palmar (flights from San José, see above) on the Pan-American Highway. Also from Sirena you can walk along the beach to Madrigal on a southern direction (excellent tidepools on the way; 2 hrs. walking) and continue along the coast to Carate.

You can head inland from Sirena on a trail past three conveniently spaced shelters to Los Patos after passing several rivers full of reptiles. A wooden house in delapidated condition gives protection overnight. Its balcony is a great observation point for birds especially the redheaded woodpecker. From Los Patos you can carry on to the park border, then, crisscrossing the Río Rincón to La Palma (small hostel), a settlement near the opposite side of the Peninsula (six more hours); from which there are several "taxis" making the one-hour trip to Puerto Jiménez. An offshoot of this trail will lead you to a raffia swamp that rings the Corcovado Lagoon. The lagoon is only accessible by boat, but there are no regular trips. Caymans and alligators survive here, sheltered from the hunters. Horses can be rented cheaply at Sirena. Chiggers (*coloradillas*) and horseflies infest the horse pastures and can be a nuisance, similiarly, sandflies on the beaches; bring spray-on insect repellant.

Avoid the rainy season. Bring umbrellas (not raincoats—too hot), because it will rain. Shelters can be found here and there, so only mosquito netting is indispensable. Bring all your food if you haven't arranged otherwise; food can only be obtained at Puerto Jiménez and Agujitas in the whole peninsula, and lodging likewise. The cleared areas (mostly outside the park, or along the beach) can be devastatingly hot. Get the Instituto Geográfico maps, scale 1:50,000. Remember finally that, as in any tropical forest, you may find some unfriendly wildlife, like snakes (fer-de-lance and bushmaster snakes may attack without provocation), and herds of wild pigs. (You should find the most suitable method for keeping your feet dry and protecting your ankles; for some, rubber boots are the thing, for others light footwear which dries quickly.)

At **Ciudad Neily**, about 18 km. from the border, are the *Motel Rancho*, F with bath; *Hotel Musuco*, E with bath, F without, fan, good, clean, quiet; 4 sets of *cabinas* (all E with bath) and *pensiones* in F range. 6 km. from the border is the *Camino Real* where it is possible to camp. Here and there on the road *cantinas* sell local food. Bus Ciudad Neily to border, US$0.25. Daily bus to San José, Tracopa, from main square,

US$2.70, 7 hrs. (on Sunday buses from the border are full by the time they reach Ciudad Neily). The road goes (plenty of buses, 20 mins.) to **Paso Canoas** (*Azteca*, E, *Cabinas Interamericano* E, *Evelyn*, F, and *El Descanso* F, all with bath) on the Panama border. No fruit or vegetables can be taken into Panama. At Paso Canoas shops sell luxury items brought from Panama at prices considerably lower than those of Costa Rica (e.g. sunglasses, stereo equipment, kitchen utensils, etc.); banks either side of border close at 1600. No difficulty in getting rid of surplus colones with money changers. Bus San José-Paso Canoas, US$5.25, Tracopa terminal Av. 18, C. 4 at 0500, 0800 and 1700, not all buses go to border; Paso Canoas-San José at 0700 and 1400. Those motoring N can get insurance cover at the border for US$6 ensuring public liability and property damage. Border open 0700-1130, 1300-1700, 1800-2200. **N.B.** If you need a tourist card only to enter Panama, you are strongly advised to get it before the border, as Panamanian border officials often do not have them (**see page** 655).

INFORMATION FOR VISITORS

Documents A passport is required. For visits of up to 90 days the following do not need visas: nationals of most Western European countries, Canada, Israel, Japan, Yugoslavia, Romania, Argentina, Colombia, Panama and South Korea. The following also do not need a visa, but visits are limited to 30 days: citizens of the USA, Australia, New Zealand, Eire, Belgium, Switzerland, Finland, Iceland, Monaco, Brazil, Mexico, Ecuador, Guatemala and Honduras. Notwithstanding this, some travellers since November 1989 report that 90 days may be allowed for nationals of some of these countries e.g. USA, Belgium, Switzerland. US and Canadian citizens may enter with a tourist card, which can be purchased at airline counters for US$2 on proof of identity. Extensions may be arranged for US$1.20, but they involve a lot of red tape. All other nationalities need a visa, costing US$20, valid for only 30 days.

With any extension, you have to get an exit visa when you leave (US$12). Alternatively you can just get an exit permit, which is valid for one month. This involves going to Tribunales in San José to declare that you are leaving no dependants in Costa Rica. There is an emigration tax of US$2. For longer stays ask for a Prórroga de Turismo at Migración in San José. For this you need 3 passport photos, an airline or bus ticket out of the country and proof of funds (e.g. travellers' cheques); you can apply for an extension of 1 or 2 months, 175 colones per month. The paperwork takes three days. If you leave the country, you must wait 72 hours before returning, but it may be cheaper and easier to do this and get a new 30-day entry. Travel agents can arrange all extension and exit formalities for a small fee.

An onward ticket (a bus ticket—which can be bought at the border immigration office or sometimes from the driver on Tica international buses—a transatlantic ticket or an MCO will do) is asked for, but cashing in an air ticket is difficult because you may be asked to produce another ticket out of the country. Also, tourists may have to show at least US$300 in cash or travellers' cheques before being granted entry (especially if you have no onward ticket). Always carry a passport, or photocopy, for presentation at spot-checks. Failure to do so may mean imprisonment.

N.B. If you have been more than a few days in Nicaragua (for example, working on a brigade), you may be refused entry into Costa Rica. Nicaraguan literature is likely to be confiscated, even burnt there and then. If entering from Nicaragua, you will be forced to take a blood-test for malaria at the border point, and if you are not carrying anti-malaria tablets, officials may oblige you to buy and swallow some in their presence. There have also been cases of tourists with stamps from Eastern bloc countries in their passports being refused entry. It is less hassle to arrive from Nicaragua by air. It may however now be easier with the political changes of 1990.

N.B. also   Entrance and exit taxes, by air or land, and legislation regarding visa extensions, are subject to frequent change and travellers should check these details as near to the time of travelling as possible.

Warnings   Those arriving by air from Colombia can expect to have their persons and baggage carefully searched because of the rampant drug traffic in the area. In Costa Rica, particularly on the Atlantic coast, do not get involved with drugs: many dealers are undercover police agents.
There has been much illegal immigration into Costa Rica: this explains why Migración officials sometimes grill visitors in their hotels.

Taxes   There is an airport tax of US$5 for tourists. There is an 8% tax on airline tickets purchased in the country.

Air Services   From London: British Airways, Pan Am, Continental, or Virgin Atlantic to Miami, then by American, Lacsa, Pan Am (all non-stop), or Taca (via San Salvador) and Aviateca (via Guatemala) to San José. **Carriers from the USA** are: from Houston, Aviateca (via Guatemala), Sahsa (via Tegucigalpa), Taca (via San Salvador); from San Francisco, Taca (via San Salvador); from Los Angeles, Taca (via San Salvador), Lacsa, American (via Miami), Mexicana; from New Orleans, Lacsa, Aviateca (via Guatemala), Taca, Sahsa; from New York, Pan Am, Lacsa, American (via Miami); from Los Angeles, Lacsa, American. From Canada: Fiesta Sun, from Toronto (once a week—Sat.—non-stop charter), and from Vancouver (twice a month, Mon.). Lacsa flies to the following Central and South American destinations (other airlines on these routes in brackets): Mexico City (Mexicana, Taca, Aviateca (via Guatemala), Aeronica), Cancún, Guatemala City (Mexicana, Copa, SAM, Aeronica, Taca), Managua (Aeronica, Aviateca, Copa, Sahsa), San Pedro Sula (Sahsa), San Salvador (Taca, Aeronica, Copa), Panama City (Copa, Taca, Aeronica), San Juan (Puerto Rico—Iberia), Bogotá (SAM), Medellín, Cartegena and Barranquilla (Copa), and Caracas. Varig flies from Quito/Guayaquil, Rio de Janeiro, São Paulo (once a week). Aeronica excursion from Panama City, US$200 including 3 free nights in a good hotel and free airport transfers. Other connections from San José: Belize

City (Sahsa, Taca), Tegucigalpa (Sahsa), San Andrés Island (SAM), Kingston, Jamaica (Copa via Panama), Lima (Iberia, once a week, Fri., March to October only). **From Europe**: KLM from Amsterdam twice a week via Curaçao and Guatemala; Iberia from Madrid via Santo Domingo or San Juan, twice a week, with a once-weekly flight to Lima.

Shipping Services Shipping a vehicle from Puerto Limón to Guayaquil costs US$1,500 in a container (virtually impossible to travel with your car on the ship); arrange through an Agente de Vapores (look in Yellow Pages), US$200-500 for agents' fees and "miscellaneous charges." For shipping information, see **Introduction and Hints** at the beginning of the book.

Customs Half a kilo of manufactured tobacco and 3 litres of liquor are allowed in duty-free. Any amount of foreign or local currency may be taken in or out.

Motoring Speed limits are low (75 kmph) and there are radar speed traps. If caught, you may have your number plate confiscated and have to pay a court to get it back. Roads are slow, so leave plenty of time for your trip. Many of the nature parks are in remote areas and 4-wheel drive may well be needed; in the wet season some roads will be impassable. Car hire firms are not covered by tourist regulations and many complaints have been made to the authorities concerning their operations. If hiring a car, be very cautious. Tourists who come by car pay US$10 road tax and can keep their cars for an initial period of 30 days. This can be extended for a total period of 6 months at the Instituto Costarricense de Turismo, or at the Customs office if you take your passport, car entry permit, and a piece of stamped paper (*papel sellado*) obtainable at any bookshop. Cars are fumigated on entry (50 colones). It is now mandatory for foreign drivers to buy insurance stamps on entry for a minimum of 3 months; e.g. motorcycle, US$6 and car, US$13. If you want to travel on from Costa Rica without your car, you should leave it in the customs warehouse at the international airport at San José. For a longer period than 60 days, however, it is necessary to leave it in a private bonded warehouse. The cost is about US$10 a week, plus US$60 to arrange it through a customs agent, plus a considerable amount of paperwork. San José is the best place to get Land Rover spares. To sell a car in Costa Rica you may have to pay a duty which is equivalent to four times the market value of the car. Main fuel stations have regular and super gasoline (unleaded) US$0.40 per litre. Tyres without rims are confiscated and burnt by the Customs. It is illegal to ride in a car or taxi without wearing seatbelts. Motorcyclists must wear crash helmets. Spares are available for Japanese makes in San José. Also, try Oswaldo Breymann, Av. 7, Calle 5-7, T 21-22-74, San José, for motorcycle spares. If you have an accident, contact Policia de Tránsito, T San José 26-84-36 or 27-21-89. If you intend to drive in the country for more than 3 months, you are required to apply for a Costa Rican Driver's Licence at Av. 18, C. 5, San José.

Cycling John Gilchrist tells us that cycling is easier in Costa Rica than elsewhere in Central America; the asphalted roads are better, there is less heavy traffic and it is generally "cyclist friendly". The prevailing wind is from the north-east, so if making an extensive tour, travelling in the direction of Panama-Nicaragua is slightly more favourable. Be prepared for a lot of rain. It is perfectly possible to travel light, without tent, sleeping bag or cooking equipment.

Hitch-hiking is easy by day in the week, though there is not much traffic off the main roads. Walkers should obtain a copy of *Backpacking in Mexico and Central America* by Hilary Bradt and Rob Rachowiecki, a new edition of which was in preparation for 1991 publication.

Food Stefaan Platteau, resident in San José, tells us: *Sodas* (small restaurants) serve local food, which is worth trying. Very common is *casado*, which includes rice, beans, stewed beef, fried plantain and cabbage. *Olla de carne* is a soup of beef, plantain, corn, yuca, *ñampi* and *chayote* (local vegetables). *Sopa negra* is made with black beans, and comes with a poached egg in it; *picadillo* is another meat and vegetable stew. Snacks are popular: *gallos* (filled tortillas), *tortas* (containing meat and vegetables), *arreglados* (bread filled with the same) and *empanadas*. *Pan de yuca* is a speciality, available from stalls in San José centre. For breakfast, try *pinto* (rice and beans) with *natilla* (cream). A *soda* in Moravia (8 km. from San José), *Soda San Martín*, is highly rec. for local fare. Best ice cream can be found in *Pops* shops in San José. *Schmidt* bakeries are highly rec.; they also serve coffee. Also *La Selecta* bakeries. Eating in Costa Rica is cheap on the whole.

Drink There are many types of cold drink, made either from fresh fruit, or milk drinks with fruit or cereal flour whisked with ice cubes. Drinks are often sugared well beyond North American tastes. The fruits range from the familiar to the exotic; others include *cebada* (barley flour), *pinolillo* (roasted corn), *horchata* (rice flour with cinnamon), *chan*, "perhaps the most unusual, looking like mouldy frogspawn and tasting of penicillin" (Michael J. Brisco). All these drinks cost the same as, or less than, bottled fizzy products. Excellent coffee.

Tipping A 10% service charge is automatically added to restaurant bills, as well as 10% government tax. Ten colones per bag for porters; same for hairdressers. Taxis and cinema usherettes, nil; 10% at hotels, restaurants, cafés, bars; ten colones for cloakroom attendants.

Shopping Best buys are wooden items, ceramics, leather handicrafts and coffee.

Health Drinking water is safe in all major towns; elsewhere it should be boiled. Intestinal disorders and Chagas disease are prevalent in the lowlands although malaria has to a great extent been eradicated; malaria prophylaxis is advised for visitors to the lowlands, all the same; in Costa Rica it is available only from the Ministerio de Salud in San José (free). Uncooked foods should not be eaten. The standards of health and hygiene are among the best in Latin America. Ice cream, milk, etc. are safe.

Clothing Strapless sun-dresses are never worn in San José, but trousers are quite OK for women. Shorts are only acceptable at the beach and country club, especially for women. Women need hats only for weddings and official functions. The Costa Ricans are conservative, the points in Travellers' Appearance in the **Introduction**

particularly apply here. Please do not cause offence.

Business Hours 0800 or 0830 to 1100 or 1130 and 1300 to 1700 or 1730 (1600, government offices), Mon. to Fri., and 0800 to 1100 on Sat. Shops: 0800 to 1200, 1300 to 1800 Mon. to Sat.

British business travellers going to Costa Rica are strongly advised to get a copy of "Hints to Exporters: Costa Rica" from Export Services Division, Dept. of Trade, Sanctuary Buildings, 16-20 Great Smith Street, London SW1P 4DB.

Public Holidays 1 January: New Year's Day; 19 March: St. Joseph; Easter: 3 days; 11 April: Battle of Rivas; 1 May: Labour Day; June: Corpus Christi; 29 June: St. Peter and St. Paul; 25 July: Guanacaste Day; 2 August: Virgin of Los Angeles; 15 August: Mothers' Day; 15 September: Independence Day; 12 October: Columbus Day' 8 December: Conception of the Virgin; 25 December: Christmas Day; 28-31 December: San José only.

N.B. During Holy Week, nearly everyone is on holiday. Everywhere is shut on Fri., Sat., and Sun., and most of the previous week as well (in San José and Cartago only a small percentage of businesses and services close Mon.-Wed. and Sat. of Holy Week; almost all transport stops on Good Friday only).

Standard Time is 6 hrs. behind Greenwich Mean Time.

Currency The unit is the colón, sub-divided into 100 céntimos. The old coins of 5, 10, 25 and 50 céntimos and 1 and 2 colones, and notes of 5, 10 and 20 colones are being phased out. New coins in use are for 25 and 50 céntimos and 1, 2, 5, 10 and 20 colones. Public telephones now use 2, 5, and 10 colón coins. Paper money in use: 50, 100, 500 (new, orange-coloured) and 1,000 colones. (5,000 and 10,000 colon notes have not yet been issued, although they are planned).

Exchange of US dollars (etc) must be effected in a bank, and for bank drafts and transfers commission may be charged (set by the banks themselves). Most tourist and first class hotels will change dollars for guests only. A small black market for dollars exists although it remains illegal to exchange in the street. It is almost impossible to exchange any other major currency in Costa Rica; only the Banco Lyon, S.A., will do so (e.g. Barclays sterling cheques) but at very poor rates.

For Customs the metric system of **weights and measures** is compulsory. Traders use a variety of weights and measures, including English ones and the old Spanish ones.

Electric Current 110, 60 cycles, A.C. (U.S. flat-pin plugs).

Mail by sea from the UK takes from 2-3 months and 3 to 5 days by airmail. Airmail letters to Europe cost 24 colones; to North/South America, 22 colones; to Australia, Africa and Asia, 28 colones. "Expreso" letters, 17 colones extra, several days quicker to USA and N. Europe. Registered mail, 30 colones extra. All parcels sent out of the country by foreigners must be taken open to the post office for clearance (packaging available from The Bookshop in San José). *Lista de Correos* charges 8 colones per letter, and will keep letters for 4 weeks. The contents of incoming parcels will be the subject of plenty of paperwork, and probably high duties.

Telephone and Cable Services Long-range radio-telephone service are run by the Instituto Costarricense de Electricidad and by Cía. Radiográfica Internacional de Costa Rica, whose HQ is at San Pedro. Local cables, though, are sent from the main post office in San José, Av. 1/3, C. 2. A telephone system connects San José with the country's main centres. The Government's wireless station at San José communicates with Mexico, Guatemala and El Salvador. A Radio and Telephone Ground Satellite Station was opened at Aserrí in January 1982. Calls abroad can be made from phone booths; collect calls abroad may be made from special booths in the telephone office, Av. 5, C. 1, San José. A daytime telephone call to the UK costs US$3 a minute, US$2 Fri. 1900 to Mon. 0700; to USA and Canada, US$1.60-3.80 per min., US$0.65-1.50 at night (2200-0700) and weekends, depending on to which state or province; to Australia, Africa, Asia, US$5 per minute. Public telex booth at Radiográfica S.A., Av. 5, C. 1 (telex CR 1050); the telex must show your name and Tel. no. or address for them to advise you; also public FAX service, to receive, 100 colones (FAX +506-231-609 or +506-337-932); to send, US$5.50 per page to Europe, US$4 per page to USA.

Newspapers The best San José morning papers are *La Nación* and *La República*. *La Prensa Libre* is a good evening paper. *Libertad*, weekly newspaper (socialist). *El Debate* is another good weekly. *La Gazette* is the official government weekly paper. *Tico Times* (Fri.) in English.

Broadcasting 6 local TV stations, many MW/FM radio stations throughout the country. Local Voz de América (VOA) station. Many hotels and private homes receive one of the 4 TV stations offering direct, live, 24-hr TV from the USA (Canal 19, Supercanal, Cable Color and Master TV-channels 56, 58, 60—all US cable TV can be received in San José on the 2 cable stations).

Association football is the **national sport** (played every Sunday at 1100, May to October, at the Saprissa Stadium). There are golf courses at San José and Puerto Limón. There is sea-bathing on both Atlantic and Pacific coasts (see text). The Meseta is good country for riding; horses can be hired by arrangement directly with owners. Most *fiestas* end with bullfighting in the squares, an innocuous but amusing set-to with no horses used. Bullfights are held in San José during the Christmas period. There is no kill and spectators are permitted to enter the ring to chase, and be chased by, the bull. Much wildlife in the Guanacaste and northern jungle areas. There is good sea-fishing off Puntarenas and in the mouth of the Río Chirripó, on the Caribbean side near the Nicaraguan border; inland river-fishing has been ruined by dynamiting.

The information offices of the **Instituto Costarricense de Turismo** are by the Plaza de la Cultura, entrance on C. 5, Av. Central/2, San José (T 22-10-90), open 0900-1700 Mon. to Sat. All tourist information is given here. Take complaints about hotel overcharging to the Instituto. There is a free weekly magazine, *The San José Gourmet*, dealing with tourism and restaurant news.

We are most grateful for a complete review of the Costa Rica section to Simon Ellis (San José), Eva Danulat (Victoria BC), Dr Palmer Acheson (Montreal), Jim Cilek (Twin Falls, ID), Juan Cutillas (Aguascalientes), Hans Van Dijk (Hilversum, Neth.), Richard Duke (Ann Arbor, MI), Craig A. Faanes (Grand Island, NE), Herm Geraedts (Curaçao), Lea van den Heijden (Aruba), Annette van den Steen (Breda) and Marian Janssen (Rosmalen, Neth.), Bob Horsfall and Judi Johnson (Auckland, NZ), Michael Kirkensgaard (Copenhagen), Rudi Lamparter (Gaechingen, W. Ger.), Toby Lanzer (Santiago de Chile), Herbert Michaud, Geoff Richardson (Scarborough), Joseph Syfrig (Riehen, Switz.), Eileen Synnott and Paul Gurn (Waterbury, CT) and Karen Morgensen Wessberg; also to other travellers whose names are listed in the general Central America section.

PANAMA

INTRODUCTION

THE S-SHAPED ISTHMUS OF PANAMA, 80 km. at its narrowest and no more than 193 km. at its widest, is one of the great cross-roads of the world. Its destiny has been entirely shaped by that fact. To it Panama owes its national existence, the make-up of its population and their distribution: two-fifths of the people are concentrated in the two cities which control the entry and exit of the canal. Panama covers 77,082 square km. The Canal Area, formerly Zone, is being gradually incorporated into Panamanian jurisdiction; this long process began in 1964, when Panama secured the right to fly its flag in the Zone alongside that of the USA, and is due for completion, with Panamanian operation of the Canal, by 2000.

Only about a quarter of the country is inhabited and most of it is mountainous, with shelvings of lowland on both its 1,234 km. of Pacific and 767 km. of Atlantic coastlines. The country's axis is, in general, SW to NE, but the mountain chains do not conform to this and run NW to SE. At the border with Costa Rica there are several volcanic cones, the boldest of which is the extinct Barú, 3,383 metres high. The sharp-sided Cordillera de Talamanca continues SE at a general altitude of about 900 metres, but subsides suddenly SW of Panama City. The next range, the San Blas, rises E of Colón and runs into Colombia; its highest peaks are not more than 900 metres. A third range rises from the Pacific littoral in the SE; it, too, runs into Colombia and along the Pacific coast as the Serranía de Baudó.

Good fortune decreed a gap between the Talamanca and San Blas ranges in which the divide is no more than 87 metres high. The ranges

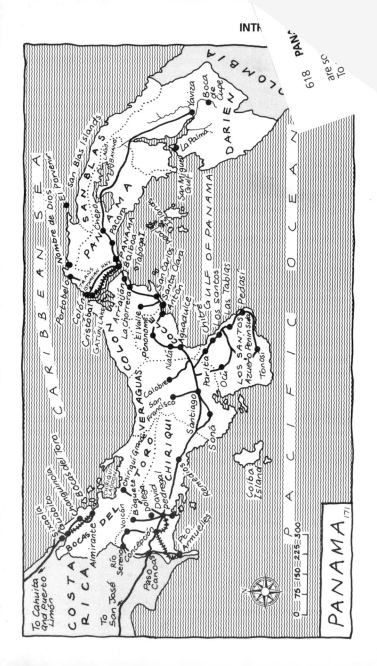

PANAMA

placed that the gap, containing the Canal, runs from NW to SE. reach the Pacific from the Atlantic we must travel eastwards, and at dawn the sun rises over the Pacific.

Climate Rainfall is heavy along the Caribbean coast: more than 3,800 mm. a year in some places, with huge but brief downpours between April and December. Temperature in the lowland ranges from 21°C (70°F) at night to 32°C (90°F) by day. The result is deep tropical forest along the coast and up the sides of the ranges of Panama, though little remains forested. The rain begins to shade off towards the crests of the mountains (10° to 18°C), and is much less along the Pacific, though there is no scarcity of it anywhere. At Balboa it is only 1,727 mm. a year, and the tropical forest gives way to semi-deciduous trees and converted areas of savanna between the Pacific and the mountains. The wet season is called *invierno*—winter, the dry, *verano*—summer.

History The history of Panama is the history of its pass-route; its fate was determined on that day in 1513 when Balboa first glimpsed the Pacific. Panama City was of paramount importance for the Spaniards: it was the focus of conquering expeditions northwards and southwards along the Pacific coasts. All trade to and from these Pacific countries passed across the isthmus.

Panama City was founded in 1519 after a trail had been discovered between it and the Caribbean. The Camino Real (the Royal Road) ran from Panama City to Nombre de Dios until it was re-routed to Portobelo. An alternative route was used later: a road built from Panama City to Las Cruces, now swallowed up by Gatún Lake; it ran near Gamboa on the Culebra Cut, and traces of it can still be seen. Las Cruces was on the Chagres river, which was navigable to the Caribbean, particularly during the rainy season.

Intruders were early attracted by the wealth passing over the Royal Road. Sir Francis Drake attacked Nombre de Dios, and in 1573 his men penetrated inland to Las Cruces, captured its treasures and burnt the town. Spain countered later attacks by building strongholds and forts to protect the route: among others San Felipe at the entrances to Portobelo and San Lorenzo at the mouth of the Chagres. Spanish galleons, loaded with treasure and escorted against attack, left Portobelo once a year. They returned with European goods which were sold at great fairs held at Portobelo, Cartagena and Veracruz. There was feverish activity for several weeks as the galleons were loaded and unloaded. It was a favourite time for attack by enemies, especially those with political as well as pecuniary motives. Perhaps the most famous was the attack by Henry Morgan in 1671. He captured the fort of San Lorenzo and pushed up the Chagres river to Los Cruces. From there he descended upon Panama City, which he looted and burnt. A month later Morgan returned to the Caribbean with 195 mules loaded with booty. Panama City was re-built on a new site, at the base of Ancón hill, and fortified. With Britain and Spain at war, attacks reached their climax in Admiral Vernon's capture of Portobelo in 1739 and the fort of San Lorenzo the next year. Spain abandoned the route in 1746 and began trading round Cape Horn. San Lorenzo was rebuilt: it is still there, tidied up and landscaped by the US Army.

A century later, streams of men were once more ... Chagres and down to Panama City: the forty-niners on th ... newly discovered gold fields of California. Many perished ... to hell", as it was called, and the gold rush brought into bei ... across the isthmus. The Panama Railroad from Colón (ther ... wo streets) to Panama City took four years to build, with great loss of life. The first train was run on 26 November, 1853. The railway was an enormous financial success until the re-routing of the Pacific Steam Navigation Company's ships round Cape Horn in 1867 and the opening of the first US transcontinental railroad in 1869 reduced its traffic.

Ferdinand de Lesseps, builder of the Suez Canal, arrived in Panama in 1881, and decided to build a sea-level canal along the Chagres river and the Río Grande. Work started in 1882. One of the diggers in 1886 and 1887 was the painter Gauguin, aged 39. Thirty km. had been dug before the Company crashed in 1893, defeated by extravagance and tropical diseases (22,000 people died). Eventually Colombia (of which Panama was then a Department) authorized the Company to sell all its rights and properties to the United States, but the Colombian Senate rejected the treaty, and the inhabitants of Panama, encouraged by the States, declared their independence on 3 November, 1903. The United States intervened and, in spite of protests by Colombia, recognized the new republic. Colombia did not accept the severance until 1921.

Before beginning the task of building the Canal the United States performed one of the greatest sanitary operations in history: the clearance from the area of the more malignant tropical diseases. The name of William Crawford Gorgas will always be associated with this, as will that of George Washington Goethals with the actual building of the Canal. On 15 August, 1914, the first passage was made, by the ship *Ancón*.

The history of Panama then became that of two nations, with the Canal Zone responsible only to the President of the USA. As a result of bitter resentment, the USA ended Panama's protectorate status in 1939 with a treaty which also limited US rights of intervention. However, the disparity in living standards continued to provoke anti-US feeling, culminating in riots in 1964 and the suspension of diplomatic relations for some months. During this period, a small, commercially-oriented oligarchy dominated Panamanian politics, although presidential successions were not always smooth and peaceful.

In 1968 Dr Arnulfo Arias Madrid was elected president for the third time, having been ousted twice previously. After only ten days in office he was forcibly removed by the National Guard which installed a provisional junta. Brig. General Omar Torrijos Herrera ultimately became Commander of the National Guard and principal power in the junta, dominating Panamanian politics for the next 13 years. Constitutional government was restored in 1972 after elections for a 505-member National Assembly of Community Representatives, which revised the 1946 constitution, elected Demetrio Basilio Lakas Bahas as president and vested temporary extraordinary executive powers in Gen. Torrijos for six years. Torrijos' rule was characterized by his pragmatic nalism; he carried out agrarian reform, yet satisfied business interests; he had close links with left wing movements in Cuba, El Salvador and Nicaragua, yet reached agreement with the USA to transfer sovereignty of the Canal of Panama. In 1978 elections for a new National Assembly were held and the new representatives elected Dr Arístedes Royo Sánchez as president. Gen. Torrijos resigned as Chief of Government but retained the powerful post of Commander of the National Guard until his death in an air crash in 1981. There followed several years of rapid governmental changes as tension rose between presidents and National Guard leaders.

Elections were held in May 1984, resulting in a narrow (and contested) victory for the government candidate, Nicolás Ardito Barletta, who took office in October 1984 for a six-year term but was removed from office by military pressure in September 1985. He was replaced by Eric Arturo Delvalle. Sr. Delvalle's attempts to reduce military influence in government, concentrated principally in the hands of General Manuel Antonio Noriega Morena, led to his own removal by General Noriega in February 1988. Sr. Manuel Solís Palma was named president in his place. Elections were held in May 1989 but the civil unrest which immediately followed led to their annulment by the military; both the ruling party and an opposition coalition had claimed an overwhelming majority of votes.

General Noriega appointed Francisco Rodríguez as provisional President in September. However, in December, General Noriega formally assumed power as Head of State, which provoked a US military invasion to overthrow him. He finally surrendered and was taken to the USA for trial on charges of drugs trafficking and other corruption offences. Guillermo Endara Galimany, who was widely believed to have won the May elections, was installed as President. The Panamanian Defence Forces were immediately remodelled into a new Public Force with a two-year limitation on the commander's term of office and compulsory retirement after 25 years' service. Over 150 senior officers were dismissed and many were arrested.

After the overthrow of General Noriega's administration, the US Senate approved a US$480m aid package to provide liquidity and get the economy moving again. A further US$500m aid package was requested to enable Panama to clear its arrears with multilateral creditors and support the Panamanian banking system. Negotiations with commerical bank creditors were started in May; arrears having built up to US$1.6 bn.

The former Canal Zone was a ribbon of territory under US control extending 8 km. on either side of the Canal and including the cities of Cristóbal and Balboa. The price paid by the United States Government to Panama for construction rights was US$10m. The French company received US$40m. for its rights and properties. US$25m. were given to Colombia in compensation for the transfer of the French company's rights. The total cost at completion was US$387m. Panama long ago rejected the perpetuity clause of the original Canal Treaty. In April 1978 a new treaty was ratified and on 1 October, 1979 the Canal Zone, now known officially as the Canal Area, was formally transferred to Panamanian sovereignty, including the ports of Cristóbal and Balboa, the Canal dry docks and the trans-isthmus railway, but the US still retains extensive military base areas. Until the final transfer of ownership in 2000 the Canal administration is in the hands of the Comisión del Canal, on which the USA retains majority representation. At the beginning of 1990, a Panamanian was appointed acting administrator of the Panama Canal in succession to an American who had held the post since 1979.

The People   The population (2.4 million in 1989) is mostly of mixed blood but there are communities of Indians, blacks and a few Asians. About 52% are urban dwellers. Most of the rural population live in the 6 provinces on the Pacific side, W of the Canal. There is only one rural population centre of any importance on the Caribbean: in Bocas del Toro, in the extreme NW. Annual population growth is 2.2%. The birth-rate is 28.0 and the death-rate 5.4 per thousand; 14% are illiterate. Of the sixty Indian tribes who inhabited the isthmus at the time of the Spanish conquest, only three have survived: the Cunas of the San Blas Islands, the Guaymíes of the western provinces and the Chocóes of Darién. Only a few of the indigenous Indians can speak Spanish.

In Bocas de Toro half the population speaks Spanish, half speaks English.

Numbers of African slaves escaped from their Spanish owners during the 16th century. They set up free communities in the Darién jungles and their Spanish-speaking descendants can still be seen there and in the Pearl Islands. The majority of Panama's blacks are English-speaking British West Indians, descended from those brought in for the building of the railway in 1850, and later of the Canal. There are also a number of East Indians and Chinese who tend to cling to their own languages and customs.

The Economy   Panama's economy has traditionally been founded on income derived from services rendered to incoming visitors, taking advantage of its geographical position, its banking centre, and Canal employees and US military personnel spending money in the Republic. However, this contribution is lessening proportionately as the country develops new sources of income: tourism, industry, copper, etc.

Apart from the Canal, the other traditional mainstay of the Panamanian economy is agriculture, which contributes about 10% of gdp. About 25% of the population works in agriculture. Agrarian reform has begun, and has brought the post-1968 governments much support from tenant-farmers and squatters. 53% of the land is forested, and development here could also bring added wealth into the country, at the same time helping to reduce the country's dependence on services. Recently the Government has taken a more significant role in industry and now owns sugar mills and cement plants. The main industry is food processing and there are textile and clothing concerns and chemicals, plastics and other light industries. Petroleum products are the only industrial export.

Vast deposits of copper have been found at Cerro Colorado and if fully developed the mine could be one of the largest in the world. There is also copper at Petaquilla, Cerro Chorca and Río Pinto. Large coal deposits have been found at Río Indio. The country also has gold and silver deposits. So far no oil has been discovered, but exploration is taking place.

One of the most dynamic sectors of the economy is banking. Since 1970 offshore banks have increased from 20 in number to 130 with the establishment of liberal conditions and the abolition of currency controls. In the mid-1980s, total assets amounted to over US\$40bn, while deposits were around US\$35bn. However, in 1987-88, political uncertainties severely affected the international banking centre. Loss of confidence led many banks to close their offices and move to other offshore centres such as the Bahamas or the Cayman Islands, the level of assets declined, and deposits fell by up to 25%. In 1990 the new government announced that banking regulations were to be amended to prevent money laundering.

Following a rapid accumulation of foreign debt by the public sector in the late 1970s and early 1980s, the debt service burden became intolerable. Panama received assistance after 1983 from the IMF and the World Bank in support of its fiscal and structural adjustment programme, while commercial banks have both rescheduled existing loans and provided new money on easier terms. As a result of the 1988 financial crisis, Panama fell into arrears to all its creditors; consequently, capital inflows were halted; the IMF declared Panama ineligible to borrow and the World Bank cut off loan disbursements. Moreover, the US economic blockade which began in 1988 directly caused a 24% fall in gdp that year.

Government Constitutional reforms were adopted by referendum in April 1983. Legislative power is vested in a unicameral, 67-member Legislative Assembly which is elected by universal, compulsory adult suffrage for a term of five years. Executive power is held by the President, assisted by two Vice Presidents and an appointed Cabinet. Panama is divided into nine provinces and one autonomous Indian reservation. Provincial governors and mayors of towns are appointed by the central authorities.

Communications There are now about 9,719 km. of roads, of which 3,236 km. are paved. Road building is complicated by the extraordinary number of bridges and the large amount of grading required. The road running from Colón to Panama City is the only paved one crossing the isthmus, and the Pan-American Highway connecting Chepo and Panama City with the Costa Rican border is paved throughout.

Education Education is compulsory up to the age of 14. English is the compulsory second language in the schools.

COLON, THE CANAL AND THE ISLANDS

Landfall on the Caribbean side for the passage of the Canal is made at the twin cities of Cristóbal and Colón, the one merging into the other almost imperceptibly and both built on Manzanillo Island at the entrance

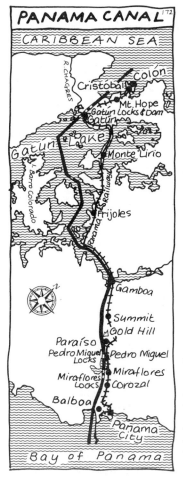

of the Canal; the island has now been connected with the mainland. Colón was founded in 1852 as the terminus of the railway across the isthmus; Cristóbal came into being as the port of entry for the supplies used in building the Canal.

Cristóbal Ships usually dock at Pier No. 9, five mins. from the shops of Colón. Vehicles are always waiting at the docks for those who want to visit Colón and other places. Cristóbal Yacht Club has a good restaurant.

Colón, population 123,000, the second largest city in Panama, was originally called Aspinwall, after one of the founders of the railway. Despite its fine public buildings and well-stocked shops, it has some of the nastiest slums in Latin America, and is generally dirty. It has been described as having a "rough, but wonderful honky-tonk atmosphere." Annual mean temperature: 26°C.

Warning Mugging, even in daylight, is a real threat in both Colón and Cristóbal. We have received repeated warnings of robbery in Colón, often within 5 minutes of arrival. The two main streets and some of the connecting ones are guarded by armed Panama Public Force men; you are strongly recommended not to leave their range of sight. In March 1990, a curfew was in force in Colón.

There is a Free Zone at Colón which offers facilities for the importing, free of duty, of bulk goods for re-export to neighbouring countries after packaging; it is not possible to take your purchases out of the zone; you must arrange for them to be taken to the airport before you leave (or you must smuggle them out). The zone is closed on Saturdays and Sundays. (If with your own car, pay a minder US$1 to look after it while in the zone).

There are good roads to Coco Solo nearby, to France Field, and to Fort Davis and the Gatún Locks, some 11 km. away.

The tourist should see the Cathedral between Herrera and Av. Amador Guerrero (open afternoons only), and the statues on the promenade known as the Paseo Centenario (Av. Central). The historic *Hotel Washington* is worth a look. For local products, try Isthmian Curio Shop, between Calle 10 and 11, and Sombrería Aldao, on Front Street, for panama hats.

The beach drive round Colón, pleasant and cool in the evening, takes less than 30 minutes.

Hotels *Washington*, A, there is a small casino; *Carlton*, B, is the next best hotel; *Sotelo*, B, also has casino; *Andros*, C; *Plaza*, C; *García*, C; *Astor*, D. These rates are without meals, whose average price is US$5-8. *Pensión Plaza*, Av. Central, is clean, cheap, D. *Pensión Anita*, Av. Guerrero y Calle 10, E (more with bath), very friendly; *Pensión Acrópolis*, E, clean and comfortable; *Pensión Andros Annex*, E, comfortable and safe; *Pensión Kingston*, E. If destitute try the Salvation Army.

Principal Restaurants *Cristóbal Yacht Club; La Nueva China*, Av. Central and Calle 8, a/c; good Chinese food also at *La Fortuna*; *VIP Club* in Front Street; YMCA restaurant, right across from the railway station; *Tarpon Club*, at the Gatún Spillway.

Taxi Tariffs vary, but are generally not high and may be agreed on in advance. Most drivers speak some English.

Cabarets Club 61, Av. Bolívar. No cover charge. Three shows nightly at 2000, 2300 and 0100. Club Florida, 3 shows nightly. Café Esquire.

Cinemas Teatro Lido, across from YMCA on Bolívar, and Teatro Rex, Calle 5 and Av. Central.

Clubs Golf (18 holes) at Brazos Brook Country Club. Rotary Club, weekly lunches.

Exchange Chase Manhattan Bank; Citibank; Banco Nacional de Panamá; Caja de Ahorros; Lloyds Bank International (Bahamas)—ex BOLSA—agency in Colón Free Zone, at Calle 15 & D. Open 0800-1300, Mon. to Fri.

Cables Tropical Radio Telegraph Co., Av. Roosevelt.

Post Office In Cristóbal Administration Building, on corner of Av. Bolívar and Calle 9.

Shipping a vehicle All ships leave from Coco Solo Wharf; to Colombia, **see page** 653. To the USA costs between US$1,800-2,600.

Bus Service At least every hour to Panama City: US$1.75, 2 hours, from bus terminal at Calle 13 and Av. Bolívar, including express bus.

Trains On weekdays there are 4 trains a day and on Sat and Sun. and holidays 3, to Panama City from Colón. Journey time 1 hr. 25 mins., US$1.25. Schedules given under Panama City **Rail**. Colón station is at Calle 11 and Front Street, near the shopping area. The journey is interesting, with intermittent views of Canal, ships and jungle. The track and rolling stock are poorly maintained.

Air Services Local flights to Panama City: Mon.-Fri. at 0700 and 1600 from the France Field Airport.

Trips from Colón: *Portobelo* is 48 km. NE of Colón by sea or by road. Columbus used the harbour in 1502 and it was a Spanish garrison town for more than two centuries. Drake died and was buried at sea off the Bay of Portobelo. Three large stone forts face the entrance to the harbour. There can be seen old Spanish cannon, and the treasure house where gold from Peru brought over the Las Cruces trail from Panama

City was stored until the galleons for Spain arrived. There are ruins of various forts, a waterfall, and mountain views (no information available locally). In the Cathedral is a statue of the Black Christ; it was being shipped from Spain to the Viceroy of Peru, but the ship was wrecked in the bay and the statue salvaged by the natives. The image is carried through the streets at 1800 on 21 October; afterwards there is feasting and dancing till dawn. Local rainfall, 4,080 mm. a year. Population 1,980.

Buses from Colón to Portobelo, every hour from 0700; leave from Calle 13 and Av. Bolívar, US$1.30 single. Portobelo can be visited from Panama City in a day by taking an early train to Colón, then go straight to the bus for Portobelo: on the return, take a bus from Portobelo to Sabanitas, at the junction with the Transisthmian Highway (US$1) and catch a bus back to Panama City (US$0.90)—take this bus route from Panama City if you wish to avoid Colón. Many beaches on the way from Colón, such as Cangrejo, about 8 km. Playa Langosta, 17 km. from Portobelo, is also recommended (toilets, bar, restaurant). María Chiquita beach has a bathing pavilion managed by the government tourist bureau, 45 minutes from Colón, US$0.60.

From Colón, visit also the old French canal, modern Canal township of Margarita, Gatún Locks (one hour). The locks are open to visitors every day 0800-1600; they can enter the lock area and take photographs, while guides explain the Canal operation. (Bus from Colón to Gatún locks, US$0.20.) Visitors can cross the locks at Gatún, and also ride through virgin jungle where wild pigs, iguanas, land crabs and snakes scuttle across the road.

Fort San Lorenzo, on the other side of the Canal at the mouth of the Chagres river, is a 16th-century fort with 18th-century additions, reached from Gatún locks by road to Fort Sherman in the Canal Area. From Fort Sherman one must drive, hitch-hike or walk 10 km. to the fort; the 18th-century part, on the top of cliffs, commands a fine view of the mouth of the Chagres river and the bay below. It was sacked by Henry Morgan and by Admiral Vernon; one of Vernon's cannon with the GR monogram can be seen.

Isla Grande, just off the coast, can be reached by boats hired from a car park, and a bus service; there are two hotels: *Isla Grande*, A p.p. in huts scattered along an excellent sandy beach, meals extra, and *Jackson's*, cheaper, also huts. The island is a favourite of scuba divers and snorkellers. Popular with the Army at weekends.

San Blas Islands An interesting trip can be made to the San Blas archipelago, which has 365 islands ranging in size from tiny ones with a few coconut palms to islands on which hundreds of Cuna Indians live. The islands, off the Caribbean coast E of Colón, vary in distance from the shore from 100 metres to several kilometres.

The Cuna are the most sophisticated and politically organized of the country's three major groups. They run the San Blas Territory virtually on their own terms, with internal autonomy and, uniquely among Panama's Indians, send their representative to the National Assembly. They have their own language, but Spanish is widely spoken. The women wear gold nose-and-ear-rings, and costumes suggestive of ancient Egyptians. They are outside the Panamanian tax zone and have negotiated a treaty perpetuating their long-standing trade with small craft from Colombia. Many men work on the mainland, but live on the islands.

Photographers need plenty of small change, as set price for a Cuna to pose is US$0.25. *Molas* (decorative handsewn appliqué for blouse fronts) cost upwards of US$5 each (also obtainable in many Panama City and Colón shops). Agencies (e.g. Agencia Giscomes in Panama City) run trips to El Porvenir where the planes land, Wichub Huala, Nalunega and Corbisky, all close to each other (hotels on first 3, one-day tour US$110, one night at *Hotel Anai* on Wichub Huala, US$40 for each additional), bookable at the major Panama hotels. These trips are inclusive of food and sightseeing. Take your own drinks, beer costs US$1. Flight leaves Paitilla airport at 0600, returning next day at 0630; if you can collect 9 people to fill the plane, you can leave at 0800 and return next day at 1600. The airline serving the islands, Aviones de Panamá (T 64-1677), can provide further information, and also runs trips to the Chocó Indians of the Darién jungle. Ansa flies at 0800, returning same day at 1630, US$49.35.

There are occasional boats to the San Blas islands from Colón, but there is no scheduled service and the trip can be rough. Alternatively, go to Portobelo (see above) and try for a boat from there, 9 hrs. to Porvenir.

As the crow flies the distance across the isthmus is 55 km. From shore to shore the Canal is 67½ km., or 82 km. (44.08 nautical miles) from deep water to deep water. It has been widened to 150 metres in most places. The trip normally takes 8 or 9 hours for the 42 ships a day passing through.

About 10 km. from Cristóbal, up the Chagres river, is the Gatún Dam, built to impound its waters. The 422 square km. Gatún Lake serves as a reservoir to hold sufficient water in the channel and for use in the locks during dry spells. A high level reservoir, Lake Alajuela (formerly the Madden Dam), feeds the lake and maintains its level, 26 metres above the sea. A ship ascends into Lake Gatún in three steps or lockages. Each of the twin chambers in each flight of locks has a usable length of 305 metres, a width of 33½ metres, and is about 21 metres deep. The flights are in duplicate to allow ships to be passed in opposite directions simultaneously. Passage of the Gatún Locks takes about an hour. Gatún may be reached by bus or train from Colón.

The largest section of the Canal is in Gatún Lake. In the lake is **Barro Colorado** island, to which the animals fled as the basin slowly filled. It is now a biological reserve for scientific research. Visits can be arranged with the Smithsonian Institute in Ancón, US$10 including boat, audio-visual display and lunch; take a Gamboa Summit bus from near Plaza 5 de Mayo (0605 or 0630) to the Dredging Division dock at Gamboa (US$0.65), from where the boat leaves. Trips go on Mondays only for 5 people. The excursion is highly recommended for seeing wildlife, especially monkeys. For longer stays, write to the Director, Smithsonian Tropical Research Institute, Box 2072, Balboa, Panamá. Administration, T 62-30-49. hours 0800-1145, 1315-1515.

After travelling over the lake for 37 km. and then through the narrow rock defile of the Gaillard or Culebra Cut for 13 km. to Pedro Miguel Locks, the descent to sea-level begins. Culebra Cut can be seen from

Contractor's Hill, reached by car (no buses) by turning right 3 km. past the Bridge of the Americas, passing Cocoli, then turning left as signed. The first stage is a descent into Miraflores Lake, 16½ metres above sea-level. The process is completed at the Miraflores Locks, 1½ km. further on. The road beyond Cocoli goes on to Posa, where there are good views of the locks, the cut and former Canal Zone buildings. Opposite Miraflores Locks is a swing bridge which only operates when traffic is heavy (e.g. on long weekends). The Canal channel continues to Balboa and the Pacific. An odd fact is that the mean level of the Pacific is some 20 cm. higher than the Atlantic, but the disparity is not constant throughout the year. On the Atlantic side there is a normal variation of 30 cm. between high and low tides, and on the Pacific of about 380 cm., rising sometimes to 640 cm.

Most people are surprised by the Canal. Few foresee that the scenery is so beautiful, and it is interesting to observe the mechanics of the passage. There are now reported to be tourist trips through the canal Tuesday and Thursday, US$35, check with Agencia Giscomes in Panama City. Otherwise since the Panama City-Colón train journey does not afford full views, travellers are advised to take a bus to the Miraflores Locks (open 0900-1700, best between 0600-1000 and 1430-1800 if you want to see shipping—the museum and model of the canal, formerly in the Department of Transport at Ancón, has been moved here). If travelling by train, get out at Pedro Miguel (no station at Miraflores), and take a bus from there, US$0.35. About 250 metres past the entrance to the Locks is a road (left) to the filtration plant and observatory, behind which is a picnic area and viewing point. Bus from Panama City to Miraflores Locks leaves from near Plaza 5 de Mayo (direction Paraíso or Gamboa), 15 mins., US$0.65. Ask driver to let you off on the main road, from where it's a 10-min. walk to the Locks. Taxi to the Locks, US$10 per hour. An alternative is take the train to Gatún and view the Gatún Locks and dam. Another good way to see the Panama Canal area is to rent a car.

The very best way to see the Canal is by boat: it is possible to traverse the canal as a linehandler (no experience necessary) on a yacht; the journey takes two days. Yachts are allowed through the canal on Tues. and Thur. only. The yacht owners need 4 linehandlers. Go to the Yacht Club in Balboa, and ask people hanging around the bar. The Club offers good daily lunch special for US$2.15. Good place to watch canal traffic. 50 metres right of the Club is a small white booth which has a list of boat departures for the next day; ask here if you can go to the dock and take the motor boat which shuttles out to yachts preparing for passage. Ask to speak to captains from the launch and see if they'll let you "transit".

Balboa The ship usually berths at Pier 18. Panama City is about 3¼ km. from the docks, an average of 10 minutes by taxi.

Balboa stands attractively between the Canal quays and Ancón hill, which lies between it and Panama City. It has been described as an efficient, planned, sterilized town, a typical American answer to the wilfulness and riot of the tropics.

The Canal administration building (with fine murals on the ground floor) and a few official residences are on Balboa Heights. At the foot of Balboa Heights is Balboa, with a small park, a reflecting pool and marble shaft commemorating Goethals, and a long parkway flanked with royal palms known as the Prado. At its eastern end is a theatre, a service centre building, post office and bank. Farther along Balboa Road are a large YMCA (where only male employees of the Canal Company can stay, but where all comers may eat, various churches and a Masonic temple.

Banks Citibank; Chase Manhattan Bank.

Telegrams INTEL; Tropical Radio & Telegraph Co. Public Telex booth.

Post Office Av. Balboa and El Prado.

Travel Agency: Chadwick's, in YMCA building, excellent, English spoken, T 52-29-72.

Excursions There is a launch service to **Taboga Island**, about 20 km. offshore (return fare US$5). Taboga is reached in about an hour from Pier 17-18 in Balboa (check the times in advance). There are 2 boats daily during the week and 3 boats on Sat. and Sun. The island is a favourite year-round resort; its pineapples and mangoes have a high reputation and its church is the second oldest in the western hemisphere (admission to beach US$0.50, covered picnic huts extra).

The trip out to Taboga is very interesting, passing the naval installations at the Pacific end of the Canal, the great bridge linking the Americas, tuna boats and shrimp fishers in for supplies, visiting yachts from all over the world at the Balboa Yacht Club, and the 4-km. Causeway connecting Fort Amador on the mainland with three islands in the bay. Part of the route follows the channel of the Canal, with its busy traffic. Taboga itself, with a promontory rising to 488 metres, is carpeted with flowers at certain seasons. There are few cars in the meandering, helter-skelter streets, and only one footpath as a road. Swimming is fine, though you may have to pay US$0.50 to use the beach in front of the hotel.

The first Spanish settlement was in 1515, two years after Balboa's discovery of the Pacific. It was from here that Pizarro set out for Peru in 1524. For two centuries it was a stronghold of the pirates who preyed on the traffic to Panama. Because it has a deep-water, sheltered anchorage, it was during colonial times the terminal point for ships coming up the W coast of South America. El Morro, at low tide joined to Taboga, is at high tide an island; it was once owned by the Pacific Steam Navigation Company, whose ships sailed from there. For a fine view, walk through the town and up to the top of the hill with a cross at the summit, to the right of the radar station (there is a shady short cut, ask locals). When surveying the view, don't miss the pelican rookery on the back side of the island; it is an easy walk down.

Hotels *Taboga* and *Chu*, B, beautiful views, own beach and bar.

It is a longer trip by launch—some 75 km.—to the **Pearl Islands**, visited mostly by sea-anglers for the Pacific mackerel, red snapper, corvina, sailfish, marlin, and other species which teem in the waters around. High mountains rise from the sea, but there is a little fishing village on a shelf of land at the water's edge. There was much pearl fishing in colonial days. **Contadora**, one of the smallest Pearl Islands, has become quite famous since its name became associated with a Central American peace initiative.

Contadora has *El Galeón Hotel*, A, and the very luxurious chalet complex known as *César Park Contadora Resort and Casino*, L, nice location on beach, T 50-4033. Return air ticket from Paitilla, US$12.75 by Aeroperlas, T 69-4555. Good skin-diving and sailing, 3-hour boat trip. Beware the sharks. Three day package tour to Contadora, US$150 for 2, recommended. Argonaut Steamship Agency, Calle 55 No. 7-82, Panama City, T 64-3459, runs launch cruises.

Ancón curves round the hill N and E and merges into Panama City. It has picturesque views of the palm-fringed shore. The following walk, proposed by Andrew M. Smith of Panama City, takes in the sights of Ancón: walk to the top of the hill in the morning for views of the city, Balboa and the Canal (conveniences and water fountain at the top); the entrance is on Av. 4 de Julio (Av. de los Mártires). Return to Av. 4 de Julio and take a clockwise route around the hill, bearing right on to Balboa Road (Av. Estado de Jamaica), passing YMCA, Chase Manhattan and Citibank, until you reach Stevens Circle where Cuna Indians sell *molas* . Here is the Post Office and a cafeteria. Then walk down the Prado lined with royal palms to the Goethals Memorial and up the steps to the Administration Building to see the murals of the Construction of the Canal (entrance free, identity must be shown to the guards). Follow Heights Road until it becomes Gorgas Road. You will pass the headquarters of the Smithsonian Tropical Research Institute (where applications to visit Barro Colorado Island are made) and, among trees and flowers, the US Army Hospital, formerly Gorgas Hospital for tropical diseases. Gorgas Road leads back to Av. 4 de Julio, but look out for the sign to the Museo de Arte Contemporáneo (open Mon.-Fri. 0800-1230, 1430-1800, Sat. 0800-1200), before Av. 4 de Julio. 2 libraries are open to the public: that of the Smithsonian Tropical Research Institute in the Canal Area, opp. Plaza 5 de Mayo, and that of the Panama Canal College, underneath the Bridge of the Americas.

At the foot of Ancón Hill the Instituto Nacional stands on the 4-lane Avenida 4 de Julio (Tivoli). The University City is on the Transisthmian Highway. Opposite the campus is the Social Security Hospital.

PANAMA CITY

Panama City, capital of the Republic, has a population of 1.2 million. It was founded on its present site in 1673 after Morgan had sacked the old town, now known as Panamá Viejo, 6½ km. away by road. Most of Panama City is modern; the old quarter of the city—the part that Spain fortified so effectively that it was never successfully attacked—lies at the tip of the peninsula; both it and Panamá Viejo are being extensively restored.

Note Some of the street names have recently been changed, which may make finding your way around a little difficult. The locals are likely still to refer to the streets by their old names, so if in doubt ask. Also, few buildings display their numbers, so try to find out the nearest cross street.

Panama City is a curious blend of old Spain, American progress, and the bazaar atmosphere of the East. It has a polyglot population unrivalled

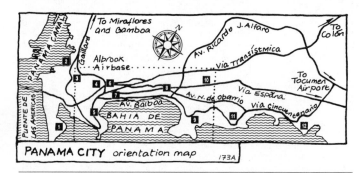

PANAMA CITY orientation map   *173A*

Panama City Orientation: Key to map

1. Fuerte Amador; 2. Docks; 3. Balboa; 4. Ancón; 5. Santa Ana; 6. Caledonia; 7. La Exposición; 8. Bella Vista; 9. Paltilla; 10. El Cangrejo; 11. Atlapa Convention Centre; 12. Ruins of Panamá Viejo.
.... area of detailed map.

in any other Latin American city. For the sober minded, the palm-shaded beaches, the islands of the Bay and the encircling hills constitute a large part of its charm. The cabarets and night life (very enterprising) are an attraction to those so inclined.

Most of the interesting sights are in the old part of the city and can easily be reached by foot, taxi, or bus. A good starting place is the Plaza de Francia, in the extreme S. In this picturesque little Plaza, with its red poinciana trees, is a memorial obelisk (topped by a cock) to the French Canal pioneers, and a monument to Carlos Finlay, the Cuban who discovered the cause of yellow fever. Facing the Plaza are several colonial buildings and the Palace of Justice, where the Supreme Court meets. Behind it runs part of the old sea wall—Las Bóvedas (The Dungeons)—built around the city to protect it from pirates. Flush under the wall, at the side of the Palace of Justice, are the old dungeons, with thick walls, arched ceilings and tiny barred windows looking on to the Bay (they have been converted into art galleries and a handicraft centre by IPAT, the tourist authority). Behind the French monument, in a recess in the walls, is a series of large tablets recording, in Spanish, the early attempts to build the Canal. The French Embassy faces the Plaza. There are steps up this old wall to the promenade—the Paseo de las Bóvedas—along its top, from which there is a fine view of the Bay of Panama and the fortified islands of Flamenco, Naos, and Perico. Beyond are Taboga and Taboguilla, tinged with blue or violet. Just beyond the end of the promenade is the Club de Clases de la Guardia Nacional, a barracks, previously the Club Unión, the city's leading club, which is now housed in a new building in the residential area.

A little way from the Club de Clases, along Av. A and to the right, are the ruins of Santo Domingo church, which has been restored and is now open to the public at times. Its flat arch, made entirely of bricks and

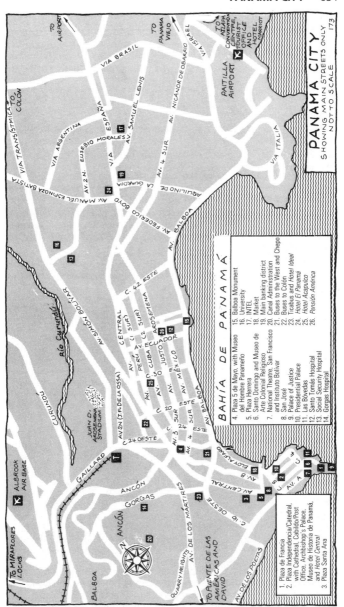

PANAMA CITY
SHOWING MAIN STREETS ONLY
NOT TO SCALE
173

BAHÍA DE PANAMÁ

1. Plaza de Francia
2. Plaza Independencia/Catedral, with Cathedral, Cabildo/Post Office, Archbishop's Palace, Museo de Historia de Panamá, and *Hotel Central*
3. Plaza Santa Ana
4. Plaza 5 de Mayo, with Museo del Hombre Panameño
5. Plaza Herrera
6. Santo Domingo and Museo de Arte Colonial Religioso
7. National Theatre, San Francisco and Instituto Bolívar
8. San José
9. Palace of Justice
10. Presidential Palace
11. Las Bóvedas
12. Santo Tomás Hospital
13. Social Security Hospital
14. Gorgas Hospital
15. Balboa Monument
16. University
17. INTEL
18. Market
19. Main banking district
20. Canal Administration
21. Buses to the West and Chepo
22. Buses to Colón
23. Ticabus and *Hotel Ideal*
24. *Hotel El Panamá*
25. *Hotel Acapulco*
26. *Pensión América*

mortar, with no internal support, has stood for three centuries. When the great debate as to where the Canal should be built was going on, a Nicaraguan stamp showing a volcano, with all its implications of earthquakes, and the stability of this arch—a proof of no earthquakes—are said to have played a large part in determining the choice in Panama's favour. At the Santo Domingo site is the interesting Museum of Colonial Religious Art, open Tues.-Sat. 1000-1530, Sun. 1500-1730 (adults US$0.50, children US$0.25, closed for extensive rebuilding since 1987).

Panama City's main street, the Av. Central, runs NW from the old city, then turns N and (less than 2 km. further) NE and sweeps right and almost parallel with the shore through the whole world (its name changes to Av. España and finally to Vía España). On the right, at the intersection with Calle 3, is the National Theatre, built in 1907, and recently restored. Up Calle 3 on the right is San Francisco church (colonial, but modernized), and the Instituto Bolívar, where the Liberator proposed a United States of South America during the Bolivarian Congress of 1826. On Av. Norte, running along the Bay, is the President's Palace (La Presidencia), the most impressive building in the city. It is locally known as Palacio de las Garzas, or herons, which are kept in a fountain area there. It was the residence of the Spanish Governor during colonial days. Av. Norte goes on to the colourful public market, on the waterfront. On Av. Norte are the wharves where coastal boats anchor and fishermen land their catches (but watch out for thieves).

Av. Central runs on to the Plaza Independencia, or Plaza Catedral. This Plaza, with busts of the Republic's founders, is the heart of the colonial city. Facing it are the Cathedral, the old Cabildo (which has now become the Central Post Office), the venerable *Hotel Central* and the Archbishop's Palace. The Cathedral has twin towers and domes encased in mother-of-pearl. The Post Office was the headquarters of the French during their attempt to build the Canal. Also in the Plaza Catedral (in the town hall) is the Museo de Historia de Panamá from colonial times to Torrijos' days in power, US$0.25 (open Tues.-Fri., 1000-1600, Sun. 1500-1800, closed for lunch). Beyond the Cathedral, Calle 8a runs S to the church of San José, which has a famous organ and a magnificent golden baroque altar, originally installed at a church in Panamá Viejo; the golden walls were resourcefully covered in mud by nuns to disguise them during Morgan's famous raid.

On Av. Central, to the right, in the second block beyond the Cathedral, is the church of La Merced, burnt in 1963 and now completely restored. It was near here that the landward gate of the fortified city stood. Further along the now curving Av. Central is the small Plaza Santa Ana, a favourite place for political meetings. Its church is colonial. Not far away is Sal si Puedes, "Get out if you can", a narrow street swarming with vendors, and Panama's Chinatown; don't linger round here late at night, best before 1930.

Some blocks E is the Caledonia district, where live the descendants of the British West-Indian blacks brought in to build the railway and the Canal. Caledonia is the Harlem of Panama City, exotic and unassimilated; whites are said to be unwelcome. Mugging is very frequent, even in daylight.

Much further along Av. Central, on Plaza 5 de Mayo (at Calle 22A Este), is the old railway station, now the Museo Nacional del Hombre Panameño, with a good display showing the origins of the populations of Panama (Tues.-Sat., 1000-1530, Sun. 1500-1730, US$0.50), and almost opposite is the Plaza De Lesseps. This part of the city is known as La Exposición because of the International Fair held here in 1916 to celebrate the building of the Canal. Calle 35 Este leads down to the Av. Balboa along the waterfront. The Santo Tomás hospital is here and on a promontory jutting out from this popular promenade is a great monument to Balboa, who stands on a marble globe poised on the shoulders of a supporting group, representing the four races of man. Many of the best hotels are in Bella Vista, also one of the main business areas, and the chief restaurant area is, appropriately, El Cangrejo ("the crab").

On Independence Day, 3 November, practically the whole city seems to march in a parade lasting about 3½ hours, centred in the old part of the city. Colourful, noisy, spectacular. Another parade takes place the following day.

Warning Thieves abound, and muggings are frequent. It is not safe to walk on any streets alone after dark (i.e. after 1730). Keep valuables in money belt, or otherwise hidden, and don't carry a bag of any sort if possible. Also you shouldn't take a taxi which has 2 people in it already. Be careful when putting luggage into a car. (All the same, most Panamanians are friendly and helpful.) Marañón (around the market), El Chorrillo (W from Santa Ana to Ancón hill) and Caledonia can be particularly dangerous; never walk there at night and take care in daylight, too. For this reason, be very careful when booking into a hotel or *pensión* between Calles 9 and 30, i.e. W of Plaza Herrera (where most of the cheap ones are to be found). **N.B.** In March 1990 a curfew was still in force in the capital following the events surrounding the depositon of Gen. Noriega.

Hotels Note a 10% tax on all hotel prices. All hotels are air-conditioned.

Hotels in our L range include: *El Marriott Panamá*, Vía Israel, T26-4077, 5 minutes from centre, restaurant, pool, health spa, etc; *El Panamá*, Vía España, 111, T23-1660; *El Continental*, also on Vía España, T64-6666, in the business district, pool, night clubs, restaurants, but noisy till 2230 from organ music (a Wurlitzer). In our A range, and belonging to the same group as *Continental* are *Granada*, Av. Eusebio Morales, T62-4900, also with casino, pool, restaurant; *La Siesta*, near Tocumen airport, T20-1400, free transport to airport, pool, tennis, casino; *Europa*, Vía España y Calle 42, T63-6911, A, opp. Teatro Bella Vista, another casino hotel, restaurants and pool, rec; *Gran Hotel Soloy*, Av. Perú, T27-1133, A; *Internacional*, Plaza 5 de Mayo, T62-1000, A, convenient for the shopping district; *El Ejecutivo*, Calle Aquilino de la Guardian, T64-3333, A, pool.

In our B range: *Vera Cruz*, Av. Perú, without breakfast, new, clean, good, but rooms at front noisy; *Doral*, Calle Monteserín (T 62-5144), a/c, TV, cold water, rec. as safe, although not in safe area, cheaper commercial rates available; *Costa Inn*, Av. Perú y Calle 39, T 27-1522; *Roma*, Av. Justo Arosemena, T27-3844; *Centroamericano*, Av. Ecuador, T27-4555 and *Gran Hotel Lux*, Av. Perú, T25-1950.

Colón, Calle 12, Oeste and Calle "B", C with shower (cheaper without), a/c, erratic water supply; *Acapulco*, Calle 30 Este (near *Hotel Soloy*), T 25-3832, between Avs. Perú and Cuba, C, a/c, clean, comfortable, TV, private bath, restaurant, conveniently located, rec.; also around corner from *Soloy*, *Residencia Turístico Volcán*, Calle 29, D with shower, a/c, clean; *California*, Vía España y

C.43, C with bath, a/c, TV, restaurant (breakfast US$1.75); *Central*, Plaza Catedral (22-6080), D with bath, E shared bath, safe motorcycle parking, good cheap meals in restaurant, lots of South American travellers, you can bargain if staying more than a week. *Caracas*, Plaza Santa Ana, C, with bath, a/c, TV, central, convenient, unprepossessing area at night; *Riazor*, Calle 16 Oeste, near *Ideal*, C. 17 Oeste, D, a/c with bath, good value, cheap restaurant downstairs next to the Ticabus terminal, therefore well placed as you arrive late from Costa Rica on the bus. *Herrera*, Plaza Herrera, basic, noisy but quite clean, E, good meals in restaurant downstairs at about US$1.50 p.p. Ten mins. from airport (nearest) on right is *El Continental*, D, air conditioned, shower, bar, excellent and easy to reach from the city, the docks, or Panamá Viejo, free bus service to airport; *Parador*, 5 km. from airport at first traffic lights, D, clean.

Cheaper accommodation can be found in *pensiones*: *América*, Av. Justo Arosemena and Av. Ecuador, D-C, back rooms best to avoid street noise, communal bathrooms, safe, clean and pleasant (airport bus stops outside); *Las Palmeras*, Av. Cuba between C.38-39, T 250811, E, safe, clean; *Foyo*, Calle 6, No. 825, near Plaza Catedral, clean (but there are mice—hang up food), E, noisy on street but good and central (reduced rates for weekly or monthly stays); the restaurant nearby is OK and cheap but closes at 1700 and on Sun.; *Panamá*, Calle 6, 8-40, E, fan, noisy, reasonable (best rooms have balcony overlooking street), safe, but cockroaches. *Mi Posada*, Calle 12 y Av. Central (Plaza Santa Ana, dangerous area), F, cheap, OK; many (unlisted here) on Av. México; *Nacional*, Av. Central 22-19, near Plaza 5 de Mayo, E with fan, basic, no hot water, many permanent residents; *Colón*, Av. Central, 30 Calle, E, clean, safe but noisy in the front rooms; *Pacífico*, Calle Carlos Mendoza (dangerous area), E, fans, laundry facilities; *Vásquez*, Av. A, 2-47, close to the Palace of Justice, quiet, friendly, nice rooms and view of ocean and sand, E; *Rivera*, Av. Calle 11 Oeste, 8-14, off Av. A, pleasant and friendly, but noisy, E (monthly rates available).

Apartments for rent at *Las Vegas Apartotel*, Calle 55 y Av. E.A. Morales, T 69-0722, B, rec; *Apartotel Suites Alvear*, Vía Argentina 2, T 69-4055, B.

N.B. It may not be easy to find accommodation just before Christmas, as Central Americans tend to invade the city to do their shopping, nor during Carnival. In the higher parts of the city, water shortages are common in summer, and electricity cuts are common in late summer everywhere.

Camping There are no official sites but it is possible to camp on some beaches or, if in great need (they agree, but don't like it much) in the Balboa Yacht Club car park. It is also possible to camp in the Hipódromo grounds (11 km. E of the city, on Vía España) but there are at present (1990) no facilities; this is allowed if you are waiting to ship your vehicle out of the country. Also possible, by previous arrangement, at La Patria swimming pool nearby, and at the Chorrera (La Herradura) and La Siesta beaches on the Pan-American Highway.

Restaurants (apart from hotels). Good are: *Lesseps*, Vía España y C. 46, La Cresta, French restaurant and bar; *Sarti's* (Italian food), Calle Ricardo Arias 5; *Panamar*, end of Calle 50, specializes in seafood; *La Mejicanita*, Av. Justo Arosemena; *Pez de Oro* (Peruvian) superb *mariscos*, and fish, and good wine, Calle 2, El Cangrejo; *Las Rejas*, Vía Brasil, just off Vía España; *Las Américas*, Calle San Miguel, Obarrio. *La Casa del Marisco* (sea food) on Av. Balboa, is open-air. *Cocina Vasca* (sea food) Calle D, in El Cangrejo, really excellent, US$18-20 for a full meal. Also in El Cangrejo, *El Cortijo*, between Eusebio A. Morales and Vía Argentina on Calle D; *Tinajas*, on Calle 51, near *Ejecutivo Hotel*, Panamanian food and entertainment, rec. Two French restaurants: *Casco Viejo*, nr. Plaza Francia, behind French embassy, and a luxurious one in Las Bóvedas dungeons (US$15-20 a head). *Le Bistrot*, Centro Comercial La Florida, Calle 53, expensive.

Other restaurants include: *El Trapiche*, Vía Argentina, Panamanian food, good; *Manolo*, Vía Argentina; *Piscolabis*, Transisthmian Highway, Vista Hermosa district, local food, reasonable; *El Jorrón*, Vía Fernández de Córdoba, Vista Hermosa district, local food, reasonable and good; *La Tablita*, Transisthmian Highway, Los Angeles district, reasonable; *Nápoli*, Av. Estudiante, corner with Calle 16, Italian, good and cheap, and many other good Italian places. *1985*, C. Eusebio A. Morales, Swiss; *Madrid*, Vía España near UK Consulate, Spanish and local food, comida daily for US$2.60; *Marbella*, Av. Balboa y Calle 39, Spanish, small; *La Cascada*, Av. Balboa and Calle 25, seafood, rec., enormous helpings, open air, "doggy bags" welcome, first drink free, waterfall/lifesize animal décor, good service, menus in charming English to take away, highly rec.; the same management runs *Las Costallitas* on Vía Argentina, same menu (which takes ½ hr. to read!), same reasonable prices; *El Dorado*, Calle Colombia 2, good service, excellent seafood, rec.

Vegetarian: *Mireya* Calle Ricardo Araneo and Calle Ricardo Arias, near **Continental Hotel**, good value, rec.

Many good Oriental places. *Matsuei*, Japanese, excellent, pricey; *Lung Fung*, Transisthmian Highway and Los Angeles, very popular with Chinese residents for Sat. and Sun. Cantonese-style brunch, very good food and value; *Mandarin*, Chinese, excellent, fair prices; *Kwang Chow*, in the Sal si Puedes area of Av. Balboa, sells Tsingtao beer, rec.; *Gran China*, Av. Balboa, between Calles 26 and 27, Chinese, good value; *Palacio Imperial*, C.17 above Ticabus terminal, Chinese, good and cheap; *Bajwa's Shamiana*, Galerías Marbella, Paitilla, T 63-8586, Indian, US$15 p.p., fair. *Jimmy's*, Paseo Cincuentenario just beyond Atlapa Centre, Greek; *Chipré*, Av. Central y C. 11 Oeste, rec.

Krispy, Macdonalds, Frutilandia, Dairy Queen, Hardee's, Burger King and *Kentucky Fried Chicken* all have their branches; *La Viña*, corner C. 6 Oeste and Av. A (no sign), behind Post Office, good, cheap; also *La Esquina*, Av. A y C. 12 Oeste; *Niko's Café*, just off Vía España opposite Rey's Supermarket, good meals at reasonable prices, good sandwiches; *La Conquista*, Calle J, up Av. Central. *La Cresta* (good food from US$1), Vía España and Calle 45. Two good restaurants on Avenida Central are *A & P* and *Yimy*, the first opposite the National Museum, the second near Chase Manhattan and Bank of America. *Café El Exagerado* serves very good meals at reasonable prices; *Markany*, Av. Cuba y Av. Ecuador, good snacks. *Café Coca Cola*, Av. Central and Plaza Santa Ana, pleasant, reasonably-priced; *Café Jaime*, corner of Calle 12 and Av. Central, for good *chichas* (natural drinks). There are good pavement cafés along Av. Balboa.

Shopping The most expensive shops are on Vía España; Av. Central is cheaper but less safe. *Casa Salih*, Av. Central 125, try local perfume Kantule from San Blas islands; *Casa Fastlich*, Av. Central at Plaza 5 de Mayo, good local jewellery; *Nat. Méndez*, Calle Jota 13, near Av. Tivoli, for Colombian emeralds and pearls; *Curiosidades Típicas de Panamá*, Av. 4 de Julio y Calle J. B. Sosa, for local craft work; *Mercado Artesanal Gago*, next to Gago supermarket on corner of Vía España y Vía Brasil, competitive prices; *Curiosidades Panameñas*, Calle 55 near *Hotel El Panamá*, local crafts; *Panamá Típico*, Via España y Calle La Perejil, same again; *Indutípica*, Av. A y Calle 8 Oeste (opp. San José church), for *artesanía*, friendly. *Inovación* is a gift shop in the *Hotel El Panamá* complex on Via España, has wide selection of new and used *molas*; *Crossroads*, Calle E. A. Morales, by *Granada Hotel*, more "typical" goods; *Joyería La Huaca*, Av. Central y Calle 21, genuine precolumbian ojects for sale upstairs. Good selections also in main hotels. Gago, El Rey, Super 99 and Machetazo (on Central) supermarkets are said to be the best. Mercado Público, near Presidential Palace, for all general items (bargain for everything except food). There is a store (Army-Navy) on Av. Central, near Plaza 5 de Mayo, which sells camping and hiking equipment. There are many laundromats around Plaza Catedral, where wash and dry will cost about US$2.

Duty-free imported luxuries of all kinds from all nations (technically only for US military personnel). Panamanian items include *molas* (embroidered blouse fronts made by Cuna Indians, e.g. Emma Vence, T 61-8009); straw, leather, wooden and ceramic items; the *pollera* circular dress, the *montuno* shirts (embroidered), hats, the *chácara* (a popular bag or purse), the *chaquira* necklace made by Guaymí Indians, and jewellery; good selection at Artesanías Nacionales, in Panamá Viejo.

Bookshops English books at *Librería Argosy*, Vía Argentina y Vía España; *Menéndez*, Av. Justo Arosemena y C. 36, good selection, some in English; *Gran Morrison* shops, Vía España (near Calle 51 Este and *Hotel Continental*), Av. 4 de Julio, Transisthmian Highway, El Dorado, limited selection of English books. *National University Bookshop*, on campus between Av. Manuel Espinosa Batista and Vía Simón Bolívar, very good, wide selection (including some in English).

Photographic Equipment Camera Center, on Tivoli at 4 de Julio (P.O. Box 7279); Foto Internacional, on main street. Panafoto, Av. Central by Plaza 5 de Mayo. Foto Enodi, Via Porras, Kodak slides developed in a day. Developing in one day in Foto El Halcón, Calle 55 alongside the *Hotel El Panamá* . In some places you will get a free film.

Local Transport Taxis have no meters; charges are according to how many "zones" are traversed (about US$0.75-US$2). Try to settle fare beforehand if you can. Note that there are large taxis (*grandes*) and cheaper small ones (*chicos*). Taxis charge US$12 for a 2½-hr. tour to Miraflores locks and the Canal Area. There are numerous small buses nicknamed *chivas* (goats). These charge US$0.15, are not very comfortable but run along the major streets (e.g. Av. Central as far as Calle 12, Av. Perú and Av. Justo Arosemena; all buses go to Bella Vista—the business section—except those marked Tumba Muerta or Transístmica). Travel into the suburbs costs more. Yell " *parada* " to stop the bus.

Car Rental At the airport (Hertz, Avis, Econorent); rates about US$30/day, special rates if reservations made abroad (e.g. Toyota, 1 day, unlimited mileage, US$13 inc. insurance). Cars in good condition. Other offices on Vía España.

Motorcycle Club Road Knights, at the Albrook Air Force base (T 86-3348), very welcoming; allows international motorcyclists to stay for free for up to 2 weeks, has repair and maintenance workshop.

Cabarets and Discotheques Hotel *El Continental*; *Playboy de Panamá*, Calle 55, El Cangrejo; *Bunny Club*, Jerónimo de la Ossa; *Oasis*, Vía Brasil; *Los Cuatro Ases*, Calle L. Recommended discos: *Open House*, near Ejecutivo Hotel, *Bacchus*, Vía España and *Magic*, Calle 81; *Las Molas*, entrance to Chase Manhattan Bank, Vía España, Los Angeles district, small band, rural decor, drinks US$1.50; *Unicornio*, Calle 50 y R. Arías 23 is night club with discothèque and gambling; reasonable prices, will admit foreigners for US$3 a week. *El Bon Ton* and *Camelot*, Río Abajo. *La Parrillita*, Av. 11 de Octubre in Hato Pintado district, is a restaurant in a railway carriage. *El Pavo Real*, off Calle 50 Oeste in Campo Alegre, hard to find, pub selling British beer (at a price), darts board, popular with expats.

Theatres and Cinemas There are occasional performances at the National Theatre (folklore sessions every other Sun., 1600, check dates). Atlapa Convention Centre. The usual air-conditioned cinemas (US$2.50 except Balboa cinema, near Stevens Circle, US$2). National University cinema, US$1.50 for general public, wider variety than in city cinemas. Foreign films must, legally, have Spanish sub-titles.

Casinos In the main hotels, at Unicornio on Calle 50, and at airport.

Bathing Piscina Patria (the Olympic pool), take San Pedro or Juan Díaz bus, US$0.15. Piscina Adán Gordon, between Av. Cuba and Av. Justo Arosemena, near Calle 31, 0900-1200, 1300-1700 (except weekends to 1700 only). Admission US$0.50 (take identification), but beards and long hair frowned on (women must wear bathing caps). Many beaches within 1½ hours' drive of the city. Fort Kobbe beach (US$0.50, bus from Canal Area bus station US$0.40) and Naos beach (US$1, Amador bus from same station, US$0.30, then 2 km. walk along causeway) have been rec.; both have shark nets, but at low tide at the former you must go outside it to swim! Vera Cruz beach is not recommended as it is both dirty and dangerous (all are dangerous at night).

Golf Panama Golf Club; courses at Summit, Amador and Horoko; Coronado Beach Golf Club (open to tourists who get guest cards at Coronado office on Calle 50).

Horse Races (pari-mutuel betting) are held Sat., Sun. and holidays at the Presidente Remón track (bus to Juan Díaz, entry from US$0.50 to 2.50). Cockfights are held on Vía España, near the road that leads to Panamá Viejo, every Sun., same bus but get out at crossing with Calle 150.

Instituto Panameño de Arte, Av. de los Mártires near Palacio Legislativo, art gallery. Open 0900-1200, 1500-1800 except Sun.

Exchange The Chase Manhattan Bank (US$0.65 commission on each cheque); Citibank; Lloyds Bank International (Bahamas) Ltd. (ex-BOLSA) Calle Aquilino de la Guardia y Calle 48, Bella Vista (also El Cangrejo agency), offers good rates for sterling (the only bank which will change sterling cash, and only if its sterling limit has not been exhausted); Bank of America; Banco de Colombia; Swiss Bank Corporation. Thomas Cook travellers' cheques only exchangeable at Banco Sudameris and Algemene Bank Nederland; Deutschmarks exchanged at Deutsch-Südamerikanische Bank. Panamanian banks, open 0800-1300, closed Sat., except for Banco General which takes Bank of America and Thomas Cook travellers' cheques. American Express, Banco Union building, 12th floor, Av. Samuel Lewis, T 635858, Mon.-Fri. 0800-1700 (US$0.10 commission on each cheque). **Note**: many banks closed down their Panamanian operations in 1988; if requiring banking services from your own country, check in advance which institutions still have offices in Panama.

If travelling N stock up on dollars as they are hard to obtain, but essential for exchange, in the rest of Central America.

Free market for almost all currencies, and good rates for all South American currencies. *Cambio* on Av. Central near *Hotel Internacional*. The US dollar is the normal circulating medium in Panama.

Embassies and Consulates : Costa Rican, Edif. Plaza Regency, Piso 2, Vía España, T 642980. **Nicaraguan**, Av. Federico Boyd y Calle 50, T 23-0981; **Salvadorean**, Vía España 125. **Guatemalan**, Vía España 128, about Calle 55, open 0800-1300. **Venezuelan**, Banco Unión Building, Av. Samuel Lewis. **Colombian**, Calle 52 (E. A. Morales) No. 5, 1 block from Vía España and Calle 52, open 0800-1200; the **Chilean** and **Ecuadorean** embassies are housed in the same building.

US, Av. Balboa and Calle 37; P.O. Box 1099. T 27-1777. **British**, Torre Swiss Bank, Calle 53, Zona 1, T 690866, Fax (507) 230730, Apartado 889. **French**, Plaza Francia, T 28-7835. **W. German**, Edif. Bank of America, Calle 50, T 23-02-02; **Netherlands**, Edif. ABN Bank, Calle M.M. Icaza, nr. Vía España, T 64-72-57; **Swedish**, Edificio Melinda, Vía Argentina 25, Panama 5, T 64-7655. **Swiss**, Av. Samuel Lewis y C. Gerardo Ortega, Ed. Pronasa, T 64-9731, P.O. Box 499. **Israeli Embassy**, Ed. Grobman, C. Manuel María Icaza, 5th floor, P.O. Box 6357, T 64-8022/8257.

Customs for renewal of permits and obtaining exit papers for vehicles in Ancón, off Curundu Road, near Albrook U.S. airbase.

Hospitals US Army Gorgas Hospital, Balboa is only for US military personnel, except in emergency. The private clinics charge high prices; normally visitors are treated at either the Clínica San Fernando or the Clínica Paitilla (both have hospital annexes). For inoculations buy vaccine at a chemist, who will recommend a clinic; plenty in La Exposición around Parque Belisario Porras. Dentist: Dr. Daniel Wong, Clínica Dental Marbella, Ed. Alfil (Planta Baja), near Centro Comercial Marbella, T 63-8998.

Worship Services in English at St. Luke's Episcopalian Cathedral, Ancón. Bahai temple, 11 km. out on Transisthmian Highway, in the Ojo de Agua district. Modern; worth seeing for its architecture. Taxi round trip for US$5, with an hour to see the temple, can be arranged.

Post Office Plaza Catedral, Calle 6 and Avenida Central. Also Calle 30 E, nr. Av. Balboa, and at the University. Parcels sent "poste restante" are delivered to Encomiendos Postales Transístmicos, behind the Sears store on Simón Bolívar; tax has to be paid on the value of the goods. If asked for a tip, feign inability to understand!

Cables All America Cables & Radio, Inc., Calle 228, No. 12-17; Tropical Radio Telegraph Co., Calle Samuel Lewis. T 3-7474. Intel, Edificio Avesa, Vía España (open 0700-2300 weekdays, from 0800 Sat and Sun.) Public telex booth available TRT office. Excellent long-distance telephone by Intel and Tropical Radio. Charges can be transferred to UK.

Travel Agency Viajes Panamá S. A., Av. Justo Arosemena 75, T 25-1838/4466, 27-4166, repeatedly rec., English spoken, helpful with documentation. Chadwick's, see under Balboa, above.

Tourist Bureau Information office of the Instituto Panameño de Turismo (IPAT), in the Atlapa Convention Centre, Vía Israel opp. *Hotel Marriott* (0900 to 1600) issues good list of hotels, *pensiones*, motels and restaurants, and issue a free *Focus on Panama* guide (available at all major hotels, and airport). Best **maps** from Instituto Geográfico Nacional Tommy Guardia (IGNTG), on Vía Simón Bolívar, opp. the National University (footbridge nearby, fortunately), take Transístmica bus from C. 12 in Santa Ana: physical map of the country in 2 sheets, US$3.50 each; Panama City map in many sheets, US$1.50 per sheet (travellers will only need 3 or so). At the back of the Panama Canal Commission telephone books are good maps of the Canal Area, Panama City and Colón.

Buses Ticabus, with office on ground floor of *Hotel Ideal*, Calle 17 Oeste, run air-conditioned buses to San José, about US$25; also to Managua (3 a week, US$40, overnight stop in San José where you must reserve seat to Managua). Air conditioners rarely work. (Tickets are refundable; they pay on the same day, minus 15%.) Impossible to do Panama City-San José in one day on public transport. Buses going north tend to be well booked up, so make sure you reserve a seat in advance, and never later than the night before you leave. Buses to the W of the country (and also Chepo) leave from a terminal at the corner of Av. A and Av. Balboa (Av. 6 Sur), behind a 13-storey block of flats (no sign). Buses to all Canal Area destinations (Balboa, Summit, Paraíso, Kobbe, etc.) leave from Canal Area bus station (SACA), behind Plaza 5 de Mayo. Bus Panamá-Chepo US$1.20. Panamá-Colón 1¾ hrs., US$1.75, from Calle 26 Oeste y Av. Central, opp. San Miguel church. To Kobbe Beach by bus ½ hr., US$0.40 on US military territory (Pacific side). Panamá-David, 6 hrs., US$10.60, express US$15, 5 hrs. 1200 and 2400 (Transchiri, from Calle 17 Este and Balboa).

Rail Four trains daily Mon.-Fri. Panamá-Colón at 0440, 0645, 1520 and 1740.

Return Colón-Panamá, 0440, 0655, 1535, 1725. Sat. and holidays: Panamá-Colón, 0830, 1235, 1750, and Colón-Panamá, 0640, 1045, 1600. No service on Sundays. Station on Av. de los Mártires, 1 km. NW of Plaza 5 de Mayo, not a pleasant area at night. Steel-car trains run roughly parallel to the Canal, of which there are excellent views, especially of Gatún Lake, crossed by a causeway. The track is in poor condition, as are the trains. Journey takes 1 hr. 25-50 mins. Single costs US$1.25. For information, T 52-7720.

Airport Tocumen, 27 km. Taxi fares about US$20, colectivo US$8 p.p. (if staying for only a couple of days, it is cheaper to rent a car at the airport, e.g. from Econorent). For about US$3 (should only be US$1.20) driver takes you by Panamá Viejo, just off the main airport road. Travellers whiling away hours at the airport can visit the delightful nearby village of Pacora, a few km. off the Pan-American Highway. Bus marked Tocumen to airport, every 15 mins., from Plaza 5 de Mayo, US$0.35, one hour's journey. Bus ("El Chirrillo") to Panama City from the crossing outside the airport (US$0.30), 45 mins. There is a 24 hour left-luggage office near the Avis car rental desk for US$1 per article per day (worth it, since theft in the departure lounge is common). There are duty-free shops at the airport but more expensive than those downtown. There is a small airport at La Paitilla (take a number 2 bus going to Boca La Caja, from Av. Balboa at Calle 40), nearer Panama City, for domestic and private flights.

Excursions A visit is usually paid, along the beachside highway, to **Panamá Viejo** and its ruins, 6½ km. away. On the way you can visit the Justo Arosemena Institute in the Paitilla district. Panamá Viejo, founded in 1519 by Pedrarias, was the point where gold from Peru was unloaded and kept in the King's store-house. There it was loaded on to mules and transported across the Isthmus to Nombre de Dios and Portobelo for shipment to Spain. In January, 1671, Henry Morgan looted and destroyed the city. Because the old site was hard to defend, the city was refounded on its present site.

Today the visitor can wander among the ruins of the Cathedral, its plaza with moss-covered stone pillars and what remains of the old government buildings. The King's Bridge, the starting point of the three trails across the Isthmus, still stands. Past the Plaza and near the sea is what remains of San José, where the golden altar and walls were. At one side are the dungeons. The whole area is attractively landscaped and floodlit. Taxi from the centre, US$1.50; bus US$0.15 from Vía España or Av. Balboa, Nos. 1 and 2.

In Panamá Viejo is the Artesanía Nacional shop, for handicrafts (more expensive than elsewhere). There is also a free display of folk dancing on six Saturdays in the dry season, which is well worth seeing.

See Balboa (page 627) for trips to Taboga Island and Pearl Islands. A good excursion—a 2-hr. drive through picturesque jungle—is to Lake Alajuela (formerly Madden Dam). The drive runs from Balboa along the Gaillard Highway and near the Canal. Beyond Fort Clayton there is a fine view of the Pedro Miguel and Miraflores locks. Beyond Pedro Miguel town a road branches off to the left to Summit (Las Cumbres), where there are experimental gardens containing tropical plants from all over the world (closed Mondays) and a small zoo containing native wild life. (The trip to Summit may be made by buses marked Gamboa, every 1-1½ hrs., from near Plaza 5 de Mayo, US$0.35; the Paraíso bus will also take you to the Miraflores and Pedro Miguel locks.) The road to Lake Alajuela (37 km.) crosses the Las Cruces trail (old cannon mark the spot), and beyond is deep jungle (if walking the trail, take machete and compass and arrange boat across the Chagres river at the end of the trail well in advance). A large area of rain forest between Gatún Lake and Lake Alajuela has been set aside as **Parque Nacional Soberanía** (trails for walking). The Park has an information centre at the Summit Garden. For excursion to Portobelo, **see page 624** .

The Madden Dam (Lake Alajuela) is used to generate electricity. A trip through part of the Canal by launch *Fantasía del Mar* costs US$16 for adults, US$8 for children, and lasts about 4 hours. A trip to Lake Alajuela by taxi is only worth while if there are enough people to fill the taxi.

The return from Lake Alajuela to Panama City can be made by the Transisthmian Highway. In Las Cumbres the restaurant *La Hacienda* serves native dishes.

WEST FROM PANAMA CITY

The Pan-American Highway runs westwards from Panama City through Concepción to the Costa Rican border (489 km.), and is well graded and completely paved. The Highway begins at the Puente de las Américas across the Canal at the Pacific entrance. The bridge, 1,653 metres long and high enough to allow all ships to pass under it, has 3 lanes, a 4-lane approach from Panama City and a pedestrian pavement all the way (muggings have occurred on the bridge in broad daylight, so be careful!).

Where the road W crosses the savannas, there are open pastures and fields where clumps of beautiful trees—largely mangoes and palms—alternate with grass.

The first place you reach, 13 km. from Panama City, is the small town of Arraiján (6,600 people). On 21 km. by 4-lane highway (toll US$0.50) is La Chorrera (37,000 people); an interesting store, Artes de las Américas, has items in wood, etc. A branch road (right) leads 1½ km. to a waterfall. On 20 km., among hills, is the old town of Capira; good food next to Shell station run by Chinese. We pass through the orange groves of Campana (where a 10-km. road climbs to **Cerro Campana National Park**; no lodgings), and then twist down to Río Sajalises (bathing) and the low-level plains. On through Bejuco and Chame to the town of **San Carlos** (Hotels: *Río Mar*, C; *El Palmar*, B), near the sea; good river and sea-bathing (beware jelly fish). Not many restaurants in San Carlos, but there are plenty of shops where food can be bought. Between San Carlos and Chame are two beaches, Nueva Gorgona (*Cabañas Ocean Blue*, C,) and Coronado. **Playa Coronado** is the most popular in Panama, even so it is rarely crowded. Hotels: *Playa Coronado*, C, secure, clean, restaurant, showers, bar, camping, owner White Russian, friendly, rec.; *Playa Coronado Golf Club*, B, villas; *Cabañas El Coquetón*, cabin up to 6 persons US$40 per day; all prices increase at weekends. Minibus Panama City-San Carlos, US$2.70, San Carlos-David, US$9.30. Beyond San Carlos is the Río Mar beach, with a good seafood restaurant.

Five km. on a road (right) leads after a few km. to a climb through fine scenery to the summit of Los Llanitos (792 metres), and then down 200 metres to a mountain-rimmed plateau (7 by 5½ km.) on which is comparatively cool **El Valle**, a small summer resort. 4 km. before El Valle is a parking spot with fine views of the village, waterfall nearby. (*Hotel Campestre*, B; *Cabañas El Potosí*, friendly; *El Greco Motel*, D; *Pensión Niña Delia*, E, no single rooms; private houses nearby rent rooms, F with meals; accommodation hard to find at weekends.) Soapstone carvings of animals, and straw birds, for sale. The town's Sunday market has become touristy and expensive, but the town itself is a good example of what life away from the cities is like. Gold coloured frogs can be seen here, including at the main hotel. There are many good walks in the vicinity, for instance to the cross in the hills to the W of town.

We leave Panamá Province at La Ermita and enter Coclé, whose large tracts of semi-arid land are used for cattle raising.

Santa Clara, with its famous beach, 115 km. from Panama City, is the usual target for motorists: fishing, launches for hire, and riding (Hotels: *Muu Muu*, B; *Vista Bella*, A, per cabin, for weekend). About 13 km. beyond is Antón (5,100 people): it has a special local type of *manjar blanco*. There is a crucifix here which is reputed to be miraculous. (*Hotel Rivera*, D, Km. 129.; *Pensión y Restaurante Chung*, on Highway, F with bath, basic, friendly, moderately-priced food.) On 20 km. is the capital of Coclé: **Penonomé** (10,715 people), an old town even when the Spaniards arrived. An advanced culture here, revealed by archaeologists (things found are in National Museum, Panama City, also Museo Conte here), was overwhelmed by volcanic eruption.

Hotels *Dos Continentes*, C with shower, a/c, restaurant; *Pensión Los Pinos*, on left of Highway to Panama City, E with bath and fan (D with a/c); *Pensión Motel*; *Pensión Ramírez*, E with bath, Calle Juan Arosemena near church and Parque; *Pensión Dos Reales*, Calle Juan Vásquez, E, basic, noisy).

Just under a km. N of Penonomé is Balneario Las Mendozas, on street of the same name, an excellent river pool for bathing in deep water. In another 18 km., is **Natá** (5,060 people), an important place in colonial days; old church (Iglesia de los Caballeros, 1522) and other colonial buildings. A few km. beyond we enter the sugar area and come to (10 km.) **Aguadulce**, 14,240 people (bus from Panamá, US$4.50); native pottery for sale; large salt-beds nearby. Hotels: *El Interamericano* (D, a/c); *Pensión Sarita*, E p.p., and others (it may be possible to sleep by the fire station). On the way to (22½ km.) Divisa, just beyond the large Santa Rosa sugar plantation, a road leads off right to the mountain spa of Calobre, 37 km. from Aguadulce; the hot springs are, however, a good hour's drive away, on a very rough road; grand mountain scenery.

From Divisa a road leads (left) into the Azuero Peninsula through Parita (25 km., 6,554 people; colonial church), and **Chitré** (40 km., 23,150 people), capital of Herrera Province (bus from Panama City, US$6, 4 hours; from Divisa, US$1, ½ hour); Herrera museum in centre of town. The *Feria de Azuero*, held late each April, is worth seeing.

Hotels *El Prado*, D, friendly; *Rex*, D (good restaurant next door), on main plaza; *Pensión Azuero*, Calle Manuel Correa, F, usually full; *Pensión Granada*, E (bargain), on road to Los Santos, basic; *Pensión Lilly*, E wth bath, cold water, clean, road to Monagrillo; *Toledo*, C. **Restaurant Popular**, Manuel Correa, good, cheap; **Restaurant Las Tejas**, on main square, small, good juices.

Swimming pool on road to Monagrillo, US$0.25 (closed lunchtime). Tourist agencies in Panama City can arrange trips to La Arena, ¾-hr. walk from the centre of Chitré, which is the centre for Panamanian native pottery. However, this walk takes you past an army camp, you may be asked for your papers and it may be tiresome if they find you have been in Nicaragua.

Los Santos (8,730 people), an old and charming town in Los Santos Province, has a fine church containing many images. The History Museum on plaza is small but interesting, in lovely house and garden. (*Pensión Deportiva*, E, no single rooms, private showers; *Hotel La Villa de Los Santos*, C, a/c caravans, with swimming pool and good restaurant.) ***Las Tablas*** (7,070 people), capital of Los Santos (Hotels: *Oria*, out of town, C; *Piamonte*, C; *Pensión Mariela*, opposite, Calle Belisario Porras, E, basic, O.K.; *Pensión Marta*, E; swimming pool near National Guard barracks, US$0.25), has a picturesque and famous *fiesta* at Carnival time, just before Lent. Bus from Chitré, US$1, ½ hour (bus Las Tablas-Panama City leaves at 0930, US$6, 4½ hrs.). From Divisa to Las Tablas is 67 km.; the road runs on nearly 13 km. to the port of Mensabé. From Las Tablas it is possible to take a bus to ***Pedasí*** (leaves when full, US$2, 1½ hrs., very bad road) which has beautifully empty beaches with crystal clear sea 3 km. from town. *Pensión Moscoso*, E with shower, good, friendly (only place in town), meals arranged by owner at nearby bar. Most things in Pedasí, a peaceful colonial town, are run by the Moscoso clan, including, it seems, a charming wild fowl reserve near the beach, with storks and herons. You can drive from Las Tablas to Pedasí by an inland route: take the unsigned road to Flores, a small tropical village (no hotel), after which the road deteriorates to Tonosí and thence to Cañas. Between Cañas and Pedasí the road is good again; a sign points to the black-sand beach of Puerto Venado (small restaurant). After Pedasí, heading back to Las Tablas, a right turn at a white house goes to a beautiful, quiet beach (cross currents can make swimming dangerous, however).

About 53 km. W of Chitré, by road into the mountains, is ***Ocú*** (2,610 people), an old colonial town whose inhabitants wear traditional dress during the *fiesta* for its patron saint, San Sebastián, 19-24 January.

Hotel *Posada San Sebastián*, E.

Travel Ocú can be reached from David (see below) by taking a bus to the Ocú turning on the Pan-American Highway (US$4) and a colectivo from there (US$0.50). One bus a day to Chitré, and several minibuses from Chitré to Panama City, US$6. From Chitré, a bus can be taken to Las Minas in the mountains, and then another to Ocú, stay the night and take a bus on to Santiago.

The road from Divisa to Santiago, the next town, 37 km., runs across the Province of Veraguas, the only one which has seaboards on both oceans. It is very dry in the summer. ***Santiago*** (32,560 people), capital of the Province (bus from Penonomé, US$3, from Aguadulce, US$2), is well inland; one of the oldest towns in the country, in a grain-growing area (very good—and cheap—macramé bags are sold in the market here). Nearby is San Francisco; it has a wonderful old church with wooden images, altar pieces and pulpit.

Hotels in Santiago: *Motel Gran David*, on Pan-American Highway, D, a/c, TV, shower, clean, rec.; *Pensiones Continental*, *Central* and *Jigoneva*, all on Av. Central, close together, all E; *Pensión San José*, Av. Central (edge of town on Panama City road), E with bath and fan, good (good *pizzería* next door); *Piramidal* on Pan-Am Highway, D, a/c, TV, shower, clean, quiet, good pool, rec.; *Santiago* near the Cathedral, clean, D with a/c, T.V. and shower. *Fortuna*, D, Chinese-run, safe, a little unfriendly. Swimming pool near town centre, US$0.75.

W of Santiago is La Mesa, with a beautiful, white colonial church. The bad road through Soná (43 km., 5,000 people) in a deep fertile valley to Guabalá, near Remedios the country's largest stock-raising centre, has been replaced by a direct paved highway from Santiago to Guabalá. This saves a couple of hours. From Guabalá to David is 92 km.

17 km. W of Guabalá, on the highway, is a hotel just outside Las Lajas, D, with restaurant. No hotels in Las Lajas itself. Las Lajas has good beaches (no facilities, 2 bars, costly shade for cars—shark-infested waters). To get there take a bus from David to the turn off (US$2), then walk 3 km. to the town, from where it is 10 km. to the beach (taxis only, US$5).

David, 71,830 people, capital of Chiriquí Province, rich in timber, coffee, cacao, sugar, rice, bananas and cattle, is the third city of the Republic. It was founded in colonial times and has kept its traditions intact while modernizing itself. The town has a fine park and beautiful neighbourhoods. Airport (flights to Panama City and Changuinola). International fair and *fiesta*, 19 March.

Hotels *Siesta Motel*, B, on edge of town on the Pan-American Highway; *Fiesta*, B, on Pan-American Highway, good pool (US$2 for non-residents); *Nacional*, C, restaurant, pizzería, swimming pool (US$2 for non-residents), tennis court, rec.; *Pensión Fanita*, a/c rooms with bath, F, clean, noisy, basic, food fair. *Iris* in central square, D with bath and fan (a/c more), rec.; *Pensión Colonial*, clean, E; *La Fortuna*, ½ block from plaza, F, cold showers, fairly clean; *Hotel Valle de la Luna*, E, reasonable food; *Pensión Costa Rica*, Av. 5 Este, Calle B Sur, E with shower, F, in small, noisier rooms, toilet and fan, ask to see room first, some are very small; *David* and *Madrid* also E. Most cheap hotels are on Av. 5 Este.

Restaurants Many around central Parque Cervantes. *Parriada El Portal*, excellent but expensive; *J.C. Car Rental*, opp. *Hotel Nacional*, rec.; *McPato*, fast food; *Las Brasas*, café. *Don Dicky*, very good 24-hr. café, meals, friendly. Good cheap food at *Rocío*, Av. 5 Este. A few cheap places round bus station and the market. *Balneario Risacua*, on the Pan-American Highway, N end of town (follow Av. 6 Este to the river), has restaurant, very nice.

Entertainment Discotheques: *Brandy and Wine*, Av. 5 Este, nr. Fuerzas de Defensa building, young clientèle; *Jorón Sebede*, more national music, older set, both rec. Plaza and Imperial cinemas, by Parque Cervantes.

Car Hire Fecar, T 75-3246, reasonable.

Local Transport Urban buses US$0.20; agree taxi fares in advance.

Museum Regional and national history at Av. 8 Este, entry US$0.25.

Costa Rican Consulate above Citibank.

Post Office Calle C. Norte, 1 block from Parque Cervantes. **Cables** Intel, Calle C. Norte, telex and long-distance telephone.

Immigration just off Av. Central.

Tourist Office IPAT, Av. 3 Este, between Calle Central and A Sur, unfriendly; ask for details of hot springs in the vicinity.

Bus from Panama City: apart from Ticabus, ordinary buses, US$10.60 (7 hrs.), about every hour from 0700 to 1900, plus express buses at 1200 and at midnight, 5½ hrs., US$15 (try Transchiri, Calle 8, 7A-23). The municipal bus terminal is in Av. 3 de Noviembre. An alternative way to Panama City is to Santiago (US$6) and then to Panama City (US$6). There is a bus to San Isidro (Costa Rica) at 0600 and 1300, 6 hrs., US$8, and to San José (Costa Rica), one bus at 0800 (US$10) that leaves from outside the *Pensión Costa Rica*. Regular minibus to Boquete from bus station (US$1.20) 1 hr. Frequent "*frontera*" buses, US$1.50, 1½ hrs. Bus station in north of town.

Note: If driving S, stock up with food in David: it is much cheaper than in Panama City. It is difficult to change Costa Rican colones in David, but the Store Romero in main square gives a good rate of exchange.

Inland from David are the sparsely forested highlands of Chiriquí, rising to 3,474 metres at the extinct Barú volcano. The region favours coffee, fruit and flowers and is very beautiful, with mountain streams for bathing and fishing. A great variety of wildlife flourishes in the area. There is some camping. There is a road from David, through Dolega (swimming pool, good carnival 4 days before Ash Wednesday), to the mountain village of **Boquete**, at 900 metres, on the slopes of Chiriquí. It enjoys a spring-like climate the year round and has many attractions: good lodging and board, excellent river bathing, fishing, riding, and mountain climbing, but it is an expensive place. Around is a beautiful panorama of coffee plantations, orange groves, and gardens which grow the finest flowers in the country. Plenty of good walks, including paved road to summit of Barú volcano. It is possible to cash travellers' cheques in the small bank in plaza. *Feria de las Flores y el Café* held each year early April.

Hotels *Panamonte*, C, full board, in very attractive surroundings, rec. *Villa Lorena Cabañas*, US$50 per day for 4 people. Cheaper hotels: *Fundadores* and *Central*, both D; *Pensión Marilos*, D, English spoken, very clean and well run with excellent, cheap food; *Pensión Wing*, F; *Pensión Virginia*, F for cheapest rooms, clean, friendly, English spoken, good and cheap restaurant downstairs. *Coffee Bean*, a café on road into town, very friendly, English-speaking owner (they have a lioness—Elsa—caged!). Plenty of cheap eating places.

After David, a dirt road turns off to the right to Las Palmas, a pleasant orange-growing village which welcomes tourists. Just before the village is a waterfall where a single column of water falls into a pool, delightful for swimming and camping.

The road and a railway go from David to **Concepción** (24 km.; 11,830 people—*fiesta* end of January), from where one can visit the beautiful Highlands to the N (US$11 bus fare—Transchiri—from Panama City, US$0.50 from David). A road runs 29 km. N to **El Hato del Volcán** (Hotels: *Dos Ríos*, C; *California*, D; *Pensión Omaya*, E; *Pensión Hung Wang*, F—no singles. Plenty of cheap eating places) and on to Río Sereno

(*Hotel Los Andes*, D, good; private cars can cross into Costa Rica here, immigration at frontier post) or to **Cerro Punta** (*Hotel Cerro Punta*, C, good, attractive restaurant; *Pensión La Primavera*, E-D, no singles; several restaurants). There are mountain lakes nearby. Bus David-Volcán, US$2.30. At Bambito there is a luxury hotel which serves good but expensive meals, it has swimming pool, horse-riding, trout farm (in the off-season very good bargains can be had here). From Volcán to Cerro Punta (US$0.95 by bus) the road follows the Chiriquí Viejo river valley. Just beyond Cerro Punta lies the Finca Rogelio Rodriguez Argüello (only a 4-wheel drive vehicle can get to it), where Sr. José will show you the haunts of the quetzal; see the quetzal also at the Finca Fernández in the **Volcán National Park**, to which there is a good asphalt road. Cerro Punta itself, in a beautiful valley at 2,130 metres devoted to vegetables and flowers, has many fine walks in the crisp mountain air. One such is a 6-8 hour hike, mostly downhill after an initial climb, to Boquete (the track is clear in places and there are a few signs showing the direction and time—ambitious—to Boquete); the last part is down the Río Caldera canyon. Don't hike alone, take a machete and sufficient provisions for 2 days in case of mishap, wear ankle boots, and notify someone before leaving and on arrival. This hike is also recommended for bird watching. Concepción is 30 km. from the Costa Rican border at Paso Canoas by road (the border is open 0700-1200, 1400-1800, 1900-2200— remember Panama is 1 hr. ahead of Costa Rica).

Chiriquí Railway, S from Concepción to Puerto Armuelles, with passenger trains, one a day in each direction, irregular. There is also a "Finca Train", 4 decrepit, converted banana trucks, leaving at 1500 for the banana *fincas*, returning, by a different route, at 1800. No charge for passengers. Minibuses also leave all day for the *fincas*. Freight service only to David and to Pedregal.

Puerto Armuelles (12,975 people), is the port through which all the bananas grown in the area are exported. Puerto Armuelles and Almirante (Bocas del Toro) are the only ports in Panama outside the Canal area at which ocean-going vessels habitually call and anchor in deep water close inshore; there is now an oil transit pipeline across the isthmus between the two places.

Hotels *Pensión Balboa*, on waterfront, E, pleasant; *Pensión Trébol*, E, 1 block from waterfront. Plenty of cheap eating places, e.g. *Enrique's*, Chinese, good; *Club Social*, on water, ask any taxi, chicken and rice dishes.

THE NORTH-EASTERN CARIBBEAN COAST

Across the Cordillera from David, on the Caribbean side, are the once thriving but now depressed banana ports of **Bocas del Toro**, on the SE tip of Colón Island, and Almirante, on the SW side of Almirante Bay, the central office of the Chiriquí Land Company (the Panamanian subsidiary of The American Banana Company). Some of the plantations, destroyed by disease, have been converted to *abacá* and cacao, but are now being planted again, especially near **Changuinola** (airport with bank, open on Sat. till 1200). Unlike Almirante, which is a busy port, dirty and disorganized, Bocas del Toro deserves a visit (*fiesta* end September):

peaceful, quiet, English spoken by most of the black population. The protected bay offers all forms of water sport and diving, beautiful sunrises and sunsets, and, on land, tropical birds, butterflies and wild life. Excursions can be made to the islands of the archipelago (Bastimentos—see below, Carenero, Solarte), to Isla del Cisne, a bird sanctuary, and to the Islas Zapatillas, for beaches and fishing. Another tour is to a cacao plantation on Isla Cristóbal. Note that many of the names here relate to Columbus' landfall here on his fourth voyage in October 1502 (Carenero was where he careened his ships, Bastimentos where he took on supplies, etc.). The area has a rich buccaneering past, too. For details on tours; Ligia (Lee) Paget—to whom thanks for information are due, Turismo y Artesanías Bocatoreñas, Apdo Postal 5, Bocas del Toro (T 78-9309/9248), or Wilberto Martínez, Panama Nature Tours, Box 1223, Cristóbal, Colón (T 42-1340).

Hotels At Bocas del Toro; *Bahía* (D); *Pensión Peck*, F (Miss Peck is a charming hostess); *Botel Thomas*, on the sea, from D, T 78-9428/9309, Apartado 5, Bocas del Toro (postcards for sale). You will be met by hoteliers on arrival. At Changuinola: *Changuinola*, D, near airport; restaurant near market has rooms, also D; restaurant *El Caribe*, nr. airport, rec.; also nightclubs (*54* best), cinema and theatre. At Almirante: *Hong Kong*, D with a/c, cheaper without, *San Francisco*, E with bath, both very clean; *Pensión Colón*, E, basic, overpriced, uncertain water supply, friendly English-speaking owner; *Viajero*, E, secure—all hotels noisy. Bocas del Toro province is about 25% more expensive than the rest of Panama.

Transport Boat Almirante-Bocas del Toro, Tues., Thur., Sat. 0725, 1¼ hrs., US$0.50, *Isla Colón*. From Almirante, take ferry or *Almirante* launch (Mon., Wed., Fri. 0930) to Chiriquí Grande, 5 hrs. if lucky, US$7.50, from where a spectacular road runs over the mountains, passing the Cricamola Indian Reservation and the Fortuna hydroelectric plant, to connect with David, bus 3 hrs., US$6 (ferry Chiriquí Grande-Almirante Tues., Thurs., Sat. 1100, 5 hrs., US$0.80; *Hotel Buena Vista* in Chiriquí Grande, E; other accommodation on seafront). Alternatively Bocas del Toro and Changuinola can be reached by Aeroperlas, or Alas Chiricanas, both from Paitilla Airport (US$41) and David (US$21). There is a road from Changuinola to Almirante (buses every ½ hr. till 2000, US$1); a road is planned from Almirante to Chiriquí Grande.

Railways The banana railways provide links between Guabito on the Costa Rican frontier, Changuinola and Almirante. Trains leave Almirante 0735 and one later, for Changuinola (US$0.40, 45 mins., rec.), but only one on Thur., and one Sat. continuing to Guabito. Train stops often.

Excursion On Thurs. and Sun. the *Isla Colón* ferry leaves Bocas del Toro at 1300 for Bastimentos Island, a small community of blacks with a marvellous beach; good snorkelling about ½-hr. walk from the jetty. Return 1800, no charge.

Entering Panama from Costa Rica

The border at Sixaola-Guabito is open 0700-1100, 1300-1700, but only on Mon.-Thurs. can you guarantee with any certainty that officials will be on hand. Malaria test on entering Panama, entry charge US$10 (receipt given), 30 days given if you already have a visa, 5 days' entry card if not, US$2 (extensions at Changuinola airport immigration, opens 0830—5 passport photos, photographer nearby charges US$7 for 6). Advance clocks 1 hr. entering Panama.

No accommodation in Guabito; bus to Changuinola US$1, ¾ hr (every ½ hour until 2000). If seeking cheap accommodation, cross border as early as possible in order to get as far as Almirante.

DARIEN AND HOW TO GET TO COLOMBIA

By Land The Pan-American Highway runs E 60 km. from Panama City to the sizeable town of **Chepo**, full of friendly blacks. From Chepo the Highway has been completed to Yaviza, 240 km. from Panama City; it is gravel from Chepo until the last 30 km. which are of earth (sometimes impassable in rainy season). 35 km. E of Chepo it crosses the new Lago Bayano dam by bridge (the land to the N of the Highway as far as Cañazas is the Reserva Indígena del Bayano). The road will eventually link Panama with Colombia. (Bus to Chepo from Panama City leaves from Plaza 5 de Mayo.)

Darién East of Chepo is Darién, almost half the area of Panama and almost undeveloped. Most villages are accessible only by air or river and on foot. At Bahía Piñas is the *Tropic Star Lodge*, where a luxury fishing holiday may be enjoyed on the sea and in the jungle for over US$1,000 a week. (Information from *Hotel El Panamá*.)

The Darién Gap road will not be open for some years, so the usual way of getting to Colombia is by sea or air. It is possible to go overland: the journey is in fact more expensive than going by air, and while still challenging, the number of travellers going overland is increasing. The main villages (Yaviza, Pucuro, Paya and Cristales) have electricity, radios and cassette decks, canned food is available in Yaviza, Pucuro and Paya (but no gasoline), only the Chocó Indians and the Cuna women retain traditional dress. Prices are rising steeply and friendliness is declining; the route is also used for drug trafficking, with its attendant tensions. Venturers are advised to get *Backpacking in Mexico and Central America* (Bradt Publications, new edition expected in 1991), which contains special maps covering the whole route and background information on Indians, fauna and flora. Maps of the Darién area can be purchased from the Ministro de Obras Públicas, Instituto Geográfico Nacional Tommy Guardia, in Panama City (US$5, reported to contain serious mistakes). Talk to knowledgeable locals for the best advice. The best time to go is in the dry months (Jan.-mid April); in the wet season (from May) it is only recommended for the hardy. Organized jungle tours to Cuna Indians, Chocó Indians and the Río Bayano costing from US$65 to over US$300 can be purchased through Mar Go Tours, Aptdo 473, Balboa. The journey as described below takes about 7 days to the first house in Colombia.

There are 5 buses from Panamá to Yaviza between 0600 and 1200, US$15, 10 hrs. This service has its problems, the road is bad and may be washed out after rains. Find out before you leave how far you can get. Alternatively there is an irregular boat, about three times a week. The only sleeping accommodation is the deck and there is one primitive toilet for about 120 people. The advertised travel time is 16 hours, but it can take as much as 28. There is only one hotel at **Yaviza** (*Three Américas*, E, basic, meals available but not very sanitary); there is a TB clinic run by a Canadian (who appreciates classical music), and a hospital. Crossing the river in Yaviza costs US$0.25. From Yaviza it is an easy walk, with two river crossings by dugout, US$1 each, to Pinogana, 2 hrs on foot (small and primitive) and by motor dugout from Pinogana to Boca de Cupe (about US$15 p.p.). Or you can take a boat from Yaviza to El Real (US$10), stay at the Touricenter of Gringo Gery (very nice and friendly people) and from there a motor dugout to

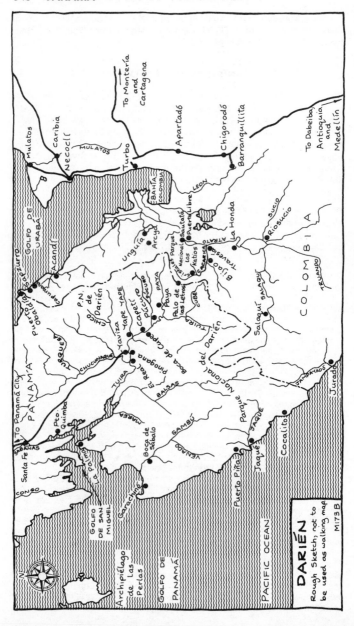

Boca de Cupe, about US$12 p.p., (if possible, take a banana dugout, otherwise bargain hard on boats). There are also boats from Panama City (at the harbour by the market in the old town) to El Real for US$12 p.p. inc. meals. Boats from El Real are not very frequent and may only go as far as Unión de Chocó or Pinogana.

Stay the night at **Boca de Cupe** with a family; food and cold beer on sale here. You can go with Chocó Indians to Unión de Chocó, stay one or two days with them and share some food (they won't charge for lodging). Chocós are very friendly and shy, better not to take pictures (US$5 after bargaining). In Boca de Cupe get your exit stamp and keep your eye on your luggage. Lodging in Boca de Cupe for US$12.50 with Antonio (son of María who helped many hikers crossing Darién, but who died in 1989). From Boca de Cupe to Pucuro, dugout, between US$15 and US$30, to Paya (if river level high enough) US$60.

Pucuro is a Cuna Indian village and it is customary to ask the chief's permission to stay (he will ask to see your passport). Visitors usually stay in the assembly house. People show little interest in travellers there; stop with your luggage. From Pucuro you can walk through lush jungle to Paya, 5-6 hrs. (guide costs US$20, not really necessary, do not pay in advance), which was the capital of the Cuna empire. From Pucuro to Paya you have to cross the river 4 times.

In **Paya** you may be able to stay in the assembly house at the village, but it is mandatory to go 2 km. away eastwards to the barracks. You can stay there, rec. (passport check and baggage search), and for a small fee you will get meals. The Cuna Indians in Paya are more friendly than in Pucuro. From Paya there are two routes.

First, from Paya, the next step is a 4-6 hr. walk to Palo de las Letras, the frontier stone, where you enter Los Katios, one of Colombia's National Parks (see below). On reaching the left bank of the Tulé river (in 3 hrs., no water between these points), you follow it downstream, which involves 7 crossings (at the third crossing the trail almost disappears, so walk along the river bed—if possible—to the next crossing). About ½ hr. after leaving this river you cross a small creek; 45 mins. further on is the abandoned camp of the Montadero, near where the Tulé and Pailón rivers meet to form the River Cacarica. Cross the Cacarica and follow the trail to the Inderena (Colombian National Parks) hut at Cristales (7 hrs. from Palo de las Letras). Guides Paya-Cristales (they always go in pairs), US$50. If you insist on walking beyond Montadero, a machete, compass and fishing gear (or extra food) are essential; the path is so overgrown that it is easier, when the river is low, to walk and swim down it (Cristales is on the left bank, so perhaps it would be better to stick to this side). The rangers at Cristales (friendly) may sell you food, will let you sleep at the hut, cook, and will take you by dugout to Bijao (or Viajado), 1½ hrs., for around US$10 (they will try to charge US$30). At Bijao ask for the Inderena station, where you can eat and sleep (floor space, or camp). From Bijao a motor dugout runs to Cacarica (also called Puerto América) for US$30 (3 hrs.), from where motorboats go to Turbo for US$10 (in scheduled boat—if it stops; if not it'll cost you about US$130 to hire a boat). One *residencial* and a shop in Cacarica. There is nowhere to get your Colombian entry stamp in Turbo; you can try in Apartado several km. south, but you will probably have to wait until Cartagena and then explain yourself in great detail to DAS there. The problems with this route are mostly on the Colombian side, where route finding is difficult, the undergrowth very difficult to get through, and the terrain steep. Any rain adds greatly to the difficulties.

The **Katios National Park** (**Warning**: entry by motorized vehicle is prohibited), extending to Colombia to the Panamanian border, can be visited with mules from the Inderena headquarters in Sautatá (rangers may offer free accommodation, very friendly). In the park is the Tilupo waterfall, 125 metres high; the water cascades down a series of rock staircases, surrounded by orchids and fantastic plants. Also in the park are the Alto de la Guillermina, a mountain behind which is a strange forest of palms called "mil pesos", and the Ciénagas de Tumaradó, with red monkeys, waterfowl and alligators.

The second route from Paya is a stenuous hike up the Paya river valley through dense jungle (macheté country) for about 12 hours to the last point on the Paya (fill up with water), then a further 3 hours to the continental divide where you cross into Colombia. Down through easier country (3-4 hrs.) brings you to Unguía (accommodation, restaurants) where motor boats are available to take you down the Río Tarena, out into the Gulf of Urabá, across to Turbo. This trip should not be taken without a guide, though you may be lucky and find an Indian, or a group of Indians making the journey and willing to take you along. They will appreciate a gift when you arrive in Unguía. Hazards include blood-sucking ticks, the inevitable mosquitoes and, above all, thirst.

Dr Richard Dawood, author of *Travellers' Health: How to Stay Healthy Abroad*, and photographer Anthony Dawton, crossed the Darien Gap at the end of the wet season (November). We are pleased to include Dr Dawood's health recommendations for such a journey: **Heat** Acclimatization to a hot climate usually takes around 3 weeks. It is more difficult in humid climates than in dry ones, since sweat cannot evaporate easily, and when high humidity persists through the night as well, the body has no respite. (In desert conditions, where the temperature falls at night, adaptation is much easier.) Requirements for salt and water increase dramatically under such conditions. We had to drink 12 litres per day to keep pace with our own fluid loss on some parts of the trip.

We were travelling under extreme conditions, but it is important to remember that the human thirst sensation is not an accurate guide to true fluid requirements. In hot countries it is always essential to drink beyond the point of thirst quenching, and to drink sufficient water to ensure that the urine is consistently pale in colour.

Salt losses also need to be replaced. Deficiency of salt, water, or both, is referred to as heat exhaustion; lethargy, fatigue, and headache are typical features, eventually leading to coma and death. Prevention is the best approach, and we used the pre-salted water regime pioneered by Colonel Jim Adam and followed by the British Army; salt is added to all fluids, one quarter of a level teaspoon (approx 1 gram) per pint—to produce a solution that is just below the taste theshold. Salt tablets, however, are poorly absorbed, irritate the stomach and may cause vomiting; plenty of pre-salted fluid should be the rule for anyone spending much time outdoors in the tropics.

Sun Overcast conditions in the tropics can be misleading. The sun's rays can be fierce, and it is important to make sure that all exposed skin is constantly protected with a high factor sun screen—preferably waterproof for humid conditions. This was especially important while we were travelling by canoe. A hat was also essential.

Food and Water Diarrhoea can be annoying enough in a luxurious holiday resort with comfortable sanitary facilities. The inconvenience under jungle conditions would have been more than trivial, however, with the added problem of coping with further fluid loss and dehydration.

Much caution was therefore needed with food hygiene. We carried our own supplies, which we prepared carefully ourselves: rather uninspiring camping fare, such as canned tuna fish, sardines, pasta, dried soup, biscuits and dried fruit. In the villages, oranges, bananas and coconuts were available. The freshly baked bread was safe, and so would have been the rice.

We purified our water with 2 per cent tincture of iodine carried in a small plastic dropping bottle, 4 drops to each litre—more when the water is very turbid—wait 20 minutes before drinking. This method is safe and effective, and is the only suitable technique for such conditions. (Another suggestion from Peter Ovenden is a water purifying pump based on a ceramic filter. There are several on the market, Peter used a Katadyn. It takes about a minute to purify a litre of water—Ed.) It is also worth travelling with a suitable antidiarrhoeal medication such as Arret.

Malaria Drug resistant malaria is present in the Darien area, and antimalarial medication is essential. We took Paludrine, two tablets daily, and chloroquine, two tablets weekly. Free advice on antimalarial medication for all destinations is available from the Malaria Reference Laboratory, T (071) 636 8636 in the UK. An insect repellent is also essential, and so are precautions to avoid insect bites.

Insects Beside malaria and yellow fever, other insect-borne diseases such as dengue fever and leishmaniasis may pose a risk. The old fashioned mosquito net is ideal if you have to sleep outdoors, or in a room that is not mosquito-proof. Mosquito nets for hammocks are widely available in Latin America. An insecticide spray is valuable for clearing your room of flying insects before you go to sleep, and mosquito coils that burn through the night giving off an insecticidal vapour, are also valuable.

Ticks It is said that ticks should be removed by holding a lighted cigarette close to them, and we had an opportunity to put this old remedy to the test. We duly unwrapped a pack of American duty-frees that we had preserved carefully in plastic just for such a purpose, as our Indian guides looked on in amazement, incredulous that we should use these prized items for such a lowly purpose. The British Army expedition to Darien in 1972 carried 60,000 cigarettes among its supplies, and one wonders if they were for this purpose! The cigarette method didn't work, but caused much amusement. (Further discussion with the experts indicates that the currently favoured method is to ease the tick's head gently away from the skin with tweezers.)

Vaccinations A yellow fever vaccination certificate is required from all travellers arriving from infected areas, and vaccination is advised for personal protection.

Immunization against hepatitis A (with gammaglobulin) and typhoid are strongly advised.

Attacks by dogs are relatively common: the new rabies vaccine is safe and effective, and carrying a machete for the extra purpose of discouraging animals is advised.

In addition, all travellers should be protected against tetanus, diptheria and polio.

You can get some food along the way, but take enough for at least 5 days. Do take, though, a torch/flashlight, and a bottle of rum for the ranger at Cristales. It is highly recommended to travel in the dry season only, when there is no mud and fewer mosquitoes. If you have time, bargains can be found.

Taking a motorcycle through Darién is not an endeavour to be undertaken lightly, and cannot be recommended. Ed Culberson (who, in 1986 after two unsuccessful attempts, was the first to accomplish the feat) writes: "Dry season passage is comparatively easy on foot and even with a bicycle. But it simply cannot be done with a standard sized motorcycle unless helped by Indians at a heavy cost in dollars...It is a very strenuous, dangerous adventure, often underestimated by motorcyclists, some who have come to untimely ends in the jungle." Culberson's account of his Journey (in the October 1986 issue of *Rider*) makes harrowing reading, not least his encounter with an emotionally unstable police offical in Bijao; the 29-mile "ride" from Pucuro to Palo de las Letras took 6 days with the help of 6 Indians (at US$8 a day each).

By Sea There are about two boats a week from Colón for San Andrés Island (**see** page 662), from which there are connections with Cartagena; the *Johnny Walker* takes 30 hours, costs US$20, including food, but the service is very irregular and travellers have sometimes waited over a week in vain. Boats also leave, irregularly, the Coco Solo wharf in Colón (minibus from Calle 12, 15 mins., US$0.30) for Puerto Obaldía, via the San Blas Islands. There is also a light plane at 0600 from Panama City to Puerto Obaldía 3 times a week (Mon., Wed., Fri.) for US$37 single, Aerolíneas Nacíonales (SAANSA, T 26-78-91, book well in advance). There are boats from Puerto Obaldía (after clearing Customs) to Turbo, on the Gulf of Urabá, US$15 p.p., 10-18 hrs. (take shade and drinks), from which Medellín can be reached by road. Walk from Puerto Obaldía to Zapzurro for a dugout to Turbo, US$10. It seems that most of the boats leaving Puerto Obaldía for Colombian ports are contraband boats. There are also (contraband) boats from Coco Solo, Colón, to the Guajira Peninsula, Colombia. 70 tough hours (minimum). 3-day journey, US$25, uncomfortable, and entirely at your own risk; captains of these boats are reluctant to carry travellers (and you may have to wait days for a sailing—the customs officials will let you sleep in the wind-shadow of their office, will watch your luggage and let you use the sanitary facilities). Once in Colombia, it's a 6-7 hr. ride on top of a truck to Maicao, where you must take a US$0.85 colectivo ride to the Venezuelan border to go through Colombian entry formalities. A passenger travelling in a contraband boat had some problems in the DAS office about getting an entrance stamp: they wanted official papers from the boat's captain showing that he brought him in. You have to bargain for your fare on these boats. Accommodation is a little primitive. There is a good *pensión* in Puerto Obaldía: *Residencia Cande*, nice and clean (E) which also serves very good meals for US$1.50. Book in advance for meals. Also in Puerto Obaldía are shops, Colombian consulate, Panamanian immigration, but nowhere to change travellers' cheques until well into Colombia (not Turbo). Alternatively one can get from Puerto Obaldía to Acandi on the Colombian side of the border, either by walking nine hours or by hiring a dugout or a launch to Capurgana (US$60), thence another launch at 0715, 1 hr., US$3. Several *pensiones* in Capurgana. To walk to Capurgana takes 3-4 hrs., guide not essential (they charge US$20); first to go to La Miel (2 hrs.), then to Zapzurro (20 mins.), where there are shops and cabins for rent, then 1-112 hrs. to Capurgana. Most of the time the path follows the coast, but there are some hills to cross (which are hot—take drinking water). From Acandi frequent but irregular boats go Turbo (US$8, 3 hrs.).

Dale De Graaf of Grand Rapids, Minn. and Paul K. Kirk of Stockton, Calif. have sent us details of an **alternative route** through the Darién Gap to Colombia: Although not quick, it is relatively straightforward (spoken Spanish is essential). Take a bus from Panama (Plaza 5 de Mayo) to Santa Fe, a rough but scenic 6-8 hours (US$8, 3 a day, check times). In Santa Fe it is possible to camp near the national guard post (no *pensiones*). Then hitch a ride on a truck (scarce), or walk 2 hrs. to the Sabanas River at Puerto Lardo (11 km.) where you must take a dugout or launch to La Palma, or hire one (US$5, 2 hrs.; also reached by boat from Yaviza, US$3, 8 hrs.—bank changes travellers' cheques in La Palma). **La Palma** is the capital of Darién; it has one *pensión* (friendly, English-speaking owners, F, pricey, with cooking and laundry facilities, or see if you can stay with the *guardia*). Wait for a flight to Jaqué (US$25, you may have to return to Panama City with the plane first—no one seems to know), near Puerto Piña, 50 km. N of the Colombian border. Alternatively, at the Muelle Fiscal in Panama City (next to the main waterfront market, near Calle 13), ask for a passenger boat going to Jaqué.

The journey takes 18 hours, is cramped and passengers cook food themselves, but costs only US$10. Jaqué (pop. 1,000) is only reached by sea or air (the airstrip is used mostly by the wealthy who come for sport fishing); there are small stores with few fruit and vegetables, a good *comedor*, one *hospedaje* (but it is easy to find accommodation with local families), and camping is possible anywhere on the beautiful 4 km. beach. The guard post is open every day and gives exit stamps. Canoes from Jaqué go to Jurado (US$20) or Bahía Solano (US$45, 160 km., with two overnight stops) in Chocó. The first night is spent in Jurado (where the boat's captain may put you up and the local military commander may search you out of curiosity). There are flights from Jurado to Turbo. Bahía Solano is a deep-sea fishing resort with an airport and *residencias*. Get your Colombian entry stamp here. Flights from Bahía Solano go to Quibdó, US$18, connecting to Cali, US$30 (with Satena), or Medellín (all flights have to be booked in advance; the town is popular with Colombian tourists). On this journey, you sail past the lush, mountainous Pacific coast of Darién and Chocó, with its beautiful coves and beaches, and you will see a great variety of marine life.

N.B. It is not easy to get a passage to any of the larger Colombian ports as the main shipping lines rarely take passengers. Those that do are booked up well in advance. The Agencias Panamá company, Muelle 18, Balboa, represents Delta Line and accepts passengers to Buenaventura (US$90). Anyone interested in using the Delta Line ships should book a passage before arriving in Panama. The only easy way of getting to Colombia is to fly. Copa, SAM and Lacsa fly to Medellín, Cartagena and Barranquilla.

Shipping agencies have not the authority to charge passages. Many travellers think they can travel as crew on cargo lines, but this is not possible because Panamanian law requires all crew taken on in Panama to be Panamanian nationals.

Colombia officially demands an exit ticket from the country. If you travel by air the tickets should be bought outside Panama and Colombia, which have taxes on all international air tickets. If you buy air tickets from IATA companies, they can be refunded. Copa tickets can be refunded in Cartagena (Calle Santos de Piedra 3466—takes 4 days), Barranquilla—2 days, Cali or Medellín. Refunds in pesos only. Copa office in Panama City, Av. 3 Sur, Calle 39 Este. One traveller has told us that the Colombian consulate at Panama City required him to buy a Miscellaneous Charges Order (US$100) which was not required at Cali airport (Colombia). Those who do not want to go to Panama can fly from San José (Costa Rica) to San Andrés and on to Cartagena cheaply.

Shipping a Vehicle from Panama to Colombia, Venezuela or Ecuador is not easy or cheap. The cheapest we have heard of is US$500, but this was arranged in the home country (Netherlands). Inair, T 66-11-98, are very helpful and offer a variety of destinations, e.g. Curaçao (US$2,000 for Land Rover and driver). The best advice is to shop around the agencies in Panama City or Colón to see what is available when you want to go. Both local and international lines take vehicles, and sometimes passengers, but schedules and prices are very variable. With a great deal of luck you might get one of the sugar boats bringing cargo to Aguadulce (**page** 641) to ship you and your car to Colombia. One traveller was lucky and it cost him only US$100. Another arranged to ship his car (within 24 hours) to Guayaquil for US$400 plus US$75 per day for passengers, a 4 day trip. The Captain later agreed to take the car on to Valparaíso, Chile, for no extra charge.

Sometimes, if enough vehicles are collected together, it is possible to charter a boat to Buenaventura from the Zócalo (Nuevo Panamá). One secret here is to go to the Hipódromo in Panama City because there are usually enough cars there to form a party at least once a month. The groups will then rent a local freighter (a customs agent is necessary for the group, and this is included in the price). It is considered the best way to go south, and drivers and cars arrive at the same time. The regular shipping companies are not interested in this business, so they raise prices to discourage customers. In addition to freight charges there are, of course, handling charges of about US$25. Very few lines take passengers; if you do succeed in getting a passage it may cost as much as US$180. (A plane ticket to the port of arrival can cost up to US$150.) Lykes Line (head office: New Orleans) runs a fortnightly ship to Cartagena (preferable—car costs US$1,520) and Barranquilla in Colombia. Lykes takes passengers but it is more expensive than flying.

A cheaper alternative to the above-named lines is to try to ship on one of the small freighters that occasionally depart from Coco Solo Wharf in Colón, which allow you to travel with your car. Obviously there is a considerable element of risk involved though the financial cost is far lower. Shipping a bicycle, with rider, from Colón to Cartagena on a freighter cost US$100 in 1990. In Balboa shipping arrangements can be made at Agencias Panamá, whose office is located just outside the entrance to Pier 18; they act as agents for most shipping lines. It is possible to sleep in your car when loading at Pier 18; there is a good and cheap restaurant inside the dock.

Once you have a bill of lading, have it stamped by a Colombian consulate. The consulate also provides tourist cards. They require proof, in the form of a letter from your Embassy (or the Embassy representing your country in Panama) that you do not intend to sell the car in Colombia, though this requirement is usually dispensed with. Then go to the customs office in Panama City (Calle 80 and 55) to have the vehicle cleared for export. After that the vehicle details must be removed from your passport at the customs office at the port of departure. In Colón the customs office is behind the post office. The utmost patience is needed for this operation as regulations change frequently, so do not expect it to be the work of a few minutes.

Some small freighters go only to intermediate ports such as San Andrés, and it is then necessary to get another freighter to Cartagena; a couple had to wait for a week in San Andrés to make the connection. From Colón to San Andrés takes 2 days and from San Andrés to Cartagena takes 3 days. There are two boats plying regularly between Colón (Pier 3) and San Andrés that are big enough for vans, but there is no schedule; they leave when they finish loading. There are also two regular boats between San Andrés and Cartagena; each stays in port about 15 days, but it can be longer.

Customs formalities at the Colombian end will take 1-3 days to clear (customs officials do not work at weekends); check in advance if a *Carnet de Passages* is required. Make sure the visa you get from the Colombian consulate in Colón is *not* a 15 day non-extendable transit visa, but a regular tourist visa, because it is difficult to get an extension of the original visa. Clearance from the Colombian consul at the Panamanian port of embarkation may reduce the bureaucracy when you arrive in Colombia, but it will cost you US$10. In Colombia you can pay an agent US$15 to deal with the paperwork for you, which can reduce the aggravation if not the waiting time. It is understood that Cartagena is much more efficient (and therefore less expensive) as far as paperwork is concerned.

Do not ship or fly your vehicle to Ecuador without the *Carnet de Passages*, or you may be held up for up to two weeks at customs, and only allowed to continue to Peru with a police escort!

It is also possible to ship a vehicle to **Venezuela**. A correspondent in 1989 took a VW microbus from Cristóbal to Puerto Cabello (more usually La Guaira) for US$550, via Vencaribe (a Venezuelan line), agent in Cristóbal: Associated Steamship, T 52-12-58 (Panamá), 45-04-61 (Cristóbal). There are several agencies in Colón/Cristóbal across the street from the Chase Manhattan Bank and next door to the YMCA building. Formalities before leaving can be completed through a travel agency—recommended is Continental Travel Agency, at the *Hotel Continental*, T 63-61-62—Rosina Wong was very helpful. Another 1989 correspondent had a similar experience with an AMC Eagle 4-door estate, 4 WD, same cost via Vencaribe. There are additional costs for paperwork (a Sr. Henríquez is a recommended customs agent) and "Servillantes" opposite *Hotel Carlton* (Colón) very helpful for storage prior to shipment.

Warning The contents of your vehicle are shipped at your own risk—generally considered to be a high one! One reader who escaped theft had chained two padlocked, wooden boxes to the car seats.

Air-freighting a Vehicle: Most people ship their vehicles from Panama to South America but some find air-freighting much more convenient. Generally it is faster and avoids many of the unpleasant customs hassles, but is more expensive. Prices vary considerably. The major carriers (Avianca, Ecuatoriana) charge about US$3,000 for a VW bus, US$1,500 for a 4-wheel drive Subaru station wagon, but the cargo lines and independents can offer more reasonable prices (US$800 to US$1,250). Prices and availability change from month to month depending on the demand by regular commercial shippers. You are generally not allowed to accompany the vehicle. Taking a motorcycle (BMW R100RS) from Panama to Medellín by Copa: driver US$110, bike US$0.62 per litre (charged either by volume or by litre). Líneas Aéreas Caribe (LAC) cargo line may fly your motorcycle to Bogotá for US$300 and has been known to allow rider to accompany. Contact Cargo International at the cargo terminal, Panama City airport. Drain oil and gasoline, and remove battery before loading; the bike goes in with just an inch to spare so you must expect a scratch or two. Mr Barham at the Copa office is most helpful. Having bought your passenger ticket, and checked bike in at Copa Cargo, old Tocumen airport, go to customs in Ancón (**see page** 638) with your entry permit and freight papers, and pay US$4.20 to have stamp cancelled in passport. Then take your airweighbill to the Colombian Consulate for stamping 3 hrs. before flight time. Allow 2 days in Panama. Retrieving the bike in Colombia, although costing very little, will take from 0900 to 1630 for paperwork.

INFORMATION FOR VISITORS

Documents Visitors must have a passport, together with a tourist card (issued for 30 days and renewable for another 60) or a visa (issued for 90 days). Holders of visas require exit permits unless they stay in Panama less than 48 hrs.; holders of tourist cards (US$2 from Panamanian consulates, Ticabus or airlines, valid 30 days, renewable in Panama City) do not need exit permits. **Customs at Paso Canoas**, at the border with Costa Rica, have been known to run out of tourist cards. If not entering Panama at the main entry points (Tocumen airport, Paso Canoas), expect more complicated arrangements. Neither visas nor tourist cards are required by nationals of Costa Rica, the Dominican Republic, El Salvador, Western Germany, Honduras, Spain, Switzerland and the UK, but if the stay in Panama exceeds 30 days they must obtain an exit permit from the authorities in Panama City. Finnish visitors do not need a visa provided they have an onward ticket out of the country. The procedure for obtaining an exit permit is: take your passport to the Ministerio de Hacienda y Tesoro, Av. Perú y Calle 35 E, to obtain a *Paz y Salvo* form (US$0.25); then go to Oficina de Migración, Av. Cuba y Calle 28 E, where the *Paz y Salvo* will eventually be stuck into your passport, and you are given an exit stamp covering the week beginning on the date you went to the office.

US and Japanese citizens need a visa (US$5 to the former, US$20 for the latter, produced in the same day); Australians need a visa (US$10) and Canadians need one (US$10). Tourist cards may not be issued to citizens of Communist countries, India and Pakistan, who must have visas. Onward tickets are required, with the exception of travellers in their own vehicles (hitch-hikers in vehicles may get away without being checked). Once in Panama, you cannot get a refund for an onward flight ticket unless you have another exit ticket. Copa tickets can be refunded at any office in any country (in the currency of that country). **Note**: You may be asked to show that you have at least US$150, or US$10 for each day of intended stay if that exceeds 15 days, before being allowed in. (However, several people have told us that the Panamanian customs are not always that strict in this respect. On the other hand, young Europeans have been strip-searched on arrival by air.)

Taxes An airport tax of US$15 has to be paid by all passengers. If you stay longer than 30 days, the tax rises to US$30. There is a 4% tax on air tickets purchased in Panama.

Air Services From London: British Airways, Pan Am, Continental or Virgin Atlantic to Miami, then by American, Pan Am, Copa, AeroPerú, or LAB to Panama City. From elsewhere in North America: New York City, Pan Am, Ecuatoriana; from Los Angeles, Varig, LAN-Chile, Taca (via San Salvador); from Houston, Continental, Taca. From Mexico, connections with Lacsa via San José, Taca via San Salvador, or via Miami. From Central America, Copa, Iberia (Guatemala City; also to Santo Domingo), KLM (Guatemala City and to the Netherlands Antilles), Copa, Lacsa (to San José, to connect with its Central American network and Los Angeles/Mexico/Miami/New Orleans/ San Juan-Puerto Rico routes), Sahsa and Aeronica (to Managua, San Salvador, Mexico, San José). Copa also flies to Kingston, Port-au-Prince and Santo Domingo. From South America, Lacsa (Barranquilla, Caracas), Copa, (Barranquilla, Cartagena, Medellín). To Bogotá via Medellín by SAM, be at airport very early because it can leave before time; also to Cali with Avianca. Other carriers are LAN-Chile, Avianca, Ecuatoriana, Varig, Avensa, Lloyd Aéreo Boliviano, SAM, Aerolíneas Argentinas, LAP, AeroPerú. From Europe, Iberia, KLM.

Customs Even if you only change planes in Panama you must have the necessary papers for the airport officials. Cameras, binoculars, etc., 500 cigarettes or 500 grams of tobacco and 3 bottles of alcoholic drinks for personal use are taken in free. The Panamanian Customs are strict; drugs without a doctor's prescription and books deemed "subversive" are confiscated. In the latter case, a student's or teacher's card helps. **Note**: Passengers leaving Panama by land are *not* entitled to any duty-free goods, which are delivered only to ships and aircraft.

Internal Air Services There are local flights to most parts of Panama by the national airlines Copa and Ansa.

Motoring Coming in by car from Costa Rica, passport is stamped for 3 days for a car or motorcycle at frontier (passengers get 30 days). Then go to David or Panama City for extensions. Entry costs US$5.20 (no change given!) plus US$1 for fumigation. Exit calls for 4 papers which also cost US$4.20 (obtainable, as are extensions for entry permits, from Customs in Ancón, off Curundu Road, near Albrook air base). Taking a car with Panamanian plates to Costa Rica requires a lot of paperwork, e.g. proof of ownership, proof that the vehicle has not been stolen, etc. A travel agency e.g. Chedwick's in Balboa, will arrange this for you, for US$30. Rental cars are not allowed out of the country; they are marked by special license plates. Low octane gasoline costs US$1.90 per gallon, super grade US$1.98. For motorcyclists, note that a crash helmet must be worn. **Note** that you may not take dogs into Panama by car, though they may be flown or shipped in if they have general health and rabies certificates; dogs and cats now have to spend 40 days in quarantine after entry.

Warning It is virtually impossible for a tourist to sell a car in Panama unless he /she can show (with help from the Consulate) that he/she needs the money for a fare home. Import duty on the sale will have to be paid. There is an office with English-speaking staff in the same building as the Diablo Height supermarket (in the street across the railway from the main entry of Albrook air base), which deals with license plates, transfer of titles. A great many US service personnel use this facility. There is a bulletin board outside.

What to Eat Best hors d'oeuvre is *carimañola*, cooked mashed yuca wrapped round a savoury filling of chopped seasoned fried pork and fried a golden brown. The traditional stew, *sancocho*, made from chicken, yuca, dasheen, cut-up corn on the cob, plantain, potatoes, onions, flavoured with salt, pepper and coriander. *Ropa vieja*, shredded beef mixed with fried onions, garlic, tomatoes and green peppers and served with white rice, baked plantain or fried yuca. *Sopa borracha*, a rich sponge cake soaked in rum and garnished with raisins and prunes marinated in sherry. Panama is famous for its seafood: lobsters, corvina, shrimp, tuna, etc. Piquant *seviche* is usually corvina or white fish seasoned with tiny red and yellow peppers, thin slices of onion and marinated in lemon juice; it is served very cold and has a bite. *Arroz con coco y tití* is rice with coconut and tiny dried shrimp. Plain coconut rice is also delicious. For low budget try *comida corriente* or *del día* (US$1.50 or so). Corn (maize) is eaten in various forms, depending on season, e.g. *tamales*, made of corn meal mash filled with cooked chicken or pork, olives and prunes; or *empanadas*, toothsome meat pies fried crisp. Plantain, used as a vegetable, appears in various forms. A fine dessert is made from green plantain flour served with coconut cream. Other desserts are *arroz con cacao*, chocolate rice pudding; *buñuelos de viento*, a puffy fritter served with syrup; *sopa de gloria*, sponge cake soaked in cooked cream mixture with rum added; *guanábana* ice cream is made from sweet ripe soursop.

Tipping at hotels, restaurants: 10% of bill. Porters, 15 cents per item. Cloakroom, 25 cents. Hairdressers, 25 cents. Cinema usherettes, nothing. Taxi drivers don't expect tips; rates should be arranged before the trip.

Health No particular precautions are necessary. Water in Panama City and Colón is safe to drink. Yellow fever vaccination is recommended before visiting Darién. Malaria prophylaxis for that area is highly recommended. It is currently very difficult to obtain chloroquine in Panama; stock up before arrival. In fact, stock up with all medicines, they are very costly in Panama. Hospital treatment is also expensive; insurance underwritten by a US company would be of great help.

Clothing Light weight tropical type clothes for men, light cotton or linen dresses for women, for whom the wearing of trousers is quite OK. The dry season, January-April, is the pleasantest time. Heavy rainfall sometimes in October and

November.

Hours of Business Government departments, 0800-1200, 1230-1630 (Mon. to Fri.). Banks: open and close at different times, but are usually open all morning, but not on Sat. British Embassy: 0800-1330 and 1430-1630 Mon. to Fri. Shops and most private enterprises: 0700 or 0800-1200 and 1400-1800 or 1900 every day, including Sat.

Business interests are concentrated in Panama City and Colón.

British business travellers are advised to get "Hints to Exporters: Panama", on application to the Export Services Division, Department of Trade, Sanctuary Buildings, 16-20 Great Smith Street, London SW1P 4DB.

Public Holidays 1 Jan.: New Year's Day; 9 Jan.: National Mourning Shrove Tuesday: Carnival. Good Friday; 1 May: Labour Day (Republic); 15 Aug.: (Panama City only, O); 11 Oct.: National Revolution Day; 1 Nov.: National Anthem Day (O); 2 Nov.: All Souls (O); 3 Nov.: Independence Day; 4 Nov.: Flag Day (O); 5 Nov.: Independence Day (Colón only); 10 Nov.: First Call of Independence; 28 Nov.: Independence from Spain; 8 Dec.: Mothers' Day; 25 Dec.: Christmas Day.

O=Official holiday, when banks and government offices close. On the rest—national holidays—business offices close too. Many others are added at short notice.

Festivals The *fiestas* in the towns are well worth seeing. That of Panama City at Carnival time, held on the four days before Ash Wednesday, is the best. During carnival women who can afford it wear the *pollera* dress, with its "infinity of diminutive gathers and its sweeping skirt finely embroidered", a shawl folded across the shoulders, satin slippers, tinkling pearl hair ornaments in spirited shapes and colours. The men wear a *montuno* outfit: native straw hats, embroidered blouses and trousers sometimes to below the knee only, and carry the *chácara*, or small purse. There is also a splendid local Carnival at Las Tablas, west of Panama City.

At the Holy Week ceremonies at Villa de Los Santos the farces and acrobatics of the big devils—with their debates and trials in which the main devil accuses and an angel defends the soul—the dance of the "dirty little devils" and the dancing drama of the Montezumas are all notable. The ceremonies at Pesé (near Chitré) are famous all over Panama. At Portobelo, near Colón, there is a procession of little boats in the canals of the city.

There are, too, the folk-tunes and dances. The music is cheerful, combining the rhythms of Africa with the melodic tones and dance-steps of Andalusia, to which certain characteristics of the Indian pentatonic scale have been added. The *tamborito* is the national dance. Couples dance separately and the song— which is sung by the women only, just as the song part of the *mejorana* or *socavón* is exclusively for male voices—is accompanied by the clapping of the audience and three kinds of regional drums. The *mejorana* is danced to the music of native guitars and in the interior are often heard the laments known as the *gallo* (rooster), *gallina* (hen), *zapatero* (shoemaker), or *mesano*. Two other dances commonly seen at *fiestas* are the *punto*, with its promenades and foot tapping, and the *cumbia*, of African origin, in which the dancers carry lighted candles and strut high.

The Guaymí Indians of Chiriquí province meet around 12 February to transact tribal business, hold feasts and choose mates by tossing balsa logs at one another; those unhurt in this contest, known as Las Balserías, are allowed to select the most desirable women.

Official time : GMT minus 5 hrs.

Currency Panama is one of the few countries in the world which issues no paper money; US banknotes are used exclusively, being called balboas instead of dollars. There are silver coins of 50c (called a *peso*), 25c, 10c, nickel of 5c (called a *real*) and copper of 1c. All the silver money is used interchangeably with US currency; each coin is the same size and material as the US coin of equivalent value. You can take in or out any amount of foreign or Panamanian currency.

Living is costly, although food is much the same price as in Costa Rica. Military personnel buy their supplies at low prices in special stores. These facilities are not available to tourists. The annual average increase in consumer prices fluctuates in line with US trends.

Weights and Measures Both metric and the US system are used.

Electricity In modern homes and hotels, 220 volts. Otherwise 110 volt 3 phase, 60 cycles A.C.

Foreign Postage Great care should be taken to address all mail as "Republic of Panama" or "RP", otherwise it is returned to sender. Air mail takes 3-5 days, sea mail 3-5 weeks from Britain. Rates (examples) for air mail (up to 15 grams) are as follows: Central, North and South America and Caribbean, 30c; Europe, 37c up to 10 grams, 5c for every extra 5 grams; Africa, Asia, Oceania, 44c; all air letters require an extra 2c stamp. Parcels to Europe can only be sent from the post office in the El Dorado shopping centre in Panama City (bus from Calle 12 to Tumba Muerta).

Telecommunications The radio station at Gatún is open to commercial traffic; such messages are handled through the Government telegraph offices. The telegraph and cable companies are given under the towns in which they operate. **Telex** is available at the airport, the cable companies and many hotels. Rate for a 3-minute call to Britain is US$14.40, and US$4.80 for each minute more.

Telephone calls can be made between the UK and Panama any time, day or night. Minimum charge for 3 min. call: US$10 station to station, but person to person, US$16 on weekdays, US$12 on Sun. plus tax of US$1 on each call. To the USA the charge is US$4 for 3 mins. Phone to Australia costs US$16 for 3 mins. (US$13 on Sunday).

Inter-continental contact by satellite is laid on by the Pan-American Earth Satellite Station. The local company is Intercomsa.

Press *La Estrella de Panamá* and *La República* (Spanish) are the largest daily newspapers; also *La Prensa*, *El Panamá América*, *Crítica Libre* and *El Siglo* . *Colón News* (weekly—Spanish and English). The US Army publishes the daily *Tropic Times* ; its Friday edition has advertisements about cars and other items for sale. It can be found in clubs etc. on the US bases.

Language Spanish (hard to understand), but English is widely understood.

We are most grateful for Panamian information to Harry Clemens (Panama 5), Jamie Butler (Petersfield), Ligia (Lee) Paget (Bocas del Toro) and A.F. Siraa (Miami); also to other travellers whose names are listed in the general Central America section.

SAN ANDRES AND PROVIDENCIA
COLOMBIA

Since the Colombian island of San Andrés is such a popular stop-over point between Central America and mainland South America, we append a description of the island here.

COLOMBIA'S Caribbean islands of the San Andrés and Providencia archipelago are 480 km. north of the South American coast, 400 km. southwest of Jamaica, and 180 km. east of Nicaragua. This proximity has led Nicaragua to claim them from Colombia in the past. They are small and attractive, but very expensive by South American standards. Nevertheless, with their surrounding islets and cays, they are a popular holiday and shopping resort. Colombia itself encompasses a number of distinct regions, the most marked difference being between the sober peoples of the Andean highlands (in which the capital, Bogotá, is built) and the more light-hearted *costeños*, or people of the coast. The islands belong in the latter category, but, owing to their location, have more in common with the Caribbean's history of piracy, planters and their slaves than with Colombia's rich imperial past. The original inhabitants, mostly black, speak some English, but the population has swollen with unrestricted immigration from Colombia. There are also Chinese and Middle Eastern communities. The population in 1988 was officially put at 35,000, but it could now be about 65,000.

History and Economy Before the European explorers and pirates came upon the islands, Miskito fisherman from Central America are known to have visited them. The date of European discovery is subject to controversy; some say Columbus found them in 1502, others that Alonso de Ojedo's landing in 1510 was the first. The earliest mention is on a 1527 map. Although the Spaniards were uninterested in them, European navies and pirates recognized the group's strategic importance. The first permanent settlement, called Henrietta, was not set up until 1629, by English puritans. The first slaves were introduced in 1633, to extract timber and plant cotton, but in that century, pirates held sway. Henry Morgan had his headquarters at San Andrés; the artificial Aury channel between Providencia and Santa Catalina is named after another pirate of that time. Although more planters arrived in the eighteenth century from Jamaica, England agreed in 1786 that the islands should be included in the Dominions of Spain. In 1822 they

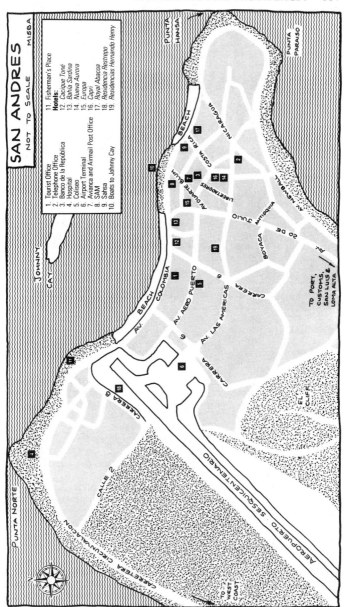

SAN ANDRES
NOT TO SCALE

1. Tourist Office
2. Telephone Office
3. Banco de la Republica
4. Hospital
5. Coliseo
6. Airport Terminal
7. Avianca and Airmail Post Office
8. SAM
9. Sahsa
10. Boats to Johnny Cay
11. Fisherman's Place

Hotels:
12. Cacique Toné
13. Bahía Sardina
14. Nueva Aurora
15. Europa
16. Capri
17. Royal Abacoa
18. Residencia Restrepo
19. Residencias Hernando Henry

became Colombian possessions. After the abolition of slavery in 1837, coconut production replaced cotton and remained the mainstay of the economy until disease ruined the trade in the 1920s. In 1953, San Andrés was declared a freeport, introducing its present activities of tourism and commerce.

Apart from these areas, the main products are coconuts and vegetable oil. The main problem is deteriorating water and electricity supplies (in most hotels the water is salty—a desalination plant was installed in 1987). Being a customs-free zone, San Andrés is very crowded with Colombian shoppers looking for foreign-made bargains. Although alcoholic drinks are cheap, essential goods are extremely costly, and electronic goods are more expensive than in the UK.

Festivals 20 July: independence celebrations on San Andrés with various events. Providencia holds its carnival in June.

San Andrés

San Andrés is of coral, some 11 km. long, rising at its highest to 104 metres. The town, commercial centre, major hotel sector and airport are at the northern end. A picturesque road circles the island. Places to see, besides the beautiful cays and beaches on the eastern side, are the Hoyo Soplador (South End), a geyser-like hole through which the sea spouts into the air most surprisingly when the wind is in the right direction. The west side is less spoilt, but there are no beaches on this side. Instead there is The Cove, the island's deepest anchorage, and Morgan's Cave (reputed hiding place for the pirate's treasure) which is penetrated by the sea through an underwater passage. At The Cove, the road either continues round the coast, or crosses the centre of the island back to town over La Loma, on which is a Baptist Church, built in 1847.

Hotels In the upper bracket (B and up), *Gran Internacional*, Av. Atlántico, No 1A-49, T 3043, air conditioning, swimming pool, 3 restaurants, largest on the island; *Nueva Aurora*, Av. de las Américas No. 3-46, T 3811, fan and private bath, pool, restaurant; *Bahía Marina*, road to San Luis, swimming pool, good restaurant; *Abacoa*, Av. Colombia, with bath and air conditioning; also *Royal Abacoa*, on same avenue at No. 2-41, good restaurant, T 4043; *Bahía Sardinas*, Av. Colombia No 4-24, T 3587, across the street from the beach, air conditioning, TV, fridge, good service, comfortable, clean, no swimming pool; *Cacique Toné*, Av. Colombia, Carrera 5, deluxe, air conditioning, pool, on sea-front; *Tiuna*, Av. Colombia No. 3-59, air conditioning, swimming pool; *Capri*, Av. Costa Rica No. 1A-110, with bath and air conditioning, good value. In our C range: *Isleño*, Av. La Playa, great sea view; *Galaxia*, Av. Colón, T 3013, with breakfast, bath, fan, smelly; *El Dorado*, Av. Colombia No. 1A-25, T 4155, air conditioning, restaurant, casino, swimming pool; *Coliseo*, Av. Colombia No. 1-59, T 3330, friendly, noisy, good restaurant; *Europa*, Av. 20 de Julio No. 1-101, with bath, clean. *Mediterráneo*, Av. Los Libertadores, D, clean, friendly, poor water supply; *Las Antillas*, Av. 20 de Julio No. 1A-81, D with bath and fan, clean, safe, good water (including for drinking), good value.

Residencias Hernando Henry, D, restaurant, fan, clean, good value, on road from airport; *Residencia Restrepo*, "gringo hotel", near airport—turn left to beach, then left, second left at fish restaurant and it's a hundred metres on left (no sign), noisy ("share a room with a Boeing 727"—till midnight), much cheaper than others, F, or less for a hammock in the porch, clean, some rooms with bath, breakfast US$0.50, other meals US$1.50, good place for buying/selling unwanted return halves of air tickets to/from Central America or the Colombian mainland. Campsite at South End said to be dirty and mosquito-ridden.

Restaurants *Oasis* (good), Av. Colombia No. 4-09; *La Parrillada* (Argentine), good meals at US$4; *Popular*, on Av. Bogotá, good square meal for US$4; comida corriente at *Don Joaco's* for US$2, good fish. *Mercapollo*, good value; *San Andrés* and *High Seas* are also recommended for cheap, typical meals; *Fonda Antioqueña Nos 1 and 2*, on Av. Colombia near the main beach, and Av. Colombia at Av. Nicaragua, best value for fish; *Miami*, special for US$3; excellent fruit juices at *Jugolandia*, Calle 20 de Julio; *Jugosito*, Av. Colombia, 1½ blocks from tourist office towards centre, cheap meals; *Mundo Acuático*, snacks of fresh fish and papaya for US$1, cheaper beer, soft drinks and mangoes. *Fisherman's Place*, in the fishing cooperative at north end of main beach, very good, simple. Fish meals for US$2.50 can be bought at San Luis beach.

Island Travel Buses circle the island all day, US$0.25 (more at night and on holidays). Taxis round the island, US$8; to airport, US$3; in town, US$0.60; *colectivo* to airport, US$0.50.

Boat transport: Cooperativa de Lancheros, opposite *Hotel Abacoa*.

Vehicle Rental Bicycles are a popular way of getting around on the island and are easy to hire, e.g. opposite *El Dorado Hotel*—usually in poor condition, choose your own bike and check all parts thoroughly (US$1.10 per hour, US$6 per day); motorbikes also easy to hire, US$3.60 per hour. Cars can be hired for US$15 for 2 hours, with US$6 for every extra hour.

Culture San Andrés and Providencia are famous in Colombia for their music, whose styles include the local form of calypso, soca, reggae and church music. A number of good local groups perform on the islands and in Colombia. Concerts are held at the Old Coliseum (every Saturday at 2100 in the high season); the Green Moon Festival is held in May. There is a cultural centre at Punta Hansa in San Andrés town (T 5518).

Exchange Banco de la República, Av. Colón, will exchange dollars and travellers' cheques; Banco Cafetero will advance pesos on a Visa card. Aerodisco shop at airport will change dollars cash anytime at rates slightly worse than banks, or try the Photo Shop on Av. Costa Rica. Many shops will change US$ cash; it is impossible to change travellers' cheques at weekends. (Airport employees will exchange US$ cash at a poor rate.)

Marine Life and Watersports Diving off San Andrés is very good; depth varies from 10 to 100 feet, visibility from 30 to 100 feet. There are three types of site: walls of sea-weed and minor coral reefs, large groups of different types of coral, and underwater plateaux with much marine life. 70% of the insular platform is divable. Names of some of the sites are: The Pyramid, Big Channel, Carabela Blue, Blue Hole, Blowing Hole, The Cove and Small Mountain/La Montañita.

Diving trips to the reef cost US$50 with Pedro Montoya at Aquarium diving shop, Punta Hansa, T 6649; also Buzos del Caribe, Centro Comercial Dann, T 3712; both offer diving courses and equipment hire.

For the less-adventurous, take a morning boat (20 minutes, none in the afternoon) to the so-called Aquarium (US$2 return), off Haynes Key, where, using a mask and wearing sandals as protection against sea-urchins, you can see colourful fish. Snorkelling equipment can be hired on San Andrés for US$4-5, but it is better and cheaper on the shore than on the island.

Pedalos can be rented for US$4 per hour. Windsurfing and sunfish sailing rental and lessons are available from Bar Boat, road to San Luis (opposite the naval base),

1000-1800 daily (also has floating bar, English and German spoken), and Windsurf Spot, *Hotel Isleño*, T 3990; water-skiing at Water Spot, *Hotel Aquarium*, T 3120, and Jet Sky.

Beaches and Cays Boats go in the morning from San Andrés to Johnny Key with a white beach and parties all day Sunday (US$1.90 return, you can go in one boat and return in another). Apart from those already mentioned, other cays and islets in the archipelago are Bolívar, Albuquerque, Algodón/Cotton (included in the Sunrise Park development in San Andrés), Rocky, the Grunt, Serrana, Serranilla and Quitasueño.

On San Andrés the beaches are in town and on the eastern coast (some of the most populated ones have been reported dirty). Perhaps the best is at San Luis and Sound Bay.

Providencia

Providencia, commonly called Old Providence (3,000 inhabitants), 80 km. back to the north-northeast from San Andrés, is 7 km. long and is more mountainous than San Andrés, rising to 610 metres. There are waterfalls, and the land drops steeply into the sea in places. Superb views can be had by climbing from Bottom House or Smooth Water to the peak. There are relics of the fortifications built on the island during its disputed ownership. Horse riding is available, and boat trips can be made to neighbouring islands such as Santa Catalina (an old pirate lair separated from Providencia by a channel cut for their better defence), and to the northeast, Crab Cay (beautiful swimming) and Brothers Cay. Trips from 1000-1500 cost about US$7 p.p. On the west side of Santa Catalina is a rock formation called Morgan's Head; seen from the side it looks like a man's profile.

On Providencia the three main beaches are Manchincal Bay, the largest, most attractive and least developed, South West Bay and Freshwater Bay, all in the South West.

Like San Andrés, it is an expensive island. The sea food is good, water and fresh milk are generally a problem. Day tours are arranged by the Providencia office in San Andrés, costing US$30 inclusive. SAM fly from San Andrés, US$35, 25 minutes, up to five times a day, bookable only in San Andrés. (Return flight has to be confirmed at the airport, where there is a tourist office.) Boat trips from San Andrés take 8 hours, but are not regular.

Hotels Most of the accommodation is at Freshwater (Playa Agua Dulce): *Cabañas El Recreo* (Captain Brian's), *Cabañas El Paraíso*, *Cabañas Aguadulce* and *Hotel Royal Queen*; *Ma Elma's* recommended for cheap food; at Santa Isabela on the north end of the island, *Flaming Trees Hotel*, clean, restaurant, good value, but a long way from the beach; at Smooth Water Bay, *Dutch Inn* (full board) and several houses take in guests. Camping is possible at Freshwater Bay. Truck drivers who provide transport on the island may be able to advise on accommodation.

Cartagena and Barranquilla

Mention should be made here of the two Caribbean cities on the mainland to which access is made from San Andrés, Cartagena and Barranquilla.

Cartagena, old and steeped in history, is one of the most interesting towns in South America, and should not be missed if you are taking this route. As well as the historical sites, Cartagena also has a popular beach resort at Bocagrande, a ten-minute bus ride from the city centre. Cartagena de Indias, to give it its full name, was founded on 13 January, 1533, as one of the storage points for merchandise sent out from Spain and for treasure collected from the Americas to be sent back to Spain. A series of forts protecting the approaches from the sea, and the formidable walls built around the city, made it almost impregnable. All the same, it was challenged again and again by enemies. Sir Francis Drake, with 1,300 men, broke in successfully in 1586. The Frenchmen Baron de Pointis and Ducasse, with 10,000 men, sacked the city in 1697. But the strongest attack of all, by Sir Edward Vernon with 27,000 men and 3,000 pieces of artillery, failed in 1741 after besieging the city for 56 days. It was defended by the one-eyed, one-armed, one-legged hero Blas de Lezo.

A full description of the city, with its churches, forts, colonial streets and other attractions, is given in *The South American Handbook*.

Barranquilla (also described in detail in *The South American Handbook*) is Colombia's fourth city, with almost 2 million people. It is a modern, industrial sea and river port on the west bank of the Magdalena, one of the country's main waterways. The four-day Carnival in February is undoubtedly the best in Colombia.

Information for Visitors

Documents A passport and an onward ticket are always necessary. Nationals of the following countries do not need visas or tourist cards: Argentina, Austria, Barbados, Belgium, Brazil, Costa Rica, Denmark, Ecuador, West Germany, Finland, Holland, Ireland, Israel, Italy, Japan, Liechtenstein, Luxemburg, Netherlands Antilles, Norway, Peru, Portugal, St Vincent and the Grenadines, South Korea, Spain, Sweden, Switzerland, Trinidad and Tobago, UK, Uruguay. All other countries need visas or tourist cards (free). Normal validity for either is 90 days; extensions for a further month can be obtained in the capital, Bogotá (DAS—immigration authorities, Carrera 27, No. 17-00, or any other DAS office—other addresses below; cost US$10, can take up to 3 days). Whether you need a tourist card or visa depends on your nationality, so check at a Colombian consulate in advance. Tourist cards are issued by Corporación Nacional de Turismo (CNT) offices (in New York, or Caracas, for instance) or by Colombian airlines or authorized foreign carriers.

Visas are issued only by Colombian consulates. A visa is required by US citizens (for example), who must be prepared to show 1 photograph, an onward or return ticket, as well as a passport (allow 48 hours). Alternatively, in the USA only, Avianca issues tourist cards (transit visas), valid for 15 days, costing US$10—these cards are renewable only by leaving the country. In Miami insist at the Consulate, as they will assume that you can work it all out through the airline. Citizens of Asian, African, Middle Eastern and Socialist countries (including Cuba, Nicaragua and East Germany), must apply at least 4 weeks in advance for a visa. You may find that your onward ticket, which you must show before you can obtain a visa, is stamped "non-refundable". If you do not receive an entry card when flying in, the information desk will issue one, and restamp your passport for free. Visitors are sometimes asked to prove that they have US$20 for each day of their stay

(US$10 for students). Note that to leave Colombia you must normally get an exit stamp from the DAS.

NB It is highly recommended that you have your passport photocopied, and witnessed by the DAS (about US$0.20) or a notary. This is a valid substitute, and your passport can then be put into safe-keeping. Also, photocopy your travellers' cheques and any other essential documents. For more information, check with DAS or your consulate.

How To Get There By Air San Andrés is a popular stopover on the routes Miami, or Central America to Colombia. By changing planes in San Andrés you can save money on flight fares. Avianca flies to Miami, SAM to Guatemala City and San José, Costa Rica, Sahsa to Tegucigalpa and Panama City. Note that Panama, Costa Rica and Honduras all require onward tickets which cannot be bought on San Andrés, but can be in Cartagena. SAM will not issue one way tickets to Central America. You buy a return and the SAM office on the mainland will refund once you show an onward ticket. The refund (less 15%) may not be immediate. Avianca and SAM have flights to most major Colombian cities: to Bogotá and Medellín with SAM (you can arrange a 72-hour stop-over in Cartagena).

Airport Information San Andrés airport is 15 minutes' walk to town (taxi US$3 p.p.). All airline offices are in town (Avianca and SAM on Av. Duarte Blum, Sahsa on Av. Colombia), except Aces at the airport. There is a customs tax of 15% on some items purchased if you are continuing to mainland Colombia.

There is an airport exit tax of US$15, from which only travellers staying less than 24 hours are exempt. When you arrive, ensure that all necessary documentation bears a stamp for your date of arrival; without it you will have to pay double the exit tax on leaving (with the correct stamp, you will only be charged half the exit tax if you have been in the country less than 30 days). Visitors staying more than 30 days have to pay an extra US$15 tax, which can only be avoided by bona-fide tourists who can produce the card given them on entry. There is a 15% tax on all international air tickets bought in Colombia for flights out of the country (7% on international return flights). Do not buy tickets for domestic flights to or from San Andrés island outside Colombia; they are much more expensive. When getting an onward ticket from Avianca for entry into Colombia, reserve a seat only and ask for confirmation in writing, otherwise you will pay twice as much as if purchasing the ticket inside Colombia.

Sunday flights are always heavily booked. In July and August, it is very difficult to get on flights into and out of San Andrés; book in advance if possible. Checking in for flights can be difficult because of queues of shoppers with their goods.

If flying from Guatemala to Colombia with SAM, via San Andrés, you have to purchase a round-trip ticket, refundable only in Guatemala. To get around this (if you are not going back to Guatemala) you will have to try to arrange a ticket swap with a traveller going in the other direction on San Andrés. There is, however, no difficulty in exchanging a round-trip ticket for a San Andrés-Colombian ticket with the airline, but you have to pay extra.

Flights To Colombia British Airways has a twice-weekly service from London to **Bogotá**, via Caracas. Airlines with services from continental Europe are Air France, Iberia, and Lufthansa. Avianca, the Colombian national airline, flies from Frankfurt via Paris and Madrid. Frequent services to and from the USA by Avianca and American.

Avianca flies from Miami and Newark to **Cartagena**; the same airline flies from **Barranquilla** to Miami (as does American), Newark, Aruba and Curaçao.

Customs Duty-free admission is granted for portable typewriters, radios, binoculars, personal and ciné cameras, but all must show use; 200 cigarettes or 50 cigars or 250 grams of tobacco or up to 250 grams of manufactured tobacco in any form, 2 bottles of liquor or wine per person.

How To Get There By Sea Cruise ships and tours go to San Andrés; there are no other, official passenger services by sea. Cargo ships are not supposed to carry passengers to the mainland, but latest reports suggest that many do. If you want to leave by sea, speak only to the ship's captain. (Any other offer of tickets on ships to/from San Andrés, or of a job on a ship, may be a con trick.) Sometimes the captain may take you for free, otherwise he will charge anything between US$10-25; the sea crossing takes 3-4 days, depending on the weather. In Cartagena, ships leave from the Embarcadero San Andrés, opposite the Plaza de la Aduana.

Car Rental National driving licences may be used by foreigners in Colombia, but must be accompanied by an official translation if in a language other than Spanish. International drivers licences are also accepted. Carry driving documents with you at all times. Even if you are paying in cash, a credit card may be asked for as proof of identity (Visa, Mastercard, American Express), in addition to passport and driver's licence.

Hotels There is a tourist tax of 5% on rooms and an insurance charge, but no service charge, and tipping is at discretion. The more expensive hotels and restaurants also add on 10% VAT (IVA). The Colombian tourist office has lists of authorized prices for all hotels which are usually at least a year out of date. If you are overcharged the tourist office will arrange a refund. Most hotels in Colombia charge US$1 to US$6 for extra beds for children, up to a maximum (usually) of 4 beds per room.

Food Colombia's food is very regional; it is quite difficult to buy in one area a dish you particularly liked in another. Of the Caribbean dishes, Cartagena's rice with coconut can be compared with rice *a la valenciana*; an egg *empanada*, consists of two layers of corn (maize) dough that open like an oyster-shell, fried with eggs in the middle, and try the *patacón*, a cake of mashed and baked plantain (green banana). *Huevos pericos*, eggs scrambled with onions and tomatoes, are a popular, cheap and nourishing snack for the impecunious—available almost anywhere. Throughout the country there is an abundance of fruits: bananas, oranges, mangoes, avocado pears, and (at least in the tropical zones) *chirimoyas*, *papayas*, and the delicious *pitahaya*, taken either as an appetizer or dessert and, for the wise, in moderation, because even a little of it has a laxative effect. Other fruits such as the *guayaba* (guava), *guanábana* (soursop), *maracuyá* (passion fruit), *lulo* (*naranjilla*), *mora* (blackberry) and *curuba* make delicious juices, sometimes with milk added to make a *sorbete*—but be careful of milk in Colombia. Fruit yoghurts are nourishing and cheap (try *Alpina* brand; *crema* style is best).

Drink *Tinto*, the national small cup of black coffee, is taken ritually at all hours. Colombian coffee is always mild. (Coffee with milk is called *café perico*; *café con leche* is a mug of milk with coffee added.) *Agua de panela* is a common beverage (hot water with unrefined sugar), also made with limes, milk, or cheese. Many acceptable brands of beer are produced. The local rum is good and cheap; ask for *ron*, not *aguardiente*, because in Colombia the latter word is used for a popular drink containing aniseed (*aguardiente anisado*).

Warning Great care should be exercised when buying imported spirits in shops. It has been reported that bottles bearing well-known labels have often been "recycled" and contain a cheap and poor imitation of the original contents. This can be dangerous to the health, and travellers are warned to stick to beer and rum. Also note that ice is usually not made from potable water.

Tipping Hotels and restaurants 10%. Porters, cloakroom attendants, hairdressers and barbers, US$0.05-0.25. Taxi-drivers are not tipped.

Shopping Local handicrafts are made from coral and coconut. Otherwise shopping is concentrated on the duty-free items so readily available. Typical Colombian products which are good buys: emeralds, leatherwork and handworked silver.

Currency The monetary unit is the peso, divided into 100 centavos. There are coins of 50 centavos (rare) and of 1, 2, 5, 10, 20 and 50 pesos; there are notes of 10, 20, 50, 100, 200, 500, 1,000, 2,000 and 5,000 pesos. Large notes of over 1,000 pesos are often impossible to spend on small purchases as change is in short supply, especially in small cities, and in the morning. There is now a limit of 500 on both the import and export of pesos. To change pesos back into dollars on departure (to a maximum of US$100), you need to keep the exchange slips received from banks.

Travellers' cheques are not easy to change in Colombia; the Banco de la República prefers to change those of no more than US$20. Owing to the quantity of counterfeit American Express travellers' cheques in circulation, travellers experience great difficulty in cashing these cheques except in main cities, where the procedure is often slow, involving finger printing and photographs. The best advice we can give is to take Thomas Cook's or a US bank's dollar traveller cheques in small denominations. Sterling travellers' cheques are practically impossible to change in Colombia. The few, legitimate *casas de cambio* give rates slightly worse than the banks, but are much quicker. Also in circulation are counterfeit US dollar bills in denominations of US$50 and US$100; US$20 bills are therefore more readily accepted. As it is unwise to carry large quantities of cash, credit cards are widely used, especially Diners' Club and Visa; Master Charge is less common, while American Express is only accepted in high-priced establishments in Bogotá. Many banks advance pesos against Visa (eg Banco Cafetero) or Mastercharge (eg Banco de Occidente, Banco Industrial de Colombia), but in early 1989, the government is considering imposing a surcharge on this service.

Security Carry your passport (or photocopy) at all times.

Avoid money changers on the street who offer over-favourable rates of exchange. They often short-change you or run off with your money, pretending that the police are coming. Beware of counterfeit dollars and pesos.

Colombia is part of a major drug-smuggling route. Police and customs activities have greatly intensified and smugglers increasingly try to use innocent carriers. Travellers are warned against carrying packages for other people without checking the contents. Penalties run up to 12 years in none too comfortable jails, and the police sometimes behave very roughly towards those they choose for a spot check at airports; complaints have been made in this connexion to the Colombian authorities. All young travellers are suspect, so be very polite if approached by policemen. If your hotel room is raided by police looking for drugs, try, if possible, to get a witness to prevent drugs being planted on you. Colombians who offer you drugs may well be setting you up for the police, who are very active on the north coast and San Andrés island.

If someone accosts you on the street, saying he's a plain-clothes policeman or drugs officer, and asks you to go to his office, offer to go with him to the nearest policeman (the tourist police where possible) or police station, or to your hotel if it's dark. He may well be a "confidence man" (if he doesn't ask to see your passport, he almost certainly is). These conmen usually work in pairs.

Health Emergency medical treatment is given in hospitals: if injured in a bus accident, for example, you will be covered by insurance and treatment will be free. Take water sterilizer with you, or boil the water, or use the excellent mineral waters, when travelling outside the capital. Choose your food and eating places with care everywhere. Hepatitis is common; have a gamma-globulin injection before your trip. There is some risk of malaria and yellow fever in the coastal areas;

prophylaxis is advised.

Climate And Clothing Tropical clothing is needed in the hot and humid climate of the coast. Average temperature on the islands is 27-31°C.

Tourist Seasons On the Caribbean coast and San Andrés and Providencia, high season is 15 December-30 April, 15 June-31 August.

Working Hours Monday to Friday, commercial firms work 0800-1200 and from 1400-1730 or 1800. Government offices follow the same hours on the whole as the commercial firms, but generally prefer to do business with the public in the afternoon only. Embassy hours for the public are from 0900-1200 and from 1400-1700 (weekdays). Bank hours in San Andrés are 0800-1130, 1400-1600 Monday to Thursday, 1400-1600 Friday only. Shopping hours are 0900-1230 and 1430-1830, including Saturday.

Public Holidays Circumcision of our Lord (1 January), Epiphany* (6 January), St Joseph* (19 March), Maundy Thursday, Good Friday, Labour Day (1 May), Ascension Day*, Corpus Christi*, Sacred Heart*, SS Peter and Paul* (29 June), Independence Day (20 July), Battle of Boyacá (7 August), Assumption* (15 August), Discovery of America* (12 October), All Saints' Day* (1 November), Independence of Cartagena* (11 November), Immaculate Conception (8 December), Christmas Day (25 December).

When those marked with an asterisk do not fall on a Monday, or when they fall on a Sunday, they will be moved to the following Monday.

Time Zone Eastern Standard Time—5 hours behind GMT.

Useful Addresses DAS (immigration authorities) are at the San Andrés airport, T 5540. (In Cartagena, DAS is just off Av. Crisanto Luque, near La Ermita at the foot of La Popa hill, T 64649; take "Socorro" bus, very helpful. In Barranquilla, DAS, Calle 54 No. 41-113.) San Andrés Police, T 6450; Red Cross, T 3333; Panamanian Consulate, Av. Atlántico No. 1A-60, T 6545. Other diplomatic representation in Barranquilla, Cartagena, or Bogotá.

Weights And Measures Metric; weights should always be quoted in kilograms. Litres are used for liquid measures but US gallons are standard for the petroleum industry. Linear measures are usually metric, but the inch is quite commonly used by engineers and the yard on golf courses. For land measurement the hectare and cubic metre are officially employed but the traditional measures *vara* (80 centimetres) and *fanegada* (1,000 square *varas*) are still in common use. Food etc is often sold in *libras* (pounds), which are equivalent to ½ kilo.

Electric Current 120 volts AC. Transformer must be 110-150 volt AC, with flat-prong plugs (all of same size). Be careful with electrically heated showers.

Postal Services There are separate post offices for surface mail and airmail. Send all letters by airmail, for surface mail is very unreliable. Avianca controls all airmail services and has offices in provincial cities (Catalina Building, Av. Duarte Blum in San Andrés). Correspondence with UK is reported to be good. It costs US$0.25 to send a letter or postcard to the US, and US$0.27 to Europe; a 1 kg. package to Europe costs US$13 by air (Avianca).

Telecommunications Systems have been automated; the larger towns are interconnected. Inter-city calls and cables must be made from Telecom offices unless you have access to a private phone (Telecom in San Andrés: Av. Américas No. 2A-23). Long-distance pay 'phones are located outside most Telecom offices, also at bus stations and airports. They take 20 peso coins. 1 peso coins for ordinary 'phones may be bought in 20 peso packets from Banco de la República. Fom the larger towns it is possible to telephone to Canada, the USA, the UK, and to several of the Latin American republics. International phone charges are high (eg US$33 for 3 minutes to Australia, US$22 to Europe), but there is a 20% discount on Sunday; a deposit is required before the call is made which can vary between US$18 and US$36 (try bargaining it down), US$1 is charged if no reply, for person-to-person add an extra minute's charge to Canada, 2 minutes' to UK; all extra minutes' conversation cost ⅓ more. Collect, or reversed-charge, telephone calls are only possible from private telephones; make sure the operator understands what is involved or you may be billed in any case.

Tourist Information In San Andrés, Corporación Nacional de Turismo (CNT), Avenida Colombia No. 5-117, in front of *Hotel Isleño*, English spoken, maps, friendly, helpful. CNT has its headquarters at Calle 28, No. 13A-15, **Bogotá** (T 283-9466); it has branches in every departmental capital and other places of interest (in   **Cartagena**, Carrera 3 No. 36-57, Plaza Bolívar, T 43400; in **Barranquilla**, Carrera 54 No. 75-45, T 454458). They should be visited as early as possible not only for information on accommodation and transport, but also for details on areas which are dangerous to visit.

CNT also has offices in **New York**: 140 East 57th St, T 688-0151; **Caracas**: Planta Baja 5 Av. Urdaneta Ibarras a Pelota, T 561-3592/5805; **Madrid**: Calle Princesa No. 17 Tercero Izquierda, T 248-5090/5690; and **Paris**: 9, Boulevard de la Madeleine, 75001 Paris, T 260-3565.

Notes

Notes

CLIMATIC TABLES

The following tables have been very kindly furnished by Mr. R. K. Headland. Each weather station is given with its altitude in metres (m.). Temperatures (Centigrade) are given as averages for each month; the first line is the maximum and the second the minimum. The third line is the average number of wet days encountered in each month.

MEXICO, CENTRAL AMERICA & CARIBBEAN

	Jan.	Feb.	Mar.	Apr.	May	June	July	Aug.	Sept.	Oct.	Nov.	Dec.
Acapulco, Mex.	29	31	31	31	32	32	32	32	31	31	31	31
3m.	21	21	21	22	23	24	24	24	24	23	22	21
	0	0	0	0	2	9	7	7	12	6	1	0
Guatemala City	23	25	27	28	29	27	26	26	26	24	23	22
1490m.	11	12	14	14	16	16	16	16	16	15	14	13
	2	2	2	5	8	20	17	16	17	13	6	2
Havana	26	27	28	29	30	31	31	32	31	29	27	26
49m.	18	18	19	21	22	23	24	24	24	23	21	19
	6	4	4	4	7	10	9	10	11	11	7	6
Kingston	30	29	30	30	31	31	32	32	32	31	31	30
7m.	22	22	23	24	25	25	26	26	25	25	24	23
	3	2	3	3	5	6	3	6	6	12	5	3
Managua, Nic.	30	30	30	32	32	31	31	31	31	31	30	30
46m.	23	24	26	28	27	26	26	25	26	24	24	24
	0	0	0	0	6	12	11	12	15	16	4	1
Mérida, Mex.	28	29	32	33	34	33	33	33	32	31	29	28
22m.	17	17	19	21	22	23	23	23	23	22	19	18
	4	2	1	2	5	10	11	12	13	7	3	3
Mexico City	19	21	24	25	26	24	23	23	23	21	20	19
2309m.	6	6	8	11	12	13	12	12	12	10	8	6
	2	1	2	6	9	14	19	18	17	8	3	2
Monterrey, Mex.	20	22	24	29	31	33	32	33	30	27	22	18
538m.	9	11	14	17	20	22	22	22	21	18	13	10
	3	3	3	4	4	4	4	3	8	5	4	4
Nassau	25	25	27	28	29	31	31	32	31	29	28	26
10m.	17	17	18	20	22	23	24	24	24	22	20	18
	6	5	5	6	9	12	14	14	15	13	9	6
Panama City	31	31	32	32	31	30	30	31	30	30	29	30
36m.	21	21	22	23	23	23	23	23	23	22	22	23
	4	2	1	6	15	16	15	15	15	16	18	12
Port-au-Prince	31	31	32	33	33	35	35	35	34	33	32	31
41m.	23	22	22	23	23	24	25	24	24	24	23	22
	3	5	7	11	13	8	7	11	12	12	7	3
Port of Spain	30	32	31	32	32	31	31	31	32	31	31	30
12m.	20	21	21	21	23	23	23	23	23	22	22	21
	11	8	2	8	9	19	23	17	16	13	17	16
San José,	24	24	26	27	27	27	26	26	27	26	25	24
Costa Rica	14	14	15	16	16	16	16	16	16	15	15	15
1172m.	1	0	1	4	17	20	18	19	20	22	14	4
San Juan, PR	27	27	27	28	29	29	29	29	30	30	28	27
14m.	21	21	22	22	23	24	24	24	24	24	23	22
	13	7	8	10	15	14	18	15	14	12	13	14
San Salvador	30	31	32	32	31	30	30	30	29	29	29	29
700m.	16	16	17	19	19	19	18	18	19	18	17	16
	0	3	2	5	12	20	21	20	18	14	4	1
Santo Domingo	28	28	29	29	30	30	31	31	31	31	30	29
14m.	20	19	20	21	22	23	23	23	23	23	22	21
	7	6	5	7	11	12	11	11	11	11	10	8
Tegucigalpa,	25	27	29	30	30	28	28	28	29	27	26	25
Hond.	14	14	15	16	18	19	17	17	17	17	16	15
935m.	4	2	1	3	14	18	10	10	17	16	8	4
Willemstad	28	29	29	30	30	31	31	31	32	31	30	29
23m.	24	23	23	24	25	26	25	26	26	26	24	24
	14	8	7	4	4	7	9	8	6	9	15	16

WEIGHTS AND MEASURES

Metric	**British and U.S.**

Weight:

1 kilogram (kg.) = 2,205 pounds

1 pound (lb.) = 454 grams

1 metric ton = 1.102 short tons
= 0.984 long ton

1 short ton (2,000 lb.) = 0.907 metric ton
1 long ton (2,240 lb.) = 1.016 metric tons

Length:

1 millimetre (mm.) = 0.03937 inch

1 inch = 25.417 millimetres

1 metre = 3.281 feet

1 foot (ft.) = 0.305 metre

1 kilometre (km.) = 0.621 mile

1 mile = 1.609 kilometres

Area:

1 hectare = 2.471 acres

1 acre = 0.405 hectare

1 square km. (km²) = 0.386 sq. mile

1 square mile (sq. mile) = 2,590 km²

Capacity:

1 litre = 0.220 Imperial gallon
= 0.264 U.S. gallon

1 Imperial gallon = 4.546 litres
1 U.S. gallon = 3.785 litres

(5 Imperial gallons are approximately equal to 6 U.S. gallons)

Volume:

1 cubic metre (m³) = 35.31 cubic feet
= 1.31 cubic yards

1 cubic foot (cu. ft) = 0.028 m³
1 cubic yard (cu. yd.) = 0.765 m³

N.B. The *manzana,* used in Central America, is about 0.7 hectare (1.73 acres).

TEMPERATURES CONVERSION TABLE

°C	°F	°C	°F	°C	°F	°C	°F
1	34	11	52	21	70	31	88
2	36	12	54	22	72	32	90
3	38	13	56	23	74	33	92
4	39	14	57	24	75	34	93
5	41	15	59	25	77	35	95
6	43	16	61	26	79	36	97
7	45	17	63	27	81	37	99
8	46	18	64	28	82	38	100
9	48	19	66	29	84	39	102
10	50	20	68	30	86	40	104

The formula for converting °C to °F is: °C x 9 ÷ 5 + 32 = °F.

ECONOMIC INDICATORS

COUNTRY	US$ GNP per head (1988)†	%change pa (1980-89)†	Annual Inflation*	Exchange rate/US$
BELIZE	1,460	0.7%	0.7% (11)	2.0
COSTA RICA	1,760	0.2%	14.5%(3)	90.4
EL SALVADOR	950	-1.8%	23.5%(12)	8.0
GUATEMALA	880	-3.1%	14.5%(11)	4.4
HONDURAS	850	-1.7%	11.4%(12)	4.6
MEXICO	1,820	-1.4%	24.5%(4)	2,858
NICARAGUA	764	-4.7%	1,174.0%(12)	320,000
PANAMA	1,880	0.1%	0.2%(1)	1.0

† Source: World Bank
*Latest month in brackets: Belize, El Salvador, Guatemala, Honduras, Nicaragua all 1989; Costa Rica, Mexico, Panama 1990.
Exchange rates at 30 June 1990; Nicaragua introduced a new currency, the córdoba de oro, on 1 July 1990, at par with the US dollar.

INDEX TO PLACES

684

WILL YOU HELP US?

We do all we can to get our facts right in **The Mexico & Central American Handbook.** Each chapter is thoroughly revised each year, but the territory covered is vast, and our eyes cannot be everywhere. A new highway or airport is built; a hotel, a restaurant, a cabaret dies; another, a good one is born; a building we describe is pulled down, a street renamed. Names and addresses of good hotels and restaurants for "budget-minded" travellers are always very welcome. We would especially like to receive diagrams of walks, national parks and other interesting areas to use as source material for the Handbook and other forth-coming titles.

Your information may be far more up-to-date than ours. If your letter reaches us early enough in the year it will be used in the next edition, but write whenever you want to, for all your letters are used sooner or later.

Thank you very much indeed for you help.

Trade & Travel Publications Limited
6 Riverside Court
Riverside Road
Lower Bristol Road
Bath BA2 3DZ. England

INDEX TO ADVERTISERS

INDEX TO TOWN AND REGIONAL MAPS

THOMAS COOK TRAVELLERS CHEQUES

REFUND ASSISTANCE POINTS

Visitors to Mexico and Central America should telephone Thomas Cook Princeton USA (+1 609) 987-7300 (collect) – 24 hour service – or during normal business hours, contact:

Thomas Cook Travellers Cheques Ltd
Campos Eliseos 345-1 Piso
Col Polanco
11560 Mexico City
Mexico

Tel: 202-0048, 5381-5825

Customers will be provided with full details of the nearest convenient local agent.

Visitors to South America and the Caribbean area should also telephone Thomas Cook Princeton USA (+1 609) 987-7300 (collect) – 24 hour service – for assistance.

In many Latin American countries there is a vigorous parallel (black) market for both travellers cheques and US Dollar notes. (This may be with or without Government permission). Rates are usually slightly better for notes but travellers cheques are obviously safer, which is especially important when theft is becoming more common.

You should shop around for rates since these may vary considerably. Hotel rates in particular tend to be poor.

Do not take currencies other than US Dollar. If accepted at all, the rate will be poor.

In some countries, only specific bank branches may deal in foreign exchange and you may have difficulty obtaining local currency when far from capital cities.

Mexico City — Rio de Janeiro
Caracas — Bogota
Lima — Santiago
San Juan — Havana
Asuncion — Sao Paolo
Panama City — Quito
San Jose — Guayaquil
Buenos Aires — Santo Domingo
Managua — Guatemala
Montevideo —

THE HOTTEST
IN LATIN AMERICA.

Iberia gives you the hottest all-round service to Latin America.

With more flights to more places than any other airline. Plus a network of internal flights.

Iberia Preference Class, the hottest business class, means seat selection

when you book, separate check-in desks, through check-in to final destination, and exclusive lounges at most airports.

In flight, seating in a separate cabin offers the comfort and space of traditional first class: on our 747s you'll be right up-front, and only two abreast. The service is distinguished by impeccable attention to detail – there's even an on board library.

Ask your business travel agent to book the hottest service to Latin America.

WARM TO THE EXPERIENCE.

London 071-437 5622; Manchester 061-436 6444; Birmingham 021-643 1953; Glasgow 041-248 6581; Dublin 0001 779846.

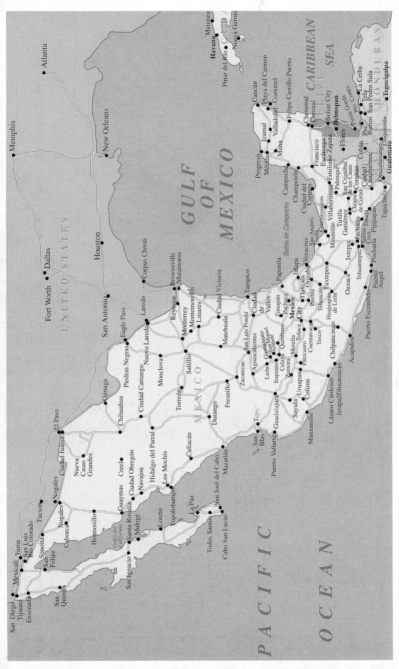